ARCHIVES

OF THE

STATE OF NEW JERSEY

FIRST SERIES

Vol. XXX

VOL. II OF CALENDAR OF WILLS

This volume was prepared and edited by authority of the State of New Jersey, at the request of the New Jersey Historical Society, and under the direction of its Committee on Colonial Documents. That Committee at present is constituted as follows:

ARCHIVES OF THE STATE OF NEW JERSEY

FIRST SERIES: VOL. XXX

DOCUMENTS
RELATING TO THE
COLONIAL HISTORY
OF THE
STATE OF NEW JERSEY,

CALENDAR OF NEW JERSEY WILLS

VOLUME II
1730–1750

EDITED, WITH AN INTRODUCTORY NOTE ON THE EARLY TESTAMENTARY LAWS AND CUSTOMS OF NEW JERSEY

William Nelson and
A. Van Doren Honeyman

HERITAGE BOOKS
2019

HERITAGE BOOKS
AN IMPRINT OF HERITAGE BOOKS, INC.

Books, CDs, and more—Worldwide

For our listing of thousands of titles see our website
at
www.HeritageBooks.com

A Facsimile Reprint
Published 2019 by
HERITAGE BOOKS, INC.
Publishing Division
5810 Ruatan Street
Berwyn Heights, Md. 20740

International Standard Book Numbers
Paperbound: 978-0-7884-0041-4

PREFACE

THIS SECOND volume of "Abstracts of Wills" of New Jersey is published long after the first volume, known as Vol. XXIII of the "New Jersey Archives," (First Series), owing, in part, to peculiar circumstances. The MSS. for it, which was prepared with much labor by employed abstracters at Trenton, was about ready for the printer when the great Paterson fire of 1902 destroyed it in the office of the late Mr. William Nelson, then the New Jersey Historical Society's Corresponding Secretary and Editor of the work. After a long time and much additional expense the entire copy was replaced under Mr. Nelson's direction, but he was unable to edit it previous to his death (in 1914), nor has the Society been able to print it until the present time.

The preceding volume of "Abstracts" was intended to include all wills and administrations up to and during the year 1730. But the present Editor discovered numerous omissions in 1730 probates, and included them in this volume, which is, therefore, entitled as beginning with that year. Other omissions in the reproduced MSS., between the years 1731 and 1750, have also been supplied. There are likewise included herein abstracts of wills, which, bearing the date of 1750, were probated later. In all, particulars of about 3,025 testaments, intestacies or guardianships are included in this volume, besides the few in the Appendix.

In order to compress the large number of entries for the twenty-one years actually embraced in these pages and to keep within the legislative appropriation applicable to the work, two sizes of small but perfectly clear type have been employed.

The spelling of proper names of persons and places, including abbreviations of Christian names, are believed to follow the original. These often vary in the same abstract, but are printed as found, although as many names, especially in inventories, are nearly undecipherable, errors of transcription in some cases have, doubtless, been unavoidable. In the "Index of Names of Persons," however, an endeavor has been made to straighten out the misspellings to a certain extent, so as to classify well-known proper surnames under present-day orthography. This seemed to be necessary in order to simplify the search for usual proper names.

A critical user of the volume may observe that the abstracts, which were made by different persons, are not based upon a perfectly harmonized plan; but, as in all cases the essential facts are stated, this cannot be a matter of moment.

In preparing the copy for the printer the Editor, as a matter of course, could not verify the accuracy of the MSS., but has endeavored to have the printing correctly follow it, and, to some extent, has harmonized the work of the abstracters.

Where wills, administrations, etc., were regularly recorded at Trenton, the book and page where the record may be found are stated. In such cases, to find the *original* wills, including inventories, etc., the printed three volumes published by the Secretary of State in 1912-'13, entitled "Index to Wills," must be consulted. Where originals were simply filed as papers, but not recorded, as happened with many wills and all inventories, the reference given is to the number of the filing case in which the original papers may be found.

The books of record and all original papers in the matters noted are preserved in the well-lighted basement of the Secretary of State's office at Trenton, with a polite and trained official in charge.

It may be of interest to some readers not familiar with the exact value of a few of the terms or expressions employed in various of the wills and inventories to state them. The word "yeoman" was in common use to signify a freeholder. The "£" (pound), which, with shillings and pence, constituted the lawful basis for the calculation of financial accounts, is to be valued at about $2.50, although its purchasing power in that day was probably five times what it now is. The double-year dating, which may look confusing to some readers, arose from the fact that in America, as in England, while the historic year ended December 31, the legal year ended on March 24, and this continued until 1750. Therefore, in reading, for example, a date such as Feb. 4, 1740-1, it is to be considered that the real year was 1741 historically, but 1740 legally. Unfortunately, all the wills, inventories, etc., noted in this work, between Jan. 1 and Mar. 24, do not bear a double-year date, as they should. No attempt has been made to alter the MSS. printed from in this respect, except in a few instances where the correct double dating was a matter of certainty.

It may be noted also that, unless otherwise stated, the amounts of inventories of estates are always of personalty only; that in various wills the word "brother," as used, has an uncertain meaning, and may refer to brother-in-law, step- or half-brother, or to a member of the same religious denomination; and that where names of testators in the bold face type are spelled in some alternate manner, it signifies that in the same document, or some corelated document, proof of such variation occurs.

A glance over the "Index of Names of Persons" at the end of the volume would seem to indicate that the names include a pretty large proportion of all the adult population of the State during the twenty-one year period covered by this work. A careful searcher will also find hundreds of cases where are stated one's exact neighbors (usually owning adjoining lands), and in many instances the names of every member of a family. It is the latter feature which will make this work of interest to searchers in genealogical lines.

We do not call attention to the unusual or curious wills to be found in these pages; there are few such. The chief interest and value of the volume are in the early names of persons and places, and in the particular dates relating to both living and deceased citizens of New Jersey at this early period. The record of these names and dates cannot fail to prove of permanent use to both present and future generations of students of the history of the old-time families of our State.

In the matter of early names of places a glance at the "Index of Place-Names" will show many old Indian and Dutch-derived names, either long since gone out of existence or greatly corrupted by time. For example, the following (many erronously spelled): Carrostoga, Covehaukin, Cuckowder, Gemocenepa, Hadgy, Leopeatenung, Machiscotuxin, Manatico, Manusking, Markashoop, Matchesqatonk, Mohoppony, Naughlomsoon, Ramenesin, Rapeketon, Sessoconneta, Shabbacunck, Steenraapje, Tatamus, Wickohoe, Wintepoc, Whopemenchonhhong, Zuckaruning.

It would require about two more volumes similar to this one to carry on the Abstracts of Wills to the year 1804, when the records at Trenton ceased and wills thereafter were recorded in each county. It is to be hoped such volumes may be published under State auspices at some time in the future.

A. V. D. H.

Plainfield, N. J., August, 1918.

ERRATA

Page 87. Strike out last entry on page, "Caruthers, James," as being a duplicate, in part, of first entry on same page.

Page 98. Lines 11 and 12. "Nathaniel Harned and Robert Dennes, fellow bondsmen," belong at the end of the preceding paragraph.

Page 99. Line 3. Strike out "Thomas Cox, witness," as a duplicate statement.

Page 160. Line 5. Strike out entire line.

Calendar of New Jersey Wills

NOTE.—The books cited as Libers 1, 2, 3, etc., are of West Jersey wills. Those cited as Libers A, B, C, etc., are of East Jersey wills. Where matters beside recorded wills, such as inventories, accounts, etc., are noted, the originals may be found in the proper boxes (arranged by counties), reference to which is made in the volumes (three volumes) entitled "Index to Wills," published by the Secretary of State in 1912 and 1913, which should always be consulted in case originals are to be referred to. All original matters herein abstracted are to be found in the Secretary of State's office at Trenton.

1742-3, Feb. 4. Aaronson, Benjamin, of Mansfield Township, Burlingston Co., yeoman; will of. Brothers Joseph and Aaron, sisters Elizabeth Gibbs and Sarah Atkinson. Cousins William and John, sons of Joseph Atkinson. Real and personal estate. Executors—brother Aaron and brother-in-law Joseph Atkinson. Witnesses—Job Talman, George Ash, John Hammell, Jr., Isaac DeCow medius. Proved April 6, 1743. Lib. 4, p. 356.

1742-3, March 3. Inventory of the personal estate, £38.16, made by Robert Rockhill, David Rockhill and Benjamin Shreve.

1741, Dec. 14. Aaronson, John, of Mansfield Township, Burlington Co., yeoman; will of. Children—Benjamin, Joseph, Aaron, Thomas, Elizabeth and Sarah. Grandsons—John Atkinson and his brothers and sisters. Negroes—Phillis and Ester. Real and personal estate. Wife Mary sole executrix. Witnesses—Benja. Talman, Francis Thompson, Elizabeth Talman, Isaac DeCow medius. Proved March 3, 1742. Lib. 4, p. 357.

1742-3, March 3. Inventory of the personal estate, £498.6.10¾, includes bonds, bills and note £230.2.8½, and negro children £30, made by Robert Rockhill, David Rockhill and Benjamin Shreve.

(Not dated) Abbott, John, of Nottingham Township, Burlington Co., yeoman; will of. Children—John, Timothy, Samuel, Mary Williams, Ann Biles, Jane Burr, Rachell Abbott, Elizabeth Williams and Sarah Abbott. Servant boy Arthur Woolard. Land adjoining Robert Pearson on the south side of Crosswick Creek. Wife Ann sole executrix. Witnesses—Robert Pearson, Rachel Pearson, Thomas Pearson. Proved April 12, 1740. Lib. 4, p. 228.

1735, Nov. 29, Abbott, Samuel, of Salem Co., yeoman, guardian, appointed Aug. 23, 1734. Resignation of, in favor of Clement Hall of Salem, merchant. The petition of the ward, Mary Walcott (daughter of Samuel Walcut of Penns Neck, Salem County) is attached to the original paper. Copy dated 22 January, 1735. Lib. 4, p. 50.

1741, July 21. Acken, Thomas, of Elizabeth Town and Ash Swamp, Essex Co.—will of. Wife Mary. Sons—Joseph, John, Samuel and

Robert. Daughter—Mary Little. Grandchild—John Acken son of son John. Real and personal estate. Executors—friends Isaac Frasey and Samuel Hinds. Witnesses—John Scuder, Ezekiah Hubbell, Nath'll Hubbell. Proved Feb. 10, 1747–8.

1747–8, Feb. 10. The executors within named having refused to act and the widow being also deceased, Elizabeth Lambert, principal creditor, appointed administrator.

1751, July 13. James Lambert, husband of the abovesaid Elizabeth, testifies to the foregoing. Lib. E, p. 134.

1745, Aug. 28. Ackerman, Abraham, of Bergen Co., "infant of 14 yrs. and upwards." Guardian—Hellebrant Lizier of Bergen Co., yeoman. Fellow bondsman—John Nevill, Esq., of Perth Amboy. Bergen Wills, 235B.

1738, April 23. Ackerman, Johannis, of Hackinsack, Bergen Co., shoemaker—Will of. Wife Jannetie Executrix, and to have the real and personal estate during widowhood. Co-executors of my "menorenne children," and assistants; my brother-in-law Hillebrant Lizier and cousin Lawrence Abrams Ackerman, both of Hackinsack. Sons, David (the Bible as a birthright), Niclas, Gilyn and Abraham to have all lands after decease or remarriage of the widow. Daughters, Hillegont (married), Trintie, Maritie and Antia. Witnesses—Joost Vanboskerck, Corns. WynKoop, David Demarest, Sen. Proved 19 August, 1745. Lib. D, p. 324.

1749, Nov. 18. Acton (Acten), Benjamin, of Salem, Salem Co., tanner—will of.

Item 1. "I give to my last wife's three daughters, which she had by her former husband, Wm. Sheals, £10 a piece out of my personal estate when they arrive to the age of 18 years, or marriage."

Item 2. "My son John Acton, my new house and lot, tanyard and stock, likewise the house and lot, which formerly belonged to Wm. Sheals, likewise a wood lot (25 acres) I bought of Wm. Chamber."

Item 3. "Son Joseph Acton to have the house and lot where I live, likewise the lot (1 acre) bought of Daniel Mestayer, and his wife, near the Bridge, likewise 50 acres of woodland reserved from the plantation I sold to Samuel Nicholson." Item 4. "My right of 100 acres of Cedar swamp belonging to me and Edward Lumas to be sold and the money with the overplus of my personal estate to be equally divided between my two sons above named. I deem Wm. Barret's mortgage part of my personal estate." Executors—Sons John and Joseph Acton. Signature with a seal. Witnesses—John Whittall, Samuel Parker, Josiah Kay. Sworn and affirmed 30 Dec., 1749. Lib. 6, p. 399.

1749-50, Jan. 8. Inventory, £1718.17.0, includes bonds, bills and notes, £807.8.0, clock and "Screwtore" £17, plate £14.13.3, "47 pair of pumps, £12," parcel of old books £4.4.0, "the wearing apparel late belonging to Rachel late wife of the s'd deceased, £9," cattle £21.15.0. "To rent due from Sam'l Abbott, same appeared £12.0.0." Appraisers—Ranier Vanhist, Josiah Kay.

1733, April 23. Adames, John, of Woodbridge, Middlesex Co., labourer; will of. Wife Agnas Adames, whose maiden name was Agnas Nisbet, now in Ireland. Son, Thomas Adames, who is with his mother. Real and personal estate. Executors—friend, Samuel Moores, and brother, Charles Adames. Witnesses—John Waller, Nicholas Stilwill, William Thorne. Proved July 17, 1734. Lib. B, p. 522.

1732-3, January 12. Adams, Thomas, of Freehold, Monmouth Co., cooper; will of. Wife, Margery. Four eldest children mentioned, but not named. Executors—friends, James Robinson and John Henderson, of Freehold. Witnesses—Walter and Joseph Wilson and William Hankinson. Proved January 26, 1732-3. Lib. B, p. 379.

1731, March 31. Addams, Jedediah, late of Evesham, Burlington Co., miller. Margaret Adams declines administration.

1731, April 1. Bond of Judah Allen as administrator; Thomas Hackny fellow bondsman, both of Evesham, yeoman. Lib. 3, p. 99A.

1731, April 5. Inventory of personal estate, £47.17, made by Thomas Middleton and Thomas Hackney.

1742, June 26. Addams, Jeremiah, of Great Egg Harbour, Gloucester Co., yeoman; will of. Wife, Mary. Children—David, Mary, Sarah, Rebecca, Joseph, Jeremiah. Executors—the wife and son David. Witnesses—Nehemiah Leeds, Elizabeth Lee, Richard Philpotts. Proved Nov. 25, 1742.

1742, Aug. 7. Inventory of the personal estate, £165.1.0, made by Joseph Leeds and Robert Smith. Burlington Wills, 3421-4C.

1742, Aug. 20. Aeten, John, of Somerset Co.; will of. Wife Elizabeth. To oldest son John and his heirs forever the "large Dutch folio Bible" and lands beginning at Raritan River at Peter Cowenhoven's line, thence to Hendrick Fisher's land. Residue of lands to son Thomas. Daughter—Elizabeth Smith, who has children, Mary Sebrant, and Eleanor Sebrant. Executors—sons John, Thomas and friend Hendrick Fisher. Signed "John Aatten (his mark)." Witnesses—Peter Cowenhoven, Evan Preston, Aaron Davis (his mark). Proved 13 March, 1743. Lib. D, p. 136.

1746, May 17. Akin, John, of Essex Co. Bond of Elizabeth Akin, widow, as administratrix; Joseph Wood, yeoman, fellow bondsman. Witness—Josiah Broadwell. Lib. D, p. 385.

1739, Dec. 17. Alberson, Abraham, of Gloucester, Gloucester Co.; will of. Sons—Abraham, Ephraim and Joseph Alberson, to have equally "all of my plantation whereon I live." Daughter—Rebecca Beverly. Executors to have the rest of estate, real and personal for bringing up of three sons, Aaron, Levi and Jonathan Alberson, until they will be 14, and then to put them out to some trade. After they attain 21 years, executors to pay them 10 pounds apiece. To son-in-law (step-son) Richard Chew £10, when he will be 21. Executors—sons Abraham and Joseph Alberson. Witnesses—Joseph Low, William Hampton, John Kaighin. Proved 18 Feb., 1744.

1745, Dec. 10. Letters Testamentary were granted. Lib. 5, p. 136.

1739, Dec. 6, (filed 1744). Inventory of the personal estate of Abraham Alberson senior (£193.4.6), includes negro Tom, £5, 30 lbs. of wool and 12 lbs. of worsted, beef, pork and lard. Appraisers—John Mickle, Joseph Low.

1745-6, Feb. 14. Alberson, Abraham, of town of Gloucester, Gloucester Co. yeoman. Int. Sarah Alberson, admx. (her mark). Thomas Clement of the same place, "cordwainer," bondsman. Witnesses—John Hampton, John Ladd. Lib. 5, p. 463.

1745-6, Jany. 18. Inventory of personal estate (£51.18.0), includes "salt pork, beaf, hogs, lard £4.10.0." Appraisers—John Hampton, John Thorne.

1748, Sept. 22. Alberson, Simon, of Newtown, Gloucester Co. Int. Joseph Ellis, admr.; Samuel Harrison, bondsman, both of place aforesaid. Witness—J. Scattergood. Lib. 6, p. 13.

1748, Sept. 19. Inventory of personal estate (£73.11.0), includes cash in hands of Josiah Alberson for rent £43, bond due from Joseph Low, cash in hand of Jacob Alberson and Joseph Ellis, 13 sheep. Appraisers—John Kaighin, Isaac Alberson.

1759, Feb. 2. Account of Jacob Stokes, adm. of Joseph Ellis, Esq., late of Gloucester Co., deceased, who was admr. of Simeon Albertson, late of same County. "So much thereof paid by the said Joseph Ellis" to Thomas Ellis, Jonah Albertson, William Edgar, Ann Hampton, John Keasley, Thomas Edgerton, Peter Sonmon, John Hampton, William Edgerton, etc., amounting to £61.10.

1744-5, 22, 12th mo. (Feb.) Alberson, William, of Newton, Gloucester Co., yeoman; will of. To son William and his heirs forever, "all the land and meadow I bought of John Kasley and the meadow I bought of Thomas Dennises, excepting the Lower Branch, also my two tracts of outland." To son Simeon Alberson and his heirs forever, "the lower part of my plantation where I live, bounded by Newton and the Fork Creek, near the house of John Mickle; also my cedar swamp, my son Simeon to pay each of my daughters Sarah and Ann £30 and my son Nathan £10, for the same when they will be 21." Son John Alberson to have the residue of land within the township of Newton, "he to pay my son Nathan, when 21, £20, to whom I give my 60 odd acre lot on a branch of Timber Creek, called 'Stephens Run.'" "I commit the tuition, care and estate of my children unto my uncle Josiah Alberson and my friend Ebenezer Hopkins." Executrix—wife Jane Alberson. Witnesses—Joseph Low, Andrew Tate, Elizabeth Smith, Jos. Cooper. Proved 16 April 1745. Letters granted July 25, 1746. Lib. 5, p. 220.

1745, 1st mo. (March), 25 da. Inventory (£858.4.4), includes watch and apparel, £54.13.3, bonds £174.1.2½, saddle-bags, remnant of cloth, ½ doz. teaspoons, £2.4.6, negro-woman and child, £40, 11 horses, 34 cattle, oxen £214. Appraisers—Jos. Cooper, Josiah Alberson.

1745, May 9. Albertson, Gilbert, of Gloucester, Gloucester Co., mariner. Admx., Jane Alberson, widow. Thomas Clement, bondsman, of the place aforesaid. Witnesses—Robt. Smith, J. Scattergood.

1749, May 22. Inventory of personal estate, £969.0.11. Includes bonds, notes and accounts of William Albertson, Thomas Edgerton, William Hugg, William Sell, Daniel Calving, Andrew Erickson, William Riggin, William Genard, Gabriel Dowel, Benjamin Stephenson, Thomas Holstone, Jonas Veneman, Lawrence Peterson, William Peterson, Andrew Holstone, Thomas Peterson, Abraham Stats, Samuel Moffett, John Heritage, William Tremble, Samuel Homby, James Holliday, William Dollerson, Aaron Bennett, Erick Johnson, William Roman, Jeremiah Hand, Isaac Hand, David Fitzgerald, Recompence Hand, Simeon Albertson, John Mackintosh, Walter Melton, Isaac Albertson, Francis Haddock, James Cusick, Jacob Albertson, Henry Siddon, Samuel Hazard, Peter Davis. Appraisers—Thos. Clements, Sam. Harrison, Junr.

1746, August 9. Alburt, Adam, of Amwell, Hunterdon County. Inventory of personal estate (£252.5.9), includes, 1 anvil and smith's tools; carpenter's tools; several Dutch Books, etc.; made by Philip Ringo and Teunes Habbah (or Hoppagh).

1746, August 13. Bond of Peter Rockafeller and Godfree Peters of Amwell, as administrators of the estate. Teunes Hoppagh, of Amwell, surety. Witness, Philip Ringo.

1748, June 8. Account of administrators, mentions names of Rut Johnson, Johannes Louks, Andrew Reed, John Quick, Casper Archaback, Charles Hoff, Jr., Philip Ringo, Peter Overfelt, Anthony Fisher, John Taylor, John Wester of Philadelphia, Jacob Swallow, Meani Vanvoras, Jacob Moore, Jacob Erwine, Philip Sine, Garret Williamson, John Opdyke, Benjamin Abbot, Benjamin Canby, Jeromas Horn, Mathias Smith, Anne Ketchin, Francis Toular (or Foular), schoolmaster, Aron Mateson, Tunas Hapough, Samuel Ketchin, James Abbot, Robert Mildram, Francis Quick, Derrick Vanvaughton and Bartholomew Hoboam. Hunterdon Wills, 185J.

1744, Dec. 4. Aldridge, Thomas (see Eldridge).

1740, June 11. Alford, David, of Woodbridge, Middlesex Co., tanner; will of. Son, Benjamin. Mentions lands bought of John Heard Esq., Richard Jones, Benjamin Martin, John Parker, John Bishop, Sam'll Leues, Jun'r, Sam'll Moores, John Insle, Timothy Tuttle, David Donham, Robert Thornell. Daughters—Sarah, Mary and Margaret. Children all minors. Mentions lands bought of Jonathan Insle, Elisha Frazee, Ephraim Lockheart and Robert Ayers. Executors—wife Mary Alford, Benjamin Martin and Petter Martin. Witnesses—Jonathan Inslee, Jonathan Inslee, Jun'r, and Jno. Herriot. Proved April 19, 1748. Lib. E, p. 160.

1748, April 18. Inventory of personal estate, £162.00.8, incl. debts due by Sam'll Barns and Sam'll Pray; made by Jonathan Inslee and Benjamin Allword.

1748-9, Feb. 9. Allcott, William, of Northampton, Burlington Co.; will of. Wife, Ann. Sons—Anthony and William. Other children mentioned but not named. Real and personal estate. Executors—wife and son Anthony. Witnesses—Thomas Eayre, John Hiller, John Burr, Jun'r. Proved Feb. 25, 1748. Lib. 6, p. 37.

1748-50, Feb. 22. Inventory of personal estate, £134.17.6; made by Samuel Woolston and John Hiller.

1731, Jan. 31. Allen, Benjamin (over 16 years old), eldest son of Judah, of Evesham, Burlington co., yeoman. Letters of guardianship of granted to William Sharo, of Evesham. Burlington Wills, 2057C.

1746, July 9. Allen, Benjamin, Jr., late of Evesham, Burlington Co. Inventory of the personal estate of, £92.12; made by William Sharp and James Cattell.

1746, July 19. Bond of Deborah Allen, widow, as administratrix of the estate of. Samuel Sharp, yeoman, and William Sharp, weaver, both of same place, fellow bondsmen. Lib. 5, p. 430.

1732, March 29. Allen, Daniel, of Egg Harbour, Gloucester Co., yeoman. Inventory of personal estate, £42.11.0, made by widow, Mary

Allen, administratrix. Appraised by William Cordray and Roturn Badkack.

1732-3, Jan. 2. Account of estate, £59.5.0, made by Mary Allen, showing payments to Richard Clymer, John Hinchman, Henry Brown, James Steelman, James Sommers, Andrew Steelman.

Gloucester Wills, 149H.

1732, March 18. Allen, David, of Shrewsbury town, Monmouth Co., yeoman; will of. Wife, Hannah. Children—Jedidiah, Ralph, Elizabeth and Rebecca. Executors—wife, friend George Williams and cousin Jacob Lippincott. Witnesses—Joseph Allen, Benjamin Corliss and Jacob Dennis. Proved May 28, 1735.

1735, May 9th and 16th. Inventory of personal estate, £514, incl. 50 neat cattle; 87 old sheep and 42 lambs; 12 horses and mares; bond from Tole Macolla; in Henry Lawrence's hand; in Hugh Porter's hand; in Benjamin Parker's, John and Preserve Lippincott's hands. Made by John Eatton, John Redford and Jacob Dennis.

Liber C, p. 35; 621-4M.

1731, Jan. 25. Allen, Deborah, late of Evesham, Burlington Co. Bond of William Sharp and Rebecca his wife as administrators (Rebecca Sharp being one of the daughters of Deborah Allen, late wife of Judah Allen, yeoman, late of Evesham). William Parke and James Shearing, all of Burlington Co., fellow bondsmen. Witnesses—Hugh Sharp, Martha Parke, Richard Parke. Lib. 3, p. 175.

1740, May 23. Allen, Ebenezer, of Shrewsbury, Monmouth Co. Bond of Hannah Allen, widow, as administratrix. George Allen of same place, yeoman, bondsman. Witnesses—Robert Hude and Thomas Bartow.

1740, May 16. Inventory of personal estate, £75.19.00, incl. bond of Joseph Patterson, due from David Jecocks; made by Benjamin Parker and John Seares. Liber C, p. 340; 881-4M.

1740-1, March 16. Allen, Elizabeth, of Elizabeth Town, Essex Co., widow. Inventory of personal estate, £30.19.01¾, incl. debts due from wife of John Drew, and bond from Jonathan Allen; made by Benjamin Trotter and John Potter.

1741, Nov. 30. Bond of Jonathan Allen, son, yeoman, as administrator. John Hyndshaw, of Woodbridge, Middlesex Co., bookbinder, fellow bondsman. Lib. C, p. 466.

1747, December 20. Allen, Ephraim, of Shrewsbury town, Monmouth Co., will of. Wife, Mary. Children—Joseph and Lydia. Grandson, John Allen. Executors—wife and friend Job Cook. Witnesses—Emmanuel Woolley, Benjamin Woolley, Stephen Cook and Amariah Slocum. Proved December 28, 1747. Executors, being Quakers, affirmed. Lib. E, p. 143.

1747, December 24. Inventory of personal estate, £189.00.11; made by William Jackson and Daniel Williams.

1747, March 2. Allen, Ezekiel, of Shrewsbury town, Monmouth Co., yeoman; will of. Wife, Amy. Children—Obadiah, Nathan, Joshua, Elizabeth, and Aaron. Executors—wife and brother, Jedidiah Allen. Witnesses—Joseph Potter, Thomas Negus, John Allen and Jacob Dennis. Proved March 14, 1747, by Joseph Potter and John Allen, Quakers. Executors, Quakers, affirmed same day.

1748, March 15. Inventory of the personal estate, £257.01.02. Made by Joseph Wardell and Joseph Potter.

1739, Feb. 20. Allen, Isaac, of Salem County, blacksmith. Int. Admx., Mary Allen (relict of). Bondsman, Benjamin Allen. Both of aforesaid County. Witnesses—Rich'd Wood, Dan'l Mestayer.

Lib. 4, p. 198.

1739-40, Feb. 16. Inventory (£270.9.21½) "praised at Alaways Creek, Salem County," includes cattle and horses, "anvil, stock in smith shoop," bellows and vise. Appraisers—Richard Wood, Abraham Moss.

1750, Dec. 3. Allen, John, Esq., of city of Burlington. Hannah Allen, widow, renounces administration and requests that same be granted her son, John Allen, Esq.

1750, Dec. 8. Bond of John Allen, of Hunterdon Co., Esq. as administrator. Bennet Bard and Joseph Hollinshead of city of Burlington, Esqrs. fellow bondsmen. Lib. 7, p. 29.

1748, November 12. Allen, Jonathan, of Shrewsbury town, Monmouth Co., yeoman; will of. Children—Hezekiah (eldest son), Bathsheba (eldest daughter), Naomi, James, Exercise, Sarah, Mary, Hannah, David (youngest son). Executors—friend Joseph Corleis and son-in-law John Woodmanse. Witnesses—John Redford, Joseph Potter and Jedidiah Allen. Proved November 26, 1748. Executors (Quakers) affirmed.

1748, November 19. Invéntory of personal estate, £178.16.7, incl. bonds of James Allen, Thomas Finemor, William Mitten, Josiah Parker and Hezekiah Allen, and nursery of apple-trees; made by Joseph Potter and John Williams.

1749, May 1. Account of estate by executors. The plantation sold for £1281; property right for £25. Cash paid to following—Joseph Wardel, Hezekiah Allen, John Woodmansey, Derious Lippincott, James Allen, William Brewer, Charles Mackey, Jedidiah Allen, Hannah Allen, David Allen, Peleg Slocum. Lib. E, p. 245.

1731, June 24. Allen, Juda, of Evesham, Burlington Co., yeoman; will of. Son, Benjamin (under age). Daughters—Rebakah, Elizabeth, Mary and Abigail. Meadow, formerly Clark Rodman's and land purchased of Judiah Adams. Executors—wife and sons-in-law William Sharp and Edward Clamans. Witnesses—Francis Hogsett, Arthur Borradaill, Mahlon Stacy. Proved July 20, 1731.

1731, Aug. 2. Inventory of personal estate, £437.1.11; made by Thomas Noolin, Joseph Fenimore and Benjamin Moore.

1731-2, Jan. 31. Benjamin, son and heir of Judah Allen, and orphan of about 16, elects William Sharp as guardian, to whom letters of guardianship are issued. Lib. 3, pp. 146, 177.

1747-8, February 20. Allen, Lydia, daughter of Ephraim Allen of Shrewsbury, Monmouth Co., nuncupative will of. Brother, Joseph. Mother, Mary Allen. Cousins—Lydia Parker and Alice Goodbody. Signed by Rachel Dennis and Lydia Parker, March 1, 1747-8. Proved by Rachel Dennis and Lydia Parker (Quaker), who testify that Lydia Allen died at twelve o'clock at night, Monday, February 22nd (?).

Lib. E, p. 144.

1732, December 2. Allen, Nathan, of Upper Freehold, Monmouth

Co., Esquire; will of. Wife, Martha. To son, Nathan, plantation and grist mills, also land adjoining Aaron Robins and Benjamin Applegate. To son Benjamin, plantation bought of Benjamin Lawrence, Jr., bounded according to lease to William Norton, also the fulling mill. Daughters—Martha and Margery (under sixteen). Wife sole executrix. Witnesses—John Tantum, Jr., Ambrose Feild and Samuel Rogers. Proved by John Tantum, Quaker, January 30, 1738.

Lib. 4, p. 154.

1738, 11th. d., 11th. m. (Jan.). Inventory of estate, £1194.15.1, incl. one negro man and two boys, a negro woman and one girl; made by John Tantum and John Middleton.

1748, September 10. Allen, Nathan, of Upper Freehold, Monmouth Co., yeoman; will of. Wife, Sarah. Son, John (or Nathan John). "Mother, Martha Decow." Sister, Martha Lawrence. Executors—wife and friend Robert Lawrence. Witnesses—Moses Robins, John Mount and William Lawrence. Proved October 1, 1748. Lib. 5, p. 531.

1748, March 26. Allen, Ralph, of Shrewsbury town, Monmouth Co.; will of. Wife, Mary. Children—Rebecca, Judah and Elizabeth, under fourteen years of age. Executors—brother Jedidiah Allen and cousin Joseph Allen. Witnesses—William Cook, Timothy Hance and Jacob Dennis. Proved April 27, 1748. Lib. E, p. 166.

—— ———. Inventory of the personal estate, £191.11.3; made by Joseph and Jacob Corlies.

1732, January 14. Allen, Samuel, of Amwell, Hunterdon Co., yeoman; will of. Wife, Martha, sole legatee and executrix for bringing up of children whose names are not given. Witnesses—Charles Woolverton (?), John Carr, George Fox and Samuel Green. Proved May 3, 1733. Executrix a Quaker.

1732, February 19. Inventory of estate, £97.5.0, incl. what was found in the weaving room, loom, tubs, etc.; fifteen head of cow kind; twelve head of swine; eight head of horse kind; one servant man; made by Charles Woolverton and Samuel Green.

1734, May 15. Account of Samuel Arnold and Martha, his wife, late Martha Allen, executrix of will of Samuel Allen. Mentions Joseph Higby, William Montgomerie, Stephen Pidcock, Daniel Howel, Elizabeth Reed, John Mullin, William Dugdale, Thomas Woollverton, Thomas McClehan, Isaac Herrin, Joseph Reed, Isaac Arey, Richard Hough, Christian Cornelius, Francis Bowes. Lib. 3, p. 298; 100J.

1744, March 13. Allen, Thomas, of New Hanover, Burlington Co., labourer. Administration on estate granted unto Thomas Miller, yeoman; John Stewart, yeoman, fellow bondsman. Lib. 5, p. 100.

1745, Nov. 30. Inventory of personal estate, £42.10.7; made by John Stewart and Jos. Steward.

1744, December 8. Allen, William, of Allentown, Monmouth Co., hatter; will of. Wife, Anna, sole legatee. Executors—wife, Jacob Lawrence and Thomas Lowrie. Witnesses—Bartholomew West, Charles Jolley and William Lawrence. Proved January 29, 1744-5.

Lib. 5, p. 77.

1744-5, January 27. Inventory of personal estate, £132.10.11, incl. one dozen wool hats, not finished, thirty-four blocks, smoothing iron, bows and stamper, twenty-one beaver skins; made by William Lawrence and Bartholomew West.

1750, Jan. 13. Allen, Zachariah, of Woodbridge, Middlesex Co., yeoman. Bond of Elizabeth Allen, his widow, as administratrix of estate. Samuel Crow, same place, carpenter, fellow bondsman. Witness—Ebenezer Saltar.

1750, Jan. 14. Inventory of personal estate, £36.1.2; made by Richard Jones and Abraham Johnston. Lib. E, p. 473.

1750, Jan. 25. Vendue list; articles bought by Eliza. Allen, Abraham Morgan, Joseph Howten, John Price, John Eastwood, Jonathan Harnet, Edward Potter, Joseph Michel, Andrew Hamton, William Comtan, John Duning, John Alwood, Sam. Axtel, Phebea Johnston, George Heard, Ebenezer Saltar, Dugal Cambel, Jonathan Ensley, John Wilson, Henry Langstaff, George Manham, Sam Martin, Steven Connan, James Pike, James Eddey, Thos. Williams, Rousa Eastwood, Sarah Kelley, Benjamin Eastwood, Sam'll Crow, Benjamin Jones, Zedakiah Bonham.

1750, Jan. 29. Debts owing to estate from John Herriot, John Vanderhoven, William Gilman, Rybben Potter, Richard Cutter, Zedekiah Bonham, Benjamin Martin, Sarah Comptan, Mary Combs, Nath'll Harned, Timothy Bloomfield, Frazee Ayers, James Ross, Abraham Monee, Samuel Preston, James Willson, Sarah Martin, Benj. Alford, Malachi Fitz Randolph, Abraham Ayers, Charles Ford, Justice Smith, Wm. Thornell, Dr. Pierson, Rich'd Mackalee, Eliakim Martin, Dr. Christie.

1732, May 4. Alling, Samuel, of Newark, Essex Co., Esq.; will of. Wife, Sarah, to have pasture at Denison Cove. Children—Samuel, Thomas, Ezechell, Elizabeth Curry, Sarah Dod, and Eunice Sergeant. Land joining lands of Joseph Rogers, John Ogden, John Bruin and James Wheeler. Executors—sons Samuel and Thomas Alling. Witnesses—Jo. Cooper, John Crane, John Currey. Proved Aug. 3, 1732. Lib. B, p. 301.

1750, Feb. 13. Alling, Thomas, of Essex Co. Bond of Hannah Alling, widow, as administratrix on estate of her husband; Timothy Johnson of Newark, fellow bondsman. Lib. E, p. 501.

1730, Feb. 19. Allison, Richard, of Burlington Co., sadler; will of. Wife, Ann, to have real and personal estate to educate children. Son, Richard, all books. Daughters—Elizabeth and Ann, each to have a silver tankard. Executors—wife and brother Rowland Ellis. Witnesses—Joseph Heulings, Benj'n Marriott, Dinah Bard. Proved August 2, 1731. Lib. 3, p. 296.

1734, ———. Account of Anne Allisson and Rowland Ellis, executors, who have paid debts due to James Veres, Ebenezer Large, Sam'l Scattergood, Thomas Hendry, Wm. Collins, Thomas Shreve, Paul Watkinson (all funeral charges), Elishep Allisson and estate of Joseph Pidgeon; in all £158.3.2. Debts due estate from Mathew Willson, Sam'l Brown, Sam'l Maxhue, Sam'l Farington, Wm. Cramer, Estate of Francis Collings, John Rothmall (who has removed into some remote part of Penn.), Hezekiah Willson.

1741, April 13. Allison, Richard, son of Richard Allison of City of Burlington, cooper, about 15 years of age, elects Robert Spencer of Trenton as his guardian. Lib. 4, p. 213.

1732, Aug. 23. Allton, William, of Elizabeth Town, Essex Co., bricklayer; will of. Children—Elizabeth, Sarah, and William (all under age). Brother, Erasmus Allton, and his daughters Phebey and Sarah. Real and personal estate. Executors—wife Deborah and friends John Shotwell and John Moriss. Witnesses—Job Pack, Benjamin Pack, Benjamin Marsh. Proved Dec. 7, 1732. Lib. B, p. 341.

1732, Nov. 23. Inventory of personal estate (£164.07.08), incl. bonds of Erasmaus Allton J'r, John Shotwell, Samuel Marsh, and a gold ring; also debts due from Jos. Marsh, Peter Noe, Job Pack, John Morriss; made by Jeremiah Bird and John Winaines.

1732, July 27. Allwood, Henry, of Baskingridge, Somerset Co., yeoman; will of. Wife, Sarah, sole executrix, and to have the personal estate "to bring up the children." Sons—John, Harry and Danyell, to have all lands; John, the oldest, to have first choice. Two daughters, not named. Witnesses—Daniel Sutton, James Wilkison, Moses Rolfe. Proved 12 May 1733. Lib. B, p. 407.

1732-3, Feb. 27. Alston, John, of Woodbridge, Middlesex Co., blacksmith; will of. Sons—John and Benjamin. Daughter, Mary, under age. Real and personal estate. Wife, Rebecca, sole executrix. Witnesses—John Rotan, Sam'll Rolph, David Alston. Proved Aug. 1, 1733. Lib. B, p. 452.

1743, May 31. Alston, John, of Woodbridge, Middlesex Co., Gent'n; will of. Wife, Mary Alston. Son John's son Benjamin to have meadow bought of John Stewart, joining Moses Bishop and Will'm Brittain's lands. Sons—David, Jonathan and Thomas. Daughters—Ann and Mary, and her daughter Lyda Bishop. Grandchildren—Susanna and Alexander Lee. 53 acres joining Michael Moores land; 54 acres joining Jonathan Bishop's land; land bought of Jno. Dilly; land joining lands of Michael Moore and Sam'll Jaquess. Executors—sons David and Jonathan. Witnesses—William Pangburn, Richard Wilkison, Charles Force. Proved July 9, 1743. Lib. D, p. 65.

1734, Aug. 29. Alton (Allton), Erasmus, of Elizabeth Town, Essex Co., brickmaker; will of. Children mentioned, but names not given; all minors. Real and personal estate. Executors—wife Rebeckah and brother-in-law Gershom More. Witnesses—Joseph Shotwell, John Morriss, Joseph Alton. Proved May 19, 1736. Lib. B, p. 99.

1736, May 22. Inventory of personal estate, £158.15.02, incl. negro boy; made by Jacob Thorn and Jos. Shotwell.

1743, Oct. 2. Alward, John, of Woodbridge, Middlesex Co., yeoman; will of. Children—John, Mary, Euphemy, and Rachel, all under age. Wife, Anne, sole executrix. Real and personal estate. Witnesses—Oswald Foord, Robert Dennes, William Kent. Proved April 10, 1745.

1745, April 2. Inventory of personal estate £63.19; incl., 17 Ghees, knives and forks, and debts due from John Eastwood, Benjamin Allward, Samuel Foord.

1745, April 15. The widow Anne having died without proving the will, administration on estate granted to Benjamin Allward, the brother, and Oswald Foord, brother-in-law, both of Woodbridge.

1745, April 15. Administration bond signed by Benjamin Allward, Oswald Foord and Sam'll Foord.

1746, May ——. Account of Oswald Foord and Benjamin Allward as administrators; showing payments made to William Foord, John Kent, John Smith, William Kent. Lib. D, pp. 259, 261.

1745, Sept. 18. Alwood, Daniel, of Piscataway, Middlesex Co., being eighteen years of age, makes choice of Obadiah Ayers of same place to be his guardian. Lib. D, p. 334.

1745, Sept. 19. Amon, Jacob, of Essex Co., labourer. Bond of Azzikam Case as administrator. David Jones and John Sip, yeomen, fellow bondsmen. Lib. D, p. 333.

1735, June 16. Amos, Philip, of Bucks Co., Province of Pennsylvania, innholder. Administration granted unto his widow, Anne. Thomas Croasdale of Burlington, innholder, fellow bondsman. Witnesses—Sam'l Bustill, Abia Cottman. Lib. 4, p. 30.

1731-2, January 25. Anderson, Andrew, of Hopewell, Hunterdon County, yeoman; will of. Wife, Elizabeth, sole legatee. Executors—wife and Enoch Anderson, Jr. Witnesses—Jacob Anderson, Francis Vannoey and Cornelius Ferrell. Proved February 7, 1732.

1732, April 3. Inventory of personal estate, £59.3.0; made by Francis Vannoey, and Abraham Anderson a Quaker. Lib. 3, p. 272.

1733, June 20. Anderson, John, of Freehold, Monmouth Co., Esquire; will of. Eldest son, John, Jr., to have 300 acres of land at Manalpan, part of tract received by deed of gift from John Reid, Esquire, December 8, 1701, part of which land has since been released to testator by Mary and James Miller, by their attorney, John Kinsey, April 12, ——, bounded by James Anderson's land, Mount Brook, Kenneth Anderson's land, and Middle Run. Also to said son, "my Negro Man named Andrew, with all my large navigation books, the large copper furnace and the silver cup." Son James to have 300 acres at Manalpan, in Freehold, bounded by Robert Cumming, Clear Brook, Manalpan River; also negroes Jack and Kate and "my silver hilted sword." Son Kenneth to have land at Manalpan, bounded by Mr. Bartow; also negro Hary and "my scymeter, gold signet ring," etc. Son Jonathan to have land at Manalpan, the testator's bed and "my silver snuff box with what shall hapen to be in it at my decease;" also negro Toney. Daughter Margaret to have £50, negro Judey and great Bible. Daughters—Helena, Anna, Elizabeth and Isabella. Residue among children, "except the craft that shall be then on the ground," to sons Kenneth and Jonathan. Executors—sons John, James, Kenneth and Jonathan. Witnesses—William Tennant, Robert Cumming and John Anderson. Proved April 8, 1736.

1736, April 23. Inventory of estate, £332.00.00, incl. "warrant to the treasurers," £28.14.7; 56 sheep; 26 swine; 11 horses and mares; 32 cattle; about 400 bushels of wheat; 60 bushels of rye; 50 bushels Indian corn; a pair of foils; prospect glass and compass box; "a nocturnal and sheep shears and three bells;" made by Robert Cumming, Joseph Newton and John Anderson.

1746, March 28. Anderson, John, of Bethlehem, Hunterdon Co., husbandman; will of. Wife, Hannah. Sons—Cornelius, John and Andrew. Devises 325 acres of land. Daughters—Mary and Martha Anderson, when of age. Granddaughter—Anna More. Plantation in Hopewell where mother now lives. Executors—wife, son Cornelius and friend Robert Laning. Witnesses—Robert and Ann White. Proved June 17, 1746. Liber 5, p. 242.

1746, June 4. Inventory of personal estate, £263.11.7, made by Robert White.

1760, August 21. Account of Cornelius Anderson and Robert Lanning, two of the executors of estate, mentions George Tayler, Samuel Ketcham, Eliza. Stevenson, Samuel Johnson, Cornelius Low, Joseph Parks, Benjamin Allen, Samuel Harris, John Burrows, Richard Anderson, Nathaniel Forster, Elia. Anderson, Philip Ringo, Garr'd Williamson, Robert White, Captain John Anderson.

1730, December 3. Anderson, Joshua, of "Madenhead," Hunterdon County, Es. Qr.; will of. Wife, Anjel, his dwelling and plantation. Eldest sons—Joshua and John, land in Hopewell adjoining land of William Briant. Sons—Benjamin, Isaac, Jacob, Abraham. Daughter Catherine and her children. Daughter, Hannah. Cedar swamp in Maryland to be divided among eight then living and they to discharge debt in the Loan Office. Executors—wife, son Abraham and neighbor Theophilus Phillips. Witnesses—Jasper Smith, Enoch Andrus and Giles Worth. Codicil of same date directing sale of house and plantation if wife see cause. Proved October 28, 1731.

Lib. 3, p. 163.

1730-1, January 5. Inventory of personal estate, (of Joshua Anderson Sen'r) £749.15.7, including debts of William Landers, Thomas Coleman, Daniel Biles and Thos. Brodreet; made by Jasper Smith and Jas. McKinly.

1750, March 9. Andrews, Ebenezer, of Burlington Co. Administration on the estate of, granted unto Mary Andrew, widow. Henry Warrington and James Cattell fellow bondsmen. Lib. 7, p. 103.

1750-1, Feb. 21. Inventory of the personal estate, £249.19.6; made by James Eldridge and James Cattell, includes servant man and negro boy, £27.

1751, Feb. 28. Thomas Andrews resigns his right in the property of his son Ebenezer in behalf of said Ebenezer's two eldest daughters, Hanah and Phebe Andrews. Witness—brother-in-law, Thomas Lippincott.

1741, December 8. Andrews, Mary, "late of Madera." Bond of John Stevens, mariner, of Perth Amboy, as administrator of the estate; Fenwick Lyell, Esquire of Perth Amboy, fellow bondsman.

Monmouth Wills, Lib. 6, p. 466.

1721, 13d., 6mo. Andrews, Mordecai, of "Littel Eggharbour," yeoman, will of. Children—Mordecai, Alice Mathews, Edith Allen and Mary Cramer. Real and personal estate. Executors—wife Mary and son Mordecai. Witnesses—Elizabeth Willitts, Jonathan Taler, Richard Willitts. Proved Nov. 4, 1736.

1736, ———. Letters testamentary granted unto Mary Andrew, widow, in absence of Morcecai Andrews, the son. Lib. 4, p. 74.

1736, June 19. Inventory of personal estate, £103.6.6; made by Jacob Andrews.

1750, April 2. Andrews, William, of Monmouth County. Inventory of the estate, £61.04.04, incl. a loom and 3 acres of rye; made by Thomas Cox and Joseph Robins.

1750, April 13. The widow, Mary Andrews, renounces right of administration in favor of John Andrews. Witnesses—David and Rebecca Gordon.

1750, April 23. Bond of John Andrews, cooper, of Monmouth County, as administrator of the estate. David Gordon, of same, farmer, fellow bondsman. Witnessed by William Phillips. (John Andrews, a Quaker).

1730, Jany. 10. Andrisse, Abraham, of Bergen, Bergen Co., miller; will of. Sister, Catryn. Brothers—Nicklaes and Mayhiel. Sister, Saara, wife of Casparis Prier. Land includes grist mill. Executors—brother-in-law, Casparis Prier, and Sara his wife. Witnesses—Morgan Smith, John Hendry, Pr. Marseliss. Proved 29 Jan. 1732.

1733, Sept. 4. Casparis Prier qualifies as executor. Lib. B, p. 466.

1740-1, Feb. 4. Androvet (Andro Vat), Daniel, of New Brunswick, Middlesex Co., cooper. Inventory of personal estate, £281.5.8; incl. notes of Caleb Haviland, Thomas Wilson, Cornelius Sallms, Abraham Letts, Joshua Cresson, Isaac Jones, James Ross, Thomas Wright, Mr. Hude, Jno. Pettingers, Richard Pettinger, Mr. Burges, Mr. Lane, Brant Clawson, David Dennis, John Dennis, Sam'll Pitts, John Stilwell, Mr. Francis Bower, John Tingles, John Mills, Peter Androvet, John Fountin, Peter Plancher, Francis Corrie, William Griffin, Thomas Montgomery, Will'm Williamson, Jun'r, John Gedeman, Jacob Ouke, Walder Burnet; also bonds in hands of John and Peter Androvet on Staten Island, Thomas Montgomery, John Rylie, Will'm Wood. Inventory by William Walling and Jen. Sperling.

1740-1, Feb. 12. Administration, granted to Hannah Androwvat, the widow; Isaac VanZant, of New Brunswick, fellow bondsman. Witnesses—John Bartow and Wm. Walling. Lib. C, p. 405.

1741, October 2. Andrus, Enoch, of Trentowne, Hunterdon Co.; will of. Son, John; son, Enoch, house and lot bought of Peter Bard on west side of York Road; son, Eliakim, 200 acres over Sanpink, which Eliakim was in possession of. Son, Jeremiah, 200 acres of land he was possessed of. Son, Joshua, 6 acres on east side of York Road, "where the brew house is now standing," and 200 acres in tract testator bought of Dr. Kidwalader (Cadwalader). Overplus of 600 acres to son-in-law Benjamin Stevens to dispose of for a debt said Stevens owed to Francis Boose for testator. Residue of estate to son Enoch and daughters, Caturn, Sarah and Rachel. Portions of daughters Elizabeth and Mary to discretion of executors. Executors—sons Enock and Joshua, and sons-in-law Benjamin Stevens and Ralph Smith. Witnesses—John Bainbridge, William Philips and Joseph Philips. Proved October 8, 1741. Lib. 4, p. 323.

1730, Oct. 30. Annelly, Edward, of City of Philada, glazier. Letters of administration on estate granted to James Inskeep of City of Burlington, weaver. Joseph Hewlings, of same place, cordwainer, fellow bondsman. Lib. 4, p. 183.

1744, 26th d. 1st mo. (March), Antram, Isaac, the Elder of Springfield, Burlington Co.; will of. Wife, Jane. Children—Abigail, Mary, Sarah, Mercy, Jane, Hannah, and Thomas, the last four under age. Land in Springfield bought of James Moore and Nathan Folwell, which Folwell bought of John Hutchin, and a tract adjoining Thomas Curtiss and John Antrum, "which I bought of Robert Hunt," also tract bought of John Norcross. Wife sole executrix. Witnesses—Samuel Hall, Nathan Folwell, John Osmond. Proved May 25, 1744.
Lib. 5, p. 29.

1731, Jan. 4. Antram, John, of Northampton, Burlington Co., husbandman. Children—Joseph, John, Stephen, Zacharias and Patience. Real and personal estate. Executor—friend Jonathan Wright. Witnesses—John Craig, John Deacon, Thomas Davis. Proved Feb. 1, 1731. Lib. 3, p. 177.

1731-2, Jan. 28. Inventory of estate, £200.2.10½; including negro woman and her child £33; made by Henry Burr, Caleb Raper and John Deacon.

1736, Dec. 29. Antrum, James, of Mansfield, Burlington Co., yeoman; will of. Wife, Mary. Sons—James and John. Daughters—Elizabeth, wife of Joseph Garwood, and Mary, wife of Thomas Biddle. Land adjoining Thomas Potts, John Beck, Joseph Shreve, Talman's land and Isaac Antram. Executors—sons John and James. Witnesses—John Aaronson, Richard Gibbs, William Satterthwait, Jun'r, Isaac DeCow, medius. Proved Nov. 17, 1739. Lib. 4, p. 193.

1739, Dec. 3. Inventory of personal estate, £117.15.6; made by Job Talman and Benja. Talman.

1741, May 11. Antrum, James, of Mansfield, Burlington Co., yeoman. Int. Administration to John Antrum. Joseph Garrett and Thomas Biddle, of Mansfield, yeomen, fellow bondsman. Lib. 4, p. 288.

1741, May 2. Inventory of personal estate, £230.6.6; made by Benja. Talman and Francis Gibbs.

1732, Nov., 4th d. Antrum, Thomas, of Springfield, Burlington Co., yeoman; will of. Eldest son Isaac at 21 years of age 150 acres bought of "my father John Antrum." Son, Dan'l, 80 acres purchased of Dan'l Smith and 81 acres known by the name of Barker's land. Son, Thomas, 8 acres of meadow purchased of Joshua Smith. Daughters—Martha, Mary and Rachel (minors). Land adjoining brother Isaac Antrum and Nathan Folwell. Executors—wife Sarah and brother Isaac Antrum. Witnesses—Peter Woolf, Sam'l Scattergood, Dan'l Zealy. Proved 5th d., Jan., 1732. Lib. 3, p. 237.

1747, March 4. Applegate, John, of Perth Amboy, and Cranberry, Middlesex Co. Hannah the widow refuses to administer on the estate and requests that Benjamin Applegate the eldest son be appointed. Lib. E, p. 136.

1747, March 4. Bond of Benjamin Applegate as administrator. Zebulon Applegate, fellow bondsman.

1747-8, Feb. 8. Account of what administrator has paid to James McKnight, Stephen Warne, Benjamin Applegate, Sen'r, Lewis Peairs, John Davison (blacksmith), Thomas Applegate (blacksmith), Samuel Spence, William Rives (for coffin), Moses Hull, John Feavell, Thos. Morris, Thos. Morford, Peter Perrine, Joseph Applegate, William Applegate.

1748, March 5. Inventory of personal estate, £79.14.6; made by Jacob Janson and Thomas Applegate.

1732, November 7. Applegate, Richard, of Middletown, Monmouth Co., yeoman; will of. Wife, Rebecca. Children—John, Abigal, Elizabeth, Joseph, Hannah, Rebecca, Johannah and William. After wife's death or marriage, all land to son William, when of age. Executors—wife and friend George Crawford. Witnesses—William Andrews, William and Darkus Hughes. Proved at "Crossweeks in Upper Freehold," January 20, 1732-3. Lib. B, p. 377.

——— ———. Inventory of estate £124.2.9, incl. silver seal; made by James Bowne, minor, Samuel Ogborne and Thomas Davies. Additional goods, £0.12.00, incl. an old gun and canoe.

1743, Dec. 15. Applegate, Thomas, of Perth Amboy, Middlesex Co., yeoman; will of. Wife, Ann Applegate. Children—Thomas, John, James and Andrew. Land in Fairfield, New England; salt meadow in Middletown; 150 acres in Shrewsbury; land in Cohansey. Executors —friend Lewis Pierce, of Perth Amboy, yeoman, and son, John Applegate. Witnesses—Peter Perrine, William Dye, Aaron Clayton. Proved Jan. 30, 1743.

1744, July 19. John Applegate qualified as executor, Lewis Peairs having refused to act. Lib. D, p. 161.

1742, May 27. Appleman, Peter, of Somerset Co., yeoman; will of. Wife, ———. Son, Baltas and his heirs "the land whereon he now liveth." Son, John, "the loom whereon he now works" and the large Bible. Rest of the estate divided between two "obedient sons John and Matthew," who are executors and trustees. Signed—Peter-the-Appleman [his mark]. Witnesses—David King, Tunis Smith, Ma' W. Brown. Proved 6 Aug., 1745. Lib. D, p. 311.

1745, Nov. 6. Inventory of Peter Appleman of the Northwest Precinct of Somerset Co. Personal estate, £210.3.5; made by Thomas Aten, Jr., and Jacob Eoff.

1741, Nov. 27. Archard, John, of "Greenage Township," Gloucester Co., yeoman; will of. Eldest son Jacob to have dwelling place. Youngest son, John, land bought from the Mortons. Swamp, marsh and meadow on Racoon Creek divided equally between them. Daughters—Catrin, Marey and Sarah. Wife, Marey, executrix. Executor —John Scatakly (Sketchley). Witnesses—Thomas Adams, Margaret Davanportt (affirmed), Isaiah Davenportt (affirmed). Proved 19 July, 1745. (Original will unrecorded). Gloucester Wills, 318H.

1744, Feb. 11. Inventory of personal estate, £179.1.10, includes 13 horned cattle, £42. Appraisers—Lawrence Lock, Alexr. Randall.

1745, July 19. Mary Archard commissioned admx. of estate.

1744, May 8. Archer, Gunner, of Greenwich, Gloucester Co., yeoman; will of. Wife, Elioner. Son, Andrew, to have home plantation, ½ of meadows, marshes and a tract of land (65 acres) joining John Archers. Son, Israel, the plantation called Boat hook and other half of aforesaid property. Daughters—Elizabeth Matson and Magdelane Archer. Executors—son Andrew and Henry Gray. Witnesses—Jno. Sketchley, John Wheeler, Philip Grace. Proved 13 Nov. 1744. Lib. 5, p. 71.

1744, Oct. 24. Inventory of personal estate, £163.14.10. Appraisers —Thomas Bickham, John Jones.

1732-3, January 16. Armitage, Enoch, of Hopewell, Hunterdon Co., blacksmith; will of. Wife, Hannah. Son, Reuben, to have plantation of 258 acres. Daughters—Mary Titus and Lydia Green. Son, John Armitage "or his children in England." Son, Reuben, executor. Witnesses—William Robinson, John Hunt and John Morgan. Proved May 9, 1739. Lib. 4, p. 179.

1738, February 21. Inventory of personal estate, £181.12.9, including a gun.

1731-2, 1st mo., 2nd. Arney, John, of Upper Freehold, Monmouth Co.; will of. Wife, Elizabeth. Son, Joseph. Daughters—Mary Arney, Rebecca Biddle, Sarah Wardell. Sons-in-law—Joseph Biddle and Samuel Wardell. Grandchildren—Elizabeth Biddle, Joseph and Elizabeth Wardell. Executor—son Joseph. Witnesses—David Branson, William Furlong and Judith Lamb. Proved March 5, 1732.
Lib. 3, p. 282.

1748, Jany. 21. Arrell (Erall), William, Junr., of Township of Deptford, Gloucester Co., yeoman. Int. Richard Arrell, of Philadelphia, Pa., Admr.; John Parks, of Gloucester Co., fellow bondsman.
Lib. 7, p. 45.

1748-9, Jany. 20. Inventory of personal estate (£369.13.1) includes cattle £47.16.0. Appraisers—John Sparks, John Wilkins.

1749, Nov. 10. Arvin, David (Irwen), of Township of Greenwich, Gloucester Co., yeoman; will of. Son, John. Daughter, Ruth Ward. Executor—Son John "Garvin." Witnesses—Robert Braman, John Bright, Wm. Weatherby. Proved 12 Feb., 1749.

1749, Feb. 12. Inventory of personal estate (£78.09.00), includes goods in hands of Ruth Ward, and rent due in hands of William Fisher. Appraisers—Robert Massett, William Weatherby, Junr.

1748, Apr. 23. Ashbrook, John, of Gloucester Township and Co., yeoman; will of. Wife, Mary, to have personal estate to bring up children and sons to trade when 14. Executors—Wife and brother-in-law, Daniel Hilman with full power to sell unto James Valentine of Gloucester Co., "labourer" a deed of conveyance for plantation (consideration (225), except the "burying place" of ½ acre. Executors to deduct what money the sd. Valentine paid to Commissioner of the Loan office. Witnesses—William Davis, William Smallwood, John Hampton. Proved 30 May, 1748. Lib. 5, p. 500.

1748, Apr. 29. Inventory (£359.14.3) includes plantation, £225. Appraisers—William Clark, William Davis.

1737, Apr. 7. Ashead, Amos, of Waterford, Gloucester Co., yeoman. Int. His widow, Cicely Ashead, Admx. Moses Ashead, yeoman, son of Amos, and John Kay, Esq., of same place, bondsmen. Witness—Joseph Rose. Lib. 4, p. 95.

1736-7, Mar. 1. Inventory of personal estate, £74.16.8. Appraisers—John Kay, Jon. Kaighin.

1747-8, Feb. 29. Ashead, John, of Township of Waterford, Gloucester Co., yeoman; will of. Eldest son, Amos, when 21, to have £100. Second son, Thomas, to have, at 21, the same. Daughter, Elizabeth, at 18 or marriage, to have £20. An expected child. "All my sons shall be put to learn some trade at the age of 14 years." Sole executrix—wife Mary. Witnesses—Thomas Middleton, Benjamin Holme, Hezk. Williams. Affirmed 21 March, 1747. Lib. 5, p. 410.

1747-8, Mar. 17. Inventory of personal estate (£151.13.6) includes horses, cattle and sheep, £50. Appraisers—Josiah Kay, Benjamin Holme.

1740-1, 11 mo. (Jany.), 7 da. Ashead, Moses, of Waterford Township, Gloucester Co. Brother, John, to have the "plantation I live on." Niece, Rachel Haines. Niece Hephsibah Haines. Mother-in-law (step-mother) Sissily Ashead. Mother-in-law's daughter, Mary Easly. Sister, Ann Haines. Sole executor—Brother-in-law, John Haines. Witnesses—William Foster, Joseph Qippett. Proved 7 April, 1741. Lib. 4, p. 270.

1740-1, Mar. 6. Inventory of personal estate, £104.7.0. Appraisers—John Burroughs, William Foster.

1736, August 19. Ashton, Elizabeth, wife of John Ashton of Upper Freehold township, Monmouth Co.; will of. Former husband, Thomas White, deceased, purchased of testatrix's sisters, Exercise and Elison, land bequeathed to them by "my father, Jacob Cole." Land disposed of by will of Thomas White. Son, Levi White, upland devised to testatrix by her father's will. Son-in-law, Isaac Hance. Will signed by testatrix and her husband, John Ashton. Witnesses—Jeremiah and Rebecca Stillwell and Robert Lawrence. Proved July 28, 1737. Lib. C, p. 172.

1731, July 19. Ashton, James, of Freehold, Monmouth Co. Bond of John Ashton, of Freehold, Esquire, as administrator of estate. Jeremiah Stillwell, of Shrewsbury, gentleman, fellow bondsman. Witnesses—Robert Lawrence and Lawrence Smyth. Lib. B, p. 227.

1743-4, Jan. 10. Ashton, John, of Upper Freehold; will of. Wife, Catherine, £20, in satisfaction of her dower. Daughter, Elizabeth. Proprietary rights to son-in-law, Jeremiah Stillwell. Daughter, Rebecca. Land near Thomas Taylor in Upper Freehold, and near Millstone brook, to be sold; proceeds to Elizabeth and Rachel Stevens, children of deceased daughter Rachel. If said grand children die, then to children of testator's daughters, Elizabeth and Rebecca. Daughter, Hannah, land in Middletown, "that was my deceased sister Mary's." Executors—son-in-law, Jeremiah Stillwell, and cousin Joseph Throckmorton. Witnesses—John Manners, James Ashton and Robert Lawrence. Proved June 1, 1744. Lib. D, p. 144.

1739, Aug. 21. Ashton, Mary, of Upper Freehold, spinster. Bond of Jeremiah Stillwell of same place, yeoman, as administrator of estate. Cornelius Van Horne, of same, yeoman, fellow bondsman. Witness, Rachel Harrison. Lib. C, p. 289.

1739, Sept. 29. Inventory of estate, £117.5.3, incl. silver tankard, 5 silver-spoons, gold rings, notes of Robert Imlay, David Stout, William Thorn, John Lawrence, Jr., William Wilkins, deceased, Evan Griffen and Isaac Stelle; made by Joseph Applin and Isaac Stelle.

1749-50, March 22. Asson, William, of Hanover, Burlington Co. Administration on the estate granted to widow, Hannah Asson; Jonathan Hough, of Springfield, fellow bondsman. Lib. 7, p. 30.

1749-50, Mar. 24. Inventory of personal estate, £69.11.0, made by John Croshair and Sam. Emley.

1750, Mar. 4. Account of Hannah Asson, widow, who has paid amounts to William Harrison, Francis Shinn, Benjamin Shreve, Joseph Shinn, Stephen Adams, James Shinn, William Budd, John Boyne, John Marshall, Peter Pintset, Joseph Wright, Ezekiel Wright, Hezekiah Jones, George Briggs, Joseph Bowker, Caleb Shreve, Richard Bowker, Thomas Sands, James Wilkinson, Isaac Ivins, William Davis.

1742, Aug. 20. Aten, John (see Aeten, John).

1743-4, Feb. 4. Aten, John, Jr., Raritan, Somerset Co., yeoman; will of. Wife, Jane, to have home-farm and personal estate during minority of oldest son John, who receives the Dutch Bible. Sons—John, Roelof and Thomas to have the lands equally, "all of which lands were willed to me by my father John Aten." Daughter, Catlyne. Executors—Roelof

Nevius, Thomas Aten and Fulkert Sebring. Witnesses—Hendrick Staats, Derck Sebring, John MacNeill. Proved 21 May, 1744. Lib. D, p. 141.

1744, May 29. Renunciation of Fulkert Sebring as executor. Witness, Nath'l Cooper.

1749, Sept. 25. Inventory of personal estate, £216. 6. 9; made by Derck Sebring, Roeleff Nevius, Thomas Aten and Hend'k Fisher.

1750, Aug. 20. Atkins, John, of Newtown, Gloucester Co., fuller. Int. Isaac Kay, yeoman, admr. Richard Matlack, yeoman, fellow-bondsman. All of said County. Witness—J. Scattergood.

Gloucester Wills, 449H.

1750, Aug. 16. Renunciation—"Haddonfield—I fully decline taking out a Lator of Administration upon the A State of John Adeing deceased. (Signed) John Beals."

1749, Dec. 26. Atkinson, John, of Trenton, Hunterdon Co., yeoman; will of. Wife, Martha, all estate to enable her to support children, "which now are most of them young." Wife executrix. Witnesses—David Dunbar, Christian Wilson and Joseph Yard. Proved March 28, 1750. (Executrix, Martha, a Quaker). Lib. 6, p. 330.

1749, Jan. 5. Inventory of personal estate, £36.4.0; made by John Jones, David Dunbar and Joseph Yard.

1751, July 10. Account of executrix, mentioning James Curry, Charles Axford, Catherine Williams ("for digging dec'd and son's grave,"), Messrs. Read and Furman, Joseph Paxton, William Cooke, Benjamin Shreve (in behalf of Preserve Brown), Dr. Cadwalader, Mary Okely (for rent), John Rikey and Joseph Rogers.

1746, Sept. 16. Atkinson, Michael, of Springfield, Burlington Co.; will of. Wife, Hope. Sons—Jonathan, Levei, Jobe and Amos, all under age. Daughters—Elizabeth, Marsey and Rachel. Expected child. Lands in New Hanover, bought of Bennet Bard and Thomas Budd. House built by Robert Gillam. Executors—wife, son Jonathan and Francis Shinn. Witnesses—Joseph Atkinson, John West. Proved Nov. 6, 1746.

Lib. 5, p. 303.

1746, Oct. 18. Inventory of personal estate, £425.9.3; made by Henry Cooper and John West.

1738, Jan. 7. Atkison, Thomas, of Northampton, Burlington Co., yeoman; will of. Wife, Sarah. Children—John, Thomas, Christian Willson, Jean Jones, Sarah Hares. Grand-children—Walker and Alse, children of my son Francis, late deceased. Real and personal estate. Wife sole executrix. Witnesses—Henry Reeves, Martha Shinn, Tho. Shinn. Proved Sept. 5, 1739. Lib. 4, p. 184.

1744, April 17. Atlee, William, of Trenton, Hunterdon Co., Esquire; will of. All estate to wife Jane, "willing her to bring up the four children God has blessed us with," viz., William Augustus, Samuel John, Amelia Jane and Joseph Edwin, "till they are of age." "Whereas I have reason to believe I have a daughter by a former wife now living in England, I desire my dear wife will send her a gold ring as a token of remembrance of me." Wife executrix, and friend Ralph Loftus to assist. Witnesses—Wm. Lindsay (Missionary), Caleb Ransted and James Rutherford. Proved May 7, 1744, by William Lyndsay, Clerk and James Rutherford. Lib. 5, p. 38.

1744, May 12. Inventory of estate, £347.7.10½, including goods in shop, cloth, hats, tobacco, cutlery, and general merchandise; silver hilted sword and belt, 600 lbs. tobacco, house and lot in Trenton, and 9½ acres bought of William Bell. Appraised by W. Morris, Jos. DeCow and Thomas Palmer.

1745, May 12. Account of Jane Atlee, Administratrix of estate, mentions, use of house for funeral at Philada.; Mr. Biddle; William Morris, Captain Atwood, Thomas Barnes, Francis Lewis of New York, Walter Hetherington, Mary Peace, John Jenkins, Francis Giffing, Joseph Price, Thomas Barns, George Davis, James Harrow, David Dunbar, servant Richard Sharson, house and lot sold Mrs. Ackey Lambert, James Rutherford.

1742, July 28. Attwood, Jacob, of "Maneuton," Salem Co., carpenter; will of. Wife, Christian. Brother, Abraham Attwood; his son, John Attwood; his sister (niece of testator) Susannah Lord (widow). Executors—William Hankook, Joseph Sharp, both of Salem County. Witnesses—Isaac Sharp, Jeremi. Wood, Cathrin Wood. Proved 23 Feb., 1744.

1744, Feb. 23. Letters testamentary issued to Isaac Sharp, one of executors named in the will. Lib. 5, p. 205.

1744, Jany. 10. Inventory, £255.16.7. Appraisers—William Burratt, William Nicholson.

1750, Sept. 3. Account. Payments to Ann Person, Thos. Thompson, Peter Peterson, John Smith, Edward Test, Jane Peterson, Charles Coneway, Lucas Peterson, Thos. Haine, Daniel Smith, Mary Hawken, Daniel Menhar, ——— Shuger, Jane Browne, Christian Atwood, Abraham Atwood.

1732, Jan. 26. Augur, Thomas, of Newark, Essex Co. Administraion on estate granted to widow Gertrie Augur. Lib. B, p. 358.

1748, May 16. Austen, Cornelius, of Cumberland Co. Int. Martha Austen, widow, administratrix. Fellow bondsmen, Jehiel Wheeler of Fairfield and Abraham Reeves of Hopewell, Cumberland Co. Witnesses—Elizabeth Cotting, Elias Cotting. Lib. 6, p. 18.

1748, May 16. Inventory of personal estate, £115.14.3. Appraisers—Abraham Reeves, Jehiel Wheeler.

1748, Oct. 19. Austen, Martha, of Cumberland Co. Int. Late Executrix of Cornelius Austen of Fairfield, County aforesaid. Administrators—Sarah Austen and Jehiel Wheeler. Fellow bondsmen—Abraham Reeves, Isaac Preston. Witnesses—Thomas Fryer, Hance Woolson. Lib. 6, p. 77.

1748, Oct. 8. Inventory of personal estate, £129.9.0. Appraisers—Abraham Reeves, Isaac Preston.

1736, Feb. 19. Austin, Mary, of Evesham, Burlington Co.; will of. Children—Amos, Martha, William, Jonathan, Francis, Sarah, Ann and Hannah. Real and personal estate. Executors—sons Amos and William. Witnesses—William Borton, Sam'll Atkinson, Ruth Atkinson. Proved Dec. 23, 1739. Lib. 4, p. 214.

1739, 1st d., 8th mo. Inventory of personal estate, £178.9; made by Caleb Haines and William Sharp.

1747, Sept. 11. Avis, Bartholomew, of Evesham, Burlington Co., sawyer. Administration granted to Francis Dudley of same, yeoman. Joseph Hollinshead, Esq., of Burlington, fellow bondsman. Lib. 5, p. 435.

1747, Sept. 14. Inventory of personal estate, £9.15.10; made by Thomas Hackney and Daniel Parker.

1734, Aug. 19. Axtell, Daniell, Esq., of Greville Street, in the Parish of St. Andrews, Holborn, Middlesex Co., England; will of. Sons —Daniel, William and Joseph. Names Phillis Ellis and her daughter of the Island of Jamaica. Real estate in New York, New Jersey and Island of Jamaica. Executors—Wife Mary, and Andrew Johnson of Amboy. Witnesses—Elizabeth Handley, Rob't Handley, Jno. Greenhill, of Inner Temple, London, Gent. Proved Oct. 8, 1735.

1736, May 28. Copy of above will sent from London. Lib. C, p. 95.

1749, Aug. 29. Axtell, Thankful, of Mendom Township, Morris Co., widow; will of. Children—Ebenezer, deceased son Thomas, Thankful Brigs and Rebecca Cook; grandchildren—Daniel, son of Thomas and Hannah, his wife, their expected child, and Ichabod Edmester. Executor—Son Ebenezer. Witnesses—William Axtell, Henry Axtell and Brice Riky. Proved Sept. 28, 1749. Lib. E, p. 334.

1749, Nov. 21. Axtell, William, of Mendom, Morris Co., "cord winer;" will of. Wife, Hannah, to have whole estate until the children—Henry, William, Benjamin, Silas and Johanna Axtell—will be of age. Executors and trustees—Wife, brother Henry Axtell, Elihu Baldwin. Witnesses—Nathan Linkon, William Lenard, Joseph Dod. Proved 30 May, 1750. Lib. E, p. 407.

1750, May 13. Renunciation of Hannah Axtell, Executrix named in will. Witnesses—Joseph Dod, William Lenard.

1743, June 1. Ayres, David, of Woodbridge, Middlesex Co., yeoman; will of. "In my 35th year." Sons—Martin and Enoch Ayres, both under age. Father and mother—Joseph and Phebe Ayres. Sister—Dilly Potter. Brothers—Daniel and Enoch Ayres. Real and personal estate. Executors—brother Daniel and friends Gershom Martin and William Mackdaniel, all of Woodbridge. Witnesses—Samuel Martin, Mulford Martin, Nugient Kelly. Proved July 28, 1743. Lib. D, p. 73.

1743, July 25. Inventory of personal estate, £86.12.1, made by William Sharp of Woodbridge, and Alexander Thomson of Piscataway.

1744, Sept. 25. Ayers, Joseph, of Woodbridge and Matuchen, Middlesex Co., yeoman. Inventory of personal estate, £144.19.11; made by David Faurot and Alexander Thomson.

1744, Oct. 1. Administration on estate granted to Elizabeth Ayers, the widow, and Joseph Ayers, the eldest son. Sealed by Jacob Ayers, bondsman, in the presence of John Smyth. Lib. D, p. 180.

1745, Sept. 12. Ayers, Obidiah, of Baskingridge, Somerset Co., guardian of Daniel Allword, a minor of 18 years. Lib. D, p. 334.

1736, April 13. Ayers, Robert, of Salem Co., yeoman. Bond of Sarah Ayers, of Salem Co., administratrix of the estate. Inventory [61.6.6. Lib. 4, p. 57.

1740, Sept. 25. Ayers, Robert, of Woodbridge, Middlesex Co., yeoman; will of "being in the 35th year of my age." Sons—Frazy and Robert, both under age. Three daughters, no names given. Expected

child. Real and personal estate. Salt meadow bought of uncle, John Ayers, deceased. Executors—wife Hummus, brother Obadiah Ayers and friend Jonathan Dennis, all of Woodbridge. Witnesses—John Roy, Joseph Martin, Eliakim Martin. Proved June 4, 1741.
Lib. C, p. 413.

1732, April 25. Ayers, Thomas, of Woodbridge, Middlesex Co., yeoman; will of. Children—Abraham, Sarah, Peter, Mary, Levie, and Rachel, all under 17 years of age. 60 acres of land between lands of John Campbel and John Wilkison. Executors—wife Mary, and brothers John and Obediah Ayers. Witnesses—Elinor Morgan, Jonathan Shepherd, Jno. Sarjant. Proved June 12, 1732. Lib. B, p. 287.

1732, June 12. Inventory of personal estate (£205.2.9) incl. debts due from Wm. Edenfield, Hendrick Breese and John Bell; made by Moses Rolfe and Jno. Sarjant.

1740, Dec. 21. Ayers, John, of Cohansey, Salem Co.; will of. Wife Secily. Children—Samuel, John, Mary, Steven. Executor—Joseph Reve. Witnesses—Seeth Bowen, William Jones, Temprance Ayars. Proved April 24, 1741. Lib. 4, p. 283.

1744, Nov. 5. Ayres, Isaac, of Salem County, weaver. Int. Admr., Nathaniel Dominy, Junr., ("nearest of kin and principal creditor") of Suffolk County, New York, yeoman. Bondsman—Jonathan Holmes, of Cohansey, Salem County, farmer. Witnesses—Burton Penton, Chas. O'Neill. Lib. 5, p. 56.

1744, Oct. 22. Renunciation: "Whereas Isaac Ayres, formerly of Easthampton, Suffolk County, New York, weaver, lately dyed at Cohansey, Salem County, New Jersey, intestate, having no wife, so that the administration of his goods belongs to his nearest of kin, but we Benjamin Erys, Junior, William Erys, Clemens Erys and Elizabeth Domony, brothers and sisters of said deceased, all of Easthampton, renounce the administration of said estate in favor of Nathaniel Domony, Junior of Easthampton, he being the husband of one of the sisters of the said deceased. Witnesses—David Mulford, John Davis."

1744, Nov. 8. Inventory, £46.3.11. Appraisers—Samuel Miller, John Miller.

1750, Dec. 4. Ayres, Moses. Inventory of "Captain Moses Ayres," late of Baskingridge, Somerset Co. (£376.17.11), including sword, £0.17.6, powder horns and shot bags, £2.6.2; made by John Roy, Levi Lewis.

1750, Dec. 19. Renunciation of Jane, widow of Moses Ayres, in favor of her son-in-law (step-son) Nathaniel Ayres, eldest son and heir of Moses Ayres.

1750, Dec. 19. Administration on estate granted to Nathaniel Ayres. Fellow bondsmen—Daniel Morris, Benjamin Lewis. Lib. E, p. 469.

1733, Dec. 14. Bacon, Abel, of Bacon's Neck, Cohansie, Salem Co., yeoman; will of. Wife, Mercy, to have during life plantation on Bacon's Neck, "being ½ of my father's (the late William Bacon's) plantation." Son, William Bacon, to have same at her death, "also the other moyety of my said late father's plantation now in the possession of my mother-in-law, Mary Bacon, devised to her by my said father during her life. My messuage and 3 acres in the town of Greenwich, Salem County, in the occupation of John Lovering, cordwainer, I devise to my daughter Sarah Bacon, at marriage or at the age of 21 years." Gifts to Cousin Benjamin Bacon. Executors —Wife, and my kinsman Benjamin Bacon. Witnesses—Jere. Bacon, John Ware, John Bacon (Quaker). Affirmed 10 January, 1733.

1733, Jany. 10. Letters testamentary granted to Benjamin Bacon, the surviving executor therein named. Lib. 3, p. 395.

1733, Dec. 26. Inventory, £156.9.6. Appraisers—Josiah Fithian, James Dixson.

1731, Aug. 1. Bacon, Jeremiah, (of Salem Co., but place not given); will of. Daughter, Hannah, to have house and lot in Greenwich, Salem County. Son, Nathaniel; wife; daughter, Lettisha. Executor—brother-in-law, Richard Wood. Witnesses—James Axford, Ann Grant, Jno. Goodwin. Proved 9 Aug., 1731.

1732, May 27. Letters Testamentary granted to Richard Wood, the executor therein. Lib. 3, p. 195.

1731, Aug. 6. Inventory (£235.0.1) of Jeremiah Bacon, sadler of Salem; includes saddles at Cohansey. Appraisers—Richard Smith, Jno. Goodwin.

1747-8, Jany. 11. Bacon, Jeremiah, of Salem Co. Inventory, £14.6.0. Appraisers—Howell Powell, John Bacon (Quaker). Salem Wills, 390A.

1747, Jany. —. Account. Cash paid Aaron Pagitt, Hanna Bacon, Thomas Walling, John Bacon, Howell Powell, Alexander Smith, Richard Wood, Ebenezer Miller, (Attr. to James Goold).

1740, Feb. 6. Bacon, Samuel, of Salem Co., yeoman. Int. Admx., Hannah Bacon. Bondsman, Philip Dennis. Both of said County. Witnesses—Uriah Bacon, Danl. Mestayer.

1740-41, 12 mo., 16 da. Inventory (£21.3.6.) includes "one Taylor's goos," etc. Appraisers—John Bacon, Philip Dennis. Lib. 4, p. 267.

1747, Jany. 25. Bacon, Samuel, Sr., of Salem Co., yeoman. Int. Admr., Jeremiah Bacon. Bondsman, John Bacon. Both of Cohansey. Witness—Jno. Andrews. Lib. 5, p. 424.

1743-4, Jan. 19. Baest, Henry, of Amwell, Hunterdon Co., yeoman: will of. Wife, Mary. Son, Johanes. Elizabeth Reace, to have a heifer bought of Philip Ringo. Sons, Godferree and Henry, minors. Son, Joseph. Daughter, Ann Hoppay, and her husband, Tunes Hoppay. Son, Johannes, to have plantation in Amwell and land bought of Peter Overvelt. Executors—sons Johanes and Joseph. Witnesses—Godfree Petters, Garr'd Williamson and Philip Ringo. Proved February 20, 1743-4. Lib. 5, p. 19.

1750, Aug. 10. Bailey, Robert, of Lebanon Township, Hunterdon Co., yeoman; inventory of estate, £217.14.2, including 180 acres of land; made by Isaiah Young and Patrick Brown.

1750, Aug. 26. Bond of Annable Bailey, of Lebanon Township, widow, as administratrix of her said husband's estate. James Woods and John Forster, of Lebanon, sureties. Hunterdon Wills, 275 J.

1732, Feb. 12. Bainbridge, John, of Maidenhead, Hunterdon Co., gentlemen; will of. Directs that tomb be erected over his grave "and on it be put the day and year of my death and my age, which was seventy-four years the second day of November last," and also a tomb over wife's grave, who died March 25, 1731, in her 67th year. Son, Edmund. Daughter Elizabeth's eldest son, commonly called John Yard, to be taught to read, write, etc. Daughters—Mary, Rebeckah and Elizabeth. Grandson, Edmund Bainbridge, a minor. Son, John, to have residue of estate, including one-sixteenth part of a Proprietary Right in West Jersey. Executors—kinsman Theophilus Phillips, and son John Bainbridge. Witnesses—Stephen Jones, William Phillips and Joseph Phillips. Proved March 1, 1732. Lib. 3, p. 261.

1732-3, February 24. Inventory of estate, £367.12.6, including bond in hands of Robert Lawrence; made by Joshua and John Anderson.

1747-8, Feb. 5. Baird, John, of Middlesex Co.; will of. Eldest son, William Baird; other children mentioned but not by name. Executors—wife, Avis Baird, brothers, Andrew and Zebulon Baird and Peter Boune. Witnesses—James Molicans, Samuel Barclay, Ann Smith. Proved July 5, 1749. Lib. E, p. 310.

1747, 8 mo. (Oct.), 18 da. Baits, Jonathan, of Township and County of Gloucester, yeoman; will of. "Mother to have my plantation and land during life." Three sisters—Abigail Greenaway, Martha Ward and Mary Baits. Executors—mother and brother, George Flanagin. Witnesses—Thomas Cheeseman, Richard Cheeseman, Isac. Jenings. Proved 9 Nov. 1747.

1747, Nov. 9. Letters testamentary granted to Elizabeth Baits, the executrix named in the will. Lib. 5, p. 485.

1747, Oct. 31. Inventory, £104.10.0. Appraisers—John Hillman, Thomas Cheeseman.

1755, June 16. Account of Elizabeth Bates, executrix, shows payments to Hanah Lippincott, Jonathan Ellis, William Clarke, Francis McMurray, Mary Morgan, John Matlack, Jr., Anthony Nichols, Samuel Somers, Robert Worrell, Elizabeth Robert, Thos. Redman, Wm. Griscombe, John Dilkes, Jacob Clement, Abram Inheap, Thos. Newell, Wm. Alberson, Josiah Alberson, John Maxwell, John Hunchman, Ladd & Scattergood, James Henchman, William Cooper, John Hewston, Susannah Williams, John Inheap, Benjamin Collins, Tho. Webster, John Collins, Jr., John Thorne, Joseph Tomlinson, Thos. Atmore, Amy Collins, Ruth Adams, George Wilson, William Hilman, William Cheasman, Eliz. Hammitt, John Gile, James Tow, Robert Rollinson, Isaac Hammett, Eliz. Bates; amounting to £122.4.10.

1730, April 9. Baker, Henry, Sen'r, of Elizabeth Town, Essex Co., tanner; will of. Children—Henry, Nicolaus, Deborah, Joanna, Susannah, Margaret, Elizabeth, Sarah, Lydia and Hannah. 50 acres joining lands of George Jewel, Benjamin Lyon and Benjamin Bond; also 6 acres joining meadow of Richard Baker, deceased. Tools for carrying on trade of shoemaker or cordwainer. Grandchildren—Lawrence and Susanna Baker, children of son Jacob deceased. Executors—wife Lydia and son Henry. Witnesses—Jonathan Dickinson, Ephraim Price, Peter Hagawout. Proved April 7, 1735. Lib. C, p. 117.

1737, Nov. 28. Baker, Lawrence, of Richmond Co., province of New York. Bond of John Brashen, of New York City, as administrator; Henry Berry, fellow bondsman. Witness—Lawrence Smyth.
Middlesex Wills, Lib. C, p. 181.

1730, April 6. Baker, Timothy, of Maidenhead, Hunterdon Co.; will of. Wife, Susannah. Eldest son, Samuel; other sons—Mathis, Timothy and Thomas. Daughters—Mary, Grace Colman and Ruth. Home plantation to son Timothy. Executors—John Smith and Jasper Smith. Witnesses—David Cowell, Samuel Mead and Hannah Carter. Proved June 9, 1747. Lib. 5, p. 364.

1732-3, Feb. 9. Baldwin, Benjamin and Elizabeth, of Newark, Essex Co. Inventory of personal estate, £98.15.09; made by John Cooper and John Morris.

1732, Feb. 17. Administration granted to Moses Ball and David Young; Eliphalet Johnson, fellow bondsman. Lib. B, p. 383.

1738, Dec. 6. Baldwin (Balding), Elnathan, of Hopewell, Hunterdon Co., yeoman; will of. Wife, Kezia. Daughter, Ruth Burt. Son, Stephen, to have plantation of 100 acres, he paying legacies to: Moses, Thomas, Joseph and Elnathan Baldwin. Plantation bought of Caleb Kerman to be sold and proceeds to testator's five youngest sons. Witnesses—Nathaniel Moore, Enoch Armitage and Edward Hart. Proved May 9, 1739. Lib. 4, p. 175.

1748, Nov. 10. Baldwin, Isaac, of Newark, Essex Co., cooper. Bond of Zachariah Baldwin, of Hanover, Morris Co., as administrator. Obadiah Bruen and Timothy Johnson, of Newark, fellow bondsmen. Lib. E, p. 220.

1748, Nov. 10. Account. Payments to Thomas Stiles, Samuel Baldwin, Zopher Beach, and Doctor Turner; "to Jacob Baldwin for five eighth parts of Isaac Baldwin's estate, namely, Jacob Baldwin, and by a power of attorney from John Mitchel and my sister Sarah Mitchel his wife, Mary Baldwin and Patience Baldwin my sisters, and Matthew Baldwin my brother, to Abraham and Israel Baldwin, and to myself, one of the brethren," Israel Lyon, David Shipman, Nathaniel Camp, Benjamin Winchill.

1748-9, Feb. 10. Inventory of personal estate, £123.02.08; made by John Robards and David Shipman.

1732-3, Jan. 28. Baldwin (Balding), John, of New Brunswick, Middlesex Co. Inventory of personal estate £83.11.6.; made by Tho. Harmar, Jacob Onsel.

1732, Aug. 6. Bond of Hannah Baldwin, "relick," as administratrix. Peter Blanchard, of Rocky Hill, Somerset Co., fellow bondsman. Lib. B, p. 294.

1732, Dec. 18. Baldwin, John, Jun'r, of Newark, Essex Co., yeoman; will of. Children—Silvanus, Ebeneazer, Jonas, Moses and Hannah Baldwin, all under age. Real and personal estate. Executors—wife Lydia and Daniel Baldwin, Junr., of Newark, yeoman. Witnesses—David Howell, Moses Ball, J. Style. Proved Jan. 31, 1732-3.

1732-3, Jan. 31. Lydia Baldwin and Daniel Harrison qualify as executors. Lib. B, p. 371.

1736-7, Jan. 17. Baldwin, Lidea, of Newark, Essex Co. Nuncupative will of widow of John Baldwin, who made his will dated Dec. 18, 1732, leaving as legatees wife Lidea, and daughter Hannah Baldwin. Said Lidea in presence of Moses Harrison, Zopher Beech and Lidea Peck, all being of lawful age, on the 11th day of January bequeathed to her only daughter, the aforesaid Hannah, £60. The residue to be divided among all her children. Witnesses—Moses Harrison, Zopher Beech, Lidea Peck.

1736, Feb. 21. Administration granted to Moses Ball, the uncle, and Daniel Harrison, the brother. Lib. C, p. 151.

1736-7, March 7. Inventory of personal estate, £258.08.11; made by Sam'll Farrand and Joseph Harrison.

1750, Aug. 6. Baldwin, Nathaniel, of Newark, Essex Co.; will of. Wife, Ester. Sons—Elijah, Robert, Joseph and Jonathan. Land joining lands of Sam'll Johnson, David Ogden and Nehemiah Crane, near the water hole; meadow bought of Thomas Longworth; land in the neck joining lands of Stephen Baldwin, Nathaniel Johnson, Obadiah Brown, Samuel Penington and David Ogden. Daughters—Eunice Beach and Jane Clisby. Land bought of Caleb Baldwin and his brother joining lands of Stephen Baldwin. To the Rev. Mr. Aaron Burr, £20. Executors—son Elijah and Joseph Beach. Witnesses—Wm. Turner, Silvanus Baldwin, Silas Baldwin. Proved Nov. 8, 1750. Lib. E, p. 504.

1748, July 25. Ball, Caleb, of Hanover, Morris Co., gentleman; will of. Wife, Sarah. Sons—Isaiah (to have 100 acres bought of Peter Imlay); Joshua (the land he lives on); Caleb (the home-place land on the south side of Forge Pond, and 26 acres adjoining W. land bought of Peter Imlay), and above named sons to have the forge, saw-mill and stream equally; Ezekiel (80 odd acres on both sides of "Wepemy River" where the old saw-mill stood, as appears by deed of Joseph Lindsley); and Mathew. Daughters—Abigail Johnson, Eliner, Jane Perry, Mary Bates, Sarah, Lydia, Ann, Deborah and Keziah Kitchel, deceased (had heirs). Executors—Wife Sarah and sons Isaiah, Joshua and Caleb. Witnesses—David Kitchel, Timothy Tuttle, Elijah Gillett. Proved 29 Aug. 1748. Lib. 6, p. 34.

1733, April 24. Ball, Joseph, of Essex Co.; will of. Wife Elizabeth, to have 8 acres at Wheeler's point, joining lands of Joseph Canfield and David Person. Children—Daniel, Joseph, Samuel, Isaac, Jonathan, Hannah Ball and Rebecca Baldwin. 50 acres of land upon Third River; lands joining lands of John Moriss, Thomas Ball, Moses Ball, Thomas Alling and Daniel Harrison; also land on Maple Island Creek. Executors—brother Moses Ball and son Daniel Ball. Witnesses—Daniel Sergeant, Jonathan Sergeant, David Ogden, Jun'r. Proved May 14, 1733. Lib. B, p. 427.

1747, Nov. 17. Ball, Mary, of Newark, Essex Co., widow; will of. Cousin—Mary, wife of Christopher Seely. Sisters—Abigail Hencock, Rachel Samson, Sarah Tichener, Hannah Shingilton, and Elizabeth Day. Executor—Stephen Baldwin. Witnesses—John Ogden, Jon'n Sergeant. Proved Jan. 13, 1747-8. Lib. E, p. 117.

1747, March 28. Ball, Moses, of Newark, Essex Co.; will of. Cousins Caleb Ball, John Ball, Joseph Peck, Timothy Peck, Sarah Peck, Marcy Dowd, and her sister Elizabeth, and Ruth Seward. Children of brother Joseph Ball, deceased, Isaac only excepted, to have land bought of Nathaniel Bowers. Children of brother Thomas Ball (one named Amos). Cousins—Moses Harrison, Daniel Harrison and Moses Baldwin. Land on the cove bought of John Gardner. Children of brothers Caleb, Joseph, and Thomas Ball, and children of sisters Abigail Harrison and Lidea Peck. Remainder of real estate to Samuel Alling, John Ogden, Jun'r and Stephen Baldwin in trust for the Presbyterian Society of Newark for the support of the ministers. Executors—wife Mary and Stephen Baldwin. Witnesses—James Nuttman, John Stratten, Jon'n Sergeant. Proved May 8, 1747. Lib. E, p. 36.

1747, May 14. Inventory of personal estate, £357.10.00; made by Jonathan Sergeant and Nathaniel Johnson.

1748-9, March 3. Account of executor, Stephen Baldwin of Newark, showing payments to Mr. Grant (for head stone) Mary Ball, Mary Sealy, Doctor Farrand, arbitration with Henry Lyon, John Crane, Isaac Ogden, Abigail Hencock, John Ogden Sen'r, Joseph Riggs, Elizabeth Brewin, Obadiah Brewin, John Alling, Sam'll Huntington, Samuel Johnson, Eli'h Baldwin, Eli'h Crane, Sam'll Plum, Daniel Harrison, Moses Harrison, John Ogden, Sam'll Alling, Mr. Woodruff, Mr. Cocker, David Ward, Doct'r Preckhet, John Dreen, Sam'll Baldwin, Eben'r Baldwin, Aaron Baldwin, Doct'r Turner, David Ball, Joseph Peck, John Johnson, Capt. Johnson, Jonas Baldwin, Elikim Seward, Jonathan Serjeant, Nath'll Bawldwin, John Ball, Daniel Harrison, Sarah Peck, Ruth Seward, Timothy Peck, Mercy Doud, Elizabeth Estel, Balls and Harrison legacies; lands sold to Sam'll Johnson, Sam'll Ball, John Crane, James Nicholson. Articles sold at vendue to John Johnson, Eleazer Brewin, Nathaniel Anderson, Ezekiel Ball, Mr. Burr, Robert Crane, Henry Martin, Job Brown, Jonathan Ward; bonds of Doct'r Turner, Joseph Tichener, David Day, ——— Carter, ——— Vreelandt, John Day, Samuel Parkhurst, Samuel Dalglish, Anderson and Crane, John Gard, Ben'j Perry, Timothy Baldwin and Jonathan Pierson.

1742-3, March 19. Ball, Thomas, of Newark, Essex Co., blacksmith; will of. Children—Timothy, Aaron, Nathaniel, David, Ezekiel, Jonas, Thomas, Amos, Moses, Apphia, wife of Simon Searing, Mary and Rachel Ball, the last two at 18 years. Real and personal estate. Executors—wife Sarah and son Timothy. Witnesses—Nathaniel Bonnell, Jun'r, Nathan Baldwin, Benj'n Bonnel. Proved Nov. 29, 1744. Lib. D, p. 197.

1744, Nov. 14. Inventory of personal estate, £378.10.8; made by Stephen Browne, Jno. Osborn, Isaac Crane.

1739, Aug. 14. Ballenger, Thomas, of Evesham, Burlington Co., yeoman. Letters of administration to Elizabeth Ballenger; Joshua Ballenger, fellow bondsman; both of Evesham. Lib. 4, p. 171.

1739, Aug. 14. Inventory of personal estate, £417.10.4; made by Thomas Evins and William Foster.

1747, Feb. 12. Ballinger, Amariah, of Gloucester Co.; will of. Wife and son, Isaac, to have upper part of plantation beginning on Steal's line to "line between me and my cousin, Amariah Ballenger." Daughters—Sarah, Margret and Elizabeth, all under 18. Son Isaac, when 21, to have plantation in Township of Evesham, Burlington Co. Executors—Joshua Ballinger and Gabriel Davis. Witnesses—Joseph Ballenger, John Aderly, Thomas Essary. Proved 8 Nov., 1748. Lib. 6, p. 252.

1748, Oct. 31. Inventory, at "Township of Debtford," £668.18.6.

1753, May 25. Account of Joshua Ballinger and Gabriel Davis, Executors of Amariah Ballinger. Moneys paid to Levi Peirce, John Evans, John McColloch, John Ladd, Jane Sparks, Henry Treadaway, John Stiles, Neal McNeil, Joseph Goldy, Joseph Scattergood, Isaac Ballinger, Richard Cheesman, John Marshall, John Blackwood, Habakkuk Warder, John Peirce, John Dilkes, John Snowden, Amos Haines, David Roe, Amariah Ballinger, Henry Wood, Thomas Sparks, John Sedden, Samuel Dukemaneer, Richard Wistar, Thomas Redman, Henry Elwes, Nathaniel Delap, Hannah David, Matthias Aspden, Henry Sparks, Eliz. Ballinger, Henry Ballinger, Rebecca Edgell.

1727, March 8. Ballinger, Henry, of Evesham, Burlington Co.; will of. Children—Mary Rethmel, Elizabeth Willard, Esther Bartlett, Rebecca

Hannah, Ruth, Thomas, Amariah, Henry, Josiah and Joseph. Real and personal estate. Executor—son Amariah. Witnesses—Jonathan Eldridge, William Hollinshead, Jacob Heulings, Justice. Proved April 10, 1733.
Lib. 3, p. 285.

1733, March 27. Inventory of personal estate, £30; made by Jonathan Eldridge and Andrew Conarrow.

1739, Nov. 29. Balm, John, of Elizabeth Town and Rahway, in Essex Co. Bond of St. George Talbot, of New York, as administrator, being principal creditor; William Thompson, cordwainer, and John Thompson, innkeeper, fellow bondsmen, both of Perth Amboy. Land in Raway mortgaged to Rev. William Veasey of New York for £264.11.10; assignment of same made to St. George Talbot at his request. Lib. C, p. 298.

1739, July 21. Inventory at "Raway" of personal estate, £1773.17.06½, incl. a picture of the deceased at length, a picture when a boy, and several others; a "schreen" of five leaves claimed by Mr. Talbot, a negro wench and child, a German indentured servant named John Mulmilhicy; made by Moses Rolfe, John Craig, Eze. Bloomfield.

1739, July 23. Second inventory of £133.09.05, incl., bonds of Joseph Bird, Ben. Gray, Sam. Bonnel, Joseph Alton, Sam. Fraze, Job Wright, Noah Bishop, Edw'd Barber, Rich'd Lambert, James Jackson, Joseph Bun, widow Rickets; notes of Eliphalet Fraze, Tho. Gin, Richard Whitehead, Sam. Oliver, Job Prance, Ric'd Taylor, Wm. Winans, John Howel, Jacob Thorn, Joseph Haynes, David Stewart, Jonas Greenway, Sam. Jacques; book debts of Richard Jones, Rubien Bird, Jonathan Winans, Cornelius Hart, Tho. Bloomfield, John Marsh, Widow Musrow, Lewis Winans, George Marshall, E. Bloomfield, Sam. Cole, John Stephens, Wm. Woodruff, Petter Noe, Dan. Lane, Ben. Eisey, Joseph Woodruff, Jno. Radly, David Steward, Tho. Bunes, Sam. Fraize, James Fraize, Patrick Mickmaners, Benj. Kelsey, Tho. Jeffers, Wm. Niblit, Johanes ———, Wm. Danoldson, Jonathan Marsh, Jacob Thorn, Sam. Farren, John King, John Love, Sam. Brant, James Marshall, Ric'd Clark, Alex. Blak, Job Bird, Nat. Hough, Joseph Spencer, Sam. Moore, David Oliver, Tho. Nicholson, Effrom Terrel Sen'r, Ric'd Hall, Sam. Cole, Joseph Alton, John Winans, Daniel Terrel, Wm. Marshall, Petter Simons; made by Rev. Edward Vaughn, George Encott, Andrew Joline.

———, ———, —. Account of St. George Talbot, administrator. Payments to Mr. Alexander, Mr. Pintard, Henry Gartwright, Mr. William Chetwood, James Marshall, Eliphalet Frase, John Stevens, Stephen Borrow, Jno. Wright, Abram Clarke, Mr. Kennedy, Mrs. Rockets, Mr. Moore and John Hicks in the Sup. Court, Mr. Nichols, post master of New York, Effey Bradley, Thomas Clarke, Esq., alderman, Samuel Bonnel, Jeffery Jones, Mary Ricketts, David Stuart, Mr. Vease.

1739, May 26. Banta, Jacob Hendrickse, of Hackensack, Bergen Co., yeoman, will of. Wife, Cornelia. Real and personal estate in Bergen Co. Son, Hendrick. Land at New Hempstead for £30. Witnesses—Derrick Blinkerhoff, Elizabeth Blinkerhoff, Robert Livesey. Proved 25 Nov. 1748. Lib. E, p. 221.

1732, Jan. 25. Banta, Wiert, of Hackinsack, Bergen Co., weaver; will of. Wife, Marie, Executrix. Children, Wiert (eldest son), David, Hendrick, Jacob (youngest son), Rachel and Ledia. Brother, Hendrick Banta and brother-in-law John Zabowrisky, both of Hackinsack, "tutors and administrators of all my minorene children as also executors and assistants of my said wife;" youngest child not 13. Land and tenements on the Hackinsack (where I live) and land on the "great swamp;" meadows on the west side of Hackinsack River. Witnesses—David Demorest, Sen., Joost Vredenburgh, Johannis Bougart, Robert Livesey, Jacob Banta. Proved 16 June, 1733. Lib. B, p. 441.

1740, Dec. 13. Barber, Samuel (of Pilesgrove), Salem Co., yeoman. Int. Admr., Daniel Barber. Bondsman, Eliakim Carle, yeoman. Both of said County. Witness—Elizabeth Jones. Lib. 4, p. 262.

1740, Dec. 15. Inventory, £24.0.11. Appraisers—Benjamin Duvall, Hugh Moore.

1741, June 1. Account by Daniel Barber. Moneys paid to David Garrison, Chas. O Neil, Aquilla Barber, Dr. Vanlecre, Zacheus Dunn, Benjamin Bispham, Roger Huckings, Abraham Barber, George Miller, Jeremiah Wood, and "counsel fee to John Coxe, Esq., to defend an action brot. agst. this accomptant at Salem by Joseph Hughs."

1744, July 16. Barckalow, Derrick, of Freehold, Monmouth Co., yeoman; will of. Wife, Jane. Children—William, Cornelius, Daniel, Aeltie, Weycoff, Helena, Jane and Mary. (Last three daughters evidently unmarried). Granddaughters—Elizabeth and Jane Suydam. Executors—sons William, Cornelius and Daniel. Witnesses—Tunis Denis, Gisbart Van Mater, William Wikoff and Jno. Henderson. Proved August 16, 1744. Lib. D, p. 170.

1744, August 14. Inventory of estate, £199.17.0; made by Tunis Denis, Gisbart Van Mater and William Wikoff.

1731, Dec. 29. Barclay, John, of Perth Amboy, Middlesex Co. John Barclay, the son, relinquishes right to administer estate in favor of William Bradford.

1731-2, Jan. 1. Bond of William Bradford, of New York, stationer and principal creditor, as administrator; Andrew Hay, of Perth Amboy, fellow bondsman. Lib. B, p. 240.

1731-2, Jan. 3. Inventory of personal estate, £275.7.3, incl. accounts due estate from Robert King, Esq., John Kinsey, Jun'r., Fenwick Lyell, Daniel Grandine, Robert Lawrence, Philip Kearny, George Emot, Wm. Jamison, Coll. Parker, Benjamin Price, Lawrence Smith, Evan Drummond, Thomas Gordon, dec'd, George Willocks, dec'd; bond of William Young; made by John Mathie and Harman Stout.

1744, Nov. 14. Barcleson, John, of Salem County. Int. Admr., Andrew A. Barcleson, of Penns Neck, Salem County, yeoman. Bondsmen—William Barcleson, Samuel Whitehorne, both of said County. Witnesses—John Eaton, Wm. Pennock (?) Lib. 5, p. 90.

1743, April 9. Inventory, £49.1.0 includes Swedish books, £0.10.0. Appraisers—John Eaton, Joseph Hawkes.

1732, Oct. 9. Bard, Peter, of Burlington Co.; will of. "At the first opportunity for London, a letter shall be sent to Mr. John Monteaud, who will give information as to whether my father, Benoist Bard, be living, and, if so, £50 is to be remitted to him in France." Children—Benoist, Peter, Samuel, John, William, Mary and Rebecca. Real and personal estate. Wife, Dinah, sole executrix. Witnesses—Edmund Cowgill, Jun., Edward Shippen. Proved Aug. 16, 1734. Lib. 3, p. 427.

1734, Nov. 11. Barker, Francis, of Northampton, Burlington Co., founder. Letters of administration to Joshua Briggs; John Doe and Richard Roe, fellow bondsmen; all of Northampton.

Burlington Wills, 2663C.

1749, Aug. 18. Barker, John, of Salem County. Int. Admrs., Ester Barker and William Barker, both of said County. Witnesses—John Stewart, Nich. Gibbon. Lib. 7, p. 36.

1743, 24th day, 7th mo. (Sept.) Barker, Joshua, of city and Co. of Burlington, saddler; will of. Wife, Martha. Children—Caleb, John, Elizabeth and Abigail, all under age. Land on High Street, adjoining Caleb Raper and widow Powlgreen. Executors—brother Caleb and Joshua Raper. Witnesses—Jonathan Lovett, William Sorsby, Isa. DeCow. Proved Nov. 1, 1745. Lib. 5, p. 185.

1734, July 29. Barker, Robert, of Burlington Co.; will of. Mentions Elizabeth Ann, daughter of Edward and Katherine Peirce, of Burlington. "£30 to be expended for my burial." Executor—cousin Ralph Barker, who is also named residuary legatee. Witnesses—Tho's. Shaw, Thomas Wetherill, Isa. DeCow. Proved May 10, 1736. Lib. 4, p. 60.

1749, Sept. 7. Barkley, James, of Hunterdon Co., will of. Wife, Jenut. Daughter, Agnis. Executors—John Kelly, John Todd and Joseph Hair. Witnesses—Daniel Oliver and John Palmer. Proved February 8, 1749-50. Lib. 6, p. 338.

1739, Aug. 25. Barnes, Thomas, of Trenton, Hunterdon Co., yeoman; will of. Wife, Elizabeth. Son, Thomas, to have one-half of lot and a house formerly belonging to Jeptha Smith in Trenton. Son, John, other half of lot and stable, and one-half of shalop called the "Elizabeth." Daughters—Mary and Rachel. Wife, executrix. Witnesses—Wm. Atlee, John Allen, Jr., and Daniel Hendry. Proved April 9, 1740. Lib. 4, p. 227.

1733, April 9. Barratt, Thomas, of Mannington Township, Salem Co., yeoman; will of. Wife, Elizabeth, sole executrix and to have all of the moveable estate for the bringing up of my children and the use of the plantation where I live until my son Thomas Barrett will be 21." Then he to pay his sisters, Rachel and Elizabeth, (at 18 or marriage) £20 each. In case of death of son Thomas in non-age, plantation to descend to my daughter Quinn Barratt. Said Quinn Barratt at 18 or marriage to have 200 acres on Salem Creek, bounded on Andrew Peterson's plantation. Have given power of attorney to John Powell to sell share of 700 acres near Lewis Town. Witnesses—Richard Graves, William Barratt, Dan. Mestayer. Proved 10 May, 1733. Lib. 3, p. 323.

1733, April 27. Inventory of Thomas Barratt, Senr., £189.6.2. Appraisers—Bartholomew Wyatt, Joseph Woodnutt.

1747, Feb. 26. Bartleson, Andrew, of Penn's Neck, Salem Co. Int. Admx., Sarah Bartleson, widow. Bondsman—William. Vanneman. Both of said County. Witness—John Eaton. Lib. 5, p. 423.

1747-8, Jany. 15. Inventory (£126.11.7½) includes "horse and armour, £13.4.0," "Sweed book and others, £1.1.0"; also "the ¼ part of Thomas Cahill's time." Appraisers—John Eaton, William Vanneman.

1750, March 26. Bartleson, William, of Salem County. Int. Admx., Sarah Bartleson. Bondsman, Peter Peterson. Both of Penn's Neck of said County. Witness—Samuel Whitehorne. Lib. 7, p. 38.

1749-50, March 23. Inventory (£99.0.4) includes "his riding horse, saddle and bridle," and "apparrel and armour." Appraisers—Alen Congleton, Samuel Whitehorne.

1750-1. March 1. Additional inventory, £2.14.40. Appraisers—Thomas Carney, Samuel Whitehorne.

1751, June 18. Account of Jeremiah Baker and Sarah, his wife, of Penn's Neck, administrators of William Bartleson, of Mannington, late deceased. Paid James Barkley, Rebecca Peterson, Nichs. Gibbons, Samuel Whitehorne. Receipts are from John Whittal, Michael Miller, Archibald Hamilton, Andrew Peterson, Junr., George Stark, Andrew Peterson, Senr., Catharine Crawford, Christopher Linmire, George Trenchard, James Dunbar, Joseph Hawks, Peter Peterson, John Procter, Matthias Nealson, Thomas Stanley, Elisha Basset, Gunla Felgate, Alen Congelton.

1736-7, 17th day, 1st mo. (March). Barton, Edward, of Mansfield, Burlington Co., weaver; will of. Executrix—wife Margaret who is to have land adjoining William Coats, Daniel Wills and Samuel Bunting. Jonathan, eldest son now living, land lying between John Harvey and William Pancoast, Jun'r, and land near Thomas Curtis. Other sons—David and Aaron. Daughters, Meribah and Mary Field. Expected child. Witnesses—Elizabeth Harvey, Elizabeth Ellis, Richard Gibbs. Proved May 2, 1737. Lib. 4, p. 104.

1737, 20th day, 2nd mo. (April). Inventory of the personal estate, £412.14.1; made by John Harvey and John Buffin.

1740, 23rd day, 10th mo., (Dec.). Barton, Jonathan, of Mansfield, Burlington Co., yeoman; will of. Wife Mary, and expected child. Brothers—David and Aaron. Sisters—Mary Field, Meribah and Sarah Barton. Real and personal estate. Wife sole executrix. Witnesses—George Folwell, Job Ridgway, Jun'r, William Pancoast, Jr. Proved Jan. 24, 1740. Lib. 4, p. 266.

1734, April 20. Basker, Joseph, of Salem Co., wool comber. Int. Admx., Sarah Watson. Bondsmen—Samuel Holmes, John Doe, all of said County. Witnesses—Richard Smith, Danl. Mestayer.
Lib. 3, p. 413.

1745, Sept. 19. Basset, Daniel, of Piles Grove, Salem Co.; will of. Wife, Mary. Eldest son, Daniel Basset, to have plantation joining Adam Labarer's mill, also lot at Newport, Pa. Youngest son, Zebedee, to have home plantation. Legacies to daughters Elizabeth, Hannah, Sarah, Mary and Amy. An expected child. Executors—wife Mary, and son Daniel Basset. Witnesses—Elisha Basset, Deborah Dunn, Thos. Farrell. Proved 3 Feb., 1745. Lib. 5, p. 253.

1745. Nov. 2. Inventory (£252.7.0) includes bonds due from Sarah Holl, Ann Davis. Appraisers—Roger Huggins, David Davis.

1729, 2nd mo. (April), 22nd da. Basset, William, of Pilesgrove, Salem Co., yeoman; will of. Wife, Rebeckah, sole executrix and to have all estate. Witnesses—Zacheus Dunn, Samuel Graves, William Birkett. Proved 25 Oct., 1733. Lib. 3, p. 385.

1733, Oct. 10. Inventory (£113.13.8) includes oxen, sheep, etc. Debtors—James Donlap, Joseph Clerck. Appraisers—Roger Huggins, David Davis.

1731, Aug. 31. Bassnit, Sarah, of Town and Co. of Burlington, widow; will of. Dau., Mary, under age. Cousins—Samuel, Sarah Ann and Mary Bustill, Sarah and Elizabeth Pearson, Wm., Thos. and Elizabeth Furnis. Sister, Sarah Borradaile, 400 acres in Hunterdon Co. lying between branches of Rarington, near Zuckaruning, "which I had of my bro. Mathew Gardnier," and lot on High Street, adjoining William Hagues and Sam'l Scattergood. Executors—brother Isaac Pearson and friend Caleb Raper. Witnesses—James Hancock, John Saunders, Sam'l Scattergood. Proved June 10, 1734. Lib. 3, p. 419.

1731, Nov. 22. Inventory of personal estate, £84.18.5; made by Samuel Scattergood and Robert Smith, includes debts due from John Gibs, Susannah Yard, John Butcher, John Stokes, Silence Bucher, James Quest, Mathias Garner, Elizabeth Proser, Thomas Staples, Peter Ross, John Richardson, John Deacon, John Hudson, Joseph Ridgeway, Grace Bustill, Joseph Thomas, Mary Seyler, Solomon Smith, William Gale, Hanah Gibbs, Susanah Robason, Susanah Moon, Jane Richardson, Hanah Pearson, Joanah Carter, Arthur Burdill, John Barton.

1744, Aug. 11. Basto, Thomas, of Somerset Co., "labourer." Inventory of personal estate, £20.12.11. Notes of Derrick Marlot, Garret Bem, Peter Cassiner, James Carty, Abrm. Bodine, Isaac Smalley, Francis Cossart. Appraisers—Abraham Bodine, James Graham. Affidavit before Ralph Smith. "John Anderson" on back of Inventory.

1744, Aug. 28. Administration granted to William McDaniel (Mackdonel) of Somerset Co., yeoman, Fellow bondsman—Daniel Donaldson Dunster, of same County. Marked "Not signed by Wm. Mackdonel." Lib. D, p. 173.

1745, Aug. 20. Inventory of personal estate, £3.5.0, made by Abraham and James Graham.

1733, Oct. 31. Bate, Joseph, of Waterford, Gloucester Co., yeoman; will of. Wife, Mercy, sole executrix, with assistance of son-in-law John Hillman. Daughter, Abigail, and son, Benjamin, minors. Son Thomas. Witnesses—Thomas Stokes, Rachel Stokes, John Kay.

1734, 3d mo. (May), 28 da. Codicil. Witnesses—John Kay, (Quaker), Elizabeth Wood (Quakeress). Proved 30 Dec. 1734. Lib. 3, p. 433.

1734, Oct. 9. Inventory, £98.15.05½. Appraisers—John Kay, Francis Hogsett, William Saminson (?).

1750, Feb. 12. Bate, Mary, 14 years and upwards, daughter of William Bate, Gloucester Co., ward. Guardian—Jonathan Zane, of County aforesaid, merchant. Witness—Luke Tuckniss. Lib. 6, p. 375.

1737, Apr. 1. Bate, William, of Gloucester Co., yeoman. Int. Widow, Esther Bate, admx. Wm. Alberson and John Mickle, of County aforesaid, bondsmen. Witnesses—Jacob Alberson, Joseph Rose. Lib. 4, p. 94.

1737, Mar. 31. Inventory, £135.15.00. Appraisers—John Mickle, Abraham Alberson.

1734, September 14. Bates, John, of Upper Freehold, Monmouth Co., husbandman. Bond of William Norton of same place, yeoman, administrator. Edward Griffith, of same place, yeoman, fellow bondsman. Witnesses—Joseph Ross and Samuel Bustill. Lib. 3, p. 414.

1731, Sept. 21. Bates, Joseph, of Gloucester Co., yeoman. Int. Widow, Elizabeth, Admx. Bondsman—John Brown of Town and County of Gloucester, shopkeeper. Lib. 3, p. 140.

1731, May 18. Inventory, £66.14.5. Appraisers—William Sharp, John Hillman.

1748, Feb. 5. Bates, William, of Mansfield, Burlington Co., yeoman. Inventory of personal estate, £101.10.6; made by William Pancoast and David Rockhill.

1748, Feb. 21. Letters of administration to Jeremiah Bates, yeoman. William Pancoast, yeoman, fellow bondsman. Lib. 6, p. 331; Lib. 7, p. 97.

1738, Jan. 6. Bayard, Peter, of Essex Co., merchant; will of. Father-in-law, Henry Wileman; mother, Rachel. Brothers—John and Samuel. Sisters—Helena, wife of John Debois, and Elizabeth Wileman. Real and personal estate. Executrix—wife Eve. Witnesses—Henry Coerten, Heres Wendover, Geo. Lurting. Proved Apr. 25, 1744. Lib. D, p. 132.

1733, Aug. 25. Bayley, Henry, of Amboy, who deceased July 31, 1733. Bond of Penelope Bayley, widow, as administratrix. Jacob Johnson, of Middlesex Co., fellow bondsman. Lib. B, p. 457.

1733, Aug. 29. Inventory of personal estate, £66.8.9; made by John Whitlock, house carpenter, and John Letts, yeoman, both of Middlesex Co.

1750, Aug. 23. Baynton, Mary, of City of Burlington, widow; will of. Sister, Ann Wheeler, sole executrix; son Benjamin to have sister's part of tract on Delaware River called Loepeatenung. Nephew, Joseph Pidgeon. Son-in-law, John Baynton, and his daughter Mary. Cousin, Elizabeth Stapleton. Church in Burlington to have £10. God-children—Joseph and Rowland Ellis, Mary, Sarah and Ann Cullum, Dinah Wheat, William Spencer and Grace Bustill.

1750, Aug. 24. Codicil. Rev. Mr. Collin Campbell to be executor in case sister dies before Benjamin is of age. Witnesses—Jos. White, Junr., Mary Campbell, Mary White. Proved Dec. 19, 1750. Lib. 6, p. 390.

1742, Dec. 11. Baynton, Peter, of City of Philada., merchant; will of. To be buried by wife at Philada. Sons—John and Benjamin, both under age. Father-in-law, John Budd. Sister, Ruth Banfield and her son Peter. Sister-in-law, Ann Wheeler. Aunt, Elizabeth Devit. Cousins—James and Elizabeth Derkinderen. Mary Sedeway of Rhode Island, kinswoman of my late wife. Late apprentice, John Stapleford. Friends, Benjamin Pollard, of Boston, Joshua Maddox and Thomas Bourn. Legacies to poor of Philada.; to poor communicants of Episcopal Church in that City; to Church at Burlington; to ten poor widows, three in Burlington and seven in Philada.; also to god-children, viz. Ann, daughter of Daniel Jones; Mary, daughter of Joshua Maddox; Thomas, son of Charles Willing; Samuel, son of Samuel Massell; and Sarah, daughter of Alexander Woodrops. £250 towards building a New Episcopal Church in Philada. House and lot on North side Arch Street, "which I bought of William Pywell;" house and lot in Burlington "I bought of Simon Nightingale." Executors—wife Mary, son John, and friends Joshua Maddox and Thomas Bourn of Philada. Witnesses—Colin Campbell, Mary Campbell and Rebecca Bard. Proved March 14, 1743-4. Lib. 5, p. 15.

1750, June 9. Beach, Epenetus, of Newark, Essex Co.; will of. Children—Ezekiel, Joseph, Elisha, Eppenetus, Jabez, Hannah, Phebe, Rachel, Sarah, Mary Lois and Tabitha, "last ten under age." Wife, Phebe. Real and personal estate. Executors—brother Josiah Beach; sons Joseph and Ezekiel. Witnesses—Isaac Browne, Samuel Beech, Jeremiah Halsey. Proved Aug. 8, 1750. Lib. E, p. 445.

1750, Aug. 8. Josiah Beach and Joseph Beach decline the executorship.

1737, October 22. Beadles, Elisha, of Trenton, baker; will of. "Knowing the dangers of the sea." Wife, Mary. If child by wife, Mary, it shall have house and lot in Trenton when of age, "likewise a house and lands called the Lower House, situate in the parish of St. Michels, in the East in the County of Munmoth in wals" (Wales); one-third of a house and land in Ponty Poole in said county, lately belonging to Elisha Beadles, the testator's father, now in possession of testator's brother, Nathaniel Beadles. Wife, executrix. Witnesses—Thó. Barnes, Wm. Atlee, James Gould. Proved August 20, 1741. Lib. 4, p. 301.

1745, 30th of 9th mo. (Nov.). Beakes, Stacy, of Trenton, Hunterdon Co.; will of. Wife, Mary. Only son, Stacy (minor), a lot bought of David Martain, sheriff, land purchased of Mahlon Kirkbride. Daughters, Lidia, Ruth and Mary Beakes when aged 21. Son, Stacy, to learn trade when aged 14. Land that belonged to testator's uncle, Mahlon Stacy, which testator's father, Atkinson, and testator's mother, promised the testator, to be sold and money to Mahlon Kirkbride to pay for land bought of him. Executors—wife and brother, Gideon Bickerdick. Witnesses—Edm'd Beakes, Nathan Beakes, William Robinson. Proved August 11, 1746. The executors, Quakers. Lib. 5, p. 264.

1745-6, 14th of 11th mo. (Jan.). Inventory of the estate, £383.6.2, includes joiner's furniture, and in the shop: 90 molding plains; 20 plains of divers sorts; chisels, gouges, saws, lathe, etc.; 1,000 ft. Black walnut; 4,000 ft. pine, cedar and gum boards, etc. Obligations of Hugh Farguson, Samuel Depue, Abel Jenne, Jun'r, Richard Howell, Daniel Cox, Samuel Johnston, Bartholomew Rowley, Cornelius Ferrill, John Smith, Archabel McCarty. Appraised by W. Morris, Wm. Plaskett, Charles Axford.

1755, March 11. Account of Gideon Bickerdike, executor, mentions Cornelius Ferril, John Smith, Archibald McCarty, Richard Howell.

1743, March 20. Beanford, William, of Hopewell, Hunterdon co. Bond of Frances Beanford, administratrix, with John Phillips and Cornelius Anderson, all of Hopewell, as fellow bondsmen.

1742-3, March 5. Inventory of the estate, £70.15.2; made by John Phillips and Cornelius Anderson.

1746-7, Jan. 27. Account shows debts paid to William Pierson, Andrew Reed, Enoch Anderson, Thomas Burroughs, William Branford of Phila., Edward Hunt, George Clifford, Frederick Vanoye, Eliez'r Morgan, Cornelius Anderson, Humphrey Hughs, John Phillips, John Lee, Andrew Mershon, James Bigger, Samuel Lee, William Moore, James Adams, Jon. Reed, Samuel Ketcham, Danl. Coxe. Hunterdon Wills, 161 J.

1744, Nov. 5. Bee, Ephraim, of Greenwich, Gloucester Co., yeoman. Grandson, Ephraim Lloyd, to have all real estate; in case of his death, without issue, same to become property of cousin, Ephiram Bee, and, if he dies without issue, cousin Thomas Bee and in case of his decease without issue, cousin Jonathan shall have it. Executors—son, John Loyd, and friend, Alexdr. Randell. Witnesses—John Bright, Thomas Braman, James Holden. Proved 7 Jan., 1744; probat. 20 July, 1745.
Lib. 5, p. 140.

1744, Dec. 3. Inventory, £19.11.1. Appraisers—Thomas Braman, John Bright.

1747, Feb. —. Account (£21.10.6), includes moneys paid to Thomas Holden, Robert Brayman, Gabraell Rambo, James Holden, John Bright, Ephraim Bee, Samuell Paull.

1749, Feb. 18. Bell, John, of Morrisses (Maurice) River, Cumberland Co.; will of. Wife, Mary, to have the plantation until son, Robert, will be 21, and ½ the marsh of 30 acres over the river, joining Leamings, providing she remains unmarried. Sons: John, to have plantation formerly belonging to Abraham Jones on the south side of Manusking; Thomas, the land formerly belonging to Johannes Hoffman; likewise land and "cripple" belonging, formerly, to Hance Steelman; likewise land and "cripple," formerly Joseph Jones', not redeemed, he to have the money if redeemed; Henry, land and marsh held in partnership with the Leamings, excepting 30 acres. Personal estate to four sons, and to Mary Bell, Junior, Agnes Bell, an expected child, and wife, excepting Robert, whose share "shall fall into the hands of his mother." Additional bequests of a Cedar Swamp (John to have below, Robert above, Sharp's Mill); ½ of the new mill, purchased of Samuel Iszard to be sold. Executors—wife, Mary; son, Robert, Aaron Leaming. Witnesses—William McGlaughlin, Richard Shaw, John Reed. Proved 20 June, 1749. Lib. 6, p. 12.

1749, May 26. Inventory of Cap'n John Bell's personal estate, £2343.3.6. Appraisers—John Purple, John Cormick.

1749, May 29. Renunciation of executorship by Aaron Leaming. Witnesses—John Purpple, Thomas Peterson.

1735, Oct. 4. Bellton (Bellten), Jonathan, of Township of Waterford, Gloucester Co., cordwainer; will of. Ephraim Tomlinson, of Gloucester Township and Co., sole executor. Wife, Mary. Infant son, Hezekiah Belton. Daughters, Lyndonia and Mary Belton, "to have the proceeds from the labor of my prentice shoemaker, Daniel Calvin (a mulatto) until he will be 31 and my said daughters to be apprenticed "to some religious and discreet master and mistress and learn to read the Bible and housewifery." Son-in-law (supposed step-son), Joseph Mapes. Son, Petter Champion. Witnesses—John Shivers, Josiah Shivers, Michael Grumley. Affirmed 7 April, 1737.

1736, 9 mo. (Nov.), 26 da. Renunciation of Ephraim Tomlinson as executor. Witnesses—John Way, William Way. Lib. 4, p. 96.

1737, Apr. 7. Administration granted to Mary, widow of Jonathan Belton. John Shivers, bondsman. Witness—Joseph Rose.

1736, May 6. Inventory (£185.11.7), includes 224 pounds of bacon, "shumakers tools," sole leather, 16 cattle. Appraisers—Tobias Holloway, John Shivers.

1749, Aug. 25. Bender, Robert, of Township of Greenwich, Cumberland Co. Bond by John Brick, of Township of Stow, Cumberland Co., and Alexander Moore, of Township of Deerfield, merchant, administrators.

1749, Aug. 25. Susanna Bender, of Township of Greenwich, Cumberland Co., widow and relict of Robert Bender, renounced administration. Cumberland Wills, 20 F.

1733, Sept. 9. Bennet, Jacobus, of Middlesex Co. Inventory of personal estate £77.9.6; made by four freeholders of New Jersey, chosen by widow, Abigail Bennet, viz., Elia. Burger, Adriaen Bennet, Cornelius Bennet, Chrisstoffel Probasco.

1734, Aug. 19. Bond of Jacobus and Jacob Bennet, dated May 3, 1730, for £1,000, held by Cornelius Vanderhoven, of Kings Co., New York, receipted in full. Witnesses to bond—John Bennet, Mare Manion; witness to receipt, Jan Vaendervoort. Middlesex Wills, 797-800 L.

1732, Sept. 15. Bennet, James, of New Brunswick, Middlesex Co., yeoman. Bond of Abigail Bennet, widow, as administratrix. William

Davenport and Henry Berry, Jun'r, both of Perth Amboy, fellow bondsmen. Lib. B, p. 300.

1738, March 1. Bennet, John, of Evesham, Burlington Co., sawyer. Letters of administration to Susanna Bennet, widow. George Morris, of Mansfield, yeoman, fellow bondsman. Lib. 4, p. 155.

1747, Aug. 22. Bennet, John, of Northampton, Burlington Co., yeoman. Letters of administration to Mary Bennet, widow. Thomas Reves and Patrick Reynolds, yeoman, of Burlington Co., fellow bondsmen. Lib. 5, p. 362.

1747, Aug. 22. Inventory of personal estate, £116.7; made by Patrick Reynolds and Saml. Gamble.

1744, April 20. Benson, Johannes, of Bergen Co. Bond of Elizabeth Benson, of Bergen Co., administratrix, and Ryck Leidecker, of same County, fellow bondsman.

1744, May 9. Inventory of estate, £125.17.3; made by Elizabeth Benson, and appraised by Hendrick Banta and John Zabriski. Lib. D, p. 128.

1746-7, March 7. Beriman (Baryman, Bereman), Thomas, of Cohansey, Salem Co., yeoman; will of. Wife, Martha, use of whole plantation until my son, John, will be 20. In case of his death before 20, and after the decease of wife, estate shall go to six daughters: Annabel Johnson, Rachel Benet, Perthenia Reeves, Elizabeth (under age), Zurviah (under age) and Hannah (under age). Executors—wife, Martha, and son, John Beriman. Witnesses—Eliakim Carll, Sen., Joseph Brick, Patrick Mitchel. Proved 14 June, 1749, before Elias Cotting, Surrogate of Cumberland County.

1749, July 14. Letters testamentary granted to Martha Beriman (signed Martha Baryman). Lib. 6, p. 294.

1749, July 14. Inventory of personal estate, £211.7.0. Appraisers—Samuel Moore, Eliakim Carll.

1739, March 20. Berry, Henry, of Monmouth County, carpenter. Bond of John Berry, of Monmouth, as administrator. Andrew Crawford, of same county, and Henry Berry, of Perth Amboy, fellow bondsmen. Henry Berry, eldest son of deceased, renounced right to administer, in favor of his brother John Berry, March 20, 1739; renunciation witnessed by John Kelly and Thomas Bartow. Lib. C, p. 325.

1740, July 18. Inventory (£20.4.9), incl. carpenter's and joiner's tools; made by Samuel Ker, Joseph Ker, David English.

1749, Oct. 11. Berryman, John, of Burlington Co. Inventory of personal estate, £33.2.5½; made by Thomas Atkinson and John Foster; includes book accounts of Roger Fort, Marmaduke Fort, Jenet Eldredge.

1749, Oct. 19. Margaret Berryman, widow, renounces administration in favor of Benjamin Bispham, principal creditor. Bond of Benjamin Bispham, of Bridgetown, merchant. Robert Hartshorn and Thomas Atkinson, fellow bondsmen. Lib. 6, p. 324.

1730, Dec. 8. Bibby, Richard, of Chesterfield, Burlington Co., labourer. Bond of Mary Bibby, widow, as administratrix. Samuel Radford, yeoman, fellow bondsman. Lib. 3, p. 140.

1730-1, Jan. 4. Inventory of personal estate, £43.19.7; made by William Wells and John Middleton.

1748, June 10. Bickham, Henry, 19 yrs. and upwards, son of Richard Bickham, late of Gloucester Co., ward. Guardian—Samuel Shivers, of Racoon Creek, Gloucester Co. Gloucester Wills, 638H.

1748, June 21. Petition to Charles Read—"That our nephew, Hendry Bickham hath made choses of Samuel Shivers for his Garden, etc."
Signed. Thomas Bickham, Martin Bickham.

1739, 9 mo. (Nov.), 21 da. Bickham, Richard, of Gloucester Co., yeoman; will of. Eldest son, Henry Bickham, when 21, to have easterly side of plantation to easterly corner of Thomas Bickham's land; thence to Oule Pond, down to Delaware River. Son, Richard Bickham, to have rest of plantation when 21, etc. Above sons, Henry and Richard to have "Seader Swamps." Legacies to daughters, Sarah, Ann and Mary Bickham, when 21. Executors—Wife, Mary, and Abraham Chattin. Witnesses—Walter Fawcet, Martin Bickham, William Wood. Affirmed 14 July, 1740. Gloucester Wills, 251H.

1740, 4 mo. (June), 23 da. Inventory, £251.14.00. Appraisers—Thos. Wilkins, Martin Bickham.

1748, Nov. 1. Bickham, Martin, of Greenwich, Gloucester Co., yeoman; will of. Wife, Sara, daughter of Robert Gerrard. Children—all under age, spoken of but not by name. Executors—wife and Samuel Shivers. Witnesses—Samuel Hopper, John Hanby, Mary Key. Proved Feb. 16, 1750. Lib. 7, p. 149.

1750-1, Feb. 4. Inventory of estate, £56.14.2, made by Thomas Bickham and William Gerrard.

1744, July 10. Bickley, Abraham, of (Burlington) Province of New Jersey, bricklayer. Administration granted to Peter Hodgson, of Philada., gent. Mary Andrews, spinster, and Wm. Paschall, sadler, both of same, fellow bondsmen. Lib. 5, p. 36.

1746, July 21. Inventory of personal estate includes £160, being amount received for 1150 acres of land in Hunterdon Co., taken in execution at the suit of Mary Andrews and sold to her.

1746, July 21. Account of Pet'r Hodgson, showing payments to Mary Andrews, Jno. Cox and Bennet Bard.

1748, Aug. 19. Bickley, Mary, of City of Burlington, widow. Administration to Charles Willias, of City of Philada., blacksmith. Isaac DeCow, Esq., and Ruchard Wright, gent., both of same, fellow bondsmen. Lib. 7, p. 94.

1748, Sept. 27. Inventory of personal estate, £192.6.4; made by R. Wright and Isa: DeCow. Includes negro man and an old woman, £30; two silver coins, £9.15.6 and tayloring outfit.

1749, May 15. Bickley, Samuel, of Philadelphia, Pa.; will of. Wife, Margaret. Children—Abraham, William, Peter, Mary. Two lots in Philadelphia; tracts in County of Kent, Delaware. Executors—James Polegreen, of Philadelphia, gent., wife Margaret, son Abraham. Witnesses—Jno. Finney, Gideon Griffith, David Finney. Proved June 17, 1749.

1750, April 11. Margaret Bickley, administratrix of estate of Samuel Bickley, "late of Newcastle, deceased, dyed at Newcastle." Lib. 6, p. 285.

1738, July —. Bickley William, of City of Burlington, yeoman; will of. Sister, Elizabeth Powlgreen. House and lot on High Street, City of Burlington, now in possession of Samuel Bustill, Jun'r, and meadow adjoining Jonathan Wright, Daniel Smith and Caleb Raper. Wife, Mary, sole executrix. Witnesses—John Craig, James Hancock, Ralph Peart. Proved Jan. 16, 1739. Lib. 4, p. 219.

1740, July 24. Inventory of personal estate, 361.14.2; made by Joseph Heulings and Jos. Scattergood.

1733, Nov. 14. Biglow, John, of Hanover, Hunterdon Co.; inventory of estate, made at request of his widow, Abigail Biglow, £118.12.3, including a sword and stone, 7s.6d; a corbin and pistols, £1.5.0; a Bible and some small books, £8. Made by Gershom Mott and Jonathan Stilles.

1733, Nov. 21. Bond of Abigail Biglow, widow, as administratrix. Samuel Crosman, of same place, bloomer, and John Budd, of same, gentleman, sureties. Witnesses—Sarah Budd, Thomas Biglow.

Hunterdon Wills, 84 J.

1728, April 6. Bilderback, Albert, of Penn's Neck, Salem Co., husbandman; will of. Wife, Margaret, to have the estate until children will be 21. If she marries, estate devised to sons Daniel and Peter Bilderback; if either die without issue, his share to descend to son John Bilderback (not 16). Daughters—Sarah, Jane, Margaret (not 21). Executors—Wife, Margaret, and brother-in-law, Senick Senickson. Witnesses—Josiah Pennington, John Denny, John Richmond. Proved 5 May, 1732. Lib. 3, p. 210.

1731-2, Jan. 5. Inventory, £114.7.0½, of farm stock, etc. Appraisers—John Seneck, Hance Bilderback.

1740, April 3. Bilderback, Peter, of Salem Co., yeoman. Int. Admx. Sarah Bilderback ("relict of"). Bondsmen—Timothy Rains, John Savoy, all of said County. Witness—Obadiah Loyd.

1740, March 22. Inventory, £16.2.6. Appraisers—Tim. Rain, John Savoy. Salem Wills, 557 Q.

1740, May 29. Biles, John, of Maidenhead Township, Hunterdon Co., yeoman; will of. Wife, Elizabeth. Daughter, Sarah Biles; two sons, John and Charles Biles, land where testator lived. Executors—wife and brother, Alexander Biles. Witnesses—George Rozel, Samuel Lee, Mary Carpenter. Proved July 22, 1740. Lib. 4, p. 247.

1740, July 1. Inventory of personal estate, £157.17.6; made by John Price and John Hunt.

1740, March 30. Biles, Samuel, of Nottingham, Burlington Co., tanner. Bond of Mary Cary, widow, of Trenton, Hunterdon Co., as administratrix. Isaac Pearson, of Burlington, Esq. and Thomas Wetherill of same, gent., fellow bondsmen. Lib. 4, p. 227.

1740, April 8. Inventory of personal estate, £1305.14.2; made by John Middleton of Nottingham, yeoman, and Frettwell Wright, of Burlington, farmer.

1733-4, March 19. Bills, Nathaniel, Jr., of Monmouth County, single man. Bond of Gershom Bills, of Shrewsbury, cordwainer, as administrator. David Allen, of Shrewsbury, cordwainer, fellow bondsman. Witnesses—Samuel Sonman, William Madock.

Monmouth Wills, 529M.

———, ———. Inventory of the estate (£73.0.0), includes bond of Richard Gardiner. Made by William Goodbody and Joseph Gifford, who were sworn Sept. 9, 1734.

1738, April 19. Bird, Jeremiah, of Elizabeth Town, Essex Co., yeoman; will of. Children—Joseph, Abigail FitzRandolph, Mary King, Prudence Gedis, Hannah Atkinson, Martha Bird and Rachel Kellsey. Real and personal estate. Executors—wife, Abigail, and son-in-law, Joseph FitzRandolph. Witnesses—Edward Vaughn, John Terrill, Anne Terrill. Proved May 5, 1738.

1738, May 5. Joseph FitzRandolph, Quaker, qualified as executor.
Lib. C, p. 194.

1738, 5th mo. (July), 11. Inventory of personal estate (£461.09), includes bonds of John Fraze, Samuel Moor, Benjamin Crowel, William Porter, John Radley, Sam'll Frazee, Josiah Terrill, Ben. Frazee, Richard ———, Eliphalet Frazee, Thomas Scuder, Thomas Abbott, John King, Hendrick ———; made by Joseph Shotwell and Eliphalet Frasee.

1740, Sept. 22. Bird, Joseph, of borough of Elizabeth, Essex Co., yeoman; will of. Children—Samuel, Ruben, John and Abigail Bird. Executrix—wife Elizabeth. Real and personal estate. Witnesses—Benony Frazee, Stephen Borrowes, John Terrill. Proved Oct. 6, 1740.
Lib. C, p. 353.

1749, July 4. Bishop, Abigail, widow, late of Township of Hopewell, Cumberland Co. Int. Phebe Bishop, James Davise, administrators. Fellow bondsmen—Daniel Davise and Samuel Lomas, of the Township of Deerfield, Cumberland Co., farmers. Witnesses—Abraham Reeves, Junior, Elias Cotting.

1749, June 29. Inventory of personal estate, £102.4.11 (£101.16.11, original). Appraisers—Thomas Sayre, Benjamin Lupton.
Cumberland Wills, 22 F.

1742-3, March 19. Bishop, Daniel, of Cohansey, Salem Co., yeoman; will of. Wife, Abigail, use of plantation, etc. Son, Nathan Bishop (when 21), house and barn, "and all that land and marsh that my father gave to me; also ½ of marsh I bought of Anne Grant, known as 'Jewel's Marsh;' also ½ of land bought of Elias Cotting, joining the river and situate between his line and Joshua Barksted's, containing 227 acres; also ½ of salt marsh, 25 acres, near Tindal's Island, bought of Elias Cotting." Son, Daniel Bishop, when 21, to have other half of the above and woodland bought of Anne Grant. Daughter, Elizabeth Bishop, when 18, 150 acres (bought of Elias Cotting) which John Terry lives on. Daughter Phebe, when 18, 150 acres, bought of Elias Cotting. Daughter Abigail Bishop (not 18). Executors—wife and Moses Bishop. "Whereas some persons claim under Joshua Barksted's right a part of the land I bought of Elias Cotting, therefore my executors are authorized to defend any action by such." Witnesses—Nathaniel Bishop, Benjamin Lupton, Thomas Sayer. Proved 30 April, 1743.
Lib. 4, p. 374.

1743, March 29. Inventory (£130.10.6,) includes cattle, sheep, swine, etc. Appraisers—James Robinson, Jonathan Holmes.

1749, June 12. Bishop, Moses, of Township of Hopewell, Cumberland Co., yeoman; will of. Wife sole executrix. Sons, Moses and Levi, land and marsh. Daughters—Esther, Mary, Rachel and Eunice (all under 18). Witnesses—And'w Hunter, Mary Perry, Rob't Nichols, Joseph Bishop. Proved 8 July, 1749. Lib. 6, p. 296.

1748-9, March 6. Bishop, Nathaniel, of Cohansey, Cumberland Co., yeoman; will of. Wife Mary. Sons—Isaac and Preston (to have houses, lands, marshes equally), Jeremiah, Zephaniah, and Nathaniel. Daughters—Mary Lupton, Abigail, Elizabeth and Hannah. Land bought of Daniel Bishop. Executors—Wife, Mary, and Annanias Sayre. Witnesses—John Preston, Moses Bishop. Proved 1 April, 1749. Lib. 6, p. 108.

1748-9, March 11. Inventory of personal estate, £122.8.4. Appraisers—Jonathan Holmes, Samuel Miller.

1745-6, Feb. 15. Bishop, Noah, of Woodbridge, Middlesex Co., blacksmith; will of. Wife ———. Daughters—Mary, Sarah, Lydia, Hannah and Ruth. Son—Noah, and his two sons, Noah and Japhet. Real and personal estate. Executors—son, Noah, and friend, David Alston. Witnesses—Jonathan Connet, David Stile, Thomas Alston. Proved June 20, 1750. Lib. E, p. 423.

1749, July 4. Bishop, Phebe, ward, "of 14 years and upwards," daughter of Daniel Bishop, late of Township of Hopewell, Cumberland Co. Guardian—James Davise. Bondsmen—Daniel Davise, Sam. Lummus, all of Township of Deerfield. Witnesses—Abraham Reeves, Jr., Elias Cotting. Cumberland Wills, 25F.

1741, Aug. 14. Bishop, Thomas, of Northampton, Burlington Co., yeoman; will of. Children—Thomas, John, Joshua, William, Ann Smith, Mercy, Elizabeth Warrington, Hannah Prickett and Mary Atkinson. Granddaughter, Sarah Gaering, under age. Lands adjoining Thomas Hains, Joseph Wills, Philo Leeds and Brook Stop "the Jades." Executors—sons-in-law, Henry Warrington and Jacob Prickett. Witnesses—Isa. DeCow, Thomas Wetherill, Jos. Scattergood. Proved Aug. 2, 1746. Lib. 5, p. 257.

1746, Aug. 1. Inventory of personal estate, £318.16.8; made by Samuel Woolston and Thomas Haines.

1747, Feb. 10. Bishop, Thomas, of Bordentown, Burlington Co., skinner. Administration to Joseph Borden, of same, merchant. Joseph Thorne, of Chesterfield, yeoman, fellow bondsman. Lib. 5, p. 437.

1744, Oct. 22. Black, John, of Springfield, Burlington Co., farmer. Administration to Thomas Black. William Black, fellow bondsman; both farmers of Springfield. Lib. 5, p. 54.

1744, Nov. 24. Inventory of personal estate, £812.1.5½; made by Michael Newbold, John Rockhill, Benjamin Shreve.

1747, March 18. Blackford, John, of Piscataway, Middlesex Co., yeoman; will of. Wife, Ruth. Sons—John, Nathaniel and Jeremiah. Real and personal estate. Executors—sons, John and Nathaniel Blackford. Daughters—Sarah Chantler, Susanna (wife of Moses Astin), Mary Laing and Ann. Witnesses—Isaac Chantler, Samuel Drake. Proved March 30, 1749. Lib. E, p. 286.

1749, April 1. Inventory of personal estate, £82.4.6; made by Samuel Drake and John Pound, Jun'r.

1738, Nov. 27. Blackman, Josiah, of Northampton, Burlington Co., blacksmith. Int. Whereas Mary Blackman, widow; mother, Mary Tuckness, widow; sister; Richard Blackman, brother, Isaac Dawson, hatter, and Jane his wife, sister of deceased, do live in Province of Penna., they renounce their right of administration unto James Hancock, of Burlington, peruke maker. Witnesses—John Craig, Joshua Henssey, Enoch Roberts, Solomon Kemble, John Harper, David Gummery.

1738, Dec. 7. Bond of James Hancock, of City of Burlington, peruke maker, as administrator. William Petty and Job Lippincott, yeomen, of same place, fellow bondsmen. Lib. 4, p. 151.

1730, April 6. Blanchard, John, of Elizabeth Town, Essex Co. Administration granted to John Blanchard, of Essex Co. Jos. Meeker, Jun'r, Wm. Robison and Andrew Joline fellow bondsmen.

Lib. B, p. 158.

1730, April 29. Inventory of personal estate (£732.10.05) includes bonds due from Alexander Scot, Peter Eastman, John Hayward, Samuel Whitehead, Jacob Piat, John Lambert, Samuel Wheten, Amos Goodin, John Morehouse, Samuel Day, Benjamin Ogden, Cozine Andris, Michael Rutter, James and William Cole, Jeremiah Osbourn, Jeremiah Osbourne, Jun'r, Jonathan Gilbert, Richard Hall, Daniel Goble, Joseph Tharp, Joseph Codington, Thomas More, Mathew Connet, Henry Connet, Joseph Jennings, John Carter, Job Pack, William Watson, Hendrick DeCamp, James Doughty, George Pack, Erasmus Allton, William Robinson, Isaac Whitehead, Silas Pearce, Thomas Hampton, Roberd Lardner, Conradus Winains, John Winains, George Gibbs, Daniel Goble, Jun'r, Roberd Goble, Nicolas Classon, William Winains, Jun'r, Noah Bishop, Thomas Pope, Thomas Gearing, William Allton, James Bishop, Amos Roberds, Joseph Rogers, Joseph Grummond, Henry Jaquish, Thomas Force, Samuel Littel, James Clarkson, Nath'll Stilwill, John Tremble, James Cole, Jun'r, Andrew Chreigh, Jun'r, Jonathan Gilbort, Joseph Gray, John Wilkinson, Thomas Bates, Thomas Rogers, William Baremore, Isaac Price, Abram Shotwell, widow Hall, William Cole, Jun'r, John Chreigh, Amos Goodin, Gershom Frazee, Thomas Clark, James Stone, Benjamin Gray, William Strayhearn, John Ryno, Jun'r, Francis More, Samuel Mils, Jeremiah Stilwill, William Robinson, James Rigs, Ephraim Sale, Jeffery Jones, John King, John Frazee, Thomas Buisson, John Winains, Jun'r, David Stuerd, Roberd Howell, Daniel Terrel, John Darby, Ephraim Terrel, John Tucker, Ephraim Frazee, Joseph Bird, Josiah Terrel, Joseph Ludlum, Isaac Frazee, Margaret Rolph, David Powell, John Chanders, Caleb Woodruff, Elnathan Rolly, Peter Elstone, Jun'r, John Hayward, John Rolph, Miles Williams, Jacob Earle, John Rayman, Joseph Coddington, Roberd Morse, Joseph Spencer, John Eastwood, Gershom More, Eliphalet Frazee, Jonathan Marsh, Richard Pangburn, Stephen Osbourn, John Jennings, Widow Winains, William Darby, John Allstone, Roberd Pool, James White, Daniel Marsh, Benja. Shelly, Jasper Totten, John Robinson, Mathias Swem, Benja. Darby, Adam Lee, Jonathan Freeman, John Oliver, John Strayhearne, Sam'll Norris, Jeremiah Osbourn, William Dyer, Samuel Wheating, Joseph Williams, Joseph Shotwell, James Frazee, Margaret Frazee; also silver made by Robert Ogden and James Hamton.

1747, June 20. Blanchard, John, Esq., of Elizabeth Town, Essex Co.; will of. Wife, Mary, sole legatee. Real and personal estate. Executors—Wife, Mary, and brother-in-law, John Halstead Esq. Witnesses—Wm. Chetwood, W. Stebs, Geo. Emott. Proved May 4, 1748.

Lib. E, p. 188.

1747, Oct. 30. Jonathan Hampton makes complaint that Mary Blanchard and John Halstead, executors of above will, refuse to bring the same to the Prerogative office; they are therefore cited to appear at the Secretary of State's Office at Perth Amboy, March 21st, next, to bring the will and have it duly proved. Lib. E, p. 101.

1748, March 19. Executors decline to act and desire that the administration be granted to Jonathan Hampton, principal creditor.

1748, May 4. Bond of Jonathan Hampton, of Elizabeth borough, yeoman as administrator. Ellis Crisy, fellow bondsman.

1743, May 16. Blanchard, Philip, of Allaways Creek, Salem Co., yeoman; will of. To sister, Elizabeth, wife of Joseph Ware, my plantation (150 acres) at Alaways Creek, she paying £10 each to Jeremiah Powel's children: John, Elizabeth and Mary Powel, when they will be 21, or at marriage. Executors—Brothers-in-law, Joseph Ware and Jeremiah Powell. Witnesses—Joseph Ware, Andrew Gardiner, Dan'l Mestayer. Proved 20 May, 1743. Lib. 4, p. 363.

1748, Sept. 20. Bloomfield, Ezekiel, of Woodbridge, Middlesex Co.; will of. Wife, Margaret. Nephew, Ezekiel Bloomfield, 10 acres in Essex and Middlesex Counties, joining Edward Frazee's land, he to pay his brothers, Ebenezer and Jeremiah Bloomfield, and sisters, Hannah, wife of Jonathan Wright, and Ursula, their legacies. Brothers—Timothy, Joseph and Benjamin. Sister, Mary, wife of Obadiah Ayers. Sister-in-law—Eunice, wife of Joseph Bloomfield, my brother. Mary, wife of James Wilkinson. Mary and Catharine, daughters of my brother, Jeremiah, deceased. Executors—Wife, Margaret, and brother, Timothy Bloomfield. Witnesses—William Burnet, Tho's Skinner, Tho's Bartow. Proved Feb. 11, 1748. Lib. E, p. 261.

1746, Nov. 18. Bloomfield, Jeremiah, of Woodbridge, Middlesex Co., farmer. Sarah Bloomfield, the widow, renounces her right of administration in favor of Richard Bloomfield, principal creditor. Witnesses—Jonathon Thickston, Benjamin Allword, Sam'll Preston.

1746, Dec. 5. Bond of Richard Bloomfield, of Woodbridge, as administrator. Samuel Martin, yeoman, fellow bondsman. Lib. D, p. 441.

1746, Dec. 10. Inventory of personal estate, £81.00.11, includes cash received from Sarah, widow of Samuel Martin; made by Samuel Preston and Benjamin Allword, both of Middlesex Co.

1744-5, Jan. 29. Board, Cornelius, of Bergen Co., yeoman; will of. Trustees to sell lands in Essex and Morris, purchased of Wm. Davenport, and all land "above the small tract that I formerly sold to the Oggdins, called the 'Falls in the County of Bergen.'" Wife, Elizabeth. Eldest son, James, and his heirs, the home-plantation at Ringwood, on the west side of Long Pond River; likewise small tract lying between said place and Philip Pico, on east side of said River. Son, David, and his heirs, that part of my plantation in the Fork of the Long Pond River and the eastermost part of the Iron Works, or Furnace River. Son, Joseph, and his heirs. Daughters—Elizabeth, Shusanah, Sarah and Martha. Executor—son, Joseph. Trustees—Jonathan Davis and Joseph Bartram. Witnesses—Robert Sturgeon, Joseph Bartram, Gerrit Fitzgarril. Proved 15 Sept., 1747.
Lib. E, p. 97.

1747, Oct. 1. Administration granted to James Board, eldest son, as Joseph Board, Executor named, was 10 years old and Elizabeth, the widow, had renounced her right. Fellow bondsmen—Joseph Bartram, of Ringwood, Jonathan Davis, of Newark, Essex Co. Witnesses—David Ogden, Uzal Ogden. Lib. E, p. 100.

1747, Sept. 27, (filed 11 Dec. 1760). Inventory of personal estate (£633.4.9), includes sword, £1, 2 negroes, £100, wheat, notes, bonds, and book debts as follows: John Phillips, Zacharia Baldwin, Caleb Ward, Elisha Kent, Nathaniel Cogswell, Ebinezar Kilburn, John Baldwin, Mary Howel, Adam Dickason, John Cambel, Christopher Frampton, Samuel Salter, Nathaniel Calkin, Martha Potts, Josiah Baldwin, James Chadwick, Daniel Dod, Stephen Coartland, Richard Day, David Michal, George Ryason, Jr., Caleb Person, John Bruin, Joseph Bruin, George Ryason, Sr., Mathew Scain, Paul Lenard, Archibel Glandining, Robert Arvin, John Howil, Wm. Hains, Josiah Church, Robert Dummin, Jacob Mead, Samuel Johnson, John Johnson, Thos. Johnson, Jesse Ford, Coonrod Lions, Abraham Mowris, Joseph Hogan, Wm. Taylor, Domini Cornili, Owin Rablin, David Johnson, Samll. Catham, John Richards, Jacob Wess, Oliver Hadden, John Hill, Jacob Pitsort, Thos Day. Appraisers—Joseph Bartram, Jacob Insoez (?), David Ogden, Jr.

1737, May 4. Boarton, Joseph, of Town and Co. of Burlington, farmer; will of. Children—Mary, Sarah, John and Rachel all under age. Real and personal estate. Executors—wife, and John Wright in Carrostoga. Witnesses—Anthony Baker, Mary Baker, John Craig. Proved Oct. 8, 1737. Lib. 4, p. 118.

1737, 30th day, 5th mo. (July). Inventory of personal estate, £163.8; made by Thos. Scattergood and John Craige.

1737, Oct. 8. Sarah Spencer, late Sarah Borton, administratrix (in absence of John Wright) affirms to above inventory.

1747-8, Feb. 22. Bodine, Jacob, Jun'r, of Hunterdon Co. Inventory (£118.7.9), includes 105 bushels of wheat. Appraisers—John Handershot, Jacob Shipman.

1748, May 23. Bond of Catherine Bodine, widow, administratrix; John Bodine and Nicholas Shipman, fellow bondsmen.

1748-9, Feb. 22. Inventory, £118.7.9.

1748, Aug. 11. Account. Cash paid John Haneshot, Johannes Sharp, John Budd, John Haman. "The deceased dyed posesed of a tract of land of one hundred eighty-three acres held by Lease from John Budd, Esq. and Sarah, his wife, for the term of ninety-seven years, to comence from the first Day of November in the year of 1746 at the yearly rent of three Spanish pistoles and a half and four shillings and Seven pence curant money of America." (Signed), Cathrin Bodine, Admx. Witnessed by Brice Riky.

1754, April 3. "Jacob Bodine's Inv. of Huntn. or Morris" (£65.8.8.), signed John Hendershot, Jacob Shipman, Roelof Roelofson. Same day, account of cash paid to Michael Hilabrant, Roelof Roelofson, Andrios Killian, John Haneshot, Johanes Sharp, John Budd, John Haman, Frederick Shipman, Burbra Curts, Peter Cramer, Michael Deller, Thos. Neal, Andrios A. Mark, Cornelius Bodine, Peter Van Nest, Dortier (Doctor?) Spitsor, Frederick Shipman, Brice Riky, Abram Dewit, John Evans, John Vandewater, John Riky, Sarah Budd, Danl. Vanwagener, Wm. Winn, John Hendershot.

1754, June 18. Settlement of personal estate of Jacob and Nicholas (children of Jacob Bodine, Jr., late of Lebanon, deceased), wards of Cornelius Bodine, Hunterdon Co. All accounts relating to the estate came into the hands of Rullif Rolefson, Morris Co. by his marrying Cathern, late widow of the above said Jacob Bodine, deceased. Witnesses—Brice Riky, R. Smith. Morris Wills, 21 N, 208 J.

1740, Feb. 23. Bodine, John, of Essex Co.; will of. Wife, Margaret. Sister, Elizabeth. Real and personal estate. Executor—brother Abraham Bodine. Witnesses—Geertje Krom, Jeremiah Douty (Doaty), Teunis Middagh. Proved June 26, 1741. Lib. C, p. 424.

1747, April 9. Bodine, John, of Rariton Landing, Middlesex Co., trader. Bond of Peter Bodine, his father, as administrator. William Williamson and George Vroom fellow bondsmen. Witnesses—John Deare, John Vroom. Lib. E, p. 24.

1735, May 14. Boels, Thomas, of Freehold, yeoman; will of. Bequeaths £40 to overseers of poor of "Lower Freehold or Topenamus," "the interest to imploy in the learning of poor children to read, forever." Sister, Dorcas Bradford, and her husband, Andrew Bradford. Sister Sarah's eldest sons. Brother-in-law, Robert Ellis, if living. Sister Priscilla's son, Robert Ellis. Sister Sarah Nixon's son; if he dies, one-third to go to the instructing of children in doctrine of the Church of England of which the minister for Topanames and church wardens to be trustees. Executors—sisters, Dorcas Bradford and Sarah Nixon, and brother-in-law, Robert Ellis. Witnesses—Andrew Crawford, James Wilson and Margaret Robinson. Proved October 16, 1735. Lib. C, p. 35.

1735, Oct. 17. Inventory of estate, £2117.13. 1¼, includes 64 bound books, seven negroes, and "a sickly Indian girl 12 years old called Tukkoho." Made by John Reid, Gideon and Andrew Crawford.

1746, Oct. 6. Bonnel, Joseph, of Borough of Elizabeth, Essex Co., yeoman; will of. "Being advanced in years." Wife, Martha. Children—David, Joseph, Phebe (wife of Noadiah Potter), Keziah (wife of Ebenezer Sturgis) and Martha (wife of John Dickinson). Daughters of son Nathaniel, deceased, viz., Temperance, Joana, Mary, Nancy, Phebe, all under age. Daughter-in-law, Martha, wife of Benjamin Lyon. Brother, Benjamin Bonnel, to have a weavers loom. Lands joining lands of Thomas Baker, David Bonnel, Henry Pierson and Samuel Headley. Executors—sons-in-law, Noadiah Potter, Ebenezer Sturgis, and son David. Witnesses—Benjamin Lyon, John Clark, David Tallon, John Wade 3rd, Samuel Lunn, Ebenezer Sturgis, Jun'r. Proved March 22, 1747-8. Lib. E, p. 154.

1747-8, March 17. Inventory of personal estate, £803.19.06; made by Timothy Whitehead and John Potter.

1736, June 19. Bonnel, Nathaniel, of Elizabeth Town, Essex Co., carpenter; will of. Children—Abigail Norris, Sarah Thompson, Mary Chanler, Nathaniel, Isaac and James. Three children of daughter, Hannah Broadwell deceased; names not given. Land joining lands of John Crane, John Clark, deceased, William Broadwell, William Jones; 140 acres by Scotch Plains, joining lands of Richard Beech and John Shadwell. Executors—wife, Mary, and son, Nathaniel. Witnesses—Jeremiah Mulford, William Jones, Benj'n Bonnel. Proved Sept. 13, 1736. Lib. C, p. 141.

1736, Sept. 20. Inventory of personal estate, £80.15.02; made by John Megie and Elijah Davis.

1745, April 19. Bonnel, Nathaniel, of Elizabeth Town, Essex Co. Bond of Joseph Bonnel, Esq., father, as administrator. John Crane, Esq., fellow bondsman. Lib. D, p. 268.

1745, April 2. Inventory of personal estate, £230.15.10½; made by Benjamin Bonnel and John Tooker.

[1733]. Boon, Peter (Salem Co., but no place or date named). "I give to my son, Peter Boon, 150 acres out of the 1000 in the Bout, 2 prs. of silver buttons, one bed, one iron pot, one Gunn, to be kept until he comes of age; the rest of the estate except one brown heifer I give to my mother Catherin Savoy. All the rest of the moveables to be at the discretion of my dear brother and executor, Andrew Boon, and he shall have the whole estate in case of the death of my son Peter." Witnesses—Henry Wallas, John Savoy. Proved 27 July, 1733, before surrogate of Salem County. Lib. 3, p. 373.

1733, May 12. Inventory (£60.18.0) of Peter Bown (Boon); made by Henry Wallas, Canneales Cannealson (Cornelius Cornelison).

1748-9, Jan. 7. Boon, Peter, of Penn's Neck, Salem County; will of. Executors—Cornelius Corneliuson and Jacob Pedrick. "They shall have my gun and the rents of my plantation whereon Charles Conaway lives, during six years from the time he was to pay rent." "I give to Cornelius Corneliuson my oxen, which were a legacy from my grand-father, Cornelius Corneliuson by his will." Witnesses—Thos. Carney, Michael Miller, Samuel Whitehorne. Proved 5 April, 1749. Lib. 6, p. 264 (duplicate pages in this Vol.)

1749, Apr. 3. Renunciation by Jacob Pedrick as executor. Dated at Penn's Neck.

1749, April 5. Inventory (£15.14.6.) includes pr. of oxen £7. Appraisers—Thos. Carney, Samuel Whitehorne.

1739-40, Feb. 27. Boone, Andrew, of Township of Penns Neck, Salem Co.; will of. "Two eldest sons: Peter and Andrew Boone to have equally my Lowest Plantation; that part next the river, where my old House is, I give to Peter, the other to Andrew." "My two youngest sons: Tobias and Cornelius Boon, to have equally the land I bought of Penn." "My sons Peter and Andrew shall pay to my brother Peter's son his due according to my brother Peter's will." Wife (not named) and daughter, Garter Boone. Executors—Wife, and Dobson Wheeler. Witnesses—John Savoy, Abigail Thackra, James Butterthworth. Affirmed 4 June, 1740. Letters testamentary granted to Ellena Boon, Executrix. Lib. 4, p. 239.

1740, April 1. Inventory (£176.5.7½) includes "his armor and apparel, linen and woolen yarn, loom and tackling, worsted stuff and yarn, swine, cows with calves, ewes and lambs, ½ of siene canoe," etc. Credits: bonds, etc., of Martin Mink, Robert Jones, Thomas Tackery, Michael Likam. Appraisers—Tim. Rain, Tho. Miles.

1748-9, Jan. 24. Booth, James, of Hopewell Township, Cumberland Co., weaver; will of. Sisters—Issable Booth, Agnes McClong, Esther McMungall, Margaret Wood and Elizabeth Nealy. Cousin—John Nealy (not 20), son of Joseph Nealy. Executors—Josiah Parvin and Joseph Peck. Witnesses—Samuel Moore, James Johnson, Peter Long. Proved 2 February, 1748. Lib. 6, p. 259.

1748-9, Jan. 31. Inventory of personal estate (£215.14.6) includes sword, gun and powder, and bonds in judgment upon John Findley, James Robinson and Aron Ayars. Appraisers—Saml. Moore, Charles Clark.

1730-1, Jan. 26. Borden, James, of Freehold Township, Monmouth

Co., yeoman. Joseph Burcham writes to Samuel Bustill to prove the will of James Borden; Joseph Burcham being indebted, "unto my mother-in-law, Mary Borden."

1730-1, Feb. 17. Robert Laurence and James Lowrie, executors named in above will, renounce their right. Addressed to Samuel Bustill, Esquire, at Burlington. (Letters of administration with the will annexed were granted to the widow, Mary Borden, a Quaker, February 22, 1730-1. For will, see preceding volume of Wills, Archives XXIII, p. 46.)

Monmouth Wills, 315-20 M.

1747, Sept. 8. Borden, John, of Bridgetown, Burlington Co., carpenter; will of. Estate, real and personal, to brother-in-law, Joseph Lewis. Executor—Uncle Henry Mitchell. Witnesses—Joseph Mullen, Alex. Robinson, Jno. Duncan, John Mullen. Proved Oct. 24, 1747.

Lib. 5, p. 370.

1748, June 19. Borden, Richard, of Middletown, mariner. Esther Borden, widow, renounces right of administration, in favor of John Stillwell, of same place, one of principal creditors. Witnessed by Edward Burrowes. Lib. E, p. 195.

1748, June 22. Bond of John Stillwell, administrator. Edward Burrowes, fellow bondsman.

1748, June 24. Inventory of estate (£104.18.8), incl. bonds and debts due from John Morford, Johannes Tice, Richard Brittain, John Hance, Jacob Billyou, James Pillyan, Peter Barker, John Allen, Matthias Mount, Samuel Bowne, John Layton, Jonathan Holmes and estate of Henry Tilton, deceased. Made by Thomas Morford, Esquire, Thomas Mount and Samuel Tilton, yeoman.

1749, June 20. Account of estate mentions Philip Kearney, Esquire, attorney; James Johnston; Thomas More of New York; John Porter; John Williams.

1737, May 4. Borton, Joseph, of City of Burlington, farmer; will of. Wife, Sarah. Children (all under age)—Hannah, Mary, Sarah, John, Rachel. Executors—wife and John Wright. Witnesses—Anthony Baker, Mary Baker, John Craig. Proved Oct. 8, 1737.

1737, July 30. Inventory, £163.8.0; made by Thomas Scattergood and John Craig. "Sarah Spencer, late Sarah Borton, executrix."

Burlington Wills, 2991-4C.

1735-6, Jan. 20. Boskerk, Peter, of Bergen Co., gent.; will of Wife, Tryntje, all real and personal estate during life and after her decease, as follows: The tract of land (600 acres) at New Hackinsack, at present in occupation of sons Lawrence and Johanes. To son Lawrence, the northeastern half (300 acres), bounded on Peter Demarie, S.E. by Teneck's Path and "land sold by me to my son Johannes," S. W. by Jacob VanBoskerk, N.W by the Road. Son, Johanes, the southeastern part of above mentioned 600 acres, bounded S.W by Benjamin VanBoskerk, N. W. by Teneck's Path, N.E. by David DeMarie, S.E. by Overpeck's Creek. Son, Andries, land and salt meadow (60 acres), "part of the estate whereon I now live" with a direct course to the Bay, S.E. to the Kill Van Kull, with the mills thereon. Son, Jacobus, rest of home plantation in Bergen County. Daughters—Jannetje (wife of Cornelis Corsen), Willemtje (wife of Abraham Shotwell), Antje (wife of Peter Tramelje), Rachel (wife of William Daniel). Executors—son, Andries, and son-in-law, Cornelis Corsen. Witnesses—Nicholas Veghte, Denis VanTuyl, Abraham VanTuyl.

———, January 21. Codicil, wherein changes are made in the distribution of personal estate, which includes slaves, Susan, Dian, Jenny,

Kuff. Same witnesses. Proved 8 Sept. 1738. Lib. C, p. 208.

1738, Oct. 10. Inventory of personal estate (£542.07.10), includes bonds of sons and sons-in-law (named in will); also bond of Calib Jeffers, mortgage from John Rolph, etc. Made by Hendrick Kroegen and Denis Van Tuyl.

1730-1, 23rd day, 12 mo. (Feb.). Boulsby (Bowlsby), Thomas, now of Burlington Co., yeoman; will of. "Whereas in Oct. 1727 there was surveyed unto me in Hunterdon Co. 1550 acres of land, 500 of which I sold to Abraham Hulings of Burlington, Esq. I now order the remainder to be sold to pay my debts." Son, Thomas, now in old England, land on branch of Rairington (Raritan) River in Hunterdon Co. Son, George, land lying between Whipeney Town and Mary Bullis. Son, John, to have his full quantity of my land. Father-in-law, Sam'll Barker, in his will gave land to my children—Elizabeth, Martha, Jane and Richard—200 acres in West Jersey. Executors—Son, John, and friend, Abraham Hulings, Esq. Witnesses—Jno. Allen, Sam'l Bickley, Thos. Scattergood, Sam'l Scattergood, Nathaniel Wilkison. Proved March 18, 1730. Lib. 3, p. 121.

1730-1, March 17. Inventory of personal estate, £82.2.6; made by James Billyeld, Nathaniel Wilkison and Titan Leeds.

1740-1, Feb. 25. Boulton, Sarah, of Mansfield, Burlington Co., widow; will of. Children—Isaac, Edward and Sarah Siders (Sidders). Grandaughters—Sarah and Rachel Cowgall and Sarah Sidders. Real and personal estate. Executor—son, Isaac. Witnesses—James Craft, Jun., Judy Adams, Thomas Scattergood, Jun. Proved Dec. 15, 1744. Lib. 5, p. 68.

1731, Sept. 27. Bourne (Burn), Patrick, of Haddonfield, Gloucester Co., laborer. Int. Admr., Thomas Teweywebb, of County aforesaid. John Hinchman, bondsman. Witnesses—Edwd. R. Price, Saml. Harrison.

1731-2, Jan. 8. Inventory, £16.03.11. Appraisers—Jno. Hinchman, Joseph Collins. Gloucester Wills, 133 H.

1748, —— ———. Bowen, Isaac, of Fairfield Precinct, Cumberland Co.; will of. Wife, Phebe, to have benefit of all lands and marsh (cedar swamp excepted), until sons Clephon and Isaac will be 21. Daughters—Phebe, Esther, Susannah. Executors—wife, Phebe, and David Westcott. Witnesses—Thomas Bateman, Abraham Sayres, Job Bateman. Proved 2 Sept., 1748.

1748, Aug. 29. Inventory of personal estate (£86.5). Appraisers—Ephraim Daton (his mark), Jehiel Wheeler. Lib. 5, p. 504.

1747, Oct. 12. Bowen, John, of Cohansey, Salem Co., yeoman; will of. Sons, Joseph and Samuel Bowen, to have equally land in Cohansey joining Esqr. Brick. Other sons—Isaac, John and James Bowen. Daughters—Lidya, Joana, Abigail, Hannah. Son, William Bowen, to have plantation I live on, also marsh joining Cohansey Creek, between the marsh of Samuel Harris and Nicolas Johnson; also 25 acres of marsh upon Stoe Creek, bought of Horner; also cedar-swamp, (1½ acres) in Broad Neck, known as Green Swamp, joining swamp of Samuel Brown, deceased; also right in dry swamp joining the same. Executors—wife, Rachel, and son-in-law, Neihemia Hoggbon. Witnesses—Noah Wheaten John Swinney, Jr., Job Shepherd, Jr. Proved 30 Nov., 1747. Lib. 5, p. 394.

1747, Nov. 24. Inventory, £123.08.03. Appraisers—John Remonten (Remington), Job Shepherd, Jr.

1735, April 18. Bowen, Richard, of Salem Co., yeoman. Int. Admr., Mary Bowen (widow). Bondsman, William Wright, of County aforesaid. Witness—Edw'rd R. Price. Lib. 4, p. 16.
1735, Feb. 25. Inventory, £16. Appraisers—Wm. Wright, Edwd. Hancock.

1742, Feb. 10. Bowen, Samuel, of Cohansey, Salem Co. Int. Admr., Martha Bowen (relict). Bondsmen—Seth Bowen and Stephen Bowen, all of Cohansey. Witness—Chas. O Neill. Lib. 4, p. 379.
1742-3, Feb. 12. Inventory (£87.11.2) includes cattle, horses, sheep, grain. Appraisers—Job Shepherd, Jr., John Rementon (Remington).

1745, Sept. 3rd and 17th. Bowler (Boller), Garrat, Junior, and Anna his wife. Inventory of personal estate (£22.16.03), includes carpenters' tools and debts due from Thomas Gale, Henry Bennett, William Brittan, Richard Rooe, Moses Lamburt, Joshua Hornor, Francis Williams and Josiah Howard. Made by Josiah Steward and Joshua Horner. Lanslot Lambert, administrator. Sworn Sept. 21, 1745. (Administration not found). Monmouth Wills, 1199-1204M.

1747-8, March 13. Bowne, James, of Middletown, yeoman; will of. Eldest daughter, Rachel Bowne. Second daughter, Sarah Bowne. Third daughter, Anna Bowne. Fourth daughter, Leah Bowne. Only son, Philip Bowne. Other daughters—Huldah, Edith and Margaret Bowne. To brother, Obadiah Bowne, land at Barnegat, inherited from testator's father, James Bowne. Executors—friend James Mott, brother Barzillai Newbold, and daughter Rachel Bowne. Witnesses—Thomas Cooper, Mathias Johnson, Patrick Foy, Samuel Bowne, Jr. Proved April 2, 1750. Lib. E, p. 377.
1750, March 31. Inventory of estate left in County of Burlington, £37.6.3; made by Thomas Black and Benjamin Shreve.
1750, April 4. Inventory of estate, £715.12.9; made by John Cooper and Edward Taylor.

1736, Jan. 10. Bowne, Nehemiah, of Shrewsbury, yeoman; will of. Wife, Deborah. Brothers—Peter Bowne, Andrew and Daniel Bray. Daughter—Mary Fisher, under 18 years. Executors—friends Thomas Tilton and Walter Herbert (Harbour). Witnesses—John Herring, Coast Miars, Sarah Worth. Proved February 16, 1736. Lib. C, p. 148.
———, ———. Inventory of estate of £116.14.0, includes cash received from Benjamin Keney; made by Henry Herbert and William Lawrence. Filed June 13, 1737.

1726, April 28. Bowne, Obadiah, gentleman, of Monmouth Co. Inventory of personal estate £577.4.0), appraised by Gersham Mott, Andrew Wilson and Samuel Ogborn, includes articles "in the Weaver's Shop." Among items—Five Pictures, "Oyl Colours;" a carbine and two pair of pistols; 24 grown cattle; 20 young cattle; yoke of oxen; 100 sheep; 16 horses; Bible and Large Concordance; Heylin's Cosmography; History Council of Trent; Second and Third Institutes; ten negros; two old wiggs. (For will of Obadiah Bowne, see previous volume of Wills, Archives XXIII, page 54).

1740, June 23. Boyce (Boice), Jacob, of Piscataway, Middlesex Co., yeoman. Bond of Neiltie Boyce, widow, of Somerset Co., as administratrix. Thomas Bowman, of Hunterdon Co., yeoman, fellow bondsman. Witness—James Smyth. Lib. C, p. 348.

1747, Nov. 7. Boyce (Boice), Mary, of Middlesex Co. "Whereas Jeremiah Field and said Mary, his daughter, then Mary Rappleyea, administrators on estate of George Rappleyea, late husband of said Mary, held bonds given by Jacob Boyce for debts due estate; and whereas said Mary later intermarried with one Jacob Boice, and said Jeremiah Field and said Mary Boyce have since deceased;" Jeremiah Field, eldest son of said Jeremiah, requires citation of said Jacob Boice to renounce right of administration on the estate of his wife. Witness—Isaac Dye.

1747, Nov. 13. Jeremiah Field, of Middlesex Co., granted administration on estate of his sister, Mary Boice. Benjamin Field, fellow bondsman. Lib. E, p. 102.

1730, Nov. 7. Boyer, Arthur, of Alloways Creek, Salem Co., sadler; will of. Sisters—Mary (wife of William Smith), Elizabeth (wife of Hugh Clifton), and Martha (wife of Gabriel Wood), to have ½ acres of land apiece in the town of Salem between John Surages and Peter Turner. Personal estate and rest of real estate to sisters, Mary Smith and Martha Wood. Executor—brother, William Smith. Witnesses—Ebenezer Eglington, Thos. Mitchell, Alexr. Simpson. Sworn and affirmed, 22 Dec., 1731. Lib. 3, p. 209.

Inventory (£58.16.6.) includes saddler tools and some curried leather. Appraisers—William Hunt, Alexr. Simpson.

1748, Oct. 17. Boylestone, Benjamin, of Morris Co. Int. Admr., Richard Gardner, Junior, of Morris Co., yeoman. Bondsman—Richard Fitz Randolph, of Perth Amboy, carpenter. Witness—Thos. Bartow. Lib. E, p. 251.

1748, Nov. 24. Inventory (£3.3.0), includes "tooth Drawers," 1 shilling. Appraisers—David M. Camly, Reuben Knape.

———, ———. Account; payments to Patrick M. Cashlin, Burklos Co., Lamuell Westburn, Richd Gardner, Nehemiah Rodgers, Elijah Collins, Robt. Turner, Patrick M. Caushlin, Rubin Knap, David M. Camly, Henry Simpson.

1745, Nov. 18. Brackney, Matthias, of Chester, Burlington Co., yeoman; will of. Sons—Matthias, John and Joseph, all under age. Daughters—Elizabeth Bevis and Hannah. Real and personal estate. Executors—wife, Frances, and son-in-law, Thomas Bevis. Witnesses—Sam'l Atkinson, Ruth Bispham, Joseph Bispham. Proved Sept. 13, 1746. Lib. 5, p. 417.

1746, 12th day, 4th mo. (June). Inventory of personal estate, £76.5.10; made by Saml. Atkinson and Henry Warrinton.

1746, Aug. 23. Account of Joseph Brackney, executor of Frances Brackney of Chester, widow, which said Frances was executrix of Matthias Brackney, showing payments to Samuel Wickward, Benj. Heritage, Wm. Sharp, Joshua Humphries, Henry Warrington, Samuel Atkinson, John Pare, Tho. Middleton, Joshua Bispham, Esq., Solomon Eldridge, Matthias Brackney.

1739, August 11. Bradberry (Broadberry), John, Capt., of Acquacknonck, Essex Co., miller; will of. Wife ———. Son, Richard, land on Third River, joining lands of Cornelius Loberson, Bastian Van Geassels. Daughters—Susanna and Elizabeth. Children of daughter, Mary Berry, deceased, viz., Mary and William. Executors—son-in-law, John Ludlow, and friend, Samuel Rattan. Witnesses—Rachel Vrelandt, Margaret Vreelent, Franseeyntyie Vreelant. Proved Sept. 7, 1742. Lib. C, p. 536.

1742, Sept. 17. Samuel Rutan, yeoman, declines to act as executor.

1742, Oct. 19. Inventory of personal estate, £1210.17.06; made by Joseph Johnson, Thomas Longworth and John Ogden, Jun'r.

1747, Sept. 11. Bradford, William, of Cohansey, Salem Co., husbandman; will of. Wife, Mary. Daughter, Reymond Bradford, to have 25 acres (being survey at the head of Peter Long's swamp); also 5 acres of salt marsh in John Belleas's survey. Son-in-law, Benjamin Parvin, 25 acres (being ½ of a survey, joining John Bennits; also 25 acres "on the south side of my survey." Son, William, to have residue of real estate. (Children are minors). Executors—son, William Bradford, and son-in-law, Benjamin Parvin. Supervisor—Ensign David Ogden. Witnesses—Thomas Hase (Hays), Ephraim Daten, Sn., Theophilus Elmer. Proved 25 March, 1749.

1749, May 24. Letters Testamentary granted to Executors. Lib. 6, p. 114.

1749, March 25. Inventory of personal estate, £86.1.4. Appraisers—Thomas Bateman, David Westcott, both of Fairfield precinct.

1739, June 3. Bradway, John, of Alloways Creek Precinct, Salem County, cordwainer; will of. Son, John, when 21, to have 50 acres at head of Cohansie, bought of Daniel Davis and Arthur Davis. Wife, Mary. Daughter, Hannah. Children of brother, William Clark. Executrix—wife, Mary, with son, John, when he will be of age. Witnesses—William Weatherby, Simon Sparks, Thomas Sparks, Richard Sparks, Nathaniel Box. Proved 25 Aug., 1739. Lib. 4, p. 203.

1739, June 14. Inventory (£176.11.8) includes one sword, 18 sheepskins and sole leather, calf skins in the hair, dry kids and leather in the tan vats, wheat and corn, etc. Appraisers—Jonathan Bradway, William Weatherby.

1744, Jany. 8. Bradway, Jonathan, of Allaways Creek, Salem Co., guardian. Ward, Bradway Casbey, orphan son of Edward Casbey, late of Salem, and of Elizabeth, his wife, also deceased. Witnesses—Ed. Rad Price, Jo. Scattergood. Lib. 5, p. 76.

1748, Dec. 7. Bradway, Joshua, of Salem Co., miller. Int. Admr., Aaron Bradway, yeoman. Bondsman—William Ridley; both of said County. Lib. 6, p. 49.

1748, Dec. 13. Inventory, £380.15.9. Appraisers—Samuel Wood, Thomas Sayre.

1739, Aug. 21. Bragg, Roger, of Salem Co., school-master. Int. Admr., Clement Hall, of Salem Town and County, merchant. Witnesses—Nathan Tarbell, Danl. Mestayer. Lib. 4, p. 199.

1739, 6 mo. (Aug.) 20 da. Inventory (£100.10.7.) includes "apparill and watch" £14.10.6. 159 pwt. 10 gr. of gold a 5/6, £43.16.9, and "advance on said gold, 3/— a pound, £6.11.6.; debts of Richard Granos, dec'd, and George Colson. Appraisers—Benja. Acton, Daniel Brandreth, Ranier Vanhiel.

1742-3, March 5. Brandford, William, of Hopewell, Hunterdon Co.; inventory of personal estate of, £70.15.2; made by John Phillips and Cornelius Anderson.

1743, March 26. Bond of Frances Branford, as administrator. John Phillips and Cornelius Anderson, of Hopewell, sureties. Witnessed by Robert Laning.

1746-7, January 27. Account of Frances Brandford mentions: Bartholomew Anderson, William Peirson, Andrew Reed, Enoch Anderson, Thomas Burroughs, William Branson, of Philadelphia, Edward Hunt, George Clifford, Frederick Vanoye, Elizabeth (or Eliez'r) Moresan (or Morgan), Cornelius Anderson, Humphrey Hughs, John Philips, John Lee, Andrew Mershon, James Bigger, Samuel Lee, William Moore, James Adams, Jonathan Reed, Samuel Ketcham, Daniel Coxe.

Hunterdon Wills.

1744, Oct. 11. Branson, Thomas, of Springfield, Burlington Co.; will of. Wife, Elizabeth. Children—David, Joseph, Jonathan, Lionell, William, John, and Sarah Owen. Grandchildren—children of Zachariah Robins and Mary his wife, and of William Rogers and Elizabeth his wife. Grandaughter, Abigail Rogers. Grandson, Thomas, son of John Branson, tract lying on "Shanandow river" in Virginia, "which I laid out to Thomas Alexander and one called 'Scotch Robin.'" Executors—sons, Thomas and John. Witnesses—James Antram, James Maclatche, John Osmond. Proved Nov. 21, 1744.

Lib. 5, p. 60.

1744, 3d mo. (May), 26. Brant, Samuel, of borough of Elizabeth, Essex Co., blacksmith; will of. Son, David, lands bought of Jeremiah Bird and Richard Lambert. Son, Lues (minor), lands bought of Lues Winans and William Winans, joining land of John Shotwell. Daughters—Hannah and Abigail Brant, both under age. Executors—wife, Susannah, brother, William Brant, and friend, Joseph Shotwell, of Rahway. Witnesses—Samuel Marsh, John Tooker, Josiah Winans. Proved Oct. 25, 1744. Lib. D, p. 189.

1744, Oct. 25. Samuel Marsh, Quaker, affirmed to his signature, and Joseph Shotwell, Quaker, qualified as executor.

1744, Nov. 3. Inventory of personal estate (£207.16), includes debts due from Andrew Bloomfield, David Steward, Benjamin Peck, John Terril, Richard Clark, Benjamin Moore, Richard Jones, Joseph Allton, Robert Pool, Isaac Winans, Thomas Scuder, William Porter, Robert Morss, Jun'r, Joseph Morss, Jacob Thorn, Daniel Lain, Benoni Frase, Benjamin Kelsey, John Ilslie, John Tucker; made by Samuel Marsh and Eze. Bloomfield.

1743, May 23. Braven, Newcomb, of Salem Co., mariner. Int. Admr., Hugh McAdam, principal creditor. Bondsman—William Maxfield. Both of Salem County, yeomen. Witnesses—Saml. Vanhist, Chas. O. Neill. Lib. 4, p. 371.

1743, May 23. Renunciation. Mary Ann Braven, relict of Newcomb Braven, in favor of Hugh McAdam.

1743, Sept. 17. Bray, Mary, of Chester, Burlington Co. Administration granted to Jonathan Thomas, of Waterford, Gloucester Co., yeoman. John Doe, fellow bondsman. Lib. 4, p. 371.

1743, Oct. 6. Inventory of personal estate, £4.16.10; made by John Pimm and Ephraim Coxe.

1731, Aug. 7. Brayman, Benjamin, of Greenwich, Gloucester Co., yeoman; will of. Son, Robert Brayman, plantation I live on, 8 acres of upland or swamp bought of Samuel Vaniman on Clamell Creek; also right to tract (100 acres), bounded south by land formerly Thomas Brights, on the east of Great Mantie's Creek. Son, John Brayman. Son, Thomas Brayman, 50 acres upon Nahansion Branch; also swamp on Great Mantie's Creek, between Fisher's land and land of Thomas Bright. These sons to have carpenter tools. Daughter, Sarah Brayman, undivided 64th part of Proprietary Right in West Jersey. Grandson, Benjamin Brayman, 50 acres above Ephiram Bee's land, and 6 acres of swamp on Great Mantie's Creek, bounded on Thomas Bright's land. Grandson, Jonathan Brayman, rights that remain to lands and swamp on Great Mantie's Creek; also plantation fronting on lower side of Great Mantie's Creek, "which my son Benjamin Brayman, lately deceased, dwelt upon." Daughters, Mary Holden and Rebecca Ares. Son, Robert, to be guardian of grandsons Thomas Bee and Benjamin Holden until they are of age. Sole executor—son, Robert Brayman. Witnesses—A. Randall, David Venaeman, James Dickson. Proved 26 April, 1733. Lib. 3, p. 293.

1733, Apr. 5. Inventory, £136.16.5½. Appraisers—Andrew Long, A. Randall.

1748, May 26. Breach, John, of Newton Township, Gloucester Co., yeoman; will of. "To Mary Chambers £100." Brothers, Simon, Peter and Thomas Breach, to have rest of estate, real and personal. Executors—brothers Simon and Peter Breach. Witnesses—John Thorne, Isaac Alberson, Hezh. Williams. Proved June 21, 1748. Lib. 5, p. 516.

1748, 4 mo. (June) 6 da. Inventory, £115.6.2. Appraisers—Robert Stephens, John Thorne.

1731, 4 mo. (June), 16 da. Breach, Simon, of Newton Township, Gloucester Co., yeoman; will of. Sons, John and Simon, to have 300 acres below the Great Road that leads to Gloucester and Salem, divided between them when Simon will be 21. Personal divided between wife, Mary, and four daughters Ann, Mary, Jane and Sarah, as they come to be 21. "If my wife be with child and it is a son that lives, he and my son Peter shall have that land (75 acres), between the said road and King's Run. If a daughter, then my son Peter shall pay her £20, when she comes to the age of 21 years." Executrix—wife, Mary. Witnesses—Rebekah Beverly, William Dennis, John Kay. Proved 23 Sept., 1731. Lib. 3, p. 156.

1731, Aug. 13. Inventory (£150.02.06), includes carpentry tools, negro, sheep, cattle. Appraisers—John Mickle, Abraham Alberson.

1740, Dec. 2. Brearley, Joseph, of Maidenhead, Hunterdon Co. Inventory of personal estate, £198.4.1; made by Samuel Hunt and John Ely.

1740-1, Jan. 19. Renunciation of Phebe Brearley, widow of Joseph Brearley of Maidenhead, in favor of Benjamin Brearley, brother of deceased, for the administration. Witnesses—Gregory (or George) Rozel and Alex: Biles.

1740, Jan. 23. Bond of Benjamin Brearley, of Maidenhead, yeoman, as administrator. John Ely, of Trenton, yeoman, and John Allen of Trenton, sadler, sureties. Lib. 4, p. 266.

1731, Sept. 16. Brearley, Sarah, of Maidenhead, in West Jersey, widow, being very sick; will of. Cloathing to Sarah Watson, Ruth Gumly and Ann Biles. Daughter, Sarah Watson. "I give and do freely remit to David Brearley my thirds of the plantation up the River." Personal estate to children, viz: John Biles, Elicksander Biles, John Brearley, David Brearley, Joseph Brearley, Benjamin Brearley, Sarah Watson and Ruth Gumly. Executor—John Brearley. Witnesses—Aaron Hews, Ashman Carpenter, Sarah Tear. Proved Oct. 27, 1731. Lib. 3, p. 161.

1731, Oct. 23. Inventory of personal estate, £149.7.1; including "an olde sorde." Made by John Anderson and Richard Stevens.

1744, 13th day, 4th mo. (June). Brian, Benjamin, of Northampton, Burlington Co.; will of. Wife, Mary, sole executrix. Mary, dau. of John Clifton, bond due from s'd Clifton. Grandchildren—Sarah and Mary, children of Wm. and Mary Stockton. Lands in Bridgetown, whereon Edward Jennet now dwells; 100 acres in fork of Rancocus Creek; land adjoining Josiah White and Abraham Warrington; ⅛ share in saw mill. Witnesses—Nathaniel Cripps, Samuel Cripps, John Osmond. Proved Feb. 13, 1747. Lib. 5, p. 399.

1749, 2 mo. (April), 13 da. Brian, Daniel, of Newton, Gloucester Co., laborer; will of. Estate equally to Robert Stephen, John Stephen, Joseph Michell, Isaac Michell and Archable Michel, all of same place. Sole executor—Robert Stephen. Witnesses—Joseph Ellis, John Littledeaile, Jun., John Kaighin. Proved 20 Sept., 1749. Lib. 6, p. 271.

1749, Sept. 19. Inventory, £40.9.0. Appraisers—Joseph Ellis, John Eastlack.

1743, 7th day, 9th mo. (Nov.). Brian, Rebecca, widow and executrix of Thomas Brian of Northampton, Burlington Co., deceased; will of. Daughters—Elizabeth (wife of Daniel Haines); Rebecca (wife of John Hank), and her eldest dau., Hannah; Sarah, wife of John Fenimore, and Ann. Son, John, his daus., Ellener and Ann. Grandchildren—Thomas, William, Uriah and Rebecca, children of son Abraham, deceased. Sheddock, eldest son of grandson Heron Brian. Sister, Sarah Dimsdall, deceased. Real and personal estate. Executors—son, John, and son-in-law, Daniel Haines. Witnesses—Will Petty, Isaac Hancock, Thomas Scattergood. Proved April 21, 1747. Lib. 5, p. 318.

1747, April 21. Inventory of personal estate, £459.11.6; made by James Lippincott and Peter Andrews.

1741, Oct. 16. Brian, Samuel, of Northampton, Burlington Co., yeoman; will of. Sons—Joseph and Jacob, both under age. Dau., Elizabeth Hugh. Real and personal estate. Executors—wife, Elizabeth, and brother, Joseph Hulings. Witnesses—Peter Andrews, Rebecca White, Alles Moore, Martha Shinn, Tho. Shinn. Proved Feb. 6, 1741. Burlington Wills, 3317-22C.

1741, Dec. 19. Inventory of personal estate, £47; made by William Murrell and William Buddell.

1734, 20th day, 3rd mo. (May). Brian, Thomas, of Northampton, Burlington Co., yeoman; will of. Wife, Rebeckah, sole executrix. Children—Benjamin, Samuel, Abraham, Elizabeth (wife of Daniel Haines), Sarah (wife of John Fenimore), Rebeckah and Ann. Sarah, widow of my son Thomas Brian. 400 acres bought of Francis Collins. Witnesses—John Burr, Henry Burr, Ju'r, Robert Vicary. Proved May 29, 1735. Lib. 4, p. 18.

1735, May 28. Inventory of personal estate, £544.6.9; made by Samuel Woolman and John Burr.

1749, Oct. 27. Briant, Andrew, of Borough of Elizabeth, Essex Co., yeoman; will of. Wife, Elizabeth. Children—John, Cornelius, Samuel, Andrew, and Mary Briant, all under age. Real and personal estate. Executors—friend, Charles Hole, schoolmaster, and brother, Simeon Bryant. Witnesses—Samuel Brooks, Daniel Pierson, Martha Post. Proved Dec. 2, 1749. Lib. E, p. 350.

1740, Mar. 25. Brice, John, of Salem Co., yeoman. Int. Admr., Ananias Sayre. Bondsman—Thomas Wethman (Weithman), yeoman. Both of said County. Lib. 4, p. 226.

1740, ———, —. Inventory, £28.7.0. Appraisers—Rich. Gibbon, Thos. Waithman.

1744, 12th d., 9th mo. (Nov.). Brindley, Elizabeth, of Shrewsbury, Monmouth Co.; will of. Grandsons—Vincent and George White, minors, money due testatrix from Thomas Holms; if they die, to children of testatrix's son, Daniel Lippincott. Granddaughters—Elizabeth, Andrea and Ann Lippincott, clothes, "which I had before I married William Brindley. Great bible to granddaughter, Elizabeth. Executors—cousins Joseph Corlies and Hezekiah Williams. Witnesses—John Webley, Stephen Wardell, Sarah Williams. Proved June 7, 1748, when Joseph Corlies, executor, a Quaker, was affirmed; the other executor, Hezekiah Williams, "not being in the said Province, as is said." Lib. E, p. 195.

1748, June 13. Inventory of estate, £77.18.0; made by Webley Edwards and Levi White.

1743, Oct. 10. Brinley, William, Junior, of Shrewsbury, Monmouth Co. Renunciation of widow, Kezia Brinley, addressed to "Mr. James Talman at his plantation," the chief creditor

1743, Oct. 12. Bond of James Talman, of Shrewsbury, as administrator. Pontius Stelle, of Perth Amboy, fellow bondsman. Witnesses—Thomas and Basil Bartow. Lib. D, p. 91.

1743, Oct. 15. Inventory of estate (£246.7.0), includes "Marrenors Books and Instrements," gun, negro man, share of a boat. Made by Isaac Hance and Thomas Lippincott.

1746, Oct. 5. Account of administrator mentions: Thomas Akins, Thomas and Josiah Holms, Samuel, Thomas and Jacob Lippincott, John Mill, William, Kezia, Thomas and John Brinley, Samuel Pintard, John, Sr., John, Jr., James and William Curlis, Webley Edwards, David Rolong, Emanuel and William Wolley, Isaac and Thomas Hance, Walter Harbort, Thomas White, Josiah Holstead, John Sears, Judiah, John and Seth Allin, Benjamin Luis, Amos White, Jr., Martin, Peter and Isaac Vandike, Mary Burdin, Timothy Aikin, Ephraim Parson, Richard Rogers, Abraham White, Amos Chanler, Nathaniel Parior, Doctor Eatton, Richard Fitzrandolph, Joseph Forman, Jacob Dennis, Stephen Cook, Doctor Harbour, Amos Chamber, Thomas Winrite, Sarah West, George Williams, Isaac Vicoros.

1742-3, March 10. Brinson (Brunson), Barefoot, of Somerset Co., yeoman; will of. Wife, Mary, executrix. Oldest son, John. Executor—Thomas Lawrence, Esq., of Philadelphia. Witnesses—Jos. Stout, Tho. Leonard, Robert Rolfe. Proved 13 May, 1748. Lib. 5, p. 472.

1732, Jan. 5. Britten, Richard, of Windsor, Middlesex Co. Bond of Samuel Rogers, of Allentown, Monmouth Co., gentleman, as administrator. Isaac Stelle and John Row, of Allentown, gentlemen, fellow bondsmen. Witnesses—Joseph Kinnan and Mary Borden.

Middlesex Wills, 533M.

1733, April 5. Brittin (Britten), Daniell, Sen'r, of Woodbridge, Middlesex Co.; will of. Son, Daniell, and his children, Nicholas and Elizabeth Britton. Sons, William and Benjamin, both under age. Daughters, Mary and Elizabeth, at 18 years. Grandson, Daniel, son of John Moores. Daughter, Deliverance, and her children, viz., James, Sarah and Elizabeth Moore. Land in Perth Amboy; lands bought of William Elstone, Moses Rolfe, Peter Codricke, Noah Bishop, John Jaquiss; land joining David Donham, Jun'r. Executors—wife, Elizabeth, John Moores, and son, William Britton. Witnesses—Charles Wright, Benjamin Codington, David Donham, Jun'r. Proved April 28, 1733. Lib. B, p. 400.

1736, Dec. 11. Britton (Brittain), Daniel, of Perth Amboy, Middlesex Co. Bond of Apphia Brittain his widow as administratrix. Moses Rolfe, Esq., fellow Bondsman. Lib. C, p. 136.

1748, Dec. 31. Britton, William, of Woodbridge, Middlesex Co., yeoman. Bond of Sarah Britton, his widow, and Samuel Moore, of Raway, as administrators. Edward Crowell, Esq., fellow bondsman.

Lib. E, p. 232.

1732, July 19. Broadwell, Richard, of Elizabeth Town, Essex Co., yeoman; will of. Children—John, David, Lydia, Sarah, Rachel, and Margaret Broadwell, all under age. Father-in-law, Nathaniel Bonell, and Samuel Chandler to take care of little daughters, Rachel and Margaret. "Plantation I purchased of Jonathan Allen on the north side of the great island by Woodruffs Creek." Executors—son, John, and brother, William Broadwell. Witnesses—Charles Hole, Mary Broadwell, Arnall Jolly. Proved Sept. 2, 1732. Lib. B, p. 348.

1732, Aug. 23. Inventory, £117.19.08, includes debts due from William Broadwell and John Baker; made by Samuel Potter and Jonathan Allen.

1745, May 9. Broadwell, William, of Elizabeth Town, Essex Co.; will of. Wife, Jane, plantation at Connecticut Farms. Sons—Josiah, William and Henry, all under age. Daughters—Mary Darling, Susannah Day, Jane, Ann, and Hester Broadwell, last three under age. Saw mill on and near Pissaick River in Essex and Morris Counties; land in Morris Co.; land in Elizabeth Town, joining lands of Benjamin Trotter, Nath'll Bonnell, Peter Willcock, John Magee, Jonathan Allen and John Chandler. Executors—sons Josiah and William. Witnesses—Jeremiah Ludlam, William Jones, John Pierson. Proved March 29, 1745. Lib. D, p. 372.

1745, March 14. Inventory of personal estate, £149.00.09; made by Daniel Day and John Potter.

1732-3, Feb. 18. Brock, Francis, of Woodbridge, Middlesex Co. Inventory of personal estate, £15,19.6; made by John Clarksone and John Shotwell.

1734, May 31. Administration granted to John Clarkson, and John Shotwell. Lib. B, p. 586.

1749, May 28. Broderick, Edmund, of Burlington, labourer. Administration granted to Abraham Heulings, of City of Burlington, merchant. John Bacon, of same, gent., fellow bondsman.

Lib. 6, p. 332; Lib. 7, p. 98.

1747, May 25. Brokaw, Abraham, of Somerset Co., miller; will of. Wife, Mary. Sons—Isaac, Bergone, Abraham, George, Christopher and John. Daughters—Catherine Vannest, Mary Defreest, Jane and Engeltje. Plantation of 306 acres on Millstone River, said plantation to be divided among six sons. Also ½ of a grist mill and 2 acres belonging thereto. Executors—son-in-law, Jeronimus Vannest, and "Cosyne" John Brokaw. Witnesses—Pieter Strycker, John Vanneste, Maregritje Bruwer. Proved 9 Sept., 1747, and Oct., 1747.
Lib. E, p. 93.

1747, Aug. 19. Inventory of real and personal estate £1356.8.8, includes large Dutch Bible, £3; silver cup, £1.4.; "Christofel's wearing apperrel, who being deceased," £1.2; "Engeltje's wearing apperrel, who being deceased" £5; steer belonging to Mary Deforsest, £1.15; half of grist mill, with 2 acres, £234.8.9; bond of Isaac Brokaw, £3.10. Made by Peiter Strycker, Burgon Hof.

1740, Nov. 14. Brokaw, John, of Somerset Co. Inventory of real and personal estate, includes lands sold to "Jeronemy Horne at New Shennick, Richard Pecal, lands adjoining John Staats, 300 acres upon Millstone River, "212 acres whereon Bergone Brokaw now lives," negroes Jack, Simon, Jacob, Herry, Old Betty, Hannah, Eva, Little Betty, silver cup and silver tencker, 38 oz @ 8 p., £15.4, copper chafondish £1, 1 gun, 2 swords and 1 silver Peyck, £5.15, large Dutch Bible £5. Bonds of Ross and Stanburey, Elyach and John Pound, Jeronimy Horne, John Cocks, Jacob Corsen, Lodewyke Wortman, Mary Covert, uncle Peter, John Sweck's note. Made by Corneleus Van Horne and Coenrat Teneyck.

1741, Aug. 3. Renunciation of Sara, widow of John Brokaw, in favor of her son John.

1741, Aug. 12. Administration granted to John Brokaw, oldest son of John Brokaw, late of Somerset Co., yeoman. Fellow bondsman, Jno. Van Middleswortt.
Lib. C., p. 426.

1738, Dec. 6. Brookes, John, of Chester, Burlington Co., yeoman. Inventory of personal estate, £229.4.51, made by Thomas Hackney and James Sherwin.

1738, Dec. 23. Administration granted to Catharine Brookes, widow. James Allen, of Northampton, and James Sherwin, of Chester, both yeomen, fellow bondsmen.
Lib. 4, p. 152.

1730, May 29. Brookes, Timothy, of Salem Co.; will of. Son, Timothy, to have land and plantation. Brother, Zebulon. Wife, Mary, sole executrix. Witnesses—Keziah Ayars, Joshua Ayars, Nathaniel Jenkins. Proved 1 April, 1731.
Lib. 3, p. 135.

1731, June 19. Peter Turner, administered on estate in place of Mary Brooks.

1733, Aug. 20. Brookfield, Job, of Elizabeth Town, Essex Co. Administration to Sarah Brookfield, widow.
Lib. B, p. 208.

1733, Aug. 25. Inventory of personal estate, £56.00.09; made by John Morris and Nathan'll Mitchell.

1733, ———, —. Accompt of Sarah Brookfield, administratrix and widow, showing payments to Jane Tongrelove, Matthias Hetfield, Gersham Higgins, William Garthwait, Robert Littel, William Donaldson, Andrew Joline, William Williamson, Samuel Whitehead, Benjamin Davis, Sarah

Morse, John Keyt, Henry Gathwaite, John Morriss, William Ogden, Nathaniel Mitchell, Ichabud Burnett, Jacob Deheart, Margat Grasillin, Caleb Jeffery.

1749-50, Feb. 18. Brooks, Henry, of Dearfield, Cumberland Co., yeoman; will of. Sons—Henry and Joel, to have equally 50 acres bought of Abraham Sayre; marsh of 20 1-5 acres bought of Uriah Mills, and Cedar swamp of 16 acres bought of Joseph Westcot. Brother—Josiah Brooks, to have ½ of plantation "he and I now live on, my half to be sold with the personal estate and divided among my four children, Mahattalle, Henry, Lydia and Joel." Executor—Robert Low. Witnesses—Jeremiah Buck, Daniel Royse, Isaac Miller. Proved 5 March, 1749.

1749-50, Feb. 23. Inventory of real and personal estate, £250.08.5. Appraisers—Jeremiah Buck, Joseph Daten.

1750, May —. Letters testamentary granted to executor. Lib. 6, p, 310.

1748, June 14. Brooks, Jacob, of Elizabeth Town, Essex Co. Bond of Deborah Brooks as administratrix. John Crane, Esq., fellow bondsman. Lib. E, p. 193.

1728, Dec. 3. Brooks, John, of Evesham, Burlington Co., yeoman; will of. Children—John, Dorothy, Goldy and Miriam. Grandson, Joseph Goldy. Wife's son and daughter, Matthew and Hannah Topham. Son, John, to pay my wife £20 "and she then will deliver to him the articles, dated April 10, 1722, which he hath broke." Real and personal estate. Wife, Elizabeth, sale executrix. Witnesses—Ruth Atkinson, Mahlon Stacy, Sam'll Atkinson. Proved Jan. 14, 1734. Lib. 4, p. 4.

1734, Nov. 19. Inventory of personal estate, £114; made by John Hollinshead and Sam'll Atkinson.

1738, —— ——. Brooks, John, Account of Andrew Anderson, administrator. John Brook's children, "for Dyet, Tendence, Nursing and Cloathing:"

To 13 week Dyet, Tendence, Nursing of Thos. Brooks in the Small pox	£ 3.18
To 3 years Dyet & Cloathing of Eliz. Brooks	18.00
To 2 years Dyet & Cloathing of Lucy Brooks	12.00
To 5 years Dyet & Cloathing of Esther Brooks	30.00
To 7 years Dyet & Cloathing of John Brooks	42.00
To 7 years Dyet & Cloathing of William Brooks	42.00
	£147.18

Paid debts due Joseph Rose, Sam'l Garwood, Isaac Willcox, Sam'l Lovett, Jno. Turner, Jno. Carrell, Wm. Cullom, Joseph Hewlings, Jacob Cooper, Fra. Dudley, Joseph Fenemore, Andrew Conors, Wm. Grott, Evan Thomas, Wm. Goldey, Hugh Hollinshead, Jos'a Wright, David Moffett, Matt. Brackner, Jno. Parrot. Burlington Wills, 3055-58 C.

1749, July 7. Brooks, John, of Deerfield Township, Cumberland Co. Int. Administration granted to Timothy Bateman, of Fairfield Township. Fellow bondsman—Alexander Moore, of Deerfield township. Witnesses—Elizabeth Cotting, Elias Cotting.

1749, May 2. Inventory of personal estate, £20.16.0; made by Charles Clark, Samuel Hannah. Cumberland Wills, 28 F.

1732, June 8. Brooks, Josiah, of Cohansey, Salem Co., yeoman. Int. Admx., Lucy Brooks (widow). Bondsman—Daniel Wescote. Both of said County. Witnesses—Ben. Davis, Nathan Hedge. Lib. B, p. 215.

1732, April 25. Inventory, £131.5.1. Appraisers: Daniel Wascote, William Beatman. (See also N. J. Archives, vol. 23, p. 62).

1750, March 11. Brooks, Josiah, of Fairfield Township, Cumberland Co. Int. Admx., Abigail Brooks. Fellow bondsman—Daniel Lummas. Witnesses—Elizabeth Cotting, Elias Cotting. Lib. 7, p. 425.

1750-51, Jan. 31. Inventory of personal estate, £124.10.8. Appraisers—Nathaniel Whitacar, Daniel Lummus.

1760, Sept. 5. Account of Catharine Stratton, Executrix of Jonathan, who, with his wife, were administrators of Josiah Brooks, deceased, shows cash paid to Alexander Moore, James Ayres, Richard Wood, Elias Cotting, Mary Henderson, Mathew Parvin, Robert Low, John Aeskin, Benjamin Sayre, Ephriam Buck, David Bowess (?), John Jay, Joseph Read, Benjamin Thompson, David Royle, Jacob Mulford, Ebenezer Darwin, John Johnson, W. Elmer, Isaac Fithian, John Presston, Hance Woolson, James Eayres, Daniel Bateman, Michael Bennit, Daniel Symes, Joseph Westcote, Enoch Bowen and John Bateman.

1747, Dec. 9. Brooks, Philip, of Elizabeth Town, Essex Co., yeoman. Mary Brooks, widow, declines administration and desires that her son, Samuel Brooks, be appointed. Witnesses—Andrew Briant, Elizabeth Briant.

1747-8, March 9. Bond of Samuel Brooks as administrator. John Denman, yeoman, fellow bondsman. Lib. E, p. 138.

1747, Dec. 7. Inventory of personal estate (£117.14.06), incl. five pictures in frames, negro woman and child, and debts of Jacob and Samuel Brooks due their father's estate; made by Timothy Whitehead and Charles Hole, schoolmaster.

1730, June 5. Brooks, Timothy. (See N. J. Archives, vol. 23, p. 63).

1744-5, March 7. Brooks, Zebulon, of Cohansey, Salem Co., yeoman; will of. Wife, Esther, sole executrix. Son, John, 5 shillings "or as much as will cut him off from a child's portion." Son Zebulon "land I now live on," which runs along Job Shepherd's line 40 rods, along Mr. Jenkin's line 80 rods, containing 20 acres square; likewise land upon the N. side of Greenwich Road, 2 acres of swamp joining Capt. Shepherd's line, and set of shoemaker's tools. Son, Joseph, rest of land with improvements thereon. Provisions for unborn son, if any. Plantation in the woods. Daughter—Mary. James, at 16, to be bound to Thomas Ewings, Jun., to learn blacksmith's trade; Zebulon to Thomas Parks to learn shoemaker's trade. Witnesses—Seth Bowen, Joseph Shepherd, Job Shepherd, Junr. Proved 3 Feb., 1748. Letters issued Mar. 23. Lib. 6, p. 244.

1730, June ——. Brotherton, John and Elizabeth, choose as their guardian Benjamin Smith, of Woodbridge, to whom letters of guardianship are granted. William Bunn, bondsman. Lib. B, p. 160.

1730, June 20. Brotherton, Grace, Ann, Henry, James, children of Henry Brotherton, of Woodbridge. Letters of guardianship issued to Abraham Shotwell, of East Jersey. Middlesex Wills, 481L.

1725, Mar. 29. Brower, Abraham, of Hackinsack, Bergen Co., weaver; will of. Wife, Lea Brower, executrix. Brother-in-law, James Cristy, and Pieter Demarest, tutors and administrators of my minorenne children; also co-executors and assistants. Eldest son, Petrus Brower, has received his share (½ of home-lot on the east); son, David, to have land on the west side of Little Mill brook; son, Johannis, residue of real estate, which is easterly to the land of my son Petrus. Other sons, Samuel and Daniel. Daughters—Lea, Rachel, Mary (youngest). Witnesses—Benjamin Demarest, Miklaes Bon, David Demarest. Proved 19 April, 1736. Lib. C, p. 82.

1736, April 19. Lea Brower, alias Westervelt, and Peter Demarest qualify as executors.

1748, Feb. 10. Brown, Benjamin, of City of Burlington, carpenter. Administration granted to Preserved Brown, Jun'r, of Springfield, yeoman. Julius Ewan, of same, yeoman, fellow bondsman.
Lib. 6, p. 330; Lib. 7, p. 96.

1736, Jan. 17. Brown, Charity, of Philadelphia, Pa., widow; will of. Sister, Elizabeth Jones, wife of Andrew Jones, plantation in Gloucester Co. whereon they live; after her death my nephew John Jones, son of said Andrew, to have same. Owen Owen, of Phila., house carpenter, to have lot in Mulberry Street (19 ft.) commonly called Arch Street, bounded on the west by vacant lot of mine, north with ground of Thos. Knight and Joshua Emlen. Legacies to Mary Chambers, (wife of Robt. Chambers), of Menchion Hampton, Gloucester Co., England; Ruth Karsey (wife of Charles Karsey) of Hampton; Ann (wife of Wm. Hill) of Horsley, Gloucester, England; Joseph and Charles Brown, brothers of my late husband John Brown, and my cousin, Nathaniel Chew, at 21. Brother, Thomas Chew. To the Congregation of Christ Church, Philadelphia, £20, towards finishing said church. Robert Chambers, son of said Robert and Mary his wife, one moiety of rest of estate, real and personal; other moiety to my two sisters, Mary Langley, now living at Cohansey, N. J., Elizabeth Jones and Priscilla Owen, wife of Owen Owen. Executor—Samuel Mickell, Esq., of Philadelphia, merchant. Testatrix's signature by copyist; missing in original will. Witnesses—Abraham Pratt, John Bollen, John Robinson. Proved 19 Oct., 1739. Lib. 4, p. 171.

1739, Oct. 20. Inventory of Charity Brown, widow, late of Philadelphia, decd. (£620.0.6), includes bonds from James Wills, Edward Williams, Ebenezer Tomlinson, William Tatam, Amariah Bellinger, Michael Chew, Stephen Armitt, Michael Fisher, Saml. Harrison, Gibbins Lawrence, Jacob Medcalfe, Gabriel Nowby, John Blackwood, Nathl. Tonkins, Charles Beverly, Tobias Holloway, Benj. Paschall, Henry Thorn, Sarah Norris, Geo. Young, Francis Haddock, John Eastlick, Benj. Worthington, Mary Robinson, Rich. Barrin, Jos. Jackson, Frances Simson, Thos. Woolsted, Wm. Stamton, Gabriel Nelson, Jonas Cox, Edward Humphrey, Israel Longacre, Danll. Wolly, Rich. West, Wm. Lindsey, Edwd. Readwell, Peter Marriage, Jno. Bond, Geo. Ward, Sen., Jno. Blackwood, Widdow Medcalfe, Samll. Farrier, Thos. Rogers, Wm. Peters, Jno. Peters, Ephraim Saely, Wm. Tatum, Edward Willson, Rich. Skirm, Black Christopher, Wm. Cunningham, Noal Mackneal, Ellis Davis, Sarah Wilson, Jacon Medcalfe, Thomas Bryan, Jno. Cowle, Robt. Garrard, Jno. Ogilby, Wm. Long, Geo. Sherrel, Eliza. Wainwright, Isaac Hollingham, Israel Lock.

1739, Nov. 9. Brown, Charity, late of Gloucester Co., widow, deceased (with testament annexed) during absence of Samuel Mickle, sole executor; letters of adm. granted to Owen Owen, of Philadelphia, joiner. Fel-

low bondsman—Saml. Harrison. Witnesses—Isaac Browne, Joseph Rose.
1741, Oct. 28. Brown, Charity, late of Philadelphia, widow, deceased, made her last will duly executed and thereof appointed Samuel Mickle sole executor, who renounced the same. Owen Owen was appointed admr. Whereas he died, leaving part of said Charity's estate unadministered, Priscilla, widow and executrix of the above bound Owen Owen, to administer upon what remains. Fellow bondsman—Samuel McColloch. Witnesses—Ed. R. Price, Joseph Rose.

1746, Nov. 4. Brown, Jane, of Woodbridge, Middlesex Co. In 66th year; will of. Friend, Jonathan Kinsey, Jane, eldest daughter of Benjamin Kinsey, at 21 years. Benjamin Kinsey, great Bible. Friends Meeting in Woodbridge, remainder of estate. Executors—friends, Nathaniel Fitz Randolph, of Woodbridge, blacksmith, and John Kinsey, attorney at law. Witnesses—Micajah Bunn, Hartshorne Fitz Randolph, Nugient Kelly. Proved Oct. 19, 1748. Lib. E, p. 216.

1749, Aug. 7. Brown, Jeremiah, of Mendom Township, Morris Co.; will of. Wife, Mary, to have personal estate absolutely and possession of the real estate until the children, Rhoda, Abner, Paul and Elenezer, will be 21. Executors—wife, Mary, and Brice Riky, of Somerset County. Witnesses—William Axtell, Isaac Ballet, Benjamin Linsley. Proved 30 Aug., 1749. Lib. E, p. 325.

1747, 29th day, 12th mo. (Feb.). Brown, Joanna, of Rodmantown, Burlington Co., widow; will of. Daughter, Ann. Grandchildren—Ephraim, Mary, Hannah and Hope Haines. Personal estate. Executors—friends, Sam'l Stokes, and Tho's Stokes. Witnesses—Joshua Bispham, Sam'l Atkinson. Proved April 12, 1748. Lib. 5, p. 408.
1747-8, March 12. Inventory of personal estate, £139.9.0; made by Joshua Bispham and Arthur Borradaill.

1727, 11 mo. (Jan.), 26 da. Brown, John, of Town and County of Gloucester; will of. Wife, Charity, to have all of real estate and personal excepting £200 to my sisters, Mary (wife of Robert Chambers, living in Menchion Hampton, near Strowdewater, "Gloucester Shire," Old England; Ruth (wife of Charles Karsey), of same place, and her son, Charles Karsey; Ann Brown (not knowing whether she be married or not); and my brother, Charles Brown. Wife impowered to sign deed of conveyance to George Ward, or his heirs, for the fulling mill. Sole executrix—wife Charity. Witnesses—John Wood, Priscilla Flemingham, Thomas Sharp. Proved 21 Dec., 1736. Lib. 4, p. 101.
1737, May 28. Whereas John Brown, late of Gloucester Co., yeoman, died in Philadelphia and left a last will, dated 26 Jany., 1727, and it has been proved in due form in Pennsylvania, letters of adm. within Province of New Jersey issued in due form. Lib. 4, p. 102.

1734, Feb. 26. Brown, John, of Deptford, Gloucester Co.; will of. Sons—John, Thomas, Chatfield and James, to have the real estate equally. Expected child. Daughters—Mary and Phebe. Executors—wife and friends, Alexander Randall and Joseph Young. Witnesses—Mary Chester, Gabriel Rambo, Sarah Dryver. Proved 24 Dec., 1736. Lib. 4, p. 79.
1736, Dec. 10. Inventory, £342.14.9½. Appraisers—Peter Rambo, Gabriel Rambo. Signed, Phebe Brown, executrix.
1738, Sept. 25. Account of Phebe Brown, executrix, moneys paid to

Gabriel Rambo, Wm. Aldridge, Abraham Chattin, George Cozens, Wm. Wilkins.

1731, Sept. 23. Brown, John, Senior, late of Deptford, Gloucester Co., yeoman. Int. Admr., Levi Pearce, yeoman. William Harrison, gentleman, Edward Rudolphas Price, same County, bondsmen. Witnesses—John Wright, Saml. Bustil. Lib. 3, p. 153.

1731, Aug. 17. Inventory (£401.14.0), includes Indian man and child, negro woman and boy, etc., and debts due from Thos. Bryon, William Vaughns, Thos. Mingleston (?). Appraisers—William Harrison, Henry Sparks.

1733, Sept. 17. Account of Levi Pearce, Admr., shows moneys paid to William Hudson, John Brown Fuller, John Sherburn, Ann Wheeldon, John Spring, George Ward, Jr., Bryam Conelley, James Parrock, William Bryan, James Brindley, William May, Charles Beverly, Thomas Chew, Enoch Ellison, Walter Griffiths, George Ward, Michael Fisher, Thomas Wilkins.

1735, Jan. 24. Brown, John, of Salem County. Int. Admx., Johannah Brown (relict). Bondsman—Jeremiah Baker. Witnesses—William Philpott, Danl. Mestayer. Lib. 4, p. 57.

1736, April 24. Inventory, £29.1.0. Appraisers—Jeremiah Baker, William Philpott.

1737, May 8. Brown, John, of Mansfield, Burlington Co., Doctor; will of. Dau., Elizabeth Lawrence. Each grandchild now born 20 shillings and a silver spoon. Wife, Elizabeth, sole executrix and to be guardian of grandson John, son of my son, John Brown, dec'd. Witnesses—John Rockhill, Peter Imlay, Isaac DeCow, medius. Proved Aug. 1, 1737. Lib. 4, p. 109.

1747, Sept. 10. Brown, John, of Hanover, Burlington Co., will of. Children—Clayton, Theodidia Groves, John plantation at age, he paying legacies to Samuel, Sarah and Catharine and making suitable provision for my wife Catherine, his mother. Negro Jim his freedom in 4 years. Real and personal estate. Executors—wife and brother Abraham Brown. Witnesses—William Emley, Sam'l Emley, Mary Emley. Proved July 30, 1748. Lib. 5, p. 528.

1748, July 24. Inventory of the personal estate, £629.7.4; made by Jacob Andrews and Saml. Emley, includes "One Grate Bible" and sundry other books £3.5. Cattle £209 and negroes [136.

1749, May 19. Brown, John, of Township of Hopewell, Cumberland Co., yeoman; will of. Wife to have plantation until son Isaac will be 21. Daughter, Anna Brown. Executors—wife and Jonathan Holmes, Esq. Witnesses—Daniel Mieller, Thomas Brown, Robt. Nicholls. Proved 29 June, 1749.

1749, ———, —. Letters testamentary granted to Deborah Brown, executrix named in will. Lib. 6, p. 297.

1749, June 6. Inventory of personal estate, £105.10.3. Appraisers—Abraham Reeves, Samuel Miller.

1743-4, Feb. 2. Brown, Lanslott, of Chester, Burlington Co., yeoman; will of. Wife, Joan. Grandchildren—Hannah, Ephraim and Mary Hains, all estate in Province of New Jersey or elsewhere. Executors—friends Samuel Stokes and Arthur Borradell, and if they should die before s'd grandchildren are of age, then my son-in-law Nehemiah Hains. Witnesses—Richard Matlack, John Willis, Isa. DeCow. Proved Oct. 22, 1746. Lib. 5, p. 268.

1746, Oct. 22. Inventory of personal estate, £272; made by Rob't Smith and Jos. Hollinshead, includes note due from Joshua Bispham.

1749, Jan. 27. Brown, Margaret, of Burlington Co., widow. Administration granted to Edward Brown. Job Lippincott, yeoman, fellow bondsman. Lib. 7, p. 91.

1749, Feb. 5. Inventory of personal estate, £16; made by John Monrow and Henry Cooper.

1741, Sept. 21. Brown, Mathew, of Piles Grove, Salem County. Int. Admr., Benjamin Bispham. Bondsmen—John Elwell and Reynolds Hawk of Pilesgrove, same County. Witnesses—Andw. Gardner, Chas. O. Neill. Lib. 4, p. 289.

1741, Sept. 15. Renunciation. Hannah Brown in favor of Benjamin Bispham, as Admr. Witnesses—Reynold Hawk, John Elwell.

1741, Sept. 15. Inventory (£29.15.0) mentions Joseph Morgen, Edward Hughes. Appraisers—John Elwell, Reynold Hawk.

1743, April 12. Brown, Phebe, of Deptford Township, Gloucester Co., widow. Int. John Brown, yeoman, admr. John Wood and Gabriel Rambo, of same place, yeomen, fellow bondsmen. Lib. 4, p. 379.

1743, 2 mo. (April), 2nd. Inventory (£148.10.4) includes bonds from Joshua Hewett, Nehemiah Cowgill, Peter Rambo, Will'm Williams, Gabriel Rambo, Peter Cox, Nathan Paull, Luke Gibson, Isaac Atkinson, Andrew Long, Edward Hewes. Appraisers—John Wood, Gabriel Rambo.

1743, ———, —. Account of John Brown, Admr., shows cash paid Joseph Rose, John Munyon, Gab. Rambo, Abrm. Chattin, Jno. Wood, Josa. Lord, Peter Rambo, Martha Young, Eliza. Rambo.

1749, Feb. 5. Brown, Preserved, of Hanover, Burlington Co. Inventory of the personal estate, £68.0.3; made by John Monrow and Henry Cooper, includes bonds of Thomas Stevenson and Sam'l Gaskill.

1749, Feb. 6. Mary Brown, widow and administratrix, affirms to above. Lib. 7, p. 101.

1734, March 23. Brown, Richard, of Northampton, Burlington Co., yeoman; will of. Wife, Elizabeth, sole executrix. Sons—Richard and Benjamin; latter at 21 to have benefit of plantation with mother. Daughters—Hannah Ridgway, Mary, Rachel and Esther. Daughter-in-law, Prudence Powell. Witnesses—Rob't Powell, John Lavenner, John Ewan. Proved May 12, 1735. Lib. 4, p. 19.

1735, April 21. Inventory of personal estate, £264.6.10; made by Nathaniel Cripps and James Wills.

1726, Dec. 5. Brown, Thomas, of Woodbridge, Middlesex Co., yeoman; will of. Mother, Annapel Brown. Brothers—William, Andrew and James Brown. Sister—Christian Brown. Alexander, son of Thomas Eger. Annaple, daughter of John Mootry. Real and personal estate. Executors—brother-in-law, Thomas Eggers and brother, William Brown. Witnesses—Rob't Hude, Will'm Stone, D. Stewart. Proved Feb. 9, 1740. Lib. C, p. 390.

1733, Aug. 10. Brown, Thomas, orphan (son of Thomas Brown, late of north side of Cohansey, Salem County, and Anna, his wife, also deceased) ward. Guardian, Josiah Fifthian, Esq., of same place. Witnesses—John Pruttan (?), Joseph Goulding. Lib. 3, p. 366.

1737, May 10. Brown, Thomas, of Essex Co., orphan, aged about 14 years. Bond of Daniel Tichener and Silas Halsey, yeoman, both of Newark, to be guardians. Jonathan Crane, Esq., fellow bondsman. Lib. C, p. 160.

1749, April 4. Brown, William, of Monmouth County, yeoman. Inventory of estate, £38.17.6; made by John Smith and Joseph Forman. Land and buildings not appraised; 70 acres sold out of Loan Office. Lib. E, p. 307.

1749, June 14. Ann Brown, widow, declines administering, in favor of Isaac Dye. Joseph Forman, principal creditor, witness. Bond of Isaac Dye of Middlesex County, yeoman, as administrator of estate. John Stelle, of same county, Esquire, fellow bondsman.

1730-1, Feb. 9. Browne, Daniel, of Newark, Essex Co., cooper; will of. Daughters—Mary Ward, Abigail Robards, Esther Tichnor, and Dorcas Bruen. Grandson—Joshua Ward, son of daughter, Sarah Ward, deceased. Real and personal estate. Executors—wife, Abigail, and son-in-law, David Ward. Witnesses—David Shipman, John Baldwin, Josiah Beech. Proved Jan. 11, 1732. Lib. B, p. 375.

1732-3, Feb. 26. Inventory of personal estate, £206.10.03; made by Jonathan Crane and Sam. Farrand.

1746-7, Jan. 23. Browne, Daniel, of Newark, Essex Co., weaver; will of. Wife, Mary. Children—Joseph, John, Susannah, all under age. Expected child. Real and personal estate. Executors—brother Job Brown and Samuel Camp. Witnesses—Aaron Brown, John Lyon, Thomas Price. Proved Feb. 14, 1746. Lib. E, p. 76.

1746-7, March 5. Inventory of personal estate, £155.04.00; made by John Ogden and Nathaniel Johnson.

1730, Jan. 7. Browne (Brown), Joseph, of Newark, Essex Co., yeoman; will of. Son—Job Browne, lands on Raway River, joining lands of Timothy Osborn, Daniel Baldwin, John Browne; land a gift from my father, Joseph Johnson; land on Maple Island, joining lands of brother, James Brown, deceased, Mr. Samuel Alling and brother, Stephen Brown. Son—Daniel, lands joining lands of Mr. Jonathan Crane, Jonathan Sayer, and Joseph Wood; land purchased from Jonathan and Benjamin Lindsley. Daughters—Hanah Camp and Elener Browne. Wife, Margaret. Executors—friends, Stephen Brown and John Cooper. Witnesses—David Howell, Thomas Sargent, Jonathan Sargent, Jun'r. Proved April 17, 1734. Lib. B, p. 505.

1732, Oct. 29. Bruer (Brower), John, of Somerset Co., farmer; will of. Children—John, eldest; Dirck, second; Antye, and "last and youngest son." Executors—Johanes Colyer, of Long Island, Kings Co., and Tunis Post and Hendrick Bris., both of Somerset Co. Witnesses—William Post, Samuel Bruer, Cornelius Willemje. Proved 30 November, 1732. Lib. B, p. 328.

1732, Nov. 13. Inventory of personal estate, £107.7.6; made by William Post, Jury Andries.

1749, April 13. Brush, Thomas, of Amwell, Hunterdon Co., yeoman, being sick; will of. Wife, Martha, one-third of estate. £80 due Ezekiel Rose. Son, Philip, sixty acres of land at end of 200-acre tract on which testator lived; also "a chest that was his brother, Eliphalet's." Son, Abner, 140 acres, remainder of plantation; and 100 additional acres adjoining. Daughters—Elizabeth Scidmore, Abigail Killsey, Sarah, Martha and Mary Brush. Son, Abner, executor. Witnesses—Charles Sexton, Timothy Brush and Andrew Smith, Jr. Proved May 24, 1749. Lib. 6, p. 242.

1749, April 25. Inventory of estate, £178.0.2; made by Andrew Smith, Jr., Robert Combs and Timothy Brush.

1742-3, March 21. Bryan, Abraham, of Northampton, Burlington Co., yeoman. Inventory of personal estate, £360.6.1; made by James Lippincott and William Murrell.

1743, March 24. Administration granted Mary Bryan, widow. John Fenimore, of Springfield, yeoman, and John Willis, watchmaker, fellow bondsmen. Lib. 4, p. 379.

1733, Feb. 4. Bryan, Thomas, Jr., of Burlington; will of. Wife, Sarah. Children—Haran, Samuel, Joseph, Benjamin. Mentions brother, Benjamin, and sons-in-law, Manuel and Samuel Cox. Wife, sole executrix. Witnesses—Joseph Rockhill, Robert Tuckniss, Edna Fisher. Proved March 21, 1736. "Sarah Kenney, late Sarah Bryan," affirms.

1734, March 30. Inventory, £64.5.2, made by Joseph Heulings and Nathan Lovett. Burlington Wills, 2665-72 C.

1734, June 6. Bryant, John, of Philadelphia, baker; will of. Wife Sarah. To brothers and sisters—William, Valentine, Benjamin, Sarah, Elizabeth, Anne, Mary, Alice, each one shilling. Executrix—the wife. Witnesses—Thomas Dunning, Joseph Fordham, William Parsons. Proved July 15, 1734. Burlington Wills, 2673-4C.

1748-9, February 14. Bryant, Mary, of Hopewell Township, Hunterdon Co. Inventory of estate, £158.7.6; made by Benj. Rounsavall and Samuel Stout. Bond of William Bryant, of Hopewell, as administrator. Benjamin Rounsaval, of Hopewell, surety. Witness—John Pearce. Lib. 6, p. 75.

1742-3, Feb. 10. Bryant, William, Sr., of Hopewell, Hunterdon Co., husbandman; will of. Wife, Sarah, estate for life, and then, to son Volintine, 107 acres of land "which now haith Coranal Cox's titall;" house and land where testator lived to son, Volentine. Son, William Bryant, all interest of a £100 bond given to testator for house and lot at Philadelphia, dated April 6, 1730 (or 1740). Daughters—Sarah, Elizabeth, Ann, Mary and Alice, (Mary being yet unmarried). Executors—friends, Benjamin Rounsevol and William Bryant, Jr., of same town. Witnesses—Isaac Herin, Edmond Herin and Thebald Shavar. Proved Oct. 23, 1744, by Isaac Herring, Esquire, and Theobald Shavar. Lib. 5, p. 54.

1732, Dec. 20. Bryant, William, of Hopewell, Hunterdon Co., being very sick; will of. Daughter, Joyce Tirrill. Granddaughters—Johanah Tirrill, Hilyard Tirrill. Friend, Jeams Richards. Executors—daughter, Joyce Tirrill, and Samuel Green; they to give Joseph Phillips deed for land testator sold him. Husbands of granddaughters. Witnesses—Robert Combs and Christian Clemens. On back of will: If heirs of daughters all die, estate to fall among nearest relations, Jeams Richard's children. Proved February 7, 1732. Joyce Tyrrell, executrix, sworn same day. Lib. 3, p. 258.

1732-3, Feb. 2. Inventory (£188.11.0), includes debts due from Joseph Philips and bond of Samuel Ketcham. Made by Abraham Laruwe and Robert Combs.

1749, Sept. 20. Bryant, William, of Salem County. Int. Admr., Thomas Clement. Bondsman—Daniel Mestayer. Both of said county. Lib. 6, p. 281.

1738, April 17. Buck, Ephraim, of Cohansey, Salem Co., weaver; will of. Wife, Ruth, use of house and lands until son Ephraim will be 21, which will be in 1753. Sons, Ephraim and Joseph Buck, (both minors), all houses, lands, marshes and tenements. In case Hannah Buck, daughter of my brother Henry, cannot maintain a right, by law, to that property given her in my father's will, then she shall have at 18 that land (90 acres) and marsh (10 acres) which my father bought of William Rush between Thomas Brown and John Pratten's and Robert James's land, but in case she leaves no issue, my sons shall have the same. Daughter, Abigail Buck (not 18). Apprentice, Peter Dayton. Executor—wife and Jeremiah Buck. Witnesses—Samuel Harris, Nathaniel Bishop, Nathaniel Harris, Moses Bishop. Proved 15 June, 1738. Lib, 4, p. 177.

1738, April 24. Inventory (£124.13.6.) includes cattle, negro girl, "3 lums, tackling, two pearse of combs and hooks." Appraisers—Moses Bishop, Saml. Harris.

1734, July 17. Buck, Joseph, of Cape May Co.; will of. Wife, Lydia, sole executrix. Brothers—Thomas and John Buck. Witnesses—William Johnson, Frs. Taylor, Thomas Stonebanks. Proved 9 August, 1734. Lib. 3, p. 443.

1734, July 20. Inventory of personal estate (£82.08.01), includes cattle, horses, sheep and swine. Appraisers—Ebenezer Swaine, William Johnson.

1739, Nov. 10. Buckalew, George, of Perth Amboy, Middlesex Co., yeoman; will of. Children—Richard, Jeames, George, Jonathan, William, Pressillah, Susannah and Sary. Land on Back Creek purchased of William Melvan. Executors—wife, Sarah, and brother, William Buckallu. Witnesses—William Melvin, Joseph Hall, N. Everson. Proved Dec. 3, 1739. Lib. C, p. 301.

1748, April 26. Buckley, Grace, of Penns Neck, Salem Co., widow. Int. Admr., Jenkin Grafton. Bondsmen—Michael Pedrick, Alen Conglington, all of Penns Neck. Witnesses—Samuel Whitehorne, Richd. Gibbon. Lib. 6, p. 51.

1748, April 18.—Inventory, £90.6.4 ½. Appraisers—Alen Congelton, Samuel Whitehorne.

1749, April 14. Buckley, James, of Hunterdon Co. Bond of Mary Buckley, widow, as administratrix. Henry Johnson and Geysbert Dehart, of same county, sureties. Witness—Cornelius Wyckof. Lib. 6, p. 78.

1750, May 10. Buckley, Joseph, Administration granted to Judah Folke, of City of Philadelphia, merchant. Robert Hartshorne, of City of Burlington, atty-at-law, fellow bondsman. Burlington Wills, 4609C.

1738, Dec. 15. Budd, Elizabeth, Relinquishment of Mary Shinn, Susannah Gaskill, William Budd, David Budd, Rebecca Lamb, Abigail, Elizabeth and Ann Budd to their brother, of administration on estate of their mother, Elizabeth Budd.

1738, Dec. 25. Administration granted to Thomas Budd, of Northampton, Burlington Co., yeoman. Lib. 4, p. 152.

1730-1, Feb. 21. Budd, John, of Northampton, Burlington Co.; will of. Wife, Hannah, sole executrix, and to have tract bounded by cousin Thomas Budd, brother Thomas Budd, and Michael Atkinson. Son, John, and expected child. William, son of my brother William. Church of England, £10. Witnesses—Thomas Wilson, Samuel Woolston, Thomas Budd, John Burr. Proved March 5, 1732. Lib. 8, p. 251.

1732-3, Jan. 31. Inventory of personal estate, £121.6.4; made by Samuel Woolston and John Burr, includes surveying instruments and books, also bond of William Atkinson.

1749, Sept. 6. Budd, John, of Hanover Township, Morris Co.; will of. Wife, Sarah, sole executrix, and to hold "the meadow joining Matthis Burnet from John Kineys to the Black Brook to Sam Ford's lots and to David Kitchell's land," that she may sell the same for £240. In case of her death before the sale, Timothy Tuttle and Benjamin Pierson empowered to pay legacy to my eldest son. Wife, Sarah, to have that tract called "the Pine Hammock," of 700 acres, bounded west by the Whippeninge River and meadows of Samuel Tuttle, Bates Lum, Allen Penn and Joseph Kitchell; she to sell same and pay my sons Barne and Thomas £250 each when of age. In case of death before the sale, Timothy Tuttle and Benjamin Pierson empowered to dispose of it. Wife, Sarah, to have the home place of 900 acres on both sides of Black Brook, except meadows devised above. Wife to have all lands leased or unleased joining her land in the Long Valley; also all lands in the Counties of Morris, Salem, Gloucester, Hunterdon and elsewhere, together with my land in the colony of New York held under our brother, John Cosens, with the exception of all mines, etc., reserved to me and Coz. Hump. Morrey in some deeds in "Penselvania to Jermans"; also my tract on west side of the Susquehanna, called Govr's, or Sir William Keith's mine, an account thereof being among Coz. Morreys or William Pidgeon's writings. Also my Eastern and Western shares of Proprieties of land yet appertaining. Witnesses—John Nuttman, Benjamin Peirson, William Budd. Proved 20 March, 1749-50.

1752, Sept. 20. Letters testamentary granted Sarah Scott, formerly Sarah Budd, executrix named in above will. "Prob. granted 16 May 1754" (vid. original). Lib. 8, p. 41.

1730, July 22. Budd, Thomas, of Northampton, Burlington Co., Esq.; will of. Eldest son, John, tract in Hunterdon Co., on branch of Rarington called Looneton (Lomerton; Lamington?), being surveyed for me Oct. 16, 1716, by my cousin, John Budd, of Philada., for 312½ acres. Second son, Thomas (under age) farm situated on both sides of Ancocus Creek and next to land of my bro, James Budd; also meadow I purchased of my father William Budd in Springfield, joining John Shinn. Daughters—Ann, Elizabeth and Rachel. Son, James, land bought of my sister Sarah Budd and joining land bought of Thomas Shinn. Sons—George and Levi, to be taught to read and write. Executors—John Gosling and Joseph Heulings. Witnesses—Joseph Endicott, Thomas Atkinson, Jun'r, John Budd.

1732, April 21. Codicil. Am now residing in Philada. and have intermarried with Mary, widow of John Eayre, and I bequeath to her £50 and all that part of my personal estate of which she was possessed at our intermarriage. Expected child. Witnesses—John Baer, James Bingham. Proved April 5, 1742.

1742, May 25. Petition of Margaret Budd, widow, of Thomas Budd of City of Burlington, cooper, stating that John Gosling and Joseph Heulings, executors, may be cited to appear and take upon themselves the execution of the testam't or show cause why the administration may not be granted unto Thomas Budd, second son of the deceased.

1742, June 8. Renunciation of John Gosling and Joseph Heulings as executors.

1742, June 8. Bond of Thomas Budd, of Northampton, Burlington Co., yeoman, second son of Thomas Budd, as administrator. Israel Heulings, hatter, and James Budd, cooper, both of City of Burlington, fellow bondsmen. Lib. 4, p. 303.

1742, June 21. Inventory of personal estate, £334.10.5; made by Joseph Heulings and Joseph Govett.

1746, Aug. 18. Buddell, William, of Bridgetown, Burlington Co., innholder; will of. Wife, Hannah. Friends—Nathaniel Thomas, sadler, and John Monro, both of Burlington Co., executors and guardians of my dau. Mary. Children of Thomas Clark. Son-in-law, John Clark. Sons and daughters-in-law. Lot joining Daniel Wells, which I bought of John McIntosh, and meadow bought of Josiah Southwick. Witnesses—Thos. Shinn, Junr., David Thomas, Jno. Duncan. Proved Aug. 30, 1746. Lib. 5, p. 261.

1746, Aug. 28. Inventory of personal estate, £1685.15.0 ½; made by John Burr and Samuel Woolston.

1742, April 15. Buddin, Joseph, of Chester, Burlington Co., yeoman; will of. Wife, Rebeckah, sole executrix. Son, William, minor. Witnesses—Joshua Wright, Daniel Packer, Ruth Packer. Proved Dec. 8, 1748. Lib. 6, p. 5.

1748, 21st day, 7th mo. (Sept.). Inventory of personal estate, £127.15.6; made by Joshua Wright and Abraham Perkins.

1750, Oct. 19. Bulfin, Thomas, of Salem Co. Int. Admr., Thomas Hancock, of Elzenbourgh, county aforesaid. (No bondsman recorded). Witness—Edward Test. Inventory, £14.18.0. Appraisers—Willm. Hancock, Junr., Saml. Wright, both of said county. Lib. 7, p. 36.

1742, Jan. 6. Bull, Sarah, of Town and County of Gloucester, widow. Son, Samuel Harrison, to have the plantation whereon he lives. After his decease same to his son, Samuel Harrison. Grandchildren, Joseph Harrison, Hannah Stokes, John Hinchman, William Hinchman, Elizabeth Hinchman, Samuel Clement (lot adjoining land lately Mathew Medcalfes, in town of Gloucester, he to pay his brother, Jacob Clement, £5). Granddaughter, Priscilla Harrison, to divide personal estate among my grandchildren to be named in writing. Son, William Harrison, to have the rest of lands, meadows and buildings. Executors—Sons, William and Samuel Harrison. Witnesses—John Jones, Sarah Jones, Gerves Hall (Quaker). Affirmed 20 Aug., 1744. Lib. 8, p. 190.

"Priscilla Harrison: I do order you to give these things herein named to Mary Shivers, Ann Frenlove (?), Rebecca and Ann Harrison, Abigail Hinchman, Joseph Harrison, Mary Thorne."

1741, May 4. Bullock, John, of Burlington Co., yeoman; will of. Wife, Susannah. Children—John, Joseph, William, Elenor Dennis, Elizabeth Folwell, Sarah Harrison, Ann B''rtiss, Mary Branson and Rebeckah. Daughter-in-law—Elizabeth Craig. Land surveyed by John Lawrence and land joining Wm. Emley. Executor—Son, John. Witnesses—Benjamin Kirby, William Kirby, Tho. Earl.
Lib. 4, p. 289.

1741, May 29. Inventory of personal estate, £223.11; made by Sam'l Emley and Thomas Cooke, includes bonds of Wm. Bullock and Joseph Burr.

1736, Aug. 12. Bullock, Joseph, of Gloucester Township, tailor. Bond of James Hinchman, of Gloucester Co., administrator, with Joseph Cooper, of same county, as fellow bondsman.

1736, July 22. Susanna Bullock, widow of Joseph Bullock, renounces administration of his estate in favor of James Hinchman, Esq. Witness—Gervas Hall. Gloucester Wills, 195 H.

1733, April 23. Bun. Serajah, of Woodbridge, Middlesex Co. Bond of Shobel Smith, of Woodbridge, as guardian. Benjamin Force, fellow bondsman, yeoman. Lib. B, p. 426.

1742, Sept. 5. Bunn, Sarah, of Piscataway, Middlesex Co., widow; will of. Sister—Pricilla Sutton. Martha, Sarah, Pricilla, Henry and Jacob, children of Joseph Sutton. Martha, Hester and Mary, daughters of brother Henry Langstaffe. Martha, Sarah, Ruth and Pricilla, daughters of Samuel Potter, deceased. William, Robert and Edward, three youngest sons of said Samuel Potter. Charlet, Sarah, Mary, Pricilla, Martha, John, Jun'r, and Henry, Jun'r, children of brother John Langstaffe. Cousin, William Potter. Real and personal estate. Executors—Friends and brothers, Henry and John Langstaffe and Joseph Sutton. Witnesses—John Gillman, Henry Gavitt, John Stelle. Proved Sept. 16, 1742. Lib. C, p. 549.

1742, 5th day, 6th mo. (Aug.). Bunting, Mary, of Cresterfield, Burlington Co.; will of. Son, Amos, under age. Brother, Amos Willits. Two sisters mentioned but not named. Executors—father, Rich'd Willits and brother Rich'd Willits, Jun'r. Witnesses—Rachel Lovell, Joseph Rogers, Jos. Reckless. Proved Sept. 21, 1742.

1742, 14th day, 7th mo. (Sept.). Richard Willits, Sen'r, of "Barnygat," declines executorship. Lib. 4, p. 315.

1742, Sept. 4. Inventory of personal estate, £49.12.5; made by Antho. Woodward and William Bunting.

1740-1, March 5. Bunting, Samuel, of Mansfield, Burlington Co., yeoman; will of. Executors—wife, Mary, and son, Samuel. Children—Isaac, Thomas, Ebenezer and Mary, all under age. Real and personal estate. Land joining Joseph Nicholson. Witnesses—Isaac Ivins, Sen., William Folwell, John Fenimore. Proved April 18, 1741, by Mary Bunting, surviving executrix. Lib. 4, p. 280.

1741, April 15. Inventory of personal estate, £207.8.3; made by John Butcher and William Folwell.

1741, March 6. Bunting, Samuel, of Chesterfield, Burlington Co.; will of. Wife, Mary; son, Amos, and expected child. Father, Saml. Bunting. Real and personal estate. Executors—Thos. Miller, of Hanover, and Benjamin Fowler, blacksmith, of Upper Freehold. Witnesses—Antho. Woodward, Constant Woodward, Benja. Horner. Proved April 3, 1741. Lib. 4, p. 276.

1741, April 2. Inventory of personal estate, £125.00.6; made by John Steward and Wm. Lowrie.

1732, Nov. 13. Burd, Joseph, of Hanover, Hunterdon Co.; will of. Brother, Abraham Burd; sister, Sarah Burd. Sister Sarah to have "what is due to me out of my father's estate, which is in West Chester in the government of New York." Executors not named. Witnesses—Sarah Hathaway and James Frell. Proved Aug. 14, 1733, by said witnesses, who stated that the testator signed the will a few days before he died. Lib. B, p. 465.

1731, March 3. Burdsall, Jacob, of Waterford, Burlington Co., house carpenter. Administration granted to Elizabeth Burdsall, widow, of Burlington. Thomas Coles, of Waterford, blacksmith, fellow bondsman. Lib. 3, p. 184.

1732, April 8. Inventory of personal estate, £101.5.6; made by John Kay and John Collins.

1732-3, Jan. 20. Petition of John Busby of Northampton, who states that his sister, Jane, lately intermarried with Jacob Burdsall, and said Jacob had, by his said wife Jane, one daughter, named Jane, and, a little after birth of said child, the mother died. After the death of petitioner's sister the said Jacob intermarried with one Elizabeth Cole, and, about 14 months after said intermarriage, the said Jacob also died, and now the said John Busby petitions to be made guardian of his niece. Lib. 3, p. 241.

1733, June 30. Account of Elizabeth Burdsall, administratrix of estate of Jacob Burdsall, late of Bucks Co., Province of Penna., house carpenter and, before that, of Burlington Co., showing moneys paid Mathew Allen, Joseph Borden, Evan Harris, Sarah Norris, James Wilde, Jun'r, John Chambers, James Childs, Joseph Coles, Mary Coles, Thomas Coles. Due estate from Evan Harris, of Bucks Co., and from James Stevenson, who has run away.

1732, Jan. 20. Burdsall, Jane (within age), daughter of Jacob and Jane, both deceased. Letters of guardianship granted to John Busby, of Northampton Township, Burlington Co., yeoman. Burlington Wills, 2213-16C.

1731, Oct. 20. Burger, Martin, of Monmouth Co. Bond of Ann Burger, widow, as administratrix of estate. Samuel Vincent, of Monmouth County, fellow bondsman. Witnessed by John Broughton. Lib. B, p. 235.

———, ———, —. Inventory of estate, £175.7.3¼, includes one house and 2 lots of ground at "Mate Wan Creek"; a pocket pistol, flute, 18 books and a "Book Called Josephes." Made by Walter Waltz and John Smith.

1737, May 28. Burgin (Burgen), John, of Cohansey, Salem Co., yeoman; will of. Sons, Joseph, John and Philip Burgen, to have equally real estate as they arrive at 21. Wife, Margaret. Executors—Nicholas Gibbon and Leonard Gibbon, to have use of personal estate yearly to pay and discharge the Loan office. Witnesses—John Lace (Lacey), William McMeneme, Andrew Gardiner. Proved 24 June, 1737.

Lib. 4, p. 115.

1737, June 10. Inventory (£161.7.0), includes negro man, cows, calves, 21 sheep and lambs, acre of wheat, etc. Appraisers—James Dixon, Samuel Holmes.

1732, Jan. 12. Burgois, Nichols, of Piscataway, Middlesex Co., yeoman; will of. Wife, Mary. Children—Moses, Margaret Smalley, Mary Royse and Rachel Burgois. Real and personal estate. Burying yard on home lot to be reserved for burying yard forever. Executors—son-in-law, Thomas Royse, and Benjamin Stelle. Witnesses—Benjamin Smalley, Peter Farwell, Henry Scibbow. Proved May 8, 1733.

Lib. B, p. 404.

1739, March 28. Burnet, John, of Perth Amboy, Middlesex Co. Bond of John Burnet and William Burnet, as Administrators.

Lib. C, p. 268.

1742, Oct. 29. Burr, Henry, of Northampton, Burlington Co.; will of. Sons—John and Joseph. Daughters—Elizabeth Woolman, Mary Lippincott, Sarah Haines, Rebeckah White and Martha Matlock. Negro woman, Maria, to have freedom. Real and personal estate. Executors—Samuel Woolman and Caleb Haines. Witnesses—Tho. Shinn, Revell Elton, John Woolman. Proved June 11, 1743.

Lib. 4, p. 362.

1743, 11th day, 4th mo. (June). Inventory of personal estate, £282.12.4; made by James Lippincott and John Deacon.

1746, Sept. 5. Burroughs, Jeremiah, of Hunterdon Co. Inventory of the estate (£72.6.10), including 1 gun and sword; a loom and reed; note of James Cox.

1746, Nov. 10. Bond of John Burroughs, of Trenton Township, yeoman, as administrator. John Mathews, of Hopewell Township, yeoman, surety. Witnesses—Garret Johnson and Theophilus Severns. Lib. 5, p. 463.

1744, March 9. Burroughs, Philip, of Readington, Hunterdon Co., yeoman. Renunciation of widow, Mary, of right to administer, in favor of John Burroughs, father of said Philip. Witnesses—John and Joseph Burroughs. Hunterdon Wills, 167J.

1720, June 19. Burroughs, Samuel, of Waterford, Gloucester Co., yeoman. Son, Samuel, to have the 200 acres of land I live on, bought of Richard Broomley and 100 acres on the other side of the creek, bought of John Walker, he to pay my daughter Hannah, when 21, £50, and same to my daughter Esther, when 21. Son, John, to have 400 acres, bought of Joseph Heritage and John Walker, Junior. Son, Joseph, 400 acres (150 acres bought of Godfrey Harsfilder, 150 of Samuel Coles, 100 acres of Joseph Heritage). Son, Benjamin, 100 acres purchased of Jacob Spicer, and 100 acres purchased of John Estaugh. Daughter Sarah, at 21, 100 acres bought of Hugh Sharp. Wife, Hannah, during life, 400 acres by the river side, purchased of Edward Tue and, after her death, to expected child. Wife, Hannah, sole executrix. "She to give my son Samuel three cows or to pay him £7 above which was given him by his grandfather, Jon. Taylor." But he not to possess the land before 23 years of age, except she allows it. Witnesses—Thomas Eves, Junr., John Roberts, John Kay. Proved 31 March, 1732. Lib. 3, p. 193.

1731-2, 1 (Mar.), 10 da. Inventory (£314.19.9), includes bacon, beef, wheat, rye, Indian corn, negro man, negro woman, horses, 20 cows, etc. Appraisers—John Kay, Jos. Cooper.

1743, April 28. Burroughs, William, of Salem Co., mariner. Int. Admx., Sarah Burrows (relict). Bondsman—Edward Test and John Thompson, yeomen. All of town and county of Salem. Witness—Mary Thompson. Lib. 4, p. 380.

1732, Oct. 10. Burt, Benjamin, of Somerset Co. Int. Administration granted to John Mills, cooper. Fellow bondsmen—Peter Vannest, John Freasuer (Frazer), of County aforesaid, and Alexander Mackdowall, of Perth Amboy. Lib. B, p. 305.

1732, Oct. 27. Inventory (filed 3 Sept. 1740), Ledger book-debts 18 ½ pages. "Other debts outstanding to the heirs" (£470.17.5). Bonds, bills, notes, goods, etc. (£507.4.2), includes 4 remnants of "shrowds," 19 raccoon skins, 3 gold rings and pair gold "buttens," watch, chain and seal, 4 gold rings, buttens, etc., silver tankard, etc. Made by John Fraizer, Jan. Hendryse, Anderies Teneyk.

Inventory, or List of Book Debts outstanding, due Heirs of Benj. Burt: July 11, 1726, Henry Rivers; August 28, John Midlesworth, Andres Anderson; Feby 13, 1722, Jacob Sebring, John Manley, Coll. Hooper; 1722, John Clare; 1723, Joseph Wood; 1724, Lawrance Kenny, John Richard; March 20, 1724, Mr. Browe, Albert Ammerman, (?), John Lawbers; June 24, 1725, John Dennon; July 1725, Jacobus Devore, Robt. Darck, Gersham Hall, Banjam Willcox, Cris. Lagrangey; Novr. 16, 1725, Rachiel Dennis, Isaac Crummel; Jan. 8, 1725, Isaac Anderson; May 30, 1726, Abraham Satoy; Decr. 10, 1731, Pears Swan; Dec. 14, 1730, Jack Vroom; Jan. 3, 1731, Wm. Halls; Feby. 7, 1731, John Hagabout; March 6, 1731, Abraham Vanhorn; April 3, 1732, Isaac and Cris Vroom; April 15, 1732, John Hall; Apr. 17, 1732, Hug. Nichol, Abr. Lane, Jon. Hendricks; Apr. 21, 1732, Rob. Traphagen; Apr. 24, 1732, Andrias Stoll, John Hendrick, Mr. Vroom, Jacob Vroom, John Franton; Apr. 25, 1732, Barant Limas; Apr. 26, 1732, Mich. Hendry; Apr. 26 & 27, Geo. Falioneer; Apr. 28, Lucius Sceunerhorn; Apr. 29, Bar. Limas, John Loder, Wm. Phillips; Apr. 30, James Boyd; May 2, Dumb John; May 6, Isaac Lamer, Paul Prickhaw, Isaac Ross; May 9, Jacob Tenneick; May 16, Guisbert Lane; May 19, Lias Clawson; May 23, Ned Murphey; May 24, Danl. Slover; May 26, Geo. Bowman; May 27, Peare Vanneste, Rolif Traphagen; June 3, James McCroggy; June 5, 1732, Joseph Road; June 7, Albert Jonston; June 9, John Troy; June 10, York Shire, Dumb John; June 10 & 12, Guilbert Lane; June 16, George Bowman, John King, John Stevens; June 23 & 24, John M. Farle; June 24 & 26, Hauns Vannette, Mr. Damaras, Francis Ennis; June 2, Jans Vannetta; June 28, Thos. Tate; July 1, John M. Neal; July 3, Coonrad, the Jerman; July 5, Eliz. Bennet; July 7, Hugh Nichol; July 13, John Biggs; July 19, Cor's. Bowman; July 21, Josh. Clark, John Frasier; July 24, Abra. Slover; July 26, 27, 28, Dederick VanStock; July 29, Cort. Johnston; July 31, Capn. Vanneste, Wm. Hall; Aug. 2, 1732, Paul Rickhaw; Aug. 9, John Cook; Aug. 12, Sanders Fitchet; Aug. 14, Jno. Wright; Aug. 17, Jon. Mills; Aug. 19, Samll. Steevens, Uria Eakie; Aug. 25, Wm. McCanes; Sept. 2, John Holliday; Feb. 7, Matthew Spencer; Feb. 11, Wm. Means; Sept. 13, John Applel; Sept. 16, Josias Clawson; Sept. 18, Phillip Bryan; Sept. 19, Thos. Collins, Edwd. Barber; Sept. 23, Hendk. Rosebam; Sept. 24, Brian Megur; Sept. 25, Richd. Power, John McFarland; Mar. 11, 1727; Jacob Vandebick; May 18, 1728, Mr. Lane; Novr. 27, Gorsham Hull; 1726,

Peter Kenny, Theophilus Kekham, Abr. Teetsworth; 1727, Mindard Johnston, Danl. Sebring, Isaac Governeur, Henry Vannest; 1730, Peter Beleiw; 1731, Arie Dewit, Jr., John Geterman, Junr., Andris Stoll, Cristor, the shoemaker; April 15, 1731, John Weal; May 19, Daniel Batron; June 28, Alexr. Smith; Aug. 21, Mr. Cors. Vanhorn; Sept. 4, Jon. Hagabout; Sept. 11, Roy Vroam; Sept. 9, Andrias Tenneik; Sept. 15, Wm. Johnston; Sept. 20, Dorick Malat, Mr. Layworthy; Jan., 1730, James Rutles, Hank Vanover; 1731, Ennis Whittinton, Benjam. Rounsavil, John States, Molly Hull, John Vandervoort, Cors. Middagh, Benj. Arch'd., John Lyon, John McMechil; 1732, Capt. Miller; Apr. 1730, Crisparus Vanostrand, Adols. Hardinbrook, Wm. Albortus, James McCreeg, Peter Burn, Thos. Day, John Stresier, James McCraken; 1731, Andres Coyman, Benjam Morgan; 1730, Philip Murphew, Bob. Hooper, Geo. Scamp, Dederick Fannestack, Urie Fieldure, Joseph Clark, Michl. Henery, Peter Hunter, Frederick Fleet, Mr. Legit, James Willson, Herman Shuniman, Richd. Hawkins, John Member, Martin Bakeman, William Phillips; 1731, John Pettinger; 1732, John Campbell, John Bodine.

1741, Oct. 26. Petition of Maynard Burt, gent. who has "come over to this country, having intelligence that the said John Mills has gone a common soldier to the West Indies without rendering an account of his administration, etc." Same day administration of estate granted to Maynard Burt, of Perth Amboy, gent., and brother of Benjamin Burt, deceased. Fellow bondsman—Philip Kearney. "No administration granted on this to my knowledge, this 26 Mar., 1742." (On back of bond). Witnesses—Sam. Nevill, Jno. Barton. Lib. D, p. 102.

1748-9, Feb. 11. Burt, Joseph, of Hopewell Township, Hunterdon Co.; will of. Wife, Mary. Son, Joseph when of age, to have plantation where testator lived. Proceeds from personal estate to five daughters—Margaret, Elizabeth, Sarah, Mary and Deborah, when aged eighteen years. Wife to have use of plantation during widowhood, until Joseph is of age. Son, Richard. Executors—wife, and friend and brother, Jacob Reeder. Witnesses—Thomas Hunt, Adam Egee, Edward Cooper. Proved Nov. 4, 1749. Lib. 6, p. 349.

1749, August 16. Inventory of estate (£151.15.9), includes library, £1.3.0; gun and sword. Made by Robert Combs and Thomas Hunt.

1763, Dec. 16. Account of Jacob Reeder, surviving executor of will of Joseph Burt, mentions cash paid to Dr. John Bellard, Thomas Hunt, Timothy Allen, Samuel Hunt, John Rous, George Corwine, Peter Pain, Esther Corwine, Andrew Smith, Richard Stockton, Edward Cooper, Thomas Whitson and Elizabeth, his wife being a legatee, Josiah Howell and Margret his wife, a legatee.

1739, May 29. Bustill, Samuel, of City of Burlington, atty-at-law; will of. Daughters—Sarah Ann and Mary. Grandaughter—Grace Bustill. Sister—Unity White, dec. Negroes—Dina, Parthenia, Hester, Cyrus and Cato. Bonds due from Daniel Grandines, of Monmouth Co., atty-at-law, and John Pledger, of Salem, Esq. Land in Bristol, Bucks Co., Penna., near the Quaker Meeting House. Executors—wife, Grace, daughter, Sarah Ann, and friend, John Coxe; the latter to be guardian of two daughters. Witnesses—Peter Baynton, Sr., Dr. Thos. Shaw, Cha. Read, Esq. Proved Oct. 7, 1742. Lib. 4, p. 336.

1739, Aug. 31. Bustill, Samuel, Jur., of Burlington, merchant. Administration granted to Elizabeth Bustill, widow. Thomas Budd, of Burlington, cooper, and Isaac Pearson, of same, clockmaker, fellow bondsmen. Lib. 4, p. 199.

1740, Aug. 31. Inventory of the personal estate, £178.10.6; made by Sam'l Scattergood and Nathan Lovett.

1729, 7th day, 2nd mo. (April). Butcher, John, of Springfield, Burlington Co.; will of. Daughter, Damaris, lot joining Jonathan Wright. Daughter, Rebecca Ridgway. Son, John. Katharin, dau. of John Butcher, and Mary, dau. of Job Ridgway, lot adjoining Henry Clothier. Executors—friends Edward Barton and John Harvey. Witnesses—James Thomson, Richard Ridgway, John Craig. Proved Dec. 5, 1737, at which time Edward Barton is deceased. Lib. 4, p. 124.

1748, Sept. 10. Butcher, John, Junior, of City of Burlington, innholder. Administration granted to Mary Butcher, widow. Job Ridgway, of Springfield, yeoman, fellow bondsman.

Lib. 6, p. 329; Lib. 7, p. 94.

1745-6, Jan. 29. Butcher, Samuel, Jr., of Evesham, Burlington Co.; will of. Wife, all estate, real and personal, for bringing up of daus., Patience and Phebe. Executors—friend, James Cattell, and bro., Joseph Butcher. Witnesses—Michael Linch, Sarah Pond, Gab. Blond. Proved Feb. 17, 1745. Lib. 5, p. 225.

1745-6, Feb. 15. Inventory of personal estate, £107.7; made by John Ecans and Abram Evans.

1748, Sept. 30. Butler, Jane, of Newtown, Queens Co., Long Island. Bond of Thomas Butler, of Westchester, New York, to be administrator on the estate of his mother. Gerardus Drake, fellow bondsman.

Essex Wills, Lib. E, p. 213.

1748, Sept. 30. Inventory of personal estate, incl. a negro wench in the hands of Matthew Williamson, to whom John Rolfe, Esq., claims some title, but agrees to pay £42 to the administrator.

1749, Sept. 20. Thomas Butler, of Westchester, forwards £10 to pay for letters of administration and other charges.

1748-9, Feb. 6. Butler, John, of Mansfield, Burlington Co., will of. Wife, Mary, to have all estate, real and personal, save a few cattle and that for dau., Mary Roberts. Executors—wife, and friend and son-in-law, John Deleplane. Witnesses—Thos. Leonard, William Parsons, Rob. Field. Proved Feb. 20, 1748. Lib. 6, p. 31.

1748-9, Feb. 16. Inventory of personal estate, £55.17; made by Isaac Horner and Rob. Field.

1746-7, Jan. 29. Butler, Obadiah, of Shrewsbury, Monmouth Co. Inventory of the estate, £185.17.1, made by Amos White and Jarius Hance.

1746-7, Feb. 2. Hannah Butler, of Shrewsbury, the widow, makes choice of Daniel Butler of same Township and county, cooper. Witnesses—David Croowly and Benjamin Walcott, Jr.

1746-7, Feb. 5. Bond of Daniel Butler as administrator of the estate; Jarius Hance, of same place, cordwainer, fellow bondsman.

Lib. D, p. 448.

1748, Nov. 27. Butterwort, James, of Penns Neck, Salem Co., yeoman; will of. Wife, Katherine. Son James Butterwort. Daughters—Elinor, Francis and Kathrine Butterwortt. Executors—Son, James

Butterwortt, and Samuel Linch. Proved 3 Dec., 1748. Witnesses—Peter Derickson, Thomas Pasenes (Parsons), Robt. Howard.

1748, Dec. 8. Jacob Corwaluson administered on estate of James Butterwort, with will of said Butterwort annexed. Bondsman—Robt. Howard. Witness—Samuel Whitehorne. Salem Wills, 790 Q.

1748, Dec. 7. Inventory (£70.19.3), includes sheep, oxen, and cattle. Appraisers—Robt. Howard, Thomas Pasenes (Parsons).

1750, Aug. 26. Butterwort, James, of Salem County. Int. Admr., Jacob Cornealuson. Bondsman—Thomas Tussey. Both of Penns Neck. Lib. 7, p. 27.

1750, Aug. 20. Inventory, £8.0.11. Appraisers—Robt. Howard, Thomas Tussey.

1745, April 8. Butterworth, John, of Deptford Township, Gloucester Co. Int. Admx., Ester Butterworth, widow, of same place. William Arill and Peter Rambo, fellow bondsmen. Witness—John Budd. Lib. 5, p. 108.

1745, April 9 and 10. Inventory, £103.04.02. Appraisers—Peter Rambo, William Arrell, Jun. Signed "Hester Butterworth."

1748-9, March 3. Buyce (Boyce, Boice), John, of Middlesex Co., yeoman; will of. Children—John, George, Mary (wife of Matthias Smock), Angeltie, Syntje and Catherine. Granddaughter—Sintje, daughter of son Jacob, deceased, a minor. Land bought of Aria Booram. Executors—wife, Syntje, and sons, John and George Boyce. Witnesses—George Buyce, Cornelius Bice, and B. Lagrange. Proved Sept. 27, 1749. Lib. E, p. 332.

1749, April 14. Inventory of estate, £610.19.7; made by Hend. Fisher and George Buys.

1725, May 26. Byerly, Thomas, Esq., of Woodbridge, Middlesex Co.; will of. Land purchased Jan. 26, 1705, of Nathan Tilson and Jonathan Johnson, both of the Inner Temple, London, gentlemen, in partnership with Robert Parker, Esq., of Grays Inn, Middlesex Co., Great Britain. Sisters—Margaret (widow of Bradwarthen Tindale, Esq.), Clare, Elizabeth, Arrabella and Catherine Byerly. Children of brother, Robert Byerly, deceased, viz., Robert, Phillip, Ann, Elizabeth, and Mary Byerly. To Church at Perth Amboy handsome pulpit cloth and cushion with an altar cloth, "my coat-of-arms to be wrought in each of them, with T. B. in cypher." Executors—Joseph Murray, of New York City, and John Kinsey, Junr., of Woodbridge, attorney. Witnesses—David Stewart, Margaret Dagworthy, Eliza Parker.

1725, June 1. Codicil—Friend, Thomas Jackson, £50. Witnesses—Edward Hart, Joseph Bonny, Robert Mannering. Proved March 27, 1733. Lib. B, p. 447.

1745, June 28. Caldwell, Hugh, of Township of Deptford, Gloucester Co. Daughter, Jean, not of age. Sister, Jennet Mefall. Wife's son, William Cox, and her daughter, Hannah Cox. Sole executrix—wife. Witnesses—John Brown, John Wood, Gabriel Rambo. Proved 19 July, 1745. Lib. 5, p. 176.

1745, July 16. Inventory (£338.8.9) includes 6 cows, 2 pair of oxen, 1 boat, 1 canoe, and field of green tobacco. Appraisers—Alexr. Randall, Gabriel Rambo.

1749-50, Feb. 24. Callahan (Kelahan), John, of Penns Neck, Salem Co., farmer; will of. Wife, Margrat, executrix. Children—Marey, John and Margrat. Witnesses—Alen Congelton, Jane Congelton, James Barkley. Proved 3 Sept., 1750. Lib. 6, p. 410.

1750, Aug. 25. Inventory (£164.15.3.) of John Callahan, husbandman, includes Riding horse, oxen and cattle. Appraisers—Samuel Whitehorne, Alen Congelton.

1750, Oct. 29. Callahan, Margaret, of Penns Neck, Salem Co., widow; will of. "For the settling of my estate which is the third part of the estate of John Calahan, my husband, I give my son, John, minor," etc. Daughters—Catharine Strong, Mary, and Margaret Callahan. Executor—Alen Congleton. Witnesses—Jane Groome, Solomon Almon, Samuel Whitehorne. Proved 15 Jany., 1750. Lib. 6, p. 397.

Inventory, £150.12.8. Appraisers—Joseph Elwell, Saml. Whitehorne.

1739, Oct. 24. Camfield (Canfield), Rachel, of Essex Co., about 16 years of age. Bond of Nathaniel Wheeler, Junr., as guardian. Nathaniel Wheeler, Senr., fellow bondsman, both of Newark. Witness—Thomas Clark. Lib. C p. 393.

1743, Dec. 3. Camp, John, of Cape May County. Int. Administrators—Elenor Camp and Daniel Ingersol (Engersol). Fellow bondsman, Peter Scull. All of Cape May County. Witnesses—Henry Young, Nathan Geldin, Samuel Everson. Cape May Wills, 108E.

1743, Dec. 2. Inventory of personal estate (£129.6.0) includes 7 cows, and calves, "44 galens of Rum and 7 galens of melases, 14 pounds of suger"; note of Johnasson and Elias Sampels, bond from John Champion, note from Elias Champion, "in E Lyas Gaudy hands." Appraisers—Peter Scull, Nathan Geldin (or Goldin).

1732, March 18. Campbell, Archibald, of New York, merchant; will of. Daughter, Mary, a minor. Cousins—John and Jannet Campbell, children of my deceased uncle, Capt. Dugald Campbell, both under age. Land in Orange and Ulster Counties, in the Minnisink Patent. Executors—wife, Mary Campbell, and friends, John Lemonted and William Jamison. Witnesses—Simeon Sonmaion, Joseph Haynes. Proved Jan. 15, 1735. Lib. C, p. 59.

1734, Oct. 19. Campbell, Dugal, of Woodbridge, Middlesex Co.; will of. Children—Dugel, Neile, Rachel, and Anne Campbell, all under age. Lands bought of Joseph Gillman, Thomas Pike, Moses Bishop, William Mackdaniel, James Brown, and Jonathan Dunham. Executors—wife, Rodey, William Mackdaniel of Woodbridge, and Neil Campbell of Piscataqua. Witnesses—Samuel Ayres, John Campbell, Wm. Sharp, Jr. Proved Dec. 2, 1734. Lib. B, p. 583.

1733, April 18. Campbell, John Sr., of Piscataway, Middlesex Co., mason; will of. Wife, Mary. Children—John, Duglas, James, Margaret, Janet, Ann, Neill. Executors—wife, and son James. Witnesses—Joseph Ayers, William Mackdaniel (one other name undecipherable). Proved April 18, 1733. Lib. B, p. 297.

1748, Nov. 11. Campbell, Peter, of Cumberland Co.; will of. Wife, Mary. Sons—Robert and William Campbell. Sole executor—Son, Robert. Witnesses—John Champion, Uriah Wheaton. Proved 23 Feb., 1748-9. (Sworn at Cape May). Lib. 6, p. 68.

1748-9, Jan. 12. Inventory of personal estate (£49.7.5) includes notes from John Bond, Thos. and John Edwards; account against William Scanlun, Charles Loyd, John Veal. Appraisers—John Champion, Lawrence Petterson, Senr.

1750, April 30. Campbell, Robert, late of "Tokehow," Cumberland Co. Int. Adminx., Mary Bell, of Maurice River, widow. Fellow bondsman—Lowerance Peterson of same place. Witnesses—Stephen Ayers, Elias Cotting.

1750, April 20. Inventory of personal estate, £30.19.6. Appraisers—Lowrance Peterson, John Comppion (signed "John Chapion").

Cumberland Wills, 56 F.

1745, Dec. 2. Canfield, Abiel, of Newark, Essex Co.; will of. Wife, Joanna. Son—Abiel, under age. Nephew, Jabez Canfield. Sisters—Bethya Wheeler, Rachel Cutler. Lands devised to me in will of father, joining lands of Uzal Ward, John Harrison, David Ward. Executors—brother, Ebenezer Canfield, and Isaac Lyon. Witnesses—Caleb Wheler, Isaac Ogden, David Ogden. Proved Feb. 14, 1745-6.

1745-6, Feb. 13. Ebenezer Canfield refuses to accept the executorship.

Lib. D, p. 364.

1738, Oct. 14. Canfield, Benjamin, of Newark, Essex Co., yeoman; will of. Son, Jabez Canfield, under age. Sword which was my father's. Land joining lands of ——— Crane, James Nutman, Israel Canfield, Daniel Tichnor; land willed me by my father, Joseph Canfield, in his will dated Dec. 6, 1733; land in the Great Neck, joining lands of Moses Ball, John Ogden, Mr. Pierson. Wife, Mehetabell, sole executrix. Witnesses—Wm. Turner, Joseph Truman, Thos. Jackman. Proved Oct. 23, 1738. Lib. C, p. 216.

1744, April 24. Canfield, Israel, of Newark, Essex Co., shoemaker; will of. Children—Phebe Bruen, Abigail Beach, Hannah Ward, Sarah, Thomas, David, Ephraim, Israel, and Abraham. Meadow, called Luddington, by Wheeler Creek; also club meadow; lands called Chestnut Hill and Tompkins Point. Ephraim, when of age, to pay £10 for maintenance of Presbyterian Ministry. Executors—wife, Sarah, and eldest son, Thomas. Witnesses—Nathaniel Johnson, Silas Halsey, David Bostwick. Proved Sept. 24, 1744. Lib. D, p. 178.

1733, Dec. 8. Canfield (Camfield), Joseph, of Newark, Essex Co., yeoman; will of. Children—Benjamin (to have my sword), Ebenezer, Abiell, Bethyah and Rachell. Daughter, Bethyah, to have all things given her by deed of gift March 15, 1721. Lands joining lands of James Nuttman, John Ogden, Mr. Pierson, Israel Canfield, Daniell Tichiner, and ——— Creane; also lands joining lands of John Harrison, John Wall, Mr. John Plum, Joseph Rogers; land on Maple Island Creek. Executors—son, Benjamin, and friend, John Crane. Witnesses—Jno. Cooper, Joseph Riggs, Junr., Abyah Olive. Proved Jan. 10, 1733-4. Lib. B, p. 490.

1733-4, March 4. Inventory of personal estate, £237.07.10, made by S. Cooper, Thomas Longworth.

1745-6, Feb. 7. Carhart, Robert, of Monmouth Co. William and Mary Robertson renounce right of administration on estate to Richard Franses.

1745-6, Feb. 15. Bond of Richard Franses of Monmouth County merchant, principal creditor, as administrator of the estate. Charles Morgan of Middlesex County, yeoman, fellow bondsman. Witnessed by David Robertson. Lib. D, p. 360.

——, ——, —. Inventory of the estate (£30.14.10), incl. 37 books; made by Arthur Brown, Jarrett Wall and John Brown. Filed February 15, 1745-6.

1732, Nov. 19. Carinton (Carrington), John, of Newark, Essex Co.; nuncupative will. Directs that John Meadliss, Joseph Bruin, Samuel Alling and James Keen take charge of his estate, and for their trouble to have one equal third part of the remainder, after sending two-thirds to the four children of his sister in England; if they cannot be located, to go towards founding a school for poor children in Newark. Witnesses—Jonathan Sergeant, Thomas Eagles, Hanah Meadliss. Proved Dec. 18, 1732. Lib. B, p. 359.

1732-3, Feb. 1. Administration granted to John Meedliss, Joseph Bruen, Samuel Alling and James Keen.

1732-3, Jan. 18. Inventory of personal estate, (£236.00.08), incl. debts due by widow Hanah Carrinton, deceased, and the widow, Mary Crane; made by Samuell Farrand, John Cooper.

1744, Nov. 15. Above inventory appraised by Samuel Farrand in conjunction with John Cooper, Esq. who is since deceased. Second appraisement includes bonds of Wm. Grant, John Hendrick and Sam'll Dod.

1746, May 22. Accompt of administrators showing payments to Doctor Powell, Timothy Shelly, John Stiles, Joseph Johnson, John Low, John Harrison, Joseph Webb, Samuel Cooper, Cornelius Beard, Thomas Lyon, David Ogden, Benjamin Canfield, Thomas Sergeant, John Bruin, Thos. Alling, Robert Ward, Timothy Ward, Jonathan Crane, Samuel Plum, Widow Curry, Garshum Gardner, Nath'll Wheeler, Sam'll Farrand, John Crane, Thomas Davis, Solomon Boile, Isaac Bonnell, Dan'll Crane, David Young, Nath'll Bowers, Jonathan Ward, David Ward, Peregrine Santford, John Morris, John Hambleton; debts due from James Souter, William Shours, Philip Harris, John Bartlett, Messrs. Lattough and Haines, Atto'ys for residuary legatees, William Harris.

1732-3, Jan. 20. Carl, Jonas (Jonah), of Elizabeth Town, Essex Co. Hanah Carl, of Elizabeth Town, desires that her father, Joannis Vanwinkle, be appointed administrator on estate of her husband. Witness—John Blanchard.

1732-3, Jan. 22. Administration granted to John Van Wyncle. John Decamp and John Blanchard, fellow bondsmen, both yeomen. Lib. B, p. 350.

1732-3, Jan. 31. Inventory of personal estate, £59.04.00; made by Benjamin Pettit, John Blanchard.

1739, March 14. Carle, Sarah, of Salem Co., widow. Int. Admrs., Benoni Dare and Jeremiah Fifthian. Bondsman—Nicholas Gibbon, Salem County, gent. Witness—John Hopkins. Lib. 4, p. 199.

1739, March 18. Inventory, £27.7.5. Appraisers—Nicholas Gibbon, Andw. Gardner.

1744, March 20. Carlile, John, of City of Burlington, carpenter; will of. Mother, Mary Carlile. Wife, Anne, sole executrix and residuary legatee of estate. Witnesses—Thomas Shaw, Chris'er Wetherill, Abigail Mason. Proved May 1, 1745. Lib. 5, p. 120.

1739, March 17. Carll, Abiel, Sr., of Salem County, yeoman. Int.

Admr., Abiel Carle, gent. Bondsmen—Benjamin Cripps, William Tufte; all of Salem. Witnesses—Jon. Smith, Junr., Dan. Mestayer. Lib. 4, p. 223.

1739, March 19. Inventory, £26.19.11. Appraisers—Andw. Gardiner, William Tufte.

1739, March 14. Carll, Sarah, late of Salem Co., widow. Administration granted to Benoni Dare and Jeremiah Fithian. Nicholas Gibbons, fellow bondsman, gent. Lib. 4, p. 199.

1739, March 18. Inventory of personal estate, £27.7.5; made by Nichs. Gibbon and Andw. Gardiner.

1744, Aug. 25. Carman, Caleb, of Hopewell Township, Hunterdon Co., yeoman, "being sick;" will of. Plantation where testator lived and all personal estate, except a mare colt belonging to the mare called the Potomack mare, to wife Abigail during widowhood, and then to his son, Jonathan, a minor. If Jonathan shall die under age, estate to testator's son John, and all his daughters then living. Sons, Samuel and Jasper, plantation in Morris County. Executors—wife and Jonathan Foreman, of Hopewell. Witnesses—John Fidler, Joseph Price and Christopher Search. Proved October 6, 1744. Executors—Abigail Carman and Jonathan Furman. Lib. 5, p. 48.

1741, Nov. 24. Carman, John, of Middletown. Renunciation of right of administration by the widow, Martha Carman, in favor of "my beloved brothers, Joseph Carman and John Dorsett." Witnessed by Samuel Jobs, Jr. Lib. C, p. 466.

1741, Nov. 28. Bond of Joseph Carman, yeoman, of Middletown, as administrator. John Dorset, of Middletown, yeoman, and Thomas Rattoone, of Perth Amboy, cordwainer, fellow bondsmen.

1741, Nov. 17. Inventory of estate, £89.13.8½, made by Cornelius Dooren, Jarratt Wall and Joseph Smith.

1748-9. Mar. 9. Account of estate by the administrators mentions bonds of Jacob Covenhoven and John Langdon.

1728, Aug. 20. Carman, Samuel, of Middletown Township, Monmouth Co., yeoman; will of. Wife, Sarah. Children—John, Timothy, Hannah Langlun and Richard. Executors—sons John and Timothy, who are to sell testator's plantation on Long Island called Hungry Harbour. To said sons is devised a patent right to land in Hempstead Township on Long Island. Witnesses—Richard and Jonathan Stout, and Robert Dodsworth. Proved December 15, 1729. Lib. B, p. 257.

1736, Aug. 19. Carman, Timothy, of Little Eggharbour, Burlington Co., yeoman. Administration granted to Ann Carman, widow. William Pettit, yeoman, fellow bondsman. Lib. 4, p. 71.

1736, Aug. —. Inventory of personal estate, £93.3.11; made by John Burr and Thomas Marshall, includes note of John Carman.

1737, Sept. 29. Account of Peter Risley and Ann, his wife, formerly widow and administratrix of Timothy Carman, showing payments to the Coroner and his jury "the fees on view'g the body of the dec'd, who was drown'd," and debts due to Jon. Bryan, Thos. Marshall, Peter Cavalier, Maham Southwick, Marg't Manns, John Caine, Catherine Peirce, Thos. Griffe, Robert White, Thos. Mark, Abraham Bryan, Benj'n Carman, and Jon. Carman.

1745-6, Jan. 29. Carmen, Samuel, of Woodbridge, Middlesex Co., yeoman; will of. Wife, Margaret Carmen. Children—Stephen, Samuel and Abigail Carmen, all under age. Executor—father, Richard Carmen. Real and personal estate. Witnesses—Ebenezer Saltar, James Moores, Nugient Kelly. Proved June 16, 1747. Lib. E, p. 55.

1745-6, Mar. 17. Inventory of personal estate, £118; made by Timothy Bloomfield and Zedekiah Bonham, all of Woodbridge. Witness—Richard Carmen.

1745, Aug. 16. Carmer, Nicholas, of New Brunswick, Middlesex Co., mariner; will of. Children—Thomas, Frederick, Henry, Nicholas, and Mary, all under age. Expected child. Real and personal estate. Executors—wife, Aeltie, and father, Henry Carmer, of New York City mariner. Witnesses—Wm. Farquahar, Jno. Van Norden, James Lyne. Proved Aug. 23, 1745. Lib. D, p. 317.

1739, May 24. Carpenter, Hope, of Elizabeth Town, Essex Co., yeoman; will of. Children—Edward, Hope, James (at 21 years), Phebe Ross, Jane, Mary, Rachel and Hanah Carpenter. Land joining lands of Samuel Lum, deceased, and John Porter. Executors—wife, Mary, and friend, James Crane. Witnesses—Jeremiah Crane, Jno. Osborn, Susanah Crane. Proved April 24, 1740. Lib. C, p. 333.

1740, April 24. Inventory of personal estate, £100.04.06; sworn to by executors.

1744, Oct. 1. Carpenter, John, of Hopewell, Hunterdon Co., husbandman, "being sick;" will of. Wife, Mary. Son, John, one half of farm in Hopewell, bounded by land of Timothy Titus, Jr., Charles Huff, Joseph Moore. Other half to son, Hezekiah, bounded by road to Trenton, etc. Daughters, Sarah and Mary, when of age or at marriage, one acre of land in Trenton, bounded by Henry Carter, Joseph Green and William Surman. Sons, when aged 16 to be apprenticed. Executors—wife, Mary, and her father, Major Ralph Hart. Witnesses—Ralph Hart, Jr., Jeremiah Woolsey, David Cowell. Proved April 2, 1745. Lib. 5, p. 114.

1732, Nov. 30. Carre, Louis, of Allentown, Upper Freehold township, Monmouth Co., merchant; will of. Wife, Margaret, to receive negroes, etc. Son, Louis, under age, a sword, negro called Paris, etc. Executors—wife; father, Lewis Carre; brother, John Lewis Pintard, and friend, Isaac Stelle. Witnesses—Thomas Parks, Moses Robins, Junior, and Isaac Stelle. Proved Dec. 21, 1732. Lib. B, p. 355.

1732, Aug. 23. Carroll, Henry, of Salem Co., labourer; will of. Friend, Henry Warrington, two gold rings and a silver snuff box in custody of Frances Dunlap. Francis Hogshead to pay James Eldridge. Legacies to John Warrington, William Reynolds, Thomas Moore. Witnesses—Benjamin Baxter and James Dole.(Not proved).

1732, Sept. 6. Bond of Henry Warrington, yeoman, of Chester, Burlington Co, as administrator. Joseph Rockhill, innholder, of Burlington, fellow bondsman. (Burlington), Lib. 3, p. 212.

1732, Sept. 19. Inventory of personal estate, £19.6.3; made by Joseph Stokes and Thomas Hackney.

1733, Oct. 9. Account of Henry Warrington on estate of "Henry Carrallee," late of Chester, Burlington Co., showing debts paid to James Eldridge and Thomas Moor.

1747, Dec. 24. Carruthers, James, late of Salem Co. Bond of Samuel Holmes as administrator. Andrew Gardiner, of Salem Town, fellow bondsman. Lib. 5, p. 424.

1748, April 18. Inventory of personal estate, £188.17.0; made by Anani's Sayre and Ebenezer Miller.

1747, Dec. 23. Lydia Caruthers, widow, renounces administration in favour of Samuel Homes, Esq., of Greenwich.

1748, Oct. 1. Carter, Barnabus, of Hanover, Morris Co., gentleman; will of. Sons—Barnabus (executor), Benjamin (executor), Luke and Nathaniel. Daughter—Mary Wines. Grandchildren—Susannah, Sarah (not 18), and Simon Hall. Meadows on Passiack River and a grist mill. Witnesses—Jeremiah Genung, Stephen Ward. Proved 19 Oct., 1748. Lib. 5, p. 548.

1748, April 26. Carter, Henry, of Trenton, Hunterdon Co., carpenter, being sick; will of. Wife, Hannah, one-third of house and lot in Trenton where testator lived, until youngest children are 21. Son, William, £5 when house is sold, and profits from half of said house and lot which testator purchased from David Cowell. House in Philadelphia. Other children—Susannah Chambers, Henry, Hannah, Spencer and Ann Carter. Executors—wife, Hannah, and testator's brother, Joseph Yard. Witnesses—Arthur Howell, William Surman (Quaker), and Sarah Surman (or Sarman). Proved October 2, 1750. Lib. 6, p. 428.

1748, March 29. Carter, Samuel, of Essex Co. Bond of Annah Carter, widow, as administratrix. Benjamin Carter and Benjamin Perkins, fellow bondsmen. Witness—Isaac Browne. Lib. E, p. 200.

1748, Aug. 2. Inventory of personal estate (£26.04.03), incl. notes from John Carter, Sam'll Samson, Benj. Carter, Daniel Cogswell; made by Nathaniell Bonnell and Daniel Day.

1746, Oct. 27. Carter, William, of Essex Co. Expenses distributed by Mary Carter, administratrix, amounting to £9.06.03.

1746, Nov. 21. Bond of Mary Carter, spinster, as administratrix, on the estate of her brother. John Gould and Thomas Woodruff, yeoman, fellow bondsmen. Lib. D, p. 437.

1746-7, Feb. 25. Mary Carter received from Capt. Henery Arnold, as the property of her brother, £68.19. Witnesses—Amos Williams and Daniel Taylor.

1749, Dec. 26. Carter, William, late of Fairfield Township, Cumberland Co. Int. Adm'r., Alexander Moore, of Deerfield Township, shopkeeper. Bondsman—James Ayers, of same place. Witnesses—Phinehas Carll, Elias Cotting. Cumberland Wills, 30F.

1743, Nov. 17. Carty, Felix, of Burlington Co. Inventory of personal estate, £34.2.9; made by William Murrell and Samuel Hall.

1743, Dec. 3. Administration granted to Oliver Carty; Paul Bradshaw, fellow bondsman, both of Northampton, yeomen.

1747, Dec. 24. Caruthers, James, of Salem Co. Int. Admr., Samuel Holms. Bondsman—Andrew Gardiner, of the same place. Witness—Edward Test. Lib. 5, p. 424.

1747, Dec. 23. Renunciation of Lydia Caruthers (relict) in favor of Samuel Homes, Esq., of Greenwich.

1748, April 18. Inventory (£188.17) includes "Cheany Delfe" and 6 silver spoons, gun and sword. Appraisers—Anani's Sayre, Ebenezer Miller.

1741-2, Jan. 11. Carvil, William, of Shrewsbury, yeoman; will of. Wife, Grace, executrix. £5 "to the little boy, John Cramor," and £5 "to the little boy, William, that lives with me, if they abide with me," till they are of age. Witnesses—James and Joanna Gibbins and Jean Parkins. Proved Sept. 25, 1742. Lib. C, p. 552.

1744, Jan. 19. Caseby, Bradway, son of Edward Caseby, of Salem County, ward. (Nothing further). Lib. 5, p. 76.

1733, Nov. 14. Casperson, Johannes, of Penns Neck, Salem Co., yeoman; will of. Children—John, Susanah, Catren Enlowes, Marey Boerd, Rebecca, Tobias, Anthony. Real and personal estate. Executors—son, Tobias, and Thomas Miles, of Penns Neck. Witnesses—Jeremiah Baker, Lillus Baker, Solomon Olmon. Proved Jan. 28, 1733-4. Lib. 3, p. 390.

1733-4, Jan. 28. Thomas Miles declines executorship. Witnesses—John Eaton and Jeremiah Baker. Inventory of personal estate, £68.10.9; made by Henry Wallas and John Eaton.

1734, April 30. Casperson, Tobias, of Salem Co., yeoman. Int. Admx., Judith Casperson, widow. Bondsmen—Peter Enlow, Anthony Casperson, of said county. Witness—Tho. Miles. Lib. 3, p. 410.

1734, April 29. Inventory (£123.17. ½) includes armour, riding horse, cattle, crop on the ground and "keeping Henry Vandivere 4 years." Appraisers—Peter Enlows, Thos. Miles.

1747, Feb. 8. Casson, William, of Deptford, Gloucester Co. Int. Admx., Jane Casson, widow. Gabriel Rambo, blacksmith, bondsman. Both of same county. Witness—Isaac Stephens, John Ladd. Signed "Jean Corseon." Lib. 6, p. 14.

1747, Jany. 25. Inventory, £29.05.06½. Appraisers—Isaac Stephens, Richard West.

1733, June 8. Cataline (Casterline), Barnet. Administration granted to Jennet Parker, principal creditor. Lib. B, p. 308.

1730-1, 12 mo. (Feb.), 23 da. Cattell, Jonas, of Deptford Township, Gloucester Co., yeoman; will of. Son James, land on the northeasterly side of the Run, he to pay £10 to his sister Hannah when she will be 21. Son, William, the plantation I live on, he to pay £40 to my son Jonas in five years after said William arrives at 21. Executors—wife, Mary, and Joseph Tomlinson. Witnesses—James Dilkes, John Dilkes, Const. Wood. Proved 20 April, 1731. Lib. 3, p. 124.

1730-1, 1 mo. (Mar.), 11 da. Inventory (£261.14.1½), includes large Bible, 14 cows, 4 oxen, 6 young cattle. Appraisers—Jonathan Ladd, Constantine Wood.

1747, Aug. 25. Cawood (Cawod), Thomas, Sen'r, of Perth Amboy, Middlesex Co.; will of. Children—Thomas, Benjamin (under age), Sarah Letts, Phebe and Sarah. Real and personal estate. Executors—son, Thomas, and friend, Samuel Foord. Witnesses—Abigail Brown, William Kent, Oswald Foord. Proved Sept. 14, 1747. Lib. E, p. 79.

1747, Sept. 25. Inventory of personal estate, £69.10.7; made by Oswald Foord and David Kent.

1730, Nov. 27. Chamberlain, John, of Shrewsbury, Monmouth Co. Bond of Rebecca Chamberlain, widow, as administratrix. John Morris, of Shrewsbury, yeoman, fellow bondsman. Lib. C, p. 298.

1741, Dec. 16. Chambers, James, of New Windsor, Middlesex Co., yeoman; will of. Sons—John, Robert, Elijah and Abijah, all under age. Land purchased of John Porterfield. Personal estate. Executors—wife, Phebe, and brothers, Robert and Joseph Chambers. Witnesses—Francis Chambers, Sarah Chambers, Mary Chambers. Proved Nov. 16, 1748.

1748, Dec. 1. Letters testamentary granted to Robert and Joseph Chambers, the surviving executors. Lib. 5, p. 545.

1733, April 7. Chambers, John, Sr., of Shrewsbury, Monmouth Co., yeoman. Eldest son, John, land whereon he lives, south of the Alewife brook and north of highway to Little Silver Neck, joining Peter White. Daughter, Patience Wainwright, land testator lives on and land below Lippincott's meadow, west of Content Bills and David Allen, both lots on Narrawatticund Neck. Son, Josiah Chambers, "non compos mentis." Son-in-law, Thomas Wainwright, husband of daughter Patience. Grandson, John Wainwright. Executors—son, John, and son-in-law, Thomas Wainwright. Witnesses—Joseph Parker, Jean West and Jacob Dennis. Proved May 4, 1733. Lib. B, p. 458.

1749, April 19. Chambers, John, of Chester, Burlington Co., yeoman; will of. "Being in advanced age." Grandson, John Chambers, 106 acres, 6 of them adjoining Jacob Lippincott, he paying his brother William and sister Mary each £10. Daughters—Ann, Sarah Erwin, Elizabeth Le Coney and Rebecca Walker. Children of my dau., Martha and her husband, Patrick Jones. Daughter, Ann, sole executrix. Witnesses—Thomas Worinton, Mary Worinton, Gab. Blond. Proved Nov. 9, 1749.

1749, Nov. 8. Inventory of personal estate, £66.1.4; made by Joseph Stokes and John Rudderow. Burlington Wills, 4421C.

1731, June 23. Chambers, Richard, of Shrewsbury, Monmouth Co. Administration granted to Ann Chambers, the relict. Lib. B, p. 102.

1731, May 25. Inventory of personal estate, £208.03.6, incl. a sloop and rigging; made by Stoffel Langstraat, Philip Edwards and William Brinley.

1750, Feb. 12. Chambles, James, of Salem Co. Int. Admr., Erasmus Fetters of Elsenburrough, said County, yeoman. Witness—Nichl. Gibbon. Lib. 8, p. 160.

1749, Sept. 20. Inventory (£406.12.0) includes farming stock. Appraisers—Thos. Hancock, Nathaniel Chambless.

1755, May 9, filed in the file of 1750. Account showing names of William Siddons, John Hale, Jonah Scogging, William Adams, Nathaniel Chamless, Grace Maron, Edmund Test, Daniel Hudey, John Stewart, Margaret Eaton, John Ware, William Tufte, Edward Draper, Peter Davey, William Crow, John Whittal, Erasmus Fetters, William Barker, Aaron Broadway, John Thompson, John Evins, John Andrews, Nichl. Gibbons, Marg. Galaspy, Elizabeth Dare, Jonah They, Richard Wister, Joshua Hale, Roberts

Walker, Peter Bryanbury, Thomas Handly, Samuel McClening, Marlin McGraugh, John Test, John Acton, Henry Hale, Joseph Sharp, William Finn, William Goodwin.

1750, Dec. 11. Champion, Elias, of Great Egg Harbor, Gloucester Co., "Gentel." "My four sons to have £10 a piece." Oldest son, Thomas, lands. Remainder of estate to wife to bring up the children. A heifer to William Gerel. Executor—John Ireland. Witnesses—George Drummond, John Wetherbe, Ruth Irland. Proved 23 Jany., 1750. Lib. 7, p. 371.

1750-1, Mar. 6. Inventory (£121.9.3) includes cattle and oxen. Appraisers—James Somers, George Drummond.

1733, 18th day, 10th mo. (Dec.). Champion, Mathew, of Town and Co. of Burlington, yeoman; will of. Cousins—James Dent, of Thorne, Co. of York, Great Britain; Hannah Knight, of Winteringham, near Thelby, in Lincolnshire, and Rachel, wife of Mathew Mayor, living in Yorkshire. Legacies to Friends of Quarterly and Monthly Meetings of Burlington, viz., Martha Dickson, Sarah Plowman, Elishab Allison, Duglis Hireton, Sarah Dawson, Elizabeth Guest, Ann Cowgill, Sarah (wife of Abraham Marriott), and William White. Whereas in my former will I left considerable estate to my wife to dispose of and she is since deceased, I give the same to her friends and relatives, viz., Garvis Pharo and his son James, kinsman John Scholey and his children, kinsman Thomas Ridgway's children by his first wife, kinsman William Murfin's children, kinsman James Pharo and his sister Mary Hollwell's children, John Butcher, Ju'r's, wife and their children, Mary wife of Daniel Smith and their children, viz., Robert, John, Benjamin and Catherine Calinder, brother-in-law John Murfin and John Syke's children. Real and personal estate. Executors—friends and kinsmen, John Sykes and Daniel Smith, Ju'r. Witnesses—Thomas Wetherill, Joshua Raper, Is. DeCow. Proved Oct. 21, 1735. Lib. 4, p. 38.

1735, 1st day, 7th mo. (Sept.). Inventory of personal estate, £1619.1.4; made by Is DeCow and Joshua Raper.

1748, April 19. Champion, Nathaniel, of Waterford, Gloucester Co., yeoman; will of. Wife, Mary. Children—Elizabeth, Nathaniel, Sarah, Benjamin and Thomas. Executors—wife, Mary, and Samuel Shivers. Witnesses—Josiah Shivers, John Shivers, Joseph Armstrong. Affirmed 10 June, 1748. Lib. 5, p. 524.

1748, June 9. Inventory (£235.10.0), includes horse, cattle, sheep, swine, etc. Appraisers—Josiah Shivers, John Shivers.

1748-9, Jan. 3. Champion, Peter, of Gloucester Co., yeoman. Int. Admx., Ann Champion, of Waterford, widow. William Ellis, bondsman, of same county. Lib. 6, p. 76.

1748-9, Jan. 31. Inventory (£239.5.1), includes oxen, cows and negro man. Appraisers—John Shivers, Aaron Aronson.

1732, Jan. 22. Champness, Edward, of Salem Co., yeoman. Int. Admrs., Thomas Mason, Isaac Sharp, Junr., Clement Hall, all of said County, gentlemen. Witnesses—John Barradwill, Juner (mark), John Groves, Tho. Miles. Lib. 2, p. 223.

1732, 10 mo. (Dec.), 6 da. Renunciation of Fenwick Champnis, brother of said deceased and petition of above named Admrs. Witness—Wm. Whittall. Lib. 3, p. 224.

1732, 13 da., 10 mo. (Dec.). Inventory (£36.6.0) includes bond of James Barber. Appraisers—William Vanneman, Lavais Holsten (Larance Holsted).

1733, Jan. 23. Account names. Phillip Vandinear, Thomas Mason, Clement Hall, John Whittal, John Kidd, George Pamroy and Cloud Haly.

1732, Jan. 30. Chandler, Joseph, of Salem Co., yeoman. Int. Admrs., Mary Chandler and Jonathan Smith, all of said County. Bondsman—Daniel Smith. Witnesses—John Den, Will Tyler.

1732, Jan. 24. Inventory (£141.3.6.) of Joseph Chandler of Alloways Creek, includes horses, cattle, sheep, swine, and Bible. Appraisers—Will Tyler, John Den.

1749-50, Feb. 3. Chapman, John, of Bethlehem Township, Hunterdon Co.; will of. Son, George. To Rachel Jones, for life, land where John Goheen then lived in East Nantmell Township, Chester Co., Pa. After her death plantation to "my son George, my daughter Sarah, and Hannah Jones, Ruth Jones and Lydia Jones." Residue to Rachel Jones. Executors—Rachel Jones and John Goheen. Mentions John Goheen's lease. Witnesses—Will. Marritt, William Silverthorn and John Clarke. Proved March 29, 1750. Lib. 6, p. 333.

1750, June 23. Rachel Jones was sworn as executrix.

1750, March 26. Inventory of estate, £234.17.0, including plantation of 130 acres in Chester Co., Pennsylvania. Made by William Marritt and Isaac Lanen.

1731, June 14. Chapman, Robert (Jr.), of Chesterfield, Burlington Co., yeoman. Administration granted to Susannah Chapman, widow, of Town and Co. of Burlington. Joseph Rockhill and Ralph Peart, of same, gentlemen, fellow bondsmen. Lib. 3, p. 103.

1731, New Castle. Chapman, Robert, of White Clay Creek Hundred, gent. Account of Susanna Chapman, sole executrix, having paid Thomas Lestrange, Asher Clayton, Jno. Killpatrick Smith, James James, Esq., Doctor Finney, Wm. Reed, Thomas Smith, Mr. Clayton, Joseph Orr, Josiah Lowden, Saml. Bickley, Thomas Ogle.

1731, Oct. 20. New Castle. Settled at Orphans' Court before Charles Springer, Simon Hadley, David French, James Heritage, and Robert Gorden, Esqs.

1732, Nov. 17. Chapman, Robert, Junr., of Chesterfield, Burlington Co., afterwards of Christana Bridge, New Castle Co., upon Delaware, gent. Account of William Danford, for himself and for Susanna his wife, late Susanna Chapman, administratrix of above exhibited annexed account showing further payments to James Smith, Esq., late Secretary of the Province of New Jersey, Thomas Woodward, Richard Harrison, James Vallett, Daniel Smith, Jr., William Allen of Phila., Merch't, John Stamper, Thomas Perry, Israel Pemberton, Joseph Heulings, Sarah Bourne, Preserved Brown, Jr.

Burlington Wills, 2685-98C.

1748, Oct. 28. Chapman, Robert, of Chesterfield, Burlington Co., yeoman; will of. 190 acres adjoining Jonathan Cheshire. Sons—William and John. Daughters—Martha (wife of Samuel Arnold), Rebecca (wife of Evan James) and her dau. Rebecca, and Elizabeth (wife of John Milbourn). Grandsons—William and Robert, sons of son William. Granddaughters—Mary, daughter of John Chapman, and Patience and Elizabeth, daus. of son Edward. Two eldest sons of son

Edward, and other grandchildren mentioned but not named. Friends, John and Joseph Steward. Real and personal estate. Executors—son, Edward, and friends, John and Joseph Steward. Witnesses—John Updike, George Hopkins, Sam. Harris. Proved April 28, 1749.

———, Nov. 12. John Steward and Joseph Steward, executors, testified to signature of Robert Chapman attached to above will. Lib. 6, p. 315.

1749, April 22. Inventory of personal estate, £429.4.4½; made by Judah Williams and Samuel Cheshire, includes 80 acres.

1743-4, Mar. 19. Cheesman, Richard, of Gloucester Co.; will of. Wife, Hannah. Sons—Thomas, Benjamin, Richard, William and Peter. Thomas to have land on south side of Cooper's Creek and in Township of Gloucester, "except a piece of meadow for Peter Cheeseman." Richard to have land on which he lives, on the fork of Timber Creek, Gloucester Township. William to have land on north side of Cooper's Creek, Waterford Township. Peter, land where the sawmill and wharf now stand and all my other lands in Gloucester County. Executors—Thomas, Peter and Benjamin Cheeseman. Witnesses—Andrew Ware, Daniel Richmond, Robt. Hubs. Proved 7 Sept., 1744. Lib. 5, p. 65.

1744, Sept. 14. Cheney, Thomas, of Perth Amboy, Middlesex Co., mariner. Bond of Gerard Syers, of Perth Amboy, principal creditor as administrator. Philip Kearny, fellow bondsman. Lib. D, p. 177.

1734, 23rd day, 10th mo. (Dec.). Chesher, John, Jr., of New Hanover, Burlington Co., yeoman. Wife, Sarah. Daus.—Mary and Elizabeth, both under 12. Home farm of 380 acres. Executors—wife, Sarah, and brother, Jonathan Chesher. Witnesses—Sam'l Emly, Samuel Curtis and Mahlon Wright. Proved Feb. 22, 1734. Lib. 4, p. 189.

1734-5, 14th day, 11th mo. (Jan.). Inventory of personal estate, £163.11.11½; made by Joshua Wright and John Steward.

1740, Sept. 30. Cheshire, Benjamin, of Chesterfield, Burlington Co., weaver; will of. Sister, Anne, wife of Richard Kirby, and their children—Mary, Richard, John, Jonathan, Joseph, Sam'l and Robert. Brother, Sam'l Cheshire. Sister, Sarah Lippincott. Sary and Ann, daus. of Gershom Shippee. Elizabeth and Hannah, daus. of Rachel Everingham. Elizabeth, dau. of Thos. Stevenson. Real and personal estate. Executor—bro., Jonathan Cheshire. Witnesses—William Kirby, Benjn. Kirby, Tho. Earl. Proved Nov. 19, 1740. Lib. 4, p. 259.

1740, 13th day, 9th mo. (Nov.) Inventory of personal estate, £241.14.9; made by Peter Harrison and Benjn. Kirby.

1735, April 16. Cheshire, John, of Chesterfield, Burlington Co., yeoman; will of. Wife, Ann. Children—Jonathan, Benjamin, Samuel, Ann and Sarah. Grandchildren mentioned but not named. Tract of land between William Chapman and William Kirby, and other lands. Executors—son, Samuel, and friend, John Steward. Witnesses—Abrm. Farington, Caleb Raper, Isa. DeCow. Proved Nov. 3, 1739.

1739, 1st day, 9th mo. (Nov.). John Steward declines executorship. Lib. 4, p. 189.

1739, 18th day, 8th mo. (Oct.). Inventory of personal estate, £334.1.10; made by Joshua Wright and Benjamin Robins.

1748, Sept. 9. Chesshire, George, of Burlington Co., collier. Administration granted to David Buckard of City of Burlington, collier. Joseph Hollinshead, Esq., of same, fellow bondsman.

Lib. 6, p. 327; Lib. 7, p. 94.

1748, Oct. 1. Inventory of personal estate of George Cheshire of Mount Holly, £2.17.6; made by John Adams and John Budd.

1736, Feb. 4. Chester, John, of Deptford, Gloucester Co., yeoman. Int. George Cozens, of Greenwich, Admr. Gabriel Rambo, yeoman, fellow bondsman, of same place. Witness—Joseph Rose.

Lib. 4, p. 84.

1736, Jany. 25. Renunciation of Abigail Chester, widow of John Chester.

1736, Feb. 14. Inventory, £49.15.2. Appraisers—Alexr. Randall, Gabriel Rambo.

1737, March 5. Account shows payments to John Butterworth, William Arell, Ann Fleming, Obadiah Gibson, Joshua Maddock, Abraham Vining, Charity Brown, Joshua Richardson, Francis Batten, Derity Turner, George Ward, Junr., Thomas Wilkins, John Worthington, Samuell Chester, John Carter, William Tettum, Hannah Ward, John Wood, Marg. Steelman, Alexr. Randall, Alexr. King, Ann Cooper, Edward Wilson.

1748, Dec. 27. Chester, Joseph, of Township of Deptford, Gloucester Co., laborer; will of. Brothers—William, James and Samuel; sister, Elen. Executors—John Wilkins and my brother, Samuel Chester. Witnesses—Francis Wood, Isaac Tatum. Affirmed 20 March, 1748.

1748, Jany. 11. Inventory, £30.8.6. Appraisers—Wm. Wilkins, William Wood. Lib. 6, p. 86.

1750, Oct. 6. Chetwood, John, son of Philip Chetwood of Salem, Practitioner of physic, of age of 14 years. Bond of Matthias Williamson, of Essex Co., as guardian. Peter Schuyler, of Bergen Co., and John Halstead, of Essex Co., fellow bondsmen. Witness—A. W. Waters. Essex Wills, 1729-30G.

1745, July 17. Chetwood, Phillip, of Salem Co., gent.; will of. Son, John, all estate, real and personal. Executors—son, John, and my brother Willm. Chetwood, and my sister-in-law Elizabeth Hall. Witnesses—John Pierson, Sarah Wyatt, Danl. Mestayer. Proved 29 July, 1745.

1745, Dec. 14. Letters Testamentary were granted William Chetwood and Elizabeth Hall, the executors named in the will, the other executor, John Chetwood, being an infant. Lib. 5, p. 199.

1745, July 24. Inventory (£2046.6.6¼) includes mortgage on John Rolfes' plantation; in the shop, a glass case with chyrurgeon's instruments, case and pocket; instruments, motars, pestle, scales, weights, medicines, drugs; cows at James McDonnough's; negroes; parcel of books, law, physick, divinity and hist'y. Mentions Clem Hall, Dr. Cheetwood, Thos. Hill's estate, Wm. Ryan, Henry Starks, John Millard. Appraisers—Andw. Gardiner, Robert Hart.

1734-5, Jan. 4. Chew, John, of Deptford Township, Gloucester Co., yeoman; will of. Wife, Sarah. Son Michael to have plantation. Daughters—Sarah, Hannah Dilkes, Charity Fisher. Kinsman, Joseph Chew. Executors—wife, Sarah, and son, Michael. Witnesses—George Ward, Jun., Abraham Lord, Thomas Hodge. Affirmed 27 March, 1735.

Lib. 4, p. 7.

1734-5, Jan. 14. Inventory (£250.1½) includes horse, cattle, sheep, hogs, fowls and bees. Appraisers—George Ward, Jun., Samuel McCollock.

1748, April 1. Chew, Michael, of Deptford, Gloucester Co., yeoman; will of. Wife, Amy, sole executrix, and, during widowhood, plantation whereon I live and personal for maintaining my children. In case of her marriage plantation to be sold when two youngest daughters will be 18. Brother-in-law, Samuel Paul, to be guardian of children. Daughter, Sarah. In case children die under age, plantation to go to Michael Fisher, Jun., my sister's son. Witnesses—John Wild, Ezekiel Linzey, Michael Fisher. Proved 4 Feb., 1748.
Lib. 6, p. 42.

1748-9, Jany. 11. Inventory (£187.18.9½), includes husbandry utensils. Appraisers—Joseph Hedger, Richard Chew.

1731, Aug. 21. Chew, Nathaniel, Senior, of Gloucester, Gloucester Co., yeoman; will of. Wife, Mary. Sons—Richard, to have plantation; Jeffery, 30 acres joining Thomas Munyan, bought of Israel Ward; Joseph, 9 acres of meadow bought of Israel Ward, joining John Thomlison's plantation, also 50 acres, bought of Jacob Clements joining meadow aforesaid; and Nathaniel (not 21). Daughters—Elizabeth, Taber, Susanna, Mercy, Priscilla, last two under age. Mentions Sarah Jones (not 18). Executors—wife, Mary, and son Richard Chew. Witnesses—George Ward, Jun., Henry Eliott, Michael Fisher. Proved 30 Dec., 1731.
Lib. 3, p. 171.

1731, Sept. 14. Inventory (£107.18.5), includes cows, calves, horses, hogs. Appraisers—John ———, Junior, Andrew Jones.

1749, Oct. 14. Chew, Richard, of Deptford Township, Gloucester Co., house carpenter. Int. Admr., John Sparks. John Marshall, blacksmith, bondsman, all of same place. Witnesses—John Davis and John Ladd.
Lib. 7, p. 33.

1749, Sept. 28. Inventory (£11.8.0), includes mention of Joseph Olbeson, Nathan Palle. Appraisers—Joseph Butterworth, John Davis.

1741, Feb. 1. Chew, Sarah, of Deptford, Gloucester Co. Int. Admr., Michael Chew, yeoman. Fellow bondsman—Richard Chew, all of same county. Witness—Mary Tatem.

1741, Dec. 21. Inventory (£310.9.2½), includes bonds, bills and book debts £252.7.8½. Appraisers—Richard Chew, Joseph Hedger.
Gloucester Wills, 262 H.

1740, Nov. 1. Church Jeremiah, of Cape May County, yeoman. Int. Admx., Rebeckah Church. Fellow bondsmen—Elisha Hand, John Stites, of same County. Witnesses—Jeremiah Leaming, Jacob Spicer.
Lib. 4, p. 257.

1740, Sept. 22. Inventory of personal estate (£120.08.4) includes cattle, sheep and swine. Appraisers—Elisha Hand, Thomas Beck.

1748, Feb. 22. Clammans, Benjamin (over 19 years old), son of Edward, of Burlington, petitions that Samuel Stokes, of Chester, he his guardian, to whom letters of guardianship are issued.
Burlington Wills, 4351C.

1737, Oct. 10. Clap, John, of Freehold, innkeeper. Inventory of estate,£108.13.6; made by James Reynolds, Henry Van Hook and Thomas Tomson.

1737, Oct. 12. Bond of Joseph Forman, trader, of Monmouth County, as administrator of estate. James Reynolds, of same County, yeoman, fellow bondsman. Lib. C, p. 181.

1727, Aug. 20. Clark, Alexander, of Freehold, yeoman; will of. Wife, Sarah. Children—William, Richard, John, Benjamin, Mary and Elizabeth, all under age. Executors—wife, her brother Cornelius Van Horn, of Freehold, and William Lawrence, Jr., of Middletown. Witnesses—John Reed, Thomas Kinnan, Dorothy Nesbit and William Lawrence, Jr. Proved Sept. 8, 1730. Monmouth Wills, 447M.

1741, April 30. Clark, Ann, of Freehold, widow; will of. Bequests to—Janet Huttin; Ann Watson, "who now lives with me;" Ann Jolly, daughter of William Jolly; William Brown; Richard Bates; George Walker's children; Ann Barclay, daughter of John Barclay; John Huttin; John Reid, now of Upper Freehold; James, son of James Reed. Mentions, "my deceased husband's will." Executors—friends, Timothy Lloyd and George Walker, yeomen. Witnesses—Sarah Crawford, Richard Bates, Joseph Forman.

1746, May 30. Codicil, which gives date of will as April 13, 1741. To Hannah, wife of John Hutton, all that was bequeathed to Janet Huttin. Ann Watson, who is now Ann Brown. Mary Watson, daughter of Richard Watson, deceased. Margaret Brown, daughter of William Brown. Witnesses—Obadiah Huntt, Jr., Elizabeth Forman and Joseph Forman. Proved May 2, 1747. **Lib. E, p. 39.**

1742, Sept. 30. Clark, Benjamin, Jr., of Windsor, Middlesex Co., yeoman; will of. Children—Benjamin and Ann, both under age. Brothers, James and John Clarke. Plantation bought of Isaac Fitz Randolph, at Millston River; also plantation and mansion at Stony Brook; land laid out to me in a West Jersey right. Executrix—wife, Margaret. Witnesses—James Oldden, Ursula Shippey, William Worth. Proved Feb. 13, 1743. Lib. D, p. 129.

1742-3, Feb. 24. Inventory of personal estate, £659.7.9.; made by Ezekiel Smith, William Worth, Benja. Doughtye.

1732, April 20. Clark, Elizabeth, of Freehold, Monmouth Co., widow. Administration granted to Lawrence Smith. Lib. B, p. 247.

1749, Feb. 14. Clark, Isaac, of Morris Co. Int. Admx., Mary (his widow). Bondsman—Alexander Roberts. Both of Hanover in aforesaid county. Lib. E, p. 368.

1741, Oct. 3. Clark, John, of Gloucester Co. Int. Admx., Mary Clark, Tuckaho. No bondsman. Witnesses—Niell Mcneil, John Willett.

1741, Oct. 3. Inventory, £14.18.0. Appraisers—Neill Mcneil, John Willett. Sworn at Cape May, 3rd Oct. 1741. Gloucester Wills, 263H.

1750, May 21. Clark, John, of Trenton, Hunterdon Co. Bond of Hannah Clark, of Trenton, widow, as administratrix. Daniel Tool, of same place, surety. Witnessed by Martin Appleby. Lib. 7, p. 34.

1748, Sept. 6. Clark, Jonathan, of the Borough of Elizabeth, Essex Co., cordwinder; will of. Children—Mathias, Sarah, David, and Jonathan Clark, all under age. Real and personal estate. Executors

—brothers, and friends John Potter, weaver, and John Clark, cordwinder. Witnesses—Jonathan Allen, Caleb Osborn, Junr., Jno. Osborn. Proved Oct. 14, 1748. Lib. E, p. 405.

1734, Sept. 16. Clark, Matthew, of New Windsor, Middlesex Co., yeoman. Bond of Benjamin Clark, Jr., administrator, with James Clark and John Doe, of said county, as fellow bondsmen.

1734, June 1. Inventory, £258.7.0, made by Eliakim Hedger and Giles Worth. Middlesex Wills, 853 L.

1733, May 14. Clark, Richard, of Freehold, Monmouth Co., yeoman; will of. Wife, Anne. John Barclay, of Perth Amboy, £10. Kinsman, Richard, son of Andrew Baits, deceased. William, son of John Brown late of Chessquaiks. Isabel Fish, daughter of Charles Fish, of Freehold. Eldest son of George Walker, of Freehold. Anne Barclay, daughter of John. Executors—wife, Anne, and friends, Timothy Lloyd and George Walker, yeomen of Freehold. Witnesses—Thomas Redford and Jno. McConnell. Proved May 30, 1733. Lib. B, p. 463.

1742, Aug. 17. Clark, Richard, of the Borough of Elizabeth, Essex Co., ship-carpenter; will of. Children—Hannah, Richard, Abigail, Elizabeth, Henry, John, and Jonathan. Land purchased of Sayre, of about 200 acres. Real and personal estate. Executors—sons, Richard, Henry and Jonathan. Witnesses—Edward Willmott, Edward Griffing, Nath'll Hubbell. Proved May 17, 1743. Lib. D, p. 58.

1743, May 16. "I Richard Clark being very sick for a long time, and still weak, desire my brothers to act without me." Witness—James Clark.

1742, Sept. 14. Inventory of personal estate (£40.06.05), incl. bond of Jonathan Clark; made by William Clark, George Ross.

1743, May 20. Clark, Richard, Sen'r, of the Borough of Elizabeth, Essex Co., yeoman; will of. Children—Richard, Elisha, James, Ruben, Samuel, Thomas, Rachel (wife of William Lawrence), Jemima (wife of Daniel Kellsey), and Abigail Clark, at 18 years. Five sons under age. Land in Raway, which my father, Richard Clark, bought of Samuel Olliver; land joining lands of Joshua Marsh, Abraham Clark, Andrew Hampton, and John Craig; land taken up in right of Caleb Curwithy. Grandson, John Mills, son of daughter Hannah, deceased. Executors—wife, Hannah, and son, James. Witnesses—Abraham Clarke, John Craig, John Terrill. Proved Nov. 5, 1743. Lib. D, p. 97.

1743, Nov. 2. Inventory of personal estate (£113.08.08), incl. bonds of Joseph Kelsey, Nathaniel Clarke and John Lee; made by Abraham Clarke, and George Ross.

1731, May 31. Clark, Thomas, of Bridgeton, Township of Northampton, Burlington Co.; will of. Children—Thomas, John, Samuel, Ephraim, Margaret, Martha and Hannah. Lot in Town of Burlington I bought of Thomas Wetherill, and land on Ancokus Creek, also Northampton River. Wife, Hannah, sole executrix. Witnesses—Oddy Brock, John Tonkins, Jr., John Burr. Proved July 5, 1731. Lib. 3, p. 143.

1731, June 30. Inventory of personal estate, £305.00.5½; made by John Burr and Thomas Budd.

1728, Oct. 20. Clark, William, of Township of Gloucester, Gloucester Co., yeoman; will of. Wife, Mary. Children—William, Sarah,

John, Joseph, Benjamin, Richard, Mary, Thomas. Executor, son William. Witnesses—Sarah Norris, Isaac Kay, John Kay. Proved Sept. 19, 1733.

1733, Aug. 31. Inventory, £96.0.0, made by John Kay and Isaac Jennings. Lib. 3, p. 375.

1742-3, March 15. Clarke, Benjamin, Sen'r, of Stoney Brooke, Middlesex Co., yeoman; will of. Children—James, Ann Cooper, Elizabeth Lord, Mary Braley and John. Real estate in Somerset Co. Executors—sons James and John Clarke. Witnesses—Benja. Yard, William Kinnison, Joseph Oldden. Proved June 5, 1747. Lib. E, p. 52.

1747, May 28. Inventory of personal estate, £159.10.7; made by Edm'd Beakes, John Oldden, John Stockton.

1732, June 15. Clarke, Daniel, of Chester, Burlington Co., yeoman. Inventory of personal estate, £78.5.8; made by John Milborn and William Sharp.

1732, June 28. Bond of Hannah Clarke, widow, as administratrix. John Milburne, of Chester, and William Sharpe, of Evesham, yeoman, fellow bondsmen. Burlington Wills, 2217 C.

1736, Jan. 10. Clarke, John, of Deptford, Gloucester Co., laborer. Int. Admr., Peter Rambo, yeoman, county aforesaid. Witnesses—Joseph Rose, John Doe. Gloucester Wills, 197H.

1737, Jany. 5. Inventory (£16.16.9), includes "charges for looking after him." Appraisers—Peter Rambo, Peter Mattson.

1744-5, March 9. Clarke, John, of the Borough of Elizabeth, Essex Co., yeoman; will of. Children—Jotham, Daniel, Phebe (wife of Joseph Hetfield), and Sarah Clark. Real and personal estate. Executors—wife, Deborah, and son, Jotham. Witnesses—Benjamin Wade, Samuel Wade, Benjamin Bonnel. Proved June 17, 1745. Lib. D, p. 298.

1732, May 22. Clawson, Abraham, of Somerset Co. Administration on estate granted to his widow, Elizabeth. John Gifford, bondsman. Lib. B., p. 256.

1728-9, March 24. Clawson, John, of Elizabeth Town, Essex Co., mason. Administration granted to Jean Clawson, the widow. Joseph Williams and Edward Thomas, fellow bondsman. Witness—Wm. Dagworthy. Lib. B, p. 115.

1729, March 30. Inventory of personal estate (£349.13.05), incl. Dutch Bible, and bonds of John Morris, Michael Vreeland, Jno. Stagg, Wm. Stagg; made by Joseph Williams and Edward Thomas.

1739, June 21. Accompt filed by widow, Jane Clawson, showing payments to Roluff Van Houghton, John Dennis, Bastyone Vangeezon, Thos. Johnson, Rachel Vreeland, Samuel Winans, Jane Tongerlove, Benjn. Williams, Law. Egbert, John Lambert, Ichabod Burnet, Daniel Ross, Mad'm Brockolls, John Winans, Benjn Price, John Salnave, John Hampton, Jacob Dehart, Abraham Brockess, Jonathan Woodruff, John Davis, Andrew Joline, Wm. Britton, Hendrick DeCamp, Sam. Royse of Barbadoes, John Parker, Esq., Mayor of Perth Amboy, Thos. Jackman.

1739, June 21. Clawson, John, of Essex Co., an orphan of 14 years. Bond of Jonathan Dayton, of Elizabeth Town, as guardian. Thos. Ogden, fellow bondsman. Witness—Robert King. Lib. C, p. 285.

1744, May 4. Clawson, John, of Woodbridge, Middlesex Co., yeoman; will of. Wife, Mary Clawson. Children—Phebe (wife of Cornelius Johnson), Sankey (wife of Eliakim Martin), Anne (wife of Nathaniel Harnet), Rachel (wife of Joseph Martin, Jr.) and John Clawson. Executors—Eliakim Martin, Cornelius Johnson and friend Gershom Martin, of Woodbridge. Real and personal estate. Witnesses—Daniel Martin, Joseph Martin and Nugient Kelly. Proved April 30, 1748.
Lib. E, p. 178.

1748, April 30. Eliakim Martin and Gershom Martin qualify as executors, the other executor being deceased.

1748, April 25. Inventory of personal estate, £93.18.2; made by Jonathan Dennes and William Sharp. Nathaniel Harned and Robert Dennes, fellow bondsmen.

1733, June 1. Clawson, Josiah, of Somerset Co. Administration on estate granted to Elizabeth Clawson. Lib. B, p. 435.

1733, Jan 21. Clawson, Robert, of Woodbridge, Middlesex Co. Administration granted to James Clawson, John Clawson and Agnes Presgrove. Lib. B, p. 586.

1732, July 3. Clay, Humphrey, of Perth Amboy, Middlesex Co.; will of. Children—Humphrey, Catherine Thorn, Sarah Clay, Rebecca Wood, Hannah Thorn, Phebe Cox, Eathalenth Denton. Real and personal estate. Wife, Rebecca, sole executrix. Witnesses—John Stevens, Rob't King, Jno. Waller. Proved Aug. 2, 1732. Lib. B, p. 293.

1736, June 12. Clay, Humphrey, of Perth Amboy, Middlesex Co., mariner; will of. Son, Humphrey Clay, the estate of his grandfather, Lawrence Vangall, deceased. Real and personal estate. Executors—mother, Rebecca Clay, and Richard Fitz Randolph. Witnesses—John Stevens, John White, Thos. Bartow. Proved July 14, 1736.
Lib. C, p. 111.

1748, Aug. 25. Clayton, David, of Freehold, yeoman; will of. Wife, Ester. Children—David, Jr., Joseph, Edward, Amie (wife of Joseph Matthews), Catherine (wife of Cornelius Tomson), Hannah and Anne. Provision for maintenance of son Richard. Executors—wife, brother John Clayton, and brother-in-law Edward Taylor. Witnesses—Rebecca Morford, William Norcross and John Henderson. Proved Jan. 25, 1748. Lib. E, p. 246.

1748, Oct. 18. Inventory of estate, £222.06.04½, incl. an old weaving loom; made by William Hankerson and Richard Saddam.

1750, May 17. Additional inventory, £19.12.5¼ incl. debts due by John Henderson and widow Mary Taylor.

1748, Aug. 25. Cleayton, Parnell, of Mansfield, Burlington Co., yeoman; will of. Sons—John, Thomas, William and Parnell. Daughters—Mary, Martha and Deborah. Children all under age. Real and personal estate. Executors—brother, William Cleayton, and bro.-in-law, George Nicholson. Witnesses—George Folwell, Isaac Boulton and William Pancoast. Proved Oct. 4, 1748. Lib. 5, p. 536.

1748, Oct. 26. Inventory of personal and real estate, £797.7.5; made by Michael Newbold and Robert Rockhill.

1742, August 23. Cleayton, Zebulon, of Upper Freehold township, yeoman; will of. Wife, Mary. Children—Thomas, John, Margaret, and Leah Robins, wife of Joseph Robins. Granddaughter, (not named), daughter of son Zebulon Clayton, deceased. Executors—wife and son Thomas. Witnesses—Thomas Cox, James McKeand, Thomas David and Robert Laurence. Thomas Cox, witness. Executors Quakers. Proved May 24, 1744. Lib. 5, p. 28.

1744, April 16. Inventory of the estate, £160.14.0, incl. a negro woman and girl; made by Jacob Robins and Benjamin Lawrence.

1750, July 22. Clegg, Joseph, of New Hanover, Burlington Co., yeoman; will of. Wife, Sarah, all estate, to enable her to bring up "my poor child Elizabeth." Executor—friend, Joseph Arney, of New Hanover. Witnesses—Moses Robins, Jur., Benjamin Allen, Ephraim Robins, Henry Van Hook and Francis Williams. Proved Aug. 6, 1750. Lib. 6, p. 344.

1750, July 31. Inventory of personal estate, £106.17.6; made by Sam'l Emley and Moses Robins.

1746, July 22. Clemanes, Edward, of Chester, Burlington Co.; will of. Sons—Benjamin, Judah and Ephraim. Real and personal estate. Wife, Elizabeth, sole executrix. Friend, Thomas Hackney, trustee. Witnesses—Dan'll Morgan, Thomas Stokes, Joseph Heritage. Proved Sept. 22, 1746. Lib. 5, p. 283.

1746, 25th day, 7th mo. (Sept.). Inventory of personal estate, £146; made by Dan'l Morgan and Robert Franch.

1748, Feb. 22. Clement, Benjamin, son of Edward Clement, aged 19 years, makes choice of Samuel Stokes, of Chester, as his guardian. Bond of Samuel Stokes as guardian. Benjamin Allen, of Evesham, fellow bondsman. Lib. 6, p. 28.

1730, Jan. 13. Clesbly (Closbly), Hannah, of Newark, Essex Co., widow. Bond of Daniel Sayre of Elizabeth Town as administrator on the estate. Epenetus Beech, fellow bondsman. Lib. B, p. 183.

1730, March 19. Inventory of personal estate, £54.19.01, incl., bonds from Isaak Jones, Joseph Wheaten, Isaack Lyon, made by Stephen Browne and Christopher Wood.

1749-50, Feb. 5. Cline (Klein), Bartram, of Kingwood, Hunterdon Co. Int. Wilhelm Klein, son and heir of Bartram Cline, assigns his right to administer on his father's estate to Peter Hapach of Amwell. Witnesses, Cornelius Wyckoff, Jr., and Martin Ryerson.

1749-50, Feb. 6. Bond of Peter Hopough, of Amwell, as administrator. Martin Ryerson, Esquire, of same place, surety. Witnesses—John Arrison and Samuel Stout. Administrator sworn, signed "Pitter Habbach," in German.

1750, May 2. Inventory, £27.12.7; made by William Vanest and Isaac Bogert. Hunterdon Wills, 246 J.

1749, April 1. Close, John, of precinct of Deerfield, Cumberland Co., hatter. Int. Elinor, widow, renounces. Administrator—Samuel Parvine (signed "Parviahie") of Aloways Creek, Salem County, yeoman. Fellow bondsman—William Oakford. Witnesses—Elizabeth Cotting, Elias Cotting. Lib. 6, p. 53.

1749, April 1. Inventory of personal estate (£17.4.0) includes notes against Thomas Pearson and Patrick Murphy. Appraisers—William Oakford, Samuel Bowen.

1732, Dec. 21. Clothier, Henry, of Upper Freehold Township, Monmouth Co. Administration granted to Anne Clothier, the relict.
Lib. B, p. 350.

1732, Dec. 18. Inventory of personal estate (£439.12.3¼) includes one negro man, Cato, hides, leather and curriers tools; bills and notes of Ambrose Field, Jr., William Thorn (granted to Abraham Bonnel), William Poole, Jonathan Lovet, Edward Evans, Robert English, Samuel Keimer, Richard Britten, Peter Rantilborough (or Cantilborough), Constentine Macmanes, Daniel Hollinshead. Made by Elias Smith, Aaron Robins and Isaac Stelle.

1734, Dec. 20. Clothier, Henry, of Allens Town, Monmouth Co., currier. Account of Ann Clothier, administratrix. Inventory of personal estate amounted to £430.12.3¼. Credit side of account mentions: Edmund Beakes, Gabriel Stelle, Samuel Lovett, Joseph Kinnan, John Black, Samuel Rogers, Elias Smith, Peter Vantillburgh, Margaret Carr, Nathan Allen, Joseph Rockhill, John Quicksall, John Middleton, Joseph Borden, Benjamin Applegate, Dorothy Large, Daniel Licker, James Chambers, Abraham Wildes, Benjamin Lawrence, John Parsons, Nathaniel Stevenson, Thomas Parks, Peter Brueza, John Row, Isaac Ivins, John Newbury, Samuel Robins, Robert Stuart, William McGhee, Samuel Wright, James Laing, Rachel Fenton, George Snow, Robert Montgomerie, William Evilman, Nicholas Stevens, Thomas Farrel, Joshua Barker, Benjamin Clark, Arthur Whitehead, Ambrose Field, Nehemiah Cowgill, Richard Smith, John Laning, Doctor John Brown, Thomas Woodward, Robert English, Guisbert Hendrickson, Lewis Curree, Daniel Hollinshead, Richard Britton, Wm. Pool, Samuel Keimer, gone beyond sea; Peter Vantillburgh, Cornelius Delany, Henry Coats, Isaiah Folkes, John Collyer, Joseph Applegate, Joseph Butler, James Chambers, Benjamin Doughty, James Moon, Joseph Overton, Obadiah Hireton, George Bates, Thomas Terry, John Wood, Joseph Britton, Joseph Butler, Thomas Richards, Elisha Lawrence, John and Robert Rockhill, William Bickley, Samuel Bustill. (See Archives, XXIII, p. 98, for administration).
Lib. B, p. 350; Monmouth Wills, 485-498M.

1735-6, Jan. 28. Coate, Samuel, of Bethlehem Township, Hunterdon Co., waterman. Inventory of personal estate, £10.0.1; made by Joseph Willits and Robert Willson.

1735, Jan. 31. Bond of Marmaduke Coate' of Bethlehem, yeoman, as administrator. Joseph Willitts, of same place, surety. Lib. 4, p. 52.

1738, Feb. 27. Account of administrator includes money paid to John Coate and John Pursel, for expences during sickness of the deceased.

1749, Dec. 15. Coate, William, of Wellinborough, Burlington Co., yeoman; will of. Wife, Rebecca, use of plantation in Wellinborough. Sons—Barzilla, Israel, Marmaduke and William. Daughters—Ann, Hannah, Rachel, Mary, Bulah and Edith, all under age. Plantation in New Hanover given me by my father Marmaduke Coat. 28 acres in Springfield, bought of Jonathan Wright. Executors—wife, brother-in-law Joseph Noble, and cousin Richard Smith, Ju'r. Witnesses—Thomas Buzby, John Buzby, Robt. Hartshorne. Proved March 24, 1749. Lib. 6, p. 318.

1749-50, March 22. Inventory of personal estate, £984.18.3; made by Revel Elton, Henry Cooper and John Buzby. Includes debts due from P. Brown, Henry Cooper, Isaac Conners, Thomas Reeves, Mary Butcher, and Wm. Buzby; also 3 negroes.

1761, Jan. 13. Account of Joseph Lippincott and Rebecca his wife, which Rebecca was acting executrix of the last will of her late husband William Coate, shows payments to John Poole, William Northcross, Eliz. Cowgill, Jane Stretchbury, Henry Cooper, Sam'l Smith, Joshua Raper, Thomas Rodman, Abraham Griffits, William Sheels, John Hartsshorne, Isaac Connero, Robert Taylor, Joseph Allinson, Daniel Doughty, Hannah Atkinson, G. Blond, Richard Smith, John Buzby, James Smith, Josiah White, Doc't Shaw, James Smith (Ex'r of Saml. Lovett), Catherine Blylor, Hester Govell, Preserved Brown, Darling Conroe, Joseph Hollingshead, John Ewan, Richard Smith, Jun'r, Robert Hartshorne, Jos. Talman, Samuel Mickle.

1750, Jan. 5. Coates, Marmaduke, of Burlington Co. Int. Administration granted to Rebecca Coates, widow. Robert Hartshorne, atty,-at-law, fellow bondsman. Lib. 7, p. 102.

1749, May 7. Coats, Marmaduke, of Mansfield, Burlington Co., house carpenter; will of. Wife, Sarah, tract in the mountains at Kingwood, Bethlehem Township, to enable her to bring up child John and expected child. Plantation in Mansfield I bought of John Gibbs. Executors—wife, and brother John Coats. Witnesses—John Buffin, Ann Buffin, Joseph Pope. Proved May 31, 1749. Lib. 6, p. 300.

1750, May 7. Inventory of personal estate, £269.8.6; made by Thos. Earl and Michael Newbold.

1733, Jan. 28. Coats, Thomas, of Salem Co., weaver. Int. Admr., Samuel Wade. Bondsmen—John Doe, Joseph Ware, all of said County. Witnesses—Daniel Mestayer, Mary Mestayer. Lib. 3, p. 393.

1733-4, Jan. 11. Inventory (£24.12.1) includes "loom & wharpin boxes." Appraisers—Joseph Wear, Hugh Clifton.

1745, Aug. 26. Cochran, John, of the City of New York, joyner. Bond of Peter Cochran, of New Brunswick, principal creditor, as administrator. Jas. Neilson and Andrew Norwood, fellow bondsmen. Middlesex Wills, Lib. D, p. 316.

1745, Sept. 26. Inventory of personal estate, £52.7.7; made by William Cox and Derrick Schuyler.

1746, Aug. 8 and 11. Account of Peter Cochran as administrator, showing payments to John Guest, John VanNorden, Francis Starkey, Luke Voorhees, William Smith, Esq., at York, Isaac Stelle, Cristerfor Wamsley, Andrew Norwood, Thos. Farmer, Esq., Israel Balldwine, James Reed, Reuben Runyon.

1746, Nov. 21. Above bond revoked and administration on estate granted to Robert Cochran, brother, now of New Jersey. James Newell and Richard Roe, both of Perth Amboy, fellow bondsmen. Witness—Ryneer Vangeson. Lib. D, p. 437.

1747, April 16. Account of Robert Cochran, of the City of New York, the administrator, showing moneys received from Mr. Catherwood, Petter Byard, Ebrim Lerue, Mr. Ganter Reed, John King of Pekant River, Emanuell Cocker of Newark, John Quay, David Ward of Newark, Stephen Cortlands, John Vanse of Newark, Mr. Ludlow, Alexander Wille, Mr. Miller of Brunswick, James Nikson, John Vance, Osell Ogton, Esq., Joseph Ward of Newark, Mager Johnston, Esq., Hezekiah Johnston, John Dow, James Still, Jeremyah Tutol of Newark, David Thomas, Sam Dobens, Robert Sanford, Simon Corgear; also payments to Mr. Banard, John Foot, John Kip, Francis Waters, Ebenezer Feron, Alexander Eagols, James Lane, Mr. Herson.

1747, Nov. 1. Inventory of estate, £212.3.3; made by Robert Cochran. John Dow, of Suhant River, Bengman Coats, Thomas Ludle, fellow bondsmen.

1736, April 2, 9. Cock, John, of Waterford, Gloucester Co., yeoman; will of. Wife, Lydia, sole executrix, and to have all lands in Newton on the south side of Cooper's Creek and in Waterford on the north side of said Creek, except that part on the road from Nathaniel Champion's to Thomas Spicer's. Legacies to cousins Nathaniel Champion and Richard Bushel. Devises to brother, Alexander Morgan, all land in Waterford on the north side of Coopers Creek, (reserving that before given to wife). He to pay sister, Charity Johnson, £100. Witnesses—Jos. Cooper, Samuel Morton, Mary Molder. Affirmed 19 April, 1736. Lib. 4, p. 64.

1736, April 17. Inventory (£506.16.4), includes 44 horned cattle, sheep, 7 negro boys, negro woman, 4,000 bricks. Appraisers—Tho. Spicer, John Shivers.

1738, Dec. 25. Coddington (Codington), John, of Woodbridge, Middlesex Co., yeoman; will of. Wife, Elizabeth. Children—John, Richard, Elizabeth Marsh, Hanah Price, Rachel, Mary and Daniel Codington. Real and personal estate. Executor, son Daniel. Witnesses—Job Pack, Jacob Fitz Randolph, Moses Rolfe. Proved Jan. 9, 1738. Lib. C, p. 234.

1738, May 4. Coddington, Sarah, of Elizabeth Town, widow. Bond of William Winans and Samuel Oliver as administrators. Lawrence Smythe, of Perth Amboy, Esq., fellow bondsman. Lib. C, p. 194.

1738, May 1. Agreement between the heirs, viz., Moses Rolfe, Andrew Drake, Samuel Oliver, William Winans, Jonathan Frazee, James Rig, William Oliver, Elizabeth Whithead, David Conger, David Olliver, Benoni Frasee, Mary Ogden, Elizabeth Olliver, Joseph Oliver, John Oliver. Witnesses—John Ross, John Radley.

———, ———, —. Accompt of administrators showing goods sold at auction to John Radley, Jun'r, Jonathan Higgins, Richard Whitehead, Elizabeth Oliver, Mary Ogden, Moses Rolfe, David Bon Rapoe, William Oliver, James Riggs, Benjamin Frazer, Mary Moore, Joseph Oliver, Samuel Roberts, John Ross, Wm. Winans, David Conger, Mary Ogden, Jun'r, Joseph Chandler, Doctor Burnet, Elizabeth Halsey, Ephraim Terril, Jacob Carpenter, John Parker, Thomas Ogden, Widow Halsey, Timothy Pike, John Higgins, Joshua Clark, Eunice Gray; also debts due by Abraham Hatfield, William Ross, John Ross, Widow Johnson, Widow Ogden and Ephraim Terrill, Junr.

1739, July 1. Coejmans, Andries, gentleman, of Somerset Co.; will of. Wife, Geertzuid. Son, Samuel Staats Coejmans, to have £100 as a birthright; also two silver cups and large silver tankard, and £500 when he attains 21 yrs. Daughters—Johanna, Mayeke, Geerhuyd (under 21). "Lands, tenements and properties in the province of New York as in the province of New Jersey." Executors—wife Geertzuyd, brother-in-law Lewis Morris, Junior, and Brandt Schuyler of New York City. Witnesses—N. Governeur, John Broughton, Joseph Clarke. Proved 19 Dec., 10th Feb., 1741, and 1st March 1741-2. Lib. C, p. 496.

1727-8, Jan. 21. Coleman, Joseph, of Salem, Salem Co., merchant; will of. Wife, Mary, executrix, to have £200 and to execute all manner of deeds to the highest purchasers of all estate, real and personal, whether in Pennsylvania or the Jersey. Children—Ann, Mary, Elizabeth, Rebecca and Hannah Coleman. Trustees for the children—Thomas Tress and William Rawle of Philadelphia, merchants. Witnesses—Simon Warner, James Gibbs.

1731, March 4. Codicil: "I approve of the above will, puting in my son Joseph Coleman an equal shear with the rest of my children." Witnesses—Solomon Goade, B. Vining, Jos. Coleman." Proved 15 Aug., 1732. Lib. 3, p. 211.

1732, Aug. 15. Letters testamentary granted Mary Coleman.

1732, Sept. 22. Inventory, £508.2.1½. Appraisers—William Hancock, Joseph Gregorey.

1740, Feb. 17. Coleman, Mary, of Salem Co., widow. Int. Admrs., John Pierson and Anne Pierson, his wife. Bondsmen—Clement Hall, William Frazier, all of said County. Witness—Rebekah Coleman. Salem Wills, 547Q.

1740, Mar. 12. Inventory, £1766.17.11. Appraisers—Clem. Hall, Will. Fraser.

1733, Aug. 15. Coleman, Thomas, of Burlington Co., joyner and house carpenter. Wm. Coleman, of Philada., requests that one of the chief creditors of his brother's estate be appointed administrator.

1733, Aug. 21. Administration granted to Joseph Rockhill. Samuel Scattergood and Richard Roe, of Town of Burlington, fellow bondsmen. Lib. 3, p. 364.

1733, Aug. 27. Inventory of personal estate, £25.1.1; made by Wm. Bickley and Saml. Scattergood.

1735, Sept. 6. Account of Joseph Rockhill shows payments to Sarah Cutler, Samuel Scattergood, Rebecca Satterthwait, Francis Smith, William Bickley, Sarah Lovet, James Hancock, Dr. Thomas Shaw, Robert Tuckness, Silas Crispin, Naomi Killgore, Daniel Sutton, Elizabeth Prosser.

1740, Dec. ——. Coles, Joseph, of Greenwich Township, Gloucester Co., yeoman; will of. Sons—Samuel, Joseph and Benjamin, to have the plantation I live on, with ½ of the saw mill and other buildings thereon, with two tracts of land adjoining the same, one surveyed by Jacob Hewlings, the other by Jacob Richman. Brother, Samuel Coles, and Thomas Coles, Robert Zaines and John Gauslin, Junior, to be trustees to divide aforesaid lands among my sons when Samuel will be 21. Wife, Mary. Executors—wife and Thomas Spicer, Sr. Witnesses—Samuel Collins, Benjamin Cheeseman, John Gosling, Junior. Proved 27 March, 1741. Lib. 4, p. 273.

1741, March 24. Inventory (£477.3.5½), includes three negroes, 19 cattle £47, etc. Appraisers—Robert Zane, Benjamin Cheeseman.

1731, Sept. 27. Coles, Mary, of Gloucester Co., widow. Int. Admr., Joseph Coles, yeoman. Fellow bondsmen—Samuel Coles and Thomas Coles, yeoman, of County aforesaid. Witnesses—Simon Ellis, Robert Hunt. Lib. 3, p. 153.

1731, Sept. 11. Inventory of Mary Coles, widow, deceased, relict of Samuel Coles, £582.17.2 includes "Great Bibles," old guns, old sword, pistols and holsters, 3 negros, wolf-trap, etc. Appraisers—Joseph Stoaks, Amos Ashead, Tho. Spicer.

1747, Mar. 9. Coles, Thomas, of Waterford, Gloucester Co., yeoman;

will of. Son, Thomas, at 21, to have all lands, swamps and mills; also the remainder of rent of grist mill after the Loan Office is paid. Other children—Hannah, Samuel, Beesheba, Mary and Joseph. Brother, Samuel Coles, to have saw mill on Alberson's Branch in Gloucester Co., with privileges of pine lands and swamp on north side of said Branch, also on south side northward of John Town's land until son Thomas will be of age. Wife, Hannah, personal estate to bring up the children and use of home plantation. Executors—wife, Hannah, and brother, Samuel Coles. Witnesses—Thomas Cowperthwait, William Ellis, Thos. Spicer, Jun. Lib. 10, p. 413.

1748, Sept. 12. Letters testamentary granted to Hannah Coles, executrix of Thomas Coles, late of Colestown, Gloucester Co., and Samuel Coles, as named in the will.

1748, April 14 and 15. Inventory, £390.5.2. Appraisers—Thos. Spicer, Charles Farguisen.

1744, Oct. 8. Collard, John, of Middletown, yeoman. Thomas Cooper, principal creditor, enters caveat against granting letters of administration. Dated Perth Amboy. Lib. D, p. 207.

1744, Dec. 1. Thomas Cooper directs that administration be granted to Andrew Baird. Dated Middletown.

1744, Nov. 30. Inventory of estate, £25.8.4; made by "James Bowne, minor," and Thomas Cooper.

———, ———, —. Inventory "of goods of John Colard left at Robard Smiths at Egharbour," £3.17.9, consisting of clothing; made by Joseph Johnson and Robert Smith.

1744, Dec. 15. Bond of Andrew Baird as administrator of estate. John Baird, fellow bondsman.

1746, March 28. Account of estate by administrator, Andrew Baird, mentions trips to "Egharbour" and bonds paid to John Corlis, Joseph Applegate, Jarvis Farro, James Haywood, James Stout, Mordecai Anderson, William Collard and Thomas Cooper.

1746, April 6. Collins, David, of Woodbridge, Middlesex Co., sadler; will of. Mother, Ruth Redford. Brothers—John and Benjamin Collins. Real estate. Executors—John Herriot and Samuel Crow, both of Woodbridge. Witnesses—Sam'll Moores, Jonathan Harned, Richard Jones. Proved Nov. 13, 1746.

1746, Nov. 22. Above executors refuse to act. Administration granted to Benjamin Collins, one of the legatees. Samuel Crow, fellow bondsman. Witness—Daniel Clark. Lib. D, p. 430.

1750, Aug. 4. Collins, Edward, of Hunterdon Co. Bond of Rebecca Collins, of Wrightstown, Pennsylvania, as administratrix. John Williams, of Bucks County, Pennsylvania, yeoman, surety.
Hunterdon Wills, 279J.

1750, Aug. 1. Collins, George, of Upper Freehold, Monmouth Co., labourer. Bond of Catherine Howard, widow, administratrix, with Peter Sexton, of same place, yeoman, as fellow bondsman.

1750, Aug. 1 Inventory, £21.3.1, made by Joseph Clegg and Peter Sexton. Burlington Wills, 4621-4 C.

1737-8, Feb. 16. Collins, John, of New Brunswick, Middlesex Co., yeoman; will of. Children—Matthew, John, Jean, all under age. Brother-in-law, John Converse. Executors—wife, Jean, friends Gerardus Depester and Wm. Hooks of Piscataway. Real and personal estate. Witnesses—Ste'n Warne, Thomas Collins, William Collins. Proved Dec. 29, 1746. Lib. D, p. 442.

1746, Dec. 29. Bond of Jane Collins, the widow, as executrix; the other two executors refusing to act.

1746-7, March 13. Inventory of personal estate, £744.00.5; made by J. Wetherill and John Tomson.

1741, 5th mo. (July), 4th. Collins, Joseph, of Gloucester Co.; will of. Son, Benjamin, £70 and lands on north side of Kings Road that goes from Burlington to Salem adjoining lands of Sarah Hinchman and John Estaugh; also lot of 2 acres on south side of aforesaid Kings Road, between Simeon Ellis and Thomas Ellis. Grandchildren—Joseph (not 21), Priscilla (not 18), the children of my son Benjamin Collins. Daughters—Sarah and Kathren Ellis and Rebaca Clements. Executors—James Hinchman and John Kaighin. Witnesses—John Maxell, William Griscom, Thomas Varnum. Affirmed 5 Oct., 1741. Lib. 4, p. 294.

1745, July 24. Inventory (£129.9.10), names Saml. Clement and Joseph Kaighin. Appraisers—John Maxell, William Griscom.

1734, Aug. 12. Collins, Matthew, of New Brunswick, Middlesex Co. Administration granted to Janna Paine. Lib. B, p. 586.

1733, Nov. 21. Collson, Thomas, of precinct of Piles Grove, Salem Co., yeoman; will of. Leaves to brother, George, plantation where their father lived. Mentions mother, and sister Hannah Oakford. Executor—brother George Collson. Witnesses—Aquila Barber, William Westan, Thomas Barber. Proved Aug. 8, 1750. Lib. 6, p. 403.

1740, Nov. 5. Collum, William, of City of Burlington, baker; will of. Wife, Mary, sole legatee and executrix. Mentions "all my children" without naming them. Real and personal estate. Witnesses—Cha. Read, John Douglas, Isa. DeCow. Proved April 16, 1741. Lib. 4, p. 279.

1743, Nov. 9. Coltas, Joseph, of Shrewsbury Township, Monmouth Co., bootman; will of. John Curtis, sole heir and executor. Witnesses—John Parson, James Lawrence, John Tafft. Proved Jan. 7, 1743. (James Lawrence and John Curtis, Quakers). Lib. D, p. 111.

1743, Dec. 19. Inventory of estate, £79.9.6; made by James Lawrence and John Parson.

1732, Dec. 2. Colver (Colwer), John, of the Blackriver, Hunterdon Co., "cordwinder, being sick;" will of. Wife, Freelove. Eldest son, John Collwer; son, Jabsh Coulver. Expected child. Residue of estate to wife, "in this colleny or att nwinglend" (New England). Wife, executrix. Witnesses—Seth Smith, Leaddy Colver and John Bell. Proved August 20, 1733. Lib. 3, p. 368.

———, ———, —. Inventory, without date, £95.11.0; including beaver hat, felt hat and Bible. Made by David Collver and John Bell.

1733, Aug. 14. Colwell, Francis, of Freehold, Monmouth Co., labourer; will of. Children—William, Thomas, John and Henry. Executors—Walter Wall and Jeremiah White. Mentions cloth at Henry Vandebelt's. Witnesses—William Smith, Thomas Whitlock and Johnsen. Proved October 16, 1733. Lib. B, p. 470.

1733, Nov. 24. Inventory (£75.1.4) includes 6 pocket books, 26 coarse combs, 10 pair of spectacles, 29 pair scissors, 55 thimbles; indicating the deceased was dealer in notions or drygoods. Debts against Joseph Dorsit, Gershom Walling, Justice Wilson, Marget Smith, Gershom Boune, William Lawrence, James Nipper, Gyen Wotson, Timothy Loyd, Jno. Reidetaner, Widow Willit, Hendrick Vanbilt, Ro. Dodgworth, Charity Erven, George Cowenhoven, Jno. Benam, Henery Collwell, James Collwell, William Covanhoven and William Cole. Made by Thomas Whitlock and Robert Thomson.

1730, June 9. Combs, Robert, of Woodbridge, Middlesex Co., yeoman; will of. Sons—Dennis and Robert. Daughters mentioned, but no names given. Land bought of Moses Coller. Executors—Wife, Euniss, eldest son Dennis, and Henry Potter of Woodbridge. Witnesses—Richard Carman, Timothy Bloomfield, Nugient Kelly. Proved Sept. 11, 1730. Lib. B, p. 166.

1730, Aug. 29. Inventory, £135.9.1; made by Richard Carman and William Foord.

1731, May 17. Compton, John, of Woodbridge, Middlesex Co. Int. Adm'x., widow, Elizabeth Compton. Lib. B, p. 211.

1745, Sept. 3. Compton, Jonathan, of Woodbridge, Middlesex Co.; will of. Granddaughter, Sarah Bonham. Executors—Wife, Easter, brothers-in-law Peter Martin and Jonathan Martain. Witnesses—Samuel Compton, James Compton, Margret Compton, Ebenezer Saltar. Proved Feb. 24, 1747. Lib. E, p. 133.

1747, Feb. 23. Inventory, £73.3; made by Gershom Martin and Zedekiah Bonham.

1736, Dec. 13. Comron, Daniel, of Chester, Burlington Co., yeoman; will of. Children—Daniel, Abraham, Richard, John, Benjamin, Isaac and Ann. Real and personal estate. Wife—Rebecca, sole executrix. Witnesses—Richard Peirce, Michael Peirce, Richard Barrow. Proved June 22, 1739. Lib. 4, p. 188.

1739, June 21. Inventory, £235.11; made by Joseph Stokes and Thomas Lippincott.

1747, Nov. 25. Conger, David, of Piscataway, Middlesex Co. Int. Ad'mx., Dorcas Conger. Rowley Arnold, fellow bondsman. Lib. E, p. 110.

1735, Nov. 29. Conger, Gershom, Jun'r. of Woodbridge, Middlesex Co., carpenter; will of. Cousin, Gershom Cawood, at 21 years. Real and personal estate. Executors—Thomas Cawood and brother Robert Mitchell. Witnesses—James Wilkison, Jane Phillips, Jno. Sarjant. Proved Jan. 20, 1735-6. Lib. C, p. 58.

1749, Jan. 30. Conger, Job, of Woodbridge and Raway neck, Middlesex Co., yeoman; will of. Children—Enoch, Moses, Ruth (wife of Nathaniel Price), Sarah (wife of Daniel Codington), Elizabeth (wife of Reuben Hierd), Esther and Barbara Conger, both under age. Executors—Wife, Keziah (Coziah), son Enoch and friend William Moore. Witnesses—Job Pack, Benjamin Tharp, Thomas Chapman. Proved Feb. 17, 1758. Lib. F, p. 497.

1743-4, Feb. 25. Congleton, James, of Salem Co. Int. Adm'x, Bridget Congleton, widow. Bondsmen—Thomas Haynes, John McKeen, yeo-

man. All of Manington, Salem County. Witness—John Haynes
Lib. 5, p. 90.

1743-4, Feb. 25. Inventory (£39.11.6) includes loom and tackling, and 3 wheels £4. Appraisers—Thomas Haynes, John McKeen.

1731, Dec. 8. Conhass (Conhash), Isaac, "Indian King of the Jerseys"; will of. Wife—Mary, sole legatee and executrix. Witnesses—Thos. Pleadwell, John Joans. Proved April 20, 1732. Lib. B, p. 246.

1749, 16th day, 7th mo. (Sept.). Conly, Patrick, of Burlington Co.; will of. My horse to Thomas Whitten and remainder of estate to William Joans, whom I appoint executor. Witnesses—John Forsyth, Rich'd Satterthwaite. Proved March 22, 1749. Lib. 7, p. 15.

1739, May 15. Connelly (Conoly) Brian, of Newton Township, Gloucester Co., bricklayer. Int. His widow, Dorothy, Admx. Robert Hubs, fellow bondsman. All of township and county aforesaid. Witnesses—Wm. Tatem, John Ladd, Jun. Lib. 4, p. 199.

1738, Dec. 22. Inventory (£65.12.6) includes debtors: Thomas Wilkins, John Kahan, Abraham Chattin, Jonas Cox. Appraisers—Robt. Hubs, Abraham Nelson.

1738, Oct. 6. Connelly, Mickeall, of Greenwich Township, Gloucester Co.; will of. Son, William, whole estate. In case of his death before 21, cousin Dennis Cannely, now living at New Castle upon Delaware, and brother-in-law, George Clark, to have equally the same. Executors—Said cousin, Dennis Cannely and William Cobb. Witnesses—Edward Mcfarlen, John Jones. "J. J. Jur., May 25, 1741."
Gloucester Wills, 274 H.

1740, Oct. 16. Inventory of Michel Conelly, "late of Salem Co.," £44.02.08. Appraisers—Matth. Boucher, Joseph White.

1750, May 3. Connet, Benjamin, of Woodbridge, Middlesex Co., yeoman; will of. Children—James, Joseph, Anne, Katherine, Philey, Sarah, all under age. Land received from grandfather, Noe Bishop. Executors—Wife, Katherine, and brother, Jonathan Connet. Witnesses—John Burwell, David Inslee, Nugient Kelly. Proved June 13, 1750.
Lib. E, p. 418.

1746, Dec. 20. Connover, Wyckoff, of Monmouth Co. Janitie, his widow, declines to administer the estate.

1746, Nov. 17. Inventory, £439.12.4¾; made by Nicholas Johnson, Elias Goulden, John Taylor. Monmouth Wills, 1281, 1285-6 M.

1749, August 15. Conrod, John of Amwell, Hunterdon Co. Int. Adm'x, Elizabeth Conrod. David Rumbo and Thomas Stillwell of Amwell, sureties. Witnesses—Benjamin Bye and William Ball. Inventory, £72.0.0; made by Job Robins and Thomas Stillwell.
Lib. 6, p. 280.

1741-2, March 12. Cook, Edward Patterson, of town of Shrewsbury, Monmouth Co.; will of. Wife, Katherine. Land at Shark River. Children—Ebenezer (eldest son), Margaret, William, John, Thomas and Edward Paterson, all evidently under age. Executors—Wife, "my brother, Ephraim Allen and brother Job Cook." Witnesses—Stoffil Longstreet, Harman Lane, John and Peter Parker. Proved March 2, 1742. John Parker and the executors, Quakers.
Monmouth Wills, 9642 M.

1745, May 2. Cook, Samuel, of Shrewsbury, Monmouth Co., weaver; will of. Brother, Matthew Cook, house and land in New Brunswick. Sister, Susanna Cook executrix, to have personal estate. Witnesses—Samuel and Henry Leonard and Joseph Throckmorton. Proved June 14, 1745. Lib. D, p. 297.

1745, June 25. Inventory, £503.3.11; made by Job Throckmorton and Samuel Leonard.

1747, August 22. Cook, William, of town of Shrewsbury, Monmouth Co., carpenter; will of. Wife, Rebecca. "My brothers and my sister." Executors—brother, Jasher Cook, and uncle, Ephraim Allen. Witnesses—Obadiah Williams, William Cook, Jr. and Jacob Dennis. Proved Oct. 31, 1747. Executors all Quakers. Lib. E, p. 141.

1747, Sept. 14. Inventory, £235.09.09; made by Joseph and Jacob Corlies.

1742-3, Jan. 1. Cooke, Thomas, of New Hanover, Burlington Co., yeoman; will of. Wife, Abigail. Sons—William and Benjamin, and dau. Elizabeth, all under age. Son-in-law, Tho. Emley, and dau.-in-law, Ruth Emley. Real and personal estate. Executors—brother William Cooke and John Steward. Witnesses—Sam'l Emley, William Emley, William Bullock. Proved Feb. 9, 1742-3. Lib. 4, p. 352.

1742-3, Feb. 1. Inventory, £959.5.11; made by Samuel Wright, Michael Newbold and Sam'l Emley. Includes plantation in the Eastern Division, £150.

1734, Oct. 16. Cooke, William, of Northampton, Burlington Co., husbandman. Int. Inventory, £9.9.9; made by Edward Mullin and Josiah White.

1734, Nov. 9. Adm'r, Abraham Bryan, of Northampton, yeoman. John Doe and Richard Roe, of same place, gents., fellow bondsmen. Burlington Wills, 2681-4 C.

1748, Nov. 22. Cooley, Simon, of City of Burlington, miller. Int. Adm'r, William Skeels, of same. Joseph Hollinshead, fellow bondsman. Lib. 7, p. 96.

1746, Sept. 20. Cooper, James, of Coles Town, Gloucester Co. Int. Inventory of personal estate, £35.2.1; made by Jos'a Bispham and Arthur Borradaill.

1746, Oct. 11. Cooper, James, of Evesham, Burlington Co., weaver. Int. Adm'r, Thomas Coles (Cole), Waterford, Gloucester Co. Richard Cannon, of Evesham, gent., fellow bondsman. Lib. 5, p. 431.

1747, April 2. Inventory, £2.15.0; made by Joshua Bispham and Arthur Borradaill.

1730, Sept. 20. Cooper, John, of Deptford, Gloucester Co., yeoman; will of. Wife, Ann. Children—James, John, David, Mary, Ann, Sarah, Hannah; an expected child. Plantation at Alloway's Creek. Executors—wife, brother John Mickle, cousin Joseph Cooper, Jr., brother Benjamin Clark, Jr. Witnesses—Henry Elliott, Joseph Dickinson, James Sloan. Proved Feb. 16, 1730.

1730-1, Feb. 10-12. Inventory, £623.1.3¼; made by Jonathan Lad and Jos'a Lord. Lib. 3, p. 118.

1733, April 17. Cooper, John, of Middletown, Monmouth Co. Int. Adm'r, Roelof Skank. Lib. B, p. 421.

1733, August 4. Inventory, appraised at house of Roeloffe Schenck, brewer, £18.18.6. Includes notes from Robert Manns and Oliver Silverthorne, and "To his Credits in two several books set down, the one in his Tavern Book and the other in his freight book." Made by Aure Van Dorn, Jacob Vandorn and Robert Dodsworth.

1732, Nov. 16. Cooper, John, of Newark, Essex Co.; will of. Son-in-law, John Sergeant, who is under age. Brother, Samuel Cooper. Children of sister Sarah Woodruff, deceased. Children of sister Mary Ward. Eldest daughter of sister Elizabeth Frayley, deceased. Sons-in-law—Thomas and Daniel Sergeant. Real and personal estate. Executors—wife, Hannah, and son-in-law, Jonathan Sergeant. Witnesses—Sam'll Farrand, Ezekiel Alling, Nathaniel Farrand. Proved March 11, 1736. Lib. C, p. 154.

1728, Oct. 2. Cooper, Joseph, of Newtown Township, Gloucester Co., yeoman; will of. Wife, Lydia, during widowhood, plantation whereon I live and personal estate. In case of her marriage or decease, son Isaac to have home farm and land bought from John Colley and Joseph Dole, next Wm. Cooper. "Whereas I have given my son Joseph the land on which he lives, I also give him 572 acres on which George Erwin lives in the Township of Waterford, upon condition, that he pays my daughters Lydia, Hannah and Sarah £33.6.8 within four years after my decease." "Whereas I have given to my son Benjamin the plantation at Cooper's Point, on which he lives, I also give him 227 acres on the northerly side of Coopers Creek in the Township of Waterford, 5 acres in the Great Meadows adjoining Samuel Cole, 300 acres on Unknown Creek in Salem County, adjoining Neale Daniel, also meadow and upland between land of Wm. Cooper and my son, Joseph." Executors—Wife, Lydia, and son, Joseph. Witnesses—Tho. Spicer, Abigail Spicer, Wm. Cooper, John Green. Proved 8 Jan. 1731. Lib. 3, p. 173.

1731, Nov. 10. Inventory (£861.06) includes 111 Barrels of "Sidder" and 103 empty cases. Appraisers—John Kay, Tho. Spicer.

1747, Nov. 23. Cooper, Joseph, of Newtown, Gloucester Co.; will of Wife, Hannah, to have the home plantation, 430 acres (at her death brother, Isaac Cooper, to possess the same), etc. Cousins—Wm. Moode and Joseph Howell. Grandchildren—Mary, Hannah, and Lydia (minors). Children of Jacob Howell, Jun'r. Sisters—Hannah Morgan and Sarah Raper. Nephews—Joseph, Benjamin, James, Samuel and William, sons of brother Benjamin Cooper. 600 acres near head of Cooper's Creek in Waterford, Gloucester Co., occupied by John Collins, Jun. Executors—Wife and Israel Pemberton, Jun., of City of Philadelphia, merchant. Witnesses—Simon Breach, Roger Irwin, Mary Shores. Affirmed 22 Nov. 1749. Lib. 6, p. 274.

1750, Aug. 8. Inventory, £1351.16.7½; made by Thos. Spicer, Josiah Alberson.

1732, Nov. 28. Cooper, Lydia, of Newtown Township, Gloucester Co., widow; will of. Legacies to grandchildren—Mary, daughter of son Joseph Cooper; Hannah, Lydia and Rachel, daughters of son Benjamin Cooper; Thomas, Lydia and Mary Raper, son and daughters of daughter Sarah, wife of Joshua Raper; Mary, Elisabeth, Lydia and Hannah, daughters of daughter Hannah, wife of Alexander Morgan. Daughter, Lydia Cock, son, Isaac Cooper. Executors—son, Joseph Cooper, and son-in-law, Joshua Raper. Witnesses—John Preston, Nicholas Lynch, Elisabeth Mclelan. Affirmed 29 Nov. 1736.

Lib. 4, p. 77.

1736, Nov. 16. Inventory (£485.15.7¼) includes "large Bible, 49 shillings," "228¾ yds. of linnen," £28.11.10. Appraisers—John Kay, Tho. Spicer.

1737, Aug. 2. Cooper, Samuel, Esq., of Newark, Essex Co. Int. Adm'x, Experience Cooper, widow. Isaac Lyon and Daniel Tichener, fellow bondsmen. Lib. C, p. 173.

1737, Sept. 22. Inventory (£580.09.19) includes bonds due from John Plumb, Thomas Stag, Ezekiel Crane, John Reno, Jun'r, Joseph Jones, Jeremiah Baldwin, Zachariah Hall, Thomas Price, Thomas Gardner, Thomas Longworth, John Nutman, Abraham Ketchel, Josiah Crane, Joseph Peck, John Johnson at Canabrok, Henry Eling, James Souter, Edward Heden, William Homes, Nathaniel Ward, Jun'r, John Melleg, Samuel Godden, James Smith, Capt. Amos Williams, Abraham Meseker, Daniel Cogswell, France Francisco, Hance Spier, Jun'r, Joseph Bestedo, Nathaniel Crain, James Meleg, John Baldwin, Jun'r, Benjamin Shipman, John Francisco, Coll. John Cooper, Caleb Ward, Moses Harrison, Benjamin Baldwin, Josiah Gilbert, David Alling, John Ogden, David Ogden, Nathaniel Anderson, Garret Jacobus, Joseph Ball, Jonathan Ward, Simeon Vanwinkle, John Hambleton, Bornt France, John Wells, Peter Sanderson, Jacob Spier, Jonathan Davis, Thomas Stag, Hendrick France, France Cook, Nathaniel Williams, Abraham Riker, Doctor Gillet, Abraham Defoe, Nathaniel Rogers, Thomas Ward, Philip Schuyler, Steven Ward, Perrigrine Sandford, Eleazer Bruen, John Mun, Adam Belsher, Jacob Vanderhoof, Abraham Francisco, Hendrick Spier, Timothy Person, Hesel Petterson, Eliphalet Johnson, Epenetus Beech, Samuel Parkis, John Brown, Daniel Serjeants, Widow Richards; made by Eliphalet Johnson and John Ogden.

1732, Dec. 4. Cooperthwaite, John, of Chester, Burlington Co., yeoman; unsigned will of. Son, Thomas, "house I now live in and all my lands on or adjoining on North side of the road that goes into the country." Son, John, lands lying between said road and the Branch, commonly called Coles Branch, and to both sons lands in Evesham, also in Waterford, Gloucester Co. Son, Hugh. Daus-Elizabeth (wife of Abraham Shadwell); Susannah (wife of William Webster); Hannah (wife of Francis Hogshead); and Deborah (wife of Ambrous Copland). Executors—Sons, John and Thomas. Proved Dec. 30, 1732.

1732, Dec. 5. John Kay, Esq., yeoman, affirmed that John Cooperthwaite was in sound health and perfect memory, but being on a Sloop found he was too weak to sign his will.

1732, Dec. 31. John King, of Chester, farmer, deposes that he was present at the time of the last sickness of John Copperthwaite and did hear John Kay, Esq., of Waterford read distinctly a certain writing purporting to be the last will and testament of John Copperthwaite.

1732-3, Jan. 1. Hugh Coperthwaite, of Chester, yeoman, affirmed that he was present at the last sickness of his father and did hear John Kay of Waterford, Esq., read distinctly a paper purporting to be said will.

1732-3, Jan. 3. Petition of Thomas and John Cooperthwaite, sons of John Cooperthwaite, of Chester, yeoman, for letters of administrations. Bond of Thomas and John Cooperthwaite as administrators.

Lib. 3, p. 233.

1730, 11th day, 9th mo. (Nov.). Coore, Enoch, of Evesham, Burlington Co., yeoman; will of. Sister Sarah, all cows and household goods. Sister Hannah, lot in Burlington that fell to me by heirship. Another sister, name not mentioned. Nephew, Isaac Wilkins, minor. Niece, Sarah Foster, minor. Executors—brothers-in-law, Thomas Wilkins and William Foster. Witnesses—Thomas Ballinger, Sam'll Atkinson, Samuel Stokes. Proved March 6, 1731. Lib. 3, p. 185.

1731-2, 16th day, 12th mo. (Feb.). Inventory, £589.00.8½; made by Joseph Stoakes and Sam. Lippincott.

1736, July 28. Coppock, Bartholomew, of Wellinborough, Burlington Co., blacksmith. Int. Adm'x, Amy Coppock, widow. Abraham Perkins, of same, fellow bondsman. Lib. 4, p. 63.

1736, Aug. 10. Inventory, £103.3.1; made by Abraham Perkins and Peter Bishop.

1731, March 11. Corbett, Mary; will of. Grandson, John Corbett Ludlow, minor, "son of my daughter Mary and Henry Ludlow, her now husband." Debt due brother-in-law, Chief Justice Hooper. Land in New York. Executor—nephew John Morris. Witnesses—Isabella Graham, James Graham, Robert Hunter Morris. Proved March 31, 1732. Lib. B, p. 298.

1740, Oct. 22. Cordesse, Anthony, of New Brunswick, Middlesex Co., baker. Int. Adm'r, Samuel FitzRandolph, Sen'r, of Woodbridge, principal creditor. Samuel Fitzrandolph, Jun'r, fellow bondsman. Lib. C, p. 359.

1743-4, March 12. Cordry, William, of Great Eggharbor, Gloucester Co., yeoman; will of. Wife, Ann. Sons—Clement, to have plantation whereon I live between Great Gutt Creek and William Reid's land; Edmund, to have residue of said tract, also meadows southeastward over the Bay and the cedar swamp; Isaac. Daughters, Rebecca Cordry, alias Leeds, Phebe Cordry, alias Covenoven, and Elizabeth Cordry, Ruth Ireland, Easter Cordry. Executors—sons-in-law, John Leeds and Joseph Ireland. Witnesses—Joseph Leeds, Deborah Leeds, Japhet Leeds, Junior.

1746, May 27. Codicil—concerning son Isaac. Witnesses—John Leeds, John Poolen, Samuel Weaire. Affirmed 23 April, 1747. Gloucester Wills, 347 H.

1746-7, March 18. Inventory (£139.5.6) includes coopers' tools, weavers loom and tackling. Appraisers—Joseph Leeds, John Ingersul.

1740, Aug. 13. Corey, Abraham, of Hanover, Morris Co., will of. Abraham (the eldest) to have improvement of plantation in Hanover until sons David and Jonathan will be 22. Daughters—Elizabeth Day, Mary Johnson and Abigail. Executors—son Abraham and son-in-law, Samuel Day. Witnesses—Stephen Ward, William Brant, Nichlous Carter. Proved 4 Nov., 1740. Lib. C, p. 362.

1740, Oct. 28. Inventory (£90.9.6) includes claims against Caleb Ball, Benjamin Winchel, William Gardner, Joseph Headley, Henery Leacy, Joseph Leacy, Jacob Gargis, Ebenezer Mehurin. Appraisers—Barnibus Carter, Jeremiah Genung.

1738, Sept. 2. Corker, Samuel, of Bristol, Bucks Co., Pa., sawyer and carter. Int. Adm'r, Joseph Rockhill, of Bristol, gent., with Samuel Scattergood, of Burlington, N. J., merchant, as fellow bondsman.

1738, Sept. 1. Jane Corker, widow of Samuel, resigns right of administration in favor of Joseph Rockhill. Burlington Wills, 3059-60 C.

1739, Oct. 20. Corlis, Benjamin, of Shrewsbury, Monmouth Co., weaver. Int. Inventory, £84.5.0; made by Samuel Leonard, John Redford and Jeremiah Bonham. Lib. C, p. 297.

1739, Nov. 14. Adm'x, Mary Corlis, widow. Joseph Corlis, of Shrewsbury, yeoman, fellow bondsman. Witnessed by Jacob Vardell.

1748, Dec. 22. Corlise, Samuel, of town of Shrewsbury, Monmouth Co., yeoman; will of. Wife, Elizabeth, and brother, George Corleis, legatees and executors. Witnesses—Joseph Eatton, Richard Anthony and Jacob Dennis. Proved Jan. 3, 1748-9, and Elizabeth Corleis sworn in. "George Corleis, the other executor therein named, living at present in New England."

1749, December 5. George Corleis sworn in as executor.

Lib. E, p. 348.

1750, Dec. 26. Cornelison, Charles, of Penns Neck, Salem County, yeoman; will of. Wife, Ann, executrix. Son, Charles, ½ plantation (110 acres) whereon I live. Son, Andrew, the other half. When they attain age of 21, they shall pay legacies to son, John Corneliuson, and daughter, Catherine. Sons John and Andrew to be put to trades. Witnesses—William Philpot, Samuel Whitehorne. Proved 23 Feb., 1750. Salem Wills, 924 Q.

1750-1, Jan. 31. Inventory, £90.10.9; made by Samuel Whitehorne, William Philpot.

1743, Dec. 17. Cornelisse, Mathew, of Bergen Co., yeoman; will of. Daughters—Maregrit Vanorde (wife of Allebert VanOrde) and Rachel Begonem. Grandson, Matheis Cornelisse. Executor—Cornelius Wynkoop, of Hackinsack, merchant. Witnesses—Lourens L. Vanboskerk, Lourens I. Vanboskerk, Nicolaes DeMarest. Proved 31 Jan. 1748.

Lib. E, p. 251.

1748, Sept. 22. Inventory, of real and personal, (£191.4.6) includes 125 acres of land and meadow and bond from John Zabrisco; made by Cor's Wynkoop, Executor.

1742, Aug. 10. Cornelius, John, of Somerset Co., yeoman; will of. Wife, Johanna. Children—John (oldest), Elizabeth, Allen, William, Joseph and James (minor). Real and personal estate. Executor—John Corle. Witnesses—Jacob Beng, Isaac Carredo, Jno. Dalley. Proved 16 March, 1742-3. Lib. D, p. 26.

1742, Aug. 21. Inventory, of real and personal, (£40.15.3) includes one lot of land, £14, and house and lot, £5; made by Ja. Leonard and Jno. Dalley.

1742-3, Mar. 19. Widow, Johanna, renounces executorship. Witnesses—Joseph Badcock, John Berrion.

1743-4, Feb. 25. Corneliuson, Cornelius, of Penns Neck, Salem Co., yeoman; will of. Wife, Ann. Eldest son, Jacob, to have 50 acres he lives on adjoining Long Bridge, "part of the old tract whereon I live," and 40 acres joining the same and Portmorant land and John Eaton's, "as will appear by the deed that I gave him." Son, Cornelius, to have "the plantation I live on," (50 acres) with all of the buildings and 55 acres adjoining Mr. Grafton's land and Andrew Bartleson's and Andrew Boon's. Daughters—Sarah Tussey, Catherine Butterworth and Elinor Mounson. Grandchildren—Elinor Butterworth and Peter Boon. Executors—wife, and son Cornelius Cornelinson. Witnesses—John Groome, Michael Pedrick, Saml. Whitehorne. Proved 10 Nov. 1744. Lib. 5, p. 87.

1744, Nov. 6. Inventory, £67.8.1; made by Michael Pedrick, Samuel Whitehorne.

1747, Oct. 7. Cornell, William, of Hopewell, Hunterdon Co.; will of. Sons—Smith (the eldest), William (the second), John (the third), Benjamin and Edward. Daughters—Hannah, Elizabeth, Sarah, Charity, Mary and Martha. Home plantation to youngest sons, Benjamin and Edward. Other plantations to sons William and John. Executors—sons, Smith and William, and son-in-law, Edward Hunt. Witnesses—Edward Hunt, Sen'r., Jonas Wood and Reuben Armitage. Proved April 17, 1749. Lib. 6, p. 56.

1731, April 28. Corson, Christian, of Upper Precinct, Cape May Co., husbandman. Int. Adm'x, Ann Corson, spinster. Fellow bondsman, Peter Corson. Witnesses—Robert Townsend, Henry Lenord, Jacob Spicer. Lib. 3, p. 101.

1731, April 22. Inventory (£174.00.11) includes smith's tools, ¼ of a shallop, oxen, cows, etc. Appraisers—Robert Townsend, Henry Young.

1736, Dec. 12. Corson, Jacob, of Cape May Co., yeoman; will of. Wife, Amy. Sons, Jacob and Peter Corson. Son, Jeremiah Corson, 100 acres "at the place called the 'fast Landing.'" Daughters—Rachel, Amy and Martha (minors). Executors—wife, Amy, and son, Jacob. Witnesses—John Willets, Joseph Badcock, Rich. Hoe. Proved 25 April 1737. Letters granted to Naomi Corson, widow. Lib. 4, p. 103.

1737, April 4. Inventory, £153.3.2; made by Henry Young, John Willets.

1740, March 31. Corson, John, of Cape May Co. Int. Adm'x, Susannah Corson. Fellow bondsman—Isaac Binar, all of aforesaid County. Witnesses—Henry Young, John Willets. Lib. 4, p. 227.

1739, April 23. Inventory, £49.13.10; made by Henry Young, John Willets.

1731, April 29. Corson, Peter, Upper Precinct, Cape May Co., yeoman. Int. Adm'x, Deborah Corson, spinster. Fellow bondsmen, Peter Corson, Jacob Corson. Witnesses—Henry Young, Mary Corson, Jacob Spicer. Lib. 3, p. 101.

1731, April 25. Inventory (£325.4.5) includes bonds of Peter Corson, Junr, and Christian Corson. Appraisers—Robert Townsend, Henry Young.

1740, Aug. 5, Cory, Benjamin, of Essex Co.; will of. "Being listed into the King's service to go to Cuba." To eldest sons (all under age) of brothers Elnathan, John and Joseph Cory, land in Essex Co., "given me in the will of my father." Sister, Anna Cory. Executors—brothers, Elnathan and John, and friend, William Winans. Witnesses—Abijah Hubbell, Phebe Lambert, Nath'll Hubbell. Proved June 3, 1747. Lib. E, p. 51.

1732-3, Jan. 24. Cory, William, of Newark, Essex Co. Int. Adm'r, Amos Roberts. Lib. B, p. 350

1732-3, Jan. 25. Inventory (£42.10.09) includes debts due from Arthur Ward, John Day, Daniel Day, Samuel Crowel, Mr. Baley; made by Jonathan Crain, Esq., and Nath'll Whealer.

1748, Jan. 2. Coryell, Emanuel, of Amwell Township, Hunterdon Co., farmer; will of. Estate to wife and six children. Wife, Sarah, to have house testator lived in and "ferry, meadows, barns and stables," during widowhood. Oldest son, John. Executors—wife and son John. Overseers—Daniel Cooper and Job Warford. Witnesses—John Johnson, Esther Dryall and Robert Evans. Proved Jan. 23, 1748-9. Lib. 6, p. 89.

1748, Feb. 3. Inventory (£854.12.8) includes bonds of Henry Smith, John Hurst, Hugh Smith; 8 negroes; 3 guns; speaking trumpet; sheep at States Jewells. Made by Derrick Hoagland and Peter Prall.

1757, Nov. 1. Account of John Coryell, executor of will of Emanuel Coryell, mentions cash received from John Miles; money for part of house and lot at Bound Brook sold by sheriff; and money paid to Randall Hutchinson, George Hughes, Richard Hainds, John Deling, William Pearson, Jacob Ketcham, Joseph Yard, John Watson, Esther Dryall, Elizabeth Phillips, John Baumont, Abraham Vendome, Thomas Kennedy, Job Warfield, John Schoolfield, Nathaniel Foster, William Osborne, Gershom Lambert, Mary Heston, Joseph Yard, Garrard Williamson, Richard Stephens, John Hamilton, Cornelius Dawett, John Reading, Moses Vancourt, Philip Kearny, Preserve Brown, Robert Evans, Sarah Canby, Benjamin Taylor, Derick Hogeland, Aaron Mattison, William Shatterthwaite, John Neglee, Thomas Gilbert, Johannes Wallace, Job Warford, Joseph Warrell, John Waggett, Robert Thompson, John Ingham, William Lowther, Christopher Lashere, William Morris, Samuel Helcome, executors of Henry Birkir, Valentine Ent, Dennis Woolverton, Joseph De Cow, Jacob Heston, George Ely, John Cox, Benjamin Smith, a schoolmaster, Mayor, clerks, etc., at Philadelphia, Jonathan Gray, Timothy Smith, surveyor; Joseph De Cou, George Reading, Daniel Cooper, Thomas Kennedy.

1736, June 10. Cosort (Cassart), David, of Somerset Co., gent; will of. Wife, Staintiah. Son, George, to have (eventually) home farm. Son, David, lands next to Jacob Derotes. Son, Francis, 110 acres and Dutch Bible. Daughters—Mary Williamson, Susannah Canine, Elenor, Jane and Eve. Grandchildren—Hendrick Harpending, son of daughter Leah, deceased, and three children of son Jacob, deceased. Williamtiah, "former wife" of Jacob. Executors—Son, David, and Peter Williamson. Witnesses—Marius Glanvill, John Riggs, Johanas Hogland. Proved 13 Jan., 1740. Lib. C, p. 387.

1741, July 1. "Inventory, Bown Broak (Bound Brook), of the late David Casaar." Personal estate, £137.1.6; made by Jacob DeGroot, William Olden.

1747-8, Jan. 10. Cossins, John, of Springfield, Burlington Co., farmer; will of. Children—John, Samuel, Mary Foort and Mary Holt. Real and personal estate. Wife, Elizabeth, sole executrix. Witnesses—Thomas Foster, Sen'r, Amariah Foster, John Foster. Proved March 14, 1747-8. Lib. 5, p. 405.

1747-8, March 14. Inventory, £49.17.2; made by Thomas Foster and John Foster.

1735, May 19. Coulton, Richard, of Shrewsbury, Monmouth Co. Int. Inventory of estate, £23.11.5, includes joiners and turners tools, notes of Hendrick Lane, Martin Conners, James Thomson and Walter Dungan. Made by Thomas Morford, Pontius Stelle and Thomas Holms. Lib. C, p. 44.

1735, May 20. Adm'x, Mary Coulton, widow. Hugh Hartshorne, of Middletown, gentleman, fellow bondsman.

1748, Sept. 6. Couwenhoven (Covenhoven), Albert, of Freehold, Monmouth Co., yeoman; will of. Wife, Eleanor. Eleven children—William (eldest), Ruluff, Anna, Jane, Alice, Marget, Sarah, Peter, Jarratt, John and Cornelius. Executors—wife, and kinsman William Covenhoven, son of Cornelius Covenhoven. Witnesses—Jan Kouwenhoven, Matteys Pitersen and William Williamson. Proved Oct. 3, 1748 and Eleanor Covenhoven, executrix, sworn. Lib. E, p. 213.

1748, Oct. 8. William C. Kouenhoven asks to be excused from executorship.

1748, Nov. 21. Inventory (£1800.12.3) includes 203 acres of land, piece of salt meadow, negros (man, woman and 4 children), loom, oyster tongs, Bible; made by William Williamson, Willem Couvenhoven and Matteys Piterson. Signed "Neltje Couenhouen."

1735, Nov. 22. Couwenhoven (Covenhoven), Cornelius, of Middletown Township, Monmouth Co., yeoman; will of. Wife, Margaret, all estate, and the old negro woman, Hannah. Eldest son, William, negroes Sam and Tom, 156 acres of land sold to testator by William Bowne, March 1, 1704, and January 20, 1705, and 120 acres received from Daniel Hendricks, John Schenck, Garrat Schenck and Peter Weycoff, July 18, 1716. Son, Roeloffe, negroes James and Toney, and residue of land and meadow received July 18, 1716, 2½ acres received from James and Rachel Hubbard, July 27, 1706, 2 acres from Jonathan Holmes, June 23, 1719, 10 acres from John Bowne, May 4, 1703, and 125 acres from Garrat and John Schenck, Dec. 24, 1700. Son, William, to pay legacies to testator's daughters—Leah, Catherine, Yacominekey, Margaret and Rachel. Son, Roeloffe, to pay legacies to daughters—Mary, Sarah, Neelkye, Allkye, Yannikee and Anne. Executors—wife, and sons William and Roeloffe. Witnesses—Gerret Schenck, Johannis Bennet and Robert Dodsworth. Proved June 22, 1736. Lib. C, p. 107.

1750, Dec. 15. Covenhoven, (Conover), Elias, of Middletown, Monmouth Co.; will of. Wife mentioned, but not named. Children—Peter, John, Patience, Lidia, Jane, Sarah, Anne, and unborn child. Executors—brother, Peter Cownover, John Longstreet of Freehold, brother-in-law John Wall, of Middletown. Witnesses—Roelyf Covenhoven and Garritt Schenck. Proved Jan. 30, 1750. Lib. E, p. 478.

1743, July 5. Covenhoven, Jacob, of Middletown, Monmouth Co., yeoman; will of. Children—Martin, Roeloff, Jacob, Garret, Peter and John. Granddaughter—Sarah Covenhoven. Grandsons—Daniel Covenhoven, Daniel Hendrickson and Jacob Hendrickson. Executors—Roeloff, Jacob and Garret. Witnesses—Joseph Goulder, George Crawford, Elias Golden and Charles Henderson. Proved July 17, 1744. Lib. D, p. 152.

1744, Dec. 3. Inventory (£618.18.8) includes six negros, large Bible, 217 bushels Indian corn, books, 32 barrels flour; also bonds and book debts from—Aron Stryker, Joseph, John and James Dorsett, Benjamin and John Carman, Andrease Johnson, Tunis and Stephen Amack, Mathias Peterson, Andrew Bray, Harman Johnson, Joseph Cooper, Stephen Heviland, Hendrick Smock, Tunis Swart, William Williamson, George Crawford, Samuel and George Jobs, Tunis Denice, John Williams, Andrew Crawford, Thomas Harbert, Johannes and John Brewer, Joseph, Andrew, Benjamin, James and John Willson, Daniel and Thomas Seabrook, Gershom Wallen, Richard Burden, John Mount, Elias Golder, James Hutchins, William Covenhoven of Flat Lands, Samuel, Joseph, and Jacob Dennis, Job Throckmorton, Thomas and William Layton, Abraham and John Watson, Robert White, John Taylor, John Tennison, Cornelius Vandevear, William and Thomas Patten, John Mackleese, Samuel, Obadiah and Obadiah Holmes, Jr., Rulof and Jacob Covenhoven. Made by Samuel Ogborne, Hendrick Hendrickson and Edward Taylor.

1746, Oct. 24. Covenhoven, Roelof, of Monmouth Co. Int. Adm'rs, Peter Covenhoven, William Hendrickson and Tunis Denis. Hendrick Hendrickson, fellow bondsman. All of Monmouth County.

Lib. D, p. 420.

1746, Nov. 17. Inventory (£439.12.4¾) includes bills, notes, etc., of Guisbert Vanmatre, Hendrick Mires, Robert Hood and Andrew Willson and two negro girls. Made by Nicholas Johnson, Elias Golden and John Taylor.

1746, Dec. 20. Janitie Couenhoven, widow of Ruloff, declines administering. (Name in letter, "Janitie Connover"). Witnesses—Cornelius and Mary Lane.

1742, Oct. 17. Covenhoven, William, of Middletown, Monmouth Co., yeoman. Int. Adm'rs, Ann Covenhoven, widow, Rolef Covenhoven and William Hendrickson. Hendrick Hendrickson, fellow bondsman.

Lib. D, p. 11.

1742, Nov. 6. Inventory (£584.19.00) includes bonds from Jos. Dennis and John Stout, James Bowne and William Bowne, Thomas Bullman and Garsham Walling, Thomas Mount, James Bowne (minor), John Taylor and George Taylor, John Compton, John Stout Boatman, Safety Grover and James Grover, Jr., Samuel Legg and Samuel Bowne, Jos. Shephard and Jos. Stillvell, Samuel Legg and John Winter and Edward Taylor; also Dutch Bible. Made by Barnes Johnson, Nicholas Johnson and Jonathan Stout.

1746-7, Feb. 17. Covenhoven, William, Jun'r, of New Windsor, Middlesex Co., yeoman; will of. Children—William, Garret, Ann, Nelly, Sarah, David, all under age. Real and personal estate. Executors—wife, Margaret, William Covenhoven of Flat Lands, Long Island, and Albert Schank, of Pennsneck. Witnesses—Albert Schanck, Cornelius Covenhoven, Derrick Sutphen, Joseph Skelton. Proved Sept. 11, 1747.

Lib. 5, p. 367.

1730, June 26. Covenoven, Peter, Sr., of Great Egg Harbour, Gloucester Co., yeoman; will of. Wife, Elizabeth. Children—Peter, Isaiah, Thomas, Micajah, Mary, Judith. Executors—wife, and brother John Covenoven. Witnesses—Samuel Huested and John Watts. Proved Aug. 21, 1730. Lib. 3, p. 105.

1730, Aug. 17. Inventory, £46.14.6; made by Joseph Leeds and Thomas Risley.

1730-1, Feb. 5. Account by Elizabeth Covenoven, executrix (John Covenoven having renounced).

1735, April 26. Covenoven, Peter, Jr., (eldest son and heir-at-law of Peter Covenoven, late of Great Egg Harbor, Gloucester Co., yeo-

man, deceased) ward; petition of. Guardian—Jeremiah Adams of same place. Witnesses—Richard Phillpotts, Elias Steelman.
Gloucester Wills, 551 H.

1732, Jan. 9. Covert, Tunis, of Somerset Co.; will of. Wife, Mary, sole executrix, and to have whole estate. Son, John. Daughters—Jeane, Mary and "younger daughter, Harmssye." Witnesses—Tunis Post, William Taylor, Johanis Post. Proved 30 April, 1735.
Lib. C, p. 29.

———, ——. Inventory (£102.13.9) includes "negro-man Jho £50." Made by Tunis Post, Peter Selyens (?). (Filed 1735; not dated).

1743, March 15. Cowenhoven, Peter, of Freehold, Monmouth Co., yeoman; will of. Wife, Patience. Son Peter, Jr. Children—William, Elias, Hannah Antonides, Jane Williamson, Mary Schenck, Aeltje Williamson, and Anne Longstreet. Executors—sons William, Elias and Peter Cowenhoven. Witnesses—Robert Cumming, Andrew McGallerd and Jno. Henderson. Proved April 23, 1755. Lib. F, p. 259.

1755, Sept. 16. Inventory (£35.19.11), includes two negros. Made by Isaac Voorhees, Dirik Zutphen, Jr., and Isaac Sutphen.

1750, June 14. Cowgill, Nehemiah, of Gloucester Co., innholder. Int. Adm'x, widow, Esther Cowgill. Bondsman—Samuel Harrison, Esq. of same place. Witnesses—Fras. Haddock, Jos. Scattergood.
Gloucester Wills, 453 H.

1734, April 18. Cox, Eareck, of Greenwich, Gloucester Co., yeoman; will of. Wife, Ann, sole executrix, with power to sell plantation (197 acres), situate on the northerly side of Rackcoon Creek, in township aforesaid. Witnesses—John Deumey, Earsek Cox, (son of Larance Cox), Samuel Shivers. Proved 11 June 1734.

1735, Aug. 13. Inventory, £35.10.2; made by Losey Cox, Samuel Shivers.

1749, July 26. Cox, Edward, of Woodbridge, Middlesex Co., hatter; will of. Five children mentioned, but two only by name, Humphrey and Dorothy. Lands bought of Shoball Smith and John Deare, Esq. Executors—friends, John Bloomfield, the elder, and John Pierson Jun'r. Witnesses—Rich'd Cutter, William Pike, David Donham, Jun'r. Proved Sept. 13, 1749. Lib. E, p. 326.

1749, Aug. 25. Inventory, £15.15.10; made by Ichabod Smith, Sen r, and Thomas Pike.

1747, December 22. Cox, James, of Upper Freehold, Monmouth Co., gentleman; will of. Reserves to his heirs forever, one chain square of ground where his wife and others of the family are buried. John Cox, son of son Thomas, deceased, when 21, lots No. 3 and 4 in draught made by John Lawrence, April 22 and 23, 1736, being 69 acres. If said John dies, land to John's sisters, Mary Cox, lately called, now married, and Anna Cox. Son, John Cox, northern part of testator's plantation, excepting burying ground; also land adjoining Robert Lawrence. Son, Joseph, southern part of plantation, 27 acres bought of Elisha Lawrence, deceased. Four daughters of testator's daughter, Anna Jewell, deceased. Daughter, Elizabeth, land adjoining Burlington road. Sons, James, John, and Joseph, all apparel and arms. Grandson, James Cox. Daughters—Elizabeth, Alice, Rachel, Dorothy and Rebecca. Executors—sons John and Joseph Cox, and kinsman Thomas Cox. Witnesses—Samuel Stelle, John Hartshorne and John Lawrence, Jr. Proved Nov. 7, 1750. Lib. 6, p. 437.

1750, Oct. 30. Inventory of the estate of James Cox, "Senior," (£715. 13.4½) includes negroes Pink, Adam, Lydia and Vina. Made by Edward Taylor and William Tapscott. Additional goods, £29.7.6, includes debts due from Joseph Throckmorton and ——— Hankinson.

1749, Jan. 29. Cox, John, late of Deptford Township, Gloucester Co., carpenter. Int. Admr., John Wilkins, yeoman. Bondsman—William Wilkins, both of same place. Witnesses—John Mickle, John Ladd. Gloucester Wills, 448 H.

1749, Oct. 20. Inventory (£15.17.1) includes chest and tools. Appraisers—Wm. Wilkins, John Sedden.

1747, July 22. Cox, Peter, of Greenwich Township, Gloucester Co., yeoman; will of. Wife, Mary. Sons—Manuel, Peter and Moans. Daughters—Katherine, Elinor, Anickor, Mary, Martha and Marget. Sons—Abraham, Addam and John to have plantation and land equally. Executor—son, Abraham. Witnesses—Robert Maffett, William Maffatt, Isaac Stephens. Sworn and affirmed 31 Aug. 1747. Lib. 5, p. 484.

1747, Aug. 15. Inventory, £112.3.11; made by Isaac Stephens, Robert Maffatt.

1728, Sept. 27. Cox, Philip, of the Blue Hills, Somerset Co.; will of. Wife, executrix. Sons—John, Philip and Phineas. Daughter—Elizabeth. Executors empowered to sell 100 acres of land in Somerset Co., purchased of John Budd. Executor—John Kinsey, Jr. Witnesses—John Kinsey, Wm. Thomson, Joanna Kinsey. Proved 18 Aug., 1736. Lib. C, p. 115.

1737, Jan. 7. (Filing date). Inventory (£304.14.3) includes Bible, £1.5. Made by Daniel Blackford, Ephraim Dunham. Signed, "Derkes Coks, admx. (her mark)."

1749, July 8. Cox, Richard, of Wellingborough, Burlington Co. Adm'x, Elizabeth Cox, widow. Abraham Perkins and William Hewlings of same, yeoman, fellow bondsmen. Lib. 6, p. 324.

1749, July 8. Inventory, £128.2.3; made by Wil'm Heulings and Abraham Perkins.

1746, March 21. Coxe, Benjamin, of Gloucester Co., laborer; will of. Friend, John Cole, of Gloucester Co., husbandman, executor and to have whole estate. Witnesses—Jo. Harrison, Andr. Tate, William Davis, Junior. Proved 13 April, 1747. Lib. 5, p. 384.

1747, April 13. Inventory (£43.18.6) includes flat, oars, mast, sail and a canoe. Appraisers—Samuel Harrison, Andr. Tate.

1737, March 21. Coxe, Daniel, of Trenton, Hunterdon Co., Esquire; will of. Out of a tract of 5,865 acres of land on South branch of Rariton River off Smiths Brook, by Joseph Kirkbrides, William Canis and Thomas Stevenson, formerly in Amwell Township, then in Readingtown, 500 acres to testator's son, John; 400 acres to son, William; 400 to daughter, Rebecca Coxe; 350 acres to Charles, Thomas and Mary, "commonly called Charles, Thomas and Mary Coxe, children of Mary Johnson of Trenton, spinster." Out of a tract of 5,000 acres, called Morris's purchase, part of 10,000 acres surveyed by John Reading, Jr., for the testator and for Joseph Kirkbride and Thomas Stevenson in Amwell Township, 900 acres to son, John; 800 acres to son, William; 500 acres to daughter, Rebecca. Land at Mount Carmel in

Amwell and Bethlehem Townships. To son, Daniel, tract of 1,000 acres at Flat kill, Hunterdon County; 408 acres at Paquacks. Survey made for Joseph Helby. Paquaess lands. Land surveyed by Edward Kemp at Coshatung; land near Indian town, on the branches of Cohanzey River in Salem County. Land at Cohanzie, surveyed by John Budd, near Island Branch of Morris's River. Lands held with Jacob Spicer, in Cape May County. Land held with Clement Hall of Salem, merchant, at Stow Creek or Hell Neck, Salem County. Articles of agreement made February 27, 1724, between testator and Samuel Hedge of Salem Township, merchant. Land in Salem County near plantation, late of Charles Angeloes, in possession of Obadiah Loyd. Land surveyed by Richard Bull late of Gloucester County, surveyor, deceased, at Alloways Creek, Salem County. Land on Musonnetcung Creek, in Hunterdon County. Land at Prince Morris's River, Salem County. Land surveyed by Bethaniah Leeds, surveyor. Land granted to the testator and others at Western Hook. Land held with John Scott, late of Rhode Island, deceased, in Salem County. Land on Rariton, patented to Joseph Bembridge and by Dr. Bembridge, brother and heir of said Joseph Bembridge, granted unto the testator's father, Doctor Daniel Coxe, and by latter to the testator. To son, William Coxe, land in Gloucester Town and Great Egg Harbour, Gloucester County, and land in Nottingham Township, Burlington County, adjoining lands of Robert Schooley and John Cox. To son, John, land in Trenton between Shabbacunck Brook and the rere line of Hutchinsons manor. Land granted by Colonel Dungan of New York, at Crabb Meadow in Huntington Township, Long Island. To son, John, dwelling house in Trenton where testator lived and four lots adjoining, containing about one acre. To son, William, when of age, stone house in Trenton wherein Mary Johnson lived. Three-fourths of iron works and grist mill near Bordentown, held with Thomas Potts, and land near there bought from ——— Antrum, of Burlington since deceased, for digging of iron ore from. Lot in town of Burlington on east side of James Verree's lot and on Delaware River. Lot in Burlington, fronting on Delaware River, adjoining Hutchinson's or Tatham's Lot, now the Society for Propogation of the Gospell. Orchard late of Jeremiah Basse and orchard belonging to the point house, in possession of Mrs. Weyman. Lot at Tatham's Point in Burlington. Lot near John Wetheril's, since Joseph Welshe's and now John Eaton's, fronting on Delaware. Lands in Hunterdon County; 3,000 acres in Hopewell; 15,000 acres in Maidenhead; farm late in possession of Thomas Winder, lately recovered by a suit-at-law and now in possession of George Fox, adjoining land late of John Dean. Lands in Oxford Township, in the Nip Nut Country of the Colony of Massachusetts. Land called Crabb Meadow, and by the Indians called Cattawomack in Nassaw or Long Island. To son Daniel, any moneys paid in Great Britain for the schooling of testator's son, John Coxe. Executors—Joseph Murray, of the City of New York, Esqüire, attorney and counsellor-at-law; Samuel Bustill, of Burlington, attorney-at-law; testator's son, John Coxe of Trenton, attorney-at-law; and James Alexander, of the City of New York, Esquire, Counselor-at-law. Witnesses, John Dagworthy, Andrew Reed and Samuel Johnson.

1739, April 18. Codicil, Mary, daughter of Mary Johnson, of Trenton, having died since date of will. Negro girl, Flora, to Charles, son of Mary Johnson. Thomas, son of Mary Johnson. Witnesses—John Dagworthy, Andrew Reed and Samuel Johnson. Proved April 30, 1739.

The deposition of Samuel Bustill shows that on April 22, 1739, about seven in the morning, Colonel Daniel Coxe desired that the deponent and his son, Johnny, should come to him where he lay sick, etc. Gave books to son Johnny. Lib. 4, p. 157.

1734, Sept. 12. Coxe, John, Jun'r, of Willingborow, Burlington Co. Int. Inventory, £105.8.8; made by Hugh Sharp and Thomas Reeves.
1734, Oct. 4. Administration granted to Jane Coxe, widow. Hugh Sharp, Esq., and Thomas Reeves, yeoman, both of Wellinborough, fellow bondsmen. Lib. 3, p. 430.

1731, April 8. Crafford, Joshua, of Cape May Co.; will of. "I give my house and land unto my brother Benjamin Crafford's son, Eleser." Sole executor, brother Benjamin. Witnesses—John Flower, Jonathan Fourman, Thomas Hand. Proved 30 April 1733. Lib. 3, p. 340.
1733, April 25. Inventory, £53.1.0; made by Richard Downes, Elisha Hand.

1744, Dec. 5. Craft, Gersham, of Mansfield, Burlington Co., labourer. Int. Administration granted to Lydia Craft, widow. James Hancock, of City of Burlington, peruke maker, fellow bondsman. Lib. 5, p. 63.
1744, Dec. 31. Inventory, £23.19.6; made by Thomas Scattergood, Ju'r, and Wm. Heulings. Affirmed to Aug. 1, 1745, by Lydia Craft, administratrix.

1734-5, Feb. 27. Craft, Thomas, of Mansfield, Burlington Co., yeoman; will of. Son, Thomas. Sons-in-law, John Brown and David Rockhill. Their children. Land bought of Dr. John Brown. Real and personal estate. Executors—wife, Margaret, and David Rockhill. Witnesses—William Shinn, Esther Garrish, John Richardson. Proved Nov. 10, 1735. Lib. 4, p. 45.
1735, Nov. 10. Inventory, £177.18.6; made by George Morris and Richard Gibbs.

1731, Nov. 4. Crafton, Ambrose, of Salem Town and Co., "petty shopman." Int. Adm'r Benjamin Constable. Bondsman—Daniel Mestayer. Both of said County. Witnesses—F. Gandonitt, Thos. Mason. Lib. 3, p. 215.
1731, Nov. 4. Inventory (£21.13) includes "5 doz. leather ink horns, 1½ doz. boys shoes, 14 horse whips, 2 doz. wigg combs." Appraisers—Daniel Mestayer, Thos. Mason.

1736, Jan. 20. Craig, Alexander, of Trenton, Hunterdon Co.; will of. Wife, Mary, executrix. Cousin, Alexander Craig, son of William Craig, living at Bohamia, when of age. Witnesses—Benjamin Smith, William Morris, Thomas Wood. Proved June 11, 1737. Lib. 4, p. 105.
1737, May 25. Inventory (£25.7.0) includes one barber's table. Made by Alexander Lockart and Benjamin Smith.

1738, Sept. 28. Craig, Andrew, of Elizabeth Town, Essex Co., weaver; will of. Children—Andrew, John, William, Margery, Elizabeth, Mary and Martha. Grandson—Abraham Terril, under age. Lands joining lands of John Marsh and William Piles. Executors—son, John, and daughter, Margery Craig. Witnesses—Thomas Clark, Samuel Brant, William Hopkins. Proved Oct. 24, 1739. Lib. C, p. 294.
1739, Oct. 16. Inventory (£144.04.05) includes bonds of John Terrill,

Richard Clark, Jun'r, John Craig, Jona'th Hamton, Geo. Gostolow, Joseph Kilsey, Jun'r.

1739, Nov. 24. Margery Craig renounces right of acting as executrix on her father's estate. Witness—John Terrill.

1748, May 8. Craig, John, of Haddonfield, Gloucester Co., "Doctor of Physick." Sons—William, John, Ebenezer, Andrew and Joseph to have equally piece of ground in Burlington when Joseph is 21. Daughters—Mary, Elizabeth and Anna Craig to have certain moveables; Elizabeth and Anna when 18. Executors—wife, Elizabeth, and Ebenezer Hopkins. Witnesses—John Maxwell, Isaac Andrews, Wm. Griscom. Affirmed 23 Sept. 1748. Lib. 6, p. 8.

1748, 5th mo. (July), 25th da. Inventory (£510.15.6) includes book debts, £38.8.7, an eight day clock, £12, books, £8.6.9; surgeon's instruments, £1.0.0; 15 gal. of spirits, £3.0.0. Appraisers—Wm. Griscom, Isaac Andrews.

1746-7, Feb. 3. Craig, Samuel, of Monmouth Co. Int. Inventory of estate, £492.17.3, includes negro boy, silver tankard, instruments and materials for making clocks and watches and tools of each trade, and materials for finishing new house. Made by widow, Gertrude Craig, Jacob Busbie (Butbin?), William Ker and John Henderson. Lib. D, p. 458.

1746-7, March 5. Bond of Gertrude Craig, John Anderson and David Rhe, of Monmouth County, as administrators. John Henderson, fellow bondsman.

1748, Jan. 28. Crane, Daniel, of Newark, Essex Co. Int. Adm'r, James Crane, the brother. Thomas Sargeant and Sam'll Huntington, fellow bondsmen. Lib. E, p. 261.

1750, May 12. Crane, David, of Newark, Essex Co., yeoman; will of. Wife, Mary. Son, Jedediah, land joining land of Lewis Crane. Son, David, land bought of Timothy Johnson; land near Thomas Dicksons called Duckersfield; land joining lands of John Crane and Nathaniel Ward. Son, Joseph, at 21, land bought of Daniel Morice. Daughters—Abigail Johnson, Pheby Lawrence, Dorcas (wife of ——— Crane), Mary Alling, Sarah and Hannah Crane, land joining lands of Joseph Rogers and Daniel Crane. Executors—wife, Mary, Joseph Riggs and son, David. Witnesses—Isaac Lyon, Job Wood, John Ogden Jun'r. Proved June 21, 1750. Lib. E, p. 433.

1742-3, March 17. Crane, Easther, of Elizabeth Town, Essex Co.; will of. Youngest son, Samuel. Daughters—Hanna, Abigail, Easter, Sarah, Rebecca and Deborah. Real and personal estate. Executors—sons, Jacob Dehart and Benjamin Crane. Witnesses—James Harris, John Chandler. Proved Sept. 16, 1748. Lib. E, p. 212.

1732, April 20. Crane, Elihu, of Newark, Essex Co.; will of. Children—Lewis, Christopher, Charles, Elihu, Isaac, Hannah and Phebe Crane, all under age. Expected child. Friends, Joseph Canfield, David Crane and Nathaniel Dalglish, to make distribution of estate. Real and personal estate. Executors—wife, Mary, and brother, David Crane. Witnesses—Jno. Cooper, Timothy Tuttle, John Crane. Proved Sept. 28, 1732. Lib. B, p. 317.

1749, Dec. 5. Crane, Jasper, of Newark, Essex Co.; will of. Wife, Ann. Children—David, Joseph, Solomon, Sarah Barber and Hanah Kingsland. Real and personal estate. Note of Adam Massaere. Lot of corn due from Abraham Massaere. Executors—Friends, Mr. Jonathan Serjant, Mr. David Bruin. Witnesses—Thomas Eagles, Eleaner Turrel, James Billington. Proved March 21, 1749. Lib. E, p. 432.

1742, May 4. Crane, Jeremiah, Jun'r, of Elizabeth Town, Essex Co. Inventory of personal estate, £104.05.09; made by John Chandler, cordwainer and Stephen Crane, joiner.

1742, June 8. Bond of Susanna Crane, widow, as administratrix on the estate. Joseph Ogden and Gershom Higgins, fellow bondsmen. Witness—Ste'n Warne. Lib. C, p. 511.

1745-6, March 13. Accompt of Susanna Clark as administratrix on the estate of her first husband, Jeremiah Crane, Jun'r, showing payments to James Townley, John Salnave, Henry Garthwait, Sarah Hunloke, Mr. Jonathan Dickinson, Samuel Woodruff, Jonathan Allen, Doctor Burnet, William Ogden, Isaac Scalleux, Jonathan Crane, Jun'r; also notes of Effingham Townley and Michael Crane

1743, May 24. Crane, Jeremiah, of Borough of Elizabeth, Essex Co., yeoman; will of. Children—James, Mary Carpenter, Rebecca (wife of Henery Garthwaite), Susanna (wife of Thomas Broadberry), Rachel Crane, and her son, Joseph Miller (commonly so called). Grandchildren—Timothy Crane, James Carpenter, Mary, Rachel and Hannah Carpenter, and Abigail, Mary and Joanna Crane, all under age, daughters of son Jeremiah, deceased. Land bought of Henry Tuttle and John Megie; land given by father, Stephen Crane; land bought of brother, John Crane, joining lands of Isaac Schalleux, Nathaniel Crane, Stephen Crane; land bought of Azariah Crane; land joining lands of Andrew Craigge, Richard Scuder, Nathaniel Crane. Executors—son, James, son-in-law Henery Garthwaite, and Elijah Davis. Witnesses—Thomas Ross, Matthias Crane, Benjamin Crane. Proved December 8, 1744. Lib. D, p. 201.

1744, Dec. 25. Elijah Davis sees no occasion for his being an executor; so declines.

1734, Jan. 2. Crane, John, of Hanover, Hunterdon Co., yeoman; will of. "Aged and infirm." Children—John, Edmond, Amos, Mary Hamilton, Abigail (wife of Stephen Ward), and Kesiah Canfield. Land in Millbank swamp in Newark, where son John formerly dwelt; land purchased of Jacob Ford at Hanover. Land in Hanover joining land of Ephraim Price. Executors—wife, Mary, and son, Edmond Crane. Witnesses—John Cooper, Eliphalet Johnson, Joseph Day. Proved March 16, 1738. Lib. C, p. 262.

1739, May 14. Inventory, £166.03.07; made by Ephraim Price and John Ball. Witnesses—Stephen Ward, Abigail Ward.

1748, July 28. Crane, John, of Morris Co. Adm'x, Mary Crane, widow, with Joseph Leasey and Thomas Ward fellow bondsmen. Lib. E, p. 218.

1745-6, Jan. 29. Crane, Jonas (Jonah), of Newark, Essex Co. Int. Inventory of personal estate (£135.09) includes note of Daniel Brown, gold buttons, gold locket and silver dish. Made by Isaac Lyon, John Johnson Jun'r and David Ogden, Jun'r.

1745-6, Feb. 21. Adm'x, John Crane. David Ogden, Jun'r, and Humphrey Nichols, fellow bondsmen. Lib. D, p. 370.

1744, April 2. Crane, Jonathan, of Newark, Essex Co., gent.; will of. Wife, Sarah. Children—Samuel, Caleb, Elijah, Nehemiah, John, and Mary Johnson. Land formerly belonging to Mr. Treat; land bought of John Lindely; lands joining lands of Samuel Wheeler, Widow Pennington; land on Morris Creek. £6 towards supporting a Presbyterian minister. Executors—sons, Samuel and Elijah, and son-in-law, John Johnson. Witnesses—Nathaniel Wheeler, David Shipman, John Ogden Jun'r. Proved Oct. 1, 1744. Lib. D, p. 181.

1731, May 7. Crane, Joseph, of Elizabeth Town, Essex Co., "sawer"; will of. Mother, Esther Crane, of Elizabeth Town, Essex Co. Saw mill, grist or corn mill, given by father, John Crane, deceased. Brothers—Benjamin, Mathias, John and Samuel, 50 acres on Raway River given by my father. Executors—brother-in-law, David Dunham, and mother. Witnesses—Samuel Morris, Abigail Morris, Caleb Jefferys. Proved June 19, 1731. Lib. B, p. 223.

1748, Jan. 28. Crane, Joshua, of Newark, Essex Co. Int. Adm'r, James Crane, brother, Thomas Sargeant and Sam'll Huntington, fellow bondsmen. Lib. E, p. 260.

1746, Dec. 15. Crane, Samuel, of Newark, Essex Co.; will of. Daughters—Sarah, Elizabeth and Margaret, all under age. Expected child. Land on west side of Wolf Harbor; meadow on Maple Island joining land of Daniel Tichnor. Executors—wife, Ann, Isaac Lyon and Elijah Crane. Witnesses—John Crane, Jon'th Higgins, David Ogden. Proved Jan. 12, 1746-7. Lib. D, p. 449.

1749, April 22. Craven, Nehemiah, of Cumberland Co., yeoman. Son, Thomas, to have all real estate "both land and marsh," also 1-3 of the personal, and daughter, Mary, to have 2-3s. (Both minors). If both die under age, ½ of real estate to Thos. Butcher, the other ½ to Isaac Rugg. ½ of personal estate to Philip Dennis, Junior, and other ½ to Aaron Butcher. Executors and trustees—Philip Dennis and Richard Butcher. Witnesses—Charles Dennes, David Platts, John Bee. Proved 10 May, 1749. Lib. 6, p. 117.

1749, 3d mo. (May), 4th da. Inventory (£178.13.3) includes cattle, horses and sheep. Appraisers—John Bacon, David Platts.

1748, Oct. 27. Craven, Richard, of Town and County of Salem, yeoman; will of. Executors—Wife, Patience, daughter, Elizabeth, and son, John. Dwelling house and lands, (excepting hereafter disposed of) to son John and for want of heirs, to son Wheat, and, for want of heirs, to three daughters, Elizabeth, Grace and Rachel. Son, Wheat, 2 acres to join back on Sim's and Satterthwaite's lot. Daughters, when 16 years, to have 3 acres to be laid out opposite to Thomas Taylor's and Samuel Tyler's etc., joining on Kessby's fence. Sons John and Wheat to be taught to read, write and cipher, and be bound to trades at 15. (All children evidently minors). Witnesses—Daniel Huddy, Edward Kessby (Keasby) Geo. Trenchard. Sworn and affirmed, 15 Nov., 1748. Salem Wills, 739 Q.

1748, Dec. 15. John Andrews appointed administrator. Bondsman—Willm. Murdock. Witnesses—Danl. Mestayer, Nicholas Gibbon.

1748, Dec. 20. Inventory, £17.13.

1748, Nov. 28. Crawford, Archibald, Penns Neck, Salem County, cordwinder. Wife, Catteron. House in Wilmington. Children—John, Mary, Jane and Margaret Crawford. Executor—Thomas Carney. Witnesses—Rebecca Jaquat, Morris Seaa, Cha. Empson. Proved 5 Dec., 1748. Lib. 6, p. 303.

1748, Dec. 2. Inventory, £101.11.1; made by Cha. Empson, Cornelius Corneliusson.

1746, July 31. Crawford, Benjamin, of Cape May Co., yeoman; will of. Son, Richard, 100 acres (being the plantation on which testator lives); also 40 acres adjoining Christopher Lupton's. He to bring up testator's daughter, Elizabeth, until she will be 18. Legacies to son, Eliezer, and daughters Rachel, Sarah, Mary, Priscilla, Judith and Elizabeth. Executors—son, Richard, and Elisha Hand. Witnesses—Reuben Crandol, Elisha Eldredge, Richd. Ball. Proved 6 August, 1746. Lib. 5, p. 312.

1746, Aug. 12. Inventory, £224.13.7; made by John Eldredge, James Whildin.

1748, Nov. 13. Account. Moneys paid to Benj. Laughton, John Crandil, Jacob Spicer, Henry Young, Esq., John Crafford, Richard Ball, Reubin Crandal, Hannah Hamilton, Ephraim Seely, Jeremiah Hand, Ezekiel Eldridge, Ezekiel Hand, Eleazer Crawford, Elisha Eldridge, Richard Crawford, Sister Elizabeth, Daniel Hand, John Eldridge, James Whildin, John Buck, Josiah Creasey.

1739-40, March 3. Crawford, Daniel, of Salem Co., schoolmaster. Int. Adm'r, Andrew Gardiner. Bondsman—William Tufte, of said county, gent. Witnesses—Chas. O. Neill, Danl. Mestayer. Lib. 4, p. 198.

1739-40, March 8. Inventory, £51.17.3; made by Nicholas Gibbon, Joseph Bacon.

1745-6, March 15. Crawford, George, of Middletown, Monmouth Co., farmer; will of. Wife, Ester. Sons—George, Richard, William, Joshua and Job, (last three evidently under age). Daughter, Lydia, under 18. Unborn child. Executors—son, George, and friends, Joseph Stillwell and James Mott. Witnesses—Samuel Ogborne, Joseph Shepherd and William Craddock. Proved May 10, 1745. Lib. D, p. 279.

1745, May 16. Inventory, £381.12.1; made by Samuel Ogborne, Dennis Swart and Joseph Shepherd.

1741, Jan. 27. Crawford, James, of Trenton, Hunterdon Co., cordwainer. Int. Bond of Martha Crawford, widow, as administratrix. James Bell and Charles Axford, of Trenton, carpenters, sureties. Witnesses—Jno. Clark and W. Hetherington. Lib. 4, p. 340.

1748, Dec. 2. Crawford, Sarah, of Freehold, Monmouth Co., widow. Int. Adm'rs, William Crawford and John Berry. James Newell, fellow bondsman. Lib. E, p. 220.

1745, May 24. Cresse, John, of Cape May Co. Int. Admx., Priscilla Cresse. Fellow bondsman—Jeremiah Hand, all of County aforesaid. Witnesses—Robert Cresse, Nathl. Jenkins, Jun. Cape May Wills, 116 E.

1745, May 2. Inventory, £123.0.5; made by Jeremiah Hand, Nathl. Jenkins, Junr.

1733, May 1. Cresse, Lewis, of Cape May Co. Int. Admx., Abigail Crese. Fellow bondsman—Ephraim Edwards, all of County aforesaid. Witnesses—John Jones, Wm. Barlow, Jacob Spicer, Junior.
Cape May Wills, 64 E.

1733, April 18. Inventory, £52,13.02; made by John Jones, Ephraim Edwards.

1747-8, March 23. Second inventory, £138.18.0; made by Elijah Hughes, John Eldredge.

1748, May 12. Cripps, Benjamin, of Salem, guardian of Jonathan Woodnuts, son of Richard, of said County. Bondsmen—John Buzby and Samuel Cripps, both of Burlington, yeoman. Salem Wills, 769 Q.

1746-7, Feb. 27. Cripps, Grace, widow of Nathaniel Cripps, of Northampton, Burlington Co.; will of. Daughters—Ann (wife of Jacob Webber), and Hanah (wife of John Buzbey), and her children, Hanah, Grace, John and Ann. Personal estate. Executor—son-in-law, John Buzbey. Witnesses—Thomas Buzby, Samuel Hank, Gab:Blond. Proved May 25, 1750. Lib. 6, p. 379.

1752, Jan. 14. Inventory, £169.5.4; made by Thomas Buzby and John Stokes, includes money due from Samuel Cripps.

1734, Sept. 27. Cripps, John, of Northampton, Burlington Co., husbandman. Int. Inventory of personal estate, £136.17.3; made by Benjamin Brian and James Lippincott.

1735, June 21. Adm'x, Mary Cripps, widow. James Lippincott and Richard Roe, yeomen, fellow bondsmen, all of same. Lib. 4, p. 23.

1746, 9th day, 10th mo. (Dec.). Cripps, Nathaniel, of Northampton, Burlington Co., farmer; will of. Wife, Grace. Children—Samuel, Benjamin, Virgin (wife of John Powell), Hannah (wife of John Buzby), and Ann (wife of Jacob Webber). Mary, dau. of a son John, dec'd, at age to have legacy left "by my sister Theophila." Solomon, James, Samuel and John, sons of a dau., Theophila Gaskin. Grandsons—Jacob, Christopher, John and Joseph Powell. Brick house near Bridgetown and 60 acres adjoining. 30 acres, called Foxe's meadow, adjoining Benjamin and Abraham Brian, Patrick Reynolds and Mahlon Pigg's Landing. 16 acres on South Branch of Machiscotuxin. 100 acres on Matchesqatonk. Lot adjoining Zerobabel Gaskin. Executor—son, Samuel. Witnesses—Abraham Griffith, Tho:Sbinn, Jno. Duncan. Proved Feb. 2, 1746. Lib. 5, p. 300.

1749, Aug. 2. Crispin, Silas, of City of Burlington, taylor; will of. Wife, Mary, house and lot wherein testator dwells. Children—Thomas, William, Samuel, Sarah, Mary, Anne, Elizabeth and Abigail. Negro, Dinah. Real and personal estate. Executors—wife, and brother-in-law, Thomas Wetherill, Jun'r. Witnesses—Thos. Atkinson, Sam'll How, Jun'r, Row'd Ellis. Proved Sept. 23, 1749. Lib. 6, p. 311.

1750, Sept. 7. Crockford, George, of Burlington Co., carter. Int. Hannah Crockford, widow, requests administration on estate of her husband be granted to Benjamin Bispham, principal creditor.

1750, Sept. 8. Bond of administration of Benjamin Bispham, of Northampton, Merch't. Thomas Shinn, Jun'r, and Jonathan Thomas, yeomen, fellow bondsmen. Lib. 7, p. 287.

1750, Sept. 8. Inventory, £130.12.2; made by George Briggs and Thos. Atkinson; includes notes of John Bracken and Philip Wickerd.

1752, April 29. Account of Benjamin Bispham showing payments to Brigs Rossel, Joseph Scattergood (a judgment), Edward Mulen, Joseph Lamb, Caleb Shinn, Daniel Packer, John West, Brigs and Atkinson, Joseph Onge (a judgment), Josiah Gaskill, John Moncow, Hannah Indecut, Zerubabel Gaskill, Thomas Shinn, Benj'n Bispham, Joseph Hollinshead. The Vendue list shows cash paid by Robert King, Philip Wickerd, Amos Shinn, Wocker Atkinson, Caleb Schref and John Springer.

1749, April 7. Croeson (Kroeson), Cornelius, of Somerset Co. Inventory of personal estate (£324.06.0) includes negro man £45, negro woman £40, negro girl £20. Made by Zabulon Brown, William Tobell. Somerset Wills, 433 R.

1731, Nov. 4. Crofton, Ambrose, of Salem, Salem Co., petty chapman. Int. Adm'r, Benjamin Constable, of Salem. Daniel Mestayer, fellow bondsman. Inventory, £21.13.0; made by Daniel Mestayer and Thomas Mason. Lib. 3, p. 215.

1739, Dec. 22. Cromall (Cromwell), John, of Upper Precinct of Cape May Co.; will of. Wife, Ruth, to have ½ of real and personal estate. Son, Olifer Cromal, the other half. Executors—wife Ruth, and son Olifer. Witnesses—Will. Ball, William Allen, Barns Sifin, Joseph Woodward. Proved 11 January, 1739. Cape May Wills, 98 E.

1740-41, Mar. 22. Letters testamentary granted to Ruth Cromall, executrix.

1740, May 24. Inventory, £50.18.0; made by Jeremiah Hand, Moses Crosle.

1750, June 13. Crook, John, of Gloucester Co., joyner. Int. Adm'x, Beata Crook. Fellow bondsmen—Thomas Denny, Andrew Hopman, all of Gloucester Co. Witnesses—John Ladd, Jo. Scattergood. Lib. 8, p. 386.

1750, June 8. Inventory (£49.8.2) includes "Carpinders tools." Appraisers—Andrew Hofman, Jas. Hinchman.

1749, April 18. Crosman, Joseph, of Mendum Township, Morris Co. Int. Adm'r, Ebenezer Byram of same place. Bondsman—John Deare of Perth Amboy.

1749, April 22. Renunciation of Abigail, widow. Witness—Mary Thomson. Lib. E, p. 298.

1749, April 13. Inventory (£39.10.0) includes shoemaker's bench, lapstone, etc. Appraisers—Henry Clark, Joseph Hinds

1732, Dec. 6. Crosman, Robert, of New Hanover Township, Hunterdon Co., yeoman. Hannah Crosman, widow of Robert, states that principal creditor of estate is her late husband's "only brother Samuel Crosman, in this country," and asked Samuel be granted letters of administration. Witnessed by John Wilshear.

1732, Dec. 10. Inventory (£28.17.9) includes a Bible and sermon book; made by Ebenezer Mahurin and Joseph Coe.

1732-3, Jan. 6. Adm'r, Samuel Crosman, of New Hanover Township, yeoman. Joseph Hinds, of same place, yeoman, surety. Hunterdon Wills, 71 J.

1739, May 23. Cross, John, (Rev.), of Baskingridge, Somerset Co.;

will of. Wife, Deborah, home plantation during widowhood ("with the white servants, negroes, stock and crops thereon, and out of the profits to give the children good English learning"). Oldest son Robert; other children (names not given), and an expected child. Daughters to have 1-4 less than the sons. "In case of the death of all of them in their non-age, the oldest daughter of my brother William to have £50, my youngest brother Nathaniel £300, and Robert, the eldest son of my brother Hughes, £80. The residue of estate to be divided among the rest of these brothers' children." Provides for John Minthorn, "the lad that now liveth with me"; mentions one Edward Rigs, and that John Ayres, Samuel Rolfe and John Hoey shall settle affairs with the congregation. Also that John Reding, one of the Governor's Council of this Province, take the plantation near the meeting-house in Hopewell, and, "if he sees fit, buy it of Mr. Cox for the good of my children." The plantation near Baskingridge meeting-house devised to the congregation for a parsonage, the conveyance being dated with these presents. Executors—John Reding and Hendrick Fisher, of Piscataway. Witnesses—John Chambers, George Davidson, Brice Ricky. Proved 20 Oct., and 15 Dec., 1748.

Lib. E, p. 227.

1740, July 9. Crowell, Barnabas, of Cape May Co., yeoman; will of. Wife, Abigail. Son, Barnabas, to have all lands. Daughter, Martha Havens. Rest to my six children—Barnabas, Elisha, Daniel Crowell, Marey, Lydia and Sarah Crowell. Witnesses—Nathaniel Hand, Joanna Hand, Abiah Ross. Proved 30 March, 1748. Lib. 5. p. 453.

1748, Feb. 14. Crowell, Benjamin, of Somerset Co. Int. Administration on estate granted to widow, Elizabeth. Bondsman—John Craig, her father, of Middlesex Co., yeoman.

1749, Feb. 14. Bond of John Craig, adm.de bonis non of Elizabeth Crowell, dec'd. Fellow bondsman—Samuel Oliver, Junior, "both of the Borough of Elizabeth, yeoman." Lib. E, pp. 264, 363.

1749-50, Jan. 2. Inventory (£187.9.6) includes bonds and notes from Philip and William Kerney, Vincent Bodine, John Hall, James and Robert McQuown, William Case, Robt. Allen, Wm. Todd, Jno. Van Clean, Tho. Harding, Simon Stoughton, Jno. Henery, Junr., Hendrick Misener, Case and Helen Bill, Ephm. Lockheart, Moses Craig, Albert Decline, Geo. Remers, Isaac and John Lefever, Jonathan Winans, Tho. Jeffery, Reid Whitehead, Junior, Ephm. Terrell, Senr. Made by John Terrill, Thomas Clark. John Craig, adm.

1747, Dec. 26. Cruize, James, of Chesterfield, Burlington Co., glazier. Int. Adm'r, John Forsyth, yeoman. Sam'l Farnsworth, fellow bondsman. Lib. 5, p. 436.

1736, ———, —. Cubberly, James, of Burlington Co. Account of the estate (£11.31.16 3-4) by John Cubberly, acting executor.

Burlington Wills, 2903-6 C.

1735, Sept. 28. Culing, (Van Culien) Catherine, of Deptford, Gloucester Co.; will of. "I bequeath my third of my first husband's estate to my daughter Mary and for the rest of the moveables of the estate my desire is that they be divided equally between them" (no names mentioned). Witnesses—Peter Rambo, Thomas Sutton. Proved 16 April 1736. Lib. 4, p. 55.

1735, Nov. 29. Inventory of Catherine Van Culien, widow (£133.17.6), includes ½ barrel of Shad, £00.08.0, milk vessels and bottles, £1, 9 cows and hay, £18, 12 barrels of "syder," £3. Debtors—John Overend, Stephen Mullekey, John Mattson, son of Peter. Appraiser—Peter Rambo, Deptford, yeoman, who swears that the other appraiser, name not mentioned and who does not sign, consented to the making thereof.

1736, Nov. 2. Account of Mary Matson, spinster, daughter and administratrix of Catherine Culin, late of Deptford, Gloucester Co., shows moneys paid to Wm. Monington, Francis Batten, John Clark, George Avis, Gabriel Rambo, Mary Gordon, Mary Glentworth, George Ward, Jun., John Raines, Peter Matson, John Mattson, etc., amounting to £136.5.6.

1750, Aug. 20. Cull, Edward, of Gloucester Co., laborer. Int. Adm'r., James Hamilton, cordwainer. John Sparks, fellow bondsman. All of same place. Witnesses—John Rumford, John Ladd.

1750, Aug. 13. Inventory, £32.10.0; made by Jones Coxe, John Sparks.

1752, Dec. 6. Account "By funeral charges as coffin, winding sheet, digging the grave, inviting the neighbours and entertainment, £5." Debtors, John Sparkes, Joseph Marshall. Gloucester Wills, 454 H.

1748-9, 11 mo (Jan.), 7 da. Cullier, Benjamin, of Manington, Salem Co., husbandman; will of. Wife. Sons—John (at 21 to have plantation where John Kempster lives and marsh joining the creek towards Preston's) and Samuel (at 21 the plantation I live on and marsh between James' line and Mary Cullyer's). These sons to be put to trades at 14. Daughter, Rebecca, not 18. Sole executor, cousin Henry Stubbins. Witnesses—William Marshall, John Kempster, Alexr. Simpson. Affirmed 10 March, 1748-9. Lib. 6, p. 293.

1748-9, 11 mo. (Jan.), 19 da. Inventory (£162.1.1) includes dwelling, swine, wheat and rye, etc. Appraisers—Benjamin Cripps, James Mason.

1733, Jany. 18. Cullyer, Samuel, of Manington, Salem County, yeoman; will of. Brothers, William and Benjamin Culyer, executors, and to have lands and marsh equally. Certain moveables to sister, Priscailia Culyer, and John Kid, Junior. Witnesses—Bartholomew Hyatt, William Barratt, Sarah Mason. Affirmed 5 April, 1734.
Lib. 3, p. 417.

1734, April 5. Inventory (£10.16.4) includes "hors, bridel, saddel and A parill." Appraisers—Thomas Wright, John Husd.

1733-4, Feb. 11. Cullyer, William, of Manington, Salem Co., husbandman; will of. Wife sole executrix. Daughters—Elizabeth, Martha, Isabell and Sarah Cullyer. Witnesses—Mary Miller, Alexander Miller, Alexr. Simpson. Affirmed March 1734.
Lib. 3, p. 421.

1733-4, Feb. 27. Inventory (£148.17.1) includes cattle and a servant-man. Appraisers—Alexr. Miller, Alexr. Simpson.

1731, March 10. Currey (Curry), Thomas, of Newark, Essex Co., taylor; will of. Children—Samuel, John, Sarah, Joseph, Elizabeth and Eunice Curry. Real and personal estate. Executors—father-in-law, Mr. Samuel Alling, and wife, Elizabeth. Witnesses—Jno. Cooper, John Clements, Ezekiel Alling. Proved Aug. 3, 1732. Lib. B, p. 303.

1732, April 25. Curtis Thomas, of Hanover, Burlington Co., yeoman. Int. Administration granted to John Curtis. Benjamin Kirby, fellow bondsman; both of the Province of New Jersey. Lib. 3, p. 190.

1732, April 25. Inventory, £124; made by Samuel Wright and Benjamin Kirby.

1732, Dec. 25. Curtis, Thomas, of Mansfield, Burlington Co., yeoman; will of. Wife, Elizabeth, personal estate. Eldest son, John, "he having the greatest part of my plantation entailed upon him by my father." Children—Elizabeth, Jonathan, Joseph, and Ann, wife of Thomas Pancoast. Grandson—Joseph Pancoast. Meadow bought of James Craft and "land surveyed to me by my father's right of property," also meadow bought of Robert Hunt and Joseph Shreve. Executors—wife and sons Jonathan and Joseph. Witnesses—Joseph Pancoast, Thomas Folkes, Jun'r, and John Pancoast. Proved May 17, 1748 by Jonathan and Joseph Curtis surviving executors. Lib. 8, p. 32.

1748, 17th day, 3rd mo. (May). Inventory, £28; made by Thos. Folkes and John Pancoast.

1748, Jan. 30. Curtis, Thomas, of Hunterdon Co.; will of. Wife, Els, the house she then lived in. Son, Thomas, half of testator's land. Son, Benjamin, other half of land. Three daughters, not named. Wife and son Thomas, executors. Witnesses—Timothy Hixson, Elisabeth Bird and Lawrence Huff. Codicil April 26, 1749. Son Benjamin to have house after wife's decease. Proved May 11, 1749. Lib. 6, p. 55.

1749, May 23. Inventory (£91.2.6) includes 3 hives of bees. Made by John Arrison and Aaron Seyou (or Scyor). Signed by Alse and Thomas Curtis.

1737, 14th day, 2nd mo. (April). Cutler, Sarah, of City of Burlington, widow; will of. Children—Elizabeth, wife of John Mullin, Sarah, wife of Joseph Rockhill, and William. Personal estate. Executors—son William and friend Samuel Lovett. Witnesses—Caleb Raper, Joshua Parker, Thos. Scattergood. Proved July 23, 1737. Lib. 4, p. 63.

1723, 4th day, 11th mo. (January). Cutler, William, of Burlington, bricklayer; will of. Children—William and Sarah. Son-in-law, John Edwards, and dau.-in-law, Elizabeth Edwards. Land near Joseph White on River Dellay bought of Hugh Huddy. Real and personal estate. Wife, Sarah, sole executrix. Witnesses—Sm'll Lovett, Benj. Wheat, Tho: Scattergood. Proved ——— —, 1731. Lib. 3, p. 331.

1741, Nov. 2. Cutler, William, of New Hanover, Burlington Co., husbandman. Int. Administration granted to James Shinn of Burlington, yeoman. Samuel Scattergood, of Burlington, merchant, fellow bondsman. Lib. 4, p. 316.

1741, Nov. 24. Inventory, £36.10.6; made by Michael Atkinson and John West.

1741, Dec. 9. Dagg, John, of Cape May Co. Int. Admr., Richard Downes, Esq. Fellow bondsman—Ebenezar Johnson. Witnesses—Nathaniel Foster, Fras. Taylor. Cape May Wills, 102 E.

1741, Dec. 4. Inventory, £34.6.2; made by Ebenezer Johnson, Frans. Taylor.

1731, Oct. 26. Dagworthy, William, of Elizabeth Town, Essex Co., inn-holder. Int. Bond of Sarah Dagworthy, widow, as administratrix. Edward Thomas and William Williamson, fellow bondsmen. Lib. B, p. 235.

1731, Dec. 29. Inventory (£400.06.05) includes 3 Bibles, 3 Books of Common Prayer, other books, pleasure slay, servant boy named Daniel, boat called the "Dorothy." Made by Andrew Joline, James Hampton and Gershom Higgins. Witnesses—John Salnave, Thos. Jackman.

1747-8, Feb. 10. Dahles, (Dallas), Herman, of Hunterdon Co.; will of. (Original in German). Wife. Testator's mother to continue with widow. Son, William; daughter, Margaret. Wife and Jeromes Manges, executors. Witnesses—John Doleing, Jerom. Horne and Tunis Quick. Proved March 23, 1747-8. Catherine Daughles, the executrix, sworn March 23, 1747-8. (Original will translated by John Doeling). Lib. 5, p. 470.

1747-8, March 18. Inventory (£137.16.0½) includes a gun and sword. Made by Godfrey Peters and Peter Rockifeld.

1733, Sept. 18. Dalbo, Mary, daughter of Charles Dalbo, late of Greenwich, Gloucester Co., ward. Christopher Taylor, of same place, guardian. Witness—Mary W. Renolds. Gloucester Wills, 163 H.

1748, Dec. 10. Dalbro, Andrew, of Penns Neck, Salem Co., yeoman; will of. Wife, Maudalena. Sons—Charles, Gabriel and John Dalbo, the land (325 acres), whereon I dwell, to be divided equally after my wife's decease, Charles to begin at Horse Creek and take in the house; Lawrance, "with power to take his brother Israel as an apprentice to learn the trade of a wheel Whrite"; William (5 shillings) and Andrew Dalbo (5 shillings). Daughter, Sarah Helm (5 shillings). Executors—sons Charles and Gabriel. Witnesses—William Wilder, Martin Morton, Robt. Howard. Lib. 6, p. 101.

1748, Dec. 26. Inventory (£172.6.11) includes "cash, horse, bridle, sadle armour, appariell, a flott, £54.3.11," cattle, £62.17. Appraisers—Samuel Linch, John Helm.

1748-9, March 9. Dalbro, Andrew, of Salem Co. Int. Adm'rs, Catherine Dalbo and Lawrence Dalbo, both of Penns Neck, said County. Witnesses—Wm. Barker, Nich. Gibbon. Lib. 6, p. 323.

1748, March 8. Inventory (£119.17.4) includes "cash in the hands of" Gabriel Dalbo, John Dalbo, William Dalbo, Jonas Skeen, Timothy Rain, Jacob Iler, Casper Lock, Jacob Cole, Jeremiah Wood, Philip Grace, Daniel Weatherby, Bartholemew Carroll. Appraisers—John Helm, John Van Culin.

1750, Sept. 19. Account. By moneys paid Thomas Parsons, Samuel Shivers, Ranier Vanhist, Nichs. Gibbon, Caleb Coupland, Andrew Hoffman, James Thompson, William Hall, Thomas Duell, Lawrence Dalbo, William Barkers, Thomas Keen, Elisha Basset, Samuel Morgan, Mathew Gile, Robert Howard.

1732-3, ——— 19. Dalding, John, of New Brunswick. Inventory, £83.11.6; made by Thomas Farmer and Jacob———.

Middlesex Wills, 693 L.

1745, Aug. 23. Dall, John, mariner, late mate of the "Snow Heathcott," belonging to Perth Amboy, Robert Farmer, master. Inventory of personal estate (£15.18.9), incl. four ruffled shirts, 2 wigs, a stone ring and a Bible. Made by Fran; Braiser, Sam'll Borrowe, James Newell.

1745, Aug. 23. Adm'r, James Newell, principal creditor of the estate. Andrew Robinson and Elizkim Higgins, fellow bondsmen, all of Perth Amboy. Lib. D, p. 314.

1749, March 30. Danford, James, of Nottingham, Burlington Co., "who departed this life Sunday the 26-March." Samuel Danford relinquishes right to administrater on estate of his brother to his sister, Elizabeth Baxter.

1749, March 31. Bond of Elizabeth Baxter, of Trenton, Hunterdon Co., as administratrix. William Duckworth, of same place, fellow bondsman. Lib. 6, p. 78.

1749, April 1. Inventory at Bordentown, £83.4.6; made by Peter Imlay and Philip Marot; includes note of Wm. Danford and debts due by Ebenezer Robinson, Sam'l Danford, Jos. Steward, Wm. Wood, Ben Fowler, Sam'l Farnsworth, Edw'd Black, Jos. Borden, Jos. Wood, Sen'r, Sam'l Rogers, Wm. Rush, John Bunting, John Steward.

1745, April 6. Danford, Samuel, of Maidenhead, Hunterdon Co., yeoman; will of. Sons, William, Samuel and James, and Samuel's two sons. Granddaughter, Mary Pittman. Son-in-law Richard Pittman, executor, he to receive "my son Aaron's" clothing. Witnesses—William Watson and James Clarke. Proved July 6, 1745. Witnesses and executor Quakers. Lib. 5, p. 158.

1737, Oct. 28. Daniel Aaron, (orphan of 14 yrs.), of Salem Co., ward. Guardian—Edward Hancock, of said County, yeoman. Witnesses—Abel Nicholson, Danl. Mestayer. Lib. 4, p. 124.

1735, April 26. Daniel, John, of Cohansie, Salem Co., yeoman; will of. "My body to be decently buried by my mother and to have a funeral sermon preached by Mr. Pearson, missionary of Salem, for which I allow £3." Sarah Padget (daughter of Francis Padget, my intended wife). John Lorrin's children. Mary Cherry. Remainder of estate, real and personal, to Thomas Walling, senior of said place, gentleman, who is to be sole executor. Witnesses—David Shepherd, Thomas Timmons, William Brand. Proved 2 May, 1735. Lib. 4, p. 13.

1735, April 29. Inventory, £59.9.10; made by Josiah Fifthian, Owen Janey.

1737, Oct. 28. Daniel, William, of Salem Co. An orphan of 16 years. Guardian—William Hancock, Esq., said County. Witnesses—Abel Nicholson, Danl. Mestayer. Lib. 4, p. 122.

1746, Dec. 27. Daniels, Clement, Sr., of Cape May Co., will of. Wife, Mary. Daughter, Martha Savage. Sons—Clement, Thomas and Randal Daniels, to have equally cooper tools, cedar swamp and marsh, excepting five acres adjoining Wigenses Branch, "which I give to my grandson, John Daniels." Executors—sons, Clement, Thomas and Randal. Witnesses—Robert Townsend (Quaker), Felix Fitz Summons (Quaker), Nathaniel Morrison. Proved 30 Jan., 1746.

1746-7, Jany. 30. Letters to Clement and Randal Daniels. Lib. 8, p. 334.

1746-7, Jany. 30. Inventory (£43.19.3) includes cooper tools. Appraisers—John Leonard, John Ireland.

1734, Apr. 3. Danielson, Jacobus, of Salem Co., yeoman. Int. Adm'x, Mary Danielson. Bondsmen—Cornelius Cobnoram, John Doe. All of said County. Witnesses—John Eaton, James Rutherford. Lib. 3, p. 410.

1734, Apr. 3. Inventory (£41.5.8) includes "parshill of Sweads Books." Appraisers—John Eaton, Cornelius Cobnoran.

1734, Nov. 9. Darbyshire, John, of Salem Co., cooper, Int. Adm'r, Matthew Morrison. Bondsman—Obadiah Loyd. Both of said County, yeoman. Witnesses—Dan. Mestayer, Rich. Roe. Salem Wills, 467 Q.
1734, Nov. 10. Inventory, £9.10; made by Will. Dorrance, Francis Dunlap.

1747-8, Feb. 1. Dare, William, of Cohansey, Salem Co.; will of. Wife, Elizabeth. Son, William, to have plantation (100 acres) on which he now lives and ½ of the salt marsh purchased of Samuel Barnes; the other half to my son, John Dare. Daughters—Mary Jessop and Hannah Ogden, to have equally the salt marsh purchased of Mr. Budd. Five of my children, William, John, Elisabeth Preston, Rachel Westcott and Sarah Westcott, to have equally two tracts of Cedar swamp (100 acres at Lebanon below Bever Dams, 15 acres upon Morrices River), and all real and personal estate without the limits of this County. John to have all lands (100 acres) and the plantation (75 acres) on which I now live in the Indianfield survey; also that part of the Cedar swamp at Lebanon above Bever Dams. Executor—son John. Witnesses—Ebenezer Westcott, John Ogden, David Ogden. Proved 6 Dec., 1749. Lib. 6, p. 282.

1738, Nov. 1. Darkin, Hannah, of Salem County, ward. Petition: "Friend Joseph Rose, Salem, November 1st, 1738: These are to certifie to thee that I of my own free will and desire and likewise by the consent of my stepmother Hannah Darkins, and consent of my couzen, Sarah Wyatt, do make and choose my uncle, Richard Smith, to be my guardian and desire thee would let him have Letters of Gardianship, and to the above we have hereunto set our hands the day and year above written. Dr. of Joseph Darkin late of Elsinborough, yeoman. (Signed) Hannah Darkin, Hannah Darkin, Widddo, Sarah Wyatt." Lib. 4, p. 150.

1739, April 14. Darkin, Joseph, of Salem Co., Int. Adm'x, Hannah Darkin (relict). Bondsman—John Darkin. Both of said County. Witness—Saml. Abbott. Lib. 4, p. 199.
1738, 6th mo. (Aug,), 23rd da. Inventory (£690.0.1) includes 3 negroes, £89.19, and cash in hand of Richard Smith. Appraisers—Samuel Abbott, Lewis Morris.

1750-1, Jany. 21. Daten, Ephraim, Jr., of Fairfield township, Cumberland Co. Int. Administrator, Joseph Daten. Fellow bondsman—Silas Newcomb, of aforesaid County. Witnesses—John Dowdney, Elias Cotting. Lib. 7, p. 425.
1749, Dec. 7. Inventory, £84.15.6; made by Robt. Hood, Edward Lummes.
1750-1, Jan. 21. Inventory, £151.14; made by Ebnesar Bower, Silas Newcomb.
1750-1, Jany. 7. Renunciation as administrator of Ephraim Daten, the elder (father of Ephraim, deceased) of Fairfield township, Cumberland Co. Witnesses—Nathaniel Hewet (?), David Daten.

1742, Sept. 4. Daton (Deaton), Jacob, of Salem Co. Int. Adm'r, Samuel Purviance, of Alloways Creek, principal creditor. Bondsman—William Fraser, Esq., Salem Town and County. Witness—Thos. Jones.

1742, Sept. 3. Renunciation of Ann Deaton, widow. Witness—Henery Farr. Lib. 4, p. 377.

1742, Sept. 3. Inventory, £9.17; made by Henery Farr, Benja. Holme.

1749-50, Jany. 20. Dauson (Dawson), William, of Alloways Creek, Salem Co. Int. Adm'r, Daniel Smith. Bondsman—Job Shepherd. Both of said place and county. Witness—Francis Teste. Lib. 7, p. 27.

1749-50, Jany. 15. Renunciation of Margaret Dawson (relict). Witnesses—Job. Shephard, Jun., James Cromwell, Francis Test.

1749-50, Jany. 26. Inventory (£41.11.4) includes looms and tackling and pair of worsted combs, £8.2.0. Appraisers—Job Shepherd, Francis Test.

1735-6, Jan. 29. Davenport, William, of Perth Amboy, Middlesex Co., yeoman; will of. Children—Phebe, Martha, Charity, Dorothy, Robert, Mary, Thomas, William. Real and personal estate. Executors—wife, Bridget, and friend, Andrew Johnston, Esq. Witnesses—Robert King, John White, John Gifford, John Gifford, Jun'r. Proved April 23, 1736. Lib. C, p. 87.

1736, Sept. 30. Davies, John, of Middletown, Monmouth Co., yeoman; will of. Wife, Abigail, all estate to bring up my children, if she hath another; if not, for herself and child Elizabeth. If wife marries, estate to "my two children." Executors—brother, Thomas Davies, and friend, Thomas Cooper. Witnesses—Thomas Cooper, David Burdge and William Hartshorne, Junior. Proved November 4, 1736. Lib. C, p. 132.

1736, Oct. 19. Inventory (£100.03.06) includes a canoe, a brass "chaphendish," large Bible, an old sword and belt. Made by William Hartshorne, John Maklisses and James Bowne.

1731, Sept. 22. Davis, Benjamin, of Chester, Burlington Co., innholder. Int. Inventory of the personal estate, £130.3.1; made by Joshua Grainger and Thomas Hackney.

1731, Sept. 27. Adm'x, Esther Davis. Thomas Hackney, William Coxe and Francis Hogsett, all of same, yeomen, fellow bondsmen. Lib. 3, p. 154.

1732, Feb. 27. Davis, Benjamin, of Salem Co. Int. Admr's, Esther Davis and Benjamin Davis. Bondsman—John Bishop. All of said county. Witnesses—Joseph Ryley, Danl. Mestayer. Lib. 3, p. 290.

1732, Dec. 30. Inventory (£355.18.3) includes one shallop, £35, 1 gun and negro man, £5.4, cattle, horses and sheep, £156.8.0, grain on the ground, etc. Appraisers—John Bishop, Joseph Ryley.

1736, Dec. 17. Davis, Benjamin, of Salem Co. Int. Admr's, John Thompson and Edward Trenchard. Bondsman—Robt. Hart, gentleman, of said County. Witnesses—Danl. Mestayer, John Doe. Lib. 4, p. 108.

1736, May 10. Inventory (£28.6.9) includes gold rings, sword, Bible, etc. "Sun, Mathew Mathakel, books and instruments, £5.10." Appraisers—Richard Woodnett, Robert Hart.

1748, April 6. Davis, David, of City of Philada., mariner. Administration granted to Lydia Davis, widow. Joseph Thomas and Richard Fordham, both of City of Burlington, shipwrights, fellow bondsmen. Lib. 5, p. 438.

1748, April 6. Inventory taken at Black Creek Forge, £171.7.11; made by Jno. Imley and Thos. Folkes, both of Bordentown. Debt—bond of James Murgatroyd.

1736, May 12. Davis, Elias, of Salem Co., yeoman. Int. Admr, Charles Davis, gent. Bondsmen—Benoni Dare and Thos. Waithman, gent. Witnesses—Josiah Fithian, Dan Mestayer. Lib. 4, p. 66.

1736, April 27. Inventory, £52.18.6; made by Thos. Waithman, Benoney Dare.

1749, July 5. Davis, Elizabeth, of Piscataway, Middlesex Co., widow. Int. Bond of Isaac Faurot, her son, as administrator of her estate. Henry Langstaff, fellow bondsman. Lib. E, p. 309.

1749, June 16. Inventory, £27.13.4; made by Henry Langstaff and Phineas Potter.

1739, March 25. Davis, Isaac, of Township of Pilesgrove, Salem Co., yeoman; will of. Wife, Elizabeth, to have all negroes (two men and one woman), and the use of "the home plantation during widowhood; and after her decease I give it to William Crawley, son of my daughter, Eleanor Crawley." If said Eleanor Crawley should not have any male heirs to live 21 years, then said plantation, after her decease, to return to Davis Bassett. Daughter, Rachel Morgan, to have plantation (260 acres) she lives on, which is held by two deeds, but in case of her death it shall descend to her son Isaac, and if he dies before possession, to her other male heirs. In want of such heirs, Samuel Morgan, son of my daughter Elizabeth Morgan, to have the same. Daughter, Abigail Bassett, and Elisha Bassett to have 19 acres of Cedar Swamp. Daughter, Hannah Nelson, to share equally in moveable estate. Executors—wife, Samuel Morgan and Elisha Bassett, "and I desire them to deliver that deed which belongs to Anthony Nelson and which I have in keeping, when he will be 21." Witnesses—David Fristane, John Richman, Jacob Richman. Sworn and affirmed 1 June, 1739. Lib. 4, p. 185.

1739, April 20. Inventory (£253.18.5) includes notes of Paul Garron, Patrick McGills, cash due by Samuel Moren, two negroes, etc. Appraisers—Samuel Elwell, Abraham Nelson.

1747, April 2. Davis, James, of Newark, Essex Co.; will of. Children—Mary, Rebecca, Thomas, Margaret and Sarah Davis, all under age. Real and personal estate. Negro, William William. Executors—wife Phebe, brother Jonathan Davis, and friend David Bruin. Witnesses—Sam'll Blume, Ja's Nicholson, Tho's Price. Proved May 14, 1747.

1747, May 16. David Bruin renounces executorship. Lib. E, p. 210.

1747, May 19. Inventory (£243.10.03) includes bonds of Robert Morss and John Morris; made by Isaac Lyon and David Ogden, Jun'r.

1749, July 4. Davis, James, of Deerfield township, Cumberland., Co., guardian of Phebe Bishop (an infant of 14 years and upwards), daughter of Daniel Bishop, yeoman, late of Hopewell township, County aforesaid. Fellow bondsmen—James Davise, Daniel Davise and Samuel Lomas, all of the same place. Witnesses—Abraham Reeves, Junior, Elias Cotting. Lib. 6, p. 100.

1734, 7 mo. (Sept.), 3 da. Davis, John, of Township of Pilesgrove,

Salem Co., yeoman; will of. Sons—Thomas and John, the plantation whereon I live, in the township of Pilesgrove, but in case one dies in non-age, the whole shall fall to the surviving brother. My part of a plantation in Penns Neck, bought by me and my brother David of my brother Malichi, to be sold for the payment of the same. Daughters—Mary, Phebe (£3.15 due from James Hudson) and Charity (all minors). Executors—wife and my brother, David Davis. Witnesses—William Brick, Joshua Garrison, Benjamin Birch. Sworn and affirmed 16 May, 1735. Lib. 4, p. 25.

1735, May 16. Inventory, £180.9.4; made by Elisha Bassett, Samuel Elwell.

1737, Oct. 12. Davis, John, of Pilesgrove, Salem Co., yeoman; will of. Wife, Ann, all of my estate, real and personal, until her youngest child will be 21. Executors—wife and Roger Huggens. Witnesses—John Law, Mary Law, Nathaniel Box. Sworn and affirmed 30 Jany. 1737. Lib. 4, p. 143.

1737, Nov. 12. Inventory (£84.16.5) of John Davis, cordwinder, includes 2 servants (a man and his wife), £18, and shoemaker tools, £1.12. Appraisers—Thos. Baker, Thomas Graves.

1745, March 20. Davis, Jonathan, of Trenton, Hunterdon Co., yeoman, "at present sick and infirm"; will of. Wife, Elizabeth. Five sons of brother, Elnathan Davis, viz: Elnathan, Jonathan, Nathan, Samuel and John. To said brother's son Jonathan, folio Concordance, set out by Clement Cotton. Executors—Charles Clark, Esquire, and testator's wife. Witnesses—Bartholomew Rowley, John Collier and Jno. Clark, Esquire. Proved April 17, 1746. Lib. 5, p. 235.

1746, April 25. Inventory (£51.14.2) includes large Bible. Made by John Burroughs and Jno. Clark.

1731, May 25. Davis, Malachi, of Salem Co., yeoman; will of. Wife, Rebecca, to have estate until son John will be 21. If son John should die in minority, my wife shall enjoy the real estate, and at her death the eldest son of John Davis, the eldest son of David Davis, and the eldest son of John Brick, shall possess the same equally. Executors—wife, brothers, John Davis and David Davis, and John Brick. Witnesses—Jere, Bacon, William Wasson, Enoch More. Sworn and affirmed 21 April, 1735. Lib. 4, p. 15.

1735, April 8. Inventory, £246.12; made by Samuel Elwell, Elisha Basett.

1736, Aug. 14. Account of John Brick and David Davis, surviving executors. "Monies paid the funeral charges and for the coffin of the dec'd, and of his wife who dyed very soon after him," £9. To Mary Dare for nursing the dec'd's child, 1 year, £9. Monies paid to Renier Vanhyste, Elizabeth Long, Marg. McFall, Ann Richman, Winifred Lecroy, David Davis, Benj. Birch, Edwd. Shepherd, Saml. Elwell, Elisha Bassett, George Fling, Wm. Murdock, Peter Turner, Hermanus Alricks, Benj. Acton, Geo. Miller, Richard Grafton, Geo. Monroe, of Newcastle, John Jones, Clemt. Plumsted, John Thompson, Owen Flanegan, John Hunt, Esq., James Gold, Esq., Wm. Shaw, Esq., Newcastle, Isaac Hudson, Rad. Price, John Stowe, Moses Campbell, Thos. Mason, John Brick, Clement Hall. Total, £536.10.5.

1737, Nov. 9. Account. Monies paid to Clemt. Hall, Philip Chetwood, Jon. Jones, Attorney for Isaac Hudson, Peter Turner, Mary Dare, James Gould. Total, £369.17.11¾.

1732-3, Jan. 7. Davis, Samuel, of Newark, Essex Co., yeoman; will of. Children—Ebenezer, Timothy, Samuel, Mary, Elizabeth, Jane and Eunice, all under age. Land lying between Lieut. Samuel Cooper and self that belonged to John Goden. Land joining lands of Thomas Sergeant and John Plum, which formerly belonged to George Harrison. Executors—wife, Abigail, and friend, Joseph Bruin. Witnesses—Daniel Sergeant, John Plume, Jno. Cooper. Proved Jan. 31, 1732-3. Lib. B, p. 360.

1732-3, March 6. Inventory, £84.12.05; made by Jno. Cooper, John Morris.

1732, May 15. Davis, Samuel, of Woodbridge, Middlesex Co., mariner. Int. Adm'rs, Edward Barber and Mary, his wife, and Margaret Davis. Lib. B, p. 251.

1736, Oct. 12. Davis, Thomas, of Piscataway, Middlesex Co. Int. Adm'x, Elizabeth Davis, of Piscataway. Henry Langstaff and Henry Berry, Jun'r, fellow bondsmen. Lib. C, p. 126.

1738, May 27. Davis, Thomas, of Newark, Essex Co.; will of. "Being aged and infirm." Son, Thomas, unmarried, house bought of Daniel Dod; son, Jonathan, land joining lands of Daniel Dod, Joseph Bruen, John Bruen, and Jonathan Sayer; son, Stephen, land bought of Daniel Dod and Mathew Canfield, land joining lands of Nathaniel Ward and the Baldwin's meadow; son, James, land bounded by lands of Samuel Farrand and Indian purchase lands. Son-in-law, John Vanderpool, and daughter, Apphia, his wife, land on Raway River, joining lands of widow Abigail Davis and Griffith Ginkens. Daughters—Sarah, wife of Thomas Ball, and Mary, wife of John Wilcock. Executors—sons Jonathan and James. Witnesses—Eliphalet Johnson, Emanuel Cocker, Jonathan Sergeant. Proved Feb. 7, 1738. Lib. C, p. 258.

1738-9, Feb. 13. Inventory (£280.09.09½) includes silver tankard and other plate, and 5 negroes, £120; made by Eliphalet Johnson and Thomas Longworth.

1741, Jan. —. Davison, Daniel Brinton, of Prince Town, Somerset Co.; will of. Friend, Frances Horner, land and house in Prince Town, and at her death to my cousin Daniel, son of my brother Josiah Davison. Luce and Hepsibath, daughters of Joshua Anderson. Executors—friends, Mr. James Hude and John Dagworthy. Witnesses—Arch'd Douglass, Thomas Anderson, Obediah Winter. Proved March 18, 1746-7. Witnesses all being absent at the date of proving, Jedediah Higgins makes oath to the hand-writing of the testator. Lib. E, p. 2.

1746-7, March 18. Above named executors having refused to act, administration on the estate granted to the brother, Josiah Davison. Jedediah Higgens, fellow bondsman. Witness—Rich'd Williams.

1749, April 15. Inventory, £148; made by Joseph Skelton, Jno. Dalley. Josiah Davison.

1744, July 30. Davison, John, of Perth Amboy, Middlesex Co., merchant and school-master. Int. Sarah, the widow, declines the administration, and recommends William Walton, Jun'r, of New York City, merchant, as administrator. Witnesses—Rich'd Saltar, Jun'r, and Jacob Ten Eyck. Lib. D, p. 169.

1744, Aug. 17. Adm'r, William Walton, Jun'r. Anthony White, fellow bondsman.

1740, Jan. 2. Dawlis, William, of Amwell, Hunterdon Co., yeoman, "being very sick"; will of. Sons William and Hormon to provide for their mother, Margaret Dawlis. Son, William, the grist mill vulgarly called the New Mill, and the field behind John Mullen's house, with half the meadow. Son, Harmon, the grist mill called the Old Mill. To Honust Yaugers four children, £50; if Honust Yauger dies before children are of age, then money to the mother of said children, Susanna Yauger. Testator's daughter, Susanna Yauger, wife of said Honust. Executors—Philip Ringo and Godfrey Peters, of Amwell, yeoman. Witnesses—Peter Fisher, Joseph Bast and Christopher Search. Proved June 15, 1741. Lib. 4, p. 308.

1741, June 11. Inventory (£257.5.8½) includes bond of William Dawlis, Jr.; made by Cornelius Ringo and Joseph Bast.

1747, Sept. 2. Dawson, Robert, of City of Philada., shopkeeper. Int. Adm'r, James Benezet and George Emlen, Jr, of same, merchants. Robert Hartshorne, atty-at-law, of City of Burlington, fellow bondsman. Lib. 5, p. 434.

1729, July 29. Day, Alexander, of Amwell Township, Hunterdon Co., yeoman. Int. Inventory of the estate (£57.8.0) includes a Bible; debts of Jonathan Paine and Josiah Prichet. Made by George Fox and Charles Woolverton, at the request of Thomas Canby, of Solsbury, Bucks County, Pa. Lib. 3, p. 34.

1729, Aug. 1. Martha Day, widow of Alexander Day, renounced her right of administration.

1729, Aug. 3. Bond of Thomas Canby, of Bucks County, Pa., yeoman, and Thomas Wetherill, of Burlington County, New Jersey, yeoman, as administrator of Alexander Day. Witness—Daniel Mestayer.

[Foregoing mentioned Vol. 23, Archives, but without these particulars].

1750-1, Jan. 16. Day, George, of Essex Co., bloomer. Neomi Allen, late widow of George Day, and Jacob Allen, renounce their rights of administering the estate, and desire that Jacob Ford, of Morris Co., be appointed.

1750-1, Feb. 23. Adm'r, Col. Jacob Foord, Esq., principal creditor. John Deare, of Perth Amboy, fellow bondsman. Lib. E, p. 497.

1742, Mar. 11. Day, Jacob, of Hackensack, Bergen Co., mason; will of. Wife, Elizabeth, to have a certain obligation (£27.7.6), dated 13 of July, 1739, "under the hand of my father." Six children (not named). Executors—Jacob Banto and brother, Abraham Day. Witnesses—William Sandtfordt van Emburgh, Jas. McKinley. Proved 12 April, 1743. Lib. D, p. 31.

1744, Nov. 19. Inventory, real and personal, estate (£355.11) includes 2 negroes, £13; made by Rick Lidecker and Johannes Bense. Witnesses—Isaac Dey, William Ellis, John Zabrisk.

1744, March 20. Dayton, Abraham, of Salem, Salem Co.; will of. Gifts to Hannah Graves, John Graves, Junr, Sally Graves, and to "the young child called Joseph." "I give Edy Graves five shillings, likewise all my tools, to defray the charges of my burial." Hanna Graves empowered to recover all debts and a penal Bill, and one thousand weight of tobacco in the hands of Burton Penton. Witnesses—Edward Seymour, George Colson, Mary Hart. Sworn and affirmed 26 April, 1745. Lib. 5, p. 496.

1745, Dec. 19. Letters granted Anna Graves, sole executrix.

1733, Aug. 21. Dayton, Ephraim, of Cohansie, Salem Co., yeoman, guardian of Peter Dayton, son of Samuel Dayton of the North side of Cohansie, deceased. Witnesses—Saml. Bevus (?), Andrew Jones. Lib. 3, p. 366.

1750-1, March 20. Dayton, Isaac, of Morris Co., clothier. Int. Admr, Col. Jacob Foord, of said County. Bondsman—John Deare, of Perth Amboy.

1750-1, March 14. Renunciation of Anne, of Hanover, Morris Co., widow. Lib. E, p. 497.

1751, July 15. Inventory, £8.15.8; made by Timothy Tuttle, Joseph Wood.

Accounts paid: Ben Trogar, Wm. Winds, James Frost, Timothy Johnes, John Ford, Joseph Harriman. "Memo. The price of plantation with sum interest added sold Ebenrs. Stiles sd. plantation, £84.0.5, to the price of a fuling mill begun but not finished, sold to Conar Clother, £26."

1744, Nov. 3. Dayton, Peter, of Cohansey, Salem Co., yeoman; will of. Wife, Hannah. All lands to daughter, Lusey Dayton, at 18 or marriage, but in case of her death under age, or without an heir, my cousin David Dayton to possess the lands. "My mother, if she lives, to have the bringing up of my daughter." Executor—Jonathan Platts. Witnesses—John Pagett, William Daniel, Thomas Pagett. Proved 8 Dec., 1744. Lib. 5, p. 98.

1744, Dec. 5. Inventory, £156.15.1; made by Richard Butcher, Thomas Pagett.

1739, Oct. 15. Deane, Andrew, of Salem, Salem Co., school master. Int. Adm'r, David Fitzrandolph. Bondsman—Robert Hart, of the same place. Witnesses—Dan Mestayer, Mary Mestayer. Lib. 4, p. 200.

1747-8, March 3. De Bonrepos, David, of the Borough of Elizabeth, Essex Co., cordwainer; will of. Sons—David, John and Alexander. Other children, but names not mentioned. Real estate in Woodbridge, Middlesex Co. Executors—wife Mary, Daniel Moore and William Moore. Witnesses—Samuel Connet, Hester Rogers, Samuel Terron, schoolmaster. Proved April 5, 1748.

1748, May 18. Adm'x, Mary De Bonrepos. William Moor, fellow bondsman. Witness—Hester Rogers. Lib. E, p. 187.

1748, July 22. Inventory, £435.05; made by John Lambert, Samuel Hinds.

1749, Dec. 13. Debow (Debowe), Frederick, of Middletown, Monmouth Co.; will of. Wife, Margaret. Daughter, Susanna Debow, under 18 years. Brother, James Debow, and John, son of deceased brother John Debow. Executors—wife, brother James and friend John Taylor. Witnesses—James McGhee, Catherine Macclesse and Mary Banks. Proved May 31, 1750. Lib. 2, p. 89.

1747-8, March 18. Debowe, Jacob, of Middletown, Middlesex Co., yeoman; will of. Children—James (eldest son), Frederick and John. Executors—sons Frederick and John. Witnesses—John Boune (minor), Priscilla Marsh and Samuel Bowne, Junior. Proved February 2, 1748. Lib. E, p. 253.

1749, May 8. Inventory, £65.10.3; made by Nathaniel Leonard and Skelton Johnson.

1749, February 8. Debowe, John, of Middletown, Middlesex Co., yeoman. Bond of Alice Debowe, the widow, and Skelton Johnson, as administrators. Samuel Legg, of Middletown, fellow bondsman. Lib. E, p. 263.

1750, April 14. Inventory, £124.18.7; made by Samuel Bowne, Jr., Samuel Legg.

1734, March 11. De Cow, Francis, of Burlington. Int. Adm'x, Sarah De Cow, widow. Lib. 4, p. 1.

1735, June 28. De Cow (De Cou), Jacob, of Mansfield, Burlington Co., yeoman; will of. Children—Isaac, Susannah, Rebecca, Jacob, Easter, Eber and Elizabeth. Brother, Isaac, £30, "which he got of John Hogg of Holden, he being my father's trustee, the money belonging to me notwithstanding my said brother got the same by a forged letter." Real and personal estate. Executor—son Isaac. Witnesses—Jonathan Wright, David Rockhill, Mary Rockhill. Proved March 1, 1735. Lib. 4, p. 54.

1735-6, Feb. 28. Inventory estate of Jacob DeCow, who deceased Feb. 21, 1735-6, £135.2.3; made by Jonathan Wright and David Rockhill.

1732, Jan. 16. DeFeurott (Faurot), Henry, of Piscataway, Middlesex Co. Int. Adm'x, Elizabeth Fearott.

1739, May 6. De Graaw, Gerrit, of New Brunswick, Middlesex Co.; will of. Children—Walter (house and lot in New York), Gerrit, Johannes, Catharina, Gysbertje, Anna, Maria, and Cornelia, wife of Hendrick Bogaert. Bond for £75 of son-in-law, Mr. Ryall of New York City, to Johannes Jamison, deceased. Daughters married at New York, Catharina and Cornelia. Distilling furniture. Houses and lands in New Brunswick. Debt due Iszac Kip. Executors—Gerrit DeGraaw, and son-on-law, Derck Van Aersdale. Witnesses—Abraham Heyer, Benjamin van Cleave, Lucas Voorhees. Proved June 12, 1739. Lib. C, p. 283.

1749-50, March 7. Degroot, Jacob, of Somerset Co., yeoman; will of. Wife, Fythie, real and personal estate during widowhood; at her re-marriage or decease oldest son John and his heirs to have the home-farm and all other lands, "except a certain piece and all the meadows, which lyes in Somerset Co., joyning Bound Brook, and the meadows of Lafert Sebring and likewise joynes land of Peter Williamson," which meadows shall be divided equally between John, Jean and Margaret. Likewise lots fronting Raritan Road, next to land that Robert Clawson lives on. "To Margaret DeGroot, daughter of my brother John, £100 when of age." Executors—wife Fythie, son John, son-in-law Lafert Sebring, and Derick Van Veighten, of Somerset Co. Witnesses—Tobias Van Norden, Hendrick Harpending, Elias V. Court, Junr. Proved 21 May, 1750. Lib. E, p. 403.

1750, May 14. Inventory (£909.15.6) includes sword, cut-lash and pistols, Dutch Bible, negro-man Sip, £20. Made by Derick Connine, Peter Williamson.

1733, June 14. Degroot, John, of Hackinsack, Bergen Co., yeoman; will of. Eldest son, Jacob; son, Johanes, the home plantation for the sum of £250, paying to his sisters and brother Jacob, Margerit Banta and Hannah Banta, £50 each. Children of my son Garret Degroot, viz: John, Peter and Margaret. Executor—Son, Jacob DeGroot. Witnesses—Jacob Degroot,. Agenishe Degroot, Richard Edsall. Proved 11 April, 1735. Lib. C, p. 25.

1734-5, Feb. 9. Degroot, John, of Hackinsack, Bergen Co., yeoman; will of. Wife, Frances. Daughter, Margrit. Executors—"my well beloved friends father Samuel Moore, and brother Johanes Sebese Banta." Witnesses—Jacob Degroot, Samuel Edsall, Richard Edsall. Proved 11 April, 1735. Lib. C, p. 27.

1733, Sept. 11. Demsey, Timothy, of Penns Neck, Salem Co., yeoman; will of. Son, John, to be kept at school until May next, when he will be twelve years old, then bound to the tailors trade. A heifer to Christian Leiten, daughter of Andrew Leiten, to be delivered to Margaret Lambston. Executors—wife, Ann, and Thomas Miles. Witnesses—Charles Johnson, John Colahan, Samuel Buckley, John Mecum. Proved 29 Sept. 1733. Lib. 3, p. 384.

1733, Sept. 25. Inventory (£137.17.5) includes riding horse, armour, and apparel, £14.2.6, cattle, boat, swine. Appraisers—Fenwick Sinick Sinicker, William Mecum.

1733, Dec. 18. Denn, John, of Salem Co., yeoman. Adm'r, Lea Denn (relict). Bondsmen—Abel Nicholson, Charles Oakford, all of Salem County. Witnesses—Joseph Darkin, Dan. Mestayer. Lib. 3, p. 386.

1733, Nov. 30. Inventory (£273.7.7) includes "a still worm and still in the still house," wheat, rye, cattle, etc. Appraisers—Abel Nicholson, Joseph Darkin.

1749, Feb. 2. Denn, Leah, of Alloways Creek, Salem Co. Int. Adm'x, Leah Denn. Bondsman—John Denn of the same place. Witnesses—Richd. Wistar, Nich. Gibbon. Lib. 7, p. 38.

1747, Jany. 9. Dennes, Charles, of Cape May, Cape May Co., gentleman; will of. Wife, Priscilla. Sons-in-law, John Cresse (minor) and Joseph Ludlam. Son, Charles Dennis, to have plantation at Cohansey, Salem County, at the upper end of the place called Beacken's Neck, joining land of Nehemiah Craven and land of Jonathan Stathem. Executors—brother, Philip Dennis, and Charles Davis. Witnesses—Henry Young, John Mackey and Elizabeth Mackey. Proved 16 May, 1749. Letters granted to Philip Dennis in Cumberland Co. Lib. 6, p. 223.

1749, May 15. Inventory, £136.13.9; made by Henry Young, Joseph Ludlam.

1737, Aug. 26. Dennis, John, of Haddonfield, tailor. Int. Adm'x, Sarah Norris, of Newton, Gloucester Co., dealer. Fellow bondsman—Jonathan Axford, of same County, yeoman.

1737, July 20. Renunciation of Mary, widow of John Dennis, as Adm'x. Witnesses—John Kay, Sarah Kay. Gloucester Wills, 219 H.

1737, Oct. 28. Inventory, £9.6.6; made by Jno. Hinchman, John Kaighin.

1739, July 14. Dennis, John, of Elizabeth Town Point, Essex Co., inn-holder; will of. Wife, Mary, sole legatee. Real and personal estate. Executors—wife Mary, and friends Jonathan Hampton of Staten Island, New York, yeoman, and Thomas Jackman of Elizabeth Town. Witnesses—Thomas Hall, Caleb Woodruff, Anne Cana. Proved Aug. 22, 1739. Lib. C, p. 289.

1739, Aug. 20. Jonathan Hampton and Thos. Jackman renounce executorship. Witnesses—Robert Drummond and Thos. Hill.

1735, March 31. Dennis, Samuel, of Salem Co., yeoman. Int. Adm'x, Anne Dennis (widow). Bondsmen—Joseph Test, John Bacon, all of same place. Witnesses—Danl. Mestayer, John Doe. Lib. 4, p. 1.

1735, March 17. Inventory (£118.17.4) includes Bible, 6 cattle, swine, surveyor's compass, chain and dividers. Appraisers—John Bacon, Abiel Carll.

1736, June 14. Account. Monies paid Wm. H. Clement Hall, Peter Turner, Saml. Fithian, Abiell, Carll, Ananias Sayre, Wm. Watson, John Brick, Edwd. Test, Saml. Clark, Ebenezer Miller, Noah Wheaten, Isaac Fithian, John Loverin, Leonard Gibbon, Joseph Test, John Weckes.

1741, Nov. 3. Dennis, Samuel, of Shrewsbury, Monmouth Co.; will of. Wife, Anne. Children—eldest son Samuel, Lewis, Anne, Mary and Margaret. Executors—brother, Jacob Dennis, and wife Anne. Witnesses—John Hepburn Jr., David Hildreth, Patrick Drugan and Mary Palmer. Proved Aug. 27, 1746. Lib. D, p. 456.

1744, Nov. 13. Denny, Thomas, of Greenwichtown, Gloucester Co., farmer. Int. Adm'r, Thomas Denny. Fellow bondsman—John Jones, all farmers and of same place.

1731, July 31. Deriemer, Isaac, of Somerset Co., glaser. Administration on estate granted to Peter Deriemer. Lib. B, p. 227.

1731, Oct. 7. Inventory (£315.12.9) includes large Dutch Bible, negro-girl Florah, £30; negro man Harry, £50; girl Dean, £40; boy Thom, £15; negro woman Joan with 2 children, £25; girl Hagg, £20. Appraisers—Henry VanDick, Daniel Nuner.

1743, Oct. 25. DeReimer (DeReemer) Isaac, of New Brunswick, Middlesex Co. Int. The widow, Geertje, declines the administration, and desires that John van Nuys, principal creditor, be appointed.

1743, Oct. 29. Bond of John Van Nuys as administrator. Luykes Voorhies and Jas. Vannuys, fellow bondsmen, all of New Brunswick. Lib. D, p. 93.

1743, Nov. 1. Inventory, £16.2.11; made by Dirck Schuyler and Dirck VanAersdalen.

1733, April 10. Derwin, Ebenezer, of Salem Co., yeoman. Int. Adm'x, Elizabeth Derwin. Bondsmen—Zacharias Santell, John Jones, all of said County. Witness—Mary Hawkins. Lib. 3, p. 300.

1733, April 3. Inventory (£111.8.6) includes carpenter's tools, £4.14. "five pounds of Newingland money, £2," bond of Thomas Gold, 1732, for "one hundred and four pounds Newingland money, value in this country, £40." Appraisers—Zehariah Santell, Gideon Concklin.

1747-8, 22nd day, 12th mo. (Feb.). Devenish, Joseph, of Northampton, Burlington Co., yeoman; will of. Cousins—John and Joseph Hilliard, Elizabeth and Martha Atkinson, and Jane Parker. Hannah and Esther, daus. of friend Samuel Woolman. Lands in Northampton loft me by my father, Barnet Devenish, and also that I bought 11th day, 3rd mo., 1702, of John and Martha Hilliard. Executor—cousin Edward Hilliard, son of my sister Martha. Witnesses—John Stoakes, Peter Phillips, Samuel Woolman, John Woolman. Proved March 2, 1747. Lib. 5, p. 406.

1747-8, 2nd day, 1st mo. (Mar.). Inventory, £49.10; made by John Stoakes and John Woolman.

1744-5, Feb. 6. Deverex (Deverix), Philip, of Gloucester Co., yeoman. Int. Adm'x, Sarah, his widow. Fellow bondsmen—William Hugg and Andrew Redmond. Witnesses—Robert Anderson, Francis Haddock, John Ladd. Lib. 5, p. 86.

1744-5, Jan. 30. Inventory, £600.5.11. Appraisers—Andrew Redmond, Isac Jennings.

1775, Jany. 6. Account. "William Tremble, who became adm'r in right of his wife Sarah, late Sarah Deverix, wife of Philip Deverix." Money paid to Dinah Glover, Mary Matlock, Abigail Hinchman, John Gill, James Hinceman, Andrew Redman, Jacob Hugg, John Howill, Timothy Matlock, Peter White, Anne Estlake, James Hambleton, Isaac Jennings, Thos. Clement, Wm. Payday, Ebenezer Zains, Robert Down, Saml. Rain, T. Atkinson, Philip Doyle, Isaac Williams, Wm. Kimsey, Joseph Harrison, John Jones, Priscilla Harrison, Dennis Organ, John Marshall, Robert Anderson, Gabriel Byron, Richard Lynden, Joseph Marshall, John Franklin, John Sparke, John Hewston, Philip Deverix, Robert Down, Frances Haddock, amounting to £677.16.10¾.

1747, April 30. Dewitt, John, of the Borough of Elizabeth, Essex Co., Esq. Int. Adm'x, Ann Dewitt, the widow. Wm. Chetwood and George Lurting, fellow bondsmen. Witness—Matt. DeHart. Lib. E, p. 36.

1744, Oct. 22. Dey, James, of Machaponex, Middlesex Co.; will of. Wife, Margaret. Daughters—Mary and Sarah. Three children by my second wife, Margaret, no names mentioned. Executors—sons James and Lorance, and son-in-law Peter Perrine. Witnesses—Joshua Edwards, Sarah Edwards, William Laird. Proved Nov. 26, 1745. Lib. D, p. 348.

1745, Nov. 23. Inventory, £254.2.6; made by John Perine and William Laird.

1744, Dec. 17. Dibble, Thomas, of Salem Co. Int. Adm'rs, James Caruthers and Alexander Moore, creditors. Both of Cohansey. Bondsman—William Murdock, of Salem County, innkeeper. Witnesses—Wm. Pennock, Chas. O. Neill. Lib. 5, p. 422.

1748-9, Feb. 11. Dickason, Jonathan, of Manington, Salem Co., husbandman, will of. Wife, Dorothy, executrix. Son, John Dickson, when 21, equal share of real and personal estate with his brother, Nathaniel Dickson. Executor—Son, Nathaniel. Witnesses—James Mason, Mary Popino, Alexr. Simpson. Sworn and affirmed 10 March 1748. Lib. 6, p. 292.

1748-9, Feb. 4. Inventory (£217.17.10) includes cattle and grain in ground. Appraisers—James Mason, William Nicholson.

1739, June 21. Dickinson, Fenwick, of Township of Piles Grove, Salem Co., yeoman; will of. Wife, Eleanor, sole executrix. Sons John and Joseph (not 21). Daughter Susannah. Four youngest children, (not of age)—Abraham, Isaac, Isabell, Eleanor. Daughter, Sarah. Witnesses—George Dickison, Henry Paullin, Jacob Richman. Proved 19 Dec., 1739. Lib. 4, p. 214.

1739, Dec. 4. Inventory (£299.0.3) includes cattle, horses, sheep, hay, etc. Appraisers—Elisha Bassett, Samuel Elwell.

1751 (Filed). Account of Thomas Murphy and Eleanor, his wife, late Elinor Dickinson, executrix of last will of Fenwick Dickinson. Moneys paid Samuel Angelo, Joseph Dickinson, Thomas Parke, Edward Horster, Mary Gray, Jonathan Dickinson, Nathan Merring, James Robinson, John Jones, Danl. Mestayer, Doctor Lenox, Benjamin Bispham, Saml. Morgan, David Garrison, Frederick (blacksmith), Jeremiah Wood; bond from Isaac Thompson (insolvent); another insolvent bond of Wm. Crawleys, Devereux Driggus, Thom. Graham. Bringing up of Ellenor Dickinson, 5 years, Elizabeth Dickinson, 8 years, Isaac Dickinson, 6 years, Abraham Dickinson, 4 years, Joseph Dickinson, 2 years (each at £10).

1747, Sept. 16. Dickinson, Jonathan, of Borough of Elizabeth, Essex Co., clerk; will of. Wife, Mary. Children—Jonathan, Abigail (wife of Jonathan Sergeant), Temperance (wife of John Odell), Elizabeth (wife of Jonathan Miller), Mary (wife of John Cooper), and Martha. Real and personal estate. Executors—sons-in-law-Jonathan Sergeant and John Odell. Witnesses—Gershom Higgins, Cornelius Hetfield, Enos Ayers. Proved Oct. 13, 1747. Lib. E, p. 108.

1737, April 16. Dickinson, Joseph, of Monmouth Co., yeoman. Int. Adm'r, Zebulon Dickinson. Lib. C, p. 159.

1737, March 27, April 9. Inventory, £16.01.6; made by John Williams and Amos Pettit, chosen by the widow, Hannah Dickinson. States it was of estate "of Joseph Dickinson, late of Shrewsbury."

1750, Dec. 3. Dildine, Francis, of New Brunswick, Middlesex Co.; will of. Children—Abraham, John, Elizabeth, Catherin and Helenah, all under age. Executors—wife, Mary, friends Luke Voorhees and Peter Cochran. Witnesses—William Hall, John Griggs, Jacob Weisen. Proved Feb. 26, 1750. Lib. E, p. 510.

1750-1, March 13. Inventory (£161.12) includes "one half dozen guilt pictures;" made by D'k Schuyler and D'k Vanveighten.

1733, May 10. Dilley, Jonathan, of Woodbridge, Middlesex Co. Int. Adm'rs, Jonathan Dilly and Edward Crowel. Lib. B, p. 406.

1739, May 23. Dimsdale, (Damsdale), Sarah, of Haddonfield, Gloucester Co., widow; will of. Executors—John Dillwin, of Philadelphia, merchant, and Joseph Kaighn, of Newton, Gloucester Co., yeoman. £300 upon special trust, as follows:—Interest of £100 to brother Joseph Collins; after his death to his daughters Sarah, Katherine and Rebacka. To sister, Elizabeth Southwick, interest of £100, and after her death to her children, Maham and Sarah, equally. Rebecka Bryan, sister, £100, and after her death to her child or children, as she may appoint; also £50 bond of her late husband, Thomas Bryan. Legacies to nieces, Katherine Ellis (wife of Thomas Ellis), Rebecka Satterthwait, Mary Jackson, Katherine Ellis (wife of William Ellis), Priscilla Ares and Elizabeth Williams; also to nephew, William Buckley, and to Francis Collins, son of John Collins. £25 to members of Haddonfield Monthly meeting. Cousins—Katherine Ellis (wife of Thomas Ellis), Priscilla Ares, Sarah Ellis (wife of Simeon Ellis),

Rebecca Clements and William Buckley. Witnesses—Edward Turner, Sarah Winter, Eliza. Estaugh. Proved 9 Nov., 1739. Lib. 4, p. 208.

1739, Oct. 26. Inventory (£1280.16.8½) includes cash, £76.18.6, wearing apparel, £71.15.9, library of books, £4.5.6. Appraisers—Timo. Matloack, Jon. Kaighin.

1740, Aug. 8. Dingee, Charles, of Great Egg Harbor, Gloucester Co. Int. Adm'r, Charles Dingee, of Chester County, in Pennsylvania. Fellow bondsman—James Eldridge, of Burlington, yeoman.

1740, 4 mo. (June), 20 da. Renunciation of Judith, widow. Witnesses—Edmon Somers, Gervas Hall.

1740, 5 mo. (July), 31 da. Renunciation of Christopher, son of Charles Dingee as admr., in favor of his next eldest brother, Charles Dingee. Witnesses—Jos. Fisher, Simon Hallock. Lib. 4, p. 250.

1745, Feb. 19. Dirdorff, Antony; will of. (Original in German). Whereas our Children are all begot of one father and mother, they shall have an equal share in the division. Land sowed of my children upon the old place. Wife to live on land where the testator then dwelt by his son Christian, as long as she pleased. Son Christian bought the land with the testator. Son Christian and daughter Christina. Witnesses—Hans Peter Jager, Wilhelmus Wertz and Johannes Peter Laashent. "Yet to notice, that the division in money shall be as at first above said from the eldest to the youngest in order till they have it; now we children have all agreed and witness this with our hands as follows: Hinrich Dirdorff, Peter Dirdorff, Bernhardes Achenbach, Johannes Dirdorff, Antony Dirdorff, Christian Dirdoff, Willem Ecker and Christina Dirdorffin. Done at an wile the 19th of february 1745 is this Testament confirmed.'"

1746-7, March 2. Christian Grassold, the translator, testified to the English translation of the original will, at Philadelphia, before William Allen, Recorder. Proved March 15, 1746-7. (Hunterdon Co.) Lib. 5, p. 321.

1746-7, March 14. Christian Dirdorff, of Amwell, renounces right of administration as no executor was named in will, in favor of Christian's son, Peter Dirdorff. Witness—Abraham Zutphin.

1747, May 6. Bond of Peter Dirdorff, of Hunterdon Co., yeoman, as administrator, and Rudolph Hurli, of same place, yeoman.

1735-6, March 23. Disbrow, Benjamin, of City of Perth Amboy, Middlesex Co. Int. Margaret, the widow, declines to administer the estate, and makes a quit claim to John Disbrow, cordwainer. Witnesses—Sarah Disbrow, Oba'd Huntt, Junr.

1736, May 15. Bond of John Disbrow, the brother, as administrator. Joseph Johnson and Griffin Disbrow, all of same place, fellow bondsmen. Lib. C, p. 95.

1749, Aug. 12. Disbrow, Henry, of Cranberry, Middlesex Co., carpenter; will of. Wife, Katharine Disbrow. Children—Daniel (land I bought of Andrew Gordon), Henry, William, Joseph, Katharine, Anne, all under age. Executors—friend Frederick Buckalew, Junr., of Cranberry, and brother-in-law, Hendrick Hendrickson of Middletown. Witnesses—Ste'n Warne, Joseph Disbrow, Hen. Moore. Proved Nov. 13, 1749. Lib. E, p. 343.

1749, Nov. 3. Inventory (£313.17.7) includes Bible, negro woman and boy, mare given to wife by Benjamin Disbrow, her brother-in-law. Made by John Barclay, Peter Gordon, Luycas Schenck.

1743, April 30. Disbrow, William, of Hopewell Township, Hunterdon Co., cordwainer; will of. Sister, Hannah Applegait. Cousin, Hannah Applegait. Brothers—Benjamin and Joseph Disbrow. Executors—brother, Joseph Disbrow, and friend Zebulon Stout, of Somerset County. Witnesses—Daniel Stout, Jno. Hyde and Gizebert Lane. Proved June 27, 1743. Lib. 4, p. 367.

1743, June 18. Inventory (£59) includes a house and three acres of land and one house not finished; books; carpenter's tools and a sword. Made by David Stout and John Waycoff. Debts due from John Disbrow, John Stout, Aaron Vanhook, Echebard Lee, Benjamin Stout, George Park, Henry Disbrow, Thomas Burrowes, John Fitch and Joseph Stout, Jr.

1748, April 5. Account mentions John Hyde, Vinsin Runen, Andrew Reed, Robert Hooper, Joseph Packston, Robert Rosebrook, James Leonard, Benjamin Disbrow, Zebulon Stout, Samuel Stout, Robert Hooper, Henry Disbrow, Joseph Merrel, Dr. Cadwalader, Widow Doughty, Sarah Disbrow, Andrew Johnson, Colonel Stout.

1748, Dec. 5. Ditty, Hugh, of Penns Neck, Salem Co., tailor; will of. Wife, Hannah. Real and personal estate. Children—John, Thomas, Martha and Margret. Executors—wife, and James Guttery of White Clay Creek, in the County of New Castle. Witnesses—James Gonart, James Barkley. Proved 13 Dec., 1748. Lib. 6, p. 92.

1748, Dec. 12. Inventory, £87.2.9; made by Alen Congelton, Jonathan Driver.

1738-9, Jan. 2. Dixon, James, of Greenwich, in Cohansey, Salem Co., yeoman; will of. Wife, Rebecca. Daughters—Sarah (to have the house and lot where I live on the East side of Main Street, Greenwich, after her mother's death), Rachel and Isabel (my lot on the West side of the Main St. in Greenwich, equally). Three acres of lot joining Josiah Fithian may be sold. Executors—wife, Charles Dennis and Philip Dennis. Witnesses—Nichs. Gibbon, Samuel Fithian, John Green. Proved 15 Jan, 1739. Lib. 4, p. 217.

1739-40, 1 mo (Mar.), 17 da. Dixson, Daniel (son of Anthony Dickson, yeoman, and Mary his wife, late of the south side of Cohansey, Salem County), ward. Guardian—Ebenezer Miller. Witnesses—Richard Wood, Josiah, Samuel and Isaac Fithian. Salem Wills, 684 Q.

1740, May 29. Dobbins, Joseph, of Newton, Gloucester Co., tailor. Int. Adm'r, Timothy Matlack, of Haddonfield, yeoman. Fellow bondsmen, James Hinchman, Esq., and Thomas Coles, gent., all of County aforesaid. Lib. 4, p. 239.

1740, May 13. Renunciation of John Dobbins, as adm'r of his brother Joseph Dobbins. Witnesses—James Jeffries, David Donogan.

1739-40, Feb. 8. Inventory, £39.4.9. Appraisers—Ja. Hinchman, Thomas Coles.

1732, Feb. 15. Dod, Jonathan, of Newark, Essex Co. Int. Adm'x, Hannah Dod, the widow. James Nuttman, cooper, fellow bondsman. Witnesses—Joseph Peck, Moses Ball. Lib. B, p. 388.

1733, June 21. Doddington, Thankful, of Essex Co. Int. Adm'r, Charles Townley. Nathaniel Mitchell, fellow bondsman. Witness—Ebenezer Lyon. Lib. B, p. 421.

1749, Nov. 29. Dodridge, Philip, of Woodbridge, Middlesex Co., yeoman; will of. Mother ——— ———. Devises lands joining lands formerly of Adam Lees, Solomon Hunt, Joseph Oliver, Charles Wright, John Skinner deceased, to be divided in 19 years among his children, no names given. Executors—wife, Lydia, and friend Nathaniel Fitz-Randolph, blacksmith. Witnesses—Ruth Pack, Meribah Dodridge, John Moores. Proved Jan. 12, 1749. Lib. E, p. 359.

1749, April 3. Dolberg (Dolber), Nicholas, of Greenwich, Gloucester Co., yeoman; will of. Plantation whereon I live at the lower end of Billins Port to Andrew Long's children—Moses, Jonathan, Mary and Elenor. Plantation which I purchased of the sons of Samuel Vanaman, deceased, to the five children of Jonas Cox, Isaac Cooper to be guardian of the aforesaid children. Other tract of land to William Lasberry and Hester, the wife of Daniel Cooper. £5 to wardens of the church at Raccoon Creek. Legacies to Mary and Sarah, daughters of Jonas Cox, and Sarah, daughter of Gunner Swanson. Executors—Andrew Long and William White. Witnesses—Nicholas Justison, Thomas Parker, Alexr. Randall. Proved 20 April, 1749. Lib. 6, p. 87.

1749, April 11. Inventory (£256.8.2) includes ship carpenter's tools, £3.18.0. Appraisers—Wm. Mickle, Alexr. Randall.

1749, April 10. Dole, John, of Great Egg Harbor, Gloucester Co., yeoman. Int. Adm'r, Joseph Dole. Fellow bondsman—Japhet Leeds; both of same place. Witness—Revell Elton.

Lib. 6, p. 331; Lib. 7, p. 88.

1748-9, March 14. Inventory (£94.8.4) includes bonds against Samuel Scull, Joseph Stone, James Robison, George May, Joseph Dale, and book account against Samuel Church. Appraisers—Joseph Ireland, Japhet Leeds.

1749-50, March 5. Donaldson, James, of Somerset Co., cooper; will of. Real and personal estate to be divided equally among brothers, Robert, William and Joseph Donaldson. Executors—Peter Berrien, of Somerset Co., gentleman, and Samuel Neilson, of New Brunswick, merchant. Witnesses—Daniel McCurrey, Daniel Brittan, Robt. Rolfe. Proved 22 May, 1750. Lib. 6, p. 421.

1749-50, March 12. Inventory (£146) includes small Bible and psalm book, 5s., gun, sword and cartouch box. Made by Ja. Leonard, John Berrien.

1736, Sept. 27. Done, George, of Upper Freehold, Monmouth Co., weaver. Int. Adm'r, Samuel Rogers, of Upper Freehold, merchant. Thomas Hunloke and Isaac Pearson, of Burlington, yeoman, fellow bondsmen. Witnesses—Joseph Rose and Richard Kennedy.

Lib. 4, p. 73.

1733, Mar. 25. Doremus, George, of Saddle River, Bergen Co., yeoman; will of. Wife, Marritie. Oldest son, Cornelius (not 21). Rest of my children—John, George and Hendrick (not of age). Executors—sons Cornelius, and wife's brother, John Berdan, Jr. "It is my will further that my brother, Thomas Doremus, and my wife's brother, Vernant Berden, shall be joint executors with the others." Witnesses—Johanes Doremus, Isaack Kip, Corneles Kip. Proved 20 Oct., 1733. Lib. B, p. 475.

1746-7, March 16. Dorn, Alice, of Monmouth Co., single woman. Int. Adm'r, Cornelius Dorn, of Monmouth County, yeoman, brother

of deceased. John Clark, yeoman, fellow bondsman. Lib. E, p. 1.
1747, March 25. Inventory, £56.3.5¾; made by Daniel Hendrickson and John Stillwell.

1738, Feb. 1. Dorrington, John, of Elizabeth Town, Essex Co. (son of Thomas, deceased), an orphan about 15 years of age. Bond of John Megie as guardian. Joseph Megie, fellow bondsman. Witnesses—W. Chetwood, Thomas Hill. Lib. C, p. 270.

1731, June 3. Dorrington (Donnington), Thomas, of Elizabeth Town, Essex Co., mariner; will of. Wife, Thankful. Children—Abigail and John. Expected child. Elinor, wife of John Woodruffe. Real and personal estate. Executors—Charles Townley and Nathaniel Mitchell. Witnesses—John Chandler, Stephen Crane, Abso'm Ladner. Proved June 12, 1733. Lib. B, p. 430.

1741, Sept. 26. Dorsett, Joseph, of Middletown, Monmouth Co., yeoman; will of. "Being weak and infirm." Wife, Elizabeth, to have negro woman, Dinah. Other negroes. Land devised to testator by his deceased son, Samuel, to be sold. Children—Rachel, John, James, Martha, Elizabeth and Joseph. "If son John dies of his present sickness." Grandson, Andrew Dorsett, minor. Executors—friend, James Mott, and sons John and James Dorsett. Witnesses—Joseph Smith, James and Martha Walling. Codicil, same date. "If Joseph dies of present sickness." Elizabeth, daughter of son Joseph. Same witnesses. Proved October 29, 1741. Lib. C, p. 457.
1741, Nov. 17. Inventory (£436.5.6½) includes negro woman and child, negro girl, 2 negro children. Made by Cornelius Dooren, Joseph Smith and Jarrat Wall.

1741, Sept. 10. Dorsett, Samuel, of Middletown, Monmouth Co., yeoman; will of. Wife, Rachel, one-half of land during widowhood, "afterwards to my child or children" (not named). Father, Joseph Dorsett. Land adjoining Joseph Smith. Executors—friends Joseph Dorsett, James Mott and John Dorsett. Witnesses—James Dorsett, Joseph Dorsett, Jr., and Thomas Bullman. Proved October 29, 1741. Lib. C, p. 454.
1741, Oct. 22. Inventory, £146.06.3 1-3; made by Cornelius Doren and Jarratt Wall.

1740, Dec. 16. Doubleday, William, of Salem Co., yeoman. Int. Adm'r, Elias Cotting. Bondsman—John Hunt. Both of said County. Gentlemen. Witnesses—Chas. O Neill, Danl. Mestayer. Lib. 4, p. 262.
1740, Dec. 24. Inventory (£16.0.1) of William Doubleday "of Cohansey." Appraisers—Josiah Fithian, Abraham Reeves.
——, ———. Memorandum of book debts, etc.: William Mulford, Peter Batman, Moses Bishop, John Bowins, William Josling, Silas Newcomb (note payable from James Johnson), Nathan Tarbell (from William Barlow), John Jones, Peter Sowter, John Sherrer, John Brook. Vouchers on said estate by Capt. Cotting."

1746, March 11. Doughty, Benjamin, of Prince Town, Middlesex Co.; will of. Wife, Abigail and son, Benjamin, house and plantation, occupied by Joseph Morrow. Executors—wife, and friends Thomas Leonard, Esquire, of Somerset, and James Leonard, of Kingstown, Middlesex County. Witnesses—William Mounteer, Joseph Morrow and Noah Gates. Proved May 2, 1747. Hunterdon Wills, Lib. 5, p. 501.

1747, April 17. Inventory (£2086.7.5) includes old silver tankard, £4; goods Benjamin Doughty bought of Thomas Whitehead; old Sambo, £5; Sarah and child, £40; negro girl, £20. Bills and bonds—John Bainbridge, Jr., Robert Barnet, Robert Montgomery, James Price, Nehemiah Howel, James Howel, William Olden, Thomas Leonard, Charles Miller, James Whitehead, Jesse Waller, Jon. Waller, John Brown, John Parker, Jon. Desburry, Jon. Huff, Richard Huff, Mathias Swaim, George Bonaface, Joseph Longley, Richard Iveson, James Vance, Joseph Barber, William Olden, Richard Stockton, James Wilmot, Archibald Shorton, Thomas Richards, Jonathan Ketcham, William Bell, William Bryant, Even Harris, William Monteer, William Willin, Edward Bunill, Joseph Pearson, William Jolley, Isaac Fitchrandle, Thomas Price, Thomas Groom, William Brittain, Thomas South, Benjamin Jolley, Dolle Hagersman. Elizabeth Fries, Nicholas Lake, Nathan Havelan, Thomas Scholey, John Covenhoven, William Bunting, Jonathan Croxson, James Doan, Zacharia Bonam, Daniel Brittain, Thomas Fleming, Isaac Randle of Newtown, Pennsylvania, William Deval, Jon. Rylie, Thomas Dunkin, Kathrin Clark, Jon. Howell, Jon. Riddle, Jon. Calleman (a negro), Christopher Conner, Nicholas Able, Hugh Talbot, Daniel Carmack, Jos. Davis, Benjamin Laurance, Jr., William Devale, Jon. Parks, Jonathan Runian, Nicholas Christopher, Robert Spencer, Jos. Morril, Mathew Giles, Barnet Stroud, Jon. Cunnungham, Richard Birk, James Keley, Benjamin Corle, Robert Wheatly, Thomas Stillwell, Edward Pedrick, Elenor Mory, James Danbridge, James Hides, Edward Hopper, James Stewart, Elis Luther, Martha Ferrill, Francis Larkin, George Birkhead, Thomas Morford, William Maise, Jon. Dohoday, Jon. Shields, Jon. Grigs, Evan Harris, Thomas Stevenson, William Offit, Richard Robbins, Robert Fish, Samuel Smith, John Bainbridge, Edward Bunil, Jon. Shaw, Richard Stockton. Inventory made by Edmund Beakes, Jedidiah Higgins, and Aaron Hughs; filed in Hunterdon County.

1750-1, Jan. 4. Doughty, Elias, of Mansfield, Burlington Co., yeoman; will of. Father and mother. Brothers—John, Jacob and Thomas. Elias and Elizabeth, children of brother Thomas. Susannah Taylor. Personal estate. Executor—friends George Taylor. Witnesses—John Gibbs, Benjamin Gibbs, Joseph Pope. Proved Jan. 18, 1750.
Lib. 6, p. 395.

1751, April 7. Inventory, £59.7.5; made by Joseph Pope and Benjamin Gibbs. Includes debts due from Philip Marot, George Taylor and Jacob DeCow,

1737, 2nd d., 5th mo. (July). Doughty, Jacob, of Bethlehem Township, Hunterdon Co.; will of. Wife, Amy; son, Daniel, and daughter Deborah. Wife, executrix. Witnesses—Samuel Stockton and Mansfield Hunt. Proved August 11, 1737. Lib. 4, p. 110.

1737, Aug. 1. Inventory (£479.11.0) includes plate, £25; plantation, £200; Bible, £1; "creatures in Thomas Leonard's hands." Made by Joseph Wilits and Joseph King.

1730, Sept. —. Douw, Andries, of Raretons, Somerset Co.; will of. Children—Volckert, Wilhelm, Johannis, Dorothy. Executor—son Volckert. Witnesses—William Hall, Richard Hall, Edward Murphy. (Will not proved).

1746, June 12. Summons to Fulker (Volckert) Douw to produce the will of his father, which he had suppressed since his death (about 1736), and in which he leaves a legacy to his daughter Dorothy, now wife of William Hall. Somerset Wills, 86 R.

1736, Sept. 29. Dove, Alexander, of Freehold, Monmouth Co.; will of. Wife, Jane, executrix. Children—Samuel, Jane, Margret, Mary, Isabel, Elizabeth and Hannah. Land in Amboy purchased of George Wolek, deceased. £5 put at interest "for the upholding of the Church." Witnesses—James Dey, James McKnight and John Buckalew. Proved November 30, 1739. Lib. C, p. 299.

1740, March 26. Inventory (£278.7.00) includes mortgage of George Hulets, George Woolley and Joseph Wilson; bonds of John Thompson, Walter Wilson, Kenneth Anderson, Michael Ereckson, Jonathan Anderson and Thomas Hay. Made by John Chambers and John Barclay.

1747, July 30. Down, Robert, of Gloucester Co., yeoman. Int. Adm'x, Jemina Down, widow. Fellow bondsman—Anthony Sharp, yeoman, of same place. Witness—Hannah Ladd. Lib. 6, p. 17.

1747, 4th mo. (June), 29th da. Inventory (£299.16.11) includes bonds from Jacob Hugg, Thomas Kimsey; debts from John Ladd, John Smallwood, Joseph Goldeye; 8 day clock, £14; cows, wheat, rye, etc. Appraisers—Anthony Sharp, Jos. Lord.

1749, June 12. Downey, Dennis, of Burlington Co. Int. Adm'r, Thomas Hooten, of Burlington. Elijah Bond, of Trenton, Hunterdon Co., fellow bondsman. Lib. 6, p. 78, bis.

1747, March 28. Downs, Richard, of Cape May Co.; will of. Wife, Elizabeth. Unto Downs Edmons, grandson, and his heirs, all lands and tenements forever, he to pay £20 to his brother Richard Edmons, when 21. Part movables to daughter, Mary Edmons, and rest to grandchildren, Robert Edmon's children, and Randal Hute's children (that he had by his first wife Hannah Downs). Executors—Elisha Hand, Nathaniel Foster, Esq., both of Cape May. Witnesses—Josiah Cresse, Benjamin Shaw, Obed. Shaw. Proved 12 May, 1747.
Lib. 5, p. 526.

1747, May 1. Inventory of "Capt. Richard Downs" (£192.11.8) includes cattle and oxen. Appraisers—John Shaw, George Stites.

1748, Nov. 13. Account. Moneys paid to Elijah Hughes, Thomas Johnson, John Garlick, Lory Hand, Uriah Hughes, Barnabas Crowele, Ebenezer Swaine, Ebenezer Johnson, George Stites, Jeremiah Leaming, Downes Edmuns, Elisha Crowele, John Robinson, Robert Edmunds, Zachariah Sickles, Josiah Cress, William Cooper, John Buck, Mary Edmunds, Samuel Leonard, Elizabeth Downs, the widow of the deceased, Robert Edmunds, Amey Edmunds, Rachele Hewit, Joseph Fancher (who married with one of the grandchildren of the deceased), Henry Young, Elisha Hand, etc., amounting to £264.12.7.

1741, July 4. Downs, William, of Cape May Co., mariner; will of. Uncle Richard Downs, Esq., of Cape May, all real and personal estate, "but if my brother should come to this country, my will is that he should have and enjoy my house and land." Sole executor—uncle Richard Downes. Witnesses—Robert Edmonds, Abigail Dagg, Fras. Taylor. Proved 9 Dec., 1741. Cape May Wills, 103 E.

1741, Aug. 8. Inventory (£77.11.8) includes "¼ of a skooner" (£40). Appraisers—John Dagg, Francis Taylor.

1747-8, March 23. Doyl, Phillip, of Deptford, Gloucester Co., weaver; will of. Executors—brothers-in-law, Robert Stephens and Isaac Stephens, with power to sell all lands, houses, etc. in Gloucester Co. and elsewhere, and to put money therefrom at interest for use of son, Robert Doyl, when 21, excepting legacies as follows—To my cousin Thomas, son of Thomas Edgerton, £7 at 21., Haddonfield Meeting House, £6 for a burial ground. If son Robert dies under age, estate shall go to my brothers-in-law Robert Henery, and Robert and Isaac Stephens. Witnesses—John Breach, John Frankin, Jno. Jenkins. Sworn and affirmed 4 May, 1748. Lib. 5, p. 488.

1748, April 3. Inventory, £261.3.8 ; made by Simon Sparks, John Breach.

1742, Sept. 16. Drake, Andrew, of Piscataway, Middlesex Co., yeoman; will of. Children—Randle (FitzRandolph), George, Jeremiah, Edward, David, Johana Manning, Susannah Smalley, Mary Lee, Lydia, Sarah and Catherine Drake. Lands bought of Moses and Jean Sutton and James Pyatt. Executors—wife, Hannah, son Jeremiah, brother-in-law John Clarkson and friend Benja. Stelle, Jun'r. Witnesses—Benja. Stelle, Hendrick Vroom, Jun'r, Marey Thomson. Proved Dec. 2, 1743. Lib. D, p. 104.

1743, Nov. 29-30. Inventory, £430.15.8 ; made by Joseph Fitzrandolph and Gideon Merlett.

1742, April 12. Drake, Benjamin, of Maidenhead, Hunterdon Co. Inventory of estate, £136.16.10, including loom and tacklings. Made by Mathew Hickson and Reuben Armitage. Hunterdon Wills, 154 J.

1742, April 16. Bond of Sarah Drake, widow, as administrator. Fellow bondsman, Benjamin Drake, of Hopewell, yeoman. Witnesses—Reuben Armitage, Archibald Horne.

1746, Feb. 7. Drake, David, of Piscataway, Middlesex Co.; will of. Wife, Sarah. Daughters—Susannah, Sarah and Mary Drake, all under age. Land leased of William Potter. Executor—brothers Jeremiah and FitzRandolph Drake. Witnesses—Isaac Stelle, John Jones, Benja. Stelle. Proved March 30, 1747. Lib. E, p. 8.

1747, March 30. The executors named in will refuse to act, and widow declines administration, but recommends John Pound, Jun'r, and Edward Drake, of Somerset Co., the principal creditors, as administrators.

1747, March 30. Bond of John Pound, Jun'r, and Edward Drake as administrators. Isaac Manning and Elijah Pound, fellow bondsmen. Witness—Jonathan Dunn.

1747, April 1. Inventory, £143.13 ; made by Thomas Machfarson and George Marlet.

1749, May 8. Account, showing lands sold to Sam'll Drake, Moleson FitzRandolph, Jeremiah Drake, FitzRandolph Drake, Widow Jones; also judgments against Francis Lewis, Andrew Johnston, John Vail, Jonathan Dayton.

1750, July 27. Additional account. Bonds of Josiah David, George Lang, Benj'n Stiles, Simon Walker, Cornelius Moore, Daniel Ayers, Jacob Ayers, John David, James Clarkson, John Deare, Joseph Barto, George Drake, Edward Drake, Nathaniel Manning, Thos. Johnson, Joseph Clawson.

1733, April 1. Drake, Francis, Sen'r, of Piscataway, Middlesex Co., yeoman; will of. Wife, Patience. Children—Rachel Runion, Martha, Betty, Francis, Benjamin, James, Henry and Joseph (all minors).

Grandson, Ephraim Drake. Real and personal estate. Executors—brother-in-law, Joseph FitzRandolph, kinsmen Edmund Dunham, Jun'r, and Moses Martin. Witnesses—Henry Skibbow, Isaac Drake, Moses Burges. Proved April 27, 1733. Lib. B, pp. 398, 400.

1733, April 26. Inventory, £48.3.2; made by Andrew Drake and William Hooles.

1749, Sept. 11. Joseph Fitzrandolph and Moses Martin, two of the executors, with the consent of Patience Drake, the widow, made choice of Azariah Dunham as executor in room of Edmund Dunham, deceased.

1750, July 13. Drake, Gershom, of Piscataway, Middlesex Co., blacksmith; will of. Children—Philip, Cathrine and Sarah, all under age. Executors—wife Rachel, and friend Samuel Dunn of Somerset Co. Real and personal estate. Witnesses—William Clawson, Peter Bebout, Reunt Runyon. Proved July 31, 1750. Lib. E, p. 443.

1750, July 25. Inventory, £337.01.6; made by David Fitzrandolph and Eb. Tingley.

1750, July 21. Drake, John, of Hopewell Township, Hunterdon Co., yeoman; will of. Wife, Rachel. Three daughters, Frances, Ruth and Mary Drake. Son, John Drake, land which testator received from his father; land bought from John Coxe. Sons Charles and Benjamin. Executors—brothers Francis and Thomas Drake, and friend Willson Hunt. Witnesses—Richard Evins, Zachariah Drake and Edward Cooper. Proved October 25, 1750. Hunterdon Wills, 280 J.

1750, Oct. 29. Inventory (£222.18.11) includes one negro fellow, £55; hive of bees; gun and sword. Made by Reuben Armitage and Richard Evins.

1756, March 23. Account mentions Edward Burrows, Dr. Dewit, Fras. Fowler, Henry Wolsey, Azariah Hunt, Thomas Drake, Edmond Drake, Benjamin Ketcham, Nevill Winn, Thomas Vandike, Richard Evans, Andrew Titus, Reuben Armitage, Henry Vankirk, Henry Wolsey, Eliza Runion, John Wolsey, Edward Cooper, Andrew Morgan, Isaac Eaton, Samuel Henry, Reed and Furman, Luffort Waldron, Jos. Tindall, Daniel Drake, Theo. Severns.

1740, April 7. Drake, John, Sen'r, of Essex Co., yeoman; will of. Children—Benjamin, Isaac, Abraham, Samuel and Sarah Fulson. Grandchildren—Abraham, John, Philip, and Gershom Drake; Samuel, Thomas and Mary Davis, children of daughter Mary, deceased. Daughter-in-law, Patience Drake. Edward Slater, Allizhiah Skebbo, Elizabeth (wife of Benjamin Hull, Esq), Filiratea (wife of Benjamin Martain), Moses FitzRandolph, Christian Rebout, the poor of Piscataqua. Executors—grandsons, Samuel and Jonas Drake, and their mother, Hannah Drake. Witnesses—James Manning, Grace Manning, David Drake. Proved Sept. 29, 1741. Lib. C, p. 442.

1741, Sept. 30. Hannah Drake, wife of Isaac Drake, renounces the executorship on account of age and other inability. Witnesses—John Blackford, Jun'r, Jacob Thorp.

——, ———. Inventory, £5.03; made by David Sutton.

1735, Feb. 23. Drake, Josiah, of Middlesex Co. Int. Bond of John Berrien, merchant, of Somerset Co., as administrator. Andrew Hay, of Perth Amboy, innkeeper, fellow bondsman. Lib. C, p. 71.

1742, Nov. 6. Drake, Philip, late of Piscataway, Middlesex Co., yeoman, having property in divers places. Adm'x, his widow, Christian. Fellow bondsmen—Gideon Merlett, John Pound. Lib. D, p. 15.

1734, April 13. Draper, Thomas, of Nottingham, Burlington Co., taylor. Administration granted to Catherine Draper, widow. Robert Pearson, Esq., and John Middleton, yeomen, fellow bondsmen.
Lib. 3, p. 394.

1734, April 22. Inventory, £182.19.7; made by Edw'd Beakes and Guisbert Hendrickson. Includes books, clock and case.

1735, March 15. Petition of Edward and Elizabeth, children of Thomas, over 14, as both parents are deceased, that John Tantum, Sr., and John Tantum, Jr., be appointed their guardians.

1749, April 10. Driver, Jonathan, of Penns Neck, Salem Co., shoemaker. Int. Adm'x, Elizabeth Driver. Bondsman—Alen Congelton. Both of Penns Neck in said County. Witnesses—James Barkley, Nich. Gibbon. Lib. 6, p. 281.

1749, April 7. Inventory (£106.13.8) includes cattle, horses, two boats, "5700 staves and 20 coards of wood." Appraisers—Alen Congelton, James Barkley.

1736, Dec. 13. Drummond, Evan, of Middlesex Co.; will of. Brother, William Drummond. Real and personal estate. Executors—Hon. John Hamilton, Esq., Andrew Johnston. Esq., James Hude of New Brunswick, Esq., and Mr. Andrew Hay. Witnesses—Adam Hay, Tho. Bartow, Thomas Jaffray, Mary Delapp. Proved March 24, 1736.
Lib. C, p. 139.

1748, Jan. 7. Drummond, Gawen, of Monmouth Co. Int. Adm'r, his brother, Robert Drummond, of same county. Bond of Robert Drummond, of Shrewsbury. Josiah Halstead, of same place, yeoman, fellow bondsman. Witnesses—Anthony and Elizabeth Dennis.
Lib. E, p. 268.

Inventory (£184.11.11) includes one gun, two pistols, sword and bayonet. Made by Stoffil Longstreet and William Jackson. Filed Sept. 27, 1749.

1733, July 7. Drummond, John, late Earl of Mellfort, deceased. Petition of John Porterfield of Trenton, New Jersey, in behalf of Alexander Porterfield, Esquire, of Duchall, in the Shire of Renfrew, Scotland, brother to the petitioner, setting forth that John Drummond, late Earl of Mellfort, was indebted to the petitioner's said brother.

1733, July 4. Bond of John Porterfield, of Trenton, Esquire, as administrator of estate of the Right Honorable John, late Earl of Melfort. Fellow bondsman, John Hyndshaw, of Hunterdon Co., yeoman.
Hunterdon Wills, 87 J.

1748, Jan. 7. Drummond, John, of Monmouth Co. Int. Adm'r, Robert Drummond, of same County, the widow having renounced.
Lib. E. p. 268.

——, ———. Inventory of estate of John Drummond, late of Shrewsbury, £8.16.9; made by Jeremiah Borden, William Price and Thomas Bell. Additional inventory, £26.4.10, made by William Davis and Thomas Bell, (filed September 27, 1749).

1749, Dec. 22. Dubois, Barent, of Pilesgrove, Salem Co., yeoman; will of. Wife, Jacomyntie. To son, Jacob Dubois, house and shop and 6 acres; son, Jonathan Dubois, bond of Robert Dars. Children—

Katharine Ellwell, Solomon, David, Isaac, Gerret and Abraham. Executors—wife and eldest son, Jacob Dubois. Witnesses—Louis Dubois, Henry Van Metere, Benjn. Worton. Proved 20 Feb., 1749.
Lib. 7, p. 264.

1749-50, Feb. 12. Inventory (£269.15.7½) includes horses, cattle, wheat, on the ground, shoemaker's tools, negroes, etc. Appraisers—David Davis, John Creag.

1765, ———. Account of Jacob Dubois, executor of the last will of Jecomtie Dubois, executrix of the last will of Barnett Dubois, deceased.

1750, May 24. Duboys (Deboys), Charles, of Amwell Township, Hunterdon Co., weaver. Int. Inventory of estate, £106.8.5, including a Bible. Made by Jno. Opdycke and William Williamsone.
Lib. 7, p. 36.

1750, June 7. Bond of Agnes Duboys, of Amwell, widow, as administratrix, and John Opdycke, of same place, trader. Witness—Theo. Phillips.

1751, July 3. Account. Mentions Daniel Larew, Dr. Coleback, Wm. Montgomerie, Henry Ringo, John Aller, John Hull, Isaac Fitchet, Phillip Peters, Andrian Kenny.

1736, Oct. 18. Dugdale, William, of Piscataway, Middlesex Co.; will of. Children all under age; no names given. Sister, Margaret Hunt, of Dublin, Ireland. Real and personal estate. Executor—wife Jane. Witnesses—Alexand'r Moore, Elizabeth Moore, John Dies. Proved April 21, 1741. Lib. C, p. 406.

1747, Dec. 29. Dukemaneer, John, of Deptford, Gloucester Co., husbandman; will of. Sons—John, Thomas and Samuel. Latter to have the plantation during full time due me in my lease from Luke Gibson. Daughters—Mary Bryan, Sarah Day, Francis Gilfrey, Susanah, Hannah and Elizabeth. Executor—son, John Dukemaneer. Witnesses—Obidiah O. Gibson, Joseph Gibson, Junr., Michael Fisher. Affirmed 19 Feb., 1747. Lib. 5, p. 412.

1747-8, Feb. 16. Inventory (£80.1.6) includes cattle, sheep, rye and corn in the field. Appraisers—Michael Fisher, John Hopper, Jun'r.

1740, March 29. Dumont, Peter, of Somerset Co., yeoman; will of. Son, John, the large Dutch Bible. To him and his heirs £50 in payments by the four sons, Hendrick, John Baptes [Baptist], Peter and Rynear, when the youngest son then living will be of age; likewise to son Abraham. Lands to be divided equally between Hendrick, John Baptes, Peter and Rynear. Daughters—Cattelintje (wife of Christian Lagrange), Margaret (wife of George Bergen), Gerrette and Jannetie. Executors—sons John, Abraham, John Baptes, brothers-in-law Rynear and Nicholas Veghten. Witnesses—Dirck Van Veghten, Henry Van Middleswaert, John Broughton. Proved 17 July, 1744. Lib. D, p. 155.

1744, July 12. Dumont, John, declines to serve as executor of the will of his father, Peter Dumont. Signed by Abr. Dumont, John Dumont.

1749, Aug. 21. Duncan, Elizabeth, of Salem Co. Int. Adm'r, John Duncan. Bondsman—William Maxfield. Both of said County. Witnesses—Elizabeth Berker, Nich. Gibbon. Lib. 6, p. 281.

1749, Aug. 23. Inventory, £81.4.6; made by Abner Sims, James Tyler.

1748, July 13. Duncan, James, of Alloways Creek, Salem Co. Int.

Adm'x, Elizabeth Duncan. Bondsmen—Thomas Lacky, John Duncan, all of same place. Witnesses—Wm. Chandler, Nich. Gibbon.

Lib. 6, p. 51.

1748, July 27. Inventory (£93.2.2) includes cattle, horses, servant-man by indenture, etc. Appraisers—Daniel Smith, James Tyler.

1748, Jan. 9. Duncan, John, of Salem Co., weaver. Int. Adm'r, John Smith. Bondsman—John Andrews. Both of Salem County, yeomen. Witnesses—William Chandler, Nich. Gibbon.

Lib. 6, p. 52 (dates and names mixed).

1748, Jany. 10. Inventory, £52.2.2; made by Jn. Andrews, William Chandler.

1742, Aug. 11. Dunham, Benajah, of Piscataway, Middlesex Co. Nuncupative will. States that "on Monday last, being 9th of August, about five hours before his death," he gave to sons Benajah and Martin lands, etc., and they were to be kind to his wife. In presence Edmund Dunham, Ephraim Dunham, Phineas Martin, John Martin. Witnesses—Jonathan Martin, Azariah Dunham, Elisha Whitehead.

Lib. C, p. 530.

1742, Aug. 23. Dorothy Dunham, widow, declines to act as administratrix, and recommends her sons, Benajah and Martin, as administrators. Witness—Azariah Dunham. Bond of Benajah and Martin Dunham.

1750, May 31. Dunham, Benajah, of Piscataway, Middlesex Co., yeoman, who deceased May 24, 1750. Int. Inventory, £172.19.7; made by David FitzRandolph and Jonathan FitzRandolph, Jun'r.

1750, June 1. Administration on the estate granted to Hannah Dunham, widow. Phineas Dunn and Peter Wodden, fellow bondsmen.

Lib. E, p. 409.

1751, May 14. Account. Payments to Elijah Dunham, Dr. John vanBuren, Cornelius Low, John Holton, James Wilson, Mary Smalley.

1731, May 28. Dunham, Edmund, of Piscataway, Middlesex Co.; will of. Children—Benajah, Edmond, Jonathan, Ephraim, Mary Smalley, Hannah Davis. Nephew, John Thomson. Land in New England. Executrix—wife, Mary Dunham. Witnesses—Sam Walker, Hugh Dunn, Hugh Dunn Jun'r. Proved April 10, 1734. Lib. B, p. 496.

1749, June 4. Dunham, Edmund, of Piscataway, Middlesex Co., yeoman; will of. Wife, Dinah Dunham. Children—Nehemiah, Daniel, Stephen, Peter, Dinah (wife of Joseph Dunn), Elizabeth, Mary, Rachel and Catrine Dunham. Lands bought of Benjamin Manning, Darby Soapland, Alexander Mackdowell; lands bought with Jeremiah Dunn, John Langstaff, Jun'r, and Henry Langstaff, Jun'r; lands my father bought of Benjamin Hull, John Harrison, Benjamin Higgins. Executors—son Nehemiah, and cousin Azariah Dunham. Witnesses—Ephraim Dunham, Benajah Dunn, Jonathan Dunham. Proved July 13, 1749. Lib. E, p. 312.

1739, Feb. 12. Dunham, Hezekiah, of Middlesex Co. The widow, Elizabeth Dunham, declines to administer, and recommends John Dunham, a brother, as administrator. Witnesses—Benajah Dunham, David FitzRandolph, Peter Woden.

1739, Feb. 14. Bond of John Dunham of Piscataway, a brother, as administrator. Peter Wooden, fellow bondsman. Witness—Sarah Hodgson. Lib. C, p. 322.

1739, March 25. Dunham, John, of Piscataway, Middlesex Co., yeoman; will of. Wife, ——— . Son, Elijah. Other children, but no names given. Lands bought of Gedion Marlat and of executors of Richard Sutton. Executors—uncle Jonathan Dunham, brother Hezekiah Dunham, brother-in-law Samuel Dunn, Jun'r. Witnesses—Benajah Dunham, Edmund Dunham, Elizabeth Brimley. Proved Oct. 16, 1740. Lib. C, p. 355.

1740, Oct. 15. Inventory, £184.00.5 (the testator having deceased 13th of Sept., 1740); made by David Fitzrandolph, Edmund Dunham.

1740, Oct. 16. Bond of Jonathan Dunham and Samuel Dunn, Jun'r, as executors, the other executor named in will being deceased.

1747-8, Jan. 31. Dunham, Jonathan, of Woodbridge, Middlesex Co., yeoman; will of. Wife, Mary Dunham. Six children, under 15 years of age; Benjamin, only child mentioned by name. Bond of Gershom Moore. Real and personal estate. Executors—friends Robert Fitz-Randolph, Charles March, David Donham, Jun'r. Proved Jan. 3, 1748. Lib. E, p. 237.

1748, Jan. 25. Inventory, £166.13.11; made by John Moores, Jonathan Frazee.

1750, May 17. Dunham, Martin, of Piscataway, Middlesex Co.; will of. Wife, Martha. Children—Nathan, Phineas, Mary, Ester and Rachel Dunham all under age. Lands bought of Josiah Davis, joining Jonathan Dunham and John Martin at Seeder Brook. Executors—Cousin Phineas Dunn and brother-in-law Peter Woden. Witnesses—Elisha Smalley, Jonathan Fitzrandolph, Jun'r, Jonathan Dunham. Proved June 8, 1750. Lib. E, p. 415.

1750, May 30. Inventory, £157.17.2; made by David FitzRandolph and Jonathan Fitzrandolph, Jun'r.

1736-7, Feb. 28. Dunham, Mary, of Piscataway, Middlesex Co.; will of. Children—Benajah (to have great Bible), Edmund, and Hannah Davis. Grandchildren—Elizabeth, Mary, James and Elisha Smalley, Jonathan Martin, Jun'r, and Mary Sutton. Son, Edmund, sole executor. Witnesses—Jeremiah Dunn, Ben. Dunn, John Dunham. Proved August 13, 1742. Lib. C, p. 531.

1750, Feb. 2. Dunham, Mary, of Woodbridge, Middlesex Co., widow. Int. Adm'r, Jonathan Dennis, her father, of Woodbridge, yeoman. Reuben Porter, of Woodbridge, yeoman, fellow bondsman. Lib. E, p. 480.

1748, May 19. Dunlap, Francis, of Township of Pilesgrove, Salem Co., yeoman; will of. Wife, Rebecca, executrix, to have personal estate and use of house and land while my widow, and until youngest child will be of age. Daughters—Mary and Bathsheba, to have plantation (200 acres) whereon I live. Executor—Samuel Purviance. Witnesses—James Currie, Alexr. McDowell, Patrick Grey. Proved 15 May, 1749. Lib. 6, p. 361.

1749, May 5. Inventory (£64.8) includes cash in hands of Jno. Miler, Francis Hampton, Thom. Erley (?), Jno. Kennedy, Wm. Hudson, David Goff, Wm. Elwell, Tho. Hutchinson, Richard Dunstan. Appraisers—James Currie, Henry Earl.

1736-7, Jan. 31. Dunn, Hugh, of Piscataway, Middlesex Co., yeoman;

will of. Children—Hugh, Jeremiah, Zachariah, Benjamin, Phineas, Ruth and Rebecca. Land in Piscataway bought of John Barrowe, formerly in the siezen of Thos. Higgins; land bought of Benjamin Higgens; meadow joining Henry Langstaff's land; 130 acres purchased of Benjamin Harrison, sold to my brother Joseph Dunn; land in Somerset County; land joining land of Benjamin Wooden; meadow joining John Wolegas' pasture. Executors—friends Joseph FitzRandolph and Edmund Dunham, both of Piscataway. Witnesses—Jonathan Dunham, Moses FitzRandolph, Jeremiah Randolph. Proved Feb. 16, 1736-7. Lib. C, p. 146.

1742, Dec. 6. Dunn, John, of Penns Neck, of Salem Co., yeoman. Int. Adm'x, Sarah Dunn (relict). Lib. 4, p. 378.

1742, Dec. 3. Inventory (£212.5.0) includes cattle, £66.6, wheat, rye, barley, flax unthreshed and unbroke, £15, "9 barrels of syder, £4," carpenter's tools, £1. Appraisers—Edmund Wetherby, Martin Skeer.

1750, April 23. Dunn, Jonathan, of Middlesex Co. Int. Adm'rs, Rebecca Dunn, of Middlesex Co., and Samuel Dunn, of borough of Elizabeth. Macaiah Dunn, fellow bondsman. Lib. E, p. 384.

1750, April 6. Inventory, £339.18.3; made by David Fitzrandolph and Ebenezer Drake.

1748, Dec. 20. Dunn, Joseph, of Essex Co.; will of. Wife, Hannah. Children—James, Hezekiah, Benajah, Benjamin (at 21), Joseph, Martha, Rachel, Elizabeth and Hannah. Real and personal estate. Executor—son Joseph. Witnesses—John Bescherer, Jonathan Dunn. Proved Jan. 2, 1748. Lib. E, p. 236.

1749, May 10. Dunn, Joseph, of Peapack, Somerset Co. Inventory (£185.4.10) includes notes from Bennaih Dunn, Hezekiah Dun, debts of Joseph Carson. Made by Alexander Aikman, John McDaniel. Somerset Wills, 120 R.

1744, Nov. 9. Dunn, Samuel, of Piscataway, Middlesex Co., yeoman; will of. Wife, Hester. Eldest son, Samuel Dunn, of Somerset Co., and his children. Sons—Jonathan, and Micayah. Rosannah Dunn, eldest daughter of son Sam'll. Samuel Dunn, son of son Jonathan, at 21 years. Grandson Samuel, son of my daughter Mary, wife to Peter Runyon, at 21 years. Marcy Dunn, daughter to son Micayah. Daughter, Hester, wife of Nehemiah Dunham. Sister, Elizabeth, widow of John Runyon. "My Pallatine servant man." 130 acres in Piscataway, bought of John Barrow. Land left me by my father. Executors—sons Samuel and Jonathan. Witnesses—Isaac Stelle, John Parker, Benj. Gross. Proved Dec. 24, 1744. Lib. D, p. 211.

1744, Dec. 26. Inventory, £232.5.1; made by David Fitzrandolph and Joseph Blackford.

1745, June 2. Dunstar, Daniel Donaldson, of Somerset Co., gent.; will of. Trustees of estate Andrew Johnston of Perth Amboy, Robert Hunter Morris, Esq., Chief Justice of New Jersey, survivors and survivor of them and their heirs. Legacy to Elizabeth Hay, daughter of Andrew Hay, deceased. Provision for maintenance and education "of the children I have by her." Proceeds of estate to be divided among them when of age; surplus share devised to "my eldest son and his heirs." Witnesses—John Barberie, Elisha Parker, Jno. Stevens.

1748, Oct. 24. Codicil. "I intend the 1792 1-10 acres of Pine Right bought by James Alexander and Robert Hunter Morris of the Society for me to be within this will, tho part of it be not conveyed to me as yet by them." Same witnesses. Proved 18 Aug., 1749.

1750, March 26. Receipt for the original will out of Secretary's office by Ja. Alexander. Lib. E, p. 322.

1739, July 17. Duran (Duron), Charles, of Second River, Essex Co., physician. Int. Adm'x, Katherine Duran. John King, fellow bondsman. Lib. C, p. 286.

1739, June 7. Inventory, £69.11.03; made by John Low and John King.

1748, July 18. Durstan (Durston), Mary, of Woodbridge, Middlesex Co. Whereas Mary Campbell, daughter of Archibald Campbell late of New York, merch't, to whom the administration belongs is a minor, she hath chosen Joseph Royall to be her guardian, while she remains under 17 years of age.

1748, ——— —. Bond of Joseph Royall, of New York, gent., as administrator. James Hude, of New Brunswick, fellow bondsman. Witness—Elisha Parker. Lib. E, p. 200.

1750, Oct. 1. Dye, John, of Perth Amboy, Middlesex Co.; will of. Wife, Anne. Children—John, David, William, James, Vinson, Joseph, Anne, Katherine. Debt owing to Capt. Samuel Leonard. Real and personal estate. Executors—sons John and William, and son-in-law Lawrence Dye. Witnesses—Peter Perrine, Stephen Warne, Sarah Davison. Proved March 8, 1750. Lib. E, p. 496.

1732, May 18. Dyer, James, of Ash Swamp and Elizabeth Town, Essex Co. Int. Bond of John Rolph, principal creditor, who, at the request of Elizabeth Dyer, the widow, was appointed administrator. Thomas Rattoone, fellow bondsman. Lib. B, p. 255.

1732, May 26. Inventory of estate found in Bucks Co., Pennsylvania, (£90.01.06), includes bonds of Wm. Hatchner, George Dirdle, Thomas Woolsten; made by Joseph Wildman and Evelydus Longshore.

1732, June 10. Inventory of personal estate found in East Jersey, £38.11; made by Jonathan Freeman, Hendricke DeCamp and James Frazee.

1732-3, Jan. 11. Dyer, John, of Greenwich, Salem Co., Doctor; will of. Executors—friends John Ware and Thomas Withman, with power to sell estate and pay debts, and divide the remainder between them. Witnesses—James Watters, Henry Sharpe, James Carruthers. Proved 24 Jan., 1732. Lib. 3, p. 273.

1732-3, Jan. 2. Inventory (£70.5.10) includes cattle, swine, horses, etc. Appraisers—Josiah Fithian, James Dixon.

1741, Nov. 16. Eakman, Charles, of Upper Freehold, Monmouth Co. Sarah Eakman, the widow, resigns her right of administration in favor of Joseph Forman. Witnesses—Richard Stevens and Cornelese Vanhoren.

1741, Nov. 25. Administration granted to Joseph Forman, principal creditor, merchant. Bond, with John Deare, Esq., of Perth Amboy, fellow bondsman. Lib. C, p. 465.

1741, Dec. 14. Inventory, £40.10.10; made by Robert Gordon and James Mackmin.

1750, Oct. 18. Earle, Edward, of Seacacoss, Bergen Co., gentleman; will of. Eldest son, Edward, 1-3 of home plantation forever; son John 1-3, son Philip 1-3; adjoining lands of Reynier VanGeren, the division line to run with equal breadth to Hackinsack River. Son Antlebee £300 in five years after decease. Son Robert £200. (Both designated later as "younger sons.") Daughters, Mary (wife of John Nelson), Elizabeth Davis and Hester. Granddaughters, Elizabeth Davis and Elizabeth Nelson. Mentions obligation to Jacob Outwater. Executors—John Earle, brother William Earle and kinsman Daniel Smith. Witnesses—William Earle, Morris Earle and Jas. McKinley. Proved 12 May, 1755.

1755, May 12. Jorn Earle and Daniel Smith qualify as executors. Lib. F. p. 273.

1755, May 8. Inventory, £442; made by Phillip Smith, Job Smith.

1748, Dec. 28. Earle, Mary, of Gloucester Co., widow. Int. Adm'r, John Tomlinson. Fellow bondsman—Joseph Tomlinson. Lib. 6, p. 14.

1748, Dec. 23. Inventory, £114.3.8; made by John Hillman, Michael Fisher.

1732, Sept. 23. Earle, William, of Springfield, Burlington Co., yeoman; will of. My son-in-law, John Webb of Jamacka, did bequeath £40 per annum to my wife Elizabeth during her life and, provided it may be recovered, I devise same to my children—William, Thomas, Mary wife of Jonathan Burden, and Martha wife of Thomas Shinn. Real and personal estate. Witnesses—Joseph Whitas, Robert Gillam, John Wright. Proved May 10, 1733.

1733, May 10. William Earle, of Springfield, eldest son, appointed administrator as in will no executors appointed. Lib. 3, pp. 306, 307.

1740, June 9. Earll, William, of Springfield, Burlington Co.; will of. Wife, Mary. Daughter Elizabeth (under age). Elizabeth Sharp, "dau. of my wife." Sisters—Martha Shinn and Mary Burden. Cousins—William (son of brother Thomas) and Earll (son of Thomas Shinn). Real and personal estate. Executors—brothers Thomas Earll and Thomas Shinn. Witnesses—Francis Venicomb, Margaret Barton, John Osmond. Proved July 22, 1740. Lib. 4, p. 248.

1740, July 7 and 8. Inventory, £619.19.10½; made by Samuel Wright, John Burr and Richard Kirby. Additional appraisement includes bonds of John Machintosh, Jones the lawyer, Thomas Cadwallett, £4. Wm. Earll had with his wife Mary, by marriage, £88.14.10, and obligations of Job Ridgway, Thomas Garwood, John Prickets, Wm. Alcot, John Small, Andrew Conrow, Timothy Middleton and Wm. Sharp.

1756, April 13. Account of Thomas Earll, surviving executor, shows payments to Jos Clayton, Deborah Watson, Rich'd Bennet, John Stockton, William Cook, Rob't Hulate, Jane Leeds, Rich'd Smith, Thomas Haines, Daniel Smith, Caleb Raper, Abraham Brown, Richard Brogden, Mary Earl, John Adamsrout, John Osmand, Benj'n Horner, Isaac DeCow, Francis Vinnecomb, John Jones, Jonathan Fowler, Wm. Montgomerie, Aaron Lovett, Ralph Peart, Michael Atkinson, Thomas Slowman, George Studhart, John Lamb, Bara. Newbold, Owen Owen, Josiah White, James Wainwright, Joseph Rose, Isaac Ivins, Richard Bonge, Joseph Rockhill, Jos. Reeves, Fran Schooley, Ann Bishop, Robert Gardner, John Brown, Brian Daniel, Rich'd Bennett, James Hancock, Rich'd French, Jacob Anders, Sam'll Scattergood, Mathew Ribinson, Thomas Earl, Peter Sumnam, Joseph Lamb, William Rogers, Thomas Hunlock, Thomas Staples, Isaac Pearson,

William Potter, Thomas Shaw, George Taylor, John Pimm, Samuel Lovett, Israel Pemberton, Daniel Smith, William Chapman, William Mott, Elizabeth Potter, John Chapman, John Biddell, John Osman, Patrick Reynolds, Peter Rose, Joseph Richards, Stephen Williams, Safety Borden, Joseph Reckless, Job Lippincott, Silas Crispin, John Tantum, William Duckworth, Benjamin Jones, John Munrowe, Julius Evans, John Igehson, Hannah Atkinson, Martha Robison, Wm. Earl a legacy, Joseph Gray, Casper Wister, Samuel Gambel, Isaac Conro, Jonathan Borden, John Crage, Meis Hais, Margare Barton, William Robison, Jonathan Thomas, Zach'a Rosele, Earl Shinn, Abraham Carpenter, John Lewis, Lewis Beles, Benjamin Springer, Joshua Shreeves, Rob't Webb and bonds of Smoath, Stedman and Robinson.

1734, Oct. 4. Eaton, Benjamin, Sen'r., of Salem Co.; will of. Son, Benjamin, 3½ acres on which the "tan fatts" stand, the lot and tenement where I live, after wife's decease, 32 acres of marsh, 40 acres of upland in Pens-cow-neck, and 150 acres in Pens Neck I have in mortgage from Mathias Johnson. Daughters—Sarah (eldest, 100 acres on which she lives), Ann (£100. to be paid by my son Benjamin when he will be 21). Executors—wife, Margaret, and son Benjamin. Witnesses—Bridget Vance, Ellener Canade, William Pryce. Proved 7 Dec., 1734.

1734, Dec. 7. Letters granted to Benjamin Eaton, surviving executor. Lib. 4, p. 5.

1734, Nov. 9. Inventory (£300.1.5) includes 3 old Bibles, and "a parcel of bark for the tanning tread." Appraisers—Jno. Pledger, Isaac Scatterthwait.

1748, April 21. Eaton, John, of Penns Neck, Salem Co., husbandman; will of. Wife, Sarah. Eldest son, John Eaton, Junr., the plantation, 140 acres, whereon Peter Peterson lives. Mentions "the causeway next to the plantation whereon I live," and "the old cart road that leads through the iron mine towards Cornelius Corneliuson's." Daughter, Elizabeth. Son, Henry Eaton, at 21, to have the plantation whereon I live. Mentions lot land at New Castle Town, formerly belonging to John Burgraf, fronting the river Delaware. Hance Alderson and Elizabeth Townsend to live with son Henry during their servitude. Executors—son Henry, daughter Elizabeth Eaton, and James Barkley. An "N. B." states that if children die without issue, estate shall be divided equally between John Eaton, the son of Simon Eaton, and Thomas Harrett, son of John Harrett. Witnesses—Samuel Whitehorne, Jenkins Grafton, John Smith. Proved 30 April, 1748. Lib. 6, p. 441.

1748, April 27 and 28. Inventory (£231.18.1) includes "riding mare, cash, apparrel and armour," £32.15.7; 3 pair of oxen, cattle, green rye in the ground and flax, gun, two swords, etc. Appraisers—Ranier Vanhise, Alen. Congelton.

1748, July 12. Additional inventory, £20.7.7; made by Alen. Congelton, Jeremiah Baker, appraisers.

1748, Aug. 23. Credits in hands of Samuel Whitehorne. Appraisers—Sinnick Sinnickson, Alen Congleton.

1748, Nov. 16. Swine and cash in hands of Peter Garner. Appraisers—John Groome, Samuel Whitehorne.

1749, May 27. Cash in hands of Thomas Emble and Nicholas Nealson.

1749, June 9. Account. Moneys paid Nicholas Gibbons, Doctor Robt. Thompson, Joseph Hawks, Richard Slape, Peter Jaquat, Archibald Crawford, Michael Miller, George Monroe, John Brown, Daniel Mestayer, Sarah Bartleson, John Griffith, Peter Garner, Nicholas Nealson, Matthias Nealson, James Dunbar, Jeremiah Baker, Samuel Whitehorne, Michael Pedrick, Charles Empson, Thomas Emble, Charles Empson, John Dilmore, Edward ford, Michael Miller, George Monroe, John Brown, Daniel Mestayer, Sarah Eaton, Elizabeth Eaton, John Eaton, Henry Eaton, Jonathan and Elizth. Grist, John Smith, Ranier Van Hist, John Mounson, Larrance Donnavan, James Barkley, Thomas Carter, Paul Kemp, Peter Enloes, Peter Vanneman, George Scott, Epharim Cox.

1743-4, March 23. Eaton, Robert, of Amwell, Hunterdon Co.; will of. Friend and nephew, William Fish, executor and heir to testator's plantation, stock, etc. Testator's wife (not named). Witnesses—John McGlaughlin, Elizabeth Thatcher and Jane Barns. Proved April 10, 1744. Lib. 5, p. 25.

1744, March 31. Inventory (£48.2.6) includes "one great Bible." Made by John Phillips, John McGlaughlin.

1745, Dec. 2. Eatton, John, of Shrewsbury town, Monmouth Co., yeoman; will of. Wife, Joanna. Son, Thomas, £600, big Bible, dictionary, Nelson's Justice and testator's sword and pistols. Son, Joseph, small gun, small dictionary, church history and 10 shillings, he having received land by deed or gift. Wife to have use of plantation where testator lived, called Strawberry Neck, and use of land bought of William Brendley. Six daughters—Valera Lecount, Sarah, Lydia, Elizabeth, Joanna and Margrit, to have land bought of Jonathan Right in Hunterdon or Morris County; land bought of Abraham Vickos; plantation where testator lived; land bought of William Brindley and land bought of Hezekiah Allin. Executors—brother-in-law Joseph Wardell, and son Thomas Eatton. Witnesses—James Grover, Levi White, Samuel Lippincott. Proved May 11, 1750, by Levi White and Joseph Wardell (both Quakers). Lib. E, p. 485.

1736, 9th day, 8th mo. (Oct.). Eayres, Richard, of Evesham, Burlington Co., yeoman; will of. Wife, Elizabeth. Children—Richard, Thomas and Margaret Wills. Son-in-law, Ralf Brock. Land in Hopewell, "alias Trent Town"; land called Coexink; land bought of Robert Chapman near John Shin, and land bought of Bathanna Leeds. Son, Richard, sole executor. Witnesses—William Garwood, Thomas Jennings, Gab. Blond. Proved May 20, 1738. Lib. 4, p. 134.

1738, June 20. Inventory, £478.12.2; made by Philo Leeds and Edward Mullin. Includes Bibles and other books, servant boy and £60 in hands of Ralph Brock.

1747, Oct. 16. Edge, Daniel, of Hanover, Burlington Co., carpenter. Int. Adm'r, Joseph Branson, of same, carpenter. Joseph Woodward, of Upper Freehold, fellow bondsman. Lib. 5, p. 435.

1744, Dec. 24. Edgerton, Joseph, of Gloucester Co.; will of. Wife, Grace, and daughter, Abigail Edgerton (not 18), to have equally all estate. Wife, Grace, executrix. Witnesses—Joseph Cooper, Wm. Varman, Ann Stephens. Affirmed 28 Jan., 1744. Lib. 5, p. 83.

1744-5, 11 mo. (Jan.), 25 da. Inventory, £164.3.5; made by Jno. Kaighin, Robert Stephens.

1750, Aug. 20. Edsall, Samuel, of Hackinsack, Bergen Co., gentleman; will of. Son, John, £50 and "a French buckaneer gun and my saddle horse." Son, Jacobus, £40, stalion and saddle, and "the little gun." Son, Samuel, "to be put to school till he be fit to be put to a merchant." Legacies to daughters Elizabeth, Mary, Frances, Catrine, Anne, and "to each of my little twins." Executors—wife, Mary, Majr. Freeland, and son-in-law, Jobe Smith. Witnesses—John Paterson, James Moore, Jas. McKinley. Proved 24 Sept., 1750. Lib. E, p. 453.

1750, Aug. 28. Inventory (£506.7.3) includes 13 milch cows; negroes—Sabine, £40; Johntie, £50; Cuff, £60, Nan, £50, Phebe, £45, Frank, £45. Made by John Day and Michael Smith.

1734, April 27. Edwards, John, of Town and Co. of Burlington, bricklayer; will of. Sister, Elizabeth (wife of John Mullen), and Rebeckah their daughter. Brother, William Cutler. Real and personal estate. Executors—wife Mary, and Sarah Cutler, "my mother." Witnesses—Joseph Hewlings, Neal Gallagher, Tho. Worrall. Proved Nov. 16, 1734. Lib. 3, p. 441.

1734, May 15. Inventory, £121.9.11; made by Joseph Hewlings and Sam'll Lovett.

1748, Aug. 25. Edwards, Owen, of Chesterfield, Burlington Co., yeoman; will of. Eldest son, John. Plantation where I live, left me for a term of years by my father-in-law, to be let out for the benefit of my four children—Susanna, Arthur, Amy and Mary. Executor—brother-in-law, Joseph English. Witnesses—Will'm Taylor, Benjamin English, Geo. Bliss. Proved Aug. 20, 1748. Lib. 6, p. 305.

1748, Aug. 27. Inventory, £211.7.4; made by Sam'll Shrouds and Will'm Taylor. Includes bond from Jno. Warren and note of Sam'l Farnsworth, Jur.

1739-40, Feb. 20. Edwards, Philip, of Shrewsbury town, Monmouth Co., yeoman; will of. Wife, Elizabeth. To son, Webley, land west of Longbranch Path and half of Salt Marsh on Goose Neck. Youngest son, Philip. Daughters, Elizabeth Follwell, Mary Edwards,, and Margaret Edwards (not yet 16). Executrix—wife; friend, John Eaton, overseer. Witnesses—John Miln, William Craddock, Patrick Devlin and Jacob Dennis. Proved August 4, 1740. Lib. C, p. 351.

1739-40, March 9. Inventory, £480.10.00; made by Samuel Leonard, Thomas Lippincott.

1733, Jany. 4. Edwards, William, of Cape May Co., yeoman; will of. Wife, Anne, sole executrix, and to have real and personal estate. Witnesses—Henry Stites, Junior, Timothy Brandrof, Richard Robins, Junior. Proved ——, 1749. Lib. 6, p. 340.

1749-50, March 1. Inventory, £43.4.1; made by Frans. Taylor, Joseph Lord.

1749-50, March 20. Administration granted to Joseph Savage of Cape May, the widow, Anne, having renounced her right as executrix. Fellow bondsman—Joseph Lord. Witnesses—Henry Young, Fras. Taylor.

1749, Aug. 26. Egberts, Peter, of Essex Co., gentleman; will of. Brothers—John and Waling Egberts. Sisters—Antje and Else Egberts. Real and personal estate. Executors—John Vinsent and Abram Brooks. Witnesses—John Degarmo, Cornelius Van Geisen, Peter De Garmo. Proved Sept. 11, 1749. Lib. E, p. 367.

1733, July 10. Eglington, Ebenezer, of Gloucester Co., husbandman. Int. Adm'r, John Eglington, his brother, of Ellensbourgh, Salem Co., the widow, Elizabeth, having renounced her right. Witnesses—Timothy Eglington, Susannah Lord. Lib. 3, p. 347.

1733, July 24. Inventory (£45.3.9) includes debts due from Robert Armstrong, Thomas Addams, John Mercy, James Smith, Elias Lashamast, Daniel Tracy, William Skinner and William Hewit. Appraisers—John Matson, Ephraim Bee.

1731, March 31. Eglington, Edward, of Greenwich, Gloucester Co., yeoman; will of. Wife, Sarah. Eldest son, Timothy. Daughter, Elizabeth Read, 30 acres joining land of John Jones, Esq., on the head of the north branch of Homan's Creek. Son-in-law, Isaac Lord, the 50 acres on which he lives. Executors—Sons Samuel Driver and Ebenezer Eglington, they to have equally the residue of estate, real and personal. Witnesses—Elinor Eglington, A. Randall, Jonathan Driver. Proved 22 Sept., 1731. Lib. 3, p. 157.

1731, April 16. Inventory (£24.2.0) includes cooper and shoemaker's tools, £1.06. Appraisers—Israel Ward, A. Randall.

1731, Sept. 20. Letter from son, Ebenezer, that he cannot appear to prove will.

1733, Jany. 25. Account of Saml. Driver, as executor. Moneys paid to Mr. Antho. Hooper, Alexander Randall, Saml. Harrison, Esq., John Gilmer, George Shinn, Israel Ward, John Brown, Sarah Eglington, John Ladd, Esq., Edward Peirce, Esq.

1733, Aug. —. Eglington, Ephraim, of Gloucester Co., yeoman. Int. Adm'rs, Timothy and Sarah Eglington. Fellow bondsman—Jacob Cosens, yeoman. Witness—Thomas Glasson. Lib. 3, p. 100.

(For inventory and account, see under next item).

1731, April 15. Eglington, Samuel, of Gloucester Co., yeoman. Int. Adm'r, Timothy Eglington, yeoman. Fellow bondsman—Jacob Cosens, both of county aforesaid. Witness—Thos. Glasson.

Gloucester Wills, 164 H.

1731, April 16. Inventory of the goods and chattles of Ephraim and Samuel Eglington (£69.19.0) includes 1 wood boat and sails, £18. Appraisers—Israel Ward, A. Randall.

1733, Aug. —. Account of administrator of Ephraim and Samuel Eglington, both late of the township of Greenwich, Gloucester Co., husbandmen.

1733, May 5. Eires [Ayres?] John, of Somerset Co. Inventory, £15.5.8; made by Julius Johnson, Thomas Borde.

Somerset Wills, 37 R.

1732, Dec. 1. Eldredge, Elisha, of Cape May Co.; will of. Brother, Ezekiel Eldredge, sole executor and to have whole estate, real and personal, he to pay my brother, Samuel and William £10, John £15, Jacob a cow, and my mother £5. Sisters—Lydia Eldredge, Bethia Parsons and Sarah Stiles. Witnesses—Huson Huse, Barnabas Crowell, James Flood. Proved 5 Jan., 1732. Lib. 3, p. 237.

1732, Dec. 25. Inventory (£44.8.9) includes half interest in a shallop, £12. Appraisers—Thomas Ross, Richard Stites.

1733, Mar. 19. Account of executor. Moneys paid to Huson Huse, Sarah Spicer, Thomas Ross, Lemuell Swain, James Flood, Richard Stites, John Eldridge, John Jones, Barnabas Crowell, William Eldridge, Sarah Spicer; pair of oxen delivered to Lydia Eldridge; two cows delivered to

Bethia Parsons; one cow and a calf delivered to Jacob Spicer; one cow and a calf delivered to Sarah Spicer, etc.

1739, Oct. 30. Eldredge, Ezekial, of Cape May County, Int. Administration on estate granted to Elizabeth, his widow, and Ezekiel, son of deceased. Fellow bondsmen—Ephraim Edwards, John Eldredge. Witnesses—Samuel Eldredge, Robert Parsons, Jacob Spicer.

Lib. 4, p. 200.

1764, Nov. 7. Account of Elizabeth Norton and Ezekial Eldredge, administrators of the Estate of Ezekial Eldridge. Moneys paid to Henry Young, Esq., Jonathan Pratt, John Eldredge, Joseph Page, Nathaniel Hand, Elisha Hand, Elijah Hughes, Sarah Parsons, Levi Eldredge, Nathan Eldredge, Elisha Eldredge, James Eldredge, Silas Eldredge, Nathaniel Forster, Joseph Buck, Elizabeth Norton, Ezekiel Eldredge, etc., amounting to £395.2.0. Mentions that Nathaniel Forster, Jr., is husband to the late Mary Eldredge, and (1760) that Joseph Buck is husband of the late Elizabeth Eldredge.

1743, Jany. 7. Eldredge, Levi, of Cape May Co. Int. Adm'x, Elizabeth Eldredge, his widow. Fellow bondsman—John Eldredge. Witnesses—Henry Young, James Whilldin. Cape May Wills, 114 E.

1743-4, Jan. 6. Inventory (£61.7.7) includes cattle and horses. Appraisers—John Eldredge, James Whillden.

1748, Nov. 25. Account of Elizabeth Skillinger, late Elizabeth Eldridge, Admr'x. Moneys paid Robert Parsons, Nathan Hand, John Eldridge, James Welding, Ezekiel Mulford, Elisha Hand, Charles Golehar, John Hand, Jacob Spicer, Richard Shaw, Henry Young, Elisha Eldridge.

1742, Sept. 23. Eldredge, Samuel, Esq., of Cape May Co., yeoman; will of. Wife, Mercy. To eldest son, Samuel, plantation I live on, lately exchanged with Mr. John Stillwell, of Cape May County; also 100 acres adjoining James Page of the place aforesaid; also the southern half of Oyster Point and my negro man York. He to pay my youngest daughter, Sarah Eldredge, £10, when she will be 17. Son, Aaron, to have 100 acres purchased of Messrs. John Parsons and Christopher Church (both deceased), and executors to Nathaniel Norton said land joining that of John Craford and Zebulon Swains; also 87 acres of woodland, bought of Capt. William Thinn in trust for the West New Jersey Society in England, adjoining the abovesaid 100 acres; also the northern ½ of Oyster Point, adjoining to Cold Spring Creek, purchased in part of Collo. Jacob Spicer, deceased, and in part of Nathaniel Norton's executors aforesaid; also my right at Gosen Creek and the Cedar Hammocks in Cape May County. Son, Jacob, to have 100 acres purchased of Daniel Mulford, formerly Robert Bells of Cape May, deceased, adjoining Robert Parsons; also the town lots adjoining William Simkins and Caleb Newton, fronting on Delaware Bay; also my right of meadow, beach and upland at Wolf Point at the Great Pond, adjoining to Richard Stites' land. All my sons to enjoy the lands when they come to seventeen years of age, respectively. If wife shall be delivered of a son, he shall have plantation at Piles Grove in Salem, which I bought of Isaac Vanmetere of said County, adjoining Harman Richman and Abraham Nelson; if a girl should be born, said plantation at Piles Grove, Salem County, shall be sold and the money divided among all my daughters. Movable estate to be equally divided among the children after 1-3 is given to my wife Mercy, who shall have the use of ½ of the plantation I now live on, and the Oyster Point, during her widowhood, for the bringing up of the children to the age of 21. Executors—wife, Mercy, and son, Samuel. Witnesses—Abiah Ross, Jacob Spicer, William Ross. Proved 22 May, 1745.

1745, June 11. Letters granted to Samuel Eldredge. Lib. 5, p. 122.

1744-5, Mar. 12. Inventory, £141.10.8; made by John Eldredge, Elisha Hand.

1735, Sept. 14. Eldridge, Jonathan, of Evesham, Burlington Co., yeoman; will of. Sons—Jonathan, Joseph, Obediah and James. Negro boy, Will. Real and personal estate. Executors—wife Elizabeth, Thomas Hackney and William Tomlinson. Witnesses—Sam'll Atkinson, Dan'll Sharp, John Higby. Proved March 2, 1736. Lib. 4, p. 86.

1736-7, Feb. 4. Inventory, £89.7; made by Abraham Haines and Caleb Haines. Includes compass and other surveying instruments.

1741, March 19. Elkinton, Joseph, of Northampton, Burlington Co., yeoman. Daughters—Frances aged 20, and upwards, and Amy, about 18, pray that Revel Elton may be appointed their guardian. Lib. 4, p. 302.

1736, 20th day, 6th mo. (Aug.). Elkinton, Thomas, of Northampton, Burlington Co.; will of. Wife, Mary, sole executrix. Son, Joshua, and other children mentioned but not named. Daniel Wills to have deed for lot in Mt. Holly next William Murrils. Witnesses—Archibald Silver, Jon. Deacon, Samuel Laning. Proved Nov. 25, 1736. Lib. 4, p. 76.

1736, Nov. 24. Inventory, £122.15.2; made by Samuel Laning and Archibald Silver.

1737, Jan. 12. Ellis, George, of Evesham, Burlington Co., miller. Inventory, £151.1; made by Thomas Coles and Nehemiah Cowgill.

1737, Jan. 17. Administration granted to Sarah Ellis, widow. James Wild, of Waterford, Gloucester Co., yeoman, fellow bondsman. Lib. 4, p. 126.

1750, July 19. Ellis, Jacob, of Haddonfield, Gloucester Co., yeoman. Int. Adm'r, Simeon Ellis, Esq. Fellow bondsman, John Hinchman, both of same place. Lib. 7, p. 32.

1750, July 10. Renunciation of Cassandra, widow, as admx., in favor of her father-in-law, Simeon Ellis. Witnesses—Jno. Hinchman, Jr., Henry Hubbs.

1750, July 19. Inventory (£207.7.7) names "Levy Alberson's time, £17.14." Appraisers—John Burroughs, John Hinchman, Junior.

1737, Jan. 10. Ellis, Joseph, of Newton Township, Gloucester Co., yeoman, guardian of Richard (over 14), son of Jon. Wright, late of said County, yeoman. Bondsman—John Kaighin. Lib. 4, p. 126.

1744, Nov. 17. Ellison, Enoch, of Gloucester Township and County, innholder; will of. Wife, Hannah, during widowhood, all estate, except 1-2 acre of ground for a burying-ground "for all Christian people." At her death or marriage, estate shall go for use of poor of Township of Gloucester. Executors—Isaac Jennings, Esq., and William Davis, yeoman. "N. B. The half acre of ground for the burying place shall be on the west side of the house enclosing the body of Dennis Dodman within the same." Witnesses—George Ward, Edward Williams, Michael Fisher. Proved 12 March, 1744.

1744, Dec. 26. Renunciation of Isaac Jennings and William Davis as executors. Witnesses—Coz. (?), Richard Caddey, James Tylee, Jacob Clement.

1744, Jany. 5. Inventory, £17.7.4; made by Jno. Kaighin, Ebenezer Brown.

1746, Oct. 31. Administration granted to James Tylee. Fellow bondsmen—Tho. Thorne, Jacob Gamble. Lib. 5, pp. 298, 299.

1746-7, Feb. 21. Letters. "Whereas Hannah, widow of Enoch Ellison is now deceased," etc. (Signed) Edward Reed Price.

1747, Dec. 26. Accounts due from Wm. Davies, William Harrison, Isaac Key, Edward R. Price. Moneys received from Samuel Harrison, Esq., High Sheriff of Gloucester Co., for sale of land, £71.10.0. (Signed) Henry Sparks, William Hugg.

1739, May 9. Ellison (Ellason), Joseph, of New Brunswick, Middlesex Co., yeoman; will of. Daughters—Annah, Marey (at 14 years), and Martha. Daughter-in-law, Ann. Real and personal estate. Executors—wife Martha, Thomas Ellason and Joshua Smalley. Witnesses—Benj'n Webley, William Chesman, Jun'r, Mary Smally. Proved June 9, 1739. Lib. C, p. 281.

1719, March 5. Ellison, Richard, of Freehold, Monmouth Co., yeoman; will of. Wife, Ellse. Children—Daniel, Richard, Samuel, Ruth, Mary, Susanna and Sarah. To daughter, Sarah, "one hollowe which lyeth about hallf a mill from Afrems Wollintins southward." Executor—son, Daniel. Witnesses—Mary Pelton, Mary Wood and Ithamor Pelton. Proved at Crosswicks, in Upper Freehold, December 23, 1732, by Ithamar and Mary Pelton. Lib. B, p. 257.

1719, April 2. Inventory, £14.7.6; made by Thomas Sutton and Jonathan Hamton.

1750, May 11. Elston, William, of Woodbridge, Middlesex Co.; will of. Children—William, Elizabeth, Ledy, Sary, and Payshance Elston, all under age. Expected child. Lands in Elizabeth Town and Woodbridge. Executors—wife, Sary, and brother, Spencer Elston. Witnesses—Michael Moore, Isaac Prall, Abraham Elston. Proved June 18, 1750. Lib. E, p. 422.

1746, May 12. Elstone, Peter, of Woodbridge, Middlesex Co., yeoman; will of. Wife, Ruth. Five daughters, no names given. Son, Peter, his wife Elizabeth and their children, viz., Peter, James, Benjamin and Daniel; lands in Woodbridge and Rahway. Grandson, Samuel, son of John. Son, Benjamin, and his five sons, meadow on west side of William Spencer's meadow that was formerly Jonathan Dillies; salt marsh bought of John Jaques. Executors—son Benjamin, and friends John Skinner and William Britten. Witnesses—Richard Walker, John Jaquess, David Donham, Jun'r. Proved June 6, 1746. Lib. D, p. 394.

1746, June 6. Benjamin Elstone qualified as executor, the others having refused to act.

1737, June 11. Elwell, John, of Salem Co., yeoman. Int. Adm'r, Robert Jenkins. Bondsman, John Doe. Both of said County, yeomen. Witnesses—Edwd. Peirce, Danl. Mestayer. Lib. 4, p. 114.

1739-40, Jan. 5. Elwell, Samuel, of Township of Pilesgrove, Salem

Co., yeoman; will of. Wife, Famzen. Sons—Jacob, to have grist mill and the 60 acres where he lives; Samuel, 100 acres of my plantation after my wife's decease, if she remains my widow, likewise the remainder to my son Abraham. Daughters—Rachel (wife of Wm. Brick), Susanna (wife of John Ray), Elizabeth, Famzen, Coziah, Phebe, Molley and Tobitha. An expected child. Cedar swamp. Executors—wife and son Jacob, who are empowered to sell the 50 acres purchased from William Paulin. Witnesses—Matthew Brown, John Elwell, John Mulford, Jacob Richman. Affirmed 16 Feb., 1739.

Lib. 4, p. 219 (imperfect; see original).

1739-40, Feb. 6. Inventory, £126.9.6; made by William Paullin, Abraham Nelson (mark).

1749-50, March 16. Ely, George, of Trenton, Hunterdon Co., yeoman; will of. Wife, Jane; sons Joshua and George, executors. Servant, Martha Crawford. Grandson, George Price, under fourteen years of age. Testator's six children: Joshua, George, Joseph, Mary Green, (widow), Sarah (wife of John Dagworthy), and Rebecca (wife of Eliakim Anderson). Witnesses—Joseph Warrell, Esquire, Daniel Stevenson and Arthur Howell. Proved Sept. 12, 1750. Lib. 6, p. 432.

1750, July 21. Inventory (£481.16.6) includes hunting saddle, gun, pike, sword and belt. Made by Nathan Beakes and Arthur Howell, the former a Quaker.

1732, Feb. 3. Ely, John, of Trenton, Hunterdon Co., yeoman; will of. Wife, Frances, the house and farm at Trenton during widowhood. Son, William. Eldest son, John, the house and plantation at Assunpink, in which John then lived. Daughters—Mary and Elizabeth, when of age. Executors—wife, and sons John and William. Witnesses—George Ely, James Gould, Christian Bell. Proved Feb. 10, 1732. Lib. 3, p. 256.

1733, April 10. Inventory, £185.13.6; made by James Gould and George Ely.

1732, Emans, John, of Gravesend, in or near the township or precinct of Wallpack, Hunterdon Co., merchant; will of. Wife, Elinor, to have care of estate until youngest child of age, then to be divided among children namely, Nicholas, Rachel, Elinor and Catharine. Nicholas to have horse, bridle, saddle, gun and sword. Negro man, Sambo. Testator's dwelling house called "Gravesend." Executors—wife Elinor, and son Nicholas. Witnesses—Abraham Vankampen, Cornelius Westbrook, John Rice. Proved May 17, 1732. Lib. 3, p. 196.

1732, June 22. Inventory (£743.0.6) includes four negroes. Made by Samuel Green and Abraham Vankampen.

1758, Oct. 9. Account of Edward Robeson and Elinor his wife, late Elinor Emans, executrix of will of John Emans. Mentions Jno. Crook, Nicholas Emans, Benjamin Smith, Johanes Depugh, Edward Tompson, Jno. Vanvleght, John Hardenbergh, Gilbert Levingstone, Garret Decker, Bruer Decker, Cornelius Hornbeck, Jacobus Van Dyke, Temo. Smyth, Heleke Conner, Nicholas Low, William Doughty, Jarman Pick, Ab. Vankampen, Everet Burguss, Gadus Hendenbergh, Samuel Green, Jacob Dewit, Cornelius Delameter, Johanes Durnon, San. Chambers, Lambert Brink, Isaac Vanoraghan, Conrad Elfender, Johanis Eltington, Urian Taper, Jno. Mathews, Chas. Broadhead; maintenance and schooling of Rachel, Elinor and Catherine, the eldest of whom was about six years of age at decease of the testator.

1732, Dec. 16. Emley, William, of New Hanover, Burlington Co., yeoman; will of. Children—Thomas, William and Ruth, all under age. Real and personal estate. Wife, Abigail, sole executrix. Witnesses—Thos. Wright, Sam Emley, James Dennis. Proved March 5, 1732. Lib. 3, p. 276.

1732-3, Jan. 23. Inventory, £208.2.2; made by Joshua Wright and Thomas Wright.

1727, March 3. Emott, William, of New York City, merchant. Administration granted to Judith Emott, the widow. Maire Morin and Ester Fresneau, fellow bondsmen. Witness—Mariana Morin. Lib. B, p. 11.

1743, Nov. 11. Encloes (Enlows, Inloes) Peter, of Penns Neck, Salem Co.; will of. Lands to be equally divided among three sons: Peter, Joseph and Anthony. Three daughters (only two named)—Ales Gill Johnson and Elizabeth Philpot. Executors—Edmond Wetherbe, Cristian Enlows, Martain Skeer and son, Peter Enlows. Witnesses—Jeremiah Baker, Earick Gill Johnson, Charl. Cornelluson. Proved 28 Nov., 1743.

Whereas Edmund Wetherby and Martin Skeer having refused to act and Peter Enlows is not of lawful age, letters of administration granted 28 Nov., 1743, to Erick Gill Johnson and John Gill Johnson of Penns Neck, Salem County. Lib. 5, pp. 50, 51.

1743, Nov. 26. Renunciation of Edmond Weatherby and Martin Skeer. Witness—Michael Lambson.

1743, Nov. 28. Administration Bond of Erick Gill Johnson and John Gill Johnson. Bondsman—Jeremiah Baker, all of Penns Neck. Witnesses—Wm. Pennock, Chas. O'Neill.

1743, Nov. 28. Inventory, £188.4.1; made by Jeremiah Baker, John Philpot.

1744, March 22. Withdrawal of caveat of William Tuft against sd. estate.

1746, March 3. Account. Monies paid Samuel Vanhis (for keeping and nursing a young child of Peter Enloes), John Phillpot, Magdalin Sinnicks, Charles Ensille, Sinnick Sinnickson, Charles O Neill, Benjamin Tindal, James Barkley, Thomas Welch, Earick Gill Johnson, John Gill Johnson, Joseph Harris, Richard Crunk, John LeFever, Owen Flanagen, George Grimes, William Crage, Edmond Wetherby, Nicholas Herman, William Tuft, Richard Ashdon, Charles Simpson, John Marshall, Hugh Maganow, Robert M. Harlin.

1748, July 14. Endecott, Joseph, of Northampton, Burlington Co.; will of. Mother, Hannah Endicott. Children all under age. Real and personal estate. Executors—wife, Ann, and friend James Wills. Witnesses—Benjamin Brown, Thomas Byrkinshier, Jun'r, Tho. Shinn. Proved March 1, 1748-9. Lib. 6, p. 257.

1748-9, Feb. 27. Inventory, £103.16.5; made by Michael Woolston and Thomas Budd.

1746-7, Feb. 14. Endicott, Joseph, Sen'r, of Northampton, Burlington Co.; will of. Wife, Hannah, sole executrix. Sons—Joseph and John. Daughters—Elizabeth Dillavoue living in Penna. and Ann Gillam, of Northampton. Grandson—Joseph Bishop of Northampton. Real and personal estate. Witnesses—Josiah Gaskill, Benjamin Brown, John Grimes. Proved May 29, 1747. Lib. 5, p. 522.

1747, May 28. Inventory, £194.2.6; made by Thomas Haines and James Wills.

1737, April 2. English, James, of Cape May, Cape May Co., yeoman. Int. Adm'r, William Greer, of Cape May, yeoman. Fellow bondsman—Peter Boynton, of Burlington, merchant. Witness—Joseph Rose. Cape May Wills, 88 E.

1737, Apr. 13. Inventory (£117.5.9) includes "3 hats, 10 silk hanckiers," deer skins and furs, articles of merchandise. Appraisers—James Statham, John Willits.

1743, Sept. 7. Engly, Samuel, of "Gloster" Co. Inventory, £85.9.5; made by Joseph Heritage and Daniel Elwell.

1743, Oct. 1. Administration granted to Mary French, mother of deceased. Robert Engly, Sen'r, and John Engly, both of Burlington Co., fellow bondsmen. Lib. 5, p. 50.

1747, Jan. 31. Errickson, Andrew, Sr., of Morrisse's River, Salem Co., mariner; will of. Wife, Modlena. Sons—Andrew, to have 350 acres at the east end of the 1,100 acres; Samuel, 200 acres, joining Andrew's. Daughters—Christiana Peterson, 200 acres; Sarah Huings (Ewins), 350 acres, beginning at the Bay, so on to the back line; Rebecca, the place that was Peter Peterson's, Sen., in the tract of Chester-town on Morrisse's River. Executor—son, Andrew. Witnesses—Charles Belitha, William McGlaughlin, William Kneebun. Proved 24 May, 1748. Lib. 5, p. 482.

1748, May 18, 19. Inventory (£671.18.2) includes 2 servants and an old negro (£23.5.0), 86 head of cattle (£150.5.0), 9 head of horses (£17.10.0), 50 head of sheep (£10), hogs (£10), "a shalloope" (£100). Bonds of William Rawson, Samuel Burn, Hezeciah Love, John Sealey's note of hand, John Jones, Neele MacNeele (?). Appraisers—Joseph Reeves, John Peterson.

1736, Dec. 3. Eslick (Eslik, Estlack), John, of Newton, Gloucester Co.; will of. Son, Daniel Eslike. Daughters—Hester, Elizabeth, Sarah and Hannah. Executors—sons John and Samuel Eslik. Witnesses—Tobias Holloway, Francis Haddock, Gabriel Newby. Affirmed 23 Feb., 1743.

1743, Feb. 28. Letters testamentary to John Estlake, the surviving executor. Lib. 5, p. 131.

1743, Dec. 10. Inventory (£263.10.04) includes "1 wigg £0.17.06," service, 7½ months, of William Price £5, 3 years' service of Jon. German £12, "some goods lodged by the sd. John Eslack with his daughter Ester Martain (not appraised)," "one Roley Coley and 1 dough trough, old Bible, etc." Appraisers—Jno. Kaighin, Jos. Kaighin.

1742, 8 mo., 5th da. (Oct.). Estaugh, John, of Haddonfield, Gloucester Co.; will of. Wife, Elizabeth (daughter of John Haddon, late of St. George, Southwark, in Great Britain, deceased), executrix and to have whole estate. Witnesses—Nehemiah Andrews, Samuel Engle, William Erwin. Affirmed 28 March, 1743. Lib. 4, p. 357-B.

1749, Feb. 7. Estell, Daniel, of Hunterdon Co. Int. Adm'rs, Elizabeth and Thomas Estell. Lib. 7, p. 46.

1743, Feb. 18. Estlack, Samuel, of Newton, Gloucester Co., yeoman.

Int. Adm'r, Ann, widow. Fellow bondsman, Simon Breach of same place. Witnesses—Robert Stephens, Francis Haddock. Lib. 5, p. 86.

1743, Jan. 2. Inventory (£89.12.0) names Thomas Attmore, John Kaighin, Elizabeth Bright, Jabell Vanniman, Abigail Petro, Gabriel Rambo, Garroll Vanniman, James Arans, Richard Brinner, Jack Lord, Anthony Hooper, Joseph Estlack, Wm. Mickle, William Kimsey, George Avis, James Hinchman Petro, Thomas Holden, Alexander Randall, Charles Rylee.

1730, Nov. 4. Estland, Ann, of Cohansey, Salem Co., widow; will of. Grandson, Mark Reeves, at 17 to have all gold, silver, plate and ½ of remaining part of estate, the other half to go equally to grandchildren, viz.: Joseph, John and Martha Reeves, when 17. Executor—son, Joseph Reeves. Witnesses—Dickason Shepherd, John Shepherd, Stephen Shepherd. Proved 26 April, 1735. Lib. 4, p. 26.

1735, April 17. Inventory (£278.16.1) includes 32 cattle and 11 sheep. Appraisers—Dickason Shepherd, Moses Shepherd.

1745, Nov. 28. Estlick, William, of Greenwich, Gloucester Co., yeoman. Int. Adm'r, Francis Estlick, yeoman. Fellow bondsman—Robert Gerrard, of county aforesaid, yeoman. Witnesses—Thomas Scattergood, Jos. Scattergood. Lib. 5, p. 185.

1745, Nov. 25. Inventory, £75.5.2; made by Alexr. Randall, Robert Gerrard.

1763, Mar. 8. Account of Admr. of "William Eastlacke." Cash paid to Joshua Lord, Thomas Coombs, William White, Mathew Farrell, Dennis Glassit, Thomas Holden.

1749, July 25. Evans, David, of Piles Grove, Salem Co., clerk; will of. £10. to the Presbyterian congregation at Piles Grove, to be paid within one year after decease to Isaac Van Meeter, Eleazar Smith, John Rose, Barnet Dubois, Lewis Dubois, Jacob the son of Barnet Dubois, Abraham Niewkirk and Jacob, the son of Lewis Dubois, or unto any two of them and unto none else. Son, Samuel, £27., and to each of his children: Hannah, Israel and Ann, 20 shillings. Wife, Ann, sole executrix, and "to have the remainder of my estate and everything justly due me by inheritance within the Dominions of Great Britain." Witnesses—James Dunlap, John Dunlap, James Dunlap, Junior, Richard Moore, James Creag. Proved 9 March, 1750. Lib. 7, p. 252.

1750, Feb. 21. Inventory (£413.8.3) includes books, book cases, carpenter's tools, maps "and other small things in the study," negro wench, £25, etc. Appraisers—William Alderman, Jacob Dubois. Proved 9 March, 1750.

1746, Oct. 14. Evans, John, of Evesham, Burlington Co.; will of. Mother, Elizabeth Evans. Children—Joseph, William, John, Jane, Rachel, Hepzibah and Beulah. 7 negroes. Land bought of Robert Engle and Andrew Conore, and tracts adjoining James Eldridge and Thomas Andrews. Executors—wife Ruth, brother Thomas Evans, brother-in-law John Brick. Witnesses—Jacob Heulings, James Eldridge, Gab: Blond. Proved Feb. 5, 1746-7.

1746-7, 21st day, 11th mo. (Jan.). Thomas Evans declines to serve as executor. Lib. 5, p. 305.

1746-7, 27 and 28 days, 11th mo. (Jan.). Inventory, £906.10.9; made by Sam. Lippincott, James Eldridge, William Foster.

1750, Oct. 22. Evans, Nathaniel, of Salem Co. Int. Adm'rs, James Evans and Jacob Evans, both of Alloways Creek, said County. Salem Wills, 925 Q.

1750, Oct. 22. Inventory, £114.14.10; made by Jn. Nicholson, Daniel Smith.

1748, Feb. 15. Evans, Thomas, of Chester, Burlington Co., yeoman; will of. Wife, Sarah. Sarah Hoskinson, servant. Plantation on Egg-harbour Road beyond the Blue Anchor, adjoining Jacob Spicer. Legacy left son Thomas by his grandfather, John Naylor. Executors—sons Thomas and Jacob. Witnesses—William Allin, Jacob Lippincott, William Sorsby. Proved Aug. 19, 1749. Lib. 6, p. 299.

1749, Aug. 18. Inventory, £126.11.7; made by John Roberts and Enoch Roberts. Includes bonds of John Carter and Thomas Kinnard.

1750, August 25. Evell, Jacob, "late of Morris County." Int. Bond of Susannah Rope of Bucks County, Pennsylvania and Michael Myers, as administrators. Fellow bondsmen—George Rope of Morris County, and Jacob Sook of Bucks County, carpenter. Witnessed by Obadiah Howell. Endorsed, "Jacob Evell, Hunterdon County." Hunterdon Wills, 283 J.

1747, Jan. 2. Evens, John, of Salem Co., shallopman. Int. Adm'r, Jacob Moor, yeoman. Bondsman, Samuel Moore. Both of Cohansey, said County. Witnesses—Edward Test, Nich. Gibbon. Lib. 5, p. 425.

1747-8, Jan. 7. Inventory (£97.1.6) of "effects of John Evings, deceased," includes "one quarter and half of a shallop called the Dolphin, and his part of rigging £26," 7½ bushels of salt, gun, and Bible. Appraisers—Ananias Sayre, Josiah Parwin.

1738, 26th day, 4th mo. (June), Eves, John, of Evesham, Burlington Co., yeoman; will of. John and Joseph (sons of brother Samuel), Thomas (son of brother Thomas), and Hudson (son of Thomas Middleton). Friends—Joshua Humphries and John Campin. Real and personal estate. Wife, Mary, sole executrix. Witnesses—Sam. Lippincott, John Alten, Freedom Lippincott the younger. Proved March 25, 1740. Lib. 4, p. 226.

1739, 24th day, 1st mo. (March). Inventory, £239.9.7; made by Sam. Lippincott and Joseph Stokes.

1749, 23rd day, 7th mo. (Sept.). Eves, Mary, widow of John Eves, of Evesham, Burlington Co.; will of. Son, John Hudson, and daughter Mary Middleton, executors and to have all estate. Witnesses—Benjamin Crispin, Samuel Stokes. Proved Dec. 22, 1749. Lib. 6, p. 272.

1749, 18th day, 12th mo. (Feb.). Inventory, £136.14.5; made by Benjamin Crispin and Joshua Ballinger.

1747, Aug. 25. Evilman, Robert, of Middlesex Co., cordwainer. Administration granted to John Evilman, of Monmouth Co. Lib. E, p. 78.

1747, Aug. 24. Statement of debts due to Robert Brown, James Aston, Mathew Collens, David Gillaland, Stephen Warner, Daniel Robins, Robert Wiles, William Cheasman, Dunken Cammel, Charles Jolley, James Jewel, Samuel Rogers, Andrew Jonston, Andrew Kettels, William Dear, £101.9.4.

1747, Oct. 29. Inventory, £53.3.6; made by Thomas Combs and Robert Brown.

1731, Aug. 11. Ewin, John, of Springfield, Burlington Co.; will of.

Sons—Absolam and Ambrose, all real estate when of age. Personal estate to wife, Mary, who is sole executrix. Witnesses—John Budd, Thomas Willson, Abigail Shin, Hope Atkinson, Elizabeth Shinn. Proved Oct. 12, 1732. Lib. 3, p. 218.

1732, Oct. 19. Inventory, £106.16; made by James Shinn and John Budd.

1744-5, Jan. 7. Ewing, Thomas, Sr., of Cohansey, Salem Co., yeoman; will of. Wife, Mary, use of 3 acres of land purchased of Charles Davis, between my dwelling house and Mathias Fithian's; use of 13½ acres of marsh on Stow Creek. At her marriage or decease, son Maskell to have same. Son John to have (at 21), 50 acres purchased of Samuel Holmes, together with 5 acres called the Dick Marsh. Other children—Thomas, Mary, Joshua, Samuel and James. Executor—son, Thomas. Witnesses—Thos. Maskell, Robert Ewing, Richard Ball. Proved 7 April, 1748. Lib. 5, p. 426.

1747, March 11. Inventory, £169,05.00; made by Thos. Wathman, Thos. Maskell.

1749, April 7. Ewing, William, of Cohansey, Cumberland Co., husbandman; will of. Brother, James Ewing. Executor—brother-in-law, Charles Dennis, Junior. Witnesses—Nehimiah Craven, John Richardson, John Bee. Proved 1 May 1749. Lib. 6, p. 121.

1749, May 1. Inventory (Greenwich township, Cumberland Co.), £152.15.02; made by John Butler, Samuel Fithian.

1732, Nov. 30. Eyres (Ayres?), John, of Somerset Co. Int. Adm'r, Andries Woertman. Lib. B, p. 328.

1739, Nov. 22. Fagan, Philip, of Upper Freehold, Monmouth Co. Int. Margaret Fagan, the widow, renounces right of administration in favor of Zebulon Cook, chief creditor. Witness—John Imlay. Administration granted Nov. 26. Lib. C, p. 298.

1739, Nov. 29. Inventory of personal estate (£29.02.8), includes judgment obtained before Justice Richard Stevens against John Ellison. Made by John Imlay and Richard Borden.

1736, Sept. 20. Fairs, John, of Mansfield, Burlington Co., bricklayer. Int. Administration granted Mary Faris, widow. Richard Gibbs, of same, yeoman, fellow bondsman. Lib. 4, p. 73.

1736, Sept. 24. Inventory, £40.3.6; made by Thos. Newbold and Richard Gibbs.

1740, 1st day, 4th mo., June. Falkenburg, Heinrich Jacobys, of Little Eggharbour; will of. Son Jacob (minor). Real and personal estate. Wife Mary, sole executrix with friends Edward Andrews and John Wills to assist her. Witnesses—John Woolman, George Bliss, John Wills. Proved June 16, 1743. Lib. 4, p. 362.

1747, 24th day, 3rd mo. (May). Farnsworth, Daniel, of Burlington Co., yeoman; will of. Daughter, Hannah, wife of Owen Edwards, and their son John, under age. Samuel, son of brother Samuel. Real and personal estate. Executors—friends Marmaduke Watson and Jos. Curtis. Witnesses—Benonie Gregory, Jonathan Quicksall, Jos. Borden, Ju'r. Proved June 13, 1747. Lib. 5, p. 326.

1747, June 12. Inventory, £148,14.10; made by Thos. Folkes and Jonathan Quicksall.

1749, May 9. Farnsworth, Nathaniel, of Chesterfield, Burlington Co., yeoman; will of. Wife, Anne. Children—Amiriah and Rachel, both under age. Plantation in Bordentown. Executors—friends Thomas Folks and Peter Imlay. Witnesses—Benoni Gregory, Ju'r, Moses English, Geo. Bliss, Ju'r. Proved May 16, 1749. Lib. 6, p. 310.

1749, May 13. Inventory, £185.14.2; made by Isaac Horner and Rob. Field. Includes debts due from Thomas Duglas, Samuel Thoen, Mathew Wright, Joseph Tilton, Robert Ashton, Anthony Lea, Joseph Rockhill, Benj'n and William French, Thomas Griggs, Estate of Sam'l Farnsworth, dec., Damares Farnsworth, John Butterfield, Jacob Taylor, Edward Wheatcraft, Preserved Brown, John Thorn, John Updike, John Flintham.

1745-6, 1st day, 11th mo. (Feb.). Farnsworth, Samuel, of Chesterfield, Burlington Co., yeoman; will of. Children—Nathaniel, Samuel, Mary Corliss, Susanna Warren, Ann, Sarah Updike and Hannah. Land in Nottingham bought of Preserved Brown, and tract on Croswick Creek, lying between my brother Daniel and Joseph Bording; also Proprietary rights. Executors—wife Damaris and son Samuel. Witnesses—John Thorn, Thomas Folkes, Jos. Wright. Proved Dec. 2, 1747. Lib. 5, p. 373.

1747, Dec. 2. Inventory, £251.2.6; made by John Thorn and Thos. Folkes. Includes bonds of Samuel Farnsworth, John Imlay, Benjamin Field, Samuel Radford, John Thorn, William Black, Nathaniel Farnsworth and "one great Bible."

1745, Nov. 25. Farr, Henry, of Salem Co. Int. Adm'x, Hannah Farr. Bondsmen—Daniel Smith, Richd. Sharpe. All of said County. Witnesses—Danl. Mestayer, Mary Mestayer. Lib. 5, p. 241.

1745, Nov. 30. Inventory, £35.5.8; made by William Chandler, Edward Test.

1747, Sept. 3. Farrand, Samuel, of Newark, Essex Co.; will of. Children—Daniel, Samuel, Ebenezer, Nathaniel Joseph, Sarah, Phebe, Hannah and Elizabeth. Land joining land of Samuel Ward, deceased. Executors—wife Hannah, and sons Samuel, Ebenezer, Nathaniel and Joseph. Witnesses—Zach'r. Hall, Timothy Dod, Isaac Dod. Proved Jan. 2, 1750. Lib. E, p. 489.

1731, July 16. Faucett (Fossett), John, of Greenwich Township, Gloucester Co., yeoman. Adm'r, Grace Fossitt, widow. Fellow bondsmen—Samuel Rain, John Doe. Gloucester Wills, 139 H.

1731, July 3. Inventory (£107.4.3) includes debts due to the estate abovesaid, by Governour of Phila (£22.10.0), Samuel Hail, David Ceplin, Thomas Bickham. Appraisers—Gunnar Archard, John Jones.

1733-4, Jan. 25. Fearman, Hannah, of Chesterfield, Burlington Co., widow; will of. Children—Jonathan, David, Hannah, Mary and Alice. Daughter Patience Fearman, residue. Executor—son Jonathan. Witnesses—Isaac Horner and Eleanor Horner. Proved May 4, 1734. Lib. 3, p. 418.

1734, April 27. Inventory, £43.6; made by Isaac Horner and Robert Taylor.

1744, Nov. 14. Fellgate, Samuel, of Salem Co. Int. Adm'x, Gunlow Fellgate, widow, of Pennsneck. Bondsmen—William and Andrew Barckleson. Witnesses—Wm. Pennock, Danl. Mestayer, of the same place, yeoman. Lib. 5, p. 91.

1744, May 5. Inventory (£41.18.8) of Samuel Felgate of Penns Neck, tailor. Appraisers—John Eaton, Samuel Whitehorne.

1732, May 16. Fenton, Enoch, of Town and Co. of Burlington, butcher; will of. Children—Enoch, Eleazer, Vesta and Rachel, all under age. Brother and sister—Jeremiah and Elizabeth Fenton. By agreement am to receive an estate in fee from John Finney and Mary his wife of lands in Springfield. Real and personal estate. Executors—wife, Rachel and friend Samuel Scattergood, latter to be guardian of children. Witnesses—Sam'l Bustill, Jos. Rockhill, Joseph Rose, John Jones. Proved Sept. 2, 1732. Lib. 3, p. 212.

1732, Aug. 31. Inventory of the personal estate, £542.7.2½; made by Silas Crippin and George Eyre. Includes bonds of Benjamin Crispin, Edward Barton, Samuel Bunting, Benjamin Barets, John Kembel, Joseph Meneer, Samuel Gaskill, Joshua Owen and Benjamin Merriot; bills of Bartholomew Gibson, Mathew Wilson, Philip Thomas, Thomas Johnson, John Perkins, William Hews, Thomas Framton, Anne Rutter, Jonathan Wright, Peter Ranton, Peter Woolf, Joseph Smith, John Simons, John Borradaile, Thomas Henry, Thomas Kembel, William Boulding, Edward R. Price, John Neal, Peter Bishop. Book debts: John Lyons, Daniel Smith, Jun'r, Benjamin Wheat, Richard Yeo, Peter Bishop, John Parsons, Rowland Ellis, John Bowlby, David Lippingate, Isaac Pearson, Matthias Gardiner, Silas Crispin, Robert Storks, Caleb Raper, Thomas Henry, Benjamin Kembel, Thomas Hunlock, Esq., Widow Allison, Peter Bard, Esq., Phelix Cartne, Widow Bass, John Gilbert, Thomas Shaw, George Wright, Edward Pearce, Richard Smith, Sen'r, Jonathan Wright, Ralph Smith, Andrew Gallager, William Maxfield, William White, Daniel Smith, Sen'r, Joseph Welsh, James Moon, Edward Cogle, Jun'r, William Taylor, James Inskeep, Henry Dell, Philo Leeds, James Smart, Andrew Galloway, Thomas Russell, John Hogden, John Shinn, George Wilkoxen, Joseph Pearson, John Barton, Jonathan Scott, John Gibbs, Isaac Anthram, Francis Smith, John Mullen, James Streeton, Ebenezer Large, Richard Robison, William Cutler, Samuel Smith, Joseph Hewlings, John Kinard, Joseph Reeves, Caleb Emerson, Joseph Ridgway, Thomas Coleman, John Ogburn, Thomas Huntley, James Veree, Joseph Rockhill, Mary Hewlings, Parson Wagman, Jeremiah Fenton, Joseph Thomas, John Edwards, Widow Pidgon, Samuel Bustill, Esq., Samuel Butcher, Obediah Eldredge, Elizabeth Songhist, William Snowden, Elizabeth Presse, William Bickley, Solomon Smith, Edward Kembel, Matthew Wood, Thomas Butcher, Ralph Peart, John Allen, Esq., Peter Fern, James Killegrove, George Gess, Peter Merron, John Fennimore, Simon Nightingaile, Richard Smith, Jun'r, Joshua Raper, Catherine Smith, Negro Ned, Benjamin Butterworth, George Eyre, David Hogden, Joshua Woolstone, Daniel Hogden, Henry Clothier, George Saterthwate, David Rockhill, Thomas Shreve, George Willis, George Noble, Robert Wild, Charles French, William Pattison, James Handcock, Mary Blackham, James Tomson, Joseph Morton, Thomas Postgate, Thomas Ageman, Joshua Barker, Doctor Rodman, Robert Smith, John Nightingaile, Roger Merrick, Bartholomew Gibson, Joshua Owen, Robert Lard, Robert Hill, James Lippincott, William Lindaile.

1732, Dec. 1. Fenton, Jeremiah, of Northampton, Burlington Co., yeoman. Int. Inventory of the personal estate, £142.00.1; made by Joseph Woolston and Charles French.

1732, Dec. 9. Administration to Sarah Fenton, widow. Joseph Woolston, blacksmith, and Charles French, yeomen, fellow bondsmen. Lib. 3, p. 226.

1747, August 4. Fenton, John, of Freehold, Monmouth Co., innholder; will of. Wife, Mary executrix. Children—Robert, and Rachel Johnston. Witnesses—James Robinson, Robert Hood and John Nath'n. Hutchins. Proved October 21, 1747. Lib. E, p. 121.

1734, Sept. 26. Ferguson, John, of Trenton, Hunterdon Co., gentleman. Administration granted to Elizabeth Ferguson, of Trenton, the widow. Hunterdon Wills, 101 J.

1734, Nov. 13. Account of debts due: Dr. John Dagworthy, John Commings, Edward Redolphs Price, William Dun (a carpenter), John Edwards (a bricklayer), Ebenezer Pettey (a carpenter), Landrissa Baker, Elizabeth Ketcham, William Martin (taylor), Robert Schooley, Richard Lovett, James Trent, James Gary, Jacob Baillergeun, William Hough, Joseph Reed (merchant), Colonel Peter Bard, Francis Maybury, Colonel Daniel Cox, Enoch Anderson, Sr., James Tucker, Henry Worley (miller), James Gould, Jeremiah Foster, Francis Giffing, Nathaniel Russell, Joshua Anderson of Maidenhead, Doctor Josiah Patterson, James McBurney, Alexander Lockhart, Alexander Crague, Samuel Johnson, Hugh Mitchell, Christopher Romine, Edward Fisher, Daniel Horsey, John Curie, William Barraclift, Enoch Anderson, Jr., William Osborn, Abraham Dickson, Cornelius Ringo, James Abernathy, James Robinson, John Page, Robert Montgomery, Chamber, Sen'r, Ann Kinions, Mr. Roberts (schoolmaster), Dennis Boile, William Lander, Terrin Swiney, Nehemiah Howell, Mr. McKinley, Joseph Yard, David Dunbar, Benjamin Hough, John Osbourn, John Ackerman, Francis Gardiner, John Francis, William Pearson, Thomas Palmer, John Severns, Richard Loveland, Mary Johnson, Robert Major, William Snowden, Henry Bellergeane, Joseph Higbey, Widow Severns, William Spencer, John Hindshaw, Robert Wright, William Philips (smith), Mr. Anderson of Bristol, Samuel Bustill, Charles Clark, Margaret Richardson, Mr. Whitehead, Stacy Beeks, Elliakim Anderson, John Reeds (his son), Francis Costigan (attorney), Mr. Mott, Mr. Murry, John Nowlan, John Murffin, Peter Justice, Alexander Downey, Mr. M:kenley, John Conorow, Josiah Apleton, Joseph Kirkbride, Sr., Hugh Bowen, Samuel Atkins, Abraham Temple, John Reed of Maidenhead, Joseph Pearson of Maidenhead, Ralph Smith, Benjamin Brayle, William Eaton of Bucks, Daniel Bellergeane, Neal Leverston, Robert Blackwell, Even Eleven (cooper), Martha Harding, Jeremiah Burros, Randel J. Daniel, Captain Scuder, Jonathan Wright, John Axford, Jeremiah Anderson, Andrew Ellett, Benjamin Price, Caleb Carman, Titus Lemore, Zebulon Stout, John Anderson of Hopewell, Samuel Baker, Jeremiah Smith, Robert Sander, John Demer, Joshua Anderson, Sarah Pew, Widow Howell, William Merrell, Elizabeth Anderson, Joseph Price, Hugh (the schoolmaster at Reuben Pownell's), Thomas Burros, Richard Arnold, Abel Jenny, James McKains, Thomas Hough, William Dunam, Susannah Crimins, William Wardell, Elener Salter, Robert Allison, John Elliot, Rose Wood, John Everett, William Bell, John Riche, Robert Right, George Leagan, Jeremiah Foster, Samuel Coat, Joshua Anderson, James Allen, Thomas Moor, Thomas Palmer, John Ackerman, James Trent, Dunkin O Killian, John Porterfield, Mrs. Coats, Gallis Franiser, Samuel Cumer, Robert Spencer, Richard Harris, Sarah Roger, Thomas Moor, Jonas Wood, Andrew Adams, William Laning (blacksmith), Bartholomew Corwain, Ann Pidgeon, Thomas Linter (carpenter), Cornelius Sleeht, Thomas Fling (glazier), John Carter, Christopher Acklin, John Colom, Mr. Hay, Robert Coleman, Timothy Dowlin,

John Cross, Charles Ore, Simon Ackers, Alburtus Ringo, William Forster, Charles Ryle, Martha Cousens, Hugh Flanengham, John Woolard, Elisha Burd, Michael Blessed, Henry Orlocker, William Reed of Hopewell, Sarah Parris (or Sarris), Richard Merrill, Thomas Reed of Hopewell, Edward Shepard, John Warberton, William Morris, Thomas Cross, Edmund Bainbridge, William Simons, Jonathan Stout, Abraham Wilds (tanner), James Bell, Captain John Anderson, Isaac Anderson, Mrs. Hatch, David Price, Mrs. Jenney of Pensilvania, William Bile, Widow Anderson of Maidenhead, James Chamber, Ralph Hart, John Anderson (Joshua's son), Robert Laning.

1734, Nov. 13. Account of goods of Doctor John Furguson in hands of Elizabeth, his widow, £8.8.10, includinga gun, one Bible and 2 other books. Made by Jos. De Cow and Samuel Johnson.

1732, Dec. 23. Fetters, Thomas, of Salem, Salem Co., yeoman. Int. Adm'r, Erasmus Fetters, cordwainer. Bondsmen—Richard Haynes, weaver, and Nathan Mering, tailor. All of same place. Witnesses—Jno. Jones, Clemt. Hall, Robt. Hart. Lib. 3, p. 224.

1747, April 2. Field, Jeremiah, Sen'r, of Piscataway, Middlesex Co. Int. Inventory of personal estate (£443.14), incl. 4 negroes; made by William Olden and Isaac Dye.

1747, May 4. Bond of son, Jeremiah Field, yeoman, as administrator. Benjamin Field, yeoman, fellow bondsman. Witness—John Lyell. Lib. E, p. 34.

1745, Dec. 13. Field, John, of Hopewell, Hunterdon Co., within the Corporation of Trenton, yeoman; will of. "Being very sick." Wife, Sarah. Children—Daniel, Nathaniel, Isaac, Elizabeth, Providence, and Seth. Son, Seth, residuary legatee and executor. Seth to take care of testator's son John. Witnesses—Andrew Foster, Roger Woolverton and Andrew Smith. Proved August 11, 1746. Lib. 5, p. 259.

1746, June 7. Inventory (£180.2.7) includes 3 guns and 3 swords. Made by Andrew Smith and Roger Woolverton.

1749, Oct. 2. Field, Joseph, of Middletown township, Monmouth Co., yeoman; will of. Wife, Mercy. Sister Charity's son, Joseph Heyt. Sister Jamimee's two sons, Thomas and William Betts. Brother-in-law, Joseph Newton, who has children. "My beloved child, Mary Lawrence Campbell, daughter of John and Mary Campbell, both deceased." Brother, Thomas Field, who has children. William Field, son of brother Thomas. Executors—wife, brother-in-law Richard Betts, John Bowne, Justice, and Richard Fitz Randolph. Witnesses—Pr. Le Conte, William Lawrence Carpenter, Henrich Gugluts, Rachel Wooley, Margaret Lawrence. Proved Nov. 3, 1749. Lib. E, p. 361

1749, Nov. 15. Richard Betts, of Newtown, New York, renounced right of executorship before Joseph Sackett, of Queens County, New York.

1749, Nov. 29. Inventory of the estate, £160.10.6; made by Elias Covenhoven and John Tipple.

1749-50, Jan. 29. Mercy Field, executrix, Quaker, affirmed.

1749-50, Feb. 2. Richard FitzRandolph, executor, Quaker, affirmed.

1749-50, Jan. 30. Inventory of goods the widow had when she became Joseph Field's wife, £138.12.0, including negro men Norris (£40), and Pero (£50). Made by Elias Covenhoven and John Tipple.

1749-50, Jan. 31. John Bowne declines to serve as an executor.

1732, 12th day, 2nd mo. (Apr.). Field, Nathaniel, of Chesterfield, Burlington Co. Int. Inventory of the personal estate, £56.9.6; made by John Middleton and William Thorne. Includes Bible, and debts of Benjamin Wright, John Pitman, John Bunting, Francis Fowler, Nathaniel Warner, William Thorn and Nathan Allen.

1732, April 14. Bond of administration of Thomas Betts. William Thorne, yeoman, fellow bondsman, both of Nottingham. Lib. 3, p. 190.

1733, March 17. Account. Payments to Joseph Rockhill, Margaret Carre, Rob't Chapman, Francis Fowler, John Middleton, Joseph Borden, John Tantum, Joshua Raper, Anne Clothier, Elizabeth Fowler, John Tantum, Jr., Elizabeth Coan, Sam'l Rogers, John Anderson, Ambrose Field, Elias Smith, William Thorn, Preserved Brown, Jr., Sam'l Shords, Benj'n Doughty, John Bunting, Richard Oskimm, Benja. Cheshire, James Johnson.

1748, July 22. Fish, Casper, of Waterford, Gloucester Co., yeoman; will of. Sons—Michael (to have 16 acres of my land purchased of the heirs of Benjamin Wood, fronting on Delawar River, whereon he lives); Elias (not 21 and to be apprenticed). Daughters—Rebeca, Mary and Eleanor. Sons John and Isaac. Sole executor, son John. Witnesses—Saml. Spicer, James Willard, Israel Fish. Affirmed 3 Sept., 1748. Lib. 5, p. 511.

1748, Sept. 1. Inventory (£153.04.6) includes gun, sword and holbert, and boat. Appraisers—Saml. Parr, James Willard.

1748, Oct. 21. Fish, Michael, of Waterford, Gloucester Co., yeoman; will of. Daughter, Martha, at 21, to have land; not 10 yrs. of age. Daughters—Deborah and Elizabeth, when 18. Executor—brother, John Fish. Witnesses—Benjamin Wood, Samuel Spicer, Israel Fish. Proved 28 Dec., 1748. Lib. 6, p. 24.

1748, Dec. 26. Inventory (£45.9.1) includes bonds of Matlock, Andarson, Hom. Appraisers—Saml. Farr, Benjamin Wood.

1747, May 14. Fish, William, of Somerset County; will of. Son, John, plantation in Amwell, when of age, paying his brother William, £20, when of age. Son John, when of age. Daughters—Sarah, Anne, Rebecca, Mary and Elizabeth. An unborn child. Five daughters under age. Wife, Mary, and friend James Clark (Quaker), executors. Witnesses—Ephraim Marritt, Hannah Runyan and Edmund Beakes. Proved June 2, 1747. (Hunterdon Wills), Lib. 5, p. 513.

1747, May 29. Inventory (Capt. Wm. Fish's Inventory), £379.14.0, including 2 large Bibles, one gun, Captain's pike, powder and powder horn. Made by Edmund Beakes and Aaron Hewes.

1742, Dec. 3. Fithian, Jonathan, of Salem County. Int. Adm'r, Jonathan Fithian, Junior. Eldest son, of Cohansey, farmer. Bondsman, Jonathan Fithian, Esq., of said County. Witnesses—Wm. Barker, Chas. O Neill. Lib. 4, p. 378.

1742, Nov. 23. Inventory, £180; made by John Woolsey, Jeremiah Foster.

1737, Aug. 3. Fithian, Jonathan, of Cohansey, Salem County, Esq.; will of. Wife, Sarah. Sons—Jonathan to have 100 acres near the head of Cohansey, bought of Col. Daniel Cox; also 50 acres purchased of Benjamin Salyer; David, 100 acres near the head of Cohansey, purchased of Cornelius Newkirk; also my new dwelling with all my other tenements, lands, marshes, etc. Daughters—Phebe (wife of Wil-

liam Stratton), Sarah (wife of Thomas Baitman). Executors—wife and son, David Fithian. Witnesses—Daniel Wescott, William Bradford, Izrael Petty, John Jones. Proved 29 April, 1743. Lib. 5, p. 12.
1743, April 18. Inventory (£445.10.6) includes guns, swords, cattle, sheep, swine, leather and shoemaker's tools. Appraisers—William Bradford, John Jones.

1733, Aug. 21. Fithian, Josiah, Esq., of Cohansey, Salem Co., guardian of Thomas Brown, son of Thomas Brown, late of the north side of Cohansey, yeoman, and Anna his wife also deceased. Witnesses—John Prutten, Joseph Gouldin. Lib. 3, p. 366.

1741, March 31. Fithian, Josiah, of Cohansey, Salem Co., Esq.; will of. Wife, Mary, remaining part of estate of Nicholas Johnston, deceased, during life and then same to go to my daughter, Mary Fithian. Son, Jeremiah, land in Greenwich at the lower end of Spring Run, N. W. to Pine Mount Run, (excepting 4 acres for my son Joseph Fithian), beginning at the upper corner of my land by James Gould's lotts; also 10 acres of salt Marsh joining Samuel Fithian; also land at the bridge on Farny Branch; also salt marsh (30 acres) joining Cohansey Creek. Son, Samuel Fithian, remainder of land and marsh appertaining to Hadgy Neck; also the house and lot in Greenwich, he paying what money is due to Samuel Fithian, the elder. Son, Joseph Fithian, land on Town Branch; also salt marsh (20 acres) joining Jeremiah's; also land and marsh from James Dickson's line to Spring Branch, along the land of Nicholas Gibbon, Esq., Thomas Walling, William Watson and James Dickson, deceased, up the course against Joseph Reny house; also marsh below Mulberry Point. Daughters—Ester Fithian and Hannah Selley. Executor—son, Samuel Fithian, and Elias Cotting to assist. Witnesses—James Johnson, Abraham Reeves, James Reeves. Proved 24 April, 1741. Lib. 4, p. 284.
1741, April 13. Inventory, £281.16.6; made by Abraham Reeves, John Rementon.

1749, May 29. Fithian, Matthias, of Cumberland Co., carpenter; will of. Son, Humphry, sole executor, and to have the plantation I now live on. Personal estate divided among rest of nine children and Hannah Mills, daughter of Isaac Mills of the County aforesaid. Son, Daniel, deceased. Sons William and Ephraim to be put out to learn a trade. Witnesses—Obadiah Wood, Joseph Fithian, Jno. Bee. Proved 24 Oct., 1749. Lib. 6, p. 340.
1749, Oct. 24. Inventory, £177.19.08; made by Maskell Ewing, Thos. Maskell.

1732, Jan. 27. Fithian, William, of Greenwich, Salem Co., carpenter; will of. Brothers, Samuel and Mathias Fithian, executors, and to have estate equally. Witnesses—Susannah Pearce, John Green, Arthur Cannon. Proved 16 Feb., 1732. Lib. 3, p. 268.
1732-3, Feb. 15. Inventory, £116.19.11; made by Saml. Davis, John Green.

1734-5, Jan. 25. Fitzgerald, (Fitzgarill) Edward, of Salem Co. Int. Adm'r, John Mills. Bondsman, Joseph Simkens. Both of said County, yeoman. Lib. 3, p. 435.
1734, Feb. 6. Inventory (£59.13.8) "of Edward Jeril (Fitzgerald),

Cohansey, carpenter. Deceased at the hous of John Millis, in Cohansey." Appraisers—Isaac Mills, Matthias Fithian.

1735, Feb. 11. Account. Moneys pd. to Richd. Butcher, David Platts, Peter Long, Jas. Carruthers, Ebenezer Miller, Peter Turner, John Brick, Thos. Slatham, Jas. Dickson, Aaron Mulford, Danl. Mestayer, Wm. Watson, Jonathan Slatham, Alexd. Smith, Philip Vickers, Thos. Berryman, Jon. Bacon, Henry Pierson, Jon. Fitzpatrick, Chas. Fordham, Justice Fithian.

1731, Dec. 13. FitzRandolph, Benjamin, of New Brunswick, Middlesex Co., joiner; will of. Daughter, Sarah, at 21. Real and personal estate. Executor—brother, Samuel FitzRandolph. Witnesses—Thomas Fleming, Elizabeth Coddington, John Cholwell. Proved Dec. 16, 1731. Lib. B, p. 241.

1743, July 13. FitzRandolph, Benjamin, of Six Mile Run, Middlesex Co., yeoman; will of. Real and personal estate. Wife, Margaret, executrix and sole legatee. Witnesses—Peter Soullard, John Williams, Walter Burnett. Proved Nov. 27, 1746. Lib. D, p. 439.

1750, May 7. FitzRandolph, Edward, Sr., of Woodbridge, Middlesex Co.; will of. In 44th year of his age. Wife, Phebe, remainder of legacy that now lies in the hands of her father's executors. Sons—James and Edward, both under age. Five daughters under age, but no names given. Nephew, Edward Thorn, eldest son of my sister Mary Jackson, at 22 years. Executors—brothers Nathaniel and Hartshorne FitzRandolph. Witnesses—William Brown, Esek Fitzrandolph, Nugent Kelly. Proved June 18, 1750. Lib. E, p. 420.

1748, 4th mo. (June), 23d, FitzRandolph, Hugh, of Perth Amboy, Middlesex Co., shipwright; will of. Brothers and sisters—Richard, Edward, Robert, Nathaniel, Esek, Hartshorne, and Mary. Mary's portion in trust for her children. Real and personal estate. Executors—brothers Richard, Edward and Nathaniel. Witnesses—U. Parker, Edward James, Henry Dennis. Proved June 25, 1748. Lib. E, p. 270.

——— ,——— —. FitzRandolph, Isaac, of Monmouth County. Hannah Fitz Randolph (signed Hanah Randolf), asks that Samuel Dove be appointed administrator. Lib. E, p. 451.

1750, August 23. Bond of Samuel Dove (brother of widow), of Monmouth County, yeoman. John Cox, of same County, fellow bondsman.

1741, Jan. 22. FitzRandolph, Joseph, of Woodbridge, Middlesex Co. Int. Administration granted to Samuel FitzRandolph, Jun'r, the father. Lib. C, p. 470.

1741, 5th mo. (July), 9d, FitzRandolph, Joseph, of Woodbridge, Middlesex Co., yeoman; will of. Children—Nathaniel, Asher, Jeremiah, Joseph, Margaret, Sarah, all under age. Land bought of Samuel Dennis, April 21, 1737, joining land of Solomon Hunt; land bought of Samuel Alling, joining Edward Freeman and ——— Vangual; land in possession of widow Isabella Randolph; lands purchased of Moses Rolph and Job Wright at Rahway, Oct. 16, 1736. Monthly Meeting at Woodbridge, £6. Executors—wife Abigail, friends Jacob FitzRandolph and Joseph Shotwell, Jun'r. Witnesses—Jonathan Moore, Samuel Moffat, Anee Moffatt. Proved Aug. 24, 1741.

1741, Aug. 24. Joseph Shotwell, executor, refused to act. Lib. C, p. 429.

1749, Jan. 25. FitzRandolph, Joseph, of Piscataway, Middlesex Co.; will of. Children—Thomas, Ephraim, Joseph, Grace Manning, Rebeckah Mathes, Prudence, Paul, Jeremiah and Sarah, at 18 years. Grandson—Jacob FitzRandolph. Baptist Congregation in Piscataway. Real and personal estate. Executors—son Joseph and friend Isaac Stelle. Witnesses—John Van Bueren, Benjamin FitzRandolph, Benja. Stelle. Proved May 4, 1750. Lib. E, p. 394.

1738, Jan. 16. FitzRandolph, Sarah, of Middlesex Co., widow. Int. Adm'r, John FitzRandolph. Lib. C, p. 236.

1745, July 24. FitzRandolph, Thomas, of Piscataway, Middlesex Co., weaver; will of. Children—David, Jonathan, Dinah Dunham, Luranna Whitehead. Executors—Jonathan Dunn and Azariah Dunham. Witnesses—David Dunham, Daniel Dunham, Ruth Dunham. Proved Oct. 25, 1745. Lib. D, p. 343.

1745, Oct. 24. Inventory (£46.5.11) includes bond from David Fitzrandolph; made by Phinehas Dunn and Bennajah Dunn.

1746, May 27. Fitzsimmons, Maynard, of Gloucester Co. Int. Adm'r, Isaac Alberson, of Newton Township, Gloucester Co., yeoman. Fellow bondsman—Jacob Alberson, yeoman, Gloucester, Edwd. Rs. Price, Jo. Scattergood. Gloucester Wills, 332 H.

1744, Oct. 12. Fleet (Vliet), Geertie, of Six Mile Run, Somerset Co., (relict of John Fleet, late of said place); will of. All real and personal estate to grandson, John Fleet, of said place, yeoman. Daughters Maritie (wife of Adrian Hageman, of same place, yeoman); Geertie (wife of Simon Wyckoff, of said place, yeoman); Rebecca (widow of Adrian TenEyk, late of Reading's Town in Hunterdon Co.); Sarah (wife of Johannes Voorhees at the Fish Kills in Dutchess County, N. Y.). Grand-daughter, Dircktie, (wife of Theodorus Snedeker of Kackiat, Orange Co., N. Y.). Executor—Simon Wyckoff. Witnesses—Willem Williamson, Laurens Vankleef, Joseph Vankleef. Proved 6 Oct., 1750. Lib. E, p. 455.

1741, July 2. Fletcher, James, of Town and Co. of Burlington, yeoman; will of. Sisters—Lucie, Mary and Hester Fletcher. Friend, George Colling, and friend, David Hildreth, whom I make sole executor. Real and personal estate. Witnesses—John Flintham, Benjamin Farington, Jno. Ditchfield. Lib. 4, p. 295.

1733, Oct. 29. Fling, Morris, of Salem Co., yeoman. Int. Adm'r, John Wright. Bondsman—Ranier Gregory. Both of said County. Witnesses—John Norton, Danl. Mestayer. Lib. 3, p. 362.

1743, Dec. 6, Flower, William, of Town and Co. of Burlington, laborer. Int. Administration granted to Oddy Brock. Joseph Scattergood and Joseph Hewlings, fellow bondsmen. All of City of Burlington. Lib. 5, p. 7.

1743, Dec. 6. Inventory, £15.00.6; made by Joseph Hewlings and Jos. Scattergood. Includes bond from Sam'l Hunt to Dan'l Smith in trust for Martha Flower, dated May 18, 1740.

1748, July 24. Floyd, Richard, of Deptford, Gloucester Co.; will of. Legacies to William Ingland (my servant lad and to have his freedom), and to Elizabeth Sell. Brother, Walter Floyd. Cousins—William Floyd and Margat Mearrady. Executors—Brother, Walter Floyd, and Thomas Kimsey. Witnesses—Edward Willson, Thomas Reves, Sarah Reves. Affirmed 10 Aug., 1748. Lib. 6, p. 104.

1748, Aug. 9. Inventory, £184.15.1; made by James Whital, Edward Wilson.

1748, Aug. 16. Renunciation of Thomas Kimsey, executor. Witnesses—Henry Stephens, John Mickle.

1736, Aug. 30. Flyng, Michael, of Salem Co. Int. Adm'r, Robert Vance. Bondsman—Benjamin Acton, Esq. Both of said County. Witnesses—Thos. Parke, Danl. Mestayer. Lib. 4, p. 108.

1736, Aug. 30. Inventory, £6.4; made by Lewis Morris, Thos. Parke.

1737, Dec. 24. Fogg, Daniel, of Alloways Creek, Salem Co.; will of. Wife, Anne. Sons—Joseph (a piece of my plantation (1 acre) where his house is built; also 10 acres adjoining Matthew Morrison); Daniel (rest of my land and plantation). Sons Samuel and Erasmus Fogg, when 21, and Charles. Daughters—Hannah, Lucy, Sarah, Margaret and Ann. Executors—wife and son. Daniel. Witnesses—William Penton, Sr., William Penton, Jr., Richard Bradford. Proved 27 Nov., 1745. Lib. 5, p. 255.

1745, 9 mo. (Nov.), 22 da. Inventory, £189.16; made by Benj. Holmes, Saml. Thompson.

1732-3, Jan. 30. Fogg, Samuel, of Salem Co., yeoman. Int. Adm'r, Samuel Fogg. Bondsmen—Edward Quinton, John Patrick. All of said County, yeoman. Witnesses—John Den, Will Tyler. Lib. 3, p. 288.

1732-3, Jan. 22. Inventory (£143.8.9½), at Alloways Creek, includes cattle, horses, sheep, molasses, hides, leather, shoemaker tools. Appraisers—Will Tyler, John Den.

1739, Jan. 15. Folkertze, Phillippus, of Somerset Co., yeoman; will of. Wife, Mettie. Sons—Folkert, Johannis, Phillippus, Joseph and Dirck (who is to have the home land). Daughters—Rebecka, Annatie. Executors—Brother, Dirck Folkertse, son Johannis, and son-in-law Cornelis Middelswart. Witnesses—Folkert Rapalie, Dirrik Rappaljee. Peter Leffertze. Proved 17 June, 1740. Lib. C, p. 342-345.

1740, June 19. Renunciation of Derrick Fulkers, Somerset Co., as executor. Witnesses—George Brice, Richard Folkers.

1749, March 29. Folsom, Israel, of Piscataway, Middlesex Co., yeoman; will of. Children—Sarah (wife of Thomas Reder, of Bethlehem, (taylor), Mary and Rachel. Lands purchased of Peter Winant and widow Sarah Hull. Executors—daughter Mary, and Robert Matthews of Piscataway. Witnesses—John Burnet, Absalom Wiggins, Charles Wilson. Proved April 15, 1749. Lib. E, p. 293.

1749, May 2. Folsom, Sarah, of Piscataway, Middlesex Co., widow; will of. Children—Joseph and Trustrum Hull, Anne (wife of John Skilinan), Elizabeth (wife of John Clawson), and Eunice (wife of Phineas Dunn). Grandsons—Moses, son of Moses FitzRandolph; Benjamin, son of Jeremiah Dunn; Mesheek, son of Benjamin Hull; Benjamin, son of Jacob Hull. Granddaughter, Zerviah, daughter of Mulford Martin. Executor—son-in-law, Jeremiah Dunn. Witnesses—

Benjamin FitzRandolph, Rachel FitzRandolph, Jonathan Dunham. Proved May 22, 1749. Lib. E, p. 302.

1749, May 19. Inventory (£181.2.9) includes bonds from Israel Folsom, Moses FitzRandolph and Thos. Walker. Made by Edmund Dunham and Azariah Dunham.

1723, 14th day, 4th mo. (June). Folwell, Nathan, of Mansfield, Burlington Co., weaver; will of. Wife, Sarah, sole executrix. Children—Nathan, John, George, William, Mary, Hannah and Elizabeth, all under age. Lands bought of William and Abraham Brown. Witnesses—Gervas Hall, Sarah Hall, Tho. Scattergood. Proved Feb. 20, 1731. Lib. 3, p. 180.

1733, April 30. Fontine, (Fontyne), Charles, of Somerset Co., yeoman; will of. Wife, Eleanor. Oldest son, Charles, land upon Raritan River, Somerset Co., "adjoining where my son Johannes now lives, which joins land of my son Abraham." Other children—Maritje, Leah, Reynier, Jacob. Executors—Sons Charles, Reynier, Johannes, Jacob, Abraham, and son-in-law, Cornelius Suydam. Witnesses—Chrisstofell Probasco, Adam Johnson, Wm. Ouke.

1733, April 30. Codicil. Son, Abraham, to live on plantation one year after death of testator. Same witnesses. Proved 17 May, 1734. Lib. E, p. 508.

1742-3, March 1. Fontine, Charles, of Somerset Co., yeoman; will of. Wife, Catherine. Home plantation on Raritan River. Brothers and sisters—Rynier, John, Jacob, Abraham, Mary (wife of Cornelius Suydam) and Lea (wife of John Smock). Legacies to mother, Lena Fontine, after wife's re-marriage or decease; also to Eleanor Buys and her daughter Sythee (minor). Executors—wife, Catherine, and brothers John, Jacob and Abraham Fontine. Witnesses—Hendrick Smock, William Williamson, Wm. Ouke.

1749, Sept. 2. Codicil. Wife, Catherine, to receive increased legacy and to pay £125 above the amount stated in will to Eleanor Buys, now wife of Jacques Fontine. Witnesses—Wm. Ouke, Lena Suydam, Maria Suydam. Proved 29 Nov. and 2 Dec., 1749. Lib. E, p. 353.

1750, Oct. 5. Fontine, Charles. (See Fountayn, Charles).

1749, Sept. 4. Fontine, (Vantine), Reneir, of Perth Amboy, Middlesex Co., yeoman; will of. Wife, Ghirthie. Children—Charles, Rineir, John, Abraham, Leanah and Sarah, all under age. Grandson, Reneir. Real and personal estate. Executors—brother Abraham Vantine, and brother-in-law John Borrum (Booram). Witnesses—Luycas Schenck, William Dye, Ste'n Warne. Proved Oct. 21, 1749. Lib. E, p. 336.

1749, Oct. 20. Inventory, £126.13.6; made by Luycas Schenck and William Dey.

1749, Dec. 10. Additional inventory amounting to £39.3.9.

1759, March 12. Account of Abraham Fontyn, executor, £265.6.6, showing payments to John Booram, Jacob Wykoff, Stephen Warne, Charity Fontine, Lewis Perce, Charles Fontine. Bond of Barent Wageman.

1759, March 15. Account of John Booram, executor, showing payments to Doct'r VanBuren, John Waller, Humphrey Mount, Thomas Applegate, Isaac Voorhies, Paul Miller, Esq., Thomas Doty, Jos. Hewlett, John Piat, Luke Smock, John Applegate, B. Legrange, Esq., Catherine Schuyler, Francis Costigan, Esq., Elisha Parker, Esq., John Romyne, Sam'll Weston,

James Reed, Philip Kearny, Esq., John Pridmore, Joris Brinkerhoof, Jacob Vandevanter, Gilbert Barton, Jacob Wykoff, Mathias Johnson, Thomas Montgomery, Just. Nude, Luke Schenck, Wm. Dye, Rynier Fontine, Jun'r, Charity Fontine, Thomas Doty, Charles Fontine. "4 gal. wine, and 1 gal. rum" for the funeral.

1749, May 7. Foort, Roger, of New Hanover, Burlington Co., yeoman; will of. Wife, Anne. Children—John, Joseph, Joan, Hester, Edith, Roger and Marmaduke. Real and personal estate. Executors—son Marmaduke, and friend John Monro. Witnesses—Edward Weaver, Francis Shinn, John Burr, Jun'r. Lib. 6, p. 47.

1749, May 13. Inventory, £138.12.2; made by Aaron Robins and John Croshaw.

1750, Jan. 24. Account of Marmaduke Fort, having paid debts to Thomas Price, Nathaniel Thomas, William Buddell, Solomon Shinn, Edward Weaver, John Croshaw, John Monrow, Henry Cooper, James Shinn, Hope Atkinson, Julius Ewan, Robert Farrell, Jonathan Taylor, James Southwick, William Fox, Thomas Allinson, William Robinson, Casper Horner, George Briggs, Edward Gaskill, Thomas Shinn, John Burr, Jun'r, Thomas Conarro, James Wills, Jonathan Thomas.

1736, Nov. 9. Forbes, John, of Monmouth Co. Int. Adm'r, Andrew Johnston, of Perth Amboy. William Skinner, of same city, fellow bondsman. Witnessed by Lawre Smyth. Lib. C, p. 127.

1736, Nov. 13. Inventory (£210.13.9) includes silver watch and chain, gold hair ring, silver spurs and buckles, gowns, cassocks, scarves, wigs, hats, silk, worsted and thread stockings, gloves and pumps, snuff box, mail-pillion, negro man (£50); due from Congregation of St. Peter's Church in Freehold, £22.10.0; from the Congregation of St. Paul's Church in Shrewsbury. Made by John Morris, William Nichols, William Madock.

1734, Aug. 16. Force, Benjamin, of Woodbridge, Middlesex Co., yeoman; will of. Children—Thomas, Benjamin (living in New England), Charity Freeman, and Hannah (wife of John Noe). Grandsons—Henry and Thomas Palmer Force, sons of son Thomas. Lands formerly belonging to William Bunn, joining lands of Joseph Bloomfield, John Noe, Jun'r, John Morris, John Wilkison; land on Rahway meadows joining Daniel Brittain, John Jaquashies, John Dillies, John Trueman; land purchased of Hugh Marsh, which he bought in 1670; lands joining Daniel Thorp, Jonathan Dillies, Jonathan Bishop. Executors—friends Jacob Thorn, Ebenezer Johnson and John Noe, Jun'r. Witnesses—J. Stevens, John Bishop, Thomas Force, Jun'r. Proved Nov. 30, 1734. Lib. B, p. 580.

1736, June 5. Force, Thomas, of Woodbridge and Raway, Middlesex Co. Int. Adm'x, Mary Force, his widow. Jonathan Freeman, fellow bondsman. Lib. C, p. 111.

1742, Sept. 30. Ford, Nathaniel, of Morris Co., joiner; will of. Executors to sell house and land at Aquackamung, Essex Co., purchased of Gerret Debo. Wife, Mary, executrix. Eldest son, Nathaniel. Son, John. Daughter, Joan. Son, James. Trustee—Joseph Bartram. Witnesses—Jacob Mead, Martin Berry, Poulus Berry. Proved 27 March, 1745.

1744-5, March 7. Inventory (£56.12.6) includes 2 English Bibles, Dutch Testament, gun and sword. Appraisers—Philip Schuyler, Peter Post.

1745, March 27. Letters testamentary granted to Mary Lock, late Mary Ford, executrix. Lib. 5, p. 110.

1731, April 19. Ford, Thomas, of Chester, Burlington Co., yeoman. Int. Elizabeth Ford, widow, requests that administration be granted to such person as the Judge of the Prerogative Court shall appoint. Witnesses—Robert Dennis, Mahlon Stacy.

1731, April 26. Adm'r, Thomas Coles, of Gloucester Co., yeoman. Joseph Rockhill, innkeeper, of Burlington, fellow bondsman. Lib. 3, p. 100.

1731, May 10. Inventory, £88.2; made by Joseph Heritage and Thomas Hackney. Includes Bible and negro boy.

1732, Feb. 27. Account. Paid executor of Isaac Blanchard, John Fordham and Hannah his wife, Edw'd Rudolph Price, John Bowne.

1740, May 5. Foredam (Fordam), Charles, of Greenwich, Salem Co., cordwainer. Int. Adm'x, Elizabeth Foredam, widow. Bondsmen—Nicholas Gibbon, Annias Sayres. Both of same place. Witnesses—John Swinney, Dan. Mestayer. Lib. 4, p. 235.

1740, June 12. Inventory (£133.17.4) includes cattle, sheep, swine, 13 acres of winter wheat, sole leather and shoemaker's tools. Appraisers—Ananias Sayre, Thos. Waithman.

1741, Dec. 31. Forman, Aaron, of Freehold, Monmouth Co., trader; will of. Wife, Ursilla. Children—George (eldest son, under age), Lewis, Andrew, Robert, Priscilla, Lydia and Phebe. Executors—wife, brothers Jonathan and John Forman, brothers-in-law Samuel Craig and William Madock. Witnesses—Samuel Throckmorton, Samuel Leonard, Jr., Ambrose Stille. Proved Feb. 12, 1741. Lib. C, p. 479.

1746, Sept. 30. Forman, Ezekiel, of Upper Freehold, Monmouth Co., yeoman; will of. Wife, Elizabeth. Farm bought of Richard Brittain. Children—Samuel (eldest son), Thomas, Aaron, Mary, Hannah and Elizabeth. Executors—wife, brother Jonathan Forman, brother-in-law Daniel Seabrook, and friend Elisha Lawrence, Esquire. Witnesses—Jemes Tapscott, George Danser, John Chasey, William Madock. Proved October 22, 1746. Lib. D, p. 421.

1746, Oct. 28. Elisha Lawrence declines to act as executor.

1746, Oct. 28. Inventory (£831.9.0) includes servant man, 2 negro girls, 2 old guns. Made by James Tapscott and Edward Taylor.

1747, May 13. Forman, John, of Freehold, Monmouth Co., blacksmith; will of. Wife, Jane, to remain on home plantation, to which is added 366 acres of woodland adjoining land taken up by Sarah Reap and Samuel Leonard, until eldest son, John, is of age. Negro girl Jin. Eldest daughter, Mary, wife of Joseph Throckmorton. Son, Samuel, 198 acres in Upper Freehold, adjoining Dr. Johnstone and Joseph Holman, deceased. Daughters—Eleanor, Hannah, Margaret, Rebekah and Anne. Son, John, to continue the smith's trade. Original shares or rights of Propriety to be held until youngest child is of age. Executors to execute deed to Daniel Emans for saw mill and 100 acres. Executors—wife, brother Jonathan Forman, brothers-in-law William Madock and David Rhe, and son-in-law Joseph Throckmorton. Witnesses—Daniel Van Mater, Daniel Grandin and George Forman. (Name of David Rhe, as executor, crossed off in original). Codicil: November 12, 1748. A son, James, having been born since making will, provided for. Daughter, Mary, wife of Joseph Throckmorton. Agreement with Daniel Emans concerning saw mill and land cancelled. Witnesses—Gysbert Van Mater, Samuel Mount, William Madock, Junior. Proved March 9, 1748. Lib. E, p. 272.

1735-6, Feb. 7. Forman, Jonathan, of Chesterfield, Burlington Co., yeoman. Int. Inventory of the personal estate, £39.11.2; made by Isaac Horner and Robert Taylor.

1735, Feb. 26. Adm'x, Hannah James. Isaac Horner and Benjamin Horner, both of Chesterfield, fellow bondsmen.

Burlington Wills, 2821-24 C.

1748, Dec. 31. Forsman, Jacob, of Greenwich, Gloucester Co., yeoman; will of. Daniel (land whereon I live), William (my dwelling house and ground in Willins Town, New Castle County). Daughter, Ellenor, during life, profits of my house and land on Great Mantua Creek. Two-thirds of moveable estate to be divided among five daughters (not named). Executors—wife, Mary, and Alexr. Randall. Witnesses—John Pinyard, Sr, William Pinyard. Sworn and affirmed, 1 March, 1748. Lib. 6, p. 93.

1748-9, Feb. 2. Inventory (£150.15.8) includes cooper's and carpenter's tools. Appraisers—John Pinyard, Junior, Mathew Tomlinson.

1748, Dec. 23. Forster (Foster), Job (over 14 years old), of Newark, Essex Co. Bond of Ephraim Wheeler, of same place, yeoman, as guardian. Lib. E, p. 244.

1731, Feb. 21. Forster, Stephen, of Woodbridge, Middlesex Co., mariner. Int. Adm'rs, Margaret Forster and John Watson. Lib. B, p. 242.

1720, May 27. Forsyth, Matthew, of Chesterfield, Burlington Co.; will of. Son, John, and other children, mentioned but not named. Real and personal estate. Executors—wife, Rebecca, son John, and friend John Tantum. Witnesses—William Satterthwaite, Samuel Satterthwaite, Joseph Reckless. Proved Oct. 13, 1733. Lib. 3, p. 380.

1733, May 19. Inventory, £244.17.6; made by Isaac Horner and William Satterthwaite.

1749, Dec. 27. Forsyth, Matthew, of Chesterfield, Burlington Co., carpenter; will of. Wife, Marcy. Children—Joseph, Jesse (under age), Mary, Sarah, Rebecka; an expected child. Real estate in Bordentown. Executors—Isaac Ivins, brother John Forsyth. Witnesses—Samuel Satterthwaite, Wheeler Clark, Benjamin Busson. Proved March 22, 1749-50.

1749-50, March 1. Inventory, £176.6.11; made by John Buffin, Robert Rockhill.

1749-50, March 2. Isaac Ivins, one of the executors named, refuses to serve.

1766, Feb. 1. Account of the estate. Burlington Wills, 7953-64 C.

1732, Dec. 6. Foster, Andrew, of Hunterdon Co., weaver. Int. Inventory of estate (£15.07.0) includes mare purchased of Joseph Howell. Made by John Emley, Samuel Willson, Jr., and Daniel Doughty.

1733, May 6. Adm'rs, Samuel Willson, Sr., and Samuel Willson, Jr., of Hunterdon County, yeoman. Hunterdon Wills, 89 J.

1735, March 4. Foster, Benjamin, of Newark, Essex Co. Int. Johanna Foster, the widow, declines to administer. Witnesses—Joseph Wood, David Ogden.

1735, March 5. Adm'rs, John Shurmer and Samuel Shurmer, principal creditors, of New York, merchants. Andrew Hay, of Perth Amboy, fellow bondsman. Lib. C, p. 71.

1748, 28th day, 11th mo. (Jan.). Foster, Isaac, of Burlington Co.; will of. Children—Benjamin, Leason, John, Sarah, Mary and Esther, all under age. Real and personal estate. Thomas Middleton, of Nottingham, executor and guardian of all children. Witnesses—John Lawrence, Gisbert Hendricson, Samuel Sykes. Proved Jan. 4, 1748. Lib. 6, p. 29.

1748, 1st day, 12th mo. (Feb.). Inventory, £25.19.10½; made by John Lawrence and Samuel Sykes.

1748, Dec. 31. Foster, Job, of Newark, Essex Co., being upwards of 14 years, makes choice of Ephraim Wheeler, of Newark, to be his guardian. Lib. E, p. 244.

1748, April 12. Foster, Johanna, of Piscataway, Middlesex Co., widow. Int. Bond of Benjamin Foster, currier, as administrator on estate of his mother. Benjamin Bloomfield, of Woodbridge, tanner, fellow bondsman. Lib. E, p. 504.

1748, April 12. Inventory of personal estate, £78.4.4; made by Henry Langstaffe and Phineas Potter.

"Benjamin Foster doth depose that Johanna Foster made a will four years ago; she afterwards disposed of her lands and sent to Samuel Walker for her will to destroy it. Walker informed her it could not be found."

1750, April 14. Foster, John, of Newark, Essex Co. Int. Hannah Foster renounces the right to administer the estate of her husband in favor of Nathaniel Wheeler, Jun'r.

1750, April 19. Adm'r, Nathaniel Wheeler, Jun'r. James Nicholson, fellow bondsman. Lib. E, p. 504.

1739, June 4. Foster, Joseph, of Newark, Essex Co., weaver; will of. "Being administrator on the estate of my deceased father, Nathan Foster." Mother, Mary Foster. Sisters—Abigail Harrison, Mary, Sarah and Damanis Foster. Brother—Job Foster. Expected child. Land my father purchased of Ebenezer Lyon Jan. 28, 1724-5. Executors—wife, Bethiah, Benjamin Crane of Newark, and uncle Joseph Lyon. Witnesses—Samuel Beach, Israel Crane, Nehemiah Grumman. Proved Aug. 18, 1742. Lib. C, p. 533.

1742, Aug. 24. Inventory, £270.00.03; made by Christopher Wood and Benjamin Lyon.

1737, Dec. 22. Foster, Nathan, of Newark, Essex Co. Inventory of personal estate (£181.08.07), includes young negro, £20. Made by Stephen Browne, Christopher Wood.

1737, Feb. 25. Mary Foster, widow, renounces her right to administer in favor of her son.

1737, Feb. 27. Adm'r, Joseph Forster, the son. Ezekiel Crane, fellow bondsman. Lib. C, p. 190.

1747, Nov. 28. Foster, William, of Mannington, Salem Co., farmer;

will of. Daughters—Mary (eldest), Rebecca (second), and Elizabeth (youngest). Wife, Ann, sole executrix. Witnesses—Archibald Hamilton, James Deaton, Patrick Gray. Proved 12 Dec., 1747.
Lib. 5, p. 415.

1747, Dec. 11. Inventory, £94.8.4; made by Hance Bilderback, Jonathan Dickinson.

1750, Aug. 8. Account (signed "John Howman") shows moneys paid to Benj. Taylor (Vaneculaw's bond), Casper Sacks (bond), Rich. Gibbon, Matts. Holshon, Isaac Savoys, Jacob Coles, Lawrence Polson, Mercy Wilder, Joseph Hawks, Cha. Empson, Thomas Parsons, Eliza. Driver, Henry Peterson, Andrew Vaneman, Gabriel Galbo, Andrew Grace, Charles Dalbo, Robert Howard, Alexander King, Jacob Cornelison, Sarah Peterson, John Pitman, Martin Morton, Ezekiel Hardin, Thos. Clayton, Caleb Caplen.

1750, Oct. 5. Fountayn, Charles, of Somerset Co., son and heir of Jaquess Fountayn. Asks to show cause why the will of Jaques Fontayn should not be proved. Lib. E, p. 455.

1732, Jan. 16. Fourot, Henry, of Piscataway, Middlesex Co. Adm'x, Elizabeth Fourot. Lib. B, p 347.

1732, Oct. 27. Inventory, £161.0.0; made by Henry Langstaffe and ——.

1731, April 19. Fowler, John, Jun., of New Hanover, Burlington Co., blacksmith. Int. Inventory, £294.5.7; made by Richard Harrison and John King.

1731, Sept. 8. Adm'x, Elizabeth Fowler, widow. Joshua Wright and John Steward, yeomen, of same place, fellow bondsmen. Lib. 3, p. 137.

1732, Jan. 10. Account. Payments to John Arney, William Cook, Sam'l Wardell, Israel Pemberton, Samuel Rogers, William Chapman, Samuel Woodward, Joseph Myers, John Tantum (for 2 coffins), Wm. Beaks, James Hancock, John Schooley, Joseph Reckless, Rob't Chapman, Isaac Harrow, Eliza. Lawrence, Sam'l Embley, John Rumford, John Bunting, Geo. Satterthwaite, Wm. Woodward, Wm. Harrison.

1732, Nov. 24. Fox, Mary, of New Hanover, Burlington Co., widow; will of. Children—Thomas, William, Elizabeth and Lemuel, all under age. Dau., Elizabeth, to be placed with sister Sarah until she is 16. Real and personal estate. Executors—friends John Burr and John Crosman. Witnesses—William Davis, Samuel Edge and John Budd. Proved Dec. 23, 1732. Lib. 3, p. 232.

1732, Dec. 14. Inventory, £194.3.7; made by Preserved Brown and Samuel Curtis.

1744, Jan. 17. Fraser, William, of Providence, one of the Bahama Islands. Adm'r, John Watson, of Perth Amboy, principal creditor.
Lib. D, p. 227.

1742, April 28. Frazee, Benoni, of Borough of Elizabeth, Essex Co., carpenter; will of. Wife, Elizabeth. Children—Edward, George, Henry and Sarah, all under age. Land joining land of Richard Jones; land bought of Samuel Frazee, joining land of William Porter. Executors—Samuel Oliver, John Marsh, Jr., Jonathan Frazee of Woodbridge. Witnesses—John Rolph, Richard Jones, Samuel Scuder. Proved June 19, 1742. Lib. C, p. 511.

1731-2, Jan. 3. Frazee, Edward (Capt.), of Elizabeth Town, Essex Co.; will of. Eldest daughters—Elizabeth Crow, Sarah Craig and

Humus Heirs (Hears); three youngest daughters—Effiah, Mary, and Mercy Frazee. Side-saddle given to dau. Mary's mother, Marcy, by her deceased grandmother, Mary Olliver. Real and personal estate. Executors—friend Ezekiel Bloomfield, and brother-in-law David Olliver. Witnesses—John Terrill, John Frazee, Benony Frazee. Proved June 6, 1733. Lib. B, p. 410.

1733, June 14. Inventory, £102.17.05; made by Wm. Robison and Peter Simons.

1748, Jan. 10. Frazee, Elizabeth, widow of Benoni Frazee, of Essex Co.; nuncupative will of. John Lee, boatman, made oath 'that the decedent being very sick, and her daughter "a poor ailing child," she desired her to have the best bed,' etc. Lib. E, p. 232.

1748, Jan. 5. Inventory, £90.18.01½; made by Eliphalet Frasee and Richard Jones.

1748, Jan. 10. Adm'r, Jonathan Frasee, of Woodbridge, Middlesex Co. Michael Moore, fellow bondsman. Witness—John Lee. Lib. E, p. 232.

1749, Jan. 24. Account. Payments to John Lee, "for taking care of the children and making a cot for Edward," Wrightling Edwards, William Springer, Joseph Shotwell, Elizabeth Hampton, Samuel Oliver, David Hatfield, William Grant, John Mot, Richard Miles, Gershom Moores, Stephen Burres, Doctor Ichabod Burnet and John Marsh.

1740, Feb. 12. Frazee (Fraser), George, of the Borough of Elizabeth, Essex Co., gentleman; will of. Body to be interred near my father and mother on Staten Island. George, son of brother William Fraser, estate in Europe or America. Executors—Philip Kearny, of Middlesex Co., gent., and Elias Grazilier, of Elizabeth Town. Witnesses—Gershom Higgins, Joseph Hetfield, Tho. Jackman. Proved Feb. 25, 1740. Lib. C, p. 396.

1741, Aug. 26. Frazee, James, of the Borough of Elizabeth, Essex Co.; will of. Wife, Ann. Mother, Margrett Frazee. Three daughters under ten years of age; no names given. Margaret Chanders, at 18 years. Expected child. Executors—William Brown, John Skiner, Benoni Frazee. Witnesses—John Rolph, Richard Jones, Benjamin Crowell. Proved Sept. 26, 1741. Lib. C, p. 437.

1741-2, Jan. 28. Frazee, Margaret, of Woodbridge, Middlesex Co., widow; will of. Children—Eliphalet, Esther (wife of William Brown) and Elizabeth (wife of Samuel Barns). Children of daughters Mary, Ruth, and Phebe, deceased. Children of son James, deceased. Child of daughter "Posthume," deceased. Executors—son Eliphalet, and sons-in-law William Brown and Samuel Barns. Witnesses—Jno. Waller, Samuel Stone, David Inslee. Proved June 19, 1747. Lib. E, p. 57.

1749, May 20. Frazee, Mercy, of Essex Co. Orphan upwards of 14 years. Samuel Oliver, guardian. William Springer, fellow bondsman. Lib. E, p. 298.

1749-50, Jan. 24. Freeman, Edward, of Woodbridge, Middlesex Co., yeoman; will of. Children—Moses, William, Benoni and Katherine Ross. Real and personal estate. Executors—wife, Elizabeth, and son Benoni. Witnesses—Joseph Shotwell, Daniel Shotwell, Josiah Davis. Proved May 16, 1750. Lib. E, p. 400.

1739, Nov. 23. Freeman, Samuel, of Somerset Co., carpenter. Int. Adm'r, John Freeman, only son and heir. Fellow bondsman—Simon Wyckoff. Witnesses—Rachel Harrison, Tho. Bartow. Lib. C, p. 297.

1739, Nov. 26. Inventory, £198.14.0; made by Jan Stryker, Jan Wyckof. Debtors—Geo. Brazier, William Ouke, Derick Schuyler, Jacob Jannary, Hendrik Fisher, Tomanse Williamson, Andrie Norwood, Moses LauZada, Abraham Schuler, John Wicof, Peter Wicof, John Bennit, Thomas Andrison, Will. Wood, Lyla Hoagland, Niclas Williamson, Thomas Quick, John Manty, Isac Kip, Jacob Mananda, John Rose, Symon Vanasdalla, Stofil Vanasdalla, Garrit Durland, John Shubar, Cornedus Vananglak, John Swiker, Daniel Hendrickson, Hendrick Vanlanat.

1746, July 5. Freeze, Abraham, of Maidenhead, Hunterdon Co.; will of. Brothers—Isaac and Joseph. Naomi Biles, daughter of John Biles, deceased, residue of estate when eighteen, if she dies in minority, then to her mother, Elizabeth Bils. Friend Elizabeth Biles, executrix. Witnesses—Sarah Overton, Alexander Biles, Martha Biles. Proved June 28, 1749. Elizabeth Moore, late Elizabeth Biles, executrix, sworn same day. Lib. 6, p. 273.

1749, June 17. Inventory (£32.16.0) includes debts due from Elizabeth Besteder and Timothy Becker (?). Made by Josiah Furman and Thomas Burroughs, Jr.

1737, March 11. Freeman, Thomas, of Trenton, Hunterdon Co. Adm'x, Grace Freeman, his widow. Daniel Coxe, Esq., and Daniel Coxe, Jr., Esq., fellow bondsmen. Burlington Wills, 3013 C.

1747, Sept. 10. French, Benjamin, of Bordentown, Burlington Co., joyner; will of. Wife, Martha, and son Richard. Real and personal estate. Executor—brother William French. Witnesses—Joseph Tillton, Sam'l Farnsworth, Ju'r, Thos. Folkes. Lib. 5, p. 375.

1747, Sept. 19. Inventory, £278; made by Thos. Folkes, Jno. Imlay, Sam'll Shourds, Jur. Includes house and lot in Bordentown, and 10 acres adjoining Wm. French.

1740, June 21. French, Edward, of Evesham, Burlington Co., yeoman. Int. Administration on estate granted to Thomas French, of same, yeoman. Lib. 4, p. 243.

1740, June 21. Inventory, £39.7.9½; made by John Means and Joseph Heritage.

1745, 24th day, 7th mo. (Sept.). French, Richard, of Mansfield, Burlington Co.; will of. Wife, Mary. Children—Richard, Thomas, Benjamin, Jonathan, William, Elizabeth (wife of William Schooley), Mary (wife of Preserved Brown), Rebeckah (wife of Benjamin Shreve), Sarah (wife of William Marling), and Abigail (wife of Jacob Taylor). Real and personal estate. Executor—son William. Witnesses—William Sunderland, Benjamin Shreve, Sam'l Harris. Proved Nov. 9, 1745. Lib. 5, p. 196.

1745, 25th day, 8th mo. (Oct.). Inventory of the personal estate, £542.14.8; made by Samuel Wright, Michael Newbold and Barzillai Newbold.

1747, April 17. French, Richard, of the Borough of Elizabeth, Essex Co., yeoman; will of. Children—Richard, John, Robert, Sarah (wife of Amos Butler), Elizabeth (wife of Samuel Anderson), and Joanna,

Phebe and Ann, last three under age. Sons of son Richard; no names mentioned. Land on Turkey Road bought of William Broadwell, deceased. Executors—wife, Elizabeth, Charles Hole, schoolmaster, and Joseph Willis, blacksmith. Witnesses—James Hindes, Joshua Marsh, Daniel Potter. Proved July 17, 1747.

1747, July 29. Elizabeth French, the widow, declines to act. Witness—Zerobubel North. Lib. E, p. 169.

1747, July 25. Inventory of personal estate (£120.04.06), includes bonds of Samuel Robinson, Jacob Wright, the widow Elizabeth French, Richard French, Jun'r, Samuel Woodruff, merchant. Made by John Stits and Daniel Potter.

1732, Aug. 29. French, Thomas, of Northampton, Burlington Co. Account of Thomas French and James Wills executors, showing payments to William Collum, Jno. Briggs, Ann Lamb, Daniel Wills, Wm. Murrell, Rich'd Smith, Dorothy Large, Wm. Allcott, Wm. Cramer, Joseph Hilliard, Thomas Bishop, Edward Shippin, Richard Jones, Jonathan Wright, John Briggs, Thos. Griffith, William Bishop, John Anderson, Samuel Woolston, John Budd, Titan Leeds, John Brown, Michael Woolston, Joseph Stephen, Jacob Lamb, Isaac DeCow, Mary Wood, Thomas Bryan, James Wills, Charles French (in full of his legacy), Enoch Fenton (in full of his wife's legacy), Joshua Woolston (in full of his wife's legacy), Thomas French (one of the sons, his legacy), Sarah French, Charles French, Ju'r. In accomptants hands £12 to be paid Samuel and Rachel Wickward, two of the legatees at 21 years. Burlington Wills; (reference not found).

1745, 26th day, 6th mo. (Aug.). French, Thomas, Sr., of Chester, Burlington Co., yeoman; will of. Wife (not named). Sons—Joseph and Robert. Daughter Mary's four sons. Real and personal estate. Executors—sons Robert and Thomas. Witnesses—Joshua Bispham, Nathan Middleton, Sam'l Atkinson. Proved Nov. 1, 1745, by Thomas French, at which time Robert French disclaimed. Witnesses—Sam'l. Atkinson, Joseph Heritage. Lib. 5, p. 190.

1745, Oct. 17. Inventory of the personal estate, £215.7; made by Joseph Heritage and Sam'l Atkinson.

1749, April 17. Friend, Charles, of Penns Neck, Salem Co., yeoman; will of. Cousin, Andrew Friend, at 21, to have all estate. If he dies under age, his brother, Isaac Friend, to have the same. Andrew to live with my executor, John Holman, until he will be 17, and then apprenticed to a tailor. Witnesses—Robt. Howard, Elinor Hawkes, Mary Wilder. Sworn and affirmed, 26 April, 1749. Lib. 6, p. 300.

1749, April 24. Inventory, £65.1½; made by Robt. Howard, Jacob Cornelison.

1737, March 8. Friend, Johannes, of Penn's Neck, Salem Co., husbandman; will of. Sons—Andrew and Charles, executors, and to have equally the plantation (330 acres) on which I live. "In case Matias Skaaging don't pay £30. for the plantation he lives on, then said sons shall enjoy the same; also 270 acres in the County of Gloster, Greenwich township." Other sons—Neals, Ephraim and John. Daughters—Nanne, Mary and Sary (who has a daughter). Witnesses—Andrew Hallcop, Cristena Stallop, Sary Bilderbak. Proved Feb. 1, 1737-8. Lib. 4, p. 144.

1737-8, Jan. 12. Inventory, £93.11.3.

1743, Sept. 1. Fritch, Phillip, of Salem Co. Int. Adm'r, Hans Michael, miller, and John Michael, of the head of Alloways Creek, yeoman. Bondsman—Abner Penton, Salem, gent. All of said County. Salem Wills, 687 Q.

1743, Sept. 3. Inventory, £36.14.3; made by Saml. Purviance, Peter Dufell.

1743, Sept. 20. Additional inventory, £5.10. Same appraisers.

1739, Dec. 4. Frost, John, of Shrewsbury, Monmouth Co. Edithy Frost, the widow, resigns right of administration. Witnesses—John Forman, John Seares, Samuel Leonard. Lib. C, p. 299.

1739, Dec. 5. Inventory, £22.8.1; made by Samuel Leonard and Jon. Seares.

1739, Dec. 12. Josiah Halstead, receipt for a coffin (£1); witnessed by Patrick Devlin.

1739, Dec. 15. Adm'r, Julius Sutton, of Monmouth County, principal creditor. Aaron Forman, same County, fellow bondsman.

1739-40, Feb. 22. William Bills, receipt for rent, a barrel of cider for the burial and screws for the coffin. Witnessed by Samuel Leonard. John Eatton's name mentioned.

1727, Jan. 16. Frost, Thomas, of Perth Amboy, Middlesex Co., yeoman; will of. Land purchased of the Minister and Church Wardens of St. Peter's Church. Children of my three brothers, Robert, James and William Frost; each of the six children at 21 years. Executors—wife, Elizabeth, Rev. William Skinner, Robert King and John Barclay, gentleman. Real and personal estate. Witnesses—John Sharp, John Thomas, Richard Aikeand. Proved March 22, 1731-2. Lib. B, p. 245.

1744, Jan. 5. Fryer, Anthony, of Town and Co. of Burlington, gent.; will of. Sister's son, Samuel Rawlins, living in City of Landon. William Sorsby, of City of Burlington. Anthony, son of Matthew Allen, my executor. Witnesses—Joseph Stokes, Robert Bishop, John Morris. Proved Jan. 24, 1744. Lib. 5, 75.

1749, April 5. Fullerton, James, of Somerset Co., farmer; will of. Children—James, Mary, Elizabeth, Jean and John (all minors). Executors—Ephraim Lockheart and William Loggan (Logan). Witnesses—John M. Gallird, Robt. Shannon, Mary M. McDowel. Proved 13 April, 1749. Lib. E, p. 291.

1749, April 18. Inventory (£198.18.4) includes a gun and sword (£1.10), "William Jones' book debts £102.3," 3 bonds £15, £40, £12. Debtors—Mr. James McKray, Wilker, Robert Barclay and Christopher Holme. Appraisers—Ralph Smith, William Colwell.

1736, March 15. Fullerton, John, of Essex Co., clerk. Int. Elizabeth Fullerton renounces administration of her husband's estate. Witnesses—Francis Nealson, Rob't Crommelin.

1736-7, March 18. Adm'rs, Edward Vaughn, clerk, and Anthony Duane, merchant, principal creditors. Witness—William Skinner. Lib. C, p. 159.

1732, May 6. Furman, Samuel, of Hopewell, Hunterdon Co.; will of. Wife, Elizabeth, plantation for life; then to son Josiah. Sons William, David and Jonathan. Son, Josiah, executor. Witnesses—Jemina Hunt, Mary Houghton, Thomas Houghton. Proved August 2, 1732. Lib. 3, p. 206.

1732, June 13. Inventory (£62.16.5) includes a Bible. Made by Thomas Houghton and Joseph Price.

1749, Dec. 16. Furman, Thomas, of Amwell Township, Hunterdon Co., yeoman; will of. Wife, Elizabeth. Sons—John and Ralph, minors. Mother, Hannah Furman. Brother, Samuel Furman. Sisters—Rebecca and Sarah Furman. Executors—brother Samuel Furman and wife's brother, John Hart. Witnesses—John Steel, Samuel Carman and Christopher Search. Proved March 12, 1749-50. Lib. 6, p. 328.
1749-50, Feb. 2. Inventory (£340.14.7) includes a sword and plantation of 115 acres. Made by Jonathan Furman and Thomas Hunt.
1764, May 22. Account. Mentions Mary Stevens, Thomas Kitchin, John Hageman, Joseph Wright, Moore Furman, James Bennet, Stephen Baldwin, Jacob Ball, Dinah Pettitt, Jonas Sutton, John Porter, John Allen, John Lamberd, William Ruttinghout, William Barag, Jacob Swallows, Charles Hoff, Garrett Williamson, Johanis Case, John Lewis, Peter Allair, Rebecca Furman, John McGreigh, Jonathan Furman, Benjamin Shuttleworth, Thomas Hunt, Some Cody, John Hawkings, Samuel Fleming, Henry Landis, Jacob Arnwine, Samuel Furman (the father), Francis Quick.

1733, 2nd mo. (April), 2nd da. Gadsby, Sarah, of Cooper Creek, Gloucester Co.; will of. Sons—Josiah Shivers (married); he to have the house in which I live, and to pay my daughter, Hannah Shivers, £10 annually for five years); John and Samuel Shivers (married). Daughter, Mary, wife of Thomas Bate. Sole executor—son, John Shivers. Mentions her "husband John Shivers" and a John Colling. Witnesses—Mary Champion, Jonathan Belton, John Kay. Affirmed 14 July, 1733. Lib. 3, p. 350.
1733, 5th mo. (July), 13th da. Inventory of "Sarah, widow of Thomas Gadsby, late of Cooper's Creek in Waterford, Gloucester Co." (£131-02-2) includes negroes, Nancy £40, Hager (girl) £10. Appraisers—John Kay, Jonathan Bellton.

1731, Dec. 7. Gaill, Mary, widow of Samuel Gaill, of Great Egg Harbor, Gloucester Co.; will of. Daughters—Heaster Risley, Mary Addoms and Diana Risley. Gifts to Meary, daughter of Diana Risley, Jeremiah Risley and Mary Homan. Executors—son John and David Covenovin; they to divide the estate among my children and two of my grand-children (Thomas and Micaijah, children of Peter Cownovin deceased). Witnesses—Peter White, David Williams, Stephen Morris. Proved 26 January, 1731. Lib. 3, p. 175.
1732, March 29. Inventory, £73.19.2; made by Peter White, Stephen Morris.

1748, April 2. Gale, David, of Egg Harbour, Burlington Co., yeoman. Int. Inventory of the personal estate, £119.15; made by John Dearndale and William Brookfield.
1748, April 7. Adm'x, Mary Gale, widow, of Little Egg Harbour. Abel Gale, of same, fellow bondsman. Lib. 5, p. 439.

1730, Sept. 19. Gale, Samuel, of Great Egg Harbor, Gloucester Co., yeoman; will of. Wife, Mary, sole executrix, and to have plantation swamps at Landing Creek and Swamp Bay, back lands and personal estate during life. At decease plantation to be rented for the benefit of grand-daughter, Mary Risley, until her brother Samuel Risley will be of age. In case of his death without issue, the estate to descend to the next heirs of his mother, Diana Risley. Legacies to mother Dina Geall, brother David Geal, nephew Able Geall (to be paid 3 years after he will be of age). Executors: after my wife's decease—John Cowneovar and Benjamin Ingersul (my neighbors). Witnesses—John Covnover, Benjamin Ingersull, Stephen Morris. Sworn at Sharon, Burlington Co., 31 July, 1749.

1744, April 25. "Stephen Morris and Benjamin Ingolson testified that Samuel Gale left a legacy to Abil Gail, son of David Gail in the presence of the aforesaid witnesses. Stephen Morris (who wrote the will) saith not, and Benjamin Ingolson saith not. The will was delivered to John Cownover till called for." (Signed) James Somers, (Justice of the Peace). Gloucester Wills, 420 H.

1733, March 11. Gandouett, Francis, of Salem Town and County, gent.; will of. Wife, Anna, sole executrix, to have personal estate, she paying to son, Francis Gandouett, when 21, half value thereof. Said son to be put in care of his grand-father, Samuel Smith, until of age. Witnesses—John Pierson, Thos. Cooke, Danl. Mestayer. Proved 20 March 1733. Lib. 3, p. 406.

1734, April 1. Inventory (£147.3.8) includes "drugs and medicines and small things," £3.17.6; case of bottles, a pare of scales, brass mortar, £0.18; law books and other books, £31.10; "Coyler's Dictoanery and Supliment," etc. Appraisers—Thos. Mason, Ranier Vanhist.

1748, June 27. Gandy, John, late of "Morris's River," Cumberland Co. Int. Adm'x, Susanna Gandy, widow. Fellow bondsmen—Joseph Lord, late of Cumberland Co., and Joseph Savage of Cape May. Lib. 6, p. 19.

1748, June 25. Inventory (£130.7.9) includes cattle, horses and swine. Appraisers—Joseph Lord, Joseph Savage.

1748, June 27. Gandy, Samuel, late of "Morris River," Cumberland Co. Int. Adm'x, Hannah Gandy, of Gloucester Co., widow. Fellow bondsmen—Joseph Lord, late of Cumberland Co., and Joseph Savage, of Cape May County. Lib. 6, p. 18.

1748, June 21. Inventory (£389.06.5) includes cedar timber and shingles; also cattle, horses, sheep and swine, £268.11.0. Appraisers—John Willets, Joseph Savage.

1748, May 21. Gandy, Thomas (no place mentioned) but of Cumberland Co.; will of. Wife. Son, Aaron, land in line with Isaac Garrison's land, to the mouth of a small creek that puts out of the "great tide pond" on the north side; thence till it intercepts John Ogden's land; then along Daniel Ogden's line, bounding therewith to Isaac Garrison's land. Also ½ of undivided marsh below Ware Creek, belonging to Thomas Gandy. Son, David, my other land and marsh. Daughters—Patience (married), Catherine, Sarah (married), Mary, Phebe, Hannah, Priscilla, Rebecca, (last three to be bound out to learn trades) and Naomy. Executors—son-in-law Nathan Shaw, John Ogden. Witnesses—Daniel Ogden, Elizabeth Ogden, Isaac Garrison. Proved 5 September, 1748. Lib. 6, p. 506.

1748, Aug. 31. Inventory (£180.12.3) includes cattle, horses, swine and books (£16.4.6). Appraisers—Henry Pierson, Daniel Ogden.

1749, April 5. Gardiner, Andrew, Town and County of Salem, "Doctor of Physick"; will of. Wife, Hope. Son, James, to have lot and marsh in Manington purchased of John Rolfe and lot in the same place bought of William Chandler. Daughter, Elinor, the Gardiner land in the Town of Greenwich. Son, Henry. Executors—wife and brother-in-law, Obidiah Robins. Witnesses—Abiel Carll, Saml. McChannan, Geo. Trenchard. Proved 20 April, 1749. Lib. 7, p. 261.

1742, 5th day, 6th mo. (Aug.). Gardiner, Joseph, of Chesterfield, Burlington Co.; will of. Children—John, James, Katherine and Anne, all under age. Negro girl to be free at 30. Land in Bordentown I bought of Richard Skirm. Executors—wife Katherine, and brothers-in-law Thomas and John Ridgway. Witnesses—Amos Willitts, Joseph Rogers, Jos. Reckless. Proved Sept. 15, 1742. Lib. 4, p. 329.

1742, Sept. 15. Inventory, £576.17; made by William Bunting and Sam'el Woodward, includes 4 Bibles and other books.

1731, May 28. Gardiner, Mathew, of Wellingborrow, Burlington Co., mariner; will of. Children—Thomas, Abraham and Mary, all under age. Kinsman Joseph Furnis and sister's children. Land now in possession of John Allen and George Willis, and house and lot in possession of William Snowden; also land on River Delaware adjoining Johnson. Executors—wife, Sarah, and friend Richard Smith, Jun'r, of Burlington, merchant. Witnesses—Robert Lucas, Robert Lucas, Jun'r, Sam. Scattergood. Proved Sept. 3, 1731. Lib. 3, p. 148.

1731, Aug. 3. Inventory, £260.8.11; made by Robert Lucas and Sam. Scattergood. Includes quadrant scale, Callinder and Atkinson's Epitomy; also hay in partnership with Tho: Hunlock; bond from Jos: Overton and Sam'l Wilson, and a negro man Simon.

1749, May 23. Gardner (Gardiner), Richard, Sr., of Morris Co. Int. Adm'r, Richard Gardner, Jr., yeoman. Bondsman, Richard Fitz Randolph, of Perth Amboy.

1749, May 18. Renunciation. Subscribers give consent to Richard Gardner to administer on his father's estate. Witnesses—Hannah Gardiner, Rachel Collard, Eljih Collard.

1749, May 29. Inventory (£85.18.6) includes silver ware, £2.8.0; a box iron and goose, 12 shillings. Appraisers—Samuel Crowell, Jon. Herring.

1750, April 25. Account. Paid to Patrick Macaslin, Isamuel Washbourn, Peter Courter, Abram Winfeald, Jon. Yarrenton, Samuel Gale, Joseph Lawrence, Richard Michel, Peter Decker, William Mountgomery, Isaac Tarsort. Morris Wills, 19 N.

1733, July 15. Garlick, Joshua, Jr., of Cape May Co., yeoman. Int. Adm'r, Joshua Garlick, Sr. Fellow bondsman, John Garlick, both of aforesaid County. Witnesses—Jacob Spicer, Silvanus Garlick. Lib. 3, p. 357.

1733, July 21. Account (£50.04.4) includes cattle and sheep. Sworn before Jacob Spicer, Surrogate.

1746, Apr. 20. Garlick, Joshua, of Cape May Co., yeoman; will of. Wife, Lucy, to have wool and leather at Elisha Hand's, and all my flax if she lives at Cape May. Mentions wife's daughter, Sarah Brooks. Son, John, and grandson Richard Stites (son of my daughter Abigail Stites), to have equally my right in the plantation belonging to the "Prispeteren Society." Daughters—Abigail Stites, Phebe Smith, Rebecca Johnston (had children), and grandson, Abenor Church (under age). Cattle at Cohansey, and bond due from Ebenezer Johnson, to my daughter Abigail Stites and her son Richard. Executors—

Daughter, Abigail, and grandson, Richard Stites. Witnesses—David Cresey, Ephraim Edwards, Elijah Hughes. Proved 6 Aug., 1746. Lib. 5, p. 313.

1746, Aug. 6. Inventory of personal estate, £38.11.6; made by Jeremiah Hand, Ephraim Edwards.

1750, Sept. 26. Garral, Rebecca, of Alloway's Creek, Salem Co.; will of. Children—John, Mary, Hannah, Susanah. Executor—Benjamin Thompson. Witnesses—Amos Penton, Nathaniel Thompson, Isaac Thompson. Proved Dec. 8, 1750. Lib. 6, p. 412.

1749, April 12. Garrison, Frederick, Junior, of Salem. Int. Adm'r, Joshua Garrison. Bondsman, Daniel Garrison. Lib. 6, p. 279.

1749, April 17. Inventory (£18.1.6) taken at Pilesgrove, Salem County. Appraisers—Joseph Champneys, Daniel Garrison.

1749, March 14. Account. Monies paid Willm. Conkelyn, Joseph Tasey, Danl. Garrison, Joseph Champneys, Nicholas Gibbon, Abdon Abbit, Archibald McColtestor, Alexander Moore.

1747, March 10. Garrison, John T., of Salem County. Int. Adm'x, Elizabeth Garrison. Bondsman, Abraham Garrison. Witnesses—Thomas Nichols, Nich. Gibbon. Lib. 6, p. 50.

1747, March 9. Inventory, £78.18; made by Abraham Garrison, Thomas Nichols.

1745, Dec. 23. Garritsen (Gerritsen), Jacobus, of Somerset Co., yeoman; will of. Wife, Sara, the use of real and personal estate during widowhood to bring up the two children. Son, Jacobus, to have the home-plantation in Somerset Co., if he is of age at remarriage or decease of widow, and to pay daughter, Sara, £200. If these children die under lawful age without issue, their portions shall go to "my brothers and sisters and to my wife's brothers and sisters." Executor—brother, Rem Gerritsen. Overseers—brother, Samuel Gerritsen, and "brother-and-law," John Koerte. Witnesses—Willem Cornel, William Williamson, Isaac Voorhest. Proved 3 June 1746. Lib. D, p. 391.

1746, June 5. Inventory (£492.11.3) includes 30 acres of wheat, £30; negroes—man "Toom," £50 and girl, Pegge, £40; Dutch testament with silver clasps 3s. Made by Lucas Voorhees, Nicholas Veghte, William Cornel. Obligations, £274.

1744, 22nd day, 5th mo. (July). Garwood, Thomas, of Evesham, Burlington Co.; will of. Wife, Margaret, sole executrix. Children—William, John, Daniel, Thomas, Isaiah, Mary, Sarah, Elizabeth, Ann and Ester. Land adjoining Michael Branins. Witnesses—John Collins, Michel Branin, William Foster. Proved April 23, 1745. Lib. 7, p. 163.

1750, 24th day, 6th mo. (Aug.). Gaskill, Samuel, Jun'r, of Northampton, Burlington Co., wheelwright; will of. Daughter, Meribah. Real and personal estate. Executors—wife and Samuel Cripps. Witnesses—Ebenezer Mott, Adam Farquhar, Jun'r, Henry Jones, Jun'r. Proved Jan. 9, 1750. Lib. 7, p. 88.

1750, 8th day, 11th mo. (Jan.). Inventory, £116.6.8; made by Josiah Southwick and John Ewin.

1748, 6 mo. (Aug.), 21st da. Gerrard, Robert, of Greenwich Township, Gloucester Co., yeoman; will of. Real and personal estate to be sold (except two lots in Philadelphia for wife Margret). Money from the sale to be divided into twelve equal parts for the wife (2 parts) and children: William, Sarah (wife of Martain Bickham), Margret (wife of John Sparks), Elizabeth (wife of John Chew), Thomas, Givin (daughter), Miles (not 21), Jain (not 18), Damsin (not 18), and Hackels (not 18). Executors—wife, son William, and Joshua Lord. Witnesses—Wm. Wilkins, Edward Hollinshead, Garret Vanaman. Sworn and affirmed, 22 Oct., 1748. Lib. 6, p. 79.

1748, 8 mo. (Oct.), 11, 12 and 13 days. Inventory (£460.06.10) includes negro man and his bed, £60; Bible, £1; cattle and sheep, £39.05; rye lent to John Sparks, blacksmith; Indian corn to Martain Bickham. Appraisers—Jacob Cozens, Wm. Wilkins.

1744, June 4. Gibbon, Leonard, of Salem Co., gent.; will of. "I give equally to my sons Leonard and John Gibbon, when of age, my tract of land called Mount Gibbon. The personal estate to be sold (except my negro Sambo, his wife and children) and the interest money necessary with the rents from the plantation shall be for the maintaining and schooling of my said sons, who at 14, shall be apprenticed," etc. If both die under age and without issue, tract and personal estate devised to brother Nicholas Gibbon, "whom I appoint executor, with William Hancock to act in case of death with my said sons." Witnesses: Lewis Jones, Hannah Bate, Isaac Browne. Affirmed 4 July, 1744. Lib. 9, p. 2.

1744, July 4. Letters testamentary granted to Nicholas Gibbon, one of the executors, (Leonard and John Gibbon not being of lawful age).

1744, July 2. Inventory of "Leonard Gibbon, Esq.," (£585.00.6.) includes cattle, £87.5; wheat, £87.6.3; silver tankard; large Bible and Nelson's Justice, £4; negro called "Will," £32. Appraisers—Benoni Dare, Ranier Vanhist, Esq.

1750, April 3. Gibbs, Francis, of Mansfield, Burlington Co., yeoman; will of. Wife, Elizabeth. Children—Richard, Francis, Elizabeth and Mary. Real and personal estate. Executors—Benjamin and Joseph Talman. Witnesses—Caleb Scattergood, Thomas Thompson, Job Talmann. Proved May 9, 1750. Lib. 6, p. 345.

1750, May 8. Inventory, £319.3.4½; made by John Antram and Job Talman. Includes bonds and bills due from John Thorn, Wm. French, Isaac Cogel, James Pugsley, Thos. Hays, John Imlay, Peter Kerlin, Jonathan Scattergood, John Buffin, Joseph Atkinson, John Atkinson, Matthew Forsyth, Caleb Scattergood, Joseph Branson, James Bell, Daniel Parker, John Hutchin, Wm. Ricketts.

1752, Oct. 23. Account of the executors showing payments to Richard, Elizabeth and Francis Gibbs, Joshua Gile, Jos. Scattergood, Thomas Woodward, William Pancoast, Job Ridgway, Alex'r Grant, Joseph Pope, Benj. Gibbs, Jos. Atkinson, Pet. Hersey, Jos. English, Ann Shaw, John Antram, Henry Delalush, John Allen, John Buffin, John English, Isaac Gibbs, Jun'r, Jos. Wright, Peter Kurlin, Jas. Pugges.

1742-3, Jan. 18. Gibbs, Isaac, of Mansfield, Burlington Co., yeoman; will of. Wife, Ann, 1-3 of moveable estate, she paying Rebeckah, widow of Richard Gibbs, £10. Children of son, Richard, dec'd—Isaac, Joseph, Rebeckah and Susannah; the sons to have plantations adjoining Joseph Pope, John Bufing and Michael Newbold. Children—Francis, Isaac, John and Sarah Dickinson. The children of son Isaac

Gibbs, by his first wife, viz., Benjamin, Hanah, Sarah Hutchin, Mary, Marcey, Jonathan, Joshua, Susannah, Isaac and Rebeckah. Children of son John, viz., Robert, Martin, Elizabeth, Edward and Richard. Executors—son, Francis, and Joseph Pope. Witnesses—William Pancoast, Caleb Scattergood, Joshua Scattergood. Proved June 23, 1750.

1749, —— —. Joseph Pope declines to accept executorship. Lib. 6, p. 318.

1749, Sept. 22. Inventory, £805.18; made by Benja. Tallman and Jos. Talman.

1750, June 16. Bond of Joseph Pope, yeoman, of Mansfield, as administrator of estate, left unadministered by Francis Gibbs. William Skeeles, fellow bondsman.

1767, July 20. Account of Samuel Black, one of the executors of Joseph Pope, dec'd, who was surviving executor of Isaac Gibbs, Sen'r, of Mansfield. Payments to J. Scattergood, Peter Harvey, Benj. Talman, Wm. Picketts, Benjamin Gibbs, F. Hammel, Eliz. Cowgill, Ann Cowgill; and legacies paid Jno. Allen in right of his wife, Rebeckah, Jno. Hutchin in right of his wife, Benj., Jno. and Mary Gibbs, Raworth Beck in right of his wife, Jno. Hammel, Jun'r, in right of his wife, Joshua, Susannah, Isaac, Jun'r, and Rebecca Gibbs, executors of F. Gibbs, Sarah Dickinson, Isaac, Martin and Rob't Gibbs, Eliz. Davenport, Edw'd, Isaac and Rich'd Gibbs.

1737, Feb. 20. Gibbs, Richard, of Mansfield, Burlington Co., yeoman. Administration on estate granted to Rebecca Gibbs, widow. Joseph Pope and Archibald Silver, of Burlington, yeoman, fellow bondsmen. Lib. 4, p. 127.

1737, Feb. 20. Inventory, £113.16.8; made by Benjamin Talman and William Pancoast, Jun'r.

1739, July 18. Account of Rebecca Gibbs, widow, having paid moneys to Mary Rockhill, William Collum, Benjamin Carter, Nathan Lovett, Barzilla Newbold, James Antrum, Margaret Barton, Francis Gibbs, James Brown, John Buffin, Joseph Pope, Mary Smith, Jr., Preserved Brown, Jr., John Harvey, George Morris, Isaac Gibbs, Peter Turlin, John Beck, Edward Bolton, Paul Marchant, Joseph Rose, George Ash, Thomas Hunlock, Richard Smith, Jun'r, Caleb Raper.

1738, Oct. 1. Gibson, James, formerly of Dublin in the Kingdom of Ireland, now of Middletown, Monmouth Co., merchant; will of. To be buried at the English Church in Shrewsbury at discretion of friend, Mr. George Taylor, of Middletown, merchant. One half of estate to mother, Anne Gibson, of City of Dublin, widow; if dead, then to testator's brother, Benjamin Gibson, of Dublin, merchant, and sister Anne Gibson. Other half of estate to Mr. George Taylor. Executors—friends James Hutchins and John Bowne, minor, both of Middletown, Esquires. Witnesses—Nicholas Johnson, Lambert Willson, Charles Henderson. Proved Dec. 22, 1738. Lib. C, p. 232.

1738-9, Jan. 29. Inventory (£126.0.03¼) includes 2 pieces of garlick, 28 yards of calliminko, 19 yards muslin, 13 yards Stroudwaters, 13 yards crape, 27 cotton handkerchiefs, large English Bible, 11 augers, 12 gimblets, haberdashery ware, a gun, Woods Institutes and other books (£2.0.0), bond of Thomas Willet, William Patten and James Conner, 2 English plows, an old fiddle. Made by Nicholas Johnson, Joseph Goulder and Teunis Swart.

1738-9, March 3. John Bowne declines to serve as executor.

1741-2, Feb. 16. Gibson, Luke, of Deptford, Gloucester Co., yeoman;

will of. Wife, Sarah. Eldest son, Luke, to have plantation (300 acres); also the grist-mill and 100 acres adjoining, he to pay legacies to my daughters, Mary, Sarah, Rebekah and Hannah, when they will be 23. Remaining lands upon Mantua Creek to be divided equally among my sons, Caleb, William and Joshua. The plantation, adjoining land of John Brown, deceased, upon a branch of Woodbury Creek, to be sold. Executors—wife, and son, Luke Gibson. Witnesses—Obadiah Gibson, Thomas Leeds, Michael Fisher. Affirmed 6 Feb., 1774. Lib. 5, p. 79.

1744-5, Jany. 17. Inventory (£222.15.2) includes wheat and rye, utensils in the grist-mill, corn in the ground, cattle and hay. Appraisers—Isaac Stephens, Obadiah Gibson.

1741-2, 1 mo. (March), 2nd da. Gibson, Obadiah, of Deptford, Gloucester Co., yeoman; will of. Wife, Mary, the estate, "desiring her to pay the interest of the bonds which I put to use to John Lord's estate towards schooling the children, the same to be paid her children equally." If unborn children they to have my lands, otherwise, at wife's decease, same shall be my brother's, Joseph Gibson's, excepting legacies he shall pay to my brother Luke and two sons of my brother John Gibson. Executors—wife and Joseph Lord. Witnesses: William Carson, Silvester Sharp, Michael Fisher. Proved 20 Feb., 1748. Lib. 6, p. 105.

1748, 10 mo. (Dec.), 26 da. Inventory (£—) includes Bible and books, (£1.4). Appraisers—Habakkuk Ward, Moses Ward.

1733, Nov. 6. Giffion, David, of Wallpack, Hunterdon Co., husbandman. Int. Adm'r, Thomas Brink, of Wallpack, gentleman.

1733-4, March 15. Inventory of estate of "David Giffin," weaver, £30.4.0, including, a gun, and 7½ pounds weight thread for weaving at 2s. per pound. Made by Derick Karmer and Ruliph Brink. Witnessed by John Hyndshaw. Hunterdon Wills, 102 J.

1742, Aug. 28. Gifford, John, of Perth Amboy, Middlesex Co., who deceased Sept. 1, 1742. Bond of John Gifford, the son, and Samuel Borrowe, son-in-law, as administrators. John Thomson and Alexander Carnes, fellow bondsmen. Lib. C, p. 536.

1744, Aug. 14. Inventory (£633.19.3) includes notes of Jas. Dudley, of North Carolina, Ephraim Jones, Edward Ryans, John Boker, Thomas Johnston, Henry Dally, Robert Lucas, John Stevens Jaques, Richard Buckalew, Thos. Cook, James Dickinson, Wm. and Mary Hiders, George West, Abraham Kierslake, Henry Molhall, Joseph Gaywill, Thos. Lawrence, Henry Verney, John Williams, Paul Painter.

1745-6, Jan. 27. Account. Debts paid to James Baily, Isabella Clark, Will. Jordon, Jos. Wright, Margaret Duddel, Peter Rutgers, Ant. Rutgars, Annely and Lewis, Wm. Thompson, Elisha Inslee, Jos. Coe, Francis Brasier, Henry Inglis, Samuel Moore, Joseph Marsh, James Newel, David Elston, James Abrams, Charles Gifford of London, Obediah Ayres, Doctor David Hays, Thos. Fox, Will. Burnet, Jno. Watson, Alex. Carnes, Rich'd Buckalew, Alex'r Thompson, James Haywood, And'w Johnston, Thos. Bartow, Ben. Dally, John Hull, Jon. Nisbit, J. Gifford, Philip Kearny, Thos. Johnston, Thos. Lawrence, John Williams, James Dudly, Edward Ryan, Robert Lucas, George West, Abraham Kierslake, Henry Molhall.

1744, June 25. Gilchrist, Marion, of Woodbridge, Middlesex Co., widow of Robert Gilchrist, deceased; will of. Negroes, Solomon, Mary and Cornelius, for civil behaviour and obedience to me in my old age, to have their freedom, as specified in indenture from John Mootry. Rev. Mr. John Gilchrist, Minister of the Gospel in Parish of Bederule, in Shire of Roxborough, in North Brittain, one third of my estate. Alexander Grierson, in the Parish of Debrayshire, of Gallaway, in North Brittain, one third of estate. John, son of John Cowan, deceased, of Diswenton, in the Parish of Kirkmahoe, Shire of Nidesdale, in North Brittain, one-third of estate, but in case of his death to his brothers or sisters. Executors—friends Robert Hude, Esq., and Thomas Edgar, merchant. Witnesses—Edward Crowell, James Brown, George Brown. Proved July 17, 1745. Lib. D, p. 307.

1735, Dec. 5. Gildemeester, Christopher, of Perth Amboy, Middlesex Co. Int. Adm'rs, Henry Schleydorn and Cadwallader Williams, both of New York. Evan Drummond and John Deare, fellow bondsmen. Lib. C, p. 57.

1742, May 10. Above administrators being strangers and not having administered the estate, Samuel Nevill, eldest brother of Sarah Gildemaster, widow, appointed administrator. John Nevill, fellow bondsman. Lib. C, p. 506.

1735, Feb. 20. Gildermeester (Gildemaster), Sarah, of Perth Amboy, Middlesex Co., widow. Int. Adm'r, John Nevill. Lib. C, p. 70.

1743, April 11. Gill, John, of Newtown, Gloucester Co., yeoman. Int. Adm'x, Ann, his widow. Bondsmen, Joseph Thackery, Joseph Heritage, Junior, all of same place. Witness—Thomas Gill. Lib. 4, p. 379.

1743, Dec. 3. Inventory (£238.3.0) includes cattle £75.10.0. Appraisers —Joseph Heritage, Junior, Joseph Thackray.

1749, March 30. Gill, John, of Haddonfield, Gloucester Co., yeoman; will of. Granddaughter, Mary (land joining John Maxells in Haddonfield). Grandsons—Thomas (land adjoining his sister's lot), and John (land adjoining his brother's), children of my daughter Hannah, wife of Thomas Redman. Mary and Mercy, daughters of my son John Gill, lots described by Jacob Heulings, the 13 of 4th mo., 1747, joining their father's land. Wife, Mary, sole executrix and to have residue of lands at Haddonfield and the meadows by Josiah Kay's. Witnesses—John Maxell, John Hillman, Jun., Daniel Hillman, Jun. Affirmed 6 June, 1749. Lib. 6, p. 231.

1732, Feb. 19. Gillam, (Gilham, Guilham), Robert, of Springfield, Burlington Co., yeoman (whose will was dated March 27, 1728). Account of Jonathan Wright and Thomas Scattergood, Ju'r, executors, showing payments to Solomon Smith for the coffin for deceased and for one of his children, Jonathan Wright, Samuel Bickley, Dr. John Brown, Ebenezer Large, Wm. White, Rowland Ellis, Caleb Raper, Wm. Collum, John Parsons, Jona. Fowler, James Thomson, Daniel Smith, Jun'r, Wm. Cook, Sam'l Scattergood, Rich'd Smith, Sen'r, John Dawson, John Schooley, Wm. Cutler, Thomas Scott, Ex'r of Abraham Scott. (For will, see N. J. Archives, vol 23, p. 185).

1732, Feb. 19. Matthew Willson, of Springfield, yeoman, and Ann his wife, late Ann Gillam, widow, residuary legatee of Robert Gillam; receipt for their share of estate. Burlington Wills, 2427-43 C.

1747, Dec. 5. Gillam, Robert, of Northampton, Burlington Co.; will of. Daughter, Ruth, the clothes that was her mother's (my former wife), that are at the house of Joseph Lippincott. Brother, John Gillam. Real and personal estate. Executors—wife, Grace, and Joseph Lippincott. Witnesses—Peter Andrews, Joseph Lippincott, John Grimes, Ju'r, John Gillam. Proved Jan. 16, 1747-8.

Lib. 5, p. 493.

1747-8, Jan. 15. Inventory, £129.1.4½; made by James Lippincott and Peter Andrews.

1733, Nov. 9. Gillchrist, Robert, of Woodbridge, Middlesex Co., gent.; will of. Wife, Marion. Legacies to Presbyterian Meeting-houses at Woodbridge and Perth Amboy; to Rev. John Pierson, Rev. Gilbert Tennent, Evienes Dromment, Esq., and John Dear, for their civility, and charge of my deceased son, James; also to Andrew Hay and Thomas Jackman Fontyme. Wife, sole executrix; Robert Hude, John Mootrie and James Brown, all of Woodbridge, assistants. If wife dies without a will, residue of estate to be sent to cousin John Gillchrist, minister of Beedearowell, in Shire of Roxborough (Scotland). Mentions brother James and cousin, Robert Gillchrist . Witnesses—Edward Crowell, "Yon Die," Ad. Hude. Proved Jan. 25, 1733.

Lib. B, p. 481.

1750, Feb. 16. Gillchrist, Thomas, of Salem Co. Int. Adm'rs, Daniel Murfy and Margaret Murphy, late Margrett Gilchrist. Bondsman, Adam Clark. All of Penns Neck, Salem County. Witnesses—Danl. Mestayer, Nich Gibbon. Lib. 8, p. 93.

1749, Jan. 22. Inventory (£37.13.6) taken at Penns Neck, includes his armour, £4.10; 13 swine, 15 shillings. Appraisers—Jacob Cornealesson, Ezekiel Hardin.

1743, May 30. Gillham, Lucas, of Mansfield, Burlington Co., husbandman. Int. Ann Gillham, widow, renounces administration, and requests that John Gilham, of Northampton, husbandman and brother of deceased, may be appointed administrator. Witnesses—Hannah Indicott, Patrick Byrne.

1743, May 30. Inventory of the personal estate, £65.3; made by Edward Mullen and Thomas Foster.

1743, —— —. Account of John Gillam, administrator. Paid Sam'll How, Wm. Murrel, Ruben Eldridge, Sam'll Atkinson, John Richardson, Sam'l Powell, Jonathan Hough, Zebulon Brown, Thos. Shinn, Ester Brown, Patrick Burn, John Lawton, Joseph Endcott, William Buddell, Solomon Curtis, Daniel Smith, Jacob Johnson, Michael Mackivoy, William Folwell, Elizabeth Shinn, William Morris. Burlington Wills, 3707-16 C.

1733, Jan. 21. GillJohnson, Giles, of Salem County. Int. Adm'r, Errick GillJohnson. Bondsmen—Oney Sefrus Stanley, John Sinnick. All of said County. Witnesses—Sinick Sinnickson, Dan. Mestayer.

Lib. 3, p. 392.

1733, Jan. 21. Inventory (£54.10.0) includes riding horse, guns and sword; accounts brot. against Alse Pennington, James Whitten, Joseph Lues, Jacob Patten, John Stanley. Appraisers—John Sinnick, Oney Sifrus Stanley.

1731, Jan. 27. Gillman, John, of Piles Grove, Salem Co., yeoman. Int. Adm'r, Benjamin Acton, of Salem town, merchant. Bondsman, John Doe. Witness—John Rolfe. Lib. 3, p. 204.

1731, Jan. 27. Inventory (£71.18.2) includes cattle and calves. Appraisers—Obediah Loyd, Malachy Davis.

1741, May 25. Gilman, Charles, of Woodbridge, Middlesex Co.; will of. Children—James Clarkson Gilman and John Gilman, both under age. Sisters—Mary Gilman, Christian Freeman, Susannah Moor. Real and personal estate. Executors—wife, Sarah, and father-in-law, James Clarkson. Witnesses—Samuel Crowell, Moses Bishop, Will'm Sarjeant. Proved June 20, 1741. Lib. C, p. 422.

1741, June 8. Inventory, £116.7.6; made by John Moobrey and Abraham Tappen.

1744, June 8. Account of James Clarkson, executor, who has paid debts to Joseph Bloomfield, Jonathan Randolph, John Heard, John Morris, John Fletcher, Jonathan Freeman, Sicil Sergeant, Jacob Oakee, Francis Costigan, Jonathan Kinsey, Abraham Tappen, Sam'll Moore of Raway, Nath'll Randolph, blacksmith, Moses Collier, Benony Freeman, Joseph Donham, David Alford, John Robinson, John Gifford, John Mutrey, Peter Kymbal, Fenwick Loyal, John Pangborn, Benjamin Bloomfield, Goen Eddy, Thomas Evans, James Wilkison, John Low, John Noe, Jun'r, Patrick McKevers, Sam'll Moore, John Waller, Henry Cuyler, Henry Freeman, Wm. Burnet, James Tomson, Richard Williams, John Freeman, Thomas Edgar, James Hude, Sam'll Crow, Obadiah Eyres, John Robinson, David Perkins, Isabella Randolph, Richard Carmen, Rev'd Skinner, Sam'll Randolph, Nath'll Randolph, Benj. Kinsey. Debts due estate from Joseph Eyres, Matthew Bunn, David Herriot, Michael Moore, John Herriot, Ephraim Lockhart, John Shotwell, Jonathan Dennis, Eliphalet Jones, Henry Moore, Timothy Bloomfield, John Morris, Jun'r, Samuel Nevil, James Thompson.

1745, May 26. Account of William Gilman, who married the widow of said deceased, includes bonds due to Isabael FitzRandolph, Thos. Hadden, Henry Freeman, Ursila Parker, Gershom Conger "for cloathing and learning to the two sons for about eight years."

1747, June 23. Account. Bond of Elisha Parker and Charles Gilman to Marion Gilchrist. Bond of Elisha Parker and Benj'n Bloomfield to Henry Freeman.

1733, June 5. Gilman (Gillman), Joseph, of Woodbridge, Middlesex Co. Int. Adm'x, Elizabeth Gilman, his widow. Lib. B, p. 409.

1749, Feb. 27. Givin, Thomas, of Essex Co. Int. Adm'x, Rebecah Givin, widow. Daniel Pierson, Esq., fellow bondsman. Lib. E, p. 552.

1750, March 9. Goble, Daniel, of Morristown, Morris Co., yeoman; will of. Sons—Daniel and John (of age); Benjamin, Stephen and William (minors). Daughters—Sary Leonard, Hannah Axtell, Jemime, Elizabeth, Mary and Martha Goble (four unmarried and not 18). Real and personal estate. Executor—brother, Robert Goble, and Ruben Winget. Witnesses—Benjamin Conger, Simeon Goble, Caleb Fairchild. Proved 5th April, 1750. Lib. E, p. 409.

1736, April 30. Godfrey, Andrew, of Cape May Co.; will of. Wife, Elizabeth, the plantation to live on during widowhood, after which son James and his heirs to have the same. Sons Philip and Andrew to have equally a tract lying up Great Egg Harbour River. Legacies to daughters Anne (eldest), Tibitha, Rebecca and Rachel. Executors—wife, Elizabeth, and son James. Witnesses—Jacob Garretson, Peter

Corson, John Leonard. Proved 15 July, 1736. Letters granted Aug. 24. Lib. 4, p. 63.

1736, May 24. Inventory (£357.6.9) includes negro man Dag (£14), negro man (£25), 37 cattle (£53.16.00), 40 sheep, 3 horses, 23 swine. Appraisers—Henry Young, John Willets.

1732, Dec. 16. Goforth, George, of Burlington Co., mariner; will of. Wife, Jane, and son, William, all my lands, provided they come into the Province to claim it within five years after my decease; otherwise to go to my brothers and sisters—John Goforth, William, George and Susannah Robinson. Executor—brother William Robinson. Witnesses—John Jones, James Moon, John Willdin, Is. DeCow. Proved Jan. 22, 1732. Lib. 3, p. 242.

1735, July 26. Goldin, William, of Tuckaho, Cape May Co., yeoman. Int. Admr, Nathan Goldin, yeoman. Fellow bondsman—Joseph Goldin, yeoman. Both of the County aforesaid. Witnesses—Henry Young, Elias Gandy, Jacob Spicer. Lib. 4, p. 23.

1735, July 26. Inventory (£51.06.0½) includes cattle (£15.10.0), lumber in the swamp, and pine boards. Appraisers—Henry Young, Elias Gandy.

1749, March 23. Goldy, Joseph, of Gloucester Township, Gloucester Co., guardian of David, 14 yrs. and upwards, son of Daniel Wills, late of Burlington Co., merchant. Bondsman, Jonathan Thomas. Witness, Rob. Smith. Gloucester Wills, 444 H.

1731, 3 mo. (May), 25 da. Goodwin, John, of Salem, bricklayer; will of. Wife, Susanna, executrix, and whole estate during widowhood, she paying debts with the help of my son, Joseph, as executor, when he will be 21. Daughter, Mary Jones, that part of the home lot, beginning front (60 ft.) at Thomas Mason's line. Joseph all the front from my aforesaid daughter's corner; also the new house and barn with all the land and marsh. Son, John, when 21, shall have front from Joseph's corner, together with the old house and shop. Youngest sons, Thomas and William, when of age, remaining land joining Isaac Satterwaith. Witnesses—James Axford, James Butterfield, Elisabeth Axford. Proved 16 May, 1733. Letters issued to Susannah Goodwin, (in the absence of Joseph Goodwin, the other executor). Lib. 3, p. 316.

1733, May 11. Inventory (£184.6.4½) includes cattle, oxen, sheep and lambs. Debtors—Saml. Morgen, Samuel Thompson, Jona. Wadington, Ranier Gregory.

1742, July 10. Goodwin, Joseph, of Salem Co. Int. Adm'x, Sarah Goodwin (relict), of Salem. Bondsmen—Joseph Hayens, of same town and county, carpenter, and Robert Townsend, of Cape May, gent. Witnesses—Wm. Fraser, Bn. Judah. Lib. 4, p. 376.

1742, July 12. Inventory (£250) includes cattle, horses, sheep and servant. Appraisers—Thos. Thompson, Willm. Peake.

1744, March 13. Account. Cash paid Joseph Sharp, John Scoggin, Eliz. Jones, Joseph Sharp, Exr., John Hall, Exr., John McKenny, William Murdock, Jonathan Driver, Isaac Sharp, Robt. Hart, Thos. Hoskins, Charles Reding, Peter Ryal, Wm. Chandler, Rachl. Shields, John Rolph, Charles Conner, Saml. McClanning, Wm. Gregg, Sarah Turner, Phebe Saterthwaite, Benjamin Eaton, Revd. M. John Pierson, Abner Penton, Roger Sherron, Ann Nicholson, Danl. Bradrifth, William Crabb, Ann Macket, Thos. Thompson, Wm. Murdoch, John Scogin, Wm. Tate, Erasmus

Fetters, Cornl. Hart, Danl. Huddy. Cr., by insolvent book debts, viz: Thos. Rice, Hugh Merly, Malakiah Long, Jos. Ware, Wm. Racoson, Zacha. Field, Richd. Craven.

1739-40, March 19. Gordon, Charles, of Freehold, Monmouth Co., yeoman; will of. Son, Peter, remainder of land at Matcheponix, purchased of George Loffly and John Gordon. Sons, Charles and David, the home plantation, David's part to include house and orchard. Daughters—Lyda and Elizabeth. Son, John. Granddaughter, Mary Ker. Executors—friends William and Samuel Ker. Witnesses—Timothy Lloyd, Archibald Craige, John Campbell. Proved April 8, 1740. Lib. C, p. 328.

1739-40, March 24. Inventory, £175.3.10; made by David Rhe, John Anderson, Joseph Forman.

1744, Dec. 8. Gordon, Jannet, of Perth Amboy, Middlesex Co., widow of Thomas Gordon, Esq., deceased; will of. Mudy, son of my son Andrew Gordon. Lewis Carree, son of my daughter Margaret Stelle. John, son of my daughter Mary Brown. Granddaughter, Katherine Kearny. Grandson, Thomas Stelle at 21. Rev. William Skinner of Perth Amboy, £25. Mrs. Catherine Lyell, my tea furniture. Mrs. Jane Lyell, my dressing table. 500 acres I had from son Thomas in Middlesex Co.; 400 acres in Elizabeth Town; 300 acres, called Mount Arrarrat, purchased of John Ireland. Executor—son, John Gordon. Witnesses—James Newell, Andrew Robinson, Lawr. Smyth.

1744, Dec. 9. Codicil. Eldest son of son Thomas to have daughter Stelle's share. Executors—Rev. William Skinner and son John. Witnesses—Alexr. Mackdowell, Mary Mackdowell, Lawrence Smyth. Proved Jan. 12, 1744.

1744-5, Jan. 12. John Gordon qualified as one of executors, being Quaker. Lib. D, p. 222.

1740, June 11. Gosney, Ann, of Woodbridge, Middlesex Co., gentlewoman; will of. Children—John, and Thomas Atkinson, Sarah, Hannah, Mary and Elizabeth. Susanna and Rachel Atkinson, daughters of son John. Ann, daughter of son Thomas. Grandson, Timothy Atkinson, large unbound Bible. Apprentice, Rebecca Dean. Real and personal estate. Friends' Meeting House, £5. Executors—son Thomas, William Brittain and Nathaniel FitzRandolph, smith. Witnesses—John Bloomfield, Philip Doddridge, Jonathan Toms. Proved Jan 13, 1740. Lib. C, p. 375.

1731, May 17. Gosney (Govsney, Gausney), John, of Woodbridge, Middlesex Co., yeoman; will of. Brother, Henery Gausney, farm I live on. Executors—wife, Anne, and friend Edward Crolle. Witnesses—Paul Tharp, Job Conger, Wm. Robison. Proved July 12, 1734. Lib. B, p. 520.

1748, Sept. 6. Gould, Anne, of Trenton Township, Hunterdon Co.; will of. Son, Samuel Leonard; son, Morris Leonard; negro boy, called Primus; daughter, Ann Eldridg. Children—Nathaniel Leonard, Morris Leonard, Elizabeth Gould, Francis Gould. Daughter, Elizabeth Gould, to have two negro girls, called "Cate" and "Little Ginne," also a chest of drawers at my mother, Francis Horner's. Daughter, Francis Gould, £100, in hands of my mother, Francis Horner, and negro woman Ginne, negro boy Jack, negro girl Rose and chest of drawers at Henry Lotts; also five acres of land in Trenton Township, at the Cross Roads, near William Mott's school house, where a log house stands. Reversion to testator's son, Samuel Leonard's eldest son. Residue to daughters, Elizabeth and Francis Gould. Executors —daughter Elizabeth Gould and William Mott. Witnesses—Zachariah Heward, Mary Wills, Esther Heward. Proved Feb. 15, 1748-9. Lib. 6, p. 59.

1748-9, Feb. 15. William Mott renounced executorship, authorizing Joseph Wanell (?) and Abraham Cottnam, attorneys-at-law, to exhibit his renunciation. Witnessed by John Chambers.

1748-9, Feb. 18. Inventory (£226.2.6) includes a negro woman, Ginne, £30; cash lent to Francis Horner, £100; negro, Jack, £30; negro, Cate, £28; negro, Rose £25; negro, Prime, £25; negro, Ginne, £18; Samuel Leonard's bond. Made by Peter Lott and Stephen Rose.

1743, July 2. Gould, James, Esquire, of Trenton, Hunterdon Co., attorney-at-law. Int. Adm'rs, Anne Gould, the widow, and Alexander Lockart of same place, gentleman.

1754, May 7. Bond of George Tucker, of Hunterdon County, blacksmith, Samuel Tucker of same place, merchant, and Joseph Hollinshead of the City of Burlington, Esquire. George Tucker as administrator of estate of James Gould, Esquire. Remaining unadministered by Anne Gould, late administratrix, at time of death of the said Anne. Hunterdon Wills, 163 J.

1731, Dec. 29. Goulden, James, of Woodbridge, Middlesex Co., yeoman; will of. Son, Richard, under age. Expected child. Real and personal estate. Executors—wife, Mary, Richard Herriman. James Thompson. Witnesses—John Blake, Mich'll Vaughton, Martha Byfield. Not proven. Lib. B, p. 292.

1745, Nov. 28. Goulding, George, of "Rhoad Island," merchant. Int. Adm'r, John Story, of Little Eggharbour, Burlington Co., yeoman. Edward Rd. Price, fellow bondsman. Witnesses—Ephraim Story and Jos. Scattergood. Lib. 5, p. 185.

1741, Dec. 21. Graham, William, of Salem County, laborer, Int. Adm'r, William Graham, "only cousin appearing to be in the Province aforesaid," of Piles Grove, yeoman. Bondsmen—Alexander King, yeoman, and Edward Hughes of same place, carpenter. Witness—William Tuft. Lib. 4, p. 316.

1708, 24th day, 10th mo. (Dec.). Grainge, Matthew, of Nottingham, Burlington Co., yeoman; will of. Land adjoining Caleb Wheatley, which I reserved when I sold my plantation, 23rd day, 10th mo. (Dec.), 1708. Samuell Wright, Senior, of Nottingham, batchelor, sole legatee and executor. Witnesses—Caleb Wheatley, Ruben Powell, William Emley. Proved June 7, 1740. Lib. 4, p. 240.

1743, June 6. Grandum, John, of Cape May Co. Int. Adm'x, Catharina Grandum, widow. No bondsman. Witnesses—Stephen Young, Philip Godfrey.

1742-3, Mar. 4. Inventory (£49.1.3) includes Testament (£0.6.0), winter grain on the ground, the lease of 150 acres of land for 4 years, which was purchased. Appraisers—John Townsend, Silvanus Townsend. Cape May Wills, 109 E.

1715, June 17. Grange, Catherine, of Nottingham, Burlington Co., spinster; will of. Elizabeth, dau. of Samuel Wright of Nottingham, the latter executor and residuary legatee. Benjamin Davis, servant of Samuel Wright. Wm. Emley, of Nottingham, yeoman, £5 in trust for Women's Meeting of Chesterfield. Witnesses—Caleb Wheatley, Sarah Readford, William Emley. Proved Jan. 10, 1737. Lib. 4, p. 125.

1743, May 6. Grant, David, of Somerset Co., yeoman; will of. Wife, Martha. Children—Marey, Grant and John. Grandchildren—Jeannet, Martha, Margaret, David and Mary Parker (minors). Son, Grant, all estate and to pay the daughter, Marey, and grandchildren legacies bequeathed to them. Executors—wife, Martha, and son, John Grant. Witnesses—Robrt. Kirkpatrick, Alexdr. M. Cullagh, Brice Rikey. Proved 27 October, 1743. Lib. D, p. 94.

1744, Jan. 30. Gray, Henry, of Greenwich Township, Gloucester Co., merchant; will of. Wife, Esther, present Estate I now live upon or until my daughter, Sarah Gray (alias Harriss) will be 18. Executor—Robert Zane, Senior. Witnesses—Wm. Wilkins, Isaac Atkinson, Thomas Wood. Affirmed 13 Feb., 1744. Lib. 5, p. 138.

1744-5, Feb. 8. Inventory, £152.10.6; made by Hance Steelman, Thos. Wilkins.

1748, March 24. Gray, John, of Gloucester Co. Int. Adm'x, Ann, his widow. Bondsmen—Gilbert Alberson, yeoman, of same place and William Spafford, of Philadelphia, merchant. Lib. 6, p. 16.

1748, March 17. Inventory, £113.0.10½; made by John Sedden, Abr. Chattin, Junior.

1749, Nov. 29. Account of Anne Patisson, late Ann Gray, adm'x of her husband, John Gray, late of Gloucester, merchant. Cash paid to Dr. Gray, Edwd. Richardson, Henry Sparks, William Kimsey, William Hambleton, Margaret Garrett, James Woods, Jno. Brown, Thos. Woods, Estate of Thos. Norbury, deceased, Margery Webb, Abra'm Chattin, Junior, Capt. Gus. Hufton, Robt. Boggs, Jos. Laed Elgr, for letter of administration, Levy Pearce, Jam's Hincksman, George Allen, Jno. Blackwood, Thos. Sparks, Willm. Spafford, Jam's Whitehead, Jam's Cooper, Moses Ward, Thos. Kimsey (acct. as per Abram. Chattin, Jun.), Jam's Thomas, Francis Hadock, Christy Greenherst, Abrah'm Chatten, Sen., Deborah Gosch, Dehoris Farrell. Bills due Estate of Capt. Jas. Smith, William Hugg, George Morris, Archibald Ingraham, Alexander Beale, Thos. Taylor, Jno. Sparks, Elias Cabell.

1737, July 18. Gray, Joseph, of Elizabeth Town, Essex Co., mariner. Int. Bond of Eunice Gray, the widow, as administratrix on estate of her husband. Benjamin Gray, of Woodbridge, and George Badgly, of Elizabeth Town, fellow bondsmen. Witness—Ebenezer Lyon. Lib. C, p. 172.

1740, Aug. 10. Gray, Joseph, of Woodbridge, Middlesex Co., yeoman; will of. Children—Benjamin, Nathaniel, Ebenezer, Andrew, Hannah Cole, Eunice Tingley, Mary, Ann and Abigail Gray. Lands bought of John Lea, Justice Bloomfield and joining lands of Joseph Olliver, Benj'n Rolfe, Richard Walker. Executors—wife, Elizabeth, and son Ebenezer. Witnesses—Eze. Bloomfield, Richard Walker, Moses Rolfe. Proved Dec. 5, 1740. Lib. C, p. 364.

1750, June 1. Gray, Nathaniel, of Borough of Elizabeth, Essex Co., weaver; will of. Children—Nathaniel, Jeneres, William and John.

Land joining lands of Jacob Degarmo, Joseph Phrazee. Executors—wife, Martha, and Benjamin Pettit. Witnesses—Silvanus Oakley, John vanZeckles, William Jones. Proved Nov. 9, 1750. Lib. F, p. 14.

1735, Feb. 13. Gray, Richard, of Newton Township, Gloucester Co., yeoman; will of. Legacies to granddaughters—Hannah, Sarah, Mary and Ann when 21, children of my daughter Ann, wife of Samuel Burroughs, yeoman, of County aforesaid. Mentions Robert Kearld. All lands to my son, John, whom I appoint executor with my son-in-law, Samuel Burroughs. Witnesses—Sarah Norris, Jonathan Ellis, Amos Ashead. Affirmed 4 Feb., 1736. Lib. 4, p. 86.

1735-6, March 13. Inventory (£48.1.2) includes debts from Margery Webb, Robert Kerld, Aaron Upin. Appraisers—John Kay, Amos Ashead.

1747, April 19. Greacon, John, of Mushiticove in Queens Co., New York; will of. Friend, William Lawrence, silver shoe buckles. Friend, Joseph Coles, Sen'r, and his sons, Joseph and Caleb Coles, remainder of estate. Real and personal estate. Executors—friends William Lawrence and Joseph, son of Joseph Coles. Witnesses—Derick Albertson, Coles Mudge, Thomas Cheesman. Proved March 6, 1750-1. Lib. E, p. 491.

1735, Jan. 15. Green, Daniel, of Salem Co., yeoman. Int. Adm'x, Anne Green (widow). Bondsman—Dennis Carrol. Both of said County. Witness—Alexander Miller. Lib. 4, p. 56.

1735, Jan. 16. Inventory (£38.7) includes grain and farming utensils. Appraisers—John Wetherbee, Alexander Miller.

1732, Nov. 27. Green, John, of Wellingborrow, Burlington Co., yeoman; will of. Wife, Jane, to enjoy plantation until my eldest son, Thomas, is 21. Children—Joseph, Jacob, Elizabeth, Martha and John, all under age. Land on Ancocus Creek, adjoining Joshua Humphries, and 300 acres in Hunterdon Co., called the Lotting. Executors—wife, Jane, brother John Stokes, and friend Samuel Woolman. Witnesses—Thomas Reeves, Sarah Reeves, Saml. Scattergood. Proved Dec. 15, 1732. Lib. 3, p. 228.

1732, Dec. 15. Inventory, £226.18.2; made by Thomas Reves and Revel Elton.

1737, July 21. Green, John, of Perth Amboy, Middlesex Co. Int. Adm'r, Stephen Warne, of Perth Amboy, Noah Barton, fellow bondsman. Witness—James Hooper. Lib. C, p. 171.

1741, June 18. Green, Richard, of Trenton Township, Hunterdon Co., yeoman; will of. Wife, Mary, and brother, William Green, executors. One half of plantation to wife, until children are of age. Son, William, 220 acres of plantation where testator then lived, on the King's Road, next to Delaware. Son, Richard, 100 acres bought of Isaac Reader, and remainder of old plantation. Personal estate to wife until daughters, Rebecca and Christian, are of age. Son, George, land in Amwell Township, in care of John Hawkings; also 50 acres bought of Peter Lott, where George Hatten lived. Witnesses—Isaac Reeder, Isaac Hutchinson, Thomas Sutton. Proved November 20, 1741. Lib. 4, p. 321.

1741, July 31. Inventory, £467.7.4; made by Charles Clark and Benjamin Green.

1747, April 9. Green, Thomas, of Chesterfield, Burlington Co., wool comber. Administration on estate granted to Michael Newbould, of same, Esq. William Skeele, of same, fellow bondsman. Lib. 5, p. 432.
1747, May 21. Inventory, £193.4.1; made by Samuel Wright and Benjamin Shreve.

1744, Jan. 1. Greenoak, John, Sr., of Newtown, Queen's Co., Nassau Island, son and heir of John Greenoak, Sr., mariner, of same place, petitions to administer his father's estate in New Jersey.
1744, Jan. 23. Inventory, £80.0.0; made by Joseph Moore and William Moore.
1744, Dec. 8. Thomas Lawrence, Joseph Hallet and Mary, his wife (lately the widow of John Greenoak, Sr.), all of Newtown, who, in the will of the latter dated July 30, 1724, were appointed his executors, renounce service.
1744, Dec. 22. Affidavit by Judah Wood (60 years old), in Queen's Co., Nassau Island, to effect that John Greenoak, Jr., of Newtown, was the son of John Greenoak and Mary, now wife of Joseph Hallet.
Burlington Wills, 3718-24 C.

1747, April 20. Gregg, Ann, of Salem Co., widow and relict of William Gregg, of Christiana Hundred, County of New Castle, upon Delaware; will of. Son, Jonathan Woodnut, £50, to be paid him at 21, also my largest Bible. Son, Henry Woodnut, a lot (2 acres) in Greenwich, at Cohansey, Salem County, which was given to me by my former husband Richard Woodnut; also £50 and my small Bible. Sister, Rachel, wife of Jonathan Womsly. Mentions Ann, wife of Samuel Gregg, and three daughters of William Gregg, viz: Elisabeth, Hannah and Margary Gregg. Youngest son, Abraham Gregg, the remainder of estates in the County of New Castle. Executors—Samuel Gregg of Christiana Hundred (to whom I entrust my youngest child to bring up, educate and apprentice) and Benjamin Cripps, of Salem County, to see my will duly performed, and my former husband's, Richard Woodnut's, in the county of Salem; also whom I intrust to bring up my two eldest children to educate and put to trades. Witnesses—Thomas Yeatman, Sarah Yeatman, William McCausland. Affirmed 1747, May 7. Lib. 5, p. 380.
1747, Aug. 14. Inventory (£266.0.9½) includes rent due out of plantation leased to Daniel Garrison and Wm. Russel. Appraisers—Elias Cotting, Chas. O Neill.
1748, May 12. Account. Monies paid Wm. Barker, innholder at Salem, Margaret Bullick, Elizabeth Barker, wife of William Barker, Daniel Mestayer, surrogate of Salem, George Trenchard, Richd. Woodnutt and Tho. Thompson.

1746-7, Jany. 10. Gregg, William, of County of New Castle on Delaware and Christiana Hundred, miller; will of. Wife, Ann. Two-thirds of profits of estate real and personal left to executors for bringing up of children and to defray the cost until son, Harmon, will be of age. Land to be divided, beginning on south side of Red Clay Creek, up said creek to mouth of the Run that comes down from Henry Green's to John Hanfield's line, leaving 2 acres on each side of the mill for mill land. Sons—Harmon (to have land on the north side) and William (land on the south side). The grist mill to my sons—Harmon, William, Joshua and Jacob, equally. Three younger sons, Joshua, Jacob and Abraham, £200. when they will be 21 and to be put to trades between 14 and 16 years of age. Legacies to daughters, Elizabeth, Hannah and Margary (not 18) when 20 years old. Executors—wife, Ann, and son Harmon. Trustees—"My two

Brethren," Samuel Gregg and George Robinson. Witnesses—George Alford, Henry Green, Jacob Hollingsworth. Sworn and affirmed 13 April, 14 Aug., 1747. Salem Wills, Lib. 5, p. 397.

1748, Aug. 14. Letters of administration granted to Samuel Gregg, brother of the deceased, during the minority of Harmon Gregg, the surviving executor. Bondsmen—Dan'l Brandreth, Chas. O'Neill. Witnesses—Wm. Barker, Dan. Mestayer.

1740, June 9. Gregory, Joseph, of Salem, yeoman; will of. Adm'rs, William Barker and Elizabeth, his wife, daughter of said Joseph Gregory. Bondsmen—Thomas Mason, David Randolph, all of said County. Witnesses—Hannah Gregory, Danl. Mestayer. Lib. 4, p. 241.

1740, June 10. Inventory (£326.10) includes house, lot and marsh, £200. Appraisers—Joseph Goodwin, David Randolph.

1748, May 23. Griesmeyer, Simeon ,of Salem Co. Int. Adm'r, Richard Wistar. Bondsman—Caspar Wistar. Both of said County. Witnesses—Martin Saltar, Nich. Gibbon. Lib. 6, p. 51.

1748, May 25. Renunciation of Susannah Griesmeyer, widow. Witnesses—John Horhasd (?), Martin Saltar.

1748, Oct. 18. Inventory, £64.19.7; made by Isaac Oakford, Benj. Thompson.

1735, Feb. 9. Griffith, John, of Perth Amboy, Middlesex Co. Int. Adm'x, Elizabeth Griffith, his widow. Thomas Skinner, fellow bondsman. Lib. C, p. 70.

1746, Aug. 23. Griffith, Morgan, of Bridgetown, Burlington Co., yeoman; will of. Wife, Mary, sole legatee and executrix with Samuel Cripps and Auddy Brock. Witnesses—William Keys, John Ewan, Jehu Claypoole. Proved Sept. 22, 1746. Lib. 5, p. 273.

1746, 13th day, 7th mo. (Sept.). Inventory, £30.2.3; made by John Ewan and Jehu Claypoole.

1728-9, March 4. Griffith, Robert, of Colebrook Dale, Philada. Co., mason; will of. Wife, Alice, sole executrix. Children—Sarah, Mary, Thomas, Joseph, Ann and Margaret. Estate in Frankfort and interest in Colebrook furnace in Philada. Co. Witnesses—Robert Durham, Evan Morgan. Proved June 11, 1733.

(Burlington Co.), Lib. 3, folio 367.

1744-5, Feb. 6. Grimes, John, of Northampton, Burlington Co., yeoman; will of. Jane Neally all debts due me in Province of Virginia. £5 towards finishing Church near Bridgetown in Northampton. Real and personal estate. Executors—brother, William Grimes, and Patrick Renolds. Witnesses—Samuel Woolston, Sen'r, John Bishop, John Woolston, Jr. Proved Aug. 20, 1745. Lib. 5, p. 156.

1745, Aug. 19. Inventory, £42.7.1; made by Samuel Woolston and John Osmond.

1748, Feb. 1. Grist, Jonathan, of Penns Neck, Salem Co. Int. Adm'x, Elizabeth Grist. Bondsman—John Eaton. Both of same place. Witnesses—Ephraim Worthington, Nich. Gibbon. Lib. 6, p. 323.

1748-9, Feb. 6. 7. Inventory (£115.10.3) includes cattle, £23, "part of a flatt" and cord wood, £22.9.6. Appraisers—Alen Congleton, Samuel Whitehorne.

1736, Oct. 8. Grow, William, of Gloucester Co., yeoman; will of. House wherein I live and 20 acres of land to Samuel Hugg, (son of John Hugg, Esq., deceased) when 21. Executors—Joseph Thackera and Isaac Jennings of same county. Witnesses—Richard Barron, Richard Fry, Enoch Ellison. Proved 16 Nov., 1736. Lib. 4, p. 75.

1736, Nov. 1. Inventory (£13.15.0); made by Saml. Harrison, Enoch Ellison.

1744, Feb. 25. Gruffith (Griffith), Walter Jr., of Newton, Gloucester Co., cordwainer. Int. Adm'r, Walter Gruffith, of Gloucester township and County. Bondsman—Henry Sparks. Witnesses—Daniel Eastlake, Henry Siddons. Lib. 5, p. 180.

1743, Oct. 25. Inventory (£12.16.6) includes shoemaker's tools, £0.11.6. Appraisers—Jno. Kaighin, Robert Stephens.

1743, March 26. Guest, John, of Middlesex Co.; will of. Wife ———. Son, John, at 21 years, to have house and lot. Desires sloop to be sold. Executor—father, John Guest. Witnesses—Peter Collas, Lewis Guest, Henry Dally, John Salnave. Proved May 24, 1743. Lib. D, p. 64.

1741, Dec. 15. Guisbertson (Gisberson), John, of Upper Freehold, Monmouth Co., yeoman. Int. Adm'r, John Guisbertson, of Upper Freehold, yeoman. Robert Smith, of City of Burlington, Esquire, fellow bondsman. Lib. 4, p. 316.

——, —— —. Inventory of the estate, £21.06.00; made by Joseph Emans, Richard Comton and Moses Robins. Exhibited December 15. 1741.

1749, Feb. 27. Gwin, Thomas, of Essex Co. Int. Adm'x, Rebecca, his widow. Daniel Pierson, Esq., of same county, fellow bondsman. Lib. E, p. 552.

1742, Dec. 29. Gwinn, Patrick, of Mansfield, Burlington Co., laborer. Inventory, £9.12.6; made by John Buffin and Francis Gibbs.

1742-3, Jan. 3. Adm'r, Michael Buffin, yeoman. John Doe, fellow bondsman, both of Mansfield. Lib. 4, p. 378.

1734, April 3. Hackett, David, of Salem Co., yeoman. Int. Adm'x, Elizabeth Hackett, widow. Bondsmen—Will'm Hunt, James Mason. All of Salem County. Witnesses—John Norton, Danl. Mestayer. Lib. 3, p. 411.

1734, 1 mo. (Mar.), 29 da. Inventory (£74.6) includes cattle, £24. Appraisers—William Hunt, James Mason.

1733, July 27. Hackett, Thomas, of Salem Co., yeoman. Int. Adm'rs, Richard Smith and John Pledger. Bondsman—Clement Hall. All of Salem in said County. Witnesses—John Norton, Philip Chetwood. Lib. 3, p. 360.

1733, July 27. Inventory, £13.7; made by Thos. Mason, Clem. Hall.

1737, Feb. 23. Hacket, William, of Salem Co., yeoman. Int. Adm'r, Robt. Hart, gent. Bondsman—Richard Woodnutt. Both of Salem County. Witnesses—James Caruthers, Dan. Mestayer. Lib. 4, p. 143.

1732, Oct. 14. Hadden, Ephraim, of Woodbridge, Middlesex Co., carpenter. Int. Adm'r, Thomas Haddon, of Woodbridge. Thomas Skinner, fellow bondsman. Lib. B, p. 305.

1736, July 12. Hagathy, Dennis, of Great Egg Harbor, Gloucester

Co., husbandman. Int. Adm'r, ———. Bondsmen—Thomas Hendry of Burlington, merchant, and Thomas Heulings of same place, cordwainer. Lib. 4, p. 64.

1734, Oct. 3. Haige (Haigue), William, of London, merchant. Administration on estate granted to James Steel, of Philadelphia, gent. Isaac DeCow and Thomas Wetherill, of City of Burlington, Esquires, fellow bondsmen. Lib. 3, p. 430.

1747, July 6. Lynford Lardner, of City of Burlington, appointed administrator on estate left unadministered by James Steel. Robert Hartshorne, atty-at-law of City of Burlington, fellow bondsman. Lib. 5, p. 433.

1742, Dec. 6. Haines, Ann, of Morris Co. Inventory (£83.11.3) includes large Bible £1, 10 acres of wheat, £4. Appraisers—Brice Riky, Thomas Miller. Morris Wills, 35 N.

1750, Oct. 9, (filing date). Account. Paid to Jonathan Dottey, Wm. Richey, David Riggs, John Morrison, James Miller, John Sutton, John Bullian, Saml. Rolfe, Edward Riggs, Dan'l Sutton, Aaron Brown, Obadiah Ayers, Benjamin Lewis, Wm. Sutton, John Ayers, Benja. Hull, Cathrine Primrose, Nathl. Rolfe, Moses Dottey, Dan'l Morris, Timothy Houton, Zeek. Sutton, John Dotty, John Roy, Saml. Dalglish, Rebecca Haines, Marey Gates, Daniel McGown, John Hooey, Wm. Beard, Saml. Brown, Mrs. Britan, George Mills, Henry Haynes, Rebecca Haynes, Saml. Heaton, George Park, Thos. Elison, Joseph Stiles, John Linbey, Jabish Jarvis, William McCarey, Steven Barnes, Isaac Names, Isaac Pricket, Israel Riky, Abraham White, Thos. Little, Robt. Right.

1748, Aug. 16. Haines, Elizabeth, of Burlington Co. Int. Adm'r, Daniel Haines, of Springfield, yeoman. Edward Rudolphus Price, Esq., atty-at-law, fellow bondsman. Lib. 6, p. 327; Lib. 7, p. 93.

1749, Sept. 11. Haines, Francis, (wife of William Haines), of Northampton, Burlington Co., (with consent of husband); will of. Eldest son, Thomas Bonell, £40 of my former estate. Son, John Bonell, and two grandchildren, Robert and Frances, son and dau. of my dau. Hannah, wife of Jeremiah Haines. Son, Samuel Bonell, executor and residuary legatee. Witnesses—Nehemiah Reeves, Nathan Haines, John Burr, Jun'r. Proved Aug. 21, 1750. Lib. 6, p. 371.

1742-3, Jan. 18. Haines, John, of Evesham, Burlington Co., yeoman; will of. To be buried near my wife, Anna, whom I appoint sole executrix. Daughters—Rachel and Hepsiba, both under age. Real estate and right in Hains' saw mill. Witnesses—Caleb Haines, William Foster, Enoch Haines. Proved Feb. 16, 1742. Lib. 4, p. 359.

1742-3, 3rd day, 12th mo. (Feb.). Inventory, £259.18.10; made by Caleb Haines and William Foster.

1731, June 18. Haines, Jonathan, of Evesham, Burlington Co., yeoman. Account of Mary Haines, executrix, showing payments to Benjamin Paschal, Jon. Head, Jon. Peacock, Jon. Gosling, Darling Conarrour, Solomon Smith, Dan'l Wills, Jon. Craig, Jon. Snoden, Jon. Burr, Dorothy Larges, Wm. Park, Rich'd Climer, Rich'd Parks, Thomas Lindley, Wm. Cullum. (For will, see N. J. Archives, Vol. 23, p. 200). Burlington Wills, 1693-1700 C, 2126-30 C.

1743, Feb. 20. Haines, Lawrence. Int. Adm'r, Joseph Weaton.
Lib. 5, p. 21.

1731, Sept. 13. Haines, Nehemiah and John, sons of Jonathan Haines, being each above 14 years, make choice of Wm. Haines and Caleb Haines, of Northampton, to be their guardians.
Burlington Wills, 2123 C.

1745, 9th day, 6th mo. (Aug.). Haines, Nehemiah, of Rodmanton, Chester Township, Burlington Co., yeoman; will of. Son, Ephraim, real estate, and at 21 he is to pay his two twin sisters, Hannah and Mary each £25, they having been provided for by their grandfather, Lancelot Brown. Daughter, Hope, under age. Executors—wife, Ann, with friend Joshua Humphris. Witnesses—Joshua Bispham, John Cox, Sam'l Atkinson. Proved Sept. 30, 1745. Lib. 5, p. 168.

1745, 23rd, 24th days, Sept. Inventory, £387.4.6; made by Sam'l Atkinson and Joshua Bispham.

1744, Dec. 17. Haines, Richard, of Evesham, Burlington Co., yeoman; will of. Sons—Abraham, Richard, Carlile, Enoch and Bethanah. Daughters—Mary Matlack, Rebecca Matlack, Rachel Allison, Sarah (wife of Edward Hillier), and widow, Elizabeth Newbury. Children of dau., Mary Matlack. Real and personal estate. Executors—wife, Mary, and dau., Elizabeth Newbury. Witnesses—Lucy Springer, Benjamin Allen, Gab. Blond. Proved April 12, 1746, by Elizabeth Newbury, surviving executrix. Lib. 5, p. 236.

1746, 11th day, 2nd mo. (Apr.). Inventory, £218.15.10; made by Thomas Wilkins, William Foster and William Sharp.

1748-9, 2nd day, 11th mo. (Jan.). Haines, Samuel, of Northampton, Burlington Co., yeoman; will of. Children—Thomas, Sarah, Lydia, Jacob and Samuel, all under age. Lot in Mt. Holly and other real estate. Executors—wife, Lydia, and friend John Woolman. Witnesses—Revell Elton, Nathaniel Haines, Elizabeth Mumppervat. Proved Jan. 26, 1748. Lib. 6, p. 21.

1748-9, 25th day, 11th mo. (Jan.). Inventory, £592.13.9; made by Revell Elton and Joseph Burr.

Haines (see Haynes).

1740, May 18. Hains, Daniel, of Allen Town, Monmouth Co.; will of. Daughter, Hannah Hains, to be brought up at discretion of executors. James, son of brother James Hains. Daniel, son of brother Stephen Hains. Ann, Sarah, Ruth and Phebe, daughters of sister Ann. Sarah, daughter of sister Sarah. Daniel, son of sister Phebe. Executors—Stephen Johnes and Abiel Davis. Witnesses—James Johnston, Moses Robins, Junior, and John Foord. Proved June 10, 1740.
Lib. 4, p. 241.

———, ———, —. Inventory (£484.15.11) includes parcel of bark, tanner's tools, 47 hides of sole leather, 13 hides of upper leather, 76 calf skins, 18 upper leather hides in the fat, 3 kip skins, etc.; also 1,000 ft. boards. Made by John Middleton and Moses Robins, Jr.

1740, ———, —. Account. Payments to Thomas Cahill, for schooling legatee, Edward Stevenson, Elizabeth Hutchinson, for instructing Hannah in tailor's trade, Richard Carnes, Bethia Ketcham, ——— Everitt, William Pidgeon, Benjamin Briton, William Whitehead, David Covide, Gideon Vikerdike, Thomas Sutton.

1731, Dec. 5. Hains, Hannah, of Gloucester Co., widow; will of. Daughters—Sarah, wife of John Snowden, and Mary, wife of John Wood. Grandchildren—James Whiteall, Hannah, Sarah, James, Henry, Jeremiah, Mary and Alice Wood, Liddia, Hannah and William Snowden. Executor—son-in-law, John Wood. Witnesses—Jos. Lord, Richard Bickham, Ju'r, Wm. Wilkins, Constantine Wood. Affirmed 26 Dec., 1732. Lib. 3, p. 233.

1732, Nov. 29. Inventory of Hannah Hains, of Woodbury Creek, Gloucester Co., (£137.15.10) includes bonds of John Snowden, Richard Bickham, Ju'r, Tho. Wilkins, Thomas Bickham, rent due, for Redbanke, from Richard Bickham, Jur. ("from Hainses and John Wood, executors"), and a servant-boy, £20. Appraisers—Wm. Wilkins, Constantine Wood.

——, ——, —. **Hains, Silas,** of Hanover, Morris Co., tailor; will of. Wife, Ruth (2nd wife). Children—Silas and Jemima Hains (minors). An expected child. Mentions "brother Samuel Haine's widow, and children" also "inheritance supposed to be fallen to me on Long Island." In case children, Silas and Jemima, should die minors, household goods I had with former wife shall be returned to Mr. Daniel Taylor. Executors—Rev. Mr. Daniel Taylor, of Newark, and Joseph Tuttle, of Hanover, Morris Co. Witnesses—Elijah Gillette, James Hayward, John Tompkins. Proved 2 Feb. 1742.
Morris Wills, 3 N.

1743, Sept. 27. Receipt for Silas Hains' will and Richard Wood's admin'n bond to be carried to Burlington. (Signed) David Stout.

1748, Sept. 27. Hall, Burgess, of Bordentown, Burlington Co., mariner; will of. Wife, Abigail, all estate, real and personal, during widowhood. Daughters—Martha Freach, Ruth and Abigail. Executors—wife, and Robert Field, Sen'r. Witnesses—Rees Roberts, Robert Ashton, Geo. Bliss, Jun'r. Proved Aug. 31, 1749. Lib. 6, p. 313.

1749, Aug. 7. Inventory £215.19.9½; made by Thos. Folkes and Isaac Horner. Includes debts due by George Palmer, Elihugh Lee, Jacob Hooker, Rees Jones, Joseph Wood, Jun'r, Rob't. Ashton, Joseph Roberts, Preston Manlaw, Charles Taylor, Job Warford, James Pugsley, Edward Kimbal, James Denness, John Ashton, Daniel Davis, John Goldsmith, Patrick Campble, John Lorton, Joseph Field, James Powell, Richard Parker, Sam'l Barwell, Oliver Carty, Thomas Holmes, Mathew McCarty, Mathew Farrell, Francis Simson, Edward Chapman, Rob't. Taylor, John McKim, James Butler, James Fagon, Rees Roberts, Ocke Halanes.

1735, Nov. 29. Hall, Clement, of Salem Town and County, merchant, petitions to be guardian of Mary Wolcott. Former guardian, Samuel Abbott, appointed 23 Aug., 1734. Witnesses—Joseph Tomlinson, Saml. Bustill. Lib. 4, p. 50.

1741, Oct. 30. Hall, Clement, Town and County of Salem, Esq.; will of. Wife, Elizabeth. Sons—William Hall, my dwelling and 8 acres in the town of Salem, being part of the 16 acre lot devised by my father to my brother Nathaniel Hall; also 50 acres at the Town's End joining William Hall's land; John, 8 acres of said land, being the lower moiety of the sixteen acre lot; also all my land in Cows Neck; and Ashton, the plantation in St. George Hundred, purchased of James Byard. Daughter, Anne Hall, at 18 or marriage, to have £300. Remainder of real estate (plantation tracts and lots) and rights and shares of Proprietary Land to be sold and the monies

divided among wife and children, William, John, Ashton and Ann Hall. Executors—uncle, Clement Plumstead, cousin William Plumstead, brother William Hall and my wife, Elizabeth. Witnesses—Phil. Chetwood, Stephen Carmick, Danl. Mestayer. Proved 7 June, 1742. Letters testamentary granted to William Plumstead, William Hall and Elizabeth Hall, three of the executors named.
Lib. 4, p. 381.

1748, June 15. Hall, Henry, of Somerset Co. Administration on estate granted to Eleanor Hall, of County aforesaid. Fellow bondsman—John Garretson (signed "John Garrison"). Lib. E., p. 193.
1748, June 15. Inventory (£111.17) includes one gun and sword, £1.14; 1 negro boy, £26; negro girl, £16. Made by John Garrison, Henry Stevens.

1747, May 16. Hall, John, of Salem Co., yeoman. Int. Admx., Anne Hall, widow. Bondsmen—James Chamless, Saml. Purveyance. All of said County. Witnesses—Edward Test, Danl. Mestayer.
Lib. 5, p. 325.

1742, Aug. 3. Hall, Samuel, of Salem Town and County, shopkeeper; will of. Brother, John Hall, executor and sole legatee, except five shilling to brother Daniel Hall. Witnesses—Wm. Siddons, John Pledger, Wm. Pennock. Sworn and affirmed 19 Aug., 1742.
Lib. 4, p. 314.

1723, Aug. 26. Hallenbeek, John, of Elizabeth Town, Essex Co., yeoman; will of. Wife, Wellimtye. Children—Catherine, Rachel and Jane Hallenbeek. Real and personal estate. Executors—father-in-law, Peter Vanbuscarrick, and wife. Witnesses—Justus Falckner, Nicholas Utter, Isaac Blanchard. Proved July 11, 1737.
1737, July 12. Administration granted to Willemtye Shotwell, late Willemtye Hallenbeek. Lib. C., p. 168, 169.

1736, March 31. Halstead, Caleb, of Middlesex Co., about 16 years of age, selects as his guardians John Halstead, of Elizabeth Town, yeoman, and Joseph Marsh, of Perth Amboy, shipwright. Witnesses—John Deare and Perit Lester. Lib. C, p. 76.

1734, May 23. Halstead, Timothy, of Elizabeth Town, Essex Co., yeoman; will of. Eldest son, Timothy, and his five children, each £5. Other children—Jacob, Jonis, John, Hannah (widow of Jacob Mitchell), Abigail Painter, Charity Haywood, Elizabeth Halstead, Rebecca Higgins. Daughter, Amey, £152, payable by bonds of Timothy Town, Barnet Christopher, Peter Sloot, Peter Andrewvet, Jonis Halstead; James Haywood and Henry Garthweight to see it paid. Executors—all the legatees. Witnesses—Joseph Man, Nathaniel Crane, Jun'r, Abs'm Ladner. Proved March 1, 1734-5.
1734-5, March 1. Jonas Halstead, Timothy Halstead, Rebecca Higgins and Elizabeth, wife of Jonathan Allen, called in the will Elizabeth Halstead, qualify as executors. Lib. C, p. 19.

1740, Aug. 15. Halton, Charles, of Greenwich, Gloucester Co., yeoman. Int. Adm'r, Zachariah Peterson (during minority of John Halton, only brother of deceased). Bondsman—Edmund Lord. Witness—Edward Noble. Lib. 4, p. 197.
1740, July 21. Inventory, £76.11.7; made by Edmund Lord, John Jones.

1736, April 2. Halton, Hance, of Rackoon Creek, Gloucester Co., yeoman; will of. Wife, Briget. Sons—John, the plantation (120 acres) on which I live; Lawrence, the 100 acres joining the aforesaid land. Also they to have equally the land (100 acres) I bought of Lawres Halton and the meadows (14 acres) on said Creek, and 50 acres bought of Samuel Shivers. Lawrence to have meadows (5 acres) bought of Paul Gerron, and 50 acres bought of Lawrence Paulson. Daughters—Mary, Sarah and Rebecka Halton. Sole executor—son, Charles Halton. Witnesses—Micheall Conelly, Zarias Peterson, John Jones. Proved 21 March, 1736. Lib. 4, p. 92.

1736, May —. Inventory, £66.3.5; made by Zarias Peterson, John Jones.

1739, Feb. 9. Halton, James, of Greenwich, Gloucester Co.; will of. Wife, Katharine. Son, James Halton, executor, and to have whole estate. Daughters—Christeena Guest, Mary Silly and Magdalena Gill. Witnesses—Erick Cox, Lawrence Paulson, John Jones. Proved 30 April, 1743. Lib. 4, p. 359.

1742, Dec. 4. Inventory (£92.6.2) includes "cattle, cotton and sider trough." Appraisers—John Jones, William Guest.

1740, Aug. 15. Halton, Lawrence, of Greenwich, Gloucester Co., yeoman. Int. Adm'r, Zacharias Peterson, in place of John Halton, a minor brother. Bondsman—Edmund Lord. Witness—Edward Noble.

1740, Aug. 9. Inventory (£67.12.1) includes working tools and old lumber, books and book debts. Appraisers—Edmund Lord, Zarias Peterson. Gloucester Wills, 254 H.

1738, July 10. Ham, William, of Shrewsbury, Monmouth Co. Int. Admx., Grace Ham. William Carvell, of Shrewsbury, fellow bondsman. Witnesses—Gabriel Stelle and John Redford. Monmouth Wills, 545 M.

1746, Jan. 3. Hamilton, Archibald, of Penns Neck, Salem Co., schoolmaster; will of. Wife, Judith, executrix, and to have during widowhood household goods and interest of bond due by Daniel Penton. Daughter, Catrine Penton. Witnesses—Olliver Webb, Nicholas Philpot, Sr., Nicholas Philpot, Jr. Proved 22 Dec., 1747.

1747, Dec. 21. Inventory (£72.8.7) includes large Bible, £1.1. Appraisers—Jeremiah Baker, Josias Penunton. Salem Wills, 829 Q.

1735, Nov. 7. Hamilton, Col. John, Esq., of Perth Amboy, Middlesex Co.; will of. Wife, Elizabeth, sole executrix, and all estate both real and personal. Witnesses—P. Kearny, Jno. Broughton, Susanna Kearny. Proved March 21, 1747. Lib. E, p. 138.

1742, Nov. 22. Hamilton, William, of Salem Co. Int. Adm'x, Mary Hamilton, relict. Bondsman—John Jones, atty-at-law, Thomas Carny, yeoman. All of same place. Witnesses—Tim. Rain, Chas. O Neill. Lib. 4, p. 377.

1742, Nov. 22. Inventory (£60.6.9) includes gun, sheep and cows. Appraisers—Thomas Carney, Benja. Cullen.

1743, May 30. Hamilton, William, of Cape May County. Int. Adm'x, Hannah Hamilton, his widow, Quakeress. Fellow bondsman—John Paige. Witnesses—Enoch Lewis, Benjamin Houlden. Lib. 4, p. 380.

1743, April 30. Inventory of estate of "Doctor William Hamilton" (£32.3.1), includes broad cloath coat, black vest, leather breeches (£2.10.0); blew coat, double breasted vest and old breeches (£1.10.0); old red great coat, old banyan, 13 gloves and old wig, cane and belts, small papers containing some pils, rasins and powders, "the value whereof is not well known to the appraisers, but conceive they are worth £1.10.0," box of small Viels, some empty and some containing some waters, spirits, salts, etc., "the value of them not well known to the appraisers, but conceive them worth £1.0.0," an amputating knife and saw, 2 saw plates, some other chirurgin's instruments, case of chirurgin's instruments, case of lancets. Debts due from James Townsend, Silvanus Townsend, Estate of John Grandam, Estate of John Stites. Appraisers—Aaron Leaming, Elisha Hand.

1745, March 29. Account. Cash paid to Lydia Taylor, Joseph Rose (surrogate), Elisha Hand, Enoch Lewis, Samuel Stevans, Jacob Spicer, David Culver, Henry Young, Benj. Holdin, William Mulford, Aaron Leaming, Henry Stites (Justice of the Peace).

1734, 2nd day, 3rd mo. (May). Hammel, John, of Town and Co. of Burlington, gent.; will of. Children—John, William, Michal (wife of Michael Freasland), Mary (wife of Peter Rose) and Elizabeth Thomson. Real and personal estate. Daughter, Elizabeth Thomson, sole executrix. Witnesses—Jno. Raworth, Thos. Scattergood, Thos. Scattergood, Jun'r. Proved Sept. 18, 1734. Lib. 3, p. 428.

1748, Sept. 15. Hammit, William, of Gloucester Co. Int. Adm'x, Elizabeth Hammit, widow. Bondsman—Thomas Cheeseman. Lib. 6, p. 328.

1748, June 23. Inventory (£174.8.0) includes cash due from Thos. Chessman, Henry Roe, William Smallwood, Richard Cheeseman. Appraisers—Thos. Cheeseman, William Cheeseman.

1748, June 22. Hampton (Hamton), Andrew, of Elizabeth Town, Essex Co., yeoman; will of. Children—Andrew, Abner, Jacob, Hannah and Margaret, last three under age. Plantation given me by my father, Andrew Hampton, deceased, of Elizabeth Town, joining lands of Thomas Clark and John Terrill; land bought of John Ryno at Ash Swamp, Middlesex Co. Executors—wife, Mary, and friend Joseph Cory. Witnesses—John Pike, Abraham Clark, Jona. Hampton. Proved Dec. 26, 1748. Lib. E, p. 233.

1748, Nov. 18. Inventory (£311.00.04) includes bonds from John Terrill, Sam'll Brooks, Andrew Bryant, Samuel Olliver, Elnathan Cory, Nath'll Clarke, Ro. Drummond. Made by Thomas Clark and Jona. Hampton.

1746, Sept. 11. Hampton, Hannah, of Elizabeth Town, Essex Co., spinster, upwards of 14 years. Bond of Samuel Olliver, yeoman, as guardian. Moses Vanname, of Perth Amboy, mariner, fellow bondsman. Lib. D, p. 403.

1731, Oct. 27. Hampton (Hamton), James, of Elizabeth Town, Essex Co., yeoman; will of. Wife ———, two-thirds of estate. Children—Jonathan and Lydia, both under age. Land called Frazee's meadow, lying between Passaick and Dead Rivers; plantation lying to northward of James Clark's land. Executors—son, Jonathan, and friend John Spinning. Witnesses—Thomas Hills, Thomas Clark, Andrew Joline. Proved May 23, 1732. Lib. B, p. 263.

1732, April 24. Inventory (£299.03.02), includes sheep sold to James Hindes Jun'r, books sold to Ebenezer Johnson, and bonds due from Phillip Donman, Jno. Salnave, Humphrey Sholes, James Clarke, R. Higgins, Jno. King, Nath'll Bonnell, Jun'r, Sam'll Clarke, George Johnston, Benjamin Watkins, Joseph Tooker. Made by John Salnave.

1744-5, March 5.—Hampton, Jonathan, of Rahway, Essex Co.; will of. Eldest son, Abraham, of Staten Island, land joining lands of Peter Tremleys and Garret Post. Son, Jonathan, negro man and clock, after the death of his mother-in-law. Daughters—Margaret Styles, Mary Oliver, Sarah, Johanna and Hannah Hampton. Son-in-law, John Bird. Land joining lands of John Marsh and Daniel Lane. Executors—wife, Elizabeth, and son Abraham. Witnesses—John Badgley, Euphema Badgley, Edward Vaughn. Proved April 13, 1745. Lib. D, p. 262.

1747-8, March 21. Hampton (Hamton), Mary Ann, widow of Jonathan Hamton of Essex Co. Int. Joseph Hindes, Jun'r, (with consent of Jonathan Hampton), administrator. Jonathan Hampton, fellow bondsman. Lib. B, p. 138.

1748, May 19. Hampton, Thomas, of Gloucester Township and County, boat or flatt-man; will of. Legacies to brothers—Edward, husbandman, John, yeoman, and William, husbandman. Sisters—Rosanna Albertson (has daughters Judith and Nancy, both under age), Mary Zain, Sarah Bogs and Judith Anderson. Executors—father, William Hampton, yeoman, of County aforesaid, and brother, William Hampton. Witnesses—Richard Arell, John Hider, Michael Fisher. Proved 30 Dec., 1748. Lib. 6, p. 255.

1748, Aug. 20. Inventory, £304.11.1; made by John Hider, Michael Fisher.

1738, Oct. 1. Hamton, Andrew, of Elizabeth Town, Essex Co., tailor; will of. Wife, Margaret, the money due her from Josiah Terrill. Children—Johannah Lambert, widow, Elizabeth Oliver, Thomas, Andrew, John, and Margaret Hamten. Land joining land of Thomas Clark; land I bought of James Hind. Executors—Joseph Tooker and Thomas Clark. Grandsons—Isaac Terrill, Jonathan Hampton. Witnesses—Joseph Clark, John Terrill, Mary Clark. Proved Jan. 30, 1738. Lib. C, p. 247.

1738-9, Jan. 18. Inventory (£170.04) includes debts due from Jonas Wood, Leonard Miles, Joseph Hetfield, Peter Simons, widow Mitchel. Made by John Spining and Andrew Joline.

1728-9, 24th d of 12 mo. (Feb.). Hance, John, of Shrewsbury, Monmouth Co.; will of. Wife, Elizabeth. Son, Thomas, the testator's sloop. Residue of estate among all my children, son Thomas excepted, and son John to have £5 more than the rest. Daughters to have £5 less than sons. Executors—brother, Isaac Hance, and Gabriel Stelle. Witnesses—Preserve Lippincott, Aron Robins and Amos White. (No record of probate. In the record the preceding probate date is August 5, 1732). Lib. B, p. 297.

1746, August 25. Hance, John, Senior, of Freehold, Monmouth Co.; will of. Wife, Willemtie. Eldest son, John. John, Antie, Aart, Willemtie, David, Jannetie, Marya and Leenaa, children of son John. John, Willemtie, Sary and Peter, children of eldest daughter, Jannetie. Willentie, John, Marya, Cornelias, Catryntie and Jametie, children of youngest son, Hendrick. Daughter, Marya. Executors—Roelof Schenck (son of John Schenck) and William Williamson, blacksmith. Witnesses—John Van Kerck and John Schenck. Proved Nov. 14, 1746. Lib. D, p. 432.

1746, Oct. 9. Inventory (£657.18.6) includes bonds of Richard Sudam, Peter Schenck, Samuel Car, John Van Mater, John Hance, Leffert Leffertson, Cornelias Van Hengelen, William Williamson, Mr. Erickson, William Logan,—Thorn, Teunnis Awmack. Made by Peter Bowne and John Van Kerck. Additional inventory, £4.16.3; made by William Clark and Peter Bowne.

1746, July 15. Hance, Thomas, of New Brunswick, Middlesex Co., mariner; will of. Children mentioned but no names given, all under age. Executors—wife, Abigail, and friend John Lyle. Witnesses—William Blane, Nathaniel Ogden. Proved Aug. 13, 1746. Lib. D, p. 401.

1746, Oct. 28. Inventory, £95.16.2; made by Nathaniel Ogden and Petries Slegt.

1734, Aug. 5. Hancock, Edward, of Alloways Creek, Salem Co., guardian of John Hopper, son of Benjamin Hopper, late of same place, weaver. Lib. 3, p. 425.

1737, Oct. 28. Hancock, Edward, of Salem Co., yeoman, guardian of Aaron Daniel, an orphan 14 yrs. Witnesses—Abel Nicholson, Danl. Mestayer. Lib. 4, p. 124.

1739, April 9. Hancock, Edward, of Alloways Creek, "alias Munmouth River," Salem Co., husbandman; will of. Wife, Hanna, for the bringing up of the children, the use of all real estate during her widowhood; also benefit of plantation given me by my father's will, purchased of Jeremiah Powell, until my son Edward attains 21. Daughters—Elizabeth and Lidia Hancock at 16, my part of that plantation in Pens Neck, unless my wife and brother, William Hancock, see fit to sell the same, and put the money at interest for them. Daughters—Hannah and Grace Hancock at 16, plantation and tract of land I purchased of Benjamin Allen. Executors—wife and son, Edward. Witnesses—Charles Davis, Wm. Siddons, John Jones, Chas. Connor. Affirmed 3 Oct. 1739. Lib. 4, p. 204.

1739, May 14. Inventory, £303.4.6; made by Samuel Hancock, James Allen.

1744, Oct. 23. Hancock, Job, of Salem Co., tailor. Int. Adm'r, Bradbury Stretch "as related and principal creditor." Bondsman—Thomas Hancock. Both farmers in said County. Lib. 5, p. 55.

1744, Nov. 9. Inventory (£118.14.3) includes Bible, £0.9.0. Appraisers—Jonathan Bradway, James Chambless.

1739, Nov. 5. Hancock, Nathaniel, of Alloways Creek, Salem Co., yeoman; will of. To daughter, Mary Hancock (not 16), all estate. Her grandmother, Mary Chandler, to have the use of all lands, except the timber, for the bringing up of said daughter; if the said Mary Chandler dies, Joseph Stretch, Junior, to act in her place. If said daughter should die under 16, without lawful issue, estate shall be divided equally among my own brothers and sisters. Executors—Daughter, Mary Hancock, and brother-in-law, Joseph Stretch, Junior.

Witnesses—Joseph Stretch, Senior, David Loper, Richard Bradford. Affirmed 1 May, 1740. Lib. 4, p. 232.

1740, 2 mo. (Apr.), 3 da. Inventory, £154.4.1; made by Wm. Hancock, Jonathan Bradbury.

1733, Dec. 18. Hancock, Richard, of Salem Co., yeoman. Int. Admrs., Joseph Bacon and Charles Oakford. Bondsman—Joseph Darken, yeoman. All of said County. Witnesses—John Norton, Danl. Mestayer. Lib. 3, p. 386.

1733, Dec. 3. Inventory, £102.13; made by Abel Nicholson, Joseph Darkin.

1740, March 11. Hancock, Samuel, of Salem Co., yeoman. Int. Admx., Rebecca Hancock, relict. Bondsman—Samuel Fogg, John Fitzpatrick, all of said County. Witnesses—John Hunt, Joseph Ward. Lib. 4, p. 269.

1740, March 11. Inventory (£214) taken at Alloways Creek, includes cattle and horses, £99.18. Appraisers—John Fitzpatrick, Joseph Ward.

1737, Oct. 28. Hancock, William, Esq., of Salem Co., appointed guardian of William Daniel (16 years). Witnesses—Abel Nicholson, Danl. Mestayer. Lib. 4, p. 122.

Hancock (see Handcock).

1732, Feb. 8. Hand, Benjamin, of Cape May Co.; will of. Wife to have ½ of plantation and the new house during widowhood. At remarriage or decease, son Isaac (who has the other half and the old house), to have the whole, also cane and shoe buckles. Daughters—Patience and Phebe Hand. If a child should be born, son, and daughter Patience, shall pay the child a certain number of pounds. Executors—wife, Ruth, and son Isaac Hand. Witnesses—James Flood, Bezabel Osborn, Nathan Osborne. Proved 20 March, 1732. Lib. 3, p. 340.

1732-3, Feb. 19. Inventory (£188.2.10) includes yoke of oxen, 12 cows, 35 sheep, 30 1-4 of rum, ½ of a shallop. Appraisers—Nathaniel Resco, Robert Townsend.

1732, Nov. 7. Hand, Cornelius, of Cape May Co., yeoman; will of. Wife, Deborah, to have the use of all land during widowhood. Son, Cornelius (not 21), to possess same forever. Daughter-in-law, Deborah Taylor, one-third part of one-third of moveable estate. Executors—wife, and my honorable father-in-law, Henry Young. Witnesses—Nathaniel Rusco, Jacob Garrison, Shamgar Hand. Proved 31 March, 1733. Lib. 3, p. 338.

1732, Nov. 18. Inventory (£141.00.03), includes negro boy (£20), cattle, sheep and horses (£67.11.06).

1748, Nov. 30. Hand, George, Junior, of Cape May Co.; will of. Wife, Mary, use of plantation and mill, during widowhood, to bring up the children. Son, Jeremiah Hand, the homestead house and land, and a piece of marsh at Fishing Crick, and ½ of piece of land at head of Green Creek. Son, Elias, land at Ash Swamp, the mill and 4 acres of marsh between William Mathews and Recompense Hand; also ½ of land at head of Green Creek, and five miles of Beach. Daughters—Sarah, Ahrhoda and Naome. An expected child (if a boy to have £20, paid by my son Jeremiah Hand). Executors—Brother, Thomas Hand, and my wife, Mary. Witnesses—Daniel Hand, Edward Church, Nathan Hand. Proved 16 May, 1749. Lib. 6, p. 367.

1749, Apr. 10. Inventory (£130.18.3), includes cattle, sheep, horses and swine. Appraisers—Richard Crafford and Elisha Hand.

1732, Oct. 4. Hand, Jeremiah, of Cape May Co., yeoman; will of. Wife. Cousin, George Hand, former son of my brother George Hand, ½ of the "home stall land" I live on, next to my brother Recompence. John Hand, son of John Hand, the remainder of said land. They to possess the five mile beech with 90 acres of land near Greene Creek branches, with 15 acres of marsh near the "Seader Homakes." Brother, Recompence and his children two-thirds of moveable estate. Legacies to cousin Mary Hand, brother Thomas and his children. Executor—George Hand, Senior. Witnesses—John Hiatt, James Flood, Richard Downes. Proved 26 Feb., 1732-3. Lib. 3, p. 260.

1732, Oct. 7. Inventory, £30.10.0; made by Nathaniel Rusco, William Mathews.

1733, May 27. Account. Moneys paid to Eliza. Hand (widow), Recompence Hand, John Jones, Saml. Bustill, Rebecca Garlick, Peter Hand, James Flood, Richard Downes, Jeremiah Hand, Jacob Spicer, Nathaniel Prusco, William Mathew, George Crandal, John Crandal, Trustam Hedges, Christopher Foster, Ebenezer Swaine, George Hand, Mary Hand.

Letter of Richard Downes, who wrote the will, dated Cape May, Feb. 26, 1732-3, explains what will meant. Sworn before Jacob Spicer, Justice.

1736, Apr. 27. Hand, John, of Cape May Co. Int. Adm'r, Elisha Hand. Fellow bondsman—Ebenezer Newton, both of County aforesaid. Witnesses—Thomas Hand, William Simkins, Jacob Spicer, Junior. Lib. 4, p. 65.

1736, Apr. 24. Inventory (£198.0.11) includes cattle, hogs and geese. Appraisers—Ebenezer Newton, Thomas Hand.

1738, June 7. Account. Payments to Nathl. Norton, Thos. Hand, James Page, John Crandall, Thos. Ross, John Hand, Ebenezer Newton, Mercy Hand, (widow), Jane Hand, Rachel Hand (daughters), Thos. Buck, etc., amounting in all to (£147.4.7). Cape May Wills, 86 E.

1743, June 1. Hand, John, of Cape May Co. Int. Adm'x, Elener Hand. Fellow bondsman—Robert Townsend, of County aforesaid. Witnesses—Clement Conicle, Jeremiah Hand. Cape May Wills, 111 E.

1742, Jan. 28. Inventory of personal estate, £92.06.5; made by Moses Crosly, John Ireland.

1744, ———, —. Account. Moneys paid out by William Morceland and Elener his wife: Loan office, Joseph Roas, Henry Stits, Esqr., Joseph Maps, Richard Smith, Silvanes Townsend, Robert Townsend, George Holenshead, John Ireland, Henry Young, Esqr., "Colnor and Jury to vew the dead body," Moses Crosle.

1747, May 20. Hand, John, of Cape May Co. Int. Adm'r, Silas Hand. James Whildin, fellow bondsman, both of County aforesaid, gentlemen. Witnesses—Elijah Hughes and Jeremiah Hand. Lib. 5, p. 457.

1747, Aug. 1. Inventory of personal estate, £119.01.3; made by Elijah Hughes, Barnabas Crowell, Junior.

1744-5, Feb. 9. Hand, Mercy, of Cape May Co.; will of. Certain moveables to sons Elisha and John Hand, to daughters Abigail Buck, Mary Paige and Jane Whilldin, and to son-in-law, Richard Smith. Son, Isaiah Hand to have negro man Will, on condition, etc. Elishu Hand, youngest son (not of age). Residue to sons Silas, Isaiah and Elishu. Executors—Elisha Hand and Richard Smith. Witnesses—Barnabas Crowell, Junior, Ezekiel Mulford, Senior, Samuel Eldredge, Jacob Spicer. Proved 5 Feb., 1745-6. Lib. 5, p. 244.

1745, Dec. 3. Inventory, £92.16.10; made by Elijah Hughes, Barnabas Crowell, Junior.

1732, Feb. 13. Hand, Sary (Sarah), of Cape May Co., widow; will of. Son, Jacob, ½ of my rights for houses, lands, goods, etc., to which I am rightfully entitled by my husband's last will; the other half to my son Jeremiah. Executor—friend, Nathanel Rusco. Witnesses—James Flood, Jeremiah Hand, Hester Hewit. Proved 10 May, 1733. Lib. 3, p. 333.

1731-2, Feb. 16. Hand, Thomas, of Cape May Co., yeoman; will of. Wife one-third of lands during widowhood. Sons—Thomas, the home lands at Fishing Creek; Jacob, all lands and meadow at Gosen; Jeremiah, £10, Aaron £10, to be paid by my son Thomas. Son, Leuey, £5, to be paid by son Jacob. Legacies to daughters—Leusey, Mary, Lidey, Jerusey. Executors—wife and George Hand. Witnesses—Richard Downes, Jeremiah Hand, Jeremiah Church. Proved 27 May, 1732.

1733, May 27. Letters to George Hand, the surviving executor. Lib. 3, p. 311.

1733, Apr. 26. Inventory (£68.03.0) includes cattle (£40.18.0). Appraisers—John Flower, John Hughes.

1738, July 27. Account. Moneys paid to Jacob Spicer, Samuel Bustill, Francis Bevis, Christopher Foster, Richd. Downs, Jon. Hughs, Mary Hand, Ruth Crowell, Joseph Lord, Nathaniel Foster, George Crandall, Nathan Osborne, Nicholas Stillwell, Andrew McFarland, Recompense Hand, William Smith, Tristam Hedges, Christopher Foster, Jeremiah Hand, etc.

1733, March 31. Hand, William, of Cape May Co. Int. Adm'r, Shangar Hand. Fellow bondsman—Nathaniel Rusco, all of County aforesaid. Witnesses—William Mathews, Jacob Spicer, Jacob Spicer, Junior. Cape May Wills, 70 E.

1732, Nov. 18. Inventory (£58.02.08) includes cattle (£31.02.08). Appraisers—Nathaniel Rusco, Jacob Garrison.

1732, Nov. 13. Hand, Zelophehad, of Cape May Co., yeoman; will of. Wife, Sarah, one-third of personal estate and £5 more for maintaining an expected child. Also, use of all lands and of negro man until sons Nathaniel and Daniel will be 21. Son, Onezemus, to be provided for by my wife until Nathaniel and Daniel are of age; then they to possess equally the plantation whereon I live. Nathaniel to have the southwesterly half next to William Seagraves, Daniel the northeasterly side joining Cornelius Hand's land. Legacies to wife's son, Jacob, and to my daughters Susannah, Jerusha, Deborah (all unmarried), and an expected child. Executors—wife, Sarah, and Nathaniel Rusco. Witnesses—Thomas Hewet, Shamgar Hand, Elisabeth Hand. Proved 10 May, 1733. Lib. 3, p. 334.

1732, Nov. 28. Inventory (£90.14.0), includes cattle, sheep, swine, horses (£55.01.06). Appraisers—John Shaw, Jacob Garrison.

1737, Oct. 28. Account of Nathaniel Rusco, Executor. Moneys paid to Jeremiah Hand, Thomas Stoneback, Thomas Hand, Joshua Shaw, Thomas Hewett, Benjamin Johnson, Ruth Hand, Ananias Osborn, James Cresse, John Garlick, Peter Hand, Henry Young, Aaron Leaming, Henry Stites, George Crandall, Ebenezer Swaine, Robt. Cresse, John Cress, Jacob Spicer, Nathan Osborn, William Seagrave, Elizabeth Crowell, Lemual Swaine, Doctor Flood, John Shaw, ——— Jones, Jerusha Hand.

1732, Feb. 4. Handcock, John, of Mansfield, Burlington Co.; will of. Wife, Anne, sole executrix. Children—William, John, Edward, Joseph and Godfrey. Real and personal estate. Witnesses—Jonathan Scott, Henry Scott, Bartholomew Gibson, George Eyre. Proved April 10, 1733. Lib. 3, p. 400.

1734, April 6. Inventory, £84.18; made by Barthol. Gibson and Edward Kimble.

1749, Jan. 5. Hankins, Richard, of New Brunswick, Middlesex Co., carpenter. Int. Janet Hankins, widow, declines administration and recommends her brother-in-law William Hankins as administrator. Witnesses—Will'm Cook, Sarah Brown. Lib. E, p. 358.

1749, Jan. 12. Bond of William Hankins as administrator. John Stewart, (Steward) fellow bondsman, both yeomen of New Brunswick.

1753, Feb. 22. Inventory of estate of Richard Hankins, who deceased Dec. 9, 1749, £59.10.6; made by Ephrain Dunham, John Stewart, Thomas Combs, Matthias Halldron. Account shows payments to Duncan Campbell, Abraham Ouke, Francis Holman, Dirk van Veghten, Folkard Bennet, Hendrick Vanduzen, Peteres Slegt, Jas. Hay, Andrew Johnston, Frederick Outgilt, Ephraim Dunham, Jun'r, Daniel Hankins, Johannes Fisher, Elisha Dunham, Mathias Holdren, Nath'll Rolfe, Josiah Barent, Jos. Forman.

1745, April 20. Hankins, William, of Winsor, Middlesex Co.; yeoman; will of. Children—John, Zachariah, Jonathan, Richard, Daniel, Mary and Lydia. Real and personal estate. Executors—wife Mary, brother Samuel Parent, and friend Benjamin Sutton. Witnesses—Robert Holmes, James Reynolds, Samuel Thropp. Proved June 7, 1745. Lib. 5, p. 117.

1744, March 10. Hankinson, John, of Freehold, Monmouth Co.; will of. Sisters, Hester Vankirk and Hanner Anderson. Cousin, An Cox, daughter of sister Lida. Witnesses—Thomas Hankinson, Jr., Thomas Cox and John Campbell, Jr. Proved May 29, 1747, when Kenneth Anderson and William Vankirk, husbands of two of the legatees, were sworn as administrators with will annexed. John Campbell, Jr., yeoman, fellow bondsman. Lib. E, p. 47.

1748, April 15. Inventory (£131.18.3) includes debts of Stephen Bogart, Joseph Wilson, William Madock, John Forman, Henry Van Hook and William Van Kerk. Made by David Rhe and John Henderson.

1736, Sept. 7. Hannah, Thomas, of Trenton, Hunterdon Co., laborer. Int. Bond of Francis Bowes, of Trenton, Esquire, as administrator. Samuel Bustill, of Burlington, Esquire, surety. Witnesses—Sarah Ann Bustill and Joseph Rose. Hunterdon Wills, 111 J.

1748, July 18. Hargrove, George, of Burlington Co. Int. Mary Hargrove, widow, and Elizabeth Brown, principal creditor, request that David Rockhill be appointed administrator. Lib. 6, p. 326.

1748, July 19. Inventory of the personal estate, £73.7; made by John Rockhill and Jonathan Shreeve.

1748, July 29. Bond of David Rockhill, of Burlington Co., yeoman, as administrator. John Rockhill, of same, yeoman, fellow bondsman.

Lib. 7, p. 92.

1748, May 16. Harney, Walter, of Reading Township, Hunterdon Co.; will of. Wife, Elizabeth. Daughter, Mary Harney, when married. Children of John Reading, of Amwell Township. Executors—wife, and friend John Reading, Jr., of Amwell. Witnesses—Abraham Zutphen, Hendrick Vannest, Robert Calcitt. Proved August 1, 1748.

Lib. 5, p. 505.

1748, July 28. Inventory, £194.6.8; made by David Berton and Abraham Zutphen.

1750, Nov. 23. Harper, William, of City of Philada., merchant. Int. Alice Harper, widow, and David Harper, eldest son of deceased, renounce, their right to administer in New Jersey to Thomas Harper, another son.

1750, Dec. 1. Bond of Thomas Harper, of Philada., merchant, as administrator. John Baynton, of same, merchant, fellow bondsman.

Burlington Wills, 4675-7 C.

1730, Feb. 17. Harriman, John, of Elizabeth Town, Essex Co., yeoman; will of. Son-in-law, John Hendricks, small Bible. Daughter, Hannah Hendricks, large Bible. Granddaughters—Hannah, Sarah and Lydia Hendricks, and to all other children of John and Hannah Hendricks land lately purchased of Joseph Willson, and seven acres joining land of Jacob Mitchell, deceased. Son-in-law John Clarke, and daughter Abigail Clarke and their children, Abigail and John, plantation joining lands of Benjamin Pierson, Benjamin Meeker and Capt. Ebenezer Lyon; land I purchased of my father-in-law, Isaac Whitehead, of Elizabeth Town, deceased; land in partnership with my brothers Richard and Stephen Harriman; lands joining lands of Benjamin Parkhurst, deceased, William Ogden and Capt. Daniell Price. Elizabeth Harriman, daughter of brother Richard. Brother, Joseph Harriman, accounts with John Lyon. Children of brother, Joseph Harriman, viz., John Harriman, instrument for surveying lands; Hannah Harriman, silver spoon; David Harriman, silver tumbler, and silver spoon to another of his daughters. Brother, Stephen Harriman, meadow joining meadow of Ephraim Price and Nathan Whitehead; his daughter, Joanna, one cow; his son, John, land I purchased of Benjamin Parkhurst, deceased, joining lands of Thos. Ogden and Richard Harriman; his other daughters each a silver spoon. Housekeeper, Deborah Price. Executors—Benjamin Price, Jun'r, and brothers Richard and Stephen. Witnesses—William Clarke, Daniel Parson (Pierson), Samuel Whitehead. Proved March 22, 1730.

Lib. B, p. 202.

1732, Oct. 20. We, Joseph Price, Silvester Cole and John Wade, are held in bonds for Richard Harriman and Benjamin Price, surviving executors. Note.—John Harriman bequeathed to Deborah Coale, wife of Silvester Cole, late Deborah Price, £25. Witnesses—Daniel Meeker, Sarah Sayer.

1750, Dec. 13. Harris, Anna, of Fairfield Precinct, Cumberland Co., widow of Thomas Harris, late of said precinct. Sons—Thomas, Caleb and Jeremiah. Granddaughter, Anna Harris. "Children in my house and family with me all that woolen cloth already made for clothing, each child to have as intended by me known to my daughter Sarah Ogden and granddaughter Anna Harris." Daughter, Sarah Ogden, wife of Thomas Ogden, residue of estate. Executor—son-in-law, Thomas Ogden. Witnesses—David Fithian, Henry Wescote, Benjamin Stratton, Junior. Proved 27 Dec., 1750. Lib. 7, p. 74.

1750, Dec. 21. Inventory (£148.17.9) includes cattle, sheep, hogs, wheat on the ground. Appraisers—David Fithian, Jeremiah Buck.

1745, May 22. Harris, Isaac, of Salem Co., yeoman. Int. Adm'x, Marey Harris. Bondsmen—Henry Seely and David Stratten, all of Salem County. Witnesses—Daniel Alderman, Danl. Mestayer. Lib. 5, p. 215.

1745, May 7. Inventory (£94.2.5) includes cattle and horses. Appraisers—Daniel Alderman, Jonathan Ogden.

1749, Oct. 24. Harris, Thomas, of Fairfield Precinct, Cumberland Co.; will of. Wife, Anna, during widowhood, ½ of improvements within Beller's Survey, both of upland and marsh, and benefit of produce upon homestead, wheat in the barn at Deerfield, and on ground at home. Son, Caleb, the other ½ of improvements within Beller's Survey, both of upland and marsh. Son, Thomas, ½ of lands at Deerfield, excepting 86 acres designed for son Isaac, and on which he lived and died, which is to be given to his sons—Isaac (not 21) and Thomas (not 21); also to my son Thomas one moiety of salt marsh, the homestead and the marsh within Beller's Survey. Son, Jeremiah, other half of the land at Deerfield. To grandsons above mentioned, improvements on the Society's land. To Anna, Mercy, Mary and Esther Harris, daughters of my late son Isaac, benefit of lease which I gave to Abraham Garretson. Daughter, Sarah Ogden, to share with her three brothers in residue of the estate, Caleb improving his part under conduct of executors. Executors—sons Thomas and Jeremiah. Witnesses—David Ogden, Isaac Preston, David Fithian, Joseph Seelye. Proved Dec. 20 (1749; but no year mentioned). Lib. 6, p. 295.

1749, Dec. 19. Inventory (£298.2) includes negro man (£50), cattle, sheep and hogs (£76.06.0). Appraisers—Jeremiah Buck, Joseph Seelye.

1732-3, Jan. 11. Harrison, Abraham, of Newark, Essex Co. Int. Hannah Harrison, widow, declines to accept the administration and requests that Daniel Pierson and David Williams be appointed.

1732-3, Jan. 11. Bond of Daniel Peirson as administrator. David Williams, fellow bondsman. Witness—Edward Thomas. Lib. B, p. 345.

1737, March 13. Harrison, Daniel, of Newark, Essex Co.; will of. Children of daughters Lydia Baldwin and Abigail Farrand, both deceased. Sons—Moses and Daniel, land formerly given testator by deed of gift, joining lands of Joseph Harrison and Joseph Johnson, and land in the Great Neck, joining land of John Plum. Grandson, Jonathan Harrison. Executors—sons Daniell and Moses. Witnesses—Sam'll Farrand, David Ogden, Aaron Richards. Proved Dec. 26, 1738. Lib. C, p. 240.

1738-9, Jan. 23. Inventory, £37.15.01; made by Eliphalet Johnson and Thomas Longworth.

1740, Apr. 2. Harrison, Elizabeth, widow of John Harrison, Junior, Esq., Rocky Hill, Somerset Co.; will of. House and lot at Perth Amboy given by the will (of 2 March, 1723) of her husband, John

Harrison, to be sold by executors and money divided among my four children—Benjamin Higgins, Benjamin Harrison, Sarah Loakison (who has a daughter Sarah under 21) and Grace Harrison. Mentions daughters Rachel Harrison, wife of Benjamin Harrison, Mary Higgens and Nance Harrison. Grandchildren—Edward Higgins, Eliza and Sarah Warden. Executors—sons Benjamin Harrison and Benjamin Higgins. Witnesses—Lewis Moore, Thomas Soden, Thos. Yates. Lib. B, p. 185.

1747, March 30. Harrison, John, of Somerset Co. Int. Adm'r, brother, Henry Harrison. Fellow bondsman—Dollin Corle. Lib. E, p. 10.

1747, July 27. Harrison, Peter, of New Hanover, Burlington Co., weaver; will of. Children—Isaac, Joseph, Thomas, Sarah Fox, Mary, Ruth and Deborah. Tract bought of Wm. Sexton's executors, viz., John Steward and Ann Sexton. Plantation formerly belonging to my father, Richard Harrison. Executors—wife, Sarah, and son Thomas. Witnesses—Joseph Rogers, William Rogers, Thos. Earl. Proved Jan. 16, 1747. Lib. 5, p. 389.

1747, Feb. 10. Inventory, £577.14.5½; made by Benjamin Kirby and Sam'l Emley.

1739, Dec. 20. Harrison, Richard, of New Hanover, Burlington Co., yeoman; will of. Wife, Alse. Children—William, Peter, George, Richard, Ruth Starkey and Sarah Rogers. Grandaughter, Rebeckah Harrison. Executors—son, Peter, and Joseph Rogers. Real and personal estate. Witnesses—William Kirby, Benjamin Kirby, Samuel Wright. Proved Oct. 5, 1742. Lib. 4, p. 317.

1742, Sept. 28. Inventory, £271.6; made by Benjn. Kirby and Sam'l. Emley.

1742, Nov. 6.—Dec. 24. Receipts of payments to Alice Harrison, Sarah Rogers, Richard Harrison, Ruth Starkey, William Harrison.

1731, June 1. Harrison, Samuel, of Gloucester Co., guardian of William Hugg, eldest son of Joseph Hugg of same county, inn-holder. Lib. 3, p. 142.

1738, 28th of 7th mo. (Sept.). Harrow, Isaac, of Trenton, Hunterdon Co.; will of. Wife, Temperance. Son, James Harrow. Executors—wife, and friends Anthony and William Morris. Witnesses—Henry Carter, Joshua Appleton and John Yard. Proved April 6, 1741. Lib. 4, p. 277.

1740-1, Jan. 24. Inventory (£440.17.2) includes an eight-day clock, two maps, Bible; articles in the plating mills, work shop, blade mill; 5 scyths; water engine. Lent to Benjamin Yard, a hammer, etc. In coal house, 900 bushels of coals, £9. Lot bought of Jas. Trent. Made by Francis Giffing, William Atlee, Benjamin Smith.

1735, March 25. Hart, Jane, an orphan upward of 14 yrs., daughter of John Hart, Salem County, ward; guardian John Pledger. Lib. 4, p. 8.

1738, Sept. 2. Hart, Jane, of Salem County, spinster. Int. Adm'r, Robert Hart, of town and county of Salem, merchant. Bondsman—John Jones, attorney-at-law of same place. Witnesses—Richard Smith, Danl. Mestayer. Salem Wills, 629 Q.

1748, March 3. Hart, Jane, of Salem Co., spinster. Int. Adm'r, Charles Hart. Bondsman—William Barker, all of said County, gentlemen. Witnesses—Dan. Mestayer, Davd. Morris. Lib. 6, p. 52.

1749, Nov. 10. Hart, Jeremiah, of Turkey, Borough of Elizabeth, Essex Co.; will of. Son, Daniel, land joining lands of Elnathan Cory, Ephraim Eakly and the parsonage. Daughters—Elizabeth, Deborah and Anna Hart, all under age. Executors—wife, Sarah, and brother Samuell Crowell. Witnesses—Abraham Hendricks, Ezekiel Mulford, Jonathan Mulford. Proved Jan. 16, 1749. Lib. F, p. 25.

1742, Jan. 21. Hart, Nathaniel, of Hopewell, Hunterdon Co., yeoman; will of. Wife, Elizabeth. Residue of estate to children except the two boys Ephraim and Moses to have £10 more than the girls. Eldest son, Ephraim. Daughter, Ann, large Bible. Daughter, Elizabeth. Executors—wife, brother Joseph Hart, and John Hart, son of testator's brother Edward Hart. Witnesses—George Woolsey, Edward Hart and Cornelius Sholdren. Proved March 5, 1742. Lib. 4, p. 361.

1749, July 2. Hart, Ralph, of Trenton, Hunterdon Co., yeoman; will of. Sons Benjamin and Samuel, home plantation in Trenton; Benjamin to have part on south side of road that goes to Maidenhead; Samuel on north side of road, with dwelling house and orchard. Eldest son, Ralph, testator's sword and walking cane. Sons, Josiah and Benjamin. Grandson, John Carpenter, son of daughter Mary, large Bible, at decease of testator's wife. Daughters—Sarah, wife of Robert Akers; Mercy, wife of Joseph Tindall; Martha, wife of Robert Laining, Jr.; Elizabeth, wife of Joseph Jones; Abigail, wife of Stephen Laining. Residue of estate to wife, Sarah. Executors—wife, and sons Ralph and Samuel. Witnesses—Samuel Hunt, William Phillips and Joseph Phillips. Proved August 22, 1749. Lib. 6, p. 274.

1749, Sept. 5. Inventory of estate of "Major Ralph Harts, Esq," (£366.14.4) includes sword and cane, £10.05; large Bible and other books, £2; cattle, horses, mares, colts, £87.10. Made by Thomas Moore and Abraham Temple (or Teple).

1739, Dec. 4. Hart, Robert, of Salem Town and County, merchant, guardian of William Ridley (aged 18). Witness—H. Stubbins. Salem Wills, 642 Q.

1745, Sept. 13. Hart, Robert, of Salem Township, Salem Co., merchant; will of. Wife, Jane, to have additionally to her dower £50 and the house, during widowhood, in Salem, where she and my children live. Son, John Hart, messuage and lot in Salem next my aforesaid dwelling. Son, William Hart, messuage and lot in Salem over against John Goodwin's. Daughter, Lilly, messuage and 10 acres in Salem bought of Hugh Clifton. 18 acres of marsh in Cowneck in sd. Township to three aforesaid children. Residue of lands to son Joseph. Executors—wife, Jane, and son, Joseph. Witnesses—Peter Turner and his wife, Sarah Turner, Charles Brockden. Proved 15 Oct., 1745. Letters granted to Jane Hart, executrix named, (in the absence of Joseph Hart, infant under age). Lib. 5, p. 204.

1762, March 10. "Whereas the said Jane Hart since taking the executorship hath died," etc., "and the said Joseph Hart hath renounced his right, Feb. 15, 1762," John Hart, of Philadelphia, a son of Robert Hart, of Salem Township and County, appointed administrator upon the estate. Bondsman—John Buzby, of Wellingborough, Burlington County, yeoman. Witness—Saml. Allinson.

1745, Dec. 12. Inventory (£1107.0.1½) includes horse, saddle, armour, watch and apparel, plate in gold and silver, wine, ware in the "beaufet," clock and case, 33 handkerchiefs, horses, mares, colts, cattle, negro man and negro child (£44). Appraisers—Wm. Hancock, Ranier Vanhist.

1742, Aug. 7. Hartshorne, Hugh, of Middletown, Monmouth Co.; will of. Wife, Catherine. To daughter of Alice and Joseph Applegate, £30 if she gives security in case executors are troubled concerning land sold by testator to Jonathan Burge, which land was formerly in possession of John Bayly, deceased. Home plantation of 300 acres to wife; bounded by John Leppit, Nicholas Johnson, George Taylor. Also to wife negro girl, Nancy, and two other negroes; riding chaise, etc. Lot in Middletown between George Taylor and Nicholas Johnson. Meadow on Waycake Creek. Son, Robert, house where Robert White lives, with land adjoining on north side of street; excepting land reserved by testator's father, by will, for a burying-ground. If congregation of English Church of Middletown will give executors title to two acres before testator's door, he will devise to them half an acre at Groom's Lane, part of land devised to son Robert, adjoining the widow Leppit. Son, Robert, 6 acres in Great Meadow at Shoal Harbor, adjoining widow Burrows. Silver tankard to son Robert, after wife's death. Provision for negro Jack. Daughters—Margaret White, Catherine Bowne (and her daughter Lydia Bowne), Rebecca Nixon (and her children), Sarah Vanbrackle, Mary, Mercy and Elizabeth Hartshorne. To said seven daughters, part of a lot in Amboy purchased of James Alexander. Granddaughter, Lydia Bowne, half of lot at Barangate, bought of James Bowne. Son-in-law, Robert White. Son, Robert, lot in Amboy, adjoining Richard Fitzrandolph, bought of Zachariah Weeks. Executors—wife, son Robert, brother William Hartshorne, brother-in-law Joseph Field, and nephew William Hartshorne, Jr. Witnesses—George Crawford, Joseph Stillwell, Charles Henderson. Proved October 18, 1742. Lib. D, p. 42.

1742, Oct. 29. Inventory (£699.07.7) includes Harrington Oceana, Thomasius's Dictionary and Dalton's Justice; folio Bible; Barclay's Apology in English and one ditto in Dutch; 2 guns; beam, weights and scales in shop; surveyor's compass and chain; one drum; weaver's loom; quill wheel and warping bars; 42 sides of leather; cheese press; silver tankard; 7 negroes; 1 Gunter's scale; guaging rod and pair of dividers; 2 vols. Hodgson's Mathematics; one pettiaugre with masts, sails, oars and all her oyster rigging and furniture, (£5.10.0); 3 doz. drinking glasses. Made by Joseph Stilwell, gentleman, Nicholas Johnson, yeoman, and Samuel Ogborne, Esquire.

1743, Nov. 26. William Hartshorne declines to serve as executor.

1735, Jan. 16. Hartshorne, Richard, of Middletown, Monmouth Co., mariner; will of. Sister, Margaret Mott. Brother, William Hartshorne, executor, who is to pay testator's other brothers and sisters. Witnesses—Peter Sasery, Miles Weekes, Richard Fitz Randolph. Proved November 19, 1736. Lib. C, p. 127.

1745, Nov. 25. Hartshorne, William, of Middletown Township, Monmouth Co.; will of. Wife, Elizabeth. Daughter, Rachel. Son, William, belt and staff that was testator's fathers. Son, Thomas, silver tankard that was testator's second wife's. Daughters, Mary and Rachel. Three younger children, John, Esek and Rachel. Son, Thomas, 200 acres, where Thomas dwells, adjoining the dam of the pond of his "tan-flats," adjoining ——— Davis. Children—Mary, Rachel, John, Esek, William, Margaret, Hugh and Robert. Executors—wife, and sons William, Thomas, Hugh and Robert. Witnesses—James Bowne, Patrick Feoye, Patrick McEntee, Henry Troot.

Codicil of August 25, 1746. Son, William, having died, bequest made to William's children Katherine and Richard Hartshorne. Witnesses—John Miln, Patrick Feoy and Richard Saltar. Proved March 10, 1747, when Thomas, Hugh and Robert Hartshorne, executors, being Quakers, were affirmed.. Lib. E, p. 204.

1745-6, March 17. Hartshorne, William, Junior, of Monmouth Co. Int. Bond of Mary Hartshorne, widow, as administratrix. John Reid, Esquire, and Thomas Hartshorne, of Monmouth County, fellow bondsmen. Witnesses—William and Robert Hartshorne, Patrick Feoy, Samuel Holmes, Helena Reid. Lib. D, p. 371.

1746, April 10. Inventory (£386.17.1¾) includes bonds and notes of Samuel Legg, Henry Marsh, Zebulon Clayton, Estate of Hugh Hartshorne, Baly's Dictionary, 2 volumes System of Mathematicks, Bible, Cole's Dictionary, 2 compasses, chain, case of instruments and scales, a servant man sold at six months credit for £20, 1 pettiauger and sails, (£4); wood boat, red cedar timber, (£130); cattle at Barnegat sold to John Lawrence. Made by John Brown and John Taylor.

1731, July 3. Hattfield, Edward, of Greenwich, Gloucester Co., tailor. Int. Adm'r, John Middleton, of the same place, yeoman, and Katherine, my wife, late the widow of Edward Hattfield. Witnesses—Saml. Bustill, Joseph Rase. Gloucester Wills, 140 H.

1731, June 30. Inventory, £2.17.10; made by Gusta Locke, A. Randall.

1731, July 3. Oath. "Katherine, relict of Edward Hattfield, now the wife of John Middleton, deposes that soon after the death of her husband she was compelled to kill one cow, worth 50 shillings, for the sustenance of herself and four small children, she being then big with child."

1739, Jan. 21. Havens, Daniel, of Shrewsbury, Monmouth Co., yeoman; will of. Wife, Christian. Children—George, Anna, Daniel, John, Mary, Margrett, Christian and Ann. Executors—wife, and son George. Witnesses—John Herring, Peter Trauerri, William Masters, William Cosgrave. Proved March 25, 1740. Lib. C, p. 325.

1740, May 6. Havens, John, of Shrewsbury, Monmouth Co., yeoman. Int. Elizabeth Havens, widow, declines administration of the estate and recommends Pontius Stelle, Esq., executor of the last will of Gabriel Stelle. Witnesses—Henry Herbert, George Havens.

1740, May 9. Adm'r, Pontius Stelle, of Perth Amboy, principal creditor. Richard FitzRandolph, fellow bondsman. Witness—Robert Lane. Lib. C, p. 340.

1742, Dec. 21. Hawke, Hezekiah, of Pilesgrove, Salem Co. Int. Adm'r, Benjamin Bispham, principal creditor, of Penns Neck. Bondsman—William Barker of Salem. The widow, Johanna, having renounced her right 9 Dec., 1742. Lib. 4, p. 378.

1742, Dec. 14. Inventory, £36.12.2; made by William Alderman, John Mayhew.

1739, Nov. 12. Hay, Adam, of Woodbridge, Middlesex Co., "Doctor of Physick;" will of. Daughter, Martha Putland Hay, at 18 years. Brothers—James and Charles Hay. Sisters—Ann Hay and Hester Putland. Cousin—Ann McCullah. Mother-in-law—Mrs. Penthiselea Putland. Real and personal estate. Executors—wife, Merial, brother

Charles Hay of London, and friends Doctor James Henderson of New Yorke and David Martine, late of Trenton, Esq. Witnesses—Edward Vaughn, Penthiselea Putland, Chris. Dening. Proved June 3, 5, 1741. Lib. C, p. 416.

1739, Aug. 6. Hay, Andrew, of Perth Amboy, Middlesex Co.; will of. Children—Elizabeth, William, Andrew and John, all under age. Real and personal estate. Executors—wife, Agness, and friends Andrew Johnston, Lewis Johnston and Thomas Bartow. Witnesses—John Hamilton, Esq., Fenwick Lyell, Peter Savery, Elinor Williams. Proved Jan. 14., 1739. Lib. C, p. 312.

1742, Nov. 8. Haynes, Ann ("Ann Burrell, otherwise called and known by the name of Ann Haynes"), of Somerset Co., widow; will of. Children—Samuel (oldest), James, Benoniah, Aaron, Henry and Rebeca. Mentions Daniel Dottey, the great Bible, a large book in folio. Works of the Revrd. Mr. Perkens, money that son Benoniah had out of New England, and land lately bought in the Western division of this Province, to be paid for out of the personal estate by Henry and Rebeca. Henry to have the land and Rebeca the personal "as shall be an equal half with him." Henry and Rebeca, all title to certain tract of land situate in Haverstraw, N. Y., and to be at equal charges in recovering the same by law. Executors—John Ayers, Esq., and Moses Ayers, Esq. Witnesses—Silvanua Conant, Timo. Stoughton, Brice Rikey. Proved 8 Dec., 1742, and 6 Jan., 1742-3. Lib. D, p. 19.

1742-3, Jan. 13. Renunciation. Moses Ayers refuses "having anything to do with that estate." Witnesses—Elisha Ayers, Silas Ayers.

1750, March 26. Haynes, Ann, of Salem Town and County, widow. Int. Adm'r, John Whittal. Bondsman—William Sydden (Siddons). Both of place aforesaid. Witness—Josiah Kaighn. Lib. 7, p. 37.

1723, Jan. 15. Haynes, Benjamin, of Salem Co., weaver; will of. Wife, Ann, executrix, to have personal estate and 18 acres purchased of Tho. Mason. Sons—Joseph, 100 acres joining my brother Joseph Haynes' land in Manington precinct, Salem County, he paying his sister, Mary Ann Haynes, £10, when she will be 18; Benjamin, acre of land purchased of Thomas Harris, joining John Killits lot; John, the land and house I live in, joining James Wiggins' lot, he to pay my daughter Hannah, £10, when she will be 18. Executor—son Joseph Hall. Witnesses—James Wiggins, Joseph Morris, Jno. Goodwin. Affirmed 2 June, 1733. Lib. 3, p. 372.

1733, May 8. Inventory, £86.5.1; made by Benj. Acton, John White.

1734, April 23. Account. Moneys paid to Daniel Mestayer, Surrogate at Salem, Clement Hall, Thomas Mason, Philip Chetwood, Abel Nicholson, Lewis Morris, Peter Turner, Joseph Morris, Thomas Haynes, Francis Gandonot, Roger Sherron, Samuel Wade, Thomas Stow, Thomas Cook, Samuel Abot, John White. Moneys due from Joseph Haynes, "who is run away," William Steward, Andrew Sinnick, John Goldsmith.

1747, June 29. Haynes, Benjamin, of Salem Town and County, carpenter. Int. Admr's, Charles Reading, William Murdock. Bondsmen—Thomas Thompson, William Barker, all of Salem County, yeomen. Witnesses—Robert Thompson, Danl. Mestayer. Lib. 5, p. 422.

1740, June 23. Haynes, Daniel, of Salem Town and County, carpenter. Int. Adm'x, Hannah Haynes, widow. Bondsmen—Benjamin Haynes, John Mason, all of said County. Witness—Thos. Price. Lib. 4, p. 244.

1740, June 23. Inventory (£466.6.0) includes horse, saddle, carpenter's tools; also bonds (£205.3.4). Appraisers—John Mason, Edward Test.

1750, March 26. Haynes, John, of Salem Town and County. Int. Adm'r, John Whittall. Bondsman—Josiah Kay. Both of aforesaid place. Lib. 7, p. 39.

1750, June 18. Hayward, Ebenezer, of Perth Amboy, Middlesex Co.; will of. "After payment of debts if anything remains I bequeath it to the School for Indians where I have been instructor under the direction of the Honorable Society for Propagating Christian Knowledge." Executor—Mr. John Brainard, Minister of the Gospel among the Indians. Witnesses—Wm. Tennent, Elihu Spencer, John Brainard. Proved July 17, 1750. Lib. E, p. 441.

1745, August 23. Heath, Andrew, of Amwell, Hunterdon Co.; will of. Wife, Mary. Sons—Andrew, John, Richard, David and Timothy. Daughters—Elizabeth Ketchum, Mary, Catharine and Sarah. Executors—wife, and son Andrew. Witnesses—Ephraim Quinby, Daniel Ketchum and John Lewis, M. D. Proved Oct. 5, 1745. Lib. 5, p. 209.

1747, April 6. Heath, Richard, of Bethlehem, Hunterdon Co. Int. Inventory; made by Jno. Coats and Peter Schmuck.

1747, April 10. Bond of Mary Heath, of Bethlehem, as administratrix. Daniel Ketcham, of same place, yeoman, surety. Witnesses—William Peirson, Joshua Howell, Mary Heath (a Quaker). Lib. 5, p. 459.

1757, May 16. Account of Mary Park, formerly Mary Heath, administratrix of the estate. Mentions Jno. Farnsworth, Jos. Linn, William Hendrickson, John Coat, Archibald Hanna, David Drake, Hezekiah Bonham, Samuel Bonham, Patrick Nixson, John Hull, Thomas Evans, Henry Coat, Robert Blair, N. Farnsworth, Luther Colvin, John Oaks, Mary Farnsworth, Nath'l Forster, Samuel Large, Samuel Large, Jr., Jno. Wiler, Lazarus Adams, Nathaniel Colman, Morris Glanwell, Jacob Whelmer, Abraham Bonnell, Peter Cambell, Godfrey Melick, William Schooley, Samuel Schooley, Jno. Reading, Jno. Moody, William Corbet, Robert Haslet, Cornelius Low, William Montgomery, Thomas Wolverton, A. Bonnell, Robert White, Nath'l Pettit, Roger Terrill, John Park, Daniel Ketcham, Godfrey Rich, Nath'l Forster, Jos. Merrill, Philip Chapman, William Bates, Samuel Willson, Peter Smock, Jas. Harker, Daniel Pegg, Henry Oxley.

1733, May 5. Hedge, Nathan, of Salem Town and County, tailor; will of. Mother, Rebecca Cox, executrix and sole legatee. Real and personal estate. Witnesses—Roger Huckings, Robert Watherbe, Alexdr. Simpson. Affirmed 15 August, 1733. Lib. 3, p. 373.

1733, June 12. Inventory (£45.13.10) includes bonds of Joseph Graves, John Surge and Francis Doyle. Appraisers—Thomas Taylor, Joseph Gest.

1731, May 12. Hedge, Samuel, of Cohanscy, Salem Co.; will of. Wife, Ann, sole executrix, and to have 1000 acres in Mannington in said County, joining Jacob Attwood's land on Salem Creek, and on Arthur's, Bovier's and Bartleson's land, being part of 15,000 acres surveyed by Benjamin Acton, the 10 da., 4 mo., 1709; also 190 acres at Alloways Creek; also 8-acre lot in Salem on the lower side of my brother Nathan's 24 acres; also 16-acre lot of woodland, and two-acre lot joining William Followell's and Nathan Hedges' lot, where the house stands, in consideration that she discharge a bond given by my father, Samuel Hedge, to William Biles, of Bucks County, Pa. ("that is to say ¼ due on my account, ¼ on William Hedge, deceased, ⅛ on John Hedge, deceased, for the which sum I gave a bond to Nathan Hedge to pay." If not paid the land to return equally to my son, Samuel Hedge, and my daughter, Rebecca Hedge). Personal estate to wife for paying debts and bringing up the children. Son, Samuel Hedge, 600 acres in Mannington; also my shares on Phoenix Grove, Salem Creek, near Hellgate; also ½ of a 16-acre lot in Salem, joining Nathan Hedge and William Followell's lots. Daughter Rebecca, the other half of said lot; also 500 acres in Mannington, joining where William Murfey dwelt. Mother, Rebecca Cox, to have 50 acres in Mannington. Witnesses—Abiel Cearll, Joseph Wheaten, Thos. Hendy. Proved 2 March, 1731. Lib. 3, p. 182.

1731, Feb. 29. Inventory (£189.6.3) "of Samuel Hedge of town of Greenwich, Salem County, gent." Appraisers—Leo. Gibbon, Abiel Carll.

1747-8, March 13. Heggeman (Heggerman), Denis, of Somerset Co., yeoman; will of. Wife, Mary. Real and personal estate. Children—Adrian, Barnett, Elizabeth and Margarette (all minors), and, if a child be born, to share. Executors—Brother, Adrian Heggerman, Abraham Striker and John Van Dyke (John Van Dyck, Junior, in letters testamentary). Witnesses—Garret Williamson, Petrys Voorheis, Roelof Van Dike. Proved 31 March, 1748. Lib. E, p. 171.

1747-8, March 23. Inventory, real and personal (£665.13) includes 133 acres of land with improvements, and field of green wheat, cattle, gun, sword and powder horn. Made by Lucas Voorhees, Roelof VanDike.

1743, Jan. 12. Heins, Lawrence, of Salem Co., combmaker. Int. Adm'r, Joseph Wheaton. Bondsman—David Platt. Both of Cohansey. Witnesses—James Fourness, Chas. O Neill.

1743, Jan. 12. Inventory (£10.12.6) includes rent due in hands of Obadiah Wood. Appraisers—Thos. Parke, David Plats.

Salem Wills, 582 Q.

1740, Nov. 3. Helm, Hermonos (Hermanus, Manus), of Greenwich, Gloucester Co., husbandman; will of. Sons—Israel, the 100 acres whereon he lives (surveyed to him by Thomas Miles); John, 66 acres, whereon he lives, also 30 acres of marsh purchased of Disha Phenemon (in case of his death without issue, my sons Okee and Andrew Helm to have equally aforesaid property and the tract whereon I live). Wife, Catteren Helm, to remain there "during her pure widowhood." In case of their death without issue tract to descend to my surviving son. Son, Joseph, 100 acres on a branch of Trumpeter's Creek, joining Hendrickson's land. Daughters—Mary, Catteren and Dinah (married). Israel Lock, one shilling in full for his wife's part of my estate. Executors—wife, Catteren, and son Okee. Witnesses—Wm. Mickle, Gerret Vanaman, John Vanaman. Proved 26 Nov., 1740. Letters granted July 18, 1741. Lib. 4, pp. 260, 261.

1740, Nov. 20. Inventory (£207.17.3) includes silver tankard, £12. Appraisers—John Vaneman, Wm. Mickle.

1744-5, Jan. 20. Helm (Helmus), Okeynus (Okinus), of Greenwich, Gloucester Co.; will of. Son, Andrew, home plantation on Rackoon Creek; in case of his death without issue, same to descend to my son Gabriel, with all my lands at Pennsneck; if he dies without issue, to my youngest son Okeynus (a minor). Eldest son, John Helm, five shillings (besides what has been given him). Daughter—Magdalena.

Executor—son-in-law, Andrew Hendrickson. Witnesses—Hendrick Hendrickson, John Jones, Peter Cox. Proved Oct. 26, 1750.
Lib. 7, p. 151.

1750, Oct. 11, 13. Inventory, £129.7.8; made by Tim. Rain, Mathew Gill.

1753, Feb. 7. Account. Moneys paid to William Guest, John Jones, Andrew Helmer, Erick Reynolds, Matthew Gill, Magdalen Sely, John Halton, Timothy Rain, John Ladd, Ebenezer Cook, Joseph Scattergood.

1750, Aug. 11. Helms, Andrew, of Greenwich, Gloucester Co., yeoman; will of. Sisters, Catherine and Mary, ½ of 19 acres, purchased of Joseph Armitt. Brother, Joseph. Executors—mother, Catherine Helms, and my brother, John. Witnesses—Alexr. Randall, Andrew Long, Ann Cox. Proved 9 Oct., 1750.

1750, Oct. 6. Inventory, £127.19.6; made by Alexr. Randall, Andrew Long. Lib. 7, p. 23.

1743, Oct. 7. Henderson, James, of New York City; will of. Children—Tessia (wife of Alexander Moore), Margaret, Elizabeth, Catherine, Eve and Mary Henderson. Land on Prince Street, joining land of Anthony Duane; land in Albany, Ulster Co., New York. Executors—wife, Tessia, and daughter Margaret. Witnesses—Peter Renaudet, William Bascome, John Kelly. Proved April 25, 1745. Lib. D, p. 274.

1734, Jan. 22. Hendricks, Baker, of Elizabeth Town, Essex Co., an orphan aged about eighteen years. Bond of David Smith, trader, as guardian. Jacob DeHart, yeoman, fellow bondsman. Witness—Pontius Stelle.

1738, Dec. 6. Bond of Jacob DeHart, mariner, as guardian. John Thomson, of Perth Amboy, yeoman, fellow bondsman. Lib. C, p. 225.

1727, November 16. Hendricks (Hendrickson), Daniel, of Middletown, Monmouth Co., gentleman; will of. (See N. J. Archives, vol. 23, p. 222. The inventory is there omitted, but given below).

1728, May 23. Inventory of the estate of "Captain" Daniel Hendricks (£1130.08.00½) includes 2 swords, male pillion and portmantle, 2 pistols, large Bible and 6 smaller books, nippers, tooth drawers, negro Joe (£35), negro lad Peter (£40), negro Bob, (£65), negro woman Dinah and child (£50), negro woman Kate, (£10), 36 sides leather; 8 cattle hides, horses, mares, colts, stallion, gun, flour at Van Guelder's mill; also bonds and debts of Johannes and Jacobus Swart, Cornelius Wecoff, Joseph Goldin, William Bowne, Mordecai Gibbons, Thomas Johnson, Robert Patterson, Benjamin Cooper, John Mount, Horman Vansandt, John Powell, Mark Farrar, Gerrett Bowler, William Parent, Richard Compton, Sarah Throckmorton, Gerrett Covenhoven, John Ruckman, Cornelius Wecoff, Thomas Smyth, John Fenton, Gershom Wallen, Bartholomew Marsh, Joseph Morgan, Andrew Johnson, James Hyde, Thomas Stillwell, John Vaughan, widow Hophmire, Alexander Wellson, John Morford, Simon Leopardus, John Whitlock, Hendrickus Kipp, Hendrick Hendrickson. Made by William Lawrence, Jr., Samuel Ogborne, Johannes Luister and Giesburt Hendrickson. Monmouth Wills, 677 M.

1733, July 5. Hendricks, John, of Elizabeth Town, Essex Co. Int. Bond of Ebebezer Johnson as administrator. Thomas Clarke, fellow bondsman. Witness—Sarah Dagworthy. Lib. B, p. 435.

1733, Jan. 13. Inventory (£482.05.05), includes large Bible, Psalm

Book, gold and silver rings, bonds of James Ogden, John Reid, Andrew Joline, John Cask, Richard Alford, William Gunner, Henry Person, William Patterson, John Low, Isaac Bonnel. Made by Justice Andrew Joline, Justice Robert Ogden, John Emitt.

1734, June 3. Hendrickson, Hendrick, Sr., of Middletown Township, Monmouth Co. Int. Inventory (£193.14.3) includes silver hilted sword, pair of pistols, sun dial, tankard, negro man and woman, "pleasure sled shod with iron." Made by Hendrick Hendrickson, Nicolas Waycott, Robert Dodsworth.

1735, Oct. 9. Adm'r, Hendrick Hendrickson, Jr., of same place, son of deceased. John Deare, of Amboy, fellow bondsman. Witness—Lawrence Smyth. Lib. C, p. 44.

1749, Sept. 21. Hendrickson, Henry (Hendrick), of Greenwich Township, Gloucester Co.; will of. Wife, Geena, "this old place, which I now live on;" after her decease same to descend to my son Jonas, and 100 acres lying on the other side of Timber Creek. Sons—Andrew, the place he lives on, also 70 acres on this side of Timber Creek, near Hance Urins' land; Henry, the place I bought of Lawrence Lock, also 86 acres I bought of John Mickel. Daughters—Bridget Lock, Madlena Lock, Sarah Dinney and Geena. Executors—sons Jonas and Henry. Witnesses—Isaiah Davenport, Charles Lock, Swan Lock. Proved 19 Dec., 1749. Lib. 6, p. 358.

1749, Nov. 23. Inventory (£435.00.5) includes cooper tools, "Syder, mattheglum and casks" (£5.14.0), young cattle. Appraisers—Isaiah Davenportt, Charles Lock.

1740, Oct. 11. Hendrickson, John, of Middlesex Co., yeoman. Int. Bond of Hendrick Hendrickson, the eldest brother, William Cowenhoven and Henry Disbrow, as administrators on the estate. Jonathan Stout, fellow bondsman. Lib. C, p. 355.

1744, Jan. 14. Henry, Alexander, of City of New Brunswick, Somerset Co., merchant; will of. Wife, Elizabeth. Children—John, James, Alexander and William (all under age), and an expected child. Real and personal estate. Wife, Elizabeth, executrix during widowhood. Other executors—William Ouke, James Neilson and James Lyne, all of said City, gent. Witnesses—Anne Kearny, John Henry, Aaron Van Cleave. Proved 18 March, 1744. Lib. D, p. 249.

1750, July 26. Henry, John, of Bedminster Township, Somerset Co., yeoman; will of. Wife, Anne, the estate for the benefit of herself and two youngest children, one-third to wife, and the remainder among the children ("including my wife's child by a former husband"), John Henry, Sarah Henry, Margaret Henry, and Mary Venobles. Wife, Anne, and Ephraim Lockheart, executors. Witnesses—John McGallird, John Colwell, Nicholas Mooney. Proved 21 August, 1750. Lib. E, p. 447.

1750, Sept. 12. Inventory, real and personal, (£562.17.9) includes 153 acres of land, with house and barn (£306), and debts due from James Adams, William McKeney, Congregation at Bedminster. Made by William Colwell, Robert Rousbrough.

1759, May 2. Settlement of estate and division among the heirs, the widow to have one-third, the other two-thirds among the four children. Signed—Ann Henry, John Henry, Sarai Adams, Mary Venebles, Margret Henry. Witnesses—Barbry A. Miller, Joseph Feach.

1732, Dec. 30. Hepburn, Edward, of Piscataway, Middlesex Co. Int. Adm'r, William Hepburn. Lib. B, p. 345.

1744-5, Jan. 28. Hepburn, John, Junior, of Freehold, Monmouth Co., yeoman; will of. Provision for father, John Hepburn, Senior. Brothers and sisters—James Hepburn, Naomi Castener and Elizabeth Jolley. John and James, sons of James Hepburn. John and James, sons of Charles Jolley. Executors—brother, James, of Windsor Township, and friends Thomas Lawrie and James Montgomery, Junior, both of Upper Freehold. Witnesses—James Debowe, John Evelman and John Silver. Proved February 4, 1745. (Thomas Lawrie a Quaker). Lib. 5, p. 218.

1745-6, Jan. 30. Inventory of estate of John Hepburn, Junior, "late of Allenstown" (£540.2.7), includes a Bible and Concordance, bonds of Benjamin and John Vancleft. Made by William Corles, Jr., and William Lawrence.

1764, Jan. 17. Account. Mentions legacy of James Jolly paid to his executor, Joseph Borden; legacy left to John Jolley, who died before testator. Cash paid to Charles Jolley, John and Joseph Foreman, Peter Schenck, Mathias Peterson, Thomas Cadwallader, David (or Doctor) Mills, Jeremiah and Naomi Castner, John Burnet, Daniel Robins, John and Robert Laurence, John Dare, William Hood, Francis Chambers, Peter Buckallow, Peter Le Conte, Stephen Warner, Henry Rall, Anthony Swain, Richard Hutchinson, Thomas Severns.

1747, August 11. Herbert, Daniel, of Middletown, Monmouth Co., yeoman; will of. Wife, Amy. Mother, Mary Cooper, a widow. Wife to have goods she brought testator and that since given her by her grandfather, Safety Grover. Children—Jonathan, (a minor), Mary, (a minor). Brother, David Herbert. Executors—wife, and friends John Taylor and Joseph Stillwell, of Middletown, gentlemen. Witnesses—Samuel Legg, Joseph Patterson, Junior, and John Nathan Hutchins. Proved September 23, 1747. Lib. E, p. 82.

1745, August 3. Herbert, Henry, of Manasquan, Town of Shrewsbury, Monmouth Co., yeoman; will of. Wife, Elizabeth. Son, Henry, lands on Manasquan River. Daughter, Hannah. Son, Isaac, land, carpenters' tools and gun. Executors—wife, and son Isaac. Witnesses—John Pearce, William Pearce, Jon. Herring and John Newman, Junior. Proved December 2, 1745. Lib. D, p. 352.

1745, Nov. 31. Elizabeth Herbert, widow, resigns her right as executor, by reason of great age and other infirmities. Witnesses—John Pearce, Cornelis Harrell.

1745, Nov. 31. Inventory, £182.01.06; made by John and William Pearce.

1745-6, March 1. Herbert, James, of New Brunswick, Middlesex Co.; will of. Sons—Richard, Daniel and James. Real and personal estate. Executors—wife Margaret, brother Richard Herbert, and Reuben Runyon. Witnesses—Thos. Hance, Cornelys Van Aersdalen, Daniel Herbert. Proved Oct. 17, 1746. Lib. D, p. 417.

1746, April 21. Inventory (£156.6) includes Bible, "book of Architex," and an account against Thos. Larrance; made by Luykes Voorhees, Thomas Hance.

1749, May 3. Hern, William, of Cumberland Co.; will of. Friend, Jonathan Smith, executor and sole legatee. Witnesses—Nathl.

Jenkins, Junr., Joseph Page, Anthony Elverd. Proved 17 May, 1749, at Cape May. Lib. 6, p. 67.

1749, May 17. Inventory, £21.9.8; made by Nathl. Jenkins, William Smith.

1733, June 21. Herriman (Harriman), Stephen, of Essex Co. Int. Bond of Johanna Herriman as administrator. Jonathan Dayton, fellow bondsman. Lib. B, p. 421.

1712, Dec. 10. Hertie, Conrardus, of Orange Co., New York, husbandman; will of. Executors—Jacobus Cole, my brother-in-law and Michael Vries Land, my wife's uncle. Eldest son, Johannes. Jacob Hertie, gun for his right of next heir of blood. Wife, Lunkie, use of real and personal estate during life for the "bringing up" of our children. 'Whereas I repute myself the sole and lawful heir to my deceased father's estate and that he died intestate, leaving several sums of money, which the above named Gortie, my mother, put to interest, whereunto I reckon to be the sole heir, do recommend my executors to recover the same, if possible, and the ½ part I give to my wife with the condition that she bequeaths the same to our children at her decease, the other ½ to be put to interest for our children's use, and to be divided equally among them as they become of age.'

'Whereas by the will of Mathias France, dated the 7th of July last I am one of the Executors, together with Thomas France, and interest in that part of said estate, which was given to the heirs of said Gortie, wife of Mathew France, and my mother, whereof I reckon myself the sole heir, my executors are empowered to receive and dispose of my part of the estate, ½ to wife during life, the other half to be put to interest for the use of our children and divided as they become majors.' Signed at Scranlingburgh in Hackensack, Bergen Co., N. J. Witnesses—P. Anconniere (Peter Fanconniere), Johanes Philus Rugeni, James Christ, Philip Peter Granberger. Proved 12 November, 1733.

1733, Nov. 12. Michael Vreeland qualifies as executor. Lib. B, p. 472.

1742, Oct. 16. Hetfield, Abraham, of the Borough of Elizabeth, Essex Co., tanner; will of. Wife, Margaret. Children—Abraham, John, David, Samuel, Elias, Jacob, William, Sarah and Phebe, last seven under age. Land bought of Baker, son of John Hendricks, deceased, joining land of John Ross, Esq.; land joining land of Samuel Winans; lands bought of Isaac Hetfield, Stephen Meeker, Johannas Winans, Cornelius Hetfield and Ephraim Sale at Woodruffs Creek, joining land of Edward Sale; land called Stoffells Creek; land given me in my father's will; land bought of John Winans called Horse Shoe; land in partnership with Matthias, Joseph and Jacob Hetfield. Executors—friends William Winans and Robert Ogden. Witnesses—Cornelius Hetfield, Jacob Hetfield, Thos. Jackman. Lib. D, p. 286.

1746, Nov. 5. Hetfield, Jacob, Jun'r, of Elizabeth Town, Essex Co., upwards of 16. Bond of Samuel Hetfield, yeoman, as guardian. Witness—John Smythe. Lib. D, p. 425.

1745, July 4. Hetfield, Margaret, of the Borough of Elizabeth, Essex Co., widow; will of. Daughters—Sarah and Phebe Hetfield. Sons—Abraham, John, David, Samuel, Elias, Jacob and William, last three under age. Real and personal estate. Executors—son, Abraham, and Matthias Hetfield, Esq. Witnesses—Benjamin Spinning, Abraham Woodruff, John Ross.

1745, July 26. Codicil—Daughter Phebe, the largest trunk. Witnesses—William Winans, Philip Blacklidge, John Ross. Proved Sept. 7, 1745. Lib. D, p. 329.

1740, April 23. Heulett, John, of Shrewsbury, Monmouth Co., yeoman. Int. Adm'x, Zibiah Heulett, his widow. Nathaniel Parker and Jacob Dennis, all of same place, yeomen, fellow bondsmen. Monmouth Wills, 909-10 M.

1731, Dec. 13. Heulings, Abraham, of Burlington Co. Int. Adm'x, Mary Heulings, widow. Joseph Heulings, cordwainer, and Charles Tonkin, husbandman, both of Burlington, fellow bondsmen. (See Mary Heulings, infra). Lib. 4, p. 168.

1731, Dec. 15. Inventory of the personal estate, £378.2.11; made by Jos. Rockhill and Sam. Scattergood. Includes sword.

1735, Aug. 16. Additional inventory, includes bonds and bills of Rachel Tonkin, Ed. R. Price, Thomas Budd, Joseph Brittain, B. Butterworth, Joseph Yard, Benjamin Wheaton, John Borradaile, Elisha Reves, Ester Belews, Edward Norton, Isaiah Foulks, Peter Rambo, James Smarts, Daniel Leeds, Joseph Thomas, William Makintosh.

1731, March 10. Heulings, Jacob, Jr., of Chester, Burlington Co.; will of. Children—Abraham, Joseph and Hannah, all under age. Brothers' and sisters' children. Negro boy, Sambo. Lands joining Joseph Fenimore, Thomas Allen and Peter Phillips. Executor—father-in-law, Benjamin Moor, and brothers Joseph and William. Witnesses—Henry Dell, William Peachee, Sam'll Atkinson. Proved Jan. 15, 1731-2. Lib. 3, p. 186.

1731-2, Feb. 8. Inventory, £219.6.9; made by Robert Lucas and Joseph Fenimore. Includes negro woman, £10, Bible and other books.

1741, Aug. 6. Heulings, Joseph, of City and Co. of Burlington, cordwainer; will of. Wife, Anne. Only son, Abraham, under age; if he die without heirs estate to descend to Isaac, Susanna, Bathsheba, Martha and Mary, children of bro., Abraham, also to children of brothers Jacob and William, and of sister Elizabeth Bryan, and to Ruth, dau. of William and Hannah Snowden. £25 to Richard Smith, Sen'r, for use of nephew, Israel Heulings. Church of St. Anne's at Burlington £10. 1050 acres in the mountains bought of John Bowlby. Executors—brother William, and friend Paul Watkinson. Witnesses—John Budd, Ben't Bard, James Budd, Row'd Ellis. Proved April 3, 1744. Burlington Wills, 3725-32 C.

1744, May 14. Inventory, £337.8.11; made by Sam'l Lovett and Anthony Elton.

1732, March 10. Heulings, Mary, of Burlington, who was administratrix of Abraham Heulings, deceased. Administration of estate granted to Joseph Heulings and Charles Tonkin. Samuel Scattergood and Joseph Rockhill, all of Burlington Co., yeomen, fellow bondsmen. Lib. 3, p. 248.

1739, 10 mo. (Dec.), 5 da. Hewes (Hews), Edward, of Oldmans Creek, Salem Co.; will of. Legacies to wife, Hannah; sons, Elihu (when 21) and Benjamin (when 21); daughters, Tabitha (when 18) and Hannah (when 18). Plantation to said sons equally. Eldest son to be bound out at the age of fourteen and a-half to my brother,

Aaron Hewes, to learn his trade. Benjamin to be bound out at fourteen to my brother, Joseph Hews, to learn his trade. Executors —wife, Hannah, and my brother, James Hews. Witnesses—Dobson Wheeler, Rebecca Pitman, Aaron Hewes. Proved 21 April, 1741. Lib. 4, p. 282.

1740-1, March 20. Inventory, £359.11.4; made by Elisha Bassett, David Davis.

1735, 2 mo. (Apr.), 25 da. Hewes (Hews), Thomas, of Oldmans Creek, Salem Co.; will of. Wife, Mary, to have personal estate and use of house and plantation until three children will be of age. Then sons, Joseph and Thomas, to have plantation and each to pay £20 to their sister. Executors—wife and my brother, Edward Hewes. Witnesses—Sarah Rain, Jeremiah Barnet, Jane Bickham. Affirmed 26 May, 1735. Lib. 4, p. 28.

1735, 3 mo. (May), 10 da. Inventory (£172.5) includes "½ of a boat and conew, £14.3." Appraisers—James Hewes, Thomas Pedrick.

1733, 2 mo. (Apr.), 7 da. Hewes (Hews), William, of Oldmans Creek, Salem Co.; will of. Wife, Sarah. Legacy to daughter, Ruth. Son, Edward, to have dwelling house and plantation, woodland and meadow "adjoining to James, with a slip of land 20 rod broad to be taken from the lands I bought of James Logan, to run parallel with formerly Pinick's line, in all about 210 acres." Son, Thomas, remainder of that land (194 acres) bought of James Logan, where he now lives, and six acres of meadow down the Creek. Executors—wife, Sarah, and sons Edward and Thomas. Witnesses—Mikel Pedrick, Thos. Pedrick, Philip Pedrick. Proved 22 May, 1733. Lib. 3, p. 320.

1733, 3 mo. (May), 16 da. Inventory, £134.5.2; made by Michel Pedrick, Thomas Pedrick.

1732-3, Feb. 12. Hewett, Randall, of Cape May Co., yeoman; will of. Wife one-third of personal and use of one-third of land, house, negro man Tom and mulatto boy Jonah, during life. Son, Randall, 140 acres out of the tract I live on next to Thomas Hewet on the north side; also 40 acres additional at the head of the same land. Son, Reuben, 60 acres on the north side of Thomas Hewet's, formerly William Whitlock's; also 20 acres of back land. Son, Joseph, 180 acres on south side of tract I live on; also 60 acres of back land. Moveable estate to sons Jacob, Nathaniel and Ebenezer. Witnesses—John Hughs, Lewis Crese, Nathaniel Rusco.

1733, June 27. Randal Hewett son of deceased, granted letters of Administration as will of father did not name an executor. Lib. 3, p. 345.

1733, Apr. 26. Inventory (£582.2.10) includes weaver's loom (£5), cattle, sheep, swine (£111), negro man and a "Melato," (£36), ½ of small shallop. Appraisers—Richard Downes, John Hughes.

1740, May 20. Hewitt, Caleb, of Greenwich, Gloucester Co., carpenter. Int. Adm'r, William Hewitt, Jun'r. Fellow bondsman, William Hewitt of same place, yeoman. Witness—Alex'r Randall. Lib. 4, p. 238.

1739, Sept. 29. Inventory (£117.1.1½) includes carpenter tools. Appraisers—Robert Zane, Alexr. Randall.

1731, Jan. 7. Hewlings, Mathew, of Wellingboro, Burlington Co.; will of. To Solomon Curtis all my land in Northampton at age.

Executors—uncle Joseph Heulings. Witnesses—Robert Stork, Joseph Wetherill, Isaac DeCow. Proved March 10, 1737. Lib. 4, p. 131.

1750-1, 9th day, 1st mo. (Mar.). Higbee, John, of Burlington Co. Int. Inventory, £43.18; made by Abraham Haines and Robert Engle.
1750, March 20. Adm'x, Mary Higbee, widow. Robert Engle and Robert Pond, of same County, fellow bondsmen. Lib. 7, pp. 52, 103.

1746-7, March 7. Higbee, Joseph, of Trenton, Hunterdon Co. Int. Bond of Joseph Higbee, of Trenton, as administrator. Elijah Bond, of Trenton, surety. Witnesses—Jno. Hutton, Theo. Severns. Lib. 5, p. 459.

1732, July 25. Higgens, Benjamin, of Somerset Co. Int. Adm'rs, John Chambers, Joseph Badcock. Lib. B, p. 292.

1736, Dec. 1. Higgins, Richard, of Essex Co. Int. Adm'r, Peter Leconte, of Monmouth County, "Phisyhan," Phebe Higgins, the widow, having renounced. Lib. C, p. 136.
1736, Dec. 1. Inventory (£63.01.01) includes bond of Thomas Williams, dated Dec. 25, 1724, bond of Court Myers in hands of Rob't Lawrence, also "articles of good luck" amounting to £41.13.08. Appraised by Joseph Lippincott, Thomas Eatton, Paul Hill, Rob't Reynolds.
1737, June 20. Account of things sold at Standley Whites'. Purchasers—Thomas Eatton, Robert Savige, Zebulon Dixson, John Hoskins, Joseph Huet, Standley White, Peter Le Conte. Made by Thomas Gleane, vendue master.
1738, Sept. 16. Account. Ezekiel Bonyot, messenger to Elizabethtown, to acquaint testator's son of his illness. Trip to Goodluck to take inventory. John Hance, Thomas Williams, Court Myres.

1746, Jan. 8. Higgins, William, of Elizabeth Town, Essex Co., blacksmith and boatman. Int. Jerusha Higgins, widow, renounces her right to administer, and desires that Gershom Higgins, father of the deceased, be appointed. Witness—John Ross, Mathias Baldwin.
1746, Jan. 10. Gershom Higgins, blacksmith, administrator. John Blanchard, Esq., fellow bondsman. Lib. D, p. 445.
1746-7, Jan. 11. Inventory, £52.07.06; made by John Ross and Cornelius Hetfield.
1747, April 6. Accompt. Payments to William Burnet, Abraham Hetfield, Samuel Woodruff, Mr. Thomas Barto.

1731, Dec. 31. Hildreth, David, Sr., of Cape May Co., yeoman; will of. Wife, Elizabeth, plantation I live on (186 acres, mortgaged in the Loan Office) during widowhood or until son, Joshua, shall be 21. But if she remains my widow, to have use of ½ of same during life. Land lately surveyed joining Indian Neck to be paid for at Loan Office, and divided equally among four sons, Jonathan, Joseph, James and David, together with piece of land joining thereto. Son, Noah, to have £5 when 21, and daughter, Mercy, the same at 18, or when married. Wife, Elizabeth, sole executrix; Henry Young, Esq., assistant. Witnesses—Aaron Leaming, Nathaniel Jenkins, Junr., Elizabeth Ludlim. Proved 20 March, 1732-3. Lib. 3, p. 312.
1732, Nov. 2. Inventory (£95.15.0), includes cows, calves and sheep. Appraisers—Nathaniel Rusco, John Shaw.

1749, Dec. 18. Hill, Elizabeth, of Amwell, Hunterdon Co. Int. Inventory of estate (£98.9.0) includes negro girl, £28; Bible, £1; part of deceased's portion in Samuel Hill's hand. Made by John Garrison and Benjamin Stout. Lib. 7, p. 41.

1749, Dec. 29. Adm'r, Samuel Hill, of Amwell, yeoman. Benjamin Stout, of same place, yeoman, surety. Witnessed by William Ball.

1746, May 28. Hill, Paul, of Amwell, Hunterdon Co. Int. Renunciation of Phebe Hill, the widow, and James Hill son of Paul Hill, in favor of Samuel Hill. Witnesses—Jon. Job and James Job. Adm'r, Samuel Hill, of Amwell, yeoman. John Taylor and John Job, of same place, yeomen, sureties. Lib. 5, p. 430.

1746, Nov. 18. Inventory; made by John Peatt and John Garrison. Includes two negroes, $80, 2 guns.

1741, Sept. 24. Hill, Thomas, Esq., of Town and Co. of Salem; will of. Wife, Margaret, to have lot of ground in Salem, purchased of Elizabeth Surridge, containing 22 ft. front; also marsh adjoining on the S. with Clement Hall's marsh, and on the west with Thomas Thompson's marsh; also plantation, 200 acres, at Pilesgrove, on which Obadiah Lord lives. Daughter, Elizabeth Hill, at 18, all real estate not before mentioned, but, if she happens to marry and die without issue before said age, same shall go to her lawful husband. If my daughter should die in non-age all real estate and personal before devised to her to be equally divided among my three sisters, Rebecah, Hannah and Sarah Hill, and my cousin, Samuel Mason's, two daughters, Sarah and Elizabeth Mason. Executors, out of the profits of the real and personal estate bequeathed to daughter, "shall maintain her in a handsome manner." Executors—wife, and brothers-in-law Isaac and Joseph Sharp. Witnesses—John Eglington, E. Axford, Geo. Trenchard. Affirmed 22 Oct., 1741.

1741, Dec. 10. Letters granted to Marg. Hill and Joseph Sharp. Lib. 4, p. 324.

1741, Dec. 15. Renunciation of Isaac Sharp, one of the executors. Witnesses— ——— Carmick, Chas. O. Neill.

1743, April 13. Inventory (£3563.1.11) includes 11 ounces of silver at 6-8, £3.13.4; rent due by Geo. Clark; due by Benja. Acton on lease for five years to Wm. Weatherby; ditto due on lease for 5 yrs., 5 mo., 12 d. to Johannes Hall; ditto due by do. on lease to Obadiah Loyd, 5 yrs. 8 mo.; the 1-5 part of his father's estate in hands of Benj. Acton, £659.14.1¾. Rents due at place of Pale Garion's; ditto, Obadiah Loyd, William Tate; ditto where Docter Garderner now lives, before Thos. Hill came of age, 13 years; ditto where Willm. Winton now lives, 13 yrs.; ditto where Aaron Marsh now lives for 13 yrs. Appraisers—Benj. Bispham, Robert Hart.

1755, ———. Account. (Indexed, but not found).

1749, Sept. 18. Hiller, Uriah, of Northampton, Burlington Co. Int. Inventory, £110.12.9; made by James Lippincott and Samuel Woolston.

1749, Oct. 19. Adm'x, Sarah Hiller. Thomas Eayres and Samuel Woolston, fellow bondsmen; all of Northampton. Lib. 6, p. 325.

1724-5, Jan. 6. Hilliard, Marthah, of Northampton, Burlington Co.; will of. Children—John, Edward, Hester Lodge, Joseph, Elizabeth, Jane and Martha. Granddaughter, Mary Webb. Personal estate. Executor—son Edward. Witnesses—Richard Eayre, Zachariah Rosell, John Briggs. Proved Nov. 10, 1735. Lib. 4, p. 45.

1735, Nov. 10. Inventory, £58.2.6; made by Zachariah Rosell and Sam'll Shinn.

1748, March 22. Hinchman, Abigail, of Town and Co. of Gloucester, widow. Int. Admr's—Samuel Harrison, Junr., yeoman, and Joseph Harrison. Bondsman—Samuel Harrison, Esq. All of same place. Witness—John Thorne. Lib. 6, p. 14.

1747-8, March 12. Inventory, £278.8.7; made by John Thorne, Samuel Harrison.

1742, July 10. Hinchman, Jacob, of Gloucester Co., miller; will of. Daughter, Mary (not 21). Wife, Abigail, executrix; James Hinchman assistant. Witnesses—William Hugg, Ja. Hinchman, Kezia Willett. Affirmed 2 Aug., 1742. Lib. 4, p. 366.

1742, July 15. Inventory of Jacob Hinchman, of Newton Township, miller (£268.7.7.) includes bonds of William Hugg, Ebenezer Brown, Isaac Hollingham, Thomas Edgertom, Joseph Thackary, Thomas Clemment, Joseph Low, Thomas Hinchman, William Smallwood, Amos Archer, Robert Hubs, Francis Haddock, Adam Sommers, John Thorne. Appraisers—Samuel Harrison, William Hugg.

1748, May 21. Hinchman, James, of Newton Township, Gloucester Co., gent.; will of. Wife, Kezia, profits of plantation where we live and, after her decease, ½ of same to Isaac Hinchman. Legacies to Hinchman Talman, when 21; in case of his death, without brother or sister, his father and mother to have the same. To my sisters, Jane Jones, Letitia Thorn and Abigail Kaighn. Executors—wife and James Talman. Witnesses—Thomas Thorne, P. Sommans, Hezh. Williams. Affirmed 2 Nov., 1750. Sworn 26 Dec., 1750. Lib. 6, p. 423.

1750, Oct. 22. Inventory (£2121.6.4½) includes negroes, £285, books, £3.15. Appraisers—Samuel Harrison, Samuel Clement.

1727, April 5. Hinchman, Joseph, of Newton Township, Gloucester Co., yeoman; will of. Wife, Sarah. Children (all under age)—Thomas, Deborah, Mary, Emey, Hannah. Executrix—wife. Witnesses—John Thorne, James Hinchman, John Kay. Proved Sept. 22, 1731. Lib. 3, p. 155.

1731, Aug. 12. Inventory, £114.10.6; made by Sarah Hinchman (the widow) and James Hinchman.

1731, Jan. 4. Hinchman, Joseph, of Newton Township, Gloucester Co., butcher; will of. Wife Phebe. Children—James, Isaac (under age). Land in Newton Township left him by his father. Executors—wife and Joseph Cooper. Witnesses—James Moore, James Mickell, John Whiteall. Proved June 9, 1731.

1731, April 23. Inventory, £261.4.6½; made by John Eastlake and Robert Zane. Lib. 3, p. 126.

1731, Sept. 26. Hinds, James, of Elizabeth Town, Essex Co., yeoman; will of. Daughters, Mary and Deborah, large silver tankard, marked I. D. H. upon lid. Daughter, Elizabeth, four silver spoons marked I. A. H. Daughter, Patience, silver tumbler with a French crown on the bottom and marked I. D. H. at 18 years. Daughter, Sarah, three silver spoons marked I. A. H. at 18 years. Sons—James, John and Joseph. Land joining lands of Thomas Clark, which I purchased of Ephraim Clark; lands purchased of Ebenezer Lyon, Deborah Moris, Richard Higens, and Edward Spining; land joining land of Samuel Marsh, purchased of Will. Oliver. No lands to be sold until sons come to 26 years. Son, John, my great Bible. Executors—son, James, and friends John Spining and Ebenezer Johnson. Witnesses—James Humdoy, Abraham Clarke, Joseph Clarke. Proved Oct. 26, 1731. Lib. B, p. 236.

1722, Nov. 19. Hoff, Derrick, of Maidenhead, Hunterdon Co.; will of. Children—William, Sary Anderson, Richard, Thomas, Powel, John, Charles, Joseph, Benjamin, and Sarah. Residue to all children, except Mary Gary. Executors—sons Powel and John. Witnesses—John Albade, Rut Johnson and Hannah Johnson. Proved Dec. 22, 1730. Lib. 3, p. 108.

1748, April 7. Inventory of the estate, £117.3.5, includes debts due from Benjamin Mapel, Thomas Van Dyke, Jonathan Lake, Jr., Samuel Nelson, Daniel South, William Couenhoven, Daniel Accor, Jon. Lake, Peter Huff, Jno. Brunson, Jon. Smith, Benjamin Emons, Jos. Higgins, William Jonson, William Watelbe, William Walker, Jno. Ronalds, Jacamiah Denton, Thomas Duer, Obadiah Holmes, Jon. Hull, Benjamin Van Horne, Thomas Ronalds, Andrew Jonston, Thomas Sodon, William Larison, estate of Barfoot Brunson, Francis Holanshed, Josiah Pricet, James Ogelbe, Jon. Van Pelt, Aaron Van Pelt, Jon. Huff, Jon. Sodon, Nathanile Ozsborn and William Swain.

1749, Nov. 16. Hoff, Powell, of Hopewell, Hunterdon Co., yeoman; will of. Children—Hannah, Richard, Rachel and Isaac. Executor—son Richard. Witnesses—Thomas Sutton, Richard Phillips and John Redford. Proved Feb. 28, 1750. Lib. 7, p. 53.

1750-1, Feb. 27. Inventory £18.16.4; made by Timothy Titus and Richard Phillips.

1732, Feb. 13. Hoff, Tunis, of Somerset Co., weaver; will of. Wife, Jane, sole executrix, and real and personal estate, including house and lot at "Rockey Hill," "she to pay to my eldest son, Richard, the sum of 20 shillings." Witnesses—Joseph Leigh, Joseph Badcock, Jane Badcock. Proved 2 April, 1733.

1733, April 2. Jean Hoff, the executrix, qualified. Lib. B, p. 391.

1742, Oct. 30. Hoff, William, of Middletown Township, Monmouth Co., yeoman; will of. Wife, Elizabeth, executrix. Son, William. Daughter, Catherine Dorset, and "three youngest children." Witnesses—James Mott, Jarratt Wall, Garsham Walling. Proved Nov. 20, 1746. Lib. D, p. 435.

1746, Dec. 11. Inventory of the estate, £386.04.0, includes 2 guns and negro man. Made by James Mott and Gisbert Vanbrackel.

1745, Aug. 12. Hoffman, Andrew, of Salem Co., yeoman. Int. Adm'r, Benjamin Bispham. Bondsmen—William Murdock, Chas. O Neill. Witnesses—John Jones, Danl. Mestayer. Lib. 6, p. 18.

1745, Aug. 7. Renunciation of Catheron Hofman, relict of Andrew Hoffman, in favor of said Benjamin Bispham. Witnesses—Tim. Rain, Chas. O Neill.

1745, Aug. 7. Inventory of estate, £22.8.10; made by Chas. O Neill, Tim. Rain.

1747, May 19. Account. Monies paid to John Helm, William Vaneman and Mathew Gill.

1741, July 28. Hoffman, John, of Reading Township, Hunterdon Co.; will of. Wife, Margaret. Eldest son, Henry. Helena Plantenberg, daughter of Mathias Plantenberg, by testator's daughter Maria. Children—Henry, Frederick, John, William, Jacob and Helena. Son, William, to have £40 more than rest. Plantation in Reading Township on south branch of Rariton River, where testator lived. Executor—brother-in-law, Christian Harshall, and Joseph Hankinson. Witnesses—David Bartron, Allen Ross, John Reading, Jr., and John Crasioll (or Christopher Krull). Proved November 21, 1748.
Lib. 6, p. 227.

1748, Aug. 13. Inventory (£391.19.3) includes books, 2 guns and sword, bonds, etc. Made by John Reading, Jr., and David Bertron.

1743, Sept. 23. Hoffman, John, of Greenwich, Gloucester Co., yeoman; will of. Wife, Mary, the plantation (304 acres) I live on until son Daniel will be 21; then ½ to be his, also half of land marsh and swamp from Oldman's Creek to head of said tract. Son, John, when 21, to have the other half. 100 acres of land in Salem Grove, Salem Co., on Oldman's Creek to be sold. Daughters—Margaret, Drusilla and Susannah. Children all minors. Executors—wife, brother-in-law Erick Reynolds, and cousin Thomas Denny, Jr. Witnesses—James Garron, George Hues, Paul Garron. Proved 16 May, 1749.
Lib. 6, p. 282.

1749, May 8. Inventory (£152.11.11½) includes "his reeding books," £2.3.9, bonds, etc. Appraisers—William Weatherby, George Hues.

1735, Nov. 8. Hogg, John, of New York. Int. Adm'r, Robert Hogg, of New York, merchant, a brother. William Donaldson and John Tomson, both of Middlesex County, yeomen, fellow bondsmen. Witnesses—Margaret and Lawra Smyth. Lib. C, p. 50.

1736, July 12. Holbrooke, John, of Salem Co., ship-carpenter. Int. Admr's, Clement Hall, Joseph Hawkes, gent. Witness—John Doe.
Lib. 4, p. 66.

1736, July 14. Inventory (£69.0.8) includes bonds of John Neals, Jno. Burd, Thos. Bicoms (?), Martin Minks, John Jaquatt, Henry Wallis, Charles Halton, John Neals, Junior, Peter Inlo, William Biddel, John Johnson, Marey Richards, David Roach, Errick Derrick, Isaac Conroo, Robert Candey's bill. Appraisers—John Eaton, Henry Wallis.

1743, 17th of 6 mo. (August). Holcombe, John, of Amwell, Hunterdon Co., yeoman; will of. Wife, Elizabeth. Son, Samuel, place said son lives on, described in testator's deed for same. Grandson, John Holcombe, son of Samuel, the place called Hoppers, as by deed for same to him. Son, Richard, the plantation bought of John Way, when he is of age. Place (John Comfort's adjoining land) to grandson John. Jacob, son of son Samuel. Daughters—Grace Calvin (wife of Philip Calvin), Mary Holcombe, Julian Holcombe. To grandson Jacob, son of Samuel Holcombe, land in the Rocks, bought of Richard Armitt. Granddaughter Elizabeth, daughter of Philip and Grace Calvin, when aged eighteen. To the poor of Buckingham Meeting. Brother Jacob Holcombe's children. Executors—wife and testator's brother, Jacob Holcombe. Mention of Robert Heath. Witnesses—Benjamin Canby, Emanuel Coryell, Charles Cross. Proved August 31, 1745. (Executors Quakers). Lib. 4, p. 371.

1743, Sept. 24. Inventory (£333.16.2) includes Bible and other books;

in the cave chamber, 13 hogsheads rye, 19 barrels of cider, with casks and lumber, Jo. Wood s time, gun and powder horn. Bonds, bills and debts due estate: George Medlar, Simon Pasher, Jacob Francis, Frederick Reesfenborge, John Bonis, William Oakes, Isaac Oakes, William Springle, David Carver, John Mundy, James Richard, Nathan Watson, Benjamin Wilcocks, Hugh Howell and Sampson his son, Andrew Heath. Made by John Emley, Charles Woolverton, Daniel Doughty.

1747, 13th of 7 mo. (Sept.). Account. Moneys paid Stephen Comfort, Benjamin Smith, Henry Smith, Richard Haines, Frank Lewis, Jno. Wells, Paul Kester, James Hill, Abraham Godson, ——— Foreman, Acksah Lambe, William Montgomery, R. Canby, William Ruttenhouse, Jno. Watson, Richard Parsons, Jo. Rose, Enoch Anderson, Jno. Thather, M. Lowther, Emanuel Coryel, A. Ringo, Geo. Cary, Jno. Yard, Samuel Barber, John Carr, Isaiah Quinby, Robert Esmey, Henry Smith, Simon Packer.

1731, Aug. 2. Holden, Jane, of Cape May Co. Int. Adm'r, Joseph Holding. Fellow bondsman—William Johnston. Both of County aforesaid. Witnesses—Henry Noden, Jacob Spicer, Jacob Garrison. Lib. 3, p. 139.

1730, Dec. 7. Inventory, £34.14.8; made by William Johnson, George Taylor.

1749, Nov. 3. Hole, Charles, of the Borough of Elizabeth, schoolmaster; will of. Children—Charles, Daniel, John, Sarah Marsh, Elizabeth and Lucretia Hole, the last under age. Land purchased of Joseph Marsh last Spring. Wife, Sarah. Executors—son-in-law, Joshua Marsh, and friend Andrew Craig. Witnesses—William Peirson, John Davis, Jun'r, Elizabeth Peirson. Proved Dec. 7, 1749. Lib. E, p. 352.

1748, May 6. Hollings, Lorence, of Waterford, Gloucester Co., yeoman; will of. Sons, Lorence and Michael, all real and personal estate, they paying legacies to my sons Abraham, Israel, Joseph, and Marcus, when they will be 26 years of age, respectively, and to my daughter Dinah, when 21. Marcus to go to a trade. Daughter, Dinah, minor. Executor—brother, Michael Hulings, of City of Philadelphia, Pa., shipwright, and son, Abraham Hollings. Witnesses—Thos. Spicer, Jun'r, Israel Fish, Saml. Spicer. Sworn and affirmed, 4 June, 1748. Lib. 5, p. 451.

1748, June 3. Inventory (£266.16.6) includes cattle, horses, negro woman (£10.10.0), a float (£12), boat (£3). Appraisers—Alexdr. Morgan, Saml. Spicer.

1730, Feb. 26. Hollingshead, Daniel, of Rocky Hill, Somerset Co. Int. Adm'r, Thomason Hollingshead, his widow. Lib. B, p. 191.

1731, ———, —. Inventory (£257.16.6), includes silver quart tankard, pr. of old double bellows for a smith, ditto new, old iron, Tippeo, an old negro-man, £26, Jack, £25, Lelia, £30, Jack, a boy £20, Bellinda, £8, Dido, £15. Made by Henry Neale, John Corle.

1747, Dec. 30. Hollinshead, Elizabeth, of Somerset Co., widow [of William]. Adm'r, John Corle, Esq., of Somerset. Fellow bondsman —John Deare, of Middlesex County. Lib. E, p. 117.

1739, Dec. 14. Hollinshead, John, Ju'r, of Evesham, Burlington Co., yeoman; will of. Children—Joseph, Benjamin, John and Martha. Plantation given me by my father, and one bought of my uncle and aunt, and cousin William Hollinshead; also meadow adjoining house where William Hollinshead, Jun,r, formerly lived. Bonds due from William Hollinshead, Jun'r, and Andrew Conaro. Executors—wife, Mary, and brother-in-law Abraham Haines. Witnesses—Jno. Hollinshead, Edward Hollinshead, Sam'l Atkinson. Proved March 12, 1739-40. Lib. 4, p. 221.

1739-40, 1st day, 1st mo. (Mar.). Inventory, £458.7.1; made by Saml. Atkinson and Henry Warrington.

1741, July 7. Hollinshead, William, Jun'r, of Chester, Burlington Co.; will of. Wife, sole executrix. Children—Jacob, Mary, Jerusha, Bethsheba and Anthony. Plantation whereon Thomas Farley now dwells, given me by my father and mother. Witnesses—Thomas Gill, Grace Rudderow, Sam'l Atkinson. Proved Aug. 11, 1741. Lib. 4, p. 291.

1742, Sept. 3. Hollinshead, William, Esq., of Somerset Co.; will of. Wife, Elizabeth. Children—Elenor, William, Robert, Daniel, Francis and Elizabeth (all minors); an expected child. Mentions servant Margrett Walker, her child, and a "melatto girle, Kate." Real and personal estate. Executor—John Corle. Witnesses—Roelof Couenhoven, Denis Hageman, Adriaen Hegeman. Proved 3 March, 1749. Lib. E, p. 365.

1741, Nov. 30. Holloway, Tobias, of Newton, Gloucester Co. Int. Adm'r, Mary Holloway (his widow). Fellow bondsman—Samuel Harrison, Esq., same county. Witness—Wm. Sorsby. Lib. 4, p. 316.

1741, May 19. Inventory (£312.5.6) includes Ed. Melnor's two bonds, notes of John Whiteалls and Samuel Harrison, Bible and other books, 12 milch cows, sheep and lambs, servant man and boy (£13), rent due from John Ladd. Appraisers—Joseph Ellis, Samuel Harrison.

1747, Dec. 24. Holman, Elias, of Upper Freehold, Monmouth Co., yeoman; will of. Wife, Mary. Children—Robert, William, Mary and Zilpha. Executors—son Robert, Elisha Lawrence and John Anderson. Witnesses—Thomas Hankinson, John Reid, James Mason. Proved January 27, 1747-8. Lib. E, p. 122.

1747-8, Jan. 22. Inventory (£489.18.3) includes 40 acres of wheat and rye, 24 loads of hay, 400 bushels of wheat in barn and mill, 120 bushels rye and oats in sheaf, 7 bbls. beef 310 bushels of Indian corn, gun, negro (£50), servant boy (£10), 300 lbs. tobacco (£3.15.0), debt due from Joseph Borden. Made by Gawin Watson, Robert Holmes, Joseph Cheesman, John Reid.

1740, Sept. 10. Holman, Joseph, of Upper Freehold Township, Monmouth Co., yeoman; will of. To be buried in burying place of my father. Wife, Thamson. Sons—Joseph, Robert, Aaron, John, Richard and Francis. Daughters—Thany (wife of Robert Granatt), Martha, Mary and Phebe. Loom to Richard; musket to Francis, the youngest son and minor. Executors—wife, sons Joseph and Robert, and Goyn Wattson. Witnesses—David Lee, Joseph Hankins, John Clarke. Proved Sept. 26, 1741. Lib. C, p. 489.

1741, Sept. 26. Gawin Watson of Perth Amboy renounces executorship. Witnesses—David Lee and Thomas Bartow.

1740, Sept. 26. Holman, Joseph, of Freehold, Monmouth Co.; will of. Wife, Grace. Nephew, Joseph Grevat. Debts due David Lee. Executors—wife and David Lee. Witnesses—Robert Grevat, Adam Woolley, Joseph Hankins. Proved February 11, 1741. Lib. C, p. 435.

1747, April 15. Holman, Richard, of Monmouth County, weaver. Inventory of estate, £15.10.7; made by Antony Swaine and Samuel Job. Includes cash received from David Vahan, Judith Stout, Absolom Hankins, Samuel Thorp, John Reed, Daniel Perine and Thomas Hankins. Lib. E, p. 189.

1748, May 31. Adm'r, Francis Holman of Middletown, yeoman, brother of deceased. Anthony Swaine, of same place, yeoman, fellow bondsman.

1748-9, Jan. 23. Account. Bills paid to Robert Corvet, John Die, Joseph Die, John Liming, Zachariah Robings, John Morford, Aarent Hoelmon, Grace Hoelman and James Reed.

1750, Nov. 8. Holmes, Elizabeth, of Upper Freehold, Monmouth Co. Int. Adm'r, Joseph Holmes, of same place, yeoman. John Lawrence, of same place, attorney-at-law, fellow bondsman. Lib. 7, p. 43.

1737, June 4. Holmes, (Rev.) Jonathan (son of Jonathan), of Middletown, Monmouth Co., yeoman; will of. Sister, Deliverance Bowne, of Freehold, £300. Half brothers and sisters, each 5 shillings. £400 to Baptist Society of Middletown, whereof John Pew and Gerret Wall are deacons; the interest for the maintenance of the ministry, meeting houses, buildings and repairing. Executors—Samuel Holmes, James Mott and James Tapscott. Witnesses—Obadiah and John Holmes, and Mary Roberts. Signed "Jon'n Holmes, Min'r." Proved June 29, 1738. Lib. C, p. 199.

1738, July 20. Inventory at houses of Samuel Holmes and Jonathan Holmes (£224.9.3), includes 130 apple trees at 4d., and a hogshead at James Mott's. Made by Robert Tilton and Joseph Dorsett.

1738, Oct. 18. Inventory No. 2 at house of Samuel Holmes in Middletown (£56.5.8) includes chest and 8 volumes of "Spectators" and 1 dictionary; other books; 12 rasors and 2 old ones; snuff mill; 12 jack knives; 2 brass sun dials; homespun linen jacket and breeches; new coat, vest and breeches; snuff colored coat, vest and breeches; light colored broad cloth coat, with cape; 12 white shirts; 2 maps of the world; 5 maps of parts of the world; ½ pound of tea, supposed to be liver wort tea; 3 Dublin newspapers. Made by John and Joseph Dorsett.

1738, Nov. 13. Inventory No. 3, at house of Jonathan Holmes in Middletown (£5.10.6), includes light natural wig (£2.15.0); black ditto, worn (£0.10.0); large old book and Psalm book. Made by Joseph and John Dorsett.

1735, Aug. 12. Holmes, Obadiah, of Salem Co., yeoman. Int. Adm'r, Jonathan Holmes. Bondsman—Samuel Clark, of said County, yeoman. Witness—Samuel Holmes. Lib. 4, p. 49.

1735, Aug. 12. Inventory, £115.19.2; made by Thomas Read, Abraham Reeves.

1744, Dec. 24. Holmes, Obadiah, of Middletown, Monmouth Co., yeoman; will of. Children—Deliverance Smith, Jonathan, Obadiah, James, Samuel, Mary Mott, Joseph and John. Have given to son Joseph, by deed of gift, February 10, 1721, land purchased of David Stout; also by deed dated Sept. 23, 1704, to said son part of land in Crosswicks, which testator purchased of his father, Jonathan Holmes, deceased. To son Joseph, part of land, between two tracts above mentioned, and remainder at Crosswicks in Upper Freehold Township, lands bounded by Burlington Path, and John Smith. Son, John, home plantation, bounded by Ramenesin Brook, commonly called Hop

Brook, and lands late of Major James Hubbard, deceased. Brother, Jonathan Holmes. Son, Samuel Holmes. Son, John Holmes. Executors—sons James, Samuel and John. Witnesses—Jonathan Holmes, John Bowne, Junior, Elias Cowenhoven, George Reid, Junior. Proved April 16, 1745. Lib. D, p. 265.

1749-50, March 10. Holmes, Samuel, of Town of Greenwich, Cumberland Co.; will of. Real and personal estate to be equally divided between my cousins, Jonathan Holmes, Esq., and Obadiah Robbins, of County aforesaid, and hereby ordain them executors. Witnesses—Elizabeth Randolph, Obadiah Wood, Ebenezer Miller. Proved 28 March, 1750. Lib. 6, p. 289.

1750, March 26. Inventory, real and personal, (£583.18.7) includes "rum, molasses, shuger and dry goods" (£204.11.04). Appraisers—Ananis Sayre, John Brick, Jun.

1750, Sept. 22. Holmes, Thomas, of Shrewsbury, Monmouth Co., yeoman. Int. Adm'r, Josiah Holmes, of Shrewsbury, mariner, only son of deceased. Richard FitzRandolph, of Perth Amboy, carpenter, fellow bondsman. Lib. E, p. 453.

1732, Oct. 13. Holsert, Benjamin, of Freehold, Monmouth Co., yeoman; will of. Wife, Hanake. Eldest son, John, loom and utensils, and "a book that one Van Brockel is the author of." Estate divided between children, male and female, but are not named. Executors—wife, son John, and friend Garret Scanck. Witnesses—Johannes Heyer, John Johnson, Wal. Wallz. Proved May 26, 1733. Lib. B, p. 457.

1742, Aug. 23. Holstin (Holstein), Larans (Lorance), of Pilesgrove, Salem Co.; will of. Sons—Lorance (to have the home farm with 25 acres of marsh I bought of John Chambs and ½ of my personal estate), Mathias and Andrew (five shillings each, if demanded). Daughters—Elizabeth (½ of the personal), Mary, Sara and Susana (five shillings each upon demand). Executor—son Lorance. Witnesses—Gabriel Peterson, William Vanneman, Peter Vanneman. Proved 26 Jan., 1750. Lib. 7, p. 250.

1750, Jan. 25. Inventory, £8.19; made by Peter Vanneman, William Vanneman.

1738, Jan. 18. Holton, Charles, husbandman, of Pennsneck, Salem Co., yeoman. Int. Adm'r, John Barkleson. Bondsman—William Vanneman, yeoman, of said County. Witnesses—Henry Wallis, Dan Mestayer. Lib. 4, p. 180.

1738, June 19. Inventory, £70.12.9; made by Henry Wallas, William Vanneman.

1732, Nov. 4. Homan, Jacob, of Greenwich, Gloucester Co., farmer; will of. Mother to have personal estate and brother, Peter Homan, to be executor and have 128 acres of land and 4 acres of meadow on Rackoon Creek. Witnesses—Catrin Culin, Ellener Forton, Gabriel Enochson. Proved 20 Sept., 1733. Lib. 3, p. 376.

1733, Sept. 19. Inventory, £59.3.6; made by Henry Hendrickson, John Jones.

1743, Feb. 24. Home, Archibald, of New Jersey; will of. Entire estate bequeathed to his brother, James Home, Esq., of Charlestown,

South Carolina. Executors—Robert Hunter Morris, Thomas Cadwalader, Esq., and brother James. Witnesses—Joseph Paxton and Moreton Appleby. Proved Oct. 1, 1744. Lib. 5, p. 47.

1746, April 21. Hoogelandt (Hogelandt), Dirrick, of Middlesex Co., farmer; will of. Wife, Annatie. Children—Hendrick, Derrick, Annatie, Sarah and Maria. Expected child. Sister, Antie Quick. Brother Adrian's son, Hendrick Hooghland. Legacies specified in will of my father. Executors—brother, Abraham Hoogelandt and Dirrick Folckersen. Witnesses—Wm. Walling, Elbert Stoothoof, Henry Cortelyou. Proved Aug. 8, 1746. Lib. D, p. 399.

1746, Aug. 7. Inventory (£527.19.10) includes cash in hands of Jeames Nelson, six pair "Pillebards." Made by Wm. Walling and Henry Cortelyou.

1740, Nov. 9. Hoogland, Adrian, of Amwell, Hunterdon Co., yeoman; will of. Wife, Yaucauminche, and son, Henry, all estate; Henry a minor. Executors—Yaukum Heulick, and Derrick Hoogland, both of Somerset County, yeomen. Witnesses—Cris. Search, Derrick Hogeland, Cornelius Johnson. Proved Dec. 11, 1740. Lib. 4, p. 261.

1740, Dec. 2. Inventory (£138.15.4) includes 4 pair leather britches, Dutch Bible, Dutch Testament, 2 swords, 2 guns, note of Thomas Stevenson. Made by Derrick Hogeland and Philip Ringo.

1738, Jan. 27. Hooper, Robert Lettis, of Perth Amboy, Middlesex Co., gent.; will of. Wife, Sarah. Children—James, Isabella and Robert Lettis Hooper. Land purchased of Charles Dunster, Esq., deceased, in Perth Amboy. Money due me from estate of Richard Ryeraft, of Barbadoes, Esq., deceased. Executors—Reynold Hooper and Richard Wiltshire, both of Island of Barbadoes, Esqs., and Joseph Murray, Esq., of New York City, wife Sarah, son James, and daughter Isabella. Witnesses—Rebecca Legatt, Jno. Webb, P. Kearny. Proved Feb. 19, 1738. Lib. C, p. 410.

1742-3, 8th day, 11th mo. (Jan.). Hooten, Thomas, of Evesham, Burlington Co., Esq.; will of. Wife, Mercy. Children—William, Benjamin, John, Thomas, Samuel and Mary. Daughter Anne's children, viz., Deborah, Mary and Margret. Dau. Elizabeth's children, viz., Sarah, William and Elizabeth. Real and personal estate, including negro servants. Bond granted by my wife as Mercy Bates to Richard Haines, Junr, and bond of £60 granted to Thomas Bates. Sam'l Loyd to pay for land he has bought of me. Witnesses—Sam'l Atkinson, Ruth Atkinson, Samuel Atkinson, Jun'r.

1744, Oct. 4. Codicil. Sam'l Loyd having paid for the land, same to go as personal estate. Executors—sons William and Benjamin. Witnesses—Joseph Eves, Sam'l Atkinson. Proved Oct. 30, 1744. Lib. 5, p. 57.

1744, 27th day, 8th mo. (Oct.). Inventory, £187.3.5; made by Samuel Eves and William Evans.

1748, Dec. 23. Hopewell, Elizabeth, of Evesham, Burlington Co.; will of. Children—John, Joseph, Christian, Rachel, Elizabeth, Sarah and Hannah, each £30, besides what was bequeathed them by their father. Real and personal estate. Executor—son Daniel. Witnesses—John Pinn, Sam'l Clement, Sam'l Atkinson. Proved Feb. 4, 1748. Lib. 6, p. 27.

1744, 21st day, 7th mo. (Sept.). Hopewell, Nathaniel, of Evesham,

Burlington Co.; will of. Children—John, Daniel and (following under age) Joseph, Benjamin, Nathaniel, Christian, Rachel, Elizabeth, Sarah and Hannah. Real and personal estate. Wife, Elizabeth, sole executrix; if she should die or marry, then my son Daniel and Samuel Lippincott to be executors. Witnesses—Thomas Eves, Gabriel Puneo, John Roderbes. Proved 27th day, 8th mo. (Oct.), 1744. Lib. 5, p. 59.

1744, 27th day, 8th mo. (Oct.). Inventory, £551.6.6; made by Sam Lippincott and John Pimm.

1746, April 26. Hopman, John, of Morrise (Maurice) River, Salem Co., yeoman; will of. Wife, Cathren. Son, John, one-fifth of the land whereon I now live on Morrises River, between Mannamuskee and Mananikoe Creeks. Rest of the land to be equally divided between sons Frederick, Peter, Jonas and Gabriel. "My nephew" (niece) Mary Hopman, £25 when 18. Executor—wife, Cathren, and sons John and Frederick. Witnesses—Abraham Jones, John Jones. Proved 6 May, 1748. Lib. 5, p. 480.

1748, April 6. Inventory, £90.3.10; made by William Cobb, Abraham Jones.

1734, Aug. 5. Hopper, John (son of Benjamin Hopper, late of Allaways Creek, Salem County, weaver), ward. Guardian, Edward Hancock, of said place, yeoman. Lib. 3, p. 425.

1749, Sept. 27. Hopper, John, Sr., of Deptford Township, Gloucester Co., yeoman; will of. Daughters—Elizabeth and Rachel. Sons—Samuel, land in the forks of Mantua Creek; John, the plantation whereon I live. Executors—Joseph and John Tomlinson. Witnesses—William Harrison, Samuel Harrison, Michael Fisher, Jo. Harrison.

1749, Sept. 27. Codicil. Sons John and Samuel to pay £6. to my daughter Elizabeth Bickham in six years, and £6. to be divided equally between her children. Same witnesses. Affirmed 15 Jan., 1749-50. Lib. 6, p. 306.

1749-50, Jan. 25. Renunciation of Joseph and John Tomlinson as executors.

1749-50, Feb. 13. Bond of John Hopper, Thomas Bickham and Levy Pierce, all of Gloucester Co., as administrators of the above estate. Witness—John Mickle. Letters granted Mar. 29, 1750.

1749-50, 11 mo. (Jan.), 26 da. Inventory (£76.01.07) at Woodbury. Appraisers—John Witeall, Abra. Chattin.

1732, Oct. 13. Horn, Capt. William, of Amboy, Middlesex Co. Int. Adm'r, Robert Gray. John Hamilton and Doctor Adam Hay, fellow bondsmen. Lib. B, p. 305.

1743, Feb. 24. Horne, Archibald, of New Jersey; will of. All estate to brother, James Horne, Esquire, of Charlestown in South Carolina. Executors—Robert Hunter Morris and Thomas Cadwalader, Esquires, of New Jersey, and testator's said brother. Witnesses—Jos. Paxton and Moreton Appleby. Proved October 1, 1744. Lib. 5, p. 47.

1747, Oct. 26. Horne, Sophia, of the City of Edinburgh. Bond of Lawrence Smyth, attorney, to Andrew and Ann Horne, children of deceased, as administrator. Lewis Johnston, Esq., and John Smyth, Esq., fellow bondsmen, both of Perth Amboy. Lib. E, p. 101.

1748, June 2. Horner, Jacob, of Waterford, Gloucester Co., yeoman.

Int. Adm'x, Azubeth Horner, widow. Bondsmen—Thomas and Simeon Ellis, of said County. Lib. 6, p. 325.

1749, ———, —. Inventory, £230.8.9; made by Thomas Ellis.

1742, Aug. 5. Horsel, Ruben, of Salem County. Int. Adm'r, Benjamin Acton, Esq. Bondsman—William Fraser, Collector. All of said County. Witnesses—Thos. Jones, Chas. O. Neill. Lib. 4, p. 377.

1742, July 22. Inventory (£47.17.4) of Ruben Horsel, of Penns Neck, cordwainer; made by Jeremiah Baker, Thos. Miles.

1740-1, March 18. Horseman, Christian, of Middletown, Monmouth Co., Joanna Horseman, the widow, resigns right of administration. Witness—Mary Vandervar. Lib. C, p. 413.

1741, June 3. Adm'r, Dr. Peter Le Conte, of Freehold. Bernardus Ver Bryck, of Monmouth County, gentleman, fellow bondsman.

1741, June 9. Inventory, £19.11.0; made by Joseph Golden, Hendrick Hendrickson and John McKinstry.

1742, July 3. Account. Payments to Hendrick Hendrickson "for funeral," Lawrence Van Cleef, Samuel Holmes, Hendrick Brees, Tunis Post, and cash from Garret Wall.

1737, Sept. 24. Horseman, Samuel, of Upper Freehold, Monmouth Co., carter. Adm'r, Samuel Rogers, of same place, yeoman. Rebekah Horseman renounces right to administer. Lib. 4, p. 117.

1744, May 11. Horsford, Samuel, of Salem Co. Int. Adm'r, Benjamin Horsford. Bondsman—Joseph Loe. Inventory, £51.12.2; made by Joseph Loe.

1748, Feb. 25. Horsman, Marmaduke, of Upper Freehold, Monmouth Co.; will of. Wife, Mary. Daughter, Mary Paxton (evidently deceased) and her children, James and Mary Paxton. Daughters—Sarah, Abigail, Susannah and Frances. Five sons of daughter Frances, viz: Jacob, Isaac, Samuel and John Warwick, and David Harley. Great Bible to grandson, Thomas Newland. Testator's three daughters and five grandsons to keep John Wood during his life. Executors—friends Thomas Miller and William Lawrence. Witnesses—William Woodward, Anthony Woodward, Jr., and William Lawrence. Lib. 6, p. 273.

1736, Nov. 19. Hough, Thomas, of Springfield, Burlington Co., yeoman; will of. Children—Jonathan, Hannah, Mary (wife of Benjamin Cripps) and their daughter. July Evens, £5. Land joining Samuel and Caleb Shinn; also land at Mt. Holly and Bridgetown. Wife, Jean, sole executrix. Witnesses—Michael Atkinson, Hugh Cowperthwaite, Tho. Shinn. Proved March 5, 1736. Lib. 4, p. 88.

1739-40, March 7. How, Micajah, of City of Burlington, cordwainer; will of. Wife, Martha. Children—Samuel, Micajah and two daus., all under age. Real and personal estate. Executors—friend Joseph Heulings, and kinsman Israel Heulings. Witnesses—Sarah Borradaill, Isa. DeCow, John Gosling. Proved April 23, 1740. Lib. 4, p. 237.

1747, June 3. Howard, James, of Elizabeth Town, Essex Co., being seventeen. Bond of John Cory as guardian. Lib. E, p. 50.

1750, August 1. Howard, Michael, of Monmouth Co. Int. Adm'x, Catharine Howard. Monmouth Wills, 1729 M.

1742, Nov. 24. Howell, Charles, farmer, of Cohansie, Salem Co., yeoman. Int. Adm'r, John Howell, Jun'r, of South Hampton, Long Island (eldest brother) in trust for Charles, only son of testator, until he will be 14. Bondsman—Nathan Lorance, of Cohansey, Salem Co. Witness—Joseph Rose. Lib. 4, p. 378.

1742, Nov. 3. Inventory, £86.7; made by Benjn. Stratton, Ebenezer Westcote.

1742, Nov. 21. Affidavit by Nathan Laurance that he well knew John Howell, of Southampton, L. I., as father of said Charles Howell and John Howell, Jr.

1725, August 30. Howell, Daniel, of Trenton, Hunterdon Co., blacksmith; will of. Wife, Mary. Son, David, land on east side on the middle road, Trenton; lot on the west side of Kings Street, Trenton, adjoining John Severam; lot of meadow in Maidenhead great meadows, adjoining James Price's land, said lot bought of Samuel Hunt. Son, Daniel, when 21, house at Trenton which John Severin lives in; half of meadow lot in Maidenhead great meadows, bought of Ralph Hunt, Senior. Son, Joshua, 100 acres of plantation where testator lives, adjoining Ebenezer Prout and John Dean; also lot in Trenton, adjoining Josiah Howel's lot. Son, John, balance of plantation where testator lived, when of age; lot in Trenton. Daughters—Phebe, Elizabeth, Hannah, Mary and Prudence, when aged 18. Testator bequeaths "my son Daniel unto my son David that he may live with him," until he is aged 20 years; Daniel to be taught trade of glazier. Executors—son, David, and friend Nathaniel Moor. Witnesses—George Woolesey, John Carpenter, Moses Dickinson.

1732, April 21. Codicil. Son, Hezekiah, having been born since writing of will, to him a lot of land with a house, and a bond due from Hezekiah Bonham and Johanas Anderson, of Maidenhead. Witnesses—Ann Yearley, Henry Woodward and Enoch Armitage. Proved August 2, 1732. Lib. 3, p. 204.

1732, June 3. Inventory (£418) includes 24 swine, 50 sheep, negro man Jack about 50 years old (£20), negro woman and her child (£40), and bonds of Samuel Everit, Samuel Ruckman, Isaac Reeder, John Moor, Richard Morril, David Davis, Jonathan Davis, William Merril, Isaac Hutchinson, Henry Oxley, John Smith of Maidenhead, Matthew Rigby, Nicholas Roberts and Edward Hart. Made by Enoch Armitage and Jonathan Davis.

1733, Sept. 9. Howell, Daniel, of Amwell, Hunterdon Co., yeoman; will of. Eldest son, Daniel Howell, Jr. Son, John, "a mare bought from Thomas Lambert." Sons, Joseph and Benjamin, the copper furnace. Two daughters, Elizabeth and Mary, household goods, etc., "which was their mother's income from the mill and plantation," for bringing up of minor children. Sons, Daniel and John (under age), the corn or grist mill. Plantation where testator lived, fronting on the river. To daughters, Elizabeth and Mary, the plantation "at Allas Hokk in the Township of Amwell." Executors—brother-in-law, John Reading and William Rightinghousen. Witnesses—Samuel Fleming, Frances Mason, Walter Cane. Proved October 24, 1733. Lib. 3, p. 382.

1733, Oct. 24. Inventory, £309.7.4; made by Samuel Green and James Kitchin.

1732, May 4. Howell, Samuel, of Great Egg Harbor, Gloucester

Co., husbandman. Int. Adm'r, Jeremiah Addams. Bondsman—John Hinchman. Witnesses—Samuel Barns, Wm. Harrison.

1732, May 15. Inventory, £15.10.9; made by Richard Phillpot, Japhet Leeds.

1733, July 17. Account. Moneys paid to Joseph Oliver, John Hutchens, Mary Ireland, Robt. Howell (brother of intestate).

Gloucester Wills, 153 H.

1748, Nov. 13. Howland, James, of Shrewsbury, Monmouth Co., yeoman; will of. Wife, Deborah, executrix. Son, Thomas, lands he now lives on in Dartmouth in New England and £120. Son, James, lands he lives on in Dartmouth and £120. Daughter, Elizabeth. Three younger sons, Cook, George and Charles, lands in Shrewsbury. Daughter, Ruth. Refers to "new house" when completed. Witnesses—William Osborn, James Osborn, Jon. Herring. Proved Dec. 13, 1748. On February 4, 1748-9, Cook Howland, a Quaker, affirmed. Lib. E, p. 257.

1748, Dec. 27. Inventory of the estate, including a turning lathe, turning tools, part of a box of Locker s Pills, some "Jazuits Bark," gun, pillion, 3 powder horns and 3 shot bags, part of cask of powder, bonds from Britten White, William Brand, Jacob Taylor, Francis Hance, James Parker and Peter White, 10 gal. rum, 45 gals. molasses, silver tankard (£14), silver porringer (£4). Made by Gisbert Longstreet, Gershom Bills, William Osbourn.

1748-9, Feb. 4. Bond of Cook Howland, of Shrewsbury, as administrator, with will annexed. Daniel Cornell, of Shrewsbury, and Richard Fitz Randolph, of Perth Amboy, fellow bondsmen. Witnesses—John Royce, Thomas Bartow.

1745, July 19. Howman (Homan), Jasper, of Greenwich, Gloucester Co., yeoman. Int. Adm'x, Eleanor, his widow. Bondsman—John Mullike, of said county. Witnesses—Alexr. Randall, Gabriel Rambo. Lib. 5, p. 177.

1745, July 6. Inventory, £100.9.11; made by Allexr. Randall, John Munnion.

1747, Nov. 27. Hubbs, Robert, of Newton Township, Gloucester Co., yeoman; will of. Wife, Lewcy, sole executrix. Son, Charles, the plantation I live on, excepting 150 acres which are to be sold with the lands and rights I purchased of Peleg Smith, of Rhode Island, for the bringing up of my children, viz., Henry, Robert and Sarah Hubbs, who are to have remainder of personal estate as they come to age. If my wife be with child and a boy, my son Charles shall bring him up and give him at age £100 out of my plantation; if girl, £80. Witnesses—Thomas Attmore, Richard Marshall, Jos. Harrison. Affirmed 17 Feb., 1747. Lib. 5, p. 442.

1747-8, Jan. 15. Inventory (£306.10.2¾) includes monies due from John Erwin, Jona. Thomas, Jonathan Axford, Joseph M. Cleans. Appraisers—John Thorne, Jo. Harrison.

1748, Oct. 25. Hude, Robert, of Woodbridge, Middlesex Co., Esq.; will of. Robert Hude, son of James Hude, Esq., of New Brunswick, land in Woodbridge I purchased of Henry and Samuel Moores. John Lee son of sister Agnes Spencer, land formerly belonging to Daniel Robins. Andrew Bloomfield, son of my sister Mary Bloomfield, land in Papiack neck in Woodbridge. Rev. Mr. John Skinner, Presbyterian Minister of the Gospel in Woodbridge, £20, for the College purposed to be erected in New Jersey. Executors—brother, James Hude, Esq., and friend William Stone and William Brown of Woodbridge. Witnesses—Abraham Tappan, James Brown, Benjamin Tappan, David Donham, Jun'r. Proved Feb. 3, 1748-9. Lib. E, p. 256.

1748-9, Feb. 2 & 3. Inventory (£496.3) includes silver spoons, silver tankerd, several negroes. Made by James Smith, John Mobrey, James Brown.

1732, Dec. 23. Hudson, Abraham, of Cohansey, Salem Co., yeoman; will of. Wife, Deborah, sole executrix. Sons—Joshua and Benjamin (not 21). Daughter, Lydia. Brother, Isaac. In case of the death of above legatees without male issue, the Baptist Church of Cohansey (of which I am a member) shall have my land and marsh to help support a ministry among them forever. Son Benjamin to be apprenticed. Witnesses—John Brick, Junior, Isaac Wheaten, Andrew Gardiner, Nathel Jenkins. Proved 27 Feb., 1732. Lib. 3, p. 267.

1732-3, Jan. 10. Inventory (£170.0.6) includes cattle and wheat. Appraisers—Nathaniel Jenkins, Ebenezer Smith.

1736, April 2. Account of Deborah Shepherd, executrix of Abraham Hudson, late of Cohansey. Moneys paid to Isaac Hudson, Benj. Acton, Jamey Gold, Charles Fordam, Ebenezer Smith, Isaac Wheaten, Ruth Miller, Elizabeth Wheaten, Andrew Gardiner, Richard Lewis, Nathl. Jenkins, Elias Cotting, Francis Brougton, James Caruthers, John Green, Daniel Bateman, Elizabeth Randolph, Jacob Ware, Thomas Statham, Mary Wheaten, Wright and Bateman, Reeves and Holmes, David Platts, Robert Rango, Francis Simkins, John Jones.

1750, April 24. Hudson, John, of Evesham, Burlington Co., yeoman; will of. Nephew, Hudson Middleton, all my propriety right to land on Rancocus, or Northampton River, adjoining that which I sold Joseph Smith of Upper Freehold. Nathan Middleton, son of s'd Hudson, 23 plate buttons. Friend, Benjamin Crispin, all timber I bought of Macajah Wills. Friend, John Lippincott, all other timber bought of him. Children of sister, Mary Middleton, remainder of estate real and personal. Executors—Thomas Middleton and brother-in-law, Hudson Middleton. Witnesses—John Campion, Dennis Mulloy, Isaac Wilcockson. Proved May 25, 1751. Lib. 7, p. 79.

1737, Dec. 28. Hudson, Richard, of Salem Co., yeoman. Int. Adm'r, Edward Lummas. Bondsman—Abial Carll, yeoman. All of said County. Witness—William Test. Lib. 4, p. 138.

1737-8, Jan. 9. Inventory (£39.17.4) includes hat and wig (£12), silver tankard, Jonathan Ogden's and Jno. Jay's note, John Pratten's bond, cash from Isaac Mill. Appraisers—Abraham Reves, Elias Cotting.

1750, Sept. 6. Hues, John, of Gloucester County, husbandman; will of. Wife, Dorkus, executrix, Eldest son, Jervis (not 21), son Jacob, and daughter Hannah. William Wood guardian of above children, and also executor. Witnesses—James Wood, John Sanders. Affirmed 3 January, 1750. Gloucester Wills, 473 H.

1750, 7 mo. (Sept.), 20 da. Inventory, £172.11.4½; made by Wm. Wilkins, James Wood.

1750, August 24. Huff, Anthony, of Hunterdon Co.; will of. Wife, Anne. Children—John, Benjamin, Anthony and Anne. An unborn child. A colt to James Merrill for service done. Executors—wife and

John Parke. Witnesses—John Corbet and Philip Chapman. Proved Sept. 29, 1750. Lib. 6, p. 408.

1750, Sept. 15. Inventory (£86.17.9) includes gun and sword and bee hives. Made by John Nayler and John Corbett.

1747, Oct. 22. Huff (Hoff), Derrick, of Kingston, late of the City of New Brunswick, Middlesex County, blacksmith; will of. Estate to wife for maintenance of two children (daughters, but not named). Executors—wife, Ann, and friend Jedediah Higgins. Witnesses—Ja. Leonard, Thomas Atchley and Jno. Dalley. Proved March 29, 1748. Ann Huff the widow renounced as executrix in favor of Jedidiah Higgins in presence of Robert Rolfe. (Hunterdon Co.), Lib. 5, p. 448.

1750-1, Feb. 21. Inventory (£119.1.11½) includes money due from Benjamin Mapel, Thomas V. Dyke, Jon. Lake, Jr., Samuel Nelson, Nicholas Juell (or Ivell), Daniel South, William Covenovan, Daniel Accore, Jon. Lake, Peter Huff, Jon. Brunson, Jon. Smith, Benjamin Emons, Jos. Higgins, William Jonson, William Walker, William Watelbie, Jon. Ronalds, Jacomiate Denton, Thomas Duer, Obadiah Holms, Jon. Hull, Benjamin V. Horne, Thomas Ronalds, Andrew Jonston, Thomas Sodon, William Larrison's estate, Barfott Brunson's estate, Francis Holanshead, Josiah Prickett, Aaron V. Pelt, Jon. V. Pelt, Jon Huff, Jr., Jon. Sodon, Nathaniel Osborn, William Swaim. Made by Ja. Leonard, Samuel Neilson and Benjamin Maple; also mortgage paid to Mr. Kimbal. Signed by Jedidiah Higgins, one of the executors.

1755, Oct. 11. Account of Jedidiah Higgins, acting executor, mentions Francis Bowes, Samuel Johnson, David Davis, Andrew Reed, Fregift Stout, Frederick Vanlue, Peter Johnson, Matthias Vandike, Jno. Dagworthy, Thomas Ashly, John Berrian.

1736, Sept. 13. Hugg, Gabriel, of Township and County of Gloucester, bricklayer; will of. Wife, Patience, personal estate to bring up the children and to occupy the farm. An expected child; if a boy, all lands shall be his and he shall pay his sisters £30 when they are 18; if a girl the lands shall descend to my daughter Hannah, under same condition. Executors—wife and John Hinchman. Witnesses—Wm. Harrison, Henry Sparks, John Collins. Proved 9 Nov., 1736. Lib. 4, p. 74.

1736, Nov. 16. Inventory, £93.6.2; made by Tobias Holloway, Jacob Alberson.

1722, 2 mo. (Apr.), 7 da. Hugg, John, of Gloucester Township and County, Esq.; will of. Wife, Elizabeth, sole executrix. Sons—Joseph, Gabriel, John, Elias and Jacob. Daughters—Priscilla Ayres and Hannah Hugg. Land which Patrick Flamingham lived on, purchased of William White, to be sold. Home tract of 340 acres (with an island bought of John Ladd) bounded N. by my brother Elias' line from Randervour Branch at the Main Creek; 60 acres in Gloucester town bought of Edward Smouth; 500 acres purchased of Joseph Pigeon, with the neck of land that Joseph Edwards lives on, fronting Timber Creek; land adjoining John Richards, below Great Mantos Creek, together with reversions of Proprietary Rights. Witnesses—William Eddenfield, William Grow, Thomas Sharp. Affirmed 23 March, 1730.

1731, April 17. Whereas Elizabeth, wife of John Hugg, the above-named testator, died before him, special letters of administration granted to his son Gabriel. Bondsman—Wm. Harrison. Witnesses—Jno. Hinchman, Saml. Bustil. Lib. 3, p. 158.

1730-1, March 19. Renunciation by Marcy, widow of John Hugg, of right to administer.

1731, March 24. Inventory (£339.18.0) includes clock (£15), old negro (£9), timber upon Joseph Langley's land and Henry Spark's land. Appraisers—Jno. Hinchman, Isa. Jennings.

1731, ———, —. Hugg, Joseph, of Gloucester Town and County. Int. Adm'x, Ann Wheeldon of the same place. (Letters of Adm. missing). Lib. 3, 158.

1731, ———, —. Account (£363.5.6) shows payments to John Marshall, Joseph Richards, Edward Roberts, John Roberts, Easkey Marshall, Samuel Parr, Samuel Bustill, Samuel Coles, Benjamin Vineing, Thomas Gurnall, Henry Spark, James Hinchman, Samuell Harrison, Swan Warner, Peter Banton, Bartholemew Cordery, George Willcox, Thomas Todd, Mary Gordon, Edward Williams, Steven Armitt, John Trapnell, William Coleman, John Jones, Henry Combs, Alexander Stewart, Steven Armitt, Hermainus Helme, John E. Staugh, Henry Pratt, Thomas Sebors, George King, Sarah Dingdale, Francis Jones, Mr. Allen, Mr. Turner, Richard Robinson, Thomas Glintworth, Anthony Morris, James Parroch, Margaret Sharp, Edward R. Price, Joseph Lynn, Phebe Hinchman, Elias Hugg.

1731, June 11. Hugg, William (above 14 years of age), eldest son and heir at law of Joseph Hugg, late of Gloucester, inn holder, with consent of his mother, Anne Wolden, made choice of Christopher Taylor, inn holder, and Samuel Harrison, Esq., as his guardians. Lib. 3, p. 142.

1747, Sept. 4. Hughes, Constantine, of Cape May Co.; will of. Executors and sole legatees, my brothers Jacob Hughes and Ellis Hughes. They to convey all real estate in houses or lands in New Jersey or elsewhere, with my personal estate (except two negroes; brother Jacob to have Jack and brother Ellis to have London). The money arising from same to be equally divided between them. Apparel of deceased wife I give to Precila Holliday. Witnesses—Benjamin Kiersted, Jno. Alsop, W. Blake. Proved 19 Oct., 1747, before Goldsbrow Banyar, Deputy Secretary of the Province of New York. Witnesses—Benjamin Kiersted and Wm. Blake, both of the City of New York.

1747, Nov. 28. Letters granted to Jacob Hughes and Ellis Hughes, as executors. Lib. 5, p. 377.

1746, May 13. Hughes, Elizabeth, of Cape May Co. Int. Adm'r, Elija Hughes. Fellow bondsman—Elisha Hand, both of Cape May County. Witnesses—James Whilldin, Cornelius Schillinks. Lib. 5, p. 248.

1746, May 27. Inventory, £13.17.3; made by Elisha Hand, James Whilldin.

1741-2, Feb. 4. Hughes, Humphrey, Junior, of Cape May Co. Int. Adm'x, Bethia Hughes. Fellow bondsman—Elisha Hand, both of Cape May. Witnesses—George Hand, Nathaniel Hand. Cape May Wills, 106 E.

1741-2, Feb. 4. Inventory (£92.10.1) includes cattle, sheep, and leather. Appraisers—George Hand, Nathaniel Hand.

1745, Sept. 28. Account of Ezekiel Mulford of the County of Cape May, who intermarried with Bethia Hughes, late deceased, widow and administratrix of Humphrey Hughes, Junior. Moneys paid Joseph Whilldin, Eliza. Eldridge, Abigail Stites, George Hand, William Hamilton, John Flower, Samuel Emlen, Henry Young, Elisha Hand, Richard Crawford, Joseph Whilldin, Elijah Hughes, Benjamin Crawford, etc.

1744-5, Feb. 13. Hughes, Humphrey, of Cape May Co., yeoman; will of. Wife, Elizabeth, an annuity. Son, Elijah, 3 tracts of land in aforesaid County, between lands of Ebenezear Swain and Cornelius Schilinks, joining land of Zebulon Swain at the N. W. part, and one-third of my right in the five-mile Beach. Son, Uriah, 3 tracts of land at Nummes near George Stites and Jonathan Forman, also one-third of my right in the five-mile Beach. Grandson, Humphrey Hughes, all land upon Cape Island, the tract between Joseph Whillden and Robert Parsons, a tract at the Northernmost part of the land of Zebulon Swaine, and one-third of my right in the five-mile Beach, upon condition that he shall pay £20 to his brothers, John and Elisha Hughes, when they will be 21. In case of his failure to pay the £20, the lands shall be divided equally among my grandsons, Humphrey, John and Elisha Hughes. ½ of the rents of these lands shall be used "to bring them up to learning;" the other half given to Humphrey. Daughters, Martha Fithian and Judith Spicer. Executor—son, Elijah Hughes. Overseers—Jacob Spicer and Elisha Hand. Witnesses—George Hand, George Sharwood, Abiel Carll. Proved 4 Feb., 1745-6. Lib. 5, p. 240.

1746, May 27. Inventory, £264.5.0; made by Elisha Hand, James Whilldin.

1755, Oct. 14. Account. Moneys paid James Willden, Elisha Hand, Charles Dennis, Nathaniel Hand, Mary Schillinks, Joseph Willden, Phebe Foster, Benjamin Laughton, James Hedges, Henry Whitefield, Isaac Nuton, David Whillden, Levi Hand, Jacob Spicer, Mathias Fithian, Richd. Stillwell, John Kinsey, etc.

1747, Jan. 7. Hughes, John, of Salem Co. Int. Adm'rs, William Willis, William Peterson. Bondsman—Edward Test, all of Salem County. Witnesses—Samuel Whithorne, Michl. Gibbon. Lib. 5, p. 424.

1747, Dec. 11. Inventory, £59.2.6; made by Samuel Whitehorne, Thomas Haynes.

1732, Dec. 7. Hughs, William, of Evesham, Burlington Co., husbandman. Int. Ann Hughs, widow, relinquishes her right of administration in favour of Daniel Wills, Merch't, of Northampton.

1732, Dec. 9. Adm'r, Daniel Wills. John Doe and Richard Roe, of Burlington, yeoman, fellow bondsmen. Lib. 3, p. 226.

1749, June 27. Huit, Mary, of Hopewell, Hunterdon Co. Int. Inventory of estate (£7.12.6) includes debt due from Samuel Smith. Made by John Ballard and Eliezer Morgan.

1749, July 7. Adm'r, Stephen Biles, of Hopewell, yeoman. Joseph Moore, of Hopewell, surety. Hunterdon Wills, 256 J.

1736, July 20. Hulet, John, of Shrewsbury, Monmouth Co.; will of. Joseph Hulet, son of cousins William and Lydia Hulet, the plantation where testator lived, meadow on Racoon Island and testator's Propriety Right. Brother, Robert Hulet, 100 acres at or near Whale pond brook, and 4 acres meadow by William West's plantation, which testator's father purchased of Daniel Leeds. Constant Hulet, 300 acres at Assinpink, adjoining Doctor Johnston's land, and 7 acres meadow. Cousin George Hulet, residue of land and meadow at Assinpink. Cousin John Hulet, upland and meadow at Mateet Conck. Cousin Constant Hulet, £20. Cousin George Allen, £20. Cousin Adam Brewer, £20. Zachariah Gant, £30. Hannah Gant, a bed, etc. Joseph, son of Ebenezer Allen, £10. Margaret Allen, daughter of Ebenezer, £10, a bed, etc. Lydia Allen, daughter of Ebenezer, £10. Thomas White's eldest daughter, Margaret, at Rumson, a bed, etc. William Jackson's eldest daughter, a bed, etc. Preserve Potter, £30. Brother Robert Hulet, long gun and great coat. Musket to George Hulet. Adam Brewer's two eldest daughters. Walter Herbert, £10. Negro Oliver to have liberty. Executors—cousin George Allen and Adam Brewer. Witnesses—Job Cook, Theophilus Longstreet and Robert Dodsworth. Proved Sept. 21, 1736. Lib. C, p. 120.

1736, Sept. 18. Inventory, £707.7.4 1-4; made by George Williams, John Eatton and Benjamin Parker.

1740, April 23. Hulet, John, of Shrewsbury, Monmouth Co., yeoman. Int. Bond of Zibiah Hulet, the widow, as administratrix. Nathaniel Parker and Jacob Dennis, of same place, yeomen, fellow bondsmen. Witnesses—Anthony Woodward, Joseph Rose. Lib. C, p. 337.

1744, May 5. Hulet, Joseph (over 14 years old). Letters of guardianship granted to George Allen and Jacob Dennis, both of Shrewsbury. Monmouth Wills, 1171-2 M.

1731, June 7. Hull, Benjamin, of Piscataway, Middlesex Co., yeoman; will of. Sons—Benjamin, Trustram, Jacob, Reuben, Meshach, and Joseph. Real and personal estate. Executors—wife Sarah, Joseph FitzRandolph and John Skillman. Witnesses—Ben. Hull, Hugh Dunn, Abraham Drake, Jun'r, and Rachel Drake. Proved Jan. 4, 1733. Lib. B, p. 478.

1744-5, March 9. Hull, Benjamin, Esq., of Piscataway, Middlesex Co.; will of. Debts I owe to Cornelius Low, Jun'r, of Rariton Landing, merchant, and John Pound, Jun'r. Brother, Hopewell Hull, and his eldest surviving son, John. Cousin, Thomas Davis, plantation joining John Blackford; also land purchased of the Thickstons on Bound Brook over against Doctor Mercer's new mills. Cousin, Benjamin Doty, plantation formerly Samuel Blackford's joining Joseph Drake's land. Cousin, Benijah Doty. Cousin, Mary Davis, land formerly Antony Blackford's. Plantation joining land which Daniel Drake and Samuel Mackfarson bought of Thomas Bowman. Negro slaves to be freed at death of wife. John King, who formerly lived with me. Elenor, wife of Charles Rowleson, of Perth Amboy. Cousin, Samuel Davis, at 21 years. Cousin, Daniel Blackford, Jun'r, of New Milford, Somerset Co. Executors—wife, Elizabeth, brother-in-law Benjamin Martin and kinsman Arunah Runyon. Witnesses—John Pound, Jun'r, Gideon Merlett, Benjamin Gross. Proved March 27, 1745. Lib. D, p. 252.

1745, March 26. Inventory, £216.14.3; made by Gideon Merlett, John Pound, Jun'r.

1747-8, Jan. 1. Hull, Benjamin, of Pepack, Somerset Co., yeoman; will of. Wife, Rhoda, one-third of estate. Daughter, Ann, to be kept until 14. Sons—Joseph, Meshack, Reuben, Peter and Jacob (all under 14 years). Executors—Peter Martin, father-in-law, of "Pescatua" in Middlesex Co., and Jeremiah Dunn of same place. Witnesses—Job Compton, William Sutton, Jonathan Whitaker. Proved 16 Feb., 1747. Lib. E, p. 130.

1747-8, Feb. 16. Hull, Jacob, of Pepack, Somerset Co. Int. Adm'xs, Catherine Hull, of Somerset Co., and Trustrum Hull, of Middlesex Co. Fellow bondsman—Hendrick Smith. Lib. E, p. 126.

1747-8, Feb. 8. Inventory (£100.5.8) includes notes due from Moses Randal, Jeremiah Dunn, Nathanial Drake, of Morris Co., Benjamin Hull's estate. Made by John Clawson, Jacob Eoff.

1736, April 19. Humphries, Richard, of New Hanover, Burlington Co., husbandman. Int. Adm'r, John Norris, of same, labourer. Lib. 5, p. 56.

1748, June 16. Hunlock, Sarah, of City of Burlington, widow; will of. Sister Hannah Buddell. Son, Bowman Hunlock, at 21, which will be in about 4 months, all estate, real and personal. Executors—son, Bowman, and Revell Elton, Esq. John Allen, Esq., and Isaac DeCow to be trustees. Witnesses—John Neale, William Horst, Hannah Budwell. Proved July 7, 1748.

1748, July 7. Revell Elton renounces executorship in favor of the son, Bowman. Lib. 5, p. 468.

1748, July 9. Inventory, £294.9.1; made by Thomas Scattergood and John Bacon. Includes 52 ounces of plate (£30.11.11), eight day clock (£10), and negro boy and girl (£60).

1746, Aug. 24. Hunlock, Thomas, of City of Burlington, gent.; will of. Wife, Sarah, profits of my ferry for two years till son, Bowman, is 21. Daughter, Mary, 4 silver spoons formerly belonging to her sister Peggy. Grandson, John Ronder. Rudolph Price, all the money he owes me. Negro servant. Real and personal estate. Executors—wife, with Isa: DeCow and John Allen to assist her. Witnesses—Isa: DeCow, Thos. Shaw, Row'd Ellis. Proved Oct. 3, 1746. Lib. 5, p. 290.

1746, Nov. 22. Inventory, £372.16.1½; made by Jos. Hollinshead and Row'd Ellis. Includes, of books, Poulton's Statutes, Burnet's History, Dalton's Justice, Sacred Divinity, Scrivener's Guide, History of the Tartars; also three slaves, eight day clock and Dutch cabinet.

1744, Dec. 10. Hunloke (Hunlocke), Capt. John, of the Borough of Elizabeth, Essex Co., mariner; will of. Daughters—Anne and Mary Hunlocke, both under age. Half brother, Joshua Hunlocke. Daughters-in-law—Elizabeth (wife of William Smith) and Sarah Dagworthy. Real and personal estate. Executors—wife, Sarah, Samuel Woodruff and John Blanchard, Esq. Witnesses—Josiah Winans, Selvester Cole, Leonard Miles. Proved Nov. 16, 1745. Lib. D, p. 350.

1737, Jan. 11. Hunn, Adrian, of Middletown Township, Monmouth Co., merchant; will of. Wife, Phebe, sole legatee, "to bring her children up with," and an unborn child. Executors—wife, brother-in-law John Smith and Mr. James Henderson, both latter merchants in New York. Witnesses—Richard Franses, Robert Carhartt, John Kearny, Robert Dodsworth. Proved January 18, 1737. Lib. C, p. 188.

1738, March 29. Inventory (£429.9.11) includes sadler and joyner ware

(£45), 24 planes, 8 hand saws, 20 shoemaker's knives, 22 bullet moulds, 2 dozen latches and staples, ½ doz. jewsharps, 1 bit and pair stirrups, 3 lb. shaving soap; various ladies' dress goods, etc.; books, including 20 Testaments, Psalter and small book; 4 do. Watson's poems; 3 do. Sure Guide to Heaven; 8 small Common Prayers, Duty of a Justice of the Peace and other articles kept in a country store. Made by Gideon Crawford, Jno. Smith and James Rockead.

1741, Sept. 12. Hunt, Edward, "son of Ralph Hunt of Maidenhead," Hunterdon Co., deceased; will of. Brother, John Hunt, 150 acres in Hopewell, in possession of Thomas Shaw and John Duglis, tenants. Brother, Ralph Hunt, to take said land until brother John is aged twenty. Residue of estate to rest of testator's brothers and sisters. Executor—father-in-law, Phillip Phillips. Witnesses—Samuel Hunt, Abner Phillips, Alexr. Biles. Proved Jan. 16, 1741-2. Lib. 4, p. 319.

1741-2, Jan. 6. Inventory, £27.16.6; made by Theo. Phillips and Samuel Hunt.

1740-1, Feb. 11. Hunt, John, of Hopewell, Hunterdon Co.; will of. Eldest son, Wilson, a negro slave "Peet," and an account due testator from Mr. Daniel Coxe. Second son, Jonathan, plantation. Wife, Margaret, negro wench Dinah. Two daughters, Johannah and Charity. Sons, John and Noah, plantation where Richard Hudnut lived. Sons, Gershom, Daniel and Enoch, plantation where testator lived, adjoining George Smith. Executors—wife, and sons Willson and Jonathan. Witnesses—William Cornell, Gershom Moore and Reuben Armitage. Proved Oct. 1, 1748. Lib. 6, p. 82.

1748, Oct. 1. Inventory (£434.5.4) includes Bible; 28 cheeses (£2.6.8), negro wench, Dinah (£60), two guns, 12 hives of bees, negro man Peet, (£30). Made by Andrew Smith, Esquire, and Vinson Runyan.

1732, Nov. 5. Hunt, Captain Ralph, of Maidenhead, Hunterdon Co., gentleman; will of. Wife, Elizabeth. Eldest son, Edward, 150 acres of land at Hopewell, a gun, etc. Second son, Ralph, a minor, part of plantation above the King's road leading from Trenton to Brunswick, 5 acres of meadow between Samuel Hunt's widow and Powel Huff's, 4 acres of meadow at lower end of lot in great meadow; Ralph to pay legacies to testator's eldest daughter, Jemima Hunt, daughter Kezia, and son John. Third son, Samuel, part of plantation below the King's Road leading from Trenton to Brunswick; Samuel to pay legacies to testator's daughter, Elizabeth Hunt, when Samuel is aged 25 years, and to fourth son, John, when John is aged 30 years. Executors—wife Elizabeth, Major Alexander Lockhart, of Hopewell, Esquire, and Theo. Phillips, Esquire. Witnesses—John Anderson, Abraham Anderson, Jr., and James McKinley. Proved Feb. 9, 1732-3. Lib. 3, p. 279.

1732-3, Jan. 20. Theophilus Phillips, of Maidenhead, renounces as executor. Witnesses—Joshua Anderson and Jas. McKinly.

1733, June 25. Inventory (£326.04.7½) includes a servant, Laurence Lareu. Made by Charles Cook and Nathaniel Moore. Elizabeth Philips, late Elizabeth Hunt, the executrix, testifies to inventory, Oct. 24, 1734.

1741, August 15. Hunt, Ralph, of Hopewell, Hunterdon Co.; will of. Wife provided for, not named. Eldest son, Azariah, plantation, when of age, paying his brother, Nathan, £50. Youngest son, Nathan, plantation bought of testator's brother, John Hunt. Wife's sister, Charity

Furman. Two daughters, Charity and Mary. Executors—wife and Reuben Armitage. Witnesses—Jno. Guild, Ephraim Titus, Benjamin Drake. Proved Dec. 9, 1741. Lib. 4, p. 320.

1741, Oct. 29. Inventory, £212.10.0; made by Nathaniel Moore and Benjamin Drake.

1727, April 10. Hunt, William, of Manington Precinct, Salem Co., husbandman; will of. Son, John, home farm of 300 acres, "he to pay £150 between his mother and the rest of my children as they come to their respective ages," sons at 21, daughters at 18. If John dies during minority, son William shall have aforesaid plantation. In case of his death it shall belong to my youngest son, Thomas. Wife, Sarah, one-third of the personal; rest to my six children, viz., Ann, Sarah, John, Elizabeth, William and Thomas. Executors to sell 240 acres of upland joining my new dwelling plantation and that of John Vance, and 60 acres of marsh on the N. side of Vickery's Creek joining Haynes' marsh in Manington. Legacies to friends, John Smith and John Goodin, whom I appoint executors. Witnesses—Wm. Smith, Joseph Crass, Junior, Alexr. Simpson. Proved 14 Feb., 1740. Lib. 4, p. 300.

1740, Feb. 14. Renunciation. "Whereas John Goodwin (since deceased) and John Smith of the same place and county (now being absent) executors thereof, I, John Hunt, eldest son of William Hunt, renounce my right and pray that letters of administration may be granted to Clement Hall of Salem, Esq." Witness—Chas. O Neill.

Clement Hall thereupon appointed administrator. Bondsmen—William Frazier, Obadiah Loyd, all of Salem. Witnesses—John Powell, Danl. Mestayer.

1740, Jany. 16. Inventory, £197.17.8; made by Clmt. Hall, John Smith.

1733, June 4. Hunt, William, of Somerset Co. Int. Adm. on estate granted to William Plumstead.

1733, June 12. Inventory (£18.14.0) includes Bible. Made by William Spader (Speeder), Burgon Bird, William Plumstead. Lib. B, p. 444.

1748-9, Feb. 11. Hutchins, Hugh, of Mansfield, Burlington Co., yeoman. Int. Elizabeth Hutchin, widow, renounces administration, and requests the same be granted to John Hutchins. Bond of John Hutchins as administrator. Benjamin Shreeve and Francis Gibs, all of Mansfield, fellow bondsmen. Lib. 6, p. 331; Lib. 7, p. 97.

1748-9, Feb. 13. Inventory, £120.14; made by Robert Rockhill and Benjamin Shreeve.

1733, Aug. 22. Hutchinson, Duncan, Doctor of Phisick, of New Brunswick, Middlesex Co. Int. Administration on the estate granted to Elizabeth Hutchinson, the widow. (No inventory found). Lib. B, p. 455.

1744-5, March 10. Account. (£153.08.2), showing payments to Capt. Abraham Sanford, Mr. Philip French, Doctor Nicolls, Cornales Santford, Davas Smith, John Machet, Mr. Barnes, James Watson, Mrs. Longavalt, Benjamin Price, Gilbort Ash; payments from Mr. Peter Bodine, John Bodine, George Hutchinson, Adam Hay, John Byse, Mr. Farguliar, Francis Dildine, Richard Stillwill, William Martin, William Storey, Frances Drake, William Covenhoven, Cornelius Van Horn, Capt. Lennard, Robart Commin, Paul Labateaux, Jereoms Rapalia, Cristian Oandroner, Hendrick

Smock, Elisha Whitehead, Mr. Benjamin Price, "who has the Doctor's books in his care." Dated New York, 10 March, 1744-5.

1747, Oct. 19. Iliff, Edmond, of Gloucester Co., yeoman. Int. Adm'r, Joseph Scattergood. Bondsman—John Bacon. Both of the city of Burlington, gent. Witnesses—James Quest, Luke Tuekniss. Lib. 5, p. 435.

1742, July 22. Imlay, John, of Upper Freehold, Monmouth Co., carpenter. Int. Inventory, £29.11.0; made by Lucas Dwidt and Robert Steward.

1742, Sept. 18. Adm'r, Samuel Rogers, of Allentown, merchant, principal creditor. Lib. 4, p. 377.

1749, May 29. Imlay, Peter, of Mansfield, Burlington Co., yeoman; will of. Children—William, Joseph, John, Lydia, Margaret and Elizabeth. Real and personal estate. Executors—wife, Lydia, brother Robert Imlay, and sons William and Joseph. Witnesses—Agnes Thompson, Tho. Potts, Jun'r, Geo. Bliss. Proved Aug. 8, 1749. Lib. 6, p. 320.

[1749], ———, —. Imlay, Peter, eldest son of William Imlay, of Monmouth County, deceased, yeoman; over 14 years of age, asks that his friend, Tobias Polemus, of Monmouth County, yeoman, be appointed his guardian.

1749, April 8. Bond of Tobias Polemus as guardian of Peter Imlay. Lefferd Lefferson, of same place, yeoman, fellow bondsman. States that father, William Imlay, left a will. Witnesses—Peter Imlay, Luke Tuckniss. Lib. 6, p. 373.

[1750],———, —. Petition of Peter Imlay, over 14 years of age, eldest son of William Imlay, yeoman, deceased, states that his father died intestate. Asks that his friend, Jacob Lawrence, be appointed his guardian.

1750, Nov. 29. Bond of Jacob Lawrence, of Burlington Co., yeoman, as guardian of Peter Imlay. Tobias Polemus, of Monmouth County, fellow bondsman. Luke Tuckniss, witness.

1741, April 9. Imlay, William, of Upper Freehold, Monmouth Co., yeoman. Int. Inventory of the estate (£437.6.2), includes great silver spoons, clasps and buckles, pair of old gold buttons; large Bible, two small Bibles and other books, gun, bond of Robert Imlay, negro man, woman and child (£80.00.02), 2 negro girls (£45). Made by Richard Stevens, Robert Imlay and Cornelius Vanhorne. Lib. 4, p. 279.

1741, April 10. Adm'rs, Rebecca Imlay, the widow, and Peter Imlay, of Mansfield, Burlington County, Esquire. Robert Imlay, of Upper Freehold, yeoman, and Samuel Woodward, of Chesterfield, Burlington County, yeoman, fellow bondsmen.

1746, Nov. 5. Account of Stephen Pangburn and Rebecca his wife, late Rebecca Imlay, administratrix, and Peter Imlay, administrator. Cash paid to John Tantum, Ezekiel Furman, Samuel Woodward, Robert Imlay, William Watson, Safety Borden, Peter Imlay, Gab. Stelle, Robert Steward, Zebulon Cook, Stephen Jones, Abiel Davis, Elizabeth Brown, John Shaw, William Meghee, Thomas Everingham, Moses Robins, Junior, William Barker, William Tapscott, Joseph Borden, Joseph Forman, Elizabeth McMain, Jeremiah Stillwell, James Haywood.

1734, Sept. 14. Inglis, Thomas, of Perth Amboy, Middlesex Co., innkeeper; will of. Son, James; other children mentioned but not named.

Real and personal estate. Executrix—wife, Mary. Witnesses—Jno. Webb, Richard Hewes, John Gifford. Proved April 22, 1735.

Lib. C, p. 28.

1732, April 1. Inskeep, Joseph, of Waterford, Gloucester Co.; will of. Mother, Mary Inskeep. Brothers—John, James and Abraham. Children of my brother, John Inskeep. Brother Abraham to pay sister, Mary Hewlings, the £50 my father ordered me to pay her in seven years after his death. Real and personal estate. Brother, William Hewlings, executor. Witnesses—Tho. Evans, Sam Eves, Sam. Lippincott. Proved April 26, 1732. Lib. 3, p. 190.

1732, 24th day, 2nd mo. (April). Inventory, £121.19.6; made by Thomas Evens and Sam. Lippincott.

1750, Dec. 16. Insley, Elisha, of Woodbridge, Middlesex Co., shipwright; will of. Children—Elisha, John and Gach, all under age. Executors—wife, Elizabeth, brother Jonathan Insley, and father-in-law Thomas Gach. Witnesses—John Pike, Will'm Stone, David Donham. Proved Feb. 26, 1750. Lib. E, p. 487.

1740-1, Jan. 6. Ireland, Amos, of Egg Harbor, Gloucester Co., yeoman; will of. Son, Amos, to have whole plantation and "beech and seader swamps." Daughters—Katherine and Sarah Ireland. Executors—Able Schull. Witnesses—Isaac Addams, David Scull, Peter Counoum (Conover), Saml. Church. Proved 14 Jan., 1745.

Lib. 5, p. 214.

1745, Oct. 24. Inventory (£179.3.8) includes book accounts "hunting John Smith, Dr. £1.10.0," Robert Morss, Peter Risley, Isaac Cavenover (Covenhoven), Daniel Scull, Jacob Ireland. Appraisers—Nathan Lake, Daniel Scull.

1749, Oct. 31. Account. Moneys paid Nathan Lake, Danl. Scull, James Johnson, Jacob Ireland, Recompence Scull, William Hope, Mary Addams, Esther Risley, Mercy Adams, Stephen Morris, John Griffith, William Griscombe, Benjamin Harker, Daniel Ireland, Peter Covenhoven, Thomas Varnum, William Cooper, Joseph Dale, Edmond Cordeary, Isaac Addams, Isaiah Scull, Elizabeth Lee, Josiah Covenhoven, Samuel Church, Christopher Lucas, John Griffith.

1732, June 23. Ireland, James, of Great Egg Harbour, Gloucester Co. Adm'r, Joseph Ireland. Japhet Leeds fellow bondsman. Both of same place.

1732, June 19. Inventory, £35.15.0; made by Japhet Leeds and Japhet Leeds, Jr.

1732, May 24. Petition of Daniel and Amos Ireland that their brother, Joseph, be given power to administer the "very small estate" of their brother, James. Burlington Wills, 2301-6 C.

1747, Jan. 4. Irish, Nathaniel, "now dwelling in the Township of Bethlem, Hunterdon County;" will of. To be buried near his brother, George Cruikshank, at Sauchon. Sister, Elizabeth Lee, of the Island of Montserrat, and her three daughters, Sarah, Elizabeth and Jane. Nephew, William Irish; niece, Sarah Irish. To testator's natural daughter, born of Ann Santee, named Ann, a plantation on which she lived called Private Neck, on the West Branch of Delaware River; also part of a plantation, part of a survey at mouth of Sauchon Creek, reserved when testator sold plantation to George Cruikshank. To said daughter a negro woman named Martilla, and her daughter, a negro girl Betty. Natural son, Johnny, living with testator. Executor—William Allen, Esquire, of Philadelphia. Date at end of will, February 29, 1747. Witnesses—George Mitchell, Jno. Chapman, Robert Ballantine. Proved April 18, 1748. Lib. 5, p. 440.

1748, Dec. 23. Inventory (£1247.14.0) includes 1-4th of tract of land held by lease in company with Messrs. Allen & Turner, for the term of fourteen years, and part of a furnace and forge thereon erected. One fourth of furnace, valued at £375; charcoal, fourth part, £55; grist mill, £25; sawmill, £7.10; teams and carriages, £32.10; goods in store £12.10; negroes, £150; smiths' tools, £3; pig iron, £400. Estimate of estate and stock of Messrs. Allin and Turner, furnace, forge, buildings, etc., being in Bethlehem Township; Furnace, £1500; charcoal in stock, £220; grist mill, £100; sawmill, £30; two horse teams and carriages, £130; goods in store, £50; eighteen negroes, £600; smiths' tools, £12; pig iron on the bank, £1600; forge with stock of coals, £600. Made by Samuel Johnson and Jona. Robeson.

1744, July 19. Isaacs, Abraham, of New York, merchant. Int. The widow, Hannah Isaacs, declines administration, and recommends Jacob Isaacs, the eldest son. Witnesses—Frances Polock and Samuel Cox.

1744, July 27. Bond of Jacob Isaac, of New York, merchant, as administrator. ("Sworn on the Books of Moses, being a Jew"). Pontius Stelle, fellow bondsman. Middlesex Wills, Lib. D, p. 168.

1759, Nov. 5. Jackson, James, of Woodbridge, Middlesex Co., yeoman. Int. Bond of Mary, the widow, and Hartshorne FitzRandolph, as administrators on the estate. Richard FitzRandolph, fellow bondsman. Lib. E, p. 461.

1750, 9th mo. (Nov.), 7th d. Inventory of personal estate, £80.4; made by Sam Moores and Abram Tappan. Memorandum of bonds, bills and book debts due from Samuel Allen, Obediah Ayres, Patrick Arvine, Benjamin Alston, William Alexander, Daniel Arvine, Thomas Alston, Joseph Ayres, David Alston, Spencer Alston, Peater Alston, William Bloodgood, Moses Bishop, Nathaniel Blumfield, Sam'll Burd, Ezekiel Blumfield, Mathew Bunn, Henery Berry, Andrew Brown, John Berpo, Samuel Barrons, Micajah Bunn, Thomas Brown, Benjamin Blumfield, Richard Bishop, Richard Blumfield, Frances Bunn, Andrew Blumfield, Jediah Brooks, Miles Bunn, John Brooks, David Berpo, Samuel Blumfield, William Bishop, Robert Butler, Noah Bishop, Living Bairmore, Jorge Badgle, Joseph Burd, John Burns, Mordecoy Barton, Simon Bogar, Timothy Blumfield, Jeremiah Blumfield, Jeames Collens, Samuel Cole, Benja. Colens, Richard Carmen, Jeames Clarkson, Lourance Carter, Samuel Congar, Benjamin Connet, William Conly, Jonathan Connet, Rubin Clark, Jorge Childs, Samuel Coddington, Andrew Kearny, Gershom Conger, Richard Cutter, Robart Comes, Copathite Copalon, William Cutter, Joseph Cutter, Edward Croel, Samuel Croel, John Davis, Thomas Duglas, Jonathan Dunham, Elisha Dunham, Joseph Dunham, John Donland, Samuel Davison, John Donham, Abraham Drake, William Dannels, William Davis, Catheron Dunham, Matthew Davis, Jacob Deney, Jonathan Daniels, David Dunbar, David Dunham, Jeames Eddy, Benjamin Ensley, Goying Eddy, Samuel Alston, William Fraisley, Gilbert Foulter, John Flecher, Edward Fitchsomans, Vuseton Froast, Henery Freeman, John Force, Benony Freeman, Thomas Finch, William Ford, Samuel Force, Isac Freeman, John Freeman, Samuel Ford, William Gilman, Ebeneazer Gray, Hezekiah Goodfellow, John Gaddes, David Hay, Samuel Hale, Thomas Horner, Robart Hude, David

Herrod, William Hider, Jorge Herod, John Hobkins, Elnathan Halley, Rubin Hiard, William Hogins, Martha Holby, John Hoggins, Robart Hays, Foster Harason, Micael Homan, Thomas Higgens, Nathanell Hadden, Samuel Jaquish, Thomas Johnson, Thomas Inglish, John Johnson, William Jackson, Jonathan Inslee, Benjamin Ensle, Efraim Jones, Joseph Insle, David Insle, John Jackson, Benjamin Jones, Eliflet Jones, Benjamin Kinsy, Spencer Kelley, Jeames Karney, John Cent, David Kelley, William Kent, David Kent, John Kelley, Nujant Kelley, John Kelley, Jun'r, Jonathan Kinsey, Jeames Kelley, John King, Samuel Lewis, John Lovit, William Ladnor, Abel Levis, Ritchard Lambart, Jeames Martain, Samuel Moores, Samuel Martain, Robart Mitchel, John Morris (of Elesstown), Jeames Mores, Mical More, John Morris, Jun'r, Benjamin Morris, Samuel Moore, Jonathan Moores, John Moores, Joseph Martain, Daniel Moores, Ketrol Monday, William Maglocklin, Mathew Miller, Benjamin Moore, Justis Morris, John Noe, Robart Noble, Peater Nap, Jeames Nevil, John Pangborn, Jarot Oman, Joseph Olever, Job Pack, Jun'r, Job Pack, Fourman Pike, William Pike, Edward Parke, Samuel Pitt, Benjamin Perdon, Edward Potter, Josiah Parker, Rubin Potter, Jeames Price, Samuel Randolph, Jun r, Robert Randolph, Jacob Randolph, Jun'r, Jeames Randolph, Jeames Robison, Samuel Rodes, William Robison, John Ramsdon, John Rainno, Ritchard Rundals, Edward Ritche, William Ranals, Hugh Roos, Edward Randolph, John Reaves, Samuel Randolph, Jun'r, Antony Runals, John Runals, Thomas Roos, John Roobard, Benjamin Skiner, William Smith, Darby Sylaven, Robart Sharp, Mathew Sharp, Joseph Shotwell, Sen'r, John Stilwell, John Smith, Edward Stoutter, Nickelos Shotwell, John Steavens, Thomas Skaw, John Speadwell, Joseph Smith, Jorge Stead, Tristram Sobe, Ichabod Smith, William Sutcleaf, Joseph Shotwell, William Stone, John Shotwell (tailor), David Stuart, William Taillor, Abraham Tapham, Solomon Thorp, Jeames Thomson, William Thornal, Jonathan Thoms, John Thoms, William Thorp, Odel Turnear, Samuel Terren, John Thorp, Benjamin Thornal, Elexsander Thomson, Samuel Thomson, Jacob Thorp, Benjamin Thorp, Josiah Tarren, John Thackston, John Updike, Mathew Veal, John Van Camp, John Veal, Cornealous Van Cleaf, Samuel Walker, Ritchard Wright, Joseph Williams, Sylas Walker, John Wright, John Waller, Job Wright, Benjamin Wheaton, Edward Wilkson, Joseph Wheaton, Simon Walker, Ritchard Walker, Jeames Wilkason, Edward Heresman, John Hereman, Mott Issleton, John Bishop, Jun'r, Samuel Brant, Steaven Insle, Abraham Pain, Zebulon Pike, Nathaniel Bunn, Benjamin Pangborn, William Thomson, Zebulon Thorp, Job Conger, Jun'r, Thomas Horner, Jacob Deng, Nickelos Shotwell, William Maglock, Sen'r, Jeames Clarkson, Samuel Davison, Jonathan Kinsey.

1742, Nov. 8. Jackson, Robert, of Mansfield, Burlington Co., yeoman; will of. Brother, John, sole executor, and he, with sister Mary (wife of Daniel Sutton), all estate real and personal. Witnesses—Samuel Oldale, Jno. Raworth. Proved Dec. 1, 1742. Lib. 4, p. 335.

1732, July 18. Jacocks, James, of Cape May Co., mariner; will of. Cousins—James Swaine (when 21, the plantation I live on at Cape May), Mary, Sarah, Daniel, Nezer, Ruth (one sheep running at Samuel Swaine's), Silas (my Bible); they all being the children of my sister, Mary Swaine. My friend, Judah Swaine, (a gun); my brother, Jonathan Swaine, my right to a tract of land at Cape Fear, to dispose of to which son he thinks best, After Swaine, or Liffelet Swaine. Cousin, Jemima Beal, a cow and calf running at her father's at Cape Fear. Cousin, Jonathan Swaine, at Cape Fear, my old gun; and all the cattle to be divided among his brothers that are left, he having his equal part. Executor—my brother, Ebenezer Swaine. Witnesses—Samuwell Swaine, Jarusha Swaine, Reuben Swaine. Proved 18 August, 1732. Lib. 3, p. 314.

1732, Aug. 5. Inventory (£32.10.0) includes "a mare and all other living creatures and two guns (£8.01.0)," "whailing craft, tuls and all sundries of old iron (£2.03.02 3-4)." Appraisers—Nathaniel Foster, Samuwell Swaine. States: "This is an inventory of James Jacock's estate, deceased at Cape May on July the 21th, 1732."

1749, April 19. Jagard, Thomas, of Deptford, Gloucester Co., yeoman; will of. Wife, Ann, during widowhood the personal estate and use of the plantation for the maintenance of my children; my son Robert at 21 to hold the same, and he to pay £30 to his sister, Ann, when he has been in possession of the plantation two years. Five acres of Cedar swamp upon a branch of one called Jericho, in Gloucester Co., to be sold. Executors—wife, Ann, and my brother, James Jagard. Witnesses—Richard Heritage, George Flamingan, Michael Fisher. Proved 29 May, 1749. Lib. 6, p. 284.

1749, May 4. Inventory, £134.6.11; made by Richard Heritage, George Flamingan.

1746, May 13. Janeway, Jacob, of Somerset Co., merchant; will of. Whole estate in America or elsewhere to be disposed of by the executors at discretion. Residue, after payment of debts, bequeathed to wife, Sarah, for her support and the education of the children, viz., William, George and Sarah. Executors—wife, Sarah, and Bernardus Legrange. Witnesses—Adrian Hoogland, John Hagewordt, Isaac Powell. Proved 6 June, 1747. Lib. E, p. 86.

1747, Oct. 13. "Received out of the Secretary's office the original will of Jacob Janeway." (Signed) "Barnardus Lagrange."

1760, Aug 23. Obligation of John Hagawoudt, Somerset Co., admr. de bon. non of Jacob Janeway, Sarah Janeway, executrix, now being deceased. Fellow bondsmen—Elias VanCourt and Adrain Hoogland.

1760, Feb. 9. Inventory of "remaining estate" (£80.17.11) includes a Dutch Bible, £3, an English Bible £0.10s., etc. Made by Elias V. Court, Florian Houglan.

1747, Nov. 19. Jaquat, John, of Penns Neck, Salem Co., yeoman; will of. Sons—Paul (eldest), ¼ of my land, marsh, swamp and meadow joining Charles Buckley's line; Peter, ¼ of the like joining Daniel Garrison's line; Hance (when of age in three years), ¼ of the like and my plantation whereon my sons Peter and Paul now live; Joseph (when of age, which will be in five years) an equal ¼ of the like, but he shall not clear over the King's Road. Daughters—Rebecca Jaquat and Mary Elwell. Executors—son-in-law, Joseph Elwell, and my daughter, Rebecca Jaquat. Witnesses—Solomon Almon (Allomon), Peter Boon, Samuel Whitehorne. Proved 5 Dec., 1747. Lib. 5, p. 395.

1747, Nov. 30. Inventory, £54.2.6; made by Samuel Whitehorne, Jacob Pedrick.

1748, Dec. 23. Jaquat, Peter, of Penns Neck, Salem County, yeoman; will of. Wife, Jane, sole executrix and to have whole estate. Witnesses—Joseph Elwell, Hanna Jaquat, Samuel Whitehorne. Proved 31 Dec., 1748. Lib. 6, p. 97.

1748, Dec. 29. Inventory (£36.12) includes "his part of the old flatt & ½ of the old boat," old sails, cord wood and staves. Appraisers—Samuel Whitehorne, Joseph Elwell.

1751, Jan. 4. Jaques, Henry, of Woodbridge, Middlesex Co., mariner; will of. Wife, Rebeccah. Children—Samuel, David, Ruth, Henry, Moses (all under age). Debts due from people in North Carolina. Plantations in Essex and Middlesex counties. Tract of land in Maryland. Executors—wife, and brother-in-law Benjamin Rolph. Witnesses—Peleg Mumford, Rachel Martin, Joseph Shotwell. Proved Jan. 18, 1750-1. Lib. E, p. 474.

1735, March 4. Jarman (Germon), John, of Town and County of Salem, blacksmith; will of. Wife, Martha, sole executrix and to have whole estate. Witnesses—John Simms, Daniel Rumsey, Danl. Mestayer. Proved 22 Jan., 1738. Lib. 4, p. 179.

1738 (1737 ?), March 18. Jeanes, Henry, of Salem Co.; will of. Son, Henry, my "now dwelling plantation." In case of his death without lawful issue, same to descend to my four daughters: Anna, Jean, Christianna and Margrat (none of age). Use of real and personal estate to go towards the "bringing up" of my children. If they die without heirs same to descend to my cousins, John and Mary Test. Executor—"my only two brothers," Joseph Test and Matthias Lambson. Witnesses—Thos. Jaullin, George Fish, Daniel Lambson. Proved 1 March, 1737-8. Lib. 4, p. 147.

1738, April 7. Inventory (£223.14.9) includes 2 cows at Hugh Nail's, 1 cow at Allen Congleton's, 1 cow at William Smith's at Manington, negro wench (£18). Appraisers—Sinnick Sinnickson, Martin Skeer.

1749, July 3. Jecocks, Jonathan, "sometime since of Shrewsbury, late of Virginia." Bond of Joshua Bond, of Shrewsbury, Monmouth Co., yeoman, a creditor, as administrator of the estate. Thomas Jecocks, of Shrewsbury, yeoman, and William Brinley, of same place, fellow bondsmen. Witness—Richard Morris, Junior. Lib. E, p. 309.

1750, July 9. Jecocks, Thomas, Junior, of Shrewsbury, Monmouth Co.; will of. Executors—wife, Mary, and James Irons. Father, Thomas Jecocks, to be maintained. Sister, Leah. Brother Jonathan's daughter, Tabitha. Sister, Grace Jecocks. Witnesses—Peter Romaine, Philip Tippy, Arthur Rowland. Proved August 25, 1750. Lib. E, p. 533.

1747, Oct. 16. Jeffery, William, of Shrewsbury, Monmouth Co., yeoman; will of. Wife, Mary, lands at Manasquan. etc. Eldest son, William, half of plantation testator lives on at Deal, with half of meadow belonging to it on Raccoon Island, and half of pine land bought of Benjamin Lewis. Son, Daniel, other half of plantation, etc., and to care for his insane sister, Phebe. Meadow at Poplar Swamp brook. After marriage or death of wife, lands at Manasquan to sons Thomas, John, Joseph and Jeremiah. Youngest son, David, under 14 years. Daughters—Grace, Jemima and Elizabeth. Executors—friends, William Jackson and Job Cook. Witnesses—Benjamin Lewis, Daniel Woolley, (Quaker), Jacob Dennis. Proved May 19, 1749. Lib. E, p. 310.

1749, May 22. Inventory (£372.11.09) includes a gun and shot, 4 hives of bees, 49 sheep, 48 head of cattle, a tame "Dow." Made by Stoffel Longstreet and Emanuel Woolley.

1733, May 24. Jenkins, Henry, of Springfield, Burlington Co., plasterer. Int. Margaret Jenkins requests that Samuel Wright be appointed administrator on her husband's estate.

1733, May 28. Bond of Samuel Wright, of New Hanover, yeoman. John Denn and Richard Fenn, both of same, yeoman, fellow bondsmen. Lib. 3, p. 369.

1733, June 9. Inventory £34.0.4; made by John Ogborn and Michael Atkinson.

1734, May 28. Account of Samuel Wright, showing payments to William Morrell, Elizabeth Shinn, Thomas Shreeve, Dr. Thomas Shaw, Nicholas Powell, Sam'l Scattergood.

1749, Oct. 24. Jennens (Jennings), James, of the Township of Deerfield, Cumberland Co., yeoman. Int. Administratrix—Rebecca Jennens, widow. Fellow bondsman—Peter Bateman, same place. Witnesses—Ephraim Seeley, Elias Cotting. Lib. 6, p. 344.

1749, Oct. 24. Inventory (£85.3.9) includes cattle, horses and sheep. Appraisers—Robert Hood, Peter Bateman.

1748, Nov. 21. Jenney (Janney), Amous, of New Jersey. Bond of William Yeardley, of Bucks Co., Pennsylvania, as administrator of the estate. Benjamin Biles, of Trenton, surety. Witnesses—Joshua Howell and Theo. Severns. Hunterdon Wills, Lib. 6, p. 78.

1740, Oct. 7. Jennings, John, of Perth Amboy, Middlesex Co. Int. Mellison Jennings, the widow, renounces her right to administer the estate of her husband in favor of John Moore, of Woodbridge, yeoman, principal creditor. Bond of John Moore. Andrew Robinson, of Perth Amboy, blacksmith, fellow bondsman. Lib. C, p. 355.

1749, March 30. Jennings, Mary, of Elsinburrow, Salem Co., widow; will of. Son-in-law, James Jennings. Daughter-in-law, Margrett Jennings, a cow at Clem Hall's. Granddaughter, Jean Dickey. Rest of estate divided equally between my grandchildren and Margrett Jennings, "whom I also will to Deborah Smart to be brought up according to her father's desire." Son, Robert Dickey, executor. Witnesses—Nathan Smart, James Allen, Mary Sencher. Proved 6 April, 1749. Lib. 6, p. 358.

1749, 2 mo. (Apr.), 6 da. Inventory (£72.8.11) includes 10 hd. of cattle, £22. Appraisers—Nathan Smart, Aaron Bradway.

1748, Sept. 10. Jennings, Redmon, of Salem Co. Int. Adm'x, Mary Jennings. Bondsmen—Israel Lawrence, William Hudson. All of Pilesgrove. Witnesses—Ann Gibbon, Michl. Gibbon. Lib. 6, p. 49.

1748, Sept. 10. Inventory (£67.12.8) of "Redmon Genins, "late of Piles Grove, includes "7 cow kind," (£20.15). Appraisers—Thomas Graves, William Worton.

1731, Dec. 6. Jerney (Jernie, Jernee), John, Sr., of Manasquan, Shrewsbury township, Monmouth Co., yeoman; will of. Wife, Elizabeth. Grandson, son of eldest son John, deceased. Sons, James and Peter, land testator lived on, between lands of Thomas Ellis and John Havens. Executors—wife, son James, and Peter Traverrie. Witnesses—Thomas Ellison, Nehemiah Bowne, Thomas Bills, James Stanley. Proved December 4, 1738. Lib. C, p. 265.

1738, May 29. Inventory (£310.13.6) includes a young negro wench

(£25); an old negro wench (£00.10.0). Made by Peter Traverrie and Thomas Ellison.

1749, Dec. 27. Jesop, John, of Gloucester Co. Int. Adm'x, Margaret Jesop, widow. Bondsman—Robert Stephen, of Newton in said County, yeoman. Lib. 7, p. 42.

1749, 10 mo. (Dec.), 2 da. Inventory, £188.6.7; made by Isaac Stephens, Deptford Township, Gloucester Co. and Richard West.

1752, Jan. 10. Account. Moneys paid John Whiteall, John Blackwood, James Wood, John Marshall, John Davis, Thomas Coombess, William Wood, Jonathan Fowler, Willm. Hudson, Timothy Matlock, Joseph Scattergood, Elizabeth Craig, Robert Stephens.

1732, Dec. 19. Jewell, George, of Elizabeth Town, Essex Co., gentleman; will of. Sarah Jewell, daughter of Jane (widow of Nathaniel Ross), late of Elizabeth Town, deceased. Granddaughters—Sarah Wheaton, Elizabeth Heady (daughter of son George Jewell), Mary Wade and Sarah Mitchell. Grandson—Benjamin Spinning, land called Bakers landing, by the well of Nathaniel Bonnel, Jun'r, upon condition that executors or administrators of Benjamin Spinning, late of Elizabeth Town, deceased, pay to my estate £7. Daughter—Mary Marsh, land purchased of Samuel Melyne. Grandsons—George and John, sons of son John Jewell, deceased. Son George to reserve firewood for Isaac Jewell, labourer. Executors—son George, son-in-law Nathaniel Mitchel, and Ebenezer Lyon. Witnesses—Thomas Ross, Job Brookfield, Thomas Chapman. Proved Aug. 31, 1734. Lib. B, p. 566.

1735, April 29. Inventory, £4.12.03; made by Abs'm Ladner and Charles Townley.

1744, Aug. 29. Jewell, George, Jun'r, of Borough of Elizabeth, Essex Co., yeoman; will of. "Being bound on a voyage to Island of St. Christopher's." Land joining the parsonage and land of David Smith. Sister—Mary Harbour, of S'nt Christopher's. Aunt Elizabeth Kersey, of same place. Aunt Elizabeth Mitchell and her daughter, my cousin, Mary Mitchell. Executors—friend Henery Garthwait, and cousin James Mitchell. Witnesses—Edward Griffing, Joseph Sayre, Thomas Chapman. Proved May 5, 1747. Lib. E, p. 42.

1727, April 26. Job (Jobs), John, of Somerset Co., yeoman; will of. Wife, Sarah. Land to be sold. Eldest son, William Job. Wife to have bringing up children testator had by her. All children by first wife to care of executor. Four daughters—Mary, Elizabeth, Martha and Carcha Job. Residue to three sons, William, John and James Job. Executor—brother, William Job. Witnesses—Daniel Hollinshead, William Hollinshead, Thomas Ring. Proved Oct. 17, 1733. Lib. 3, p. 378.

———, ———, —. Inventory (£354.2.6) includes one negro boy, "a core of sheep, and bees." Made by John Manners and John Garrison.

1737, May 16. Account of William Jobs, executor, filed on this date by John Taylor, executor of said William Jobs. Mentions Joseph Stout and William Williams.

1747, Jan. 3. Job, Samuel, (place not stated); will of. Son, Samuel. Other children mentioned but not named. Executors—wife, Rachel, John Anderson and John Morford. Witnesses—John Muirhead, James Keen, Gilbert Barton. Proved Jan. 29, 1747-8.

1747-8, Jan. 29. John Morford alone qualifies as executor, the others having declined. Middlesex Wills, Lib. E, p. 125.

1748, Jan. 5. Account. Payment to Tomson Hoolman, Gilburt Barton, William Ross, Francis Hoolman, John Williams, James Patterson, James Wilson (executor of John Applegate), Charles Cossin, Matthias Mount.

1748-9, March —. Account. Debts due to Patrick Vance, Robart Holms, Humphrey Mount, Benjamin Applegate, John Kar, Thos. Harburd, John Coxe, attorney, John Hite. Money received from Peter Wilson, Paul Miles, John Dear, Andrew Gerding.

1744, August 20. Jobs, Rachel, of Freehold, Monmouth County, widow of George Jobs; will of. Son, Samuel Jobs, £100, with interest from February 22, 1725, being legacy left testatrix's son George by his father, George Jobs, and paid by said Samuel. Five daughters—Rachel Spence, Mary Fenton, Dorcas Walker, Deborah Tomson, and Elizabeth McCoy. Two sons—Samuel and George. Executor—son Samuel. Witnesses—George Jobs, Junior, John Jobs, Noah Gates. Proved March 3, 1747-8. Lib. E, p. 140.

1747-8, March 3. Bond of John Morford, of Perth Amboy (executor of Samuel Job, who was left executor of Rachel Jobs' estate) as administrator on estate of Rachel Jobs. Samuel Jobs and George Job, Jun'r, fellow bondsmen.

1737, May 16. Jobs, William, Jr., of Amwell, Hunterdon Co., yeoman. Int. Bond of John Taylor, yeoman, of said county, as administrator. Thomas Houghton, of same place, yeoman, surety. John Taylor to be administrator during minority of Jas. Jobs, only brother of the deceased.

———, ———. Inventory (£57.16.0) includes a stallion. Made by Thomas Houghton. Hunterdon Wills, 117 J.

1736, March 18. Jobs (Job), William, of Amwell, Hunterdon Co., freeholder; will of. Nephew, William Job; residue to rest of testator's brother's children, John, James, Christopher and Martha Job. As to Mary Reeder's part, if Joseph Reeder will give up deed of lands from testator to him, etc. The two youngest girls, Jerusie and Sarah Jobs, household goods, and they and the two youngest boys to live with their mother and husband, William Excien. Executors—friends John Taylor and Daniel Lake, and testator's nephew, William Job. Witnesses—Thomas Houghton, Francis Gano, John Minor. Proved April 28, 1737. Lib. 4, p. 100.

———, ———, —. Inventory (£474.12.4) includes bonds of William Jobe, Jr., Joseph Reeder, John Jobe, William Hankins, Robert Comes and John Morris; one negro woman. Made by Thomas Houghton.

1743, March 20. Johnson, Anne, of Woodbridge, Middlesex Co., single woman. Int. Adm'r, Joseph Bloomfield, principal creditor. Ezekiel Bloomfield, fellow bondsman. Lib. D, p. 124.

1743, ———, —. Account. "To nursing deceased in my house," and to Anne Ower "for nursing in her own house."

1744, May 4. Inventory, £27.15; made by David Donham, Jr., and Sam'll Jaquess.

1736, Jan. 24. Johnson, Ebenezer, of Elizabeth Town, Essex Co.; will of. Children—Ebenezer, Thomas, John, Sarah, Elizabeth and Abigail, all under age. Expected child. Real and personal estate.

Executors—wife, Sarah, and David Ogden, attorney. Witnesses—William Ross, John Magee, Jane Ross. Proved May 7, 1737.
Lib. C, p. 173.

1750, Feb. 2. Johnson, Erick, of Penns Neck, Salem Co. Int. Adm'x, Margaret Johnson. Bondsman—Peter Bilderback. Lib. 9, p. 92.

1750-1, Jany. 31. Inventory (£140.9) includes horse, bridle, saddle, armour, "2 boats with all their Riging (£20)," wheat in stack. Appraisers—Jeremiah Baker, Andrew Sinnickson.

1746-7, Feb. 17. Johnson, Henry, of the Borough of Elizabeth, Essex Co., labourer. Int. Inventory of personal estate, £40.11.03; made by Isaac Manning and John Pound, Jun'r, of Piscataway. Adm'r, Thomas Johnson of Somerset Co. Isaac Manning and John Pound, Jun'r, fellow bondsmen. Lib. D, p. 453.

1732, March 10. Johnson, John, of Manington, Salem Co. Int. Admr's, William Johnson and Edward Johnson, gent. Bondsman—Benjamin Acton. All of said County. Witnesses—Benjamin Alford, John White.. Lib. 3, p. 291.

1732, Sept. 17. Inventory (£36.5) includes carpenter's tools and whip-saw. Appraisers—John White, Daniel Haynes.

1733, ———, —. Account (£51.14.10) includes monies paid to John Davis, Benjamin Acton, Thomas Mason, Peter Turner, Richd. Haynes, Warwick Randal, Joseph Test, Robert Hart, Ann Haynes, William Siddons.

1734, April 24. Johnson, John, of Monmouth Co. Int. Admr's, Barns Johnson and Nicholas Johnson. Lib. B, p. 586.

1730, Aug. 18. Johnson, Margaret, of Salem, widow and executrix of Robert; will of, etc. (See N. J. Archives, Vol. 23, p. 263).

1732, Sept. 1. Johnson, Nicholas, of Cohansey, Salem Co., yeoman; will of. Wife, Mary, sole executrix, and to have the use of the plantation during widowhood, or until my sons Nicholas and Othniel will be 21. Said sons to have equally my lands and marsh together, paying £50 to my son Nathaniel (youngest), whom I order to have a good trade. Legacies to my daughters—Sarah Haries, Hannah Peterson, Ann Smith, Temperance and Sarah. "The two last named to have their legacy each at 18, or marriage." Witnesses—Nathaniel Jenkins, Robert James, John Dowdney. Proved 27 Feb., 1732-3. Lib. 3, p. 270.

1732-3, Jan. 25. Inventory (£313.3.4) includes cattle, sheep, horses, wheat, barley, flax, bonds due estate and some iron. Appraisers—Nathaniel Jenkins, Abraham Reeves.

1744, Nov. 28. Johnson, Nicholas, of Penns Neck, Salem Co., yeoman; will of. My brother, Garret Johnson, plantation I live on. Personal estate equally to my said brother, and to Margaret and Elizabeth Johnson. Executors—Sinnick Sinnickson, and my brother, Garret Johnson. Witnesses—"Only Sephins Stanly" (mark), Edward Gorman, Roger Sherron. Proved 6 Dec., 1744. Lib. 5, p. 82.

1744, Dec. 6. Letters to Sinick Sinnickson, one of the executors. "Garret Johnson the other executor at this present time very sick and likely to dye."

1744, Dec. 4. Inventory (£58.3.11½) includes black cattle, 30 swine, 14 sheep, corn and hay. Appraisers—James Barkley, Andrew Sinnickson.

1744, Dec. 13. Additional inventory, £1.1.6; same appraisers.

1748, Nov. 5. Johnson, Paul, of precinct of Maurice River, Cumberland Co. Int. Adm'x, Rebecca Johnson. Fellow bondsman—Joseph Lord. Both of same place. Witnesses—Matthias Johnson, Margaret Morphey. Lib. 6, p. 77.

1748, Oct. 12. Inventory (£99.08.6) includes a silver tankard, razors, 26 head of cattle, 6 horses, 8 sheep. Appraisers—Joseph Lord, John Petterson.

1733, Jan. 10. Johnson, Rhina, of Salem Co., spinster. Int. Adm'r, Matthias Johnson. Bondsmen—Sinick Sinnickson, John Doe. All of Salem County. Witnesses—Clem. Hall, Dan. Mestayer. Lib. 3, p. 391.

1748, Aug. 30. Johnson, Rut, of Somerset Co., yeoman; will of. Wife, Ann. Son, John, after her decease to have homestead plantation (excepting the grave yard). Son, Garrerd, plantation adjoining to or near Delaware River whereon he now lives. Daughters—Eve Huff, Winefred Huff, Anne Updike, Christian Smith, Elizabeth Covanhovan and Mary Schenck. Legacies to Elizabeth Huff, daughter of John Huff. Grandsons—John (son of John Johnson), and Joseph, Cornelius and Rut (sons of Gerrard Johnson). The grave yard to be reserved forever as a burying-ground "for my offspring and to be in care of my son John and his heirs." Executors—sons John and Gerrerd Johnson. Witnesses—Francis Wallace, William Binge (Quaker), Joseph H. Hendrickson, Nathaniel Fitz Randolph. Proved 24 April, 1749. Lib. 6, p. 234.

1749, Apr. 3. Inventory (£6,719.17) includes cattle, horses, negroes (£398.17.6) and bonds (£6,016.7.3). Made by Edmd. Beakes, Captain John Price.

1728, Nov. 21. Johnson, Samuel, of Cape May Co., yeoman; will of. Wife, Charity, executrix and use of all lands until she remarries, or until son, Samuel, shall be 21. Land at Goshen, alias Mackrel Neck, in Cape May County, whereon I live, I devise unto son, Samuel Johnson. Daughters—Sarah, Hannah, Phebe, Charity and Susannah, to be paid as they arrive respectively at age of 18 years or at marriage. Witnesses—Daniel Walker, Benjamin Mareux, Henry Stites, Junior.

1729, April 8. Codicil. Daughter Phebe being dead, her share to go to my other four daughters. Witnesses—Anr. Leaming, Cornelius Schillinks, Junior. Proved 13 and 27 May, 1732. Lib. 3, p. 201.

1732, Feb. 9. Inventory (£124.18.04) includes cattle, sheep and swine, etc. Appraisers—Benjamin Hand, Henry Stites, Junior.

1732, June 5. Johnson, Samuel, of Elizabeth Town, Essex Co. Int. Inventory of personal estate (£175.07.09), includes mention of Daniel Meeker, Obad, Lewis, Wm. Broadwell, Henry Garthwait, David Thomas, Jacob Seebring, Jos. Williams, William Garthwaight, Jno. Megie, Jas. Potter, Thos. Feare. Made by Charles Hole and Samuel Potter.

1732, June 6. Administration granted to Mary Johnson, the widow, Daniel Potter, fellow bondsman. Lib. B, p. 261.

1734, Dec. 8. New bond of Mary Davis (now married to Nathaniel Davis), formerly Mary Johnson, the widow, as administratrix. Nathaniel Davis and William Broadwell, yeoman, fellow bondsmen.

1735, Nov. 26. Johnson, Samuel, of Newark, Essex Co. Int. Inventory of personal estate (£95.16.11); made by Thomas Longworth and Nathaniel Johnson.

1736, Oct. 13. Bond of Hannah Johnson, the widow, as administratrix on the estate, Nathaniel Johnson and Isaac Lyon, fellow bondsmen. Lib. C, p. 126.

1750, June 8. Johnson, Samuel, son of Samuel Johnson of Essex Co., deceased, being 14 years of age and upwards. Petition that Thomas Canfield and John Roberts may be appointed his guardians.

1750, Aug. 11. Bond of Thomas Canfield and John Roberts as guardians. Ephraim Canfield and Thomas Johnson, fellow bondsmen. Witness—David Ogden, Jun'r. Lib. E, p. 500.

1732, March 7. Johnson, Thomas, of Elizabeth Town, Essex Co., gentleman; will of. Daughters—Debora Smith, Sarah Canfield, Hannah Keen. Real and personal estate. Executors—wife ———, and son Ebenezer. Witnesses—Andrew Joline, Sarah Dagworthy, Daniel Makmekell. Proved May 23, 1732. Elizabeth Johnson qualifies as executor with her son. Lib. B, p. 262.

1748-9, March 8. Johnson, William, of Cape May Co.; will of. Wife, Abigail, sole executrix and to have all lands and personal estate during life, after which same shall be given to my nephew, Amos Johnson. Witnesses—Timothy Hand, Ezekiel Hand, Elijah Hughes. Proved 16 May, 1749. Lib. 6, p. 73.

1749, April 29. Inventory, £57.16.3; made by George Stites, Joshua Shaw.

1743, Dec. 12. Johnston, Augustus, of Middlesex Co., being about 14 years of age. Bond of Lewis Johnston, Esq., of Perth Amboy, his uncle, and Bathsheba Robinson, of Rhode Island, late Bathsheba Johnston, his mother, who are appointed his guardians until he arrives at 21 years. Lib. D, p. 107.

1738, July 3. Johnston, David, of Upper Freehold, Monmouth Co.; will of. Wife, Mary. Children—David (eldest son, in Scotland), John, Hannah, Mary and James. Executors—son James, and James Grover of Middletown. Witnesses—Robert and William Imlay, James Debowe and Robert Montgomerie. Proved October 12, 1738. Lib. C, p. 214.

1738, Oct. 7. Inventory of the estate (£242.13.0) includes bonds of Isaac Stelle, Jacob Lane, William Imlay, Thomas Everingham, William Duglass, William Wilkin's bill. Made by James Cox, John Ashton, Robert Imlay and William Duglass. Additional inventory, (£1.8.0), made Dec. 23, 1738, by Richard Fitz Randolph and Samuel Borrowe.

1723, Nov. 14. Johnston, Eupham, daughter of John Johnston, of Perth Amboy, Middlesex Co.; will of. Sister, Margaret Smyth, and her children, Eupham and James Smyth. Eupham, daughter of brother Andrew Johnston. Friend, Mary Forster. Mary, daughter of William Harrison, late of Amboy. Executors—father, John Johnston, and brothers John and Andrew Johnston, and sister Mary Johnston. Witnesses—Ad. Hude, J. Stevens, Isabella Graham. Proved Oct. 11, 1732. Lib. B, p. 324.

1731, Oct. 29. Johnston, John, of Perth Amboy, Middlesex Co.; will of. Children—John, Andrew, Margaret Smyth, Jennet Parker, Mary and Lewis Johnston. Children of George Johnston. James Johnston, son of son James, deceased, farm on Hop River called Scots Chester in Monmouth County. Farm at Matchaponix that was formerly Robert Barclay's; 400 acres by patent dated June 20, 1688; farm on Sanpink River at Crosswicks on which James Silver now lives, of 400 acres; 2,180 acres in Bergen County; land which belonged to Michael Hawdon, lying by Major Brockhool's, to hold in partnership with George Willocks. Executors—wife, Eupham, sons Andrew and Lewis Johnston and sons-in-law John Parker and Lawrence Smyth. Witnesses—Evan Drummond, John White, J. Stevens.

1732, Aug. 18. Codicil. To Mary Forster, daughter of Miles Forster, my friend, 500 or 600 acres on Passaick River between land of John Parker and Lawrence Smyth. To the widow and children of son John, 1000 acres in Evans Pattent in Province of New York. To Johnston, son of William Harrison, 5,800 acres in Bergen County, at 21 years. Executors—Rev. W. Skinner and James Alexander. Witnesses—Evan Drummond, Daniell Donalson Dunstar, Richard Fitzgerald. Proved Nov. 17, 1732. Lib. B, p. 320.

1731, August 16. Johnston, John, Junior, of Monmouth Co.; will of. Wife (not named) to have furniture, plate, little negro girl, Hannah, etc. Children—John, Mary, David, Jamison and Hannah, to be maintained and educated until of age. Executors—wife, her father David Jamison, Esquire, brother Andrew Johnston and friends William Jamison, John Throckmorton and John Reid, gentlemen. Witnesses—William Crawford, John Tipple and Lawrence Smyth. Proved April 13, 1733. Elizabeth and Andrew Johnston, as executors, qualified same day. Lib. B, p. 434.

1730, August 8. Johnston, Mary, of Freehold, Monmouth Co.; will of. Son, John Johnston. Son, James Johnston, executor, and to have lands at Crosswicks, which were bequeathed to testatrix by her parents, Joseph and Hannah Grover, by wills dated December 7, 1688, and May 8, 1690, respectively. Above lands, purchased by testatrix's mother from James Johnston, October 16, 1690, on east side of testatrix's husband's land on Doctor's Creek. Witnesses—William Kinnan, James Poullown and Richard Douglass. March 15, 1732-3, David Johnston, husband of the above Mary, then deceased, declares he gave full liberty to make said will. Witnesses—William Kennan, James Poullon. Proved May 7, 1733. Lib. D, p. 292.

1742, Dec. 8. Johnston, Mary, of Middlesex Co.; will of. Brother, Lewis Johnston, lands devised by sister Euphemia. Nephews—John Smyth, Johnston Harrison, John Johnston (son of brother John), Lewis Smyth and Lawrence Smyth, my share of my father's estate. Niece, Mary, daughter of John Tingle, deceased. Niece, Euphemia Smyth, and nephew. Andrew Smyth, at 21 years, or to surviving brothers and sister. Executors—brother Lewis Johnston and brother-in-law Lawrence Smyth. Witnesses—William Davis, Thomas Robinson, Andrew Robinson, John Smyth. Proved May 15, 1744. Lib. D, p. 134.

1733-4, Feb. 27. Johnston, William, of Shrewsbury, Monmouth Co., yeoman; will of. Wife, Elce. Children—James, Mary and Sarah. Executors—Benjamin and David Johnston. Witnesses—Joshua Edwards, Mary and George Wooley. Proved May 20, 1733. Lib. B, p. 431.

1741, June 18. Joline, Andrew, of Borough of Elizabeth, Essex Co., gentleman; will of. Son, John, debts due me from Matthias Baulding, taylor, of £20, and John Brookfield, £10. Daughter—Mary (wife of John Blanchard), and their children, Andrew, John, Ann and Mary Blanchard, all under age. Real and personal estate, including a number of negroes. Executors—wife, Mary, and son John. Witnesses—Ephraim Sale, George Nicolls, Thos. Jackman. Proved Feb. 13, 1741. Lib. C, p. 485.

1747-8, March 24. Jones, Andrew, of Precinct of Fairfield, Cumberland Co. Int. Adm'r, Joseph Jones. Fellow bondsmen—Thomas Whiteker and John Whiteker, of place and county aforesaid.

1747-8, March 22. Inventory (£31.18.2) incmludes loom and tackling. Appraisers—John Whitecar, Thomas Whitecar. Cumberland Wills, 1 F.

1733, May 13. Jones, Ann, of Township of Waterford, Gloucester Co., widow; will of. Sons, John and Henry, 5 shillings each. Personal estate to be sold and the monies divided equally among my daughters—Mary Jones, Ann Shute, Rebecca Holms, Elizabeth Rudderow, Edith and Sarah Jones (youngest). Executors—son-in-law, John Rudderow, and Thomas Stoaks. Witnesses—Cicely Ashead, Benjamin Collins, Amos Ashead, Moses Ashead. Sworn and affirmed 29 July, 1740. Lib. 4, p. 249.

1740, July 28. Inventory, £54.6.0; made by Moses Ashead.

1748, April 17. Jones, Benjamin, of New Hanover, Burlington Co.; will of. Daughters—Sarah and Mary, each £50 at 18. Brothers—Spencer and Richard Jones, each 5 shillings. Son, Benjamin, land lately bought of Hezekiah Wilson. Executors—wife, Jane, and kinsman Jonathan Fox. Witnesses—Patrick Field, John Jones, Wm. Cooke. Proved May 10, 1748, by Jonathan Fox, surviving executor. Lib. 5, p. 487.

1748, May 7. Inventory, £265; made by Samuel Wright and Thos. Earl. Includes a servant man £6.1.

1760, April 4. Account of Jonathan Fox, executor, having paid executors of Dan'l Smith, also Thomas Newbold, Caleb Shreeves, George Kendall, Henry Jones, mason, John Buffin, John Marshall, Benj'n Oney, Josiah White, Samuel Wright, William Murrell, William Jones, James Shreeve, Isaac Ivins, William Cooke, Jno. Crusher, Barzillai Newbold.

1750, Aug. 3. Jones, Benjamin and Mary, over 14 years of age, son and dau. of Benjamin Jones, dec'd. Bond of guardianship by Joseph Arney, of New Hanover, yeoman. Jonathan Thomas, of City of Burlington, innholder, and Thomas Woodward of Monmouth Co., fellow bondsman. Burlington Wills, 4691-7 C.

———, ——, —. Jones, Daniel, (will not found, or record of same).

1750, 1st mo. (Mar.), 31 da. Renunciation of William Cheeseman of executorship of above will.

1749-50, Feb. 26. Inventory (£144.2.0;) made by Joshua Stokes, William Bates.

1757, March 23. Letters testamentary granted Naomi Jones, Executrix. Salem Wills, 528 Q.

1735, Nov. 8. Jones, David, of Town and County of Gloucester, cordwainer. Int. Adm'r, John Whiteall (during the minority of Susanna and Alice Jones children of the said deceased) cordwainer.

Bondsman—John Eastlake (mark), weaver, all of the County aforesaid. Gloucester Wills, 181 H.

1734, Sept. 11. Inventory (£25.12.9) includes "shoomaker's seat," etc. Appraisers—John Eastlake, Saml. Harrison.

1743, April 9. Jones, Edmond, of City of Burlington, joyner. Int. Inventory of the personal estate, £49.9.5; made by Joseph Heulings and Israel Heulings. Includes case of drawers to be had of Isaac DeCow and a wooden house on Rob't Smith's grounds in Water St. (£5).

1743, April 26. Adm'r, John Raworth, of same, glover. Jacob Heulings and Israel Heulings, of same, yeoman, fellow bondsmen. Lib. 4, p. 379.

1749-50, Feb. 11. Jones, Henry, of Waterford, Gloucester Co.; will of. Sons, Jeremiah and Henry Jones, all lands equally. Daughter, Ann Haynes. Executors—wife, Naomi, and William Cheeseman. Witnesses—George Weed, John Stokes, Joseph Browning. Affirmed 4 April, 1750. Lib. 8, p. 365.

1745, April 3. Jones, Isaac, of Northampton, Burlington Co., sawyer; will of. Friend, Gabriel Blond, my gun. Friends—Solomon, son of Carlile Haines, and Mary, dau. of William Parke, remainder of estate. Witnesses—Isaac Taylor, John Springer, Gab. Blond. Proved June 16, 1745.

1745-6, Jan. 16. Adm'x, Mary Park, spinster. William Sharp and Jonathan Haines, all of Evesham, fellow bondsmen. Lib. 5, p. 429.

1734, April 8. Jones, John, of City of Burlington, joyner. Int. Adm'r, James Richardson, of same. Burlington Wills, 2747-8 C.

1734, Jan. 8. Inventory, £5.2.3; made by Isaac DeCow, Ju'r, and Patrick Brannin. Includes ———, in hands of Edmond Jones.

1735, Nov. 11. Jones, John, of Cohansey, Salem Co., yeoman; will of. Wife, Hannah, sole executrix, and during life profits of all goods and chattels, which at her death shall be divided equally among my three children—John, Samuel and Elizabeth. Other three children—Andrew, Joseph and Elinor, wife of Samuel Barnes, having received their respective portions. Witnesses—John Fithian, James Bunell, Josiah Weakes. Proved 25 Nov., 1735. Lib. 4, p. 48.

1735, Nov. 21. Inventory, £19.16; made by John Fithian, William Bradford.

1739, Oct. 16. Jones, John, of Salem, schoolmaster; will of. Son-in-law, Job Hancock, a piece of land between the house I live in and land of Joseph Wade, deceased. Son, John Jones, rest of my land with buildings thereon. Wife, Mary, executrix and the house I dwell in with the land thereto, and the personal estate for the bringing up of my son. Witnesses—Jacob Townsend, John Young, Nathan Smart. Proved 5 Nov., 1739. Lib. 4, p. 206.

1739, Nov. 9. Inventory (£46.9.6) includes note of hand upon George Crow. Appraisers—Thomas Gillingham, Wm. Siddons.

1740, April 26. Jones, John, of Salem, Salem Co., innkeeper; will of. £10 to mother, Mary Jones. In case of her death same to be divided between my sisters, Elinor Jenkins in Bristol, and Elizabeth Jones. My sister, Ann Mullan, now living in Philadelphia. Friend, Thomas

Hinds. Wife, Elizabeth, sole executrix, and to have residue of estate. Witnesses—Edward Test, John Williams, Joseph Carroll. Proved 2 May, 1740. Lib. 4, p. 233.

1746. Inventory (£968.15.8) includes eight-day clock; negro woman, £20; white maid (time?), £10; negro boy, £30; servant man (time?), £10. Made by Clem. Hall, Edward Test.

1746, Oct. 20. Jones, John, of Salem Co., Att-y-at-law. Int. Adm'x, Mary Jones, widow. Bondsmen—Thomas Thompson, Thoms. Goodwin. All of said County. Witnesses—Stephn. Cormick, Danl. Mestayer. Lib. 5, p. 457.

1735, Jan. 9. Jones, Katharine, of Perth Amboy, Middlesex Co., spinster. Int. Adm'r, Adam Hay, Doctor of Medicine. Andrew Hay, vintner, fellow bondsman. Lib. C, p. 61.

1736, Mar. 26. Inventory, £6.5.5; made by Joseph Leigh and Henry Bossy.

1749, June 24. Jones, Marcus, of Salem Co. Int. Adm'r, John Holmes, of Alloways Creek. Bondsman—Samuel Thompson. Witnesses—Benj. Thompson, Michl. Gibbon. Lib. 6, p. 281.

1749, June 24. "The subscribers give the right of administration into the hands of our son, John Holme. Benj. Holme, Rachel Holme. Witness—Saml. Thompson, Benj. Thompson."

1749, June 24. Inventory, £154.17; made by Saml. Thompson, Benj. Thompson.

1743, Oct. 15. Jones, Samuel, of Monmouth Co. Int. Adm'rs, Thomas Jones and Robert Cumming, of same county. William Thomson of Perth Amboy, fellow bondsman. Lib. D, p. 92.

1743, Oct. 17. Inventory, £45.4.6; made by Gawin Watson and James Dye.

1744, Oct. 13. Account. Bonds, bills, etc., of John Rochead, Robert Davison, Robert Cumming, William Preston, John Frances, William Hughes, William Laird, Thomas Laird, Thomas Jones, Senior, Ellis Jones and Samuel Jobs.

1748, July 30. Jones, Thomas, of Trenton, Hunterdon Co. Inventory, £9; made by Robert Spencer.

1748, August 17. Adm'r, Isaac Green, of Trenton, Robert Spencer, of Trenton, surety. Hunterdon Wills, 218 J.

1747, May 5. Jones, William, of Piscataway, Middlesex Co.; will of. Wife, Ann, sole legatee and executrix. Witnesses—Affia Manning, Mary Manning, Jno. Stelle. Proved June 10, 1747. Lib. E, p. 53.

1747, Aug. 7. Inventory (£171.4.4), includes silver buckles and gold buttons, silver tea spoons, Bible and Testament. Made by Jno. Croker and James Drake.

1750, Feb. 16. Jouet, Daniel, of Borough of Elizabeth, Essex Co., gentleman; will of. Grandson—Cavelier Jouet, at 21, my great English Bible and gold head cane; grandson, William Trotter, plantation in the parish of St. Andrews on the Island of Jamaica, with the negroes. Other grandchildren—John Cavelier Trotter, and Catharine, Sarah and Elizabeth, all under age, gold buckles, silver snuff box and gold ring. Nephew, William Dixon, large French Bible. Land in

Essex Co. Executrix—wife, Mary. Witnesses—John Keyt, William Barker, Ichabod Burnet. Proved March 21, 1750. Lib. F, p. 184.

1732, July 4. Jouet, Mary, of Elizabeth Town, Essex Co., widow; will of. Grandson, William Dixon, moneys due me from Thomas Woodruffe, Nathaniel Crane, Joseph Haer, Daniel Clarke, Richard Miller, all of Elizabeth Town, and a small silver mug. Daughter, Elizabeth Ladner, and her daughter Mary. Sons—Daniel and Peter. Grandson—Daniel Jouet. Executors—son, Daniel, grandson William Dixon, and son-in-law Absalom Ladner. Friend, Rev. Mr. Edward Vaughn, to be overseer. Witnesses—Jane Tongrelon, Mary Emott, Geo. Emott. Proved Nov. 25, 1732. Daniel Jouet and Absalom Ladner qualified as executors, William Dixon not being of age.

Lib. B, p. 326.

1744-5, March 14. Jurejanse (Jurianse), Garret, of Bergen Co., yeoman; will of. Wife, Beletje. To three children of my eldest son, Jurejan Gerretse, deceased, named Gerrit, Altje, Beletie, one-half of three lots on the south of Altje Dedrick's and on the north of Marselious Pieterson; also ½ part of land joining Johannis Gerretse VanWagenen and Johannis VanHoute; also ½ of right to meadow within the Bridge Creek; also one-third part lying over the Bridge; also ½ part of the meadow by the mill, joining, N. E., Arent Lowrencey (the whole containing 5 ½ morgans); also one-third of land at Aghquaquenock, S. of land bought of Jurian Pieterse, provided their mother, Gritje, the widow of my son Jurejan Gerretse, shall have the same during widowhood for maintaining them (the grandchildren), until the youngest will be of age. Son, Cornelious Gerretse, the other half of the aforesaid lands; also the outward garden formerly belonging to Guert Korten, lying N. W. of Matheys DeMott, and S. of Johannis Vanwagene; also the lot formerly belonging to Hendrick Osterum. Son, Johannis Gerretse, land formerly belonging to Balthus Bayard; also my inside garden; also ½ of the land which joins Johannis Gerretse Van Waganen and Johannis VanHoute; also ½ of meadow within the Bridge Creek, he to have the home plantation after the decease of the widow. Son, Dirck, to have full liberty to live in the said home. Also, son Dirck to have two-thirds part (90 rods) of the land at Agquakaunack, joining the land devised unto the heirs of my son, Jurian, deceased; also the tools belonging to the trade of a wheelwright. The claim to the commons, or undivided lands in the township of Bergen, to be divided among the sons and heirs of the deceased son. Legacies to daughters Elizabeth (wife of Maghiel Vrelant), and Leah (wife of Jacob VanWagenene); also lands on the S. and N. W. of Thomas Frederickse, at Aguakaunack. Executors—wife, Beletje, and sons Cornelious and Johannis. Witnesses—Peter Marselis, Zacharias Sickels, David Abeel. Proved 8 April, 1749.

1749, Apr. 8. Cornelius Jurianse and Johannis Juranse qualify as executors. Lib. E, p. 277.

1746, Aug. 7. Jurianse, Altje (single woman), of Bergen Co. Int. Administration on estate granted to her brothers, Harman Jurianse and John Jurianse, of Essex Co. Fellow bondsmen—Nicholas Gerebrant, Garret Thomase, yeoman, all of Essex County.

Bergen Wills, 241 B.

1740, July 15. Justin, Andrew, of Salem Co., gent.; will of. Daughter, Ann Cornelineson, to have land and marsh I live on, formerly John Yanimor's in Penns Neck, Salem County. In case of her death and that of her heirs, said plantation to go to the grandchildren—Marey Scott and Elinor Willin. My said daughter to have ½ of my lot in Willingtown, beginning in Second St.; the other half to my grandchild, Marey Scott. The marsh in New Castle County to be divided equally between them, provided said Mary Scott does not marry Hugh Curel. Rest of my land in New Castle to be sold to pay debts. £3 to my daughter, Catherin Willen. Executors—Charles Cornelius, and my daughter Ann. Witnesses—William Philpot, Alen Congleton, Jeremiah Baker. Proved 19 Aug., 1740. Lib. 4, p. 254.

1740, Aug. 13. Inventory, £76.6.3; made by Jeremiah Baker, William Philpot.

1749, April 30. Kaighin, John, of Newton, Gloucester Co., yeoman; will of. Wife, Abigail, the personal estate and house and lot in Haddonfield, and my two houses and lots on the east side of Second street, or Moyamensing Road, "as the said street extends from the City of Philadelphia" for the maintenance of my children until 21, respectively. Daughter, Sarah, to hold the said house and lot, and my sons, John and Samuel, to hold the aforesaid two houses and lots. Executors—wife, Abigail, and my brother-in-law, James Hinchman. Witnesses—Caleb Sprague, Robert Stephens, Joseph Cooper. Proved 14 June, 1749. Abigail Kaighin sworn in as executor July 4, 1749. Lib. 6, p. 230.

1748, May 10. Kaighin, William, of Town and County of Gloucester, husbandman. Int. Adm'x, Abigail Kaighin, widow. Bondsman, Samuel Harrison, of said County. Witnesses—John Ladd, John Mickle. Lib. 6, p. 16.

1748, May 3. Inventory, £62.14.4; made by Saml. Harrison, John Kaighn.

1749, May 7. Kaighn, Joseph, of Newton, Gloucester Co.; will of. Wife, Mary, sole executrix, and to have the personalty absolutely and benefits of the real estate until my children, Joseph, John, James, Isaac and Elizabeth, attain 21. Real estate—80 acres on Delaware River, where Edward Hampton lives; home farm (30 acres) southwest of Isaac Cooper's field, which his father bought of Joseph Dole, to the line, lately of Tobias Griscomb; 100 acres west of the meadows, lately of Stephen Newby's; a field northof Joseph Mickle's meadow, joining Arthur Powell's; land south of Daniel and William Cooper, west by Delaware River. To son, John, land in the City of Philadelphia. Witnesses—Joseph Morgan, Wm. Griscom, Joseph Cooper. Affirmed 7 Aug., 1749. Lib. 7, p. 5.

1731, Oct. 4. Kay, Benjamin, of Gloucester Co., miller; will of. Brothers—Isaac, Josiah and John. Sister—Sarah. Legacies to daughters of my brother John; to daughters of my sister, Elizabeth Wood, deceased; to sons and daughters of my brother Josiah; to Elizabeth and James Morris, children of my sister Sarah Morris. Executor—my brother, John Kay. Witnesses—John Thorne, Gervas Hall, Amos Ashead. Affirmed 30 Dec., 1731. Lib. 3, p. 192.

Inventory (£116.7.9) includes Bible, Testament, bonds and bills. Appraisers—William Ellis, Amos Ashead.

1740-1, 12 mo. (Feb.), 20 da. Kay, John, of Waterford, Gloucester Co., yeoman; will of. Wife, Sarah, house we live in, and the land "as far as the tree we go over to Thomas Ellis' house." Elizabeth

Fearn to serve her during her indenture. Son, John, to have my house in Evesham, where Nathaniel Hopewell lives, he paying £20 to Samuel Smith, of Salem County, or to the children he had by his wife, Mary, the daughter of John Appleton; he to sign a title to John Cleverly for the land I sold him in Hanover. Daughter, Sarah Norris, my brick house in Philadelphia, and the house she lives in, in Hattenfield, and that land adjoining to Simeon Ellis by the bridge in the road, bounded by Jonathan Axford's land; also all my land unsold in Mauris (Morris) County. Granddaughter, Elizabeth (daughter of my daughter Sarah Norris), ½ acre joining her mother's lot in Haddonfield. Grandson, Josiah, son of my son Josiah Kay, 1 acre in Haddonfield. Son, Isaac, to have the house he lives in, the mill and all my land on that side of the creek; also that on the north side of the branch (300 acres); also that piece of meadow adjoining Jonathan Axford; also that warrant of survey for 500 acres and the reversion of the house and land given to my wife during her life, upon condition that he will pay to my son John £300, and my son Josiah £100, within four years after my decease. Granddaughters, Abigail (the wife of Robert Hunt), Mary (the widow of Josiah Cole), Elisabeth (the wife of Elias Tay) and Hannah Wood, land equally between the two branches of Rackoon Creek, they performing Samuel Collins' lease and paying £20 to their brother, Benjamin. My warrant of survey for 400 acres in the care of Isaac DeCow I give to my son, John Kay, whom I appoint my executor. Residue of my estate to be divided among my children—John, Josiah, Isaac, Sarah Norris, and my said four granddaughters. Witnesses—Benjamin Collins, Thomas Stokes, John Ashead. Affirmed 15 Sept., 1741. Lib. 4, p. 312.

1741-2, Feb. 10. Inventory (£384.5.4) includes bonds, bills, notes and interest due thereon, £232.13.5. Appraisers—Jas. Cooper, Jno. Kaighin.

1748, July 3. Kealy, Edward, of Piscataway, Middlesex Co., cooper; will of. Wife, Christian. Daughter, Mary, under age. Real and personal estate. Executors—friends Garshum Marten, William McDaniell of Woodbridge, and John Hepburn of Piscataway. Witnesses—Richard Taylor, Alex'r Thomson, Josiah Davis. Proved April 7, 1749. Lib. E, p. 289.

1749, April 3. Inventory of personal estate, £95.12; made by Abraham Shotwell, of Piscataway, and John Campbell, of Woodbury.

1749, May 6. Kearney, Catherine, of Middletown Township, Monmouth Co.; will of. To daughter, Mary Shippey, negro girl Bridget, testatrix's brocade gown and wedding ring. Daughter, Catherine. Son, Thomas, negro boy Cork. Son, James, negro boy Ireland, and negro woman Leucy. Granddaughters, Catherine, Mary and Anna Kearney, daughters of John Kearney. Daughter's (Mary Shippey's) children. Friend, Marget, daughter of Marget Judges, £10, when aged 18. Sister, Mary Conun. Mentions Hannah Cotrell. Executors—sons Thomas and James, and friend John Taylor, Esquire, of Middletown Township. Witnesses—Aarent Dyrcken van Haaren, John Cottrell and Thomas Bullman. Proved Nov. 27, 1749. Lib. E, p. 346.

1745, Feb. 18. Kearney, Thomas, of Monmouth Co., merchant; will of. Wife, Catherine, annuity, furniture, silver, negroes, etc. Eldest son, John, has received money and slaves. Son, Thomas, 750 acres where testator lived, called Key-grove, bounded N. by the bay, E. by land late of Christopher Wormsley and land called Canasko, S.

by land late of Gershom Mott, deceased, W. by Lupakitonque Creek and Rapeketon brook. Said land was bought from John Bowne July 21, 1714, John Johnstone, Esquire, Sept. 18, 1714, and John Bowne, Jan. 15, 1715. If Thomas dies without male issue, land to son John and his male heirs, or to male heirs of son James. If no male heirs, then to testator's son Thomas's first born grandson and his male heirs, he and they retaining the name of Kearney additional to their surnames in the family. To son, Thomas, land bought, November 19, 1717, from Elisha Lawrence; land in Middletown, bought of John Willson and wife Hannah, April 28, 1719; 40 acres bought of Lawrence Smith, February 28, 1717. Also right of Propriety bought November 18, 1717, of Richard Saltar. Half of saw mill brook and saw mill house. Daughter, Catherine Kearney. Son, James, land in Middletown Township, called Brown's Point, bounded N. by bay, E. by Lupaketonque creek and Rapaketong brook, S. by Obadiah Bowne and William Bowne, deceased, W. by lands late of Lydia Bowne, deceased, and Whingson brook and creek, Obadiah Holmes, Jonathan Holmes and Mattewan bay, same as granted to testator by John Bowne July 21, 1714, Abram Watson August 21, 1717, Richard Saltar November 18, 1717. Daughter, Mary, wife of Joseph Shippen of Philadelphia, merchant. Executors—wife, and sons Thomas and James. Witnesses—James Mott, Joseph Carman, Gysbert Van Bracle and Nicolas Cottrell. Proved April 14, 1747. Lib. E, p. 25.

1748, July 25. Kearnes, Nicholas, of Bethlehem, Hunterdon Co. Int. Adm'r, William Corne. Lib. 7, p. 92.

1740-1, March 12. Kearny, Michael, of Perth Amboy, Middlesex Co.; will of. Son, Philip, one-half of Howell lot in Kent Co., on Delaware. Daughters—Mary Vanhorn, Isabella, Sarah, Euphemia, Arrabella, and Graham Kearny, last two under age. Son, Michael, provided for by Lewis Morris, Esq. Land I purchased formerly belonging to James Armour, opposite Perth Amboy City; land Lewis Morris gave his daughter Sarah Kearny. Executors—daughters, Mary Vanhorn, Isabella and Sarah Kearny. Witnesses—Jon. Miln, Elizabeth Stodgill, Patrick Devlin. Proved March 9, 1742.

1744, ———, —. Letters to Isabella Kearny and Mary Vanhorn, two of the executors; Sarah, the other executor being deceased and the other daughters under age. Lib. D, p. 149.

1744, Jan. 28. Keasbey (Casbey), Bradway (son of Edward Casbey of Salem County and Elizabeth his wife, also deceased), being 14 yrs. and upward, ward. Guardian—Jonathan Bradway of Alloways Creek. Witnesses—Ed. Rad Price, Jo. Scattergood. Salem Wills, 428 Q.

1733-4, Feb. 9. Keasbey, Edward, of Town and County of Salem; will of. Son, Broadway Keasbey, that 16 acre lot against Thomas Taylor's, joining widow Wiggins' lot and 20 acres joining Richard Smith's from the end next Salem Town, and ½ acre joining Mathew Keasbey's lot; also the rent of my house and lot where James Vance lives, to be paid by my executors when he will be 21. In case of death, son Edward shall have the same to be paid in like manner; also the residue of my real estate, the profits of which shall be for maintaining my sons until of age. If he dies without lawful issue, same shall descend to my son Bradway, and his lawful heirs. In case of no such issue, my said sons' brother, Mathew Keasbey, shall have the same. Personal shall be divided equally between said sons when 20 years of age. To Elizabeth Kellit, £5. Executors—son Edward, my brother Matthias Keasbey, and Richard Smith. Witnesses—Benjamin Vining, Thomas Taylor, Edward Johnson, Jno. Jones. Sworn and affirmed 8 March, 1733-4. Lib. 3, p. 401.

1733-4, March 8. Renunciation of Richard Smith, one executor. Witness—Jno. Jones.

1733-4, Feb. 18, 19. Inventory (£451.8.9½) includes a parcel of bricks, 120 oxen, four cows, nine yearlings, four do., 13 cows, 30 sheep, 19 acres of wheat. Appraisers—Joseph Darkin, Lewis Morris.

1733-4, March 8. Letters testamentary granted to Mathew Keasby, in absence of Edward Keasbey and Richard Smith.

1737, 10 mo. (Dec.), 10 da. Keasbey, Mathew, of Town and County of Salem, joiner; will of. Son, John, at 20 to have the house and lot that Thomas Thompson lives in; my wife Sarah to have the benefit thereof. Daughter, Mary, when 18, the lot at the lower end of the town, which was formerly James Sherron's. Executors—wife, Sarah, and Jonathan Broadway. Witnesses—Nathan Smart, Hugh Clifton, Alexander Simpson, Daniel Haynes. Affirmed 31 Dec., 1737. Lib. 4, p. 140.

1737, Dec. 23. Inventory (£768.12.10) includes cattle and cash due for cattle (£208.8.6), servant boy and negro boy, servant girl. Appraisers—Joseph Darkin, Lewis Morris.

1740, May 26. Keasby, Edward (son of Edward Keasby, of Salem County, said petitioner's mother having since died), 14 years old, ward. Guardian—Thomas Rice, of Salem, gent. Witnesses—John Jones, Clem. Hall. Bond signed by Thos. Thompson, Daniel Haynes. Lib. 4, p. 195.

1750, April 30. Keen, Erick, of Township of Maurice River, Cumberland Co. Int. Adm'x, Catherain Keen, widow. Fellow bondsman—Gabriel Isard, of the same place, yeoman. Witnesses—Elizabeth Cotting, Elias Cotting. Lib. 7, p. 45.

1750, May 16. Inventory (£50.12), includes cattle and sheep. Appraisers—Gabrill Isard, Abraham Jones.

1750, Sept. 11. Keen, Jonas, of Salem County. Int. Account of Lawrence and Catherine Dalbo, Admrs. Monies paid to Francis King, John Howman, George Cote for William Hall, Rainer Vanhist for William Bettel, James Hinchman for Neh. Cowgill, Jacob Pedrick, Wm. Pedrick, Thomas Wilkins for Timothy Rains, Thomas Duell, Thos. Wilkins for Thos. Pedrick, Andrew Hoffman. Salem Wills, 1011 Q.

1749-50, Feb. 24. Kelahan, John, of Penns Neck, Salem County, farmer; will of. Wife, Margaret, executrix, and to have full use of estate during life, provided she will keep house for our children and not make any after charge, they following their business according to her directions, and at her decease freely give up her right to her thirds to be divided equally among our lawfully begotten children, viz: Marey, John and Margrat. If wife claims her thirds son John shall have £20 above his sisters' share. Witnesses—Alen Congelton, Jane Congelton, James Barkley. Proved 3 Sept., 1750. Lib. 6, p. 410.

1750, Aug. 25. Inventory (£164.15.3) includes riding horse, oxen, cows, etc. Appraisers—Alen Congleton, Samuel Whitehorne.

1739-40, Feb. 13. Kellsey, Joseph, Sen'r, of Elizabeth Town, Essex Co., planter; will of. Two youngest sons, Benjamin and Daniel, land joining lands of Jonathan Miller and John Radley's mill. Eldest son, Joseph. Daughters—Lidia Winans, Marey Cutter, Hannah Badgley, Mary Olliver, Ruth Ellstone and Phebe Wood. Executors—John Terrill, James Badgley, Joseph Wood. Witnesses—William Crage, Nathaniel Messenger, Mary Hand. Proved July 1, 1742.
Lib. C, p. 591.

1742, July 1. John Terrill, of Elizabeth Town, declines to act as executor.

1745, May 6. Kelly, James, of Elizabeth Town, Essex Co.; will of. Devises one-half estate to wife, Sarah, and one-half to Presbyterian church in Wesfield. Witnesses—William Clark, Charles Clarke. Proved Feb. 9, 1746. (No executors). Lib. D, p. 451.

1746-7, Feb. 10. Administration granted to Sarah Kelly, his widow. Samuel Pray, cordwainer, and Obadiah Ayres, carpenter, both of Woodbridge, fellow bondsmen.

1746-7, Feb. 11. Inventory, £9.10; made by Zedekiah Bonham and David Compton. Witness—Daniel Alward.

1746-7, Feb. 11. Account of the administratrix (£19.12.7), showing payments to William Clarke and Charles Clarke.

1753, April 4. Additional account of the administratrix, showing gain of £1.17.6.

1738, June 7. Kemble (Kembell), Peter, of Middlesex Co., boatman. Int. Adm'r, Peter Kemble. Andrew Johnston, Esq., fellow bondsman.
Lib. C, p. 197.

1732, June 20. Keney (Kenny), Thomas, of Elizabeth Town (Whipenny), Essex Co., blacksmith. Int. Bond of John Keney, of Hanover, Hunterdon Co., cordwainer, as administratrix. Edward Thomas, of Elizabeth Town, innholder, fellow bondsman. Witnesses—Samuel Whitehead, George Newman. Lib. B, p. 261.

1732, Oct. 11. Inventory, £23.00.06; made by Andrew Joline and Edward Thomas.

1733, June 22. Kenney, Samuel, of Elizabeth Town, Essex Co. Int. Adm'x, Pheby Kenney, the widow. John Higgins, fellow bondsman.
Lib. B, p. 422.

1748, Aug. 22. Kenny (Kenney), David, of Reading Town, Hunterdon Co., yeoman; will of. Wife, Jean. Children—Peter, Adrian and Ida. Executors—brother, William Kenny, and friend George Biggs. Witnesses—David Cock, Isaac Kip, Rinear Vansickel. Proved Nov. 1, 1748. Lib. 5, p. 542.

1748, Oct. 19. Inventory (£377.14.8½), includes negro man, £15, negro lad, £15. Made by David Cock and Isaac Kip.

1766, June 17. Account of George Biggs, executor, mentions, John Broughton, James Jobs, Samuel Fleming, Jury Hapach, Trentjie Van Wagneses, Cornelius Low, John Van Sickle, Jr., Rike Vanderbelts, Isaac Van Nawken, John Van Sickle, Paul Flag, Baultus Pickle, Pet. Kenny, cordwainer, John and George Reading, William Coxe, Joseph Yard, George Murry, Jacob Crasto, Andrew Brown, James Jobs, William Searross, David Able, Christofel Brissey, Garret Van Wagonon, Aaron Lonsadee, Peter Low, Philip Ringo, Charles Hoff, Jr., Johans Ten Brook, Peter Kimble, William French, Andreas Tenick, Adrian Atte, Edward Herrington and Jane his wife (late widow of testator for nursing children and in right of her dower), Andrew Stall, Peter Devore, Abram Smith, Eliz. Kenny, Jacob Carson, John Stoll, Jr., Cornelius Kenny.

1744, Sept. 12. Kenny, Timothy, of Woodbury, Gloucester Co., school master; will of. Clothes, etc., to Richard Kenny, in Philadelphia, to be inquired for at Samuel Richshy's upon Society Hill. Wife, Ruth, and her daughter a shilling apiece. Books to John Wilkins' two sons. To his daughters Rachel and Ruth Snowden a whole piece of chins, now in hands of Grace Chattin. 10 shillings to fence in the new burying-ground, (where I am to be buried). Knee buckles to Sarah Wilkins; my gold headed cane to Sarah Snowden. Executors—John Wilkins and John Snowden and they to have the residue of my estate equally. Witnesses—Thomas Kinsey, Junior, John Marshall, Lidia Snowden. Affirmed 22 Oct., 1744. Lib. 5, p. 69.

1744, Oct. 22. Inventory (£54.7.1) includes 7 gold pieces (£24), silver buckles, gold headed cane (£1.15.0), silver headed cane. Appraisers—Robert Downs, John Sparks.

1742, Sept. 13. Kerr, John, of Salem Co. Int. Adm'x, Sarah Kerr (relict). Bondsman—Aaron Hill, cordwainer. All of Piles Grove in said County. Witnesses—Wm. Crabb, Chas. O Neill. Lib. 4, p. 377.

1742, Sept. 13. Inventory (£139.8.9) includes cattle, wheat, corn, one servant (£18). Appraisers—David Davis, Henry Paullin.

1741, April 9. Ketcham, John, of Hunterdon Co.; will of. Executors—friends Benjamin ——— and Nathaniel Hart. To wife of Rulof Traphagan or her children. Residue to testator's daughter, Liana Ketcham, a minor. Testator's sisters—Martha Knowles and Elizabeth Titis. Testator's mother (not named) a legatee. Witnesses—Joseph Stout, Roger Merrel, Mary Reder. Proved Feb. 16, 1741-2. Lib. 4, p. 354.

1748, Oct. 10. Ketcham, Jonathan, of Middlesex Co.; will of. Children—Phebe, Mary, Daniell, Josiah and Hester Ketcham, all under age. Real and personal estate. Executors—wife, Mary, and brother David Ketcham. Witnesses—John Tyson, Sarah Tyson, Mary Ketcham. Proved Nov. 3, 1748. Lib. 5, p. 218.

1748, Nov. 15. Inventory, £122.6.2; made by John Throckmorton and John Scobey.

1754, Feb. 25. Account of David Ketcham and Mary Smock (lately Mary Ketcham) the executors, showing payments to Andrew Johnston, Richard Francis, Joseph Forman, Samuel Leonard, Hendrick Hendrickson, Garret Walls, Isack Emans, Jno. Combs, Fradrak Buckalew, William Smith, Jun'r, James Abraham, George Williams, James Pattin, Thomas Loyd, Alexander Scobe, John Hurd, William Smith Sen'r, Jno. Scoby, Jno. Tone, Moses Peterson, James English, Thomas Bray, Phebe Huns, Josiah Parent, Griffin Disbiry, Charles Morgin, Micaiah Ketcham, William Morgin.

1733-4, Jan. 28. Ketcham, Samuel, of Trenton, Hunterdon Co., house carpenter. Int. Inventory (£177.2.0) includes bond of Joseph and William Greens. Made by Richard Scudder and Charles Clark.

1733-4, Feb. 8. Adm'x, Hannah Ketcham, of Hunterdon County. Charles Clark, of same county, gent., surety. Witnesses—John Holcombe and Andrew Reed. Lib. 3, p. 387.

1736, March 16. Kidd, John, of Salem Co., yeoman. Int. Adm'x,

Martha Kidd (relict). Bondsman—Wm. Hunt. Both of said County. Witnesses—Wm. Hall, Danl. Mestayer. Lib. 4, p. 114.

1736-7, March 12. Inventory of John Kidd of Mannington, Salem Co., £56.10; made by Wm. Hall, William Hunt.

1750, Oct. 16. Kidd, John, of Mannington, Salem Co., yeoman; will of. Sons—Abraham and Isaac, to have plantation I live on, the western part joining Joseph Sharp's upland. Son, William, during life to have use and profits of ½ of the land I have devised to my son Isaac, but if the said William dies before his wife Anne, Isaac to pay her 40 shillings annually for ten years. Son, Jacob, five shillings. Personal estate to be divided equally among my said four sons and my daughters—Anne (wife of Edward Johnson), Elizabeth (wife of James Halton), and Mary (wife of John Wood). Executor—Adam Leberg, of Piles Grove, miller. Witnesses—William Tuft, John McKim, Danl. Mestayer. Proved 25 Jan., 1750-1. Lib. 7, p. 262.

1750-1, Jan. 21. Inventory (£118.12.2) includes cattle, sheep, wheat, etc. Appraisers—John Smith, David Seley.

1755, Oct. 17. Account. Monies paid Thomas Thompson, Samuel Johnson, John Smith, William Lyth, Nicholas Gibbon, Mount Sheep, William Scott, Thomas Hanly, John Hanley, John Thomas, James Mason, John Halford, William Harvey, Eliz. Smith, John Thompson, David Seely, Richard Wesler, William Tuftt, William Barton, Thomas Dowell, Robert Haynes, James Halton, Jacob Kidd, John M. Kimp.

1732-3, Jan. 18. Killburn (Kilburn), Ebenezer, of Hanover Township, Hunterdon Co. Elizabeth Kilburn, the widow, renounces her right to administer, in favor of Amos Killburn and John Johnson, Jr. Witnesses—Joseph Hinds and Jno. Budd. Bond of Amos Kilburn, of Hanover Township. John Johnson, Jr., and Samuel Crosman of same place sureties. Witnesses—James Primrose, Joseph Hinds and Jno. Budd. Hunterdon Wills, 75 J.

1732, Dec. 8. Killey, David, of Middletown, Monmouth Co., yeoman; will of. Wife, Anna. Son, Joseph, half of Propriety Right bought of John Reid, Esquire. Son, David, plantation where testator lives. Daughter, Anna Matthews. Executors—wife, and sons Joseph and David. Witnesses—Joseph Forman, Elizabeth Forman and William Madock.

1735, Dec. 26. Codicil. Witnessed by William Jones, Thomas Leonard and William Madock. Proved Sept. 17, 1737. Lib. C, p. 177.

———, ———, —. Inventory, £169.6.0; made by John Throckmorton, Job Throckmorton, John Taylor.

1744, Dec. 17. Kimble, Edward, of Springfield, Burlington Co., yeoman. Int. Adm'x, Martha Kimble. Lib. 5, p. 69.

1744, Dec. 21. Inventory £309.1.5; made by Elnathan Stevenson, John Budd and George Eyres. Includes bonds of Zebulon Brown, John Kemble, Andrew King, and John Dutchfield. Notes of Edward Price, John Gray, Martin Springer and John Fenimore.

1746, March 9. Account showing payments to Jos. Scattergood (for letters of administration), Thos. Tuly, Richard Smith, Jr., John Bigan, Edward Noble, Thos. Shaw, Richard Smith, Sen'r, Samuel Smith, Hugh Hartshorn, Jos. Richards, Daniel Smith, Rob't Smith, William Hewlings, Isaac DeCow, Ju'r, Jacob DeCow, Ben. Kemble, John Canady, Thos. Homan, Thos. Atkinson, Zebulon Brown, Francis Simpson, Joseph Allinson,

James Wills, Thomas Holmes, Ben. Butterworth, William Gardiner, Sam'l Rogers, Sam'l King, Thos. Staples, Elnathan Stevenson, James Inskeep, Samuel Hall, Elizabeth Johnson, Thos. Merideth, Ben. King, Obediah Irton, Ann Wheeler, Margaret Budd, Mary Raper, Joshua Raper, Thos. Budd, Sam'l How, William Lindon, Josiah White, Israel Hewlings, Bartholomew Gibson, Rob't Hartshorn, Mary Tuly (executrix of Thos. Tuly, deceased, being part of bond executed by Edward Kemble and Sarah Hunlock, executrix of Tho's Hunlock).

1735, June 7. Kimmins, Ann, of Nottingham, Burlington Co. Int. Inventory of the personal estate, £20.4; made by William Tindall and John Tantum.

1735, June 16. Adm'r, Samuel Danford. John Tantum, fellow bondsman, both of same, yeoman. Lib. 4, p. 21.

1735-6, March 2. Account. Payments to John Tantum for the coffin, Dr. Rutledge, William Tindall, Thomas Williams, Francis Bowes.

1750, Sept. 20. Kimsey, James, of Gloucester Co. Int. Adm'x, Mary Kimsey, widow. Bondsman—Samuel Harrison, of same place. Witness—Tim. Rain. Lib. 7, p. 42.

1750, June 25. Inventory, £3.8.6; made by James Talman, William Hugg.

1744, 6 mo. (Aug.), 15 da. Kimsey, Thomas, of Woodbury, Gloucester Co., husbandman; will of. Wife, Ann, sole executrix. Son, James. Witnesses—Thomas Kimsey, Adam Hatfield, William Wood. Gloucester Wills, 356 H.

1747, June 19. Inventory, £118.14.3; made by Peter Rambo, Abraham Chattin.

1750, Oct. 8. Kimsey, William, of Timber Creek, Gloucester Co., husbandman; will of. Wife, Deborah. Sons—Jonathan, Thomas and William (all minors), and to be "under the care and tuition of my brother Thomas Kimsey and to be bound to a trade when of suitable age." Executors—wife, Deborah, and my brother, Thomas Kimsey. Witnesses—Robert Down, John Down, John Milles. Affirmed 1 Jan., 1750-1. Lib. 7, p. 25.

1750, Dec. 30. Inventory (at Township of Deptford), £129.13.14½; made by Abra. Chattin, Tos. Harrison.

1749, March 5. Kindal, John, of New Hanover, Burlington Co., labourer. Int. Bond of Phebe Kindal, widow, as administratrix. Bennet Bard, of City of Burlington, gent., fellow bondsman. Lib. 7, p. 90.

1750, March 13. Inventory, £32.3.4; made by Joseph Woolston and Solomon Watkins.

1737, Aug. 17. King, Abraham, of Newark, Essex Co. Int. Adm'x, Susannah King, the widow. John King, yeoman, fellow bondsman. Witnesses—John Foster, Jacobus Bargan. Lib. C, p. 175.

1739, Nov. 20. King, Elizabeth, of Monmouth Co., widow; will of. Son, Harmanus, 102 acres, bounded by Edmund Beakes, Crosswicks Creek and Peter Sonman. Son, William, plantation where testatrix lives, bounded by Crosswicks Creek and Anthony King. Daughter, Mary, £20 towards paying debt testatrix's husband was bound for

(her) husband at Philadelphia. Children—Hannah, Elizabeth, Samuel and Joseph, when of age. Executors—sons (Anthony, crossed off), John, Benjamin, Harmanus and William. Witnesses—John Quicksall, Daniel Robins and Edmund Beakes. Proved March 31, 1741.
Lib. 4, p. 306.

1741, March 30. Inventory (£460.11.03) includes debts, bonds, etc., from Harmanus, Thomas, Anthony, Benjamin and William King, William Woodward and John Quicksall. Due from Jon. Barker at his mill, 5,000 ft. pine boards. Made by John Quicksall and Robert Montgomerie.

1735, Nov. 8. King, Francis, of Nottingham, Burlington Co., yeoman. Int. Inventory of the personal estate, £197.7.8; made by Edw'd Beakes and Thos. Miller.

1735, Nov. 20. Adm'x, Catherine King, widow; John Thorne, Jr., fellow bondsman. Lib. 4, p. 41.

1748, Oct. 3. King, Francis, over 14 years of age, son of Francis King of Nottingham, Burlington Co., yeoman. Guardianship to Joseph Thornes, of Chesterfield, yeoman. John Bunting, Jun'r, of same, fellow bondsman. Lib. 5, p. 515.

1739, Oct. 15. King, John, of Upper Freehold, Monmouth Co., yeoman. Int. Inventory of estate (£503.13.4) includes servant girl, (£7); 27 sheep, 10 cows, 2 steers, etc., bonds of Francis Garvis, Anthony and Benjamin King. Made by Joshua Wright, John Ashton, Edmund Beakes, John Steward. Lib. 4, p. 200.

1739, Oct. 19. Adm'rs, Elizabeth King, the widow, and Anthony King, son. Obadiah Ireton, of Burlington, yeoman, fellow bondsman.

1747-8, Feb. 22. King, John, of Piscataway, Middlesex Co. Int. Adm'x, Anderiah King. Benjamin Doty, fellow bondsman.
Lib. E, p. 127.

1748, Feb. 25. Inventory, £45.19; made by Isaac Manning and John Pound Jun'r.

1749, Aug. 31. Account showing debts due to Mr. Lagrange, Thos. Clawson, Peter Sharp, Lawrence Reuth, Thomas Poole, William Worrall, Marcey Smalley, John Leforge, Benjamin Doty, William Jones, Charles Robison, Daniel Barto, Nathaniel Blackford, John Whitehead, David Laing, Amariah Bonham, Joseph Sutton, James Barto, James Alexander, And'w Johnston, Esq. Cornelius Low, Justice Thomson, John Pound. Signed by "Anderiah Grimes, late Anderiah King," and George Greems.

———, ———, —. Account of sale of land to Benjamin and Benajah Doty, for £129.15. Paid Solomon Comes, Mr. Alexander.

1746, Nov. 27. King, Robert, Esq., of Perth Amboy, Middlesex Co. Int. Adm'r, widow, Judith King. Elias Grazeillier, fellow bondsman. Lib. D, p. 438.

1746-7, Feb. 16. Inventory, £171.9; made by Tho's Fox and Rich'd Fitz-Randolph.

1748, June 12. The widow, Judith, administratrix of Robert King, being deceased, administration on the estate granted to Elias Grazillier of the Borough of Elizabeth, cousin german to the decedant. Th'o. Fox, fellow bondsman. Lib. E, fol. 194.

1745, Dec. 10. King, William, of limits of City of Burlington, yeoman; will of. Brothers—Samuel and Joseph. Sisters—Mary Ireton,

Hannah and Elizabeth King. Nephew, William Ireton. Real and personal estate. Executors—brother, Obadiah Ireton, and friend Thomas Miller. Witnesses—Ebenezer Gaskill, Benj'n Kemble, Edward Noble. Proved Jan. 1, 1745-6. Lib. 5, p. 212.

1745, Dec. 30. Inventory, £444.3.4; made by Joseph Pearson and Tho's Atkinson.

1741, July 29. Kingsland, Edmund, Esq., of Bergen Co.; will of. Wife deceased. Children—William, Edmund Rodger, Isaac, John, Elizabeth (wife of Geo. Leslie), Mary, Anna, Hester, Catherin. William to have 300 acres of land, which he lives on near New Barbadoes Neck, adjoining John Schuyler, mines excepted; also one-third of meadows and cedar swamps adjoining aforesaid. Son, Edmund Rodger, to have residue of estate upon the New Barbadoes Neck, undivided, lying between Pissaick and Hackensack Rivers (mines excepted), he to pay my sons John and Edmund Kingsland £300 each within two years after decease, as also to my daughters Mary, Anna, Hester and Catherine £150 each four years after decease. "If he refuses to perform my will to my children one year after my decease, then my son Isaac to assume same, paying to Edmund Kingsland £500 within two years" and so on. In case all sons refuse, then the executors to dispose of estate and proceeds to be paid in sums, as before devised, unto each of my said children, and to Geo. Leslie for my daughter, Elizabeth, his wife. Large silver tankard to daughter Mary. Anna to have small silver tankard; Hester and Catherine each to have 6 silver spoons. Mentions mines and lands upon New Barbadoes Neck, shares of mines upon Secacus, held from Mr. Pinhorn, deceased, two cedar swamps, shares of meadows upon Bergen side, together with the eleventh part of all the Commons of Bergen (now in dispute), belonging to me, held in right of Mr. Pinhorn, deceased. Same to be divided into 9 equal parts for my children. Son, William, not to be called to an account for any debt due me concerning the leasing of my plantation after the death of his mother. Executors—sons Isaac, Edmund Rodger, and George Leslie. Witnesses—Charles Morgan, John Vandeventr, Thomas Morgan, Will'm Morgan.

1742, July 26. Codicil. Personal bequests, and daughter Mary to serve as executor in place of son, Isaac. Witnesses—Geo. Lurling, Ephraim Vangelder, Charles Oasborn. Proved 6 and 12 May, 1743.

1743, May 6. Edmund Rodgers Kingsland and Geo. Leslie qualify as executors, Mary Kingsland having renounced. Lib. D, p. 48.

1747-8, March 7. Kinnan, Joseph, of Upper Freehold, Monmouth Co., cooper; will of. Wife (not named) appointed executrix. Children—John, Ann and Luce. Witnesses—Robert Imlay, Stephen Pangburn, William Dunterfield. Proved April 2, 1748. Anne Kinnan, the executrix, sworn same day. Lib. 5, p. 469.

1736, August 28. Kinne, Peter, of Reading Township, Hunterdon Co., yeoman; will of. Wife, Ida. Eldest son, William, big Dutch Bible. Son, David. Eldest daughter, Willeminsa Devore, and her eldest child. Youngest daughter, Elenor Biggs. Grandson, Peter Kinne, surviving son of testator's son Adrian. Executors—friends William Krom and Hermanus Tildine. Witnesses—Marten Ryerson, Edward Beatty, Teunes Coole. Proved August 6, 1745. Lib. 5, p. 162.

1734, Dec. 4. Kinsey, John, of Woodbridge, Middlesex Co., yeoman;

will of. Children—John, Benjamin, Sarah Pritchard, Hannah Bourn, Johannah FitzRandolph, Elizabeth FitzRandolph and Jonathan. Grandsons—John Kinsey and John Kinsey FitzRandolph. Son-in-law, Nathaniel FitzRandolph. Daughter-in-law, Experience Moores. Executors—wife, Grace, and son John. Witnesses—Samuel Allen, Jane Brown, Jno. Sarjant. Proved May 5, 1735. Lib. C, p. 31.

1750, July 4. Kinsey, John, Esq., late of Philadelphia. Int. Adm'r, Philip Kearny, Esq. Robert Lettis Hooper, Esq., fellow bondsman. Middlesex Wills, Lib. E, p. 430.

1753, July 11. Bond of James Kinsey, of Philadelphia, eldest son, as administrator on estate remaining unadministered by said P. Kearny; said deceased at time of death being a widower and his children under age. Philip Kearny, Esq., could by law only administer the estate until one of said children was duly qualified by age. P. Kearny, fellow bondsman. Witnesses—P. Kearny, Jun'r, Jno. Webb. Lib. F, p. 127.

1733, Oct. 14. Kirby, Richard, of Newhannover, Burlington Co., yeoman; will of. Wife, Anne. Children—Mary, Recompense, Richard, John, Jonathan, Joseph, all under age. An expected child. Line to be run from Isaac DeCow's to the new mill north of Thomas Wright's land. Real and personal estate. Executors—wife, and brother William Kirby. Witnesses—John Steward, Tho. Wright, David Starkey. Proved March 5, 1740. Lib. 4, p. 269.

1741, Feb. 24, 25. Inventory of the personal estate, £482.7.3; made by Samuel Wright, Tho: Earl and Isaac Ivins. Includes specialties from Francis Davenport.

1745, June 25. Kitchen, Henry, of Amwell Township, Hunterdon Co., yeoman; will of. Wife, Ann, annuity, to be paid by Samuel and Wheeler Kitchen. Son, Samuel, 200 acres of land at Pohatcung; land in the great swamp and one-half of saw mill. Son, Wheeler, 300 acres at Pohatcung. Son, Joseph, 100 acres at Pohatcung and land in great swamp. Son, Henry. Son, Richard, old plantation in Amwell, bought of Samuel Green. Executors—wife, and brother Thomas Kitchen. Witnesses—Jean Robins, George Baylis, John Lewis. Proved August 12, 1745. Lib. 5, p. 160.

1744, Jan. 29. Knowles, Stephen, of Cape May Co. Int. Adm'r, Jacob Spicer. Fellow bondsman—John Eldredge. Both of County aforesaid. Witnesses—John Smith, Henry Young. Cape May Wills, 118 E.

1744-5, Jan. 2, 7. Inventory of personal estate, (£34.07.08½); made by John Eldredge, Robert Parsons.

1746, July 25. Account. Moneys paid to Daniel Crowell, Charles Gallehaughn, Hollener Gallehaughn, Samuel Crowell, Jacob Hughes, Eliza. Evans, Reuben Swaine, John Paige, Elisha Hand, Silas Lupton, Benjamin Stites, Ebenezer Johnson, Barnabas Crowell, Joseph Paige, Cornelius Schillinks, Aaron Leaming, Richard Downes, John Oakford, Joseph Whillden, David Whillden, John Bancraft, John Eldredge, Nathan Hand, Anthony Elvird, Sarah Spicer, Samuel Eldredge, Enos Schillinks, Henry Young, John Grandal, Joseph Scattergood, Ezekiel Mulford, Elijah Hughes, Nathaniel Norton, Benjamin Crawford, Abigail Stites, Joshua Stites, Barnabas Crowell, Benjamin Laughton, Samuel Bancraft, Daniel Stilwill, etc.

1746, May 29. Kones, Nicholas, of the Mountains in Somerset Co.;

will of. Wife, Cathrine. Sons—Jacob (oldest), Michael ("whom I ordain my sole executrix of this my last will and testament and heir of all lands, etc., I now live on"), and Adam. Daughters—Barba Menton, Margret Harsough, Elizabeth Ranger, Mary Harpending. Executors—Robert Bolmer, Thomas Aten. Witnesses—John Bolmer, Albert Bolmer, P. (Patrick) Boyle. Proved 15 Oct., 1746.
Lib. D., p. 414.

1746, Oct. 14. Inventory of personal estate, £45.6.7; of real estate, 106 acres, £75; made by George Auston, John Kastner.

1744, Jan. 13. Kookandall, Jacobus, of Walpack Township, Morris Co., yeoman; will of. Mother, Sarah Kookandall, to be maintained out of the estate during widowhood. £200 to be divided equally, after ten years, among seven of my brothers and sisters, viz: Margaret Free, Dena Decker, Marica Fanning, Nathaniel, Christina, Abraham, and Sarah Kookandall. My wife, Aleday, and my three children, Jacob, Sarah and Abraham Kookandall, to have equally rest of my estate. Executors—my uncle, Peter Kookandall, living at Fish Kill, Orange Co., New York, Saml. Green, of Grinedge Township, Morris Co., husbandman. Witnesses—Adam Dingemanse, Andrus Dingman. Proved 8 April, 1746. Lib. 5, p. 232.

1746-7, Feb. 17. Kouwenhoven, William Ws., of Windsor Township, Middlesex Co., yeoman; will of. Wife, Margret. Children—William (eldest and under age), Garret, Ann, Nelly, Sarah, David. Executors—wife, William Covenhoven, of Flatlands, Long Island, Albert Schenck. Witnesses—Albert Schenck, Cornelius Covenhoven, Derrick Sutphen, Joseph Skelton. Proved Oct. 29, 1747. Lib. 5, p. 376.

1747, June 17. Inventory, £280.2.0; made by Derrick Sutphen, Joseph Skeleton and Cornelius Covenhoven.

1748-9, March 2. Kroesen, Cornelis, of Burlington Township, Burlington Co., yeoman; will of. Wife, Catharine, and daughter Adriana, all real and personal estate. Wife, sole executrix. Witnesses—Andries Meyer, Jun'r, Cornelius Meyer, Casparus Schuyler, Jun'r. Proved April 8, 1749. Lib. 6, p. 66.

1749, April 7. Inventory of the personal estate, £324.6.1; made by Zebulon Brown and William Follwell.

1733. March 29. Kyp (Kipp), Henry (Hendicus), of Middletown Township, Monmouth Co., yeoman; will of. Wife, Williamkee. Charles Hubbs and Major Leonard, creditors. Land in Freehold. Executors—Benjamin Vancleave, of Freehold, Honnas Lyester and Cornelius Waycoffe, of Middletown. Witnesses—Cornelius Couwenhoven, Hendrick Hendrickson, Robert Dodsworth. Proved April 16, 1734. Lib. B, p. 501.

1734, April 20. Inventory of the estate, appraised at the house of Jacob Waycoffe, Middletown (£28.11.0), includes money scales and weights, 22 lasts, shoemaker's tools and bench, box full of books, two swords. Made by William Bowne, Elias Covenhoven, Henricus Hendrickson.

1734, May 10. Additional inventory, taken at Freehold (£400.18), includes a Dutch Testament; plantation of 200 acres sold for £395. Made by Walter Wilson, John Morris, Andrew Crawford.

1735, Oct. 9. Inventory of other goods not found before, £1.18.0; made by Samuel Job, Hendrick Suydam, John Henderson.

1737, August 2. Account. Mentions bonds, etc., of Charles Hubbs, Samuel Leonard, Peter Lyster.

1730, 11 mo. (Feb), 4 da. Ladd, John, of Deptford, Gloucester Co., yeoman; will of. Wife, Elizabeth, to have 300 acres in Greenwich Township, near Stephen Jones'. Sons—Eldest, Samuel, deceased (had children), Jonathan, deceased (had children), and John, youngest, to have the home land (500 acres), Proprietary Rights to take up land in Burlington and town of Gloucester, and all other lands. Granddaughter—Mary Parker, 875 acres near Neshaning Creek in Amwell Township, Hunterdon Co. In case of her death without issue, same shall be divided equally between my son John and my daughter, Katherine Ladd, who shall possess the 300 acres called Raven Rock above the falls on or near the Delaware River, in Amwell Township, Hunterdon Co., together with 506 acres near Mantoes Creek, Deptford Township, Gloucester Co., and 300 acres near Allmon Creek, Deptford Township. Executors—wife, Elizabeth, and son John Ladd. Witnesses—Jacob Usher, Joseph Drinker, Rowland Rice, Thomas Potter.

1733, June 1. Codicil. Whereas my wife, Elizabeth, is deceased, the said 300 acres in Greenwich Township shall descend equally to my son John Ladd and to my daughter Katherine Ladd. Witnesses—Clement Hall, Malachi Davis, Rachel Black. Affirmed 20 March, 1739; 10 May, 1740. Lib. 4, p. 224.

———, ———, —. Inventory (£432.6.8) includes silver & gold money (£22.13.1½), carpenter's tools, corn in ground, oxen, 13 cows, 5 calves, etc. Appraisers—Samuel Lippincott, Joshua Lord.

1731, 2nd mo. (Apr.), 5th da. Ladd, Jonathan, of Deptford Township, Gloucester Co., yeoman; will of. Wife, Ann, sole executrix and to have the income from personal and real estate until children are of age. Son, Samuel, to have the plantation. Daughter, Elizabeth, and an unborn child (if a son to have the plantation in case of Samuel's death without lawful issue). If all children die without issue under age, then my cousin, Joseph Ladd, second son of my deceased brother, Samuel Lad, to have the aforesaid plantation, he to pay £30 to his three sisters, Sarah, Debrough and Kathron. Legacy to Sarah Lad, cousin. Supervisors—my brother-in-law, Samuel Lippincott, and John Wood. Witnesses—William Vaughn, Thomas Potter, Josa. Lord. Affirmed 10 June, 1731. Lib. 3, p. 132.

1737, March 30. Ladd, Joseph, of Gloucester Co., ward, petition of. Gloucester Wills, 434 H.

1735, March 9. Ladd, Mathew, of Deptford Township, Gloucester Co., cordwinder; will of. Brother, Joseph (when 21) my plantation on Timber Creek and all my lands. Sisters—Deborah and Katherine Ladd (both under 21). Executors—esteemed friends and uncles, John Ladd and Joseph Parker. Witnesses—William Shute, Mary Grifits, Saml. Sharp. Affirmed 9 March, 1736.

1736, March 9. Letters Testamentary granted John Ladd in the absence of Joseph Parker, etc. Lib. 4, p. 90.

1728, Oct. 16. Laing, John, of Piscataway, Middlesex Co.; will of. Children—John, David, Sarah, Elizabeth, Margaret, Ann, Martha, Mary, Christian, Isaac, Abraham, and Jacob, all under age. £10 towards building a Meeting House. Executors—wife, Elizabeth, brother William Laing, and Abraham Shotwell. Real and personal estate. Witnesses—William Nicholas, Benjamin Smith, William Webster. Proved June 14, 1731. Lib. B, p. 217.

1742, 5th mo. (July), 22. Laing, Samuel, of Piscataway, Middlesex Co.; will of. Monthly meeting at Woodbridge, £8.8. Son, John, at 21 years. Wife ——— Laing. Real and personal estate. Executors—friends John Shotwell, John Vail, Jun'r, Stephen Vail. Witnesses—Sarah Smith, Abraham Shotwell, John Hepburn. Proved Aug. 9, 1742. Lib. C, p. 527.

1735, June 13. Laing, William, of Piscataway, Middlesex Co., yeoman; will of. In the 55th year of his age. Children—William, John, Samuel, George, Benjamin, Jane and Anne. Land in Essex Co. 100 acres at Woodbridge, joining lands of Isaac Drake. Salt meadow, joining old Bloomfields and Samuel Moore's corner. Mortgage on Charles Gillinan's plantation. Deed of gift to youngest son, Benjamin, March 15, 1734. Executors—son, Samuel, daughter Jane, and friend John Kinsey. Witnesses—Isaac Drake, Samuel Drake, Daniel Drake. Proved Jan. 23, 1735-6. Lib. C, p. 42.

1731, Feb. 13. Lamb, Jacob, of Northampton, Burlington Co., yeoman. Account of Anne Lamb, widow and executrix, showing payments to Peter Bard, Esq., Rich'd Eayre, Ju'r, Rich'd Smith, Jun'r, John Prickett, Samuel Bustill, Joseph Wills, Eliza. Humphrys, Charles Weston, Zachariah Rosell, Henry Clothier, Ann Alcott, Thomas Hunlock, George Willis, Joseph Endecott, Wm. Prickett, Mr. Edw'd R. Price, atty-at-law (in full of his fees for prosecuting an action ag'st Gervas Hall in the Supreme Court), Mathew Champion. (For will, see N. J. Archives, Vol. 23, p. 279).

1749, July 8. Lamb, Joseph, of Somerset Co., clergyman; will of. Wife, Sarah, "all that land I had with her at marage situate in Glossenbery and Wethersfield in Conectecot Govermt in New England." Son, John David Lamb (not 21), to have all lands. Daughters—Lydia Clark, Elizabeth Wade, Patience Beidle, Sarah Badgly, Marcy and Jemime Lamb. Executors—wife, Sarah, and Moses Ayres. Witnesses—John Ayers, Samuel Brown, Brice Rikey. Proved 8 August, 1749. Lib. E, p. 317.

1748, Nov. 18. Lambert, Hannah, of Borough of Elizabeth, Essex Co.; will of. Sons—Solomon and David. Grandsons—John and Samuel Lambert. Granddaughters—Joanna and Margaret Lambert. Real and personal estate. Executor—friend Isaac Winans. Witnesses—John Baker, Joshua White, Jonathan Hampton. Proved Dec. 22, 1748. Lib. E, p. 230.

1748, Nov. 23. Inventory of personal estate, (£232.06.09), includes cash due from John Spining. Made by Thomas Clarke, Jona. Hamton.

1750, May 22. Account showing payments to Joseph Hanes, Thomas Givin, Thomas Coddington, Thos. Clarke, Ephraim Terrill, Jun'r, Sam'll Lambert and David Lambert (for keeping Solomon).

1737, Oct. 6. Lambert, John, of Elizabeth Town, Essex Co., yeoman; will of. Wife, Hannah, to care for my infirm son, Solomon. Other sons—John, Richard and David. Grandson—John Lambert (son of my eldest son John), lands purchased of Capt. Ebenezer Lyon, Samuel Miller, Richard Miller, Jonas Wood and Benjamin Bond, Esq.; land at Piles Creek which my father, Roger Lambert, purchased of Barnabas Wines; land purchased of William Darby; land my father purchased of John Decent. Executors—wife, Hannah, and friend John Spinning. Witnesses—Jonathan Woodruff, Ephraim Terrill, Jun'r, Thomas Chapman. Proved Nov. 10, 1738. Lib. C, p. 222.

1746, Nov. 30. Lambert, Margaret; will of. Brother, Thomas Cadwallader, executor, and his children, Martha, John, Lambert and Mary Cadwallader, to have plantation where William Duglis lived. Cousins —Hannah Adams and Peggy Stevenson. Lands belonging to estate of testatrix's father to her three sisters, Elizabeth Biles, Hannah Cadwallader and Achsah Lambert. Witnesses—D. Martin, Benjamin Biles, John Jones. Proved July 14, 1749.

Hunterdon Wills, Lib. 7, p. 11.

1732, 12th day, 12th mo. (Feb.). Lambert, Thomas, of Nottingham, Burlington Co.; will of. Wife, Ann, in lieu of dower, £500. Grandchildren—Thomas and Margaret Biles, tract in Amwell, Hunterdon Co. Sisters—Hannah Hodge and Ruth Adams. Nephews—Samuel, Thomas and Benjamin Biles. By decease of my bro., John Lambert, I became heir at law to a plantation in Bucks Co., Penna., which I have sold to Thomas Yardley, of same Co. Remainder of estate to my four daughters—Elizabeth Biles, Hannah, Achsah and Margaret, whom I appoint executrices. Witnesses—Isaac Watson, John Williams.

1732, 12th day, 12th mo. (Feb.). Codicil. Sister, Hannah Hodge, of Philada., widow, all my right to a certain tract in New Hanover. Same witnesses. Proved June 12, 1733. Lib. 3, p. 327.

1733, 27th day, 6th mo. (Aug.). Inventory of the personal estate, £4837.5.9; made by Edmd. Beakes and Wm. Biles. Includes purse, apparel and watch, £170.1.7; plate, £17.16; servants—James Price, Margaret Warner, Kathrin Poland, Francis Lewis, Hendrix Pout; negroes, Jemy, Dick, Hagar and mulatto boy, and an Indian called Peter. Bonds and bills in the desk, £1766.1.7.

1735, Dec. 19. Lambson, Thomas, of Penns Neck, Salem Co., yeoman; will of. Wife, Ann. Son, Mathias, all my lands, he paying £40 apiece to my sons Michael and Daniel. Legacies to daughter, Elenor Pennington, son Thomas and daughter Mary Elwell. Remainder of personal estate divided among my three sons, Mathias, Michael and Daniel. Executors—wife, and son Mathias. Witnesses—John Philpot, Mathias Johnson, Earick GillJohnson. Proved 4 Jan., 1735.

Lib. 4, p. 61.

1735, Dec. 31. Inventory (£112.10.1) includes cattle and fodder, silver shirt buttons. Appraisers—Sinick Sinnickson, Thos. Miller.

1732, Dec. 29. Lane, Anthony, Esq., of Perth Amboy, Middlesex Co. Int. Bond of Robert Burnett, of Perth Amboy, as administrator. Adam Hay, fellow bondsman. Lib. B, p. 340.

1750-1, Feb. 5. Langerfelt, John, of Lebanon twsp., Hunterdon co. Inventory of the personal estate, £291.6.0, made by Ralph Smith and Baltis Pickel.

1750-1, Feb. 20. Administration granted to Christian Langerfelt, widow, with Baltis Pickel as fellow bondsman.

1756, May 31. Accounts (two) of the estate by his widow, Christian Lambert, late Christian Langerfelt. Hunterdon Wills, 298 J.

1733, Feb. 5. Langevelt (Longfield), Cornelius, Esq., of Raritan,

Middlesex Co.; will of. Son, Henry, and his son, Thomas Longfield. Grandson, Thomas, eldest son of son-in-law Thomas Lawrence of Philadelphia, to have my daughter Rachel's portion. Grandson, John, son of son-in-law William Cox, the portion of daughter Catherine. Or to the second son, Thomas. Grandchildren—Cornelius, Obediah, Thomas and Mary, children of daughter Elizabeth, deceased, late wife of Obediah Bowne of Monmouth Co., Esq., deceased. Wife, Mary, sole executrix. Land I bought of heirs of Robert Barclay, Esq., dec'd, in conjunction with Mr. John Johnston, dec'd, and George Willocks, dec'd. Son, Henry, lands by deeds of Feb. 22, 1720, and May 12, 1731. Witnesses—Peter Sonmans, Sarah Sonmans, Thomas Stilwell. Proved Dec. 24, 1734. Lib. B, p. 577.

1734-5, Feb. 21. Inventory of personal estate, £889.0.0; made by Edward Antill and Dirck Schuyler.

1735, March 27. Langley, Thomas, of Salem Co., yeoman. Int. Adm'x, Mary Langley (relict of). Bondsman—Nathaniel Jenkins. Both of said county. Witnesses—John Green, Danl. Mestayer. Lib. 4, p. 2.

1734-5, Feb. 17. Inventory (£58.9) includes cattle, sheep and swine. Appraisers—John Remington, Nathl. Jenkins.

1735, Dec. 20. Account of Mary Langley "of Cohansey." Paid to John Shaw, Recompense Hand, John Green, William Watson, Samuel Fithian, Francis Simpkins, John Blackwood, Joseph Wheaten, Charles Campbel, John Brick, Peter Long, John Peck, John Wright, Stephen Mulford, Benjamin Mulford, Mr. Matthew, Mr. Clement Hall.

1749, April 13. Lanning, Samuel, of Burlington Co. Inventory of the personal estate, £67.19.6; made by John Deacon and John Antram.

1749, April 19. Administration on estate granted to Anne Lanning, widow of Northampton. George Elkinton, of same, yeoman, fellow bondsman. Lib. 6, p. 332; Lib. 7, p. 98.

1747, Feb. 26. Larew (Larou, Laraw), Abraham, of Hopewell, Hunterdon Co., within the corporation of Trenton, yeoman; will of. Wife, Harmekie. Children—Abraham, Isaac, Jacob, Susannah (wife of Cornelius Slack), Altie, Catran and Mary. Executors—wife, and son Abraham. Witnesses—Robert Akers, William Wood, Andrew Smith. Proved Feb. 15, 1749-50. Lib. 6, p. 303.

1749, Feb. 14. Inventory of the estate (£391.8.9) includes gun and sword. Made by Andrew Smith and Robert Akers.

1732, Jan. 24. Larew (Laroue, Larue), David, of Hopewell, Hunterdon Co., yeoman. Int. Inventory of estate (£116.1.6) includes bonds, etc., of Richard Farman, Robert Comb, William Larrans, Robert Acres, Thomas Morrel, Joseph Reed, John Hunt, John Titus, Edward Borrous. Made by Andrew Smith and Joseph Price.

1732, Feb. 6. Bond of Abraham Larue, of Hunterdon Co., as administrator. Peter Larue and Daniel Larue, of same place, sureties.

1734, May 18. Account. Mentions Peter Larue, Isaac Larue, Thomas McClehan, Joseph Reed, Robert Acres, Henry Haldern, Thomas Yardley, Joseph Price, Executors of Daniel Howell, Roger Woolverton, James Larue, Robert Combs, Daniel Larue, John Phillips, George Ely, Francis Chamburst, Thomas Smith, Jonathan Smith, Sarah Hooffe, Andrew Smith. Also moneys paid to following, as distributive parts of the estate: James,

Daniel and Peter Laroue, Jane Praull, Isaac Laroue and Abraham Laroue, the accountant. Lib. 3, p. 287.

1750, 28th day, 5th mo. (July). Large, Samuel, Jun'r, of Chesterfield, Burlington Co.; will of. All estate to my daughters, Sarah and Mary; but if they should die under age then ½ to the children of my two brothers and sisters, and the other half to the children of William Murfin. My maid, Mary Rick, to be bound to a taylor's trade. Executors—brother, Robert Large, and brother-in-law William Murfin. Witnesses—Abra'm Brown, Joseph Thorn, Deborah Bunting. Proved Aug. 6, 1750. Lib. 6, p. 342.

1750, Aug. 28. Inventory of the personal estate, £240.6.8; made by Abraham Brown and William Bunting.

1749, April 7. Larrison, William, of New Brunswick, Middlesex Co.; will of. Children—James, William, Thomas, John and George Larrison. Real and personal estate. Executors—son, John, and son-in-law David Stout. Witnesses—Jediah Higgins, Samuel Neilson, Ro. Rolfe.

1749, April 7. Codicil. Daughters—Elizabeth Stout, Martha Hide, Mary Higgnis, Rebeckah Brittain, Deborah Shippey and Keziah Vantilborrow. Witnesses—Jediah Higgins, Samuel Neilson, Ro. Rolfe. Proved May 30, 1749. Lib. 6, p. 70.

1736, Oct. 30. Laurence, Edward (son of George, of Greenwich, Gloucester Co., deceased), ward; petition of, with the consent of his mother, Elizabeth Laurence, "much indisposed." Guardian—Mr. Timothy Raines, Penns Neck, Salem Co. Lib. 4, p. 67.

1742, Dec. 6. Law, John, of Salem Co., yeoman. Int. Adm'r, Benjamin Bispham, Penns Neck, store-keeper and principal creditor. Bondsman—Elisha Basset, of Piles Grove, farmer. Witness—Thos. Jones. Lib. 4, p. 378.

1742, Dec. 6. Renunciation. Mary Law, relict of John Law, in favor of Benjamin Bispham as adm'r.

1742, Dec. 1. Inventory, £28.12; made by Elisha Basset, Thos. Graves.

1736, June 10. Lawrence, Joseph, of Middlesex Co., about 16 years of age. Bond of Joseph Rolph, of Essex Co., and Thomas Rattoone, of Middlesex Co., as guardians. Lib. C, p. 101.

1739, June 23. Lawrence, Joseph, of Manasquan, in Shrewsbury, Monmouth Co., yeoman; will of. Wife, Rachel. Son, William. Four youngest sons, Joseph, James, Benjamin and Elisha, meadow on the beach this side the Great Hill against Matetakung river. Wife's sons, John and David Curtiss, part of lands at Barnegat beach. Propriety Right to eight children—Hannah, William, Faith, Joseph, James, Sarah, Benjamin and Elisha. Executors—wife, and sons Benjamin and Elisha. Witnesses—Elisha Stout, Isaac Herbert, Peter Parker, Henry Newport, William Worth. Proved May 12, 1743. Lib. D, p. 56.

1743, April 25. Inventory of the estate, £38.9.3; made by Elisha Stout and Peter Parker.

1737, May 26. Lawrence, Robert, of Somerset Co., glazier. Int. Bond of Thomas Haddon, of Woodbridge, carpenter, principal creditor, as administrator on the estate. P. Kearny, fellow bondsman. Lib. C, p. 161.

1733-4, March 19. Lawrence, William, of Nottingham, Burlington Co., waterman. Int. Inventory of the personal estate, £48.17.3½; made by Cha: Clark and Tho. Barnes.

1734, May 7. Deborah Lawrence, widow, renounces her right to administration on estate to uncle, Thomas Burroughs, and Aaron Jenkins, two of the principal creditors.

1734, May 27. Administration granted to Thomas Burroughs and Aaron Jenkins. Charles Clark, of Hunterdon Co., cooper, fellow bondsman.

1734, Dec. 20. Account of administrators showing payments to Joseph Yard, Mr. Kinsey, Francis Bowes, Esq., Thomas Yardley, Sam'l Bustill, Alexander Woodrop, Wm. Morris, Thomas McClehan, and a judgment against deceased at the suit of Thomas Lawrence and Thomas Sober.

Burlington Wills, 2727-44 C.

1741, Feb. 20. Lawrence, William, of Middletown, Monmouth Co.; will of. Being in the eighty-fourth year of my age. Grandson, William, son of Richard Lawrence, deceased, 36 acres at Barnegat, being part of Thomas Cooper's lot. Grandson, William, son of John Lawrence deceased, 100 acres on Hop river. Granddaughter, Jane Lawrence, daughter of John, deceased, 80 acres adjoining Peter Tilton's. Daughter, Elizabeth Hartshorne, half of Propriety Right and land near Metecunk, and large Concordance. Daughter, Hannah Herbert; land and next great Bible. Son, Thomas, largest old Bible, surveyor's instruments and £5. Two eldest grandsons, 20 sh. Executors—brothers Joseph and Benjamin Lawrence, son-in-law William Hartshorne, daughter Elizabeth, and son Robert. Witnesses—James Seabrook, Thomas Cooper, Andrew Bowne, William Hartshorne, Junior, Thomas Hartshorne. Proved Nov. 22, 1750. Robert Lawrence, Esquire, one of the executors qualified same day, "three of the others being dead."

Lib. E, p. 523.

1751, May 11. Inventory of the estate (of "William Lawrence, Esquire") taken at the house of Robert Hartshorne, in Middletown (£16.2.0), includes 11 silver spoons. Made by Samuel Bowne and Thomas Hartshorne.

1740, August 30. Lawrie, James, of Upper Freehold Township, Monmouth Co., yeoman; will of. Son, William, land in Upper Freehold, where said son dwells, bought of Anthony Woodward, Senior, gentleman. Children of son William—James, William, Thomas and Elizabeth. Son, Thomas, plantation near Allentown, where Thomas dwells. Eldest daughter, Sarah. Younger daughter, Elizabeth. £2 to Quakers Meeting House near Crosswicks Bridge. Books to said four children. Executors—sons William and Thomas. Witnesses—Benjamin Fowler, William and Thomas Lawrie. Proved Nov. 3, 1741.

Lib. 4, p. 297.

1740, Nov. 12. Inventory of estate, ("of James Lawrie, carpenter"), £59.15.0; made by Benjamin Fowler.

1741, March 10. Lawson, Roger, of Trenton, Hunterdon Co., tailor; will of. Son, John. Eldest son, James; other children, Rodger, Elizabeth, and William. Executor—Andrew Reed of Trenton, merchant. Witnesses—Alexander Chambers, Joseph Morrow, Charles Hoff, Jr. (Not probated).

1742, May 8. Another will of Rodger Lawson, of Trenton, tailor. Children—John, James (eldest son), Rodger, Elizabeth, William. "Indentures which are upon my son William and my daughter Elizabeth may be dis-

posed of by George Lawson, to pay himself for their passage from Ireland." Executor—Andrew Reed, of Trenton, merchant. Witnesses—Thomas Swaffer, Gilbeart Gaa and Charles Hoff, Jr. Proved May 24, 1742.
Lib. 4, p. 339.

1744, July —. Account of executor, mentions John Clark, William Plaskett, David Martin, Esquire, William Moore, Colonel Daniel Coxe (by Jno. Coxe, Esquire), Davis & Lawson, Jno. Allen, Isaac Huchinson, Robert Spencer, Francis Bowes, James Shey (or They), Theo's. Severns, John Hart, Jr., William Morris, James Rutherford, George Davis, Stacy Beakes, Joseph Paxton, Joseph Higby, Charles Axford.

1733, April 9. Laycon, Andrew, of Deptford, Gloucester Co., yeoman. Int. Adm'r, Michael Lycon. Bondsman—Thomas Thackery. All of aforesaid county, yeomen. Gloucester Wills, 170 H.

1733, March 29. Laycon, Zacharias, of Gloucester Co., will of. Brothers—"Mounce" (his eldest daughter Catherine when 21 to have the plantation), Michael (his eldest daughter one of my best beds), and Nicholas, appointed executor and to pay the money due the Loan office, and to have the residue of my estate. Witnesses—Michael Laycon, Dinah Cox, Constantine Wood. Affirmed 8 June, 1733. Gloucester Wills, 170 H.

1733, April 9. Inventory (£24.16.6) includes bed given to Ellen Lycon, "sith and sword," Bible and books. Appraisers—William Wilkins, Constantine Wood. Signed by "Dinah Cox, Admx."

1733, June 8. Dinah Cox, Adm'x of the within named Zacharias Lycon deceased, upon articles left unadministered by Michael Laycon, his brother.

1733, ——— 10. Inventory of Andrey and Zakryas Leken, both brothers, deceased, Deptford, Gloucester Co. (£56.3.0). Appraisers—Benjamin Wait, Edward Willson.

1750, May 9. Layton, John, of Morris Co. Int. Adm'x, Anne Layton (relict of). Bondsman—Jacob Carle, of Morris Co.
Lib. E, p. 397.

1750, May 21. Inventory, £190-13-11; made by Samuel Brown, Timy. Stoughton.

1740, Sept. 14. Layton, Thomas, of Lower Freehold, Monmouth Co. Int. Inventory of the estate (£170.1.0) includes bonds of Christopher and Peter Romine, Anthony Pintard, Jacob Emons, Francis and John Masters; negro man (£0.10.0); negro woman (£5), negro boy Mink (£35), negro boy Titus (£35), 2 guns. Made by John Williams, John and Thomas Layton.

1740, Sept. 16. Bond of Joseph Williams and Peter Romyn, of Lower Freehold township, yeomen, as administrators. John Williams and Lawrence Vanclieffe, of same place, yeoman, fellow bondsmen. (Joseph Williams having married Sarah, and Peter Romyne married Rachel, daughters of the deceased). Lib. 4, p. 256.

1750, Oct. 12. Layton, Thomas, of Somerset Co., yeoman. Int. Administration on estate granted to William Layton, brother. Fellow bondsmen, Richard FitzRandolph. Lib. E, p. 457.

1750, Oct. 12. Renunciation of Ledey, widow of Thomas Layton, in favor of deceased's brother, William Layton. Witness—John Layton.

1750, Oct. 25. Inventory of personal estate, £30.3.0; made by Ebenr. Finley, Timo. Stoughton. 131 R.

1731, April 10. Layton, William, of Freehold, Monmouth Co., yeoman; will of. Wife, Mary, land, negroes, etc., for life. Cousin, William Layton, Junior, son of testator's brother, Samuel Layton, of Freehold, yeoman, land bought of William Scott. Executors—friends Jonathan Forman, Esquire, and William Madock, trader, of Monmouth County. Witnesses—James Stanly, George Seemur and Mary Romine. Proved May 15, 1735. Lib. C, p. 33.

1734, Feb. 5. Inventory of estate (£104.17.0) includes negro man and woman (£40). Made by Joseph Throckmorton, David Cleayton, Joseph Taylor.

1743, Oct. 15. Leaming, Aaron, Sr., of Cape May Co., yeoman; will of. Wife, Lydia. Son, Jeremiah Leaming, to have all the land whereon I live, between the land of David Cresse and John Shaw's Creek, beginning at the easternmost corner of said land at Cresse's Creek, running up said Creek to David Cresse's land, then to the head of my said land to land surveyed for me by Henry Young, Esq., bounded by the lines of said survey across the heads of David Cresse's, James Cresse's and Nathan Hand's lands, until it comes to a direct line northeast to an oak tree in the Great Savannah, near the road side, which goes from said land where I now live to the Bay Side. Son, Aaron Leaming, Junior, all my lands at the Bay Side, between the land of the heirs of Lewis Cresse, deceased, and the land of Nathan Hand; also all the above mentioned survey not herein given to my son Jeremiah, made by Henry Young, Esq. Sons, Jeremiah and Aaron, the saw mill on Manatico at Prince Maurice's River, Salem Co.; also my lands near the said river in Salem County, or any of the Branches thereof, and at the Beach and Island, known as Nummy's Island. Daughter, Elizabeth Leaming, all my land and marsh at Goshen, between Dennis Creek and Goshen Creek; one tract of 200 acres which I purchased of Yelverton Crowell; another tract and marsh purchased of the West New Jersey Society; also all other lands which I surveyed by virtue of a right of Propriety; also all other lands I own, lying between Dennis Creek and Goshen Creek, and Cedar swamp and marsh near Beaver pond, which is of the land surveyed for Colonel Daniel Coxe and Jacob Spicer, till it comes to Denises' Creek. The residue of my land, marsh and cedar swamp at the southward or eastward of Stipson's Island, East Creek, or any of the branches thereof, between that and Cape May, and all my land, marsh, timber and Beach belonging to Seven and Five Mile Beach, and my Proprietary Rights not returned and recorded, I bequeath equally to my three children, Aaron Leaming, Junr., Jeremiah and Elizabeth. Executors—my three children Aaron, Junr., Jeremiah and Elizabeth. Witnesses—Thomas Eldridge, William Eldridge, Esther Eldridge. Proved April 20, 1747. Lib. 6, p. 266.

1747, April 16, 17, 18. Inventory of personal estate (£1174.18.8), includes: cash (£163.18.2), 12 negroes (£316), a compleat set of the Statutes at Large, mostly gilt and bound in quarto (£24), other law books (£32.6.), books of Phisick (£3.1.6), books of Divinity, Logick, Learning, History, Divertion, etc. (£17.10.6). Debts due from Sam Land, Geo. Keen, John Ross, Att'y, (recovered from David Forman), 19 horses and mares (£99), 8 pr. oxen, 192 cows, steers and other cattle (£329.17.0), 83 sheep (£20.15), one gun, 5 pistols, two cutlasses and a sword (£3.7), 2 watches, 3 anchors for a sloop, maritime implements, etc. (£76.16.2). Appraisers—Elisha Hand, Richard Crafford.

1728, March 20. LeBoyteuix, Gabriel, of Piscataway, Middlesex Co.; will of. Daughters—Catherine and Mary. Real and personal estate. Executors—wife, Constance, and son Paul LeBoyteuix. Witnesses—William Williamson, Peter Williamson, Alexander McDowall. Proved April 10, 1734. Lib. B, p. 499.

1748-9, Feb. 13. Leckey, Thomas, of Salem Co. Int. Adm'r, John Smith of Elsenbury, Salem County. Witnesses—Thos. Rue, Michl. Gibbon.

1748-9, Feb. 13. Inventory (£92.13.1) of Thomas Leckey, of Elsenbrough. Appraisers—William Chandler, Thos. Rice. Lib. 6, p. 323.

1742, Oct. 11. Lee, Adam, of Woodbridge, Middlesex Co. Int. Inventory of personal estate, £125.19; made by Ezekiel Bloomfield, Esq., and William Brown.

1742, Oct. 12. Bond of John Lee, the brother, and William Spencer and Agnes his wife, the mother of said deceased, as administrators on the estate. William Britton, fellow bondsman. Lib. D, p. 10.

1743, Sept. 6. Lee, Joshua, of New Windsor, Middlesex Co. Bond of Hannah Lee, his widow, and Samuel Dove, of Freehold, yeoman, as administrators. Stephen Warne, fellow bondsman. Lib. D, p. 83.

1743, Sept. 9. Inventory of personal estate (£105.12.6), includes bonds and bills due from Isaac FitzRandolph, Jonathan Gibben, Samuel Throp, Robert Fary, John Mount, Daniel Hankeson, John Throp, and his father. Made by Benjamin Sutton, John Morford and John Row.

1748, Dec. 15. Leeds, Deborah, of Great Eggharbour, Gloucester Co., widow. Administration on estate granted to John Leeds and Japhet Leeds. Abild Leeds, yeoman, fellow bondsman. All of Great Eggharbour. Lib. 6, p. 330; Lib. 7, p. 96.

1744, July 17. Leeds, Felix, of Burlington Co., yeoman. Int. Inventory of the personal estate, £772.14.7; made by Thomas Haines and Samuel Woolston.

1744, July 18. Administration granted to Hannah Leeds and Isaac Leeds. Sam'l Woolston, fellow bondsman. All of Burlington Co. Lib. 5, p. 50.

1747, Dec. 19. Leeds, Isaac, of Northampton, Burlington Co., yeoman; will of. Mother, Hannah Leeds, Brothers—Abraham and Titan. Plantation joining Thomas Haines and Benjamin Brown. Executor—brother Abraham. Witnesses—Samuel Woolston, Thomas Bishop, Jno. Duncan. Proved Feb. 23, 1747. Lib. 5, p. 403.

1736, Feb. 5. Leeds, Japhet, of Great Egg Harbor, Gloucester Co., yeoman; will of. Wife, Deborah. Sons—Robert, land bought of Benjamin Jennings near a brook, formerly called Wigwam Creek, southeast to Holly Swamp brook; John, land, 200 acres, bought of his uncle Felix Leeds, by the south branch of Landing Creek; Japhet, the plantation I live on by the Bay northwest to Maple Swamp; Nehemiah, land adjoining Jeremiah Addams; James (youngest son), land bought of Benjamin Jennings, adjoining his brother Robert's; and Daniel, not 14. Daughters—Mary, eldest (alias Somers), Sarah, Deborah, Dorothy, Ann and Hannah. Cedar swamps on Bever Run and Proprietary Rights to the sons. Executors—sons John and Japhet. Witnesses—Jeremiah Adams, Abel Scull, Isaac Addams. Affirmed 15 Dec., 1748. Lib. 6, p. 10.

1748, Nov. 4. Inventory, £213.17.3; made by Abel Scull, Joseph Johnson.

1741, April 29. Leeds, Thomas, of City of Burlington, cooper; will of. Paull Watkinson, present "clark" of Church of Burlington, lot and house where I now live, he paying to Revel Elton, of Northampton, and Ann his present wife, my cousin, £10. Legacies to Mary (present wife of Paul Watkinson); the minister of the Church at Burlington; Samuel Lovett, shoemaker, and Mary, his present wife; Anthony Elton, shoemaker, the wife of Edward Cowgill; Mary, wife of Richard Yoe and the three daus. she had by Bethanah Leeds, viz., Elizabeth, Ann and Lucretia; John Sanders, "charemaker;" Elizabeth Pomptlett, late of Burlington; old Robert Nailer and Dority his wife; Edmund Jones, a lame joyner—all living in Burlington. Joseph Heulings, shoemaker, and Ann, his present wife, my Great Bible. Overseer of the highways of said City of Burlington, £4, towards moulding said highways. John Stockton, an old man in Springfield. Remainder of estate for poor folks and widows. Executors—John Allen, Esq., of Burlington, Paul Watkinson and Joseph Hulings. Witnesses—Simon Nightingale, Nicholas Toy, Isaac Hewlings, Jacob Sullivan, Isa. DeCow.

1742, Feb. 20. Codicil. The legacy given to Elizabeth, wife of Benjamin Kemble, not to be paid, but the money he oweth me to pay the rent for the Minister of Burlington Church. £3 to be added to legacy of Joseph Hulings. Legacies to the three youngest children of Benjamin and Elizabeth Wheats, viz., Hannah, Dinah and Abigail. Witnesses—Caleb Raper, Joshua Raper, Isa. DeCow. Proved July 15, 1743. Lib. 4, p. 368.

1743, July 5. Inventory of the personal estate, £178.13.5; made by Saml. Lovett and John Budd. Includes cash in the hands of Joseph Hulings, bond due from Benj. Kemble and Anthony Elton to go to the use of the Church, and an old Sword.

1735, June 20. Leeds, William, of Middletown Township, Monmouth Co.; will of. Body to be buried by the body of his mother. Wife, Rebecca. Eldest brother, Thomas Leeds. Helpless brother, Daniel. Wife's children—Rebecca, Gracy and Ebenezer Applegate. Abigail Applegate, daughter of Richard Applegate. Jemimah Leeds, eldest daughter of Philo Leeds. John Leeds, of Egg Harbor. Elizabeth Chambers, daughter of Thomas Chambers, of Shrewsbury. Jacob Applegate. After decease of wife and brother Daniel, real estate to go to the Venerable and Honorable Society for the Propagation of the Gospel in Foreign Parts, for a perpetual glebe for use of a clergyman of Church of England to preach to the inhabitants of Middletown and Shrewsbury. Executors—Captain John Throckmorton, James Hutchings and John Bowne, Esquires. Witnesses—James Gibson, Richard Gibbons, John Coleman, Trustrum Inglis.

Codicil (without date). Witnesses—John Ruckman, Els Grover, Thomas Bodenham, James Rice. Proved Nov. 20, 1739. Lib. C, p. 308.

1739, May 1, and February 18, 1739-40. Inventory of the estate (£209.15.½), includes bond of Ebenezer Applegate, large Bible, the Conductor Generalis, book of Common Prayer, Dutch loom, quilling wheel, rattle brushes and Swift's three shuttles; servant man named Thomas (£1); Dutch plow, cash in hands of Jehanas Polhemuls. Made by James Grover, Samuel Ogboren, Jehanas Swart.

1749, March 30. Leek, Recompence, of Deerfield, Cumberland Co.;

will of. Wife, Martha. Sons—John (20 shillings within one year), Samuel (100 acres, purchased of David Sayer's, joining Joseph Peck's line), Recompence, Junior, and Nathan (190 acres, purchased of Benj. Davison, Burlington Road, adjoining Thomas Nickalls and David Stratton's land). In case of death without lawful issue, survivor to enjoy same. Daughters—Abigail, Elizabeth, Sarah, Rachel and Hannah, all under age. Executors—wife, Martha, and sons Recompence and Nathan, who shall bring up and provide for the four last named children. Witnesses—William Stratton, Robert Dare, Benj. Worton. Proved 18 Nov., 1749. Lib. 6, p. 287.

1749, Nov. 16. Inventory of personal estate (£201.15.8) includes cattle, and horses (£68.18.0), wheat on the ground. Appraisers—Charles Clark, Robert Dare.

1749, Nov. 18. Certificate by Martha Leek that she is satisfied with the will. Witnesses—Charles Clark, Benj. Worton.

1748-9, March 3. Leforg, John, Jun'r, of Piscataway, Middlesex Co., weaver; will of. Children—John, Nathaniel, David, Frances Blackford, Sarah Leforg (under age). Real and personal estate. Executors—wife, Sarah, John Bound, Jun'r, and John Leforg, the third. Witnesses—Reune Runyon, Samuel Mackfarson, Zachariah Bonham. Proved March 30, 1749. Lib. E, p. 288.

1748-9, March 15. Inventory of personal estate, £106; made by David FitzRandolph, and Reune Runyon.

1740, June 12. Leigh, Joseph, of Perth Amboy, Middlesex Co., butcher. Int. Bond of Philip Kearny, Esq., as administrator. John Doe, fellow bondsman. Lib. C, p. 346.

1734, June 13. Leland, Adam, of Boston, in New England, merchant. Administration on estate granted to Edward Pierce, of City of Burlington, Esq. John Doe and Richard Roe, of same, gents, fellow bondsmen. Burlington Wills, Lib. 3, p. 420.

1739, April 17. Leonard, Henry, of Shrewsbury Township, Monmouth Co., gent.; will of. Wife, Lydia. Son, Henry, land where testator lived bounded by John Throckmorton, Esquire, Edward Taylor, deceased, whortleberry bog, son Samuel, David Kelly; also part of old mill, alias five acre bogg mill and lands. If son, Henry, has no male issue, then to son Thomas. Daughter, Mary, £50 when aged 27 years. Son, Samuel, old saw mill or Mine brook mill. Daughters, Sarah, bond from testator's son, Samuel, dated February 8, 1734, witnessed by John Fawcett and son Thomas Leonard. Daughter, Susannah, bond of son Samuel. Salt meadow at Mateetcunck. Red brook mill to son Thomas. Son, Henry, mare bought of Obadiah Herbert. Daughter, Susannah, green plush bridle and saddle made by James Parker. Daughter, Parthenia Cook. Daughter, Margaret. Son, Henry, land surveyed for him by Jacob Dennis. If wife does not accept dowry of £25, testator's daughter, Elizabeth, to be excluded from share of residue of estate. Executors—brother, Samuel Leonard, brother-in-law Thomas Morford, and sons Samuel and Thomas. Witnesses—John Throckmorton, Junior, John Taylor, Robert Dodsworth. Proved Feb. 11, 1739-40. Lib. 3, p. 317.

1739, July 25. Samuel Leonard, named as an executor of his brother, declined to serve.

1739, May 8. Inventory of the estate (of "Henry Leonard, Esquire"), includes 2 negroes and their bedding, (£63), note of Michael Kearny, Esquire, bond of John Cleyton, of Capefare. Made by Anthony Pintard, Aa. Forman and David Kelley.

1748-9, Jan. 11. Leonard, Morris, of Trenton, Hunterdon Co., yeoman; will of. Real estate in Trenton to his mother, Ann Gould, and to his sisters, Mary Taylor, Frances Gould and Elisabeth Gould. Executrix, the mother. Witnesses—Peter Lott, Daniel Howell, William Green. Proved Feb. 15, 1748-9. Lib. 31, p. 258.

1742, Nov. 14. Leonard, Samuel, of Shrewsbury, Monmouth Co., will of. Wife, Elizabeth. Sons, Joseph and Thomas, lands at Black river and in Burlington County. Unborn child. Residue of estate to wife and daughters (not named). Executors—John Eatton and Joseph Wardell. Witnesses—Margaret Wardell, Joseph Eatton, John Wardell. Proved Feb. 16, 1742. (John and Joseph Wardell, Quakers). Lib. D, p. 68.

1742, Dec. 20. Inventory of the estate (£376.19.06) includes servant man (£10.17). Made by Adam Brewer and Joseph Parker.

1732, Dec. 11. Leonard, Stephen, Esquire, of New Hanover, Hunterdon Co., yeoman. Inventory of estate, including 3 perukes, wooden surveying compass, a musket, 2 powder horns, Dalton's Justice, 16 small books of Divinity, one old clock and other brass, negro Peter (£12), parcel of iron ore in the forge, some loose tools in the forge. Made by Joseph Prudden and Caleb Fairchild.

1732-3, Jan. 6. Bond of Comfort Leonard, of New Hanover, widow, as administratrix. Samuel Crosman and Joseph Hinds, of Hunterdon County, yeoman, sureties. Lib. 3, p. 240.

1733, Sept. 14. Additional inventory includes debts due from Benjamin Hathay, John Nutman, Jonathan Stiles, Isaac Thomas, Morres Morrison, John Johnson, Humphrey Davenport, John Davenport, Solomon Munson, William Meler, Thomas Clarck, James Miley, Seth Hall, Benjamin Beach, Eunis Kilborn, Cristeen Johnson Jr., Samuel Crosman, Joseph Johnson, William Bradford, Joseph Ludley (or Lindley).

1748, Nov. 7. Lestrang, James, of Manington, Salem Co., weaver. Int. Adm'r, Andrew Ball. Bondsman—Davd. Morris. Witnesses—Danl. Mestayer, Michl. Gibbon. Lib. 6, p. 49.

1748, Nov. 8. Inventory (£24) includes "To Susaney from Roy's Bord," 10 shillings. Appraisers—John Smith, Archable Hamilton, (mark).

1742, Sept. 15. Letts, Francis, of Middlesex Co.; will of. Sons—John, Abram, Peter and Francis. Francis Letts, Jun'r, eldest son of son William, deceased. Jeams, son of son Francis. David, son of John Bissord. Real and personal estate. Executors—wife, Mary, sons Francis and Peter. Witnesses—Henry Moore, Elisha Dunham. Proved Nov. 29, 1742. Lib. D, p. 88.

1739-40, Feb. 27. Letts, William, of Middlesex Co., yeoman; will of. Children—Francis, John, Margratt and Mary Letts. Land joining Peter Sonmans, deceased, and Peter Tys, which I purchased of Ephraim Dunham. Executors—wife, Antie, and cousin, Peter Bokelow. Witnesses—Sam'll Walker, Peter Letts, N. Everson. Proved April 16, 1740. Lib. C, p. 330.

1732, Nov. 30. Lewis, Edward, of Basking Ridge, Somerset Co. Administration on estate granted to Alice Lewis. Lib. B, p. 319.

1740-1, Feb. 28. Lewis, James, of Bordingtown, Burlington Co.; will of. Wife, Abigail, sole executrix. Son, James, under age. Lots in Bordingtown bought of Joseph Jay and Charles Taylor; also plantation near Neshaminy, Bucks Co., Penna. Witnesses—Samuel Shourds, John Clayton, Thomas Folke. Proved March 28, 1741.

Lib. 4, p. 274.

1742-3, Feb. 15. Lewis, John, of Manington, Salem Co., husbandman; will of. Wife, Ruth, dower. Children—Joseph, Sarah, Elizabeth, Mary and John, rest of the estate equally, as they come of age. Brother, William Roberts, trustee of the said children during their minority. Executor—son Joseph. Witnesses—Alexr. Simpson, Barnabas Ashley. Sworn and affirmed, 26 March, 1743. Lib. 5, p. 51.

1743, Dec. 3. Whereas Joseph Lewis aged about thirteen years, or thereabouts, was appointed sole executor in his father's will, letters of administration were granted to William Roberts (trustee). Bondsmen—John Roberts, James Holladay. Lib. 5, p. 52.

1742-3, March 4. Inventory (£178.14.9) includes servant man and woman (£11), field of wheat, cattle, horses. Appraisers—Bartholomew Hyatt, Othniel Tomlinson.

1744, May 11. Lewis, John, of Deptford Township, Gloucester Co., shingle maker; will of. Executors—Joseph Hedges, of Gloucester Township, yeoman, and Peter Marriage, of Deptford, Gloucester Co., laborer. Former to have 132 acres of that land called Squankum, Gloucester Co., and one-third of the personal; latter to have all my other improvements, land and cedar swamps, and two-thirds of the personal. Witnesses—Dad. Roe, James Valentine, Michael Fisher. Proved 11 June, 1744.

1745, Oct. 17. Letters issued to aforesaid executors. Lib. 5, p. 133.

1744, May 23. Inventory, £98.10.1; made by Michael Chew, Michael Fisher.

1746, Sept. 10. Lewis, Mary (late Mary Bickham), of Gloucester Co. Int. Adm'r, Samuel Lewis, of Chester Co., Penna., yeoman. Bondsman—Abraham Chattin, of aforesaid County.

Gloucester Wills, 333 H.

1733, Dec. 21. Lewis, William, of Elsenburgh, Salem Co., labourer. Bond of, to Thomas Mason, of Salem, merchant, for £5.15.10.

1734, Nov. 29. Bond of Thomas Mason, as administrator of the estate of William Lewis, with John Doe and Richard Doe, of Salem, gentlemen, as fellow bondsmen.

1734, Dec. 26. Inventory of the estate, £2.3.0; made by Joseph Darkin and Edward Test. Salem Wills, 497 Q.

1740, April 14. Light, Mary, of Middletown, Monmouth Co. Bond of Peter Le Conte, of Freehold, physician, principal creditor, as administrator. Joseph Eatton, of Shrewsbury, physician, fellow bondsman. Lib. C, p. 332.

1740, April 16. Inventory of the estate (£16.10.3) includes bonds of Benjamin Willson and Benjamin Chesterman. Made by James Hutchins and Hannus Swart.

1741, April 16. Account mentions cash paid Joseph Eatton, Jacob

Trueax, William Deveny, Benjamin Chesterman and George Reid. Cash from Benjamin Willson.

1748, April 7. Liming, William, of Upper Freehold, Monmouth Co., yeoman; will of. Wife, Deborah. Children—Daniel, John, Deborah, Lidah, Elizabeth and Sarah. Executors—wife, son Daniel and John Cox. Witnesses—John Liming, Junior, James Reid and Joseph Cunningham. Proved Jan. 20, 1748. Lib. 6, p. 26.

———, ———, —. Inventory of the estate; £106.03.11; made by John Trout and Joseph Cunningham, Junior.

1749-50, March 7. Lindsly, John, of Morristown, Morris Co., Esq.; will of. Sons—Stephen (eldest), Junia, Caleb, John, Levi (minor), Demas (minor), Philip (minor). Daughters—Phebe and Hanna. Real and personal estate. Executors—My brother, Daniel, and my son Junia, both of Morristown. Witnesses—Caleb Fairchild, Thomas Miller, Timo. Johnes. Proved 5 April, 1750. Lib. E, p. 411.

1750, April 2. Lindsly (Lindsley), Stephen, of the Borough of Elizabeth, Essex Co. Int. Administration granted to Phebe Lindsley (relict), of the County of Morris. Bondsman—Joseph Wood, Jr. Lib. E, p. 408.

1750, April 3. Inventory of personal estate (£488.18.05), includes bonds of Abel Day, Joseph Wood, Ebenezer Holleburd, David Powers, Daniel Roberts, John Prodden, Ebenezer Allen, Jona. Allen, Abner Beach, Adam Blackman, Thomas Johnson, Cornelius Cain, John Welshar, John Forster, Thomas Allason, Thomas Rite. Also debts due from Mathew Connet, Thomas Morgan, John Pears, Zopher Bedford, Jacob Allen, Isaac Ball, John Muchmore, Abraham Stagg, Samuel Ross, John Carter, George Day, Henery Von Vollaman, William Miller, Sarah Hart, James Dody, Daniel Day. Made by Nath'll Bonnel, Benjamin Carter.

1745-6, March 8. Line, William, Jun'r, of the Borough of Elizabeth, Essex Co., yeoman; will of. Wife, Elizabeth. Children—Joseph, William, John, Mary, Rebeckah, Katherine and Martha. Real and personal estate. Executors—son, Joseph, and John and Benjamin Miller. Witnesses—Joseph Atin, John Davis, William Nicholas. Proved May 9, 1746. Lib. D, p. 382.

1746-7, April 22. Inventory of personal estate, £100.18.03; made by John Vail, John Shotwell, Jun'r.

1746-7, Jan. 15. Linn, John, of Somerset Co., yeoman. Int. Administration granted to the widow, Margaret, and Joseph Linn, the son. Fellow bondsmen—William and Alexander Linn, all of Somerset Co. Witnesses—Bryan Leferty, Tho. Bartow. Lib. D, p. 445.

1746-7, Jan. 7. Inventory of personal estate, £179.12.0; made by Bryan Leferty, Adam Reemer.

1747-8, Jan. 22. Account. Paid to Denil Haly, Petter Smith, Petter Kembel, Loran S. Sliger, Nathl. Cooper, Evan Lesada, John Tinbrock, Cornaloues Low, Thomas Halam, Mr. James Alexander.

1748, Aug. 28. Lippincott, Ann, of Northampton, Burlington Co., widow; will of. Children—Job, Samuel, Patience Folwell and Elizabeth Gaskill. Daughter—Ann Gaskill. Executors—sons Job and Samuel. Real and personal estate. Witnesses—John Atkinson, Jonathan Jess, Tho. Shinn. Proved Sept. 9, 1748. Lib. 6, p. 110.

1748, Sept. 6. Inventory of the personal estate, £341.7.4; made by James Lippincott and Revell Elton. Includes bonds and notes due from Edward Gaskill, Oddy Brock, Walter Harbert, James Southwick, Samuel Cripps, Amos Shiver, John Brock, Joseph Gaskill, Edward Wever, Joseph Ruchards, Jobe Lippincott, Joseph Shinn, James Shinn, Henry Reeves, Thomas Kimbal, Jonathan Gaskell, John Powel, Josiah Southwick, Samuel Gaskell, Thomas Foster, John West, John Fort, Jolive Evan.

1741, July 8. Lippincott, Daniel, of Shrewsbury, Monmouth Co., yeoman; will of. Wife, Genet. Only son, Preserve, under age. Daughters—Elizabeth, Andria and Ann. Land adjoining Abraham White; meadow on Long Neck. Executors—wife, uncle George Williams, and friend Joseph Parker. Witnesses—Abraham White, George Woolley, John Fisher, Jacob Dennis. Proved Oct. 7, 1741. Lib. C, p. 446.

1743, 4th day, 4th mo. (June). Lippincott, Freedom, Jun'r, of Evesham, Burlington Co., yeoman. Int. Inventory of the personal estate, £230.10.3; made by Thomas Hooten and Daniel Bates.

1743, June 16. Administration granted to Hannah Lippincott, widow. Samuel Lippincott and Thomas Wilkins, fellow bondsmen. Lib. 4, p. 381.

1734, Aug. 4. Lippincott, Jacob, of Chester, Burlington Co., yeoman; will of. Sons—Richard, Thomas, Ezekiel and Jacob, all under age. Real and personal estate. Wife, Mary, sole executrix. Witnesses—John Means, Robert French, Joseph Heritage. (Not proven). Lib. 4, p. 243.

1740, June 21. Inventory of the personal estate, £151.11.2; made by John Means and Joseph Heritage.

1745, May 27. Lippincott, John, of Shrewsbury, Monmouth Co., yeoman; will of. Wife, Sarah, plantation where testator lived, bounded by his second son Jacob's land, during her life; then to son Jacob. Eldest son, Thomas. Son, Jacob, land adjoining Peter White. Third son, Joseph. Fourth son, John, plantation where said son lives at Norrawaticunk, for life, and then to testator's grandson, John Lippincott, eldest son of John; entailed to male heirs. Negro woman, Hester, to be free, and her five children to be free when aged 35 years. Daughters—Margaret, Mary, Faith, Deborah, Anne and Sarah. Executors—three eldest sons, Thomas, Jacob and Joseph. Witnesses—James Parker, Thomas Crafts, Anthony and Jacob Dennis. Proved May 25, 1747. (James Parker, a Quaker). Thomas and Jacob Lippincott, executors (Quakers), qualified same day. Lib. E, p. 206.

1747, May 11. Inventory of the estate (£411.08.00) includes negroes Ishmael, Primus, Hagar, Bess and Oliver, to serve 6, 11, 13, 17 and 19 years respectively, (time at £200). Made by Isaac Hance and Jacob Dennis.

1737, Sept. 9. Lippincott, Preserve, of Shrewsbury, Monmouth Co. Int. Bond of Gabriel Stelle, of Perth Amboy, Esquire, as administrator. Andrew Johnston, Esquire, of Perth Amboy, fellow bondsman. Lib. C, p. 175.

———, March 16. Lippincott, Restore, of Northampton, Burlington Co., husbandman; will of. Wife, Martha. Grandson, Joseph Lippincott, my long gun. Grandsons—Restore Lippincott, Daniel and Jonathan Jess. Daughters—Rachel Dawson, Abigail (wife of James Shinn), Rebecca (wife of Josiah Gaskill), and Elizabeth (widow of

George Shinn). Two old negroes to have their freedom. 100 acres in New Hanover upon Rancocers Creek near James Shinn's mill. Son, James, sole executor. Witnesses—William Parker, John Parson, Tho. Shinn. Proved Aug. 8, 1741. Lib. 4, p. 310.

1741, July 25. Inventory of the personal estate, £154.18; made by Benjamin Brian and John Butcher. Includes Bible and other books.

1747, Nov. 4. Lippincott, William, of Shrewsbury Township, Monmouth Co., carpenter; will of. Wife, Esther, executrix. Brother, Wilbur Lippincott. Witnesses—John Morris and William Bills. Proved April 5, 1748. Monmouth Wills, ——.

1747, Nov. 19. Inventory of the estate (£221.19.6 1-3) including riding chair and harness. Made by Joseph Kelley and Abraham Tilton.

1731, Oct. 9. Littell (Little), Anthony, of Elizabeth Town, Essex Co., yeoman; will of. Children—Absalom, Abraham, Andrew, Anthony, Andoniah, Amoz, Abigail, Mary and Ruth Little. Daughter, Elizabeth, daughter of my former wife Elizabeth, deceased. Lands joining lands of Joshua Clark, Joseph Conkling, Joseph Holsea, Eliakim Chorey. Executors—wife, Mary, son Absalom and friend Matthias Hetfield, cordwainer. Witnesses—Thomas Chapman, Dan'll Sayre, David Crane. Proved Jan. 5, 1733-4. Lib. B, p. 484.

1733-4, ——, —. Inventory of personal estate, £64.17.06; made by Abs'm Ladner, N. Mitchell.

1750, Jan. 14. Little, John, of Shrewsbury, Monmouth Co.; will of. Wife, Hannah. Son, John. Son, Thomas, deceased. Granddaughter, Isabell Little, daughter of son Thomas; granddaughter, Isabell Little, daughter of son John. £200 to Trustees of Presbyterian Church of Monmouth County. Executors—friends John Anderson and David Rhe, both of Freehold. Witnesses—Joseph Potter, Andrew McDowell and John Nath'n Hutchins. Codicil made February 12, 1750, same witnesses. Proved March 8, 1750. Lib. E, p. 292.

1743, Jan. 19. Liviston, Dan'l, "at the North Branch of Rarriton and County of Summerseat," blacksmith; will of. Wife, ——. Children—Robert, Danl., John, Cathrine, Peggy, William and Malcom (last three designated as the three younger children). Son-in-law, James Andrew. Mentions Wm. McDonald, miller, and John Collier, a tenant. The home farm to be held "so long as the family keeps together." Rents to be paid to Mr. Alexander, his attorney. Executors—son, Robert, and Gisbert Lane, living at the North Branch of Rariton, Somerset Co. Witnesses—Danl. McEowen, James Andrew.

(On back of will): "Left here by Duncan McCoy, who said he would get it proved." Not probated. Somerset Wills, 63 R.

1747, Oct. 16. Lloyd, Thomas, of Perth Amboy, Middlesex Co., yeoman. Int. Bond of Bridget Lloyd, his widow, as administratrix. John Throckmorton and John Lorton, fellow bondsmen. Witness—Elizabeth Lloyd. Lib. E, p. 100.

1747, Oct. 19. Inventory of personal estate (£112.6.7) includes 123 pounds of butter, £3.10.9. Made by Charles Morgan and John Bowne.

Lloyd (see Loyd).

1742, Sept. 8. Lock, Jestah, of Greenwich Township, Gloucester Co., yeoman; will of. Wife, Magdelen, the personal estate, and "to give my daughters as she sees proper." Sons—Andrew, all my lands excepting the land I gave to my son, Swan Lock, with 8 acres of meadow on Rappah Creek, Gloucester Co.; Zebulon and Jestah, at 21, to have equally the rest of the land I purchased of John Ladd. Executors—wife, Magdelen, and son, Andrew. Witnesses—Deborah Veneman, Jonas Lock, William Guest. Proved 4 Nov., 1742. Lib. 4, p. 323.

1742, Nov. 3. Inventory (£122.12.4) includes book (£1), 100 bu. of Indian Corn (£10), cattle (£34.10.0). Appraisers—William Guest, Hance Steelman.

1731, June 9. Lock, Peter, of Gloucester Co., yeoman; will of. Wife, Mary. Children—Lawrence (eldest), Charles, Jones, John, Jasper, Peter, Mary, Susannah (the last six under age.) Executors—wife, and son Lawrence. Witnesses—Mounce Keen, Jacob Mattson, John Jones. Proved July 16, 1731. Lib. 3, p. 145.

1731, June 28. Inventory, £111.16.8; made by Gunnar Archard and John Jones.

1744, Sept. 8. Lockheart (Lockart), Alexander, of Trenton, Hunterdon Co., Esquire; will of. Wife, Mary. Son, Daniel Coxe Lockheart. Executors—wife, and friend John Coxe, of Trenton. Witnesses—Mary Bond, Elijah Bond and Jno. Jenkins. Proved Sept. 4, 1749. Lib. 6, p. 349.

1749, Dec. 28. Logan, John, of Gloucester Co., laborer. Int. Admr'x, Evy Belanger. Bondsman—Japheth Leeds. Both of Egg Harbor, county aforesaid. Gloucester Wills, 430 H.

1749, May 3. Logan, William, of Hunterdon Co., yeoman; will of. Wife, Sarah. Youngest daughter, Mary. Other children—Anne, Staffle, William and Sarah. Executors—Ephraim Lockheart and Richard Porter. Witnesses—James McCrea, Ralph Smith and John McGallird. Proved May 8, 1749. Lib. 6, p. 306.

1749, May 9, 10. Inventory of estate of William Logan, "late of Ridden Town" (Readington), (£424.9.2), includes a pleasure "slay," two yoke of oxen, two guns, large Bible, books; 270 acres of land leased from Mr. James Logan of Stenton, in Philadelphia County, (£200), planks at Joshua Nichols; money due from Patrick Brown, John Bodine, Alexander Hunter, James Woods' part of the fulling mill, and John Allen. Debts due from Thomas Lane, Cornelius Weacoff, John Weacoff, Cornelius Skinner, Samuel Bernardt, Derrick Morlat, John Reed, Staffel Vock, Ephraim Lockheart, John Vandwenter, Nathan Dally, John Mallick, John Andrews, James Andrew, Duman McQuoan, John Faze, Abraham Dally, Andreas Wortman, William Bay, Jonathan Delley and Valentine Faze. Made by Joshua Nichols and William Jones.

1752, Dec. 27. Account of executors mentions Anthony White, William Logan of Philadelphia, Hendrick Hendrickson, Tunis Vandever, Cornelius Wycoff, William Alexander, Peter Boun, Hugh Tompson, Aaron Longstreet, Robert Cummins, Joseph Furman, Estate of Thomas Noble, Samuel Johnson, James Wood, Jacob Angell, Jacob Tennicke, William Osborn, James McCoy, John Broughton, John Collins, John Vandeventer, Doctor Liddle, Jacob Cline, Doctor Vanwagener, John Vansickle, Mary Buckley, Mr. Guilard, John Allan, Cornelius Low, John Walker, Thomas Helam, John Coleman, John Henry, Robert Simpson, John Langerfelt, John Spencer, James McGill, Maur's Glanviel, Archibald Marryon, Ralph Smith, Joshua Nichols, James Wood, William McKenney.

1749, July 13. Lollard, John, of Gloucester Co., laborer. Int. Adm'r, William Hill, of Waterford, farmer. Bondsman—John Estlack, Newton, yeoman. All of said County. Witness—Luke Tuckniss. Lib. 6, p. 333.

1749, July 10. Inventory, £52.13.5; made by John Estlack.

1750, June 5. Account. Goods sold at vendue: Max Field, Edward Bush, Isaac Mickle, William Ellis, Nathan Pratt, Joseph Ellis.

1748-9, March 15. Long, Elihu, of Mannington, Salem Co., yeoman; will of. Children—Abner, Daniel, Malachi and Rebecca Long, the plantation (50 acres) I live on, equally when they arrive to the age of 21 years. Executors shall bring up and educate children until fifteen and then bind them to trades. Executors—William Siddons and Mary, his wife. Witnesses—William Chandler, Thos. Rice, Geo. Trenchard. Sworn and affirmed, 3 of April, 1749. Lib. 6, p. 362.

1749, April 4. Inventory (£191.18.8) includes negro boy (£20), horses and colts, oxen, cows, etc. Appraisers—Edward Keasbey, William Chandler.

1743, Nov. 14. Long, William, of Cohansey, Salem Co., husbandman; will of. Sons—Joseph (eldest) and Elihu. Daughter—Elizabeth, wife of Abraham Cunningham. Witnesses—Margaret Abel, Nathan Shaw, George Willis. Proved 10 Jan., 1743-4. Salem Wills, 305 Q.

1743-4, Jany 10. No executors being named in the will, Joseph Long and Alexander Cunningham appointed to administer the estate. Bondsman—Andw. Gardiner. Witnesses—William M'Manamy, Chas. O. Neill.

1743, Nov. 29. Inventory, £40.12.5; made by Hugh Dunn, Nathan Shaw.

1741-2, March 11. Longfield, Mary, of New Brunswick, Middlesex Co., widow of Cornelius Longfield. Daughters—Rachel Lawrence and Catherine Cox. Friend, widow Foret, alias Lebon. Real and personal estate. Executor—son, Henry Longfield. Negro woman, Sucky, to have her freedom. Witnesses—Edw'd Antill, Joseph Philips, Wm. Antill. Proved March 25, 1747. Lib. E, p. 4.

1731, ———. Longhurst, Henry, of Burlington. Inventory, £105.0.0 (value of contents of a country store); made by Richard Smith, Jr., and Samuel Bickley. Burlington Wills, 2311-2 C.

1739, December 1. Longstreet, Theophilus, of Shrewsbury Town, Monmouth Co., yeoman; will of. Wife, Mercy. Eldest son, Richard, plantation he lives on, on Manasquan river, old gun and £50. Second son, Gilbert, plantation where he lives on same river. Third son, Aury, land at Rariton, where he lives. Fourth son, Theophilus, land in said town on Long Branch and Raccoon Island. Daughters—Yonica, Catherine, Mary, Sarah, Moica and Anne. Executors—four sons. Eldest daughter, Yonica, to have old loom. Witnesses—John Little, Thomas Wainwright, Jon. Seares and Jacob Dennis. Signed, "Stoffel Langstraat." Proved March 1, 1741. Lib. C, p. 491.

1742, Feb. 15. Longworth, Thomas, of Newark, Essex Co.; will of. Children—Thomas, Martha, John, Mary, Isaac, Samuel, David (last four under age). Land purchased of Thomas Ludington, joining lands of Jonathan Pierson, Isaac Lyon, David Shipman. Executors—wife,

Dorcas, and son Thomas. Witnesses—Daniel Pierson, Joseph Riggs, Jun'r, David Ogden. Proved Nov. 25, 1748. Lib. E, p. 223.

1723, Oct. 5. Loofbourrow, John, of Middlesex Co.; will of. Children—John, Nathaniel, Thomas, Mathew, Hannah, Katherine, Ruth. Eldest daughter at 14 years. Granddaughter, Ruth, at 18 years. Lands at Paysiack neck, Staten Island; 60 acres in Woodbridge; at Rariton, joining lands of Ezekiel Bloomfield. Bonds of Cornelius Johnson, of Staten Island, Richard Stilwill, of New York, Samuel Allen, of Newark. Executors—friends John Vail and John Kinsey, Jun'r. Witnesses—Daniel Shotwell, Henry Brotherton, J. Kinsey. Proved Jan. 29, 1732. Lib. B, p. 362.

——, ——, ——. Loofbourrow, John, of Perth Amboy, Middlesex Co.; will of. All estate to be at my wife's disposal. Eldest son, Wade. Witnesses—Thomas Inglis and William Harrison.

1749, March 30. Gannatta Harrison, of full age (widow), made oath to the signature on the will.

1749, April 12. William Harrison, one of the witnesses, made oath to the signature as being that of the testator. Lib. E, p. 271.

1728, Dec. 27. Loots, John, of Hackinsack, Bergen Co., farmer; will of. Wife, Helena, sole executrix, and to have whole estate during widowhood. Sons—Johannis (eldest), the land in the Hills, and Paulus, land "on Tien Neck," and to share equally the meadows. Legacies to daughters, Tryntje and Geesje. Daughter-in-law, Aeltje Westervelt, £25 (being her portion of her father's estate). Witnesses—Jacob Hendreckse Banta, Hendreck Hendreck Banta, Robert Livesey. Proved 1 March, 1744. Lib. D, p. 239.

1744, Nov. 23. Lorance, Nathan, of Cohansey, Salem Co., yeoman; will of. Wife, Elizabeth, one-third of moveable estate; at her marriage or decease same shall be equally divided among my three youngest daughters, Elizabeth, Rhoda and Violetta. Daughter, Abigail Elmore, "that tract called Flying Point (except one acre where the Baptist meeting house stands—where the Baptist members that live on the south side of Cohansey Creek shall think fit to take it"), together with 100 acres between Edmund Shaw's and Samuel Chard's, joining Barn's line to be hers and her heirs forever by her present husband Daniel Elmore, if any shall survive; for want of such heirs after the decease of said Daniel Elmore and Abigail his wife, then to any other lawful heirs of her body, who shall pay £10 to each of my three youngest daughters at their marriage or at the age of 21 years. Sons—Jonathan and Nathan, all of my lands and all my shares and rights of "Proprietye." Daughters—Elizabeth Shephard, ½ of the marsh (50 acres) in Sears Neck and £30; Rhoda, 200 acres at White Marsh, 100 acres of marsh below John Peterson's on the west side of Morris River, and £50 to be paid when she will be 20 or married; Violetta, 200 acres at White Marsh, ½ of the marsh on the east side of Dividing Creek, also £50 at 20, or marriage. Executors—sons Jonathan and Nathan Lorance. Witnesses—William Dallis, Joseph Reeves, Isaac Preston, Nathaniel Diament. Proved 24 April, 1745. Lib. 5, p. 150.

1744, Dec. 20. Inventory (£534.0.10) includes silver tankard and spoons (£20.18.9), 77 neat cattle (£146.1), negro woman (£36), horses (£31), a still and 36 gals. of spirits (£22). Appraisers—Joseph Reeves, Jonadab Shephard.

1749, March 23. Lord, Constantine (above 14 years), son of Edmond Lord, late of Gloucester Co., ward. Guardian—Joshua Lord, his uncle. Bondsman—James Lord. Both of Deptford Township, yeomen. Witnesses—Luke Tuckniss, Jos. Rockhill, Junior. Lib. 6, p. 270.

1741, May 4. Lord, Edmond, of Greenwich, Gloucester Co., yeoman. Int. Adm'x, his widow, Susanna. Bondsmen—John Raine and John Jones, both of place aforesaid. Lib. 4, p. 287.

1741, April 27. Inventory, £61.10.0; made by John Rayn, John Jones.

1732, April 28. Lord, John, of Waterford, Gloucester Co., yeoman; will of. Executors—wife, Mary, John Wood, of Woodbury Creeke, and Joseph Tomlinson. They to sell the whole estate, real and personal, ½ for my wife, the other half for the "bringing up of my children, who shall receive equally at 21 what is left of their portion." Witnesses—Joseph Tindall, Jun'r, John Kay, Sarah Kay. Affirmed 17 June, 1732. Lib. 3, p. 200.

1732, June 8. Renunciation of John Wood, one of the executors named. Witnesses—Joseph Tindall, Josa. Lord.

1732, May 20. Inventory (£369.16.11) includes 144 acres of land, with improvements thereon (£19.16.11). Appraisers—John Kay, Joseph Bate, John Collins.

1734, Jan. 8. Lord, Joseph, of Salem County, yeoman. Int. Adm'x, Alice Lord, widow. Bondsmen—John Purple, John Doe. All of said County. Witness—Richard Roe. Lib. 3, p. 434.

1734, Dec. 16. Inventory (£145.3.4) includes cattle, horses and colts. Appraisers—Thomas Hopkins, John Purple.

1735, 18th day, 3rd mo. (May). Lord, Robert, of Springfield, Burlington Co., yeoman; will of. Sons—John and Samuel. Daughter, Sarah, wife of John Tatam. Remainder of estate, both real and personal, to seven children, viz., Isaac Lord's wife and children, Abraham, Rachel, Elizabeth Borton, Robert, Joshua and Abigail. Executors—wife, Jane, and son-in-law John Borton. Witnesses—Abr'm Farington (tallow chandler), Dan. Smith, Jun'r (merch't), Is. DeCow (Esq.). Proved June 21, 1735. Lib. 4, p. 31.

1735, May 30. Inventory of the personal estate, £189.10.6; made by James Lippincott and John Butcher.

1737, May 4. Account showing payments to Isaac DeCow for making coffin, Richard Robinson, Elishab Allison, Mary Austin, Sam'll Lovett, Dan'l Smith, Jun'r, Caleb Raper, Jon. Fenimore, William Bissell, Joseph Rockhill, Joshua Barker, Rich. Smith, Jonath'n Wright, Joseph Atkinson, Rebecca Bryan, Joseph Ridgway, Sarah Antram, Joshua Owen, Jas. Antram, Sam'll Scattergood, John Buffin, Jon. Craige, Dan'l Zelley, Abigail Smith, John Ridgway, Sam'll and Mary Gibson.

1748, May 16. Lord, Samuel, of Deptford Township, Gloucester Co. Int. Adm'x, Mary Lord, widow. Bondsman—James Cattell, of place aforesaid. Witness—John Mickle. Lib. 6, p. 16.

1748, May 14. Inventory, £78.13.10; made by James Cattell, Michael Fisher.

1748, April 11. Lord, Thomas, of Monmouth Co. Int. Bond of Andrew Johnston, Esq., as administrator of the estate, with Andrew Smyth as fellow bondsman. Lib. E, p. 160.

1730, March 26. Louden (Lowden) Renier, of Precinct of Piles Grove, Salem Co., tailor; will of. Children—Robard, Rachel, Eales and one not born, to have equally, when the youngest will be 21, my real estate, consisting of house and lot in Salem occupied by Clement Haul, and 100 acres (Salem County) in the occupation of William Loper. Wife, Easter, executrix and to have the personal. Witnesses —Benjamin Davall, Joseph Loyd, Wm. Crawley. Proved 14 April, 1730. Salem Wills, 498 Q.

1730, April 13. Inventory (£75.18.3) includes cows (£28.10) and sheep (£11.5). Appraisers—John Davis, Samuel Elwell.

1731, Nov. 21. Account of "Esther Loudon," executrix. Monies paid to Mathew Ranton, Peter Evans, Esq., attorney for Jon. Brick and Eliza. Worthington.

1750, Sept. 11. Louzada, Moses, of Middlesex Co. Int. Bond of Hannah Louzada, the widow, late of Middlesex Co., now of New York City, as administratrix. Daniel McKinney and Marius Glanvil, of Hunterdon Co., fellow bondsman. Lib. E, p. 452.

1750, Sept. 27. Inventory of personal estate (£246.4.9) includes mohogany desk, 4 burnt china chocolate cups, silver watch, silver snuff box, 12 silver table spoons. Made by Dan'll McKenney and James Nuttman.

1739, Nov. 13. Love, Mary (parents not given), of Salem Co., ward. Guardian, Thomas Paget, yeoman, of said County. Witnesses—Thos. Eniley (?), Dan. Mestayer. Salem Wills, 676 Q.

1739, Dec. 3. Love, Robert (parents not given), Salem Co., ward. Guardian, John Parke. Bondsman—Sinick Sinnickson. Both of said County. Witnesses—Thomas ——— (?), Dan. Mestayer. Salem Wills, 672 Q.

1741, May 22. Loveland, Richard, of Trenton, Hunterdon Co., yeoman. Int. Bond of Mary Loveland, of Trenton, widow, as administratrix. David Dunbar, of same place, blacksmith, surety. Witnesses—Jno. Clark, Susannah Loveland. Lib. 4, p. 271.

1741, June 1. Inventory of the estate (£116.10.4) includes 3 maps and 19 pictures, 13 old pictures, 60 oz. silver (£2.2.8), a servant man's time, 2 years, 3 months (£7). Made by Joseph Peace and Andrew Reed.

1740, Sept. 30. Lovett, Aaron, of City and Co. of Burlington, yeoman; will of. Sons—Joseph and Aaron. Daughter, Mary who is under age. Lot on East side of High St., in Burlington, I bought of John Gosling, and lot on River Delaware, adjoining James Bispham, which I bought of Thomas Hooten. Executors—wife, Lydia, and father, Samuel Lovett. Witnesses—John Carlile, Israel Heulings, Sam'l Scattergood. Proved Dec. 9, 1745. Lib. 5, p. 207.

1745, Jan. 11. Inventory of the personal estate, £103.8.9; made by Israel Heulings and Hugh Hartshorne.

1750, Nov. 17. Lydia Thomas, late Lydia Lovett, executrix, affirms to s'd inventory.

1747, 14th day, 2nd mo. (April). Lovett, Samuel, of City of Burlington, cordwainer; will of. Wife, Mary, £300. Nathan, son of son Nathan, and the 3 children of son Aaron (2 sons and a dau.). Daughters—Rebecca Pearson and Sarah, wife of James Smith. Lot in City of Burlington, lying between Parson Cambel's and Pheby Satterthwait's, which I bought of Thomas Cutler, to my two grandchildren,

Samuel and Joseph Lovett. Executors—wife, son Nathan, and sons-in-law Isaac Pearson and James Smith. Witnesses—Joshua Raper, John Saunders, Isa. DeCow. Affirmed at Burlington, 1749, by Mary Lovett and James Smith, surviving executors. Lib. 6, p. 315.

1748, April 30. Lowe, Joseph, of Newton, Gloucester Co., cooper. Int. Adm'r, James Hinchman, Esq. Bondsman—Edward Rudolphus Price, of the city and County of Burlington. Lib. 5, p. 439.

1748, April 1. Inventory, £63.11.6; made by Isaac Alberson, Jacob Alberson.

1745, July 12. Lowrance (Lowner), "Johanous, of Pepack, Sumerset Co.," miller; will of. Wife, Marget. Sons—Alexander, Daniel, John. Daughters—Elizabeth Kealer, Lenah Moore, Barbra Beshearer. Mentions indentured boy, Fredrick Shoemaker; dwelling house and orchard; right and title to a mill, according to a bargain with Mr. Andrew Johnston; house that son Daniel lives in, with the cleared land belonging thereto. Signed, "Johanes Lowner." Witnesses—Michal Burger, Margret Burger, Jonathan Pitney. "We, Hendrick Smith and Jacob Eoff, are chosen indeferant by Johannes Lowrance for to be executors of my hol Estait." Proved 3 Dec., 1745. Lib. D, p. 354.

1745, Nov. 26. Inventory of personal estate, £237.17.4; made by Alexander Aikman, ——— Smitz (?).

1736, Oct. 30. Loyd, Bateman (under 14 years of age), son of John, of Piles Grove, Salem Co., yeoman. Catherine, the widow, married again, and Timothy Raines, the uncle of Bateman, petitions that he be appointed his guardian, to whom letters of guardianship are issued. Lib. 4, p. 67.

1747-8, Jan. 15. Loyd, Bridget, of Middlesex Co., widow; will of. Estate of my husband, Thomas Loyd, deceased. Son, Thomas Loyd. Real and personal estate. Executors—daughters Elizabeth and Briget Loyd, they to have remainder of estate. Witnesses—Sam'll Throckmorton, Jun'r, John Throckmorton, Sarah Throckmorton. Proved Jan. 27, 1748. Lib. E, p. 249.

1745, Aug. 28. Lozer (Lozier), Hellebrant, of Bergen Co., yeoman, guardian of Abraham Ackerman, an infant of the age of 14 years and upwards. Fellow bondsman—John Nevill, Esq., of Perth Amboy. Bergen Wills, 235 B.

1745, April 12. Lozier, Nicholas, of Hackensack, Bergen Co., shoemaker; will of. Wife, Antie, sole executrix during widowhood. Brother-in-law, Jacob Derkse Banta, and son-in-law, David Demarest, both of Hackinsack, to be tutors and administrators of the minorene children, as also assistants of the wife, and, if she dies or remarries, to act as executors. In case of second marriage, wife, Antie, to hold the whole estate secured, until the youngest child will be sixteen, that the children may be educated, etc. Then the oldest son, Anthony, to have the land where he hath formerly lived, at Steenraapje (?), that is from Hackinsack River running back westerly according to the deed thereof unto the first run beyond the hill. Son, Johannis, to have remaining part of said land. Son, Petrus, the land where he formerly lived, called the New Hook, on Hackinsack river, between Peter Alje Hendrick and Samuel Laroe. Son, Lucas, the south half part of the tract between the land of Goleyn Ackerman and Peter Alje (according to deed). Son, Derrick, the other half of the tract. Sons, Jacobus and Benjamin, the land on the plain east of Hackinsack River, with the slip, containing 63 acres (according to deed thereof). Sons, Jacob and Abraham, the home farm, with a piece of land I bought of Benjamin VanBoskirk, and the meadow bought of Wm. Day. Son, Hillebrant, "all his smith tools." Further, I have given to the children begotten by first wife, Fraintje, viz., Anthony, Jannetje, Petrus, Johannis, Mary, Hillebrant, Antje, Lucas, Jacobus and Benjamin, each £5 allowance of their mother's estate. "Oldest son, Anthony, to have my cane and 'sit place' in the church at Schralenburg." Unto children Fraintje, Hester, Rachel, Derrick, Jacob, Abraham, Lea, and Margrietje, whatsoever they may require out of my estate. Witnesses—Johannis Vanhooven, Silvester Earle, Robert Livesey. Proved 8 April, 1761. Antie Lozier qualified as executor. Lib. G, p. 419.

1745, Apr. 12. Fragment of renunciation. "Whereas Nicholas Lozier by his last will, dated 12 April, 1745, appointed Antie Lozier, Jacob Derkse Banta, and David Demarest executors, and whereas the said Jacob Derkse Banta and David De (missing) refused to take upon them the burthen."

1737-8, 11th mo. (Jan.). Lucas, Robert, of Wellingborrow, Burlington Co., yeoman; will of. Son, Benjamin. Grandson, Seath Lucas. Daughters—Hannah Gibbs, Elizabeth and Margaret. Land in Chester I bought of Lucy Bore. Executors—son, Benjamin, and daughters Hannah Gibbs and Elizabeth Lucas. Witnesses—William Heulings, Joseph Fenimore, Jun'r, Henry Nordik. Proved April 18, 1740. Lib. 4, p. 229.

1740, April 14. Inventory of the personal estate, £200.15; made by Joseph Fenimore and Peter Parker. Includes debt due from Francis Gibbs.

1736-7, Jan. 15. Ludlam, Anthony, of Cape May, Cape May Co., gent.; will of. Wife, Presela, during widowhood, use of the plantation whereon I live and ½ of the moveable estate. Daughters—Elizabeth, pair of curtains that were her aunt Sarah's; Jude and Elizabeth to have, respectively, £7.10 in gold, and ½ of right of land surveyed by Henry Young, Deputy Surveyor. Son, Providence, land at "Popler Island," Cape May, with all the mills, houses, etc., to be delivered when he will be 20; also one-third of the marsh below the "Thorowfare" in the south side of Dennis Creek, which he shall have no power to sell until he comes to the age of 30. Son, Reuben, at 20, ½ of the plantation I live on, but have no power to sell same under 30 years of age. Son, Anthony, at 20, the other half of the plantation where I live; but if my wife marries before he will be 20, then disposed of as hereafter directed; also two-thirds of the marsh below the "Thurafair" on the south side of Dennes Creek in Cape May County, but with no power to sell the same under 30 years of age. Son, Joseph, at 25, all land and marsh in Gloucester County, on the southernmost branch of Great Harbour River, commonly called Tuckaho River, but with no power to sell same under 30. "If either of my sons should die without children, the land shall be divided between the said brothers that shall be living." Rent of the mills, house and plantation to be applied to the schooling of my sons Providence, Anthony, Reuben and Joseph. Whomsoever has the mill shall grind toll free for my father and for my wife, while my widow.

Two-thirds of the personal shall be divided equally among my four sons and delivered one year after my death. Executors—wife, Presela, and my father, Joseph Ludlam. Witnesses—Joseph Ludlam, Deborah Young, Henry Young. Proved 21 July, 1737. Lib. 4, p. 111.

1737, July 13. Inventory of personal estate, £182.19.11½; made by Henry Young, Jeremiah Hand.

1731, Nov. 17. Lues (Lewis?), Edward. Inventory of personal estate (£5.19.3). Made by Ephraim Dunham, David Sutton.

Somerset Wills, 33 R.

1732-3, Feb. 28. Lum, Samuel, of Elizabeth Town, Essex Co., yeoman; will of. Children—John, Samuel, David, Hannah and Mary Lum, all under age. Real and personal estate. Executors—wife, Martha, Major Joseph Bonnell and Christopher Wood, Esq., yeoman, of Newark. Witnesses—Edward Gillman, Joseph Bonnell, Jun'r, Charles Hole. Proved March 6, 1732-3. Lib. B, p. 393.

1733, April 7. Inventory of personal estate, £191.04; made by Joseph Bonnel, Christopher Wood.

1738, Oct. 28. Lummis, Edward, of Cohansey, Salem Co., yeoman; will of. Wife, Abigail. Children—Edward, Abigail, Samuel, Sarah, Daniel and Mary, to have £1 apiece. Remainder of the estate equally to my three younger daughters—Tamson, Lydia and Elizabeth. "My sons should accept their legacies or parts herein given in husbandry implements." Executor—son, Samuel Lummis. Witnesses—Zechariah Sandwell, Hannah Seely, William Trefy. Proved 5 May, 1740.

Lib. 4, p. 234.

1739-40, Feb. 27. Inventory (£117.9.11) includes cattle, sheep, swine and wheat. Appraisers—Josiah Fithian, Nathaniel Jenkins.

1748, Aug. 6. Lummis, Samuel, of Cohansey, Cumberland Co., yeoman; will of. Wife, Deborah, sole executrix and use of my plantation until my three sons, Samuel, David and Henry, will be of age. Executrix to sell four pieces of Cedar swamp, that the expected child, when of age, may have £20, if a boy, or £18 if a girl. Also to dispose of a piece of meadow at discretion. Witnesses—Ephraim Seeley, Edward Lummus, Nath'l Jenkins. Proved 20 July, 1750.

1750, July 20. Inventory of real and personal estate (£76.13.2) includes 2 lots of cedar swamp (£20.1.1). Appraisers—Robert Hood, Jonathan Bowen.

1751, Oct. 30. Account. Cash paid Alexander Moore, Robart Hartshorn, Daniel Lummas, John Dare and Abraham Reves.

1744, April 23. Lummix, William, of Amwell Township, Hunterdon Co., yeoman; will of. Wife, Cathrine. After decease of wife, negro man Primes to be free and to have two acres of land adjoining the place of Carneles Ringoes for life. Executrix—wife. Witnesses—Benjamin Willcox, Robert Meldrum, Garret Williamson. Proved April 9, 1746. Lib. 5, p. 233.

1732-3, March 20. Lupton, Christopher, of Cape May Co. Int. Adm'x, Abigail Lupton. Fellow bondsman—Richard Downes, Esq. Witnesses—John Eldridge, Jacob Spicer, Junior, Francis Bevis.

Cape May Wills, 75 E.

1732-3, Mar. 19. Inventory of personal estate, £11.10.0; made by Benjamin Crafford, Elisha Hand.

1733, July 23. Account. Moneys paid to Richard Downes, John Hand, Francis Bevis, Isaac Flood, Elisha Hand, John Scull, Benjamin Crafford, Jacob Spicer, Nathaniel Foster, George Crandall.

1741, Dec. 7. Lupton, Joseph, of Salem Co. Renunciation. To all whom it may concern: Know ye that we, Daniel Lupton and Nathan Lupton, Executors appointed by the last will and testament of our late father, Joseph Lupton, of the County of Salem, dec'd, weaver, bearing date the thirtieth day of March, 1736, for good causes us hereunto moving, do hereby renounce and refuse all our right and title to the administration of the said will as Executors thereof, being unwilling to take the burthen of the execution of s'd will upon us. Signed by Daniel Lupton and Nathan Lupton. Witnesses—Dan. Mestayer, Chas. O. Neill. Salem Wills, 638 Q.

1749, Jan. 20. Lurting, George, Esq., of Essex Co. Int. Bond of Peter Schuyler, principal creditor, as administrator. David Ogden, Jun'r, fellow bondsman. Lib. E, p. 368.

1744, Aug. 29. Luse, Benjamin, of Roxbury Township, Morris Co.; will of. Wife, Abigail, use of estate during widowhood. Daughters—Abigail and Mary, at 18 or marriage. Sons—Joseph, Benjamin, Matthias and Eleazar, at age, to have real estate equally. Executors—wife, Abigail, my brother David Lues, and Samuel Coleman. Witnesses—Jesse Corwin, Walter Brown, Wm. Griffing. Proved 2 Nov., 1749. Lib. E, p. 338.

1744, Nov. 7. Inventory (£90.9.6) includes "bought servant, £4." Appraisers—Samuel P. Fazzer, Wm. Griffing. (Filed 1749).

1733, March 13. Lycon, Nicholas, of Deptford Township, Gloucester Co.; will of. Executrix—my friend, Dinah Cox, and she to have all of my personal estate. Witnesses—John Chester, Abigel Chester, Elias Fish. Proved 7 June, 1733. Lib. 3, p. 325.

1733, April 9. Inventory (£74.3.4) includes bonds of Michael Lycon, Peter Cox; debts due from James Wills, John Chester. Appraisers—Wm. Wilkins, Constantine Wood.

1748-9, Jan. 18. Lydee, James, of Trenton, Hunterdon Co.; inventory of estate, £70.10.1; made by Charles Clark and Arthur Howell.

1748-9, Jan. 26. Bond of Margaret Lydee as administratrix. Charles Axford, of Trenton, surety. Lib. 6, p. 75.

1738, April 8. Lyell, David, of Perth Amboy, Middlesex Co.; will of. Sons—Lorain and Thomas. Real and personal estate. Executors—wife, Mary, and brother Fenwick Lyell. Witnesses—John Loofbourrow, Andrew Robinson, Wade Loofbourrow. Proved July 9, 1742.

1742, July 9. Mary Lyell qualified as executrix, Fenwick Lyell the other executor named, having died before the testator. Lib. C, p. 526.

1737, Sept. 27. Lyell, Fenwick, of Perth Amboy, Middlesex Co.; will of. Five children (no names given). Expected child. Real and personal estate. Executors—wife ———, friends Andrew Johnston, Esq., and Mr. John Stevens. Witnesses—Jennet Parker, Martin Wilkins, Law'r Smyth.

1741, March 18. Codicil. Mary and James Lyell, born since making my will. Executors, all my children as they shall severally arrive at 19 years. Witnesses—John Smyth, Sarah Stevens, Richard Stevens. Proved July 9, 1742.

1742, July 9. Lawrence Smyth sworn as witness. Jennet Parker is deceased, and Martin Wilkins (as is said) is beyond seas.

1762, June 8. William Lyell, one of the children, qualified as executor. Lib. C, p. 523.

1733, Dec. 26. Lyndsey, Mark, of Gloucester Co., yeoman. Int. Adm'x, Rebecca Lyndsey. Bondsman—Andrew Jones. Both of said County. Witness—Alexander Morgan.

1733, Dec. 26. Inventory, £97.7.8; made by George Ward, Walter Griffith. Gloucester Wills, 169 H.

1738, May 1. Lyne, Conradt, of Bergen Co. Int. Administration on estate granted to Abraham Lyne, of said Co. Jacob Arents, of Essex Co., fellow bondsman. Lib. C, p. 194.

1738, Jan. 19. Inventory of personal estate £125.2.0; made by Philip Schuyler and Wessel Pieterse.

1747, Dec. 28. Lyon, Benjamin, of Lyons Farms, in the borough of Elizabeth, Essex Co., yeoman; will of. Wife, Martha. Children—Benjamin, Samuel, Matthias, Daniel, Moses, Rachel, Mary, Sarah and Martha. Four sons under age; Rachel and Mary married. Land joining land of Stephen Meeker and John Tunis; lands bought of William Broadwell, deceased, and Ezekiel Crane, joining lands of Benjamin Crane, Daniel Salle, deceased; ——— Morehouse, Samuel Conger; land at Ash Swamp, joining land of Nathaniel Lyon, deceased; lands bought of Joseph Lyon, Sen'r, and Henry Peirson. Grandson, Rufus Crane, son of Jonas Crane, deceased, a minor. Wife's daughters—Hannah Lum and Mary, wife of my son Benjamin Lyon. Executors—sons Benjamin and Joseph, and son-in-law Amos Day. Witnesses—Stephen Morehouse, John Perry, Charles Hole. Proved Jan. 18, 1747. Lib. E, p. 145.

1747-8, Jan. 28. Inventory of personal estate (£543.01.04), incl. silver buckles, and debts due from Ephraim Baker, Timothy Harrison, Joseph Bonnel, Thomas Winter, David Morehouse, Hezekiah Johnson, Matthew Johnson, James Carter, Daniel Thompson, Samuel Chandler, James Chandler, Josiah Lyon, Ezekiel Crane, Daniel Day, John Dilly, deceased, Peter Kuton, John Wade Jun'r, William Whitehead, Isaac Jones, Richard Broadwell, deceased, David Meeker, and note of Samuel Lum, deceased. Made by Christopher Wood and Benjamin Crane, Esq'rs, both of Lyons Farms.

1742, May 21. Lyon, David, of Newark, Essex Co.; will of. Wife, Phebe, sole executor and legatee; after her decease estate to brethren—Nathaniel, Jonah, Zophar, Jonathan and Henry Lyon. Land joining land of John Johnson. Witnesses—Josiah Quimbe, Samuel Winter, David Ogden. Proved Nov. 26, 1742. Lib. D, p. 16.

1738-9, Jan. 22. Lyon, Capt. Ebenezer, of Elizabeth Town, Essex Co., yeoman; will of. Daughter, Elizabeth, wife of Ephraim Clark, and her five children, viz., Elizabeth, Ephraim, Hannah, Ideras and Darkis Clark, all under age. Daughter, Darkis, wife of Ebenezer Stebbins. Daughter, Susana, wife of David Moorehouse. Grandson, Peter Lyon, land bought of George Jewell, deceased, at 21, unless his father, my son Benjamin, should return and need it. Grandson, Ebenezer Wade, land I bought of his grandfather, Benjamin Wade, and £3.10, to purchase two acres of land from the heirs of Daniel Burnet, deceased. Granddaughters—Elizabeth and Hannah Thompson, a trunk dated 1682, with its contents (£43.16.08), belonging to the estate of Benjamin Wade, Jun'r, for the use of his son and daughter, Ebenezer and Mary Wade, both under age; Phebe Thompson, a legacy left her by her father, John Thompson, at 18 years of age. Other grandchildren—Bethiah Winans, Mary and Ebenezer Lyon, Samuel and David McCan, Elizabeth, Ephraim, Hannah, Darkis, Henery, Riderous, Nathaniel and Ichabod Clark, David and Johaanah Moorehouse, Cornelius, Abigail and Jacob Stebbins. Land joining lands of Benjamin Meeker, John Thompson, Alexander Kene, deceased. Land that belonged to Thomas Headley. Executors—friends, David Ogden, attorney-at-law, Thomas Longworth, Isaac Lyon, Benjamin Clark, Joseph Lyon of Newark, and Joseph Tuttle of Hanover. Witnesses—Benjamin Meeker, Samuel Meeker, Thomas Jackman.

1738-9, March 17. Codicil. If son, Ebenezer, should not return in four years, his share to revert to my three daughters. Witnesses—Benjamin Meeker, Samuel Meeker, Thomas Jackman. Proved May 16, 1739.

Lib. C, p. 270.

1739, April 9. Inventory of personal estate (£465.09.08), includes bonds of Samuel Kneeland of Boston, Joshua Hunlock and Zophar Lyon; cash received from Thomas Cushing of Boston; debts due from Nath'll Price, Nath'll Crane, Mathias Burnet, Ephraim Terrill, Jotham Clark, Joseph Mun, William Martin. Made by Nathaniel Johnson, Benjamin Meeker.

1739, May 4. Benjamin Lyon, of Newark, called Benjamin Clark in will, Joseph Lyon and Joseph Tuttle decline to act as executors. Witnesses—John Hinds, Samuel Chandler, Nathaniel Dalglish, Samuel Mun.

1739, May 15. Accompt of executors, showing payments and legacies to the widow, three daughters, Ebenezer and Mary Wade, Phebe Thompson, David Moorehouse and 20 grandchildren; also to Roger French, James Bancks, Justice Mun for coffin, Eliakim Higgins, Mr. Chetwood, James Townley, Jr., Mrs. Cooper, Will'm Winans, Mr. Grazalie, Jonathan Dickinson, Jonathan Thompson, Samuel Price, Edward Willmott, Henry Garthwait, John Higgins, Ebenezer Stebbins, Peter Wennum, Mrs. Tongreloo, Stephen Hinds, Doct'r Burnett, Eunice Gray (admx of Joseph Gray), Joseph Marsh, John Pierson, John Joline, Andrew Joline, Daniel Clark, Sen'r, Nath'll Hazard, Thomas Woodruff, Nathaniel Johnson, Samuel Carter, Widow Sayres, Henry Howell, Nath'll Woodruff, Stephen Brown, Jonathan Dayton, Samuel Farrand.

1731, May 31. Lyon, Elizabeth, Jun'r, of Newark, Essex Co., spinster; will of. Nephew (niece), Sarah Miles, daughter of Leonard Mills; children of Annis Mills; children of brother Thomas Lyon; Mattoniah, son of Isaac Lyon. Personal estate. Executors—friends John Cooper and Eliphalet Johnson, Jun'r. Witnesses—Joseph Peck, Jonathan Sergeant, Jun'r, Jno. Cooper. Proved Feb. 15, 1732.

1732, Jan. 7. Codicil. Nathaniel, son of brother Isaac Lyon. Remainder of estate to all the children of Thomas Lyon, Isaac Lyon and Annis Mills. Witnesses—Ebenezer Lyon, Mary Beech, Jno. Cooper.

Lib. B, p. 383.

1732, Jan. 16. Inventory of personal estate (£58.10.04½) includes payments to Sarah Miles, Major Banner, Eliphalet Johnson, Doct r Burnet, Nathaniel Johnson, Jonathan Peirson, Joseph Browne, Mr. Bradford; cash received from David Crane.

1744, June 16. Eliphalet Johnson made oath to the truth of above inventory, the original having been in the custody of Col. Cooper, the other executor, since deceased.

1750, July 18. Lyon, James (son of Zophar Lyon, of Essex Co., deceased), over 14 years of age. Bond of Isaac Lyon and John Crane as guardians. Christopher Wood, fellow bondsman. Witness—Joseph Johnson. Lib. E, p. 500.

1744, Dec. 11. Lyon, Zophar, of Newark, Essex Co. Int. Bond of Mary Lyon, the widow, as administratrix. Christopher Wood, yeoman, fellow bondsman. Lib. D, p. 206.

1744, ———, —. Inventory of personal estate, £157.15.07; made by Nathaniel Johnson and Isaac Lyon, both yeomen.

1741, June 16. McCan, John, of Middlesex Co., fuller. Int. Bond of Hugh McCan, his brother, fuller, as administrator. John Brown, farmer, fellow bondsman. Lib. C, p. 413.

1737, Aug. 6. McCarty, Dennis, of Town and Co. of Burlington, yeoman. Int. Administration granted to Benjamin Butterworth, yeoman, and Ann, his wife (late Ann McCarty) of Springfield. William Robinson, of City of Burlington, innholder, fellow bondsman.

Lib. 4, p. 110.

1746, Mar. 19. McCarty, Dennis, of Gloucester Co. Int. Adm'r, John McCarty. Bondsman—Henry Thorne. All of said County, yeomen. Witness—Alexr. Robinson.

1746-7, March 23. Inventory, £41.0.9. Debtors—Joseph Ballinger, John Conner, Henry Roe, Richard Cheeseman, Benjamin Burd, Robert Hartshorn, Neal McNeal. Appraisers—Henry Thorne, Hugh Bartlet.

Gloucester Wills, 336 H.

1748, May 6. McCarty, Owen, of Gloucester Co. Int. Adm'r, Thomas Bates. Bondsman—Jonathan Ellis, yeoman. Witness—John Mickle.

1748, April 29. Inventory, £20.3.0; made by Jonathan Ellis, John Borton. Gloucester Wills, 336 H.

1739, Oct. 15. McClane, William, of Salem Co., wheelwright. Int. Adm'r, Simon Sparks. Bondsman—Benjamin Duvall. Both of said County. Witnesses—Jenkin William, Danl. Mestayer.

Lib. 4, p. 199.

1739, Oct. 12. Inventory (£44.18.3) taken at Pilesgrove, includes cattle and sheep. Appraisers—Benjamin Duvall, William Weatherby.

1740, Dec. 4. Account. Includes monies paid to Jas. Sharp for medicine and attendance on dec'd, John Hoffman, Ann McClain for nursing dec'd and his wife, John Hoffman, Henry Sparks, Jon. Smith, Jas. Lestrange, Isaac Sharp, Thos. Graves, Wm. Hambleton, Anthy. Wilkinson, Michael Noah, Benjn. Bispham, cash from Jon. Ashbrook, Aaron Ashbrook, Richard White. Monies paid to Benjn. Duvall, Jon. Coxe (for Jon. Jones, atty for John Hoffman).

1748, June 8. McColloch (McCulluch), Samuel, of Gloucester Township and County, yeoman. Sons—John (eldest, not 23), to have 400 acres of the homestead fronting Timber Creek, a tract, which was his grandfather's and my father's (John McCulloch's), also the meadows and two tracts of land and cedar swamps called Faraway Swamp, and all my lands formerly Montgomery's; George, at 21, to have the other part of my plantation, 200 acres, beginning at Samuel Hazard's upper corner, and the principal and interest from the sale of pine land, 220 acres, at Four Mile Branch road, also White Oak, Fish Creek and White Hall Cedar Swamps. Daughters—Mary, Elizabeth and Hannah McCulluch. Executor—son, John. Witnesses—James Cooper, David Ward, Michael Fisher. Sworn and affirmed 30 June, 1748. Lib. 8, p. 255.

1748, June 29. Inventory (£336.18.11) includes watch, cattle, horses, sheep, timber, husbandry tools. Appraisers—John Blackwood, Richard Cheeseman.

1746, Oct. 23. McCollum, Dugall, of Perth Amboy, Middlesex Co. Int. Mary McCollum, his widow, declines acting as administratrix, and recommends Michael Erickson, of Monmouth Co., yeoman, as administrator. Bond of Michael Erickson as administrator. James English, fellow bondsman. Witness—Hannah Lewis. Lib. D, p. 120.

1746, Oct. 13. McColm, Quintin (Quentin), of Piscataway, Middlesex Co., merchant. Bond of Alexander Malcolm, of Marblehead, County of Essex, Province of Massachusetts Bay, clerk and brother, as administrator of estate. Anthony White, Esq., of New Jersey, fellow bondsman. Witnesses—Alex'r Malcolm and Peter Kemble. Lib. D, p. 411.

1746, Sept. 27. Inventory of personal estate of "Master Quentin McColm, who deceased August 3, 1746," (£1842.9.5) includes silver watch, several small gold rings, stock in partnership with Mr. Kemble, bonds of Adam Fullerton, Dan. McGouens, Geo. Wm. Lawrence, Ja. Ritchie, Mr. McRea, Hugh Campbell, Jacob Tennyck.

1750, Dec. 31. McComb, Joseph, of Middlesex Co., mariner, late belonging to ship "Snow" of Belfast. Bond of Samuel Lyon, mariner, Master of the "Snow," principal creditor, as administrator. John Deare, of Perth Amboy, Esq., fellow bondsman. Lib. E, p. 470.

1747, Sept. 8. McCoy, James, living between first and second Mountains in Somerset Co.; will of. Wife, Mary. Plantation to be sold and divided equally between daughters, Margarett, Sarah and Elizabeth McCoy. "If Isaac Powell has a mind to purchase it, he can have it 20 pounds cheaper than any other man." Executors—Isaac Powell, of Bound Brook, cooper, and Alexander Lynn, of Mine Brook, shopkeeper. Witnesses—Jon. Harris, Charles Adams, Francis Peppard. Proved 16 Sept., 1747. Lib. E, p. 81.

1747, Sept. 15. Inventory of personal estate (£142.19.6) includes servant man and servant girl, £8.10. Appraisers—Jon. Harris, Joseph Colteehat.

1739, Jan. 5. McDowall, Isaac, of Perth Amboy, Middlesex Co., mariner; will of. Intending a voyage to sea. Father and mother, John and Jane Mackdowall. Expected child. Nephew, Isaac, son of brother William. Nephew, William, son of sister Elizabeth Vance. Children of brothers John and William Mackdowall. Land in Chester Co., Penn., purchased of Robert Patten. Wife, Honar, sole executrix, with the advice of Mr. Philip Kearny, gent. Witnesses—Sam'll Jaquess, Susanna Kearny, P. Kearny. Proved July 25, 1740. Lib. C, p. 348.

1742, Oct. 26. McDowall (McDowell), John, of Hackensack, Co. of Bergen, physician. Bond of William McDowall, of Mill Creek Hundred, Co. of New Castle, yeoman, and only brother, as administrator of the estate. John Thomson and James Newell, fellow bondsmen.

Lib. D, p. 12.

1742, Nov. 4. Inventory of personal estate (£355.7.2), includes silver watch and chain (£5), gold signet-ring (£2), knee-buckles, gold chain, 3 gold rings, silver tea pot, silver tankard, parcel of silver work, negroes—Floura (£16), boy Joe (£30), Jenny (£12), boy Billy (£10), boy Prince (£8). Made by John Berry, James Christy.

List of book debts—Gisbert VanBlarm, Wm. Forbes, John Berry, Cornelius Bentta, Cornelius VanDan, Henrick Boss, Abra. Vester, Francis Rivers, John Romine, Leonard Degrove, Yons Vangeeze, Jacobus Van Hessen, Claus Romine, Halebrant Luzer, Benj. Deneree, Roluff Romine, Garrett Garrett, Jacob Kipp, Jacobus Vanordan, John Poulson, Yoras Vangeeza, Lucas Lozer, Thomas Oldwater, John Romine, Jr., Daniel Romine, Cornelius Bogart, Hendrick Hopper, John VanBuskirk, Benjamin Demarest, Cornelius VanHouse, Johan. Lowrance Ackerman, Isiah Vallow, David Christy, Jacobus Bogart, Jacob Myers, Isaac Vreeland, Wm. Petersa Vand —(?), Stephen Terhon, Leana Tours, Aaria Blinkerhoof, Isaac Vanderbeek, Hendrick Varts Banta, John Andries Hooper, Albertus Terhoon, Peter Tibow, Roluff Romine, Samuel Demarest, Roluff Vester Felt, Steven Vester Felt, Abra. Camaur, Garrett VanBlackerman, Hendrick Vanallen, William Ramsey, Isaac Bogert, Adolph Juet, John Banta, Stephen Bogart, Cornelius Vesterfelt, Jube Blinkerhoof, Isaac Thomasee, Jacob Tibet Horn, Barnet Tibow, Abraham Stagg, Elias Williams, Jacob Stagg, Yorst VanBuskirk, Artie Van Pelt, David Ackermen, Isaac Stagg, Peter Kipp, William Ell, John Anderson, Garrat Hornbeck, Adrian Van Houter, Garrat VanVoss, Jacobus Lawr. VanBuskirk, Antie VanTile, Jacob DeRireaser Banta, Derick VanHorn, Hesta Banta, Tada VanWinkle, Hannes Walinsa, Peter Demarest, Aria Vanwinkle, Peter VanBlarkin, Lawrance Ackerman, Thomas Derimas, Hannes Dericksee Banta, Harma Harta, Garrett VanHorn, Cornelias Vanderhoof, Elias Williams, Jacobus Ackerman's Son, Abra. Husiman, Albert Trehoven, Abraham Coles, Harmanus Bell, Derick TerHoon, Peter Vanorder, Albert Cornell, Staats Boos, Casparus Tadsa, Albert Bordan, Garritt Hooper, Anna Tours, Cornel. Helmigha VanHouta, Hendrick Foss, Jacob VanWinkle, Edward Jeffers, Hanes Nestew, Michl. Stanford, Edwd. Earl, Henry Myers, Harmanus Gerrettsee, Abel Smith, Abraham Lerue, Jacobus Luzeer, Wm. Forbes, Andries Vanorden, Rouluff Van Houtee, Philip Mercan, Roger Kingsland, Jacobus Hartje, Christopher Beil, Nathaniel Earl, Abraham Vanbuskirk, John Christion, Abra. Ackerman, Johanes Loats, John VanVorhess, Hessall Peterson, Jacob Vallinsee, Johannes Trehoven, Hendrick Hendrickson, Cornelius Vanorlan, Hendrick Blinkerhoof, Catherine Vienbrush, Abra. Wuaklingbuss, Abra. Blueflet, Johannes Lozer, Peter Vanderbrough, Hans Eversee, David Demarest, David Brower, Barnas Demarest, Johnas Myers, Johannes Banta, Madelinta Towis, Abraham Herrin, Jacob Stagg, Coll. Bayard, Mrs. Warman, Michael Smith, Henry Patterson, Hannes Post, Louzda Shugarland, Peter Helmasa, Poulas Marsea, John Bogart, John Lee, John Morris, Lucas VanHesee, Peter Hall, John Varaway, Lucas Gearsted, John Van Drasee, Peter Dyer, Messill Domini, John Lewis, Isaac VanDrusee, Jacob VanOstren, Aria Carlah, Peet Gans' wife, John Ryers, Lawrance Van Buskirk, Cornelin Hendrick VanHouts, Johannes Stagg, Urie Thomasee, Johannes Troess, John Talaman, Johannes Blaufelt, Joseph Blaufelt, Garret Blaufelt, Samuel Gretfeet, Jacob Pardon, Peter Van Brykirk, Hannas Carel Mangel, Hannas Taddas, Simon VanWinkle, Jacob VanOstran, John Kingsland, Edmond Kingsland, John Schuyler, Johanes Stotts, Isaac Blewfelts, Hendrick Gessioner, Peter Van Skinne,

William Felt, Joseph Wood, Johanes Myers, Daniel Desark, Tunnis Healing, John VanOrda, Nicholas Stilwell, Samuel Edsell, John VanNorder, Mrs. Valow, Eliza Decay, George Stagg, Adrian Post, Jacob Spier, Thomas VanDyke, Philip Earl, John Berry, Peter Berry, Henry Petterson, Mr. Vanaland, all amounting to £392.5.9½.

Also book debts, per contra—Egbert Eckerman, Timo. Townsend, Isaac Van Giesen, Manus VanBossen, Isaac Kipp, Jacob Oldwater, Thos. Oldwater, Garret Debow, Samuel Demarest, Peter Hardey, Robt. Kirkwood, Simon Freeland, Abraham Boss, Abraham Tracey, Elias Williams, Abrah'm Myers Cohen, Isaac and Abra. DePeyster, James Burling, Jane Rolang, Lawrance Ackerman, John Blanchard, Latouch & Hains, Abra. Huisman, Rich'd Annelly, Annely & Lewis, Hendrick Bear, Samuel Edsall, James Christy, John McKinley, Jno. Banta, Francis Hendrix, Doct. Arch. Fisher, Thos. Gray, John Niccols, John Allen, David Ogden, Saml. Woodward; amounting to £257.19.3¾.

1744, August 13. McGee (McGee, Meghee), William, of Allentown, Monmouth Co., brewer. Inventory of the estate (£187.0.8) includes gun and cutlass, Bible, Book of Divinity, rye in stack, cask and utensils for brewing, malt, copper, bonds, etc. Made by William Lawrence and Charles Jolley. September 7, 1744, Amy McGhee, the widow, declared said inventory to be true. Monmouth Wills, 1177-80 M.

1742-3, Feb. 23. McGloon, Peter, of Monmouth County, laborer. Int. Inventory of the estate (£18.7.6) includes gun and sword (£4.8.6), cash due John Tise, James Wilson and Darbey Carver. Made by James Ferel, Hendrick Hendrickson, John Pew, George Reid, Junior, Isaac Vandorn. Lib. D, p. 25.

1742-3, March 5. Bond of Isaac Vandorn of Monmouth County, yeoman, as administrator. Peter Vandorn, of same County, yeoman, fellow bondsman.

1743, March 21. List of goods, sold by administrator, to Archibald Gray, Benjamin Chesterman, John Lord, William Arnal, Henry Jackson, John Bray, Peter Scanck, Philip Truex, William Robbers, George Reid, Roliph Scanck, Laurence Carstolfel, Joseph Truex, Thomas Paton, John McKinster, William Hendrickson (the sword), Andrew Bray, George Reid, Junior, William Pool, James Wilson, John Tise.

1743-4, Feb. 5. Account of administrator, includes moneys paid to Dr. Le Count, George Reid, Nancy Cruse, Hugh McCollum, James Ferel, Obadiah and Samuel Homes, William Hendrickson.

1749, Sept. 25. McIntosh, John, of Bridgetown, Burlington Co. Int. Administration on estate granted to Hannah McIntosh, widow. Patrick Reynolds and Nicholas Toy, carpenters, both of same, fellow bondsmen. Lib. 6, p. 334; Lib. 7, p. 100.

1749, Sept. 25. Inventory of the personal estate, £84.18.4½; made by Patrick Reynolds and Nicholas Toy. Includes notes of Thomas Newell and Andrew Liken.

1732-3, Jan. 6. McKay (MacKay), Daniel, of Freehold, Monmouth Co., miller; will of. Wife, Mary. Children—James, Jean and Katheran. Executors—friends Joseph Newton and Robert Cumming. Witnesses—John Shaw, Allen Rose and Charles Murrey. Proved at Crosswicks, March 7, 1732-3. Lib. B, p. 403.

1732-3, March 23. Inventory of the estate (£125.4.1½) including carpenter and joiner tools and turner's tools. Made by Thomas Hankinson, James English and John Henderson.

1750, May 28. McKeand, James, of Monmouth County. Int. Bond of Robert English and Gysbert Hendricson, yeomen, as administrators. James Jackson, yeoman, fellow bondsman. Luke Tuckniss, witness. Lib. 7, p. 28.

1736, March 2. McKeen, James, of Salem County, yeoman. Int. Adm'x, Katharine McKeen (widow). Bondsman—William Vaneman. Both of Salem County. Witness—Joseph Hawks. Lib. B, p. 114.

1736-7, Feb. 21. Inventory (£40.14.6) includes "a few old Sweed books" and sheep. Appraisers—William Vanaman, Joseph Hawkes.

1738, Sept. 28. Account of Catherine, widow and administratrix of "James McKein," late of Penns Neck. Monies paid to Jon. Wilder, Anna Alderson, Joseph Hawkes, Wm. Vanneman, Daniel Mestayer, Richard Grafton, Thos. Wright, Benjn. Acton, John Hutton, Gunlah Holton, Timothy Raine, James Lennox, Henry Wallace, Wm. Hurd, John Thomas, Thomas Thompson, Edward Saddick, Hugh McNeal, Robert Hart, George Minrow, John Eaton, Garret Vanneman, John McKeen, Rosanna Moore, Wm. Murdock, Wm. Hamilton, Cornelius Corneliuson, Sinnick Sinnickson. Total—£59.14.6.

1732, Feb. 15. McKnight, Hugh, of Salem Co. Int. Adm'x, Hannah McKnight. Bondsmen—John Paget, Thomas Paget. All of Salem Co. Witness—Joseph Worce (?). Lib. 3, p. 289.

1732, Dec. 7. Inventory (£242.4.11) taken at Cohansey, includes books (£1.3). Appraisers—John Pagett, Thomas Pagett.

1749, Jan. 25. McKnight, James, of Perth Amboy and Cranberry, Middlesex Co., schoolmaster. Int. Bond of James Wall, principal creditor, as administrator. Joseph Wilson, fellow bondsman. Lib. E, p. 361.

1750, March 31. Inventory of personal estate (£24.13.6) includes bond from Robert Davison to John Kerr, Jun'r. Made by Henry Moore, John Karson, James Wall.

1741, Aug. 22. McKnight, Malcolm, of Pensneck, Salem Co., tailor; will of. Wife, Catheren, one-third of moveables and the full use during widowhood of houses and plantation, "but if she marries she must go with her husband and leave said plantation;" otherwise, may hold it during life, then leave it to my four children—Charles, John, Malcolm and Shusanna; they to have equally remainder of moveable estate, allowing my daughter Jean, £2. All real estate at end of wife's term to be sold and money divided equally among said children, allowing my son, Charles, the money he has had since he went to Mr. Tennant's; also to have the care of his brother Malcolm. Executors—son, Charles, and James Barkley. Witnesses—William Westcott, Nicholas Johnson, Samuel Inly. Proved 4 Sept., 1741. Lib. 4, p. 312.

1744-5, Feb. 4. Inventory of part of the goods (£6.) includes credit by Hance Bilderback, his apple trees sold to Jonnas Stalkup, credit due to Peter Cormack. Appraisers—Andrew Sinnickson, Sinick Sinnickson.

1745, Sept. 2. Inventory (£217.2.6½) includes house rent due from Mr. James Barkley and credits due from William Scott. Appraisers—Thos. Eniles, Sinick Senick.

1742, Dec. 1. McMin, James, of Upper Freehold Township, Monmouth Co., cooper; will of. Wife, Elizabeth. Bonds made with Robert Imlay for land testator bought of James Debough, to be paid. Executors—wife, and friends Robert Imlay and Samuel Parent. Witnesses—John Johnston, John Imlay, Robert Lawrence. Proved January 14, 1742. Lib. 4, p. 344.

1742, Jan. 1. Inventory of the estate, £58.9.0; made by Richard Stevens and Robert Lawrence.

1749, March 12. McNeal, Neal, of Gloucester Township and Co., shinglemaker. Int. Adm'r, Joseph Hedger. Bondsman—Richard Cheeseman. Both of said County. Witness—John Mickle. Lib. 7, p. 41.

1749, March 9. Inventory, £38.7.6; made by Richard Cheeseman, John Wild.

1735, June 8. McWilliams, William, of Salem Co. Int. Adm'r, William Mucdock. Bondsman—Abial Carle. Both of said County. Witnesses—John Hunt, Dan. Mestayer. Salem Wills, 509 Q.

1746, Sept. 19. Macdonel, William, of Somerset Co., yeoman; will of. Wife, Florrance. Sons—John, William, Daniel, and Richard. All real and personal estate to be sold, one-third to wife and remainder divided among the four sons. Executors—Bryen Lafferty and Daniel McEowne. Witnesses—James Andrew, Jean Gililan, Robt. Levisstone. "It is ordered by this will that the £50 York money for which Nath. Cooper is bound for me in New York shall be first paid out of my estate." Proved 13 Oct., 1746. Lib. D, p. 411.

1746, Oct. 3. Renunciation of Bryan Lefferty and Daniel McEowen of the executorship.

1746, Oct. 14. Bond of Florance, widow, as adm'x of the estate of her husband, William Macdonel. Fellow bondsmen—Robert Wilson, John McDaniel. Witnesses—Tinnit Wilson, Wm. McDaniel. Lib. D, p. 413.

1746, Oct. 3. Inventory of personal estate, £173.19.1; made by Daniel McEowen, James McKean.

1730, Oct. 10. Macelroy, Patrick, of Chesterfield, Burlington Co., labourer; nuncupative will of. Proved by the testimony of William Woodward and Abigail Eastland, who declare that he stated, if he died in America, that Jabez Taylor, one of the sons of Robert Taylor, should be his heir. Lib. 8, p. 106.

1730, Oct. 22. Inventory of the personal estate, £23.11; made by Anthony Woodward and Edm. Beakes.

1730, Dec. 19. Bond of Robert Taylor, yeoman, of Chesterfield, Burlington Co., as administrator on estate.

1748, March 15. Mackaway, Michael, of Gloucester Co., laborer. Int. Adm'r, Edward Willson, weaver. Bondsman—Joseph Dean. Both of said County. Witness—John Mickle. Lib. 6, p. 15.

1748, March 21. Inventory (£9.0.7) includes "The Chronicles of England," and debtors—Edward Wilson, Robert Greeg, John Sparks.

1732, Nov. 24. MackDonald, Robert, of Town and Co. of Burlington, merchant. Administration on estate granted to Thomas Shaw, gent. Thomas Hunlock and Isaac Pearson, gents., fellow bondsmen; all of Burlington.

1732, Nov. —. Thomas Shaw states that it is not known that the deceased hath any kindred or relations either in this Province or any other part of America. Lib. 3, p. 221.

1732, 4th day, 10th mo. (Dec.). Inventory of the personal estate, £266.6.11; made by Richd. Smith and Robt. Smith. Includes silver snuff box and silver watch, large Bible, and debts due by Esther Furness, Simon Nightingale, Thomas Palmer, Jude Clarkson, Francis Smith, Coll. Daniel Coxe, Thomas Shreeve, Samuel Bustill, Ann Pidgeon, Isaac Pearson, Peter Bard, Esq.

1734, April 6. Account, showing payments to nurses Lovett and Wrigth, Hugh Roxs, (going to Philada. to invite friends of deceased to his funeral), Sarah James, Simon Nightingale, Samuel Bustill, Samuel Sharp, Benjamin Wheat, Joseph Murray, Esq., Edw'd Walbank, Patrick Reynolds, Patrick Ghrame, James Hancock, Francis Smith, Peter Bard, Esq., Edw'd Price, Mr. Rowland Ellis, Richard Peckover, of London, watchmaker.

1733, May 16. Mackey, John, of Cape May Co. Int. Adm'r, Jeames Hathorn. Fellow bondsman—William Johnson. Both of Cape May. Witnesses—Humphrey Hughes, Samuwell Swaine, Jacob Spicer. Cape May Wills, 76 E.

1733, April 10. Inventory of personal estate (£58.13.3½), includes "linen whele and wolen whele." Appraisers—Samuwell Swaine, William Johnson.

1741, May 29. Account of "James Hathorne," administrator of the Estate of "John Mackie." Moneys paid to Jacob Spicer, John Flower, John Jones, Ezekiel Eldridge, Wm. McGowen, Robert Swaine, John Roberts, John Jones, Wm. Seagrave, Jas. Flood, Elias Taylor, Benjamin Richison Lemual Swaine, Corns. Schillinger, Joshua Shaw, Wm. Johnson, etc.

1742, Dec. 29. Magogin, Alexander, of Salem Co. Int. Adm'x, Mary Magogin (relict of). Bondsmen—James Cury, Thomas Stonebank. All of Salem. Lib. 4, p. 378.

1742, Nov. 13. Inventory (£68.19.6) includes 3 horses and horned cattle. Appraisers—James Curry, Thomas Stonebank.

1741, Oct. 28. Magwire (Maguire), Thomas, of Gloucester Co., husbandman. Int. Adm'r, James Ward. Bondsman—Benjamin Holmes, of Waterford in said County, yeoman. Lib. 4, p. 307.

1741-2, Jany. 19. Inventory (£14.18.7) includes debtors—Thomas Cole, Thomas Rain, Henry Moring, Joseph Ellis. Appraisers—Jonathan Axford, Isaac Smith.

1734, Jan. 6. Mains (Maynes), Samuel, of Salem Co., yeoman. Int. Adm'x, Anne Maynes, widow. Bondsmen—Erick Skeer and John Doe. All of Salem County. Witnesses—Henry Wallas, Thos. Eniley. Lib. 3, p. 437.

1734, Dec. 30. Inventory, £32.10.10; made by John Eaton, Henry Wallas.

1730, May 8. Mall, Roger, of Cohansey, Salem Co., yeoman; will of. Wife, Ellenor, executrix, and to have personal estate. Sons—George, 100 acres where he lives; Robert, 5 shillings; Benjamin, 60 acres on south side of my plantation; and my two younger sons, Joseph and Rodger, 55 acres each, where I now live, when they will be 21. Witnesses—Thomas Waithman, Zechariah Sawdell, Samuel Hedge. Proved 18 Jan., 1744. Lib. 5, p. 164.

1744, Dec. 28. Inventory, £71.19; made by Josiah Parvin, John Woolsey.

1749, Oct. 21. Mallally, Bryant, of Salem Co. Int. Adm'r, Job Smith. Bondsman—William Barker. Both of said County. Witnesses—James Smith, Michl. Gibbon. Lib. 7, p. 35.

1749-50, Jan. 4. Inventory (£74.15) includes "a taylor's goos, 2 shillings." Appraisers—Hance Penton, James Smith.

1709, Aug. 2. Mandeval, Hendrick, of Peqquanock, Essex Co.; will of. Wife, Elizabeth. Children—David, Antie Brouwer, Hendrick, Johannes, Yelles (under age). Wife sole executrix. Witnesses—Jan Mead, Dyrck Dey, Henry Brockholls. Proved Dec. 8, 1732. Lib. B, p. 346.

1738, July 28. Maning, John, of Piscataway, Middlesex Co., yeoman; will of. Children—Gershom, Sarah, Martha, Ephraim, Mary, all under age, Real and personal estate. Wife, Mary. Executors—friends Benjamin Martin and Peter Martin. Witnesses—Benja. Stelle, Isaac Manning, John Dennis. Proved Aug. 22, 1745. Lib. D, p. 320.

1747, April 2. Marlet, Gideon, of Somerset Co.; will of. Wife, Penelepe, executrix. Real and personal estate to be sold and proceeds divided equally among children—Abraham, Mary, Elizabeth, Gideon and Jeremiah. Executors—Reeve Runyon and John Vail, Junior. Witnesses—George Marlett, Thomas Jacobs, Jno. Stelle. Proved 22 April, 1747. Lib. E, p. 32.

1747, April 18. Inventory of personal estate (£81.20.6), includes gun, "sord," mason's tools. Debtors—Jethro Manning, John Tuneison, Nathl. E. Roft, Hendrick Lane, Elieb Vancourt, Thomas Johnston. Appraisers—Peter Williamson, John Pound, Junior.

1734, Jan. 24. Marmion, Samuel, of Burlington, merch't; will of. Grandchildren—Benoist, Peter, Samuel, John, William, Mary and Rebecca Bard. Brick dwelling house on High Street, Burlington, now occupied by Thomas Hendry. Daughter—Dinah Bard, sole executrix. Real and personal estate. Witnesses—Is. DeCow, Edmund Cowgill, Jr., Row. Ellis. Proved May 20, 1735. Lib. 4, p. 10.

1740, Oct. 11. Marriott (Merit), John, of Springfield, Burlington Co., husbandman. Samuel Merit declines administration on estate of his brother, who died by an extraordinary accident, and requests that Joseph Atkinson, principal creditor, be appointed. Witnesses—John Butcher, Jr., and Henry Fenimore.

1740, Oct. 25. Bond of Joseph Atkinson, of Springfield, yeoman, as administrator. Samuel Scattergood, of Burlington, merch't, fellow bondsman. Lib. 4, p. 257.

1740, Oct. 23. Inventory of the personal estate, £32.17.8; made by Jos. Owen and John Butcher, Jr.

1747, Dec. 9. Marselisen (Marselis), Harman, of Piscataway, Middlesex Co.; will of. Son, John, dwelling house on Green Brook purchased of Joseph Hull, at 21 years. Son, Peter, land joining land of John Vail, in the mountains. Executors—wife, Hannah, brother Peter

Marselis, and brother-in-law, Anthony Hutchins. Witnesses—Fredrich Vermeule, Iden Marselisen, John Morselis. Proved Jan. 21, 1747-8. Lib. E, p. 119.

1733-4, Jan. 31. Marsh, Benjamin, of Elizabeth Town, Essex Co., yeoman; will of. Eldest son, Benjamin, land called Raway, given me by my father, John Marsh. Other children mentioned but not named. Grist mill, which formerly belonged to my father-in-law, John Ewen, signed over to me by William Robinson. Executors—wife, Margaret, and brother Daniell Marsh. Witnesses—John Terrill, Job Pack, Mephibosheth Marsh. Proved March 25, 1734. Lib. B, p. 513.

1734, March 26. Inventory of estate (£106.12.03), includes mortgage of land and grist mill that formerly belonged to John Ewen, deceased. Made by William Porter, John Terrill.

1745, Sept. 4. Marsh, Ephraim, of the Borough of Elizabeth, Essex Co.; will of. Wife, Anna. Children—Ephraim, Jean, Keziah and Anna, all under age. Land joining lands of Samuel Willis; lands given me by my "fathers," John Marsh and John Scuder. Executors—friends Nathaniel Hubbell and Thomas Scudder. Witnesses—William Jones, Henry Clarke, John Davis. Proved May 9, 1750. Lib. E, p. 398.

1739, Dec. 27. Marsh, John, of Elizabeth Town, Essex Co., yeoman; will of. Children—Joseph, Joshua, Jonathan, Ephraim, Daniel, Mephibosheth, David, Elizabeth (wife of Job Pack), Hannah (wife of William Miller), and Sarah (wife of Isaac Noe). Land of brother, Joseph, deceased. Grandchildren—John, William, Mary (wife of Joseph Conger), children of son John, deceased; Benjamin, Enoch, David, Sarah and Margaret Marsh, children of son Benjamin, deceased, minors. Wife, Elizabeth. Lands bought of Benjamin Pack and Philip Doldridge. Executors—sons Daniel, Mephibosheth and David. Witnesses—Peter Tranbles, David Watkins, Thomas Chapman. Proved Dec. 3, 1744. Lib. D, p. 215.

1744, Dec. 21-22. Inventory of personal estate (£529.16.02½), includes notes of Ephraim Marsh, Robert Mors, Isaac Noe, Jeffery Gons, Jonathan Marsh, Steven Harding, Margaret Marsh, Richard Wind, Caleb Hail, Henry Backer. Made by John King and William Oliver.

1748, Dec. 23. Marsh, John, of Newark, Essex Co. Administration on estate granted to Uzal Ogden, Esq., principal creditor. Ephraim Wheeler, yeoman, fellow bondsman. Lib. E, p. 231.

1745, Dec. 17. Marsh, Joseph, of the Borough of Elizabeth, Essex Co., carpenter; will of. Children—Samuel, Joseph, Elizabeth, John, Henry, David and Hannah. Real and personal estate. Executors—wife, Elizabeth, and friend Nathaniel Hubbell. Witnesses—Jonathan Marsh, Ephraim Marsh, Samuel Yamans. Proved Nov. 7, 1746. Lib. D, p. 428.

1746, Dec. 4. Inventory of personal estate, £234.18.10; made by Ephraim Marsh and Robert Meeker. Witnesses—Elizabeth Marsh, John Marsh, Nath'll Hubbell.

1746-7, Jan. 12. Marsh, Joseph, of Perth Amboy, Middlesex Co., shipwright; will of. Children—Sarah, Frances, Mordica, Joseph, all under age. Mills at Raway I have in partnership with Samuel Marsh and John Trembley; land in Perth Amboy joining land of Andrew

Robertson; land joining land of Reuben Peters. Executors—wife, Susannah, Elias Marsh, Thomas Gach and Joseph, son of John Shotwell of Raway. Witnesses—George Badgley, Sam'll Borrowe, Margaret Hews, Anne Moor. Proved March 26, 1747. Susanna Marsh a Quaker, qualified as executrix. Lib. E, p. 5.

1744, Sept. 20. Marsh, Joshua, of the Borough of Elizabeth, yeoman; will of. Wife, Susanna. Children—Joshua, Abraham (under age), Susanna Davis, Elizabeth Meeker, and Sarah (wife of John Tooker). Grandson, Joshua Tucker. Enoch, second son of brother Benjamin, deceased, when of age. Land given me by my father, June 3, 1726. Land bought of Philip Doldridge, May 8, 1731. A negro wench and her child. Executors—son, Joshua, and son-in-law John Tucker. Witnesses—John Denman, Benjamin Williams, John Cleverly. Proved Oct. 20, 1744. Lib. D, p. 185.

1744, Oct. 25. Inventory of personal estate (£369.12.01), includes bonds of Joseph Morris, Henry Ford, Abraham Shotwell, Nathaniel Baker, Joshua Morss, William Woodruff, Benjamin Hill, James Carter of New Yorke, Moses Ogden, Jacob Harte, William Miller, Jonathan Marsh. Made by Abraham Clarke, George Ross.

1746, Jan. 6. Accompt of Joshua Marsh, executor. Payments to Ephraim Terrill, Jonathan Hampton, Ickobad Burnet, Jacob Dehart, Wm. Peirson, Peter Evertse, Jona. Thompson, Robert Woodruff, Isaac Schelenex, John Crage, William Ogden, Joseph Shotwell, Sam'll Woodruff, Alexander Black, Thomas Edgar, Moses Crane, John Emot, Edward Thomas, Joseph Hinds, Richard Win, Andrew Andrewson, Benja. Marsh, John Parker, Mary Black, Abra. Marsh, David Meeker, John Davis, Joshua Marsh, Nathaniel Crane, John Cleverly, John Ross (for coffin), Thos. Clark, Wm. Springer, Jonathan Woodruff, Sam'll Clark, Justice Rolph, George Gostolowe.

1747-8, 14th day of 12th mo. (Feb.). Marsh, Margaret, of the Borough of Elizabeth, Essex Co., widow; will of. Children—Benjamin, Enoch, David, Margaret, Sarah Williams, and Mary Clark. Mortgage on plantation on which Rubin Clark lives. Real and personal estate. Executors—son, Benjamin, and friend Joseph Wood. Witnesses—Jeames Clark, Sarah Parker, Joseph Shotwell. Proved Jan. 20, 1748. Lib. E, p. 242.

1735, May 5. Marshall, Mary, of Alloways Creek, alias Monmouth River, Salem County, spinster; will of. Moveables to my mother, Sarah Marshall. Nephews—Isaac, Thomas and Richard Moss (sister Rebechah's children), and Elizabeth Blancher. Residue to three lads before mentioned. Executor—friend and brother, Abraham Moss. Witnesses—Henry Stubbins, Elizabeth Blancher, Elizabeth Barber. Sworn and affirmed, 14 May, 1735. Lib. 4, p. 14.

1735, May 12. Inventory, £315.19.8; made by Abel Nicholson, Jos. Clowes.

1749, Oct. 7. Marshall, William, of Salem Co. Int. Adm'x, Elizabeth Marshall. Bondsman—John Kampstar, of said County. Lib. 6, p. 278.

1748-9, Feb. 7. Inventory, £51.2; made by Thomas Haynes, John Kampstar.

1749, Dec. 21. Account. Monies paid to Mary Cullyer, John Nicholson, Henry Hale, James Holliday, Robert Dickey, Thomas Henley, Daniel

Moore, Mary Siddens, Wm. Siddens, John Thompson, Nicholas Gibbons, Danl. Mestayer.

1733, April 24. Martin (Martins), Isaac, of Piscataway, Middlesex Co.; will of. Sons—Abraham, Isaac and Jacob, a minor. Real and personal estate. Wife, Hannah, sole executrix. Witnesses—Benja. Stelle, Sam'll Martin, Jonathan Martin, Humphrey Foster. Proved July 19, 1733. Lib. B, p. 446.

1733, July 5. Inventory of personal estate £39.8.6; made by ———.

1749, Sept. 18. Martin (Martain), James, of South Amboy, Middlesex Co., yeoman. Inventory of personal estate, £70.4.3; made by John Burwell, David Edgar.

1750, Aug. 30. Bond of Susannah Martin, his widow, as administratrix. Benja'n. Rolph, fellow bondsman. Lib. E, p. 452.

1750-1, Feb. 3. Letter from P. Kearny, Esq., states Mrs. Martin is deceased and has infant son about two years.

1750-1, Feb. 5. Bond of Benjamin Rolph, of Woodbridge, cooper, as administrator on the estate which remains unadministered by Susannah Martin, she being deceased. Richard FitzRandolph, fellow bondsman. Lib. E, p. 480.

1741, Feb. 4. Martin, John, of Salem Co. Int. Adm'x, widow, Sarah Martin, of Greenwich. Bondsmen—William Watson, of Greenwich, William Tuft, of Salem. All of said County. Witnesses—Danl. Mestayer, Chas. O. Neill. Lib. 4, p. 376.

1743-4, March 8. Martin, Mulford, of Woodbridge, Middlesex Co., yeoman. Int. Bond of Peter Martin, the father, and Rachel Martin, widow, as administrators on the estate. Gershom Martin, fellow bondsman. Lib. D, p. 123.

1733, May 20. Martin, Samuel, of Woodbridge, Middlesex Co., yeoman; will of. Executors—wife, Sarah, and sons Thomas and Samuel, they being sole legatees. Real and personal estate. Bond from Wright Skinner. Witnesses—Anne Martin, David Ayers, Jno. Sarjant. Proved June 12, 1740. John Sarjant, one of the witnesses, deceased at time of proving.

1740, June 12. Sarah and Samuel Martin qualified as executors, the other executor being deceased. Lib. C, p. 340.

1733, Feb. 14. Martingrace, John, of Gloucester Co., laborer. Adm'r, Joseph Hedger, of said County, yeoman. Bondsman—William Barton, of Burlington Co., yeoman. Gloucester Wills, 178 H.

1733-4, Feb. 11. Inventory (£19.1.22) includes debtor, Benjamin Cheesman. Appraisers—Andrew Ware, Thomas Cheesman.

1735, Sept. 21. Marvel, Joseph, of Salem Co., yeoman. Int. Adm'r, Lewis Marvel. Bondsman—Robert Vance, yeoman. Both of said County. Witnesses—Bridget Vance, Danl. Mestayer. Lib. 4, p. 41.

1739, Jan. 5. Maskell, Constant, of Cohansey, Salem Co., yeoman. Int. Adm'x, Rachel Maskell, widow. Bondsman—Thos. Waithman. Witnesses—Thomas Ewing, Danl. Mestayer. Lib. 4, p. 198.

1739, Dec. 3. Inventory (£256.2.10) includes books (£5.11.6), horses, cows, sheep, and part of a shallop (£9.10). Appraisers—Thomas Ewing, Benoni Dare.

1732, Oct. 26. Maskell, Thomas, of Cohansey, Salem Co.; will of. Wife, Mary, sole executrix during widowhood and to have the house we live in (15 acres) South of the swamp that parts my land from Thomas Wethman's; also my clear land on the N. side. Daughter, Mary Yeuens, 100 acres. Grandson, Maskell Yeuens. Son, Constant Maskell, and Thomas Yeuens and Thomas Wethman to have equally my marsh by the creek. Son, Constant Maskell, to have remainder of my land on the East, that is to say, on both sides of the road. Witnesses—Charles Dennes, Richard Mills, Samuel Dennis. Affirmed 30 Jan., 1732. Lib. 3, p. 254.

1732, Jany. 30. Inventory (£137.18) includes riding horse, cattle, corn, etc. Appraisers—Sam. Davis, Charles Dennes.

1734, 8 mo. (Oct.), 30 da. Mason, Aaron, of Manington, Salem Co., farmer; will of. Wife, Abigail. Sons—Thomas (eldest) and Joseph (second son) to have equally plantation I live on when 21. Youngest son, Samuel, the land my father, Thomas Mason, purchased of Samuel Hedge on Fenwick's branch, joining John Kid's. Executors—wife, and son Thomas, "allowing my wife to have the use of the plantation until the said Thomas and Joseph Mason will be of age." Witnesses—William Smith, Joseph Carroll, Wm. Heckel. Sworn and affirmed 6 Nov., 1734. Lib. 3, p. 447.

1734, Nov. 6. Letters testamentary granted to Abigail Mason executrix, the other executor, Thomas Mason, being under age.

1734, 9 mo. (Nov.), 6 da. Inventory (£214.10.6) includes clock and case (£10), and horned cattle (£53.10). Appraisers—William Hunt, Clm. Hall.

1749, May 15. Mason, John, of Salem Co. Int. Adm'r, William Murdock. Bondsmen—Benjamin Cripps, Saml. Tyler. All of said County. Witness—Josiah Kay. Lib. 6, p. 279.

1749, April 26. Inventory (£615.7.5) includes riding horse, carpenter's tools, part of two yoke of oxen, "some other things at the saw mill at Morris River," etc. Appraisers—Wm. Siddons, Thos. Rice.

1746, Sept. 22. Mason, Mary. Rachel Draper, wife of James Draper of City of Philada., and daughter of Jonathan Wilson and Mary, his wife, who is late deceased intestate, does hereby request that "my cousin, Samuel Burge, may have administration of the estate of my mother, Mary Mason." Witness—Frederick Holsten.

1746, Sept. 22. Bond of administration of Samuel Burge, gent., of City of Philada., on estate. Robert Montgomerie, merchant, of Monmouth Co., fellow bondsman. Lib. 5, p. 431.

1744, Dec. 16. Mason, Samuel, of Elsenborough, Salem Co., yeoman; will of. Wife, Grace. Children—Sarah and Elizabeth. Mentions brother John and his children—Anne and Mary. Executors—daughters Sarah and Elizabeth. Witnesses—John Jones, John Darkin and Daniel Mestayer. Proved Feb. 11, 1744. Lib. 5, p. 222.

1738, April 12. Mason, Thomas, now in Philadelphia, but of the County of Salem, merchant; will of. Wife, Sarah, to have the profits of the real estate until my son John will be 21; also a lot of ground in Salem where I dwelt, parallel with the Sherron and Turner lots; also 6 acres to extend from Joseph Goodin's lot to Margaret Lane's. Son John, the residue of the estate, real and personal. In case of his death, unmarried, without issue, same shall go to my said wife forever, she paying £100 to my cousins, Hannah and Sarah Darkin. In case my wife dies before my son, his moiety of my personal estate shall be given to my brother, John Mason, he paying the said £100; in case of his death, my cousins, Ann and Mary Mason, shall have the same. At the death of my wife, if my son or his issue are not living, the house in Salem I give to Ann, the daughter of my brother John. The residue of my real estate, in case of the death of my said son and wife, I give to Mary Mason, Hannah and Sarah Darkin. Executors—wife, brother-in-law Isaac Sharp, and friend Joseph Darkin. Witnesses—Richard Smith, Thos. Hill, Robert Moulder, Robt. Hartshorne. Affirmed 6 May, 1740. Letters testamentary granted to Sarah Mason and Isaac Sharp. Lib. 4, p. 235.

1740, Sept. 8. Inventory (£1216.0.2) includes servant boy (£13), money in Ireland in Anthony Sharp's hands (£220), bills and bonds of Walter James, Richard Servis, Thomas Hill, William Tuft, Daniel Smith, John Foster, Daniel Mayture, Redmond Janings. Appraisers—Richd. Smith, Clem. Hall.

1747, March 11. Mathews, Daniel, of Newark, Essex Co. Bond of Rebekah Mathews, the widow, as administratrix on estate of her husband. Daniel Pierson, Esq., fellow bondsman. Lib. E, p. 196.

1736, Jan. 25. Mathie, John, of Perth Amboy, Middlesex Co.; will of. Grandchildren—Mathues and Margaret Sharp, both under age. Real and personal estate. Executors—daughters Margaret Hughs, Anne Allen, and friends Gabriel Stelle, of Perth Amboy, alderman, and John Hutton of Fresh Ponds, yeoman. Witnesses—John Moore, Alex'r Mackdowell, Margaret Moore. Proved April 11, 1737. Lib. C, p. 157.

1732-3, Feb. 19. Matlack, Ann, of Chester, Burlington Co., widow and executrix of William Matlack. John Matlack renounces all right to administer on estate of Ann Matlack, and also on unadministered estate of William Matlack unto his brother, Timothy Matlack. Lib. 3, p. 244.

1732-3, 19th day, 12th mo. (Feb.). Inventory of the personal estate, £119.8.5.; made by John Roberts and Thomas Middleton.

1745, ———, —. Account by Timothy Matlack, who has paid for "schooling and board" for Mary, Rachel, Rebecca and Jeremiah Matlack.

1739, Nov. 29. Matlack, George, of Chester, Burlington Co., yeoman; will of. Sons—Josiah and George. To the latter the saddle that belonged to his deceased brother, William. Children—Benjamin, Joshua, John, Thomas, Jonathan, Samuel, Martha and Elizabeth, each £5 at age. Wife's dau., Elizabeth Hancock, £5 at age. Real and personal estate. Executor—brother, John Matlack. Witnesses—Thomas Parker, Sam'l Atkinson, Michael Tolman. Proved Dec. 12, 1739. Lib. 4, p. 200.

1739, Dec. 11. Inventory of the personal estate, £240.9.8; made by Thomas Lippincott and Joseph Stoakes.

1748, Nov. 11. Matlock, Mary, dau. of William Matlock, of Burlington Co. Bond of guardianship of John Bispham. Thomas Bishop, yeoman, fellow bondsman. All of Burlington Co. Lib. 6, p. 351.

1747, Nov. 3. Matson, Mathias, yeoman, of Greenwich Township, Gloucester Co.; will of. Brothers—Andrew and Peter Matson, to have equally the money from sale of plantation where I live, on the River Delaware, below Rackoon Creek, and all my other estate. Executors —my kinsmen and friends, Mathias Matson and John Jones, both of the township aforesaid. Witnesses—Christian Steedom, Charles Hopman. Proved 22 Dec., 1747. Lib. 5, p. 499.

1747, Dec. 5. Renunciation of Mathias Mattson as one of the Executors.

1747, Dec. 4. Inventory, £8.2.4; made by Charles Hopman, Erick Derickson.

1748, ——, —. Account. Paid to John Morton, Evan Morgan, Robert Hartshorn, Thomas Williams, John Vanneyman, Charles Hopman, Nicholas Crone, Thomas Wilkins, Mary Lampland, Thomas Clayton, Morris Coner, Thomas Wilkins, Esqr., John Jones, Gunnar Cox, Swan Boon, Mathew Gill, Andrew Mattson, Henry Helvis, Timothy Rayn, John Pennel, Peter Dalbo, Lawrence Strong.

1750, Oct. 20. Matson, Mathias, of Greenwich Township, Gloucester Co., yeoman; will of. Wife, Judith. Sons—Peter (had his share of the estate); Mathias, to have the remaining part of my home plantation; William, 141 acres, formerly belonging to John Swanson, also 96 acres I bought of John Alford. Daughters—Mary, Lydiah and Cattern. Executors—sons, Mathias and William Matson. Witnesses —Jacob Lippincott, Caleb Lippincott, Abraham Lord. Sworn and affirmed, 13 Nov., 1750. Lib. 7, p. 20.

1750, Nov. 7. Inventory (£335) includes cattle, horses, sheep, corn and hay. Appraisers—Jacob Lippincott, Benjamin Cheesman.

1745, August 26. Mattison, Joseph, of Amwell Township, Hunterdon Co.; will of. Wife, Ann. Eldest son, Aaron. Wife to have use of estate for nineteen years, to bring up testator's children, viz., Aaron, John, Jacob and Jeames. Executors—wife, Ann, and brother Jacob Mattison. Witnesses—Samuel Fleming, Joseph Hegeman and William Bishop. Proved October 15, 1745. Lib. 5, p. 194.

1745, Oct. 9. Inventory of the estate (£164.5.11) includes gun, sword and belt, Bible, and servant girl's time (sold for £6.15). Made by Thomas Atkinson and Jacob Gray.

1747, Nov. 18. Account. Mentions Johanas Busenbaruch, Joseph Bast, Philip Ringo, Samuel Fleming, William Anderson, Frances Quick, Paul Hill, Paul Flock, John Mullen, Aaron Mattison, Sr., Benjamin Stout, William Force, Garret Williamson, John Conaway, Peter Fisher, Urban Kerkuff, Adrian Aten, Daniel Griggs, Abraham Schuyler, John Henderson, William Bishop, Mahlon Kirkbride, Joseph Forman.

1746, Dec. 11. Mattson, Anne (Anneky), of Deptford Township, Gloucester Co., widow. Int. Adm'r, Peter Rambo, yeoman. Bondsman—Joseph Tatem, cordwainer, of said township. Witness—Isaac Hinchman. Lib. 5, p. 459.

1746, Dec. 20. Inventory at Greenwich, Gloucester Co., £15.7.3; made by Jno. Smith, Jun., James Hamlington.

1732, Nov. 24. Maxbur, Hannah, of New Hanover, Burlington Co. Inventory of the personal estate, £25.16.3; made by Thomas Wright and Sam'l Emley. Includes debts due from Tho. Woodward, Benj. Kirby, Wm. Wilson, Rich'd Humphary, George Ferrar, Sam'l Wright, Rich'd Harrison, Abraham Brown, Peter Harrison, John Bullock, William Kirby, Isaac Forman, Nick Hill, Wm. Chapman, John Rumford,

Nahamiah Cogill, Tho. Wright, Sam'l Emley, Wm. Ketner, George Harrison, Wm. Cook, Ann Saxton, Wm. Rutter, Thomas Plat.
Burlington Wills, 2313-15 C.

1709, Nov. 1. Mead, John, of Paquaneck, Essex Co.; will of. Children—Peter, John, Jacob, Jellies, Chisstena and Else, all under age. Real estate at Paquaneck and Pomton. Executrix—wife, Margret. Witnesses—George Reyese, Henry Brockholls, Hendrick Mendfyle. Proved April 27, 1745. Lib. D, p. 276.

1745, June 3. Inventory of personal estate, £48.0.1; made by Peter Post and Jacob Titsort. Witnesses—George Reyerse, Jun., Gerrit Jacobus.

1747, June 22. Mead, Peter, of Pauquaneck, Bergen Co., yeoman; will of. Wife, Jane, whole estate during widowhood. Son, John, after his mother's decease, ½ of my real estate in Paquaneck and in Hanover, Morris Co.; also the sum of £10, or a silver cup or beeker of that value, in consideration of which he or his heirs are to pay his sisters, Martha (wife of Hendrick Brown), Margerett, Sarah and Mary, £10 each. The other half of the real estate in Bergen and Morris counties to the son-in-law, Hendrick Brown. Executors—wife, and trusty friends and brethren, Johannis Mead and Arien Jacobus. Signed "Pyeter Mead." Witnesses—Hendrick Spier, Engeltye Cadmis, Daniel Taylor. Proved 9 Nov., 1747. Jane (Janniete) Mead and Arien Jacobus qualify as executors. Lib. E, p. 437.

1749, Dec. 26. Renunciation of John Mead as executor. Witnesses—Adriaen Vanhouten, John Mead, Jun'r.

1741, Nov. 18. Meaker (Meeker), William, of Newark, Essex Co., yeoman; will of. Wife, Hannah. Daughter-in-law, Abigail, widow of son David, deceased. Grandchildren—David and Hannah Meaker, both under age, children of Abigail and son David, deceased. Real and personal estate. Executors—sons Jonathan and Isaac Meeker. Witnesses—Benjamin Lyon, Benjamin Lyon, Jun'r, Charles Hole. Proved March 5, 1744. Lib. D, p. 241.

1744-5, March 4. Inventory of personal estate, (£252.07.08), includes negro wench and her child (£38). Made by Benjamin Lyon, Joseph Lyon.

1741, July 14. Meally, Hugh, of Salem Co., yeoman. Int. Adm'x, Jane Hart. Bondsman—James Rodgers. Witness—William Hall.
Lib. 5, p. 422.

1739, Sept. 17. Mecum, William, of Pennsneck, Salem Co., gent., guardian of Mary Scoggin (14 years old). Bondsman—Thomas Miles. All of same place. Witnesses—Aaron Wood, Peter Peterson.
Salem Wills, 666 Q.

1747-8, Jan. 3. Mecum, William, of Penns Neck, Salem Co., yeoman; will of. Wife. Son, William (minor), to have my silver hilted sword, cutlass, silver headed cane, buckles, gun and Bible; also the real estate at 21, he paying £20 to my only daughter, Margaret Mecum, when she will be 21. In case of his death without issue, same shall belong to my said daughter. Mentions Peter Enlow, his apprentice. If son and daughter die without issue, and in possession of my real estate, the interest of the same forever to go to the inhabitants of the lower part of Penn's Neck for the use of a free school for the benefit of poor children and orphans. Executors—only son, William Mecum, and my trusty friend, John Marshall. Witnesses—Jane Scott, Henry GillJohnson, Peter Enlows. Proved 5 March, 1747. Lib. 5, p. 401.

1748-9, Feb. 24. Inventory (£366.4.7) includes armour, bacon and lumber, horses, Bible (£1.10), wheat, sheep, oxen and steers, cattle, swine, clock. Appraisers—Jeremiah Barker, Sinick Sinickson.

1749, May 23. Account of Wm. Mecum. To moneys paid Hannah Siddins, Ebenezer Dun, Peter Peterson, Henry Giljohnson, Edward Test, Jeremiah Baker, Sinnick Sinnickson, Robt. Thompson, Henry Gillas, William Tuft, Edward Shepard, Matthias Stark, Margret Stark, Timothy Connor, Nicholas Philpot, Hue Blackwood, Thomas Emley, Oliver Webb (for a quarter's schooling for Margret Mecum, Jun'r), and Petters Petterson. Certain bad debts due from John Moore, Geo. Flings and Arthur Tools.

1737, Sept. 5. Medcalf, Hanna, of Gloucester Town and County; will of. Children—Mathew, Rachel, William and Susanna. £50, etc., to Abraham Albirson for services. Executors—brother, William Hutson (Hudson), Joseph Cooper. Witnesses—Tobias Holloway, Job Ingraham, Mary Hollingum. Affirmed 2 Nov., 1737. Letters granted to Joseph Cooper. Gloucester Wills, 220 H.

1737, Oct. 3. Inventory (£188.1.2) includes 38 ounces of silver (£15.4.0), a piece of gold and gold buttons (£3.11.6). Appraisers—Ja. Hinchman, Tobias Holloway.

1732, 11 mo. (Jan.), 6 da. Medcalf, Jacob, of Newton, Gloucester Co., yeoman; will of. Wife, Hannah. Son, Mathew, to have all my land and meadows (200 acres) on Little Timber Creek adjoining William Harrison. If said son dies under age without issue, the premises to go to my sons William and Jacob (minors); and in case of their death childless, wife Hannah shall have the same. Legacies to daughter, Rachel, and cousin, Hester Medcalf. Executors—brother-in-law, William Cooper, Joseph Cooper and William Hudson, Junior. Witnesses—Silvanus Smout, Willm. Crosthwaite (of Philadelphia), James Armstrong.

1732, Jan. 6. Codicil. On consideration that children are small, the interest from the sale of house and lands at Gloucester may be insufficient for their support; therefore executors shall sell said 200 acres and the interest therefrom shall be for their maintenance during Mathew's minority, but, when of age, he shall have the principal. (Same witnesses).

1735, Jany. 21. Codicil. Since the above will was made my son Jacob died, and two daughters, Susanna and Hannah, have been born to me. Witnesses—William Hudson, William Moode, Abraham Bickley, Richard Buckele. Sworn and affirmed 11 Aug., 1736. Lib. 4, p. 69.

1736, Aug. 11. Letters Testamentary were granted William Hudson and Joseph Cooper (Quakers).

1736, 4 mo. (June), 25. Inventory (£650.13.5) includes debt of Walter Griffes, boats with sails and oars (£15.0.0), gun and silver tankard, servant-maid's time (£6), books (£2.10.0), bond of Robt. Stevens and Tobias Hollwell. Appraisers—John Mickle, Ja. Hinchman.

1744, Nov. 22. Meeker, Benjamin, of Elizabeth Town, Essex Co., blacksmith; will of. Children—Benjamin, Samuel, Phebe (wife of Nehemiah Ludlum), Esther (wife of Stephen Hindes), and Sarah (wife of Isaac Woodruffe). Real and personal estate. Executors—wife, Phebe, and son-in-law Stephen Hindes, and son Samuel. Witnesses—John Clarke, David Meeker, Boynton Ramsden. Proved March 11, 1750. Lib. E, p. 536.

1730, Feb. 18. Meeker, John, of Elizabeth Town, Essex Co., yeoman;

will of. Granddaughters—Sarah Griffing, Rebekah Whitehead, Hannah Talmadge. Daughter, Eunice Meeker. Sons—Robert, James and David. Grandson, John Meeker, only son of son John, deceased. Lands joining lands of Mr. John Thompson, Thomas Squire, James Hindes. Executors—sons Robert and James, and brother-in-law, Robert Ogden, Esq. Witnesses—John Hinds, Leonard Miles, Stephen Hindes. Proved March 22, 1730.

1731, April 21. Robert Ogden did depose that he did ask the testator who should enjoy the lands of David Meeker till he came of age, and he said his son James should enjoy David's part. Lib. B, p. 200.

1730-1, March 17. Inventory of personal estate, £108.05; made by Benja. Bond and John Thompson.

1730, Dec. 24. Meeker, John, Jun'r, of Elizabeth Town, Essex Co., cooper; will of. Children—Joanna, Rebekah and Mary, all under age. Expected child. Real and personal estate. Executors—wife, Joanna, and relatives, Robert Ogden, Esq., and James Meeker. Witnesses—Samuel Whitehead, Joseph Chandler, Stephen Hindes. Proved March 22, 1730-1. Lib. B, p. 198.

1731, Feb. 28. Meeker, Joseph, of Elizabeth Town, Essex Co., mariner. Bond of Phebe Meeker, the widow, as administratrix. Stephen Meeker, fellow bondsman. Lib. B, p. 242.

1732, July 14. Inventory of personal estate, (£1.249.08.05½) includes a sloop called "the Elizabeth and Patience," note from Mr. Braddit, bills of Miles Williams, James Banks, Isaac King, John Vanderpool, George Jewel, John Denis, John Hendricks, Joseph Jackson, John Wilkins, Hannah Stout, David Powers, Sam'll Wheelens, Nath'll Whitehead, Dan'll Lane, John Lurtin, George Johnston, Thomas Curry, Nicholas Arent, John Kite, Joseph Herriman, Lowerance Elberson, Nath'll Anderson, Adam Blackman, Andrew Crag, Jonathan Oliver, James Riggs, John Fraze, John Bell, Nath'll Cogswell, John Matthews, Andrew Hay, John Deers, Will'm Hudson, Larns Hartman, Joseph Lee, John Wilkins, Hendrick Vanpelt. Made by Nathaniell Johnson and Henry Lyon.

1737-8, March 1. Accompt of administratrix, showing payments to Nathaniel Hazard, Searle and Pintard, Thomas Allinger, Joseph Johnson, Jno. Rochead, Thomas Woodruff, Benjamin Canfield, Timothy Bruen, Jacob Dehart, Charles Townley, David Gomezas, Wm. Bradford, Mathias Miller, David Ross, William Woley, John Dewitt, Mrs. Mulford, Henry Pierson, Mr. Aubeyneau, John Brown, Samuel Potter, Mordecai Gomez, Thomas Day, Jno. Emott, Catharine Richardson, Thomas Noble, Thomas Hureanse, William King, James Darcy, John Earle, Joseph Tuttle, George Webb, John Williamson, James Alexander, David Ogden, John Wilkinson, Thomas Peet, John Ogden Jun'r, Deacon Woodruff, Mr. King, Josiah Gilbert, John Dagworthy, Dan'll Lane, George Johnson, Jonathan Pines, Joseph Lee, and each of the four children of the deceased.

1749, Oct. 2. Meeker, Stephen, of the Borough of Elizabeth, Essex Co.; will of. Children—Stephen, Obediah, Elizabeth, Sarah, Mary, Phebe and Rhode Meeker, all under age. Expected child. Real and personal estate. Executors—wife, Mary, and friend Joseph Lyon, Junior. Witnesses—Wm. Turner, John Johnson, David Ogden. Proved Nov. 13, 1749. Lib. E, p. 342.

Meeker (see Meaker).

1733, April 23. Megie, John, of Elizabeth Town, Essex Co., blacksmith; will of. Son, John, lands bought of Henry Tuttle and Samuell Littel. Son, Joseph, land joining land of Jeremiah Crane. Daughters—Anna (wife of John Crane), Jannet (wife of Jonathan Woodruffe), and Abigail (wife of Samuel Woodruffe). Executors—wife, Anna, and sons John and Joseph. Witnesses—Jeremiah Creain, John Chandler, William Clark. Proved March 9, 1735-6. Lib. C, p. 112.

1741, Dec. 14. Megie, John, of Elizabeth Town, Essex Co., blacksmith; will of. Wife, Martha. Sisters—Anna, Jennet, Abigail Megie and Mary Hinds. Mary Hinds, daughter of sister Mary. Kinsman, John Megie, son of brother Joseph, at 21 years. Real and personal estate. Executors—friends Stephen Crane, Elijah Davis, and brother, Joseph Megie. Witnesses—Charles Hole, Robert Meeker, Joseph Littell. Proved Jan. 22, 1741-2. Lib. C, p. 470.

1741, Dec. 14. Martha Megie, the wife, certifies that she is satisfied with her bequest.

1748, Dec. 8. Meldrum, Robert, of Amwell, Hunterdon Co.; will of. Wife, Anne. Son, John (minor), house and land. Daughter, Marget. Witnesses—Alexander Thomson, Robert Lee and George Meldrum. Proved December 19, 1748. Lib. 6, p. 81.

1749, April 15. Inventory of estate, £32.11.2; made by Alexander Thomson and Joseph Bost.

1735, Aug. 9. Mercereau, John, of Woodbridge, Middlesex Co. Int. Bond of Elizabeth and Joshua Mercereau and Andrew Craige, as administrators of the estate. Paul Mercereau and John Craig, fellow bondsmen. Lib. C, p. 44.

1735, Aug. 15. Inventory of personal estate, includes bonds from Benjamin Moore, Jacob Thorn, Jos. Rolph, Thom. Atkinson, Jno. Doe, Benjamin Rolph, Lues Deboy, Samuel Crowel, John Noe, Jun'r; also large Bible, 43 lasts, shoemaker's tools and 4 sides of leather. Made by Joseph FitzRandolph and Benjamin Coddington.

1749, Feb. 12. Merchant, Paul, of Mansfield, Burlington Co. Int. Administration on estate granted to Henry Delatush, of Mansfield, yeoman. Isaac Gibbs, of Mansfield, and Patrick McCowen, of City of Burlington, yeomen, fellow bondsmen. Lib. 7, p. 91.

1749-50, Feb. 23. Inventory of the personal estate, £33.6.1½; made by George Taylor and Benjamin Shreve.

1732, May 20. Merick, Roger, of Springfield, Burlington Co., yeoman; will of. Sons, John and Thomas, now in Bracknockshire, Wales. Real and personal estate. Executors—wife, Mary, and Thomas Potts. Witnesses—Peter Woolf, James Freeman, Titan Leeds. Proved May 2, 1733. Lib. 3, p. 299.

1733, April 30. Inventory of the personal estate, £114.7.6; made by Roger Fort and Job Ridgway. Includes debt due from Thomas Kimble.

1740, Oct. 11. Merit, John, of Springfield, Burlington Co., husbandman. Int. Administration on estate declined by the brother, Samuel Merit, in favor of Joseph Atkinson, chief creditor.

1740, Oct. 23. Inventory, £32.17.8; made by Joshua Owen and John Butcher, Jr.

1740, Oct. 25. Bond of Joseph Atkinson, of Springfield, Burlington co., yeoman, as administrator, with Samuel Scattergood, of Burlington, merchant, as fellow bondsman. Burlington Wills, 3251-6 C.

1748, Aug. 25. Merlatt, Thomas, of Somerset Co.; will of. Wife, Nelly, executrix, and to have the house and lot in Piscataway near the Bound Brook. Legacies to sons Abraham, John, Thomas and Mark. If Thomas or Mark die in non age, survivor shall have his portion, but if both die their portions shall be divided among their three sisters (not named), or their heirs. Executor—John Pound, Junior. Witnesses—Isaac Smalley, Zachariah Bonham. Proved 18 Jan., 1748-9. Lib. E, p. 241.

1748-9, Jan. 12. Filed 1752. Inventory of personal estate, £203.13.2; made by John Vail, Joseph Hall.

[Not dated]. Account of said estate, mentions Peter Kemble, Jonathan Dunham, Isaac Hoofe, Thos. Pound, Jno. VanBuren, David Lang, Zachariah Bonham, Micaiah Dunn, John Pound, Jun., Teunis Middah, Elijah Pound.

1740, Aug. 19. Merrill, William, of Hunterdon Co. Int. Pennelie Merrill, having been advised by her brother, Benjamin Stout, that "Mr. ffenix, Leyal atturney att Law Liveing at amboy," desired her to take an inventory of the estate of Will: Merrill, deceased, declined to do so and relinquished her right to administer on the estate. Dated at Hopewell, August 19, 1740. Lib. C, p. 395.

1740, Nov. 4. Bond of Jennet Parker, of the City of Perth Amboy, widow, as administratrix of the estate. Fenwick Lyell, of same place, Esquire, surety.

1750, June 25. Merry (Merrey), Ebenezer, of Woodbridge, Middlesex Co., yeoman; will of. Children—Joseph, Job, Annah, Phebe, all under age. Executors—Job Tharp and David Evens. Witnesses—Benjamin Price, Barsheba Duvall, William Kent. Proved July 27, 1750. Lib. E, p. 442.

1750, July 28. Inventory of personal estate (£113.19.3) includes moneys due from Jonathan Tharp, Mr. John Pierson, Robert Combes, Robert Donham, James Ross, William Coats, Job Tharp. Made by Joseph Freeman and Isaac Tappen.

1752, Nov. 20. Account, showing payments to Barsheba Duvall for nursing, Rev. Mr. John Pierson, Morgan Linnard, John Heard, Edward Mitchel, Edward Crowel, James Brown, Benjamin Thornell, John Morris, Jun'r, Henry Freeman, Doctor Forker, Jonathan Kinsey, George Manhom, Andrew Brown, Doctor Christey, Zedekiah Bonham, James Coddington, Doctor John Pierson, Nugent Kelly, Mary Wilkinson, Benjamin Bloomfield, Reuben Potter, William Coates, Zebulon Tharp, Jonathan Brooks, Thomas Nelson, Thomas Edgar, Alexander Freeman, Benjamin Price, Joseph Freeman, Isaac Tappen, William Kent.

1738, July 19. Mershon, Henry, of Maidenhead, Hunterdon Co., weaver; will of. Wife, Ann. Son, Houghton, plantation of 111 acres, held by several deeds, from ——— Revel, Benjamin Maple, Susannah Stockton and Daniel Cox, being a second purchase. Wife, Ann, five acres of meadow bought of said Revil, in town of Maidenhead, adjoining five acres which belonged to Hezekiah Bonham. Sons—Henry, Andrew, Peter and Thomas. Daughters—Mary, Ann, Rebeckah, Elizabeth and Sarah. Wife executrix. Witnesses—Stephen Minor, Philip Chapman, John Job. Proved Oct. 27, 1738. Lib. 4, p. 149.

1738, Oct. 25. Inventory of estate (£265.6.0) includes one servant man, £10; one negro girl, £40; twelve swarms of bees, £5; three looms and harness, £10; books £1.5. Made by Stephen Minor and Peter Mershon.
Hunterdon Wills.

1747, May 9. Mershon, Peter, of Maidenhead, Hunterdon Co., farmer; will of. Wife, Jane. Children—Andrew, Daniel, John, Aaron, Elizabeth and Ann. Profits of plantation to wife to bring up children, until they are aged fifteen years. Testator's four oldest children by former wife; two youngest sons by wife Jane. Executors—brother, Thomas Mershon, and brother-in-law John Vancleave. Witnesses—Henry Mershon, John Smith, Nathaniel Fitz Randolph. Proved June 11, 1747. Lib. 5, p. 416.

1747, July 25. Inventory of the estate (£541.9.6) includes looms and weavers' utensils (£5.18.6), a negro wench and three negro children (£77), his land and meadows (£283). Made by Henry Mershon and Nathaniel Fitz Randolph.

1731, March 29. Mestayer, Elias, of Shrewsbury, Monmouth Co., yeoman; will of. Two negroes, Stephen and Hester Steall, upon payment of one hundred pounds in five years, to be free; to aid in this they to have use of farm, implements and stock. After expiration of this time, estate to be sold and proceeds to testator's only sister, Anne Hester Villeneau, wife of John Villeneau of Spittelfield, London, distiller, during her life, and, at her death, to the poor of the French Protestant Church in Artillery Lane in the said Spittelfield. Other part of estate, not left to negroes, to be sold at once and proceeds to said sister. Executors—friends, John Auboyneau, of New York, merchant, and Peter LeConte, practitioner of physick, of Shrewsbury. Witnesses—Stoffel Langstraat, John Chamberlain, Robert Ireland. Proved June 1, 1731. Lib. B, p. 228.

1735, Dec. 27. Mickle, Archibald, of Newton, Gloucester Co., yeoman; will of. Wife, Mary, sole executrix and to have estate affer legacies paid to my brothers, Joseph and James Mickle, and to my sister, Mary Powel. Witnesses—Tobias Holloway, William Kent, Ruth Wright. Affirmed 9 Feb., 1735-6. Lib. 4, p. 52.

1735-6, Feb. 3. Inventory, £154.10.4; made by Tobias Holloway, Robert Stephens.

1736, May 3. Mickle, James, of Newton, Gloucester Co., yeoman; will of. Wife, Sarah. Brother, Joseph Mickle. Sister, Sarah Powell. James Hinchman and Joseph Kaighin of Newton, executors, and to apply the rent from plantation necessary for the bringing up of my daughter Rachel until my son Jacob will be 21. In case of death of these children under age without issue, estate shall descend to my cousin, Joseph Mickle. Witnesses—William Kent, Thomas Randall, Priscilla Ingram. Sworn and affirmed, 14 May, 1736. Lib. 4, p. 65.

1736, May 13. Inventory, £52.1.1; made by Tobias Halloway, Robert Stephens.

1741, Sept. 7. Mickle, John, of Gloucester, Gloucester Co., yeoman; will of. Wife, Mary. Sons—William, to have 411 acres on the east side of Oldman's Creek in Gloucester Co., with 37 acres of meadow and swamp on a branch of said Creek called "Allsprout;" John, at age, the plantation where I live, within the town bounds of Gloucester, also 47 acres of Cedar swamp "I took up in conjunction with

William Alberson;" Samuel, the residue of my lands, taken or untaken, by virtue of my Proprietary Rights, the same to be shared with my daughter, Hannah Ladd. My cousin, Joseph Cooper, of Gloucester Co., to have charge of the estate and education of my son John during his minority. Grandchildren—John Mickle, to have 126 acres in Penn's Neck, Salem County, adjoining Hugh's land; Hannah Mickle, £10, and the youngest child of my son William £10. Executors—sons William, Samuel and John, and son-in-law John Ladd. Witnesses—Joseph Thackray, Joseph Heritage, Job Siddon. Affirmed 12 Dec., 1744. Lib. 5, p. 63.

1744, Dec. 8. Inventory (£623.08.11) includes Bible, £2.17; negroes—Jim, £20, Tom, £40, Nell, £40, Jack, boy, £25, Tom, boy, £18, Lindee, girl, £13, Moll, girl, £10, and Roger, boy, £6; wherry, £5; cattle, £82. Appraisers—Wm. Harrison, Jacob Alberson.

1748, May 1. Mickle, Samuel, of Newton Township, Gloucester Co., sadler; will of. Wife, Letitia, executrix, and brother, John Mickle, and David Cooper, executors. Premises to be sold and £150 put to interest for education of my son, Samuel, until he will be 14. In case of his death under 21 without issue, all lands, excepting the said house and lot, my son would have had, to be divided equally among my brothers, John and William Mickle, and my sister, Hannah Ladd. Mentions tract of land in Morris County and a marsh in Egg Harbour. Witnesses—Wm. Griscom, Thomas Varnum, Jacob Stokes. Affirmed 31 Aug., 1748. Lib. 6, p. 352.

1748, May 23. Inventory (£203.14.10½) includes china Delft, sadler's tools, gold and silver buttons. Appraisers—Isaac Andrews, Wm. Griscom.

1736, March 26. Middleton, John, of Greenwich, Gloucester Co., yeoman; will of. Wife, Garthro, executrix, and to have estate, real and personal. Sons—John (eldest) and Jacob. Witnesses—William Howard, Samuel Shivers. Affirmed 17 May, 1736. Lib. 4, p. 67.

1736, April 29. Citation: To "Gertrude," widow of John Middleton to prove will of the deceased.

1736, May 3. Inventory, £43.5.2; made by Mounce Keen, Samuel Shivers.

1737, Aug. 27. Middleton, John, of Deptford Township, Gloucester Co., yeoman. Adm'x, Grace Middleton, his widow. Bondsman—Aaron Ward, of the same place. Witnesses—Peter Rambo, John Snowden. Lib. 4, p. 114.

1740-1, March 17. Middleton, John, of Burlington Co.; will of. Children—William, John, Abel, Amos, Jonathan, George, Bridget and Neomy. Grandson, George Middleton. 50 acres to be taken out of a warrant I have upon Job Booth's Right; 145 acres I bought of William Wilson; plantation in Monmouth Co. I bought of Francis Doughty; meadow joining Thomas Wetherill in Burlington; also land Thomas Wilson and his wife have for their lives. Executors—wife, Esther, and friend James Clark, of Stony Brook. Witnesses—William Bunting, William Cannaro, Edw'd Beakes. Proved May 14, 1741. Lib. 4, p. 281.

1741, April 14. Inventory of the personal estate, £1302.6.8; made by Isaac Horner and William Bunting. Includes two Bibles, Dictionary and other books.

1743-4, Jan. 6. Middleton, Jonathan, of Upper Freehold, Monmouth

Co. Int. Inventory of the estate (£345.13.2) includes, in the smith shop, 96 lb. London steel at 7d., 47 lb. Bristol steel at 6d.; bonds, etc., of Thomas Lowrie, John Foord, Abraham Tilton, Samuel Damford, John Biddle of Philadelphia, Edmund Beakes; balance on books for smith work, (£145.12.10). Made by Bartholomew West and William Miller, Quakers.

January 20, 1742 (?). Meribah Middleton, widow of Jonathan, and Thomas Middleton, brother of Jonathan, affirm that the deceased died intestate.

1743-4, January 17. Bond of Meribah and Thomas Middleton of Upper Freehold, as administrators of the estate. Bartholomew West, of same place, fellow bondsman. Lib. 5, p. 11.

1740, July 27. Midleton, Elizabeth, of Burlington Co.; will of. Sisters—Jane Richardson and Martha Rogers. Cousins—Mary and Elizabeth Midleton, Mary Staples, Ann Brown, Martha Handcock, Susanna, Mary, Phebe, Jane, and Elizabeth Richardson. Real and personal estate. Executors—brother, John Richardson, and cousin Henery Brown. Witnesses—Henry Hall, Peter Imlay, Lydia Imlay. Proved 18th day, 9th mo. (Nov.), 1740. Lib. 4, p. 258.

1740, Nov. 8. Inventory of the personal estate, £18.7.6; made by Jonathan Shreve and Peter Imlay. Includes debts due by Henery Browne, Peter Imlay, Henery Hall and John Cowen.

1740, Nov. 22. Additional inventory, £124.15.8¾. Includes bonds from estate of John Rogers, Jun'r, Estate of Joseph Grouden, Esq., John Richardson and his son John; also a Bible and Prayer Book.

1749, April 13. Mier (Meyer), Andros, of City of Burlington, yeoman; will of. Son, John, and dau., Johannah, my lands; son John to pay my dau., Cornelia, £50, and Johannah to pay my dau., Mariah, £50. Executors—wife, Frena, and son John. Witnesses—John Vansciver, John Vansciver, Jun'r, Jos. Scattergood. Proved May 4, 1749. Lib. 6, p. 334.

1740-1, Feb. 19. Milbourn, Andrew, of Hopewell, Hunterdon Co., carpenter. Int. Bond of Sarah Milbourne, the widow, as administratrix. Roger Woolverton, of Hopewell, tailor, surety. Witnesses—Archibald Horne and John Clark. Lib. 4, p. 306.

1741, May 15. Inventory of the estate (£78.19.0) includes a gun and sword, £1.10. Made by Andrew Smith and Roger Woolverton.

1747, Oct. 2. Miles, Isaac, of Cape May Co. Int. Adm'r, Jeremiah Garritson. Fellow bondsman, Peter Scull. Both of Cape May County. Witnesses—Henry Young, Benjamin Scull.

1747, Oct. 1. Inventory of personal estate (£10.19.1) includes twelve weaver's spules. Appraisers—Peter Scull, Benjamin Scull.

1748, Sept. 30. Account. Allowances, £23.7.9. Cape May Wills, 134 E.

1743, May 5. Miles, Thomas, of Penns Neck, Salem Co., weaver; will of. To Ann Owens one painted dressing box, and one silver tumbler. To Richard Ashdon and Thomas Emlin "my apparel, except two new suits, and my best hat with the stockings and all things thereto belonging." To Thomas Elwell "all the debts he oweth me." "I give £50 to erect a schoolhouse in some part of the lower part of Penns Neck." My son, Francis, at 21 to have the remainder; if he dies in non-age the interest shall be used to erect a schoolhouse and to maintain a schoolmaster. The Trustees of the place in Salem

County shall appoint where the schoolhouse shall be built, the number to be taught, and a master. Executor—son, Francis Miles, with Sinnick Sinnickson, his guardian. If the said Sinnickson should die before my son will be of age, Daniel Branderiff; and in case of his death I appoint Edmond Weterby. Witnesses—John Marshall, Joseph Gibbon, Onesiphorus Standly, John Callaham, Peter Brynberg. Proved 21 May, 1743. Lib. 4, p. 364.

Codicil. Sinnick Sinnickson appointed sole executor until Francis Miles will be seventeen, and, if my said son at 21 refuses to pay within three years the legacies mentioned in the will, the bequests to him shall become void and pass immediately to the use of the school mentioned.

1743, June 24. Letters Testamentary granted to Sinnick Sinnickson.

1743, May 18, 19, 20. Inventory (£561.8.2.¾) includes riding horse, armour, books of law, mathmaticks and other books (£17.16.2), writing desk, maps, pictures, morter, "pistle," weight and scales, iron and steel, bellows and anvil, with other smith tools, pair of steers at Thomas Gilchrist's, oxen at John Malcolm's, at James Owen's, at Owen Ryan's and at Ersack Gilljohnson's, cows and calf at John Malcolm's, at Daniel Bilderback's, and on his plantation, etc. Appraisers—Ranier Vanhist, James Barkley.

1743, June 17. Additional goods from the houses of Yewrison and Shuzanna Herman. Appraisers—William Tuft, James Barkley.

1743, June 22. Additional appraisement by John Kellachin and Peter Brynbery includes cash from Charles Scott.

1744, Feb. 5. Affidavit of Francis Miles, now at the age of seventeen years, that the several annexed writings contain the will of his father and that he will truly execute the same.

1744, Feb. 6. Account. Moneys paid to Benjn. Bispham, John Marshall, Francis Janviers, Roger Sherron, Sarah Dunn, Thomas Gillingham, Wm. Peake, Jeremiah Baker, Morris Johnson, Jacob Cornelieson, Susannah Harman, Henry Peterson, John Smith, Margate Wilder, John Fumy, Roger Sherron, Robert Hart, Ranier Vanhist, Daniel Bilderback, Elizabeth Wallis, James Owen, Isaac Sharp, Joseph Test, John Callahan, Mary Grafton, Anne Owen, James Congleton, Sarah Downing, Danl. Lambstone, Elizth. Casperson, George Monrow, Richd. Ashdon, Andrew Bartleson, John Eaton, James Barclay, John Jones, Johannes Flannegan, Danl. Bilderback, Elizth. Wright, Jos. Sharp, Charles O Neill, Abner Penton, John Demsey, John Pierson, Willm. Pennock, Catherine McKnight, Josiah Pennington, Ashdon & Emley, Jos. Test, Erick Gilljohnson, Andrew Sinnick, Tim. O Conner, Ja. Barkley, Danl. Mestayer, Thomas Elwell, Mary Grafton, James Congleton, John Mecum, Willm. Mecum, Archibald Crawford, Thomas Gillingham and Nicholas Harman.

1742, Feb. 18. Millar, George, of Pilesgrove, Salem Co., blacksmith; will of. Wife, Mary, to have use of the place I live on during widowhood for the bringing up of my sons, viz., Joost (at 21 to have the said place, 112 acres) and James (100 acres joining the same tract). The money arising from the sale of one-third of the moveables to be put at interest during the minority of my sons and used by my wife for their support and education. Executors—wife, and brother, William Millar. Witnesses—Josiah Elwell, Andrew Lock, Joseph Carroll. Proved 28 February, 1742. Lib. 4, p. 358.

1742, March 3. Inventory (£144.19.10) includes horses, oxen, etc., smith's tools, Bible, "balance of his books, £38.07.7," debt due from Samuel Morgan. Appraisers—Samuel Morgan, Thos. Graves.

1750, June 23. Miller, Charles, of Burlington Co. Administration on estate granted to John Imlay, of Bordentown, merchant. John Trapnele, of Burlington, innholder, fellow bondsman. Lib. 7, p. 44.

1739-40, 1 mo. (Mar.), 17 da. Miller, Ebenezer, of Salem Co., house carpenter, guardian of Daniel Dickson (son of Anthony Dickson, yeoman, and Mary his wife, late of the south side of Cohansey). Witnesses—Richd. Wood, Josiah Fithian, Samuel Fithian, Isaac Fithian. Salem Wills, 684 Q.

1749, Feb. 8. Miller, James (14 yrs. and upwards), son of George Miller, of Salem Co. Guardian—Jeremiah Wood. Bondsman—Bateman Loyd. Witnesses—Zechonius Wood, Frederick Hoffman. Salem Wills, 756 Q.

1736, March 26. Miller, John, of Salem Co., yeoman. Int. Adm'x, Martha Miller, widow. Bondsman—Jonathan Holmes. Both of said county. Witnesses—Abraham Reeves, Danl. Mestayer. Lib. 4, p. 57.

1736, March 25. Inventory (£155.1.1) of "John Miller, weaver," includes cattle, horses, wheat, books, etc. Appraisers—Abraham Reeves, John Remmenton.

1735-6, Feb. 14. Miller, John, of Chesterfield, Burlington Co. Int. Inventory of the personal estate, £117.0.2; made by Joshua Wright and John Steward.

1735-6, March 19. Administration granted to Ann Miller, widow. John Steward and Thomas Miller, yeomen, fellow bondsmen. Lib. 4, p. 55.

1738, June 19. Account of "Ann Muller," administratrix, showing moneys paid John Tantum for making coffin and digging grave, Doct. John Brown, John Quicksall, Wm. Cooke, Anthony Woodwatd, Wm. Chapman, Richard Smith, Benjamin Burges, George Hopkins, Richard Harrison, Miriam Fowler, Samuel Horseman, Elizabeth Newberry, Richard Martin, Thomas Roberts.

1740, Sept. 12. Miller, John, of Cohansey, Salem Co., cooper; will of. Wife, Susannah, executrix, and to have all my goods and chattels. Witnesses—James Caruthers, Abraham Reeves, Josiah Fithian. Proved 17 May, 1749. Cumberland Wills, 40 F.

1749, May 2. Inventory of personal estate, £100.1.8; made by Hugh Dunn, Caleb Ayars, Junior.

1749, June 3. Jonathan Holmes and Josiah Parvin appointed administrators. Fellow bondsmen—Caleb Ayars, Jun., and Hugh Dunn. Witnesses—James Ayars, Elias Cotting.

1749, Feb. 8. Miller, Joost (aged 14 years. and upwards, son of George Miller, Salem Co.), ward. Guardian—Jeremiah Wood. Bondsman—Bateman Loyd. Witnesses—Jechonias Wood, Frederick Hoffman. Salem Wills, 755 Q.

1725-6, March 19. Miller, Noah, of Cohansey, Salem Co., yeoman; will of. Wife, Joanah. Sons—Samuel, Noah and John. Daughters—Elizabeth, Joanna and Susannah. Home farm to be divided among the sons. Executors—wife, and son Noah. Witnesses—Nathaniel Bishop, Moses Bishop, Abraham Reeves. Proved 8 Oct., 1737. Lib. 4, p. 146.

1737, Oct. 4. Inventory (£115.13.11) includes cattle, sheep and horses. Appraisers—James Robinson, Moses Bishop.

1741, Oct. 30. Miller, Noah, of Cohansey, Salem Co. Int. Adm'x, Susannah Miller (relict of). Bondsmen—John Rementon and Samuel Clark, of Cohansey. Witnesses—Robt. Lynd, Chas. O. Neill. Lib. 4, p. 316.

1741, Nov. 2. Inventory, £122.18; made by Abraham Reeves, James Robinson.

1736, April 24. Miller, Peter, of New Brunswick, Middlesex Co. Int. Bond of Eve, his widow, as administratrix. Jacob Ouke, fellow bondsman. Witness—Thomas Harmer. Lib. C, p. 95.

1731-2, Jan. 29. Miller, Richard, Jun'r, of Elizabeth Town, Essex Co. Int. Administration granted to the widow, Sarah Miller. Lib. B, p. 242.

1731-2, Feb. 2. Inventory of personal estate (£281.01.11), includes note from Matthias Miller, bonds from Johannes Black, carpenter, George Leslie, Caleb Jefferys, Samuel Williams, David Whitehead, Peter Steelman, Daniel Ingerson, James Steelman. Made by Andrew Joline and Matthias Hetfield.

1736, Feb. 28. "On the 3rd of Jan., 1731, Richard Miller, Jr., dyed intestate, and letters of administration were granted Sarah Miller, the widow, on Jan. 29, 1731. And whereas she has since intermarried with one Elijah Davis, they have now exhibited an account of administration."

1736, Feb. 28. Bond of Elijah Davis as administrator on the estate. John Ogden and John Megie, fellow bondsmen. Lib. B, p. 242.

Accompt of Elijah and Sarah Davis, showing receipts from Mr. Andrew Joline, Searle & Pintard, Mr. Royall, Joh. Lawrence, William Gathwait, Jeane Tongasto, Mindwell Williams, John Blanchard, Thomas Clark, Andrew Crag, Steven Hinds, Joseph Tooker, Steven Crane, Daniel Meeker, Mary Marsh, John Drew, Phebe Meeker, Jonathan Dayton, Joseph Gray (for Peter Scull of Cape May), Jeremiah Crane, Jun'r, Aaron Miller, Jeams Marten, Sam'll Miller, Dan'll Clark, Joseph Megie, Sam'll Littell, Gershom Higins, Icobod Burnet, William Miller, Peter Steelman, James Steelman, James Steelman Jun'r, Zachary Blake (of New York), Matthew Hetfield, Myndert Williams.

1736, Oct. 23. Miller, Ruth, widow, of Salem Co. Int. Admr's, John Foster and Ruth Foster. Bondsman—Josiah Fithian. All of said County. Witnesses—Jacob Ware, Danl. Mestayer. Lib. 4, p. 107.

1736, Oct. 26. Inventory, £58.6.1; made by Josiah Fithian, Jacob Ware.

1749, May 18. Miller, Susannah, widow of John Miller, of Cohansey, Cumberland Co.; will of. "I bequeath my whole estate left me by my husband to my three children, Elizabeth, Susanna and Jonathan, equally." Executors—Josiah Parvin and my son, Jonathan Holmes, Witnesses—Elizabeth E. Mulford, Sarah Shepherd, Joseph Read. Proved 3 June, 1749. Lib. 6, p. 119.

1750, May 1. Miller, Thomas, of Morristown, Morris Co., weaver; will of. Wife, Margreat. Sons—James and John to have the whole estate and pay legacies to other sons and daughters, viz., Thomas, Mary and Isaac Miller (no interest to be demanded until they will be sixteen). Executors—wife, Margaret, and son James Miller. Witnesses—Zophar Gildersleeve, Daniel Walling, Caleb Fairchild. Proved 25 July, 1750. Lib. E, p. 481.

1751, Feb. 6. Renunciation of Margreat Miller, the Executrix, in favor of the said James Miller, executor. Witnesses—John Riky, John Miller.

1746-7, Jan. 29. Miller, William, of Bethlehem, Hunterdon Co.; will of. Son-in-law, Benjamin McFarlen. Son, John Black. Robert Hazlett, Robert Breaden and Francis McKemie to appraise property. Samuel Sloan to be free at testator's decease, and Benjamin McFarlin to take care of him and send him to school. Said Benjamin to take care of Mary McClean. Clothing of testator and his wife to the disposal of Francis McKenne (or McKemie), Robert Breden and Robert Hazlett, to distribute among testator's children. Residue of estate to children (?), William Miller, Benjamin McFarlin, John Black, James Young, Thomas McBroom and Daniel McClean. Executors—Francis McKemie and Robert Breden. Witnesses—Thomas Camens and Robert Hazlett. Proved Feb. 24, 1746-7. Lib. 5, p. 315.

1746-7, Feb. 3. Inventory of estate (£27.0.6), includes a Great Bible. Made by Samuel Loudin and James Cimins.

1748, Dec. 24. Milles, Michael, of Evesham, Burlington Co., yeoman; will of. Daughters—Rosannah and Sarah. Real and personal estate. Executors—wife, Sarah, and brother-in-law, Benjamin Moore, Jun'r. Witnesses—Samuel Moore, Ann Sill, John Burr, Jun'r. Proved Jan. 30, 1748. Lib. 6, p. 23.

1748, 11th day, 10th mo. (Dec.). Inventory of the personal estate, £433.5.6; made by Carlile Haines and Amos Austin.

1750, May 28. Account of Benjamin Moore, Jun'r, and Sarah Milles, showing payment to Jonathan Austin and Elizabeth Shinn for funeral charges, Timothy Matlock, Reuben Haines, William Foster, David Bassett, Job Haines, Jacob Heulings, Samuel Hale.

1732, 2nd day, 2nd mo. (April). Mills, Francis, of New Hanover, Burlington Co.; will of. Children—Joshua, William, Aurelius, James Lord, Jamima, Mary, Keziah, and Sarah, all under age. An expected child. Real and personal estate. Executors—wife, Elizabeth, and friend John Wright, Esq. Witnesses—David Davis, Magdalin Bard, James Lewis. Proved Sept. 15, 1732. Lib. 3, p. 216.

1732-3, March 17. Inventory of the personal estate, £99.7; made by William Bowker and Constantine Wood. Includes "wearing apparrill where he dyed in Pennsylvania," two Bibles and other books.

1738, Jan. 30. Mills, James, of Salem Co., tailor. Int. Adm'r, John Steward, of Alloways Creek, yeoman. Bondsman—Robert Hart, merchant, of Salem. Witness—Richd. Roe. Lib. 4, p. 180.

1738-9, Feb. 2. Inventory (£110.5); made by Clem. Hall, Robert Hart.

1747, Dec. 5. Mills, James, of the Borough of Elizabeth, Essex Co., cutler; will of. To Gideon Mills land bought of Susannah Morehouse. Thomas, son of brother Robert Mills, to be apprenticed to Isaac Nutman. Brother, Edward Mills, land in Kingdom of Ireland. Land in North Carolina. Executors—friends Isaac Nutman and David Smith. Witnesses—Matt. Baldwin, Mary Baldwin, John Ross. Proved Nov. 13, 1749. Lib. E, p. 340.

1735, April 15. Mills, John, of Indian Fields, Salem Co., yeoman; will of. Wife, Mary, during life, all my plantation and improved lands on the north side, called Rich Neck Branch, providing that she takes care and provides for my little daughter, Temperance. At her decease lands shall go to my son John, on condition aforesaid. Son, Ephraim, at age, to have lands I purchased from William Joslin. Son Seelye, 50 acres in Little Mill Branch. The marsh which I purchased of Ephraim Sayres to my five sons, John, Seelye, Ephraim, Uriah and Jedidiah, equally. Daughters—Mary, Sarah and Rebecca. Executors—wife, and son John. Witnesses—Samuel Foster, John Robinson, John Pedmore. Proved 3 June, 1735.

1735, June 3. Letters testamentary granted to Mary Mills, executrix named, John Mills being under age. Lib. 4, p. 36.

1735, May 13. Inventory, £236; made by Joatn. Fithian, Jno. Blackwood.

1740-1, March 10. Mills, John, of the south side of Cohansey "called by the name of Rich Neck," Salem Co.; will of. Wife, Pheebe, to have whole estate forever, and to put to interest £7 in two years from this date for the use of my eldest son, Jerediah, until he will be 21; likewise for my youngest son Jeremiah; both said sons at 14 to be apprenticed to a joyner's trade. Wife to have the use of my part in the salt meadow which my father bought of Ephraim Sears until sons will be of age. Executors—wife, Phebe, and Daniel Bowin. Witnesses—Hugh Luckie, Jacob Robinson, Abraham Hyatt. Proved 21 May, 1741. Lib. 4, p. 285.

1740-1, March 10. Renunciation of Danl. Bowen, one of the executors named. Witness—Elias Cotting.

1741, May 1. Letters testamentary granted to Phebe Mills, executrix.

1740-1, March 24. Inventory, £84.5.1; made by Jonathan Bowen, Abraham Hyatt.

1748, Feb. 22. Mills, John, of Stoe Creek, Cumberland Co. Int. Administratrix, Mary Mills, widow. No bondsman recorded. Witnesses—Peter Long, Elias Cotting. Lib. 6, p. 76.

1748, Dec. 30. Inventory of personal estate, £51.01.0; made by Peter Long, David Reed, both of Stoe Creek.

1749, July 12. Mills, Jonathan, of Township of Stoe, Cumberland Co., yeoman, appointed guardian of James Padgett, an infant of 14 and upwards, son of Francis Padgett, late of same place. Bondsmen —Jonathan Mills, Joseph Denn, both of the township of Stoe. Witnesses—Rebekah Padgett, Elias Cotting. Cumberland Wills, 42 F.

1744, Aug. 7. Mills, Samuel, of Elizabeth Town, Essex Co., yeoman; will of. "Being far advanced in years." Children—Samuel, John, Joseph, Mary Thompson, Hannah Scott, Rachel Stuart, Susanna Winans, Elizabeth Frazee, Phebe Clark, Sarah Lee and Jane Mills. Sons—Richard Mills, Sen'r, and Richard Mills, Jun'r, (alias James Mills); division of land between them to be made by William Porter and Abraham Clark. Executor—son, Richard Mills, the elder. Witnesses —Joseph Kelsey, John Cleverly, Daniel Kelsy. Proved March 16, 1744. Lib. D, p. 246.

1741, Aug. 10. Milnor, John, of City of Burlington, innholder; will of. Children—Isaac, John, Joseph, Thomas, William, Martha and Mary; the daughters under age. Land and houses in Penna. to sons Joseph and John. Executors—wife, Martha, and son Joseph. Witnesses—Thomas Scattergood, Jr., Will Lyndon, Francis Hague. Proved Aug. 15, 1741. Lib. 4, p. 311.

1745, July 24. Inventory of the personal estate, £76.2.1; made by Isaac DeCow and Israel Heulings.

1745, Oct. 11. Minor, Samuel, of New Windsor, Middlesex Co., weaver. Int. Bond of Hannah (Annatie) Minor, his widow, as administratrix of his estate. William Updike, fellow bondsman. Witness—John Heard. Lib. D, p. 343.

1745-6, Jan. 18. Inventory of personal estate, £152.13.5; made by James Clark, William Updike, Luke Cowenhoven.

1742, May 1. Miranda, George, of the City of Philadelphia, merchant. Bond of Ann Magdalen Miranda, widow of said deceased, as administratrix of the estate. Joseph Warrell, of Trenton, Esquire, and Thomas Bourne, of Philadelphia, merchant, sureties. (Hunterdon Wills), Lib. 4, p. 376.

1731, April 14. Mitchell, Jacob, of Elizabeth Town, Essex Co. Int. Bond of Hannah Mitchell, Nathaniel Mitchell and John Halstead, as administrators on the estate. Witnesses—Timo. Halstead, Elizabeth Halstead. Lib. B, p. 205.

1730-1, Jan. 6. Inventory of personal estate (£175.14.08) includes debt due from Richard Eastbe, Hanover. Made by Ebenezer Lyon, Jonathan Allen.

1732, Sept. 18. Mitchell, John, of Cossiam, Philada. Co., Province of Penna. Administration on estate granted to Joseph Lownds, of Cossian, yeoman. Samuel Bustill, Esq., of Burlington, fellow bondsman. Witnesses—John Hyndshaw, Joseph Rose. Burlington Wills, 2309 C.

1738, July 11. Mitchell, Nathaniell, of Elizabeth Town, Essex Co., tailor; will of. Children—James, George, William, Sarah, Mary and Elizabeth. Swamp land purchased of Aaron and Thomas Thompson; land in partnership with my brother William Mitchell; land joining land of Samuel Lambert, deceased, given me and my wife by my father, George Jewell, deceased. Executors—wife, Elizabeth, and friend William Richardson. Witnesses—Richard Miller, Samuel Miller, John Borrowes, Jun'r. Proved July 28, 1738. Lib. C, p. 204.

1738, Aug. 14. Inventory of personal estate, (£219.00.09), includes a silver porringer, and a negro man valued at £55. Made by Jon. Dayton, William Winans.

1742, Dec. 18. Mitchell, Nathaniel, of Elizabeth Town, Essex Co., orphan of about 14 years. Bond of Jonathan Allen as guardian. William Mitchell, fellow bondsman. Witnesses—James Hindes, Joseph Littell. Lib. D, p. 23.

1747-8, Jan. 22. Mocleroth (McIllrath), William, of Somerset Co. Administration on estate granted to Thomas Mocleroth, brother of deceased. Fellow bondsman—Henry Sloan. Lib. E, p. 118.

1747-8, Jan. 21. Inventory of personal estate, £68.00.2; made by David Sutton, Abraham Vantuyle.

1730-1, Jan. 8. Mollegan, James. Administration granted to Sam. Dennis, of Shrewsbury, Monmouth Co. Lib. B, p. 182.

1749, Sept. 26. Monday (Mundy), Hopewell, of Piscataway, Middlesex Co. Int. Bond of Sarah Munday, his widow, as administratrix.

Jeremiah Hemsted and John Martin, fellow bondsmen. Lib. E, p. 332.

1749, Sept. 26. Inventory of personal estate, £84.11; made by Henry Langstaff and Joshua Marvin.

1734, Sept. 2. Monday, Nicholas, of the Vineyard, Piscataqua Township, Middlesex Co., yeoman; will of. Children—Joseph, Hopewell, Thomas, Nicholas, Benjamin, John, Samuel, Abigail Gyles, Hope Blackford, Elizabeth Flat, Mary Luke, Margaret Monday. Granddaughter, Providence Blackford. Lands joining lands of John Martin, Jun'r, Joseph Martin, Henry Loveal, Mistris FitzRandolph, Nicholas Monday, Elizabeth FitzRandolph, Samuel Hulls, Nicholas Monday, Sen'r, and Jun'r, Moses Martin. Meadow I purchased of Joseph Dennis, joining lands of John Compton, Henry Potter, Daniel Hendrick. Part of land sold to me by John Dennis, Jabesh Hendrick, Wm. Taslo, Benjamin Smith, Peter Martin, John Parker. Executors—wife, Hope, and Thomas Monday. Witnesses—Peter Martin, Reziel Runyon, Tho. Broderwick. Proved Nov. 20, 1734. Lib. B, p. 574.

Monday (see Munday).

1748, June 24. Monsell, Thomas, of Cape May Co. Int. Adm'x, Deborah Monsel. Fellow bondsman—Thomas Munsell, of Cape May County.

1748, June 22. Inventory of personal estate, £23.9.2; made by John Leonard, Thomas Daniels.

———, ———, —. Account. Moneys paid Henry Young, Danl. Mestayer, Thomas Duils, Christopher Leaming, Recompence Hand, etc.
Cape May Wills, 138 E.

1733, June 1. Montgomerie, John, Esq., late Captain General and Governour in Chief of the Province of New Jersey, New York, etc. Administration on the estate granted to Charles Williams, gent. William Cosby, Esq., Captain General and Governour in Chief of the Province of New Jersey, New York, etc., fellow bondsman—Witness—Jo. Warrell. Burlington Wills, Lib. 8, p. 315.

1734, Dec. 19. Montgomery, George, of Middlesex Co. Int. Bond of John Miller, principal creditor, of New York City, as administrator. Andrew Hay, of Perth Amboy, fellow bondsman. Witness—James Hooker. Lib. B, p. 587.

1747, May 8. Moon, Peter, of New Brunswick, Middlesex Co., mason. Int. Bond of Henry Bogert, bolter, and Evert Pels, ropemaker, both of New York City, as administrators, being next of kin. Abraham Hyer, of New Brunswick, cooper, fellow bondsman.
Lib. E, p. 35.

1741, May 27. Moore, Alexander, of New Brunswick, Middlesex Co., innkeeper; will of. Wife, Elizabeth. Children—John, Alexander, Henry, William, Mary, George, and James, all under age. Real and personal estate. Executors—friends Alexander Henry and William Ouke, both merchants of New Brunswick. Witnesses—Fran. Costigan, Jan DeWitte, Thos. Harding. Proved March 21, 1742. Lib. D, p. 28.

1732, Sept. 12. Moore, Andrew, of Burlington Co., labourer. Int. Administration on estate granted to Thomas Barns, of Nottingham, innholder. Thomas Clayton, of Trenton, Hunterdon Co., fellow bondsman. Lib. 3, p. 137.

1732, Sept. 12. Thomas Barns states that Andrew Moore died at his house of a fever and that he had no kindred in these parts.

1726-7, Jan. 6. Moore, John, of Chesterfield, Burlington Co., yeoman; will of. Legacies to Thomas, son of Gershom Moore, deceased, in Maidenhead, Hunterdon Co.; to John, son of Nathaniel Moore of Hopewell, Hunterdon Co.; to Sam'll, son of Benjamin Moore, of Newtown, Queens Co., Island of Nassau; and also to eldest dau. of said Benjamin Moore. Wife, Mary, executrix. Real and personal estate. Witnesses—Samuel Fenton, Samuell Taylor, Jno. Richardson. Proved Dec. 17, 1735. Lib. 4, p. 47.

1735, Nov. 7. Inventory of the personal estate, £94.12; made by Is. DeCow and R. Wright. Includes large Bible and other books.

1730, March 13. Moore, John, of Woodbridge, Middlesex Co., yeoman; will of. Children—Benjamin, Enoch, Samuel, Daniel, William, John, Rachel, Mary, Hannah, Deborah, Sarah, Elizabeth, Hope and Frances. Real and personal estate. Lot joining land of Peter Elstone. Executors—wife, Mary, and son Benjamin. Witnesses—Joseph Conger, Joseph Oliver, Benj. Tharp, J. Stevens. Proved April 20, 1736. Lib. C, p. 85.

1739, July 6. Moore, John, of Salem Co.; will of. To the son of Jacob Moore, my brother, the bond I bought from Joseph Pack. Land bought from my brother, Samuel Moore, I freely will to said Samuel, whom I appoint my executor to dispose of my effects as follows: one yoke of oxen to my brother Jacob, a case of bottles to my sister Elizabeth Pack, and the personal to himself. Witnesses—Geo. Hanna, Josiah Parvin, Ephraim Mills. Proved 10 Oct., 1739. Lib. 4, p. 205.

1739, Aug. 20. Inventory, £38; made by Josiah Parvin, Ephraim Mills.

1736-7, Jan. 17. Moore, Lewis, of Rockyhill, Somerset Co., merchant; will of. Wife, Margaret. Estate to be sold at discretion of executors; one-third to wife and two-thirds to bring up the three children, Lewis, John and William. Executors—Alexander Moore, Gershom Shippey and John Corle. Witnesses—Jurie Brower, Joseph Kno, John Berrien. Proved 10 Feb., 1736. Lib. E, p. 144.

1736-7, Jan. 24. Inventory of real and personal estate (£782.0.4) includes one acre of land and the buildings, £125.; silver watch, £7; silver hilted sword, £4.10. Appraisers—Thos. Yates, Jurie Brower.

1732-3, Feb. 24. Moore, Matthew, of Woodbridge, Middlesex Co., carpenter; will of. Children—Nehemiah, Elizabeth, Matthew, and Sarah Skinner. Grandson—Matthew Skinner. If negro, Frank, pay £25 by Feb. 24, 1733-4 and interest for one year, he shall have right to his wife, Parthenia, and her children. Real and personal estate. Executors—Sam'll, son of James Moore, deceased, and Robert, son of John Moore, deceased. Witnesses—Samuel Lockheart, Thomas Jackson, Elizabeth Dyer. Proved April 5, 1733. Lib. B, p. 390.

1748, Dec. 23. Moore, Robert, of Manington, Salem Co. Int. Adm'x, Jane Brown. Bondsman—Robert Walket. Both of said County. Witnesses—Wm. Barker, Nichls. Gibbon. Lib. 6, p. 323.

1748-9, Jan. 19. Inventory, £8.19; made by Thomas Haynes, Alexr. Simpson.

1732, May 17. Moore, Will, of Middlesex Co.; will of. Wife and children mentioned but not named. Real and personal estate. Executors—Matthew Clarkson, of New York City, and Henry Fisher, of Raritan. Witnesses—Elizabeth DeForest, Jno. Broughton, Andrew Barclay. Proved March 23, 1738-9. Lib. C, p. 268.

1745, June 3. Moores, John, of Woodbridge, Middlesex Co., Esq.; will of. To daughter, Mary, and her eldest daughter, a negro I bought of John Noe. Children—Mary, John, Daniel, Matthew, Francis and Elizabeth, last four under age. Expected child. Farm I purchased of the executors of Benjamin Force, joining lands of Joseph Bloomfield and Jonathan Frazee; land bought of the executors of John Harrison in Perth Amboy; salt marsh by mortgage from Thomas Moore late of Woodbridge, deceased; land given me by my father and land purchased of Cousin William Moores; land bought of Serajah Bunn; land formerly belonging to my brother, Benjamin Moores, deceased; freehold right I purchased of Joseph Gilman. Executors—wife Mary, son John, and friend William Brittain. Witnesses—James Wilkinson, Sam. Jaquess, David Donham, Jun'r. Proved July 1, 1745. Lib. D, p. 302.

1739, June 15. Morehouse, David, of Elizabeth Town, Essex Co., carpenter; will of. Wife, Susannah. Children—Pheebe, Hannah, Johannah, Abigail and David, all under age. Land joining lands of Edward Sale and Bowley Ramsey. Executors—friends Matthias Hetfield and John Ogden. Witnesses—Samuel Meaker, James Chandler, Thos. Jackman. Proved Dec. 24, 1739. Lib. C, p. 314.

1739-40, Feb. 18. Inventory of personal estate (£329.17.02), includes bonds of Daniel Sayer, Henery Peirson, John Hunloke. Made by Joseph Woodruffe and David Whitehead.

1732, Nov. 5. Morehouse, John, of Hunterdon Co.; will of. Wife, Susannah. Executors—wife, and brother David Morehouse, of Elizabeth Town. Plantation to be sold and proceeds to wife, for the bringing up of children (not named). Witnesses—Jonathan Osborn, Zachariah Fairchild, Henry Lacy. Proved Jan. 10. 1732. Lib. 3, p. 240.

1732, Nov. 27. Inventory of estate, £106.16.2; made at Hanover, by Edward Sale.

1756, April 13. Whereas Stephen Morehouse, son of John Morehouse, late of Hunterdon County, deceased, hath made complaint that David Morehouse, deceased, surviving executor of the will of said John Morehouse, did not render any account of his administration, and that Matthias Hetfield, Esquire, and John Ogden, of Elizabeth Town, executors of the will of David Morehouse, have not rendered an account, citation was issued by Charles Read and the said executors appeared, April 23, 1756.

1734, Aug. 21. Mores (Morris), Joseph, of Bergen Co.; will of. The thirds of the rents of the plantation I now live on and of the rents of the land sold at New York shall be paid yearly to my mother, Rebeckah Anderson, during her life. Executors to dispose of the whole estate and after all debts paid to put the remainder for the maintenance of my wife, Elenor Mores, and her children, that is to say, "my daughter Rebeckah, my son William, my son Jocobus and my child not yet born." Each shall share equally, excepting a ½ share which I give to my son-in-law, Isaac DeReiner; but if the said Isaac shall recover my estate at the fresh water he shall have ¼ of a share. The lands at New York formerly in the possession of

William Huddlestone I give equally to my sisters, Rebeckah, Hannah, and Sarah, if they can recover the same. Executors—wife, Elenor, Thomas Dekey and Jeams Hasyard, with power to execute deeds for that which I have sold to Joan Blake at New York for a lot of land there. Signed "Joseph Morris." Witnesses—Jere Bleke, St. George Talbot, Richard Edsall. Proved 28 May, 1735. Thomas DeKay and Elenor Morris qualify as executors. Lib. C, p. 40.

1734, Nov. 25. Inventory of personal estate (£201.9.6) includes negro women Cate, £35, Jude, £30; bonds of Joan Block, William Anderson and Charles Comlein (?). Made by Samuel Edsall and Matheues Benson.

1747, May 20. Morford, Thomas, of Middletown Township, Monmouth Co., yeoman; will of. Wife, Hannah, land, negro wench Beas, etc. Son, John, land at Shoal harbor, silver tankard, etc. Son, Jerrett, 20 sh. Son, Thomas, £150, loom and tackling. Daughter, Mary, has had her share. Daughters—Sarah, Hannah and Catherine, when aged 18. Son, Joseph, under age. Executors—wife, and son Jerrett. Witnesses—George, James and Elizabeth Mount, and William Woolley. Proved June 2, 1750. Lib. E, p. 413.

1751, Nov. 4. Morgan, Alexander, of Waterford, Gloucester Co., yeoman; will of. Wife, Hannah. Sons—Joseph, to have in addition to the place whereon he lives, by previous deed of gift, land in Township of Newton, purchased of my brother-in-law, Joseph Cooper; Benjamin, the home tract, also land purchased of Samuel Burge, 23 acres in Burlington County, joining Samuel Davis and Thomas Lippincott, 34 acres of swamp purchased of Samuel Burroughs on Delaware River and the northeast side of Pensawking Creek. Daughters—Mary (wife of Edmund Hollinshead), Elizabeth (wife of William Miller), Lydia, to have her legacy in 12 months, Hannah, Sarah and Rachel to have theirs at 21. Grandchildren (minors; names not given). Executors—wife, Hannah, and son Joseph. Witnesses—George Weed, Thomas Lippincott, Junior, Saml. Spicer. Affirmed 11 Dec., 1751. Lib. 7, p. 165.

1751, Nov. 28, 29. Inventory (£1912.1.11½) includes clock (£20), map of Europe, Delft ware, "A Larum Clock & stand," 2 mulatto slaves, a woman and boy (£53), wheat, rye, hay, boat with awning, sail oars. Appraisers—Tho. Spicer, Joshua Raper.

1739, Oct. —. Morgan, Charles, of Hopewell, Hunterdon Co., yeoman. Int. Inventory of the estate (£169.09.02) includes a servant man, bond from John Cole. Made by Joseph Stout and Samuel Stout. Lib. 4, p. 184.

1739, Nov. 9. Adm'x, Elizabeth Morgan, of Hopewell, widow. Samuel Stout, of same place, yeoman, surety.

1749-50, Jan. 6. Morgan, Charles, of Middlesex Co., yeoman; will of. Children—Thomas, Charles, William, Danniel, James, Mary, Abigail, Sarah. Plantation purchased of George Lesley, where Yose Soey formerly lived, on Cheasquake Creek. Executors—sons William and Danniel, and brother-in-law Seth Ellison. Witnesses—John Bowne, Samuel Ellison, John Night. Proved April 10, 1750. Lib. E, p. 380.

1734, Aug. 12. Morgan, Elizabeth, widow of Charles Morgan, of Middlesex Co. Int. Adm'x, Joanna Paine. Lib. B, p. 586.

1748, May 12. Morgan, Morris, 18 years of age, son of Evan Morgan, late of Philada. Peter Bard, of Philada., appointed guardian. Bennet Bard, of Burlington Co., fellow bondsman. Burlington Wills, 4185 C.

1736, Aug. 16. Morgan, Robert, of Northampton, Burlington Co., schoolmaster. Int. Inventory, £54.13.6; made by Samuel Woolston and John Hilher.

1736, Aug. 24. Administration granted to Mary Morgan, widow. Samuel Woolston, yeoman, fellow bondsman. Lib. 4, p. 71.

1732, Dec. 1. Morrell, Thomas, of Hopewell, Hunterdon Co.; will of. Wife, Mary. Children—Martha, Mary, Hannah, Abigail, John and Daniel. Executors—wife, Benjamin Hixson of Amwell, and Andrew Smith of Hopewell. Unborn child. Witnesses—John Fidler, Joseph Reed, George Smith. Proved May 16, 1733. Lib. 3, p. 309.

1733, May 25. Inventory (£103.12.0) includes library, bonds of Oliver Silverthorn, John Titus, John Fidler. Made by Joseph Price and John Fidler.

1733, ———, —. Additional inventory (£11.11.0) includes debts of Joseph Price and Hugh Hendry. Made by Abraham Philip Philips.

1734, Jan. 28. Account of Robert Combs and Mary, his wife, late Mary Morrell, executrix of Thomas Morrell. Mentions Enoch Anderson, coroner of Hunterdon County for viewing body of deceased, Francis Bowes, Esquire, Jeremiah Smith, Mary Roberts, Ralph Smith, John Dagworthy, Abraham Arnes, John Smith, Andrew Smith, John Mullen, Hugh ODonel, Susannah Critchfied.

1733-4, 11 mo. (Jan), 26 da. Morris, David, of Elsenburgh, Salem Co.; will of. Son, David, at 18 to have plantation I live on with the mill and marsh; if he dies, then to my son, John Jeffreys Morris, at 18; if he dies, then to my daughter, Jane Morris; if she dies without heirs, then to male heir of my brother Lewis Morris, and, for want of a male heir, to the female. My two plantations upon Manington Creek to my wife, Jane, during life and, at her decease, the plantation Robert Connaway lives on to my son, John Jeffrey, and the plantation which was John Young's unto my daughter, Jane. Personal estate unto my wife with the rents and profits of the home farm for the bringing up of my children, until son David will be 18. Executors—wife, Jane, and my brother, Lewis Morris. Witnesses—Richard Smith, Phil. Chetwood, Nathan Smart. Sworn and affirmed, 16 Feb., 1733. Lib. 3, p. 389.

1734, 3 mo. (May), 25 da. Inventory (£861.3.2¾) includes clock, 3 negroes (£90), oxen and other cattle, large boat, cable, anchor, 5 stocks of bees. Appraisers—Richard Smith, Wm. Hancock.

1736, June 14. Account. Paid John Powel, Thomas More, Mathew Ranton, Isaac Vanmeter, Joseph Darken, Robert Hart, Jno. Redstreake, Wm. Hall, Elis Cutting, Hugh Mealey, Joseph Morris, Richard Smith, Wm. Hancock, Clement Hall, Mary Loyel, Mathew Heisbey, Joseph Test, Wm. Hancock, Jno. Ogden, Iabe Sheppard, John Jones, Benjamin Peters, Joseph Darken, Wm. McDaniel, Ann Grant, Eliz. Surridge, Jno. Masson, Thomas More, Mary Coleman, Lewis Morris, Peter Turner, Robert Dickey, John Lewis, Daniel Huddy, Thomas Masson, Edw. Peirce, Wm. Willis, David Straughn, Benj. Davis, Daniel Mestyre, Clement Hall, Joshua Thompson, Mathew Rantoms, Mary Coleman, Nathan Mirring, John Thompson, Benjamin Eaton, Wm. Tuft, Thomas Nugent, Richard Grafton, John Husted, Benja. Peter, George Ward, Joseph Sharp, George Mondever, Peter Earnick, Joseph Pledger, Abiel Carll, Daniel Fogg, Jno. Lewis, Erasmus Fetters, John Powel, Mary Nix.

1743, Nov. 10. Morris, Eneas, of Freehold, Monmouth Co. Int. Mary Morris, the widow, resigns right of administration to John Henderson, of Freehold, principal creditor. Witness—John Williams. Lib. D, p. 101.

1743, Nov. 10. Inventory, £22.4.0; made by James Robinson and Peter Clark.

1743, Nov. 12. Adm'r, John Henderson, of Freehold. James Newell, of Perth Amboy, fellow bondsman. Witness—Robert King.

1748, Dec. 16. Morris, Grace, of Elsenburgh, Salem Co.; will of. Sisters—Sarah Goodwin, Mary Goodwin, Jane Wright, Gaile, Ann and Rebackah Morris. Brother-in-law, William Goodwin, to have £94, to be paid by my brother-in-law Thomas Goodwin. Cousin, John Goodwin, son of William, £100, when 21. Executors—brother-in-law, William Goodwin, and his son John. Witnesses—Mary Gennens, Mary Senchar, Jno. Smith, Junior. Affirmed 25 April, 1749. Lib. 6, p. 266.

1749, 2 mo. (Apr.), 28 da. Inventory, £118.19.6; made by Joshua Thompson, Aaron Bradway.

1734-5, Jan. 18. Morris (Morriss), John, of Elizabeth Town, Essex Co., yeoman; will of. Children—John, Deborah and Justus, all under age. Land joining lands of John Shotwell, Erasmus Allton and Job Pack. Wife, Eliphol. Executors—friends John Shotwell, Joseph Shotwell, and son Justus. Witnesses—Jeffry Jones, Mary Shotwell, Deboriah Lane. Proved Feb. 8, 1734. Lib. C, p. 8.

1734-5, Feb. 12. Inventory of personal estate (£1165.13.04) incl. bonds due from Job Pack, John Lambert, William Robison, Isaac Lawrence, Thomas Hamton, Jonathan Winans, Lues Winans, Samuel Randolph, James Wilkison, Erasmus Allton, Nicholas V. Diks, Nicholas Clauson, Peter Simons, William Winans, Ephraim Sale, Ebenezer Price, Benjamin Tharp, Edward Yomans, John King, Alexander Scot, Ephraim Clark, Eliphalet Frasey, Robert Morss, Ephraim Sayre, Joseph Allton; book debts due from William Dagworthy, Jonathan Pine, Ben. Pack, Ebenezer Johnson, Benjamin Ogden, Nathan Whitehead, John Hendricks, Jonathan Hamton, James Hines, Richard Broadwell, John Blanchard, Charles Tucker, Daniel Dehart, Charles Townley, Timothy Halstead, John Winans, Sen'r, Benjamin Bonnel, Edward Frasey, Daniel Marsh, John Shotwell, John Terrill, Anthony Little, William Williamson, Andrew Joline, John Lamburd, Richard Win, Grant Thorp, Job Pack, Robert Howen Sen'r, William Whithead, John Atkinson, Jacob Carle, Jos. Kelsey, William Jones, Robert Bond, Jno. Bonel, Thomas Scuder, Samuel Scuder, John Chanders, Thos. Moore, Thos. Squire, Abra'm Clark, David Howel, Jos. Williams, Sam. Carter, Henry Baker, Nat. Bonel, Daniel Meaker, Jno. Willis, Will. Meaker, Jos. Lion, Sam. Lambert, Ebenezer Lion, William Struharn, Jun'r, David Steward, Jos. Ackerman, Peter Blanchard, Thomas Ross, Jacob Bonel, Richard Jones, Cornelius Hatfield, Isaac Jewel, Jno. Tucker, Ackley Williams, Thos. Ackerman, Jon'th Higins, Tho's. Clark, Ben. Spining, James Banks, Isaac Bloomfield, Thos. Price, David Powers, Thos. Robison, Robert Clarkson, Daniel Ladner, Efingham Townley, Jos. Bonel, P. Kearney, Rich'd Whitehead, Jno. Davis, Nat. Pendue, Sam. Frasey, John Lawrence, Ben. Frasey, Benajah Palmer, Maximillion Lalour, Jno. Picket, Jno. Baker, Ben. Moore, Frank Fort, Henry Touttel, Daniel Lambert, Jonathan Woodruff, Daniel Lain, Jos. Mors, Nathaniel Bud,

Jos. Rolph, Gershom Frasey, James Woodruff, Zebulon Tharp, John Tremly, Will. Dean, Jack Shotwell, Able Lee, Leffery Jones, John Shotwell Jun'r, Benjamin Drake, Noble Hamilton, John Dean, Wm. Schyler, Capt. Lockhart, Justus Bloomfield, Andrew Johnson, Peter Trembly, Dean Carney, Job Conger, Jos. Conger. Made by Samuel Brant, Jacob Thorn, Andrew Scott.

1743, April 16. Morris, Joseph, of Salem Co. Int. Admr's, Prudence Morris, the widow, and Margaret Morris, daughter. Bondsman—Joseph Sharp, gent. All of Elsenburrough, said County. Witnesses—John Strown, Chas. O. Neill. Salem Wills, 727 Q.

1748, March 30. Morris, Joseph, of Middlesex Co., yeoman. Int. Adm'rs, Elizabeth Morris and Sam'll Jaquess. Thomas Moores and John Jaquess, fellow bondsmen. Lib. E, p. 158.

1739, 11 mo. (Jan.), 4 da. Morris, Lewis, of Elsinburgh, Salem Co.; will of. Wife, Grace, the profits from a certain mill and plantation, formerly belonging to my brother David Morris, situate in Elsinburgh, until my nephew, David Morris, son of my said brother, arrives to 18 years, it being bequeathed to my said wife for the bringing up and educating of my children. Further, wife shall have the use of my estate that I live on and the personal until my eldest daughter, Sarah Morris, will be 21. Second daughter, Mary, part of the home farm, beginning at a ditch between my land and Nathan Smart's, along the casway to Rich Island, until it intersects with the division line of Samuel Mason, "together," belonging equally to my friends, Wm. Hancock, Rich. Smith, Esq., and sd. Morris, Nathan Smart and Joshua Thompson; with ½ of Rich Island and marsh, also one-third of a marsh called Money Island, she paying £30 when 21, to my eldest daughter, Sarah Morris, who shall have the westernmost part of the home farm and ½ of Rich Island and marsh with the residue of my whole estate, she at 21 paying £100 to each of my daughters, Grace, Jane, Jayl, Ann, and Rebeckah, when 18 years old. Executors—wife, and my eldest daughter, Sarah Morris. Trustee—Richard Smith. Witnesses—Ann Woodnutt, Joseph Jackson, Joseph Carroll. Sworn and affirmed 18 July, 1740. Lib. 4, p. 245.

1740, July 18. Inventory (£785.5.8½) includes remnant of blew homespun cloth, 12 yds. homespun kersey, 40 yds. linen, barley, servant man's time, servant boy do., servant maid, nine negroes (£80). Appraisers—Nathan Smart, John Mason.

1744, Dec. 19. Account. Moneys paid Saml. Morton (Exr. of Mathew Ranton), Samuel Dickinson, Joost Miller, Saml. Mck. Cleny, John Pack, James Bredin, Peter Carmick, James Sharp, Mary Allen, John Eglington, Benjamin Acton, William Barrat, Robert Hutchinson, Ebenezar Miller, Robert Dickey, Charles O Neill, Phillip Chetwood, Hugh Blackwood, Mary Jennings, James Ridley, Thomas Sheppard, William Crabb, Hugh Mealey, Jonathan Hughs, Joseph Carroll, William Mordock, William Siddons, Edward Test, Daniel Mestayer, Benjamin Eatons, Thomas Nile, John Darkin, John Mason, Benjamin Haines, Erasmus Totters, Joseph March, William Doaen, Robert Hart, Thomas Rice.

1732, March 24. Morris, William, of Nottingham, Burlington Co., merchant. At his request he and his wife, late Sarah Dury, appointed guardians of their children, William, Sarah, Anthony and Mercy

Morris (they being under age), and for any property to which they are heirs. Lib. 3, p. 256.

1741, Oct. 29. Morris, William, of Elizabeth Town, Essex Co. Petition of Mary Parrot, of Elizabeth Town. "That whereas William Morris married the petitioner's daughter and died intestate near twelvemonth ago, and his wife died soon after, the petitioner being a poor woman and having had the expenses of the funerals;" and that Mr. William Anderson, who married the mother of said deceased, did take the moveable estate, for which no return has been made, she now asks that letters of administration be granted to her instead of said William Anderson.

1742, June 2. Daniel Potter, of full age, deposed he delivered within petition to William Anderson.

1742, June 2. Adm'x, Mary Parrot, mother-in-law. Thomas Baker and William Parrot, fellow bondsmen. Witnesses—Robert Hude, Robert King. Lib. C, p. 511.

1749, May 3. Morton, John, of Greenwich, Gloucester Co., yeoman; will of. Ann Morton, my mother, executrix and to have all my estate, real and personal, during widowhood. At her decease same shall be equally divided among the children of my brother Andrew, viz.—George, Hannah, Ann, Elizabeth, Elinor and Amey; and the children of Mortee Morton, viz.—Andrew, Margett and Rebecca; and the children of my deceased sister, Ann, the former wife of Garret Vanneman, viz.—Elinor and Ann. Executor—William Guest. Witnesses—Peter Mattson, Samuel Kain, Mary Hendrickson. (Not probated).

1751, July 30. Adm'x, Hannah Morton, widow. Bondsman—Garret Vanneman. Witness—Jos. Hollinshead. Lib. 7, p. 117.

1751, Aug. 9, 10. Inventory (£441.8.2½) includes negro, £55; 11 coins, £35.15.0; Indian corn, £21.15.0; writing desk and tea table. Appraisers—William Mickle, Nathan Boys, Jun.

1752, Jan. 29. Inventory of goods belonging to the widow before intermarriage, £16.5.0; made by William Mickle, Nathan Boys.

1738, Sept. 1. Morton, Joseph, of Mansfield, Burlington Co., husbandman. Int. Ann Morton, widow, renounces right to administer in favour of Joshua Owen. Witnesses—John Butcher, Jr., and Henry Browne.

1738, Sept. 4. Adm'r, Joshua Owen, of Springfield, yeoman. John Doe, fellow bondsman. Lib. 4, p. 149.

1738, Sept. 6. Inventory, £12.11.6; made by John Atkinson and John Butcher, Jr.

1738, Sept. 26. Additional inventory, £8; made by same.

1740, Jan. 27. Account. Payments to Reuben Eldredge, Rowland Owen, John West.

1734, April 18. Moslander, Johannes, of Salem Co., yeoman. Int. Adm'x, Sarah Moslander. Bondsmen—Cornelius Moslander, Jacob Jones. All of Salem County. Witnesses—William Vanneman, Danl. Mestayer. Lib. 3, p. 412.

1734, March 23. Inventory, £34.18.8; made by Peter and William Vanneman.

1734, Nov. 12. Account. Moneys paid to Errick Skeer, Garret Vaneman, Richard Grafton, Thomas Mason, Nicholas Johnson, Peter Vaneman, Jacob Jeans, Wm. Vaneman, Mathias Holston, Cornelius Copned, Tobias

Peterson, Thomas Lambson, Thomas Miles, Henry Jeans, Peter Tranbury, Tuda Gasperson, Jacob Atwood, Sarah Scoggins, Mecum McKnight, Charles Buckley, Lucas Peterson.

1748-9, 11 mo. (Jan.), 29 da. Moss, Abraham, of Philadelphia, yeoman; will of. Eldest son, Richard, ½ of my plantation that I purchased of Mary Marshall, provided he pays £250 to my youngest son, Isaac Moss, at any time within space of five years after my decease. In case of default Isaac to have the aforesaid moyety. Remainder of my estate real and personal to Isaac, he paying £100 unto my two daughters, Rebecca and Hope, as they come of age or marry. Executors—John Stewart, of Alloways Creek, and son Isaac. Witnesses—Benjamin Kindall, Alxr. Seaton. Sworn and affirmed, 17 March, 1748. Joseph Ogden (witness). (Salem Wills), Lib. 6, p. 38.

1748-9, 1mo. (Mar.), 9 da. Inventory, taken at Alloways Creek, Salem County, £152.19; made by Henry Stubbins, Nathaniel Evans.

1732, Dec. 5. Mott, Adam, of Little Egg Harbour, Burlington Co., yeoman. Int. Adm'r, Joseph Pancoast, Jun'r, of Mansfield. John Doe and Richard Roe, of same, fellow bondsmen.

1732, Dec. 5. Joseph Pancoast states that deceased died at his house. Lib. 3, p. 222.

1732, Dec. 9. Inventory, £11.2; made by Henry Cooper and Charles Tonkin.

1730, Feb. 15. Mott, Gershom, of Middletown Township, Monmouth Co., gentleman; will of. Part of plantation (not given to son James by deed) below Long bridge, bounded by Joseph Dorset, road from Middletown to Amboy, Thomas Kerney and Barren Bog, to be sold. Land at Barnegat. Son, John, heir at law. Negroes, Jack and his wife, Jenny, to be settled on part of son James' land, to pay yearly rent of one penny. To daughter, Huldah, negro girl Cate, given her by deed. Five children—William, Gershom, Asher, James and Huldah. Had given to son, James, land and island in Chingeres Bay and salt marsh at Conescunk. Executors—sons William, Gershom and James. Witnesses—Joseph Dorsett, Samuel Job, John Dorsett, William Walling. Proved March 20, 1733. Lib. B, p. 487.

1732, Nov. 27. Mott, John, of Hanover, Hunterdon Co., yeoman; will of. Wife, Charity. Son, Gershom, nine-tenths of land, when of age. Brother, Gershom Mott, books and apparel. Wife, residue of estate ,and half profit of saw-mill. Executors—wife, and brother, Gershom Mott. Witnesses—Nathaniel Whealen, Joseph Compton, E. Style. Proved Oct. 21, 1734. Lib. B, p. 572.

1734-5, Jan. 21. Inventory (£159.14.0) includes sword and pistol, map, books, silver, half of two negroes (£30.5.6). Made by John Campbell and Adam Blackanan.

1748, Sept. 19. Mott, William, of Burlington Co. Int. Adm'r, Jonathan Hough, of Springfield. Thomas Shinn, Jun'r, of Bridgeton, gent., fellow bondsman. Lib. 6, p. 328; Lib. 7, p. 95.

1748, July 23. Mount, Moses, of Shrewsbury, Monmouth Co. Int. Adm'x, Lydia Mount, the widow. Thomas Bills, of Shrewsbury, mason, fellow bondsman. Witnesses—Moriah Van Dyke, Richard Saltar. Lib. E, p. 201.

1744, Sept. 30. Mount, Peter, of Amwell, Hunterdon Co., farmer. Int. Inventory of the estate, £17.16.9; made by Benjamin Stout, Johannis Youngblust and Peter Young.

1744, Oct. 26. Adm'r, Welhelmus Wertgen, of Amwell, farmer. Benjamin Stout, of same place, farmer, surety. Lib. 5, p. 54.

1745, Nov. 22. Account exhibited.

1747, Dec. 8. Mucklewroth, William, of Salem Co., pedler. Int. Inventory (£10.16.9) includes pocket-books, needles, combs, handkerchiefs, thread, knives, ink horns, "Jew's Harpes." Appraisers—George Avis, Daniel Smith. Salem Wills, 803 Q.

1750, Nov. 29. Mulford, Aaron, of Hopewell, Cumberland Co., yeoman; will of. Wife, Christian, one-third of my plantation. Son, Aaron, the marsh below Tindals Island. Son, Moses, the plantation whereon I dwell, he to pay his brother Daniel £10 four consecutive years after he will be 20 (deemed then of age). If Daniel dies under age, his brothers, Benjamin (not 21) and William (not 21), shall receive £20 each. Legacies to daughter, Mary. Executors—wife, Christian, and John Miller. Witnesses—Ephraim Sheppard, Samuel Bowen, Robert Nicholls. Proved 16 Feb., 1750-51.

1750-1, March 15. Letters testamentary granted to Christian Mulford, executrix. Lib. 6, p. 449.

1750-51, Feb. 8. Inventory, £292.0.0; made by Abraham Reeves, Benjamin Mulford.

1746, Sept. 18. Mulford, David, of Newton Township, Gloucester Co., tailor; will of. Wife, Sarah, executrix and to have estate to bring up "the expected child." "My new saddle to my child and its heirs." Brother, Daniel Mulford. Witnesses—John Burrough, Matthew Frear, John Craig. Sworn and affirmed 16 Oct., 1746. Lib. 5, p. 293.

1731, Nov. 1. Mulier, Joost Arianse, quietus to his father-in-law, Isaac Lemeter. Middlesex Wills, 683 L.

1748, Sept. 7. Mullagan, James, of Freehold, Monmouth Co. Int. Adm'r, George Rhe, of Freehold, weaver, brother-in-law and principal creditor. Jonathan Forman, of Freehold, yeoman, fellow bondsman. Lib. E, p. 209.

1748, Sept. 15. Inventory (£40.17.8½) includes a loom, warping bars, spooling wheel, quills, treadles and pulleys. Made by Robert Newell and William Cowenhoven.

1749, Sept. 6. Account of administrator. Mentions bonds, etc., of William Cowenhoven (son of Albert), Mr. Blackly, in Philadelphia, John Henderson, Gysbert Van Matre, Peter Cowenhoven, Dr. Lecount, David English and Sarah Read.

1747, July 6. Mullen, John, of Amwell Township, Hunterdon Co., shopkeeper; will of. Wife, Elizabeth, house, orchard and land adjoining Peter Wooliever, with meadow purchased of William Dawles; wood from plantation bought of "the Stevensons of Rye in New England." Son, William, when of age, 419 acres adjoining John Boulsboy in Morris County, by right purchased from John Beaumont. Daughter, Rebecca, when aged 18, brick house in Burlington, and 333 acres of land to be taken up as purchased from Cornelius Stephens, of Amwell. Daughter, Sarah, when eighteen, other house in Burlington, rented by Israel Hulings, and a plantation bought of James Johnston in Morris County, and a 50-acre right purchased from John Beaumont. Daughters, Elizabeth and Mary, when 18, plantation where Joseph Runyan lived, with 20 acres bought of John Vanvorst. Executors—wife, Richard Smith (son of Samuel Smith of Burlington), merchant, and Peter Prall, Sr., of Amwell, yeoman. Witnesses—Laurence Marr, Nathaniel Parker and Christopher Search. Proved August 11, 1749. Lib. 6, p. 278.

1749, Sept. 1. Inventory (£2,014.7.0) includes a negro girl, £26. Made by Job Robins and Wilson Hunt. (Job Robins a Quaker, and the executors, Quakers).

1749, Dec. 26. Munday (Monday), Joseph, of Piscataway, Middlesex Co., yeoman. Nuncupative will, but not admitted by P. Kearny, and administration granted without regard to it.

1749-50, Jan. 22. Adm'rs, Elsie Monday, his widow, and Joseph Monday, his son. David Coryel and James Gyles, fellow bondsmen. Lib. E, p. 361.

1749-50, Jan. 20. Inventory, £144.4; made by Thomas Pound and Reune Runyon.

1749-50, Feb. 6. Vendue by the administrators. Articles sold to Samuel Wilson, David Fitzrandle, Benjamin Gross, Mathew McMickle, Clary Clawson, Joseph Munday, John Long, Nathaniel Leforge, Will'm Stelle, Ebenezer Drake, Ebenezer Daniels, Elisha Smalley, Nemiah Dunham, John Haghawont, Sam'l Wilson, Jos. Runyon, Wm. Clawson, Wm. Clawson (son of Brant), Sam'll Betts, John Smalley, Nathan Flint, John Pound Jun'r, Isaac Wright, And'w Chitester, John Heborn, Andrew Smalley, Henry Randle, John Mollison, James Giles.

1750, March 31. Sundry effects divided to satisfaction of the heirs, who are Alce Monday, the widow, Joseph Munday, the son, and Benja. Gross.

1750, May 30. Account. Debts due to Andrew Myars, Cornelius Low, Gersham Drake, Rune Runyon, Peter Low's estate, Geo. Morlatt, Cornelius Clawson, Elijah Pound, Anthony Blackford, Tim'y Blumfield, Thos. Bartow, Philip Kearny, David Coriel, James Giles, Elias V. Court, Jun'r.

Munday (see Monday).

1742, 18th day, 5th mo. (July). Murfin, William, of Nottingham, Burlington Co.; will of. Children—Robert, William, Sarah and Mary. John, Daniel and Ann, children of son William. Grandaughter, Susanna Murfin. 260 acres of land surveyed the 22nd, 23rd and 24th days of May, 1738; also a Right to 200 acres in West Jersey, and 350 acres at Bethlehem, Hunterdon Co. Executors—wife, Sarah, and son William. Witnesses—John Tantum, Isaac Arey, Jos. Reckless. Proved Aug. 27, 1742. Lib. 4, p. 317.

1742, Aug. 18, 19. Inventory, £615.9.3; made by Marmaduke Watson and William Bunting. Includes two Bibles and other books (£2.9).

1747, Oct. 9. Murphy, Mark, of New Brunswick, Middlesex Co. Int. Adm'x, Phillis Murphy, his widow. James Thomson, of New Brunswick, and James Newill, of Perth Amboy, fellow bondsmen. Lib. E, p. 92.

1749, Oct. 24. Murphy, Stephen, of Northampton, Burlington Co. Int. Inventory, £77.16.6; made by James Wills and Thomas Budd.

1749, Nov. 2. Adm'x, Esther Murphy, widow. Lib. 6, p. 334; Lib. 7, p. 100.

1747, Oct. 11. Murrell, William, of Northampton, Burlington Co., yeomen; will of. Two daughters and son, Samuel, each £5. Executor —friend Henry Paxson, to have remainder of estate, real and personal, in trust for sons William, Joseph, Leamy and John. Witnesses— Patrick Reynolds, Jun'r, John Clark, Tho. Shinn. Proved Nov. 28, 1749. Lib. 6, p. 345.

1749, Nov. 25. Inventory, £65.15.3; made by Patrick Reynolds and Thos. Atkinson.

1744, May 8. Napier, Alexander, of Freehold, Monmouth Co., yeoman; will of. Daughter, Elizabeth English, £100 due from John Smith, of Freehold, trader. Grandchildren—David Watson, Mary Buckalow, Euphon (wife of Joseph Smith), Margaret, Agnes and Elizabeth Watson, and Zilpah Smith. Grandson, John Napier, when of age, lands at Middletown Point and Mount Pleasant; if grandson dies under age, to grandson, David English. Executors—son-in-law, David English, and friend John Henderson. Witnesses—John Campbell, John Irwin, James English, Joseph Ker. Proved February 5, 1744. Lib. D, p. 229.

1744, Oct. 5. Inventory (£237.7.5) includes bonds of James Napier and John Smith. Made by William Cowenhoven, John Irwin, Joseph Ker.

1748, July 18. Neale, John, of City of Burlington, carpenter; will of. Son, Joseph, Mary his wife, and their children, dwelling house on north side of Pearl St., adjoining Thomas Gardiner. Son, John. Daughters—Martha Sprague and Hannah Buddle. Lot in Salem in New England. Executor—son, John. Witnesses—Richard Smith, Mary Butcher, Jonathan Smith. Proved Aug. 24, 1755.
Burlington Wills, 4287-88 C.

1744-5, Feb. 28. Neilson, John, of Piscataway, Middlesex Co., Doctor of Phisick; will of. Daughter, Gertrude Neilson. Expected child. Real and personal estate. Executors—wife, Johanna, and James Neilson, of New Brunswick, merchant. Witnesses—Samuel Staats Coesjemans, Majesie Coejemans, Gartruyd Coejimans. Proved Sept. 9, 1745.
Lib. D, p. 359.

1732-3, March 11. Nesbitt, Samuel, of Newark, Essex Co., weaver; will of. Children—James, Samuel, John, Abigail, all under age. Real and personal estate. Executors—wife, Abigail, brother-in-law, Samuel Harrison, and friend Eliphalet Johnson. Witnesses—Jno. Cooper, Thomas Eagles, Isaac Cundict. Proved June 20, 1733. Lib. B, p. 424.

1750, April 29. Nevius, Johanis, of City of New Brunswick and Somerset Co., yeoman; will of. Wife, Susana, use of all real and personal estate in Somerset Co., excepting 100 acres at the southwest end of said plantation reserved for debts. Sons—Peterus (eldest), Marke, Johanis and Abraham (all minors). Executors—brothers Peter and David Nevius, and brother-in-law, Lucas Schenck. Witnesses—Guysbert Sutvin, Peter Van Voorhees, Gerrit Gerritsen. Proved 19 May, 1750. Lib. E, p. 498.

1750, Dec. 7. Inventory (£102.17.7) includes his arms, gun, cutlash, belt, holster and pistols, £4.10; Bible and books, £4. Made by Albert VanVoorhes, Abraham VanVoorhees, Peter VanVoorhees.

1739, 29th day, 10th mo. (Dec.). Newbold, Thomas, of Mansfield, Burlington Co., yeoman; will of. Wife, Edith. Children—Caleb, William, Mary and Hannah, all under age. Plantation in Springfield, where William Rogers now dwells, adjoining John Scholey; also plantation in Chesterfield, where John Page, Sen'r, now dwells. Executors—brothers William and Barzillai Newbold. Witnesses—William Coate, Francis Shinn, Sam. Harris. Proved Oct. 17, 1741. Lib. 4, p. 325.

1741, Oct. 17. Inventory, £2074.13.2¾; made by Samuel Wright, Benjamin Shreve and Thos. Potts, Jun'r.

1744, Dec. 10. Newby, Gabriel, of Newtown, Gloucester Co., yeoman; will of. Wife, Elizabeth. Son John (not 14) to have all lands when 21. In case of his death under age and that of my wife, estate shall descend to Stephen, son of Joseph Thackray, of place aforesaid. Executors—John Kaighin, Esq., and Joseph Ellis, of the same place. Witnesses—John Estlack, Patience Estlack, William Sarjeant. Sworn and affirmed, 27 Dec., 1744. Lib. 5, p. 73.

1744, Dec. 21. Inventory, £206.8.7; made by Henry Sparks, James Gill.

1734-5, Feb. 10. Newby, Mark, of Newton, Gloucester Co., yeoman; will of. Joseph Cooper, of Newton, sole executor, and to have in trust my plantation (250 acres) in said County, which is leased to John Newbury for three years. My sister, Hannah, wife of Joseph Thackery, to have all my estate after legacies are paid to my brothers Jacob and Isaac, and my sister Sarah Hugg when they will be of full age. Witnesses—Gabriel Hugg, Thos. Darroch, Nathan Newby. Proved 6 March, 1737. Lib. 4, p. 129.

1737, Jan. 22. Renunciation of Joseph Cooper, executor named, in favor of Joseph Thackery.

1735, 1st mo. (March), 9. Inventory (£147.4.5) includes rent received from John Newbury. Appraisers—John Estlack, Tobias Holloway.

1736, Feb. 9. Newby, Nathan, of Newton, Gloucester Co., yeoman. Inventory of the estate, £41.17.6; made by John Estlack and Tobias Holloway.

1736, Mar. 10. Bond of Gabriel Newby (brother and heir-at-law of Nathan), as administrator, with John Estlack, as fellow bondsmen. Both of Newton, yeomen. Lib. 4, p. 86.

1733, Jan. 4. Newcomb, Joseph, of Salem Co. Int. Adm'x, Joyce Newcomb (widow). Bondsman—Gabriel Glenn. All of said County. Witnesses—Mary Mestayer, Danl. Mestayer. Lib. 3, p. 394.

1732, Nov. 9. Inventory (£457.18.8), appraised at Morris River, of "Captain Joseph Newcomb, gent.," includes cattle and horses; also bonds from New England against sundry persons living there, £357.12.8. Appraisers—Gabriel Glenn, Samuel Tompson.

1739, July 26. Newell, John, of Freehold, Monmouth Co.; will of. Wife, Martha. Children—Robert (eldest son), John, Martha, Vilet, Adam and Agnes. £10 for schooling, etc., of two youngest children, Adam and Agnes. Executors—friends Timothy Lloyd and James English. Witnesses—Joseph Ker, James Reed, Joseph Forman. Proved August 25, 1739. Lib. C, p. 291.

1739, August 11. Inventory, £169.6.0; made by Joseph Forman, merchant, and Joseph Ker, yeoman, of Freehold.

1744, Feb. 6. Newey, John, of Woodbridge, Middlesex Co., cord-

wainer. Int. Adm'r, John Moore, of Woodbridge, gent., principal creditor. John Doe and Richard Roe, fellow bondsmen.
Lib. D, p. 228.

1744, Oct. 20. Newkirk, Cornelius, of Salem Co. Int. Admr's, Rachel Newkirk, widow, and Abraham Newkirk. Bondsman—Jost Miller. All of said county. Witnesses—Benjamin Bispham, Chas. O. Neill. Lib. 5, p. 56.

1744, Oct. 4. Inventory (£953.12.½) includes bonds, etc., due from Saml. Boggs, Abraham Nealson, Saml. Rain, Sam'l. and Jeremiah Foster, Isaac Vanmetre, Adam Oshel, Henry Vanmetre, John Hull, Peter Duffle, Nathaniel Moore, George Hildebrant, Daniel Westcote, Ebenezer Westcote, Robert Small, John Campbell, John Trimnal, David Loper, Ephraim Seyrs, Henry Vanmetre, Josh. Carroll, Walter Burke, Edmond Hynds; also negroes, £129.12.11, and copper still, £11. Appraisers—Davis Davis, William Paullin.

1739, May 18. Newton, Ebenezar, of Cape May Co.; will of. Wife, Elizabeth, one-third of improvement of my plantation during life; after her decease land shall be divided between my sons Calab and Isaac, they to have the improvement of two-thirds at present. Sons, Ebenezer and Nathan, equally, the cedar swamps and rest of my lands. Daughters, Sarah and Martha, to share equally with their brothers in the personal estate. Witnesses—Peter Johnson, Joseph Johnson, Israel Johnson. Proved 18 July, 1739. Cape May Wills, 93 E.

"Derby, in the county of New Haven, Connecticut, in New England July the ninth, 1739, appeared Petter Johnson, Joseph Johnson and Israel Johnson, to take the deposition of the last will of Ebenezer Newton, late deceased in Derby, etc." Signed, "John Riggs, Justice of the Peace."

1739, Aug. 10. Inventory (£340.5.9), includes "44 head of chattel and 12 calves" (£94.03.0), 3 horses, 60 sheep, 12 hogs and 13 pigs, 39 geese and 2 turkeys, wheat, corn, rye, flax, barly, oats, negro woman, whale boat and craft (11.17.00), leather, books, yarn and indigoe (£4.15.06). Appraisers—Ezekiel Eldredge, Thomas Ross.

1729, Nov. 24. Nichols, William, of Freehold, Monmouth Co., Esquire; will of. Nephew, George Murison, under age, living in New York, testator's share of lands, etc., in New York, that belonged to said nephew's mother, by will of testator's father-in-law, William Smith, Esquire, in case she had lived until a division had been made between her and her sister, who was the testator's wife, now deceased. Residue of estate in colony of New York that belonged to testator or his deceased wife, and estate in New Jersey, to wife Sarah, who is to be executrix. Witnesses—James Reid, Amice Grandin and Daniel Grandin. Lib. D, p. 61.

1750, Feb. 5. Nicholson, Abel (over 14 years old), son of Samuel, of Gloucester Co. Samuel Parr, of same county, yeoman, guardian.
Gloucester Wills, 465 H.

1740, Sept. 7. Nicholson, Joseph, of Mansfield, Burlington Co., yeoman; will of. Sister, Hannah, wife of Isaac DeCow, and their daughters, Sarah and Hannah. Brothers—George and John. Kinsman, Josiah Bunting. Sister-in-law, Mary Butcher. Father-in-law, John Butcher, all my interest in a lot on York Street, which I secured of him as my wife's portion. Uncle Samuel Bunting's children. Executors—father, John Butcher, brother and sister, Isaac DeCow, Jun'r, and Hannah DeCow. Witnesses—Jonathan Barrton, Job Ridgway,

Sam'l Scattergood. Proved 1st day, 8th mo. (Oct.), 1740. Lib. 4, p. 256.

1740, Sept. 29. Inventory £401.8.10; made by Daniel Haines and William Folwell. Includes note of hand of Ben't Bard, £5, and plantation, 105 acres, £250.

1749-50, Feb. 24. Nicholson, Samuel, of Waterford, Gloucester Co.; will of. Wife, Jane. Sons—Joseph, Samuel (to have at 21 land joining Thomas Spicer and Thomas Wood), Abel (the plantation where I live when 21; in case of his death without issue my son Samuel to have the same). Daughters—Abigail, wife of Daniel Hillman, Junior, Hannah, wife of John Hillman, and Sarah Nicholson. Executors—wife, Jane and son, Samuel. Witnesses—Joseph Heritage, William Matlack, Saml. Spicer. Affirmed 4 July, 1750. Lib. 7, p. 2.

1750, April 27. Inventory (£323) includes four negroes—woman, £18; man, £45; boy, £20; girl, £3. Appraisers—Tho. Spicer, Junior, Joseph Heritage.

1750-51, March —. Account. Payments to Benj. Collins, Jos. Heritage, Junr., Thos. Spicer, William Matlack, Saml. Nicholson, Junr., Sam. Spicer, John Ross, George Weeds, Hannah Cooper, Daniel Cooper, Isaac Andrews, Daniel Hillman, Junr., Saml. Parr, William Stones, Matthias Aspdon, Timothy Matlack, William Hudson, John Atkins, Mary Champion, Edwd. Rads. Price, John Gill, Hannah Hillman, Isaac Lippincot, Jacob Clement, John Calfrey, Jacob Burroughs.

1744, Dec. 18. Nicolls, George, of Elizabeth Town, Essex Co. Int. Elizabeth Nicolls renounces her right to administer estate of her husband, and desires that administration be granted to John Halstead, Esq. Witness—John Blanchard.

1744-5, Jan. 10. Adm'r, John Halstead, Esq., principal creditor. Eliakim Higgins, of Perth Amboy, fellow bondsman. Lib. D, p. 221.

1740, Oct. 25. Nicholson, Thomas, of Newark, Essex Co., boatman; will of. Son, George, land at Connubrook, bought of William Robinson. Other children—Mary, Elizabeth and Ann, all under age. Exexecutors—wife, Ann, and friend John Johnson, of Two-mile brook. Witnesses—Thomas Price, schoolmaster, Thomas Alling, Josiah Lyon. Proved Aug. 20, 1741. Lib. C, p. 427.

1737, May 10. Nisbet, James, late of London but now of Perth Amboy, Middlesex Co., taylor; will of. "Being weak by reason of age." Children—James, William, Thomas, Anne. Real and personal estate. Executors—wife, Sarah, and son Jonathan. Witnesses—John Nevill, John Waterman, Francis Neville. Proved April 1, 1741. Lib. C, p. 400.

1741, Feb. 25. Noble, Gertrude, of City of Burlington, widow; will of. Executor—cousin, George Eyre, to have all moneys and real estate devised to me by my deceased husband, Joseph Smith. Witnesses—Rebecca Fling, Abram Dixon, William Sorsby. Proved March 15, 1741. Lib. 4, p. 332.

1751, 2 mo. (April), 16. Norbury, Richard, of Woodbury Creek, Gloucester Co., tailor; will of. Estate to be divided equally between my mother and all my own sisters. Hanna to have pay for services done. Executor—William Wood, who shall sell my land in Woodbury. Witnesses—Andrew Sloan, Abichai Chattin, Sarah Whiteal. Affirmed 24 May, 1751. Lib. 7, p. 143.

1751, 2 mo. (Apr.), 27 da. Inventory, £45.09.0; made by Abra. Chattin, Joseph Gibson Junr.

1747, ——, —. Norbury, Thomas, of Gloucester Co. (Card indexed, "Inventory, filed 1747;" but paper missing).

1742, July 10. Norris, James, of Haddonfield, Gloucester Co., shipwright. Int. Adm'x, his widow, Sarah. Bondsmen—Thomas Atkinson, of Burlington County, and Jonathan Axford, of Haddonfield. Lib. 4, p. 376.

1735, April 10. Norton, John, Esq., of Salem Co. Int. Adm'r, Robert Hart, of Salem Co., merchant. Bondsman—Joseph Test, of said County, gent. Witness—John Doe. Lib. 4, p. 21.

1749, Oct. 24. Norton, Nathaniel, of Cape May Co., gentleman. Wife, Elizabeth, one-third of the personal and all the interest arising from the money of the children of Ezekiel Eldredge, deceased, "on account of my becoming executor of his estate by marrying his widow." Daughter, Elishaba Norton, the house I live in, one acre and two rods of land. A house and five acres of land bought of Samuel Crowell to be sold by my executors and one-third of the money given to my wife, two-thirds to my son, George Norton, and he shall have an equal part of the personal estate with my daughters Hannah and Mary Norton. Executors—wife, and brother Daniel Norton. Witnesses—Ellis Hughes, Nathan Eldredge, John Leek. Proved 4 April, 1750. Lib. 6, p. 363.

1750, April 24. Inventory of real and personal (£142.0.6), includes a house and five acres of land (£25), cattle, sheep and horses. Appraisers—John Shaw, John Eldredge.

1748, May 24. Norton, Sarah, of Burlington Co. Int. Inventory, £18.16.2; made by Thos. Cobberley and Isaac Arney.

1748, May 20. Adm'r, John Martin. Thomas Cobberley and Isaac Arney, of Middlesex Co., fellow bondsmen. Lib. 5, p. 492.

1749, Aug. 7. Account. Paid Richard Horsefield for principal and interest on bond due from Wm. Norton, deceased.

1749, April 19. Nuttman, Isaac, of Elizabeth Town, Essex Co., blacksmith; will of. Children—Phebe, Sarah, John, all under age. Real and personal estate. Executors—wife, Joanna, Edward Sale, and John Nuttman. Witnesses—Mathias Baldwin, Moses Ogden, Jonathan Dod. Proved Nov. 20, 1749. Lib. E, p. 370.

1739, May 1. Nuttman, James, of Newark, Essex Co., cooper; will of. Children—Samuel, John, James, Isaac, Ephraim (last three under age), Mary Williams, Abigail Nuttman, Hannah Sergeant. Son, Samuel, land in Hunterdon Co., where he now lives. Lands joining lands of David Baldwin, Joseph Peck, Benjamin Canfield, deceased. Lands bought of John Gardner, Thomas Huntington and Mr. Prudden. Executors—wife, Sarah, and sons John and Samuel. Witnesses—Moses Hall, Alexander Eagles, Thomas Eagles. Proved Dec. 10, 1740. Lib. C, p. 369.

1742, July 14. Oakford, Charles, of Salem Co. Int. Adm'x, Esther Oakford (relict of). Bondsmen—Samuel Abbott, Joseph Ware, farmers. All of Alloways Creek in said County. Witness—Elizabeth Huddy. Lib. 4, p. 376.

1742, 2 mo. (April), 1 da. Inventory, £269.0.10; made by Joseph Ware, Samuel Abbott.

1750, June 24. Odell, John, of the Borough of Elizabeth, Essex Co., joyner; will of. Son, Jonathan, "to be kept to learning till he hath taken his degree at college." Daughters—Joanna, Eunice, and Elizabeth, all under age. Expected child. Real and personal estate. Executors—wife, Temperance, friends Jonathan Sergeant of Newark and Timothy Whitehead of Elizabeth. Witnesses—Caleb Smith, Hezekiah Dickinson, Daniel Hole. Proved June 28, 1750. Lib. E, p. 435.

1749, Aug. 12. Ogden, Abigail (over 14 years old), daughter of Jonathan, of Salem County. Ananias Sayre, Esq., of Cumberland County, guardian. Lib. 6, p. 116.

1726, March 18. Ogden, David, of Newark, Essex Co., yeoman; will of. Children—Sarah, Abigail, Elizabeth, John, David, Usal, and Martha, last four under age. Real and personal estate. Executors—wife, Abigail, sons John and David, and sons-in-law Nathaniel Johnson, Joseph Tuttle and John Johnson. Witnesses—James Wheeler, Stephen Baldwin, John Baldwin. Proved Nov. 11, 1734. Lib. C, p. 16.

1737, May 13. Ogden, James, of Elizabeth Town, Essex Co., mason; will of. Children—James and Phebe Ogden, both under age. Real and personal estate. Executors—wife, Elizabeth, and father-in-law Edward Croel, of Woodbridge. Witnesses—Andrew Joline, John Woodruff, Ichabod Burnet. Proved June 20, 1737. Lib. C, p. 167.

1729, Dec. 15. Ogden, John, of Elizabeth Town, Essex Co. Int. Adm'rs, Mary Ogden and Ebenezer Lyon. (Omitted from previous vol. of Wills). Lib. B, p. 146.

1745, Dec. 21. Ogden, John, of Cohansey, Salem Co.; will of. Wife, Sarah. Sons—John, sole executor and to have the marsh called Hay Neck, which I purchased of Saml. Barns, and one-third of a marsh upon Dividing Creek, he paying £10 to my son Daniel Ogden; David, land and marsh belonging to the mill survey on the south side of the Creek; Daniel, 70 acres upon Rattle Snake Gutt, belonging to the survey my son Thomas lives on; Thomas, land which he lives on and ½ of my mill and pond; Joseph, the homestead and ½ the mill and pond, and one-third of the marsh upon Dividing Creek. Moveables equally among my five sons and daughter Mary. Eldest son of my son Samuel, deceased, 10 shillings. Eldest son of my son Jonathan, deceased, 10 shillings. Eldest child of my daughter Sarah Ogden, deceased, 10 shillings. Witnesses—Daniel Elmer, Azariah Cooley, Daniel Lyon. Proved 26 March, 1746. Lib. 5, p. 249.

1746, Oct. 31. Inventory, £14.1.0.5; made by Mathew Parvin, Thomas Harris, Junior.

1731, June 19. Ogden, Jonathan, of Elizabeth Town, Essex Co. Int. Bond of Elizabeth Ogden, the widow, as administratrix on estate of her husband. John Ogden, fellow bondsman. Lib. B, p. 127.

1731, Aug. 9. Inventory (£251.13) includes three Bibles and other books and negro boy valued at £84. Made by Samuel Alling and Benja. Bond.

1731, July 2. Ogden, Jonathan, of Elizabeth Town, Essex Co., tanner; will of. Son, Robert. Grandsons—John and Samuel Ogden. Great grandson, Jonathan, youngest son of grandson Jonathan, deceased. Sisters of grandson Samuel Ogden. Great-granddaughters—Sarah Griffing and Rebekah Whitehead. Plantation whereon my son Jonathan, deceased, dwelt, joining land of Joseph Ogden; land bought of Mr. Effingham Townley and David Morehouse; pasture joining lands of John Miles deceased, Mr. John Woodruff and my son, Samuel, deceased; land bought of Mr. Samuel Barret, of Boston; land joining land of Benjamin Parkhurst, deceased; meadow called Bray lot, at mouth of Homan's Creek; farm joining lands of Abraham Baker and Isaac Whitehead, deceased; meadow which was John Parker's Bay lot; land purchased of Mr. Samuel Peck, joining farm of Joseph Crane, Esq., deceased; land bought of Abraham Baker, joining land of Daniel Woodruff; 100 acres joining lands of Samuel Headley. Executors—son, Robert, friend and relation, Joseph Woodruff, Sen'r, and grandson, John Ogden. Witnesses—John Woodruff, Daniel Price, William Ogden. Proved Jan. 9, 1732-3. Lib. B, p. 351.

1732-3, Jan. 15. Inventory £63.11; made by William Winans, David Whitehead.

1735, Feb. 10. Ogden, Jonathan, of Cohansey, Salem Co., weaver; will of. Daughter, Abigail, the whole estate; if she dies without issue before twenty, all estate shall be sold and £15 paid towards the public worship of God for the "Descenting Prespeteareans of the Congregation of Greenwich." Legacies to my mother-in-law, Sarah Bishop, and Moses, Joseph, Samuel, Daniel and Nathaniel Bishop. John Shaw and his wife, Sarah, shall take my daughter Abigail and bring her up until she will be fourteen, during which time she shall be well educated, and then put to the trade of tailoring, and, when eighteen, executors shall deliver to her the lands, which shall be rented, in the meantime. Sarah Shaw to take moveables, and, in case of the death of my said daughter, she shall possess them and all my wife's clothes. "My daughter Abigail Ogden was born April 23, 1733." Executors—Abraham Reeves and Jonathan Holmes. Witnesses—James Johnson, Ephraim Buck, John Miller, Christopher Randolph. Proved 27 March, 1736. Lib. 4, p. 58.

1735, March 18. Inventory (£81.6.3) includes books, "weaver's lume and tackling," cattle and sheep. Appraisers—James Robbinson, John Miller.

1743, Nov. 21. Ogden, Jonathan, of Deerfield, Salem Co., yeoman; will of. Wife, Hannah, to have lands, meadows, etc., until my son Richard will be 21. Said properties shall be divided equally between my two sons, Richard and Jonathan, when 21. Executors—wife, and William Dare, Junior. Witnesses—Henry Seelye, Joseph Ogden, John Ogden, Junior. Proved 12 Nov., 1745. Lib. 5, p. 251.

1745, June 19. Inventory (£146.0.6) includes cattle, English grain. Appraisers—Jeremiah Foster, Henry Seeley.

1731, Feb. 8. Ogden, Robert, of Elizabeth Town, Essex Co., tanner; will of. Children—Robert, Moses, Elihu, David, Hannah (wife of Samuel Winans), Phebe, Rebecca and Mary, last three under age. Land on which my father Jonathan Ogden dwelt, joining land of Joseph Ogden, and which was given me in his last will; land joining lands of Sam'll Peck and Samuel Headley; land purchased of Effingham Townley and David Morehouse; land my father purchased of Mr. Samuel Barret, of Boston; land joining land of Joseph Crane. Present wife Phebe, from her late husband, Jonathan Bauldwin, deceased. Executors—wife, Phebe, son Robert, and kinsmen John Ogden of Elizabeth Town and David Ogden Jun'r of Newark. Witnesses—Thomas Woodruff, William Whitehead, Samuel Woodruff.

1733, Nov. 19. Codicil. Expected child. Witnesses—Jonathan Dickinson, Thomas Woodruff, Mary Jones. Proved Dec. 6, 1733.

Lib. B, p. 515.

1733, Dec. 6. Inventory £308.07.03; made by Joseph Woodruff, David Whitehead.

1714, Feb. 10. Ogden, Samuel, of Elizabeth Town, Essex Co. Inventory of personal estate, £220.14.06; made by Daniel Price and Benjamin Bond. (For his will, see Archives, Vol. 23, p. 345).

1737, Nov. —. Accompt of Samuel and Johanna Williams, late Johanna Ogden, the widow and executor on the estate of Samuel Ogden, whose will was dated Nov. 26, 1714, showing payments to Elizabeth Alexander, Isaac Price, Gershom Higgins, Joseph Osborn, John Tappen, Isaac Whitehead, Mr. Jonathan Dickinson, John Cramble, Daniel Juet, Samuel Stanborough, Henry Rolef, Will'm Looker, Thomas Baker, Ephraim Price, Abraham Baker, Doct'r Edwards, William Dixon, Jonathan Vanimbrogh, John Blanchard, wife of John Meek, Samuel Meeker. Essex Wills, 9-14 G.

1742, Dec. 25. Ogden, Samuel, of Deerfield, Salem Co., yeoman; will of. Wife, Mary, to have use of the lands until my son, Samuel, will be of age, and then same divided equally between my two sons, Samuel and Malachia Ogden. Moveables to be divided equally between my wife, Mary, and my daughter, Lorain. Executor—friend Jonathan Ogden. "Not before the signing I appoint that Mary, my wife [be] Exct'x." Witnesses—Jeremiah Foster, David Wescoat, Thomas Ogden. Proved 26 Jan., 1742-3. Lib. 4, p. 353.

1742-3, Jan. 1. Inventory, £126.18.6; made by appraisers Jeremiah Foster, Abraham Garrison.

1739, Oct. 25. Ogilvy, George, of Perth Amboy, Middlesex Co., yeoman. Int. Adm'r, William Antill, principal creditor. Lib. C, p. 294.

1750, Nov. 4. Oharro, Owen, of Bedminster, Somerset Co., yeoman; will of. Wife, Margaret, executrix. Children—John, James, Robert and Margaret (a minor). To the sons all real estate, and the 107 acres agreed for of Andrew Johnston, Esqr., "adjoining the home-farm." Executor—son John. Witnesses—John Oliphant, Matthias Lane, Moses Craig. Proved 20 March, 1750. Lib. E, p. 502.

1750, Feb. 2. Inventory (£177.18.3) includes cattle and horses, 25 acres of green wheat, dry wheat. Made by William Allen, Moses Craig.

1732, Feb. 12. Oliphant, Duncan, of Amwell Township, Hunterdon Co.; will of. Wife, Mary. Eldest son, David, the long gun, large Bible, and a book called the Conductor Generalis. Wife, entire estate to bring up children. Four sons—David, John, Ephraim and James. Three daughters—Margaret (wife of Thomas Gordon), Mary and Ann, the plantation where William Allen lived, when youngest daughter is aged 18. Executors—son, David, brother-in-law John Garrison, and friend Peter Praul. Friend, John Reading, trustee. Witnesses—Thomas Lake, William Job, Jacob Reeder. Proved August 7, 1734.

Lib. 3, p. 425.

———, ———, —. Inventory (£152.14.0) includes gun, books, Bibles and Testaments. Made by Thomas Lake and Daniel Seaburn.

1747, Nov. 3. Oliver (Olliver), David, of the Borough of Elizabeth, Essex Co., carpenter; will of. Children—David, Samuel, Jeremiah, John, Jonathan, Sarah and Elizabeth, last four under age. Lands purchased of Abel Smith and John Shotwell, at Westfield; land joining land of Joseph Bird. Executors—wife, Elizabeth, and son Samuel. Witnesses—Daniel Terrill, Joanna Lambert, John Terrill. Proved Nov. 24, 1747. Lib. E, p. 111.

1739, Nov. 1. Oliver, Samuel, of Elizabeth Town, Essex Co., yeoman; will of. Cousin, Mercy Olliver, one-third part of moveable estate at 18 years; in case of her death to go towards building of Presbyterian meeting-house. One-third of moveable estate to wife, Margret, and one-third to cousin Benoni Frazee, he to purchase a burial cloth for the use of Raway. Real and personal estate. Executors—cousin, Benoni Frazee of Raway, to act with my wife. Witnesses—William Ross, William Barber, Jane Ross. Proved June 16, 1744.

1744, June 16. Margaret Oliver, the surviving executor, qualified. Lib. D, p. 147.

1744, June 19. Inventory (£125.08), includes bonds of Jonathan Frazee and John Olliver, a Psalm Book, Common Prayer Book, and an old negro man. Made by Andrew Craige and Eliphalet Frasee.

1747, Aug. 28. Citation to the executor to appear with a copy of the will and Mr. (James) Alexander's opinion thereon. (See files, Essex Wills, 905-14 G).

1747, ———, —. A citation to the widow to appear and render an account, brought by John Oliver, brother of said deceased, and David Oliver, his brother s son, in behalf of themselves and others concerned.

1749, Nov. 17. Oliver, Stephen, of Trenton, Hunterdon Co. Int. Inventory of estate (133.3.9) includes books, two guns, and debts due from Robert Hood and John Riche. Made by Peter and Henry Lott. Lib. 7, p. 32.

1749, Dec. 19. Adm'r, Andrew Oliver, of Hopewell. Peter Lott, of Trenton, tanner, surety. Witnesses—Stephen Rose and Henry Lott.

1750, June 27. Account. Mentions George Davis, Tim. Long, Francis Hall, Thomas Boden, Daniel McCarty, Peter Lott, Jr., James Heigerman, Doctor Cadwallader, Ezekiel Smith, Doctor Moon, John Berrien, Isaac Herin, Doctor Ballard, Jno. Vantillborough, Jno. Roney, Henry Wesener, Peter Lott, Henry Lott, David Rumbo, Richard Clawson, Jos. Tindel, Jno. Burtis, William Savage, Jos. Paxton, sister, Elizabeth Oliver, father, Stephen Oliver.

1748, March 29. Oneal (Oneill), Cornelius, of Deptford, Gloucester Co., laborer. Int. Adm'x, Katherine Oneill, widow. Bondsman—John Sparks, of County and township aforesaid. Witness—James Hamilton. Lib. 6, p. 13.

1748, March 25. Inventory, £233.9.4; made by Peter Rambo, James Hamilton.

1749, Oct. 10. Account. Moneys paid Jeremiah Wood, Peter Mattson, William Fletcher, John Blackwood, William Wood, John Sparks, Elizabeth Ballinger, Sarah Wills, Abraham Chattin, Levi Peirce, John Marshall, John Mattson, John Dukeminner, Jane Waite, Thomas Kimsey, Thomas Wood, Charles Morris.

1748, Nov. 18. O'Neil, Charles, of Salem Co., clerk. Adm'r, Andrew Gardiner. Bondsman—Josiah Kay. Both of said County. Witnesses—Ann Gibbon, Michl. Gibbon.

1749, Sept. 16. Adm'r de bonis non, Joseph Rose; goods, etc., left unadministered by Andrew Gardiner, late of Salem County, Adm'r. Bondsman—Robert Hartshorne. Both of city of Burlington, attorneys-at-law. Witnesses—Jonathan Thomas, Jo. Scattergood. Lib. 5, p. 550.

1744, Sept. 5. Ong, Jeremiah, of Little Egg Harbour, Burlington Co., husbandman; will of. Grandchildren—Jeremiah, Ann, Sarah, Thomas, John and Jobe Ridgway, all under age. Real and personal estate. Executor—son-in-law, Thomas Ridgway. Witnesses—Samuel Andrews, Alse Mathis, Sarah Mathis. Proved Sept. 6, 1746. Lib. 5, p. 263.

1746, 2nd day, 7th mo. (Sept.). Inventory, £309.6.3; made by Sam'll Andrews and James Bellangee.

1733, May 4. Orchard (Archard), Andrew, of Greenwich, Gloucester Co. Int. Adm'x, Christian Orchard. Bondsmen—John Jones, Gunner Orchard. Witnesses—Ben. Bard, Joseph Ross. Lib. 3, p. 297.

1734, April 22. Inventory, £112.17.7; made by Thomas Bickham, John Jones.

Account. Moneys paid to William Ives, John Archard, John Wheeler, Magdalen Peterson.

1731, Sept. 6. Orgill, John, of Perth Amboy, Middlesex Co. Int. Adm'r, John Hamilton, Esq. Lib. B, p. 227.

1749, Dec. 23. Orin (Oran), John, of Greenwich Township, Gloucester Co., flatman. Int. Adm'x, Mary Oran, widow. Bondsman—John Hains. Witness—Hannah Cooper. Lib. 7, p. 35.

1749, 10 mo. (Dec.), 14 da. Inventory, £53.7.5; made by John Hains, Jacob Cozens.

1747-8, Jan. 18. Osborn, Roger, of Little Eggharbour, Burlington Co., yeoman; will of. Friends Meeting at Little Eggharbour, £50. My brother's son, Richard, £10. Benj. and Cornelius Osborn, James and Solomon Wilets, Jun'r, and William Wood that lived with my bro., Richard, each £10. Real and personal estate. Executors—cousin, Richard Osborn, and James Wilets. Witnesses—Hugh McCullum, John Ridgway, Edward Andrews, James Willits. Proved Feb. 28, 1748. Lib. 6, p. 304.

1748, Feb. 7. Mary Andrews, wife of Mordecai Andrews, of Little Eggharbour, being one of the people called Quakers, affirmed that she had had the care of Roger Osborn of Little Eggharbour in his last illness and that during said illness the said Roger stated to Phebe Ridgway that he had made a will, and also told said Phebe he wished certain bequests not stated in his will to be given as follows: his cousin, Richard Osborn, cloth that James Willis had brought from the fulling mill, cloth purchased of Elizabeth, wife of Samuel Andrews, a coat at Nehemiah Andrews, etc.

1748-9, 22nd day, 12th mo. (Feb.). Inventory £269.14.5; made by John Ridgway.

1748-9, 23rd day, 12th mo. (Feb.). James Bellangee stated he was with Roger Osborn when he died and he, the said Roger, spoke of the articles he had given away.

1729, Nov. 28. Osborne, Bezaliel, of Cape May Co.; will of. Brother, Ananias Osborne, sole executor and all my lands forever. Moveables to my sister Ruth, and to my brother Nathan Osborne. Witnesses—Jeremiah Hand, John Robinson, Henry Stite, Junior. Proved 28 June, 1734.

1734, March 28. "This may certifie that Ananias Osborne the within named executor" (to whom letters testamentary were granted), "desires that his brother, Nathan Osborne, may administer in his stead, provided that he shall not at any time contrive to disanulle or make void the sd. will." Signed, Ananias Osborne (his mark). Witness—Jacob Spicer. Lib. 3, p. 444.

1734, March 28. Inventory, £45.16.0; made by Moses Cross, Henry Leonard.

1745, Dec. 14. Osborne, Nathan (no place mentioned; Cape May); will of. Wife, Ann, to have ½ of all lands during widowhood. Eldest son, Richard Osborne, all my lands except the said part bequeathed to my wife, he to pay my son Nathaniel £20 when he will be 21. Sons, Nathan and John, and daughter Ruth, residue of the personal estate (the widow having one-third). Executors—wife, Ann, son Richard, and my brother-in-law, Daniel Smith. Brother-in-law, Jonathan Smith, to take my son Richard in his care, and sd. brother Daniel to take my son Nathan until they respectively arrive at 20 years. Witnesses—Geo. Jeares, Ann Osborne, Robt. Wakely. Proved 31st Jan., 1745-6.

1746, April 25. Letters granted to Ann Osborne and Daniel Smith, (the above named Richard Osborne being infant within age). Lib. 5, p. 246.

1745-6, March 1. Inventory (£120.16.8), includes cattle, horses, sheep and swine (£56.19.0). Appraisers—Jeremiah Hand, John Leonard.

1733, May 26. Osman, Samuel, of Woodbridge, Middlesex Co. Int. Adm'x, Hannah Osman. Lib. B, p. 367.

1746, 11th day, 1st mo. (Mar.). Osmond, John, of Bridgetown, Burlington Co., yeoman; will of. Children (not mentioned) all under age. Father-in-law, John Crownshaw, to assist my wife Martha as executrix, and she is to make a good deed of plantation sold to Daniel Stockton of Springfield. Witnesses—Josiah White, Abraham Griffith, Thomas Budd, John Ewan. Proved April 7, 1746. Lib. 5, p. 230.

1746, 4th day, 2nd mo. (Apr.). Inventory, £308.7.9; made by Josiah White and Henry Paxson.

1749, July 5. Osmun (Osmund), Isaac, Sr., of Bethlehem Township, Hunterdon Co., will of. Wife, Sarah, the plantation. Son, Isaac, a heifer bought of Edward Williams. Sons—Thomas and Joseph. Daughters—Sarah Mecrakin, Hannah Carr and Deborah Osmun. Executors—wife, Sarah, and son-in-law, William Mecrakin. Witnesses—Joseph Webster, David Faurot and William Emley. Proved August 1, 1749. Lib. 6, p. 277.

1749, July 14. Inventory (£133.1.11) includes a gun and 40 geese. Made by William Emley.

1750, Aug. 10. Ouke, Abraham, of New Brunswick, Middlesex Co.; will of. Wife, Annetje. Son mentioned, but not named. Daughter, Maria. Three younger children—Annatje, Sarah and Lea. Real and personal estate. Executors—Hendrick Fisher, and brother William

Ouke. Witnesses—D'k Schuyler, D'k VanVeghten, Derck VanAlen. Proved Sept. 19, 1750. Lib. E, p. 532.

1750, **Aug.** 25. Inventory, £665.12.5; made by D'k **Schuyler**, and D'k Van Veghten, Sen'r.

1733, Jan. 17. Owen, John, late of Philadelphia, tailor. Int. Adm'r, Renier Vanhist. Bondsmen—Samuel Bustill, John Doe. Salem Wills, 505 Q.

1745-6, 14th day, 12th mo. (Feb.). Owen, Joshua, of Burlington Co., yeoman; will of. Wife, Sarah. Son, Humphrey, and other children mentioned but not named; an expected child. Real and personal estate. Executors—wife, and brother Rowland Owen. Witnesses—John Butcher, John Allen, John Woolman. Proved March 21, 1745. Lib. 5, p. 228.

1745-6, March 8. Inventory, £231.; made by John Atkinson and Jos. Fenimore.

1736-7, 2nd day, 12th mo. (Feb.). Pachee (Peachee), John, of Wellingborrow, Burlington Co., yeoman; will of. Brother, William, and sisters Ann, Phebe, Sarah and Mary. Land leased to Abraham Perkins. Executor—brother, William Pachee. Witnesses—Henry Dell, Abraham Perkins, Thos. Scattergood. Proved Sept. 7, 1737. Lib. 4, p. 117.

1731, March 17. Pachee (Peachee), Thomas, of Wellingborrow, Burlington Co., yeoman; will of. Children—William, John, Ann, Phebe, Sarah and Mary. Land adjoining Jacob Perkins. Wife, Charity, sole executrix. Witnesses—Robert Lucas, Henry Dell, Sam'l Scattergood. Proved June 17, 1731. Lib. 3, p. 128.

1731, April 30. Inventory, £98.11.4; made by Robert Lucas and Joseph Fenimore. Includes 2 Bibles and old books.

1750, April 17. Pack, Job, of Essex Co. Int. Administration on estate granted to Job Pack, the son and Thomas Scuder. Lib. E, p. 383.

1748-9, Feb. 4. Padan (Paden), Robert, of Shrewsbury, Monmouth Co.; will of. Wife, Charity. Son, Thomas. Grandson, Robert Padon; if he dies under age to his eldest sister. Mary, widow of Joseph Roberts. Executors—William Jeffery, Senior, and Thomas Bell. Witnesses—John Davis, William Davis, Joseph Cook. Proved March 13, 1749. Thomas Bell, surviving executor, sworn same day; William Jeffery, Senior, "dying about three months after the said testator." Lib. E, p. 371.

1749, March 1. Inventory (£157.11.10½) includes Joseph Roberts' clothes, deer skins, negro boy. Made by John Little, Junior, and William Jackson.

1749, April 7. Thomas Paden withdraws caveat he had entered at Mr. Dennis' against proving of his father's will. Addressed to "Mr. Barto, living in Perth Amboy."

1749, July 12. Padgett, James, ward (son of Francis Padgett, late of township of Stowe). Guardian—Jonathan Mills, of same place. Joseph Denn, bondsman. Cumberland Wills, 42 F.

1745, May 22. Page, James, of Cape May Co. Int. Adm'x, Mary Page, or her heirs. Fellow bondsmen—Joseph Page, Elisha Hand, all of said County. Witnesses—John Eldredge, James Whilldin. Lib. 5, p. 121.

1745, April 12. Inventory (£87.17.2) includes cattle, horses, sheep and swine. Appraisers—John Eldredge, James Whilldin.

1728, Jan. 14. Page, John, of Welenborow, Burlington Co., yeoman. Administration on estate granted unto John Green, of Burlington Co. John Doe and Richard Roe, yeomen, fellow bondsmen. (Omitted in previous vol of Wills).

1728, Jan. 22. Inventory of the personal estate, £23.6.11; made by Revell Elton and Samuel Woolman.

1730, June 19. Account. Payments to Susannah Borden, Mary Busby, Jacob Burcham, John Whatson, William Rogers. Names of those who purchased at vendue were Jno. Fenimore, Robert Woodcock, Jno. Ward, Eliz. Stocks, Judjah Adams, Rich'd Burding, John Green, Thos. Buzbey. Burlington Wills, 2109-22 C.

1739, March 6. Pagett, Ann, of Salem Co. Int. Adm'r, William Murdock (gent.), only son of Ann Paget, widow, deceased and residuary legatee. Bondsmen—Job Shepherd, John Slackwood. All of said County, gents. Witnesses—Wm. Murdock, Dan. Mestayer, Mary Mestayer. Lib. 4, p. 223.

1739, March 8. Inventory (£262.17.1) includes 33 cattle, Bible, etc. Appraisers—Jonathan Bradway, John Blackwood.

1741, Dec. 25. Account. Monies paid to Thomas Pagett, Mary Allen, Jon. Thompson, Hugh Blackwood, Bradway Stretch, John Jones, James Gould, Clemt. Hall, Mary Coleman, Jon. Mason, Mary Yeuens, "allowance for a legacy pd. to Thomas Pagett as executor of the sd. John left him by his will"; Abraham Reeves, for subscription of John Pagett to building a meeting-house at Cohansey and for building a pew and glazing a window in Cohansie meeting house; Robert Hutchins, Robert Conway "in rights of his wife one of the daughters of the deceased"; John Smith, "his part of the deceased estate in rights of his wife, one of the daughters of the deceased."

1735, April 17. Pagett, Francis, of Cohansey, Salem Co., yeoman; will of. Wife, Isabel, during widowhood to have moveable estate and profits of plantation in consideration of bringing up children. Son, Francis, said plantation, with 190 acres of land and marsh. If he dies in nonage, his surviving brother shall have it. Eldest daughter, Sarah. Witnesses—Danl. Crawford, Rebecka Dickson, Thomas Pagett. Proved 27 May, 1735. Lib. 4, p. 27.

1735, May 19. Inventory (£97.11.6) includes cattle. Appraisers—James Dickson, Thos. Pagett.

1733, Dec. 17. Pagett, James, of Salem Co., yeoman. Int. Admr's, Jonadad Shephard and Hezekiah Love, yeomen. Bondsman—Dickson Shephard. All of said County. Witnesses—John Norton, John Rementon. Lib. 3, p. 363.

1733, Dec. 17. Inventory (£100.9.4) includes cattle. Appraisers—Dickason Shepherd, John Rementon.

1739, Aug. 9. Pagett, John, of Alloways Creek Precinct, Salem Co., husbandman; will of. Wife, Ann, to have ½ of moveable estate and the negro and white servants. Legacies to nephews—John McKnight, Moses Paget, James Paget, Abigail Shirgeon, the daughter of my eldest brother. John Paget (eldest son of my brother Thomas Paget) to have all my lands, but said wife shall have use of the same during her widowhood. Executors—wife, and my brother, Thomas Paget.

Witnesses—Jonathan Wadinton, Joseph Hancock, Richard Bradford.
1739, Aug. 11. Codicil. My nephew, John Paget, to pay the legacies bequeathed to Moses and James Pagett out of the land devised to him. Witnesses—John Smith, John Butler, Richard Bradford. Proved 5 Dec., 1739.
Lib. 4, p. 210.
1739, Dec. 4. Inventory (£535.3.7) includes cattle and horses, Indian corn and wheat in the barn, white and negro servants (£60), books. Appraisers—Job Shepherd, Josiah Fithian.

1739, Nov. 13. Pagett, Thomas, of Salem Co., yeoman, guardian of Mary Love. Witnesses—Thos. Emley, Dan. Mestayer.
Salem Wills, 676 Q.

1737, Oct. 4. Pain, Robert, of "Basken Ridge," Somerset Co., farmer; will of. Wife, Margaret, executrix. Children—Margaret, Martha (wife of William Means), Jean and Anna. Plantation and personal estate. Executor—Bryant Leverty. Witnesses—William Allen, David Grant, Patrick Willson. Proved 18 Jan., 1737. Lib. C, p. 186.

1733, April 2. Paine, Nathaniell, of Woodbridge, Middlesex Co., merchant; will of. Desires to be buried by a Minister of the Church of England. Sons Benj'n and Nathaniell Paine, of Great Britain, four houses in Tulyegat Street, Southwark, Co. of Surrey; land in Acton parish, township of Burland, Co. of Palatine of Chester; bond due from Joseph Woolley, £232; bond of brother, Ephraim Paine, whom I understand transferred himself and family to South Carolina; lands in East Jersey and New England. Executors—wife, Janna, friends John Wattson and Thomas Heddey. Witnesses—Benjamin Bloomfield, Tho. Broderwick, Richard Bloomfield. Proved Aug. 16, 1733.
Lib. B, p. 453.

1748, May 21. Palmer, Thomas, of Trenton, Hunterdon Co. Anthony Palmer declines to administer on the estate of his son, Thomas Palmer, and requests that administration be granted to Mr. John Allen, Jr. Dated, Kensington, May 21, 1748. Witnessed by William Yard. Hunterdon Wills, 223 J.
1748, May 30. Adm'r, John Allen, of Trenton. Joseph Higbee, of Trenton, surety. Witness—Abraham Cottman.

1749, Nov. 4. Pancoast, Elizabeth, of Chesterfield Township, Burlington Co., widow; will of. Children—Hannah, Joseph, John. Legacy "due to me from England according to my aunt Sarah Ogborn's will." Executor—brother-in-law, Thomas Pancoast. If he refuses to serve, brother-in-law, Thomas Folkes, to be executor. Witnesses—William Pancoast, Aaron Watson, Mary Pancoast. Proved ———.
Burlington Wills, 4539 C.

1750, May 24. Pancoast, Israel (over 14 years old), son of Joseph Pancoast, of Burlington, yeoman. Mary Pancoast, guardian.
Burlington Wills, 4721-3 C.

1748-9, Feb. 10. Pancoast, John, of Chesterfield, Burlington Co., yeoman. Int. Inventory of the personal estate, £142.6.8; made by Thos. Folkes and Joseph Thorne.
1748-9, Feb. 20. Adm'x, Elizabeth Pancoast, widow. Thomas Folks and John Butler, yeoman, fellow bondsmen. Lib. 6, p. 79.
1749, Dec. 12. Thomas Pancoast, brother of deceased, requests that Thomas Folkes, of Bordentown, be appointed administrator on estate left unadministered by his widow. Adm'r, Thomas Folkes, yeoman. William Pancoast and William Watson, yeoman, fellow bondsmen.

1749, Oct. 7. Pancoast, John, of Mansfield, Burlington Co.; will of. Son, Edin, land adjoining that of brothers William and Samuel, and late brother Joseph. Children—John, William, Asa and Hester, all under age. An expected child. Real and personal estate. Executors—wife, Mary, and Job Ridgway, weaver. Witnesses—Jacob Ridgway, Aaron Barton, Jno. Fenimorr. Proved Oct. 28, 1749. Lib. 6, p. 338.

1749, Oct. 20. Inventory, £434.8.4½; made by Jno. Fenmorr and John Harvey.

1731, Oct. 19. Pancoast, Joseph, Ju'r, of Mansfield, Burlington Co.; will of. Brothers—John, Thomas and Benjamin. My own sisters—Mary Thomison, Elizabeth, Anna, Susanna and Phebe. Cousin, William Scholy. Friend, Rachell, dau. of Isaac Horner. Real and personal estate. Father, Joseph Pancoast, sole executor. Witnesses—John Curtis, George Ash, Henry Cooper. Proved June 3, 1732. Lib. 3, p. 199.

1732, 3rd day, 4th mo. (June). Inventory, £29.17; made by John Curtis and Henry Cooper.

1749, Aug. 6. Pancoast, Joseph, of Mansfield, Burlington Co.; will of. Wife, Mary. Children—Israel, Shedlock, Garuis, Joseph, Elizabeth, Mary and Hannah, all under age. Real and personal estate. Executors—Edward Tonkins and Thomas Pancoast. Witnesses—Aaron Watson, John Butler, Micajah Reeve, Ju'r. Proved Aug. 31, 1749. Lib. 6, p. 301.

1749, Aug. 29. Inventory, £413.17.8; made by David Rockhill and Jos. Fenimore.

1750, May 24. Bond of Mary Pancoast, widow, of City of Burlington, as guardian of Israel Pancoast, of 14 years, son of Joseph Pancoast, yeoman. Thomas Rodman, Elias Hughs, Joseph Hollinshead and Jonathan Thomas, all of City of Burlington, fellow bondsmen.

1739-40, March 19. Pancoast, William, of Mansfield, Burlington Co., yeoman; will of. Children—William, Joseph, John, Seth, Sarah, Samuel, Elizabeth (wife of Marmaduke Watson), and Hannah (wife of Mathew Watson). 300 acres at Little Egg Harbour, lying between Bass River and Wading. Executors—wife, Hannah, and son-in-law, Marmaduke Watson. Witnesses—Thomas Scattergood, Ju'r, Joseph Pancoast, Jos. Scattergood.

1742, July 10. Codicil. Devises more overplus land to sons William, Joseph and John. Witnesses—Anthony Morris, Sarah Butler, Susannah Walker. Proved Aug. 28, 1742. Lib. 4, p. 333.

1740, Oct. 7. Parent, William, of Upper Freehold, Monmouth Co., yeoman. Int. Bond of Mercy Parent, the widow, and Samuel Parent, of same place, yeoman, as administrators. Corbet Smith, of same place, yeoman, and Obadiah Ireton, of Burlington, yeoman, fellow bondsmen. Lib. 4, p. 257.

1740, Oct. 9. Inventory (£137.5.6) includes 2 guns, and debts due from Corbet Smith and Joseph Robins. Made by John Lawrence and John Brown.

1739, Dec. 3. Parke, John, of Salem Co., guardian of Robt. Love. Bondsman—Sinnick Sinnick. All of said county. Witnesses—Thomas ———, Danl. Mestayer. Salem Wills, 672 Q.

1727, April 13. Parker, Elisha, of Perth Amboy, Middlesex Co., merchant; will of. 100 acres in Woodbridge sold to David Burgoies of Piscataway, Middlesex Co., husbandman, by my brother, John Parker, Esq., Sept. 21, 1725. Sisters—Elizabeth, Ursula, and Mary Parker. Nephew, Elisha, eldest son of brother John Parker, Esq. Executor—brother, John Parker, Esq. Witnesses—Js. Maxwell, Mary Forster, J. Stevens. Proved June 21, 1732. Lib. B, p. 284.

1738, Nov. 11. Parker, James, of Hunterdon Co. Int. Inventory of the estate (£118.11.0) includes a Bible and other books; 4 guns. Made by Daniel Cooper. Lib. 4, p. 157.

1738, Nov. 14. Adm'x, Mary Parker of Hunterdon County. Alexander Aikman of Hunterdon, and John Grant of Somerset County, sureties.

1749, April 17. Parker, James, of Township of Greenwich, Cumberland Co. Int. Adm'r, Charles Davis. Fellow bondsman—David Shepherd, of same place. Witnesses—Philip Dennis, Elias Cotting. Lib. 6, p. 53.

1749, March 20. Inventory (£67.13.6) includes pair oxen, 4 cows. Appraisers—Philip Dennis, David Shepherd.

1740, Dec. 19. Parker, Janet, of Perth Amboy, Middlesex Co., widow; will of. Children—Elisha, Mary, James, John, and Lewis, all under age. Real and personal estate. Executors—brother Lewis Johnston, sister Ursula Parker, and friend Robert Hude. Witnesses—Sarah Cook, Thomas Cook, Fenw'k Lyell, Esq. Proved Feb. 23, 1740-1. Lib. C, p. 393.

1731, Jan. 10. Parker, John, of Perth Amboy, Middlesex Co., gent; will of. Plantation leased to Thomas Abbott and John Wade, deceased, in Somerset Co. Land in Perth Amboy bought of Mrs. Isabell Davis and Moses Rolfe, lying in front of Andrew Herriot's door; land in Woodbridge joining lands of Mr. Peterson, Shobal Smith, and Henry Freeman; land my father, Elisha Parker, and Mr. Adam Hude bought of Nathaniel FitzRandolph and Edward FitzRandolph, to my brother, Edward Parker, at 21 years of age, on condition that his mother, my mother-in-law, Mrs. Elizabeth Parker, release her right of dower. Agreement made with Alexander Ekman, James Parker and James Caldwell for land on Pasiack River; agreement with David Sutton. Deceased brother, Elisha Parker. Children—Elisha, James, John, Lewis Johnston, and Mary, all under age. Sisters—Elizabeth Johnston, Ursula and Mary Parker. Friend Mary Forster a ring. Guardians—wife Jennette and brothers Andrew and Lewis Johnston. Executors—wife, and friends William Skinner, clerk, Andrew Johnston of Perth Amboy, merchant, and Robert Hude of Woodbridge, yeoman. Witnesses—Anne Morris, John Hamilton, John Watson.

Codicil. Friends Robert and James Hude, land purchased of their father, Adam Hude, joining lands of Elizens Barron, deceased, and John Thomson; lands bought of my sisters, Moses Rolfe and John Herriot; land lately Richard Worth's deceased; land in Perth Amboy now in possession of Joseph Leigh. Witnesses—Robert King, John Watson, Fenw'k Lyell. Proved Dec. 5, 1732. Lib. B, p. 330.

1750, March 20. Parker, John, of Somerset Co.; will of. Wife, Elizabeth. Children—James, John, Elender, Jannet (all minors). Mentions "brother Andrew and his son that is at learning," and "one hogzed of flax to be sent and divided among his brothers and sisters."

Executors—Thomas Mcmurtry and Alexander Aikman. Witnesses—Thomas McMurtre, Alexander Aikman. Proved 30 April, 1750.
Lib. E, p. 391.

1750, April 27. Inventory (£374.10.8), includes guns and sword, 97½ bushels of wheat, and bonds of David Allen, John Conn, John Barclay, Hugh Campble, James McColemby, Saml. Willson, Wm. Gaston, Wm. Clemons, Joseph Howard, Wm. Johnston, Stephen Leech, Saml. Crow, Wm. Sutton, Jacob Teval, Edward Husey, John Kimble, Ephraim Lenard, Eliab Byram, John Cole, Richard Stillwell, John Phileps, Jefoth Byram, John McDanel, Thos. McMurtry, John Bartly, John Ayres, Junr., John Lee, Teeter Misener, Uriah Rush, Alexander McCullagh. Appraisers—Brice Rikey, Hendrick Smith. Creditors—Alexander Linn, Widow Rice, Brice Rikey, Hendrick Smith, Jacob Desher.

1750, April 30. Renunciation of Thomas McMurtre and Alexander Aikman as executors. Witnesses—John Barkley, Thos. Bartow.

1750, April 30. Adm'rs, Elizabeth Parker, of Basking Ridge, widow, and James Barclay. Fellow bondsman—John Barclay.

1742, Oct. 7. Parker, Jonathan, Junior, of Upper Freehold, in Township of Shrewsbury, Monmouth Co., sawer; will of. Estate to father, Daniel Parker, and testator's brothers and sisters. Executors—Joshua Horner, of Upper Freehold, and Benjamin Oney, of New Hanover, Burlington County. Witnesses—Abraham Cleavenger and James Maconel. Proved November 9, 1742. Original will, endorsed: "The will of Jonathan Parker, deceased, who died October the 13 day, in the year of our Lord 1742." Lib. 4, p. 368.

1742, Oct. 30. Inventory (£46.12.9) includes a fox trap, 2,000 foot boards, bill due from Joshua Horner, note of Joseph Arny, and due on book accounts: John Estell, Junior, Richard Parker, Joseph Applin, John Parker, Thomas Platt, John Peirce, Nathan Starky, Content Horner, William French, Thomas Gale, Benjamin Nony, Isaac Horner, Richard Row. Made by Joseph Applin and Nathan Starkey.

1744, Nov. 24. Parker, Peter, of Shrewsbury, Monmouth Co., yeoman; will of. Wife, Elizabeth. Children—Josiah, John, Peter, Hannah Wardell. Mentions "three youngest daughters," but not by name. Tracts of land at Squancom and at Red Bank. Executors—wife, son Josiah, and Job Cook. Witnesses—Daniel Phillips and Jonathan Croxson. Proved May 7, 1745. Lib. D, p. 294.

1746, Oct. 6. Parker, Reuben, of Greenwich, Gloucester Co., yeoman; will of. Son, Robert, to have 100 acres in Burlington County. Grandsons—John and Reuben Tomes and William Bright, the land where I dwell equally, when they will be 21. Daughters—Hester, wife of Anthony Hooper, who is to have his joiner's tools; and Hannah. Executors—son-in-law, Anthony Hoopper, and Alexd. Randall. Witnesses—Joseph Carter, Thomas Boyle, Elizabeth Hires. Proved 25 Oct., 1746. Lib. 5, p. 279.

1746, Oct. 21. Inventory, £62.11.11; made by John Bright and Gabriel Rambo.

1747, Feb. —. Account. Cash to Anthony Hooper and wife, John Tomes and wife, "William Bright, son of Jeremiah, which marryed Mary, the daughter of said deceased," Peter Rambo, Margaret Gerard, Solomon Fassett, Robert Parker.

1745, Dec. 6. Parker, Samuel, of Northampton, Burlington Co., blacksmith. Int. Inventory, £159.12.3; made by Samuel Woolston and John Helter.

1745, Jan. 4. Adm'x, Elizabeth Parker, widow. James Allen, yeoman, fellow bondsman. Both of Northampton. Lib. 5, p. 428.

1750, Dec. 8. Parks, Paul, of Evesham and Goshen Neck, Burlington Co. Int. Adm'x, Hannah Parks, widow. Benjamin Brown, of Northampton, yeoman, fellow bondsman. Lib. 7, p. 101.

1750, Dec. 28. Inventory, £193.19; made by Benjamin Springer and James Cattell.

1749, June 26. Parr, John, Jr., of Morris Co.; nuncupative will of. Bequests to brothers and sisters—Cornelius, Matthias, Elihu, Eliphalet, Jess, Jemima. Witnesses—Phebe, Nathaniel and Elijah Horton. Proved Nov. 13, 1749. Lib. E, p. 340.

1749, Nov. 13. Bond of Cornelius Parr, of Morris co., yeoman, as administrator.

1750, Feb. —. Inventory, made by Elijah and Caleb Horton.

1750, Aug. 13. Account. Debts paid to Nancy Brown, Israel Swasey, Obadiah Souard, Joseph Ogden, Johannah Cathcart.

1750, Feb. 5. Parr, Samuel, of Gloucester Co., yeoman, guardian of Abel Nicholson, (above the age of 14 years, son of Samuel Nicholson late of the County aforesaid). Bondsman—Jonathan Thomas of Burlington, innholder. Witnesses—Tho. Rodman, Isaac De Cow, Junr. Lib. 6, p. 374.

1732, Dec. 4. Parson, John, Sr., of Cape May Co.; will of. Wife, one-third of the moveable estate, rest to my children. The real estate equally to sons John and Robert, excepting the place John bought. "So far my land on Long Island, I give it to my son John, and if he can get it in order he is to give his brother Robert his part." Executors—wife, and son John. (Not signed).

1732-3, June 22. Deposition of witnesses, William Mulford, Ebenezer Johnson. Proved 22 June, 1732. Cape May Wills, 61 E.

1732, Dec. 25. Inventory (£140.6.1) includes cooper's tools, etc. (£5.10.2), cattle and horses (£50.15.0). Appraisers—Richard Stites, Thomas Ross.

1732-3, Mar. 3. Adm'x, Elizabeth Parsons. Fellow bondsman—Joshua Stites. Both of County aforesaid. Witnesses—George Stites, Jacob Spicer, Junior, Jacob Spicer.

1742, Oct. 16. Parsons, Elizabeth, of Cape May Co.; will of. Daughters—Elizabeth Hand, Charity Mulford, Abigail Stites, and granddaughter Mary Edwards, to have my estate, equally. Son, Jonathan Forman, and son, Robert Parsons, to have 10 shillings apiece. Son, Joshua Stites, sole executor. Witnesses—John Stites, Elijah Hughes, Cornelius Schillinks, Junior. Proved 7 March, 1742-3. Lib. 5, p. 9.

1743, May 30. Inventory, £31.16.2; made by Elijah Hughes, Robert Parsons.

1732, ——, 4 da.. Parsons, John (Jr.), of Cape May Co., yeoman; will of. Wife, Bethia, the personal estate. Brother, Robert Parsons, the real estate and appurtenances, provided he will pay to my daughter, Sarah Parsons, £150 upon her marriage day, or when she will be of age. In case my brother Robert dies without issue, all shall return to my lawful heir, my daughter, except the value of £150, which if she has received shall be remitted to him or his order. If that money upon Long Island is recovered or received according to the will of my father, my brother Robert should have his equal part. William Mathews to have cow and calf. Executor—Ezkiel Eldredge. Witnesses—Huson Huse, John Shaw, Mary Crowell. Proved 5 Jan., 1732-3. Lib. 3, p. 237.

1732, Dec. 25. Inventory (£58) includes shoemaker's tools (£1.11.0). Appraisers—Richard Stites, Thomas Ross.

1732-3, March 19. Account. Includes Samuel Croweld, John Parsons (funeral charges). Letter with account shows oxen given to sister Lydia, 2 cows to sister Bethia Parsons, cow and calf to sister Sarah Parsons, and same to brother Jacob Parsons. Letter signed Ezekeill Eldredge, and dated at Cape May, April 23th, 1733.

1742, Jan. 5. Parvin, Thomas, of Cohansey, Salem Co., weaver; will of. Wife, Rebecca. Son, Mathew, to have "after the decease or widowhood of my said wife" the plantation in Cohansey, and my cedar swamp called Chatfield's Swamp. My four sons, Josiah, Mathew, Jeremiah and Silas, to have my Cedar Swamp at Morris River, Salem County. Daughters—Sarah, Elizabeth (wife of Moses Moore) and Hannah (wife of Thomas Sayres, Junior). Mentions grandson, Benjamin Parvin. Executors—wife, Rebecca, and son, Mathew. Witnesses—Daniel Westcote, John Coney, Jno. Padmore. Proved 18 April, 1744. Lib. 5, p. 31.

1743, Sept. 26. Inventory, £71.9.6; made by William Bradford, John Woolsey.

1730, Oct. 10. Paul, James, of Middletown, Monmouth Co., miller; will of. In consideration of favors from Obadiah Bowne, for maintenance, etc., devises estate to said Obadiah's children—Mary, Cornelius, Obadiah and Thomas. Executors—friends John Bowne (son of Obadiah, deceased), and Jeremiah White, both of Middletown. Witnesses—William Bowne, James Bowne, Junior, John Watson. Proved March 16, 1732. Lib. B, p. 388.

1750, April 17. Paul, Samuel, of Gloucester Co., yeoman; will of. Wife, Marey. Sons—John, Samuel and Jonathan, to have the real estate equally. Legacies to daughters, Sarah and Susannah (the latter to be "in the control of my said wife while she remains my widow." Executors—son, John, and Jacob Cosens. Witnesses—Alexr. Randall, Nathan Paul, Robert Braman. Affirmed 31 May, 1750. Lib. 6, p. 355.

1750, 3d mo. (May), 7th da. Inventory (£785.17.02½) includes bonds and notes of George Cosens, Joseph Wilkisson, Amy Chew, Charls Lock, Timothy Rains, John Pinyard, John Sparks, William Pinyard, Garret Veneman, Jonas Dinney, Jonas Cox, Jacob Folks, William Weatherby, Niclas Justesson, Garret Dewese, Gorge Flanagam, Robart Marfutt, Peter Rambow, Thomas Wood, William Wilkins, Daniel Weatherby, Anthony Huppet, Mathew Tomlin, John Richards, Jun'r, Laurance String, James Acret, Jun'r, Robart Nicson, Edward Holenshead, Thomas Ozgood, Thomas Chester, James Stealman, Joseph Jonson. Appraisers—Wm. Mickle, Robert Braman.

1750, Sept. 15. Paxton, Joseph, of Trenton, Hunterdon Co., merchant; will of. Wife, Mary, one-fourth of personal estate and all money due her from estate of Colonel Daniel Coxe, deceased, before her marriage to testator. Sons, William and James, all real estate. Daughter, Jane. Legacies to said three children when aged 21 years. Executors—wife, and David Cowell. No witnesses and not signed.

Dec. 24, 1750. Abraham Cotman, of Trenton, attorney-at-law, did depose that he was generally employed by Joseph Paxton. About a month or six weeks before testator's decease he gave the deponent some notes to draw his will. On the morning the testator was taken ill, to wit, September 15th last, he desired to draw the will immediately. This was done and the will read to him and read by Rev. David Cowell, one of the executors, in presence of the deponent and of James Levingston. The testator ordered the will to be drawn again, leaving out the devise relating to his brother's two sons. The deponent at 12 o'clock of the same night took the will to the testator for signing, but the latter was then speechless and unable to sign. Lib. 6, p. 414.

1751, April 10. Inventory (£4,432.7.2) comprises a long itemized list of general mdse., including dress goods, persian, holland, silk, graset, dimity, taffety, alamede, velvet, cambric, muslin, fustian, broad cloth, crape, mohair, calico, flannel, damask, buckram, camblet, shalloon, diaper; shoes and galloshes; 102 packs playing cards, £4.7.1; 16 women's cloaks; 6 laghorn hats; 4 doz. Bibles and 4 doz. Testaments; 4 doz. Psalters and 7 doz. Catechisms; 5 doz. horn books and 3 large books; 7½ doz. primers; 34 lbs. tea; 180 pewter porringers; 52 pewter tankards and quarts; 180 men's hats; 2 velvet hoods; 1,500 fish hooks; 128 lbs. coffee; 15 gross pipes; 48 lbs. Philadelphia tobacco; 324 papers York do; 222 yds. best oznabrigs; 4 barrels nails; 4½ bbls. sugar; 21 razors; 20 brass ink pots; 84 snuff boxes; 30 pair spectacles; 9 leather ink pots; 240 pair shoe buckles; 12 brass catches for tea tables; 14 papers ink powder; 1,500 bus. salt; 2 hogsheads rum and one of molasses; 1 bbl. wine; 36 firkins butter; 170 lbs. beeswax; 150 lbs. brimstone; 10 lbs. gun powder; 1 negro boy, £40; 3½ years service to come of Flora, £12; pictures, £2.5; debts due on book accounts, £1,652.8.10; debts due on bills and bonds, £435.5.3. Made by Andrew Reed and Theo's Severens.

1744, April 28. Peace, Joseph, of Trenton, Hunterdon Co., gentleman; will of. Wife, Mary. Daughter, Sarah Peace. To William Pridy and Ann Pridy. Isaac Watson to sell testator's real estate and proceeds to be divided into eight parts; for testator's wife, Mary, and son, Joseph, each two parts, balance to children, Isaac, Sarah, Johanna and Deborah Peace. Executors—wife, and brother-in-law Isaac Watson. Witnesses—Jno. Hrorock, William Sprouls, John Harding, Jr. Proved June 10, 1744. Lib. 5, p. 33.

1750, April 13. Bond of John Allen, Jr., of Trenton, yeoman, as administrator of estate of Joseph Peace, left unadministered by the executors. Thomas Tindall, of Trenton, millwright, surety.

1758, Feb. 10. Account of John Allen, adm'r, mentions Edward Stevenson (for Joseph and Isaac Peace), Captain John Anderson, John Barnes (for Joanna and Deborah Peace), Mrs. Sheard, Joseph Woodward (for boarding and schooling Joseph and Isaac Peace), George Davis, John Baldwin, Jno. Abraham Denormandy, Edward Paxton, Sarah Chubb, Benjamin Rendle, William Morris, Esquire, William Cleay, ——— Englehart, Henry Inglehart, Conrad Cotts, John Ob Dike, William Yard, Peter Lott, William Moorhead, Samuel Leonard, Jno. Axfoard, Jno. Thomson, Jno. Dagworthy, Richard Furman, Jno. Smith, Henry Carter, Mrs. Gold, Thomas Moore.

1758, Oct. 9. Bond of Sarah Chubb, of Trenton, widow, as administratrix of estate of Joseph Peace, left unadministered by John Allen,

Theophilus Severns, of Trenton, surety on bond. Witnesses—Deborah Peace and Mary Barnes.

1736, June 17. Pearse, John, of Perth Amboy, Middlesex Co. Int. Adm'x, Mary Pearse. Lib. C, p. 102.

1746, Nov. 10. Pearse, Mary, of Parish of Saint Mary LeBone, Middlesex Co. (England). Widow of Vincent Pearce, Esq., late Captain in his Majesty's Navy, deceased; will of. Sister, Mrs. Euphemia Norris, widow, a basket at Mrs. Ogleby's; land in Lintown, East New Jersey. Sister, Margaret Morris, if she marries. To the younger children of my sister, Ashfield, who were excluded in their father's will. Mrs. Mary Waggett. Real and personal estate. Executrix—Euphemia Norris. Witnesses—Eliz. Coltman, of Harley Street, in the Parish of "Marrowbone," Mary Wright of same place, Ja. Jackson of Furnivall's Inn, Holborn. Proved Jan. 23, 1746. Lib. E, p. 59.

1748, Sept. 12. Pearson, Isaac, of City of Burlington, silversmith; will of. Wife, Rebecca. Daughter, Rebecca, lot on High Street, which lies between Mary Collum and Ebenezer Large, at 21. Son-in-law, Thomas Rodman, my anvill and silversmith's tools. Daughter, Elizabeth Rodman, my silver tankard. Grandchildren—Isaac Pearson Rodman, my silver shoe buckles; John and Margaret Rodman. Heirs of my daughter, Sarah, lately dec'd. Son-in-law, Joseph Hollingshead. Legacies to the children of Samuel Scattergood, dec'd. Executors—wife, and son-in-law, Thomas Rodman. Witnesses—John Bacon, Chris'er Wetherill, Robert Hartshorne. Proved Feb. 14, 1748-'9. Lib. 6, p. 263.

1748, Sept. 12. Pearson, Thomas, of Nottingham, Burlington Co. Int. Adm'r, Robert Pearson, of same. Joseph DeCow and John Yard, of Hunterdon Co., fellow bondsmen. Lib. 6, p. 19.

1748, Nov. 17. Inventory, £289.8.9; made by George Douglass and Jos. Yard. Includes time of servant, Alexander Moor.

1745, Oct. 18. Peck, John, of Cohansey, Salem Co., weaver; will of. Wife, Rebecca, all goods that she brought to me upon marriage, provided she will give sufficient security to indemnify my executor from all demands that may be made on my estate through her as administratrix of the estate of John Wheeler, deceased; also the use of my dwelling where we now live during her widowhood. Sons—Jeremiah, John and Joseph, to have 5 shillings apiece; likewise my daughter Abigail, and my granddaughter Mary Ware. Residue of estate, real and personal, to my son Herbert Peck, whom I appoint sole executor. Witnesses—Ananius Sayre, Robert Glaskey, Richd. Ball. Proved 1 May, 1748. Lib. 6, p. 290.

1746, April 9. Inventory (£101.11.6) includes looms and tackling, £6.10; cattle, sheep and hogs. Appraisers—Samuel Moore, Josiah Parvin.

1732, March 8. Pedrick, Edward, of Woodbridge, Middlesex Co. Int. Adm'r, Henry Freeman. Lib. B, p. 386.

1748, Aug. 30. Pedrick, Joseph, of Green's Neck, Salem Co.; will of. Cousin, Thomas Pedrick. Robert Pedrick to have stock of bees. My two brothers, Jacob and Thomas Pedrick, executors, and to have residue of moveable estate. Said executors to make Peter Justice a deed for the land which I sold him. Witnesses—Mary Pedrick, Aaron Howel, Thomas Pedrick. Affirmed 8 Dec., 1748. Lib. 6, p. 90.

1748, Dec. 7. Inventory, £106.17.4; made by Samuel Whitehorne, Peter Justice.

1739-40, Feb. 4. Peirce, Edward, Esq., of Burlington. Int. Inventory of the personal estate, £182.13.4; made by Joseph Hewlings and Jos. Scattergood. Includes a parcel of law books, £12.16.6; one-third of Thomas South's bond for £90.10, being £30.3.4; ½ of James Wales' bond for £40.

1739-40, Feb. 18. Adm'x, Catharine Peirce, widow. Joseph Heulings and Joseph Scattergood, fellow bondsmen. Lib. 4, p. 198.

1749, Sept. 5. Peirce, Richard, of Gloucester Co., husbandman. Int. Admr's, Richard Comron, Joseph Osler. Bondsman—Jonathan Thomas, innholder. Lib. 6, p. 324.

Peirce (see Pearse).

1743, Sept. 22. Peirson, Caleb, of Newark, Essex Co. Int. Adm'x, Sarah Peirson, the widow. Samuel Baldwin and John Tomkins, fellow bondsmen. Lib. D, p. 90.

1732, Dec. 1. Peirson, David, of Newark, Essex Co., joyner; will of. Children—Theophilus, Mary and Susannah, all under age. Expected child. Negro boy, Titus, to be sold towards paying my debts. Lands joining lands of Ebenezer Headly and Daniel Harrison. Executors—wife, Hannah, and brother, Jonathan Peirson. Witnesses—John Crane, John Wall, J. Styles. Proved Jan. 11, 1732-3

Lib. B, p. 373.

1733, March 22. Inventory, £91.01.09; made by Timothy Tuttle and Thomas Longworth.

1736, Sept. 9. Account of Jonathan Peirson, showing payments to Sam'll Wheeler, Isaac Harrison, John Baldwin, Daniel Harrison, Joseph Ball, Thomas Alling, Hannah Ball, Joseph Riggs, David Ogden, Josiah Ogden, Joseph Burwell, Lawrence Ward, Sam'll Plum, John Stiles, Joseph Hay, James Banks, Sarah van Tillburgh, Joseph Webb, Hannah Dod (widow of Jonathan Dod), Jasper Crane, Joseph Tuttle, Gilbert Heddin, David Crane, Samuel Baldwin, Samuel Ward, Philip Cundit, John Wall, Thomas Smith, and Hannah his wife (late Hannah Pierson, the other executor).

1747, July 10. Peirson, Henry, of Cohansey, Salem Co.; will of. Son, Henry, executor, and to have all my lands and buildings, except 100 acres bounding upon Nixon and Shepherd's lines, which shall be for my son Azal. Sons—William, John, Eli, and my daughter, Amy, to have equally the money from the sale of residue of moveable estate. Witnesses—Benjamin Chard, William Casto, John Ogden.

Lib. 5, p. 391.

1747-8, Feb. 2. Inventory, £63.3.5; made by Jonadab Shepherd, John Ogden.

Peirson (see Pierson).

1749, April 25. Pelton, Ithamer, of Monmouth Co. Int. Adm'r, Richard Parker. Lib. 6, p. 332.

1749, Oct. 30. Peneton (Penetant), Timothy, of Mendom Township, Morris Co., yeoman; will of. Wife, Mary, to have the dwelling house and the lot purchased of John Carter until the youngest of my three sons (Elijah, Jonathan and Ephraim Penetant) will be of age. Executors—wife, Marey, and Joseph Dod; and they shall sell the land I bought of Joseph Thomson to pay just debts. Witnesses—Stephen Dod, Isaac Kemble, Brice Riky. Proved 22 Feb., 1749-50. Lib. E, p. 364.

1749-50, Feb. 25. Inventory (£62.13.0) includes an old Bible (£25), sword, and debts due by Josiah Cain, Nathan Crossman, John Barton. Appraisers—Joseph Hinds, Stephen Dod.

1733, April 3. Pennington, Alice, of Salem Co., widow. Adm'r, Josiah Pennington. Bondsmen—John Sinnick, Joseph Hawks. Witnesses—Alexr. Simpson, Danl. Mestayer. Lib. 3, p. 300.

1733, April 2. Inventory (£30.12.2) includes cattle, £15.8. Appraisers—Thomas Elwell, John Sinnick.

1750-51, Feb. 22. Penny, William. Int. Adm'r, John Croker, of Essex County. David Rouset, of Second river, fellow bondsman. Lib. E. p. 501.

1749, Nov. 9. Penton, Burton, of Elsinburg, Salem Co., shoemaker; will of. Legacies to brothers Abner, Amos and Daniel; to Miriam Merrin, Martha Tracey and "Henry Miller, Joust Millers." Executors—brothers Abner and Amos. Witnesses—Daniel Huddy and John Ewen. Proved Dec. 15, 1749. Lib. 8, p. 541.

1749-50, Jan. 27. Inventory £394.5.7; made by William Murdock and William Barker.

1733, Feb. 24. Penton, William, of Alloways Creek, Salem Co., yeoman; will of. Sons—Abner and Burton, to have equally the home farm; John, to be maintained out of the profits of the land; Amos, 100 acres in Alloways Creek, adjoining the widow Kelly's; William 140 acres adjoining the plantation I dwell on; and Daniel, £20. Legacies to daughters—Mary, Elizabeth, Sarah, Martha and Miriam. Executors—sons, Abner and Burton. Witnesses—Daniel Fogg, Ann Fogg, Richard Bradford. Proved 25 June, 1735. Lib. 4, p. 34.

1735, July 7. Inventory (£134.13.7) includes grain, £32, cattle, £10.6.2. Appraisers—Benj. Holmes, Daniel Fogg.

1731, Jan. 18. Perkins, David, of Wellingborrow, Burlington Co., yeoman; will of. Brother, Abraham, plantation in Wellingburrow, which came to me by will of my father, Jacob Perkins, dated Oct. 26, 1731. Sister, Rebecca, wife of Henry Nordike. Mother, Sarah Perkins. Brother, Abraham, sole executor. Witnesses—Joseph Fenimore, Henry Nordike, Sam'l Scattergood. Proved March 4, 1731-2. Lib. 8, p. 184.

1731-2, March 4. Inventory, £181.12.6; made by Joseph Fenimore and Sam'l Scattergood.

1731, May 18. Perkins, Jacob, of Wellenborrow, Burlington Co. Int. Administration on estate granted to his son, Jacob Perkins, of same, yeoman. Abraham Heulings and Joseph Rockhill, all of Burlington Co., gentlemen, fellow bondsmen. Lib. 3, p. 102.

1731, May 20. Inventory, £91.18.5; made by Robert Lucas and Joseph Fenimore. Includes cane and sword, £1.10; debt of 14 shillings from

Benja. Perkins; 8 years rent due from Benja. Perkins and Wm. Makintass, £1.

1731, Oct. 26. Perkins, Jacob, Jr., of Wellingborrow, Burlington Co., yeoman; will of. Wife, Sarah. Children—Abraham, Rebeckah, David, Mary, Ann, Susannah, Hannah, Sarah, Bethseda and Martha. Land in Chester, which I bought of John Ward March 15, 1728. Bonds due from James Smith, Esq., John Shinn and Henry Nordike. St. Mary's Church, Burlington, £10. Son, David, executor. Witnesses—Joseph Fenimore, Eliza Fenimore, Sam. Scattergood. Proved Dec. 7, 1731. Lib. 3, p. 169.

1731, Dec. 6. Inventory, £205.14.6; made by Joseph Fenimore and Sam'l Scattergood.

1750-1, Feb. 27. Perrine, Mathew, of Perth Amboy, Middlesex Co.; will of. Wife, Isebale. Children—John, Kenith, Henry and Margaret, all under age. Executors—John Anderson and William Laird of Freehold. Witnesses—Henery Perrine, Peter Perrine, Jacob Applegate. Proved March 8, 1750-1. Lib. E, p. 495.

1750-1, March 4. Inventory (£340.03.6) includes debts due from Thomas Lowrey, John Egbert, Jonathan Anderson. Made by Peter Perrine and Henry Perrine.

1748, Jan. 3. Person (Peirson), Henry, of the Borough of Elizabeth, Essex Co., yeoman; will of. Wife, Sarah. Children—Henry, John, Benjamin and Jemima, wife of James Arnet. Grandchildren—Henry, Jemima and Elizabeth Skillman, children and James, deceased. Lands bought of Benjamin Meeker, John Clark, David Morehouse, deceased, Benjamin Lyon; land joining land of Benjamin Bond, bought of Joseph Meeker, deceased; land bought of John Blanchard, May 20, 1736; land bought of Benjamin Williams, deceased; land joining lands of Stephen Brown, Abraham Baker, Isaac Crane and Joseph Crane, deceased. Executors—sons Joseph and Benjamin. Witnesses—John Hinds, Michael Meeker, Jno. Oborn. Proved Sept. 22, 1750. Lib. F, p. 341.

1739, Oct. 1. Peters, Benjamin, of Raccoon Creek, Gloucester Co., innkeeper; will of. Wife, Ann. Son, Benjamin. Daughter, Rebecca, wife of Jonathan Beaton. Executors—wife, Ann, and my brother, Rice Peters. Witnesses—Joseph Stiles, Elizabeth Stiles, Laurence Stacpole. Affirmed 4 June, 1741. Lib. 4, p. 307.

1741, April 23. Inventory (£308.12.1½) includes book debts, £153.3.0; old writing desk £3.0.0; wine £1.5.0; old shoemaker's tools, 15 shillings; rum, £5.10.0. Appraisers—Alexr. Randall, Peter Long.

1737, Nov. 11. Peterson, Gabriel, of Salem Co., yeoman. Int. Adm'x, Elizabeth Peterson (widow). Bondsman—William Penton. Both of said County. Witnesses—John Roe, Danl. Mestayer. Lib. 4, p. 139.

1737, Nov. 11. Inventory, £39.17.4; made by William Penton, Charles Balliter.

1747, May 18. Peterson, Gerrebrant, of Somerset Co. Int. Adm'r, son, Peter Peterson. Fellow bondsman—Tomas Pietersen. Lib. E, p. 39.

1747, May 14. Renunciation of Hannah (signed "Anna"), widow of Gerrebrant Peterson, in favor of their son, Peter. Witnesses—Tomas Pietersen, Hurpet Pietersen.

1741, Nov. 2. Peterson, Henry, of Salem Co. Int. Adm'x, Mary Peterson, of Morris River (relict of). Bondsman—John Bill, Esq., of said county. Witnesses—Andw. Gardiner, Chas. O. Neill.
Lib. 4, p. 316.

1741, Oct. 30. Inventory, £15.11; made by John Bell, Joseph Lord.

1733, Sept. 18. Peterson, Peter, Sr., of Morris River, Salem County, yeoman; will of. Wife, Ann. Sons—Peter, Junior, Henry, Aaron, Gabriel (to have the place where Joseph Lord lives), John and Mathias—all to have my land equally, but last named to have the place I live on. Legacies to daughters, Modlena (eldest), Rebecca Scull, Christian, Elener and Susanna Steelman (daughter of John Steelman) at 18. Andrew Erixson, Junior, to have a deed for 100 acres I sold to him. Witnesses—Henry Hickin, Charles Belitha, Moses Poolson. Proved 18 Oct., 1735.

1735, Oct. 18. As will names no executors, there were appointed as administrators, Gabriel and Mathias Peterson. Bondsman—Charles Belitha. Witnesses—Edwd. Peirce, Danl. Mestayer. All of Salem County, Gent. Lib. 4, pp. 40, 41.

1735, Nov. 4. Inventory (£188.10.6) includes cattle, £31; one Great Bible, £1.10; bonds, £120. Appraisers—Charles Belitha, Ed. Trenchard.

1737, April 18. Account. Monies paid to Andrew Erickson, Peter String, John Thompson, Silas Parvin, Elias Naudam, John Erickson, Danl. Mestayer, William Rawson, John Bell, Peter Tranberg, John Purple and Alice his wife (late Alice Lord, wife of Joseph Lord).

1740, May 9. Peterson, William, of Greenwich, Gloucester Co.; will of. Sons—Andrew and Zacheriah, executors, and to have the real estate, paying legacies to other sons Laurance and Moses (1 English shilling each), and to my granddaughter, Mary Cox, when 18, one-tenth of the full value of my free lands. In case of her death under age, the aforesaid one-tenths shall be paid to my three daughters (now living), or to their heirs. Witnesses—John Hanby, Mathew Boucher, John Orchard. Sworn and affirmed, 26 Sept., 1743.
Lib. 4, p. 375.

1731, July 17. Petterson, Christian, relict of Gabriel Petterson. Int. Inventory, £124.0.7; made by Andrew Shallcop, Henry Jeanes.

1731, Aug. 14. Sworn to by Lucas Petterson. Salem Wills, 489 Q.

1732, Oct. 13. Petticrew, William, of Burlington, carpenter. Int. Administration on estate granted to Thomas Hendry, merchant. Edward Peirce, gent., fellow bondsman. Both of Burlington.
Lib. 3, p. 218.

1748, Oct. 21. Pettit, Andrew, of Amwell, Hunterdon Co., blacksmith. Bond of Dinah Pettit, of Amwell, as administratrix. Job Robins, of same place, surety. Witnessed by Anne Rockhill. (Dinah Pettit, a Quaker). Lib. 6, p. 76.

1748, Dec. 26. Inventory, £367.11.5½; made by Job Robins, Mansfield Hunt, Amos Thatcher.

1747, Aug. 15. Petty (Pelty), William, of Burlington, woolcomber. Int. Adm'r, Richard Blackham, of Philada, blacksmith. Benjamin Kimble and Israel Heulings, yeomen, of Burlington Co., fellow bondsmen. Lib. 5, p. 434.

1748, April 23. Phillips, Joseph, of Maidenhead, Hunterdon Co.;

will of. Wife, Mary. Eldest daughter, Mary, when aged 18. £100 to each daughter. Residue to three sons (not named), under 14 years. Executors—wife, brother Theophilus Phillips, and brother-in-law Abner Phillips. Witnesses—William Philips, John Philips, Benjamin Stevens. Proved May 9, 1748. Lib. 5, p. 450.

———, ———, —. Inventory £155.10.6; made by Benjamin Stevens and John Vancleave.

1740, August 22. Phillips, Philip, Senr., of Maidenhead, Hunterdon Co., yeoman; will of. Wife, Elizabeth. Oldest son, Philip. Son, Abner, 12 acres of land on east side of the King's Road, by Samuel Hunt's line. Son, Samuel, when of age, the mansion house and plantation. Daughters—Esther and Ruth, at marriage. Youngest son, John, to remain with son Samuel until aged 16. Executors—wife, and son Philip. Witnesses—Samuel Hunt, John Van Cleave, Lewis Charles Fanuiel. Proved November 3, 1740. Lib. 4, p. 257.

1740, Oct. 24. Inventory, £249.15.0; made by Theo. Phillips and Samuel Hunt.

1748, Feb. 8. Phillips, Philip, of Morris Co. Int. Admr's, Johannah Philips, of Greenwitch, Morris Co., and Benjamin Slack, of Maidenhead, Hunterdon Co. Bondsman—John Carmen, of Greenwitch, Morris Co. Witnesses—James Anderson, Samuel Carman. Lib. 6, p. 75.

1748-9, Jan. 24. Inventory includes 190 acres of land, £160; bonds, £120; cattle, £13; horses, £18; book debts, £37.11.8. Appraisers—James Anderson, John Carman.

1750, Sept. 21. Phillips, Philip, of Morris Co. Int. Adm'r, Reuben Winget, of said County. Bondsman—Obadiah Heady (signed "Hedden"). Lib. E, p. 481.

1750, Nov. 1. Inventory, £20.7.5; made by Gideon Riggs, Thomas Darling.

1748, March 29. Phillpot, John, of Penns Neck, Salem Co.; will of. Wife, Christiana. Estate to be sold and money put at interest for benefit of my three sons—John, Earick and Abraham. Executors—wife, Christiana, and Edmond Weatherby. Witnesses—Martin Skeer, Henry Gilljohnson. Proved 23 April, 1748. Lib. 5, p. 544.

1748, April 16. Inventory (£150.3.8) includes cattle, £58.4; wheat, £21. Appraisers—Martin Skeer, Samuel Capner.

1742, Aug. 28. Phillpots, Richard, of Great Egg Harbor, Gloucester Co., tailor; will of. My land and money in England to my sister, Mary Ades, and after her to her child. "If she can keep my wife from the thirds thereof, she is welcome to it, by giving her five shillings." 20 shillings to Mr. Jenkin Jones, Baptist minister in Philadelphia. Residue and my lands here to my aforesaid sister, "living in the Parish of St. James, in Milk Street, near the signe of the ship Bristoll," and her daughter. If they do not see cause to come here and enjoy it, let it be sold, and the moneys remitted home. Executors—my brother-in-law, Walter Ades, and his wife, my sister Mary, in Bristoll; but, they being not here to act, Japheth Leeds, Junior, and Edward Doughty shall be trustees to act for them. Witnesses—Peter, Isaiah and Phebe Covenoven, Joseph Ashurst. Sworn and affirmed 4 Nov., 1742. Lib. 4, p. 348.

1742, Oct. 23. Inventory, £61.17.3; made by Japhet Leeds, William Cordry.

1749, June 4. Pierson, Ann, of Salem Town and County, widow; will of. Daughter, Mary, to have the Great Bible, negro woman Flora, two silver pepper boxes, nine large silver spoons, one set of teaspoons and £200, when of age or at marriage; the interest thereof to be used for the bringing up and education of said daughter. Sons—Henry to have £100 at interest, for his bringing up and education; John, one silver porringer, two silver salts, two small silver spoons, together with the sum of £200 to be delivered to him when of age (the £200 to be put to interest for the bringing up and educating of my son). Residue of my estate to be divided among my three children, Mary, Henry and John; the land to be delivered at their respective ages aforesaid. Executor—my brother-in-law, Joseph Sharp. Witnesses—Elizabeth Coleman, George Trenchard. Proved 1750. Lib. 9, p. 83.

———, ———, —. Inventory, (£313.18.6, but missing).

1741, Nov. 17. Pierson (Peirson), Daniel, of Elizabeth Town, Essex Co.; will of. Children—Daniel, Phebe, Sarah, Stephen, Hannah, Abigail and David. Expected child. Real and personal estate. Executors—wife, Sarah, and brothers Henry Pierson and Jonathan Crane. Witnesses—Daniel Perrine, Enoch Miller, Nath'll Hubbell. Proved April 16, 1743. Lib. D, p. 34.

1743, April 30. Inventory, £71.16; made by Andrew Craige, Daniel Perrine.

1747, Oct. 9. Pierson, John, of Salem Town and Co., clerk; will of. Wife, Ann, sole executrix, and to have personal estate with the profits of my real estate until my three sons will be 21. Sons—Coleman, at 21, to have the plantation called the Fork, which I purchased of Edmund Wetherby, also my negro boy Prime and my silver tankard; Henry, my dwelling in Salem Town, with the lot belonging, he paying £100 to his sister Mary Pierson, when she will be 21, also my negro girl and my pint silver can; Abraham, when 21, to have my house, land and marsh in the Town bounds of Salem, with 12 acres in Cow's Neck, and my silver ladle. Daughter, Mary, at 21, or marriage, to have my silver salver and negro girl, Calia. Unto the expected child (be it male or female), £100. Witnesses—Andrew Gardiner, Rebekah Coleman, Dan. Mestayer. Proved 29 Oct., 1747. Lib. 9, p. 359.

Pierson (see Pearson, Peirson, Person).

1730-1, Feb. 15. Pike, Joseph, of Woodbridge, Middlesex Co., yeoman; will of. Children—John, Sarah, Timothy and Elizabeth, all under age. Land joining the farms of James Worth and Samuel Jaques. Executrix—wife, Elizabeth. Brother, Zebulon Pike, and brother-in-law Richard Cutter, to assist her. Real and personal estate. Witnesses—Stephen Foster, Thomas Cook, Wm. Jones. Proved March 12, 1730-1. Lib. B, p. 193.

1736, July 3. Pike, Timothy, of Essex Co., aged about 16 years. Josiah Terrill, guardian. William Craige, fellow bondsman. Lib. C, p. 126.

1741, Oct. 31. Pike, Timothy, of Woodbridge, Middlesex Co., yeoman; will of. Cousin, John Pike. Sister, Elizabeth Pike, at 21 years. Brother, John Pike. Real and personal estate. Executor, uncle Zebulon Pike. Witnesses—David Heriott, Ursula Heriott, Jno. Waller. Proved Dec. 1, 1741. Lib. C, p. 467.

1736, October 20. Pilkington (Pilkinton), Gabriel, of Monmouth Co., tailor. Administration granted to George Allen of same county, yeoman. Samuel Leonard, of same county, fellow bondsman. Lib. C, p. 136.

1736, Nov. 16. Inventory (£32.11.4) includes gun and sword. Made by Adam Brewer and Benjamin Parker.

1732, Feb. 6. Pine, Jonathan, of Elizabeth Town, Essex Co., cooper; will of. Eldest son, Jonathan, my gun; other children mentioned, but not by name, all under age. Real and personal estate. Executors—wife, Phebe, and friend Samuel Searing. Witnesses—Isaac Southard, Jane Southard, John Blanchard. Proved March 28, 1733. Lib. B, p. 425.

1733, May 26. Inventory, £64.15.06; made by Benjamin Pettit and John Clark.

1729, Feb. 24. Pintard, Anthony, Senior, late of Shrewsbury, Monmouth Co., now of the City of New York, gentleman; will of. Being aged and infirm. Eldest son, Anthony. Daughters—Margaret, Florinda and Frances, house and lot in the City of New York, near the new Dutch Church. £30 to the French Church in New York; £10 to the minister, Lewis Rou. £10 to Mr. Moulinar, another French minister at New Rochel. Children—John Lewis, Samuel, Magdalen Hutchins, Catherine Searls, Margaret, Isabela Vandam, Florinda and Anna Frances. Executors—friend Lewis Carree, of New York, merchant, sons John Lewis and Samuel Pintard, and son-in-law John Searles, all of New York, merchants. Witnesses—Philip Cortlandt, John Waldron, Daniel Bontecou, Pr. Quintan. Codicil of July 31, 1731, makes provision for legacy to daughter Isabel and recites agreement made at the time of her marriage to Isaac Van Dam, son of Rip Van Dam. Witnesses—Tho: Ives, Gerrit Roos and Thomas Owen. Proved May 11, 1732. Lib. B, p. 248.

1748, March 31. Pintard, Samuel, of Monmouth Co. Int. Adm'r, Anne Pintard. James Russell, of Monmouth Co., fellow bondsman.

1748, May 4. Inventory, £35.9.0; made by William Hugan, Benjamin Kallum and Robert Thompson. Lib. E, p. 158.

1740, July 1. Pirey (Perey), William, of Alloways Creek, Salem Co., yeoman; will of. Wife, Margret. Sons—James (eldest), 5 shillings; Samuel (second), the plantation with all my lands. Daughter, Rebecah McKnight (£20). Son James' daughter, Mary Perey (not 18). Servant girls—Mary Moore and Elener Holland, both under age. Executors—son, Samuel Perey, and Thomas Evings. Witnesses—Bilby Shepherd, William Finlow, Thomas Pagett. Proved 6 Sept., 1740. Lib. 4, p. 255.

1740, Sept. 2. Inventory, £172.8; made by John Finlow, Thomas Pagett.

1742, Nov. 25. Pitcock, Stephen, of Amwell, Hunterdon Co., plantation man; will of. Two sons, John and Thomas Pitcock. Executors—friends, Thomas Kitchen and William Barnes. Witnesses—Edward Rockhill, Andrew Pettit, Jacob Knowles, Thomas Thatcher. Proved Dec. 28, 1742. Lib. 4, p. 343.

——, ——, —. Inventory £92.9.3; made by Henry Ketchin and George Fox.

1761, April 10. Account by William Barns, Thomas Kitchin, the other executor, being rendered incapable by age. Mentions William Montgomery, Benjamin Taylor, John Watson, George Fox, Charles Hoffman, for B. Smith, William Yard, James Neilson, John Wright, Walter Caine, Samuel Carey, John Lewis, Benjamin Savery, Joseph Lambert, Jerom Horne, Jeremiah Thacher, Mary Robins, Philip Ringo, Thomas Thacher, Thomas Laba, James Journay, Emanuel Carreyell, George Bayles, Benjamin Chamley, John Robins, Samuel Carey, Henry Kitchins, Jacob Knowles, Mary Adams, Josiah Prickitt, John Stevenson, John Mullin, John Wells, Nathaniel Pettit, Joseph King, Benjamin Severns.

1750, April 13. Pitney, James, of Morris Co. Int. Admr's, Susannah Pitney and Jonathan Pitney, widow and son of deceased. Bondsman—Shobal Smith, of Woodbridge, Middlesex Co. Lib. E, p. 383.

1748, Jan. 1. Pitney, Samuel, of Roxbury Township, Morris Co., gent.; will of. Executors—wife, Surviah, brother Jonathan Pitney and Nathaniel Drake, who are empowered to dispose of estate, for maintenance and bringing up of children (not named). Remainder payable to my sons at 21, to my daughters at 18. Witnesses—Jeamiah Rogers, James Martin, Benjamin Pitney. Proved 27 Jan. 1748. Lib. E, p. 250.

1748, May 14. Plaskett, William, of Trenton, Hunterdon Co., mason; will of. Wife, Margaret. Son, William (under age), house and lot wherein David Martin lived, on the east side of King's Street in Trenton, bounded by the Church lot, the kitchen of house where testator lived and Enoch Anderson's land; another lot in Trenton, purchased of Amos Janney, adjoining William Yard's land on Maidenhead Road at Stockin's Hollow. Son, John (under age), house and lot on east side of King's Street, adjoining abovesaid lot, and is testator's dwelling, bounded by Benjamin Smith's corner, and Enoch Anderson's land; and another lot in Trenton bought of George Ely, adjoining Joseph Warrel's land, containing ten acres. Daughters, Margaret, Mercy and Mary Plaskett, when of age. Executors—brother, John Lucas, and friends William Morris and Nathan Beakes. Witnesses—Thomas Barnes, Richard Margerum, Joseph Yard. Proved June 16, 1748. Lib. 5, p. 460.

1748, 16th of 4 mo. (June). Inventory, £423.11.0; made by Gideon Bickerdike and Thomas Barnes.

1748, Dec. 12. Platts, Jonathan, of Stow Creek, Cumberland Co., yeoman; will of. Wife, Jean, to have use of my plantation until my son Thomas will be 21. Son, Jonas, 50 acres of land and marsh, part in Hell Neck; also a piece of marsh, 10½ acres, in Bottel Neck on the west side of Stow Creek; also £25. Remaining part to be divided (with the ½ of my moveables) equally between my daughter, Mary Evens, and my son, Thomas Platt. Youngest son, Thomas, at 21 to have my plantation (136 acres), and 30 acres of land and swamp. Executors—wife, Jean, and son Thomas. Trustee—James Butcher. (Unsigned).

1748-9, Feb. 18. Affidavit and affirmation of Thomas Pagett and William Daniel. "That the within named testator allow the within instrument to be his will and at the doing thereof he was of sound mind; that the seal was fixed to the said will and the said testator sat up to sign the sd.

instrument and attempted the same, but died away before he could complete the same; and that David Platt was in the Room with those deponents, which would have been witness to the sd. will." Lib. 6, p. 336.

1748-9, May 16. Inventory (£199.14.1) includes bricks at John Plumbers, wheat, rye and sundries at Thomas Bucher's, at William Daniel's 1 pair of oxen, cow and calf, Indian corn, etc. Appraisers—Peter Long, H. Stubbines.

1735, March 25. Pledger, John, Esquire, of Salem Co., guardian of Jane Hart (upwards of 14 years), only daughter and heir at law of John Hart, late of Salem, merchant, deceased. "Her parents being deceased many years, having left real and personal estate."

Lib. 4, p. 8.

1743, Dec. 30. Pledger, John, Esquire, of Salem Co.; will of. The 300 acres called the Fork to be sold to pay debts and legacies. The one-third of the profits of the plantation I live on (exclusive of the part where Richard Graves lives, and where Thomas Hale did live), unto my wife during life, and one-third of the rent due from James Chambless (after legacies due to him and his brother, and sister are paid) to my wife. The dwelling house and plantation (216 acres) where I live to Edmond Weatherby and Martha, his wife, forever. My son-in-law, Joseph Siddons, to have the privilege of occupying free, for 7 years, the tan-yard set upon the above premises. Grandson, Joseph Pledger, at 21 to have the plantation (92 acres) where Richard Graves lives, and where Thomas Hale did live, if it should not be necessary to sell the same to pay debts and legacies. Legacies to wife and my daughter Elizabeth Casperson, grandchildren Joseph, Sarah and Dorothy Pledger, and to John, Joseph, and Pledger Redstreicke, after they arrive at 21 years. Executors—son-in-law, Edmond Weatherby, and Martha, his wife. Witnesses—Dan. Mestayer, William Tuft, Geo. Trenchard. Proved 4 Jan., 1743.

Lib. 5, p. 14.

1743, Jan. 9. Inventory (£582) of John Pledger, "late of Manington," includes George Fox's Journal, oxen, cows, yearlings and calves, negro man (£15), mulatto boy s time, servant woman's time. Appraisers—Benjamin Cripps, Daniel Smith.

1743, July 28. Pledger, John, Jr., of Township of Alloways Creek, Salem Co., yeoman; will of. Son Joseph (at 21) to have the home farm. Two daughters, Sarah and Dorothy Pledger (at 21), to have one-third of an undivided tract of land in the Township of Manington. Wife, Mary, the personal and the rents, provided she maintains my said children. Mary Vaughan to have a cow, if she lives with my wife until 18. Executors—wife and my father, John Pledger. Witnesses—Wm. Pennock, Jeames Johnston, Mary Vaughan. Proved 10 Oct., 1743. Lib. 5, p. 11.

1743, Sept. 29. Inventory, £350.14.2; made by Benjamin Cripps, Daniel Smith.

1733, Jan. 15. Polony, Thomas, of Woodbridge, Middlesex Co. Int. Adm'r, John Bloomfield. Lib. B, p. 586.

1748, Oct. 15. Porter, Abraham, of Gloucester Co., who made will dated 17 Dec., 1729; unadministered estate. Adm'r de bonus non, Charles Stow, of Philadelphia, innholder. Bondsman—William Coats, Burlington, yeoman. (For will and inv. see Archives, Vol. 23, p. 370).

Lib. 5, p. 532.

1733, April 14. Porter, John, of Middlesex Co. Int. Adm'rs, Philip Dodridge and William Porter. Lib. B, p. 380.

1735, Jan. 1. Porterfield, John, of Trenton, Hunterdon Co., merchant; will of. If necessary, executors to sell 200 acres out of a tract on south branch of Rariton River in East Jersey, containing 1,000 acres, bought of William Farquhar, who received same from Evan Drummond. Brother, Alexander Porterfield, of Duchall, Scotland. Lands in East Jersey received from John, Earle of Mellfort, deceased, conveyed to testator by deeds from William Corby, sheriff of Middlesex and Bernard Vanbryck, Sheriff of Monmouth County. To William Farquhar, chyrurgeon at Brunswick in this Province, the testator's nephew, one-third of the forge at Trenton, with the lands, houses, waterworks, etc., with 100 acres of land bought of George Green in Nottingham Township, a tract in said township adjoining the Pond Run, bought of Robert Eaton, and a tract in same township on Mirey Run adjoining land late of John Cox, surveyed by Samuel Green. Nephew, William Rallston, in Ayrshire. Emanuel Walker, Collector of Port Glasgow. Boyd Porterfield, grandson of testator's brother, bond due testator, dated June, 1708, for 2,346 marks Scotts, or £130 Sterling. Bond from James Stuart, of Lum loch, the testator's uncle, payable to testator's mother and by her assigned to him; this bond left with testator's brother in 1708 with power of attorney; testator is informed the bond was paid by the Earl of Glasgow; the principal was for £1,000 Scotts or £83.6 Sterling, dated about 1700, or before. If above legatees die, then legacies to next heir of the family who shall succeed to the estate of Duchall after the decease of testator's nephew, William Porterfield. Executors—John Kinsey of Philadelphia, attorney-at-law, Joseph Peace of Trenton, and William Farquhar, the testator's nephew. Witnesses—Thomas Barnes, Jr., Elisha Beadles, John Allen, Jr. Proved June 16, 1738. Lib. 4, p. 136.

1750, April 23. Post. John, of Amwell, Hunterdon Co., farmer; will of. Wife, Altie, executrix, and to receive the interest from estate until the children (John, Charity, Mary, Abraham, William and Hendrick) are of age. Executors—Peter Scank and John Precor (Brokaw) of Millstone, Somerset Co. Witnesses—Thomas Poole, Thomas Newman, Lovrence Vankleef. Proved 1 May, 1750. [On back of will "John Post's will of Somerset Co., who dyed in Hunterdon"]. Lib. F, p. 168.

1750, May 4. Inventory (£606.15.8) includes large Dutch Bible in a box with a hone, £3.17.0; sword; cross-cut saw at Jacob Powelsess, a bond, £488.1.5. Made by Pieter Stryker, Peter Perrine, Jacob Probasco; and by Peter Schenck and John Brokaw, executors.

1741, Jan. 19. Potter, Henry, of Woodbridge, Middlesex Co. Administration on the estate granted to Phineas Potter, the son. Lib. C, p. 469.

1741-2, Jan. 25. Articles sold at vendue and bought by Henry Langstaff, Wm. Foord, Reuben Potter, Eunice Shippey, Daniel Waldron, Benjamin Wooding, David Evens. Notes of Samuel Walker, Jeremiah Ogle, Duson Ogle, Isaac FitzRandolph, Josiah Barent, John Bowey, Joseph Applegate; debt due to Cornelius Wynans.

1743, April 1. Inventory (£79.01.2) includes cash paid to Andrew Van Horne. Made by Henry Langstaffe and Samuel Martin.

1746, June 28. Potter, Preserve, of Shrewsbury, Monmouth Co., laborer; will of. Wife, Catherine. Son, Thomas, two-thirds of right to take up land, bought of Robert Savage. Other children—Hannah, Robert, and Deborah, last named under age. Jacob, son of brother Joseph Potter. Executors—brother, Joseph Potter, and friend Joseph Patterson. Witnesses—Henry Herbert, William Newbray, Jon. Herring. Proved Jan. 7, 1747-8. Joseph Potter, a Quaker, affirmed as executor. Lib. E, p. 124.

1747-8, 15th d., 11 mo. (Jan.). Inventory £39.7.6; made by John Williams, cordwainer, and Joseph Potter.

1747-8, March 17. Joseph Patterson declined to serve as an executor.

1745-6, March 17. Potter, Samuel, of Hanover, Morris Co., gent.; will of. Wife, Phebe. Sons—Isaac, 50 acres at the north of the homestead; Samuel (at age), 20 acres adjoining, and to be put to a trade when 14 years old; Joseph, the remainder of the homestead and to care for his mother and younger brothers and sisters, excepting Zebeedee, who shall have £25 at age and be put to a trade at the discretion of the executors; Moses, £20 at age and when 14 to be put to a trade. Legacies to daughters—Phebe, Sarah and Jemimah, when 18. Executors—brothers, Joseph and Noediah Potter, of Elizabethtown, Essex Co. Witnesses—Joseph Meeker, Robert Schooley, Stephen Ward. Proved 2 May, 1746. Lib. D, p. 379.

1746, April 28. Inventory (£347.6.6) includes cows and calves, wheat, rye and other grain. Appraisers—Stephen Ward, Ephrm. Price, Jun'r.

1742, 16th day, 5th mo. (July). Potts, Thomas, Jun'r, of Mansfield, Burlington Co., tanner. Int. Inventory of the personal estate, £911; made by Isaac Horner and Preserved Brown. Includes stock in tanyard and shoemaker's shop, £160.8; five negroes £100; book debts supposed to be good, £352.4.7½.

1742, July 19. Adm'x, Sarah Potts, widow. Isaac Horner, of Mansfield, yeoman, fellow bondsman. Lib. 4, p. 377.

1731, Aug. 2. Poulson, Jonas, of Great Egg Harbor, Gloucester Co., husbandman. Int. Admr's, Jasper Poulson and Joseph Pearce, of place aforesaid, yeoman. Witness—Joseph Rose.

1731, Aug. 1. Renunciation of Ann Poulson in favor of said administrators "on account of their brother, Jonas Poulson, and for us take care of all the estate and the two boys and girls." Witnesses—Rob.——— (?), Dennis Dorrell.

1731, Aug. 5. Inventory, £48.16.5½ made by Robert Smith, John Darby.

1733, Sept. 4. Account. Monies paid to Levi Pearce, Jeremiah Adams, Charles Shing, John Hunlope, Peter Cavelier, ——— Lashley, Isaac Willcockson. Gloucester Wills, 129 H.

1749, Nov. 2. Powell, Arthur, of Newton Township, Gloucester Co., yeoman; will of. Wife, Mary, to have during widowhood the profits. Son, James (not 21), the plantation, and to pay my daughter, Rachel Lewis, £50 and my grandson, Samuel Kent, £25 in four years after my wife's decease or her marriage. Executors—wife, Mary, and Joseph Ellis. Witnesses—Robert Stephens, Edward Hampton, Jos. Harrison. Affirmed 30 March, 1751. Lib. 7, p. 181.

1743-4, 12 mo. (Feb.), 11 da. Powell, Jeremiah, of Alloways Creek, Salem Co.; will of. Son, John, a silver cup and to have the home farm and land in Stoe Neck. Daughters—Elizabeth, a truck that was my mother's; Mary, one silver spoon. The residue to be divided among my three above-named children. Daughters to have their part at 18 or marriage, and son his part of the moveables at 20. Cousin, Mary Mason, to have my daughter, Elizabeth, until 18. John and Elizabeth Nicholas to have my daughter Mary during her minority; also my son John until he will be 14, "that he may be put out to be a tailor." Executors—Nathaniel Chamlis and Benjamin Allen. Witnesses—Abel Nicholson, Joseph Ware, James Abbott.

1744-5, Jany 11. Codicil. The profits of all my lands shall be divided equally among my children, John, Elizabeth and Mary Powell until my son will be 18. (Unsigned). Affirmed 10 Feb., 1744.

1745, April 3. Benjamin Allen sworn as executor, Nathaniel Chamlis having renounced his right. Witness—Thomas Atherington. Lib. 5, p. 93.

1744-5, 12 mo. (Feb.), 4 da. Inventory (£124.12.4) includes cattle, horse and sheep. Appraisers—Saml. Abbott, John Stewart.

1743, May 3. Powell, John, of Salem Co. Int. Admr's, James Mason and John Nicholson, yeoman (sons-in-law of the said John Powell), of Elsenburrow, the same County. Bondsman—Edward Test. Witnesses—John Hunt, Chas. O. Neill. Lib. 4, p. 371.

1743, May 7. Inventory (£1622.0.5) includes watch, £7.10; bills, bonds and book debts, £1156.6.5; 2 mortgages on lands, £266; 34 neat cattle, £72.10; 7 horses, £17.10; one negro man, £20. Appraisers—Benjamin Cripps, William Barrat.

1733, June 20. Powell, Michael, of Newark, Essex Co., doctor. Int. Adm'r, Eliphalet Johnson. Samuel Harrison, fellow bondsman. Lib. B, p. 422.

1733, Dec. —. Inventory (£38.17.05), includes silver buckles, debts due to Doctor Nickalls, Benjamin Foster, Joseph Johnson, Alexander Henry, Sarah Buckingham, Garret Wouters, Mr. Ferrand. Made by Jno. Cooper, Elijah Gillett.

1745, Jan. 22. Powell, Walter, of Salem Co., yeoman. Int. Adm'x, Jemima Powell. Bondsmen—Thomas Harris, Isaac Preston. All of said County. Witnesses—Mathew Parvin, Dan. Mestayer. Lib. 5, p. 420.

1745, Dec. 3. Inventory (£59.3.2) includes shoemaker's tools and leather. Appraisers—Isaac Preston, Thomas Harris.

1736, Nov. 4. Powers, Richard, of Somerset Co. Int. Adm'r, Thomas Hinchman, of Queens County, New York, the widow, Ann Powers, having renounced her right. Fellow bondsman—Richard Fitz Randolph. Lib. C, p. 127.

1742-3, March 11. Inventory (£412.13) includes negro man Tom, £45; Harry, £45; negro woman, £35; large Bible; coat and breeches of silk £2; beaver hat, sword and belt, 12s.; bond of James Stout, dated 2 Aug. 1729; bonds of Hendrick Johnson, and Robt. Bolmore. Made by Jno. Van Middlesworth, Johannis Folekerse.

1732-3, Feb. 23. Prall, Cornelis, of Hunterdon Co., yeoman; will of. Wife, Esther. Executors—wife, and brother Aaron Prall. Only an unborn child. Witnesses—James Laroe, Edward Whitaker, Daniel Laroe. Proved Oct. 8, 1733. Lib. 3, p. 377.

———, ———, —. Inventory (£59.0.6) includes guns and sword. Made by Thomas Lake and Daniel Laroe.

1736, March 11. Petition of Simon Kinney, of Hunterdon County, yeoman, sheweth that he married Esther, widow of Cornelius Prall; that the child mentioned in the latter's will was born, a daughter named Mary. Petitions for guardian.

1739-40, Feb. 22. Prat, William, of Evesham, Burlington Co., blacksmith; will of. Wife, Mary, sole executrix and legatee. Witnesses—Samuel Woolman, John Neale, Jun'r, John Woolman. Real and personal estate. Proved March 1, 1739-40. Lib. 4, p. 220.

1739-40, Feb. 27. Inventory, £429.17.11; made by Revell Elton and Daniel Wills. Includes smith's tools in the shop, £22.

1739-40, Feb. 11. Pratt, Jonathan, of Cape May Co. Int. Inventory of the estate, £11.16.4; made by Barnabas Crowell and Elisha Hand.

1739-40, Feb. 23. Adm'r, Benjamin Laughton, of Cape May County. John Eldredge, of same County, fellow bondsman. Cape May Wills, 99 E.

1732, May 26. Prays, Samuel, of Perth Amboy, Middlesex Co., carpenter. Int. Adm'x, Mary Prays, the widow. Lib. B, p. 261.

1748, Dec. 16. Preston, Isaac, of Fairfield Precinct, Cumberland Co.; will of. Children—Levi, Isaac, William, John, Elizabeth, Joseph. Wife, Elizabeth, sole executrix, and to have the residue of estate for her own benefit and that of the children, or "for pious uses as her conscience and prudence shall direct." Witnesses—Jeams Johnson, William Bradford, David Westcote. Proved 27 Feb., 1749. Lib. 6, p. 301.

1749-50, Feb. 23. Inventory (£226.19.3) includes cattle, 2 horses, 18 sheep. Appraisers—David Westcote, Henry Westcote.

1731, July 31. Preston, Levi (Leavy), of Cohansey, Salem Co., yeoman. Int. Adm'x, Mary Preston, widow. Bondsman—Leavy (Levi) Preston, Senior, yeoman, of said place and county. Witnesses—Josiah Fithian, Jno. Rolfe. Lib. 3, p. 215.

1731, July 31. Inventory, £235.0.1; made by Josiah Fithian, Moses Husted. Witness—Jno. Rolfe.

1733, Dec. 14. Price, Daniel, of Elizabeth Town, Essex Co.; will of. Cousin, Joseph Price, son of my eldest brother. Brothers—Ephraim and John Price. Real and personal estate. Executors—wife, Elizabeth, and cousin Joseph Price. Witnesses—John Clark, Daniel Peirson, Sarah Peirson. Proved April 16, 1743.

1743, April 16. Joseph Price refuses executorship. Witness—Thomas Price. Lib. D, p. 36.

1745, Aug. 20. Price, Dennis, of Essex Co. Int. Adm'r, Isaac van Vleck, principal creditor. Edward Pigot and John King, fellow bondsmen. Lib. D, p. 313.

1745, Aug. 28. Inventory, taken at Second River, £18.17.04; made by Franscoys Wouters and John Kip.

Accompt. Debts due from Stacy King, Jno. Foster, Jno. Cockran's Estate, Stephen V. Cordland, Jacobus Joralaman, James Butler, Edward Vaughn, Jacob Vogstrand, David Roset, Sam'll Godwin, Nathaniel Godwin, Peter Meet, Jno. Schuyler, Tunis VanPelt, Thomas Peet, Peter Jeralaman, Jno. Jeralaman, Hilligent Gerrebrants, Ab'm Wendall, Wynant VanderPoel, George Larkins, Isaac Vreland, Gustavis Kingsland, Jno.

Hamilton, Rob't Sandford, Thomas Kadnits, Peregrine Sandford, Jno. Neilson, Henry Vreland, Ab'm Vreland, Peter Brae, John Dow, John Kingsland, Edmond Kingsland, Rodger Kingsland, Wm. Kingsland, Ab'm Kadims, Jacob Phillips, Henry Van Winkel, Thomas Dod, James Still, Sam'll Retan, Wm. Stephans, Ab'm Godwin, Jacob Pear, Thomas Larkins.

1745, Aug. 29. Price, Ebenezer, of the Borough of Elizabeth, Essex Co. Int. Bond of Mary Price, the widow, as administratrix. The Rev. Mr. John Cleverly, fellow bondsman. Lib. D, p. 328.

1745, Sept. 5. Inventory, £61.11.07; made by Henry Clarke and William Marsh.

1737, July 20. Price, Ephraim, of Elizabeth Town, Essex Co., timber-man; will of. Children—Jane (widow of Nathaniel Ross), Lidia, Ephraim, Isaac, James, Samuel, Nathaniel, Ebenezer and Daniel. Land joining lands of Henry Baker, Nath'll Ross, deceased, and kinsman Benjamin Price. Executors—wife, Jane, and kinsman Joseph Bonnel. Land to be divided in the interest of my family by kinsmen Benjamin Price, Benjamin Bonnel and Joseph Bonnel. Witnesses—Jonathan Thompson, Jonathan Clarke, Rob't Ogden. Proved July 8, 1738. Lib. C, p. 201.

1738, July 17. Inventory, £116.08.01½; made by Jonathan Thompson and Joseph Hetfield.

1741, July 2. Price, James, of Maidenhead, Hunterdon Co. Int. Bond of Thomas Price, of Maidenhead, brother, and George Ely, of Bucks County, Pennsylvania, cordwainer, brother-in-law, as administrators. Thomas Hooton, Jr., of Trenton, merchant, surety. Lib. 4, p. 311.

1741, March 8. Inventory, £275.19.3; made by Benjamin Doughty and James Worth.

1739, May 10. Price, John, of Elizabeth Town, Essex Co., yeoman; will of. "Being aged and infirm." Children—John, Thomas, Abraham, Timothy, Jemima, Anne (wife of Daniell Woodruff), Prudence (wife of Stephen Brown), Phebe (wife of Jonathan Thompson), Mary (wife of Nathaniel Crane, Jun'r). Land in Neck, joining lands of Mr. Edward Vaughn; lands on Oyster Creek and Green River; land formerly belonging to Benjamin Parkhurst, deceased. Executors—son, Thomas, and son-in-law, Jonathan Thompson. Witnesses—Daniel Price, Jun'r, Caleb Woodruff, Jun'r, Benj. Bonnel. Proved Oct. 31, 1749. Lib. E, p. 471.

1749, Oct. 24. Inventory, £24.14.06; made by Nathaniel Price and Nathaniel Ross.

1750, Jan. 9. Pricket, Isaac, of Evesham, Burlington Co. Int. Administration on estate granted to Mary Prickett, of same, widow. John Sharp, yeoman, fellow bondsman. Witnesses—Richard Connon, Luck Tuckness. Lib. 7, p. 112.

1740, Nov. 16. Prideaux, James, of New Brunswick, Middlesex Co.; will of. Son, John, of the Island of Antego, silversmith, one shilling. Daughters—Jean and Margaret Prideaux. Lena and George Edward, children of my daughter Elizabeth Mason, both under age. Executors—daughter, Elizabeth Mason, and James Wilmot. Witnesses—Jan Stryker, Peter Poumee, Mary Poumee. Proved Dec. 24, 1740. Lib. C, p. 373.

1740-1, Jan. 3. Inventory includes a negro girl, £20; negro boy, £20; negro wench, £15; house and lot of one and a half acres, £30; thirty old books, including Rules of Rithmetic, and Baptism and Confirmation, being in the hands of Jeames Vance, Isaac Vansant, Thomas Tals, Mr. Robert L. Hooper; a large Bible, in the hands of John Cammel; £3 in the hands of John Edwards; £13 in the hands of William Marreday; and £7 in the hands of William Wallis. Made by Albert Stoothoff. Henry Cortelyou, Jan Stryker, Wm. Walling.

1735, Feb. 24. Primrose, James, of Hanover, Hunterdon Co.; will of. Wife, Experience, executrix. Brother, Henry. Witnesses—John Lindly, Jr., Caleb Fairchild and James Frost. Proved Dec. 11, 1739. Lib. 4, p. 212.

1748, March 6. Prusfander (Provender), Jonathan, of Wallpack Township, Morris Co.; will of. Friend, Thomas Brink, sole executor, and to have all my goods, riding horse, saddle, young horse, and a mare in the possession of Abraham Van Campen. Witnesses—Johanis Clin, Thomas Robertson, Benjamin Smith. Proved 25 May, 1748. Lib. 5, p. 471.

1748, April 5. Affidavit before Abraham Van Campen, Justice of the Peace, by Benjamin Smith and Phillip Taylor, to make a true inventory, etc.

1748, May 25. Inventory (£19.10.0) includes carpenter's tools, 10 shillings; riding horse, bridle and saddle, £4. Appraisers—Ben. Smyth, Philip Taylor.

1749, Aug. 8. Purple, John, of Morris's River, Cumberland Co.; will of. Legacies to daus., Ponthenia Custolow, Marsey, Abyah Peterson; also to grandchildren, Catherin and Purple (children of my daughter Abyah Peterson). Grandson, Purple, to have all lands, the same to be in the hands of his mother until he will be of age. In case of his death under age, without issue, said lands shall go to his mother, Abiah Peterson, my daughter. Executors—Abyah Peterson, Mary Bell, William Jones. Witnesses—Joseph Jones, Mary Jones, Thomas Flinter. Proved 9 April, 1750.

1750, April 7. Renunciation of Mary Bell and William Jones as executors. Witnesses—Daniel Lummus, Mary Knubun.

1750, April 9. Letters granted to Abiah Peterson. Lib. 6, p. 365.

1750, April 23. Inventory (£129.17.5) includes 25 head of cattle, £55. Appraisers—Gabril Isard, Wm. Jones.

1747, July 18. Purveyance, Samuel, of Alloways Creek, Salem Co., guardian of John Redstreak (16 years old), eldest and only now living son of John Redstreak, of Penns Neck, in said County, gent. Witnesses—Joseph Rose, Jo. Scattergood. Salem Wills, 822 Q.

1734, Sept. 14. Putland, Heron, of Middletown, Monmouth Co., gentleman; will of. Wife, Penthisilia, to draw bills of exchange for England and go to England with testator's two daughters. Executors—wife, and friend, the Rev. Mr. Edward Vaughan, of Elizabethtown. Witnesses—Hugh Hartshorne, Robert White, Robert Hartshorne. Proved August 10, 1738. Lib. C, p. 207.

1728, Aug. 28. Quicksall, William, of Nottingham, Burlington Co., weaver; will of. Wife, Mary. Children—Joseph, William, John, Joshua and Sarah. Real and personal estate, including Proprietary

Rights. Daughter, Sarah, sole executrix. Witnesses—Mercy King, Francis King, William Clark. Proved Jan. 6, 1740 (at which time Martha, wife of Thos. Miller, of New Hanover, did affirm that she saw William Quicksall sign foregoing will).

1736, Aug. 21. Sarah Miller, wife of William Miller of Nottingham, late Quicksall, requests that John Quicksall may be appointed administrator. Witness—Joseph Rockhill. Lib. 4, p. 263.

1736, Aug. 21. Receipt of William Miller and his wife Sarah to John Quicksall for £20 from her father's, William Quicksall's, estate. Witnesses—Rob't Lawrence, Elizabeth Lawrence.

1740-1, Jan. 3. Inventory £113.12; made by Edw'd Beakes and Harmanus King.

1731, Oct. 7. Radford, Andrew, Esq., of Amboy, Middlesex Co. Int. Adm'r, Gabriel Stelle, Esq. Lib. B, p. 235.

1747, Dec. 8. Radford, Anne, of Burlington Co. Int. Inventory of the personal estate, £31.3.6; made by John Quicksall and John Lawrence.

1747, Dec. 9. Adm'r, Joseph Radford, of Burlington Co., yeoman. John Quicksall, yeoman, of same, fellow bondsman. Lib. 5, p. 436.

1745, July 15. Radley, Hannah, of Hanover, Morris Co.; will of. Sons—Jeams, to have (at 21) the farm lately purchased of Seth Hall, joining Barnebus Carter, Junior; Joseph (at age), the farm lately purchased of William Brant, bounded by John Crane's land in Hanover Township; John. Daughters—Sarah Hunt, Ufamah Bagley. Elizabeth Hart, Rachel, Isabella, Catrine and Hannah. Grandson, John, son of John Radley of Elizabethtown. Executors—my brother, Jonathan Allen, of Elizabethtown, and Barnabas Carter, Junior. Witnesses—Ichabod Burnet, David Burnet, Stephen Ward. Proved 20 Aug., 1745. Lib. 5, p. 166.

1744-5, Feb. 21. Radley (Raiey), John, of Hanover, Morris Co.; will of. First, "I give £5 to my loving (omission in the original). Wife, Hannah, to have all lands and improvements. Executors—wife, and Barnebus Carter, Junior. Witnesses—David Burnet, Stephen Ward, Jeremiah Gunung. Proved 28 March, 1745. Lib. 5, p. 109.

1744-5, March 19. Inventory (£199.6.7) includes cows and calves; bonds of Benjamin Moore, Ephraim Sayre, Patrick Mackmaners, Herrick Benjamin, James Carter, Saml. and Hesadiah Sampson, Nicholas Carter. Appraisers—Nathl. Bonnel, Jeremiah Jenung (Genung), Jonathan Allen.

1747, Oct. 10. Rain, Samuel, of Grenage Township, Gloucester Co., yeoman; will of. Brother, Timothy Rain, and Samuel Shivers, executors, (both of said township) and to sell the plantation where I live, purchased of Andrew Morton. But if my said brother refuses to join in the sale of the real and personal estate, then the said Samuel Shivers (with the consent of my friends Francis Batten and Benjamin Cheeseman of said township, yeomen) shall execute my will. Legacies to my brother, Timothy; his sons Samuel and Timothy (when 21); my sister Catherine's sons, Beackman, Obadiah and John Loyd (all under 21), and Hannah Hanby, widow, of same township. Witnesses—William and John Pinyard, and Samuel Middleton. Affirmed 9 Aug., 1748. Lib. 6, p. 44.

1734, Dec. 31. Raines, Robert, of Mannington, Salem Co., bricklayer, guardian of John and Jonas Scoggin, upwards of 14, children of Johanns Scoggin and Katharine, his wife, both late of Penns Neck in said County. (Note on same paper appears as follows: "Jacob Scoggin, Mary Scoggin and Elizabeth Scoggin, all under 14"). Lib. 3, p. 451.

1747-8, Jan. 8. Raines, Robert, of Salem Co., bricklayer. Int. Adm'x, Christian Rains (widow). Bondsmen—David Seely, Woolrich (signed "Oldrich") Richman, Mounce Kein, John Kein, all of said County. Witnesses—William Paullin, Wm. Hall, Michl. Gibbon. Lib. 5, p. 425.

1747-8, Jan. 7. Inventory (£694.13.11) includes plantation tools, bricklayer's and blacksmith tools, grain, negro man and woman and her child (£50). Made by William Paulin, Wm. Hall.

1739, Dec. 5. Rambo, Andrew, of Deptford, Gloucester Co., yeoman. Int. Adm'x, Catherine (relict of). Bondsman—Peter Rambo, of aforesaid place, yeoman. Witnesses—Wm. Wilkins, Joseph Rose.

1739, Sept. 1. Inventory (£141.14.6) includes "a parcel of old Sweeds Books," £1.16.0. Appraisers—Alexr. Randall, Wm. Wilkins. Gloucester Wills, 242 H.

1740, April 12. Rambo, John, of Deptford, Gloucester Co., yeoman; will of. Legacies to sons John and Gabraell, and daughter Deborah. Son, Peter, sole executor and to have rest of the estate, including plantations, and all Proprietary Rights. Witnesses—Allexr. Randall, John Fish, Beatah Lock. Proved 21 Nov., 1741.

1741, Nov. 2. Inventory, £149.19.9; made by Allexr. Randall, John Butterworth. Gloucester Wills, 271 H.

1739, Nov. 5. Ranton, Mathew, of Elsenburgh, Salem Co.; will of. To Lewis Morris, of Elsenburgh, £12, for the love and good will I bear him. To Mary Morris, daughter of Lewis Morris, and to his other six daughters, £2 apiece. £12 to the children of Richard Woodnut; £12 to my brother, William Ranton, of the Kingdom of Ireland, and to my sister Jean Ranton, of the Kingdom of Ireland; £10 to John Blackburk; £10 to Samuel Morton's sister Sarah; £5 to John McComb; £20 to my cousin, Samuel Morton. Remainder of estate to be equally divided between my brother and sister above mentioned. Executors—Lewis Morris and Samuel Morton. Witnesses—John Rampon, James Ridley, Nathan Smart. Affirmed 10 Dec., 1739. Lib. 4, p. 643.

1739, Nov. 16. Inventory, £327.0.1; made by Nathan Smart, Joshua Thompson.

1745, June 18. Raper, Caleb, of City and Co. of Burlington; will of. Wife, Mary, a brick house and lands on High and York Streets, said land given me by my father in his last will. Nephew, Caleb Raper, and his brother, Thomas, sons of my brother Joshua. Nephew, Caleb Barker, lot on York Street I bought of Richard Smith and Peter Fearon. Niece, Anne Carlile. Elizabeth, Abigail, John and Mary Barker, and Mary Smith, daughter of Thomas Smith my kinsman, deceased, each £5 at age. Cousins, Mary Sands and Elizabeth Blondeau. Friends, Peter Fearon, Peter Andrews, Elizabeth Sullivan and Abraham Farrington. Executors—wife, and brother Richard Smith, Ju'r. Witnesses—Joseph Ridgway, Joshua Delaplaine, Ju'r, R. Hartshorne. Proved Dec. 13, 1745. Lib. 5, p. 200.

1743, April 6. Rappleye, George, of Somerset Co. Int. Adm'x, Mary Rappleyea, widow. Fellow bondsman—Jeremiah Field, Esq., of Middlesex Co. Lib. D, p. 31.

1737, Aug. 16. Rappleyea, Abraham, of Somerset Co.; will of. Wife, Jean, executrix. Estate to remain in her possession until daughter, Sarah, is of age; then to be divided equally between them. In case of death of daughter under age, same to fall to the wife. If the wife dies, the daughter becomes the sole heir. Executors—George Rappleyea and Hendrick Roseboom. Witnesses—Casparus V. Noorstrandt, John Townsen, Edmond Bowman. Proved 25 Oct. and 5 Nov., 1737. Lib. C, p. 176.

1737-8, Jan. 24. Inventory of personal estate (£159.13.10) includes Testament and Psalm book bound together with silver, £1; negro boy Simon, £30; 150 bushel of wheat; 1 sword. (Unsigned).

1750-11, Jan. 18. Read (Reid), James, of New Brunswick, Middlesex Co. Int. Bond of Mary, the widow, as administratrix; William Bennet, of New Brunswick, fellow bondsman. Lib. E, p. 473.

1750-1, Jan. 17. Inventory includes pair of silver clasps, and bonds due from Charles Morgin and Ann Applegate. Made by Abraham Bennet and Folkard Bennit.

1744-5, March 15. Reath, Deborah, of Salem Co. Int. Adm'r, Nathan Solley. Bondsmen—Abiel Carle, William Tufte. All of said County, yeoman. Witness—Thomas Gillingham. Lib. 5, p. 215.

1744-5, March 4. Inventory, £24.8.5; made by Abiel Carle, Alexdr. Smith.

1737, Dec. 17. Redstreak, John, of Penns Neck, Salem Co.; will of. Eldest son, John, at 21 to have land and marsh (500 acres) known by the name of Melcome Island. In case of his death without issue, the same to my son, Joseph Redstreak, and for want of such heirs to my son, Pledger Redstreak. Son, Pledger (at 21) to have 125 acres, which was formerly the plantation of Edward Godin; also 50 acres of marsh, part of Melcome Island, joining on Fishing Creek. Son, Joseph, to have 321 acres. Son, John, to have that part of said Island now in the occupation of George Fling, and to dwell there if he chooses so to do. Wife, Elizabeth, to have the personal, and the use of the whole estate for bringing up my three children until they come to their respective lawful ages. £5 to my sister-in-law, Mary Pledger. In case of the death of said children without issue, then wife, Elizabeth, shall possess aforesaid lands, with the condition that she will pay £30 to my cousins, Rebecca Johnson and Rachel Shivers. Executors—wife, and three sons, John, Joseph and Pledger. "Before signing it is my will that my wife, Elizabeth, shall have what timber and wood for her use off of that land I purchased of Joseph Gregory." Witnesses—George Fling, John Richmond, Rebecca Richmond, Jno. Pledger. Proved 10 Jan., 1738.

1738, Jan. 10. Letters granted to Elizabeth Redstreak executrix named, in the absence of John, Joseph and Pledger Redstreak, infants.

Lib. 4, p. 182.

1738-9, March 9. Inventory (£665.1.11) includes one negro girl, £26; "syder in seller," £27.14, cattle, horses, etc.; and debtors—George Fling (for rent, £40), John Made, William Vuorey, Joseph Hawks, Matthias

Stark, Mary Colliar, Andrak Hendrickson, Johannah Brown, alias Thomas. Appraisers—Ranier Vanhist, Clem. Hall.

1731, July 29. Reed, John, of Hopewell, Hunterdon Co.; will of. Wife, Elizabeth. Eldest son, John. Son, Richard. Mentions other children, but not by name, as "son, Richard, and his brethren." Executors—wife, and son Richard. Witnesses—John Hixson, John Field and Bartholomew Corwine. Proved Oct. 27, 1731. Lib. 3, p. 162.

1731, Sept. 17. Inventory (£238.19.10) includes books, a loom, 7 reeds and tackling, a servant man. Made by Andrew Smith and John Hixson.

1746, Aug. 26. Reed, John, of Salem Co., merchant. Int. Adm'r, John Jones, of Salem Town and County, attorney-at-law. Bondsman—William Barker, of the same place, inn holder. Witnesses—Wm. Pennock, Danl. Mestayer. Lib. 5, p. 277.

1746, Sept. 20. Inventory of John Reed, late of County of New Castle. Debt due from Stephen Vandike, £23. Appraisers—Nich. Gibbon, Wm. Pennock.

1749-50, March 18. Reed, John, of Hopewell, Hunterdon Co.; will of. Wife, Susannah. Plantation to be sold when youngest child is aged 18. Children—Susannah, Nathaniel, Jemimah, Mary and Alse. Son, Nathaniel, to assist his mother until aged 21. Executors—wife, Isaac Lanning and James Deen. Witnesses—Nathan Moore, Philip Palmer, Reuben Armitage. Proved April 12, 1750. Lib. 6, p. 332.

1750, April 12. Inventory, made by Nathan Moore and Philip Palmer.

1737, April 27. Reed, Joseph, of Trenton, Hunterdon Co. Citation issued directed to Anne Reed, widow, Thomas, Andrew, Joseph and John Reed, children and next of kin of Joseph Reed, late of Trenton, to appear at Burlington, the 16th of May next, to shew cause why some of them do not take out letters of administration on the estate, and, in case of their refusal to do so, why letters should not be granted to Matthew Clarkson and Anthony Duane, as principal creditors. "If said Anne Reed or the others cannot be found, a copy of this citation to be left on door of the house or on Church door of the parishes to which they belong."

1737, May 7. Letter of John Hamilton, President of his Majesty's Council, and Commander-in-Chief of New Jersey, dated at Perth Amboy, directing Joseph Rose, at Burlington, to grant letters to Matthew Clarkson and Anthony Duane, if the widow and children of Joseph Reed refuse to administer.

1737, May 16. Deposition of Stephen Reynolds, that on May 6th he delivered the citation unto Anne, Thomas, John and Joseph Reed.

1737, May 16. David Martin, Sheriff of Hunterdon County, delivered copy of citation to Andrew Reed son of Joseph Reed deceased.

1737, May 17. Adm'rs, Matthew Clarkson and Anthony Duane, of City of New York, merchants. Andrew Johnston, of Perth Amboy, merchant, surety. Witnesses—Stephen Warne, James Smyth, Thomas Bartow.

1750-1, Feb. 14. Bond of Samuel Burling (executor of Edward Burling, who was a creditor of Joseph Reed of Trenton, deceased), as administrator of estate of Joseph Reed, unadministered by Matthew Clarkson and Anthony Duane, both now deceased. John Redford, Esq., of New Jersey, surety. Lib. C, p. 159.

1749, April 5. Reed, Thomas, of Somerset Co., yeoman; will of.

Wife, Martha, one-fourth of estate. Three-fourths "committed to Andrew and John Reed, my executors, for the bringing up of the children." Witnesses—David Chambers, James Hammond (Hamon), Francis Moriarty. Proved 24 April, 1749.

1749, June 5. Letters granted to Andrew Reed, one of the executors named in the will. Lib. 6, p. 58.

1749, April 10. Inventory (£162.15.6) includes debts due from Hugh Caplee, Alexander Annen, Jas. McGinnes, James Hammond, James Wilson. Made by David Chambers and James Hamond.

1748, Sept. 27. Reed, William, of Hopewell, Hunterdon Co., yeoman; will of. Wife, Mary. Plantation to be sold. Children to have shares of estate (boys when 21, girls at 18), but not named. Unborn child. Executors—wife, and brothers John and Joseph Reed. Witnesses—Smith Cornell, Nathan Moore, Sarah Reed. Proved Nov. 3, 1748. Lib. 5, p. 541.

1748, Oct. 29. Inventory £64.15.0; made by Philip Palmer and Nathan Moore.

1736-7, 23rd, 12 mo. (Feb.). Reeve, John, of Philadelphia, mariner; will of. Children—Peter, Hannah, Mary and Rachel. Personal estate. Executors—friend, Israel Pemberton, and brother Matthias Aspden, both of the City of Philadelphia, merchants. Witnesses—Wm. Hill, Evan Bevan, Abr. Mitchel. Proved Sept. 5, 1743. Cape May Wills, Lib. 5, p. 2.

1743, Sept. 14. Reeve, John, of Burlington. Int. Inventory of the personal estate, £1,362.5.10; made by Caleb Raper and Dan Smith. Includes 101 ounces of Plate, £50.10; shop goods, £688.0.5½; servant maid's time, £5; negro girl, £20. Burlington Wills, 3629-32 C.

1748, Nov. 11. Reeve, Joseph, of South side of Cohansey, Cumberland Co.; will of. Son, Mark, to have 100 acres of land, purchased of Hannah Pierce; also 70 acres of land, situate at Morris River, adjoining lands of Gabriel Powel and William Cobb. Son, Joseph, the home place I now live on, joining my son Mark's land; to begin at the N. end of the tide bank that runs from Gilman's place to Stores Island, thence (giving courses and naming) Ayres' line, Middlemarsh Creek, Cohansey Creek, Joseph Bacon's. Son, John, all lands westward of Joseph's land, beginning at the mouth of Little Creek above Joseph Bacon's, then up the creek to Ayres' land until it comes to Dickason Shepherd's line, then to Cohansey Creek. Son, Samuel, all lands on the south side of Middlemarsh Creek. Legacies to daughter Mary at the age of 20, and to son Benjamin (not 21), who shall be apprenticed by my executors. Sons, Joseph, John and Samuel, two tracts of land situate at Morris River, one on the east side called Dibbles Island, the other on the west side called "old Major." Remainder of real estate to be divided among my four sons, Mark, Joseph, John and Samuel. In case of death of any of them, without issue, that part shall descend to my son Benjamin. Executors—sons Mark and Joseph. Witnesses—Richd. Wood, Dickason Shepherd, Ebenezr. Miller, Jr. Proved 1 March, 1748. (Richard Wood and Ebenezer Miller affirmed). Lib. 6, p. 249.

1748-9, 12 mo. (Feb.), 1st da. Inventory (£795.10½) includes library of books, cattle, horses and bees. Appraisers—Moses Shepherd, Richard Wood. Lib. 6, p. 249.

1732, Sept. 23. Reeves, Ann, of Northampton, Burlington Co., widow; will of. Sons—Walter, William, Joseph, Elisha, Caleb and Samuel. Personal estate. Executor—son, Samuel. Witnesses—Jas. Smith, Jno. Allen, Sam'l Bustill. Proved July 31, 1733. Lib. 3, p. 356.

1733, Aug. 20. Inventory, £114.6.2; made by Revell Elton and Samuel Woolman.

1734, Dec. 20. Account of executor, showing payments to James Veree (for coffin), Wm. Collum, Mary Willis, Samuel Scattergood, Samuel Bustill, Peter Ross, Elizabeth Frampton, Thos. Elkinton, John Allen, Joseph Devenish, John Wills, Esq.

1749, Nov. 14. Reeves, David, of Alloways Creek, Salem Co., yeoman; will of. Son, David, all my lands and meadows on the east side of Salem Road, or the upper side; also 50 acres of marsh below Jonathan Wadington's. Grandson, Joshua Reeves, the remaining part of the land on Salem Road, also part of my salt marsh not before bequeathed. Daughter-in-law, Partheny Reeves, to take care of said lands until Joshua will be of age. Residue of the moveables (negroes alloted) shall be equally divided between my two granddaughters (when 18), Mary Reeves (daughter of my son David), and Elizabeth Reeves (daughter of my son Joshua). Executor—Thomas Pagett. Witnesses—James Cromey, Saml. Perry, Elizabeth Cromey. Proved 2 Dec., 1749. Lib. 6, p. 267.

1749, Nov. 28. Inventory (£188.16.8) of personal estate of "David Reeves, Senior," includes grain, and 4 negroes (£120). Appraisers—Jonathan Bradway, James Cromey.

1750, Dec. 13. Reeves, Elisha, of Gloucester Co. (late of Burlington Co.). Int. Adm'r, David Watson, Hunterdon Co., laborer. Bondsman—Elnathan Stevenson, of Burlington Co., yeoman. Lib. 7, p. 101.

Dec. 10, 1750. Inventory of Elisha Reeves, of Township of Waterford, Gloucester Co., (£45.15.2¼) includes bond of Wm. Reeves, Jun'r; notes of David Watson, George Monroe. Appraisers—Simeon Ellis, William Ellis.

1747, Dec. 31. Reeves, Joseph, of Northampton, Burlington Co. Int. Inventory of the personal estate, £59.9.10; made by James Lippincott and Samuel Haines. Includes 1,559 lbs. pork delivered to Thos. Shinn, £15.17.3; 130 lbs. pork at Richard Fenimore's at 2½; pair of scales, and gold and silver weights.

1747, Jan. 22. Adm'r, John Fenimore, of Springfield, yeoman. James Lippincott and Samuel Haines, of same, yeoman, fellow bondsmen. Lib. 5, p. 436.

1737, Dec. 2. Reeves, Samuel, of Northampton, Burlington Co., taylor; will of. Samuel, son of my brother William. Real and personal estate. Wife, Mary, sole executrix. Witnesses—Tho. Shinn, Revell Elton, Sam'l Shinn, Thomas Kemble, John Geary. Proved Jan. 19, 1737. Lib. 4, p. 127.

1737-8, Jan. 13. Inventory, £285.3.6; made by Sam'l Shinn and Thomas Kemble.

1732, Sept. 23. Reeves, Walter, of Northampton, Burlington Co. Account of Anne Reeves, executrix. Payments made to James Cooper, Thomas Tresset of Philadelphia, Isaacs Marriott of Burlinton, Rob't Wheeler, John Tatam, George Deacon, Dr. John Roberts, and Thomas Wetherill. Disbursements to the children of deceased, viz., Walter, Jonathan, William, Elisha, Joseph, Caleb, Samuel and Elizabeth. Burlington Wills, 2345-60 C.

1748, April 29. Reid, James, of Freehold, Monmouth Co. Int. Ann, the widow, resigns right of administration to Joseph Forman, principal creditor. Witness—William Cruckshank. Lib. E, p. 186.

1748, May 3. Adm'r, Joseph Forman, of Monmouth Co., gent. Witness—Thomas Inglis.

1748, May 4. Inventory of the estate, £33.14.6; made by William Hugan, Benjamin Kallum, Robert Thomson.

1745, Oct. 24. Reives (Reeves), Henry, (place not named; Gloucester Co.); will of. Executors—wife, Abigail, and my brother Thomas Reives, they to sell the real estate wheresoever. Children—Hope, James, Ann, Abraham, Henry and Mary. Widow to have use of same until the boys are 21 and the girls 18. In case of her remarriage, my brother Thomas to have care of said children. Residue of my real and personal estate shall be my wife's for the care and education of said children. Witnesses—Richard Floyd, Jonathan Fowler, Josa. Lord. Sworn and affirmed 20 Jan., 1745. Lib. 5, p. 216.

1745, Nov. 5-9. Inventory (£246.13.8) includes "A Penel given by Jonathan Reeves to Thomas Shin and assigned to Henry Reeves"; notes from Jonathan Reeves to Thomas Newel and by a second assignment to Henry Reeves; book debt from William Buddel; "one equal halfe part of a 8 cord flat with the sails and oars" (£12). Appraisers—Jonathan Fowler, Josa. Lord.

1732-3, Feb. 15. Remington, John, of Salem Co., yeoman. Int. Adm'x, Sarah Remington, widow. Bondsmen—John Goodwin, Benjamin Peters. All of said county. Witness—Mary Abbott. Lib. 3, p. 291.

1732-3, Feb. 15. Inventory (£40.19.6); made by Jno. Goodwin, Benja. Peters.

1733, March 28. Remington, Sarah, of Salem, Salem Co., widow. Int. Adm'r, John Remington. Richard Smith and Joseph Gregory, of same place, fellow bondsmen. Lib. 3, p. 297.

1733, March 30. Inventory, £47.0.0; made by Hugh Clifton and John Goodwin.

1731, Oct. 4. Renshaw, Thomas, of Gloucester Township and Co., laborer. Int. Adm'r, Richard Weldon, of the same place, mariner. Bondsman—Samuel Harrison. Witness—Edw. Rs. Price. Lib. 3, p. 153.

1738, June 9. Reynierse, Ouke, of Somerset Co., yeoman; will of. Wife, Ida, sole executrix, personal estate and home plantation in Somerset Co., during widowhood. Real estate valued in Somerset Co. at £1,610. Sons to have two-thirds; daughters one-third of said sum. Son, Reynier, to have 150 acres lying on the western side of "Milston River," binding upon Roolif Van Bront's land. Son, Cornelius, to have 100 acres in Middlebush, lying on the eastern side of Milston River. Sons, Hendrick, Aernout and Ouke, the rest of the land in Middlebush, joining the land of Cornelius upon Milston River. Daughters—Magdelana, Catherine, Ida, Aleda, Mary, Ariaentje and Femmy.

Witnesses—Dk. (Dirck) Schuyler, Jacob Ouke, Wm. Ouke. Proved 20 Jan., 1740. Lib. C, p. 383.

1740, March 6. Inventory (£380.22.8) includes cattle, £43; horses, £80; 3 slaves, £140; wheat, £119. Made by John Bookhout, Garret Garretsen.

1747, Oct. 9. Rhemer, Adam, of Somerset Co. Int. Adm'r, Catherine Rhemer, widow. Fellow bondsmen, Jacob Strite (Streight), of Somerset Co. and Lawrence Roelofs, of the County of Hunterdon. Lib. E, p. 93.

1747, Oct. 6. Inventory (£175.5.10) includes guns, sword, powder horns, "servant boy that is sick like for to die" (£0.4.2). Made by Alexander Linn, Bryan Leferty.

1750, Oct. 2. List of debts paid by Katherine Remer. To Leonard Straight, Susanna Chidester, Cornelus Low, Junr', Lourance Sluker (?), Francis Moriarty, Alexander Linn, Joseph French, Jno. Castner, Peter Smith, Frances Bukel, Barthelo Kelsey, Elizabeth Rimmer, Peter Castner.

1740, May 27. Rice, Thomas, Salem Town and County, guardian of Edward Keasby, son of Edward Keasby. (Mother has since died). Bondsmen—Thos. Thompson, Daniel Haynes. Witness—Clem. Hall, John Jones. Lib. 4, p. 195.

1743, Oct. 27. Richards, Benjamin, husbandman, of Gloucester Co. Int. Adm'r, Jeremiah Burch. Bondsman—Archibald Jolly, of Deptford Township, yeoman. Lib. 5, p. 49.

1743, Oct. 24. Renunciation of Ruth, widow of Benjamin Richards. Witnesses—John Jenkins, Richard Cheeseman.

1743, Nov. 7. Inventory, £22.4.1; made by Richard Cheeseman, Archibald Jolly.

1743, Oct. 27. Richards, Jeremiah. Adm'r, Jeremiah Burchon. Lib. 5, p. 49.

1742, April 10. Richards, John, of Freehold, Monmouth Co., ditcher. Int. Jonathan Forman and John Henderson, creditors, agree that John Forman, another creditor, may administer on the estate. Lib. C, p. 500.

1742, April 12. Adm'r, John Forman, yeoman. Ezekiel Forman, yeoman, fellow bondsman.

1742, April 15. Inventory, £21.0.6; made by John Layton and Hendrick Suydam.

1748, May 10. Richards, John, of Newark, Essex Co. Int. Phebe Richards, the widow, declines to act as administratrix, and desires that Aaron Richards, eldest son, be appointed. Witnesses—John Johnson, Uzal Ogden.

1748, May 10. Adm'r, Aaron Richards. David Richards, fellow bondsman. Lib. E, p. 260.

1748, April 1. Inventory, £190.10.02; made by Eliphalet Johnson and Jon'n Sergeant.

1749, June 13. Richards, John, of Greenwich Township, Gloucester Co., yeoman; will of. Wife, Mary. Sons—Joseph, to have the plantation after his mother's death; John, the plantation adjacent; Benjamin, 20 acres of the tract I bought of Samuel Burgis. Legacies to grandchildren, John and Mary Sweeting (under age). Executors and trustees for wife and children—John Hains, of Greenwich, and my son

Joseph. Witnesses—John Chivers, Thomas Chester, Benjn. Lodge. Proved 27 Nov., 1750. Lib. 7, p. 18.

1750, Oct. 15. Inventory, £117.18.0; made by Mathew Tontin, Moses Ward.

1750, 2nd da., 8 mo. (Oct.). Renunciation of John Hains, as executor. Witness—Jacob Cozens.

1733, April 27. Richards, Thomas, of Essex Co.; will of. Children—Thomas, Daniell and Nathaniell, all under age. Land joining lands of Daniel Dod, Jun'r, and Samuel Dod. Executrix—wife, Mary. Witnesses—David Ward, Samuel Ward, Jun'r, David Ogden, Jun'r. Proved May 14, 1733. Lib. B, p. 422.

1738, Feb. 9. Richardson, Benjamin, of Cape May Co., yeoman; will of. Wife, Elizabeth, the use of all my lands until my son, Samuel, will be 21; she to bring up and maintain my two children unless she marries before that time; then I desire my brother, Jacob Richardson, to take immediately my lands and to have the use of my other estate, which is hereafter given to my children, for their maintenance. Son, Samuel, to have all lands I live on, and to pay £20 to his brother, John, when of age. Residue of my estate shall be equally divided between my two said children and "I desire my wife to take into her hands and bring up and maintain them until each one will be fourteen years of age." Executors—wife, Elizabeth, and my brother, Jacob Richardson. Witnesses—Ephraim Edwards, James Edwards, An. Leaming, Junior. Proved 26 November, 1739. Lib. 4, p. 222.

1739, Nov. 3. Inventory (£76.2.9) includes horse, cattle, sheep, swine and fowls. Appraisers—Nathl. Jenkins, Ephraim Edwards.

1742, Sept. 17. Richardson, James, of City of Burlington, joyner. Int. Anne Richardson requests that administration be granted unto her father, Isa. DeCow.

1742, Sept. 18. Adm'r, Isaac DeCow. Richard Wright, fellow bondsman. Both of City of Burlington, gents. Lib. 4, p. 377.

1742, Sept. 18. Inventory, £42.11.2; made by R. Wright and Dan Smith. Includes debt of Thomas Budd.

1735, May 27. Richardson, Joseph, of Gloucester Co., yeoman. Int. Adm'x, Anne Richardson, widow. Bondsman—Edward Richardson and John Doe of same county, Gent. Witness—John Geary. Lib. 4, p. 17.

1735, 3d. mo. (May), 23 da. Inventory (£240.17.05) includes bonds due from Thomas Monican, Thomas Kinsey, Mary Bull and John Clark; notes by William Johnston, James Kinsey, John Stiles, John Smallwood; book debts from Walter Griffeth, Enoch Ellison, Daniel Worthington, Henry Eliet, Edward Williams, George Shirreld. Indentured: Katherine Kinshloghs, William Emesone. Appraisers—Abraham Chattin (Quaker), William Hampton.

1732, Dec. 28. Richardson, Joshua, of Deptford, Gloucester Co., yeoman. Int. Adm'x, Martha Evans. Bondsmen—John Doe and Richard Roe. Witness—John Ladd, Jun'r.

1732, Dec. 20. Inventory of Joshua Richardson, "Senior," (£12.15.6) includes cash due by Aaron Ashbrook, Martha Howel, Thomas Dorah, John Newborey; "due to Ellis Battines by William Vaughan (?)." Appraisers—William Davies, William Vahhan. Gloucester Wills, 154 H.

1732, Dec. 3. Richardson, Samuel, of Cape May Co.; will of. To my brother, Benjamin Richardson, all my land; but if my wife be now with child and it comes to age, then said land to belong to the child. If said Benjamin possesses the land, he shall pay £10 to my brother, John Richardson, within one year, and £5 to my brother, Jacob Richardson, when 21. Wife, Elizabeth, all the chattels, except my best hat, which my brother Jacob shall have when of age. Executors—wife, Elizabeth, and my brother Benjamin. Witnesses—John Jones, James Flood, Ephraim Edwards. Proved 20 March, 1732-3.

1732-3, Jany. 17. Inventory, £45.8.10; made by Nathaniel Rusco, Ephraim Edwards. Cape May Wills, 78 E.

1747-8, March 10. Richey, Robert, of Amwell, Hunterdon Co. Int. Inventory of estate (£56.0.10) includes a Bible, bonds of Stephen Baldwin, Daniel Kelsey, Edward Hunt, Bickley Welling, James Osborn. Made by Philip Cawlvin and Edward Rockhill.

1747, March 15. Adm'r, John Richeye, of Amwell. James Darompel and Edward Rockhill, of Amwell, yeoman, sureties. Witnessed by Abraham Bonnell. Lib. 5, p. 491.

1749-50, February 20. Account. Mentions Elizabeth Mullin, Andrew Mershon, Charles Bounfield, Abraham Bonnell, Joseph Paxton, Jno. ODonnell, Samuel Fleming, Jno. Rouse, Doctor John Naars, Isaac Lanning, William Roseborough, John Jobe.

1744, June 9. Richman, Herman, of Township of Piles Grove, Salem Co., yeoman; will of. Wife, Mary Elizabeth. Sons—Jacob (eldest), to have 250 acres that I bought of Elias King, where my said son dwells; also 150 acres that I bought of John Easter, joining said plantation; John, 300 acres of the tract I bought of John Easter; Uldrick, the plantation (350 acres) I live on that I bought of Joseph Clews; also 6½ acres bought of Isaac Davis, joining the mill pond and Clews joining the Creek; also the place (200 acres) bought of Nicholas Hoffman, joining the home place; also 46 acres bought of Clement Hall; also ½ acre of land and store-house on Oldman's Creek that I bought of John Rain (but if he marries Sarah Chanlier, or any of the family, his portion shall be five shillings); Michael (at 21), 300 acres that I bought of John Easter. Daughters—Margaret (eldest), Mary, Ann, Elizabeth, Maudlen and Sarah; they to have 112 acres each of the tract I bought of John Easter, with 50 acres bought of James Currie, additionally, to Sarah. 300 acres bought of Andrew and Peter Boon in Monatauny at Schoolkill in Pennsylvania, 50 acres in Gloucester County, and 50 or 60 acres at Broad Neck, Salem County, to be sold and the money divided equally among my children. The 25 acres of Cedar Swamp bought of Henry Paulin shall be divided; ½ shall belong to the home place, the other divided between John and Michael; also 3¼ acres that I bought of Timothy Rain on Oldman's Creek shall be equally divided among Jacob, John and Michael, when the last named will be 21. If any of my daughters marry with any of the Sceilley's family they shall not have one foot of my land. Executors—sons Jacob, John, Uldrick and Michael. Witnesses—William Paullin, David Davis, Elisha Basset, Thomas Duell. Affirmed 7 August, 1744.

1744, Aug. 10. Letters granted to Jacob, John and Uldrick Richman, Michael Richman, the other executor, not being of lawful age.

Lib. 5, p. 39.

1744, July 5, 6. Inventory (£712.3.10½) includes negro man, woman and four children, £102; cattle, horses, sheep, and swine, £125.18. Appraisers—David Davis, William Paullin.

1738, May 23. Riddel, Walter, of Somerset Co. Int. Administration on estate granted to Quinton McColme. Fellow bondsmen, Lawrence Smyth, Adam Hay, both of Perth Amboy. Lib. C, p. 197.

1738, May 2. Inventory of cash, goods and book debts due to the store in partnership betwixt the deceased Walter Riddell and Quintin McColme, £972.13.5; made by Peter School, Justice of the Peace, Benjamin Stirling and Stephen Campbell.

Inventory of papers belonging to deceased, Walter Riddell:

Indenture betwixt Robt. Barclay and Wm. Aikman for one-tenth part of one fourty-eight part of the Province of East Jersey, dated April 22d, 1684.

Release, The Proprietors of East Jersey to Wm. Aikman of 400 acres land, June 2d, 1688.

Deed, The Proprietors of New Jersey to Mr. Archbald Riddell and order of Survey for 200 acres land, July 28, 1685.

Release, The Proprietors of East Jersey to Mr. Archbald Riddell of 300 acres land, June 2d, 1688.

Agreement, Mr. Archbald Riddell and Mr. Tho. Aikman, Aug. 7, 1685.

Letter of Attorney, Wm. Aikman and Mr. Arch. Riddell, Aug. 7, 1685.

Agreement, Mr. Arch. Riddell and Tho. Aikman, Aug. 7, 1785.

Disposition, Wm. Aikman to Capt. Walter Riddell, Sept. 5, 1730.

Disposition, Mr. Arch. Riddell to Capt. Walter Riddell, Dec. 30, 1707.

Release, Capt. Walter Riddell to Walter Riddell, his nephew, Dec. 31, 1736.

Letter of Attorney, Capt. Riddell to Walter Riddell, Dec. 31, 1736.

Order of the Proprietors of East Jersey to survey 170 acres of Land for Walter Riddell, Aug. 9, 1737.

Extracts of Survey for Adam Hude and Andrew Johnston, etc.

Bond of Relief, Quintin McColme to Walter Riddell, Oct. 3, 1737.

Eight letters, John Johnstone to Capt. Riddell.

Six letters, John Hamilton to Capt. Riddell.

Two letters, James Douglas to Capt. Riddell.

1747, July 20. Ridgway, Richard, of Springfield, Burlington Co., carpenter. Int. Phebe Ridgway, the widow, declines to act and requests that Jobe Lippincott be appointed administrator.

1747, July 21. Adm'r Job Lippincott, of Springfield. Edward Tonkin, of same, yeoman, fellow bondsman. Lib. 5, p. 433.

1747, July 23. Inventory, £175.7; made by John Monrow and Thos. Foster. Mentions Joseph Franson, William French, William Shinn, Henry Cooper.

1747, Oct. 27. Account. Moneys paid Dr. Thos. Shaw, Geo. Gilbert (for his wife nursing deceased 2 weeks in the smallpox), Joseph Pope, Joshua Shreeve, Joseph Wright, E. R. Price, Isaac Ivins, Edward Tonkins, Henry Cooper, William Fox, Susannah Toole, William Sorsby, Anna Stockton, John Stockton (Exr. of William Buddell), Isabella Schooley, Thomas Black. Debts due from Joseph Allinson, James Shinn, Jr., William Fox, William Rogers, Benj'n Bryan.

1732, June 7. Ridgway, Thomas, of Little Eggharbour, Burlington Co., yeoman. Peter Andrews, of same, appointed guardian of Edward and Richard, two of the sons of Thomas. Lib. 3, p. 198.

1739, Dec. 4. Ridley, William, of Salem Town and Co., ward (aged 18 yrs.). Guardian, Robert Hart, of same place, merchant.
Salem Wills, 642 Q.

1749, Nov. 13. Ridley, William, of Town and Co. of Salem, carpenter. Int. Adm'x, Hannah Ridley. Bondsman—Thomas Thompson. Both of same place. Lib. 6, p. 279.

1749, Nov. 15. Inventory, £119.12.11; made by Wm. Murdock, Samuel Sims.

1738, Aug. 17. Riely, Bridget, of Gloucester Co. Int. Adm'r Mathew Topham, of City of Burlington, cordwainer. Samuel Bustill, of same, gent., fellow bondsman. Lib. 4, p. 142.

1733, Aug. 21. Inventory, £34.11.9; made by Paul Watkinson and James Richardson.

1734-5, Jan. 25. Riley, Joseph, of Cohansey, Salem Co., yeoman; will of. Son, Aaron (at 21) to have all my lands. Other three sons the personal estate "only my great wrighting book and great arithmetic book I give to my son Joseph, and the book of Marters and three Nativity books to my son Mark Riley, the History of Troy and the Book of Geogrify to my son Elihu and my Bible to my wife during widowhood;" other books to be equally divided among my three youngest sons. Wife, Rachel, use of real and personal estate until sons will be 21. Executors—wife, and brother-in-law, John Reminton. Witnesses—Moses Shepherd, John Bishop, Dacon Buck, Abraham Smith. Proved 24 Feb., 1734-5. Lib. 4, p. 9.

1734-5, Feb. 28. Renunciation of Rachel, widow. Witnesses—Moses Shepherd, Silas Freland.

1734-5, Feb. 12. Inventory (£80.18.6) includes cattle, sheep, horse and swine. Appraisers—Moses Shepherd, Abraham Smith.

1740, Feb. 15. Ring, Elias, of Hopewell, Hunterdon Co.; will of. Wife, Deborah. Children to be brought up out of estate, boy until 21, and girl until 18. Son, Nathaniel; daughter, Deborah. Wife, executrix. Witnesses—Joseph Overton, Thomas Barnes, John Allen, Jr. Proved April 7, 1741. Lib. 4, p. 278.

1741, April 6. Inventory (£371.1.0) includes negro slave, £35. Made by Thomas Barnes, Reuben Armitage, John Hart, Jr.

1730, July 31. Ringo, Peter, of Hunterdon Co., gent. Int. Inventory, £18.7.6; made by John Hunt, Cornelius Ringo, Alexander Lockart.

1730, Aug. 13. Adm'r, Philip Ringo, of Hunterdon Co., gent. Alexander Lockart, of Hunterdon Co., gent., surety. Hunterdon Wills, 65 J.

1733-4, Jan. 17. Riorteau, John, of Nottingham, Burlington Co.; will of. Son, John. Real and personal estate. Wife, Magdelen, sole executrix. Witnesses—John Tantum, Benjamin Robins, Isaac Stelle. Proved May 29, 1734. Lib. 3, p. 415.

1729, Jan. 6. Ripley, Edward, of Middlesex Co. Inventory of personal estate (£6.06.3); made by Samuel Stone and Thomas Gach. (Omitted from Archives, Vol. 23).

1728, July. Account. Margaret Ripley; for her husband's funeral.

1735, Oct. 4. Receipt of Richard Bishop, coroner, for 40s., as fees for viewing the body of Edward Ripley, who was drowned.
Middlesex Wills.

1737, May 2. Risley, Richard, Sr., of Township of Egg Harbor, Gloucester Co., yeoman; will of. Wife, Esther, sole executrix. Sons—Peter and Thomas, 300 acres on which I live, beginning at the line that divides my son Richard's plantation down to the Sound or Bay of Abcecon Creek, the latter to have the part with the dwelling, etc., as far as the King's Road. The Cedar swamps, beeches and other out-lands to aforesaid three sons equally. Daughters—Mary, Jemimah, Esther, Sarah, Rebecca. Witnesses—Frederick Steelman, John Counover, David Lindsey. Proved 17 June, 1740. Lib. 4, p. 242.

1740, May 22. Inventory, £85.3.0; made by John Counover, Thomas Risley.

1740, Dec. 25. Risley, Thomas, of Great Egg Harbor, Gloucester Co. Brothers—John Risley, of Hartford, New England, and Richard. Richard's sons, Richard, Peter and Thomas, to have lands joining their father and John Covenoven by the Bay. Nieces—Sarah (not 21) and Rebecca ("the youngest"), daughters of my brother Richard. Executor—nephew, Richard Risley. Witnesses—Japhet Leeds, Richard Philpott, Japhet Leeds, Jr. Affirmed and sworn 4 June, 1746. (Letters granted May 27, 1748). Lib. 5, p. 386.

1739, Oct. 23. Ritchie, Anne, of Perth Amboy, Middlesex Co. Int. Adm'r, John Ritchie, the husband. James Newell and Peter Savery, fellow bondsmen. Witness—John Burnet. Lib. C, p. 293.

1740, Aug. 26. Bond of George Leslie as administrator. And'w Johnston, of Perth Amboy, gent., and Peter Savery, barber, fellow bondsmen.

1737, May 7. Roberts (Robards), Hugh, of Newark, Essex Co., yeoman; will of. Wife, Mary. Children—Hugh, John, Samuel, Hannah Smith and Abigail Roberts. Children of my daughter, Rebecka Tompkins, deceased. Executors—sons Hugh and John. Witnesses—Isaac Cundit, Daniel Taylor, Elizabeth Taylor. Proved Dec. 26, 1738.

Lib. C, p. 237.

1738, Dec. 25. Inventory (£211.05.11½) includes notes from John Roberts and Hugh Roberts; made by Deacon Wheeler and Thomas Longworth.

1747, Nov. 12. Roberts, John, Sen'r, of Chester, Burlington Co., yeoman. Int. Inventory of personal estate, £421.6.4; made by Thomas Middleton and Samuel Coles. Includes 4 negroes, £122.

1747, Nov. 16. Adm'r, John Roberts, of same, yeoman. Thomas Middleton and Samuel Coles, of Evesham and Waterford, yeomen, fellow bondsmen. Lib. 5, p. 435.

1740, Feb. 8. Roberts, Mary, relict of Jonathan Roberts of Trenton, Hunterdon Co.; will of. Daughter, Jemima, wife of Solomon Maxwell; granddaughter, Abigail Morrel; daughter, Mary, wife of Robert Combs. Other daughters, Sarah, Elizabeth, Kezia. Executors—Ralph Hart and Richard Furman. Daughter, Martha, to have equal share with other four daughters. Witnesses—Jonas Wood, William Snowden, Edward Hart. Proved March 25, 1741. Lib. 4, p. 288.

1742, Feb. 19. Robertson, Thomas, of the City of New York. Int. Adm'r, Edward Fogg, of New York, merchant. Benjamin Smith, of Trenton, merchant, surety. Witness—Archibald Horne.

Hunterdon Wills, 159 J.

1749-50, Feb. 13. Robertson, William, Jr., of Middletown Township,

Monmouth Co., yeoman; will of. Wife, Mary. Children—Robert, Mary and Duncan, when of age. Brothers and sisters mentioned but not named. Executor—brother, Duncan Robertson. Witnesses—James Reid, Elizabeth Robertson, Robert Savage. Proved March 13, 1749-50.
Lib. E, p. 368.

1741, April 1. Robins, Isaac, of Hunterdon Co.; will of. Wife, Asubia. Sons—Vincent and Joseph. Six children mentioned. Executors—wife, and friends Job Robins and Amos Thatcher. Witnesses—Jacob Knowles, Lydia Thatcher, John Lewis. Proved Oct. 22, 1741.
Lib. 4, p. 322.

1741, Oct. 13. Inventory (£46.15.2) includes books. Made by W. Montgomerie, Charles Woolverton, Peter Johnson.

1747-8, Feb. 3. Robins, James, of (Allenstown), Upper Freehold, Monmouth Co., tailor; will of. Wife, Elizabeth, executrix. Son, James, 46 acres bought of Nathan Allen. Daughter, Elizabeth, 3¼ acres bought of Charles Jolley. Brothers and sisters, but not named. Witnesses—James Laing, Timothy Robins, Thomas Lawrie. Proved Feb. 22, 1747-8. Lib. E, p. 131.

1747-8, Feb. 12. Inventory, £96.3.8; made by Charles Jolley, Thomas Lawrie.

1750, March 6. Robins, John, of Gloucester Co. Int. Adm'r, Thomas Denell, Salem Co., merchant. Bondsman—Thomas Denny, of Greenwich. Witness—Danl. Mestayer. Lib. 7, p. 543.

1749-50, Jany. 27. Inventory, (£8.0.3); made by Thomas Denny, Mathew Gill. Mentions Abraham Nelson.

1739, April 14. Robins, Nathaniel, of Upper Freehold Township, Monmouth Co., yeoman. Int. Sarah the widow resigns right of administration to Jonathan Robins. Witness—James Reynolds. Jonathan Robins, of Monmouth, gives bond; James Reynolds, surety.
Lib. C, p. 269.

1738-9, Jan. 26. Inventory, £20.3.5¼; made by William and James Reynolds.

1747-8, March 12. Robins, Timothy, of Allen Town, Burlington Co., carpenter. Int. Inventory, £99.00.2; made by Thomas Lawrie and Samuel Davenport.

1747-8, March 24. Administration granted to Ruth Robins, widow. Aaron Robins, of same, fellow bondsman. Lib. 5, p. 438.

1749, May 25. Robins, Zachariah, of Upper Freehold, Monmouth Co., tanner. Int. Inventory (£844) includes mortar, 12 trenchers, 8 years' service of negro, Bristow (£25); 6 yrs. of Richard Holland's time (£5); 11 deer skins (£5.4); leather (£30.10); hides (£8.1); 52 sides of leather (£15.12); 70 hides in tan vats (£33); 117 sides of leather (£35); raw hides and skins in bark house (£32.12); hides in tan vats (£16.16); bark at Thomas Taylor's and at Hankinson's, etc. Made by Robert Lawrence and Thomas Cleayton.

1749, June 9. Administration granted to Mary and Moses Robins.
Lib. 6, p. 333.

1740, Jan. 8. Robinson, Edward, of Philadelphia, cooper. Int. Adm'r, Thomas Robinson, of City of Philada., blacksmith. Daniel Smith, Ju'r, of City of Burlington, merchant, fellow bondsman.
Lib. 4, p. 263.

1740, Jan. 8. Inventory, £22.10; made by Thos. Robinson. Includes bond from David Shreeve for £15 dated Oct. 6, 1727.

1749, April 17. Robinson, James, of Township of Deerfield, Cumberland Co., yeoman. Int. Adm'r, James Robinson. Fellow bondsman—Daniel Lomas. Both of the same place. Witness—Elizabeth Cotting. Lib. 6, p. 53.

1749, April 13. Inventory (£53.15.6) includes cattle, horses and hogs. Appraisers—Daniel Lummus, Robert Hood.

1734, May 10. Robinson, John, of Manington, Salem Co., yeoman; will of. Wife, Kathrain, and Clement Hall, executors, to divide moveable estate among children—Elizabeth, Catrain and Jean. Eldest son, John. Daughter, Margaret Robinson, plantation I possess after her mother's death. Witnesses—Lorance Wining, Rose Rutherford, James Rutherford. Proved 13 July, 1734. (Letters granted Katharine Robinson in absence of Clement Hall). Lib. 3, p. 445.

1734, July 6. Inventory, £81.8.1; made by John Huse, James Rutherford.

1748, Oct. 20. Robinson, Jonah, of Morris Co. Int. Adm'x, Susanna Robinson of said County. Bondsmen—Samuel Swazey, Junr., Morris Co., and Samuel Davis, of Brookhaven, Long Island, blacksmith. Lib. E, p. 217.

1748, Oct. 15. Inventory (£146.19.0) includes note from David Allen. Appraisers—Caleb Horton, David Luse.

1733, April 3. Robinson, William, of Cape May Co., yeoman. Int. Adm'r, Dinah Robinson. Fellow bondsman—John Smith. Both of same County. Witnesses—Daniel Norton, Jacob Spicer, Jacob Spicer, Junior.

1732-3, Jany. 10. Inventory, £64.12.6; made by Daniel Norton, John Smith. Cape May Wills, 79 E.

1749, Sept. 26. Robison, Arthur, of Middlesex Co., labourer. Int. Adm'rs, James Wilson, of Perth Amboy, and Cornelius Arvin. Witness—John Martin. Lib. 3, p. 332.

1749, Oct. 24. Inventory, £15.19.7; made by Thomas Morford and Richard Jewell.

1737, Nov. 29. Robison, John, of Cranberry, Middlesex Co.; will of. Friend, William Laird, executor and sole legatee. Real and personal estate. Witnesses—James Willson, James McKnight, Samuel Spence. Proved Dec. 16, 1737. Lib. C, p. 182.

1737-8, Jan. 21. Inventory, £46.9.3; made by John Anderson and Samuel Dove.

1740, April 7. Robison, John, of Elizabeth Town, Essex Co.; will of. Children—William, Mary, Samuel and John, all under age. £10 to Church of Christ in Westfield. Land bought of Rev. Mr. Jonathan Dickinson and Joanna his wife, laid out in right of Mr. Moline, formerly of Boston, deceased. Executors—wife, Mary, son William, and friend Henry Clark. Witnesses—William Clark, Cornelius Ludlam, Nath'll Hubbell. Proved May 21, 1740. Lib. C, p. 348.

1740, April 21. Inventory (£222.10.10) includes Bible called "Daniel's," Bible called "John's," book called "War with the Devil," sermons and other books, bonds from Ephraim Oakley, Edward Barber, Samuel Woodruff, Efingham Townley, Abraham Chandler, Daniel Ross, Senior, negro boy (£25) and negro girl (£20). Made by William Clark, William Miller, Henry Clark, William Roberson.

1740, May 21. Mary Robison renounces the executorship in favor of son, William, and Henry Clark. Witnesses—William Clark, Cornelius Ludlam.

1746-7, 9th day, 11 mo. (Jan.). Robison, Sarah, of City of Burlington, widow; will of. Sons—David and Richard, David to have £30 per year, quarterly, during his life. John Mifling's three children. George and Sarah Mifling. George and John Mifling, sons of George Mifling. Kinsman, John Mifling and Joseph Trotter. William and Jonathan, sons of my sister and her husband, Richard Smith. Ann and Elizabeth Smith. Kinswoman, Martha DeCow. Ann Pound. Samuel, son of Ralph Peart. Women Friends of Monthly Meeting of Philada. Lot of land in Philada., formerly William Lees; and other lands; also personal estate. Executors—friends John Mifling and Joseph Trotter. Witnesses—Richard Smith, Ralph Peart, Isa. DeCow.

1746-7, 9th day, 11th mo. (Jan.). Codicil. Mentions son David, sister Elizabeth Smith, Martha DeCow and Ann Pound. Same witnesses as to will. Proved Feb. 5, 1746. Lib. 5, p. 295.

1746-7, Feb. 6. Inventory, £1,503.8.9; made by Stephen Williams and Ralph Peart of Burlington, sadler. Affirmed by the son, Samuel Peart. Includes Silver Plate, weight 136.15 @ 3-6, £79.7.4; negroes, £64.

1750, Nov. 13. Roch, John, of Township of Deerfield, Cumberland Co., yeoman. Int. Adm'r, Alexander Moore. Bondsman—Samuel Leek. Witness—Elizabeth Cotting. Cumberland Wills, 64 F.

1739, Jan. 31. Rochead, James, of New York City, merchant; will of. Legacies to eldest sister, Sophia Home, in Edinburgh, Scotland, widow of Doctor Alexander Home, and her children, Elizabeth, Andrew and Agnus; to sister, Margaret Spence, widow of Mr. Thomas Spence, late of Edinburgh, writer, and her children, Agnus, Sophia and Jane Spence. Property in New Jersey, New York, New England and Maryland. Requests to be buried beside deceased brother, John, in the churchyard at "Topenomous," Monmouth Co. Executors—Andrew and Elizabeth Home, with Mr. Charles Home and George Burnet as assistants. Witnesses—Charles Home, George Burnet, Daniel Cofton. Proved Jan. 26, 1740. (Monmouth Wills), Lib. C, p. 378.

1737, Jan. 11. Rochead, John, of Monmouth Co. Int. Adm'r, James Rochead of same County, gent. Laurence Smyth, of Perth Amboy, Esquire, fellow bondsman. Witness—Adam Hay. Lib. C, p. 190.

1748, June 6. Rockhill, Edward, of Amwell, Hunterdon Co.; will of. Wife, Ann. Son-in-law, William Godly, and Mary his wife, testator's daughter; son, John; negro boy, Dick; daughters, Ann and Achsah. Executors—wife, and testator's "brothers," Parnall Clayton of Burlington Co., and William Clayton of Trenton. Witnesses—Emanuel Coryell, Job Warford, Jona. Robeson. Proved June 10, 1748. Lib. 5, p. 476.

1748, July 7. Inventory (£1.436.13.9) includes large old Bible; negro girl Cate, £40; negro boy Dick, £30; negro girl Hannah, £18; 11 Indian Blankets in store, £7.14; numerous articles of general mdse.; sundry goods bought of Preserve Brown, at Philadelphia, May 25, 1748; house and improvements, £50; sundries appraised at upper place at Bethlehem; negro boy Peter, £28; 6 hives bees; fulling mill and 50 acres of land, £124; half an old boat, £5; tract of land in Kingwood, £127.9.3. Bonds of Robert Wilson, Samuel Stevenson, Ezekiel Oliver, Henry Benet, Moses Collins, John Barbor, Edward Slayter, William Coats. Made by W. Montgomerie and Job Robins.

1762, March 15. Account. Mentions land bought of R. Smith, Samuel Carpenter's article found in John Coat's hands, John Rockhill for posting books, Robert Pearson, James Martin, Samuel Holcomb, Malon Kirkbride, Francis Bows, Catharine Meadock, Benjamin Severns, Rut Johnson, John Riddel, Francis Castakin (for Samuel Myas Cohain and Bur. Kelsey), Parnel Clayton, John Coxe, Thomas Larrance, James Burling, Edward Burling, Elizabeth Baxtor, Andrew Reed, Robert and Amos Struttel, Benjamin Price, D. Martin, Mary Rockhill, Isaac Decow, Sr., Paul Lewis, Thomas Litle, John Coxe (for cost against executors of E. Corril), Thomas Cadwalader.

1750, Feb. 25. Roe, Henry, of Gloucester Township and Co., yeoman; will of. Executors—wife, Hannah, and son Abraham. Real and personal estate to be sold; two shares to my wife, and the other children one share, but eldest son, Abraham, to have £20 above his share. Witnesses—Da'd Roe, John Pickin, Michael Fisher. Proved 13 March, 1750. Lib. 7, p. 374.

1750, March 8. Inventory (£467.18.9) includes bonds, bills, book debts, bills due from James Reynolds, William Cheeseman. Appraisers—John Willman, Michael Fisher.

1749, Feb. 15. Rogers, Isaac, son of John Rogers, of Burlington, of 14 years and upwards, prays that Thomas Gill of Chester, yeoman, may be appointed his guardian. Bond of Thomas Gill and Jos. Biddle, fellow bondsman. Burlington Wills, 4555 C.

1740, June 27. Rogers, John, Jun'r, of City of Burlington, yeoman; will of. Wife, Sarah. Children—Isaac and Rebeckah, both under age. Real and personal estate. Negro boy. Executors—wife, and friend Revell Elton. Witnesses—John Deacon, Samuel Laning, Jos. Scattergood. Proved Aug. 13, 1740. Lib. 4, p. 250.

1740, Aug. 12. Inventory, £281.0.7; made by Jacob Lippincott and John Deacon. Includes note of James Hapes.

1736-7, Feb. 25. Rogers, William, of Evesham, Burlington Co., yeoman. Int. Adm'x, Ann Rogers, widow. John Turner and John Evens, both of same, yeomen, fellow bondsmen. Lib. 4, p. 86.

1736-7, Feb. 25. Inventory, £258.9.5; made by John Turner and John Evens.

1736, Nov. 27. Rogers, William, of New Hanover, Burlington Co., yeoman. Int. Inventory, £159.11.6; made by William Davis and John Marshall.

1736, Dec. 10. Adm'x, Hannah Rogers, widow. Marmaduke Fort, of same, fellow bondsman. Lib. 4, p. 78.

1750, June 6. Rogers, William, of Piscataway, Middlesex Co., cordwainer. Int. Bond of Kittrell Mundin, of Piscataway, as administratrix. Benjamin Doty, of same place, fellow bondsman. Lib. E, p. 412.

1751, July 16. Inventory (£34.12.1) includes mention of Jonathan Dunham, John Hepburn, Thomas Davis, Thomas Lester, James Pyat, Gershom Lee, John Pound, Jun'r, John Marlatt, Joseph Vutten. Made by Joseph Drake, and Benajah Doty.

1742, Nov. 20. Rolfe, John, Esq., of Salem Co.; will of. Sons—John, plantation in Maninton precinct, Salem County, in occupation of Thomas Stowe, when my son Josiah will be 21; Josiah (at 21), house, lot and meadows I live on in the town of Salem. Daughter, Mary Rolfe, in New Castle, Pa., to be paid £50 by my son John. Son-in-law, David Ross, and Sarah his wife, my house and lot in Bridge Street, in Salem, occupied by Daniel Mestayer. Residue of personal estate (negroes allotted) to be divided between the three children when they arrive at 21. Executor—The Rev'd Mr. George Ross, Minister of New Castle, Richard Smith, James Whitton, and my son John. Witnesses—Daniel Mestayer, Robt. Hart, F. Gaudonett. Proved 9 Dec., 1732. Letters granted to Richard Smith in absence of others named. Lib. 3, p. 225.

Inventory and account indexed, but not found.

1746, April 24. Rolfe, Moses, Esq., of Somerset Co., Adm'x, Mary Rolfe, widow. Fellow bondsmen, Samuel Rolfe, of Middlesex Co. Lib. D, p. 375.

1746, May 1. Inventory of personal estate (£41.12.2) includes great Bible, £1; books, "The State of Europe," "Dr. Vincent's Explanation of Assembly," "The Doctrine of Mortification," "The Country Justice," three "Acts of Assembly," "The Justices' Guide," "Military Discipline." Appraisers—William Worth, John Sutton.

1747, April 22. Account. Moneys paid Dr. Wood, Henry Freeman, Esq.

1747-8, 13th day, 12th mo. (Feb.). Rolph, John, of the Borough of Elizabeth, Essex Co.; will of. Children—Henry, Hannah, Elizabeth and John, all under age. Expected child. Real and personal estate. Executrix—wife, Sarah. Witnesses—Samuel Smith, William Hall, Joseph Shotwell. Proved March 26, 1750. Lib. E, p. 374.

1733, May 15. Rolph, Samuel, of Woodbridge, Middlesex Co., yeoman; will of. Executors—wife, Anne, and John Alston; wife sole legatee. Real and personal estate. Witnesses—Jacob Thorn, Abraham Thorn, William Hider. Proved June 9, 1733. Lib. B. p. 429.

1748, Sept. 26. Romine, Christopher, of Shrewsbury, Monmouth Co. Rebekah Romine, the widow, resigns right of administration in favor of son, Thomas Romine, and Layten Romine. Witnesses—Christopher Romine and Robert Lee. Lib. E, p. 213.

1748, Sept. 28. Bond of Thomas Romine and Layton Romine, of Shrewsbury, yeomen, as administrators. Samuel Layten of Freehold, yeoman, fellow bondsman.

1732, April 14. Romyne, Samuel, of Six-Mile Run, Middlesex Co., yeoman; will of. Son, Nicholas Romyne, at 21. Real and personal estate. Executors—wife, Saertye, brother John Romyne, and brother-in-law, Phillip Munthorn. Witnesses—William Williamson, Sen'r, William Williamson, Jun'r, H. N. Sperling.

1732, April 15. Codicil. In case of death of wife and of son without

issue, estate to be divided between my brothers and sisters and my wife's brothers and sisters. Witness—Same. Proved Aug. 5, 1732.
Lib. B, p. 295.

1748, March 5. Rose, Ephraim, of Little Egg Harbour, Burlington Co., yeoman. Int. Inventory, £277.17.4½; made by Samuel Andrews and Joseph Parker.

1748, March 8. Adm'x, Martha Rose, widow. Samuel Andrews and Elisha Stout, of same, fellow bondsmen. Lib. 5, p. 437.

1749, June 14. Rose, James, of Fairfield Precinct, Cumberland Co.; will of. Wife, Elizabeth. Children—Phebe, Abigail Hays, James (to have the Bible), Hannah and Elizabeth. Residue of personal estate to wife. Executrix—wife, with cousin, Thomas Harris; they to put son James to trade. Witnesses—Daniel Elmer, Ephraim Daten, Jun'r, David Bower. Proved 20 Dec., 1749. Lib. 6, p. 293.

1748, Dec. 8. Rose, Timothy, of Perth Amboy, Middlesex Co. Int. Bond of Mary Rose, as administratrix on her husband's estate—John Cluck, of same place, fellow bondsman. Witness—William Rose.
Lib. E, p. 220.

1749, May 26. Inventory (£273.13) includes bonds from John Hill, Benjamin Simmons, Jacob Burchal, Daniel Greegs and Benjamin Wilson. Made by Griffin Disbrow and Nath'll Hillyear.

1750, Oct. 18. Ross, George, of Borough of Elizabeth, Essex Co., carpenter; will of. Children—John, Susanna Griffe, George, Hannah, David and Phebe. Land joining land of John Williams; lands bought of Andrew Hampton, Jonathan Miller, Caleb Jeffers, deceased, Ebenezer Sears, Thomas Woodruff and Hezekiah Woodruff. Executors—sons John and George. Witnesses—Thomas Scuder, James Still, ——— Coverly. Proved Nov. 10, 1750. Lib. E, p. 461.

1748, Aug. 23. Ross, Isaiah, of Waterford, Gloucester Co., yeoman; will of. Executors—wife, and Benjamin Holme, they to sell the plantation. Son, John, and daughters Sary and Elizabeth, to be apprenticed and to have at age equally one-third of estate; remainder to wife to bring up son, Isaiah. Witnesses—Samll. Boggs, Neil Morris, Margaret Moris. Proved 5 June, 1749. Letters granted to Ruth Ross, Sept. 16. Lib. 6, p. 286.

1748, Oct. 14. Inventory of "Isaer Ross, that Dyed the 27 day of August 1748" (£103.1.4) includes cattle and horses. Appraisers—Isaac Matlack, Daniel Fortiner.

1734, Nov. 26. Ross, John, of Woodbridge, Middlesex Co., weaver; will of. "Being in 28th year of my age." John, son of Thomas Shaw, my brother-in-law. William Mackreder and his sister, Nancy Reader. Real and personal estate. Executors—brother-in-law, James Taylor, Jun'r, of Woodbridge, weaver, and James Taylor, of Staten Island. Witnesses—Jacob Apers, Wm. Sharp, Jun'r, Israel Thornell. Proved Jan. 14, 1734. Lib. C, p. 6.

1748-9, Jan. 10. Rossell (Rezell), Nathaniel, of Maidenhead, Hunterdon Co. Int. Renunciation of widow, Elizabeth, in favor of friend, Andrew Reed, Esquire, of Trenton. Witness—Henry Mershon. Bond of Andrew Reed, merchant, as administrator. Theophilus Severns, of Trenton, merchant, surety. Witness—Benjamin Biles. Lib. 6, p. 17.

1748-9, Jan. 10. Inventory, £28.9.3; made by Henry Mershon and Theo's Severns.

1764, Oct. 1. Account. Mentions Charles Axford, Robert Taylor, Estate of Francis Bowes, Esquire, Philip Ringo, Estate of Joseph Peace, William Yard, Jeremiah Anderson.

1743, Aug. 16. Rowand, Alexander, of Waterford Township, Gloucester Co., yeoman; will of. Executors—wife, Abigail, and son John. Son, James. Surplus from sale of moveables to be equally divided among five other children—Margaret, Ann, Hannah, Isaac and Thomas (last two when 16 or 17 to learn a trade). Proved Nov. 7, 1743. Witnesses—John Hillman, Jeremiah Meteeth, Thos. Lawrence. Lib. 5, p. 4.

1743, Oct. 8. Inventory, £130.6.6; made by John Hinchman, John Hillman (Quaker).

1750, April 5. Royce, Aaron, Morris Co. Int. Adm'x, Elizabeth Royce, widow. Bondsman—John Royce. Lib. E, p. 380.

1750, April 4. Inventory, £34.7.0; made by Amos Crane, John Cole.

1739, June 13. Royse, Thomas, of Piscataway, Middlesex Co. Int. Adm'x, Mary Royse, the widow. Sam'll Barrowe and Henry Langstaff, fellow bondsmen. Witness—Robert Hude. Lib. C, p. 270.

1749, Dec. 24. Ruckman, John, of Hunterdon Co.; will of. Wife, Susannah, and William Allen, executors. Sons and daughters mentioned but not named. Witnesses—Jonathan Stout, Thomas Ruckman, Uriah Bonham. Proved Feb. 2, 1749-50. Lib. 6, p. 337.

1749-50, Jan. 25. Inventory, £86.12.6; made by Jonathan Stout and Charles Wolverton.

1767, April 15. Account of William Allen, acting executor, names Jonathan Stout, William Carrell, John Reading, Esq., G. Fox, Jonathan Pettit (for weaving), Joseph Yard, Esq., Jno. Burcham, Jno. Opdyke, Robert Evans, Andrew Anderson, Joseph Ruckman, Jacob Rush, Uriah Bonham (for writing the will), Thomas Ruckman, J. Warrel, Esq., Thomas Price (who married eldest daughter of deceased).

1727, Sept. 20. Rudderow, John, of Chester, Burlington Co., yeoman; will of. Wife, Lucy, profits of plantation I now let unto Samuel Davis. Daughter, Hannah, (wife of William Hollinshead), 50 acres I bought of Thomas Lippincott. Daughters, Mary (wife of Joshua Madaks), and Ann (wife of Samuel Davis). Grandaughter, Jane Addis. £10 towards building a church. Executor—son, John, to have remainder of estate and plantation at decease of his mother. Witnesses—William Forster, Joseph Browning, John Kay. Proved May 12, 1733. Lib. 3, p. 308.

1733, April 20. Inventory, £54.14; made by Joseph Heritage and Joseph Browning.

1736, Sept. 1. Rudman, Elizabeth, of Philadelphia Co., Penna., widow; will of. Children—Magdalen Robeson and Anna Catharina, wife of Peter Tranberg. Grandchildren—Andrew, Rudman, William, Elizabeth and Sarah Robeson; Andrew, Rebecka and Elizabeth Tranberg. Plantation situated on Schuykill river. Witnesses—Mounce Keen, Judith Mattson, Philip Chetwood. Proved Oct. 2, 1736, Bond

of Peter Tranberg, as administrator of the estate, with Mounce Keen as fellow bondsman, both of Salem Co., N. J., gentlemen.
Salem Wills, Lib. 4, p. 80.

1736, Jan. 31. Rugg, Benoni, of Cohansey, Salem Co., yeoman. Int. Adm'x, Ann Rugg, (relict). Bondsmen—John Wright, John Doe. Witnesses—Thomas Pagett, Danl. Mestayer. Lib. 4, p. 108.

1736, Jan. 25. Inventory, £64.5.9; made by Jonathan Mills, Thomas Pagett.

1739, Feb. 26. Rumford, John, of Greenwich, Gloucester Co., yeoman. Int. Adm'x, Ann (relict). Bondsmen—Thomas and Jacob Roberts, both of same place, yeoman. Witness—Robert Zane.
Lib. 4, p. 199.

1739, Feb. 11. Inventory, £733.12.0 1-3; made by Alexr. Randall, Robert Zane.

1748, Nov. 28. Account of William Weatherby and Anne his wife, late Ann Rumford. Payments to Henry Gray, George Cook, Ganner Cox, Nicholas Justico, Wm. Vanculin, Gabl. Friend, John Jones, Elias Thomas, Willm. Cobb, Michl, Homan, Wm. Griffith, William Harkley, Alexander Randall, John Stamper, John Burch, Thomas Roberts, Joseph White, Andrew Hofman, John Stow, Andrew Homan, Okannus Holme, Joseph Ross, Saml. Shivers, Michael Hofman, Andrew Mullico, Lawrence Hoffman.

1749, Jan. 18. Runalls, William, of Woodbridge, Middlesex Co., cordwainer. Int. Adm'x, Sarah Runalls (Reynolds), widow. John Donham, of Woodbridge, fellow bondsman. Lib. E, p. 360.

1746-7, March 3. Runion (Runyon), Benjamin, of Somerset Co. Int. Inventory (£101.4.6) includes gun, sword and halbert, one white stallion. Made by Zebulon Stout and Benjamin Rounsavall.

1747, Dec. 4. Bond of Mary Fish, of Somerset County, widow, as administratrix. James Clark, of New Windsor, Middlesex Co., farmer, surety. Witness—William Coxe. Lib. 5, p. 458.

1756, April 19. Account of Josiah Furman and Mary his wife, late Mary Fish, and James Clark, administrators of the estate, mentions Noel Furman, Jno. Chanders, Richard Iverson, Jos. Disborrow, Benjamin Hedges, Aaron Bateman, William Savage, Jno. Hoff, Robert Campbell, Jean Ganno, Thomas Solden, Abraham Striker, Jno. Berrian, Peter Vantilberry, Robert L. Hooper, Lewis Charles Fonnel, Thomas Soden, Jackemiah Denton, Jno. Norris, Sarah Bryant, Jno. Disbrow, Daniel McCartey, Jos. Munow (or Murrow), Samuel Nelson, Jno. Berrian, Cornelius Stevenson, Jos. Disborrow, Jacobus Voras, Jno. Hide, M. Blew, William Bryant, Zebulon Stout, Andrew Reed, Jno. Gordon, Mary Bryant, Jno. Radell, Cornelius De Hart, William Phillips, Jno. Cull, Jno. Fackendal, James Clark, Peter Moon, John Opdyke, Jno. Johnson, William Sickel, Obadiah Davison, Thomas Carehart, Jno. Runion, Eliakim Hedger.

1745, Nov. 20. Runyon, John, of (Rocky Hill), Somerset Co., yeoman. Int. Adm'x, Ann Elizabeth, his widow. Bondsman—Joseph Freeman of Woodbridge, Middlesex Co. Lib. D, p. 347.

———, ——, —. Vendue List. Richard Even, Curnerles Anderson, John McCrary, Elicom Hedger, John Hyde, George Larson, Avon Van-Houk, Charles Saxhous, Nicoles Wecoff, John Folkin, Jeromas Horn, Hendrick Vankirk, Lorance VonHook, Joseph Furman, George Coppin, Hennery Obey, William Bryant, Jerimiah Smith, Jones Wood, Capt. Stout,

Benjamin Anders, Nud Burris, Hugh Howell, Hendrick Luke, Robert Whood, John duBrow, Mary Runyon.

1745, Nov. 18. Inventory of estate (£129.14.6) includes note from David Crosher, bonds from Christiaen Corl, Vincent Runyon. Appraisers—Pieter Strycker, Hendrick Wilson, Abeah Couwenhoven.

1748, Aug. 23. Account. Payments to Dona Skiler, John Berrien, Robart Rosbogh, Thomas Groues, Thomas Whitehead, Joseph Disbery, Ezeblon Stought, Lewis Charles Faneuel, Jacob Moon, Thomas Burrows, Freemon Runyan, Mary Runyan, Abraham Cownover, Caleb Farle, Jonathon Hunt, John Tillyer, John Jublart (?), Hinson (?) Runyan, James Nelson, Benjiman Tomson, Tunis Quick, Dr. Vanuahter, James Hood, Peter Belyeu, William Oca, Benjiman Doughty, Samuell Linnard, John Mack Cray, Theo. Severns (?), Leffert Waldron, John Hide, John Heulick.

1749, Oct. 5. Runyon, Vincent, of Somerset Co., yeoman. Int. Adm'x, daughter Elizabeth. Fellow bondsmen—Nathaniel Runyon, James Campbell of Piscatua. Lib. E, p. 335.

1749, Aug. 31. Inventory, £176.10.2; made by Hendrick Willson, John Loder, Francis Hollinshead.

1751, April 25. "John Savage, who married the said Elizabeth Runyon," etc. Account of Elizabeth Savage, administratrix of Vincent Runyon. "Aug. 25, 1749, To cash for a coffin, £1.6.0. Sept. 12, 1749, cash paid for rum at funerall, £1.7.8," etc.

1744-5, March 7. Russell, Abraham, of Shrewsbury, Middlesex Co. Int. Inventory, £73.9.2; made by Samuel Scott and George Woolley.

1744-5, March 15. Bond of Mary Russell, widow, and James Russell, as administrators. Samuel Scott, of Shrewsbury, fellow bondsman. Lib. D, p. 245.

1750, May 7. Account. Includes payments to John Williams and Thomas Holmes.

1749, Dec. 4. Russill (Reeswill), John, of Trenton, Hunterdon Co. Adm'r, Joseph Warrell, Esquire, of Trenton. Abraham Cottnam, of Trenton, surety. Hunterdon Wills, 265 J.

1735, March 26. Rutherford, Allen, of Salem Co. Int. Adm'r, John Pagett. Bondsman—William Murdock. Both of Salem County, yeoman. Witnesses—Abraham Reeves, Danl. Mestayer. Lib. 4, p. 57.

1736, April 29. Inventory (£19.15.6) includes shoemaker's tools. Appraisers—James Rutherford, Thomas Pagett.

1738, May 10. Account, includes money paid Clement Hall.

1744, Nov. 17. Rutherford, James, of Salem Co. Int. Adm'r, Samuel Purveyance, of Alloways Creek, store keeper. Bondsmen—Andw. Gardiner, John Cunningham. Witnesses—George Gardiner, Chas. O. Neill. Lib. 5, p. 90.

1744, Nov. 7. Renunciation of John Cunningham, Salem County, yeoman, nearest of kin to James Rutherford, shoemaker. Witnesses—Stephen Caxmuck, Chas. O'Neill.

1744, Nov. 12. Inventory, £23.11.9; made by Robt. Walker, Alexr. Walker.

1744, July 21. Ryerson, George, of Bergen Co.; will of. Eldest son,

John. £450 to my daughters, Mary Reading, Blandina Hall, and the children of deceased daughter, Anna Wessels (by name Wessell), George, Evert, Luke, Jannitie, Helena, Antje and Mary Son, John Ryerson, the farm on which he now lives at Waggrow, Bergen Co., excepting the benefit of a brook and 2½ acres on the west side and ½ acre on the east side, at the most convenient place for building a mill. Sons, George and Luke, the two lots on which I now live at Parquanack, Bergen Co., bounded N. by Henry Brockholst, W. by Parquanack River, S. by Margrat Mead, E. by rear line of Parquanack Patent; the S. part to son George, the N. part to son Luke; also the meadows at the East end of the said lots; also my two lots in the Precinct of Parquanack, Morris Co., one of the said lots on a brook called Beaver Dam, bounded N. by Gyles Mandefield, S. by land of the late John Mandefield, W. by Abrm. Vantine and Brant Jacobus, joining E. the lot of Saml. Berrien and so between the top of the Mountain and the great meadow. A tract held in partnership with Derrick Dey in the precinct of Parquanack, Morris Co., at the upper end of the Plain at the west side of the S. line shall be sold, with my personal estate, to pay debts. The overplus, if any, to be divided into eight equal parts and given to sons John, Martin, George, Luke, daughters Mary, Blandina, Elizabeth and the eight children of my daughter Anna, deceased. Executors—sons, John, George and Luke. Witnesses—Joseph Bartram, Jacob Mead, Henry Mandefield. Proved 29 March, 1749. Lib. E, p. 283.

1741, April 23. Ryle, James, of Cohansey, Salem Co., gent.; will of. Son, James, and his first born son, all my lands during their life time; after their decease to sons John, Thomas and Joseph Ryle, who shall have the moveable estate. Executors—son, James, and Benjamin Davis. Witnesses—William Ellark, Mary Davis, Ester Davis. Proved 8 June, 1743. Lib. 4, p. 365.

1743, June 8. Inventory, £54.1.10; made by Nathaniel Whitaew, Abraham Smith.

1738, Oct. 28. Ryley, Patrick, of Piscataway, Middlesex Co. Int. Adm'x, Mary Ryley, the widow. Aaron Faitout, Sen'r, of Perth Amboy, fellow bondsman. Lib. C, p. 222.

1738-9, Jan. 17. Bond of William Jones and Anne Jones, his wife, as administrators, the widow being deceased. James Thomson and John Brown, fellow bondsman, both of Piscataway. Witnesses—Simon Walker, Neal Macgugan. Lib. C, p. 270.

1739, Feb. 26. Saint, Hercules, of Gloucester Township and Co., yeoman. Int. Adm'x, Rebecca (relict). Bondsmen—Josiah* Albertson and Jacob Roberts of said county, yeomen. Lib. 4, p. 198.

1739-40, 12 mo. (Feb.), 22 da. Inventory, £71.07.3; made by Joseph Tomlinson, Josiah Alberson.

1749, July 3. Salder, Alexander, of Burlington Co. Int. Adm'r, Charles Tonkin. Charles How, fellow bondsman. Both of City of Burlington. Lib. 6, p. 333; Lib. 7, p. 99.

1745-6, March 12. Sale (Sallee), Daniel, of Elizabeth Town, Essex Co., yeoman; will of. Wife, Orselea. Children—John, Mary, Martha, Rebecca, Sarah, Hannah and Daniel. Real and personal estate. Executors—son-in-law, James Collie, Joseph Ogden and Samuel Meeker. Witnesses—Sarah Ross, John Ross, Mary Ross. Proved Sept. 23, 1746. Lib. D, p. 404.

1746, Sept. 27. Inventory, £72.15.11; made by Edward Sale and John Ogden.

1749, Oct. 14. Sale, Thomas, of Deptford, Gloucester Co., laborer. Int. Adm'r, John Sparks, yeoman. Bondsman—John Marshall, of same place, blacksmith. Witness—John Davis. Lib. 7, p. 33.

1749, Aug. 1. Inventory, £8.6.10; made by John Tredway and John Davis.

1743, Aug. 16. Salnave, John Peter, of the Borough of Elizabeth, Essex Co. Int. Adm'x, Sarah Salnave, the widow. Thomas Hill and John Salnave, fellow bondsmen. Witnesses—Gershom Higgins, Robert Hine. Lib. D, p. 76.

1728, Oct. 8. Saltar, Elizabeth, of Freehold, Monmouth Co.; will of. Lands in New Jersey and Pennsylvania to be sold, except 50 acres on the Neck, at lower end of husband's plantation and small piece of land and the house testatrix lived in at the Iron Works. If sufficient, £10 apiece to daughters, out of the 100 acres of land given testatrix by her father. Daughters—Sarah, Lucy, Lidy and Elizabeth. Executors—friends and brothers, Elisha Lawrence, John Lawrence, John Emley, Richard Saltar, Jr. Witnesses—Robert Lawrence, Ebenezer Saltar, James Tapscott. Proved August 20, 1741.

1747-8, 1 mo. (Mar.), 17 da. Sanders, John, of Woodberry Creek, Gloucester Co., husbandman; will of. Wife, Elizabeth, sole executrix and to have whole estate to bring up my children. Witnesses—William Wilkins, John Jefferis, William Wood. Affirmed 12 April, 1748. Lib. 5, p. 503.

1748, 2 mo. (Apr.), 5 da. Inventory (£502) includes books, boat and sails, oxen and cows. Appraisers—John Wilkins, William Wood.

1748-9, Feb. 16. Sanderson, Egbert, of Newark, Essex Co., yeoman; will of. Children—Waallens, John and Peter Egbertson, Elsie (wife of Cornelius Deremus, Jun'r) and Antie Egbertson. Land bought of executors of Joseph Wheeler, joining land of Nathaniel Crane. Executors—my three sons. Witnesses—Reiner VanGiesen, Peter Garmo, Jon'n Sergeant. Proved Aug. 7, 1749. Lib. E, p. 319.

1740, Nov. 6. Sandford, Peregrine, of New Barbadoes, Bergen Co., yeoman; will of. Wife, Fiety, the whole estate for bringing up and educating the children; if she marries, to enjoy same until youngest child will be 18. "By reason of my son, William Sandford, being deprived of one of his arms, he shall have £60 for his education at the discretion of the executors." Rest of estate to be divided equally among five children, Enoch, William, Jane, Aphie, Elisabeth. Executors—wife, Fietye, brother Michael Sandford, and John Low. Witnesses—Jonathan Sergeant, John Cochran, Thos. Turner. Proved 14 June, 1750. Fietie Sandford qualified as executrix. Renunciation of John Low and Michael Sandford. Witness—Uzall Ogden. Lib. E, p. 438.

1732, Feb. 24. Sandford, William, of New Barbadoes Neck, Bergen Co., yeoman; will of. Son, Richard, ½ of cedar swamp in Bergen Co., between the rivers Pasayack and Hackinsack, with that tract of meadow between the cedar swamp and Hackinsack River, beginning at Ponka Kill, running to the swamp, thence by the side to Kingsland's line, thence to Hackinsack River, etc. Daughters, Frankie, Jenne and Anna (all under age) the other half of the cedar swamp, with the remaining part of the meadow. Wife, Mary, to have, absolutely, personal estate and 100 acres at Rahway, Essex Co., bought of Mr. William Robinson, by deed dated 24 February, 1720; also the use of the cedar swamp and meadows given to Richard, until he will be of age. Executors—wife, Mary, John King and Richard Bradberry. Witnesses—Jno. Cooper, Gisbert VanEmburgh, Maria Tomasson.

1732, Feb. 24. Codicil. Wife, Mary, may dispose of the land and use interest for the maintenance of herself and the children. 5 shillings to each of my sons, William, Michael, John, Peregrine, Robert and Peter. Witnesses—John Hill, Francis Harrison, Johannes Van Emburgh. Proved 16 April, 1733. Mary Sandford and John King qualify. John Stagg, surety. Witnesses—John Brown, Ragel Kinge.

1733, Apr. 16. Affidavit of Francis Harrison, aged 39 years, who wrote the codicil. Names daughter Sarah as being overlooked, etc., by his error. Lib. B, p. 415.

1749, Feb. 22. Sandford, William, of New Barbadoes Neck, Bergen Co., yeoman; will of. Only son, William, my plantation (300 acres) and 150 acres of meadow on the eastward part. If he dies without lawful heirs, said land and meadow to be divided equally among my surviving children. Wife, Catherine, to have the use of same during widowhood. Residue of my meadows on New Berbadoes Neck to be divided equally between wife and daughters, viz: Mary, Benington, Sarah, Elizabeth, Francis, Rachel and Catherine. To said wife the great Bible, and to daughter Sarah the silver tankard. Executors—John Low and John Vanderpool. Witnesses—James Still, John Sandford, Jon. Sergeant. Proved 7 April, 1750. John Vanderpool renounces and John Low qualifies. Witnesses—James Still, Elipt. Johnson, Thomas Alling. Lib. E, p. 408.

1750, May 31. Sandford, William, Jun'r, of Essex Co. Int. Bond of Samuel Plum, principal creditor, as administrator. James Nicholson, fellow bondsman. Both of Newark, Essex Co. Lib. E, p. 440.

1739, March 27. Sarjant, John, of Perth Amboy, Middlesex Co., innkeeper. Int. Adm'x, Sissell Sarjant. Robert Hude, fellow bondsman. Witnesses—Robert Lane, Eze. Bloomfield. Lib. C, p. 268.

1734, June 7. Satterthwaite, George, of Burlington, Burlington Co., glasier. Int. Adm'x, Rebecca Satterthwaite, widow. John Doe and Richard Roe, fellow bondsmen. Lib. 3, p. 411.

1734, March 3. Satterthwaite, Isaac, of Salem Town and Co., weaver; will of. Wife, Phebe, during life, house and plantation in the Town of Salem where I dwell; also profits of a tract of land on Cows Neck that I purchased of the Proprietor, Penn; also 20 acres of marsh that runs to Margate's lane, 2½ acres of meadow joining Peter Carmack's land, and 16 acres of woodland joining Richard Craven's; all of which shall be my son Isaac's at her decease. Also he shall have, when 21, 120 acres of upland and marsh in Cows Neck, which I bought of the Proprietor, Penn. Executors to give deed to

Peter Bard, Esq., on the payment of £108, the purchase money. Wife, Phebe, and daughters, Anne, Rebecca, Sarah and Margate, to have equally residue of personal estate when they arrive at 21. Executors—wife, and son Isaac. Witnesses—Philip Chetwood, William Thompson, Danl. Mestayer. Proved 18 Dec., 1737. Lib. 4, p. 141.

1737, Dec. 26. Inventory (£626.19.4¾) includes cash in the house, £132.9.5; cattle, £162.14; debtors—Dinah Bard, Thos. Rives, Joseph Gregory, Jane Stow, John Thompson, Edward Trenchard, Nicholas Casels, Joshua Nicholson. Appraisers—Wm. Hancock, Clement Hall.

1741, 7th day, 2nd mo. (Apr.). Satterthwaite, Mary, of Chesterfield, Burlington Co.; will of. Children—Richard, Anne, Jonathan and David. Anne to be placed with Eliz'b Watson to be a "tayloris." Jonathan to be with Joseph Bustill, and David with John Sykes, each until they are 17. Real and personal estate. Executors—friend Joseph Burr, and bro.-in-law Michael Buffin. Witnesses—Michael Vanroon, Jos. Reckless. Proved May 4, 1741. Lib. 4, p. 287.

1741, April 28. Inventory, £875.3.3; made by John Buffin and Isaac DeCow, medius. Includes negro man and girl, £63.

1731, 26th day, 6th mo. (Aug.). Satterthwaite, William, of Chesterfield, Burlington Co.; will of. Wife, Martha. Children, Samuel, William and Sarah. 220 acres I bought of George Morris, and 14 acres I bought of John Dennis, both in Mansfield. 30 acres I bought of Allen Wood in New Hanover, and 100 acres in Nottingham given me by William Biddle. Executor—son Samuel. Witnesses—Richard French, Matthew Forsyth, Jos. Reckless. Proved Oct. 12, 1747, at which time Matthew Forsyth and Richard French are both deceased.

Lib. 5, p. 366.

1740, June 28, 29. Satterthwaite, William, of Mansfield, Burlington Co., yeoman. Int. Inventory, £1075.5.8; made by John Buffin and Isaac DeCow, medius. Includes debts of Benjamin Tallman, Jacob DeCow, Mathew Forsith, Henry Brown, Daniel Bacon, Benjamin Wright, Micajah How, Robert Wright, Jacob Wysz, Edward Haines, Eber DeCow, John Maulsby, Thomas Thompson, Darby Coneley, Francis Fowler, Stephen Wright, John Newland, Isaac Ivins, Robert Webb, Charles Tonkin, Hugh Hill, Samuel Curtis, John Middleton, James Cruse, Joshuay Quicksel; also negro man, woman and girl, £95.

1740, July 17. Bond of Adm'x, Mary Satterthwaite, widow. John Buffin and Michael Buffin, both of Mansfield, yeomen, fellow bondsmen.

Lib. 4, p. 245.

1746, Oct. 16. Sautter, Michael, of Woodberry Creek, Gloucester Co.; will of. Legacies to Charles Sautter of Cohansey Creek, Christian Nauzell of Alloways Creek, Lodowick, son of Lodowick Haun, Michael, son of Christopher Cook, Elias Cook. Residue of estate to Elizabeth Sanders. Executors—John Wilkins and William Wood. Witnesses—Wm. Wilkins, Mary Wilkins, James Chatting. Affirmed 7 Aug., 1750.

Lib. 7, p. 139.

1750, 5 mo. (July), 28 da. Inventory, £160.15.4; made by Wm. Wilkins, John Hues.

———, ——, —. Account. Moneys paid James Wood, Thos. Clement, John Ladd, Joseph Scattergood, Wm. Wilkins, Dorcas Hues, Nathan Lord, Honnour Flemon, John Ramboe, Garret Dewees, Samuel Chester, Andrew Sloan, Elizabeth Sanders, Charles Sautter, John Marshall, Wm. Wood, Jno. Wilkins.

1732, Feb. 20. Savoy, Jacob, of Penns Neck, Salem Co., yeoman. Int. Adm'x, Rhina Savoy. Bondsmen—Sinick Sinicker, Thomas Miles. All of said County. Witnesses—Elias Cotting, Dan. Mestayer.
Lib. 3, p. 290.

1732-3, Jan. 29. Inventory, £63.4.4; made by Sinnick Sinnicker, Thos. Miles.

1732, Sept. 12. Saxton, William, Sr., of Freehold, Monmouth Co., yeoman; will of. Wife, Anne. Children—William (eldest son), Daniel, Peter, Charles, James, Sarah, Anne, Charity, Jemima, Elizabeth and Rebecca. Executors—wife, brother-in-law Stringam, son William and friend John Steward. Witnesses—Thomas Shaw, David Lippincott and Joshua Wright (a Quaker). Proved Nov. 11, 1732.
Lib. 3, p. 219.

1732, 28th d., 8 mo. (Oct.). Inventory (£215.8.6) includes fowling piece, cooper's tools and weaver's loom. Made by John King, Thomas Doughty, Joshua Wright.

1749, March 2. Sayre, Ananias, Esq., and David Shepherd, both of Greenwich Township, Cumberland Co., guardians of John and Hannah Walling, infants of 14 years and upwards, children of John Walling, late of the same county. Witnesses—Stephen Ayers, Elias Cotting.
Cumberland Wills, 52 F.

1742, Feb. 21. Sayre, David, of Cohansey, Salem Co., husbandman; will of. Wife, Ruth. Son, David, at the marriage of the widow to have all my lands and 16 acres of meadow purchased of Ephraim Seeley, he paying £16 to my sons Daniel and William, when they will be 21. Son, Thomas, the loom and tackling, worsted, comb, cattle and service of my apprentice, Thomas Ryley. Son, James, at 21, ½ of the saw mill with the lands and meadows thereto. Daughters—Hannah Dayton, Elenor, Ruth, Mary and Prudence when 18. Executors—wife, Ruth, and eldest son, David. Witnesses—Job Sayre, Nathaniel Whitacar, Jeremiah Buck, Jehiel Wheeler. Proved 26 April, 1742.
Lib. 4, p. 354.

1742, April 9. Inventory (£412.9.1) includes 58 head of cattle, sheep, hogs and colt. Appraisers—Thomas Pagett, Moses Shepherd.

1740-1, Feb. 16. Sayre, David, Senior, of Cohansey, Salem Co., yeoman; will of. Sons—David (eldest) five shillings; Job, the plantation I live on. Daughters—Dorothy Pagett (eldest), Hannah Plummer, Christian Mulford, Rebecca Gelaspse, and Anne Sayre. Granddaughter, Mary Platts. Executor—son-in-law, Thomas Pagett. Witnesses—Alexander Maccoy, Nathan Bacon, Moses Pagett. Proved 8 Dec., 1744.
Lib. 5, p. 95.

1744, Nov. 22. Inventory, £80.6.7; made by Richard Butcher, Jonathan Platts.

1746, May 16. Sayre, Ephraim, of Elizabeth Town, Essex Co., carpenter. Int. Elizabeth Sayre, the widow, renounces right to administer, in favor of Ebenezer Sayre, brother, and Lewis Mulford, principal creditor. Witnesses—Joseph Williams, Jonathan Sayre, Edward Griffing, Thomas Chapman. Bond of Ebenezer Sayre and Lewis Mulford. Joseph Williams, fellow bondsman. Witness—Josiah Broadwell.
Lib. D, p. 386.

1746, May 20. Inventory (£330.01.05¾) includes bonds of John French,

Joseph Linley, John Radley, Joseph Hetfield. Made by John Stils, Joseph Cory.

1729, Jan. 29. Sayre, James, of Elizabeth Town, Essex Co.; will of. Cousin, Benjamin Price, Jun'r, of Elizabeth Town. Nephews—Ezekiel, Benjamin and James Sayre, sons of brother Job Sayre, of Southampton, County of Suffolk, New York. Brother Job to care for estate until nephews come to age. Real and personal estate. Executors—wife, Sarah, and friend Benjamin Price, Jr. Witnesses—David Morehouse, Benjamin Meeker, Samuel Whitehead. Proved Oct. 24, 1732. Lib. B, p. 306.

1727, Dec. 14. Sayre, Jonathan, of Newark, Essex Co.; will of. Daughter, Hannah Sayre, executrix and sole legatee. Real and personal estate. Witnesses—Benjamin Co, Caleb Sayre, Abigail Co. Proved June 22, 1732. Hanna Ogden, late Hannah Sayre, and John Ogden qualify as executors. Lib. B, p. 286.

1736, Sept. 12. Sayre (Sayers), Richard, of Salem; will of. Sisters—Mary Pledger, wife of John Pledger, Junior, £10 and one great iron pot, given to my brother, Joseph Sayres, deceased, by my mother; Ann Johnson, likewise. Legacies to brother, Robert Johnson, at 21; cousins Richard, Thomas and Job Butcher (sons of Richard Butcher, living at Stoe Creek). James, son of James Vance, carpenter of Manington, and Tompson and Ruth Sayres (at 21). Richard Butcher to have my Proprietary Rights, excepting lot of land in town of Salem (purchased from Abiel Caril of Cohansey, glazier), which shall be for his son John when 21. Interest of £20 for propagating a free school in Salem for the education of the children of Friends. Executor—uncle, Richard Butcher. Witnesses—Joseph Goodwin, Erasmus Fetters, Joseph Carroll. Affirmed 18 Dec., 1738. Lib. 4, p. 181.

1738, Dec. 19. Inventory (£208.15.5) includes horse, chest of books, "Rume reced. from the West Indies." Appraisers—William Willice, John White, Clemt. Hall.

1741, Nov. 5. Account. Mentions Hannah Smith, William Chandler, Israel Potter, John Smith, Junr., Edward Trenchard, Vaylie Hunnell, Philip Chetwood, Leonard Gibbon, Jonathan Walmsley, Phebe Satterthwaite, Mary Willis, Jam. Caruthers, Edward Shepherd, John Goodwin, John Eglington, Nicholas Gibbon, Wm. Handcock, Joseph Goodwin, David Fitzrandolph, John Steward, Elizabeth Jones, John Turner, John Phillips, Rebecca Sherrin, Wm. Crabb, Wm. Burroughs, Mary Coleman, John Pledger, Edward Hancock, Elizh. White, Daniel Mestayer, Charles O. Neill, Clement Hall, Daniel Huddy, Benjamin Eaton, Ann Haynes, George Crow, Thos. Robinson, Thos. Hodgkin, Edward Shepherd, Joseph Goodwin, John Steward, Abraham Reeves, Saml. Holmes, Ann Woodnutt, Erasmus Fetters, Wm. Murdock, Thos. Gillingham, Peter Turner, Benjm. Crosse, Benjn. Eaton, John Rolfe.

1742-3, March 4. Scattergood, Benjamin, of Mansfield, Burlington Co., yeoman. Int. Inventory, £54.16.6; made by Francis Gibbs and George Folwell. Includes debts due from Joshiew Scattergood, William Pancoast, Sam'll How, Sam'll Hunt, Caleb Scattergood.

1742-3, March 19. Administration granted to Caleb Scattergood. Joshua Scattergood, fellow bondsman, both of Mansfield, yeomen. Lib. 4, p. 379.

1732, Nov. 16. Scattergood, Joseph, of Mansfield, Burlington Co.; will of. Brothers—Jonathan and Caleb. Sisters—Thomasine, Martha and Elizabeth, all under age. Real and personal estate. Sister, Sarah, executrix. Witnesses—John Buffin, Francis Gibbs, William Taylor. Proved Dec. 1, 1732. Lib. 3, p. 223.

1732, Nov. 30. Inventory, £42.5; made by John Buffin and Francis Gibbs.

1743, Dec. 16. Scattergood, Samuel, of City of Burlington, merchant; will of. Wife, Rebecca. Children—Thomas, Samuel, Elizabeth, Mary, Rebecca and Sarah, all under age. Wharf, storehouse and water lot in Burlington. Lot adjoining Joseph Rose and Daniel Bacon, on High Street. Land purchased of George and Gertrude Noble. Plantation whereon Joseph Reeves now dwells in Northampton Township. Two tracts in Hunterdon and Morris Counties. Executors—wife, and brothers Aaron Lovett and Joseph Scattergood. Witnesses—James Hancock, Jos. Lovett, James Smith. Proved March 5, 1743. Lib. 5, p. 23.

1730, Oct. 6. Scattergood, Thomas, of Mansfield, Burlington Co.; will of. Brothers and sisters—Joseph, Jonathan, Sarah and Tomasin, all real and personal estate. Executors—William Pancoast and Edward Barton. Witnesses—Isaac Gibbs, Jr., Francis Gibbs, Benjamin Shreve, Richard Gibbs. Proved March 25, 1730. Lib. 3, p. 123.

1731, 26th day, 1st mo. (Mar.). Inventory, £67.13; made by John Buffin and Job Ridgway.

1743, June 4. Scattergood, Thomas, of City of Burlington, carpenter; will of. Wife, Phebe. Youngest son, Joseph, 50 acres I bought of Samuel Furnis and Ralph Peart. Son, Thomas. Son, Samuel, and his children—Thomas, Elizabeth, Mary, Ann, Rebecca, Sarah, Samuel. Dau., Elizabeth, now wife of Joseph Allinson £60, and each of her children, save Thomas, 25 shillings; he to have 40 shillings. Daughter-in-law, Rebecca wife of Aaron Areson. Plantation in Mansfield containing 200 acres, and 100 acres in Nottingham, given me by my father-in-law, Christopher Wetherill. Executors—wife, and sons Thomas and Joseph. Witnesses—James Hancock, David George, Sarah DeCow. Proved March 19, 1744. Lib. 5, p. 100.

1744, March 24. Inventory, £108.16.10; made by John Bacon and Joseph Hollinshead.

1739, Jan. 12. Schenck, Garrat, of Middletown, Monmouth Co., gent.; will of. Wife, Neelkie. Son, Raeloffe, the great Dutch Bible, meadow at Conascunk meadows and the third of landing on Chingaroras Creek. Sons Raeloffe and Garrat, neck of land adjoining Capt. Reid's. Son, Koert. Son, Garrat, lot adjoining Hendrick Hendrickson, land bought of John Bowne, March 10, 1705, and testator's home plantation. Sons, John and Albert, land at Brunswick, bought of Koert Van Voorhuyse, Nov. 5, 1723. Five daughters, Mary, Alkie, Neelkie, Rachel and Margaret, land at Conascunk purchased of Hendrick Hendrickson, and 986 acres at Penns Neck bounded by Tatamus Swamp, Bear Swamp and Asinpink Creek. Grandchildren, sons and daughters of daughter Anne (evidently eight in number). Granddaughter, Nelly. Personal estate after wife's decease to testator's eleven children. Executors—wife, son Roeloffe and son-in-law Hendrick Hendrickson. Witnesses—Johannes Bennet, Roelyf Covenhoven and Robert Dodsworth. Proved Oct. 7, 1745. Roelef Schenck and Hendrick Hendrickson sworn as executors. Lib. D, p. 334.

1742, March 4. Schilinx, Cornelius, of Cape May Co., yeoman; will of. Wife, Abigail, executrix. Sons—Cornelius and Abraham; also William, to have all my lands within the County, joining land in possession of my son Cornelius on one side and lands of Barnabas Crowell, Joshua Stites and John Bradner on the other side; also the privilege my heirs have of having our grain ground toll free at the grist mill on Cold Spring Creek. Witnesses—Aaron Leaming, William Barlow, Elisha Crowell. Proved 30 May, 1743.

Cape May Wills, 112 E.

1743, March 3. Inventory, £92.14.1; made by Ebenr. Swaine, Elijah Hughes.

1746, April 14. Schillinks, Cornelius, of Cape May Co., yeoman; will of. Wife, Mary, ½ of moveable estate, ¼ of the mill and privilege of ½ of the home plantation, (it being the half which I give unto my son Henry Schillinks), during widowhood. Sons—Cornelius, ½ of the plantation whereon I live, it being the west side joining William Schelink's and ¼ of the mill; Henry, the eastermost half, joining Elijah Hughes; Enos, the ½ of my plantation at Dividing Creek, Salem County, it being the westernmost half, joining Nicholas Crosen; Daniel, the other half, it being the easternmost, joining Charles Fox. Daughters—Mary Stillwell, Lydia and Hannah Schillinks, ½ of moveable estate. Executors—wife, Mary, and son, Cornelius. Witnesses—William Schillinks, Abraham Schillinks, Mary Taylor, Elijah Hughes. Proved 21 May, 1746. Cape May Wills, 127 E.

1746, May 29. Inventory, £96.19.3; made by Elisha Hand, Elisha Crowell.

1744, March 2. Schillinks, William, of Cape May Co., yeoman; will of. Wife, Josena, executrix, and whole estate during widowhood. If a son by my said wife, and he lives to be 20, he shall possess all lands and tenements; if a daughter, she shall have all at 18. If twins, male and female, the male at 21 to pay his sister £20, but if he should die under age, the daughter at 18 to have whole estate. If two males and they live to the age of 20, they shall hold the property in joint tenantcy, or it shall be divided equally between them, or, if one die, the other to have the property absolutely. If two females and they arrive to 18, they shall hold the estate in joint tenantcy, or, if one dies, the other shall have it absolutely. If no issue, or none to attain majority, I give all my lands to my brother, Abraham Schillinks. Witnesses—Joshua Stites, Nathan Hand, Daniel Foster, Jacob Spicer. Proved 30 March, 1748. Cape May Wills, 139 E.

1747-8, Jan. 8. Inventory, £63.13.8; made by Ebenezer Swane, Elisha Crowell.

1744, 11th day, 2nd mo. (April). Scholey, Francis, of Springfield, Burlington Co., widow; will of. Children—Susannah Newbold, John, Ann Scattergood, Mary Barton, Isabel, Rebeckah, Samuel, Sarah and Jonathan. Grandchildren—John, Ann, Clayton, Rebeckah, Mary and Michael, children of my daughter, Susannah Newbold. Grandson, Jonathan Barton. Son, Jonathan, to have £20 to support and care for my negro man, Simon. Real and personal estate. Executors—sons John, Samuel and Jonathan. Witnesses—Peter Andrews, Esther Andrews, John Osmond. Proved April 23, 1750. Lib. 6, p. 322.

1749-50, March 8. Inventory, £720.12.5¾; made by Thomas Earl and Benjamin Shreeve. Includes negro wench, £31.15.

1731-2, Jan. 15. Scholey, John, of Springfield, Burlington Co., yeoman; will of. Wife, Frances. Children—John, Samuel, Jonathan, Rebecca and Sarah, all under age. Daughters—Ann Scattergood, Susanna Newbold, Mary and Isabel Scholey. Grandson, John Newbold. 135 acres in New Hanover; meadow adjoining Thos. Branson; land I bought of John Stacy, adjoining 50 acres I sold Jarvis Pharo; plantation where John Atkinson now lives; 16 acres at head of William Bougars' Swamp, bought of John Harvy in town of New Hanover; 9 acres formerly belonging to Harriet Gaunt. Wife, sole executrix. Witnesses—Zebulon Gauntt, Thomas Bevin, Bartho. Buxton. Proved Feb. 8, 1735. Lib. 4, p. 53.

1735, 10th day, 12th mo. (Feb.). Inventory, £674.16.10; made by Thomas Scattergood and Zebulon Gauntt. Includes negro youth, Simon, negro woman, Bess, and her three children.

1748, April 18. Scholey, John, of Chesterfield, Burlington Co., weaver; will of. Wife, Mary. Land I surveyed adjoining William Chapman and Godfrey Beck, to my son Jehosada. Other children mentioned but not named; left to care of their mother. Executors—friends Michael Newbold and Isaac DeCow. Witnesses—Thomas Scholey, Rebeckah Taylor, Benja. Busson. Proved May 10, 1748. Lib. 5, p. 477.

1748, May 9. Inventory, £162.11.10; made by Godfrey Beck and Thos. Black.

1766, Feb. 28. Account of Eber DeCow, executor of Isaac DeCow of Mansfield, who was executor of John Scholey. Moneys paid Hoppins and Schooley, Mary Schooley, Wm. Halloway, Sam'l Schooley, Hopkins and Black, William Chapman, Isaac Ivins, Christian Wilson, George Nicholson, Barzilla Newbold, Samuel Cheshire, Kirbey and Foster, David Wright, Samuel Satterthwaite, John Schooley, Jos. DeCow, Benjamin Busson, Sam'l Tuely, George Taylor, Samuel Ivins, Daniel Smith, Daniel Tillton, John Taylor, Benjamin Thorn, Ann Arion, William Beakes, Dan'l Doughty, Jos. Reckless, Marmaduke Watson, Isaac Price, Antho. Sykes, Caleb Shreeve, Eliz. Watson, William Hopkins, John Bunting, Widow Merrell, Thomas Ivins, John Padgo, William Ivins, James Farro, William Taylor, Peter Harvey, Benjamin Roberts, Abraham Thorne, Edith Newbold, Peter Kirl.

1732, June 19. Schooley, Robert, of Nottingham, Burlington Co., yeoman. Int. Adm'x, Katherine Schooley, widow. Samuel Danford and Thomas Williams, fellow bondsmen, all of same place, yeomen. Lib. 3, p. 199.

1732, June 25. Inventory, £30.4; made by Thomas Pitman and Robert Johnson.

1735, March 20. Account of Thomas Williams and Catherine his wife, late Catherine Scholey, administratrix. Debts paid Joseph Peace, Jno. Marlon, Rob't Bolton, Thos. Lambert.

1739, Sept. 17. Schuggen (Scoggen), Mary, (14 yrs. old), of Penns Neck, Salem Co., ward. Guardian—William Mecum, yeoman. Bondsman—Thomas Miles, gent. Both of said County. Witnesses—Aaron Wood, Peter Peterson. Salem Wills, 666 Q.

1750, March 26. Schuyler, Abraham, of New Brunswick, Middlesex Co. Int. Adm'x, Catharine Schuyler, the widow. Derick Schuyler, fellow bondsman. Lib. E, p. 399.

1733, Dec. 13. Scogen, Jonas, of Penns Neck, Salem Co.; will of. "An unworthy member of the Church of England." Wife, Sarah. Son, Jonas, at 20, to have my plantation (208 acres), he paying £10 to his sister Mary when 18. If he dies without lawful heirs, same to my daughter Mary. Son-in-law, William Vaniman (not of age). Executors—wife (Sarah), son Jonas, and friend William Vaniman, who are to put my only son Jonas to Henry Jean's for two years that he may be instructed in learning. Witnesses—Mouns Anderson, Sarah Pownell, Henry Jeanes. Proved 1 March, 1733. Lib. 3, p. 403.

1733-4, Feb. 26. Inventory (£577.15.9½) includes tables at house of Andrew Barleson. Appraisers—Thos. Miles, Henry Jeanes.

1734, Jan. 1. Scoggin, John, Jonas, Jacob, Mary, Elizabeth (last three under 14 years), children of Johannes and Catherine (since deceased), of Penn's Neck, Salem Co. Robert Raines, of Mannington, Salem Co., brick-layer, guardian. Lib. 3, p. 451.

1746, May 9. Scott, Charles, of Salem Co., yeoman. Int. Adm'r, Jeremiah Baker, of Penns Neck. Bondsmen—John Marshall, of Penns Neck, Chas. O. Neill, of Salem. Witnesses—Eliza. James, Danl. Mestayer. (Letters not issued until Aug. 10, 1747). Lib. 5, p. 420.

1749, June 9. Account. Moneys paid Robert Birney, Elizabeth Jones, Jeremiah Baker, Mary Grafton, Charles O. Neill, Grace Mason, Daniel Mestayer, Daniel Wattson, William Mecum, John Marshall, John Eaton, William Mecum, Junior, Robert Hartshorne, Joseph Rose.

1750, May 13. Scott, Elizabeth, of Gloucester Township and Co., spinster; will of. Eldest daughter, Elizabeth, executrix. Daughter—Amy, to be cared for by my sister, Joana Williams; Temperance, to be cared for by my sister Jean Hutchinson; both under 18. Witnesses—Michael Fisher, Elizabeth Roes, Bathsheba Williams. Proved 13 April, 1751. Lib. 7, p. 141.

1750, May 21. Inventory, £34.16.5; made by Peter Martin, Benjamin Liddon.

1730, Aug. 1. Scott, James, of Mansfield, Burlington Co., mariner. Int. Admr's, John Browne, Sen'r, and John Browne, Ju'r, both of same, doctors in physick. Lib. 3, p. 99.

1730, Aug. 8. Inventory, £53.11.8; made by Nathan Folwell, Joseph Shreve, Rob: Field.

1731, Dec. 2. Account of Dr. John Brown. Debts paid Joseph Brown, shallop-man, for passage of dec'd and freight of his things from Philada., Isaac Angomy, Mr. Rob't Ellus of Philada., merch't, Wm. Atwood, of Philada., merch't, att'y for Andrew Alexander, of Jamaica.

1736, Sept. 13. Scott, John, of Shrewsbury, Monmouth Co., planter; will of. Eldest son, William, land formerly Abraham Vickers', adjoining Newman's spring, George Allen and Edmond Lefetra. Also meadow called Glassmaker's Landing. Son, Samuel, house and land adjoining the old peach orchard. Sons, John and Ebenezer, under age. Daughters, Mercy Tollet and Hannah Scott. Negro girl, Johannah, to live with testator's daughter, Mehetable White. Executors—sons William and Samuel, and son-in-law George Crawford. Witnesses—William Leeds, James Grover, John Holdsworth, John Hanskins, John White, Christopher Nicholson. Proved Nov. 16, 1736. Lib. C, p. 128.

1736, Nov. 15. Inventory of £511.17.00; made by Isaac Hance, Samuel Leonard.

1735, Oct. 16. Scott, Robert, of Middletown, Monmouth Co., laborer. Int. Adm'r, James Patton. John Patton, fellow bondsman. Lib. C, p. 44.

———, ——, —. Inventory of estate (£53.15.1) includes bonds and notes of John Sudam, Henry Sudam, David Hilldrith, Joseph Aston, Anne Vandorn, William Bowne, Job Throgmorton, John Larris, Careseme Horsmans, John Tunis. Made by Peter White, Bans Jansson, John Cooper.

1746, Aug. 2. Scott, Thomas, of City of Burlington, yeoman; will of. Wife, Leah. Children—Abraham, Thomas, Brazilla, Anne, Leah, Mary and Alice, all under age. Real and personal estate. Executors—wife, and brother Henry Scott. Witnesses—Jonathan Scott, John Bigan, George Eyres. Proved Sept. 19, 1746. Lib. 5, p. 285.

1746, Sept. 19. Henry Scott declines executorship. Witness—Christopher Finigan.

1747-8, Feb. 24. Scott, Timothy, of Salem Co. Int. Adm'x, Sarah Scott. Bondsmen—Chas. Empson, Thomas Carney, Thos. Pearson, all of Penns Neck. Witnesses—Rebeckah Murdock. Lib. 5, p. 423.

1747-8, Feb. 22. Inventory, £42.9.2; made by Thomas Carny, Thomas Persons.

1743, April 17. Scudder, Benjamin, of the Borough of Elizabeth, Essex Co.; will of. Daughters—Sarah Ayres, Ruth Ross, Hannah and Elizabeth, last two under age. Four sons under age, not mentioned by name. Real and personal estate. Executors—friend George Ross, and son-in-law George Ross, Jun'r. Witnesses—Samuel Scudder, John Robards, John Cleverly. Proved April 29, 1743. Lib. D, p. 37.

1743, April 30. Inventory (£255.18) includes bonds from Samuel Brant, Jon'n Winans, John Robards, William Winans. Made by Richard Clark, Joshua Marsh.

1738-9, Jan. 13. Scudder, John, of Elizabeth Town, Essex Co.; will of. Wife, Mary. Children—John, Richard, Samuel, Thomas, Elizabeth, Kesiah, Anna, Mary, Joanna and Phebe. £10 to Presbyterian Church of Christ, in Society of Elizabeth Town, to be given on Thanksgiving Day. Land joining land of Joseph Moss in Raway; meadow purchased of Joseph Thompson in Raway. Executors—sons Samuel and John, and Ephraim Marsh. Witnesses—Joseph Woodruff, Gershom Moore, Nath'll Hubbell. Proved April 25, 1739. Lib. C, p. 278.

1739, June 27. Inventory (£410.09.10) includes negro man, three negro boys, two negro girls. Made by John Rolph, Joseph Shotwell.

1748, June 15. Scudder, John, of Trenton Township, Hunterdon Co. Int. Inventory (£179.11.0) includes bonds of William Snodden, Joshua Howell. Made by Charles Clark, Stephen Rose.

1748, June 17. Bond of Joseph Scudder, of Maidenhead, and Phebe Scudder, of Trenton Township, as administrators. Stephen Rose, of Trenton Township, surety. Lib. 5, p. 492.

1742, Sept. 23. Scull, David, of Great Egg Harbor, Gloucester Co.; will of. Brothers—Recompense (sole executor), Gideon and Isaiah

(to have equally all the lands). Father, John Scull, the personal estate. Witnesses—Able Scull, Sarah Scull, Mary Badcock. Filed 9 June, 1749.
Gloucester Wills, 441 H.

1745, March 15. Scull, John, of Great Egg Harbor, Gloucester Co., yeoman; will of. Wife, Mary, sole executrix. Sons—John (eldest), Abel, Peter, Daniel, Benjamin, Recompense, Gideon and Isaiah (last three to have all my Right to Absekon Beach). Two younger sons, Gideon and Isaiah, to have ½ of moveable estate. Sons-in-law, Robert Smith (one shilling, my daughter Margarett being in her lifetime by me advanced) and Amos Ireland (one shilling, my daughter Catherine being in her lifetime by me advanced). Daughters, Mary Lee and Rachel, wife of James Edwards. Witnesses—Thos. Carty, Return Badcock, William Mapes. Affirmed 6 July, 1748. Lib. 6, p. 2.

1748, 3d mo. (May), 14 da. Inventory, estate of John Scull who "deceased the 8th of the second month, 1748," (£103.06.00) includes 36 head of cattle. Appraisers—Daniel Ireland, James Somers.

1739, Aug. 28. Scull, Peter, of Great Egg Harbor, Gloucester Co., yeoman; will of. Wife Jane. Sons—Peter, Philip, Samuel (the home plantation and 216½ acres, one-third of which fronts upon the river line), Daniel (216½ acres between Peter and Samuel Scull, one-third upon the river line), David (likewise) and John. Daughters—Marey Lake, Pashance Truax, Elizabeth Tounsen, Ann Scull. Granddaughter—Gartrey Steelman. Executors—Nathan Lake, Samuel Scull. Witnesses—John English, Daniel Scull, Benjn. Utter, James Marsh. Affirmed 7 Nov., 1739. (Letters granted to Samuel Scull).
Lib. 4, p. 207.

1739, Oct. 8. Inventory, £101.7.6; made by Nehemiah Nicholson, Daniel Scull.

1750, May 2. Seabrook, Daniel, of Middletown, Monmouth Co. Int. Admr's, Joseph Stillwell and Edward Taylor, of Middletown. James Pew, fellow bondsman. Witnesses—Sketon Johnson, James Mott.
Lib. E, p. 393.

1750, May 12. Inventory (£212.2.6) includes old sword, fish gig, spear and net, 2 guns, negro man, £50; negro girl, £20; servant boy, £15; bonds of Wilson Hunt, Benjamin Drake, William Whitehead, 22 hides. Made by Samuel Ogborn, James Grover, Jr., James Pew.

1751, May 1. Account. Cash paid Dr. Stephen Talman, Mrs. Mary Walton, Benjamin Drake (which was due his wife), John Lippincott, Samuel Ogborne, George Taylor, Richard Crawford, John Hire, William Weakfield, James Pew, James Joy, Mary Morris, Widow Walton, William Woolley.

1750, March 29. Seabrook, Mary, of Middletown, Monmouth Co.; will of. Lands in Shrewsbury. Children—Daniel, Nicholas, Thomas, John, James, Hannah and Mary. Executors—Joseph Stilwell and Edward Taylor, of Middletown. Witnesses—James Mott, Skelton Johnson, Juda Compton, Elizabeth Forman. Proved May 2, 1750.
Lib. E, p. 303.

1749, June 24. Seagrave, William, Jr., of Deerfield Township, Cumberland Co., yeoman. Int. Adm'x, Aribella Seagrave. Fellow bondsman—William Seagrave, of Township of Piles Grove, Salem Co.
Cumberland Wills, 47 F.

1749, April 19. Inventory, £91.17.0; made by Charles Clark, Daniel Alderman.

1738, Oct. 6. Searing, Samuel, of Elizabeth Town, Essex Co.; will of. Children—Isaac, Elizabeth (wife of David Morehouse), Hannah (wife of Simeon Bryant), Samuel, John, Mary, Phebe, Sarah, and Susannah Searing, last six under age. Lands purchased of Mathias Swem and William Looker (Tooker), deceased; land joining land of Thomas Welles. Executors—wife, Rose, and friends Simeon Searing and Timothy Whitehead. Witnesses—John Odell, Nathaniel Bonnell, Jun'r, John Blanchard. Proved Oct. 26, 1738. Lib. C, p. 219.

1738, Nov. 2. Inventory, £159.13.11; made by John Wade, yeoman, and Moses Thompson, cordwainer.

1735, June 30. Searing, Simon, of Elizabeth Town, Essex Co., yeoman; will of. Wife, Alse. Son, Simeon, land joining land of Joseph Williams. Son, Joseph, land joining land of Mathias Swaim. Daughters—Sarah, Phebe and Amy Searing. Executors—brother, Samuel Searing, brother-in-law Thomas Ball, of Newark, and son Simeon. Witnesses—Timothy Whitehead, George Ross, Jun'r, Benjamin Bonnel. Proved Aug. 2, 1735. Lib. C, p. 64.

1735, Aug. 1. Inventory, £123.02.03; made by Joseph Bonnel and George Ross, Jun'r.

1748-9, March 17. Sears, John, of Shrewsbury, Monmouth Co. Int. Grisell Sears, the widow, renounces right of administration in favor of Thomas Holms, creditor. Witnesses—John and Lydia Worthley.

1749, June 15. Bond of Thomas Holms, of Shrewsbury. Timothy Akin of Shrewsbury, yeoman, fellow bondsman. Lib. E, p. 307.

1743, Feb. 4. Sebring (Seabring), Jesantie, of Somerset Co. Int. Renunciation of Cors Vroom, her eldest son, in favor of his brother Hendrick, as administrator. Witnesses—Gerit Remson (?), Rem Remson.

1743, Feb. 21. Bond of Hendrick Vroom. Fellow bondsmen—Peter Bodine of Middlesex Co. Lib. D, p. 122.

1733, June 26. Seeley, John, of Salem Co., yeoman. Int. Adm'r, John Wright, gent. Bondsman—Ranier Gregory, of Salem Co., gent. Witnesses—Clemt. Hall, Dan. Mestayer. Lib. 3, p. 360.

1733, Dec. 8. Inventory, £18.1; made by Daniel Westcote, John Ayers.

1750, Sept. 17. Seeley, John, (no place stated; Cumberland Co.). Int. Adm'r, Ebenezer Miller, Jun'r, of Cohansey, yeoman. Fellow bondsman—Robert Hartshorne, of Burlington, attorney-at-law. Cumberland Wills, 93 F.

1731-2, Feb. 3. Sergeant, Jonathan, of Newark, Essex Co. Int. Inventory (£422.18.03) includes bonds due from Thomas Sergeant, Mr. Joseph Bonnell, Robert Crane, Samuel Davis, John Mun, Joseph Wilson, John Plum, Thomas Alling, John Biglow, Samuel Camp, David Alling, Abraham Harrison, John Goddin, Peter VanTilburgh, Samuel Wheeler, Nathan'll Camp, David Howell, Joseph Prudden, Jacob Van-Winkle, John Carrington, Lidea Peck, John Low, John Hambleton, Joseph Peck, Isaac Harrison, Samuel Dod, Meribey Gardner, Gershom Gardner, Mr. John Cooper. Made by David Ogden and Sam'll Ferrand.

1732, April 13. Administration granted to Samuel Cooper and Mary, his wife. Lib. B, p. 246.

1747, May 25. Sergent, Joseph, of Bethlehem, Hunterdon Co. Int. Adm'r, Benjamin Smith, of Amwell, Hunterdon County. Job Warford, of same place, surety. Witnesses—Faith Chapman, Olive Smith. Lib. 5, p. 464.

1732, May 29. Severns, John, of Trenton, Hunterdon Co.; will of. Wife, Frances, use of new house and lot in Trenton, adjoining Samuel Johnson. Son, Benjamin. Son, Theophilus, said house in Trenton after mother's decease. Daughter, Margaret Seanders. Testator's dwelling and lot, and a fifty acre lot near the town, bought of Staniland, to be sold. Executors—wife, and friends Alexander Lockart and James Neilson, both of Trenton. Witnesses—Robert Tindall, William Pierson, Jonathan Davis. Proved July 10, 1732. Lib. 3, p. 202.

1732-3, March 4. Inventory of estate, "as appears by a list of debts as they now stand upon his book," viz.: Johanners Anderson (Enoch's son), Joshua Anderson, Jr., Richard Alison, Richard Arnold, Simon Akers, William Allen of Maidenhead, Thomas Akerby, John Abbott, John Anderson (Joshua's son), Enoch Anderson, Jr., Joshua Anderson, Sr., William Allen of Hopewell, Richard Armstrong, John Anderson, mason, Eliakim Anderson of Hopewell, Samuel Anderson of Maidenhead, Abraham Anderson (widow's son), Christopher Akley, Bartholomew Anderson, John Amons of Amwell, Ananias Allen, Robert Allison, Ralph Ashton, David Adams, William Arden, Thomas Allen, Samuel Allen of Amwell, Eliakim Anderson (Enoch's son), James Abernathy, Andrus Anderson, Abraham Anderson (Joshua's son), John Axford, Jacob Bellerjeau, Edward Barbour, Peter Bard, John Brown, Joseph Brittain, John Burroughs, Samuel Bonham, William Bryant of Stoneybrook, Edmund Beeks, Samuel Beeks, Alexander Biles, Samuel Barnes, William Bryant (the lame man), Elisha Bird, Richard Baxter, William Burtus, Sr., Daniel Bayly, Samuel Buckly, Jacob Benge, Doctor Bellergeau, George Bates of Amwell, Bearfoot Bronson, Edmund Bainbridge, Warren Barr, Doctor Brittain, John Beeks, William Bell, Thomas Burroughs, Sr., John Brown, tailor, Joseph Burleigh, Zedekiah Bonham, John Bainbridge, Jr., Francis Bowes, Peter Berian of Long Island, Thomas Biles of Bucks County, John Bainbridge, Sr., William Burroughs, Edward Baldwin, John Brayly and David, Peter Bantiff of Philadelphia, Taylor Blew, John Bennet at Mr. Bards, John Branes, William Benge, Jun'r, Jeremiah Bonham, Nehemiah Bonham, John Brightwell, John Biles, William Barracliff, John Boise of Amwell, Thomas Bates, Samuel Bedford, John Burroughs, Samuel Bunnel, James Bell, carpenter, Patrick Broderick, Joseph Brown, attorney, Benjamin Brayly, Andrew Bontinhouse, Andrew Bradford of Philada., Henry Bellerjeau, Benjamin Bard, Bruer of Allentown, Bruer of Amwell, Christopher Beckett, James Bell, taylor, Charles Clark, Ashmael Carpenter, James Carver, John Clark, Caleb Carmen, Benjamin Clyft, John Coxe, John Coats, Bartholomew Corwine, Benjamin Clark, Andrew Clealand, John Coe, John Coleman, Henry Coate, John Carpenter, William Cornwell, Thomas Coleman, James Crawley, James Collings, William Cook, Henry Carter, John Carter, blacksmith, Robert Comes, John Clowes, Alexander Craige, Joseph Cross, Matthew Cupley, James Clark, Archibald Camblee, John Collear, George Cumings, William Coats, Anthony Cook, Charles Corder, Samuel Coats, Robert Chapman, Francis Currie, John Currie, Edward Currie, James Currie, William Coxe, Thomas Curtis, Anthony Camp, John Cross, John Carter, "breekmaker," Francis Costigan, lawyer, John Dagworthy, Esq'r, Elnathan Davis, Sen'r, Elathan Davis, Jun'r, John Dean, Alexander Day, Jonathan Davis, Richard Densey, David Dunbar, Samuel Davis, Jonathan Davis, cooper, Robert Darch, William Daury, Daniel Doughty, Henry Darrington, Doct'r David Davis, Jacob Doughty, Mr. William Dun, Nathan Davis, Josiah Davison, Francis Deldine of Brunswick, Anthony Dardoff, James Dean, Timothy Dowlin, gard'r, Jonathan Davis, Jun'r, Richard Eliot, James Evens, Francis Eliott, Samuel Everett, Joshua Ely, John Eles, small, Thomas Eles, glazer, Robert Eles of Philadelphia, Roger Edmonds, John Eles, forgeman, George Eley, John Eaton, John Everet, William Eaton of Bucks County, Timothy Evans, wood carter, John Edwards, Thomas Eamans, William Easom, Andrew Forster, Gelease Frazer, Henry Folk, Joseph Furnice, taylor, Samuel Foreman, Sen'r, Samuel Foreman, Jun'r, Isaiah Foulks, Hendrick Froom (Vroom), John Frampton, Benjamin Floyd, Richard Foreman, Jeremiah French, Sam. Fitch, David Foreman, George Fox, Josiah Foreman, William Fish, Thomas Foulks, Flatt Fac'dman, Ambrose Field, Samuel Francis, Jeremiah Forster, Joseph Ford of Long Island, John Farguson, John Francis, George Furnace of Long Island, Benjamin Foreman of Philada., Thomas Fling, glazier, Forster of Woodbridge, "Little" Sam Freeman, Francis Grandowett, Mr. Captain James Gould, William Grey, the pedlar, Peter Groom, Jun'r, Thomas Graves, Mr. Daniel Grandine, Robert Green, George Guinup, Thomas Gipson, sawyer, Richard Green, James Geary, Samuel Green, Francis Gitling, Joseph Green, Jacob Goodwone, Daniel Gagers, hatter, William Gear, forgeman, Stephen Green, William Green, Noah Gates, Benjamin Green, Francis Geno, Daniel Geno, Nicklus Gale of Philada., Richard Gerves, Edward Ganett, William Griffith, Francis Gardner, Edward Green, David Howell, Thomas Higgins, Daniel Hollingsheard, Richard Harker, Alexand'r Harper, Isaac Herring, Thomas Hunt, John Hunt of Maidenhead, Ralph Hunt of Hopewell, Johannes Hendrickson, Hugh Howell, Joseph Hixson, Matthew Hixson, Martin Harding, Powell Hoff, Thomas Huntingdon, Robert Harvey, John Hoff, Nicholas Hagerty, Thomas Hoff of Hopewell, Daniel Howell of Amwell, Joseph Hart, John Holcomb, Robert Higgins, Samuel Huff, Isaac Hutchinson, John Hart, John Hunt of Hopewell, Christopher Howell, John Hixson, Samuel Hunt of Hopewell, Samuel Hunt of Maidenhead, Michael Higgins, Benjamin Harding, James Hide, Arthur Howells, Capt'n Ralph Hart, James Harpin, Edward Hunt, William Hoff, Joseph Higbee, Ralph Hunt of Stony Brook, Thomas Huntly, Joseph Houghton, Thomas Houghton, Joseph Hill, Tune Hoff, Charles Hoff, Jerome Hendrickson, Edward Hart, Doct'r Humbleton, William Hope, Thomas Hoff of Maidenhead, John Houghton, Joseph Herring, John Heaward, Delius Hegemiah, Mr. Huble, John Hide, Jasper Hunt, Joseph Harding, John Huston, Peter Hendrickson, Richard Hoard, Joseph Heans, Thomas Hendry, John Hoaldren, Thomas Hoalaway, butcher of Philadelphia, Jeremiah Hendrickson, Joseph Hoff, Jedediah Higgins, Benjamin Harrinson, Collonell Hooper, Thomas Housley, collier, John Howel, Richard Hoff, over the river, Thomas Howell of Amwell, John Head, Thomas Hunt of Hopewell, John Hoff, Powel's son, William Holdeen, Richard Hands, Joseph Ingham, the lame pedler, Joseph James, Samuel Johnson, Jenkins, Daniel Jones, Maurice Justice, Rutt Johnson, Robert Johnson, John Jones, joyner, Isaac Jones and Thomas, George Jobes, William Janas, Joseph Jones, Charles Jennes, Samuel Jones, Peter Justice, Cornelius Johnson, Theophilus Ketcham, Samuel Ketcham, John Knowles, John Knowles of Philada., John Kinsey, Esq'r, Joseph Kipp of Bristol, John Killy, Phillip Kearney, attorney, Henry Kitchin, Joseph King, William Killy, Jacob Knowles, Joshua Knowles, James Leonard,

Robert Lanning, Richard Lanning, John Lovering, Thomas Leonard, Esq., John Laewes, tinker, Adrian Lane of Whippeney, Capt'n Lester Peter Lose, Henry Lott, Fenwick Lyell, William Larenson, Peter Lott, Christopher Lupton, William Launder, taylor, Richard Loveland, Thomas Laurence of Philada., Thomas Lambert, William Laurence of Hopewell, Johannes Laurens, Joseph Longley, Joseph Linn, Isaac Lanning, Thomas Leasey, William Lommox, Joseph Lambert, Richard Lonnon, Sam Lees, Robert Lanning, Jr., John McGills, Samuel Montgomerie, Andrew Milburn, Henry Mershon, Jun'r, Henry Mershon, Sen'r, James McCombs, William Merrill, Thomas McClenney, John McCoy, William Miller, James Melvin, Richard Merrill, Thomas Morrill, William Miller at Huff's place, Hugh Moore, Mrs. Muirhead, Francis Moore, Lewis Moore, Alex'r McCallaster, little sadler, John Morehouse of Whippenny, Benjamin Morgan, Rarington Smith, George Miller, Daniel McCormick, Benjamin Merryl, William Martin, the taylor, Jonathan Moore, Abraham McDaniel, James McKinley, John Moore, Thomas Maybury, Thomas McClehan, merch't, Nicholas Miller, Francis Mayberry, Hugh Mitchell, Andrew Morgan, Charles Morgen Smith, Thomas Moore, shoemaker, Joseph More, Mr. McKiney, John Montgomerie, Morgan the minister, William Merrill, Jun'r, John McGlaughlin, Charles Mitchell, John Morehead, James McBurney, David McBride, Charles Moon, William Nitt, William Nevil, Thomas Neelous, John Nelson, Robert Nealor, Thomas Newman, Robert Nealor, Jun'r, Azekiel Olipper, Thomas Okley, Jun'r, William Osbur, Sen'r, Albert Opdike, Joseph Overton, William Osbur, Jun'r, Lawrence Opdike, Duncan Olypant, William Phillips, John Pane, Baker Phillips, Phillip Phillips, Doct'r Peterson, Theophilus Phillips, Richard Palmer, Ebenezer Provost, David Price, Cap't Phillip Phillips, John Pricely of Bristol, James Price, Sen'r, Joseph Phillips, Phillip Palmer and Edmund, Nathaniel Phillips, John Porterfield, Esq'r, Richard Phillips, Ebenezer Petty, Jonathan Pettit, John Phillips, Peter Pomme, Joseph Pitts, Jos. Parks, Jun'r, Edward Pierce, lawyer, James Price, Jun'r, Joseph Price, Mr. Thomas Palmer, parchment maker, John Pearce, John Parks, William Pearson, George Phillips, Reuben Pouner, Josiah Prechitt of Amwell, John Prickett, shoemaker, Joseph Parkes, John Palmer, John Pursly, John Pearsons of Burlington, Francis Quick, Tunis Quick, Ralph Rann, Thomas Reed, Nathaniel Rossill, Joseph Raeder, John Rogers, Daniel Robins, Matthew Rosselly, Matthew Rogers, Moses Robins, Thomas Roberts (great), John Rouse of Philada., Thomas Roberts (small), Nathaniel Randolph, Isaac Randolph, Joseph Reed, merch't, Benjamin Robinson, Phillip Ringo, Cornelius Ringo, John Richardson, Benjamin Randolph, Sen'r, Joseph Reed, carter, John Reader, Thomas Runian, Benjamin Randolph, Jun'r, John Robinson, James Robinson, Redson the doctor, John Reed of Maidenhead, Sam. Runion, Stephen Renolds, Edward Ruckell, Cobus Romine, William Reed of Hopewell, Christopher Romine, Maurice Roberts the schoolmaster, James Reny of Long Island, Elisha Robins, Peter Relve, Francis Robion, Matt. Solom of Rarington, William Snowden, Jasper Smith, Esq'r, Sue Solom of Rarington, John Schudder, William Skinner, William Spencer, William Scholey, Robert Scholey, Jonathan Stickland, Benjamin Stout, Joseph Stout, James Shores, Ebenezer Saymore, John Sutten, Aaron Shyhalk, John Smith of Hopewell, Coburs Slack, Richard Smith, John Smith, baker's son, Robert Shaw, James Silver, Silvanus Sikes, John Swift, Joseph Scott, Robert Spencer, Andrew Smith, Hugh Standland, Thomas Standland, Jepthah Smith, Cornelius Slack, John Stevens, Richard Scudder, Jeremiah Smith, Richard Stanhope, William Stanhope, Richard Stockton, John Smith (Jasper's son), Thomas Skelton of Philada., Jonathan Stout, Thos. South,

Daniel Sebring, William Strickfield, George Snow, taylor, Samuel Smith, James Starkey, Thomas Strickland, Thomas Smith (Jasper's son), Ralph Smith, Thomas Stevens, James Stevens, Thomas Shirds (Sibb's son-in-law), John Sullivan, Joseph Stout of Amwell, John Stevens of Brunswick, Benjamin Severns, Henry Slack, William Simmons, Benjamin Slack, Jonathan Stiles, Thomas Scholey, Ezekel Smith of Stony brook, Maurice Trent, Job Thomas, John Taylor, John Titus, Ephraim Titus, Timothy Titus, William Tindall, Joseph Tindall, James Tucker, Abraham Temple, Edward Tuckett, James Trent, Robert Tindall, James Terrill, Thomas Turners, Robert Titus, Robert Taylor, shoemaker, Francis Tollett, schoolmaster, John Talbot, Samuel Tucker, Mr. Vansant, Browne Vangelder, Henry Vernon, Hendrick Venoy, Smith Venscekill of Rocky Hill, John Vancleaf of Maidenhead, Henry Woely, John Woolard, Thomas Wood, merch't, Benjamin Warton, Thomas Winder, George Woolsey, William Wordell, Richard Wooliox, John White, Jonas Wood, Nathan Watson, John Willis, John Wood of Salem, Matthew Watson, Thomas Woorrell, Solomon Warder, Giles Worth, John Wright of Amwell, Richard Weathered, John Wharburton, John Willing, William Wilkins, Sen'r, John Wright of Croswix, Henry Woodward, Joseph Yard, Thomas Yardley, William Yard, Sen'r, John Yard (Wm's son), John Yard (old).

1742-3, Feb. 18. Shaa, John, of Somerset Co., bricklayer. Int. Adm'x, Mary Waldron, of New York, wife and attorney of Danl. Waldron, principal creditor. Fellow Bondsman—William Thomson, of Perth Amboy. Lib. D, p. 24.

1742-3, Feb. 21. Inventory, £24.9.10; made by Marius Glenville, Rike Vanderbilt. Goods left in hands of George Cosort.

1743, April 8. Vendue List. Sales to Mary Waldron, Ana More, John Ford, Saml. Crowell, Marious Glanvill, Elias VanComt, Saml. Carvel, Hendr. Lane, Robt. Steell, Nath. Killey, Tomas Armstrong, Wm. Carson, George Cosort, Josiah Standberry, Adoni Hoglene, Saml. Thomson.

1736, Nov. 3. Shaffer, Bernardus, of Somerset Co. Int. Adm'r, Francis Lucas, Jun., the widow, Catrin, having renounced her right. Fellow bondsmen—George Rowland. Lib. C, p. 126.

1736, Nov. —. Inventory, £35.12.1; made by Daniel Sutton and Moses Ayers.

1731, 10 mo. (Dec.), 14 da. Shakle, Thomas, of Haddonfield, Gloucester Co.; will of. £5 to Lydia Cooper and Elizabeth Estaugh. £3 to John Estaugh (money owing by Jonathan Wood when he was in my service). 50 shillings to Joseph Cooper, ("my share for fence of burying-ground at Haddonfield"). 50 shillings to Samuel Dennis. £5 to Joseph Cooper, my executor; he to send residue of my estate to Great Britain to be equally divided among children of my brother, John Shakle. Witnesses—John Estaugh, Mary Gill, John Kay. Affirmed 31 Jan., 1732. (Letters issued to Joseph Cooper Mar. 31, 1733). Lib. 3, p. 274.

1732, 11 mo. (Jan.), 23 da. Inventory (£101.18.00) includes "Sewell's History," 10 shillings; Bible, 2 shillings; a book of G. Fox, 1 shilling; old iron and shoemaker's tools. Appraisers—John Kay, Timo. Matlack.

1736, Aug. 30. Shaproon (Shabrom), Peter, of Trenton, Hunterdon Co.; will of. Friend, Duncan Oguillon, of Trenton, laborer, for regard and for services, sole legatee and executor. Witnesses—Benjamin Smith, Richard Smith, Charles Iloff. Proved June 11, 1739. Lib. 4, p. 173.

1741, 5th day, 8th mo. (Oct.). Sharp, Hugh, Esq., of Wellingborrow, Burlington Co.; will of. Wife, Rachel, lot in Burlington on Pearl Street, and £30 annually. Daughter-in-law, Rachel, wife of John Mickle. £5 to Caleb Raper, Esq., for the Monthly Meeting of Friends in Burlington. Real and personal estate. Executors—sons-in-law, William Coate and John Brientnalle. Witnesses—Peter Fearon, Ab'm Farington, Joshua Raper. Proved Jan. 13, 1742. Lib. 4, p. 356.

1742, 7 mo. (Sept.), 7 da. Sharp, John, of Amboy, Middlesex Co., carpenter; will of. Children—John, Matthew and Marion, all under age. Land formerly belonging to Daniel Brittain. Executors—wife, Sarah, son Matthew, and Richard FitzRandolph. Witnesses—Joseph Marsh, Edward Griffin, Elizabeth Griffin. Proved Oct. 9, 1742. Lib. D, p. 8.

1736, Dec. 31. Sharp, Samuel, of Evesham, Burlington Co., yeoman; will of. Son, Joseph, plantation adjoining Abraham Haines, near the Meeting House and Thomas Sharp's. Son, Samuel, land bought of my brother, Thomas Sharp. Daughter, Elizabeth, brass kettle that was her grandfather's. Children all under age. Cousin, William Sharp. Executrix, wife, Mary. Witnesses—Joseph Tomlinson, William Sharp, John Tomlinson. Proved March 2, 1736-7. Lib. 4, p. 86.

1736-7, 7th day, 12th mo. (Feb.). Inventory, £201.14; made by Thomas Wilkins.

1746, May 26. Sharp, Samuel, of Newtown, Gloucester Co., yeoman. Int. Admr's, Henry Siddon and Elizabeth his wife (late Elizabeth Sharp), and Robert Downs and Anne his wife (late Anne Sharp) of same county. Bondsman—Edward Radolphus Price, Esq., of Burlington. Witness—John Trapnell. Lib. 5, p. 429.

1749, April 23. Sharp, William, of Woodbridge, Middlesex Co.; will of. Wife, Sarah, £40 and plantation for ten years. Sons—John, Henry, William, Samuel, Langstaff, Jonathan, last five under age. Daughter, Mary Sharp, a minor. Real and personal estate. Executors—wife, Sarah, friend and brother Jonathan Dennis, and son John, all of Woodbridge. Witnesses—William Mackdaniel, James Campbell, Sen'r, Jos. Davis. Proved May 22, 1749. Lib. E, p. 298.

1749, May 10. Inventory (£110.07) includes sword, gun and "pleasure slay." Made by Ichabod Smith and Samuel Martin.

1744, April 1. Shaw, Benjamin, of Cape May Co.; will of. Wife, Margatt. Sons—Benjamin, Obidiah, Joshua, William. Daughters—Sarah and Mary. Executors—wife, Margatt, and John Shaw. Witnesses—Elisha Hand, Robert Edmonds, Marah Edmons. Proved 4 Feb., 1746-7. Lib. 5, p. 360.

1747, Aug. 24. Letters granted to Margaret Shaw, in absence of John Shaw.

1746-7, Jany. 29. Inventory of personal estate (£58.18.2) includes smith's tools. Appraisers—Elisha Hand, Richard Crawford.

1750, March 26. Shaw, Carll, of Fairfield Precinct, Cumberland Co.; will of. "I have had two wives, Hannah, the former, long since dead, and Elizabeth, my present wife, and have had issue by both." Carl (first born by Hannah), the homestead and all the land on which I now dwell, purchased of Jonathan and Nathan Lorance; he to pay my son Ryal £20, who shall have 50 acres (taken up by Proprietor's

Right, purchased of Clement Hall, deceased), also ½ of piece of land purchased of my brother, Joshua Shaw, lying on Middlerun; also one loom and half the weaving tackle, the other loom and ½ of weaving tackle to his brother Carl. Daughters, Hannah and Mary, residue of the personalty. Executor—John Ogden. Witnesses—John Jones, John Whitecur, Job Bateman. Proved 21 April, 1750. Lib. 6, p. 361.

1750, April 16. Inventory, £101.2.6; made by John Jones, John Whittecur.

1747, March 4. Shaw, John, of Freehold, Monmouth Co., yeoman; will of. Wife, not named. Sons, William and John Shaw, Jr., lands with fulling and grist mills, etc., and the furniture, etc., "that was mine in my first wife's time." Money due Richard Nixon and to Robert Ellis of Philadelphia. Son, William, pocket Bible, gold sleeve buttons, silver shoe buckles, and seal skin trunk. Son, John, silver breast buttons and large Bible. Other children—Thomas, Henry, Joseph, Robert, Sarah and Elizabeth Shaw. Son, Thomas, to have deed from his uncle, William Hankinson. Executors—brother-in-law, William Hankinson, and friends Robert Cumming and John Henderson. Witnesses—Lawrence Debow, John Andrew, William Adams. Proved May 4, 1748. Lib. E, p. 181.

1748, April 12. Inventory, £239.17.3, includes wheat, rye, etc. Made by John Bennem, John Anderson, Samuel Ker.

1746, Sept. 25. Shaw, Phebe, of Hopewell, Hunterdon Co. Adm'r, Andrew Mershon, of Hopewell, yeoman. Cornelius Holdren of Hopewell, yeoman, surety. Witness—Cornelius Anderson. Lib. 5, p. 278.

———, ——, —. Inventory, £6.16.0; made by Richard Philips and Cornelius Holdren.

1750, May 28. Shaw, Thomas, of City of Burlington, practitioner in physick; will of. Wife, Ann. Sons—Thomas and Samuel, both under age. Brother, Samuel. Brother, John, and his children. Sister, Sarah. Niece, Sarah Bickham. Brother-in-law, Gervais Burgess, £14, in case he does not recover his sight. Real and personal estate. Executors—wife, son Thomas and brother Samuel. Witnesses—Isaac Hewlings, Jun'r, John Tylee, Jun'r, Jos. Scattergood. Proved Oct. 5, 1750. Lib. 6, p. 377.

1734-5, Jan. 20. Shepherd, Daniel, of Cohansey, Salem Co., yeoman; will of. Wife, Deborah, executrix. Daughter, Sarah, my land and tenement in Cohansey; wife Deborah to have use thereof during widowhood. In case of death in nonage of said daughter, without lawful issue, above named premises shall descend to my brother Thomas. Witness—John Rementon, Elijah Bowen, Nathaniel Jenkins. Proved 26 April, 1735. Lib. 4, p. 35.

1734-5, March 10. Inventory (£212.15.3) includes cattle, horses and swine, Bible, and other books. Appraisers—John Reminton, Nathaniel Jenkins.

1742-3, March 11. Shepherd, Dickason, of Cohansey, Salem Co., yeoman; will of. Wife, Eve. Son-in-law, William Paulin, and daughter Patience, ½ of tract of land purchased of one Bolebee on Autuxet, joining end of Leancet Sockwell's land, and along south side of land that one Sturgeon dwells on, i. e., 200 acres of land and marsh to an Oyster Creek called "Sow and Piggs." Son, Stephen, remainder of said land lying upon N. W. side of Enoch and Thomas Shepherd's, joining Bedan's land; also piece of a marsh at the end where Sturgeon lives; also 200 acres of upland and marsh running down to the Bay, together with all my plantation and tract I now live on, and ½ of the tract purchased of Johnson (the other half being possessed by John Shepherd); also ½ of land and marsh on the south side of Cohansey Creek below Ayres, commonly called Smith's Islands. Son, Dickenson, ½ of land and marsh on Peter's Point; the other half heretofore given to Jonadab Shepherd, as by his deed doth appear; also land joining on the N. W. side of John Ogden, formerly belonging to Benoni Dare, and 200 acres of land and marsh joining on Jonadab's south side. The ½ of the personal estate to my son Dickinson and daughter Patience; the other ½ to my three sons, John, Stephen and Jonadab, together with my daughters, Ann and Eve. Executors—wife, Eve, and son Stephen. Witnesses—Joseph Reeve, Moses Shepherd, John Bee. Proved 28 Nov., 1749 (in Cumberland County). Lib. 6, p. 291.

1749, Nov. 21. Inventory (£142.14.10) includes books (£2.0.3), 20 head of cattle, etc. Appraisers—Abraham Smith, Mark Reeve.

1749, Feb. 26. Shepherd, Edward, of Manington, Salem Co. Int. Admr's, Peter Ryal and Thomas Handly. Bondsman—Benjamin Cripps. Lib. 7, p. 27.

1749, Feb. 27. Inventory, £89.11.1; made by Benja. Cripps, Wm. Murdock.

1749-50, Feb. 3. Shepherd, Eve, of Cohansie, Cumberland Co., gentlewoman, and widow of Dickason Shepherd; will of. Children—Stephen, Dickason, John, Jonadab, Eve Sakel, Ann and Pesiains (Patience). Executor—son, Stephen. Witnesses—Sarah Shepherd, Thomas Conner, Job Shepherd. Proved 12 March, 1749-50. Lib. 6, p. 309.

1749-50, March 6. Inventory, £74.11.5; made by Job Shepherd, Isaac Wheaten.

1747, June 17. Shepherd, Thomas, of Cohansey, Salem Co., yeoman; will of. Wife, Rachel, executrix, and to have personal estate. Sons—John (at 20), the land whereon I live and ½ of my land and marsh at Antucket, on condition that he pays £30 to my daughter Mary (at 18). Daniel, the land I purchased of John Bowen, and ½ of my land and marsh at Antucket upon the same condition. Witnesses—Job Shepherd, Joseph Shepherd, Nathaniel Jenkins. Proved 29 July, 1747. Lib. 5, p. 534.

1747, June 26. Inventory, £241.15.9; made by John Loyd, Philip Vickers.

1747-8, Feb. 6. Sherlock (Shearlock), James, of Monmouth Co. Int. Inventory, £58.19.9; made by Benjamin Fowler, John Cutler and Richard Herbert.

1748, Aug. 4. James Lawrence, administrator, sworn at Burlington. Lib. 5, p. 437.

1740, Feb. 25. Sherman, William, of Amwell, Hunterdon Co., yeoman. Int. Adm'x, Susannah Sherman, of Amwell, widow. William Montgomery, of same place, shop-keeper, surety. Witness—Archibald Horne, Jno. Park. Lib. 4, p. 288.

1741, May 1. Inventory (£85.12.2) includes debts of Jno. Wright, Jacob Frantz. Made by W. Montgomerie, Job Robins, William Allen (?).

1731, Dec. 6. Sherron, James, Esq., of Manington, Salem Co. Int. Estate left unadministered by Alexander Grant. Adm'r, Roger Sherron, only son of said James Sherron. Bondsman—John Doe, Richard Roe, Burlington. Witnesses—Joseph Rose, Saml. Bustil.

Lib. 3, p. 168.

1739, Aug. 21. Sherwin, James, of Chester, Burlington Co., yeoman. Int. Inventory, £199; made by Thomas Hackney and John Milburn.

1739, Dec. 3. Bond of Rebecca Sherwin, widow, as administratrix. Thomas Hackney and John Milbourne, both of Chester, yeomen, fellow bondsmen. Lib. 4, p. 200.

1741, May 16. Shields, William, of Salem Town and Co., carpenter. Int. Adm'x, Rachel Shields (widow). Bondsmen—Jonathan Walmsley, Esq., of said place, "shop-joyner." Witnesses—Daniel Smith, Chas. O Neill. Salem Wills, 652 Q.

1741, May 11. Inventory, £60; made by Jonathan Walmsley, Daniel Smith.

1741, March 18. Account. Cash paid William Crab, John Person, Danl. Smith, Thomas Gillingham, Martha Jerman, Chas. O Neill, William Murdock, Willm. Dawson, Saml. McCleland, Clemt. Hall, Jonathan Walmsley, Benjamin Acton, Thomas Shephard, Saml. Mason.

1745, April 15. Affirmation of Rachel Acton, late Rachel Shields.

1732, April 14. Shinn, George, of Greenwich, Gloucester Co., cooper; will of. Wife, Elizabeth, executrix and to have lands, Proprietary Rights and personal estate. Witnesses—Stephen Jones, Joseph Young, Alexander Randall. Proved June 16, 1732.

1732, May 29. Administration granted to Samuel Harrison, Esq., of Town and County of Gloucester, the widow, Elizabeth, having renounced. Bondsmen—Thos. Hunloke, Jos. Rockhill. Witness—Edward R. Price.

Lib. 3, p. 198.

1732, May 29. Inventory, £55; made by Joshua Lord, James Wills.

1736, Jan. 29. Shinn, John, of Springfield, Burlington Co.; will of. Wife, Mary. Children—Jacob and Caleb. Grandson, John, son of George Shinn, deceased. Real and personal estate. Executors—sons Jacob and Caleb, with my cousin, Samuel Shinn. Witnesses—Thomas Foster, Mary Bray, Thos. Shinn. Proved March 19, 1736.

Lib. 4, p. 91.

1736, March 17. Inventory, £244.16; made by Aaron Robins and John West.

1739, Aug. 7. Shippey, Gershom, of Windsor, Middlesex Co., yeoman; will of. Son, John, the great Bible and "Barclay's Apology" at 21. Daughters, Sarah and Ann, at 18. Real and personal estate. Executors—friends Benjamin Clarke, Jun'r, and John Clarke, yeomen (Quakers). Witnesses—Benja. Doughty, Thomas Marriot, Jun'r, Nath'll FitzRandolph. Proved Sept. 18, 1741. Lib. C, p. 439.

1744, Aug. 12. Shippy, Josiah, of Hopewell, Hunterdon Co., carpenter, "going to take a Voyge to See;" will of. Brother, Ishmael, real estate, tools, fire arms, gun and sword; he paying £12 to testator's mother. Brother-in-law, John Prise. Sisters—Elizabeth and Ursilah. Executor—brother, Ishmael. Witnesses—Sackett Moore, Benjamin Moore, John Moore. Proved Sept. 27, 1746. Lib. 5, p. 266.

1748, June 10. Shivers, Samuel, of Rackoon Creek, Gloucester Co., yeoman. Guardian to Henry Bickham (19 years and upwards), son of Richard, late of Gloucester Co. Bondsman—Beckman Loyd, of same place, yeoman. Gloucester Wills, 638 H.

1733, Sept. 22. Shoals, Humphrey, of Essex Co. Int. Adm'x, Hannah Whitehead, single-woman. Henry Haynes and John Styles, fellow bondsmen. Witness—John Ritchie. Lib. B, p. 468.

1733, June 20. Shores, Jonathan, of Newark, Essex Co., an orphan about 16 years of age. Bond of Samuel Harrison, Esq., as guardian. Eliphalet Johnson, fellow bondsman. Witness—Jno. Broughton. Essex Wills, 769-71 G.

1733, June 20. Shores, Peleg, of Essex Co. Int. Adm'r, Samuel Harrison. Samuel Peirson, of Newark, fellow bondsman. Lib. B, p. 421.

1744, Oct. 18. Shorten, Archibald, of Burlington Co., laborer. Int. Adm'r, John Grey, of Newton, Gloucester Co., farmer. Bondsman—Jonathan Axford, of Waterford, said County, farmer. Burlington Wills, 311 C.

1750, May 9. Shotwell, Abraham, of the Borough of Elizabeth, Essex Co. Int. Adm'rs, Peter Shotwell, the son and Henry Baker, principal creditor. Thomas Skinner, Jun'r, fellow bondsman. Lib. E, p. 397.

1732, Dec. 21. Shotwell, Daniel, of Woodbridge, Middlesex Co., yeoman; will of. Daughters—Mary, Martha, Susannah, Elizabeth and Margaret. Real and personal estate. Executors—sons Joseph, John and Abraham. Witnesses—Martha Caisson, Sissell Sarjant, Jno. Sarjant. Proved Jan. 30, 1735. Lib. C, p. 66.

1743, Oct. 31. Shotwell, John, of Woodbridge, Middlesex Co., yeoman; will of. Wife, Lydia. Children—Johanah Stelle, Elizabeth, Lydia, Mary, Prudence, John, Benjamin and Joseph. Land bought of John Ayres. Executors—son-in-law, Benja. Stelle, and friend Edward FitzRandolph. Witnesses—John Clarkson, Jonathan FitzRandolph, Benja. Stelle. Proved Feb. 14, 1745-6. Lib. D, p. 361.

1745-6, Mar. 6. Inventory of estate of "John Shotwell, who departed this life Nov. 16, 1745," £176.9.6; made by Joseph FitzRandolph and Jeremiah Drake.

1735, April 5. Shreve, Caleb, of Mansfield, Burlington Co., yeoman; will of. Wife, Sarah. Sons—Benjamin, Thomas, Joshua, Caleb, Jonathan and David. Daughters—Mary Gibbs and Sarah Ogburn. Son-in-law, Benjamin Scattergood. Granddaughter, Sarah, dau. of son Joshua. Goods bought at Preserved Brown's vendue. Real and personal estate. Executor—son Benjamin. Witnesses—Thomas Newbold, Barzillai Newbold, Nathan Richardson, Robert Bland. Proved Feb. 18, 1740. Lib. 4, p. 267.

1746, Oct. 22. Shreve, Caleb, of Springfield, Burlington Co.; will of. Wife, Ann. Children—Amos, Amy (wife of Josiah Gaskill), Rachel, Mary and Caleb. My cousin, Isaac Gibbs, living with me, I leave to my brother, Benjamin Shreve, whom I appoint executor and guardian of my children. Real and personal estate. Witnesses—Benjamin Carter, Robert Webb, Isaac DeCow, medius. Proved Dec. 10, 1746. Lib. 5, p. 291.

1746, Dec. 6. Inventory, £194.18.10½; made by Barzillai Newbold and John West.

1746, Feb. 23. Shreve, Thomas, of City of Burlington, innholder; will of. Wife, Elizabeth. Children—Mary Hilbourn, Hannah North, Elizabeth Tylee, Thomas, Caleb and Martha, the latter being yet an infant. Brick dwelling house on Hight Street now in tenure of my son-in-law, James Tylee. Other lands and personal estate. Executrix—wife, and sons Thomas and Caleb to assist their mother. Witnesses—Daniel Bacon, Fretwell Wright, Hugh Hartshorne. Proved July 14, 1747. Lib. 5, p. 362.

1747, Aug. 22. Inventory, £215.8.2; made by Rowland Ellis and William Lyndon. Includes silver watch, bond of Charles French, bill of Charles Tonkin, judgment against Capt. Thos. Farmer, and "moneys rec'd from the Treasury as Serg't-at-Arms, £126.8.5."

1734, Nov. 23. Sickles, Abraham, of Piscataway, Middlesex Co., yeoman; will of. Children—Abraham, Jacob (minor) and Mary Thickston. Real and personal estate. Executrix—wife, Elizabeth. Witnesses—James Campbell, William Clawson, Tho. Broderwick. Proved Dec. 19, 1744. Lib. D, p. 208.

1749, Oct. 9. Siddon, John, of Township of Deerfield, Cumberland Co., yeoman. Int. Adm'r, Zadok Thompson. Fellow bondsman—Mathew Parvin. Both of same place. Cumberland Wills, 50 F.

1732, Oct. 25. Siddon, Mary, of Town and County of Gloucester; will of. Sons—Henry (5 shillings) and Joy (to have 18 acres of land and meadow purchased of Thomas Sharp). Daughters—Sarah, Hannah (executrix) and Jane. Witnesses—John Gray, Sarah Kay, John Kay. Affirmed 27 Nov., 1735. Lib. 4, p. 44.

1735, Nov. 20. Inventory, £31.8.0; made by Ja. Hinchman, Jno. Hinchman.

1748, May 16. Sill, William, of Gloucester Co., guardian of William Sweetin (under 21), son of Andrew Sweetin of said County, deceased. Gloucester Wills, 403 H.

1746, Sept. 13. Silverthorn, Oliver, of Bethlehem, Hunterdon Co., yeoman; will of. Wife, Mary. Sons—John, Thomas and George. Executors—wife, and son William. Witnesses—Thomas Silverthorn, Edward Rockhill, Anne Rockhill. Proved Nov. 1, 1746. Lib. 5, p. 284.

1746, Oct. 25. Inventory (£119.07.04) includes sundries in old log house and cooper shop. Made by Edward Rockhill and Robert White.

1748, May 12. Account. Mentions Kemp and Palmer, Ganet Vanwagenen, Doct'r Edward Stevenson, John Bodine, Joseph Applegate, Andrew Reed, Charles Clark, David Martin, Sheriff, Bartholomew Kelsey, Robert Coborn, Joseph Parks, Samuel Hill, John Mullen.

1735-6, Jan. 10. Simkins, Ruth, of Cape May Co.; will of. "By these Presents do cutt off all former wills or deeds and appoint my son, William Simkins, sole executor and heir to all my moveable estate." Witnesses—Elizabeth Crowell, Hance Hamilton, Wm. Hamilton. Proved 1 June, 1736. Cape May Wills, 90 E.

1735-6, Feb. 16. Inventory, £8.17.6; made by Ebenezer Newton, Elisha Hand.

1743, Aug. 27. Sims, John, of Salem Co., yeoman. Int. Adm'x, Sarah Sims (widow). Bondsmen—Abner Sims, William Chanler, yeomen. All of said County. Witnesses—Benja. Eaten, Chas. O Neill.
Lib. 4, p. 371.

1743, Aug. 4. Inventory, £282.16.6; made by William Chanler, Benja. Eaton.

1729, Dec. 18. Sinicker, Johannas, of Piles Grove, Salem Co., husbandman; will of. Wife, Gartrow, one-third, and my plantation so long as unmarried, and shall maintain my son Isaac "if he remains in the condition he now is." Son, Stephen, residue of moveable estate and in plantation if my wife marries again or at her decease. In case of his death without any heir, same unto my daughter, Susannah. One shilling to my sons Isaac and Andrew, and to my daughter Bridget. Executors—wife, Gartrow, and son Stephen. Witnesses—Sinick Sinickson, John Sinickson, Willm. Peake. Proved 26 May, 1735.
Lib. 4, p. 29.

1735, May 26. Inventory, £30.18; made by Willm. Peake, Tim. Rain.

1739, Nov. 3. Sinnick, John, of Penns Neck, Salem Co., yeoman; will of. Wife, Ann, to have whole estate during widowhood. Son, John, all of my lands and tenements, and to pay £5 to my daughter Sarah and my son Sinneck Sinnickson (to whom said property shall descend in case of the death of my son John). Executors—wife, with my brother Sinnick Sinnickson. Witnesses—William Philpot, Earick Gilljohnson, Owney Stanley. Proved 1 Dec., 1739. Lib. 4, p. 210.

1739, Dec. 1. Inventory, £136.16.2; includes gun and sword. Appraisers—Jeremiah Baker, William Philpot.

1750, June 23. Sinnick, Sinnickson, of Penns Neck, Salem Co., yeoman; will of. Wife, Mary. Son, Andrew, executor and to have my plantation that I live on and my carpenter tools. £20 to my daughter Sarah, at 21 or marriage; also that plantation at the river side that I purchased of the Loan office in Penns Neck, which Richard Ashton now lives on; likewise 40 acres of woodland and swamp. If no lawful issue, same shall descend to my daughter Ann, to whom I give the place where she and her husband Peter Peterson live, joining a corner between me and Baker, including all the land belonging to me binding on Earick Gilljohnson's line and for want of lawful issue to the lawful heirs of my daughter Sarah. Witnesses—Jno. Dickson, Benjamin Bacon, Ann Vaniman, Jno. Marshall. Proved 28 July, 1750.
Lib. 6, p. 404.

1750, July 27. Inventory, £206.13.6; made by Joseph Wright Jno. Marshall.

1729, Apr. 11. Sipp, John, of Bergen, Bergen Co., yeoman; will of. Eldest son, Arya, plantation at Acquackanong, Essex Co., whereon he now dwells, containing 100 acres (in first division), bounded east by Passayack River, N. by land belonging formerly to John Spier, W. by my own land, S. a by-way between the land of Juryansee and my own; also ½ of my second division of land (50 acres) adjoining the first mentioned tract at the westerly end, N. by land of John Spier, S. by aforesaid by-way; also ½ of a tract within the bounds of Newark at the mountain, purchased of Gershom Gardner, deed dated 18 April, 1718. Son, Edee, all my lands and rights of lands divided or undivided in commonage in the town and county of Bergen with all the improvements; also the ½ of the before mentioned land in the bounds of Newark, which I bought of Gersham Gardner; also ½ of the second division at Acquackanong, containing 50 acres, at the west end of the lot bounded E. by the half given to Arya. Sons Arya and Edee (Edward) to pay £250 each to my four daughters (or their heirs), viz, Helegont (wife of Johanas Walingsee), Margaret (wife of Johanes Garitsee), Lena (wife of John Vanhorn), within six years after my decease. Wife, Anatia, executrix, and to have sole use and improvement of real and personal estate during life, as well as that part above given to my sons Ayra and Edee. Witnesses—J. Cooper, Adr. Vermeule, Robert Syckels. Proved 8 Oct., 1734. Lib. B, p. 569.

1748, Jan. 2. Skeen, Jonas, of Penns Neck, Salem Co. Int. Adm'r, Andrew Dalbo. Bondsman—Alexander King. Both of same place. Witness—Wm. Baker. Lib. 6, p. 52.

1748, Dec. 10. Inventory, £40.18; made by Alexander King, Gabriel Dalbow.

1750, April 5. Skinner, Elizabeth, widow of John Skinner, late of Woodbridge, Middlesex Co.; will of. Household goods to be priced by my sisters, Sarah Jaquesh and Esther Marsh. Five daughters, mentioned but not named, all under age. Executor—brother-in-law, Charles Marsh. Witnesses—Sarah Jaquess, Andrew Gray, David Donham, Jun'r. Proved April 13, 1750. Lib. E, p. 382.

1725, July 12. Skinner, John, Sen'r, of Woodbridge, Middlesex Co., yeoman; will of. Children—Catte, John, Daniel, Richard, Benjamin, Ann and Mary, last five under age. Land at Woodbridge. Executors —wife, Ann, and son John Skinner. Witnesses—Ezekiel Bloomfield, Esther Bloomfield, William Hidor. Proved Aug. 19, 1749. (Affidavit by William Hidor, only surviving witness to above will). Lib. E, p. 320.

1748-9, Feb. 14. Skinner, John, of Woodbridge, Middlesex Co., yeoman; will of. Wife, Elizabeth. Youngest child, Elizabeth, at 15 years, "that will be the space of 12 years and 3 months." Four daughters, now living, all under age. Expected child. Executors—friend, David Donham, Jun'r, brother Richard Skinner, and wife's brother, William Cutter. Witnesses—William Brown, Ebenezer Gray, Andrew Gray. Proved March 9, 1748-9. Lib. E, p. 264.

1748-9, March 10. Inventory (after the widow has taken her legacy of £100), £312.02.6; made by Samuel Moore and Henry Baker of the borough of Elizabeth.

1751, July 29. Additional cash, £7.19.6 (£4 being in the hands of Wright Skinner). Sworn to by David Donham, Richard Skinner, William Cutter.

1732, Dec. 15. Skinner, William, of Manington Precinct, Salem Co., husbandman; will of. "My unworthy wife, one shilling." Legacy to servant-boy, William Marshall, and John Robeson. Gifts to Mary Haynes (daughter of Sarah Simpson), and Ann, Rebecca and Martha Simpson (daughters of Alexr. Simpson and Sarah his wife). Mary Watkins to be maintained out of the estate during her life. Gifts to Sarah (daughter of John Hughs), Thomas Haynes, James Nickson, Ann Campbell, Andrew Peterson and to Daniel and John Haynes (sons of the abovesaid Sarah Simpson). Executor—my friend Alexr. Simpson, and unto him all my lands and tenements. Witnesses—

Hannah Miller, Alexander Miller, Thomas Baker. Proved 25 Dec., 1732. Lib. 3, p. 264.

1732-3, 11 mo. (Jan.), 17 da. Inventory (£222.3.9) includes cattle, £118.10, and 90 sheep, £18. Appraisers—William Hunt, Joseph Pledger.

1747, Aug. 28. Skirm, Richard, of Nottingham, Burlington Co. Int. Adm'x, Elizabeth Skirm, widow. John Allen, of Trenton, sadler, surety. Witness—Benjamin Taylor. (Hunterdon Wills), 204 J.

1727, Oct. 27. Inventory of estate of Richard Skirm, fuller, (£129.7.0) includes clock, £5, 2 Bibles, 2 guns, press papers, dye stuff and log wood, 3 bbls. of soap. Made by David Dunbar and John Yard.

1746, Jan. 12. Slaght, Cornelius, of Piscataway, Middlesex Co., yeoman. Int. Adm'x, Elizabeth Slaght, the widow. Gideon Merlett, of Somerset Co., fellow bondsman. Witness—John Pound, Jun'r. Lib. D, p. 445.

1736, Jan. 8. Sleeper, Hannah, widow of Jonathan Sleeper, of Bridgetown, Burlington Co.; will of. My share (being one-eighth) of the grist mill left me by my husband, to be divided amongst my children—Jonathan, John, Mary and Leah, all under age. Executor—Thomas Shinn, Esq., of Bridgetown. Witnesses—Peter Andrews, Simon Battin, John Geary. Proved Jan. 24, 1736. Lib. 4, p. 82.

1736, Jan. 17. Inventory, £111.5.10; made by Sam'll Shinn and Peter Andrews. Includes debt due by John Perkins.

1736, Jan. 24. Sleeper, John, eldest son of Jonathan Sleeper, of Burlington Co., and under 14. Thomas Shinn appointed his guardian. Lib. 4, p. 83.

1736, May 3. Sleeper, Jonathan, of Bridgetown, Burlington Co., carpenter. Int. Inventory, £116.2; made by Sam'll Shinn and Peter Andrews. Hannah Sleeper, widow, affirmed to above May 10, 1736.

1736, Jan. 24. Administration granted to Thos. Shinn, Esq., on estate left unadministered by Hannah Sleeper, widow, at the time of her death. John Doe, fellow bondsman. Lib. 4, p. 63.

1735, Dec. 19. Slocum, John, of Shrewsbury, Monmouth Co., ship-carpenter; will of. Wife, Susannah, use of plantation; also negro Jo. Son, John, plantation adjoining Peter Parker, Edward Pattison Cook and John Hulit. Son, Peter, land adjoining Samuel Slocum, late deceased. Son, Jonathan. Daughters—Hannah and Meribah, when aged 18. Executors—wife, and kinsman Josiah Parker. Witnesses—Bartholomew West, Nathaniel Slocum, Francis Brinley. Proved Dec. 10, 1736. Lib. C, p. 136.

1736, March 23. Inventory (£299.11.6) includes loom and tackling, white servant, £15, and negro boy, £40. Made by Peter Parker and Jacob Wardell.

1746, Aug. 16. Slocum, Jonathan, aged 15 years. Bond of Benjamin Parker, of Shrewsbury, Monmouth County, as guardian. Lib. D, p. 402.

1732, Aug. 22. Slocum, Samuel, of Shrewsbury Town, Monmouth Co.; will of. Wife, Deborah. Son, Nathaniel, land "below where negro Gibey now dwells," to my brother John's line. Son, Amasiah, land adjoining Stofild Longstreet. Son, Pelick, land adjoining John Hulit. Son, Samuel. Daughters—Eathaliah and Margaret. Testator's mother to live in his house. Executors—friend, George Williams, and Eaphram Allin. Witnesses—Mary Allin, William Cradock, John Slocum. Proved August 2, 1733. Lib. B, p. 455.

1737, July 28. Smalley, Benjamin, of Piscataway, Middlesex Co., yeoman. Int. Adm'x, Mercy Smalley, the widow. John King, of same place, fellow bondsman. Lib. E, p. 66.

1749, May 6. Smalley, Isaac, of Piscataway, Middlesex Co., taylor; will of. Wife, Hannah. My mother to live in my house. Brothers and sisters—Benjamin, Joshua, John, Susannah and Lydia Smalley. Land bought of Thomas Lewis. Executors—friends Daniel Drake and Joseph FitzRandolph, Jun'r. Witnesses—John Holton, John Molleson, Reune Runyon. Proved May 22, 1749. Lib. E, p. 304.

1749, May 19. Inventory (£38.19.7) includes Bible, and cash in the hands of John Smalley, son of Jonathan Smalley, John Dennis, William Rogers, George Lang, James Piatt. Made by John Hepburn and Zachariah Bonham.

1731, Sept. 13. Smalley, John, of Piscataway, Middlesex Co., yeoman; will of. Wife, Liddea. Sons—Jonathan, Elisha and Benjamin. Daughters and daughters-in-law to have personal estate at death of my wife. Executors—son, Jonathan, and friend Benja'n Stelle. Lands bought of Hezekiah Bonham, Joseph Gilman, and Benjamin Cull. Witnesses—William Hooks, Samuel Slater, Elizabeth Garner. Proved May 25, 1733. Lib. B, p. 408.

1736-7, Feb. 2. Smalley, Joseph, of Piscataway, Middlesex Co., yeoman; will of. Children—Isaac, Ester, Lucy, Susannah, Lideah, Joseph, Benjamin, Joshua and John, all under age. Wife, Ann. Real and personal estate. 50 acres joining land of Benjamin Hull, Esq. Executors—brother, Joshua Smalley, and friend Joseph Randolph. Witnesses—Hendrick Johnson, Benjamin Grose, Joshua Smalley. Proved March 2, 1736-7. Lib. C, p. 152.

1731, Aug. 25. Smalley, Thomas, of Piscataway, Middlesex Co., husbandman; will of. Wife, Jane. Bequests "to the poorest people in the town." Executors—Benjamin Martin, Jun'r, and Henry Skibbow. Witnesses—Peter Ferwell, John Peters, Alathea Skibbow. Proved Dec. 15, 1731. Lib. B, p. 234.

1732, Dec. 11. Smith, Abigail, of Cape May Co., widow of Thomas Smith. Int. Adm'r, Aaron Leaming. Witnesses—Saml. Bustil, Robert Davis.

1732, Nov. 17. "Ebenezer Johnson, Phebe Johnson and Abigail Johnson, children of the said deceased by her former husband, Samuel Johnson, have renounced their right in favor of Aaron Leaming." Lib. 3, p. 227.

1748, August 8. Smith, Abraham, of Upper Freehold, Monmouth Co., carpenter. Int. Inventory, £34.7.9; appraisers' names not shown. Elizabeth Smith, the widow, requests administration be granted to her father-in-law, Thomas Smith, to whom letters issue. Lib. 6, p. 326.

1744, Oct. 10. Smith, Alexander, of Greenwich, Morris Co., yeoman. Int. Adm'r, John Axford, of same place, yeoman. Josiah Appleton, cooper, and David Dunbar, blacksmith, both of Trenton, Hunterdon County, sureties. Witnesses—William Yard, Jr., Jno. Clark. (Hunterdon Wills), 173 J.

1731, Oct. 1. Smith, Anne, of Burlington Co., spinster. Adm'r, George Eyre. Thomas Bryan, fellow bondsman. Both of Town and Co. of Burlington. Burlington Wills, 2173 C.

1731, 5th day, 11 month (Jan.). Smith, Benjamin, of Woodbridge, Middlesex Co., planter; will of. Children, John (at 21); Esther (at 20 years the 6d, 11mo., 1743); Elizabeth (at 20 years the 6d, 11mo., 1745); Sarah (at 20 years the 6d, 11mo., 1747); Mary and Abraham. Land bought of John Ayers, Jun'r, and James Smith, June 11, 1722, and Feb. 21, 1729; land bought of Moses Rolph Nov. 19, 1711; land bought of Samuel Lewis and John Loofborrow; bonds from Edward Freeman and Edward Harned; cows in the care of Nathan'll Harned and Moses Freeman. Executors—wife (not named), and brothers John and Abraham Shotwell. Witnesses, Sam'll Smith, Elizabeth Laing, Thomas Young. Proved June 8, 1732. Lib. B, p. 268.

1731, Oct. 29. Smith, Benjamin, of Woodbridge, Middlesex Co.; will of. Children—Legget, Ichabod, Ephraim, Thomas, Mary and Sarah, all under 14. Real and personal estate. Executors—wife, Elizabeth, brother Ichabod Smith, and friend John Vail. Witnesses—Sam'll Moores, Peter Savery, John Gifford. Proved Dec. 26, 1732. Lib. B, p. 343.

1744, Sept. 25. Smith, Charles, of Hopewell Township, Hunterdon Co., farmer. Int. Adm'r, George Smith, of Hopewell, farmer. Jonathan Hunt, of Hopewell, farmer, surety. Witness—George Murray. Lib. 5, p. 47.

1744, Mar. 15. Inventory (£69.10.3) includes gun, sword and belt; 1 Bible, bound with brass, and 1 ditto. Made by Ralph Hunt and John Fidler.

1742, 27th day, 1st mo. (March). Smith, Daniel, of City of Burlington, merchant; will of. Wife, Mary. Sons—Daniel, Robert and Benjamin. Daughters, Katharine (wife of William Calinder), house I bought of Ebenezer Large in City of Philadelphia. 100 acres on High Street in New Hanover, which I bought of William Dean. I have agreed to sell Thomas Saint between 400 and 500 acres in New Hanover for £200, to whom deed to be given. Wife, executrix. Witnesses—William Murfin, Caleb Raper, Isa. DeCow. Proved Aug. 11, 1742. Lib. 4, p. 338.

1747, Jan. 5. Smith, Daniel, of Manington, Salem Co., carpenter; will of. Children—Seath, Anne, Solomon, John, Daniel and Benjamin, ten shillings apiece when 21. Rest of my estate to wife, Elizabeth, executrix. Witnesses—John Lumley, William Barratt. Proved 24 Feb., 1748-9. Lib. 6, p. 288.

1748-9, Feb. 22. Inventory, £345.16.11; made by William Murdock, John Barker.

1731, April 3. Smith, David, of Salem Town and Co., cooper. Int. Adm'x, Sarah Smith. Bondsmen—Clement Hall, John Doe, same place. Witness—John Rolfe. Salem Wills, 491 Q.

1731, April 27, 28. Inventory, £85.15.9½; made by John Savidge, Jno. Goodwin.

1731-2, Feb. 12. Account. Paid John Rolfe, Esq., Clement Hall, John Peck, John Johnson, Warrick Rundle, Owen Dayly, Wm. Murdock, Nathan Merem, Jos. Test, Wm. Hunt, John Colebrook. Nathan Tottin and "Laughlin Follin, who is run away."

1744-5, Jan. 16. Smith, Elias, of Allentown, Monmouth Co., yeoman; will of. Son, Josiah, debt due from Joseph Steniard of Philadelphia for lot in Allentown, less money paid Robert Lawrence. Daughters—Martha Hicks and Sarah Williams. Granddaughter, Abigail Hicks, daughter of Stephen Hicks, when aged ten; if she dies, to eldest daughter of testator's daughter, Sarah Williams, then living. Younger children—Merium, Ruth, Jacamiah and Elias. Executors—daughter, Merium, son-in-law John Hicks, and friend John Quicksell. Witnesses—Moses Robins, Bartho. West, Will Lawrence. Proved Dec. 24, 1746. Lib. 5, p. 294.

1746, Dec. 13. Inventory, £184.17.6; made by Bartho. West and Moses Robins.

1736, Feb. 5. Smith, Ezekiel, Jr., of Windsor Township, Middlesex Co., yeoman; will of. Wife, Margaret. Children—Martha, Elizabeth and Ezekiel (all under age). Executors—the wife, father Ezekiel Smith, and John Clarke. Witnesses—James Clarke, John Smith, Benjamin Clarke, Jr. Proved April 22, 1737. Lib. C, p. 161.

1742, 10 mo. (Dec.), 2nd da. Smith, Francis, of Waterford, Gloucester Co., yeoman; will of. Executors—wife, Rachel, Samuel Clemens and William Foster. Daughter, Rebeccah, £25. Home plantation to be sold before my son Aaron will be 21. He to have £25. Wife to have profits of real and personal estate until children will be of age. She to have one-third of the estate (minus Rebecah's £25) if she marries. Residue to be divided equally among sons—Aron, Thomas, Daniel, Samuel and my daughter Sarah. Witnesses—Thomas Redman, David Elwell, Benja'n Holme. Affirmed 10 Jan., 1742-3. Lib. 4, p. 352.

1742, 10 mo. (Dec.), 25 da. Inventory (£190.15.0) includes a servant lad, £10. Appraisers—Timo. Matlack, David Elwell.

1731-2, Feb. 26. Smith, George, of Northampton, Burlington Co., husbandman. Int. Hannah Smith, widow, renounces, and requests John Bennet may be appointed administrator. Lib. 3, p. 185.

1731-2, March 1. Inventory, £29.6.1; made by Tho: Shinn and Samuel Woolston.

1731-2, March 4. Bond of John Bennet, husbandman, as administrator. Thomas Shinn, Esq., and Richard Roe, gent., fellow bondsmen. All of same place.

1734, Feb. 28. Smith, Hugh, "within age," eldest son and heir-at-law of Ralph Smith, of Burlington, mariner, and Olive his wife (also deceased), makes choice of Mr. Samuel Scattergood, of Burlington, shopkeeper, and Mr. Paul Watkinson, of same, cordwainer, as guardians. Burlington Wills, 2777 C.

1750, May 11. Smith, Ichabod, of Woodbridge, Middlesex Co., yeoman. Int. Adm'rs, Reuben Potter and David Perkins, both of Woodbridge, sons-in-law of said deceased. Richard RitzRandolph, of Perth Amboy, fellow bondsman. Witnesses—Thos. Alston, Thos. Bartow. Lib. E, p. 399.

1750, May 16. Inventory includes bond of Joseph Freeman, and debts due from Sam'll Duglas and William Pangborn. Made by Joseph Shotwell and Joseph Freeman.

1746-7, Feb. 10. Smith, Isaac, of Newtown, Gloucester Co., blacksmith. Int. Adm'x, Elizabeth Smith, widow. Bondsmen—John Cox, blacksmith, and Thomas Atkinson, both of Burlington Co. Witnesses —Nathan Lovett, Jo. Scattergood. Lib. 5, p. **464.**

1746-7, Jan. 27. Inventory (£475.19.7) includes, in the smithshop, tools and bellows anvils, £43.15.10. Appraisers—John Kaighin, Jno. Cox.

1758, Sept. 29. Account of John Hinchman and Elizabeth his wife, late Elizabeth Smith, on estate of Isaac Smith. Paid to Dad. Sonmon, Saml. Collins, William Smith, John Collins, James Wills, John Gill, Philip Dide, Abel James, Joseph Mclean, Williard Burdge, John Justice, Saml. Mickle, Rebecca Heartley, John Maxwell, Joseph Morgan, Eliz. Craig. Mary Bassett, William Cranson, James Atmore, James Bate, John Kay, Thomas Edgerton, Simeon Ellis, John Hinchman, Elizabeth Woolman, Adam Somers, John Hedger, Isaac Kay, John Parock, Benjamin Frankline, James Hinchman, Timothy Matlack, Uriah Trench, William Rush, James Robson, Thomas Treadman, James Salmon, James Childs, John Bood, Samuel Lippincott, John Kaign, Mary Cooper, Isaac Jennings, Caleb Sprague, Elizabeth Estaugh, George Mifflinn, Thomas Atmore. (Total, £614.13.10).

1748, August 9. Smith, Isaac, of Upper Freehold, Monmouth Co., laborer. Int. Adm'r, Jacob Smith. Lib. 6, p. 326; Lib. 7, p. 93.

1748, ——, —. Inventory (£28.9.0) includes 4 gownes, one bonnet, pair stays, gun and sword, or cutlas. (No names signed).

1732, Oct. 30. Smith, James, Esq., late Secretary of the Province. "Inventory as the same was found at the Opening of his Scritore and Chests at the Point house in Burlington, £1282.14;" made by Jno. Allen, Isaac Pearson, Mahlon Stacy. Gold and paper money, £76.14.6. Sword, silver watch and pair of pistols, etc. Moneys due on securities in hands of Wm. Smith, and a negro boy. Burlington Wills, 2395 C.

1737, Oct. 1. Smith, James, of Northampton, Burlington Co., yeoman; will of. Wife, Mary, dwelling house and 30 acres adjoining William Haines. Daughter of son, George, late deceased. Other children, not named. Real and personal estate. Executors—friends William Haines and his son Jeremiah. Witnesses—John Butcher, Sam'l Brian, Tho. Shinn. Proved Nov. 14, 1739. Lib. 4, p. 179.

1739, Nov. 12. Inventory, £22.2; made by Sam'l Shinn and Pe't Andrews.

1734, Nov. 24. Smith, Jeremiah, of Salem Co.; will of. Wife, Sarah. Son, Jeremiah, land I live on, excepting 150 acres taken off next Mill Creek. Son, Job, at 21, tract adjoining Dan. Smith's (excepting 50 acres). Daughters—Sarah, Elizabeth and Mary. Executors—wife, and sons Job and Jeremiah. Witnesses—Francis Test, William Hogbin. Proved 9 Oct., 1735. Lib. 4, p. 43.

1735, Oct. 9. Inventory (£848.17.10) taken at Alloways Creek. Made by Francis Test, John Fitzpatrick.

1748, Aug. 23. Smith, Jeremiah, of Middlesex Co. Int. Admr's, Hepzebath Smith, the widow, and William Linn, of Hunterdon Co. The Inventory amounts to £157.01.8. Lib. 5, p. 492.

1743, March 22. Smith, John, of Alloways Creek, Salem Co.; will of. Only son, Samuel, the tract left me by my father and £20 for his schooling; wife, Mary, to have use of it during widowhood. Land bought of Michael Walker and moveable estate divided equally between my wife and my daughters, viz., Mary, Ann, Margret, Jean and Hannah (unnamed yet; but it is my desire that it may be Hannah). Land called Turkey Hill to be sold for the bringing up of my children; if wife marries, a share shall be allotted for each child. Executors—wife, my cousin Daniel Smith, of Alloways Creek, and Edward Quinton. Witnesses—Benja. Wallace, William Carr, Sam. Purviance. Proved 1 May, 1744. (No inventory). Lib. 5, p. 42.

1747-8, March 1. Smith, John, of Maidenhead Township, Hunterdon Co., yeoman; will of. Wife, Hannah. Son, John, plantation, when of age, when testator's wife is to remove to the house and plantation on west side of the Five Mile Run. Son, Thomas, when of age, plantation on west side of Five Mile Run. Daughters—Mary, Elizabeth, Susanna, Hannah, Sarah and Prescilla. Executors—brother-in-law, William Waters, and John Ely, Sr., of Maidenhead. Witnesses—Joshua Smith, William Ball, Peter Verdal. Proved May 4, 1748. Lib. 5, p. 446.

———, ——, —. Inventory (£800.10.6) includes clock, £11; 1 doz. silver spoons, £10.15.0; 2 guns and a sword; a negro man, £62.10; debt of John Jones. Made by Henry Mershon and Samuel Baker. Also bonds due the estate: John Jones, Thomas Marriett, Philip Pammer, Joseph Everitt, John Everitt, Daniel Laning, Benjamin Slecht, Joseph Titus, Mathis Baker, Sackett Moore, Joseph Jones, Jeremiah Anderson, Abner Phillips, Nathan Moore, Mathis Baker, Thomas Hooten, Alburt Updick, Andrew Morehead, Joseph Baras, Timothy Baker, John Price, Ralph Hunt, Henry Ballerien, Samuel Smith, Anthony Cook, Samuel Baker, Joshua Bawn (or Prawn).

1746-7, Feb. 19. Smith, John, of Perth Amboy, Middlesex Co., mariner. Int. Adm'x, Elizabeth Smith, widow. Thos. Skinner, baker, and Thos. Inglis, fellow bondsmen. Lib. D, p. 453.

1746-7, March 2. Smith, John, of New Brunswick, Middlesex Co.; will of. Son, John, four acres and brick yard; other children mentioned, but not named. Moses, son of my brother Moses Smith. Executors—wife, Mary, Derrick Skyler and Reuben Runyon. Witnesses—William Blane, John Stilwill, Jeremiah Stilwill. Proved March 4, 1747-8. Lib. E, p. 139.

———, ——, —. Smith, John, of Mappleton, Middlesex Co.; will of. Wife, Mary. Children—John, Peter, Edward and Jemyma Smith. Real and personal estate. Witnesses—Tho. Leonard, Hugh Scott, Geone Ore.

1749, June 7. Thomas Leonard, Esq., one of the witnesses, deposed that about 16 years ago he saw John Smith, the testator, sign and seal the same, and that Hugh Scot and Jean Ore left the Province of New Jersey several years ago, and cannot now be found.

1749, July 7. Administration on the estate granted to his widow, Mary Smith. Lib. 6, p. 64.

1749, July 17. Smith, John, of Amwellberry, Salem Co., yeoman; will of. Plantation I live on "to be divided so as to strike the middle of the land at the head next to that part left to my brother Richard, by my father," together with my town meadow and 6 acres that I bought of George Trenchard, one-third of my salt marsh at Alloways

Creek, the town lot and the remainder I purchased of George Trenchard—all to my son Richard. My plantation as far northerly as the road to Elsinburrough, with one-third of the salt marsh, to my son Hill. My town lot (12 acres) with 6½ acres joining Edward Keasby and the remainder of the Trenchard purchase and salt marsh, to my son John, at 21. Wife, Sarah, £100. Personal estate equally divided among three sons at 21, or survivors. Executors—wife, and brother-in-law, Charles Davis. Witnesses—Samuel Nicholson, Richard Smith, Geo. Trenchard. Affirmed 19 Aug., 1749. (No inventory).

Lib. 9, p. 59.

1741, July 22. Smith, Margaret, of Monmouth Co., widow. Int. Adm'r, James Napier, of Freehold, merchant, principal creditor. John Smith, of Freehold, merchant, fellow bondsman. Lib. C, p. 426.

1741, July 28. Inventory, £41.8.8; made by John Smith, William Rogers.

1734, Jan. 6. Smith, Ralph, of Burlington, boatman. Int. Adm'r, Joseph Peirce. Edward Peirce and William Bickley, gentlemen, fellow bondsmen. Burlington Wills, 2779 C.

1750, June 8. Smith, Rebecca, of Burlington Co., widow. Int. Adm'x, Ann Carlile, of City of Burlington, widow. Thomas Scattergood, Esq., of same, fellow bondsman. Lib. 7, p. 29.

1750, June 14. Inventory, £82.13.6; made by Thos. Scattergood and Elias Hughes.

1738, Nov. 11. Smith, Richard, of Salem Co., guardian of Hannah Darkin (daughter of Joseph Darkin, late of Elsinborough, yeoman), with consent of her step-mother, Hannah Darkin (the widow) and of her cousin, Sarah Wyat. Lib. 4, p. 150.

1740, Feb. —. Smith, Richard, Esq., of Elsinborough, Salem Co.; will of. Sons—John, the plantation (600 acres) called Amblebery that I live on, excepting what I shall hereafter dispose of; also 12 acres in Salem; Richard (not 21), the plantation (220 acres) that was formerly John Pain's, of Alloways Creek; also 150 acres of the plantation called Ambleberry; and Merriman (not 21), the plantation (400 acres) that George Trenchard (lived on ?), deceased, situate in Alloways Creek. Daughters—Mary, lot in Salem adjoining the house lot of Edward Test at Margate's lane (so-called); Grace, 4 acres in Salem, on the road to Alloways Creek Bridge, that Daniel Smith lives on. My daughters, Rachel and Sarah Dennis, shall share with the above named heirs in all the lands and profits due me from my right in Patomack, in the province of Virginia. Sons and above unmarried daughters shall share equally in the lands at Cohansey or elsewhere, depending between myself, John Wright and Clement Hall; also said daughters, Mary and Grace Smith, at 18 or marriage, to have £200. Negroes allotted. Executors—sons, John and Richard, dau., Mary. Witnesses—Andrew Gardiner, Jos. Clowes, Edmund Winder. Proved 11 March, 1740.

1740, March 11. Letters granted to John and Mary Smith (Quakers), (Richard Smith being 13 years old). Lib. 4, p. 271.

1740, 1 mo. (Mar.), 20 da. Inventory (£1073.10.11.1.2) includes negroes, Sharper, £20; Franck, £40; Phillis, £30; Dick, £17; Dinah, £10; cattle and sheep, £104.16. Appraisers—Samuel Abbott, Thomas Hill.

1750, Dec. 25. Smith, Richard, Jr., of Burlington, merchant; will of.

Children—Samuel, John, William Lovel, Richard, Elizabeth; grandchildren—Abigail, Sarah and Sarah Logan Smith; Joseph and James Smith. Legacy to friend Sarah Morris. Executors—sons Samuel, John and William Lovel Smith. Witnesses——Joseph Noble and Joseph Clowes. Proved ———, 1750-1.

Burlington Wills, pp. 4875-8 C.

1733, May 26. Smith, Samuel, of Burlington Co.; will of. Children mentioned but not named, all under age. Real and personal estate. Executors—wife, Elizabeth, brother Armstrong Smith, and cousin Armstrong Smith. Witnesses—Peter Bard, Thomas Leeds, Aaron Lovett. Proved July 18, 1733. Lib. 3, p. 351.

1737, 10 mo. (Dec.), 5 da. Smith, Sam'l, Esq., of Maninton, Salem County; will of. Son, Pile Smith, the plantation I live on and £50. The plantation purchased of Roger Sherron to be sold to pay charge of the law-suit now depending about Pile Grove and what remains to be equally divided among my daughters, Hannah, Elizabeth and Mary Ann. Wife, Hannah, lot in Salem where John Turner lives, use of the plantation where I live during widowhood and to share equally with said daughters in rest of moveable estate. Executors—wife, Hannah, John Kinsey, atty.-at-law in Phila., and Isaac Sharp, of Piles Grove. Witnesses—John Powell, Joseph Ward, Richard Bradford. Affirmed 27 Dec., 1737.

1738, May 30. Letters granted Hannah Smith and Isaac Sharp, in the absence of John Kinsey. Lib. 4, p. 139.

1737-8, 12 mo. (Feb.), 15 da. Inventory (£1,306.19.6) includes law books and other books, £5; negroes, Dick and Toby, £55; 6 other negroes, £100; cattle, £98; sheep and hogs, £42.18; horses, £50; pair of oxen, £48, etc. Appraisers—William Hunt, John Powell.

1748, Dec. 27. Smith, Samuel, of Elizabeth Town, Essex Co. Int. Adm'rs, Mercy Smith, the widow, and John Webster. Richard Fitz-Randolph, of Perth Amboy, fellow bondsman. Witness—Robert Fitz-Randolph. Lib. E, p. 231.

1739, June 9. Smith, Solomon, of City of Burlington, carpenter; will of. Wife, Sarah. Son, Thomas, lot on York Street. Daughter, Anne, lot on York Street and Assiscunk Creek. Son, Samuel. Lot adjoining Jonathan Wright and other lands (fully described in maps attached to will). Executors—friends, Jonathan Wright and Thomas Scattergood, Jun'r. Witnesses—Isa. DeCow, Caleb Raper, Rich'd, Smith, Jun'r, Marmaduke Watson, Edw'd Peirce. Proved Sept. 28, 1739.

1739, Sept. 9. Thomas Scattergood, Jun'r, refuses executorship.

Lib. 4, p. 190.

1739, Aug. 22. Inventory, £869.3.10½; made by Rob't Smith, Sam'l Scattergood and Jos. Scattergood. Includes goods at Edward Noble's and William Petty's. James Godfrey's time by indenture. Bonds of George Eyre and Thomas Worrell. Bills of Sam'l Gaskin, Katherine Talbold, Fretwell Wright, Joseph Pancoast. One large folio Bible; "Sacred History," in 2 vols.; "Barclay's Apology" and the "History of Thomas Ellwood's Life."

1742, Dec. 13. Jonathan Wright hath dyed since Solomon Smith, and appointed in his last will as executors Caleb Raper, Samuel Lovet and Joshua Raper who have declined to accept the executorship. Bond of Sarah Smith, of City of Burlington, widow, and Richard Smith, Jun'r, of same, merchant, as administrators on estate, left unadministered by Jonathan Wright. Lib. 4, p. 326.

1748, March 14. Smith, Solomon, of Greenwich Township, Cumberland Co., yeoman. Int. Adm'r, Daniel Fithian. Fellow bondsman—Jonathan Stathem. Witness—Timothy Brooks.
Cumberland Wills, 15 F.

1748-9, March 13. Inventory, £38.2.4; made by Jonathan Stathem, Ashbury Smith.

1731, Dec. 28. Smith, Thomas, of Cape May Co., yeoman; will of. Wife, Abigail. Sons, Thomas and Christopher Smith, my lands, equally, when of age. Son, Anthony, a double portion of my moveable estate, when of age. Daughters—Margery, Jerusha, Ruth and Alathare. Executors, "friends and brother," William Smith and Henry Young. Witnesses—Elizabeth Crowell, John Thomson, John Thompson, Jun'r. Proved 13 May, 1732. Lib. 3, p. 217.

1732, April 13. Inventory (£119.00.6) includes cattle, (£54), and "half a shalop and a cannew," (£5.15.0). Appraisers—Benjamin Hand, John Ingrum.

1741, June 20. Account. Moneys paid to Samuel Bustill, Benj. Hand, Lewis Cresse, Benj. Johnson, Richd. Buckeley, Jacob Garrison, Thos. Stonebanks, Jeremiah Hand, Jon. Robinson, Danl. Walker, Mary Paschal, Jon. Bond, Eliz. Crowell, David Cress, Jacob Spicer, Richd. Downes, John Crandall, Jon. Smith, Wm. Segrave, Sebastian List, Aaron Leaming, Jon. Thompson, Wm. Bond, Edwd. Nicholas, Randal Hewet, Phebe Johnson, Jas. Pharo, Jas. Bellangee, Lemuel Swaine, Alathar Smith, Thomas Smith, Henry Young, etc.

1732, Jan. 6. Smith, Thomas, of Evesham, Burlington Co., yeoman, deceased. Children of Sarah, his wife—Martha, Thomas, Lydia, Elizabeth and George, all under age; Sarah Smith, the mother, is lately deceased; the children request that their uncle, Francis Smith, of Burlington, cordwainer, be appointed their guardian. Lib. 3, p. 238.

1737, Feb. 19. Smith, Thomas, son of Thomas Smith of Northampton, Burlington Co., now about 18, petitions that Thos. Bishop, of Northampton, yeoman, and John Prickitt, of Evesham, sawyer, be appointed his guardians. Bonds of same as guardians.
Lib. 4, p. 126.

1732-3, March 14. Smith, Thomas, of Maninton Precinct, Salem Co.; will of. Wife, Grace, all land during widowhood; "after she ceases to be my widow," my son-in-law, Daniel Rumsey, shall possess it, he to pay £100 to my daughter-in-law, Ruth Rumsey, and to my daughters, Mary and Grace Smith, when 18. In case of death of Daniel Rumsey, lands shall be divided equally among my three said daughters, among whom shall be divided £70. Gift to brother, William Smith. Executors—wife, Grace, and Isaac Sharp. Witnesses—Thomas Haynes, William Smith, Alexander Simpson. Sworn and affirmed, 17 July, 1733. Lib. 3, p. 370.

1733, June 14. Inventory (£276.12.6) includes cattle, wheat, etc.; William Jentry's time, £5; an Indian man, 5 shillings. Appraisers—Wm. Hunt, William Nicholson.

1742, Nov. 9. Smith, Thomas, of City and Co. of Burlington, carpenter; will of. After decease of my mother-in-law, Sarah Smith, my wife, Rebecca, to have use of lot on York Street until my daughter, Mary, is 21. Sister, Ann Smith. Executors—wife, and friend Thomas Scattergood, Jun'r. Witnesses—Will Petty, Abigail Mason, Jos. Scattergood. Proved Dec. 1, 1742. Lib. 4, p. 332.

1742, Nov. 26. Inventory, £173.12.3½; made by John Bacon and Sam Scattergood. Includes bond of John Kimble; ballance of Dan Hough's note; silver watch, £5.

1748, Feb. 7. Smith, Thomas, of Greenwich Township, Gloucester Co., miller. Int. Adm'x, Sarah Smith, widow (Quaker). Bondsman—Elisha Bassett, of Township of Pilesgrove, Salem, yeoman. Witnesses—John Ladd, Hannah Ladd. Lib. 6, p. 78.

1748-9, Feb. 3. Inventory (£286.2.9) includes negro man, £35. Appraisers—Isaac Sharp, David Davis.

1739, Feb. 26. Smith, William, of Salem Co. Int. Adm'x, Mary Smith, widow. Bondsman—Edw. Trenchard. Witnesses—William Hunt, Danl. Mestayer. Lib. 4, p. 198.

1739-40, 6 mo. (Aug.), 22 da. Inventory (£194.10.7) includes cattle, grain, etc. Appraisers (no names given).

1740, July 8. Smith, William, of Manington, Salem Co., yeoman. Int. Adm'x, Mary Smith (widow). Bondsmen—James Mason, James Rutherford. Witnesses—John Jones, Dan. Mestayer. Lib. 4, p. 244.

1740, July 8. Inventory (£75.15) includes farming utensils, stock, etc. Appraisers—Thomas Haynes, James Rutherford.

1740, Sept. 27. Account. Cash paid Clement Hall, Doctor Chetwood, Tho. Thompson, Richard Graves, Daniel Mayster.

1743-4, Feb. 18. Smith, William, Senior, of Cape May Co., yeoman; will of. All of the marsh, which I surveyed, joining the cedar hammock, to be paid for out of my moveable estate, and that part of said marsh between the line fence and my son's, John Smith's, land shall be given to him with all my rights to his land. Son William, all my rights to his land. "The reason I give these sons no more is because I have given each a plantation before." Son, Richard, all my lands, surveys and rights (except what has been mentioned), provided he shall pay £100 to my son, Jonathan Smith. Sons, Daniel and Jeremiah, £60 each. Daughter, Elizabeth (wife of Samuel Foster), 5 shillings. Granddaughter, Ruth Osborn, £7 at 18. Executors—sons Richard and Jonathan. Witnesses—Michael Iszard, Mary Conner, Nathl. Jenkins, Jun'r. Proved 3 Aug., 1744.

1744, July 30. Inventory (£231.19.2) includes negro man, £25; cattle, horses, sheep, etc. Appraisers—Jeremiah Hand, Nathl. Jenkins.

1748, May 9. Smith, William, of Upper Freehold, Monmouth Co. Thomas Smith, father of deceased, being infirm, resigns his right of administration to Robert Montgomerie, principal creditor. Witness—Andrew Peairs.

1748, May 16. Bond of Robert Montgomerie of Allen Town, as administrator. Andrew Peairs, of Middlesex County, yeoman, fellow bondsman. Lib. E, p. 187.

1738, Dec. 8. Smock, Ghurtje, of Piscataway, Middlesex Co., spinster. Int. Adm'r, Hendrick Smack (Smock), of same place, yeoman. Edw. Antill, Esq., fellow bondsman. Lib. C, p. 225.

1738-9, Mar. 14. Inventory, £66.0.4; made by William Williamson and William Maxwell.

1747, May 27. Smock, Hendrick, of Middletown, Monmouth Co.; will of. Wife, Mary. Children—eldest son, John, Catherine, and Nelly Lane. Executors—Cornelius Vanderveer, Barrents Smock, Garret Schank. Negroes to sons John, Garett and Barrents. Witnesses—Hendrick Bennet, Stephen Tallman, Cors. M. Curtain. Proved Oct. 7, 1747. Lib. E, p. 90.

1747, June 12. Inventory (£581.11) includes a sword, pistol, nine Dutch books, negro wench (£30), 3 negro boys (£117) and negro girl (£16). Made by Samuel Holmes, Hendrick Bennet, Cornelius Curtain.

1747, 19th of Oct. Inventory "of the goods of Hendrick Smock and Mary Smock, deceas'd," £78.18.3; made by Cornelius M. Curtain, Hendrick Bennet.

1738, Oct. 11. Smock, Leendert, of Piscataway, Middlesex Co.; will of. Wife, Sarah. Daughters—Sytie Boice and Sarah Clauson. Granddaughter, Neiltie Tunison. Grandson, Leonard Smock. Son, John, at 21. Real and personal estate. Executors—Dollen Hageman, Aurea Booram, brother Johannes Smock. Witnesses—John Carter, Jeremiah Field, Jun'r, Johannes Swart. Proved April 12, 1739. Lib. C, p. 255.

1738, Oct. 31. Snow, George, innkeeper, of Nottingham Township, Burlington Co., will of. Sister, Phebe Osborne. Wife, Mary, executrix and residuary legatee. Real and personal estate. Witnesses—Joseph Peace, D. Martin, John Wollard. Proved April 28, 1739. Lib. 4, p. 173.

1747, August 27. Snow, Mary, of Trenton, Hunterdon Co.; will of. Sister Phebe Wright's child, £100 and negro girl Morenah. If said child dies under 18, to testator's brothers and sisters, and child of her sister, Martha More. To honored mother, £30, etc. To Rafe Hunt and his wife, the sister of testatrix, the negro woman Sue, they to bring up Morenah, the negro girl. Eldest brother, William Ausbond. Executors—brother-in-law, Ralf Hunt, and his wife Elizabeth. Witnesses—Rebekah Pangburn, Alles Emley, Stephen Pangburn. Proved Oct. 21, 1747. Lib. 5, p. 368.

1747, Oct. 25. Inventory (£325.18.9) includes debts of James Ozburn. Made by Peter Pain and Reuben Armitage.

1742, April 23. Snowden, William, of City of Burlington, hatter. Int. Adm'r, Joseph Heulings, of same, cordwainer. John Pye, fellow bondsman. Lib. 4, p. 379.

1745, Dec. 14. Bond of Richard Smith, Jun'r, merchant, principal creditor, on estate which Joseph Heulings left unadministered at time of his decease. Lib. 5, p. 192.

1745, July 30. Soaper (Soper), Richard, of Barnegat, Monmouth Co., gent.; will of. Wife, Anne. Four daughters, not named. Son, John. Executors—sons Joseph and Richard. Witnesses—David Kent, Sr., Cornelius Johnson, William Kent. Proved Oct. 4, 1746. Lib. D, p. 408.

1749, April 22. Soaper (Soper), Thomas, of Middletown, Monmouth Co. Int. Inventory (£93.7.2) includes pair of silver clasps, ink horne, gun, cutlass and caduce box, gold ring, Dutch loom and tackling, bonds of William Bennet, Phebey Huns and William Bennet, Jr., half of a boat (£30). Made by John Bowne and William Couwenhoven.

1749, April 24. Bond of John (or Johannes) Bennet, merchant, of Middletown as administrator. Daniel Flen and Mary Van Pelt, of same place, sureties. Monmouth Wills, 1667-70 M.

1743, April 1. Solley, Timothy, of Cohansey, Salem Co., yeoman; will of. Residue of estate after debts to my brother, Nathan Solley, whom I appoint executor. Witnesses—Elizabeth Jones, Ephraim Dayton, Elias Cotting. Proved 30 April, 1743. Lib. 4, p. 364.

1743, Apr. 30. Inventory (£114.13.6) includes bonds of Peter Daton and Jonathan Miles. Appraisers—Elias Cotting, Edward Lumas.

1743-4, ——, —. Account. Cash paid Elias Cotting, Chas. O'Neill, Ananias Sayre, Dr. James Johnston, Samuel Fithian, David Sayre, John Butler, Samuel Holmes, William Corry.

1743, Aug. 21. Somers, Edmund, of Egg Harbor, Gloucester Co.; will of. Wife, Mary, executrix, and to have whole estate until my son, Edmund, will be 21; at her decease plantation shall be his. Daughters—Hannah, Judith and Mary Somers (when 18) to have my land about "Mapel Swamp," together with 200 acres of marsh at Great Egg Harbor Inlet. Witnesses—Richard Somers, Judith Dinge, Abigail Somers. Affirmed 15 Sept., 1744. Lib. 5, p. 170.

1744, 10 mo. (Dec.), 13 da. Inventory, £189.10.2; made by Richard Somers, James Somers.

1737, Oct. 12. Somers, Hannah, of Great Egg Harbor, Gloucester Co.; will of. Sons—Richard (to have Bible), James, Samuel, Job, Edmond. Daughter, Millicent Townsend. Grand-children—the children of Hannah Ingerson, deceased, and Hannah, daughter of James Somers. (Memorandum. "Before signing and sealing, the half of the household goods given to the children of Hannah Ingerson, to be equally divided among them, is given only to the three daughters of said Hannah, deceased.") Executor—son, Richard. Witnesses—Daniel Ireland, Judith Steelman, Ruth Ireland. Affirmed 24 Feb., 1737-8. Lib. 4, p. 128.

1738, Jan. 7. Inventory, £278; made by Daniel Ireland, John Sculle.

1744, March 26. Somers, Job, of Egg Harbor, Gloucester Co., yeoman; will of. Sons—Job and John, to have the plantation where I live. Daughters—Hannah and Eunets. Executor—brother, Richard Somers. Witnesses—John Bond, Ezekill Harcort, Daniel Harker. Affirmed 15 Sept., 1744. Lib. 5, p. 172.

1744, 2nd mo. (Apr.), 10 da. Inventory, £130.2.0; made by James Somers, David Cownover.

1720-21, Jan. 8. Somers, John, of Great Egg Harbor, Gloucester Co., yeoman; will of. Wife, Hannah. Sons—Richard, executor, and to have the home land, excepting 400 acres on the east side of the same, upon condition that he pays £10 per annum to his mother during her life; James, 350 acres on the north-east side of Mulberry Point, where he now lives; Samuel and Job, equally, 800 acres on the northwest side of Patcons Creek; Isaac, 400 acres at Gilbort's Pon, over to the head of the mill creek; Edmond, 350 acres on the southwest side of his brother James. Sons Samuel, Job, Isaac and Edmond to pay 10 shillings per annum to their sister, Bridget, after the decease of their mother. What remains to be divided equally among my three daughters. Witnesses—Peter White, Jonathan Addomas, Thomas Green. Affirmed 14 Jan., 1739. Lib. 4, p. 216.

1734, Dec. 4. Songhurst, Editha, of Salem Town and Co., widow; will of. Estate, real and personal, to be sold and proceeds divided among my children—Mary Crow, George Crow and William Crow. Friend, Benjamin Acton, to assist my daughter Mary (the executrix) in the management until my two sons will be 21. Witnesses—Rebecah Hill, Richard Sears, Ben. Davis. Proved 10, Feb., 1735. Lib. 4, p. 62.

1733, Jan. 21. Songhurst, Edward, of Salem Co. Int. Adm'x, Editha Songhurst (widow). Bondsman—Thomas Cooke. Both of said County. Witnesses—Danl. Mestayer, Mary Mestayer. Lib. 3, p. 394.

1733, Jan. 10. Inventory, £19.2.6; made by William Shields, Benjamin Vining.

1734, April 22. Account. Monies paid Richard Haines, Peter Turner, Edward Test, Benjamin Peters, Mary Coleman.

1724, Feb. 19. Sonmans, Peter, Esq., now of London; will of. Wife, Sarah, all real estate in Europe, or in New Jersey in America, and to be sole executrix. Witnesses—Jno. Netmaker, Dr. Downing, Jno. Nevill, Will'm Cursell. Proved May 23, 1734. (Middlesex Wills), Lib. B, p. 504

1734, Jan. —. Received of Lawrence Smyth the original will of my deceased husband. Signed by John Nevil for Mrs. Sarah Sonmans. Lib. B, p. 505.

1742, May 7. Said Sarah being since deceased, administration on the unadministered estate granted to John Nevill, gentleman, who gave bond. Samuel Nevill, fellow bondsman. Lib. C, p. 508.

1745, March 25. Sooy, Joost, of Great Egg Harbor, Gloucester Co. Int. Adm'r, Arand Van Hook. Bondsman—Isaac Anderson, yeoman. Both of Hunterdon Co. Witnesses—Thos. Hunloke, Wm. Sorsby. Lib. 5, p. 104.

1745, March 25. Sooy, Sarah, of Great Egg Harbor, Gloucester Co. Int. Adm'r, Arand Van Hook. (Another paper shows Joost and Sarah Sooy had sons Joseph and Nicholas). Lib. 5, p. 104.

1746, Dec. 17. Sotten, John, of Somerset Co.; will of. Wife (not named). Children—John, Dave, Jams, Jesse, Mary, Eprem. Legacies to Aron, son of Moses Sotton and his mother; son Aron's daughter and her mother; and Peter Martin. Real and personal estate. Executors—sons John and Dave. Witnesses—George Boice, Jacob Boice, Leander Boice. Proved 20 Dec., 1750. Lib. E, p. 469.

1748, Dec. 21. Souther, Peter, of Penns Neck, Salem Co., weaver; will of. Wife, Margaret, executrix. Sons—John, William, Phillips and Charles. Daughter, Katherine. "I expect a sum of money out of my country that shall pay for the land whereon I live." Witnesses—Casper Sack, William Wilder, Robert Howard. Proved 10 Dec., 1750. Salem Wills, 919 Q.

1750, Dec. 6. Inventory, £100.14; made by Samuel Linch, Robert Howard.

1750, Dec. 10. Administration granted to Philip and William Souther. Witnesses to bond—Nichos. Gibbon, Grant Gibbon.

1748, March 4. Sparks, Simon, of Deptford Township, Gloucester Co.; will of. Wife, Jane, plantation whereon I live until my son, Henry, will be 21. Other sons—John, Richard, Thomas and Robert (not 21). Daughters—Elizabeth, Agnes and Mary. Executors—wife, Jane, and John Marshall. Witnesses—Henry Sparks, James Hamilton, Joseph Harrison. Affirmed 28 March, 1749. Lib. 6, p. 95.
1749, March 31. Inventory, £144.01.06; made by Andrew Sloan, Abr. Chattin, Ju'r.

1739, April 26. Spear, Joseph, of Boston, New England, mariner. Int. Adm'r, Evan Morgan, of Philada., merchant. Samuel Bustill, Esq., of Burlington, fellow bondsman. Burlington Wills, Lib. 4, p. 170.

1749, Dec. 9. Spencer, Agnes, widow of William Spencer, of Woodbridge, Middlesex Co.; will of. Eldest son, John Lee, money due from George Brown. Son, Abraham, bond due from Mary, widow of Thomas Force. Daughter, Agness, wife of John Burrell, and her daughter Susannah, silver spoon. Daughter, Martha, wife of Abraham Elstone, and her daughters Agness and Anne. Grandsons—Adam, Alexander and Robert Lee. Books that formerly belonged to my father and brother. Executors—son, Abraham Lee, and friend Jonathan Frazee. Witnesses—Spencer Elstone, Charles Toms, David Donham, Jun'r. Proved Dec. 29, 1749. Lib. E, p. 356.

1731, June 28. Spencer, Joseph, of Woodbridge, Middlesex Co., yeoman; will of. Executor—son, Joseph. Other children—Margaret, Katherine, Elizabeth, and John, all under age. Real and personal estate. Witnesses—Nathaniel Stilwell, Joseph Weaston, Samuel Dean. Proved Sept. 23, 1738. Lib. C, p. 287.

1738, Sept. 8. Spencer, William, of Woodbridge, Middlesex Co., weaver; will of. To Spencer Elston, son of the brother of my first wife, Elizabeth, 34 acres on Raway Road. To Abraham Lee, youngest son of, and Mary Lee, eldest daughter of, my present wife Agness. John Spencer (as he is called), son of the first wife of my deceased brother, Joseph Spencer. John, son of brother John Spencer. John, son of brother Joseph Spencer. Henry, Charles, Samuel, and Thomas Force, sons of my sister, the widow of Thomas Force. William, Abraham, and Samuel, sons of my brother-in-law, William Elstone, my first wife's brother. Executors—wife, Agness, and friend and neighbour Samuel Jacques. Witnesses—Thomas Edgar, Jonathan Frazee, Janet Edgar. Proved Jan. 22, 1743. Lib. D, p. 118.

1738, Dec. 4. Spencer, William, of Trenton, Hunterdon Co., yeoman; will of. Tract of land purchased from Robert Spencer to be sold. Bond of Garret Johnson, wherein the testator and his sons Robert Spencer and Henry Carter are bound. Wife, Susana, use of dwelling and plantation bought from Mahlon Stacy and John Hutchinson. After wife's decease, proceeds of this land to six children, two sons and four daughters, Robert Spencer, John Spencer, Hana (Hannah) Carter, Susana Robison, Ann Yard and Abigail Duten. Executors—wife, and sons Henry Carter and Joseph Yard. Witnesses—William Ely, Samuel Tooke, Jr., and William Mott. Proved January 5, 1738. Lib. 4, p. 153.
1738, Jan. 4. Inventory (£87.05) includes debts of Patrick Car and John Perce. Made by William Mott and William Ely.

1743, Jan. 10. Spencer, John, of Woodbridge, Middlesex Co., mariner. Int. Bond of Gershom Conger, his brother, as administrator. Brother-in-law, George Morris, of Woodbridge, fellow bondsman.

Lib. D, p. 112.

1715, April 10. Spey, John, of Gloucester Co., yeoman; will of. Wife, executrix, and to have the estate during life to dispose of the same at her discretion between my daughters, Mary and Ann, both of whom shall receive a legacy at marriage. Witnesses—R. Bull, Nathaniel Tylee, Richd. Whitling. Proved 27 April, 1733.

Lib. 3, p. 294.

1732, Nov. 4. Spicer, Jacob, of Cape May Co., yeoman; will of. wife, Sarah. Son, Jacob, all my lands within the Province of West New Jersey or elsewhere, also two-thirds of personal estate; but if he dies before 23, "which will be the tenth of April, or thereabout, 1739," without lawful issue, then my brother, Thomas Spicer, shall hold my land in the County of Gloucester, he to have ½ of the benefit of the fishery on my plantation in Gloucester County, during life, and same to revert to my son Jacob, in case he survives him. Executors—wife, Sarah, and son, Jacob. Witnesses—Jacob Spicer, William Coats, Joshuay Grainger, Joseph Sleigh. Affirmed 9 April, 1742.

Lib. 4, p. 318.

1731, Dec. 14. Spining, Benjamin, of Elizabeth Town, Essex Co., innholder; will of. Children—Benjamin, John, William and Humphrey, all under age. Daughter—Sarah Wheaton. Land purchased of Andrew Joline; land joining lands of Phillip Blackledge and Samuel Winans. Executors—wife, Margaret, and Andrew Joline. Witnesses—Elijah Davis, Wm. Patterson, John Salnave. Proved Feb. 28, 1731-2.

Lib. B, p. 243.

1731-2, Jan. 24. Inventory (£785.08.08) includes tankard, silver teapot, debts due from Nich's Paratt, John Gee, Frances Heart, Rob't Owen, Rich'd Higins, Geo. Jewell, John Shaw, John Burrows, John Bonnel, A. Graham, John Kyle, Mark Kellsey, Jno. Woodruff, Wm. Robinson, Dan'll Woodruff, James Hampton, Daniel Sears, Joshua Osburn, Max Labors, Rob't Little, John McKinzee, Mr. Vaughn, Aaron Ingram, Henry Tuttle, Rich'd Ryno. Made by William Donaldson, William Williamson, Return Messenger.

1749, Oct. 16. Sprague, Caleb, of Newton, Gloucester Co., gent.; will of. John Thorn, of Gloucestertown, Gloucester Co., yeoman, executor, and to have estate after paying legacies to Abigail (widow of John Kaighin, deceased), Sarah, Samuel and John, (children of the aforesaid John Kaighin), Abigail, Priscilla, Sarah (the three eldest daughters of Joseph Ellis), Sarah, Mary (daughters of John Thorn); also to the two daughters of Thomas, son of John Thorn and Mary Cheesman (daughter of Benjamin Cheeseman). Witnesses—James Keeling, Peter Breach, Isaac Andrews. Affirmed 24 Dec., 1750.

Gloucester Wills, 472 H.

1748, June 25. Sprakeling (Sparkeling), Robert, of the City of Philadelphia, "practitioner in Physick and Chirurgery," about to embark on a voyage by sea; will of. All my estate to my friend Peter David of said city, goldsmith, whom I appoint executor. Witnesses—Thos. Haward, Jno. Reily. Proved 17 Oct., 1749. Lib. 6, p. 355.

1749, Nov. 9, 10. Inventory (£219.2.7½) includes horse and mare and saddle, medicine in the shop (£6.15.3½), mortars and pestles. Appraisers—Neil Stewart, Thomas Ross, Gent.

1742, 14th day, 3rd mo. (May). Stacy, Mahlon, Esq., of Northampton, Burlington Co. Int. Mary Pownell, Ruth Atkinson and Rebeccah Wright request that administration on estate of their brother, Mahlon Stacy, be granted to Jos. Wright and Sam'l Atkinson. Witnesses—Mahlon Kirkbride, Stacy Beaks.

1742, May 17. Bond of Samuel Atkinson and Joshua Wright of Chester, yeomen. Thomas Budd, of Northampton, and Samuel Lovett, of City of Burlington, yeomen, fellow bondsmen. Lib. 4, p. 376.

1742, 16 and 18, 3rd mo. (May). Inventory, £1903.11.10; made by Thomas Shinn and James Lippincott. Includes silver tankard and cup, £9; library of books, £18; accounts between deceased and Company in the Iron Works, £820.19; negro man, £20.

1738, Dec. 26. Stagg, John, of Barbadas Neck, Bergen Co.; will of. Son Johannes, 6 shillings as my heir-at-law, he having had his part; likewise son, Cornailes, has had his full share. Sons Abraham and Jacob the land whereon they now live, being ½ of the plantation I possess, their half along the line of Garret Vanfoos. They to pay £100, and Abraham to give Jacob a deed for his half, according to a deed in his possession. Son, Isaac, the land he now is possessed of, meadows excepted, and he to pay £100. Son, George, the other half of plantation whereon I live, joining John Berry, with cattle, furniture, and he to pay £125. The meadows on Isaac's land to be divided among the four sons. Overplus of money, if any, divided among the four sons and my daughter Margaret, wife of Arie Blinkerhoof. Executors—Isaac and George Stagg. If a debt of £14 has not been paid to Mrs. Shiler on Cornailes Stagg's land, then above sum shall be paid her out of the loose estate. Witnesses—John Berry, Gerrat Vanfoos, John McDowell. Proved 29 Jan., 1738-9. Lib. C, p. 242.

1724, Nov. 6. Stagg, Thomas, of Newark, Essex Co., yeoman; will of. Five children by my former wife—Thomas, Margaret (wife of Peter Sanderson), Elizabeth, Silvester, Ann (wife of John Northcut). Residue divided between wife, Hannah, and son Nicholas Stagg, under age. Wife, Hannah, executrix. Witnesses—Thomas Husk, John Cooper, Thomas Sargent. Proved June 18, 1734. Lib. B, p. 564.

1735, March 27. Inventory, £45.08.11; made by Jno. Cooper, Henry Van Gesen.

1750, June 1. Stanborough, Elisha, of Newark, Essex Co. Int. Hannah, the widow, refuses to administer, and desires that Daniel Pierson, Esq., of Newark, be appointed. Witnesses—William Church, Samuel Stanborough.

1750, June 5. Bond of Daniel Pierson, principal creditor, as administrator. David Ogden, Jun'r, fellow bondsman. Lib. E, p. 445.

1749, Nov. 29. Stanbrough (Stanborough), Solomon, of Morristown, Morris Co., yeoman; will of. Brothers—Nehemiah and Ichabod Stanbrough. If either die in non-age then his part shall be equally divided among all the surviving brothers and sisters. Sister, Sarah, to have a cow, additionally. Executors—Ezra Halsey, Job Lorain, both of Morris Co., yeomen. Witnesses—Phillip Cundict, Benjamin Forgeson, Ezekiel Cheever. Proved 19 Dec., 1750. Lib. E, p. 468.

1750, Aug. 10. Inventory (£114.11.2) includes names of Philip Cundict, Thomas Forgeson, Zechariah Farchild, Job Coree, Ezra Halsey,

Thomas Nener Gray, John Parkes, Francis Causfren, Nemer Holaway. Appraisers—Henry Clark, Richard Carson.

1750, April 29. Stanley, John, of Middletown Point, Monmouth Co., trader; will of. Wife, Grace, choice of negro wenches, etc. Bequest to "my god-daughter, Margaret Francis," of lot of land. Eldest brother's son, if any there is, residue of real and personal estate. Executors—wife, Johns Williams, Thomas Fox, John Conway. Witnesses—Richard Franses, John Brown, Andrew Crawford. Proved June 25, 1750. Lib. E, p. 427.

1748, Dec. 6. Staples, Thomas, Jun'r, of Burlington Co., innholder. Int. Adm'r, Thomas Rogers. John Deacon and John Antram, of City of Burlington, yeomen, fellow bondsmen. Lib. 5, p. 547.

1748, Dec. 6. Inventory, £30.7; made by John Deacon and John Antram.

1749, June 28. Account. Payments to Jos. Scattergood, John Deacon, John Antrum, Joseph Biddle, John Morris, Joshua Raper (Executor of Joshua Raper), John Rogers.

1748-9, Feb. 22. Starkey, James, of New Hanover, Burlington Co.; will of. Children—Nathan, Sarah, Ruth, Edith, Mary, Alice and Phebe. Real and personal estate. Wife, Ruth, sole executrix. Witnesses—Richard Harrison, William Price, Jos. Clegg, Jur. Proved April 18, 1749. Lib. 6, p. 41.

1749, April 19. Inventory, £274.18.1; made by Saml. Emley and Benjn. Kirby. Includes bond, £100, and clock, £10.

1746, Sept. 3. Starkey, Thomas, of Hanover, Burlington Co., farmer. James Starkey declines administration on estate of his son and requests that same be granted to his son, Nathan Starkey.

1746, Sept. 3. Inventory, £223.13; made by Sam'l Emley and John Brown.

1746, Sept. 26. Bond of Nathan Starkey, of Hanover. Fretwell Wright, of Burlington Co., gentleman, fellow bondsman. Lib. 5, p. 273.

1749, April 12. Stathem, Thomas, of Cumberland Co., yeoman; will of. Wife, Mary. Dau., Catherine. Real and personal estate. Executors—wife, Mary, and son Jonathan. Witnesses—Eldad Cook, John Johnson, Jno. Bee. Proved 2 Oct., 1749. Lib. 6, p. 343.

1744, Nov. 17. Stathum, Thomas, Jr., of Cohansey, Salem Co.; will of. Wife, Keziah. Legacies to father, Thomas Stathum, to brother Jonathan, and to Cathrine Lester. Executrix—wife. Witnesses—Nehemiah Craven, Hannah Smith, Job Shepherd, Jr. Proved Jan. 20, 1744-5. Lib. 5, p. 91.

1744, Dec. 3. Inventory, £144.11.5; made by Nehemiah Craven and Job Shepherd, Jr.

1731-2, Jan. 2. Steelman, Andrew, of Great Egg Harbor Township, Gloucester Co.; will of. Wife, Judith, executrix. Sons—Frederick, 420 acres bought of John Budd, and 100 acres bought of Samuel Ward, between South River and Stephens' Creek, joining to Great Egg Harbor River; James, 450 acres adjoining John Rambo's on the west side of Great Egg Harbor River, joining upon west side of Stephens' Creek; Peter, 250 acres of the plantation I live on, joining Daniel Ireland's; Andrew, the plantation I live on, containing 250 acres, joining James Sommer's on the west side, (which my wife, Judith, shall enjoy during her widowhood). Andrew and Peter, 130 acres equally near Seader Swamp Bridge. Absecon Beach and my cedar swamps to be divided equally among my aforesaid sons, only that my wife shall enjoy them during widowhood. When the sons come to age they or either of them may buy or sell to each other and not otherwise. Daughters—Mary Somers, Judith, Susanna (last two not of age). Witnesses—Daniel Ireland, John Wells, Alexander Fish, Thos. May. Proved 5 Feb., 1736-7. Lib. 4, p. 84.

1736-7, Feb. 3. Inventory (£286.14.0) includes 83 head of cattle, £160. Appraisers—Daniel Ireland, Alexdre. Fish.

1739, Feb. 26. Steelman, Elias, of Great Egg Harbor, Gloucester Co., yeoman. Int. Adm'x, Comfort Steelman (relict). Bondsman—Amos Ireland. Witness—Richard Phillpott. Lib. 4, p. 199.

1739, Feb. 15. Inventory, £103.12.7; made by Richard Phillpott, Amos Ireland. (Names a daughter, Sarah Steelman).

1731, May 12. Steelman, Erick, of Gloucester Co. Int. Adm'rs, Tobias Bright and Bridget Steelman (spinster), of same place. Bondsman—Andrew Long. Witness—James Smith.

1731, May 11. Inventory, £79.18; made by Stephen Jones, Alexander Randall.

1733, June 20. Account. Moneys paid to Jos. Jones "for nursing and attendance on deceased in time of his sickness with small-pox;" also to Thomas Cumming (Exr. of John Baldwin, dec'd), Saml. Harrison, Esq. Sheriff of Gloucester Co., on judgment at the suit of Christopher Taylor and his wife, Michael Homan, Gabriel Enochson, Thomas Wilkins, John Fisher, of Phila., William Cobb, Dishedarius Vaneman, Andrew Matson. (Names Catherine and Mary Steelman, as daughters of deceased). Gloucester Wills, 145 H.

1734, Aug. 2. Steelman, James, of Egg Harbor, Gloucester Co., gent.; will of. Wife, Katharine, use of estate during widowhood. Sons—Andrew and Hance (who had plantation, etc.); John, the land and marsh bought of John English, where the mill stands, "at the day of his mother-in-law, Katharine Steelman's, death or marriage," he to pay £10 to my granddaughter, Susannah, the daughter of my son John; James, 200 acres where he lives that is mortgaged in the Loan office; Elias, (had plantation); Peter (not 21) (to have after the death or marriage of my widow and his mother, Katharine Steelman, the home plantation bounding upon Pattcunk's creek, also 200 acres bought of James Adams and Judah Allen, as appears by deed, also all my swamps, beach and the land bought of Peter Scull). Daughters—Susannah Kean (had portion), Mary Blackman (had portion). Executors—wife, Catherine, and son, John Steelman. Trustee—Nathan Lake. Witnesses—Nathan Lake, Edward Orser, Solomon Manery. Proved 10 Jan., 1734-5. Lib. 3, p. 452.

1734-5, Jan. 4. Inventory (£322.3.4) includes cattle and sheep, £122.4.4. Appraisers—Nathan Lake, Solomon Manaring.

1734-5, March 24. Stelle, Gabriel, late of Monmouth Co., but now of Perth Amboy, Middlesex Co.; will of. Wife, Margaret. I have mortgage belonging to William Allen in Allens Town, Monmouth Co. Son—Thomas Gordon Stelle, at 21, land near Allens Town I purchased from Henry Allen of Shrewsbury. Sons, Pontius and Isaac, brigantine I hold in partnership with Messrs. Johnston, Frazer and

Emott. Daughters—Elizabeth and Catherine, £200 at 18. Real and personal estate. Executors—wife, Margaret, son Pontius, and son-in-law Mr. Thomas Billop. Witnesses—Adam Hay, Lawr. Smyth. Proved Dec. 22, 1738. Lib. C, p. 228.

1739, May —. Margaret Stelle, the widow, and Thomas Billop, of Perth Amboy, renounce their rights of executorship. Witnesses—Rich'd FitzRandolph, William Davis. Lib. C, p. 322.

1738, Jan. 31. Stelle, Isaac, of Upper Freehold, Monmouth Co., yeoman; will of. Wife, Rachel, one-third of estate; other two-thirds to "all my children, as well sons as daughters;" to sons at 21 and daughters at 18. Three daughters, Abigail, Susanna and Elizabeth. Executors—brother, Benjamin Stelle, Jacob Dennis and nephew, Pontius Stelle. Witnesses—Gizburt Hendrickson, Lefferd Lefferson, John Willgate. Proved Sept. 10, 1741. Lib. C, p. 449.

1741, June 20. Jacob Dennis and Pontius Stelle having renounced, May 29, 1741, Benjamin Stelle, and Rachel, widow of the testator, request that administration be granted to Elisha Lawrence, of Monmouth County. Witnesses—Isaac and Benjamin Stelle, Samuel Rogers, Robert English.

1741, August 17. Elisha Lawrence, of Perth Amboy, requests that the will of Isaac Stelle be delivered to Anthony White.

1741, August 17. Renunciation of Pontius Stelle, Jacob Dennis and Benjamin Stelle as executors of Isaac Stelle, late of Allens Town. Witnesses—James Stevenson, Miles Weekes.

1741, Sept. 9. Caveat, entered by Abraham Jonneau, withdrawn.

1741, Oct. 17. Bond of Gulian Verplanck, of City of New York, merchant, as administrator. Patrick McEvers and Anthony White, of New Jersey, attorneys, fellow bondsmen. Witnesses—Lewis Johnston, D. Martin.

1741, Nov. 2. Inventory (£24.8.11) includes sword without scabbard, and bayonet, three guns, parcel of old French and English books. Made by Robert Lawrence and Samuel Rogers.

1733-4, Jan. 23. Stephens, Charles, of Amwell, Hunterdon Co., laborer; will of. Daughter, Mary, residue of estate and gold ear rings of her mother. Executors—William Lumicks and Philip Ringo. Witnesses—Godfree Peters, Hezekiah Bonham, Jr. Proved April 6, 1737. Philip Ringo, in the absence of William Lumicks, sworn. Lib. 4, p. 94.

1730, April 28. Sterborn, William, of Middlesex Co., yeoman; will of. Whole estate left to wife, Elizabeth. Witness—Edward FitzRandolph. (Not proved). Unrecorded Wills, Vol. 9, p. 273.

1749, August 18. Sterling, Thomas, of Bethlehem, Hunterdon Co. Int. Inventory, £82.19.6; made by Robert Combs and William Pettit. Additional inventory (undated) includes debts of Thomas West and Henry Burd.

1749, August 21. Johannis Buys states that his son-in-law Thomas Sterling and wife are both deceased, and desires that his son, William Buis, administer on the estate. Bond of William Boyce, of Amwell, Hunterdon Co., yeoman. John Buys, of Amwell, yeoman, surety. Witnesses—Joseph Phillips, Benjamin Hart. Hunterdon Wills, 266 J.

1735, April 21. Stethens (Stethem), Mary, of Salem Co. Int. Adm'r,

Alexander Smith, yeoman. Bondsman—Thomas Waithman, yeoman. All of said county. Witnesses—Dan. Mestayer, John Doe.
Lib. 4, p. 3.

1737, May 5. Inventory (£106.13.2) includes debtors: Robart Huchason, John How, Joseph Thompson, John Indacot, William Tuft, Thomas Wolsted, Daniel Huddy. Appraisers—Isaac Satterthwaithe, Mathew Keasby.

1737, June 4. Stevens, John, late of City of Perth Amboy, now of Rariton, Somerset Co.; will of. Present executors, the sons, Campbell (oldest) and John; sons William, Lewis and Richard to join them as they come of age. Executors to sell all houses and lots in Perth Amboy; also plantation at "Rockehill" and any part of the estate they see fit, and each one to share equally in residue at 21. Daughters—Sarah and Mary (wife of Fenwick Lyell, "had her share at marriage"). Brother, Thomas Stevens, perriwig maker, in Arundell Street, near the Strand, in London. Witnesses—Johannis Folkerse, John Scott, John Ross. Proved 5 Jan., 1737-8. Lib. C, p. 183.

1744, June 12. Stevens, Richard, of Upper Freehold, Monmouth Co., "being about to go to old Ingland;" will of. Daughter, Elizabeth, a negro wench, Fillis, living with testator's sister Elizabeth. Daughter, Rachel. Richard Stevens, eldest son of Benjamin Stevens. Brothers and sisters—Benjamin, John, Thomas, Elizabeth and Anne. Executors—brothers Benjamin and John Stevens, and John Henderson. Witnesses—Jeremiah Stillwell, Richard Parker, Henry Holiday. Proved Oct. 3, 1745. Lib. D, p. 340.

1745, Oct. 30. Inventory of the estate of "Richard Stevens, Esquire," £1830.8.8. Includes old negro man, past his labor, with his bedding and apparel, 5 shillings; negro woman and two female children and their bedding, £55; negro girl at Mr. Wales's, £30; books of sundry sorts, £10.4; one-half of wolf trap; the plantation and improvements, £1,200; note from William Britton. Made by Jeremiah Stillwell, Jacob Lawrence, Stephen Pangburn.

1742, Sept. 18. Stevens, Robert, of Northampton, Burlington Co., weaver; will of. £5 to my negro woman, Rachel. Negroes, Peter, Meriam, Dina, Charles, Deby and John, to have their freedom. Executor to have two tombstones placed at the graves of "my wife and me" in Burlington churchyard. Remainder of estate, real and personal, to Zachariah Prickett, whom I appoint sole executor. Witnesses—Patrick Byrne, Mary Ogburn, Sam'll Hall. Proved Oct. 11, 1742. Lib. 4, p. 349.

1742, Oct. 11. Inventory, £124.8.6; made by Tho: Shinn and John Osmond.

1748, Sept. 11. Stevenson, Elnathan, of City of Burlington, yeoman; will of. Wife, Sarah. Son, Cornell, 250 acres in Hunterdon Co., adjoining that I conveyed to his brother Thomas, and dwelling house built by Philip Philips. Son, Edward, 250 acres in Hunterdon Co. Son, Benjamin, land adjoining Thomas Rogers and John Antrum. Son, Elnathan (under age). Daughters—Sarah (wife of Joseph Hedger), Charity (wife of William Pettit), Ann and Elizabeth. Executors—wife, son Cornell and friend John Deacon. Witnesses—Thomas Rogers, Ju'r, John Antrum, George Eyre. Proved Dec. 13, 1748.
Lib. 6, p. 246.

1748, Dec. 12. Inventory, £256.10.7; made by Caleb Haines and John Antram.

1744, Sept. 25. Stevenson, John, Esq., of Bethlehem, Hunterdon Co. Int. Adm'x, Margaret, widow. Edward Rockhill, of same place, gentleman, surety. Witness—Thomas Cadwalader. Lib. 5, p. 62.

1744, Oct. 5. Inventory (£261.7) includes three negroes, £105; John Hawkins' bill. Made by Joseph King, John Emley, Abraham Bonnel. (John Emley a Quaker).

1748, May 10. Stevenson, John, of Gloucester Town and Co., laborer. Int. Adm'x, Sarah Stevenson, of Deptford Township, widow. Bondsman—John Carter, of said County, yeoman. Witness—John Mickle. Lib. 6, p. 15.

1748, April 16. Inventory (£38.18.0) mentions Francis Haddock, woodboat (£16), John Carter, Jun'r, John Carter, Sen'r. Appraisers—Thos. Clement, Jon. Harrison.

1751, Nov. 22. Account of Jonas Cattell and Sarah, his wife, late Sarah Stevenson, administratrix of John Stevenson. Moneys paid Jos. Kaighin for coroner's fees, £1.5.0; John Turner, John Carter, Eliza. Ballenger, Jim Matlack, Rebecca Hartley, Archd. Ingram and allowance for wood flat appraised to said Sarah, which appears to be the property of Tho. Reves (?).

1738, June 30. Stevenson, Mary, of Nottingham, Burlington Co., widow. Int. Adm'r, Rob't Rockhill. John Rockhill, fellow bondsman, both of Mansfield. Lib. 4, p. 138.

1738, July 1. Inventory, £118.4.3; made by Rob. Field and Thos. Dotts, Ju'r. Includes bills due from John Stevenson, Jona. Parker, Edw'd Stokes, Jas. Lewis, Jas. Coverley, Hugh Davis.

1736, June 5. Stevenson, Nathaniel, of Burlington Co., yeoman; will of. Wife, Mary. Thomas, John and Mary, children of brother John Stevenson. William and other children of brother Daniel Stevenson. William, eldest son of brother William Stevenson. Sam'll, eldest son of brother Thomas Stevenson. James and Nathaniel, children of brother Stephen Stevenson. Nathaniel, son of Sam'll and sister Ann Thorn. Real and personal estate. Executors—wife, and nephew John Stevenson. Witnesses—Hugh Hutchin, Jun'r, Jos. Overton, Edw'd Beakes. Proved Aug. 31, 1736. Lib. 4, p. 71.

1736, Aug. 14. Inventory, £393.10.4; made by John Tantum and John Middleton.

1748, Sept. 20. Stevenson, Thomas, of Amwell, Hunterdon Co. Int. Letter from Elnathan Stevenson asking that administration be granted to Joseph Hedger and William Pettit, he being eldest son of said Elnathan Stevenson.

1748, Sept. 22. Bond of Joseph Hedger, of Middlesex County, tanner, and William Pettit, of Amwell, yeoman. John Allen, of Trenton, sadler, surety. Witness—Elijah Bond. (Administrators Quakers).

1748, Sept. 23. Inventory (£157.1.2) includes sword; 2 hives of bees; nursery. Made by John Phillips and Robert Combs.

Hunterdon Wills, 233 J.

1746, Nov. 1. Stevenson, William, of Northampton, Burlington Co., husbandman. Int. Adm'x, Sarah Stevenson, widow. John Deacon, yeoman, of City of Burlington, fellow bondsman. Lib. 5, p. 431.

1734, Feb. 12. Steward, Charles, of Somerset Co.; will of. Sons, John and James, all real estate, together with tract in the county of Gloucester [obtained] by indenture dated 21st day, 11 mo., 1722; also land adjoining, purchased of Samuel Clement of Long Island, New York, "for which I paid and was never confirmed by any manner of conveyance." Daughter, Mary, all personal estate. Executor—Richard Van Veighten. Witnesses—Jno. Reade, Jno. Broughton, Jacob Janeway. Proved 21 March, 1734. Lib. C, p. 23.

1734, Feb. 12. Inventory. Names. John Chambers, Jacob Bodine, George Mills, Brice Richey, Widdow Allward, Nathaniel Harned, Thomas Vemstone, Barrant Shaver, Alexander Fitchet, Phillip Kearney, John Reade, Samuel Lewis, James Miller, Abraham Drake, William Sutton, James McKain, William Smith, Albert Decline, John Rose, Patrick McGee, Benjamin Dun, Nathaniel Stillwell.

1733, June 11. Steward, Joseph, of New Hanover, Burlington Co.; will of. Brothers—Girshom and John Woodel, at age. Rebeckah, dau. of George Harrison, at 18. Remainder, real and personal, to George Harrison's wife and four children. Executor—friend, Benjamin Kirby. Witnesses—Richard Harrison, Richard Harrison, Jun'r, William Harrison. Proved July 21, 1733. Lib. 3, p. 354.

1733, June 23. Inventory, £174.11.2; made by Joshua Wright and Saml. Finley. Includes five bonds for £140.15.2.

1737, Aug. 29. Account. Payments to John Tantum for making coffin, Esteer Harrison, Joshua Fretwell, Dan'l Smith, Benjamin Fowler, Wm. Chapman, Wm. Duckworth, Thomas Platt, Isaac Horner, John Cheshire, Jonathan Cheshire, Samuel Wright, Thos. Wright, William Harrison, James Pascoe, Joseph Reckless, Wm. Kirby, Joseph Arney, Samuel Wardell, David Starkey, John Rumford, Richard Harrison, Jr., Mary Brown, John Warren, Elizabeth Platt.

1733, April 6. Stewart, David, of Woodbridge, Middlesex Co., gent.; will of. Daughters—Jane and Ursila. 1250 acres of land in North Carolina, in hands of Robert West, Esq. Debts due me in Scotland. Real and personal estate. Executors—wife, Christian, and brothers John Mootree and James Brown, both of Woodbridge. Witnesses—James Thomson, Nath. Randolph, Jno. Sarjant. Proved June 9, 1733. Lib. B, p. 419.

1737, ——, —. Stiles, Isaac, upwards of 19, son of Robert Stiles of Burlington Co., yeoman (both parents being dead), makes choice of his uncle John Rudderow of Burlington Co., as his guardian. Bond of John Rudderow. Lib. 5, p. 486.

1735, Jan. 21. Stiles, Robert, above 14, eldest son of Robert Stiles of Pensawkin, Burlington Co., yeoman, prays that John Rudderow be appointed his guardian. Bond of John Rudderow. Lib. 4, p. 53.

1748-9, Feb. 27. Still, Benjamin, of Amwell Township, Hunterdon Co. Int. Renunciation of Jean Simones and Kathreen Still of right of administration. Witnesses—Zaccheus Beebe, Thomas Stilwell.

1748-9, March 16. Adm'r, Jacob Race of Amwell, yeoman. Thomas Stilwell, of Amwell, yeoman, surety. Witnesses—Henry Oxley, Titus Hixson. Inventory (£11.11.9) includes a gun and sword; cash at Tunes Quick's and Andrew Morehead's.

1750, May 15. Account. Payments to Catherine Still, for nursing, Nathaniel Parker, Dr. Ballard, suit against John Phillips, Justice Smith. Hunterdon Wills, 234 J.

1746, Oct. 22. Stillwell, Mercy, of Shrewsbury, Monmouth Co., widow of Richard Stillwell; will of. Children—eldest son, Richard; eldest daughter, Mary (wife of Captain Thomas Clark), Catharine, Elizabeth, Lydia, Deborah (wife of Richard Smith), Anne (widow of Theodosius Bartow). Land in Shrewsbury on west side of road from the church and Quaker meeting-house to "the Red Bank in said town." Executors—Daughters, Mary Clark and Catherine and Elizabeth Stillwell. Witnesses—Daniel Seabrook, Othniel Rogers, Jacob Dennis. Proved Nov. 4, 1746. Lib. D, p. 425.

1742, Nov. 17. Stillwell, Richard, of Shrewsbury, Monmouth Co., late resident of City of New York, merchant; will of. Wife, Mercy. Eldest son Richard. Eldest daughter, Mary Stillwell, to have negro girl, Lucy. Daughter, Deborah Smith, negro girl Silvia. Daughter, Catharine Stillwell, negro girl Phillis. Daughter, Anne Stillwell. Son, Samuel. Sons Richard and Samuel and daughter Deborah have been provided for. Daughter, Elizabeth Stillwell. Youngest daughter, Lydia Stillwell. Grandchildren—Mary, Richard and John Stillwell, children of testator's eldest son. Executors—wife, brother-in-law John Reid, and cousins Richard Stillwell of Staten Island and Joseph Stillwell of Middletown. Witnesses—John Reid, James Stevenson, Daniel Seabrook, Jacob Dennis. Proved June 27, 1743.
Lib. D, p. 162.

1743-4, Jan. 16-18. Inventory of estate of "Richard Stillwell, trader," £2,908.11.4, including cash, £216.17.08; silver plate, £83.18.6; silks, linens, woollens, and other wares, £694.19.7; negro man and 2 negro women, £130. Made by Jacob Dennis, John Redford, Daniel Seabrook.

1732, Sept. 6. Stites, Benjamin, of Cape May Co., yeoman; will of. Wife, Elizabeth, during widowhood, use of house and 40 acres where I live, and 10 acres of marsh near Fishing Creek, except two apple trees and land under them, which I have given to my two youngest sons; also debt due me from Shangar Hand. Son, George, the residue of my land, he to pay out of his own estate a bond due the West Jersey Society or their agent, Lewis Morris, Esq. Also he shall have all my land after my wife's marriage or death, and shall pay to each of his brothers, Benjamin and Jonathan, £20, when they arrive at 21. Daughters—Deborah Paig and Martha Ludlum. Executors—wife, Elizabeth, and son George Stites. Overseers of two youngest sons—sons-in-law, Joseph Paige and Jeremiah Ludlam. Witnesses—William Mathews, Daniel Norton, John Crandol, Ar'n Leaming.
Lib. 3, p. 335.

1732, Sept. 18. Inventory, £64.9.8; made by Nathaniel Rusco, John Paige. "Exchanged with Jeremiah Ludlam a loom, table and met hook for a barrel of cyder."

1746, Sept. 1. Stites, Henry, Junior (no place mentioned; Cape May Co.). Cousin, Zibulon Swaine, son of Zebulon Swaine, late of Cape May, deceased, sole executor, and to have all my estate, real and personal. Witnesses—Daniel Smith, Martha Smith, Willm. Evans. Proved 27 Nov., 1746. Lib. 5, p. 495.

1746, Dec. 3. Inventory of "Henry Stites, Esq.," (£174.10.0) includes horses, cattle, sheep, swine, whale boat and tackling. Appraisers—John Leonard, Joseph Savage.

1748-9, Feb. 6. Stites, Henry, of Cape May Co.; will of. Son,

Esaiah, sole executor, and to have all that tract of land and marsh whereon I live, joining Richard Smith, and the land that was formerly John Reeves; also ½ of personal estate. Daughter, Mary Skillinger, ½ of moveables. Witnesses—Richard Smith, Hannah Smith, Daniel Hand. Proved 8 May, 1749. Lib. 6, p. 62.

1749, May 25. Inventory (£159.14.2) includes cattle, sheep, swine (£100.3). Appraisers—Joseph Savage, Zebulon Swaine.

1743, June 29. Stites, John, of Cape May Co., yeoman; will of. Cousin, Abisha Stites (son of Richard Stites, of Cape May, deceased) when 20, one tract of land and marsh, between the land of Richard Shaw and John Garlick, Cape May County; likewise 50 acres I bought of the Commissioners of the Loan office (as a legacy left him by his father, I being one of the executors; provided he discharges my executrix from said legacy of £80). If he refuses the land, executrix to sell the same, pay the legacy and dispose of a cedar swamp (25 acres) at West Creek; also sell 99 acres of beach and cedar, beginning at Pond Creek, thence to the Bay, downward to Butler Fry yard, thence to Lilly Pond to the place of beginning. Wife, Prissila sole executrix, and the use of all lands unsold, until my cousin, Abisha, will be 20, and of the remaining lands not passed by my will, until my daughter Margrit will be 20. If said daughter dies childless, my cousin, Abisha, to have all lands. Witnesses—Joshua Stites, Elijah Hughes, Cornelius Schillink, Jun'r. Proved 1 Aug., 1743. Lib. 5, p. 7.

1743, Aug. 1. Inventory (£144.12.2) includes cooper tools and plantation tools (£7.12.9) and stock (£69.00.6). Appraiser—Elisha Hand.

1746, May 21. Stites, Joshua, of Cape May Co. Int. Adm'x, Abigail Stites. Fellow bondsman—Henry Stites. Witness—Cornelius Schillinks. Lib. 5, p. 248.

1746, May 7. Inventory (£199.1.6) includes cattle, horses, sheep (£96.10). Appraisers—Joseph Savage, Elisha Hand.

1729, Oct. —. Stites, Mary, of Elizabeth Town, Essex Co. Int. Inventory, £344.04.08; made by William Lines and John Littell.

1732, Jan. 29. Administration granted to John Stites. Lib. B, p. 358.

1739, Dec. 26. Stites, Richard, of Cape May Co.; will of. Son, Richard, all my lands and certain personal when he comes to 14 (excepting the use of half my lands, which I give unto my wife, Abigail, during her widowhood). Sons, Henry and Abishai, £80 at 21. Henry to be given to my brother, Henry Stites, until of age, and Abishai to my brother, John Stites, until 20. Daughters—Hannah, Zerviah and Abigail (all under 18 years and unmarried). Executors—Henry Stites, my brother, John Stites, and Abigail my wife. Witnesses—Robert Parsons, Ezekiel Eldredge, Levi Eldredge. Proved 22 May, 1740. Lib. 4, p. 238.

1740, May 15. Inventory (£446.16.2) includes cash and apparel (£242.-11.6), cattle, sheep, swine (£109.9.0). Appraisers—Elisha Hand, Joshua Stites.

1746, May 21. Stites, Zeruiah, of Cape May Co. Int. Adm'r, Richard Stites. Fellow bondsman—Elisha Hand. All of County aforesaid. Lib. 5, p. 248.

1746, April 10. Inventory, £83.7.1; made by Elisha Hand, Cornelius Schillinks.

1736, Dec. 27. Stoaks, Thomas, of Waterford, Gloucester Co., husbandman; will of. Wife, Rachel, use of plantation during widowhood. Sons—Benjamin, Thomas (to have plantation in Chester Township, Burlington Co.), Joshuway (to have home plantation, paying my son Jacob £50). Daughters—Ledia, Deliverance and Rachel (had their portions); Hannah, Cosier and Roseauner (to have legacies at marriage, or 21). Executor—wife, and brother Joseph Stoakes. Witnesses—Jon. Hollingshead, John Matlack, John Matlack, Junior, Peter Stringham. Affirmed 27 April, 1737. Lib. 4, p. 98.

1737, April 27. Renunciation of Joseph Stoakes, one of the executors.

1737, 2nd mo. (Apr.), 4th da. Inventory, £278.13.11; made by Wm. Tomlinson, Sam. Lippincott.

1745, Oct. 10. Stockton, Anna, of Springfield, Burlington Co., widow; will of. Son, William, and daughter, Anna Leeds. Grandchildren—Job, Richard and Anna Stockton. Granddaughters—Susannah, Sarah and Mary. Brother, William Petty. Mulatto, Peter Brown, to my son, Vincent Leeds and his wife. Negro, Simon, to my daughter, Anna Leeds. Executors—sons William and Vincent Leeds, and dau. Anna Leeds. Witnesses—Francis Venicomb, Mary Brian, Robert Ferrell. Proved Sept. 20, 1746. Lib. 5, p. 281.

1728, July 29. Stockton, Job, Sr., of Springfield, Burlington Co., yeoman; will of. Eldest son, Joseph, land adjoining John Woods. Son, Jobe. Son, William, land adjoining John Clark and John Stockton. Daughter, Anna, under age. Brother, John Stockton, and kinsman, Thomas Shinn, to make equal division of my land. Executors—wife, Anna, and son Jobe. Witnesses—Richard Bennit, Ann Stockton, Tho. Shinn, John Stockton, Sarah Stevenson. Proved Dec. 22, 1732. Lib. 3, p. 229.

1732, 21st day, 9th mo. (Nov.). Stockton, Job, Jr., of Springfield, Burlington Co.; will of. Brothers—Joseph and William, the plantation given me by my deceased father. Sister, Anna Stockton. Mother, Anna Stockton, a negro girl. Brother, William, sole executor. Witnesses—John Sykes, Francis Chamard, Jos. Reckless. Proved Dec. 22, 1732. Lib. 3, p. 231.

1745, Aug. 31. Stockton, John, of Springfield, Burlington Co., yeoman; will of. Sons—Daniel and David. Daughters—Rebekah Lippincott, Rachel Briggs and Mary Wetherill. Daughters-in-law—Sarah Woolston and Anna Lippincott. David, Joseph and Benjamin Butterworth, Jun'r, each £4 at age. Real and personal estate. Executors—sons Daniel and David. Witnesses—John Mackintosh, Stephen Murphy, John Osmond. Proved April 4, 1747. Lib. 5, p. 316.

1747, 3rd day, 2nd mo. (Apr.). Inventory, £170.9.2; made by Zebulon Gaunt, John Croshaw, Henry Cooper.

1741, 10th day, 6th mo. (Aug.). Stockton, Joseph, of Springfield, Burlington Co.; will of. Wife, Mary. Son, Job, 200 acres of the upper tract which joins John Wood. Son, Richard, the lower tract, which joins uncle John Stockton. Daughters—Anna and Susannah. All children under age. Executors—wife, and Isaac Antram, carpenter. Witnesses—John Warren, Francis Venicomb, John Osmond. Proved Sept. 24, 1741. Lib. 4, p. 292.

1741, 10th day, 7th mo. (Sept.). Inventory, £157.14; made by Zebulon Gaunt, John Warren, Henery Cooper. Includes servant man, £1.

1744-5, Jan. 25. Stockton, Robert, of Somerset Co., gent.; will of. Wife, Rebekah. Sons—Robert, Thomas, Job (all under age). Daughters—Susanna Mershon (eldest), Eunice, Elizabeth, Sarah and Mary (under 14). An expected child. Home plantation, running east to my brother Joseph's land, thence with John Stockton's line, side line to John Oldden. Upper plantation joining land of my brother, Samuel Stockton, deceased. Meadows running to my brother John Stockton's land. Harry, a slave, to be set free 1 May, 1746. Executor—brother, John Stockton. Witnesses—Natl. Fitz Randolph, William Worth, Samuel Stockton. Proved 15 March, 1744-5. Lib. 5, p. 104.

1739, Oct. 12. Stockton, Samuel, Esq., of Somerset Co.; will of. Wife, Rachel. Sons—Samuel (eldest), Joseph, Richard (all under age). Daughters—Ame, Rachell and Ruth (all under 21). Plantation on the King's Road; meadows adjoining land of brothers, Joseph and John Stockton; mansion and plantation on the east side of Stony brook; plantation whereon Benjamin Runyon now lives, joining Henry Freeman's land; meadows, (100 acres) on Millstone River, joining lands of Bearfoot Brunson and my brother, Richard Stockton, in Somerset Co., formerly belonging to Dr. Greenland, and now in possession of Joseph Knoks. Executrix—wife, Rachell. Executors—brother, John Stockton, and James Worth. Witnesses—William Holmes, William Worth, Lewis Charles Faneuill. Proved 12 Dec., 1739.
Lib. C, p. 304.

1739, March 20. Stockton, Samuel, of Somerset Co., aged about 15. Bond of Benjamin Doughty as guardian. John Clark, fellow bondsman. Both of New Windsor, Middlesex Co. Witness—John Forman.
Lib. C, p. 325.

1748, April 8. Stockton, Samuel, of Princetown, Somerset Co., deceased. Letter of Jos. Stout dated at Hopewell, asking that a guardian be appointed for his grandson, Joseph Stockton. Joseph Stout has sent his son with said grandson.

1748, April 9. The Petition of Joseph Stockton, aged 16 years and upwards, son of Samuel Stockton, late of Somerset County, deceased. That the father did not in life time or by will appoint a guardian over said Joseph, who is now upward of 14, and has lands given him by his father's will. Requests that his grandfather, Joseph Stout, be appointed guardian. Bond of Joseph Stout, of Hunterdon County, as guardian. Jonathan Stout, of Hunterdon County, surety. Witnesses—David and Andrew Stout. (Hunterdon Wills), Lib. 5, p. 443.

1747-8, 1st mo. (March). Stokes, Benjamin, of Burlington Co., husbandman; will of. Sisters—Lydia Haines and Deliverance Conro. Real and personal estate. Executor—Thomas Stokes, who is to have remainder of estate. Witnesses—Francis Robinson, Sam'l Atkinson. Proved April 12, 1748. Lib. 5, p. 407.

1748, April 7. Inventory, £183.4.3; made by Joshua Bispham and Arthur Borrodaill.

1743, 28th day, 10th mo. (Dec.). Stokes, John, of Burlington Co., yeoman; will of. Wife, Elizabeth. Son, John, my plantation, he paying £5 each unto my grandchildren, Elizabeth and William Blackham. Daughters—Mary Mulling and Sarah Rodgers. Executors—wife, and friend Revel Elton. Witnesses—Thomas Green, Samuel Woolman, John Woolman. Proved Sept. 11, 1749. Lib. 6, p. 314.

1749, Sept. 4. Inventory, £408.7.9; made by John Deacon and Samuel Cripps.

1738, 12 mo. (Mar.), 29 da. Stokes, Rachel, of Waterford, Gloucester Co.; widow and executrix of Thomas Stokes; will of. To Benjamin Stokes his father's best hat; Lydia (wife of Saml. Haines of Northampton), Thomas Stokes, Deliverance (wife of Darling Conrow), Rachel (wife of John Copperthwaite), each 5 shillings; daughter, Keziah, a negro girl. Son, Joshua, executor. Remainder of estate to daughter Hannah, son Jacob, daughter Keziah, son John and daughter Rosanna, to be paid at 21 or marriage. Witnesses—Henry Jones, Isaac Matlack, Sam'l Lippincott. Affirmed 20 April, 1748. Lib. 5, pp. 414-5.

1748, April 20. Inventory (£270.8.10) includes cash, £180.10.0; mulatto boy, £25; girl, 30. Appraisers—Saml. Lippincott, John Collins.

1748, Aug. 17. Stone, Samuel, Sen'r, of Woodbridge, Middlesex Co.; will of. Daughter, Mary. Wife, Mary, executrix. Real and personal estate. Witnesses—Barnabas Taylor, William Bloodgood, Daniel Ayres. Proved Sept. 2, 1748. Lib. E, p. 208.

1748, Sept. 3. Stone, Samuel, of Woodbridge, Middlesex Co., boatman; will of. Son, Samuel, under age. Daughter, Sarah. Other daughters mentioned but not by name. Real and personal estate. Executors—wife, Rebeccah, and brother William Stone. Witnesses—Jon'th Inslee, Elisha Inslee, David Herriot, Jun'r. Proved Jan. 11, 1748-9. Lib. E, p. 239.

1749, April 26. Stonebank, Thomas, of Pilesgrove, Salem Co.; will of. Executors—wife, Mary, and son John. They to have equally estate real and personal on condition said Mary shall remain my widow; otherwise all to son. Witnesses—Samuel Huett, Lewis Melbore, John Halford. Proved 13 Feb., 1750.

1750, Feb. 12, 13. Renunciation of Mary Stonebank, the executrix. Letters granted to John Stonebank.

1750, Dec. 29. Inventory (£113.1.3) includes blacksmith's tools, £25. Appraisers—Elisha Basset, Lewis Melbore. Salem Wills, 934 Q.

1732-3, 17 day, 12 mo. (Feb.). Stork, Robert, of Town and Co. of Burlington, taylor. Int. Inventory, £84.13.9; made by Thos. Scattergood and Caleb Raper. Includes silver tankard.

1733, June 21. Adm'x, Tabitha Stork, widow. Thomas Scattergood and Caleb Raper, both of same place, yeomen, fellow bondsmen. Lib. 3, p. 332.

1727, April 25. Stout, James, of Amwell, Hunterdon Co., yeoman; will of. Wife, Catherine, home plantation during widowhood, it being land testator received from Philip Elington (Edington). Son, John. Land received from Elington, Thomas Stevenson and Mr. Reading, to testator's seven sons, if unborn child is a son; if a girl, she to have £50. Sons—John, James, Joseph, David, Jacob and Jonathan. Executor—uncle, James Aston, or, if he cannot, then uncle John Aston, or cousin Joseph Stout, of Hopewell. Witnesses—William Allen, George Ash, John Manners. Proved April 26, 1731.

———, ———, —. Inventory, £46.6.3; made by John Garrison, Thomas Houghton.

1739, Nov. 10. Account of Samuel Stout, adm'r cum testamento annexo. Mentions John Manners, Geo. Ash, Jas. Hude, Lewis Moore, David Stout, Jon. Ashton. Hunterdon Wills, 70 J.

1747, June 8. Stout, James, of Hopewell, Hunterdon Co. Int. Adm'r, Joseph Stout of Hopewell. John Allen, Jr., of Trenton, sadler, surety. Witness—Joshua Howell. Lib. 5, p. 464.

1731, April 15. Stout, John, son and heir-at-law of James Stout, late of Amwell, Hunterdon Co., above 14. John Manners, of Amwell, guardian. "Seal affixed at Fort George in New York." Lib. 3, p. 142.

1749, Dec. 28. Stout, Richard, Esq., of Middletown, Monmouth Co.; will of. Son, John, land adjoining Thomas Coxe, Sarah Lippet, William Bowne, John Stout, John Pew. Son, Jonathan. Negro Harry, and Bess his wife, to be set at liberty and have use of field adjoining Samuel Tilton, for life. Negro, Prince, to be free. Negro Woman, Nanny, to be free. Moveable estate to daughters, Mary, Catherine and Rebecca, and the three daughters of deceased daughter, Esther Woolley. Executors—sons John and Jonathan. Witnesses—Matthias Mount, Silas Tilton, John Nathaniel Hutchens. Proved Jan. 17, 1749-50. Lib. E, p. 476.

1736-7, 12 mo. (Feb.), 6 da. Stowe, Jane, of Mannington Precinct, Salem Co., widow; will of. Sons Thomas and John, and daughters Mary, Elizabeth, Joanna and Jane, to have equally estate. Executors—Robt. Hutchinson, and daughter, Elizabeth. Witnesses—James Vance, Mary Ann Vance, Rachel Bradford. Proved 1 May, 1737. Lib. 4, p. 116.

1735, Jan. 9. Stowe, Thomas, of Salem Co., yeoman. Int. Adm'x, Jane Stowe, (relict). Bondsman—Clement Hall. Both of said County. Witnesses—Jno. Carmick, Dan. Mestayer. Lib. 4, p. 57.

1735, Jan. 12. Inventory (£150.8.4) includes debtors—William Oakford, Joseph Thompson, Edward Williams. Appraisers—Mathew Keasbey, Clem. Hall.

1738, Jan. 28. Administration de bonis non (of estate yet unadministered). Adm'r, Robert Hutchinson. Bondsman—William Chandler. Both of Salem County, yeoman. Witnesses—Wm. Burroughs, Dan. Mestayer.

1747, Dec. 10. Stowe, Thomas, of Salem Co., yeoman. Int. Adm'x, Sarah Stowe, widow. Bondsmen—Seth Smith and James Tyler, of Alloways Creek. Witnesses—Chas. O. Neill, Nichs. Gibbon. Lib. 5, p. 425.

1747, Dec. 2. Inventory, £102.9.3; made by Seth Smith, William Chandler.

1769, April 10. Petition of John Stowe. That he is entitled to two-thirds of the estate. That the administratrix, Sarah Stowe, hath refused to comply with said obligation; therefore petitioner prays for copy of said bond, with leave to prosecute same.

1734, June 9. Stratton, Manuel, being about 14, son and heir of Manuel Stratton, of Evesham, Burlington Co., yeoman, who died about 10 years since, after which the mother intermarried with Philip Thomas, (who has had possession of the plantation for 8 years and committed great waste), petitions that Levi Shinn be appointed his guardian. Lib. 3, p. 455.

1735, Jany. 3. Straughan, David, of Salem Co., yeoman. Int. Adm'x, Susannah Straughan, widow. Bondsmen—Mathias Johnson and Thomas Roe, of Salem County. Witnesses—Thos. Miles, Danl. Mestayer. Lib. 4, p. 57.

1735-6, Jan. 2. Inventory, £88.15.2½; made by William Mecum, Thomas Miles.

1732-3, Jan. 2. Strayhorne, William, of Elizabeth Town, Essex Co.; will of. Daughters—Rebecca, Mary and Anna. Real and personal estate. Executors—wife, Mary, and friend Ebenezer Johnson. Witnesses—Benjamin Trotter, Ebenezer Spinning, Robert Nisbett. Proved July 5, 1733. Lib. B, p. 445.

1739, Feb. 28. Street, William, of Salem Co., yeoman. Int. Adm'rs, Joshua and Aaron Bradway, yeomen. Bondsman—Joseph Hancock. All of Salem County. Lib. 4, p. 223.

1739, Nov. 24. Inventory, £78.9.4; made by Nathaniel Chamless, Samuel Hancock.

1748, 10 mo. (Dec.), 28 da. Stretch, Bradway, of Alloways Creek, Salem Co.; will of. Wife, Mary, during widowhood, profit of home plantation (600 acres), two parts of which I purchased of my father, the other part left to me by my mother. Son, John, to possess said plantation, but, if he dies without lawful issue, same to descend to my sons David and James. Son, William, the land I purchased of Philip Tyler; also oxen bought of Jonathan Davies. Daughters—Sarah, Mary and Eleanor. Wife, Mary, executrix. Trustees—Wm. Hancock and Joseph Stretch. Witnesses—Philip Tyler, Mary Vaughan, Rich'd Bradford. Sworn and affirmed, 11 May, 1749. Lib. 6, p. 356.

1749, April 18. Inventory, £364.9; made by Joseph Ware, Jonathan Bradway.

1735, March 19. Stretch, Daniel, of Alloways Creek Precinct, Salem Co., yeoman; will of. Wife, Elizabeth. Sons, Isaac and Daniel, equally plantation I live on. Daughters—Martha, Hannah, Mary and Sarah. Gifts to John, William and Richard Barker. Executors—wife, and my father, Peter Stretch. Witnesses—Nathan Shaw, John Carle, Joseph Smith. Proved 1 May, 1735. Lib. 4, p. 12.

1735, April 30. Inventory (£102.19.6) includes 3,000 staves, £4.10. Appraisers—John Carll, Joseph Stretch.

1742, 5 mo. (July), 8 da. Stretch, Joseph, Sr., of Alloways Creek Precinct, Salem Co., husbandman; will of. Sons—Broadway, part of my estate, real and personal, in Stow Creek; Joseph, land on north side of the Great Ditch on plantation where I live; Peter, land on south side of the Great Ditch and residue of moveable estate. Daughter—Sarah Ware. Executors—sons, Broadway, Joseph and Peter. Witnesses—James McGinnis, Mary Smith, Rich'd Bradford. Sworn and affirmed 28 March, 1745. Lib. 5, p. 180.

1745, March 30. Inventory (£124.1.6) includes clock, £4; Bible; smith's tools, £5.7; cattle, £50.5. Appraisers—Joseph Ware, Jonathan Bradway.

1749, July 17. Stretch, Peter, of Alloways Creek Precinct, Salem Co. Int. Adm'x, Sarah Stretch. Bondsman—Joseph Stretch. Both of said county. Witnesses—Jonathan Bradway, Nich. Gibbon. Lib. 6, p. 279.

1749, July 5. Inventory, £385.7.4; made by Joseph Ware, Jonathan Bradway.

1748, Nov. 15. String, Peter, late of Morice River, Cumberland Co. Int. Adm'x, Margaret String. Fellow bondsmen—Thomas Peterson, Abraham Jones, all of same place. Witnesses—Seth Brooks, Jr., William Josling. Lib. 6, p. 77.

1748, Nov. 14. Inventory (£52.10) includes 20 head of cattle (£20). Appraisers—Thomas Peterson, Abraham Jones.

1750-1, Feb. 16. Strycker, Peter, of New Brunswick, Middlesex Co., shopkeeper. Int. Adm'x, Anne Stryker, widow. Peter DeReimer, of Somerset Co., yeoman, fellow bondsman. Lib. E, p. 485.

1750-1, Feb. 19. Inventory, £512.04.6; made by William Ouke, and D. Schuyler.

1754, March 25. Account of Johannes Schurman and Ann his wife (who was the widow and administratrix of Peter Stryker). Payments to Luke Voorhees, Albert Voorhees, Wm. Bayord of New York, Abm. Lott, David Clarkson, Theo. VanWyck, Gabriel Ludlow, Peter Kemble, Peter Slegt.

1741, Nov. 23. Stryker, Jan (John), of Six-Mile Run, Somerset Co., yeoman; will of. Wife, Grietje, executrix; to have all estate during widowhood. Thereafter sons John, Frederick and Gerrit to have the estate, paying daughters, Dina, wife of Johannes Vanderveer, £100, and Styntje Strycker, £200. If death or marriage of wife, son John, and son-in-law Johannes Vandeveer, to be executors. Witnesses—Walter Burnet, Pitue Poumil, John Michael Sperling. Proved 6 Aug., 1747. Lib. E, p. 74.

1731, Oct. 11. Stuard, Catherine, of Amboy, Middlesex Co. Int. Adm'r, Thomas Skinner. Lib. B, p. 235.

1732, June 1. Stynmuth, Christophel, of Acquickanong, Essex Co., yeoman; will of. "Being aged and infirm." Wife, Sarah. Children—Casparus, Antie, Janetie, Benjamin, Judah, Peter, Hanah, Johanes, Garret, George, Elizabeth and Marya, land joining lands of Close Vreeland and Hendrick Garretsee; 299 acres on Passayack River joining land of Dirck Vreelandt; land bought of Hugh Roberts, March 31, 1698; meadow in Bergen Co., by Hackingsack River, joining land of Fredrick Tomasee and Garrett Van Waganon. Executors—son, Peter, and son-in-law Harman Vriansen. Witnesses—Jno. Cooper, Thomas Jurianse, Aldereck Brewer. Proved June 17, 1735. Lib. C, p. 92.

1745, Oct. 6. Sullivan, Benjamin, of Upper Freehold, Monmouth Co., currier; will of. Friend, Samuel Wright, tanner, a riding horse. Residue of estate to use of poor of Allenstown. Executor—Samuel Wright. Witnesses—David Lyell and Empson Wright. Proved December 3, 1745. Lib. 5, p. 203.

1745, Dec. 3. Inventory (£304.3.3) includes plantation, £120. Made by Moses Robins and Thomas Lawrie.

1744, Jan. 22. Sullivan, Benjamin, of Trenton, Hunterdon Co., yeoman. Mary Sullivan, of Trenton, widow, mother of said Benjamin, renounces right of administration and requests it be granted to Andrew Reed and William Surman, principal creditors. Witnesses—Maurice Justice, William Brown.

1744, Jan. 28. Bond of Andrew Reed, merchant, and William Surman, brewer, both of Trenton, as administrators. Hunterdon Wills, 176 J.

1748, June 27. Sullivan, Daniel, of Alloways Creek, Salem Co. Int. Adm'r, Benjamin Allen, of same place. Witnesses—John Lorein (?), Nich's Gibbon. Lib. 6, p. 50.

1748, July 9. Inventory, £18.7.6; made by John Pagett, Peter Stretch.

1749, May 22. Sullivan, Dennis, of Alloway's Creek, Salem Co. Int. Adm'r, William Sharp. John Barker, fellow bondsman. Inventory, £89.10.0; made by John Barker and Samuel Thompson. (Another paper indicates that William Sharp is son of Elizabeth Sullivan, who is probably the widow). Lib. 6, p. 280.

1732-3, 27 d., 12 mo. (Feb.). Sullivan, Turlass, of Chester, Burlington Co., labourer. Int. Mary Suluvan, widow, declines administration and requests that Sampson Cary, principal creditor, accept the same.

1732-3, March 16. Adm'r, Samuel Cary, of Bristoll, Bucks Co., Penna. Thomas Shreeve, of Burlington, yeoman, fellow bondsman. Lib. 3, p. 250.

1732-3, March 17. Inventory, £18.19.3; made by Thomas Davis and Elias Toy. Witnesses—Mary Solovan and Margaret Toy.

———, ——, —. Account. Payments to Jno. Brooks, Fradrick Toy, E'rd R. Price. Goods sold Jno. Brooks, En. Williams, Fraddick Toy, Wm. Hope, Jno. Johnson, N. Bye, James Higgs.

1747, Nov. 28. Sunderland, William, of Mansfield, Burlington Co.; will of. Mary, eldest daughter of Preserved Brown, merch't, at Philada.; William, son of Benjamin Shreeve; Richard, son of Benjamin French; Jason, son of William Marlen; Lewis, son of Jacob Taylor, and Thomas French, each as they come of age, £30. Remainder of real and personal to friends William and Jonathan French. Executors—William French and Benjamin Shreeve. Witnesses—William Chapman, Ju'r, Gideon Pettit, Ju'r, Sam'l Harris. Proved July 11, 1748. Lib. 5, p. 465.

1748, 13th day, 4th mo. (June). Inventory, £302.14.3; made by Dan Doughty and Thos. Black.

1741, March 20. Suplea, Bartholemew, of Greenwich, Gloucester Co., weaver; will of. Children—Jacob, John, Bartholemew, Ann, Rebeckah and Margaret, to have equally real and personal estate, 'and as for daughter Rebekah's part, executor to have care thereof until death of her husband, Robert Hamleton, the interest to be paid her annually.' I sold land to Edward Hamton, Gloucester Co., and order my son, Jacob, to execute a deed therefor. Executors—Alexander Randall and Andrew Long. Witnesses—Jeffrey Chew, Catherine Steelman, Mary Steelman. Proved 12 June, 1744. Lib. 5, p. 34.

1744, June 9. Inventory, £244.18.5; made by John Munyon, Jeffrey Chew.

1747, Feb. —. Account by Alexander Randall. Monies paid Daniel

Cooper, Jacob Suplea, Jacob Dutchey, Samuel Paul, Gabriel Rambo, Ann Yeocum, Hopewell Vokins, John Suplea, Margate Howe's late widow, Bartholemew Suplea, Rebeccah Hamleton.

1729, 10 mo. (Dec.), 12 da. Surridge, John, of Salem Town and Co., yeoman, mariner; will of. Cousin, Jonathan Suradge. Wife, Elizabeth, executrix and to have residue. Witnesses—Joseph Gregory, Mary Dare, Clement Hall. Affirmed 4 Nov., 1734. Lib. 3, p. 446.

1734, Nov. —. Inventory (£83.19.9) includes ½ of old shallop, £10. Appraisers—Bartholomew Wyatt, Richard Woodnot.

1745, Jan. 10. Sutton, Daniel, of Mansfield, Burlington Co., blacksmith; will of. Wife, Mary. Son, Daniel Jackson, ½ of plantation on Rackoon Creek, which I bought of my father-in-law, John Jackson, and Margaret his wife. Son, John Jackson, the other half. Brother-in-law, John Jackson, to give my son John the plantation he bought of Joseph Foster, and then son Daniel to have my entire plantation at age. Daughters—Catherine, Mary, Elizabeth and Jane. All my children under age. Lot on Pearl Street, adjoining Samuel Barker, left me by my father. Lot on Salem Road I bought of Thomas Clark. Executors—wife and John Jackson. Witnesses—John Weldin, Robert Sutton, Jno. Raworth. Proved May 21, 1746. Lib. 5, p. 245.

1741, April 28. Sutton, John, of Essex Co. Int. Adm'x, Mercy Sutton, widow. Joseph Smith, of Hunterdon Co., fellow bondsman.
Lib. C, p. 405.

1746, Dec. 17. Sutton (Sotton), John, of Middlesex Co.; will of. Wife ———. Aaron, son of Moses Sotten, and his mother. My son, Aaron's daughter and her mother. Other children—John, Dave, Jams, Jesse, Mary and Epram. Names Peter Marten. Real and personal estate. Executors—sons John and David Sotten. Witnesses—George Boice, Jacob Boice, Leander Boice. Proved Dec. 20. 1750.
Lib. E, p. 469.

1750, Dec. 14. Inventory, made by Joshua Smalley and James Pyatt. Includes bonds of James Fitzrandolph, John Webster, Jeremiah Dunn, George Boice, Trustrym Manning, FitzRandolph Drake, Moses Burges, Thomas Davis, Gershom Drake, John Tenbroke, Joseph FitzRandolph; also notes of Ephrim Sutton, Zachariah Sutton, Martin Dunham, Andrew Smalley, Peter Martin, Jun'r, Isaac Manning, Moses FitzRandolph, Elisha Whitehead.

1740, April 5. Sutton, Moses, of Pepack, Essex (Somerset?) Co., weaver. Jane Sutton, widow, renounces right to administer, and desires John Sutton, her eldest son, be appointed. Witness—Benjamin Manning.

1740, April 14. Adm'r, John Sutton, of Paypack, yeoman. Benjamin Shelley and Samuel Willet, both of Lebanon, Hunterdon Co., yeomen, fellow bondsmen. Essex Wills, Lib. C, p. 332.

1740, July 7. Inventory, £86.6.4; made by James Sutten, Jelbes Johnson. Debtors—Joseph Samle, Edward Luis, John Johnson, John Harris, John Bell, Hennery Beegel, Edward Jones, James Alen, Aaron Rice, Abraham Drake, Aaron Sutten, James Piat. Bond from James Pyat and Philip Cox, dated April 23, 1719.

1733, May 25. Sutton, Nathan, of Piscataway, Middlesex Co. Inventory, £1.10.0; made by Daniel Sutton and Jeremiah Drake.

1733, Aug. 22. Administration granted to Richard Sutton.
Lib. B, p. 455.

1740, Oct. 13. Sutton, Peter, of Metuchen, Middlesex Co., weaver; will of. Wife, Sarah. Brothers and sisters; no names given. Real and personal estate. Executors—wife, Sarah, James Campble and John Blackford. Witnesses—William McCreery, Alexander Thomson, Richard Sutton. Proved Nov. 1, 1740. Lib. C, p. 359.

1722, Sept. 8. Sutton, Richard, of Piscataway, Middlesex Co., yeoman; will of. Son, Nathan. Other sons and daughters, not mentioned by name. Real and personal estate. Executors—wife, Sarah, brother Daniel Sutton, and brother-in-law Peter Runyon. Witnesses—Jno. Borrowe, William Hunt, Elizabeth Borrowe. Proved Feb. 28, 1732.
Lib. B, p. 385.

1750, April 20. Suydam, Richard, of Freehold, Monmouth Co., blacksmith; will of. Wife, Sarah. Son, Richard, Jr., silver beeker, when of age. Negro man, Yarrow, to wife. Daughters—Elizabeth, Jane, Lucretia and Sarah Suydam, under age. Executors—father-in-law, Johannes Luyster, brethren Hendrick and John Suydam, friend John Williams. Witnesses—Richard Vanmater, Daniel Hay, John Henderson. Proved May 17, 1750. Lib. E, p. 41.

1747, April 6. Swain, John, of Waterford, Gloucester Co., weaver. Int. Adm'r, Thomas Buzby, of Welling borough. Bondsman—John Busby. Lib. 5, p. 429.

1747, April 18. Account. Payments to Benjamin Holmes for funeral, John Holmes, Isaiah Ross, Preserved Brown.

1733, Sept. 21. Swaine, Lemuel, of Cape May Co., whale-man; will of. Wife, Jerusha. Son, Samuel, at 21, 60 acres back of William Johnson, which land I hold by deed from the Proprietors. Son, Reuben, lands whereon I live. Daughters—Abigail, Elizabeth, Marcy, Lydia and Phebe, two-thirds of personal estate, equally. If my wife be with child and it live to maturity, said son or daughter an equal part in the personal. Executors—wife, Jerusha, and son Reuben. Witnesses—Humphrey Hughes, Ebenezar Swaine, Daniel Swaine. Proved 2 March, 1733-4. Lib. 3, p. 408.

1733-4, March 2. Inventory, £103.18.1; made by John Stillwell, Joshua Stites.

1748, Dec. 27. Swallow, Johannes, of Amwell, Hunterdon Co., yeoman; will of. Wife, Eagnes, to be maintained by testator's son, Johanes. Son, Johanes, home plantation. Son, Jacob, plantation "amongst the Rocks," bought of Seth Lowry and James Anderson, in Amwell Township. Son-in-law, Benjamin Johnson. Executors—sons Johannes and Jacob. Witnesses—Thomas Stilwell, Andrew Trimer (Tremer), Philip Ringo. Proved March 27, 1749. Lib. 6, p. 71.

1748, Dec. 30. Swallow, Johannes, Jr., of Amwell, Hunterdon Co., yeoman; will of. Wife, Elizabeth. Daughters—Eagnes and Mary; an unborn child. Plantation left testator by his father's will. Executors—brother, Jacob Swallow, and Philip Ringo. Witnesses—Peter Rockefeller, Thomas Stilwell, Jacob Ronk. Proved March 27, 1749.
Lib. 6, p. 61.

1736, Sept. 29. Swanson, John, of Greenwich, Gloucester Co., yeoman; will of. Peter Tranberg, in special trust, my plantation (300 acres) bought of Zacheus Dunn, on Oldman's Creek, to give rents and profits to my sister, Judy Mattson, during life; same to be divided equally between my cousins, Peter and William Mattson, after the decease of his mother. Cousins—Gertrude Dun, John Justis (for his schooling), Catherine, Liddy and Mary Mattson. Brother, Peter Swanson. Executor, brother Mathias Mattson, he to have residue of personal estate. Witnesses—Samuel Shivers, Jacob Mattson, Joseph Coles. Affirmed 14 Dec., 1736. Lib. 4, p. 78.

1736, Dec. 2. Inventory, £150.19.1; made by Joseph Coles, Samuel Shivers.

1744-5, Feb. 21. Swart, Johannes, of Monmouth Co., yeoman. Int. Barnes Smock and Isabella Heaviland declare before John Bowne, judge, that they heard Rebecca Swart, widow of Jehannas Swart, deceased, say to Jehannas Swart, son of Jacobus, that she would not administer on the estate, that his father may.

1744-5, February 22. Adm'r, Jacobus Swart, yeoman. James Hutchins, Esq., of Middlesex County, fellow bondsman. Lib. D, p. 238.

1748, May 16. Sweeten (Sweeting), William (over 16 years old), son of Andrew Sweeten, of Gloucester Co., yeoman, petitions that William Sell, of Gloucester Co., carpenter, be appointed his guardian. Letters issued. (Burlington Wills), 4343 C.

1737, Aug. 27. Sweeting, Andrew, of Greenwich, Gloucester Co., yeoman. Int. Adm'x, Rebecca Sweeting, (relict). Bondsman—Alexander Randall, Esq., of same place. Witnesses—Hannah Ladd, Michael Fisher. Lib. 4, p. 114.

1738, Sept. 15. Account filed with Inventory. Inventory (£78.4.6).

1747, July 6. Swinder (Swindon), Robert, of Middletown, Monmouth Co.; will of. Daughter, Nancey, under age. Son-in-law, John Delap. Apprentice boy, George Porter. Executors—brother-in-law, John Van Brakle, and friend James Mott. Witnesses—Jarrett Wall, William Wall, James Van Brakel. Proved July 24, 1747.

1747, Aug. 3. Inventory (£140.6.7½) includes tailor's tools, one sword. Made by Jarret Wall and John Bowne.

1747, Aug. 12. James Mott, of Middletown, renounces as executor. Monmouth Wills, 1437-43 M.

1737, 3 mo. (May), 21 da. Sykes, Ann, of Waterford, Gloucester Co.; will of. Samuel Coles, executor. Sister, Elizabeth Cosings. Sister's son, James Cosings (not 21); her daughter, Mary, (not 18), legacies when of age, and residue of estate. Witnesses—Susanna Coles, Benjamin Stokes, Samuel Lippincott. Affirmed June 13, 1737. Lib. 4, p. 105.

1737, May 31. Inventory, 72.2.1; made by Sam. Lippincott, John Collins.

1738, Dec. 30. Account by Josiah White.

1737, June 19. Taber, Benjamin, of Gloucester Township and Co.; will of. Wife Elizabeth, whole estate, including gold, silver, jewels, etc., and to be executrix and "universal actrix," to bring up the children until they will be fit for trades. She may dispose of plantation lately purchased by me from Thomas Munnyon, in township and County aforesaid. Witnesses—Samuel McColloch, John Edge, Will Kyd, Richard Chew. Affirmed 31 July, 1738. Lib. 4, p. 148.

1737, July 17. Inventory (£142.18.6) includes man-servant, £5; wearing apparel, £5; cash, £1; debts due him, £16.14.9; cattle, £36.5. Appraisers—George Ward, Samuel McCulloch.

1742, Sept. 13. Talbart, William, of Bordentown, Burlington Co., cooper. Int. Jennit Talbart, widow, requests that Joseph Richards, yeoman, be appointed administrator. Bond of Joseph Richards. Preserved Brown, Jun'r, fellow bondsman. Lib. 4, p. 377.

1742, Sept. 13. Inventory, £56.16.4; made by William Morlan and Benoni Gregory.

1732, Sept. 19. Talbot, Sarah, of Trenton, Hunterdon Co.; will of. Daughter, Martha Talbot, to be apprenticed to Rachel Pinyard, wife of Matthias Pinyard, sister of testatrix, to learn trade of tailoress, until 18. Executors—friends, Captain James Gould and James Trent, gentleman. Witnesses—John Anderson, Mary Oboyle, Jos. Yard. Proved Feb. 10, 1732. Lib. 3, p. 245.

1732-3, Feb. 10. James Trent and James Gould renounced executorship. Administration to John Anderson.

1736, Feb. 21. Talman, James, of Shrewsbury, Monmouth Co., yeoman; will of. Wife, Abigail. Son, James, negroes Jemmy and Joe; cattle at Toms River. Eldest daughter, Deborah Mott. Daughter, Mary, negro girl, Sall. Youngest daughter, Elizabeth, under age, negro girl, Pegg. Executors—wife, son James, brother Benjamin Talman, friends John Redford and Pontius Stelle. Witnesses—William Brinley, Edward Patterson Cook, W. Brinley, Jr., Jacob Dennis. Proved March 29, 1737. Lib. C, p. 159.

1737, May 27. Inventory (£1,581.00.11¾) includes silver plate, £15; 12 negroes, £377. Made by Jacob Dennis, Pontius Stelle, George Williams.

1739, Sept. 14. Tantum, John, Ju'r, of Nottingham, Burlington Co.; will of. Son, John. Other children mentioned, not named. Real and personal estate. Wife, Anne, executrix and to have personal estate. Witnesses—John Middleton, Walter Davenport, Parnell Cleayton. Proved Oct. 25, 1739. Lib. 4, p. 184.

1739, 12th day, 8th mo. (Oct.). Inventory, £172.2.2; made by John Middleton and Gissbert Henderson. Includes servant boy and girl, £5.

1742, Feb. 27. Tantum, John, of Nottingham, Burlington Co.; will of. Wife, Rebekah, personal estate. Son, Joseph. Daughter-in-law—Ann Tantum, widow of deceased son, John, and their children—Francis, Mary, Martha and John. Daughters—Elizabeth Worth, Mary Morfin, Ann Heulens and Sarah, wife of Jonathan Lovet. Children of dau., Mary Morfin. Grandson, Abraham Heulens. £5 to be paid Mathew and Marmaduke Watson for burying ground at Crosswicks. Mentions William Morfin. Land in Hunterdon and other real estate. Executors—wife, and brother-in-law Thomas Folkes. Witnesses—Rob't Priest, Charles Burton, Sarah Shippy. Proved Nov. 6, 1742. Lib. 4, p. 330.

1742, Nov. 6. Inventory, £263.10.3; made by John Lawson and William Wills. Includes 2 servants £18.

1744, April 12. Tappen, David, of Woodbridge, Middlesex Co., weaver; will of. Nephew, Isaac, son of Abraham Tappen, land on which I live. Executors—wife, Hannah, and friend Jonathan Frazee.

Real and personal estate. Witnesses—Mary Wright, Joseph Donham, David Donham, Jun'r. Proved Dec. 9, 1748. Lib. E, p. 225.

1732, Nov. 8. Tappen, Jacob, of Cohansey, Salem Co., yeoman, husbandman; will of. Wife, Mary, executrix, and to have during life all real estate in Cohansey; after her decease, to my daughter-in-law, Mercy Williams, and her lawful heirs; in default of such issue, to my grandson, Joseph Hodge. Witnesses—Charles Davis, George Gray, Jno. Podmore. Affirmed 5 Feb., 1732. Lib. 3, p. 278.

1732, Nov. 24. Inventory, £141.14.9; includes cattle and sheep £32.3. Made by Ebenizer Smith, Jonathan Stathem.

1749-50, March 6. Tapscott, James, of Upper Freehold Township, Monmouth Co., yeoman; will of. Wife, Margaret. Plantation to son William. Negress, Cate, to son James. Executors—son, William, and Edward Taylor. Witnesses—William Scott, Richard Harent, John Lawrence. Proved Nov. 22, 1750. Lib. E, p. 464.

1750, April 10. Inventory (£420.0.1) includes 38 paper books and 48 bound books, £5.17.00; old gun and old sword; 36 bbls. flour and 1 bbl. corn meal, £30. Made by Thomas Cox and Joseph Holmes.

1750, Aug. 1. Tate, Thomas, of Somerset Co. Int. Adm'r, Peter DeReimer. Fellow bondsman, Albert Voorhees. Lib. E, p. 445.

1750, Oct. 22. Inventory, £12.18.7; made by Abraham Hegeman, Albert Van Voorhes, Jochm. Gulick, Saml. Gulick.

1748, June 1. Tatem, John, of Deptford Township, Gloucester Co., tailor. Int. Adm'x, Sarah Tatem, widow. Bondsman—Abraham Chattin, Jun., of same place, carpenter. Witness—Jacob Heulings. Lib. 7, p. 43.

1748, May 20. Inventory, £95.4.10; made by John Chew, Michael Fisher.

1750, July 17. Account. Monies paid James Wood, John Ladd, Joseph Hugg, Jane Waite, Jonathan Fowler, John Snowden, William Wood, Andrew Sloan, Elizabeth Lord, John Blackwood, William Fletcher, William Cooper, Nathan Lord, John Jessop, James Cattell, Jonas Jagard, John Chew, Edward Richardson, Phebe Ward, Michael Fisher, Thomas Kimsey, John Jagard, Timothy Matlack, Moses Ward, Nixon Chattin, John Marshall, Habakkuk Ward, Abraham Chattin, Abraham Chattin, Jun., Richard Chew, Joseph Marshall, James Lord, William Sill (guardian of William Sweetin), Thomas Redman.

1742, May 14. Tatem, Stephen, of Deptford Township, Gloucester Co., yeoman; will of. Brother, Joseph, executor, and to have all estate, real and personal. If he depart this life before recovery of a bond (£50) under the hand of my brother William, dec., in such case I give the bond to William Tatem, son of said Joseph. (Signed Oct. 16, 1742). Witnesses—Shadrach Clement, Isaac Butterworth, William Tatem. Proved 23 Oct., 1742. (Letters granted Oct. 17, 1745). Lib. 5, p. 178.

1745, May 6. Inventory, £54.02; made by Robert Boggs, John Snowden.

1739, July 7. Tatem, William, of Deptford, Gloucester Co. Int. Adm'x, Mary Tatem, widow. Bondsmen—John Wood and George Ward, of same place. Lib. 4, p. 183.

1739, 26-27, 4 mo. (June). Inventory (£308.18.9) includes moneys due from Josiah Alberson, Thomas Kimsey, Jun'r, William Borton, Samuel McColloh, John Collins, Edward Wilson, Amos Jerland, Richard Lloyd, John Smallwood (for John Lad, Jun'r), Nichlas Juthreson, Henry Roe, William Harrison, Edward Williams, Benjamin Wood, Enoch Halsworth, Patrick Lloyd, John Stow, William Middleton, Aaron Ashbrook, John Ogilby, Robert Bryon. (Mentions payment by Willm. Tatem to Joseph Preacher, on settlement between Tatem and Samuel Bustill). Appraisers —George Ward, John Wood, Henry Sparks.

1741, Aug. 15. Account. Moneys paid Doctor Bard, Doctor Shaw, Joshua Maddox, Owen Owen (Executor of Charity Brown, dec'd), Edward Richardson, John Ladd, John Chatten, James Cooper, William Ives, Abraham Chattin, Robert Down, Thomas Kimsey, Jun'r, Solomon Smith, John Boreton, Mary Tatem, Jon. Jessup, George Scott, John Marshall, Jas. McChestnut, James Hinchman, Sarah Coxe, Rich'd Floyd, John Dilkes, Sam'l Reine, Jas. O' Bryan, Joseph Armitt, Sarah Norris, Wm. Lashley, George Shirrill, John Snowden, John Stokes, Moses Ward, Henry Stevens, Philip Devereux, Thos. Penrose, Robert Gerrard, Levi Peirce, Thomas Wilkins, Elizabeth Roberts, John Mickel, John Dilks, Peter Matson, Jacob Ware, Sam'l Raine, Ann Cooper, Andrew Hamilton.

1735, March 29. Tathem (Tatem), John, Sr., of Deptford Township, Gloucester Co., yeoman; will of. Wife, Mary, executrix, to have the use of plantation we live on, and an acre of ground near the Quaker Meeting-house, and, during life, the lower plantation. Son, William, 220 acres of land I live on according to deed of gift already given him; if he die with [out] issue, same shall go to my son, Stephen; and if he die without lawful heirs, to son Joseph. Son, John, and daughter, Patience Albeson. Assistant—Abraham Liddon. Witnesses —James Wilkins, Henry Sparks, Edward Hughes. Sworn and affirmed May 2, 1738. Lib. 4, p. 132.

1731, June 11. Taylor, Christopher, of Gloucester Co., guardian of William Hugg, eldest son of Joseph Hugg, late of aforesaid Co., innholder, with Samuel Harrison, Esq., of same County. Witnesses— Edw. R. Price, John Ladd, Jun'r. Lib. 3, p. 142.

1733, Oct. 20. Taylor, Christopher, of Greenwich, Gloucester Co., guardian of Mary Dalbo, an orphan within age, daughter of Charles Dalbo of same place and county. Witness—Mary W. Renold. Lib. 3, p. 381.

1747, Dec. 21. Taylor, Daniel, of Newark, Essex Co., clerk; will of. "Being aged and infirm." Wife, Elizabeth. Children—Daniel, Jemima, Mary, Elizabeth, David, Joseph and Job; last five under age. Real and personal estate. Executors—friends and brethren in covenant relation, Joseph Peck and David Williams. Witnesses—Abraham Soverhill, Eleazer Lamson, Sarah Lamson. Proved Jan. 23, 1747. Lib. E, p. 128.

1733, Feb. 22. Taylor, Edward, of Shrewsbury, Monmouth Co., yeoman; will of. Wife, Catharine. Son, Edward, silver cup. Sons, Edward and John, land in Freehold, bought of John Okeson. Son, James, a minor, land bought of Samuel Leonard. Sons, Thomas, Joseph and George, minors. Land bought of John Reid. Sheep at Crosswicks. Daughters—Esther, Susannah, Hannah, Catherine and Rebecca. Executors—wife, and brothers William and Joseph Taylor, and Thomas

Morphet. Witnesses—Henry and Thomas Leonard, and John Nathaniel Hutchens.

Codicil, same date. Bonds due from Peter Demun to Thomas Holmes and Daniel Tilton of Middletown. Bond Peter Demun and testator's son Edward to David Johnston. Deed from Elias Holmes. Moses Crage, John Eaton, Esquire, John Williams, Benjamin Borden. Proved June 12, 1734.
Lib. B, p. 554.

1734, June 3. Inventory (£257.9) includes a loom, and negroes (£40). Made by John Killy, John Throckmorton, Jonathan Forman.

1734, Oct. 11. Additional inventory, £67.19.04; made by David Killay, John Throckmorton, Jon'n Forman. Mentions Rev. John Fegel, Moses Craig, Isaiah Okisson.

1738, Aug. 11. Taylor, George, of Cape May Co., yeoman; will of. Wife, Lydia. Children—William, George, John, Matthias, Daniel, Lydia (all under age). Executors—wife, and son William ("now very ill"). Witnesses—Joshua Shaw, Nathan Shaw, Francis Taylor.

1738, Aug. 14. Codicil. One plantation to son William; another to son George. Witnesses—(same as above). Proved July 14, 1739.

1739, May 19. Inventory, £232.11.3; made by Ebenezer Swaine and John Stites. Cape May Wills, 95 E.

1737, Jan. 14. Taylor, Hope, of Monmouth Co., aged about 16. John Stout, guardian. Abraham Watson, fellow bondsman. Lib. C, p. 181.

1750, Sept. 10. Taylor, Hugh, of Middlesex Co. Int. Adm'x, Frances Taylor, widow. Lewis Johnston, Esq., fellow bondsman.
Lib. E, p. 452.

1750, Oct. 12. Inventory (£485.08.6) includes silver watch and eleven negroes. Made by Jno. Barclay and John Combs. Witness—John Throckmorton.

1740, July 10. Taylor, John, of Bordentown, Burlington Co., carpenter; will of. Wife, Lydia, real and personal estate to bring up my children, John, Elizabeth and Amos (all under age). Executors—wife, her father Thomas Wright, and John Thorn. Witnesses—Burgis Hall, Safety Borden, Benoni Gregory. Proved July 28, 1741.
Lib. 4, p. 291.

1741, July 27. Inventory, £96.19.4; made by Isaac Horner and Benoni Gregory. Includes carpenter's tools, £5.5.

1744-5, Feb. 15. Taylor, John, of Shrewsbury, Monmouth Co., farmer. Int. Adm'rs, Mary Taylor, the widow, and Edward Taylor, brother of deceased. Joseph Throckmorton, fellow bondsman.
Lib. D, p. 237.

1744-5, Feb. 16. Inventory (£424.15.1) includes 68 sheep, 32 swine, 14 cows and heifers, negro man and wench (£90), weaving loom; debts due from Jonathan Thickston, Edward Brooks and William Vannote. Made by Jonathan Forman and Joseph Throckmorton. (Note on reverse of inventory states articles mentioned as half belonging to deceased, were half the property of intestate's brother, George Taylor).

1748, Sept. 30. Taylor, John, of Chesterfield, Burlington Co., yeoman; will of. Wife, Deliverance. Sons—Aaron, Ezra and John, all under age. Expected child. Real and personal estate. Executors—father-in-law, Benjamin Robins, Sen'r, and kinsman Samuel Cheshire.

Witnesses—Joseph Reckless, Ju'r, Rowelth Beck, Sam'l Harris. Proved June 8, 1750. Lib. 6, p. 382.

1750, June 8. Inventory, £420.15.11; made by Thos. Duglass and Joseph Reckless. Includes bonds of Mich. Newbold, Jos. Reckless and Wm. Chapman, Jun'r.

1747, Aug. 27. Taylor, Joseph, of Freehold, Monmouth Co., yeoman; will of. Wife, Eleanor. Children—Joseph, John, Amey Strickland, Hannah Chamberlain, Anne Tomson, Rebecca Clayton, William, David, Mary, Margaret, and Eleanor. Executors—wife, son Joseph, and cousin Edward Taylor, of Middletown. Witnesses—Rebecca Mills, William Norcross, John Henderson. Proved April 27, 1748. Lib. E, p. 173.

1748, April 8. Taylor, Nicholas, of Burlington Co. Int. Adm'r, Andrew Anderson. Thomas Shaw, fellow bondsman. Both of Burlington Co. Lib. 5, p. 439.

1730 (?), Aug. 8. Taylor, Sarah, of Shrewsbury, Monmouth Co. Inventory (£420.3.4¼) includes bonds, etc., of Robert White, Hugh Hartshorne, John Mount, Zebulon Clayton, John Estell, Willson & Hortopie, William Hews, Brindley & Curlis, James & Willson, Jacob and Jonathan Robins, George Rescarick, Margaret Leonard, Gasharea & Kinnan, James Stelle. Made by John Curlies and William and Thomas Lippincott. Signed by William and Hugh Hartshorne.

1737-8, Feb. 28. Additional inventory. Bonds, etc., of William Hugs and George Molat. Made by John Curlies, Thomas Lippincott, William Hartshorne. Monmouth Wills, 803-5 M.

1749, April 3. Taylor, William, of Chesterfield, Burlington Co. Int. Adm'r, Charles Taylor, of same, carpenter. Samuel Farnsworth, bricklayer, fellow bondsman. Lib. 6, p. 331; Lib. 7, p. 97.

1749, April 6. Inventory, £121.18½; made by Wm. French and Sam'l Farnsworth. Includes debts from George Gilbert, James Powell, Jacob DeCow, Burgess Hall, Joseph Borden, Edward Blaney, Phillip Marrot, George Bliss, Robert Ashton, Samuel Harris, Charles Miller, Adam Pavey, Thomas Bishop, Thomas Douglass, Benj'n Franch, William Marlain, Jacob Hooker, Daniel Barker, Charles Vandike, John Stevenson, John Flintham, Matthew Forsyth, Mary Cleaton, Matthew Wright, John Thorn, John Trapnal, Joseph Field, Joseph Tilton, Joseph Wright, Benja. Biles, John Collins, William French. Insolvent Debtors: James Powell, Burgiss Hall, Jos. Borden, Sam'l Harris, Chas. Miller, Adam Pavey, Thos. Duglis, Wm. Morlam, Jacob Hooler, Daniel Harker, Chas. Vandike, Jno. Stevenson, Mary Cleaton, Jno. Trapnell, Jos. Field, Jos. Wright, Jno. Collings.

1749-50, Jan. 4. Account. Payments to Thomas Budd, John Ashton, George Bliss, John Horner, Safety Borden, Preserved Brown, Thomas Briggs, John Elgin, Charles Jolley, Jos. Richards, Sam'l Farnsworth, Jos. English, Jacob Taylor, Jos. Borden, Jun'r, Benoni Gregory, John Imlay (for funeral charges), Jacob Taylor, Jno. Budd, Joseph Aronson, Geo. Palmer, and Jno. Beecks (for burial of deceased at Crosswicks).

1734-5, March 15. Tees (Teaze), Robert, of Bethlehem, Hunterdon Co., weaver. Int. Inventory (£57.8.6) includes Indian goods, £4; loom and tackling, £7. Made by Robert Laning and John Moore.

1735, March 31. Adm'r, John Couan (Cowen) of Bethlehem. Robert Laning, of same place, surety. Witnesses—Andrew Lyttle, James Cowan; Will Robison.

1736, April 6. Account. Mentions Benjamin Severns, John Garrison, Samuel Johnson, Andrew Little, John Mullen, William Devall, James Mease, Abraham Vanhorn, Israel Riky. Hunterdon Wills, 105 J.

1741, Oct. 22. Tenbroek, John, of Rocky Hill, Somerset Co., yeoman. Int. Adm'x, Catherine, widow. Fellow bondsmen—George Van Nest, yeoman, and Benjamin Price, Esq., of New Brunswick.
Lib. C, p. 453.

1747, Aug. 14. Tenbrook, Wessel, of Somerset Co.; will of. Wife, Neeltje, the home-plantation (400 acres) with the negroes and stock, during widowhood. In case of marriage, executors to have same for use of the children: Jacob (the oldest), Tyerk, Johannes, Anatje and Elizabeth (all under 21). Wife, Neeltje, executrix. Executors—brother, Cornelius, Jacob Tenbrook, brother-in-law, Henry and Andreas Dewitt, Peter Nevius and John Berrien. Witnesses—Abraham Stryker, Hendrick Tader, Thomas McBryde. Proved 1st March, 1747-8.

1750, Aug. 3. "Peter Nevius qualified." Lib. E, p. 149.

1748, Dec. 1. Inventory (£563.8.6) includes horses, sheep, negroes Quack (£70), Kuff (£65), Pete (£55), Sarah and Pegg (£23), Deanna (£18); woman servant (£6). Made by Roelof VanDike, Abraham Stryker.

1753, Apr. 24. Inventory continued (£1,293.7.5) includes notes of James Hill, Isaac Schonhorsden, Hendrick Baeriene, John Sutvin, Isaac King, Peter Wienaer, Cornelius Tinbrook. Made by Roeloff Van Dike, Gerrit Dorlant.

1749, Dec. 12. Terrill, Josiah, of Elizabeth Town, Essex Co., yeoman. Int. Adm'r, Lewis Terrill, of Connecticut. John Terrill and Ephraim Terrill, both of Elizabeth Town, fellow bondsmen.
Lib. E, p. 353.

1735, April 11. Tesdal, John, of Waterford, Gloucester Co.; will of. Friends, Henry Wood and Sarah Wild, executors and legatees. Brother, George, one shilling. Mentions William Albortson. Witnesses—Mary Wood, Thomas Boner, John Green. Sworn and affirmed, 14 June, 1735.

1735, June 13. Inventory, £20.10; made by Samuel Nicholson, John Green. Gloucester Wills, 187 H.

1727, Aug. 24. Teunissen, Cornelius, of Raratan River, Somerset Co.; will of. Wife, Neelye, the home plantation on Raritan River, during widowhood. Oldest son, Cornelius, one-half of same at her remarriage or death, and to pay to my eldest daughter, Fenmeye, widow of George Fairly £300. Second son, Tunis, to have the other half and weaving looms. Peter DuMont, John Tunissen, Junior, Derk Van Veghten, to proportion said plantation equally between these sons. Tunis to pay my youngest daughter, Sarah, £300. Third son, John, the plantation on which he now lives, at the "bound brook," which was purchased of Jonathan Douty. The youngest son, Dinis, that plantation between the first and second mountains, bought of Jacob Sebring, on which my son Cornelius now lives. Residue of estate, consisting of bonds, plate, jewels, cattle, horses, slaves, etc., to be divided equally among the six children. Executors—sons Cornelius and Tunis. Witnesses—Peter Sonmans, Manuel Correll, Noah Butterton. Proved 3 Oct. and 3 Nov., 1731. Lib. B, p. 238.

1733, April 10. Tharp, Benjamin, of Woodbridge, Middlesex Co. Int. Adm'r, Thomas Edgar. Lib. B, p. 380.

1735, July 5. Tharp, Israel, of Woodbridge, Middlesex Co., yeoman; will of. Children—Jonathan, Thomas, Lydia, and Anna, all under age. Lands bought of John Beal, Shobal Smith, William Bingle and Edward Crowell. Executrix—wife, Mary. Witnesses—John Bilyou, Moses Freeman, Jonathan Shepard. Proved Feb. 13, 1735.
Lib. C, p. 68.

1736, May 31. Tharpe (Thorp), Mary, of Woodbridge, Middlesex Co., widow, and executrix of last will of Israel Tharpe. Int. Adm'rs, Thomas Thorpe and Jonathan Shepherd, both of Woodbridge. Jos. Leigh, fellow bondsman. Witnesses—James Smyth, Lawrence Smyth.
Lib. C, p. 101.

1749, May 12. Thatcher, John, of Kingwood, Hunterdon Co.; will of. Daughter, Ann, to be brought up by testator's wife, not named. Executors—brothers, James and Jeremiah Thatcher. Witnesses—Mathew Resley, Edmond Thatcher, John Arrison. Proved August 1, 1749. Lib. 6, p. 276.

1749, August 1. Susanna, widow of John Thatcher, withdraws her caveat.

1749, Aug. 15. Inventory (£47.3.3) includes gun and sword, £1.10. Made by Jaques Barkeloo and Daniel Lake.

1752, Nov. 19. Account. Mentions John Lewis, Doctor, William Montgomery, Nathaniel Pettit, Daniel Howell, Justice Montgomery, A Curtis, William Sleter, William Barnes, William Thatcher, Joseph Thatcher, Jr., Aaron Sigock (?), Isaac Rutinghouse, Charles Hoff, Jr., William Foular, Lot Ritinghouse, Jona. Furman, Jacob Swallow, Edmond Thatcher, James Allen, John Allen, Jeremiah Thatcher, Elizabeth Thatcher, Joseph Thatcher, Sr., William Allen.

1747, May 26. Thickston, John, of Middlesex Co., blacksmith. Mary Thickston, widow, renounces her right of administration, and desires that William Clawson be appointed. Witnesses—Samuel Martin, Isaac Manning.

1747, May 26. Bond of William Clawson of Essex Co., and Isaac Manning of Middlesex Co., yeomen, principal creditors, as administrators. John Deare, of Perth Amboy, fellow bondsman. Lib. E, p. 46.

1748, March 29. Thomas, John, of Deptford Township, Gloucester Co., laborer. Int. Adm'x, Prudence Thomas, widow. Bondsman—Thomas Kimsey, of same County, yeoman. Witness—John Mickle.
Lib. 6, p. 13.

1747-8, 1st mo. (Mar.), 12 da. Inventory, £82.18.2; made by John Wilkins, William Wood.

1750, June 30. Thomas, John, of Evesham, Burlington Co., single man; will of. Davis Strattan to be discharged from all debt due me. Executor—friend, Robert Braddock, who is sole legatee of all estate, real and personal. Witnesses—Elizabeth Holbird, Sarah Price, Thomas Shinn. Proved July 13, 1750. Lib. 6, p. 385.

1750, July 21. Inventory, £48.15; made by William Sharp and David Strattan.

1750, Aug. 29. Thomas, Joseph, of City of Burlington, shipwright. Int. Adm'x, Sarah Thomas, widow. William Heulings, of same, fellow bondsman. Lib. 7, p. 40.

1731, May 10. Thomas, Lewis, of Hanover, Burlington Co., schoolmaster. Int. Inventory, £15.3.6; made by John Bullock, Benjamin Kirby, John Steward. Debts due from Thomas Bevis, Thomas Branson, William Rogers, Ju'r, Francis Mills, Joseph Rogers, James Starkey, Dr. Wright, Banja. Kirby, Andrew Race, Isaac Knight, John Rumford, Joseph Holt, Steven Wright, Francis Fowler, Cornelius Clauson.

1731, May 29. Adm'r, Joshua Wright. John Steward, bondsman. Both of New Hanover, yeomen. Burlington Wills, 2175-80 C.

1738, Sept. 15. Thomas, Philip, of Evesham, Burlington Co., husbandman. Int. Hannah Thomas, widow, renounces right of administration in favor of Benjamin Moore, yeoman, principal creditor.

1738, Sept. 23. Adm'r, Benjamin Moore, of Evesham. John Doe, fellow bondsman. Lib. 4, p. 149.

1738, Nov. 27. Inventory, £58.4; made by Levi Shinn and William Sharp.

1745, Jan. 25. Thompkins (Tomkins), Elleeazer, of Newark, Essex Co., yeoman; will of. Rev. Mr. Aaron Burr, £10, for use of the Gospel. Daughter, Rachel, remainder of real and personal estate at 21; in case of her death, my brothers and sisters. Wife, Hannah. Land called Tomkins Point. Executors—brother, David Thompkins, and Joseph Harrison. Witnesses—Stephen Baldwin, Samuel Crane, William Turner. Proved Feb. 18, 1745-6. Lib. D, p. 367.

1745-6, Feb. 18. Inventory (£129.13.10) includes bonds of Sam'll Baldwin, John Ball, Nath'll Anderson. Made by Isaac Lyon and Wm. Turner.

1749, April 18. Thompson, Aaron, of Mendam Township, Morris Co. Int. Adm'x, Mary Thompson, widow. Bondsman—Ebenezer Byram, of same place.

1749, 15 Aug. Inventory (£99.10.10) includes 3 Bibles, 6 other books, and debtors: Capt. Bobbet, Joseph Dod, John Cary, Stephen Dod, Perkins Lovel, Malici Hallowy. Appraisers—Henry Clark, Ezekiel Lyon. Lib. E, p. 298.

1748, April 9. Thompson, Catharine (alias Catharine Robison), of Middlesex Co.; will of. Children—John and Moses Thompson. Real and personal estate. Executors—William Macdaniel and Mallieiah (Malachi) Randolph. Witnesses—Jonathan FitzRandolph, Ebenezer Saltar. Proved May 24, 1749. Lib. E, p. 305.

1748, April 12. Inventory (£25.08.11) includes Dutch "Wheall." Made by Gershom Martin and William Sharp.

1732, July 10. Thompson, Henry, of Mansfield, Burlington Co.; will of. Sons—Thomas and John. Daughters—Rebecca Guest and Dina Hopkins. Meadow adjoining Jacob DeCow and other lands. Executors—wife, Elizabeth, and friend John Tantum. Witnesses—Constantine Overton, Jno. Tantum, Jr., Elizabeth Tantum. Proved Dec. 2, 1735. Lib. 4, p. 46.

1735, Dec. 1. Inventory, £116.8; made by John Rockhill and David Rockhill. Includes negro girl, £8.

1740, Sept. 20. Thompson, Isaac, of Alloways Creek, Salem Co., weaver. Int. Adm'r, John Thompson, gent. Bondsman—John Hunt. All of said county. Witnesses—John Fitzpatrick, Danl. Mestayer. Lib. 4, p. 256.

1740, Sept. 20. Inventory (£6.2.6) includes loom and tackling. Appraisers—John Fitzpatrick, John Kelly.

1729-30, March 9. Thompson, James, of Town and Co. of Burlington, cordwainer; will of. Wife, Elizabeth, personal estate to bring up children, and sole executrix. Real estate. Witnesses—Sam'l Smith, Abra. Heulings, Is. DeCow. Proved ———, 1733.

Burlington Wills, 2027 C.

1732, June 24. Thompson, John, of New Brunswick, Middlesex Co., merchant; will of. Body to be buried in the church ground at Piscataway; funeral charges not to exceed £20. Wife, Mary, now in Dublin, Ireland. Son, Benjamin, in Ireland. Son, John, suit of black broad cloath and silk westcoat and breeches. Servant man, David Davies. Real and personal estate. Executors—Coll. John Hamilton of Perth Amboy, merchant, Mr. Robert King of Perth Amboy, collector, Mr. James Hude of New Brunswick, merchant, and son, John Thompson, now of New Brunswick, schoolmaster. Mr. Benjamin Price, of New Brunswick, attorney, and Mr. John Parker of Perth Amboy, attorney, to collect debts. Witnesses—Alexand'r Moore, Jno. Dally, Sam'll Belknap, David Davies. Proved Sept. 24, 1733.

Lib. B, p. 468.

1739, Dec. 17. Thompson, Joseph, of Alloways Creek, Salem Co.; will of. Wife, Sarah, use of plantation during widowhood. Sons—William, 170 acres, part of the land I live on; Joseph, 50 acres, adjoining John Hilton, also that he be apprenticed. Daughters—Elizabeth, Jane, Martha, Sarah, Grace, Mary and Susannah, the two-thirds of my moveable estate. Executors—wife, and my son William. Witnesses—Benj. Holme, Martin Garrel, William Thompson. Affirmed 25 April, 1740.

1740, May 1. Letters granted to Sarah Thompson. Lib. 4, p. 231.

1739-40, 11 mo. (Jan.), 30 da. Inventory, £137.8.2; made by Benj. Holme, William Oakford.

1749, July 4. Thompson, Joseph, of Mendam, Morris Co.; will of. Sons—Stephen (eldest) the land where I dwell, bought of John Bullan, except 10 acres on the north side of the road from Rocksitecos to Morristown, which I formerly gave to my son Aaron, deceased; David, 95 acres purchased of Josiah and David Ogden, Esqrs., together with meadow, 15 acres, purchased of Benjamin Lenard, deceased, and at 21 to have £150 out of the moveable estate, to be paid by my son Stephen. Daughter, Desire; grandson (not 21), son of my son Daniel, deceased, by Abegal Byram; the children of my son Stephen and my daughter Marey. Executors—son, Stephen, and Jeremiah Brown. Witnesses—Ezra Cary, Daniel Cary, Brice Riky. Proved 19 July, 1749. Lib. E, p. 316.

1745-6, Jan. 13. Thompson, Nathaniel, of the Borough of Elizabeth, Essex Co., yeoman. Int. Adm'r, Benjamin Thompson, uncle. Samuel Chandler and Timothy Thompson, fellow bondsmen.

Lib. D, p. 357.

1748, June 29. Inventory, £81.05.10½; made by Christopher Wood and Benjamin Crane. Witnesses—Samuel Walter, Richard Townley.

1739, Aug. 1. Thompson (Thomson), Phebe, of Essex Co., an orphan about 16. Bond of Jonathan Dayton as guardian. John Thompson, fellow bondsman. Both of Elizabeth Town, yeomen. Witness—Rachell Harrison. (John Thomson not being admitted guardian to his sister, Jonathan Dayton was chosen). Lib. C, p. 286.

1733, July 19. Thompson, Samuel, of Salem Co., yeoman. Int. Adm'x, Abigail Thompson. Bondsman—Samuel Forster. Both of said County. Witnesses—John Weale, Danl. Mestayer. Lib. 3, p. 362.

1732-3, Jan. 14. Inventory (£168.17.6) includes cattle, horses, sheep, oxen. Appraisers—Saml. Forster, James White.

1749, Dec. 17. Thompson, Samuel, of Alloways Creek, Salem Co., yeoman; will of. Wife, Edith, use of the home plantation until my son Thomas will be 21; said son to pay £12 to his brother Samuel when 21, likewise to his brother Aaron when 21. Daughters—Ann, Mary and Rebekah. The 56 acres I bought of William Atwood, merchant, of Philadelphia, to be sold. Executors—wife, and Benjamin Thompson. Witnesses—Joseph Ware, William Oakford, Hugh Blackwood. Affirmed 24 Feb., 1749-50. Lib. 6, p. 426.

1749-50, Jan. 24. Inventory (£223.0.2) includes "still and necessarys belonging to it, £21.15." Appraisers—Joseph Ware, William Oakford.

1750, June 19. Thompson, Stephen, of Morris Co., blacksmith; will of. Legacies bequeathed by my deceased father in will dated 4th July, 1749, shall be paid by my executors. Wife, Marey, to hold the home plantation until my son, Jacob, will be 21, that she may bring up and school the children. Jacob, at age, to pay legacies to my daughters, Phebe and Lydia, when they will be 18, and plantation to be divided equally between them in case of death of my son. Executors—Joseph Hinds, of Morris Co., Brice Riky, of Somerset Co., and my wife, Marey. Witnesses—Ezra Cary, Daniel Cary, Dezier Thompson. Proved 9 July, 1750. Lib. E, p. 430.

1750, Aug. 14. (Filed 8 Dec., 1757). Inventory (£514.19.8); made by Daniel Cary and Caleb Balwin. (On back of inventory: "Pade to the widdow besides, when she married").

1750, Sept. 8. List of debtors—David Allen, John Heams, Henry Clark, John Cary, Perkins Lovet, Zekel Lyon, Ebenezer Byrams, Jun'r, Japheth Byrams, Caleb Linsley, Saml. Ford, Morris Aber, John Whitehead, John Heams, Richard Carton, Timothy Penetant, Caleb Baldwin, Ezra Carey, Captn. Robet, Benjn. Leonard, Ebenezer Allen, Pipes & Browns, John Wills, Ezra Carey, Danl. Carey.

1743, Sept. 14. Thompson, Thomas, of Mansfield, Burlington Co., yeoman; will of. Wife, Agnes, personal estate and plantation during widowhood, to enable her to bring up my younger sons and daughters. Sons—John and Thomas. Executors—wife, and friend Thomas Biddle. Witnesses—John Laning, James Hammell, Isaac DeCow, medius. Proved Oct. 8, 1743. Lib. 5, p. 1.

1743, Oct. 8. Inventory, £66.16.9; made by Joseph Tallman and Nathan Potts.

1747, Dec. 24. Thompson, Thomas, of Salem Town and Co., joiner; will of. Wife, Mary, during life, use of the house I live in; then my son, Daniel, shall possess it, he paying £20 to my son Joshua, and to my daughter Mary. Executors—wife, and my brother, Joshua Thompson. Witnesses—Samuel Abbott, Eliz. Hall, Thos. Rice. (Not properly proved). Salem Wills, 844 Q.

1730, Feb. 11. Thompson, Thomas, Jun'r, of Elizabeth Town, Essex Co., yeoman; will of. Mary and Nathaniel, children of my first wife, the daughter of Nathaniel Lyon, deceased, land in common between

me and Stephen Brown. Other children—Thomas, Daniel, Sarah and Joanna, land purchased of George Harris, dec'd. Executors—wife, Sarah, and brother Jonathan Thompson. Witnesses—James Galloway, Samuel Whitehead, Jonathan Meeker. Proved April 13, 1731.
Lib. B, p. 206.

1734, May 15. Inventory, £111.18.09; made by David Whitehead and Henry Peirson.

1733, April 7. Thompson, William, of Alloways Creek, Salem Co.; will of. Sons—Joseph (had portion); William (had portion); Samuel, the home plantation, he paying £15 to my son Benjamin and £5 to my grandson Sam'l Test when they will be 21; the said Benjamin to have 20 acres on the south side of the creek and 5 acres joining the bridge. Daughter, Sarah (had portion). Rest of personal estate to son Benjamin and daughter Rebekah. One acre for use of a burying ground and a meeting-house for the people called Quakers. Executors—sons, William and Benjamin. Witnesses—Benjamin Holme, John Powel, Richard Bradford. Affirmed 25 April, 1734.

1734, April 25. Letters granted to William Thompson.
Lib. 3, p. 418.

1734, 2 mo. (Apr.), 16 da. Inventory (£146.13;) made by Benj. Holmes, Daniel Fogg.

1750, Sept. 29. Thomson, Lewis, of Freehold, Monmouth Co., yeoman; will of. Wife Sarah. Daughters—Mary and Elizabeth. Brother, Cornelius. Executors—brother, Thomas Thomson, and friend John Clayton. Witnesses—James Wilson, Rachel Willson, John Anderson. Proved October 17, 1750. Lib. E, p. 460.

1742, Oct. 4. Thorn, William, of Nottingham, Burlington Co.; will of. Son, Jedidiah, 30 acres. Son, Joseph, his present land, adjoining Abraham Tilton by the York Road. Sons—William, Thomas and Mahlon. Daughters—Mary Wright, Elizabeth Sykes and Meribah. Executors—wife, Meribah, and son Joseph. Witnesses—William Stiles, William Wetherill, Jos. Reckless. Proved Nov. 17, 1742. Lib. 4, p. 350.

1742, Nov. 5. Inventory, £222.10.7; made by John Steward and Benjamin Robens.

1734, Sept. 18. Thornborough, George, of Shrewsbury, Monmouth Co., cooper. Administration granted to Robert Ireland.
Lib. B, p. 587.

1735, July 24. Account. Mentions bond of Adam Brewer.

1735-6, Feb. 16. Thorne, John, of Chesterfield, Burlington Co.; will of. Sons—John, Joseph, Samuell, Benjamin and Thomas, all under age. Daughters—Rebecca Simmons, Kathron King, Hannah, Sarah, Mary and Debra. Real and personal estate. Wife, Kathron, executrix. Witnesses—William Murfin, John Tantum, Samuel Merrit. Proved June 14, 1737. Lib. 4, p. 106.

1737, June 6. Inventory, £200.19; made by John Tantum and William Wills. Includes silver plate £15; two Bibles and other books.

1735, May 20. Thorne, William, of Woodbridge, Middlesex Co. Int. Adm'rs, Mary Thorne and Richard FitzRandolph. Lib. B, p. 587.

1730, March 24. Thorp, Joseph, of Woodbridge, Middlesex Co., yeoman; will of. Wife, Anna. Children—Paul, land to the line my father set between my brother Benjamin and me; Jonathan, Zebulon, Job, Mary, Kezia. Grandsons—James and William. Executors—Adam Hude and Abraham Tapine. Witnesses—David Cambell, Jonathan Cambell, Jo'n Stevens. Proved Sept. 19, 1749. Lib. E, p. 328.

1750, Oct. 16. Thorp, Solomon, of Woodbridge, Middlesex Co., yeoman. Int. Adm'rs, Hannah Tharp (Thorp), widow, and William Moore. Thomas Thorp, fellow bondsman. All of Woodbridge. Lib. E, p. 458.

1733, Dec. 1. Thorpe, Joseph, of Woodbridge, Middlesex Co. Int. Adm'x, Janna Paine, widow. Adam Hay, Doctor of Medicine, and Lawrence Smyth, fellow bondsmen. Witnesses—John Hamilton, John Michell. Middlesex Wills, 819 L.

1736, Oct. 21. Thorpe, William, of Woodbridge, Middlesex Co., yeoman; will of. Children—William, Thomas, Elijah, Rebecka (widow of John Wilkison), Lydia and Barsheba. Grandson, Israel, youngest child of son Israel, deceased, at 21. Land I had of my father, Thomas Thorpe, of said town, deceased. Executors—brother, Daniel Thorpe, and son Thomas, both of Woodbridge. Witnesses—Charles Murray, Benjamin Morris, Ad. Hude. Proved March 12, 1740. Lib. C, p. 398.

1748, April 23. Throckmorton, Job, of Shrewsbury, Monmouth Co., yeoman; will of. Negress, Hannah, and her children, and negro Oliver, not to be sold. Land formerly John Williams'. Wife, Hannah. Daughter, Elizabeth. Brother, John Throckmorton. "Brothers and sisters" mentioned, but not named. Executors—brothers, John and Joseph Throckmorton, and uncle Jeremiah Stilwell. Witnesses—Sam. Leonard, John Throckmorton, Jr., William Madock. Proved May 3, 1748. Lib. E, p. 307.

1748, July 25. Throckmorton, Job, of Freehold, Monmouth Co. Frances Throckmorton, the widow, resigns right of administration in favor of her eldest son, John. Witness—Elizabeth Dennis. Bond of John Throckmorton, yeoman, of Freehold, Samuel Throckmorton, of same place, yeoman, fellow bondsman. Witnesses—Jonathan Burdy, Elizabeth Dennis. Lib. E, p. 307.

1741, Oct. 12. Throckmorton, John, of Shrewsbury, Monmouth Co., yeoman; will of. Wife, Abigail. Mother, Sarah Throckmorton. Son, Job, land bought of John Williams; lot near Wintepeck Bog purchased by testator's father from Nathaniel Leonard; lot bought of Samuel Dennis; pine right purchased of Richard Ashfield. Son, John, land in Middlesex County purchased of Robert Lucting (?) and William Bradford in New York. Son, Joseph. Daughter, Mary Leonard. Son, James, under age. Daughters, Sarah, and Eliza, under age. Son, Samuel. Executors—brothers, Joseph and Job Throckmorton and Thomas Morford. Witnesses—Parthenay Cook, William Nichols, Richard Saltar. Proved Nov. 11, 1741. Lib. C, p. 461.

1741, Nov. 10. Inventory ("John Throckmorton, Esquire"), £1259.3.7. Includes sword, 2 negro men, negro woman, negro boy (£180), 92 head of cattle, 3 guns. Made by John Campbell, Jonathan and John Forman.

1750, Sept. 19. Throp, John, of Monmouth Co., single man. Int. Inventory, £25.14.5½; made by Thomas Mount and William Vahan.

1750, Oct. 3. Adm'r, brother, Samuel Throp, of New Windsor, Middlesex County. Francis Holman, of same county, fellow bondsman.
Lib. E, p. 455.

1750, March 1. Tichener, Joseph, of Township and County of Morris, shoemaker; will of. Wife, Elizabeth. Sons—Joseph, 56 acres on the west joining to the heirs of James Primrise, deceased; James, and Daniel, equally, the remainder of my land; Moses, 51 acres in the great Swamp bought of Mr. Penn. Daughter, Jane, two-thirds of moveable estate. Witnesses—Caleb Fairchild, Sam'l Tuthill, Benjamin Conger. Proved 5 April, 1750.

1750, May 10. Administration granted to Elizabeth (relict). Bondsman—Nathaniel Ward. Lib. F., p. 7.

1751, Nov. 6. (Letter on file, from Uzal Ogden, Jr., of Newark, states that Mr. Fairchild wrote the will, but entered executors' names after testator's decease, though at his direction, and that Samuel Wade "is now married to the widow Tichener").

1732, Jan. 29. Tichener, Martain, of Newark, Essex Co., weaver; will of. Children—Susanah, Ester, David, John and Martin. Real and personal estate. Executors—wife, Susanah, and brother-in-law Moses Ball. Witnesses—John Cooper, Eliphalet Johnson, David Shipman. Proved Feb. 22, 1732-3. Lib. B, p. 387.

1738, Dec. 18. Tiebout, Henry, of Middletown, Monmouth Co. Int. Adm'r, John Tiebout, of City of New York, brother, Johannes Bennet, of Middletown, trader, fellow bondsman. Lib. C, p. 226.

1746, Jan. 12. Tillyer, John, of Somerset Co., cordwainer; will of. Wife, Susannah. Real and personal estate to be sold; one-half to be given to wife for her maintenance and bringing up of the child, the other half to be put at interest for my daughter Mary, until 18, or on the day of marriage. If Mary dies before marriage, said share to my brother William's son, Thomas. Executors—brother, William Tillyer, and Francis Feurt, of Somerset Co. Witnesses—Samuel Gulick, James Baynham, Jockam Gulick. Proved 29 Jan., 1746.
Lib. D, p. 446.

1749, Oct. 14. Tilton, Daniel, of Middletown, Monmouth Co.; will of. Children—John, Mary Ridgeway, Margaret Lawrence, Anne, Sarah, Phebe and Lydia. Money due from John Ellison. Executors—Robert and Nathan Tilton. Witnesses—Peter Tilton, Ezekiel Smith, Cornelius McCurtain. Proved Nov. 13, 1749. Lib. E, p. 428.

1749, Nov. 13. Inventory (£791.19.8) includes debt from John Neveson, Bible and 12 books, gun, silver bowl, 25 bbls. cider. Made by Samuel Holmes, John Tilton, Jedidiah Allen.

1747-8, Feb. 15. Tilton, Daniel, Senior, of Freehold, Monmouth Co., yeoman; will of. Wife, Sarah. Eldest son, Peter. Son, John. Samuel, son of testator's son Peter. Daughters, Hannah and Cathrine. Children of daughter Sarah. Youngest son, Mott. Sons, Joseph and Daniel. Executors—son, Daniel, and William Waycoff. Witnesses—Daniel Tilton, Benjamin Carman, Arthur Rowland, Joseph Tillton. Proved May 31, 1748. Lib. E, p. 190.

1731, Aug. 11. Tilton, John, of Middletown, Monmouth Co., yeoman; will of. Eldest son, Robert, part of plantation bounded by Samuel Tilton, Swimming River, etc. Son, Nathan, part of plantation bounded by land of testator's brother Peter, Samuel Dennis's saw-mill brook, etc. Youngest son, John, under age, middle part of plantation adjoining William Lawrence. Daughters—Anne, Margaret and Hester. Son, Nathan, to be overseer and guardian of his brother John. Executors—sons, Robert and Nathan, and testator's brothers, Daniel and Peter Tilton. Witnesses—Joseph Lawrence, Lucas Whit, Richard Bartlet, Jacob Dennis. Proved Oct. 9, 1731. Lib. B, p. 253.

1748, May 13. Tilton, Patience, of Nottingham, Burlington Co., widow. Int. Adm'r, Abraham Tilton, of same. John Lawrence and Joseph Thorn, both of same, fellow bondsmen.
Lib. 6, p. 325; Lib. 7, p. 91.

1731-2, Feb. 26. Tilton, Peter, of Freehold, Monmouth Co., carpenter. Int. Inventory, £89.10.10½; made by John Williams, Daniel McKay, James Patterson.

1731-2, March 4. Administration to Abel Tilton, son and heir.
Lib. B, p. 245.

1742, April 1. Account. Mentions Elizabeth Wood, Steaven Aumack, Joseph Nutens, James Maccoy, ——— MacDaniel, Silas Tilton, Peter Tilton, Silvester Tilton, Joseph Forman, drummer's suit, William Brinley, Justice Littel, Jacob Gibbins, John Fenton, John Clap, John Henderson.

1745, 8th, 2d mo. (April). Tilton, Samuel, of Middletown, Monmouth Co., yeoman. Int. Inventory (£394.01.02½) includes 39 cheases, £4.17.8; 31 casque of flower, £20.18.03; 55 bushels wheat in mill, £8.5. Made by William Miller and Thomas Lawrie.

1745, May 6. Adm'x, Patience Tilton, widow. Lib. 5, p. 113.

1748, April 20. Inventory, £83.08.0; made by Thomas Lawrie and Robert Lippincott.

1732, July 18. Tindal, Robert, of Trenton, Hunterdon Co.; will of. Aged mother, Isabel Tindal. Kinswoman, Isabel Vanroomer, daughter of Josiah Vanroomer, in Middlesex County, when 18. Susannah Vanroomer, sister of said Isabel, when 18. Friend, William Pearson, work, etc., done since partnership with testator. Friend, Phebe Howel, of Trenton. Executor—brother, William Tindal, of Middlesex County, and he residuary legatee. Witnesses—Benjamin Robeson, Maurice Justice, Jonathan Davis. Proved Oct. 25, 1732. Lib. 3, p. 220.

1732, Sept. 18. Inventory of estate, £78.11.6; made by Alexander Biles and Joseph Tindall.

1732, Nov. 17. Tindall, Isabel, of Winsor, Middlesex Co., widow of Thomas Tindall, Sr.; will of. Daughters—Isabel Vanroomer, Anne Biles (the great Bible), Sarah Bud. Sons—William, Joseph and Isaac. Grandchildren—Marey, Margaret, Elizabeth and John Pullin; also Catrin, Mary, Elizabeth, Rachel, Sarah and Anne Pearson. Real and personal estate. Executor—son, Joseph Tindall. Witnesses—Isaac Tindall, Jon. Marlen, John Beates. Proved May 15, 1733.
(Hunterdon Wills), Lib. 3, p. 310.

1732-3, Jan. 25. Inventory, £130.0.6; made by Daniel Haines and Joseph Haines.

1741-2, 12th mo. (Feb.), 7 da. Tindall, Joseph, of Waterford, Gloucester Co.; will of. Son, Benjamin, also Mary Gibson, Elizabeth Gibson and my daughter, Sary Heretage, to have 5 shillings. Granddaughters, Elizabeth Rase and Darkis Heretage, when 21, or at marriage. Executors—cousin, John Holme, and my daughter, Ruth Ross, who shall have residue of my estate. Witnesses—Marget Ayers, Alexander Hambeltown, Benjamin Holme. Sworn and affirmed, 27 Sept., 1743. Lib. 5, p. 4.

1742, Nov. 20. Inventory (£69.15.9) includes bond from Ben. Tindel to his father, Joseph Tindel, for £50; note from John Holmes. Appraisers—Robert Powell, Rowland Owen.

1739, Sept. 8. Tindall, William, of New Winsor, Middlesex Co., yeoman; will of. Children—John, Thomas, Robert, Elizabeth, Rachel and Sarah, last four under age. Land bought of Joseph Lee on Assinpink Creek. Executors—wife, Sarah, and brother Joseph Tindall. Witnesses—Richard Kerns, Martha Rogers, Johanna Page, Isaac Stelle. Proved March 25, 1742. Lib. C, p. 502.

1733, May 31. Titsort, Isaac, of Piscataway, Middlesex Co., farmer; will of. Children—Jacob, and second son, mentioned but not by name; both under age. Land due me out of estate of John Martin, late of Piscataway. Executors—wife, Elizabeth, and Samuel Dunn, of Piscataway. Witnesses—William Titsort, Moses Martin, Nugien Kelly. Proved July 6, 1733. Lib. B, p. 436.

1733, July 20. Bond of Andrew Van Horn as administrator. Gershom Martin, fellow bondsman.

1730, May 26. Toers, Jakemintie, widow of Claes Arentse Toers, of Town and Co. of Bergen. Son, Arent Clason Toers, all farming utensils. Rest of personal estate to children, viz., Arent Clase, Judith (wife of Gerrit Roos, carpenter), and Petertie Toers, unmarried. Executors—son, Arent Claes, son-in-law Gerrit Roos (in right of his wife Judith), and daughter, Pietertie. Witnesses—Nich's Bayard, Morris Light, Sam'l Bayard. Proved 9 Jan., 1744. (Arent Claes Toers qualified as executor). Lib. D, p. 235.

1737, Sept. 26. Tomlinson, William, of Waterford Township, Gloucester Co., yeoman; will of. Wife, Rebekah, executrix, and to have whole estate; ½ shall be hers and the other half I give to my three children, Samuel, William and Daniel, when 21. Witnesses—David Hide, John Kay, Joseph Tomlinson. Affirmed 29 Oct., 1731. Lib. 4, p. 122.

1737, 8 mo. (Oct.), 26 da. Inventory (£176.5.6) includes bonds, bills and accounts £20.09.00. Bible and other books. Appraisers—Sam. Lippincott, Samuel Coles.

1731, March 23. Tompkins, Joseph, of Newark, Essex Co., yeoman; will of. Nephews, children of brother John Tompkins, deceased, viz., Obediah and Iccobud. Wife, Mary, real and personal estate during life and to be executrix. Witnesses—Jno. Cooper, Robert Murdock, Bethya Tompkins. Proved May 10, 1732. Lib. B, p. 309.

1732, June 1. Inventory (£147.06.07) includes debts from Robert Hayse, Silas Halsey, Nathaniel Baldwin, Ebenezer Linsley. Made by Joseph Tuttle, John Baldwin, Jun'r.

1732, April 13. Tompkins, Mary, widow of Joseph, late of Newark, Essex Co., deceased; nuncupative will of. Josiah Ogden and Joseph Burwell declared that the will of deceased was that the two sons and two daughters of her sister, Corre, deceased, and her sister, Asubah

Day, were to have her estate. Her brothers were in her debt. Proved May 10, 1732. Lib. B, p. 310.

1732, July 4. Liberty given Joseph Day to secure the crops.

Tompkins (see Thompkins).

1747-8, Feb. 27. Toms, Jonathan, of Woodbridge, Middlesex Co., yeoman; will of. Wife, Hannah, partition given her by her father, Peter Elstone, in his last will. Children—Benjamin, Daniel and Johanah, all under age. Real and personal estate. Executors—wife, Hannah, and Jonathan Frazee. Witnesses—Michael Moore, Benjamin Elstone, Thomas Alston. Proved April 5, 1750. Lib. E, p. 379.

1742, Oct. 18. Tongrelou, Jane, of New York City, widow; will of. Nephew, Lewis Carree, at 21. Elizabeth and Jane, daughters of niece Mary, (wife of John Emott), both under age. Nephew, John Pintard, Jun'r, son of sister Katharine (wife of John Pintard). To the poor in Elizabeth, £25. Rev. Louis Row, minister of the French congregation in New York City, £15. To the poor of same congregation, £25. Land in possession of John Emott. Executors—sister, Maria Katharine Boudinot, and brother-in-law, John Pintard. Witnesses—Gershom Higgins, Will. Anderson, Geo. Emott.

1743, Aug. 3. Codicil. Now of Elizabeth Town, Essex Co., widow. Niece, Mary Emott, silver porringer. Grand-nieces, Magdalen, Jane and Elizabeth Emott. Aunt, Laretta Rosse. My two sisters. Witnesses—Samuel Man, Edward Vaughn, Geo. Emott. Proved Aug. 16, 1743. (Essex Wills), Lib. D, p. 77.

1734, July 4. Tonken, John, of Springfield, Burlington Co., yeoman; will of. Wife, Susannah. Children—Elizabeth, Edward, John, Charles, Joshua, Jacob. Wife, executrix. Witnesses—Benjamin Marriott, Hester Small (afterwards Hester Tonken), Thomas Shinn. Proved ———, 1735. Burlington Wills, 2877-8 C.

1745, Aug. 22. Tonkin, Susannah, of City of Burlington, widow. Int. Inventory, £80.13.7; made by Thomas Scattergood and William Lyndon.

1745, Aug. 23. Adm'r, John Tonkin. Samuel Scattergood and William Lyndon, all of Burlington Co., yeomen, fellow bondsmen. Lib. 5, p. 158.

1735, April 21. Tooker, Charles, of Elizabeth Town, Essex Co., yeoman; will of. Children—Charles and John. Grandson, Worner Tooker. 100 acres of land on road leading to grist mill of Samuel Oliver, deceased. Executors—brother, Joseph Tooker, friend John Spinning, and son John. Witnesses—Robert Morss, Jonas Wood, John Terrill. Proved May 6, 1740. (John Spinning and Joseph Tooker decline to act). Lib. C, p. 335.

1740, April 7. Inventory (£201.13.07) includes debts from John Halstead, Bowley Ramsdon, Joshua Halsey, John Ross, Lam. Decamp, Sam. Winans, Ben. Doud, Jos. Little, John Radley, Jun'r, Peter Tranblas, Nath'll David, Messrs Farlon and Horon (Heron), Hannah Winams, Ben. Watkins, Isaac Jewell, Ephraim Terrill, Jun'r, Thos. Headly. Made by Jonas Wood, Jona. Hampton.

1745, Aug. 26. Tooker (Tucker), John, of Elizabethtown, Essex Co. Int. Adm'x, Sarah Tucker, widow. Joseph Tucker, of Essex Co., and Eliakim Higgins, of Middlesex Co., blacksmith, fellow bondsmen.

1745, Sept. 2. Inventory, £233.1.5; made by Eliphalet Frasee and Richard Jones. Lib. D, p. 315.

1745, July 29. Topliff, Joseph, of Gloucester Co., yeoman; will of. Friend, Grace Fawcett, executrix and to have the plantation I live on and marsh by Racoon Creek; also all personal estate. Witnesses—Thomas Wilkins, Thomas Bickham, Isaiah Davenport. Affirmed 12 Aug., 1745. Lib. 5, p. 155.

1745, Aug. 7. Inventory, £143.14.8; includes debts due by bills, bonds and notes £109.11.5. Made by Thos Wilkins, Isaiah Davenport.

1747, Nov. 8. Townsend, Deborah, of Oyster Bay, Queens Co., gentlewoman; will of. Cousins, Berzalee Lovell, Noah Townsend, Deborah Barker, Rachel Lovell and Ann Farnsworth. Remainder, real and personal, to Berzalee Lovell, Deborah Parker and Rachel Lovell. Executors—Berzalee and Rachel Lovell. Witnesses—James ——— (?), Nathan'ell Farnsworth, John Flintham. Proved Dec. 12, 1747.

1747, Dec. 10. Rachel Lovell declines executorship.

(Burlington Wills), Lib. 5, p. 382.

1740, May 31. Townsend, Jacob, of Salem Co., blacksmith. Int. Adm'x, Mary Townsend, widow. Bondsmen—Joseph Goodwin, William Tufte, all of said County. Witnesses—Clemt. Hall, Danl. Mestayer. Lib. 4, p. 239.

1740, May 31. Inventory (£169.7.8) includes smith shop, 500 lbs. of iron in bars, smith's tools. Appraisers—Clem. Hall, Jos. Goodwin.

1737, 2nd mo. (April), 30 da. Townsend, Richard, of Cape May Co., yeoman; will of. Wife, Millicent. Eldest son, John, the tract of land and marsh whereon I live (my wife to have during widowhood use of the house and mill and half the barn to keep what creatures she may have on the plantation), he to pay £15 a piece to my two younger sons, Samuel and Daniel, when 21. In case of death of either, survivor to have £20. Son, Richard, 200 acres whereon he lives, he to pay two younger sons, Samuel and Daniel, £8 a piece when 21. If one dies, survivor to have £12. Son, Isaac, 200 acres, joining my son Richard on the North, which land I bought of Timothy Brandeth. Son, Silvanus, land and marsh bought of Thomas Gandy, between lands of Joseph Ludlum and Henry Young, he to pay my two younger sons, Samuel and Daniel, £8 when 21. In case of death of either, survivor to have £12. My two younger sons, Samuel and Daniel, when of age, that land and marsh (663 acres) on the west end of Peck's Beach, bought of Lewis Morris. These two younger sons to have schooling and at 15 to be put to trades. Son, Jacob, £15 when he "sets up his trade." Moveables to my daughter, Hannah Gregory, and to my daughter, Millecent Townsend, when she will be 21. Grist mill to be shared equally by sons John, Richard, Silvanus and Isaac. Witnesses—Robert Townsend, Ebanr. Swaine, Jacob Corson. Proved 29 Sept., 1737. Lib. 4, p. 119.

1737, Oct. 13. Whereas, Richard Townsend left a will naming no executor, said Millicent Townsend, widow, and John Townsend, eldest son, appointed administrators. Lib. 4, p. 119.

1737, Sept. 21. Inventory, £262.19.3; made by Henry Stites, Daniel Brandeth.

1741, Jan. 27. Toy, Frederick, of Chester, Burlington Co., yeoman; will of. Sons—Elias and Nicholas. Real and personal estate. Executors—wife, Bridget, and son Nicholas. Witnesses—James Leconey, Richard Barrow, Isaiah Toy. Provèd Sept. 9, 1743. Lib. 4, p. 315.

1742-3, March 2. Inventory, £72.9; made by James Laconey and Daniel Comron.

1745, Sept. 18. Toy, Frederick, of City of Philadelphia, mariner; will of. Peter Toy, ship carpenter, of Philada., executor, and to have all that shall be mine in West Jersey or elsewhere. Witnesses—John Stoop, Edward Barrett. Proved Jan. 20, 1747.

(Burlington Wills), Lib. 5, p. 418.

1745, July 11. Toy, Isaiah, of Chester, Burlington Co., yeoman; will of. Sisters—Margaret and Christian Toy, land bought of Elias King. Brothers—Andrew and Daniel. Real and personal estate. Executors—brother, Andrew, and sisters Margaret and Christian. Witnesses—James Toy, Francis Roberson, Thomas Staminers. Proved Oct. 29, 1745. Lib. 5, p. 189.

1745, Oct. 26. Inventory (of Isaiah Toy, who deceased Sept. 24, 1745), £115.7.6; made by Thomas Lippincott and David Walker.

1740, Jan. 30. Travers, John, of Lower Freehold, Monmouth Co., husbandman. Int. Adm'r, John Fenton, Junior, of same place, yeoman. Samuel Job, yeoman, fellow bondsman. Lib. 4, p. 267.

1740, Jan. 30. Inventory (£26.7.4) includes bills of William Cosgrove, John Fenton, James Peteson, John Foreman, John Job, John Laton, Joseph Taylor, Rachel Job, John Williams. Made by John Clayton and John Bennem.

1738, Nov. 13. Treadway, John (above 14), son of Henry, late of Deptford, Gloucester Co., ward. Guardian, Thos. Wilkins.

Lib. 4, p. 150.

1737, ——, 28. Tredway, Henry (about 16), son of Henry Tredway, late of Gloucester Co., yeoman. Ward petitions that Thomas Wilkins, of Deptford, said County, be appointed guardian; that petitioner's father by his last will appointed Constantine Wood, Esq., late of same County, deceased, guardian of his sons Henry and John.

Lib. 4, p. 93.

1749-50, Jan. 10. Tremer, Johannes, of Amwell, Hunterdon Co.; will of. Wife, Mary. Children by first wife—Tys, Toenis, Andry, Gorg, and Herbert Tremer. Children of second wife—Anna, Christina, William, Hannes, Niclas, Judit and Henrick. "I will that my 3th wife, Mary Catrina, shall live in my house." Executors—sons Tys Tremer and Andris Tremer. Witnesses—Godfrey Peters, Mathias Housell, Adam Belesfelt. Proved Feb. 22, 1749-50. Mathias and Andrew Tremer sworn as executors. Lib. 6, p. 335.

1749-50, Feb. 21. Inventory (£126.15.3) includes 3 books and a Bible. Made by John Jewel and Mathias Housell.

1734, July 23. Trent, James, Esq., of Trenton, Hunterdon Co., gent. Int. Adm'r, Nathaniel French, of Trenton, gent. Thomas Hunloke, of Burlington, Esquire, surety. Lib. 2, p. 292.

1734, July 25. Inventory, £219.13.9; Made by Alexander Lockhart, James Gould, Samuel Bustill. Includes these books: Adam's Commentary upon St. Peter; Tyrril's History of England, 3 vols.; Roberts' Merchants' Map of Commerce; The Art of Logick, by Blundeuile; The Nature of Bodys; A Defence of the Reformed Catholick; Backster on Baptism; Speidell's Geometricall Extraction; Jemeson against Hierarchy; Homer's

Iliad in Greek; Boyer's French Dictionary, abridg'd; Volumes of Tillotson's Sermons, 9 vols.; Sherlock upon Death; Boyer's Practical Discourse on Sickness and Recovery; The Third Annal of King George; The Discription of the Western Island of Scotland, by Martin; Potter's Greek Antiquitys; Kennet's Roman Antiquity; Echard's Roman History, 2 vols.; Somner's Treatise of the Roman Ports and Forts in Kent; Volume II of The Turkish History; History of the Earls and Earldom of Flanders; Keil's Introduction to Natural Philosophy; Commandini Euclid's Elements; Brown's Entring Check; A Switch for a Snake; Keith Against Barclay; Cheyne on Health and Long Life; Echard's Geography and Geographical Index; Yongue's Antidote Against Grief; French Dialogues of Death, 2 vols.; Davies' Poem on the Immortality of the Soul; An Introduction to the Reading of the Holy Scriptures, in Latin; 6th Vol. of Molier's Plays in French; Farnaby's Seneca's Tragedys; Homer's Illiad; Wilson's Trigonometry; Office and Duty of Executors; Compleat Solicitor; The Faithful Councilour; The Conductor Generalis.

1730, Dec. 1. Trent, Maurice, of Trenton, Hunterdon Co.; will of. Brother, William Trent, lot between Joseph Reed and Joseph Green, containing about ½ acre. Friend, Thomas Palmer, for valuable services, lot in Trenton, bounded east by Benjamin Smith, containing ¼ of an acre. Elizabeth, wife of Thomas Palmer. Brother, James Trent, and Thomas Palmer, executors. Witnesses—John Ferguson and Jeremiah Foster. Proved January 9, 1730-'1. Lib. 3, p. 111.

1731, April —. Inventory (£26.19) includes silver hilted sword, £1.10; pair of gold buttons, £1.10; silver watch and chain, £4. Made by James Neilson and John Dagworthy.

(Undated). List of names, with amounts, filed, evidently portion of executor's account: William Huff, John Severns, Wm. Yard, James Gould, Dan'l Coxe, Jun'r, John Porterfield, James Garey, Coll. Bard, John Vanlaer, John Hart, Wm. Waldring, Jos. Reed, Wm. Morris, Math'w Phillips, Mrs. Wardell, Maj. John Anderson, Rich'd Merrill, Thos. Barns, Sr., Dr. Hamilton, Rob't Boulton, Ralph Hunt, S'r, Terret Seester, Jon. Gray, Edw'd Hart, Wm. Spencer, Rich'd Dinsey, Alexand'r Lockhard, Rich'd Palmer, George Guinip, Edw'd Fisher, Warren Barr, Johnathan Peptitt, Blind Coats, Thos. Leonard, George Hankill, Jos'a Anderson, John Haywood, Enoch Anderson, Sr., Sam'l Bonham, John Burrus, Sam. Davis, John Jones, James Hide, Cornelius Ringo, Peter Ringo, Thos. Huff, Enoch Anderson, Jun'r, Jos. Hills, James Tucker, Phillip Kearney, Wm. Bryant, Edw'd R. Price, Thos. Clifford, ——— Keymer, Sam'l Johnson, John Dagworthy, Alexander Harper, Moses Pettit, Col'l Cox, Ann Spencer, Ann Oakley, George Mill'r, James Neilson, Peg Irish, Rich'd Loveland, James Trent, Rich'd Stanwill, David Dunbar, Wm. Lauder, Mandart Johnson, Wm. Snowden, John Parker, Abraham Temple, Peter Hendriccson, Francis Pincham, John Reading, Thomas Canby, John Stevenson, Showly Taylor, John Richardson, Thos. Allen, Wm. Cornwall, Dr. Patterson, Laurance Obdike, Rob't Laurance, Charles Huff, Thos. Winder, Lewes Moore, Ann Crace, Peter Berrian, Natt'l French, Henery Woodward, John Huff, Rich'd Roberts, Jerem'a Anderson, Isaack Anderson, Peter Yager, Abenezer Salter, Peter Vantilberough, Eliza. Chambers, Dan'l Carmack, Thos. Hendry.

1742, Dec. 1. Trent, William, of Trenton, Hunterdon Co. Int. Adm'r, Samuel Burge, of Philadelphia, sadler, for William Burge, of Philadelphia, principal creditor, or estate unadministered by James Trent, deceased. Lib. 4, p. 380.

1733, Aug. 27. Trimble (Trumbul), Thomas, of Perth Amboy, Middlesex Co. Int. Adm'rs, Janna Pain and John Parker, both of Woodbridge. Zebulon Pike, fellow bondsman. Lib. B, p. 463.

1740, 30th day, 4th mo. (June). Troath, William, of Evesham, Burlington Co., yeoman; will of. Wife, Elizabeth, rents of plantation in tenure of Richard Burden, containing 250 acres adjoining Jacob Heulings, Thomas Evans and Matta Scoxon. Isaac, son of my son Paul (after decease of my wife), 200 acres, formerly belonging to Henery Manley and leased to Richard Burden. Grandson, William Troth. Children of my daughters—Mary Prickett, Jane Garwood and Rebecca Hains. Brother, Edward Troath, living in Great Britain. Executors—sons-in-law, Zachry Pricket, William Garwood and Amos Hains. Witnesses—Richard Borden, William Whitton, Freem. Lippincott, Jun'r. Proved Aug., 1740. Lib. 4, p. 252.

1740, 9th day, 6th mo. (Aug.). Inventory, £500.9.6; made by Thomas Hooten and Freedom Lippincott.

1738, Dec. 9. Troth, Paul, of Evesham, Burlington Co.; will of. Wife, Deborah. Children—William, Isaac, Elizabeth, Mary and Jane, all under age. Real and personal. Executors—brother-in-law, Zac'ry Pricket, and friend, Thomas Busbey. Witnesses—James Springer, Jno. Brasington, Freedom Lippincott, Jr. Proved March 10, 1738. Lib. 4, p. 155.

1738-9, 6th day, 11th mo. (Jan.). Inventory, £308.17; made by Thomas Ballenger and Hudson Springer.

1729, Sept. 23. Trotter, Elizabeth, of Elizabeth Town, Essex Co. Bond of David Morehouse as guardian. Jonathan Thompson, fellow bondsman. (Omitted in Archives, Vol. 23). Essex Wills, 449-50 G.

1750, Nov. 24. Truex, Philip, of Monmouth Co. Int. Larue Jacob Trewex, Jun'r, desires that his brother, Samuel Truvex, be appointed administrator, of, as Larue lives at a distance. Bond of Samuel Truax, of Monmouth Co., yeoman. John Truex, of Middlesex Co., yeoman, fellow bondsman. Lib. E, p. 463.

1745, Aug. 26. Tucker, John, of Newark and Elizabeth Town, Essex Co. Int. Adm'x, Sarah Tucker, widow. Joseph Tooker, of Essex Co., and Eliakim Higgins, of Middlesex Co., blacksmith, fellow bondsmen. Lib. D, p. 315.

1745, Sept. 2. Inventory (£233.01.05) includes negro girl, one-half boat called "New Minne," bond of Susannah and Joshua Marsh, debts from Sam'll Haynes, William Craig, William Grant, Sam'll Robison, Sarah Bloomfield, Henry Randolph, Mary Nichols. Made by Eliphalet Frasee and Richard Jones.

1746, Sept. 11. Accompt. Payments to John and Jonathan Woodruff, Richard Jones, Thomas Woodruff, Joseph Tucker, Daniel Moor, ——— Chapman, schoolmaster, Susannah Brant, William Lawrance, Enoch Moor, Madlong Fremble, John Decamp, John Cleverly, Dr. Ichabod Burnet, Samuel Moor, Joseph Shotwell, Abraham Woodruff, Daniel Marsh, John Paintard, Peter Frenble, Mary Nichols.

1748, April 26. Tucker, Nathaniel, of Essex Co., Minister of the Gospel, at Connecticut Farms. Int. Inventory, £297.14.02; made by Mr. Jacob Green, David Bonnel.

1748, April 27. Adm'x, Sarah Tucker. Daniel Harrison, fellow bondsman. Lib. E, p. 186.

1737, Oct. 19. Tuckney, Robert, of Burlington, butcher. Int. Adm'x, Mary Tuckney, widow. William Petty, of same place, yeoman, fellow bondsman. Lib. 4, p. 121.

1746, Sept. 12. Tuley, Thomas, of Burlington Co.; will of. Wife, Mary, plantation and lands bought of Margaret Ellis and John Hancock, to bring up and educate my children, and after her decease to our son, John. Other children—Jonathan, Abraham, Sarah and Judith. Wife, executrix. Witnesses—Bartho. Gibson, Isaac DeCow, Thos. Atkinson. Proved Sept. 20, 1746. Lib. 5, p. 288.

1746, Sept. 19. Inventory, £433.7.1; made by Henry Scott and Thos. Atkinson.

1743, May 7. Tunis, Myndert, of Connecticut Farms, Borough of Elizabeth, Essex Co. Int. Adm'rs, Deborah Tunis, widow, John Tunis, Hendrick Tunis and John Jewell. Moses Jewell and Benjamin Bond, Jun'r, fellow bondsmen. Witness—Samuel Stone. Lib. E, p. 84.

1743, May 17. Inventory includes negro wench, £29; negro man, £49; bonds of Sam'll Williams, Peter Tunise, Daniel Sayre, William Mitchell, Joseph Searing, Thomas Squire, John Jewell, John Post, Joseph Willis, Enoch Miller, Hue Osborn, Mathias Burnett, Benjamin Thompson, John Joline, Joseph Marsh, Isaac Headley, James Hinds, John Looker (Tooker), William Jones, Nathaniel Davise, Joseph Williams, James Hinds, Jun'r, William Brant, Mrs. Tunise, John Tunise, William Clark, Daniel Osborn, Isaac Willis. Made by Eliphalet Johnson and Jno. Osborn.

1743, Sept. 12. Note. "Myndert Tunis was drove out in a Pettiaugur and, not being heard of, is supposed to be lost."

Tunison (see Teunissen).

1734, Feb. 14. Turner, Hannah, of Salem Co. Int., Adm'r, John Turner, gent. Bondsman—Edward Test. Both of said County. Witnesses—Danl. Mestayer, John Doe. Lib. 4, p. 2.

1739, 21st day, 7th mo. (Sept.). Turner, John, of Evesham, Burlington Co., yeoman. Int. Inventory, £308.14.8; made by Caleb Haines and William Foster.

1739, Oct. 15. Adm'x, Jane Turner, widow. William Foster, yeoman, fellow bondsman. Lib. 4, p. 171.

1740, Jan. 13. Turner, John, of Salem Co., innkeeper. Int. Adm'x, Sarah Turner. Bondsmen—Robt. Raines, Jos. Goo, Jos. Godwin. Witnesses—Jas. Smith, Junr., Danl. Mestayer. Lib. 4, p. 266.

1746, Jan. 6. Inventory (£56.15.7) includes Bible. Appraisers—Robt. Raines, Jas Goodwin.

1749, Feb. 23. Tussey, Catharine, of Salem Co. Int. Adm'r, Christopher Lynmire. Bondsmen—Samuel Lynch, John Helms. All of said County, yeomen. Lib. 7, p. 34.

1749-50, Jan. 20. Inventory (£58.19.6) includes debt of Timothy Raines. Appraisers—Samuel Linch, John Helm.

1747-8, Jan. 29. Tuttle, Josiah, of Newark, Essex Co. Int. Adm'r,

Robert Crane. Timothy Crane, fellow bondsman. Witness—David Ogden. Lib. E, p. 127.

1732-3, Jan. 23. Tuttle, Stephen, of Hanover Township, Hunterdon Co. Renunciation of Sarah Tuttle, widow, of right to administer, in favor of Joseph Tuttle and John Lindsley, Jr. Witnesses—Warren Rivers and Jno. Budd.

1732-3, Jan. 24. Bond of Joseph Tuttle, of Essex Co., and Town of Newark, blacksmith, and John Lindsley, Jr., Esq., of Hunterdon Co. James Primrose, of Hunterdon Co., surety. Witnesses—Warren Rivers and Jno. Budd. Hunterdon Wills, 98 J.

1746, April 2. Tyler, Enoch, of Salem Co. Int. Adm'r, Philip Tyler. Bondsman—John Smith. Both of Salem, yeomen. Witnesses—Josiah Kay, Danl. Mestayer. Lib. 5, p. 420.

1746, April 1. Inventory, £76.18.10½; made by Edward Test, Josiah Kay.

1732, Sept. 5. Tyler, John, of Allaways Creek, Salem Co., yeoman. Adm'x, Rachel Tyler, widow. Bondsmen—John Butler, Richard Wood. Witnesses—Saml. Bustill, Joseph Rose.

1732, Sept. 15. Petition. Whereas said John Tyler left a will, dated 23 August, 1731, appointing his son, John Tyler, executor and whereas said John Tyler being at this time a minor under seventeen, petitioner prayeth that letters be granted to her. (Signed) Rachel Tyler. (Appointed Adm'x).

1732, Aug. 4. Inventory, £334.10½; made by Abel Nicholson, Richard Hancock. Salem Wills, 413 Q.

1737, Aug. 1. Tyler, Philip, of Salem Co.; will of. Sons, Philip and Enoch, to have equally all of my lands. Executor—friend and brother, Benjamin Acton. Witnesses—Jonth. Wadington, James Sharp, Jos. Clowes. Affirmed 10 Jan., 1737. Lib. 4, p. 145.

1737, Nov. 14. Inventory (£49.4.6) includes linen at Bilbey Shepard's; 27 sheep. Appraisers—John Pagett, Jonathan Bradway.

1732, Nov. 29. Tyler, William, of Allaways Creek, Salem Co.; will of. Sons—William, the home plantation, paying £50 to daughters Editha (wife of Samuel Thompson) and Rebecca Tyler; James, plantation, 234 acres, by Simeon Warner's, which I bought of William Hall, late of Salem, deceased; Samuel, 100 acres, called Smith's Neck, formerly belonging to Daniel Smith and John Smith, deceased; William and Samuel, 100 acres at Smith's Neck, formerly belonging to John Denn, deceased. Wife, Mary, and my two daughters to have personal estate. Executors—wife, Mary, son William Tyler, and Samuel Thompson. Witnesses—John Hall, Samuel Hall, Jno. Jones. Affirmed 8 March, 1733-4. Lib. 3, p. 405.

1733-4, 1 mo. (Mar.), 7 da. Inventory, £271.13.3; made by Abel Nicholson, Thomas Taylor.

1749, June 10. Tyler, William, of Allaways Creek, Salem Co.; will of. Executors to sell as much land joining Thomas Hill, deceased, as will discharge debts. Wife, Elizabeth, to enjoy plantation until youngest daughter, Editha, will be 18; then land (not sold) divided equally among my five daughters—Mary, Grace, Rebeccah, Sarah and Editha. Executors—wife, and my brother-in-law, Samuel Thompson.

Witnesses—Sarah S. Sims, Wm. Murdock, James Tyler. Sworn and affirmed, 17 July, 1749. Lib. 6, p. 265.

1749, June 20. Inventory, £122.10; made by William Chandler, Daniel Smith.

1733, Oct. 19. Uerison, John, of Penns Neck, Salem Co., husbandman; will of. Wife, Ann. Children—John and Lorance. Executors—wife, and son John. Witnesses—Richard Shearwood, Mecum McKnight. Proved July 23, 1737. Lib. 4, p. 114.

1737, July 20. Inventory, £81.7.7; made by Earick Gilljohnson and John Sinick.

Uerison (see Yourison).

1745, June 10. Updike, Lawrence, of Maidenhead, Hunterdon Co., farmer; will of. Wife, Agnes, money in hands of Tunis Post. Sons—William, John and Tunis. Daughters—Rachel Price and Atheliah Minor. Executors—William and John Updike, and John Johnson. Witnesses—John Price, Joseph Phillips, Houghton Mershon. Proved May 27, 1748. Lib. 5, p. 474.

1748, May 7. Inventory (£434.8.4) includes negro man, £25; negro wench, £28; bond of David Stout; bill of Jacob Oakey; account against John and William Updike. Made by William Phillips and Abraham Anderson.

1742, Jan. 8. Uppom, Aaron, of Waterford, Gloucester Co., yeoman. Int. Adm'r, Elizabeth Uppom, (relict). Bondsman—Aaron Aronson. Lib. 4, p. 379.

1742, Dec. 28. Inventory, £28.4.0; made by Thomas Ellis, Aaron Aronson.

1744, Nov. 19. Urions, Johannes, of Greenwich Township, Gloucester Co., yeoman; will of. Wife, Elizabeth. Sons—Hance and John, to have equally home plantations and that piece (65 acres) adjoining Lawrence Cox's, and 12 acres of marsh upon Racoon Creek; Frederick, James and Andrew. Daughters—Catherine, Mary, Elinor Cox, and Elizabeth Cox. Executors—wife, Elizabeth, and son Hance. Witnesses—George Keen, Jestah Justisson, William Guest. Proved 10 May, 1748. Lib. 5, p. 466.

1747, June 13. Inventory, £100.19.10; made by William Guest, Lawrence Cocks.

1750-1, Feb. 26. Vahan, William, of Freehold, Monmouth Co. Cathrine Vahan, under age, asks that administration be granted her brother, Isaac Light. Witness—Samuel Mount.

1750-1, March 2. Bond of Isaac Leet, of Hunterdon Co., yeoman, (husband of Rebecca Leet, late Rebecca Vahan, daughter and coheir of William Vahan) as administrator. John Williams, of Monmouth Co., fellow bondsman. Lib. E, p. 490.

1745, March 26. Valentine, Richard, of Gloucester Co., yeoman. Int. Adm'r, Edward Redolphus Price, Esq., of Burlington. Bondsman—Samuel Harrison. Witnesses—Henry Sparks, Dan. Mestayer. Gloucester Wills, 331 H.

1746, April 21. Valentine, Richard, of Shrewsbury, Monmouth Co. Eldest daughter, Sarah. Estate divided between four daughters as they come of age. Executors—Timothy Ridgway and Thomas Cramer. Witnesses—John Potter, John Grant, Sarah Ridgway. Proved April 1, 1748. (John Grant a Quaker). Lib. E, p. 158.

1748, April 10. Inventory of the estate, £103.16.10, including bill of Thomas West and debt of Nathaniel Petet. Made by Stephen Burdsall and Richard Willets, Justice.

1741, Nov. 22. Vallat, James (Jaque), of New Windsor, Middlesex Co., husbandman; will of. Daughter, Judith McOan. Executrix—wife, Judith Vallat. Real and personal. Witnesses—Thomas Sutton, Jun'r, John Brown. Proved March 4, 1741. Lib. C, p. 500.

1749, Nov. 30. Vanarsdalen, John (Jan), of Somerset Co.; will of. wife estate during widowhood for maintenance of children, viz., Cornelis (eldest), Garret, Johannis, Isack, Maritie (wife of John Vannuise), Johanna and Sara. An expected child. After remarriage or death of wife estate to be divided equally among them. Executors—brothers, Philip Vanarsdalen and Nicholas Wyckof. I order that children by my first wife shall first have out of my estate £57, etc. Witnesses—Abraham Vanarsdalen, Josound (Johannis) Sait (Hait), Nicholas Wyckoff. Proved 26 March, 1750. Lib. E, p. 376.

1753, May 9. Inventory (£688.8.0) includes negro wench and child, £50; bonds, £465.18.0; bonds in York money, £95.18.0. Made by Saggijyus (Zaccheus) Van Voorhees, Petris Quick.

1749, March 31. Van Blarkham, Petrus, of Essex Co. Int. Adm'r, John Van Blarkham, Jun'r, eldest son, as administrator on the estate of. Gerrardus Drake, fellow bondsman. Lib. E, p. 273.

[No date]. Van Boskerck, Thomas, of Reading Township, Hunterdon Co.; will of. Wife, but not named. Son, John. Daughters—Janetie, wife of Pieter Van Norden; Gertruy, wife of Wiert Banta. Residue to children, viz., Laurens, Andries, Abraham, Pieter, Isack, Machiel, John, Margret, the wife of John Church, and Titie, wife of Andries Amack. Executors—sons Laurens, Abraham and Machiel. Witnesses—Jacobus Swart, Joost Schamp, Nicholas Wyckoff. Proved Oct. 20, 1748. Lib. 5, p. 539.

1747-8, March 1. Inventory, £136.3.10; made by John Stoll, Jr., and Isaac Krom (or Crom).

1747, May 9. Vanbrackle, Gisbert, of Middletown, Monmouth Co., cordwainer; will of. Wife, Rachel, land bought of James Mott and John Dorsett. Daughters, Anne and Rachel. An unborn child. Executors—wife, Rachel, brother Stephen Vanbrackle, friend James Mott. Witnesses—Jarratt Wall, Richard Herbert, James Dorsett. Proved May 30, 1747. Lib. E, p. 48.

1747, June 11. Inventory (£373.13.10½) includes sword and 2 guns. Made by Cornelius Dooren and Jarratt Wall.

1749, Feb. 2. Van Brackle (Verbreckle), Matthias, of Monmouth County, yeoman; will of. Children—Stephen, Matthias, James, John, Samuel. Granddaughter, Anna Vankirk. Daughters—Cornelia Vankirk, Naomi Crawford, loom and tackling belonging to weaving trade. Son, Stephen, bark-mill and currying and shoemaking tools. Granddaughter, Artilla Verbrackle. Son, Samuel, "has been long absent and know not where;" if he does not return in two years, or has issue, then £6 given to granddaughter, Artilla, to come from Samuel's share. Lands to son Stephen, excepting a burying-place on testator's home plantation, to be 30 ft. square and have fence and free passage to road leading from testator's house to John Bowne's house. Executors—son, Stephen, and John Bowne, Esq. Witnesses—William Couwenhoven, Johannes Bennet, John Nathaniel Hutchins. Proved March 24, 1749-50. Lib. E, p. 372.

1750, March 28. Inventory (£251.16.6) includes 2 guns, pistol and sword, £2.10; 2 Bibles; 1 "voyalin." Made by William Couanhoven, Johannes Bennet, Isaac Hance.

1745, March 25. Van Campen, John, of Somerset Co.; will of. Debts to be paid out of bond of £100, given by Wessel Brodhead. Wife, Tietie. Children—John, Jun'r (eldest), Isaac, Cornelius, Heyltie (wife of, Jacob Dewitt). Grandchildren—John Cock, Jun'r (under 5 years), son of daughter Janitie, deceased; John, Patris, Heyltie (children of son Jacob, deceased), provided last three discharge bond of Everson given by their father Jacob Van Compen and myself. Personal estate includes slaves, Plato and Betty. Executor—son, Cornelius. Witnesses—Albert Low, Ari Molinare, John Broughton. Proved 3 May, 1745. Lib. D, p. 282.

1745, Oct. 29. Vance, James, of Princeton, Somerset Co., innkeeper. Int. Adm'r, Thomas Noble, of New York City, merchant, principal creditor, the widow, Margaret, having renounced right. Fellow bondsman—William Burnet. Lib. D, p. 345.

1749, Oct. 21. VanCleaf, Cornelius, of Somerset Co. Int. Adm'r, his father, John VanCleef of Long Island, the widow, Femmetie, having renounced. Fellow bondsman—John Vanmiddlesworth. Lib. E, p. 336.

1749, Oct. 26. Inventory, £124.10.7; made by Abraham Voorhees, Peter Schenk, Gerrit Gerritsen.

1747, Sept. 26. Van Cleave, Benjamin, of Freehold, Monmouth Co.; will of. Wife, but not named. Eldest son, John, land whereon he lives in Freehold, purchased of Daniel Grandin and John Benham, formerly Hendrick Kips, deceased. Daughter, Elizabeth, wife of William Cownover. Son, Richard, land whereon he lives, purchased by testator from William and John, sons of Alexander Clark. Land adjoining road to Mount Pleasant. Daughter, Ellen, wife of Hendrick Van Derbelt. Son, Benjamin, land whereon he lives, bought of John Heppron, and land bought of Jehannes Coart. Daughters—Alse (wife of William Beard), and Mary (wife of John Brocaw). Executors—sons John, Richard and Benjamin, and friend John Bowne. Witnesses—David, Elbert and Arthur Williamson. Proved Nov. 12, 1747. Lib. E, p. 113.

1731, Aug. 25. Vanclief, Isaac, of Upper Freehold, Monmouth Co.; will of. Wife, Rebecca. Real estate to be sold and proceeds divided between wife and children (not named). Eldest son, £10 more, being legacy left him by his uncle, Jacobus Vanclief. Cornelius Van Horne and Joseph Forman, trustees. Brothers, Lawrence and John Van Clief. Executors to sign release to Jacob Morice for share of farm on which testator lived. Executors—wife, "brother" Joseph Forman, and friend Cornelius Van Horn. Witnesses—Richard Saltar, Jacob Morris, Mary Morris. Proved Oct. 2, 1731. Lib. 3, p. 160.

1731, Sept. 20. Inventory (amount lacking); made by Isaac Stelle and ———.

1750, April 4. Van Court, Elias, of Piscataway, Middlesex Co., cordwainer; will of. Wife, Ann, all real and personal estate as long as she lives. Children—Agness, Jane, Ann, Elizabeth, Moses, Thomas, Samuel, John and Michael, all under age. Sons, Eliass and Daniell, have had their portions. Executors—wife, son Moses, and brother-in-law Daniell Cooper. Witnesses—Benjamin Runyon, Jare Sebring, Edward Willmott. Proved Aug. 23, 1750. Lib. E, p. 449.

1750, Aug. 24. Inventory, £258.16.1; made by John Vail and Peter Williamson.

1745, July 22. Van Culin, Jacobus, of Salem Co., yeoman; will of. Grandson, Andrew Matson of Oldman's Creek, Gloucester Co. (my daughter's son), to have my land in Grenig, Gloucester Co., the money that Charles Friend and Timothy Rain owe; also £11 that Robert Pedrick owes. Son, William Vanculin. Rest of my personal estate to my wife. Executors—John Rain and grandson, Andrew Matson, both of Gloucester Co. Witnesses—Peter Peterson, An Peterson, Martin Reardon. Proved 16 April, 1747. Lib. 5, p. 385.

1746, Dec. 27. Vanculin, William, of Penns Neck, Salem Co., yeoman; will of. Executors—son, John Vanculin, Samuel Shivers of Gloucester, and John Parrack of Philadelphia, shipwright. Honored father, Jacobus Vanculin, to have during life 100 acres in Penns Neck adjoining Ash Creek whereon Robert Peddriff lives; after his decease same to be divided as the residuary estate. Said son, my wood boat. Rest of estate to my eight children—John, Jacob, William, Andrew, Catherine, Rebecca, Sarah and Rachel (my son John, eldest, to have a double share). Executors shall be the guardians of children during minority, and apply the interest of personal estate for maintenance, education, or placing them out to trades. Son, John, to be dutiful to his mother. Witnesses—Wm. Graddocke, John Forbes, John Church, Jno. Reily. Proved 19 Feb., 1746. Lib. 5, p. 498.

1746, Jan. 15. Inventory, £210.10.6; made by Tim. Rain, Benj. Bispham.

1750, July 14. Vanderbelt, Jeremiah, of New Brunswick, Middlesex Co., yeoman. Int. Adm'x, Neeltie Vanderbelt, widow. Frederick VanLowe, of Somerset Co., and Luke Voorhees, of Middlesex Co., fellow bondsmen. Witness—David Cawood. Lib. E, p. 431.

1750, July 11. Inventory, £932.01.7; made by Robert Van Noordstrant and Hans Bleekhad.

———, ——, —. Account. Bonds of Jno. VanD'rbelt, Gerrit VanDuyn, Aart VanPelt, Dan'll Thomson, Jacob VanDeventer, Hugh Blackhull, widow Wyckoff, Com'r Dehart, James Hude, Rem. Symonse, Executors of Estate of William Clarkson, Joris Brinkerhoff, Peter Remson, Theo. VanWyck, Catharine Schuyler, Derik Schuyler, Mich. Veght, Jno. VanBower, Ann Longfield, Jno. Bissel, Leffiert Waldron, Volkert Van Noordstrand, Mary Voorhees, Jno. Shureman, Dirck VanAllen, Charles Fontine, The Deacons of Flatbush Church.

1746-7, Jan. 3. Vanderhuyden (Vanderhye), Catharine, of Freehold, Monmouth Co., widow; will of. Daughter, Elizabeth, £155, etc., when of age. Sister, Gertrude Craig, her children, and children of testatrix's brother, Joseph Ward, deceased. Executors—sister, Gertrude Craig, and friend David Rhe. Witnesses—William Ker, Robert Barclay, John Henderson. Proved March 5, 1746-7. Lib. D, p. 454.

1746-7, Feb. 2. Inventory of the estate (£261.18) includes things belonging to the clockmaking or watchmaker's trade, 2 gold rings, old gold and old silver. Made by Jacob Sutvin, William Ker, John Henderson.

1733, April 25. Vandeventer, Abraham, of Monmouth Co., blacksmith; will of. Wife, Alche. Son, Peter. Wife's daughter, Mary Van Dorn, interest due from Crisyon Van Dorn. Executors—father-in-law, Cornelius Cownover, and brother Isaac Van Deventer. Witnesses—Jacob Vandeventer, Rowliff Couenhoven, John Bowne. Proved Dec. 11, 1733. Lib. B, p. 479.

1733, June 2. Inventory, £45.14.0; made by Johannis Bennet, John Bowne, Nathan Beers.

1747-8, Jan. 22. Vandeventer, Peter, of Middletown, Monmouth Co., yeoman. Hannah Vandeventer, the widow, resigns right of administration to James Willson and Joseph Dorsett, of Middletown. Witness—Thomas Bullman.

1747-8, Feb. 1. Adm'rs, Joseph Dorsett and James Willson. Lambert Johnson, of Middletown, fellow bondsman. Lib. E, p. 123.

1747-8, Feb. 2. Inventory (over £57) includes ½ a boat, £30. Made by Joseph Carman, Matthias Johnson, Nicholas Johnson.

1748-9, Feb. 22. Vandevere, Henry, of Penns Neck, Salem Co.; will of. Wife, Sarah. Lands to be sold and the money put at interest towards sustaining Jacob, my son. In case of his death, to wife. Executors—wife, Sarah, and Peter Derickson. Witnesses—Jacob Vandevere, Thomas Tussey, Thomas Cahill. Proved 12 March, 1748-9. Lib. 6, p. 289.

1748-9, March 4. Inventory, £41.12.1; made by Thomas Tussey, Jacob Vandevere.

1748, Feb. 11. Vandick, Stephen, of Salem Co. Int. Adm'x, Irane Vandick, widow. Bondsman—John Fitzpatrick. Both of Alloways Creek. Witnesses—Saml. Hedge, Nichl. Gibbon. Lib. 6, p. 322.

1748, Feb. 11. Inventory, £40.8; made by John Fitzpatrick, James Evans.

1750, Nov. 5. Account. Monies paid Robert Hartshorne, William Murdock, Nicholas Gibbon, James Hutson, John Jarman, Benja. Allen, John Jones.

1732, Dec. 1. Vandike, Charles, of Shrewsbury, Monmouth Co., yeoman; will of. John, Mary and Elizabeth, children of son Aurt Vandike, late of Island of Bermudas, deceased. Son, Thomas. Children of daughter, Gerty Remine (or Romine). Children of daughter, Angleche Vanwey. Children of son, John, late of Shrewsbury, deceased. Moveable estate to son Thomas. Executors—son, Thomas, Jacob Dennes, Richard Hartshorne, Junior. Witnesses—Daniel Tilton, Britain White, Richard Hartshorne, Junior. Proved March 11, 1734. Lib. C, p. 12.

1734-5, March 3. Inventory (£62.2.7) includes Bible and 2 other Dutch books, £1.0.0; sword and belt; bond of Corte Myers; judgment before Justice Little against Rebecca Vandycke. Made by Isaac Hance, Thomas Lippincott, Thomas and Peter White.

1732, Jan. 20. Vandike, John, of Shrewsbury, Monmouth Co. Bond of Rebecca Vandike, the widow, as administratrix. Theophilus Longstreet, yeoman, of Monmouth Co., fellow bondsman. Witnesses—Somerset Mash, Anne Morris. Bondsman—Stoffel Lanstraat. Monmouth Wills, 515 M.

1748, Sept. 3. Van Dorn, Aure, of Freehold, Monmouth Co., miller; will of. Wife, Ante. Son, Jacob, under age. Daughters, Mary, Sarah, Anne and Nelly, when married. Grist mill and land left to testator by his father, Jacob Van Dorn. Brother, Isaac, to keep his building and tan house for life; also his shoemaker's and merchant shops and cellar. Executors—friends, Garret Scanck (Schenck) and Isaac Vandorn. Witnesses—William McConckey, John Schenck, Jr., and Isaac Vandorn. Proved April 18, 1749. Lib. E, p. 295.

1748, Sept. 4. Inventory (£581.1.2) includes large Bible, small Bible and other books; two negroes, one wench, and three children, £230; pike and sword. Made by Johannis and Hendrick Bennet, Rolof Schenck.

1744, Dec. 15. Van Eate (Van Eta), Arie, of Somerset Co., yeoman; will of. Wife, Elizabeth, estate during widowhood; thereafter same equally to sons Samuel, Jacobys, John, they to give daughter, Elizabeth, £14, when youngest will be 21. Land in Morris Co. Executors—brother, Jacobys Van Etea, and Mathew Van Stee. Witnesses—Andries Stol, Frederick Bodyen, Volckert Doun.

1746, Aug. 29. Codicil. Makes provision for son Arie, born after the signing of will. Witnesses—Frederick Bodyn, Hendrick Van Stee, Volikert Doun. Proved 6 April, 1747. Lib. E, p. 19.

1747, April 2. Inventory, £154.14.10; made by Frederick Bodyn, Hendrick Van Stee.

1746, May 9. Vaneman, John, of Penns Neck, Salem Co., husbandman, yeoman. Int. Adm'r, William Vaneman. Bondsmen—Allen Congleton, Martin Skeer. All of said county, yeomen. Witnesses—Margaret Vaneman, Dan. Mestayer. Lib. 5, p. 421.

1746, May 6. Inventory, £64.12.10; made by Martin Skeer, Alen Congleton.

1748, Nov. 1. Vaneman, William, of Piles Grove Precinct, Salem Co.; will of. Wife, Magdalen. Sons—Jacob, plantation (100 acres of land and 17 of swamp) in said Precinct and county where Matthis Holten formerly lived; William, plantation I have hitherto lived on and 10 acres of marsh; Andrew, piece of rough land, 100 odd acres, joining my son Jacob's land. Daughters—Elizabeth Lorance and Rebecca Vanneman. Negro woman and child allotted. Moveable estate equally divided among the children. Executors—sons, Jacob and William. Witnesses—Mary Vaneman, Andrew Senicks, Peter Tranberg. Proved 30 Nov., 1748. Lib. 6, p. 225.

1748, Nov. 28. Inventory (£272.2.4) includes negro woman and child. £30.29. Appraisers—Senick Senickson, Samuel Linch.

1748, Feb. 21. Account. Monies paid Alen Congleton, Daniel Mestayer, Martin Skeer, Margaret Vaneman, Margaret Hill, Mary Jones.

1729, June 6. VanEmburgh, Johannis, of Bergen Co. "Doctor of Physick;" will of. Wife, Cathrina, management of whole estate during widowhood. Eldest son, Guisbert, £5 as birthright. Son, William Sandford VanEmburgh, my doctor's chest and all instruments. Rest of the estate after death of or remarriage of wife divided equally among my children, viz., Guisbert, Sarah Spier, Rachel King, William Sandford, Mary Sandford, Johannes, Cathrena, Elizabeth Bartulf and Perrigeam. Executors—Richard Edsall, and my eldest son, Guisbert. Witnesses—John Geust, Johannes Everson, Haermaen Lukes. Proved 13 Sept., 1742. (Guisbert VanEmburgh qualified as executor).

Lib. C, p. 541.

1742, Sept. 23-25. Inventory, personal and real estate (£1302.2.5), includes old sword; lot of land with house, £175; the old place, land with buildings and orchard, £200; the house lot with house on east side of the church, £50; land at "Hoghakos," £225; 10 acres down Hackinsack River, £10; negroes, Clay (85 years old), £35; boy (5 years), £15; Jane (40 years), 15 shillings. Made by David Demarest, Benjamin Demarest, Egbert Ackerman. Bonds and notes:—Demarest, William Eniss, William Santford, Elias Williamson, William Eniss, Isack Morris, John Verwey, Thomas Vandyck, Henry Myer, Sarah Vareck, Jacob Coal, John Coal, Olivier Schuller, Warnar Burger, John VanHolkerk, Jacob Vangelder, Gysbert VanEnburge.

1742, July 9. VanEmburge, Katherine, widow, of Hackinsack, Bergen Co.; will of. Children—Sarah (wife of Abraham Spier), Gysbert, Rachel (wife of John King), William Standford, Johanes, Katherine (wife of ——— Giebs) and Peregrain. Grandchildren—Guillam Bartholst, son of daughter, Elizabeth, deceased; William and Mally Sandfordts, children of my daughter, Mary, deceased; unto them equally the residue of my estate, which I have upon New Barbado Neck, according to last will of my mother, Sarah Sandford, deceased. Mr. Cornelius Wynkoop, David Demorest and Benjamin Demarest, all of Hackinsack, executors of my minorene grandchildren and assistants of all my children. Witnesses—Hendrick Sabagh, Nicholas Stillwell, David Demorest, Thos. Turner. Proved 13 Sept., 1742.

Lib. C, p. 544.

1743, Nov. 17, 19. Renunciation of David and Benjamin Demorest as executors.

1745, May 1. Inventory (£532.14) of Catharin VanEmburgh, "late of New Barbadoes." Bonds due from Gilbert VanEmburgh, Thomas Van-Dike, Frans Van Den Burgh, William Enis, John Cool, Jacob Cool, Isaac Morris, David DeMarest, Enoch Earl, John Van Boskerk, Jacob Van Gelder, Oliver Schuyler.

1733, Sept. 1. Van Gale, Lawrence, of Perth Amboy, Middlesex Co. Int. Adm'xs, Hannah Clay, Margaret Forster, Catherine Lufberry (co-heirs). Lib. B, p. 466.

1742, Aug. 27. Van Garden, Albart, of Walpack, Morris Co. Int. Adm'r, William Van Garden. Bondsman—Derrick Westbrook, of same place, yeoman. Witness—James Cumine.

1742, Aug. 21. Jannetie, relict, renounces in favor of William, eldest son. John Coxe, Esq., Proctor. Witnesses—Derrick Westbroeck, Abram Van Campen.

1746, Sept. 6. Inventory (£12.11.0); made by Benjamin Smith, of Wallpack, and Richard Howel, of same place, tailor. Includes bill of Dr. An'w Maxwell, Mar. 17, 1740, for medical visits to intestate, and debts to James Hyndshaw, Derrick Westbroeck, Jacob Kuykindael, Abram Van Campen, Harman Van Garden, Hendrick Cortrecht, Lambert Brink.

Morris Wills, 2 N.

1748-9, March 16. Vangelder, Hannah, of Amwell Township, Hun-

terdon. Int. Adm'r, Henry Oxley, of Hopewell, yeoman. Thomas Stilwell, of Amwell, yeoman, surety. Witness—Zaccheus Beebe.
Hunterdon Wills, 238 J.

1741, Aug. 20. Vangiesen, Isaac, yeoman, of Hackinsack, Bergen Co. Int. Adm'r, Henry Vangiesen, of same place. Fellow bondsman, Henry Vangiesen, of Second River, Essex Co., yeoman. Witnesses—Jno. Clark, Edward Harrold. Lib. C, p. 426.

1741, Aug. 24. Inventory (£229.5.10) includes 25 shirts (£13.12), silver hilted sword (4), ivory headed cane, large Dutch Bible (£3), Dutch books, English books, silver poringer, negro woman and children (£75). Made by Jan. Romyn, Albert Terhuyn, Hendrick VanGiesen.

1747, May 6. Vanhengle, Arnout, of Somerset Co. Int. Adm'r, Hendrick Vanhengel. Fellow bondsmen—John Jubart. Lib. E, p. 35.

1747, May 14. Inventory (£163.10.6) includes large Dutch Bible (£1), sword and "beldt" (14s), negro man and woman (£70). Made by Corneless Vanhengelen, Ouk Vanhengelen, Steffy (Christoffel) Van Aertsdalen, Daniel Hendrickson, Maertynes Hogelandt, Pouwel Aminmen (Amerman), Charles Suydam, Richard Stockton, Ren Gerritsen, Pieter Schenck.

1747, April 6. Vanhist, Rainier, of Salem Co., yeoman. Int. Adm'r, Ranier Vanhist. Bondsmen—William Barker, of said County, gent. Witnesses—Joseph Carroll, Danl. Mestayer. Lib. 5, p. 421.

1750-1, Feb. 18. Van Hook, Henry, of Upper Freehold, Monmouth Co., yeoman; will of. Wife, Deborah. Son, Lawrence, half of land near Manalapan, adjoining Thomas Hankinson; other half to Lawrence's uncle, Aaron Van Hook. Son, Benjamin, land bought of John Nesmith, at Middletown Point. When, son, Isaac is of age, testator's dwelling house and lot, in Allenstown, to be sold and money to testator's wife, and to sons, William, Samuel and Isaac. Executors—wife, and son Lawrence. Witnesses—Ephraim Robins, Benjamin Allen, William Lawrence. Proved March 7, 1750. Lib. 6, p. 419.

1750-1, March 4. Inventory (£75.8.7½) includes bond of Benjamin Allen, bills of Thomas Herbert and Nathaniel Bowman. Made by William Lawrence, Jr., Benjamin Allen.

1740, June 6. Van Hooren, Ruth, of Bergen Co.; will of. Only son, John, all land at Gemocenepa, Bergen Co., with all improvements. Daughter, Jannitje, wife of Dirck Cadmus, all land at Pemrepoch, Bergen Co., with improvements, and rights in commons of Bergen, except such as have been sold to my son. Daughters—Marytie, wife of Elias Michielje Vreelandt, and Antie, wife of Jacob Bergen. Executors—Michielje Vreelandt, his wife Marytie, Jacob Bergen, and his wife Antie. Witnesses—Johannis Vreelandt, Johannis Diederick, Hartman Blinckerhoff. Proved 8 June, 1741. Lib. C, p. 419.

1741, June 10. Inventory (£1.293.4.6) includes bonds and cash, £1,065.-19.6; negro man, £80; negro woman and child, £45. Appraisers—Lawrence VanBuskirk, Cornelius Blinkerhof.

1732-3, Feb. 26. Vanhorn, Cornailes, of Scralingbrough, Bergen Co., yeoman. Eldest sons, Cornailes, Loukes and Joannes, all land equally, each to pay £25 to their brothers and sisters being seven (if wife be now with child); eldest son, Cornailes, to pay in 8 years, Luke, 2nd son, in 12 years, Joannes, 3d son, in 15 years. Moveables equally divided among children. Executors—brothers, Loukes and Johanes

Vanhorn. Witnesses—Yan Duru (Jan Duryee), Johannes Vanboskerck, John Morse. Proved 26 May, 1733. Lib. B, p. 437.

1743, Dec. 24. Vanhorn, Cornelius, of Reading Town, Hunterdon Co.; will of. Wife, Hannah. Eldest son, Thomas, tract of land where testator lived, bought of John Bud, subject to maintaining testator's minor children. Son, Matthias, land in Upper Freehold, adjoining Thomas Leonard, Thomas Averhem, Abiah Cook and Joseph Williams, in Monmouth County, subject to payments. Eldest daughter, Cathrine Vanhorn, when aged 27; second daughter, Elizabeth Vanhorn, when aged 24. Son, Cornelius, small tract of land in Upper Croswix Creek in Burlington County, purchased of Matthew Watson, he paying money to younger brother Daniel Vanhorn, at 21. Seven sons and three daughters. Executors—son, Thomas, brother Abraham Vanhorn, and Nicholas Wykoff. Witnesses—Cornelius Wyckof, Roelof Roelofson, Methias Van Horn, Matt: Brown. Proved March 16, 1743-4.

1743-4, Feb. 3. Codicil. Testator's printing books to whole family. Elizabeth Vanhorne, side saddle which was her mother's. Witnesses—Matthew Brown, Cornelius Wyckof, Methias Van Horne. Lib. 5, p. 17.

1744, April 5. Inventory (£992.19.4) includes two Bibles and other books, two guns, two swords, servant woman's time (£12), two negro boys (£50), bills of Burges Hall, Isaac Still, John Estil, Leonard & Lawrence, Harmanns Roilefson, Jacob Shermerhorn, Hugh McCarrin, William Peppenger, Merriley Sharpsteen. Made by John Emley and Edward Rockhill.

1742, Sept. 9. Van Horne, Andrew, of Piscataway, Middlesex Co., gent.; will of. Wife, Mary. Children—Tomes, Catharine and Sarah. Executors—wife, brother James, and brother-in-law Phillip Kearny. Witnesses—James Lyne, Alexander Henry, Francis Costigen. Proved Jan. 19, 1747.

1747, May 18. Codicil provides for an equal division of estate among the wife, above children and expected child. Witnesses—James Thomson, Richard Merrell, Jonathan Stelle. Proved June 14, 1763. Lib. H, p. 241.

1733, June 23. Van Horne, John, of City of New York, merchant; will of. Executors—all my children, Cornelius, Andrew, Abraham, James, and Catharine. Land bought of Samuel Royce, John Burrows, Dockwra, Sonmans, and John Outman; lands joyning "brother" Abraham Garrett, and Henry Neald, where Edward Phillips lives, on Millston River, joyning land of Francis Elrington; land where Robert Letice Hooper lives, joyning lands of James and Thomas Leonard and Edward Phelps. Witnesses—Joh. VanSolingen, Jere. Tothill, P's Rynders. Proved Nov. 22, 1735.

1735, Nov. 9. Bond of Andrew Vanhorne, brother of John Vanhorne, Jun'r, as administrator on estate left unadministered by his father, John VanHorne. Patrick McEvers, fellow bondsman. Witness—James Hooper. (Middlesex Wills), Lib. C, pp. 51, 57.

1733, March 28. Vanneman (Van Iman), David, of Greenwich, Gloucester Co., yeoman; will of. Adm'x, Mary Vanneman, widow. Bondsman—Christopher Taylor, of same place yeoman. Witness—A. Randall.

1732-3, March 21. Inventory (£138.18.9) includes 3 Bibles and Common Prayer book. Appraisers—John Van Iman, Robert Garrard, Wm. Mickle. Gloucester Wills, 172 H.

1732, Feb. 20. Vanneman, Samuel, of Greenwich, Gloucester Co., yeoman; will of. Sons—Samuel and Jonas, the plantation (140 acres where I live); Gabriel, David and John, land upon Clamell Creek; Peter, £25. Wife, Margarett, executrix and to have residue of estate. Executors—Jacob Forsman and Alexander Randall, and to be guardians of son Peter. Witnesses—Stephen Jones, Abraham Jones, John Lock. Proved 28 March, 1733.

1732-3, March 22. Inventory (£168.3.3) includes 2 weavers looms, £2. Appraisers—John Van Iman, Stephen Jones.

1734, April 17. Account. Monies paid Wm. Ward, Dishadorus Vanneman, Peter Vanneman, Margaret Vanneman. Gloucester Wills, 174 H.

1743-4, Jan. 27. Van Neste, George, of Raritan, Somerset Co., yeoman; will of. Children—Mary, Peter, Rynear, Jean, Abraham, Hendrick and Jacob. Home plantation, of 504 acres, to be "sold at vandue amongst my children." Executors—sons Peter, Rynear, Abraham, Hendrick and Jacob. Signed "Joris Vannest." Witnesses—Da'l Don. Dunster, Rice Vroome, George Price. Proved 6 July, 1747.

Lib. E, p. 62.

1732, Jan. 22. Van Noma, Anglebert (Angelburth), of Essex Co. Int. Adm'r, John DeCamp. John Vanwinkle and John Blanchard, yeomen, fellow bondsmen. Lib. B, p. 350.

1732-3, Feb. 1. Inventory, £38.09.10; made by Solomon Bates and John Blanchard.

1739, March 21. Van Nortstrandt, Casparus, of Somerset Co., blacksmith; will of. Wife, Jane. Children—Jacob, Christophell, Jane, Ann, Arjantie and Sarah. Those under 16 years to have suitable education. Home farm, adjoining Rariton River, to be Jacob's and Christophell's. In case Daniel Donaldson Dunstar conveys a tract of land, as by obligation of 7 of Feb., 1738, said land to be paid out of personal estate, and, after wife (Jane's) re-marriage or decease, to be divided equally among the children. Executors—"brothers," Jacob Van Nortstrandt, Isaac Kipp, Aria Miller and John VanMiddlesworth, Junior. Witnesses—Jores Rappelye, Boudewoyn Dennerl, Jacob Janeway. Proved 16 May, 1744. Lib. D, p. 139.

1744, June 19. Renunciation of Isaac Kipp as executor. Witness—Isaac Kipp, Junior.

1747, Sept. 29. Van Nuys, John, of New Brunswick, Middlesex Co., joyner; will of. Children—Jacobus, Margrata, Lena, Elizabeth and Anna. Land on Tan Pit Brook. Executors—wife, Ariaentje, son Jacobus, and friends Abraham Ouke and Gerrit Stoothoof. Witnesses—Aereys Vanaesdaelen, Peter Vredenburgh, Johannes Nefyees. Real and personal estate. Proved Nov. 23, 1747. Lib. E, p. 192.

1748, Feb. 2. VanRipen, Jurie, late of Bergen Co. Int. Adm'r, Thomas VanRipen. Fellow bondsmen, John VanRipen, of Bergen Co., and Adrian A. Post, of Essex Co. Bergen Wills, 249 B.

1749, Apr. 14. VanRiper, Simeon, late of Waickran (?), Bergen Co. Int. Adm'r, Mersalus Post, of Acquanknong, Essex Co., the widow, Yonckee, renouncing her right. Fellow bondsman, George Vreland. Witnesses—Geo. Vreland, Andrian Post. Bergen Wills, 260-2 B.

1748, Aug. 29. Vanroom, Isaiah, of Middlesex Co. Int. Adm'r,

Daniel Hankins, who married one of the daughters. William Hutchinson, Esq., and Francis Holman, fellow bondsmen. Lib. E, p. 206.

1749-50, Feb. 8. Vanschuyze, John, of Co. of Burlington, yeoman; will of. Wife, Mary, personal estate. Plantation I purchased of Robert Ridgway and William Cutler to my sons, Walter and John, they paying legacies to my daughter Katherine Vervalah, the heirs of Deborah Westervelt, my daughter Jane Vervalah, and my youngest son Jacob. Plantation I purchased of Charles Read to sons Abraham and William. Daughter, Gertrude. Executors—son, Walter, and friend John Morris. Witnesses—Jacob Heays, Mary English, Casparus Schuyler. Proved Feb. 17, 1749. Lib. 6, p. 312.

1749, August 31. Van Sickelen, Reinier, of Reading Township, Hunterdon Co.; will of. Wife, Styntie. Daughter, Jannetie. Residue to wife and sons Ferdenant and Ryke, Geisbert and Hendricks, and daughters Jannetie and Marya. Executors—brother-in-law, John Sudam, and brothers Geisbert and Johannis van Sickel. Witnesses—John Van Sickle, Peter Van Sickle, John Van Boskerck. Proved March 6, 1749-50. Lib. 6, p. 326.

1749-50, March 6. Inventory (£83.14.6) includes gun and sword. Made by Jacobus Vandeerveer, Daniel Lucas.

1757, Dec. 1. Account. Mentions Jacob Smock, Johanes Van Boskirke, John Johnson, Joost Shampe, Mich. Demott, Peter Vansickelen, Dan. Crast, James Blair, Adam Arie, Nicholas Wycoff, Hannah Johnson, John Broughton, George Hall, Catherine Schuyler, William Day, Cornelius Lowe, James Job, Jacob Vanderveer, Cornelius Lane, Jacob Swart, Garret Vansickelen, H. Lane, Jacob Swartwort, Peter Lowe, Ann Stryker, Peter Slight, Herman Lane, Johanes Van Sickland, John Stall, Jerry Hoff, Doc'r Van Waggoner, John Vroom, Mich. Vanboskirk, Mary Sichlen, Geo. Beggs, Jacob Vanderbilt (for fulling mill testator sold in his life time), George Brinkerhoffe.

1742-3, March 4. Vansickle, Garret, yeoman, of Readings Town, Hunterdon Co.; will of. Wife, Margaret, executrix. Son, Garret, the dwelling place, when of age. Eldest daughter, Tonilie (or Tonjtie), the place, with half the mill, near Coart Johnson's, when of age. Daughter, Margaret, £300. If wife marries, David Cocks to be guardian of children. (Signed by Garret and Margett Vansickle). Witnesses—Abraham Tetsort, Hendrik Vandezzal, Mary Sanders. Proved Oct. 20, 1748. Lib. 6, p. 4.

1748, Oct. 12. Inventory (£519.18) includes wind mill, three negroes, two wenches. Made by Frederick Bodine, Harman Lane, Abraham Titsworth.

1749, May 24. Vansickle, Jacob, and Abraham, of Middlesex Co., upwards of 14 years, make choice of Micaiah Dunn and James Campbell, as guardians. Bond of same, both of Piscataway. Edmund Dunham and Jonathan Dunham, fellow bondsmen. Lib. 5, p. 306.

1744, Dec. 13. Van Sickles, Abraham, of Piscataqua, Middlesex Co. Inventory, £91.6.2; made by James Campbell and William Clawson.

1749, June 1. Account rendered by Elizabeth Rattan, formerly Van Sickles, widow of Abraham. Lib. D, p. 208.

1734, May 20. Vanveghten, Michael, of Raratan, Somerset Co., yeoman; will of. Wife, Jannitje, executrix, and the income from bonds, bills and debts outstanding during life. Daughters—Mary, wife of Jeremiah Field, £200; Jannitje, wife of Jacobus Hegemen, the plantation on south side of Raraton River bought of Philip Headman, now in possession of Jacobus Hegeman, also piece of low land to southward of the New River, and one-half of land and meadow at place called the great "inboght," near Catskill, in Albany County, N. Y., known by lot No. 3, and part of a large tract, formerly patented to one William Leveridge. The other half of said land to son Dirck, who is to have residue of estate. Executors—son, Dirck, and son-in-law, Jacobus Hegeman. Witnesses—Cor. VanHorne, M'w Clarkson, Jno. Chambers. Proved 24 March, 1737-8. Lib. C, p. 191.

1747, June 9. Vanveighten, Benjamin, of Rariton, Somerset Co., husbandman; will of. Wife, Sarah. Children—Cornelius (oldest), John, Reuben, Annatie, Mary, and youngest son Benjamin. Personal estate. Executors—wife, Sarah, and "John Webster, my son." Witnesses—Yesep Falkerse, John Davis, John MacNiell. Proved 26 June, 1747. Lib. E, p. 61.

1747, June 27. Renunciation of John Webster as executor.

1748, Oct. 3. VanVeghtie, Ephraim, of New Brunswick, Middlesex Co. Int. Adm'x, Catherine VanVeighten, of Albany. John Richards, of New York, fellow bondsman. Lib. E, p. 213.

1747, March 24. Van Voorhees, Peter, of Somerset Co.; will of. Wife, providing she "marry not," the house, furniture, and land belonging to it, with the lot of land in Brunswick. At her death real estate to be sold and price divided among the children: Gerret, (oldest) to have £25 over his common share. Executors and trustees —Peter Nevius, Daniel Polhemus, Hendrick Vanforhees. Witnesses—John Gordon, Nicolas Waycoff (Wycoff), Gisbert Lane. Proved 2 April, 1748. Lib. E, p. 315.

1749, May 24. Inventory (£148.9.6) includes negro-man (£18), big Dutch Bible, guns and sword. Appraiser—Oky Vorous. ("Hendk. Voorhees died before this came to the office").

1734, Sept. 3. Van Voorhies, Albert, of Somerset Co. Inventory, £133.11.6; made by Jerimijes VanDerBilt, Cornelius Bennett. (Signed also by Catrina Vorhees). Somerset Wills, 41 R.

1730, Jan. 22. VanVoorhies, Albert, of New Brunswick, Middlesex Co., yeoman; will of. Children mentioned but not named; all under age. Real and personal estate. Executors—wife, Cateyntje, and brothers Roelof and Minne VanVoorhies. Witnesses—Cornelius Cornel, Petrus Sperling, J. N. Sperling. Proved Dec. 2, 1734. Lib. C, p. 3.

1733, Sept. 20. VanVoorhies, Minne, of Middlesex Co.; will of. Wife, Lametje. Children—Luykis, Gerrit, Minniss, John, Abraham and Cattrina, all under age. Real and personal estate. Executors—Albert VanVoorhuiss, Abraham VanVoorhuiss, Derrick Schuyler. Witnesses—Hend'k Fisher, Reijck Suddem, Peter Morn. Proved Nov. 15, 1733. Lib. B, p. 494.

1732, Jan. 18. VanVoorhouse, John, of New Brunswick, Middlesex Co., yeoman; will of. Wife, Sarah. Children—John, Anne, Sarah,

Eleanor, all under age. Expected child. Real and personal estate. Executors—John Luykisse, John Schenck, Lucas VanVoorhouse, Jun'r, Minne VanVoorhouse, Derryck Schuyler. Witnesses—Cornelius Covenhoven, Aure VanDorn, Robert Dodsworthy. Proved Dec. 4, 1734. Lib. C, p. 13.

1708, Sept. 30. VanWinckel, Jacob Jacobsen, Sr., of Bergen Co., yeoman; will of. Second wife, Margaretha, executrix and whole estate during life. In case of her death, my eldest son (by Margaretha), Henry, to be executor. Minorene children to be brought up and educated before division of estate, "which by agreement I am bound to do." The ¾ of whole estate to be delivered equally to my four (?) children (begotten of my said wife, Margaretha), viz., Henry, Catherine and Samuel. The children of my first wife, Aeltie VanWinckel, viz., Jacob (5 sh. for his birthright), Margaretha, Daniel, John and Simon, to have ¼ part of whole estate. All that tract of land, which I enjoy by conveyance of Henry Teunisen Helling, with the lot I live upon, paying equal portions of the same to their sisters, I will to my sons, begotten of my wife Margaretha, with all the moveable estate for £75, ½ of said sum to the children of first wife, ½ to children of second wife. Witnesses—Henry Epken Banta, Abraham Ackerman, John Conrad Codweiss, Matthys Demoot, Elaes Gerbran.

1709, Sept. 19. Codicil. Daughter, Cathrine VanWinckel, bed with furnishings. Witnesses—Ulderick Brouwer, Cornelis Gerbrantsen, John Conrad Codweis. Proved 16 Oct., 1732. Lib. B, p. 311.

1732, Oct. 16. Hendrick VanWinckel qualifies. Fellow bondsman—Jacob Hendrickse Banta. Witnesses—Roelof Westervelt, Benjamin Westervelt.

1743, April 11. Van Winkel, Abraham, of "Equackanam," Essex Co., yeoman; will of. Children—Simeon, Fransois, Sytie, Antie, all under age. Expected child. Real and personal estate. Executors—friends Richard Bradbery, Marynes Vanwinkel, and wife, Mary. Witnesses—Marselis Post, John Vreland, George Vreland. Proved Sept. 28, 1744. Lib. D, p. 257.

1745, March 25, Apr. 3. Marianus Van Winkle and Richard Bradbery renounce executorship.

1750, March 28. Van Winkle (Van Winckle), Jacob, of Acquekenong, Essex Co., yeoman; will of. Daughter—Hannanche, under age. Ann, eldest daughter of brother Simon's son, Abraham Van Winckle. Real and personal estate. Executors—wife, Catherine, Mr. Samuel Bayard, Jun'r, of New York, and brother Marrinus VanWinckle. Witnesses—John Vrelandt, John VanVechten, James Billington. Proved May 9, 1750. Lib. E, p. 26.

1722, June 19. Van Winkle, Simon, of Acquackanong, Essex Co., yeoman; will of. "Being aged and infirm." Wife, Anna. Twelve children—Jacob, Aria, Johanus, Gideon, Simeon, Marinus, Abraham, Margrett, Trintie, Rachel, Altie and Leah. Real and personal estate. Executors—sons, Johanus and Gideon, and Johanus Cowman. Witnesses—Jno. Cooper, Arian Sip, Eder Sip. Proved Feb. 24, 1732-3. Lib. B, p. 492.

1732-3, March 6. Inventory (no amount given); made by George Gordon with consent of widow and her sons.

1734, June 8. Additional inventory was made.

1750, May 9, 11. Vaughan, Samuel, of Monmouth Co. Int. The widow, Mary, resigns right of administration to Hugh McCullom and William Liming. Witness—John Gisebartson. Bond of same. John Monrow, fellow bondsman. Witness—Luke Tuckniss. Lib. 7, p. 33.

1750, ——, —. Inventory (£34.2.4) includes 180 new rails, £0.5; a house and improvement, £3.10. Made by David Vaughan, Hugh McCullum.

1747, July 30. Vaughn, Edward, Minister of St. John's Church in Elizabeth Town, Essex Co.; will of. "Having been a missionary for many years under the Society for the Propagation of the Gospel in foreign parts, and being far advanced in years, I do hereby possess myself to die an orthodox member of the Church of England." Land in possession of John Keit, my tenant, purchased of John Lea, to remain to the use of the Church of England Minister, at Elizabeth Town and his successors, forever. James Emott, of New York City, gentleman, by his last will, dated Oct. 3, 1709, devised to his wife, Mary, his executrix, and his four sons, George, William, James, and John, all his estate; I afterward married his widow, Mary Emott, who is also since deceased. House and 12 acres of land, sold to Mr. William Ricketts. Niece, Mrs. Sarah Townley, all my plate and £100; niece, Mrs. Mary Townley, £50; brother-in-law Mr. Charles Townley; sister-in-law, Mrs. Sharpnagle, £100; sister, Mrs. Jane Godden, wife of Thomas Godden, of Leather Lane, near Holborn in London, £100. To Charles Vaughn, son of my brother, the Rev'd Mr. Robert Vaughn, Rector of Llantewell and Vicar of Llantrissan in Monmouthshire, in Wales, £100. Executors—friends Paul Richards, Esq., of New York City, and Walter Dongan, of Staten Island. Witnesses—Isaac Browne, Rob't Ogden, Nath'll Rusco. Proved Oct. 29, 1747. Lib. E, p. 103.

1748, April 21. Veghte, Johannes, of Somerset Co., yeoman; will of. Wife, Gerretje. Lands at Millstone River, Somerset Co., to be sold and proceeds given equally to wife and the daughters, Cornelia and Gerretje. Executors to hold the daughters' shares until 18. In case of death of these children, the same shall descend to the nephews John, son of my brother Nicholas, and John, son of my brother Garret Veghte. Executors and trustees—brothers Nicholas and Garret Veghte. Witnesses—Avis VanDerBilt, Christoffel Hoaghlandt, Dan'l Corsen. Proved 25 April, 1748. Lib. E, p. 162.

1735-6, March 23. Vickery, John, of Penns Neck, Salem Co., single man, yeoman. Int. Admr's, William Mecum, Margaret Mecum. Bondsman—Andrew Hendrickson. All of said County. Lib. 4, p. 57.

1735-6, March 19. Inventory (£38.6.11) being ½ of personal estate of Thomas Vickery, late of Penns Neck, father of deceased, now in hand of Margaret Mecum, wife of William Mecum. Appraisers—William Mecum, Thos. Miles. Witnesses—Charles Scott, Thomas Welsh, Samuel Buckley. Proved 21 Feb., 1738.

1738, Sept. 18. Vickery, William, of Penns Neck, Salem Co., husbandman; will of. Lands to be divided equally between sisters Jane and Margaret Vickery, upon condition that Jane shall pay £30 to Margaret when 21, in consideration of legacy left her by her father, Thomas Vickery, deceased, and fully acquit me and my heirs from said legacy. In case of her default Margaret shall have the land for-

ever, upon like condition as to Jane. Executors—father-in-law, William Mecum, and Thomas Miles. Proved ———, 1738. Lib. 4, p. 178.
1738, Nov. 30. Inventory (£108.15.5½) includes cattle, £36; wheat in the ground, £22. Appraisers—Martin Skeers, Edmond Weatherby.

1749, May 3. Vickey (Vickery), Edward, of Salem Co. Inventory, £51.11.6; made by Wm. Hall, James Mason. Salem Wills, 781 Q.

1731-2, Jany. 6. Vickey (Vickery), James, of Mannington, Salem Co., husbandman; will of. Daughter, Elizabeth Vickey, £30 to be paid by my son James in six years after he has possession of plantation I live on (which will be when he comes of age). If son dies in nonage, my brother, Edward, and his male heirs shall possess it; for want of such issue, next male heir of the Vickerys shall have it, allowing my daughter, Elizabeth, £60. Said son shall not sell the plantation unless thirty years old, and then to no one out of the Vickery family. Executors—brother, Edward, and Sinick Sinickson "to whom I give all of my lands and tenements." Witnesses—Robt. Robieson, Elizabeth Robieson, Alex'r Simpson. Affirmed 15 Feb., 1731-2. Lib. 3, p. 207.
1731-2, Jan. 14. Inventory, £47.12.6; made by John Hughs, Alexander Simpson.

1734, Aug. 20. Vining, Benjamin, of Barrenton house, near Salem, gent.; will of. Eldest son, John, to have Barrenton house and land, 800 acres, where I live, being part of lands called the "sixth lott," as lately surveyed, by Thomas Miles, beginning at head of Holiburn Creek, thence south by west to corner tree of old John Smith and John Pledger's, thence west to Mulhollow Creek (called Smith's Creek); also that "fifth lott," called Petersfield, 1060 acres, excepting 300 acres formerly sold to William Willis, and 200 acres since devised by Hugh Middleton to Sarah Hurley and her heirs; also my late dwelling at Philadelphia that Mr. Peter Baynton, merchant, lives in; also 9 acres on west side of Myamensick road, opposite eastward of Philip Johns, of Wickohoe. Son, Benjamin, and his eldest heir the remainder of the said Barrenton (sixth lot) being the westernmost part of late survey, containing 900 acres, beginning at mouth of Holiburn Creek to Millhollow Creek, till it intersects Fenwick River; also the old house and lot in Salem, east side of Bridge St.; also my house and lot in Philadelphia and water lot and wharf at Philadelphia, where my brother, Abraham Vining, lives. "Child in embro" (whether male or female) to have plantation on Mohoppony's Creek, near Salem, that John Wetherby lives on, together with the half of the grist mill; also my house and lot on north side of Chestnut Street in Philadelphia, that John Harker lives in. In case any of said children die under age, or issueless, his or her part to revert to survivors after they arrive at full age. Son, John, and his heirs to have my half gallon, eight-square silver tankard, the silver salver and a new silver spoon, marked "J. V.," also my library. Benjamin to have my three pint silver tankard, the largest silver porringer, and silver spoon marked "B. V." My unborn child my Winchester measur'd pint silver can, the next biggest silver porringer and a silver spoon, marked "M. V." The 1,000 acres in Covehaukin, or "Capt. John Neck" to be sold to bring up my children, clear of charges, to their respective ages, and the other lands in the Jerseys, after the judgment obtained against the late house and lot of Wm. Clark of Lewistown, Sussex County, and my lands (3,000 acres) of Primehook in said County, part of which is in possession of the widow Codd (the deeds whereof are in my chest); also my house and three lots at Markashoop, alias Chichester, in the possession of Capt. Welding, and the Goshen plantation in Chester County. Residue of my whole estate to my wife upon condition that "my children may be piously educated in the Rubrick of the Church of England and that my two sons may have a Grammar, Latin education and all be well taught to write well and learn Arithmetic, without any charges for their maintenance," until their respective ages of 21. Executors—wife, and sons, John and Benjamin Vining. In case of death of my wife, my brother, Abra. Vining, and Doctor Philip Chetwood, shall be guardians and trustees of my children. Witnesses—Sarah Turner, Danl. Mestayer, Philip Chetwood. Proved 13 Oct., 1735. (Letters granted to Mary Vining, John Vining and Benjamin Vining being infants). Lib. 4, p. 42.

1735, Oct. 15. Inventory (£1,243.17.3½) includes silver in plate, £42.-11.6; linen (bed and table), £35.10.2; "divinity law and phisick books," £1.8.9; clock and case in entry, "being very old;" negro slaves, men, women and children, £160; servant boy's time, £12; grain, farming animals, etc. Appraisers—Nichs. Gibbon, Ranier Vanhist.

1742, Aug. 9. Vleat, Margaret, of New Brunswick, Middlesex Co., widow; will of. Children—John, Francis, Marey, Ann, William, and Daniell, last two under age. Legacy to Philip Obrien. Executor—Elbert Stotof. Witnesses—John Bookhout, John Piatt, J. Wilmot.

1742, Aug. 9. Codicil. I desire my sons, Daniel and William, to keep house together. Witnesses—Francis Wilmot, J. Wilmot. Proved Nov. 5, 1742. Lib. D, p. 13.

1742, Oct. 26. Inventory (£201.10.7); includes cash in hands of Abraham VanVoorhous, several negroes and silver cup; made by William Walling, Reyck Sudam.

1747, Sept. 7. Voorhies, Lucas, of New Brunswick, Middlesex Co., blacksmith. Int. Adm'x, Siche (Sytye), the widow. John Boyse, yeoman, fellow bondsman. Witness—John Boice, Jun'r. Lib. E, p. 78.

1747, Sept. 30. Inventory, £107.11.2; made by Boliker Van Noordstrat. Witness—John Boice, Jun'r.

1734, Dec. 10. Vreland (Vreelandt), Abraham, of Newark, Essex Co., yeoman; will of. "Being aged and infirm." Son, Enoch, received £135 on Dec. 22, 1732; this to be his full legacy. Other sons—Jacob, Johannus, Simeon, Isaac, Abraham, and Hendrick. Daughter, Dirickee. Land joining land of Tunis Pier at Pesayack River; land bought of sons of John Fransoy, viz., Hendrick, France, Barat and Abraham Franser, on Nov. 19, 1733; land formerly belonging to Jacob VanWinkle, Jun'r, conveyed to me by Simeon VanWinkle, Oct. 17, 1715. Executors—sons Jacob and Johanus. Witnesses—Jno. Cooper, Jacob Van Winkle, William Williamsee. Proved Jan. 8, 1747-8.

1747-8, Jan. 8. William Williamsee testified to his signature, the other witnesses being deceased. Lib. E, p. 168.

1750, Nov. 4. Vreland, Michael, of Acquechenong, Essex Co., yeoman; will of. Sons—George and Michael. Seven children of daughter, Margaret, deceased. Executors—sons, Michael and Elias, and Mr. John Low. Real and personal estate. Witnesses—Gerret Gerretson, Adrian Post, Jun'r, James Billington. Proved Dec. 29, 1750. (John Low declines to act). Lib. E, p. 500.

1747, Feb. 26. Vrelandt, Elias, of Pemmerepogh, Bergen Co., yeoman; will of. Negroes, Tom and Susannah, to be sold at auction. Brother, Joris, of Pemmerepogh, to have farm at New Barbadoes Neck, Bergen Co., and to pay £450 within three months after my decease; on refusal, executors to sell the same, deducting costs and overplus, to be given to him and his heirs. Monies from sale of personal estate and the £450 to be put at interest and paid yearly to my sister Feytie, wife of Perrigren Santford; at her decease to be divided among her children. Executors—Michael, son of Harmen Vrelandt, deceased, Johannes Vrelandt, and Cornelius Gerrebrants, all of Gemonepagh, Bergen Co. Witnesses—Frans Covenhoven, Abram Van-Dursen, S. Johnson. Proved 25 April, 1748. Lib. E, p. 196.

1748, July 1. Citation. Whereas executors named have refused to act, etc., Feytie Sandford, residuary legatee, petitions that administration be granted to Isaac Lyon, of Newark, Essex Co. Witnesses—Peter Schuyler, Uzal Ogden.

1748, June 13. Renunciation of Michael Vrelandt, Johannes Vrelandt and Cornelius Garrabrant, in favor of Saphira Sandtford, sister of Elias Vrelandt. Witnesses—Uzal Ogden, Eleazor Brown.

1748, June 30. Administration with will annexed granted to Isaac Lyon, of Newark. Fellow bondsman—Peregrine Sandford, Bergen Co. Witnesses—Peter Schuyler.

1748, June 26. Inventory (£978.2.11) includes notes due from George Vreland, Wm. VanStraut, Dow (?) Cooper, Joseph Hower, Jacob Everts, Isaac Kingsland. Appraisers—Jas. Nicholson, David Ogden, Jr.

1749-50, March 21. Account. Mentions Uzal Ogden, Esq., Mr. Carter the lawyer, Dr. John Brown, David Abeel, Joris Vreland, David Ogden, Esq.

1732-3, Jan. 29. Vroliman, John, of Hanover Township, Hunterdon Co., husbandman. Letter from Jno. Budd to Mr. Peter Vantilburgh, merchant, of Newark, by Mr. Samuel Ludlam, stating he has been informed that Peter Vantilburgh is principal creditor of John Vroliman and therefore has right to administer, ("none of the kindred or sons being present that are of age"). Renunciation in name of Peter Vantilburgh attached, signed by Sarah Vantilburgh. Witnesses—Sara and Ann Ware.

1732-3, Feb. 2. Bond of Samuel Ludlum, of Hanover Township, weaver, as administrator. Jonathan Stiles, of same place, yeoman, surety. Witnesses—Richard Easton, Benjamin Carter. Hunterdon Wills, 81 J.

1731-2, Jan. 16. Vroom, Hendrick, of Kingston, Ulster Co., (New York), yeoman; will of. Wife, Deborah. Land occupied by Christopher Romeyn, in Amwell, Hunterdon Co., West Jersey. Son, Henry, a minor. Brother, Christian Vroom. Executors—wife and Andries Tenyke, of "The Rarartans." Witnesses—Johannes De Lametter, Pieter Vander Lyn, Jarman Pick. Proved May 12, 1732, before Edward Whitaker, Surrogate of Ulster County.

(Hunterdon Wills), Lib. 4, p. 59.

1748, 9 mo. (Nov.), 15 da. Waddington, Jonathan, of Alloways Creek Township, Salem Co., farmer; will of. Son, William, all my lands. Moveables equally to wife and my four daughters—Hannah, Jane, Mary and Elizabeth. Executors—wife, and my son. Witnesses—Philip Tyler, Joan Waddington, Richd. Bradford. Sworn and affirmed 15 Feb., 1748. Lib. 6, p. 287.

1748, Nov. 30. Inventory, £255.15.5; made by John Wright, James Daniel.

1731, March 12. Wade, Joseph, of Salem Town and Co., cordwainer. Int. Adm'rs, Renier Gregory, gent., and Hannah his wife (late Hannah Wade). Bondsman—Danl. Mestayer. All of said place. Witnesses—Edwd. Rs. Price, Jno. Rolfe. Lib. 3, p. 179.

1731, Feb. 23. Memorial of Samuel Wade, of Salem County, yeoman, setting forth that Joseph Wade died "in June last;" that the widow, administrator, has since married Renier Gregory, "a young man," who may waste the estate, and praying a faithful administration.

1731, 4 mo. (June), 29 da. Inventory (£491.9.6¾) includes horses, cows, sheep, swine, etc. Made by Abel Nicholson, Warwick Rundle.

1734, 5 mo. (July), 18 da. Wade, Samuel, of Alloways Creek, Salem Co.; will of. Estate to be equally divided, among my daughters, Lidya Thomlinson, Mary, Esther, Hannah and Meliscent (with slight qualification). Executors—son-in-law, Joseph Tomlinson, and daughters Mary and Esther Wade, assisted by Abel Nicholson and Joseph Clowes. Witnesses—Richard Bowen, John Steward, John Tyler. Affirmed 29 July, 1734. (Letters granted to Joseph Tomlinson and Mary Wade, Esther Wade being a minor). Lib. 3, p. 448.

1741, 8 mo. (Oct.), 21 da. Waite, Benjamin, of Woodberry Creek, Gloucester Co., yeoman; will of. Son, Benjamin, land on east side of Second Street from Delaware in Philadelphia; also plantation at Mouth of Woodberry Creek; the profits of said lands to be wife's until son will be 21. Executors—wife, Jean, and father-in-law Thomas Nickson (Nixon). Witnesses—Abraham Chattin, James Wilkins. Affirmed 18 Nov., 1741. Lib. 4, p. 321.

1741, 9th mo. (Nov.), 1 da. Inventory (£197.09.3) includes tailor's implements, etc. Appraisers—Abraham Chatten, William Wood.

1735, Nov. 29. Walcott, Mary, of Salem Town and Co., (an orphan under age) made application in 1730 that Samuel Abbott, of Salem County, be appointed her guardian. But said Samuel Abbott desires that the letter be revoked and Clement Hall, of Salem, merchant, be appointed. Witnesses—Joseph Tomlinson, Saml. Bustill. Lib. 4, p. 450.

1746-7, Feb. 7. Wales, Rev. Eleazer, of Middlesex Co., "Preacher of the Gospel of Christ;" will of. Wife, Elizabeth, executrix and sole legatee. Real and personal estate. Witnesses—Rebeccah FitzRandolph, Ann FitzRandolph, Nathaniel FitzRandolph. Proved August 8, 1750. Lib. 6, p. 401.

1750, Aug. 8. Inventory (£153.07.00) includes debts due from ——— Davison, Robert Rolfe. Made by John Stevens and Daniel Bayles, Jun'r.

1745, April 11. Walker, Benjamin, of Chesterfield, Burlington Co., fuller. Int. Inventory, £180.4; made by William Bunting and William Vause.

1745, April 18. Adm'x, Phebe Walker, widow. William Bunting and William Vause, fellow bondsmen. Lib. 5, p. 108.

1753, Jan. 22. Bond of George Nicholson as administrator on estate left unadministered by Phebe Walker, dec'd. Isaac DeCow, fellow bondsman.

1750, May 1. Walker, Daniel, late of Fairfield Township, Cumberland Co. Int. Adm'r, William Walker. Fellow bondsman—William Dalles. All of same place. Witnesses—Stephen Ayers, Elias Cotting. Lib. 7, p. 46.

1749, Dec. 23. Inventory (£86.14.1) includes hogs, cattle and sheep. Appraisers—William Dalles, Nathan Share.

1748, Feb. 14. Walker, Francis, of Woodbridge, Middlesex Co., gentleman; will of. Children—William, Benjamin, Sylas, Ashsher, Mary, Prudence and Annee, all under age. Real and personal estate. Executors—wife, Jane, son William, and Joseph Shotwell, Jun'r. Witnesses—Jonathan Kinsey, Reuben Bunn, Micajah Bunn. Proved March 20, 1748-9. Lib. E, p. 266.

1746, July 15. Walker, George, of Freehold, Monmouth Co., yeoman; will of. Wife, Gertrude. Son, George, lands bought of Richard Clark and Thomas Millige's heirs. Children—Elizabeth, Rachel, Esther, James and Ann Clark Walker, last three minors. Executors—David Rhe and William Hankinson. Witnesses—George Egger, William Norcross, John Henderson. Proved April 27, 1748. Lib. E, p. 176.

1748, May 17. Inventory (£334) includes one negro man, £40; gun and sword. Made by William Couenhoven and John Bennem.

1733, March 25. Walker, Joseph, of Manington, Salem Co., weaver; will of. Wife, Mary, her thirds. Rest of estate divided among children: Ann, Hannah, William and Sarah, as they come of age. Plantation in Pilesgrove to be sold. Executors—wife, and Richard Woodnut. Witnesses—William Hunt, Elisabeth Johnson, Alex'r Simpson. Proved 25 April, 1733. (Letters granted to Mary Walker in absence of Richard Woodnutt, the other executor). Lib. 3, p. 317.

1733, May 2. Inventory (£231.15.5) includes cattle, horses, etc.

1744-5, March 14. Walker, Phebe, widow of Benjamin Walker, of Chesterfield, Burlington Co.; will of. My two young children I commit to care of my sister, Mary Whitehead, whom I appoint executrix, with George Nicholson. Real and personal estate. Witnesses—Samuel Woodward, William Vause, Jun'r, Jno. Richardson. Proved Dec. 4, 1748. Lib. 6, p. 7.

1748, Dec. 23. Inventory, £57.16.5; made by Abra'm Brown and Will'm Vause.

1745, Nov. 13. Walker, Samuel, Capt., of Piscataway, Middlesex Co.; will of. Children—Thomas, Lucia, Mary, Sarah, James and John. Land in Piscataway, with grist mill, joining meadow of Capt. John Langstaff, deceased; land between Millbrook and Woodbridge; land joining lands of Jonathan Dunham; land rights in New England. Executors—sons, Thomas, James and John, and daughters Lucia and Mary Walker. Witnesses—John Langstaff, John Langstaff, Jun'r, and Gershom Manning. Proved April 25, 1750. Lib. E, p. 384.

1750, April 17. Inventory (£429.1) includes 3 sets of china and tea ware, 4 Bibles and other books, 2 negro men (£100), 3 negro wenches (£110). Made by Az. Dunham and Henry Langstaff.

1746-7, April 9. Walker, Samuel, of Woodbridge, Middlesex Co., mariner. Int. Adm'r, Francis Walker, the father, of Woodbridge, yeoman. William Pangborn, weaver, fellow bondsman. Lib. E, p. 166.

1750, Aug. 31. Bond of Henry Martin, of Middlesex Co., yeoman, principal creditor, as administrator on estate unadministered by Francis Walker, late deceased. William Walker, of same, yeoman, fellow bondsman. Lib. E, p. 452.

1743, March 5. Wallace, Henry, of Salem County. Int. Adm'x, Elizabeth Wallace. Lib. 5, p. 11.

1743, June 1. Walling, John, of Cohansey, Salem Co., yeoman; will of. Sons—John, the plantation (160 acres) on which I live; Jonathan, my ivory headed cane and 223 acres in Back Neck. Daughter, Hannah, at 18, ½ of moveable estate, and ½ acre, with house on it, at Bacon's Neck. Executors—Sons, John and Jonathan, with my brother, Thomas Walling, and my sister, Mary "Bowring" (Bowen). Witnesses—Charles Dennis, Thomas Stathem, Jr., (Quaker), Richard Ball. Proved 25 April, 1745. (Letters granted to Thomas Walling only, in absence of Mary Bowen and the other executors named, who are infants). Lib. 5, p. 183.

1744, Dec. 4. Inventory, £149.7; made by Charles Dennes, Benoni Dare.

1748-9, March 2. Walling, John and Hannah, wards (infants of 14 years and upwards), children of John Walling, late of County of Cumberland, deceased. Guardians—David Shepherd and Ananias Sayre, both of County aforesaid. Witnesses—Stephen Ayars, Elias Cotting. Cumberland Wills, 52 F.

1733, Jan. 21. Walling, Thomas, of Salem Co., yeoman. Int. Adm'x, Bathinpieoth Walling, widow. Bondsmen—Samuel Elwell, Abraham Nelson. All of said county. Witnesses—Danl. Mestayer, Mary Mestayer. Lib. 3, p. 393.

1732, Dec. 11. Inventory (£119.5) includes cattle, etc. Appraisers—Samuel Elwell, Abraham Nelson.

1747, Oct. 6. Walling, Thomas, of Cohansey, Salem Co., yeoman; will of. Wife, one-third of personal; two-thirds to be divided equally between my two daughters, Anna and Mary. Sons—Jonathan, my farm, called Bethel; Thomas, my four sixteen-acre lots in Greenwich, with improvements thereon, for which I have the deeds from John Daniel, deceased. Executrix—wife (Sarah). Witnesses—Thos. Waithman, Ebenez Miller (both Quakers), John Bee. Proved 7 June, 1748. Lib. 5, p. 478.

1748, May 24. Inventory (£231.15) includes cattle and sheep (£71). Appraisers—David Shepherd, Jonathan Stathem.

1750, March 8. Walling, Thomas, of Salem Co. Int. Adm'rs, Aaron Petterson and Elizabeth Walling. Bondsman—John Richmon. All of Pilesgrove.

1751, March 1. Inventory, £115.12.6; made by Jacob Richman, John Richman. Salem Wills, 826 Q.

1736, Sept. 20. Walsh, John, of Burlington Co., cooper. Int. Adm'r, Aaron Lovett. Samuel Scattergood, of Burlington, yeoman, fellow bondsman. Lib. 4, p. 73.

1749, Oct. 24. Walton, William, of New York, merchant. Int.

Adm'r, William Walton. Robert Hunter Morris, fellow bondsman. Witness—Anthony White. (Monmouth Wills), Lib. E, p. 338.

1749, 2nd mo. (April), 29 da. Ward, Aaron, of Deptford, Gloucester Co., yeoman; will of. Son, Joshua, to have plantation, out of which shall be paid £45 to my sons John, Samuel and Aaron, when 21, and to my daughters, Martha and Phebe, when 18. Executors—wife, and brother-in-law, Benjamin Holme. Witnesses—Phillis Clark, Henry Snabler, Sary Scott. Proved 5 June, 1749. Lib. 6, p. 281.

1749, May 23. Inventory of Aaron Ward, who "deceased this life 1st of May, 1749." Appraisers—William Clarke, Anthony Sharp.

1735, Dec. 31. Ward, Caleb, of Newark, Essex Co.; will of. Children—Caleb, Timothy, Theophilus, Thomas, Mary Smith, Sarah Sealley, Hanah Woodruff and Elizabeth Ward. Land joining lands of John Plum and Thomas Sergeant. Executors—wife, Mary, and son Timothy. Witnesses—John Cooper, John Van DerPoel, Griffin Jenkins. Proved April 14, 1736. Lib. C, p. 89.

1736, March 29. Inventory, £139; made by Sam'll Farrand, Joseph Bowen.

1746, Sept. 1. Ward, Caleb, Sr., of Canoe-brook, Essex Co., yeoman; will of. Sons—Caleb and Zebediah. Land I bought of Jasper Crane. Executors—wife, Hannah, and David Williams. Witnesses—Jon'n Sergeant, Daniel Campbell, Abigail Sergeant. Proved March 21, 1750. Lib. E, p. 28.

1744-5, 1st mo. (Mar.), 1st da. Ward, George, Jr., of Deptford Township, Gloucester Co., yeoman; will of. "Being by the pleasure of God lately left a widower with eight small children and now me, myself, much indisposed." Real estate equally to four sons: Josiah, George (to have the land I live on next the River Delaware), Isaac and David; all under age. Daughters—Hannah, Sarah, Elizabeth and Mary; all under age. Land joining Isaac Sharp and a lot joining my father's land. Negroes, Jack, Dinah and Tom. Mentions neighbor, James Lord. Executors—father, George Ward, brother-in-law, Samuel McCollock, and Edward Richardson, to whom I commit my son, Josiah, to be placed with James Whiteall; my son George and my daughter Sarah with James Lord; my daughters Hannah and Mary to my sister Mary Parker; and my sons Isaac and David to be apprenticed when 14. Witnesses—Edward Willson, Thos. Kinsey, Junior, Josa. Lord.

1748, 3d mo. (May), 13th da. Codicil. "Whereas I have since married, I give my wife, Martha, £100." Cousin, George McCollock. Executors—James Cooper, Samuel McColloch (instead of Edward Richardson), to whom I give power to deed unto John McColloch 63 acres of Cedar swamp. Witnesses—John Cooper, Nathan Lord, James Lord. Proved 6 June, 1748. Lib. 8, p. 215.

1748, 3d mo. (May), 25, 26. Inventory (£525.19.7) includes negro man, woman and child, £90; Bibles and other books; cattle and "boat and sale."

1758, Jany. 11. Account of James Cooper, surviving executor. Moneys paid John Dilks, John Hart, James Hinchman, John Marshall, Richd. Matlack, Michael Fisher, John Collins, James Wood, John Ladd, Abram Inskeep, John Blackwood, Elizth. Bates, Thomas Kimsey, John Chew, Daniel Hillman, Jane Bryan, Prisscilla Ingram, Joseph Tatem, Robert Baggs, James Whiteal, John Davis, John Carpenter, Joseph Marshall, Wm. Hugg, Moses Ward, Henry Meds (?), Nixson Chatten, Peter Sonmans,

Joshua Lord, James Lord, Arch'd Jolly, Robert Hartshorne, Robert Zane, Saml. Austin, Saml. Willson, John Kimsey, David Ward; bond from Joseph Turpin; note from Edward Willson; due from Daniel Leake, John Hillman, Japhet Leeds, E. Adams, George Kean, Gabriel Peterson, Thomas Denny, John Stow, Charles Haulton, John Burrows, Widow Ashwood, Joseph Heretage, Sarah Hinchman, Joseph Matlack, Joseph Low, Wm. Smith, John Howell, John Tatem, Joseph Loyd, John Plumley, Joseph Cupear, John Winton, Daniel Garrison, George Coulson, John Warrinton, Saml. Eastean, John E. Mun, John Snowden.

1747-8, March 2. Ward, George, Sr., of Big Timber Creek, Deptford Township, Gloucester Co.; will of. Wife, Abigail. Sons—George, ½ of a tract near Rowell's Branch, and a cedar swamp; David, the homestead place, ½ of land at Rowell's Branch, a cedar swamp and my Proprietary Rights. My sons' heirs equally to have all land indicated. A bond (£80) from James Valentine to be divided equally between my sons. Legacies to my own grandchildren ("excepting the children of McCollock"). Daughters—Mary, Hannah, Sarah and Martha, to have the residue of estate. "The three grand, granddaughters of my daughter Elizabeth McColloch, deceased, shall have a full share with my daughters aforesaid." Executors—son, George Ward, and Abraham Inskip. Witnesses—John Blackwood, Michael Fisher, Thomas Wood. Proved 26 March, 1748. Lib. 8, p. 222.

1747-8, March 2. Inventory, £422.17.10; made by Michael Fisher, Richard Cheeseman.

1736, Nov. 16. Ward, Henry, of Woodbury, Gloucester Co., yeoman; will of. Brothers—Aaron and Habbakuk Ward, to have my land, "and if one has more mind of all the land than the other, he shall pay one-half the value of the same." Executor—brother, Aaron Ward. Witnesses—Benjamin Waite, James Wilkins, Thomas Wilkins. Affirmed 28 March, 1737. Lib. 4, p. 94.

1736, 10th mo. (Dec.), 16 da. Inventory, £9.8.10; made by Thomas Wilkins, Benjamin Waite.

1737, May 28. Account. Monies paid Thos. Wilkins, Jon. Hopper, Jun., Michael Fisher (for Sarah Chew).

1734, Aug. 14. Ward, Israel, Sr., of Greenwich, Gloucester Co., yeoman; will of. Sons—William (the eldest) ½ of a Proprietary Right bought of Thomas Wearthel; Israel, the other equal half of said Proprietary Right; Jacob my plantation (210 acres) at Mantos Creek, bought of Eareck Cox; Samuel (when 21) the grist-mill and land thereto (20 acres) bought of John Plumly, he paying his sisters £40, but in case of his death under age the aforesaid grist-mill and land thereto shall descend to them. Executors—son, Jacob, and Samuel Shivers. Witnesses—Gabriel Enochson, Jacob Fowsman, William Hewitt. Proved 2 Oct., 1734. Lib. 3, p. 431.

1734, Oct. 2. Inventory (£136.11.6) of Israel Ward, who "deceased 19 Aug., 1734." Appraisers—Alexr. Randall, Robert Zane.

1747, Aug. 4. Account of Samuel Shivers, "sole executor." Monies paid John Jones, John Ladd, Wm. Tatem, Henry VanMetre, Elias Long, John Brown, Anthony Wilkinson, Henry Thorne.

1734, Aug. 20. Ward, Jacob, of Greenwich, Gloucester Co., yeoman; will of. Plantation (210 acres) at Mantos Creek, given me by my father, Israel Ward, the 14 day of this instant, shall be sold and the mortgage thereon paid, and money divided among my brothers and sisters. Executors—brother, Israel Ward, and Samuel Shivers. Witnesses—Gabriel Enochson, John Pinyard, Benjamin Worthington. Proved Oct. 2, 1734. Lib. 3, p. 432.

1734, Sept. 2. Inventory of Jacob Ward, "who deceased the 24 of Aug., 1734," £23.9.8; made by Alexr. Randall, Robert Zane.

1747, Aug. 4. Account of Samuel Shivers, executor. Monies paid Phebe Ward (sister of deceased), William Thorne (his proportionable part of the estate of the testator left to his wife, being one of his sisters), Levy Elwale (as part of estate of testator, left to his wife), and Israel Ward ("who hath never as yet taken upon him the execution of said will').

1740, May 22. Ward, James, of Manington Precinct, Salem Co., husbandman; will of. Wife, Jean, executrix. Son—James, my plantation adjoining Thomas Haines and £10; if he should die my daughter, Margaret Ward, shall have it; if she dies, my son-in-law, Anthony Saunders, shall possess it. Personal to be divided between my wife and daughter Margaret, allowing my wife Margaret's part for six years, and afterwards; my trustees, Benjamin Cripps and John Murray, having power to put at interest the said child's part until she will be 18. Witnesses—William Hunt, Thomas Haynes, William Smith. Affirmed 16 July, 1740. Lib. 4, p. 244.

1740, June 25. Inventory, £209.14; made by William Hunt, James Mason.

1745-6, Jan. 28. Ward, John, of Newark, Essex Co., yeoman. Int. Adm'r, Lemuel Ward, the son, yeoman, of Essex Co. Daniel Pierson, Esq., fellow bondsman. Witness—William Guest. (Daniel Pierson declared that the wife of the deceased refused to administer the estate and desired that her son might be appointed). Lib. D, p. 358.

1748, Dec. 3. Ward, John, Jun'r, of Burlington Co., labourer. Int. Adm'x, Ruth Ward, widow. Ezekiel Hardin, of same, yeoman, fellow bondsman. Lib. 6, p. 330.

1748, Dec. 3. Inventory, £21.12.10; made by Ezekiel Hardin and Thomas Hackney.

1746-7, Sept. 5. Ward, Josiah, of Newark, Essex Co. Int. Adm'x, Hannah Ward. Thomas Canfield and Samuel Ward, fellow bondsmen. Witness—David Ogden, Jun'r. Lib. D, p. 449.

1731, Dec. 27. Ward, Nathaniel, Sr., of Newark, Essex Co., yeoman; will of. Son, Nathaniel, land joining lands of Joseph Baldwin, Jonathan Baldwin, Azeriah Crane. Grandson, James Ward, son of eldest son Joseph, deceased, land called "personage," joining lands of John Cooper and David Sealey, the said James paying his three sisters, Elizabeth, Christian and Deborah, each £5; all under age. Daughter, Phebe Crane. Three daughters of daughter Sarah, deceased, viz., Mary Dalglish, Phebe Dalglish and Rachel Canfield. Three children of daughter Joanah, deceased, viz., Nathaniel, Rebeckah and Joanah Pierson. Executors—son, Nathaniel, and son-in-law Jonathan Pierson. Witnesses—John Cooper, John Richards, John Young. Proved Jan. 11, 1732. Lib. B, p. 368.

1732, Aug. 25. Ward, Nathaniel, Jr., of Newark, Essex Co., yeoman;

will of. Children—Nathaniel and Abner Ward, and Eunice Woodruffe. Real and personal estate. Executors—wife, Sarah, and son Nathaniel. Witnesses—Jno. Cooper, Caleb Ward, Sam'll Nesbett. Proved Jan. 25, 1732. Lib. B, p. 395.

1732-3, Jan. 24. Inventory (£86.17.04) includes note of James Wheeler. Made by Jonathan Person and Nathaniel Ward.

1731, Sept. 1. Ward, Samuel, of Parish of St. John's, County of Baltimore (Maryland); will of. Grandsons—Simon and Samuel Collings. Granddaughters—Ann Collins, Hannah Asbrook, and "my two grandchildren of Mary Ann Ward." Ephraim Tomlinson and Joseph Tomlinson of Gloucester Co., to be guardians of my said grandchildren and to place the legacies and use the interest until they will be of age—the boys at 21, the girls at 18. Daughters—Mary Ann Ward, Hannah and Rosanna (last two executors and to have residue of estate). Witnesses—Abraham Johns, M. Martinox, Nicholas Day. Proved 5 Nov., 1731, before Thomas Sheredine, Deputy Commissioner of Baltimore Co.

1733, May 10. Exemplified copy filed in Gloucester Co. Mentions that execution of said will in New Jersey was granted to Hannah Cooke, late Hannah Ward, and Rosanna Pearce, late Rosanna Ward. Lib. 3, p. 303.

1742, Aug. 8. Ward, Sam'll, Jun'r, of Newark, Essex Co.; will of. Wife, Rebecca. Children—Uzal and Jemima, both under age. Brothers—John, Josiah and Ebbenezer Ward. Real and personal estate. Executors—cousin, Uzal Ogden, and Samuel Huntington. Witnesses—Thomas Alling, Humphrey Nichols, Josiah Tuttel. Proved Jan. 13, 1742. Lib. D, p. 21.

1737, March 30. Ward, William, of Woodbury Creek, Gloucester Co., yeoman; will of. Int. Adm'x, Hannah Ward (relict). Bondsman—John Wood, of same place. Lib. 4, p. 94.

1736-7, 11 mo. (Jan.), 20 da. Inventory (£105.12.10) includes Robert Briant's bond; due from Thomas Leedes, Joseph Langly, Elizabeth Robinson, Joseph Gibson, George Ward, Benjamin Waite; "tailor's shears, goose, box iron and heaters." Appraisers—Wm. Wilkins, Josa. Lord.

1738, May 2. Account. Moneys paid John Wood, Abraham Chattin, Joshua Lord, William Wilkins, Aaron Ward, Jane Bickham, Habbakuk Ward, Thos. Thackera, Jas. Wilkins, George Ward, Wm. Cooper, Abraham Moss, Jon. Wilkins, Jon. Dukeminnear, Benj. Holme, Charity Brown, Jos. Howell, Thos. Kimsey, Abraham Vining, Ann Cooper, Ann Richardson.

1737, Jan. 16. Wardell, Eliakim, of Shrewsbury Town, Monmouth Co.; will of. Wife, Mary. Children—Esther, Sarah, Cathrine and Stephen. Executors—wife, John Calton (Catton), Samuel Leonard, Solomon Wardell. Witnesses—Joseph Wardell, Benjamin Corlies, Andria Webley, Jr. Proved May 4, 1738. Lib. C, p. 197.

1738, April 12. Inventory, £105.3; made by Ephraim Allen and Benjamin Corliss.

1733, May 5. Wardell, Joseph, of Shrewsbury, Monmouth Co., yeoman; will of. Wife, Sarah. Children—Eliakim, Joseph, Soloman, Joanna Eatton, Elizabeth Leonard, Samuel and Ebenezer; also son, Jacob, he to have land where testator lived, adjoining William West, Solomon Wardell and Shrewsbury River. Negro Jack and negro girl

Jeany to be free after death of testator's wife, who is made executrix. Witnesses—Samuel Dennis, Bartholomew West, Benjamin Parker. Proved May 30, 1735. Lib. C, p. 38.

1735, July 28. Inventory (£505.10) includes loom, silver ware (£29.19), 2 negroes (£40). Made by John Eatton and Samuel Leonard.

1746-7, Feb. 11. Wardell, Solomon, of Shrewsbury Town, Monmouth Co.; will of. Wife, Sarah. Children—James, Joseph, John, Elizabeth, Lydia and Sarah. Executors—wife, and Joseph Eatton. Witnesses—Bartholomew West, Jacob Wardell, Joshua Parker. Proved May 20, 1748. Lib. E, p. 219.

1748, June 7. Inventory, £277.14.8; made by John Eatton and Jacob Wardell.

1733, Jan. 19. Ware, Jacob, of Salem Co., guardian of ward, Solomon Windsor. Lib. 3, p. 399.

1749, May 19. Ware, Jacob, Jr., of Cumberland Co. Int. Adm'rs, Phebe Ware, widow, of Greenwich Township, and Thomas Ewing, blacksmith, of Cumberland Co. Lib. 6, p. 322.

1749, May 19. Inventory (£72.15.03) includes weaver's looms and tackling. Appraisers—Maskell Ewing, Thos. Maskell.

1734, May 1. Ware, John, of Cohansey, Salem Co., yeoman; will of. Wife, Bathsheba, plantation in Cohansey until my son John will be 21. Children—Hannah, Roda, Elnathan, Mary and Abigail, to have equally two-thirds of the personal as they come to age; Elnathan to have 25 acres I purchased of Abiel Carle, Junior, and 11 acres purchased of Isaac Davis, adjoining John Bacon. My land in Rhode Island (if recovered) to my children John, Hannah and Roda. Sons to be bound to trades. Executors—wife, Bathsheba, and Abraham Reeves of Cohansie, blacksmith. Witnesses—Uriah Bacon, Charles Davis, Eben'r Goold.

1734, May 7. Codicil. If son John should be dispossessed of the place I live on before Elnathan is 21, he shall be released from paying to him the £10. Witnesses—Uriah Bacon, James Caruthers, Eben'r Goold. Proved 20 June, 1734. Lib. 3, p. 422.

1734, May 16. Inventory, £170.2.2; made by Philip Dennis, Josiah Fithian.

1749, April 23. Ware, Josiah, of Cohansey, Cumberland Co., tailor; will of. To my "honoured father my beaver hat." Brother, Thomas, my silver shoe buckles, knee buckles and stock buckles. Estate to be equally divided between my aforesaid brother, my sisters Phebe, Amey and Elizabeth. Executors—Enos Woodruff and Thomas Ewing. Witnesses—Elizabeth Fordham, Phebe Ware. Proved 19 May, 1749. Cumberland Wills, 54 F.

1749, May 19. Inventory, £18.0.09; made by Maskell Ewing, Thos. Maskell.

1738, Sept. 29. Ware, Mary, of Gloucester Co., widow; will of. Daughters—Magare (the eldest, housewife of Caleb Brown); Sarah (housewife of Nathaniel Pettitt); Ruth (housewife of Nathaniel Ireland, and wife of Daniel Ireland). Granddaughters—Mary and Elizabeth (daughters of my daughter Mary, wife of John Dennis, living in Crosweeks or thereabouts); my eldest daughter's children. Margaret

Brown, wife of Caleb Brown; Martha Thomas (housewife to Abraham Thomas), and Margaret, daughter of Caleb Brown. David Williams and his wife, household goods. Executor—David Williams. Witnesses—Benjamin Ingersoll, Abraham Vangelder, Sam'l Church. Affirmed 30 July, 1739. Lib. 4, p. 202.

1739, June 16. Inventory, at Egg Harbor, £23.2.10; made by James Somers, Benjamin Ingersoll.

1732, Sept. 16. Warman, Richard, of Hackinsack, Bergen Co., merchant; will of. Wife, Martha, executrix, and to have whole estate within the provinces of New York, New Jersey and within the Kingdom of Great Brittain. Witnesses—John McDowell, James Duncan, Jacob Cornelis Banta. Proved 10 Jan., 1732. Lib. B, p. 345.

1731, July 12. Warner, Simon, of Alloways Creek, Salem Co.; will of. Executors—William Hancock and William Willis. In case of forfeiture of my plantation, now mortgaged to Clement Hall of Salem, merchant, they shall sell it and residue of money divided among my sons, William, Simon and George, as they attain 21. Also they shall pay £20 to my daughter Hannah, when 18, and £50 to my wife Susannah if the place is sold; otherwise she shall have use of it until William will be 21; and he to enjoy it until my son, Simon, will be 21, then to share it equally. Three aforesaid sons to pay £20 to their sister, Sarah. Son, George, at 21, to have 30 acres towards Salem Town, joining Wm. Tyler's land. Boys to be put to trades. Witnesses—Ranier Gregory, John Hall, William Murdock, Dan'l Mestayer. Proved 7 June, 1735.

1735, June 6. Renunciation of William Willis and William Hancock as executors. (No record of testamentary letters; inventory missing).

Salem Wills, 528 Q.

1732, Feb. 16. Warren, John, of Chesterfield, Burlington Co., yeoman. Inventory, £218.9.8; made by Wm. Cook and Tho. Newbold.

1732, 2nd day, 1 st mo. (Mar.). Rebecca Warren, widow, declines administration, and requests that son, John, be appointed.

1732, March 9. Bond of John Warren as administrator. Thomas Newbold, of Springfield, yeoman, fellow bondsman.

Burlington Wills, 2413-16 C.

1744, Feb. 12. Warrington, John, of Chester, Burlington Co., yeoman. Int. Adm'x, Hannah Warrington, widow. Simon Ellis, of Gloucester Co., and Edward Radolphus Price, of City of Burlington, fellow bondsmen.

1744, March 4. Inventory, £125.2.3; made by Thomas Ellis and Edward Clemmens. Burlington Wills, 4155 C.

1728, Oct. 29. Watkins, David, of Elizabeth Town, Essex Co., mariner. Int. Inventory (£266.17) includes gold rings, silver snuff box, silver buttons, silver buckles and girdle, silver tankard, silver tumbler, silver spoons, one negro woman and one negro boy. Made by James Hamton and Robert Ogden. (For administration, see Archives, Vol. 23, p. 493).

1736, ——, —. Accompt by Benjamin Watkins, administrator, who asks allowance for moneys paid to coroner and jury for "setting" upon the body of his brother, David Watkins, when found upon Long Island; also payments to David Thomas for making coffin, Wm. Garthwait, John Spining, Phebe Ogden, Sam'll Marsh, John Miller, Nath'll Clarke, Jacob

DeHart, Wm. Dagworthy, Jer. Higgins, Geo. Ross, Paul Thorp, Eb'r Lyon, Anthony Little, Jobe Pack, John Denis, Sarah Riggs, Jas. Colie, Eph. Terrill, Chas. Tooker, Jas. Hinds, Jun'r, Wm. Strayhearne, Giles Lewis, Jane Closon, Thos. Johnston, David Morehous, John Ross, Jona. Dayton, Sara Elsworth, Gerard Beekman, Thos. Jackman, Jas. Hamton, Jacobus Corson, Ethan Sayre, Jos. Tooker, Ich. Burnett, Jno. Davis, Eliz. Ogden, Cha. Tooker, Senior, Jno. Oliver, Sara Marsh, And. Joline, Jona. Dickinson, John Morris, Isaac Holsey, Jonathan Olliver, Timothy Halsted, John King, Wm. W'm'son, Jno. Kinsey, Sarle & Pintard, Jno. Fullerton, Ben. Howard, Daniel Clarke, Sam'll Whitehead, Jacob Pownell, Joseph Meeker, Mrs. Tongrelowe, Michael Kearny. Names children of deceased, David, Mary, Johannah, Sarah.

1736-7, March 17. Further accompt of administrators, Benjamin Watkins and Mary Hinds, late Mary Watkins. Payments to Daniel Sayre, Jonathan Daton, James Collie, John Clauson, Chas. Tucker, Jacob Bonnel, Joseph Tucker, Jere Crane, Jun'r, John Larrabee, Sam'll Mills, John Kenny.
Lib. B, p. 101; Essex Wills, 467-77 G.

1731, May 24. Watkins, David, of Elizabeth Town, Essex Co., aged about 15 years, made choice of Edward Thomas as guardian.
Lib. B, p. 211.

1749, Nov. 4. Watson, Abraham, of Salem Co., shoemaker. Int. Adm'x, Margaret Watson. Bondsmen—John Andrews, William Maxfield, all of said County. Witnesses—Leonard Gibbon, Nich's Gibbon.
Lib. 7, p. 35.

1749, Nov. 4. Inventory, £333.10; made by Wm. Siddons, Josiah Kay.

1749, Nov. 17. Watson, Isaac, of Nottingham, Burlington Co., yeoman; will of. Mother, Johannah Watson. Brothers—John and William. Sisters—Elizabeth, Johannah, Sarah and Naomi. Joseph and Isaac, sons of Joseph Peace. Deborah, daughter of Elias King, deceased, £10, and if she die under age to her two sisters-in-law, Martha and Mary. Plantation in Nottingham and Island in Delaware River, called Wood Island; land in Trenton on Sandpink Creek and Delaware River, formerly property of Joseph Peace. £10 to Meeting-house at Crosswicks, and £10 for the Meeting-house in Trenton, adjoining Joseph Clayton and John Ozburn. Executors—mother, and brother John. Witnesses—Jos. Clayton, John Johnston, Reuben Armitage. Proved Dec. 1, 1749. Lib. 6, p. 277.

1749, Dec. 9. Inventory, £578.10; made by Antho. Woodward and William Murfin.

1746, 14th day, 3rd mo. (May). Watson, Marmaduke, of Chesterfield, Burlington Co., yeoman; will of. Wife, Elizabeth, personal estate and 3 negroes. Son, Aaron, tract lying between George Taylor and Amos Wilkins. Son, Marmaduke, plantation I now dwell on. Daughter, Ann Curtis, and her daughters Diademe and Elizabeth. Executors—wife, and son Marmaduke. Witnesses—John Butler, Sen'r, John Butler, Jun'r. Proved July 24, 1749. Lib. 6, p. 308.

1748, 13th day, 6th mo. (Aug.). Watson, Matthew, of Chesterfield, Burlington Co.; will of. Daughter, Hannah, wife of John Welding, plantation I bought of William Plaskett, situated in Trenton. Wife, Hannah, executrix, and remainder of estate. Witnesses—Marmaduke Watson, James Danford, Sam'l Harris. Proved Feb. 15, 1750.
Lib. 7, p. 13.

1736, Sept. 13. Watson, Richard, of Freehold, Monmouth Co., yeoman; will of. Son-in-law, William Jolly, and testator's daughter, Jean Jolly, for their eldest son when of age. Children—Peter, James, Richard, Margaret, Euphens, Anne and Mary. Executors—brothers, William and Gawan Watson, and Joseph Furman (Forman), who are appointed guardians of children, James, Richard and Mary. Witnesses—John Lowell, William Brown, John McGalliard. Proved Sept. 22, 1736. Lib. C, p. 123.

1736, Sept. 22. Inventory (£59.11) includes loom and parcel of books. Made by Gideon Compton, Timothy Lloyd, Robert Newell.

1742, March 9. Watson, William, of Greenwich, Salem Co.; will of. Wife, Sarah. Sons—Samuel, lands next to Cohansey Creek, part of which I live on; William, land next to Samuel Fithian's, also piece of marsh I bought of James Dixson; and Isaac, lot bought of Samuel Clark and 2 acres bought of Mary Wheton. Aforesaid sons to have equally two 16 acre lots in the town of Greenwich, and the marsh on Cohansey Creek bought of Peter Banton. Two-thirds of moveable estate to be equally divided among my six daughters—Rachel Shepherd, Lurane Coffen, Sarah Martin, Hannah Wheaton and Mary and Elizabeth Watson. Executor—son, Samuel. Witnesses—Joseph Reeves, John Foster, Joseph Dennis. Affirmed 30 April, 1743. Lib. 5, p. 44.

1743, April 1. Inventory, £297.15½; made by Abiel Carll, Uriah Bacon.

1741, Oct. 7. Waye, Peter, of Monmouth Co., aged twelve years, orphan. Paul Richard, Esq., of City of New York, guardian. Joseph Warrell, Esq., Attorney-General of New Jersey, fellow bondsman. Witnesses—Robert Lawrence, Thomas Bartow. Lib. C, p. 444.

1745, May 21. Webb, John, of New Hanover, Burlington Co., yeoman. Int. Inventory, £38.4.4; made by Henry Cooper and Joshua Miller.

1745, June 1. Adm'x, Rebecca Webb, widow. Henry Cooper, of same, fellow bondsman. Lib. 5, p. 117.

1745, June 8. Account. Paid William Murrele, for making coffin, as appears by receipt from William Scattergood; debts due Isaac Ivins, Noah Wills, Edward Tonkin, Sam'l Scattergood.

1749, Jan. 17. Webb, Margery, of Haddonfield, Gloucester Co.; will of. Only son Thomas Webb, to have ½ of my dwelling and to pay his sister, Susannah Elmore, £20. Daughter, Hannah Price, to have the other ½ of dwelling. Executor—James Hinchman. Witnesses—John Marcell, Benjamin Collins, Elizabeth Craig. Affirmed 29 Oct., 1750.

1750, Oct. 7. Inventory (£113.15.09) includes "furniture over the inn-room," £13; books, £3; "furniture in the bar-room," £1.15.0. Appraisers—Samuel Clement, Jacob Clement. Gloucester Wills, 475 H.

1740, 5th mo. (July), 21st da. Webb, Thomas Peri (Perry), of Haddonfield, Gloucester Co.; will of. Houses and lands in Haddonfield to be sold. Wife, Margery, and three children, Perry, Thomas, and Hannah, to have personal estate equally. Whereas an estate and right of inheritance belongs to me in a place called "Hill," in the Parish of Sutton, County of Warwick, South Brittain, England, my will is, that they be sold and given equally to my wife and three children. Executor—John Kaighin, of same place. Witnesses—Thomas Redman, David Elwell, John Weldon. (Back of will states testator died July 29, 1741).

1741, Aug. 26. John Kaighin renounced the said executorship. Witnesses—John Douglas, E. R. Price.

1741, Oct. 5. Administration "of Thomas Perry Webb, Innkeeper" granted to Margery Webb. Bondsmen—Ja. Hinchman, Jno. Kaighin. Witness—Joseph Ross.

1741, Aug. 30. Inventory, £135.14.8; made by Ja. Hinchman, Jno. Hinchman. Gloucester Wills, 273 H.

1748, May 30. Webster, Thomas, of Township and Co. of Gloucester; will of. Wife, Sarah, all personal estate, one-third of the saw-mill, and to abide on homestead during widowhood. Sons—Samuel, the part and reversion of said homestead, and likewise tract (290 acres) on a branch of Cooper's Creek; Lawrence, that part of the homestead in the Township and County aforesaid, beginning near Reed's fence, N. between land of John Hillman and P. Webster, W. to the Big Hollow above Ephraim Tomlinson's; together with land purchased of David Davies, which he purchased of Mahan Southwick, being in the Township and County aforesaid. Daughter, Catherine (under age). Executors—wife, Sarah, John Hillman and Joseph Tomlinson, of Township and County aforesaid. Witnesses—Benjamin Bates, Joab Hillman, Thomas Wood. Affirmed 15 Sept., 1748.

1748, 5 mo. (July), 9 da. Renunciation of Joseph Tomlinson, as executor. (Inventory filed. Paper missing).

1754, ——, —. Account filed, but missing. Gloucester Wills, 409 H.

1748, Oct. 22. Weiser, Margaret, of Hunterdon Co. Int. Adm'r, Conrad Weiser, Esq., of Lancaster, Pa. Joseph Scattergood, of City of Burlington, surety. Witness—Robert H. Morris. Lib. E, p. 215.

1747-8, Feb. 29. Welch, Thomas, of Penns Neck, Salem Co., weaver. Int. Adm'r, Robert Connerway (Conaway), of Penns Neck. Bondsmen (not given). Witnesses—Samuel Hedge, Nich's Gibbon. Lib. 5, p. 423.

1747-8, March 4. Inventory, £21.1.4; made by Jeremiah Baker, Thomas Vickery.

1742, June 17. Weldon, John, of Marcus Hook, Chester Co., Pa. Int. Adm'r, John Handly, of Chester County. Attorney of Edward Brogden and Elizabeth his wife, adm'rs of John Weldon. Bondsmen —John Jones, of Salem Co., gent. Witness—Chas. O Neill. (Salem Wills), Lib. 4, p. 376.

1749, Aug. 31. Welling, Beckley, of Hopewell, Hunterdon Co. Int. Inventory (£81.0.6) includes 10 beaver hats (£15); beaver and ten blocks and a stamper (£1.5). Made by John Woolsey.

1749, Oct. 12. Adm'x, Rachel Welling, widow. John Woolsey, of same place, cooper, surety. Witness—Will: Ball. Lib. 7, p. 44.

1751, Sept. 12. Account. Mentions George Clifford, Charles Moore, Aaron Davis, Nehemiah Howell, Gisebert Lane. Administrators of Richard Skirm, John McIntyer, Robert Evin, Andrew Reed, F. Rossell. Hunterdon Wills.

1733, June 3. Welsh, Joseph, of Town and Co. of Burlington, yeoman; will of. Children—John, Sarah, Lidea Lovit, Easter and Mary, the latter under age. Real and personal estate. Executors—friends, Samuel Lovett, Richard Smith, Jr., and Caleb Raper, of same place, gentlemen. Witnesses—Thos. Shaw, Wm. Davis, Isaac DeCow. Proved July —, 1733. Lib. 3, p. 348.

1733, 9th day, 5th mo. (July). Inventory, £1164.4.11½; made by Isaac DeCow and Thomas Scattergood. Includes silver watch, £2; large Bible.

1750, Oct. 31. Wessels, Evert, of Essex Co. Int. Adm'r, Wessel Wessels, eldest son. Rinear Vangeesen, fellow bondsman.
Lib. E, p. 504.

1741, Sept. 26. West, Job, of Shrewsbury Town, Monmouth Co.; will of. Wife, Sarah. Son, William, land adjoining Whalepond brook, which testator's father, William West, designed to give testator. Two youngest sons, George and Joseph, the home plantation. Daughters—Margaret and Elizabeth. Executors—wife, brother Ephraim Allen, brother Bartholomew West, and brother-in-law William Brinley. Witnesses—John Holdsworth, Benjamin Woolcott, Robert Lippincutt, Jacob Dennis. Proved April 6, 1742. Lib. C, p. 504.

1742, April 16. Ephraim Allen and Bartholomew West, renounced executorship.

1750, Feb. 22. West, John, of New Hanover, Burlington Co., schoolmaster. Int. Adm'r, Samuel Wright, of same, yeoman. Thomas Scattergood, Esq., of City of Burlington, fellow bondsman.
Lib. 7, p. 422.

1740, May 1. West, William, of Shrewsbury Town, Monmouth Co., yeoman; will of. Wife, Margaret. Eldest son, Bartholomew. Salt meadow adjoining Henry Gren and John Hulet. Son-in-law, Ephraim Allen. Youngest son, Job. Meadow near Raccoon Island, adjoining William and Francis Jefery's meadow. Bog in Shrewsbury South River, adjoining Stephen Cook. Daughter, Catharine Cook. Ten grandchildren, children of testator's daughter, Sarah Curles, deceased. Daughter Sarah's eldest son, Stephen Cook (sic); Ebenezer Cook (sic), daughter Sarah's next eldest son. Ephraim Parker, Joshua Parker and Lydia Potter, each a heifer. Executors—son, Bartholomew, and sons-in-law Ephraim Allen and Edward Patison Cook. Witnesses—Solomon Wardell and Beriah Goddard. Proved March 15, 1746. (Bartholomew West and Ephraim Allen, Quakers).
Lib. E, p. 22.

1747, April 7. Inventory, £80.4.9; made by Joseph Parker and Jacob Lippincott.

1748-9, Jan. 7. Westcot, Ebenezer, of Fairfield Precinct, Cumberland Co., husbandman; will of. Wife, Barbary. Son, Ebenezer, that part of homestead on the west side of Ephraim Sayres east side of 150 acres formerly Jacob Garrison's), he to pay my executors £54; also one-third of my marsh, he paying as before; also upland. Sons—Foster, Samuel, Jonathan, David; those "within age" to be put to trades. Son, Joseph, residue of estate. Daughters—Abigail, Rhode, Mary, Phebe and Joanna Westcot, household goods equally, except what my wife thinks shall be needful for their improvement, while any of them are young and supported by her. Executors—wife, and son Joseph. Witnesses—Thomas Harris, Jr., David Husted, Ephraim Daten, Jr. Proved 25 Feb., 1748-9. Lib. 6, p. 261.

1748-9, Feb. 25. Renunciation of Barbery, executrix. Witnesses—Thomas Harris, Sen., Ephraim Daten, Jr.

1748-9, Jan. 27. Inventory (£145.9.11) includes farm stock, guns and sword. Appraisers—Thos. Whitecur, Jeremiah Buck.

1742, Oct. 14. Westcott, Daniel, of Cohansey, Salem Co.; will of. Wife, Elizabeth. Sons—Daniel and Henry, (to have ½ of my dwelling land and marsh), with proviso as to death of Henry. Daughter—Rachel Percel. Executor—son, Henry. Witnesses—Daniel Elmer, Walter Powell. Proved 3 Dec., 1742. Lib. 4, p. 344.

1742, Dec. 3. Inventory (£80.7.5) includes cattle and sheep, £22.9. Appraisers—Nathaniel Whitacar, Jeremiah Buck.

1743, Dec. 6. Westervelt, Jacobus, of Clooster, Bergen Co., farmer; will of. Wife, Deberah, all estate during widowhood. After her death or marriage same to my sons Jacobus and Isaac. Each son to pay £25 to their sister, Direkje. Executors—Jan. Morris and Jan Vanschyve, both of Burlingtown. Witnesses—Arije adeer Yansen, Waters Percell. Daniel Verveele. Proved Dec. 21, 1743. Lib. D, p. 108.

1734, April 17. Westland, Oliver, of Penns Neck, Salem Co., joiner. Int. Adm'r, Joseph Hawks, of Penns Neck, yeoman. Bondsmen—John Doe, Richard Doe. Witnesses—Sam'l Bustill, Sam'l Bustill, Jr. Salem Wills, 549 Q.

1735, Jan. 15. Wetherby, Robert, of Salem Co., yeoman. Int. Adm'r, Roger Huckings (Huggins), gent. Bondsman—Ranier Vanhist. Witnesses—Philip Chetwood, Dan'l Mestayer. Lib. 4, p. 57.

1735, Jan. 14. Inventory, £55.9.6; made by David Davis, Joseph Graves.

1735, Dec. 11. Wetherill, Capt. Thomas, of Piscataway, Middlesex Co.; will of. Children—John, George, William, Thomas, Ann, Hannah, Elizabeth, Mary and Catherin. 599 acres of land at Cranberry; 215 acres at Drinking Brook hollow. Son-in-law, Lawrence Hartwisk. Executors—wife, Anne, and son John. Witnesses—Samuel Walker, Jacob Burnet, Samuel Walker, Jun'r. Proved Jan. 20, 1735. Lib. C, p. 62.

1742, Dec. 29. Wetherill, Thomas, of Piscataway, Middlesex Co. Int. Adm'r, John Wetherill, Esq., eldest brother. John Doe, fellow bondsman. Lib. D, p. 18.

1748, Nov. 7. Wettenberey (Wittenberry), Jacob, of Penns Neck, Salem Co., flatman. Int. Adm'r, Charles Empson. Bondsmen—Thomas Karney, John Pitman. All of said County, yeomen. Lib. 6, p. 50.

1748, Nov. 5. Inventory (£47.1) includes 2 flats, £23.1. Appraisers—Thomas Carney, John Pitman.

1733, Aug. 3. Wheeldon, Richard, of Gloucester, Gloucester Co., mariner. Int. Adm'x, Anne Wheeldon, widow. Edward Rudolphus Price and Joseph Gregory, gentlemen, fellow bondsmen. Gloucester Wills, 173 H.

1732-3, March 20. Wheeler, Robert, of Perth Amboy, Middlesex Co., mariner; will of. Going beyond seas. Wife, Elizabeth, executrix and sole legatee. Real and personal estate. Witnesses—John Stevens, Daniel Jones, John Chapman. Proved Feb. 15, 1739. Lib. C, p. 323.

1748, Aug. 9. Wheeler, Stephen, of Newark, Essex Co. Int. Adm'r, Joseph Wheeler, brother. Ephraim Wheeler, fellow bondsman. Lib. E, p. 201.

1748, Sept. 1. Inventory (£71.06.10) includes payments to Nath'll Anderson, Mr. Bell, Sam'll Clizbee, Jos. Riggs, Thos. Longworth, Aaron Brown, Zopher Beech, Charles Woodruff, Humphrey Nikel, Samuel Parkus, Moses Clark, Ickabod Burnett, James Nichadon, Edward Pigot, William

Turner, Paul Richards of New York (executor of the Rev. Mr. Vaughn of Elizabeth Town). Made by Capt. Nath'll Johnson and Mr. Ezekiel Crane.

1730-31, Feb. 10. Wheeler, Rebeckah, of Town and Co. of Burlington, widow; will of. Grandson, Joseph Pidgon, at age, his mother's legacy due by my husband, Robert Wheeler, deceased. Executrices—daughters, Mary Carpenter and Ann Wheeler. Witnesses—Peter Bard, Esq., Isaac DeCow, Jos. DeCow. Proved Nov. 30, 1731.
Lib. 3, p. 167.

1747-8, March 16. Whilden, Joseph, of Cape May Co., yeoman; will of. Wife, Abigail. Sons—Mathew, land and marsh purchased of Isaac Whildin, and my interest in Five Mile Beach and 20 acres of Cedar Swamp; James, plantation whereon I live and 20 acres of Cedar Swamp; David, 10 acres of Cedar Swamp, also price of my negro man "Asse," and a negro woman, upon condition that he pay £5 to each of my daughters, viz., Hannah, Rachel and Loes, and £2 to my deceased daughter Mercy's children, Ellis and Judith. Grandsons—Memukin Hughes, Willman and Isecar Crafford. Executors—James Whillden and Richard Crafford. Witnesses—William Mulford, Charity Mulford, Elijah Hughes. Proved 30 March, 1748. Lib. 5, p. 454.

1748, April 26. Inventory (£347.18.10) includes farm stock and 3 negroes (£100.00.2). Appraisers—Thomas Hand, Elisha Hand.

1748, May 19. Account. Moneys paid Elijah Hughes, Elisha Crowell, Will'm Mulford, Elisha and Thomas Hand, Henry Young, Elisha Eldridge, Uriah Hughes, Ephraim Seeley, David Bancraft, Ellis Hughes, James Whilldin, Richard Crawford, Abigail Whildin, David Whilldin, Mathew Whilldin, Loes Whilldin, etc.

1728-9, 12 mo. (Feb.), 27. White, Amos, of Shrewsbury, Monmouth Co.; will of. Eldest son, Ziphphaniah, plantation testator lives on in Oramson Neck, to be divided by Jacob Dennis and Jonathan Stout. Land at Deall to be sold and, after payment of debts, balance of money to youngest sons, Andrew and Samuel, to whom is given land in Middlesex Co. Daughters, Leah Stout, Ams (Avis ?), Jennet and Hannah White; last three under age. Executors—son-in-law, Jonathan Stout, and Benjamin Woolley. Witnesses—John Lippincott, Thomas White, Hugh Jackson, William Cradock. Proved March 26, 1730. Lib. B, p. 217.

1739, Nov. 19. White, John, naval officer for port of Perth Amboy, Middlesex Co. Bond of Sissel Sarjant, widow, and principal creditor, as administratrix. Rich'd FitzRandolph, fellow bondsman. Witness—Robert Lane. Lib. C, p. 297.

1740, March 25. White, John, of Salem Co., joiner. Adm'x, Elizabeth White, (relict). Bondsmen—William Willis, Abraham Moss. Witness—Daniel Smith. Lib. 4, p. 226.

1739-40, 11 mo. (Jan.), 22 da. Inventory (£289.11) includes work done for Richard Butcher. Appraisers—William Willis, Daniel Smith.

1733, 14th d., 2nd m. (April). White, Peter, of Shrewsbury, Monmouth Co., yeoman; will of. Wife, Abigail. Eldest son, Britton, land in Shrewsbury, adjoining land of John Chambers. Sons—Peter and Benjamin. Daughters—Ruth Boude, Hannah Cook, Sarah, Dorothy, Elizabeth and Abigail White. Executors—wife, and son Peter. Witnesses—William Wooley, Robert White and Joseph Wardell, Jr. Proved May 22, 1733. Lib. B, p. 471.

1742, May 15. White, Peter, of Haddonfield, Gloucester Co., yeoman; will of. Wife, Rebeckah, £490, and bond of John Burr's, furniture and silver tankard. Legacies to brother, Joseph White, and his sons, William and Joseph, and his three daughters by his last wife; to kinswoman, Sarah North; to my adopted daughter, Judith Sumors, wife of Richard Summors and her children (under age); to kinsman, John Hall (land in Bristol); to John English; to the nine children of Timothy Matlack; to Titus Matlock. Remainder to be divided equally among my wife's children and his children, kinsman Peter White (son of Francis), Solomon Manero's wife, Catherine Harker (daughter of Thomas Green), William Cordroy, Joseph White of Bristol, and John Hall (to have all of my real estate in Kent County on Delaware), the daughter (under age) of William Snowden, Ann Hulings (daughter of Joseph White), the three daughters of my brother, Francis White. Mentions Francis White's daughter, Martha, and Rebeckah, daughter of Sarah North, and her son. Residue of estate to be divided between my brothers, Francis and Joseph White, and kinsman Peter White, son of Francis White. Executors—Timothy Matlock and Richard Summors; they to give deed to Joseph Addams for land I sold him. Witnesses—Wm. Snowden, Benjamin Weat, Isa. De Cow. Affirmed 9 March, 1743-4. Lib. 5, p. 21.

1743-4, March 7. Inventory, £1,363.18.3¼; made by Ja. Hinchman, Jos. Cooper.

1747, ——, —. Account. (Record missing).

1750, Nov. 23. White, Peter, of Middletown, Monmouth Co. Int. Adm'r, Jacob Johnson, of Monmouth County. Richard Fitz Randolph and Griffin Disbrow, of Perth Amboy, fellow bondsmen. Lib. E, p. 463.

1745, 30th, 8th mo. (Oct.). White, Thomas, Senior, of Shrewsbury, Monmouth Co.; will of. Wife, Christian. Eldest son, George, half of two plantations, one near John Lippincott's tan pits, the other whereon Constant Hulit lives. Youngest son, John, other half of plantations; land formerly Amos White's of Shrewsbury, deceased, on road from the Meeting-house in Shrewsbury to Naughlomsom. Son, Thomas, land whereon testator lives, adjoining Little Silver Brook and William Brinley. Daughters—Anna, Sarah and Elizabeth White. Grandson, Benjamin Parker. Granddaughters, Christian White and Lydia Parker. Negro man, James. Executors—wife, and sons George and Thomas. Witnesses—Peter White, Hugh Jackson, William Craddock. Proved May 25, 1747. Christian and George White, executors, Quakers, affirmed. Lib. E, p. 67.

1747, 2d, 4th mo. (June). Inventory, £515.15; made by Isaac Hance, Joseph Wardell.

1731, July 18. White, Unity, of Burlington, widow; will of. nephew, Samuel Bustill, Jun'r, £150 due by bond from Anthony Wright, of Bucks Co., Penna. Nieces—Sarah and Mary Bustill (daus. of my brother, Samuel), Mary, wife of Francis White, Jun'r, of Bristoll, and Mary (wife of Anthony Wright above named); also friend Thomas Clifford and Mary Bagley for attendance. To be interred in the churchyard of St. Mary's Church, Burlington, near the remains of my father, William Bustill. Friend, Elizabeth Jackson, of Philada. Ex-

ecutor—brother, Samuel Bustill. Witnesses—Isaac Pearson, James Thomson, Gabriel Hugg, Joseph Rose. Proved Aug. 19, 1731.
Lib. 3, p. 147.

1734, Jan. 31. Whitehead, Samuel, of Elizabeth Town, Essex Co., cordwainer; will of. Wife, Mary, sole legatee and executrix. Witnesses—Jonathan Dickinson, Thomas Hill, Geo. Gostolowe. Proved Nov. 7, 1735. Lib. C, p. 49.

1733, Dec. 15. Whittal, John, of Salem Co., yeoman; will of. Wife, Elizabeth, executrix, and to have plantation I live on. Sons—William, the plantation I formerly lived on in Piles Grove Precinct, he paying the mortgage thereof to Loan office; John, 125 acres in Mannington Precinct. Personal to wife for bringing up of my children. Witnesses—J. Gaudonett, William Wright, Samuel Angelo. Sworn and affirmed 14 Feb., 1733. Lib. 3, p. 397.

1733-4, 12 mo. (Feb.), 8 da. Inventory (£241.3.10) includes negro man, Tom, £33; negro child, Vilett, £5. Appraisers—Clem. Hall, Joseph Ware.

1735, 9 mo. (Nov.), 16 da. Whittall, Elizabeth, of Salem Co., widow; will of. Sons—William and John, executors. Daughters—Esther (executrix), Elizabeth, Rhoda. Personal estate only. (Negroes allotted). Witnesses—Ann Kidd, Richard Smith, Rich'd Bradford. Proved 31 Dec., 1740. (Letters granted to Esther Whittall, executrix, William and John Whittall being infants under age). Lib. 4, p. 262.

1739-40, Jan. 9. Inventory (£217.11.4) includes farm stock, etc., negro man (£40), negro girl (£25). Appraisers—Wm. Hancock, Joseph Ware. (Affidavit to inventory, Apr. 14, 1741, by Esther Breding, executrix).

1740, March 2. Whittall, Elizabeth, of Salem County, spinster. Int. Adm'r, James Breedin (principal creditor and brother-in-law), of Alloways Creek, Salem County. Bondsmen—John Thompson, William Tuft. Both of said County, yeomen. Witnesses—Ed. Trenchard, Chas. O Neill. Lib. 4, p. 269.

1732, 1 mo. (Mar.), 7 da. Whitton (Whitten), Catherine, of Salem, widow; will of. Brother, Edward Williams. Sister, Elizabeth Loyd and her children. Mother-in-law, Jane Williams. Joseph Darkin, £10, for use of the meeting at Salem, to be laid out in fencing and repairing graveyard. Legacies to Elizabeth Whartenby, John Richardson, Mongo Buli, Hannah Dent, and cousins—Rebecka Key, Elizabeth Simmons, Samuel Cripps. Friend, Hugh Clifton. Joel Darkin, "the bed that was Joseph Whitton's mother's to be delivered by her uncle, David Morris, when 18." Cousin, Richard Darkin (minor). Cousin, Hannah Darkin. Mentions Sarah Darkin, Mary Walcott and her sister Rhina Johnson; cousin Gwen Evans, Hannah Maclawler, Esther Anderson and Samuel Wade. Executors—Samuel Wade and David Morris, and they to have residue of estate. Witnesses—F. Gaudonett, Anna Gaudonett, Suanah Wells. Sworn and affirmed 19 May, 1733.
Lib. 3, p. 318.

1733, 3 mo. (May), 2 da. Inventory (£1,132.8.2) includes malt tub, malt mill, hair cloth, wool, 1,100 bushels malt, sundry in Philip Johnson's hands, cows, oxen and steers. Appraisers—Joseph Darkin, Bartholomew Hyatt.

1732, Nov. 3. Whitton, James, of Salem Co., yeoman; will of.

Wife, Catherine. Sons—Joseph, the plantation where I live, and in case of death and no lawful issue same to my kinsman, Benjamin Cripps, and for want of his heirs, then to Samuel Cripps and his heirs, and failing in such to the daughters of Nathaniel Cripps. If my son dies, Benjamin Cripps, if the said plantation comes into his hands, pay legacies to Sarah Jequat, Virgin Powell, Theophilus Gaskin, Ann and Hannah Cripps, the daughter of Peter and Sarah Jequat, Ann Cross, Susannah Wells, Rhina Johnson, Sarah Mason, Mary Walcot and Stephen Sinmans; also £10 for use of the meeting at Salem. Executor—son, Joseph. Assistants, Samuel Wade and Joseph Darkin. Witnesses—F. Gaudonett, Thomas Barrett, Thomas Smith, Sr.

1732, Nov. 25. Mem. My marsh in Penns Neck unto my son, Joseph Whitton. Witnesses—Bartholomew Hyatt, John Powell. Affirmed 10 Jan., 1732. Lib. 3, p. 243.

1732-3, 11 mo. (Jan.), 4 da. Inventory (£1104.17.11) includes clock, £7.10; 1,500 of malt (£181.19.6); servant man (£5); cattle (£225). Appraisers—Bartholomew Hyatt, David Morris.

1732, March 2. Whitton, Joseph, of Salem Co., yeoman; will of. Legacies to John Crips; the meeting at Salem, £10 (to be paid to Joseph Darkin for their use); Hannah and Sarah, daughters of Joseph Darkin; uncle John Darkin's three children, viz., Jael, Richard and Joseph. Also to Mary, Henry and Richard Hosier (to be paid to their father for their use), and Thomas Shepard. Residue of estate to my mother, Catherine Whitton. Executors—uncle, David Morris, and Samuel Wade, Esq. Witnesses—F. Gaudonett, Giles Gilljohnson, Michael Laimpstone. Proved 12 March, 1732. Lib. 3, p. 266.

1733, May 19. Inventory (£1,132.0.2) includes malt tub and malt mill, hair-cloth and wool, 1,100 bushels of malt and sundry of do., cattle, wheat. Appraisers—Joseph Darkin, Bartholomew Hyatt.

1731, May 14. Wiggins, David, of Salem Town and Co., cordwainer. Adm'x, Rebecca Wiggins, of Salem Town. Bondsman—Clement Hall, of same place. Witnesses—Edward Test, Jno. Rolfe.

1731, May 17. Inventory (£60.17.9½) includes leather and shoemaker's tools, £8.06. Appraisers—Benjamin Peters, Jno. Goodwin. Additional inventory, Sept. 13, £4.

1731-2, March 9. Account. Cash paid John Rolfe, Esq., Clement Hall, Sam'l Smith, Peter Turner. Salem Wills, 536 Q.

1744, Nov. 28. Wiggins, David, of Penns Neck, Salem Co., yeoman; will of. Brother, Garret Johnson, to have plantation I live on. Personal estate equally divided among my brother, Garret, and sisters Margaret and Elizabeth Johnson. Executor—Sinnick Sinnickson, and brother, Garret Johnson. Witnesses—Sephins Stanly, Edward Gorman, Roger Sherron. Proved 6 Dec., 1744. (Letters were granted to Sinick Sinnickson, Garret Johnson being very sick and likely to die).

1749, Oct. 31. Wiggins, George, late of Johnson Co., North Carolina, now of Somerset Co.; will of. Wife, Margaret. Son, John. Mentions Gershom Wiggins, son of brother John, brother Gershom, sister Rachel. Executor—brother, Gershom. Witnesses—Garret Williamson, Petrys Voorhees, John Reynolds. Proved May 8, 1750. Lib. E, p. 396.

1731, Aug. 31. Wild, James, of Gloucester Co., yeoman; will of. Wife, Rachel, executrix, and to have real and personal estate to settle and portion out my children's shares, excepting hereafter excepted. Legacies to children: James; Samuel, to have wheelwright tools; John, Sarah, Jonathan, Elizabeth, Joseph and Rachel, when they will be 21, or at marriage of daughters. Land in Burlington and Gloucester Counties. Assistant—brother-in-law, Alexander Morgan. Witnesses —Tho. Coles, Andrew Griscom, Amos Ashead. Sworn and affirmed 31 Dec., 1734. Lib. 3, p. 450.

1734, Dec. 31. Inventory (£299.1.6) includes a big Bible and other books, £1.10; plantation meadow, £200; seat in Burlington church, £1.15. Mentions Samuel Embly, Winiah Cowgell. Appraisers—Alexander Morgan, Thomas Coles.

1736, May 12. Wild, John, of Salem Co., yeoman. Int. Adm'r, John Ogden, Junior. Bondsmen—William Bradford, Thomas Harris. All of said county, yeomen. Lib. 4, p. 66.

1736, April 17. Inventory, £32.9.7; made by William Bradford, Thomas Harris, Jr.

1735, June 17. Wild, Rachel, of Waterford, Gloucester Co., widow. Adm'r, James Wild. Bondsmen—Thomas Coles, John Doe, yeomen. Witness—Abra. Cottnam. Lib. 4, p. 22.

1735, June 17. Inventory (£62.5.11) includes great Bible and other books, £1.10; notes of Samuel Embly, Noamyah Cowgell. Appraisers—Thomas Coles, Thomas Thorne.

1738, Jan. 8. Wilde, Samuel, of Waterford, Gloucester Co., wheelwright. Int. Adm'r, James Wilde, yeoman. Bondsman—William Ellis, yeoman. Both of the same place. Lib. 4, p. 154.

1742, Oct. 21. Wilder, John, of Penns Neck, Salem Co. Int. Adm'x, Margaret Wilder (relict). Bondsmen—Timothy Rain, John Savoy. Witnesses—Step'n Caxmuck, Chas. O Neill. Lib. 4, p. 378.

1742, Dec. 18. Inventory (£51.17) includes carpenter's tools. Andrew Dalbow, debtor. Appraisers—Tim. Rain, John Savoy.

1751, Oct. 26. Wilkerson, Samuel, of Cape May Co. Int. Adm'r, Ephraim Cent (Kent) of same county. No bondsman. Witnesses—John Mackey, Henry Young. (Inventory missing). Lib. 7, p. 157.

1748, Oct. 24. Wilkins, James, of Woodbury, Gloucester Co., joiner. Inventory, £50.19.6½; made by William Wood and James Cooper.

1748, Oct. 26. Adm'x, Jane Waitt, of Township of Deptford, Gloucester Co., widow. Thomas Nixon, of Philadelphia, Pa., yeoman, fellow bondsman. Lib. 6, p. 17.

1732-3, Jan. 22. Wilkins, Obadiah, of Upper Freehold, Monmouth Co. Int. Adm'r, William Wilkins, of same place, yeoman. Nehemiah Wilkins and William Kinnan, yeomen, fellow bondsmen. Witnesses —Thomas King, Richard Duglass. Lib. B, p. 377.

1732-3, Feb. 7. Inventory, £31.17.0; made by William Kinnan, John Finley, Joseph Robins. Mentions Joseph Hankins, Robert Roe, Safty Borden, Robert Montgomery, Barney Macollom.

1748, Sept. 2. Wilkins, Obidiah, of Somerset Co. Inventory includes negro, Blackwall (£60), Cate (£50), boy Dick (£25), 2 children "onto

6 mo." (£5). Made by Samuel Huluck, Abraham Polhamous, Martha Wilkens.

1768, Dec. 28. Inventory of goods of Obidiah Wilkins, deceased, administered on by Martha Wilkins, late of Hunterdon Co., deceased, now administered on by Abraham Crusee and Jonathan Combs, (£62.14.6); made by Isaac Vandyke, Abraham Tunison.

1770, May 22. Settlement of estate left unadministered includes fee to Mr. Stockton, costs paid Mr. Reed attending court 3 days.

Lib. 7, p. 58; Lib. 15, p. 17.

1729, 4th day, 12th mo. (Feb.). Wilkins, Thomas, of Evesham, Burlington Co., yeoman; will of. Wife to have negro named Frank. Son, Thomas, tract adjoining Richard Haines, Josiah Foster and Oustin's land; also one-fifth part of Propriety which is between me and my brother, purchased of John Penford. Son, William, land bought of Hugh Sharp. Son, Amos, land adjoining Sharp's. Grandson, Thomas Rakestraw. Daughters—Sarah and Rachel. Executors—sons William and Amos. Witnesses—Mahlon Stacy, Sam'll Atkinson, Ruth Atkinson. Proved Jan. 20, 1735. Lib. 4, p. 49.

1735, Dec. 17. Inventory, £201.2; made by Abram Haines and John Dearnall.

1738, ——, —. Wilkins, Thomas, of Deptford, Gloucester, yeoman, guardian of John (under 14) and Henry (about 16), sons of Henry Treadway, Gloucester Co. Lib. 4, p. 150.

1732, Nov. 19. Wilkins, William, of Upper Freehold, Monmouth Co., yeoman; will of. Wife, Alice. Children—Sarah, Deborah, Elizabeth, Alice, William, Nehemiah, Samuel and John; last two under 14. Executors—wife, son William and friend Elias Smith. Witnesses—William Kinnan, Richard Duglass, Isaac Stelle. Proved Jan. 22, 1732-3.

Lib. B, p. 381.

1733, April 18. Inventory (£86.3.6) includes one Bible. Made by Isaac Stelle, William Kinnan, Joseph Applin.

1748-9, Feb. 9. Wilkinson, James, of Woodbridge, Middlesex Co., Doctor. Int. Adm'x, Mary Wilkinson, widow. Isaac Tappen, of same place, yeoman, fellow bondsman. Lib. E, p. 261.

1748-9, Feb. 17. Inventory (£272.15.6) includes negro man, £40; negro woman and child, £40. Made by Abraham Tappen and David Donham, Jun'r.

1733, May 16. Wilkinson (Wilkison), John, of Woodbridge, Middlesex Co., mason; will of. Being in 51st year of my age. Children—Allen, Edward, Aron, John, Thomas, Patience, Charity, Rebecca and Mary Wilkison; all under age. Lands bought of David Ayers, Moses Bishop, Francis Walker; land on North branch of Raway River, joining land of Ben. Force; land bought of Noa Bishop, lying near Benjamin Coddington's corner. Executors—wife, Rebecca, and son Allen. Witnesses—Benj. Force, James Wilkison, Nugient Kelly. Proved June 6, 1733. Lib. B, p. 412.

1735, March 9. Wilkinson, John, of Greenwich, Gloucester Co., weaver. Int. Adm'r, Joseph Young, of Gloucester Co., yeoman. Bondsman—Alexander Randall, of same County. Lib. 4, p. 55.

1735, Mar. 19. Inventory (£24.3.1) includes 18 Indian baskets. Appraisers—Alexander Randall, Peter Long.

1737, March 17. Account. Paid to Francis Battin, Obediah Gibson, Susannah Lord, Abraham Chattin, Nathaniel Paull, Timothy Eglington, Alex. Randall, Roger Huckings, George Cofus, Benjamin Tindall, Rebeccah Sweetings, Sarah Cox, John Smallwood, Gunner Cox.

1740, Aug. 20. Wilkinson, Rebecca, widow of John Wilkinson, late of Woodbridge, Middlesex Co., mason; will of. Children—Edward, Charity, Rebecca, Mary (a minor). Granddaughter, Jean Wilkinson, daughter of son Aaron, deceased. Executor—son, Edward, and daughter, Rebecca Wilkinson. Real and personal estate. Witnesses—Joseph Bunn, Micajah Bunn, William Hider. Proved June 6, 1741.

1745-6, Feb. 3. Rebecca Frazee, late Rebecca Wilkinson, qualified as executrix. Lib. D, p. 165.

1739-40, Feb. 4. Willard, Henry, of Waterford, Gloucester Co.; will of. Eldest son, Joseph, when 21, to have home plantation. Legacies to son Isaac, when 21, and to daughter Mary, when 18. Executor—Thomas Spicer, Senior; he to put sons to trades. Witnesses—Alexr. Morgan, Daniel Comron, Abraham Comron. Proved 19 Feb., 1739-40.

1739-40, Feb. 19. Renunciation of Thomas Spicer, Senior. Witnesses—Tho. Spicer, Jun'r, Samuel Spicer. Administration granted to James Williard, of Waterford, Gloucester Co., yeoman, brother of deceased. Lib. 4, p. 195.

1739-40, Feb. 9. Inventory (£51.10.04) includes boat, sculls, horses, cattle, apple-mill. Appraisers—Humfrey Day, Isaac Cooper.

1748, Oct. 31. Willard, James, of Waterford, Gloucester Co., yeoman; will of. Wife, Rebecca. Sons—Thomas, and Benjamin, to have equally, when 21, all lands. Son-in-law, Samuel Spicer. Executors—wife, and son Thomas. Witnesses—John Calfrey, Francis Calfrey, Christian Fish. Sworn and affirmed Nov. 30, 1748. Lib. 6, p. 1.

1748, Nov. 28. Inventory (£338.19.9) includes boat and sail, £5; cattle and horses, £99.15. Appraisers—Henry Wood, William Stone, Jr.

1731, Nov. 23. Willard, Thomas, of Waterford Township, Gloucester Co. Sons—Henry, James, Thomas, Benjamin, Isaac and Richard. Granddaughter, Abigail, when 21 or married. Mentions "her sister." Granddaughter Mary Willard (minor), rest of the personal estate. Executors—Henry and James Willard. Witnesses—Lorence Hollings, Peter Homan, Amos Ashead. Proved 23 May, 1732.

1732, May 22. Inventory (£76.6.7) includes "two negro boys at £30 each." Appraisers—Alexander Morgan, Lorence Hollings. Gloucester Wills, 157 H.

1730-1, Feb. 26. Williams, Benjamin, of Elizabeth Town, Essex Co., yeoman; will of. Eldest sons—Benjamin and Ebenezer, both, under 14, land bought of Obadiah Valentine and the Hetfields; Thomas, land I and my brother Joseph bought of Coll. Richard Townley, deceased; Jonathan, land bought of Robert Pool, Samuel Barret of Boston and Henry Peirson. Daughters—Sarah, wife of Richard Miller, Jun'r, Margaret and Ann Williams. Executors—wife, Mindwell, friend Robert Ogden, Esq., and son-in-law Richard Miller, Jun'r. Witnesses—Jonathan Dickinson, Dan'll Sayre, Daniel Meeker. Proved March 20, 1730-1. Lib. B, p. 194.

1730-1, March 12. Inventory (£304.03.05½) includes bonds from David Dunham, Elnathan Cory, David Stewart, Major Joseph Bonnel, Leonard Miles, Joseph Price, Samuel Williams, John Willis, Miles Williams. Made by Samuel Miller and Richard Miller.

1750, Nov. 26. Williams, Benjamin, of Borough of Elizabeth, Essex Co., yeoman; will of. Children—Benjamin, Betty and Anne, all under age. Cousins—Benjamin Miller and Jonathan Davis, both under age. Land in partnership with my three brothers, Ebenezer, Thomas and Jonathan Williams, joining lands of Moses Crane, Andrew Crage, Daniell Meeker. Land bought of brother Thomas, joining lands of Joseph Ludlam, Jun'r, and ——— Little. Executors—wife, Elizabeth, friends John Cory and Joseph Cory. Witnesses—Thomas Williams, Joseph Sayre, Abraham Clark, Jun'r. Proved Dec. 18, 1750.
Lib. E, p. 466.

1744, April 30. Williams, Elisha, under 14. Bond of George Williams, of Shrewsbury, as guardian. Monmouth Wills, 1197 M.

1743, Nov. 1. Williams, George, of Town of Shrewsbury, Monmouth Co., yeoman; will of. Wife, Lydia, one-third of plantation where testator lives and one-fourth of land on Goose Neck, one-third of houses, barns, etc., excepting fulling mill, tools, etc. Eldest son, Obadiah. Second son, George, land, mill, tools, etc., belonging to fulling mill, and grist mill and press, "which was Obadiah William's," and which testator bought of the auditors. Third son, Hezekiah, land bought of John Throckmorton at Squancum; land bought of Thomas Bills on Meteeteconk Neck; land on Whale Pond Brook, bought from testator's brother Judah. Fourth son, John, land bought from testator's brother, Judah, now in John's occupation. Youngest son, Elihu, plantation whereon testator lives, land on Goose Neck. "The above bequest to his mother-in-law, my wife Lydia, being excepted during her widowhood." To son, Elihu, the fulling mill with the copper press, sheers, etc. Daughter, Hannah, £100, when aged 21 or at marriage. Wife, use of one-third of silver plate. Mulatto man to be let or set free at age of 30, etc. Executors—sons George and Hezekiah. Witnesses—Emanuel Woolley, Webley Edwards, Michael Robinson, Jacob Dennis. Proved April 10, 1744. (Webley Edwards and the executors Quakers). Lib. D, p. 174.

1744, 1st mo. (Mar.), 24. Inventory (£1,386.19.8) includes mulatto man, £20, and utensils belonging to the clothers trade. Made by Ephraim Allen, Joseph Corlies, Jacob Corlies.

1751, 4th mo. (June), 12. Account. Mentions James McCarty, Jacob Corlies, Susanna Swain, Thomas Glean, John Bedford, Ste. Talman (Doctor), Jos. Eatton (Doctor), David Hance, John Beck, Henry (the Dutchman), John Williams of Freehold, Lydia Williams, Mercy Stillwell, Jno. Lippincott, Jno. Lippincott, Jr., Jacob Dennis, Frances Borden, Daniel Seebrook, Aaron Robins, George Corlies, Rebeckah Chamberlain, Thomas Herbert, John Holdworth, James Osborn, Eliakim Wardell, Solomon Wardell, William Brinley, Jos. Allen, Ebenezer Allen, William Cradock, John Chambers, Jno. Crackson, William Brewer, Jno. Drummond, William Corlies, Gershom Bills, John Longstreet, Jo. Pang, Jos. Lippincott, Preserve Lippincott's estate, Gisbert Sutfen, Ephraim Allen, John Williams, John Mills (Doctor), John Cox, attorney-at-law, William Chamberlain, Jno. Willis, Ralph Allen, Benj. Swan, Remembrance Lippincott, Jno. Holloway, Jno. Husbans, William Taylor, Benj. Woolcott, Thomas Tilton, Samuel Worden, Ann Chambers, Timothy Willits, Hannah Slocome, Jno. Wikoff, Jeremiah Bonham, Jno. Pears, Jno. Hires, Jno. Fisher, Richard Gardner, Frances Borden, John Webley, Jno. Lippincott, Jr., Jno. Little, Esquire, Thomas Lemon, David Rulan, Jno. Woolley, Lewis Chamberlain, Derick Longstreet, Obadiah Boun, Widow Nichols, Jacob Lippincott, Lydia Leonard, Webley West, Jno. Cooper, Eatton Burros, Thomas Borden, Mort.

Vandike, Job Cook, Philip Dennis, Ste. Flemen, Robt. White, James Tucker, Thomas Borden, Jr., Emanuel Woolley, Jno. Hulet, Ste. Colvine, Richard Stout, Peter Willson, Going Watson, Thomas Richards, Richard and Robert James, Abigail Lippincott, Nicholas Winright, James Winright, Martha Winright, John Remine, Thomas Layton, Sawne Neper, Joseph Parker, Benj. Stout, Thomas Johnson and his son Thomas, Jno. Wikoff, Peter Willson, Thomas Jencoaks, James Craig, Cornelius Vandiveere, Samuel Dennis, Robert Allen, Cornelius Compton, Jno. King, Joseph Throckmorton, James Layton, Jno. Rogers, Garret Bowler, Peter Parker, Richard Meechell, William Carhart, William Taylor, Henry Perrine, Thomas Potter, John Ocoson, David Lippincott, John Burcham, John Willson, Thomas Williams, Nicholas Helens, William Wilkinson, Abram Russel, William Exceen, Edmond Lefebro, Elias Dehart, Jno. Allen, Walter Herbert, Thomas Woodmansee and his widow, Joseph Lippincott, Jacob Sutfen, James Winter, Thomas Adams, Orry Motoson, Samuel Willit, Ste. Warn, Lewis Morris (the Governor), Wm. Clark, John Willson (son of Peter), Joseph Gardner, William Lawrence, David Allen, Edward Taylor, Jno. Heavens, Jno. Chambers, Jno. Hance, Wm. Osborn, Samuel Rogers, James Grover, Jr., Lawrence Horsman, Oliver Mene, Zachariah Allen, Hendrick Kep, Jno. Hoskins, Richard Sutfen, Clem McDaniel, Edmond McAnder, William Johnson, Garret Garrison, Abel Tilton, Peter Romine, Sarah Russell, Charles Fish, Wm. Maccoy, Isaac Vickers, Jno. Taylor, Henry Newport, Luke Gyant, Jno. Vandeventer, William Letts, Samuel Carman, Elen Runnels, Christopher Leonard, Jos. Morgan, Jos. Spragg, Jno. Morford, Thos. Stillwell, Jno. Hogerlon, Thomas Sutton, Esther Leonard, Ephraim Potter, Wm. Truax, William Clark, Susanna Applegate, Matthew Ellison, Thomas Parker, William Redford, Jno. Layton, Ste. Mene, Abram Vickers, Samuel Watson, James Reid, Benjamin Talman, Robert White, Robert Harris, Jno. Holmes, Sr., Daniel Hendrickson, Benjamin Corlis, Gisbert Vanmater, Benj. Vanmater, Jno. Vancleave, Daniel Smith, Hannah Slocome, Richard Rogers, John Willson (son of Widow), John Pew, Margret Gyant, Jno. Hance, John Hires, Mary Davis, Jno. Smock, Jno. Eastwood, Thomas Hance, George Counover, Roliff Skank, Mary Parker, Sarah Heritage, Samuel Brewer, Robert Padison, Stanley White, Thomas Parks, Jno. Huse, Tunus Swort, Methias Tisen, Mary Rogers, Thomas White Rumson, James Johnson, Eliza. Lukerson, Jno. Davis, William Woolley, Benjamin Hoofmire, Sarah Parker, Abigail White, Andria Webley, Sen'r, Jno. Mills, Samuel Bown, Mary Allen, John Bullen, Thomas King, William Woodward, Jno. Fisher, Benjamin Forman, Samuel Frop, Thomas Herker, Sarah Potter, Jno. Emmons, Jno. Hampton, Orry Borum, Rachel Jobs, Archibald Craig, Ann Leonard, Eliza. Leonard, Wm. Redford, Wm. Clark, Jno. Vaun, Else Grover, Jno. Hebron, Wm. Parent, Thomas Forman, Jno. Powell, Jno. Reid, Jno. Taylor, Margret Winright, Sarah Graves, Else Winright, Jno. Forman, Ben. Borden, Wm. Gifford, James Edwards, Charles Matthews, Honos Brewer, Peter White (of Middletoun), Elen Mills, Jno. James Stelle, Widow Stelle, Samuel Form, ——— Pateson, Mordica Gibbons, Timothy Holsted, Jno. Taff, Daniel Herbert, Thomas Fenimore, James Patison, Thomas Harve, Eliza. Green, Rebeckah Cavileer, Abram Covet, Jno. Perkins, Peter Tilton, Jno. Lawrence, Edward Hardman, Obadiah, George, Hezekiah, John, Elihu, Hannah and Lydia Williams. James McCarty, the mulatto man, for his freedom dues, £20.

1749, Aug. 16. Williams, George, of Shrewsbury, Monmouth Co.; will of. Wife, Elizabeth. Children—Tylee, Edmond, George, Johanna and Obadiah. Wife's brother, John Abbott. Executors—wife, and brother-in-law John Abbott. Witnesses—Nathan Tilton, Isaac Palmer, Cor's McCurtain, Edward Price, Anthony Pintard. Proved May 7, 1750. Lib. E, p. 465.

1738, May 22. Williams, James, of Gloucester Co., sawyer. Int. Adm'r, Joseph Lynn, of Phila., shipwright. Bondsman—Thomas Hunloke, Esp., of Burlington.

1738, May 18. Renunciation of Edmund Lord of Philada., in favor of Joseph Lynn, the greatest creditor. Witness—John Carter.

1739, May 25. Inventory, £14; made by Samuel Shivers and Hans Steelman. Gloucester Wills, 234 H.

1737, Feb. 21. Williams, Joseph, of Elizabeth Town, Essex Co., yeoman; will of. Children—Mary (wife of John Denman), Phebe (wife of William Woodruff), Joseph and Daniell. Granddaughter, Remember Winans, at 18. Land bought of Nathaniel Bonnel, taken up in right of James Bullen; land purchased of John Tapping, deceased, joining land of Daniel Meeker; land bought of Col'l Richard Townley, deceased. Executors—wife, Mary, sons Joseph and Daniel. Witnesses —Ichabod Vallentine, William Jones, Thomas Chapman. Proved Jan. 30, 1738. Lib. C, p. 25.

1746, Aug. 23. Williams, Joseph, of Upper Freehold, Monmouth Co. Int. Inventory includes male negro child, £5; negro man, £50. Made by Thomas Leonard and John Ashton.

1746, Sept. 8. Sarah Williams, widow, renounces right of administration in favor of her brother-in-law, John Williams, of Amboy.

1746, Sept. 26. Bond of John Williams, of Freehold, as administrator, brother of intestate. Robert Savage, of Freehold, and James Willson, of Perth Amboy, fellow bondsmen. Lib. D, p. 403.

1734, Nov. 29. Williams, Lewis, of Elsenburgh, Salem Co. Int. Adm'r, Thomas Mason. Bondsmen—John Doe, Richard Roe. Witnesses—Saml. Bustill, John Jones.

1733, Dec. 21. Bond (£5.15.10) of William Lewis, laborer, to Thos. Mason, of Salem Town, merchant. . Witnesses—Richard Smith, Chas. O Neil.

1734, Dec. 26. Inventory, £2.3; made by Joseph Darken, Edwd. Test.

1747, Oct. 17. Williams, Miles, of Borough of Elizabeth, Essex Co., yeoman; will of. Wife, Phebe. Children—Samuel, John, Joshua (under age), Ann; other daughters mentioned but not named. Land joining lands of James Hinds, Samuel Scudder and Joseph Williams; land bought of John Halstead, Esq.; bond of Nathaniel Woodruff, of Ashswamp, weaver. Nephew, John, son of son Samuel Williams. Executors—kinsman, Benjamin Williams, yeoman, and son John. Witnesses—John Crane, John Denman, Charles Hole. Proved May 4, 1748. Lib. E, p. 183.

1748, June 9. Williams, Obadiah, of Shrewsbury, Monmouth Co. Int. Inventory (£358.07) includes debt of James Hamers; "Adam Herds, a Palatine's time," (£05), and silver tankard (£20). Made by Joseph Corlies, John Eatton, Jedidiah Allen. Lib. E, p. 200.

1748, July 1. Catherine Williams, widow, declines right of administration in favor of her father, Humphrey Wady. Witnesses—John Smith, James Hamer.

1748, July 4. Bond of Humphrey Wady, late of New England, now of Shrewsbury, as administrator. John Williams, of Shrewsbury, yeoman, fellow bondsman. Witnesses—Anthony and Elizabeth Dennis. (Humphrey Wady, a Quaker).

1746, Sept. 25. Williams, Thomas, of Upper Freehold, Monmouth Co. Int. Adm'r, son, John Williams, of Freehold. Robert Savage, of Freehold, and James Willson, of Perth Amboy, fellow bondsmen. Lib. D, p. 404.

1750, Sept. 3. Williamson, Arthur, of Freehold, Monmouth Co.; will of. Children to be educated. Wife, Mary, £60. Son, Cornelius, two parts of residue of estate. Daughter, Jemimah, the other third part. If children die in minority, estate to testator's three brothers and sisters. Executors—Mr. Cornelius Vanderveer, Albert Williamson, David Williamson. Witnesses—Jacob Covenhoven, Garret Covenhoven, Cornelius McCurtain. Lib. E, p. 457.

1750, Sept. 21. Inventory (£309) includes negro lad, £50; old negro and old wench, £25; gun and sword. Made by Cornelius Vanderveer, Elbert Williamson, David Williamson.

1747, Sept. 24. Williamson, Peter, of North Branch of Raritan, Somerset Co. Int. Adm'x, widow, Barbara. Fellow bondsman—Jonathan Hunt. Lib. E, p. 85.

1747, Sept. 19. Inventory, £79.11.9; made by Job Compton, Jacob Eoff.

1734-5, Jan. 9. Williamson, William, of Elizabeth Town, Essex Co., tailor; will of. Sons—Mathias and William, both under age. Land joining land of Edward Thomas; land and grist mill. Executrix—wife, Margaret. Witnesses—Edward Vaughn, Edward Thomas, Geo. Emott. Proved Jan. 18, 1734-5. Lib. C, p. 1.

1728, Nov. 14. Willis, George, of Town and Co. of Burlington, innholder; will of. Wife, Mary, executrix, with assistance of friends, Mr. Charles Read, of Philada., merchant, and Mr. John Allen, of Burlington, as trustees. Sons—George, John and Charles, all under age. Land in Town and Island of Burlington, adjoining Richard Wright and Isaac DeCow. House and lot where Thomas Shrieve now lives, and meadow adjoining Francis Smith. Witnesses—Isaac Pearson, Joseph Heritage, Is. DeCow.

1731, June 8. Codicil. Since making will I have bought of Henry Clothier a lot in Burlington, which I bequeath to my son Charles. Witnesses—Wm. Bickley, Thos. Hunlock, Sam. Buckley. Proved Sept. 6, 1731. Lib. 8, p. 150.

1740, Aug. 3. Willis, George, of City and Co. of Burlington, joyner; will of. Mother, executrix, and house on High street, Burlington, and meadow on London Bridge Creek, a silver tankard, etc. Brother, John, after decease of my mother, the silver tankard and £20 left me by my father. Brother, Charles. Witnesses—Ralph Peart, John Saunders, Isa. Conaro. Proved Jan. 15, 1742. Lib. 4, p. 335.

1740, July 24. Willis, John, of Alloways Creek, Salem County, carpenter. Int. Adm'r, William Willis, yeoman. Bondsmen—Edward Quinton, John Hughs. All of said County. Witnesses—Jonathan Walmsley, Dan. Mestayer. Lib. 4, p. 249.

1740, Sept. 14. Inventory (£221.13.5) includes bonds of Jonathan Hughs, Joseph Cluse, David Randel, Joseph Fogg, William Tiler; and John Tone's note. Appraiser—Isaac Sharp.

1743, Dec. 3. Willis, John, Sen'r, of Borough of Elizabeth, Essex

Co., blacksmith; will of. Wife, Mary. Children—John, Samuel, Thomas, Isaac, David, Susana Sutherd, and her children; other daughters, but not named. Land I now live on at Connecticut Farms; land my son Isaac and I bought of Har. Osborn. Executors—son, Thomas, and friend Timothy Whitehead. Witnesses—Thomas Squier, Charles Hole, Jun'r, Charles Hole. Proved Jan. 22, 1743-4. Lib. D, p. 118.

1743-4, Jan. 28. Inventory (£90.05.05) includes debt of Cornelius Ludlam. Made by Samuel Potter, yeoman, and Charles Hole, schoolmaster.

1748, Oct. 21. Willis, John, of City of Burlington, clockmaker. Int. Adm'rs, Joseph Rose, of same, atty-at-law. Charles Willis, of same, blacksmith, fellow bondsman. Lib. 6, p. 329; Lib. 7, p. 95.

1748, Nov. 3. Inventory, £31.18.6; made by Thomas Rodman and Hugh Hartshorne.

1740, June 26. Willis, William, Senior, of Alloways Creek, Salem Co., carpenter; will of. Wife, Mary, executrix. Sons—William, two tracts of land in his possession at Alloways Creek, one containing 200 acres, the other 245 acres, also ½ of my cedar swamp, 250 acres, at head of Stow Creek, and 100 acres, being part of 300 acres I purchased of Benjamin Holmes at Alloways Creek, to be laid out and joined to the place he lives on; Stephen (at 21) the plantation, 300 acres, I live on, ½ of my lands at the cedar swamp, and 200 acres I purchased of Benjamin Holmes, also my carpenter's tools. Personal estate to daughters, Elizabeth, Esther, Rachel and Lydia Willis, when 18. Witnesses—John Thompson, Sarah Duncan, Benj. Acton. Affirmed 14 August, 1740. Lib. 4, p. 251.

1740, July 5. Inventory, £368.18.7¾; made by John Mason, Tho. Hill.

1743, Aug. 18. Willits, Amos, obligation that he binds himself, his heirs, etc., to Abigail Willits after marriage that he will permit her to make her last will and testament, and to give to whom she pleases £40, and pursuant to the said authority the said Abigail Willits made her will as next follows.

1745, July 8. Willits, Abigail, of Burlington Co.; will of. Daughter, Ruth Emley, £40. Children—Elizabeth, William and Benjamin Cook. Executrix—daughter, Ruth Emley. Witnesses—John Thorn, Wm. Marlan, Benjamin French. Proved April 7, 1747. Lib. 5, p. 497.

1743, Oct. 2. Willits, James, Senior, of Little Eggharbour, Burlington Co.; will of. Wife Phebe, personal estate. Children—James and Martha, real estate. Executors—wife, son James, and brother Richard Willits. Witnesses—Joseph Lippincott, Roger Osborne, Bartho. Brixton. Proved Nov. 2, 1743. Lib. 5, p. 6.

1743, Nov. 7. Inventory, £294.3.6; made by Richard Willets and Joseph Lippincott.

1728, Jan. 3. Willocks, George, of Perth Amboy, Middlesex Co.; will of. (For will, see Archives, Vol. 23, page 512).

1735, Sept. 6. Inventory, £1,628.13.0; made by Messrs. Johnston and Parker.

1791, Feb. 25. Bond of Henry Waddell, John Lawrence and Charles Axford, trustees of estate so far as the legacy to the Episcopal churches of Shrewsbury, Burlington and Hopewell are concerned. (Legacy not disclosed in previous will abstract). Middlesex Wills, 575-609 L.

1742-3, Jan. 29. Wills, Daniel, of Northampton, Burlington Co., merchant; will of. Sons—Noah and Richard, plantation near Trenton, now in tenure of Zacheriah Haywood. Son, David, plantation in Evesham I bought of Thomas Sharp, he paying daughter Hannah £1 at age. Son, Daniel, house and lot in Mount Holly, called Blacksham's Lot and lot by the bridge, which I bought of Nathaniel Cripps, and also 160 acres in the mountains near South Branch of Rariton River, taken up for me by John Reddin [Reading]. Sons—John and George, home plantation at age. Daughters—Margaret, £150, and Hope, £50. Wife, Margarette, executrix and remainder of estate. Witnesses—Felix Leeds, Samuel Parker, Gab. Blond. Proved Dec. 5, 1747.

Lib. 5, p. 378.

1747, Nov. 17. Inventory, £1421.14.10; made by James Lippincott and Samuel Woolston.

1749, March 23. Wills, David, 14 years and upwards, son of Daniel Wills, of Burlington Co., deceased, ward. Guardian, Joseph Goldy, of Gloucester Co., yeoman. Bondsman—Jonathan Thomas, of Burlington Co., innholder. Witnesses—Rob. Smith, J. Scattergood.

Gloucester Wills, 4144 H.

1749, June 16. Wills, Jacob, of Deptford Township, Gloucester Co., yeoman. Adm'x, Deborah Wills. Bondsman—Samuel Harrison. Witnesses—Samuel Griscom, Thomas Kimsey. Lib. 6, p. 322.

1749, June 7. Inventory (£306.13) includes boat (£6), negro man named Fortune (£65). Made by George Kimble, Thos. Kimsey.

1745, 17th day, 9th mo. (Nov.). Wills, John, of Northampton, Burlington Co.; will of. "Being in the 86th year of my age." Son, Daniel, tract of land where he lives, and which I had of my father, Daniel Wills, on Burlington road and adjoining Thomas Green. Wife, Elizabeth, use of room in said house during widowhood. Son, James, and his wife Sarah, and his sons Jacob and Samuel, my ferry flat. Grandsons—John (third son of son Daniel), Daniel, Jonathan, Moses and Aaron Wills. Son, John. Children of daughter Hope Lippincott; Freedom, her eldest son, being deceased, his share to descend to his son Abel. Grandchildren—Samuel, Hope and Molly, children of Freedom Lippincott. Dau., Elizabeth, wife of Samuel Lippincott, and their children. Children of dau., Anne, wife of Jonathan Ladd, and their children, Elizabeth, Samuel and Jonathan. Children of dau., Sarah Lord. Children of dau., Rebecca, which she had by William Tomlinson, Hope, Elizabeth, Anne and Sarah. Negro woman, Denny, to have freedom and be provided for by grandson Daniel Willis. Executor—son-in-law, Samuel Lippincott. Witnesses—Revell Elton, Thomas Green, Gab. Blond. Proved Feb. 26, 1746. Lib. 5, p. 308.

1746-7, Feb. 25. Inventory, £307.10½; made by Revell Elton and John Deacon.

1736, Sept. 7. Wills, Joseph, of Northampton, Burlington Co., yeoman. Int. Inventory, £300; made by Philo Leeds and Michael Woolston.

1736, Sept. 9. Rebeckah Wills, widow, relinquishes right to administer to Daniel Wills, her brother-in-law. Bond of Daniel Wills, merchant, as administrator. Philo Leeds, fellow bondsman, both of Northampton, yeomen. Lib. 4, p. 73.

1737, May 14. Account. Payments to Benjamin Springer, Joseph Woolston, Felix Leeds, Michael Woolston, James Mills, Levi Shinn, Samuel Woolston, Darling Cannaroe, William Murrell, Joseph Rockhill, Samuel Shinn, John Lamb, Michael Sill, Patrick Reynolds, Jacob Johnson, William Goldy, William Harris, John Mich. Brand, John Milnor, Edward Hamilton, John Simons, Edward Radolphus Price, Tho. Hunlock, Gabriel Blond, Patrick Hendely, Abraham Bryan, Elizabeth Shinn, Anne Lippincott, Thomas Shinn, William Buddell, John Burr, John Hollinshead, John Webster, Richard Smith, Jun'r, Samuel Bustill.

1748, Dec. 20. Wills, Margaret, widow of Daniel Wills, merchant. Int. Inventory, £930.6.11; made by James Lippincott and Samuel Woolston. Includes debts due from Jno. Murrow, Jno. Brown, Chas. Tonkin, Benj. Inman, James Pemberton.

1748-9, Jan. 21. Bond of Noah Wills, of Hunterdon Co., yeoman, and John Hugg, of Gloucester Co., yeoman, as administrators; also administrators of estate of Daniel Wills, left unadministered by his widow. Samuel Woolston and Jonathan Thomas, of Burlington, yeomen, fellow bondsmen. Burlington Wills, 4385-8, 5551-6 C.

1739, 12th mo. (Feb.), 5. Wills, William, of Woodbury, Gloucester Co., tailor; will of. Loving friend, Alice Wood, executrix, and to have whole estate. Witnesses—John Jeffries, Thos. Wilkins, Priscilla Hugg. Affirmed 29 March, 1742. Gloucester Wills, 281 H.

1747, 7th mo. (Sept.), 20th. Willson, Edward, of Deptford Township, Gloucester Co.; will of. Wife, Sarah. Son, Sevil, my plantation; in case of his death without lawful male issue, same shall descend to my next son and his lawful male issue, and so on according to the law of Primogeniture. If sons die without lawful male issue said plantation to descend to the male issue of my brother, Sevil Wilson. Children—John (not 21), Susannah (not 21), Thomas (not 14), and Joseph. Sons to dwell together and manage the plantation at my son Sevil's discretion, until the 12 day of ninth month next after date hereof. Executor—son, Sevil. Witnesses—Edward Jesop, Thomas Reeves, Jr., Alexander Carson. Affirmed 5 April, 1750. Lib. 6, p. 347.

1750, March 28. Inventory, £253.1.2½; made by Isaac Stephens, Thomas Reeves, Jr.

1747-8, March 9. Wilson, Hezekiah, of New Hanover, Burlington Co., yeomen. Int. Adm'x, Christiana Willson, widow (Quaker). Benjamin Jones, of same, yeoman, fellow bondsman. Lib. 5, p. 438.

1747-8, March 12. Inventory, £39.17.6; made by Benj. Jones, John Warren.

1737, April 25. Willson, John, of Middletown, Monmouth Co. Int. Inventory (£246.08.5) includes 35 lbs. tobacco, negro woman and child (£45), negro man (£20), debts due from William Lawrence and Richard Gibbons. Made by George Taylor and John Teunisson. Lib. C, p. 164. Monmouth Wills.

1735-6, Jan. 27. [Earlier] inventory of (£23.4.9) includes loom and tackling, share coming from Estate of Mary Willson, mother of John Willson. Made by John Bennem and George Walker.

1731, Feb. 5. Willson, Mary, of Freehold, Monmouth Co. Int. Adm'r, John Willson, of Freehold, yeoman, eldest son. Aaron Matison, of Freehold, yeoman, fellow bondsman. Lib. B, p. 242.

1732, March 31. Inventory (£377.3.6) includes a half pike and sword (£1.4), Bible and some old books (£1.5), negroes Rose, Jack, June and Oliver (£150). Made by John Campbell, Joseph Newton, Joseph Taylor.

1731, Nov. 20. Wilson, Andrew, of Middletown Township, Monmouth Co., yeoman; will of. Wife, Ite, to have negro girl, Nan, etc.; also use of estate to maintain and educate children. Daughters—Johannah, Margaret, Mary and Martha. Son, James, 30 acres of land, bought of Samuel Ruckman; 35 acres purchased from the testator's father, John Wilson; 12 acres to be taken from land bought of Isabrant Vancleave, which lies between the road that goes to Widow Hendrickson's, and the King's Highway. Son, John, 60 acres bought of Isabrant Vancleave; 9 acres of meadow, etc. Sons, Andrew, Lambert and Peter, 96 acres, 52 acres and 11 acres, commonly called Cuckowder's Neck, bought from testator's father, and 20 acres on same Neck, bought of George Willox. Son, James, land bounded by lands of George Taylor, testator's son John, land formerly Edward Tart's, etc. Sons, Andrew, Lambert, James and Peter, four lots of meadow purchased of my father, John Throckmorton, Garret Wall, John Carman and Timothy Carman. Son, James, quit rents bought of John Reid; also upland called Mahoras Brook, lying by Jonathan Eldrith's. Executors—wife, Ite, and son James. Witnesses—Nicholas Johnson, John Willson, William Willett, Robert Dodsworth. Proved July 29, 1734. Lib. B, p. 560.

1734, Nov. 19. Wilson, Jeremiah, of Piscataway, Middlesex Co. Int. Adm'r, James Wilson. Lib. B, p. 587.

1736-7, March 15. Wilson, John, of Middletown Township, Monmouth Co., gent.; being aged; will of. Eldest son, John, loom and tackling, now in his possession. Sons, James and Andrew. Sons, Joseph and Benjamin, lands granted to them by testator by deeds of April 22, 1727. Son, Benjamin, negro man Monk, negro woman Pegg, and her son Robin. Daughter, Susanna. Daughter, Joan, box the testator kept his writings in, pewter platter that was her grandmother's and as much pewter as the rest of my daughters already married have. Granddaughter, Hannah Disbrow. Residue to daughters, Sarah, Hope, Joan, Elizabeth, Mary and Susannah. Executors—Thomas Morford, Esq., and sons, James and Benjamin. Witnesses—Lambert Willson, Benjamin Coleman, Mary Disbrow, Robert Dodsworth.

1737, Apr. 9. Codicil. Mentions son Benjamin and daughter Susannah. Witness—Robert Dodsworth. Proved May 19, 1737. Lib. C, p. 164.

1731, Jan. 22. Wilson, Peter, of Freehold, Monmouth Co., yeoman; will of. Wife, Sarah. Sons James, Thomas and Peter, each one-third of plantation whereon testator lives. Peter's share to include orchards and buildings. Executors—brother-in-law, William Hankinson and Thomas Hankinson, Jr., both of Freehold, yeomen. Witnesses—Aaron Matison, Daniel McKay, John Shaw.

1731-2, Jan. 22. Codicil. Son, Thomas, the orchard over the brook. Same witnesses. Proved March 13, 1731-2. Lib. 3, p. 188.

1732, May 30. Inventory (£163.0.4) includes gun, £1; two Bibles; negro man, Oliver, £70. Made by John Campbell, Aaron Matison, John Shaw (or Thaw).

1746-7, March 5. Wilson, Walter, of Monmouth Co. Int. Adm'rs, Jannet Wilson and David Rhe. John Henderson, of Monmouth County, fellow bondsman. Witnesses—Geartryed Crag, Thomas Bartow. Lib. D, p. 453.

1746-7, March 5. Inventory (£326.8.3) includes Indian corn, loom, gun and cutlas. Made by John Bennem and William Laird.

1749, Feb. 22. Account. Mentions, Wm. M. Gallard, Stephen Bogar (tending in time intestate had smallpox), Jane Dove, John Henderson, Owen Carack, Marget Fenton, Rachael Willson, Thomas Stephens, Thomas Bartow, Richard Sidam, Ursilla Forman, Joseph Forman, James Robinson, Matthew Rue, Widow Nicholls, Robert Savage, Jos. Newton, Peter Forman, David English, Hannah Clayton, Henry Van Hook, Samuel Jobe (vendue master), John Fenton, Samuel McConkey, Arthur Sutphin, Thomas Thomson, Jane Dove (debt undertaken by James Wilson, son of deceased), Lewis Thomson.

1736, Oct. 13. Winans (Wynants), Benjamin, an orphan about 14. Bond of William Winans, yeoman, guardian. Witness—Andrew Hay. Hunterdon Wills, 112 J.

1732, Oct. 28. Winans, Conrade, of Elizabeth Town, Essex Co. Int. Adm'r, Daniel Lane. Lib. B, p. 306.

1748-9, Feb. 20. Account; payments to Mr. Vaughn, physician.

1730-1, March 13. Winans, Isaac, of Elizabeth Town, Essex Co. Int. Inventory, £14.06.09; made by Nath'll Bonnell and Caleb Jefferys.

1731, May 29. Bond of Joseph Williams, father-in-law, as administrator. William Jones, fellow bondsman. Lib. B, p. 211.

1733, June 21. Winans, John, of Essex Co. Int. Adm'rs, Bethia Winans and Ebenezer Lyon. William Winans, fellow bondsman. Witness—Charles Townley. Lib. B, p. 422.

1734, Dec. 23. Winans (Wynans), John, of Elizabeth Town, Essex Co. Int. Adm'x, Frances Wyans. Lib. B, p. 587.

1740, May 25. Winans, John, of Perth Amboy, Middlesex Co.; will of. Sons and daughters mentioned, but not named; all under age. James Hooper, High Sheriff of Middlesex Co. Real and personal estate. Executors—wife, Anne, and brother William Winans. Witnesses—Samuel Brant, Sam'll Borrowe, J. Gifford. Proved July 3, 1740. Lib. C, p. 346.

1744, June 13. Winans, Samuel, of Borough of Elizabeth, Essex Co., yeoman; will of. "Being aged." Daughters—Hannah, Abigail, Ann, Sarah, Eunice and Zeruiah. Son, Samuel, lands joining lands of Phillip Blackledge, Benjamin Spining, Abraham Hetfield, Ebenezer Johnson, deceased, Joseph Halsey, and Charles Tooker. Son, Jedediah, land purchased of George Jewell; land joining lands of Abraham Winans, Samuel Meeker, William Winans. Executors—sons-in-law Thomas Clark and David Watkins. Witnesses—Benjamin Spinning, John Spinning, Benj'n Bonnel. Proved Oct. 3, 1747. Lib. E, p. 87.

1734, May 23. Winder, Thomas, of Hopewell, Hunterdon Co., yeoman. Int. Adm'x, Rebecca Winder, widow. Joseph Peace, of Trenton, yeoman, surety.

1734, June 4. Inventory includes bonds of Samuel Baker, ——— Parker, Thomas Newman, Frances Hague, Randle Idons, Immanuel Correl, Thomas Hoff, Abel Janney, Jr.; a canoe, new rifle barreled gun, old ditto, large fowling piece, new small gun sett off with brass, old gun and pistol, old sword, two great Bibles and three small ones, negro Ben

(£6), Toby (£30), wheat sold Benjamin Pidcock. Debtors—Joseph Peace, John McGloughlin, Peter Likin, Jonathan Cooper, Thomas Hough, Henry Slackt, Joseph Price, Joseph Higbey. Due from John Windor for wheat pr Peter Windor. 23 sheep in Pennsylvania. Made by Joseph Kirkbride, Andrew Smith, John Burroughs.

1746, March 10. Account of Rebecca Collins, late Rebecca Winder, administratrix. Mentions John Parker, William Yard, Richard Arnels (or Amels), Samuel Parker, Thomas Robinson, Richard Skirm, Eliakim Anderson, Thomas Palmer, "Flour" Greenland, James Neilson, Bennet Bard, Samuel Biles, Rut Johnson, Thomas Hamlin, Jeremiah Foster, John Andrewson, Sarah Dagworthy (for Theo. Severns), John Wills, Benjamin Canby, Mary Davis, Manuele Coryele, Ezekiel Clements, Timothy Smith, John and Thomas Winder (sons of deceased), James, Jane and Elizabeth Winder (other children of deceased), William Snowden, Timothy Smith, Joseph Kirkbride, John Burrows, Andrew Smith, Sarah Davis. Paid for taking deceased body out of the water, he having been drowned, £2; the Coroner; copy of a writing said to be a will made by deceased, but proved not to be such. Eleanor Winder, youngest child of deceased.
Hunterdon Wills, 107 J.

1733, Jan. 19. Windsor, Solomon, petitions that Mr. Jacob Ware be appointed his guardian. Salem Wills, 292 Q.

1732, March 6. Winn, William, of Gloucester Co. Int. Adm'x, Ruth Winn, widow. Bondsman—John Preston, of Waterford, husbandman.

1732, March 8. Inventory, £11.15.10; made by John Preston, Thomas Spicer. Gloucester Wills, 158 H.

1734, Dec. 26. Winter, Joshua, of Cohansey, Salem Co., yeoman. Int. Adm'r, Obadiah Winter, yeoman. Bondsman—Ebenezer Smith. Both of said county. Witnesses—Danl. Mestayer, John Doe.
Lib. 3, p. 436.

1734, Dec. 21. Inventory, £21.7; made by Ebenezer Smith, Thomas Ewing.

1738, June 2. Winter, Richard, of Newtown, Gloucester Co. Int. Adm'x, Sarah Winter, widow. Bondsmen—John Kaighin, Joseph Kaighin, of same place, yeomen. Lib. 4, p. 139.

1738, May 25. Inventory, £20.11.9; made by Tobias Holloway, John Kaighin.

1748-9, March 7. Winter, Thomas, of Newark, Essex Co. Int. Adm'r, Thomas Alling, principal creditor. Nathaniel Anderson, fellow bondsman. Lib. E, p. 269.

1722. Winter, William, of Middletown, Monmouth Co., yeoman; will of. Wife, Hannah. Eldest son, John, 4 acres of salt meadow on east side of Shoal Harbor. Second son, Andrew, land where testator lived, with land bought of James Grover. Youngest son, James. Grandson, Benjamin, second son to testator's eldest son John. Son, Andrew, currier's knife and all tools of the currier's and shoemaker's trade. Son James, great Bible and carpenter's tools. Daughters—Zerniah Borden and Rebecca Applegate. After wife's marriage or death, residue of estate to testator's two sons-in-law, Richard and Joseph Gardiner, and testator's own five children above named. Executors—sons Andrew and James. Witnesses—Richard Applegate, Richard

Gibbens, Benjamin Gibbines. Proved June 13, 1733. (Andrew Winter, surviving executor, sworn). Lib. B, p. 460.

1733, ——, —. Inventory, £99.4.6; made by John Mount, Samuel Willet, Abiel Cook. Additional inventory, £2.11.2.

1735, April 28. Winton, Joseph, of Salem Co. Int. Adm'r, Obadiah Loyd, innholder. Bondsman—Mounce Hopman. Both of Salem County, yeoman. Witnesses—Jos. Carroll, Dan. Mestayer. Lib. 4, p. 4.

1734-5, March 20. Inventory (£24.2) includes cash in hands of Matan Morrison, William Halls, Mounce Hofman, John Betellons. Appraisers—William Hall, Mounce Hofman.

1748, Oct. 13. Wiser, Margaret, of Rockyhill, Somerset Co., spinster. Int. Adm'rs, Jacob Wiser, brother, of New Brunswick, cordwainer. John Deare, of Perth Amboy, fellow bondsman. Lib. E, p. 215.

1748, Oct. 24, Dec. 3. Inventory (£43.10.9) includes bond of Christoper Wiser. Made by Isaac Voorhees and Minne V. Voorhies of New Brunswick.

1748-9, March 7. Wolf (Wolfe), Jerome, of Reading Township, Hunterdon Co. Int. Inventory (£155.17.4) includes bellows, anvil, vice and other tools, £20; smith shop and lot, £10. Made by David Vertron and Isaac Kip.

1748-9, March 17. Admr's, William Housell and Jacob Wolf of Reading town. Witness—Will: Ball. Hunterdon Wills, 241 J.

1737, 12th mo. (Feb.), 20th. Wood, Benjamin, of Hopewell, Gloucester Co., yeoman; will of. Wife, Mary. Sons—Henry, sole executor and to have the whole plantation (350 acres) at death of widow; Benjamin, the land (140 acres) where John Herris lives and ½ of "the fifth Divident" taken up for me; Henry, the other half; John (at 21) 210 acres on Manto Creek. Daughters—Mary, Elizabeth, Hannah (at 21, or marriage). Also Judith, my Bank lot in Phila.; Jane, my water lot; Abigail, the negro woman, Assar, now in her service. Mary Roberts, my wife's cousin. Witnesses—John Green, James Willard, John Kay. Proved 12 June, 1738. Lib. 4, p. 135.

1737, March 17. Inventory (£244.10.10) includes small Bible, negroes Isaac (£15), Cajoe (£30), debts of Casper Fish, Samuel Shivers, Joseph Ballinger. Appraisers—Humphry Day, Thos. Spicer.

[Not dated]. Wood, Benjamin, of Waterford Township, Gloucester Co., yeoman; will of. Wife (Rebecca), executrix, and to have place (140 acres) we live on for 18 years, when my youngest child, Wiley, will be 21; then plantation to be equally divided between my sons Isaac and Benjamin, they to pay £20 to their brothers James and Wiley Wood when latter will be 22 years old. Sons, as they arrive to 15, to be put to trades. Witnesses—Henry Wood, Henry Davis, and Henry Baldwin. Sworn and affirmed 29 Jan., 1750. Lib. 7, p. 367.

1750, Jan. 29. Inventory (£31.15) includes warrant to take up land, £1. Appraisers—Benj. Baldwin, Henry Davis, Ju'r.

1734-5, 1st mo. (Mar.), 19th. Wood, Constantine, of Woodbury, Gloucester Co., yeoman; will of. Wife, Alice. Sons—William (the eldest) home plantation; John, land fronting on Mantos Creek, bounded on lower side by land belonging to Ward and on upper side by land of William Chester; Constantine, land fronting on Mantos Creek, between land of John Chester and that of Samuel Chester; Francis, land fronting on Delaware River, between Richard Bickham's and William Arrel's, extending to Treadway's land. £10 to daughter Abigail Chew, and £15 to daughter Loetitia. Executors—wife, Alice, and son, William Wood. Witnesses—William Wilkins, Richard Floyd, Richard Bradford.

———, ——, —. Codicil. Certain privileges and moveables to wife, Alice. Witnesses—Richard Chew, John Overend, Richard Floyd. Affirmed 16 June, 1736. Lib. 4, p. 68.

1736, June 16. Inventory (£388.8.5) includes debts due from Daniel Gant, Thomas Lucy, Thomas Wilkins, Dav. Bristo, John Clifton, John Ladd, Edward Wilson, Richard Chew, Martain Bickham. Appraisers—Wm. Wilkins, Richard Bickham.

1732, Jan. 12. Wood, Gabriel, of Mannington, Salem Co., husbandman; will of. Son, Gabriel, 250 acres in Tobies Neck, part of 500 acres left in the will of Arthur Boyer. Daughter, Elizabeth Wood, 100 acres in Maninton, adjoining John Kid's, and 100 acres left by Elizabeth Mason. Son and daughter, Joseph and Hannah Wood, the personal estate equally. Brother and trusty friend, Joseph Wood, and Saml. Smith, Jr., of Maninton, executors. Added before signing: "My brother, Joseph Wood, the use of the plantation whereon I live for the bringing up of my daughter Hannah, until my son Gabriel comes to age." Witnesses—James Dunlap, William Graham, Rich'd Bradford. Proved 29 Jan., 1732. Lib. 3, p. 253.

1732, Jan. 25. Inventory, £123.16.8; made by David Davis, Mala. Davis.

1748-9, Feb. 14. Wood, Jeremiah, of Deptford Township, Gloucester Co. Int. Adm'x, Deborah Wood, widow (Quaker). Bondsman—James Wood, of same place, carpenter. Witness—Wm. Wilkins. Lib. 6, p. 78.

1748-9, Feb. 2. Inventory, £191.11.5; made by Wm. Wilkins, John Wilkins.

1752, ——, —. Account. (Paper missing).

1749, Feb. 8. Wood, Jeremiah, of Salem Co., guardian of Joost Miller, 14 years old. Bondsman—Bateman Loyd. Witnesses—Jechonias Wood, Frederick Hoffman. Salem Wills, 755-6 Q.

1744, 11th mo. (Jan.), 15th. Wood, John, of Woodbury Creek, Gloucester Co., yeoman; will of. Wife, Mary. Sons—James (the eldest), 380 acres bought of James Wills, likewise two lots bought of Thomas Wilkins and 6 acres purchased of Swan Warner; Henry, land purchased of Swan Warner, and meadow purchased of James Whiteal Jeremiah, home plantation, 100 acres, purchased of John Cox, and meadow called "Hors-shooe." These sons to have all my right in a cedar swamp called "Scotland," and all my unlocated rights. Daughters—Hannah Kimsey, Sarah Wilkins, Mary, Alice (not 18), and Lidia (not 18). Executors—wife, Mary, and son, Henry Wood. Witnesses—Jos. Lord, Sam'l Lippincott, William Wood. Affirmed 14 March, 1744. (Letters granted to executors Aug. 2, 1745). Lib. 5, p. 145.

1744, 5th, 12 mo. (Feb.). Inventory (£419.07.6½) includes debts due from John Sparks, Charles Morris, Thomas Kimsey, Jun'r., John Brown, John Wilkins, Henry Wood, John Blackwood, Jacob Middleton, Isaac Butterworth, Jonathan Fowler, Peter Rambo, Samuel Driver. Appraisers—John Hains, Josa. Lord.

1732, May 6. Wood, Jonas, of Great Eggharbor, Gloster Co.; will of. Daughters—Elizabeth, Jemima, Cathron—Expected child. Wife, Mary, executrix, and, if she should die during minority of children, then her brothers, John and Abel Scull, to have charge of estate, real and personal. Witnesses—John King, Dennis Dorelly, Elizabeth Williams, Thomas Marke. Proved Nov. 4, 1732. Lib. 3, p. 221.

1732, Oct. 24. Inventory, £185.14.3; made by Robert Smith and John King.

1745, April 1. Wood, Jonas, of Borough of Elizabeth, Essex Co., planter; will of. Children—Samuel, Anna (wife of James Clarke), Phebe (wife of Ephraim Terrill), Margaret and Sarah. Wife, Mary. Nephew, John Wood, son of brother John, deceased, land joining lands of Mephibeshoth Marsh and Daniel Marsh. Lands bought of Jacob Headfield and John Tooker, joining lands of Isaac Headfield, John Oliver, Recompense Stanbery; land joining land of Jonathan Woodruff; land bought of John Tooker, joining land of Joseph Tooker; land bought of Joseph Hariman and Isaac Headfield. Executors—brother, Joseph Wood, and Charles Tooker. Witnesses—John Baker, Israel Tyler, John Terrill. Proved April 23, 1745. Lib. D, p. 270.

1750, Nov. 6. Wood, Jonas, of Hopewell, Hunterdon Co. Int. Adm'rs, John Barcroft and Jonathan Smith, of Hopewell, yeoman. Andrew Smith, Jr., of Hopewell, surety. Witness—John Moore.
Hunterdon Wills, 290 J.

1743, Aug. 10. Wood, Joseph, of Manington, Salem Co. Adm'x, Katherine Wood (relict). Bondsmen—Joseph Fogg, Thomas Smith. All of said County. Witnesses—Chas. O Neill, Abner Penton.
Lib. 4, p. 371.

1743, Aug. 5. Inventory (£282.16.6) includes his horses, cattle, sheep, 4 servants (£25). Appraisers—Benjamin Holmes, Dan. Fogg.

1735, Oct. 9. Wood, Martha, wife of Gabriel Wood, of Salem Co., deceased. Int. Adm'r, Samuel Smith. Bondsman—John Doe. Witness—Joseph Rose. Lib. 4, p. 30.

1740, 22nd day, 3rd mo. (May). Wood, Mary, of Chesterfield, Burlington Co., widow; will of. Daughters—Margaret Stevenson and Joannah Woodward. Grandchildren—William and Mary Wood, and Parnell Cleayton. Negro man, Sam, to have freedom in three years. Executor—son-in-law, William Cooke. Witnesses—John Page, Benja. Busson, Mary Moris. Proved Nov. 17, 1742. Lib. 4, p. 349.

1742, Nov. 30. Inventory, £88.19.8¾; made by Samuel Wright and John Page. Includes cash in the hands of William Cooke and debt of Isaac Ivins.

1746-7, Feb. 21. Wood, Mary, widow of Jonas Wood, late of Borough of Elizabeth, Essex Co.; will of. Children—Benjamin Winans and Susanna, wife of Daniel Meeker. Jacob, son of Benjamin Winans. Granddaughter, Mary Bond, all goods marked "M. B." at 18. Grandson, Jacob Bond, under age. Executor—Thomas Clark. Witnesses—John Winans, Joseph Conkling, Abraham Clark, Jun'r. Proved May 13, 1747. Lib. E, p. 44.

1749, 7th mo. (Sept.), 22nd. Wood, Mary, of Woodbury, Gloucester Co., widow; will of. Sons—James (eldest) and Henry. Grandson,

Jehue Wood (not 21). Daughters—Lidia Wood, so much as will make up legacy her father left (£100), Hannah Kimsey, Sarah Wilkins, Mary Chattin, Alice Wood. Executors—sons James and Henry Wood. Witnesses—William Wood, Deborah Wood. Affirmed 9 Oct., 1749.
Lib. 6, p. 350.

1749, 7th mo. (Sept.), 30th. Inventory, £446.17.6½; made by Wm. Wilkins, James Whital.

1748-9, ——, 18. Wood, Thomas, schoolmaster, of Gloucester Co.; will of. Real and personal estate to Gabriel Rambo and his wife and their heirs for bringing up of two children, Jane and Thomas Wood, until of age. £1 to Martha Nichols, widow. Witnesses—Joseph, John and Isaac Tomlinson. Affirmed 14 March, 1748. Lib. 6, p. 84.

1748-9, 12th mo. (Feb.), 27. Inventory, £45.0.3; made by Joseph and Isaac Tomlinson.

1729, July 21. Wood, William, of Chesterfield, Burlington Co., yeoman; will of. Wife, Susanna, executrix. Mother, Mary Wood. Children—William and Ann, both under age. Brother, George Taylor. Lands adjoining John Scoley, Godfrey Beck, William Taylor and Matthew Fenwick; also land near Samuel Wardell and the mill. Mentions William Clayton. Witnesses—Asher Cleaton, John Page, Elizabeth Coar. Proved Feb. 10, 1731. Lib. 3, p. 179.

1731, Dec. 8. Inventory, £369.8; made by John Chesher, Robert Chapman, Thomas Newbould.

1733, Sept. 22. Woodmansee, Thomas of Shrewsbury, Monmouth Co., yeoman; will of. Plantation where testator lives to be sold, also interest in land in or near New London, in New England. Wife, Mary. Children—Thomas, John, David, Gabriel, James, Sarah, Elizabeth, Hannah and Margaret. Son-in-law, Ephraim Potter, and daughter, Leadea. Daughters—Abigail and Ann. Executors—John Littel and George Williams, of Shrewsbury, and testator's wife, Mary. Witnesses—Richard Higgins, John Woodmansee, David Woodmansee, Piep Doan (?), John Parker. Proved June 18, 1737. Lib. C, p. 170.

1737, Nov. 26. Inventory, £7.0.3; made by Matthias Venbrockel, Jr., and John Williams. Witness—Richard Compton.

1741, June 25. Account. Includes payments to Mr. Madock, John Davis, George Lefeter, Joseph Huit, Thomas Cooper, Simon Butler, Jonathan Jecocks (executor of Jos'h Stout), Benjamin Watkins, Ebenezer Allen, Dr. Edward Faulkner, Colonel Stelle, Samuel Leonard, John Eaton.

1748, May 12. Woodnutt, Jonathan and Henry, age of 14 and upwards, sons of Richard Woodnutt, of Salem Co., deceased, wards. Guardian—Benjamin Cripps, of Salem County, yeoman. Bondsmen—John Buzby, Samuel Cripps. Salem Wills, 769 Q.

1735, May 17. Woodnutt, Joseph, of Salem Co. Int. Adm'x, Rachel Woodnutt. Bondsman—Bartholomew Hyatt, of Salem County. Witnesses—Lewis Morris, Dan. Mestayer. Lib. 4, p. 16.

1735, 3 mo. (May), 2 da. Inventory (£293.17.6) includes cattle, sheep and lambs. Appraisers—Bartholomew Hyatt, Lewis Morris.

1738, Jan. 20. Woodnutt, Richard, of Mannington, Salem Co., bricklayer; will of. Wife, Ann, 2 acres in Greenwich, purchased of Thomas Chalkley, joining Elias Cottins, with full enjoyment of my estate until my son, Jonathan, will be 21. If wife marries, her husband shall give security for the children's part, remembering that Jonathan comes of age before my youngest son, Henry. Son, Henry, land in Mannington, in Haynes Neck; also one house and lot in Salem, mortgaged to me by William Burroughs, mariner, husband of my sister Sarah. Executors—wife, Ann, and Lewis Morris. Witnesses—Jonathan Walmsley, Grace Woodnutt, Joseph Carroll. Proved 21 Feb., 1738. Lib. 4, p. 174.

1739, April 10. Inventory (£768.11.5½) includes negro man and woman, £75. Appraisers—William Hunt, Benja. Cripps.

1743, ——, —. Account. (Paper missing).

1750, Aug. 1. Woodruff, Abraham, of Borough of Elizabeth, Essex Co., cordwainer; will of. Children—Jonathan, Benjamin and Sarah Woodruff. Real and personal estate. Executors—wife, Christian, and Mr. Thomas Scudder. Witnesses—Jon. Louve, John DeCamp, Laughlin Fallon. Proved Oct. 25, 1750. Lib. E, p. 458.

1732, June 5. Woodruff, Benjamin, of Middlesex Co.; will of. "Being taken with smallpox." Brothers—Charles, James and Ecobod, all under age. Sisters—Susanna and Sarey Woodruff, both minors. Executor—Jonathan Datton. Witnesses—Tho. Woodruff, Joseph Woodruff, Rich'd Harriman. Proved June 27, 1732. Lib. B, p. 270.

1732, June 29. Inventory, £63.04.06; made by Rich'd Harriman and Jonathan Dayton.

1747-8, Feb. 10. Woodruff, Caleb, Jun'r, of Elizabeth Town, Essex Co., cordwainer; will of. Daughter, Abigail. Expected child. Land purchased of Abraham Woodruff. Executors—wife, Abigail, and friend and relation, Robert Ogden. Witnesses—Jona. Higgins, Jona. Ogden, Sarah Woodruff. Proved Feb. 24, 1747-8. Lib. E, p. 254.

1747-8, Feb. 25. Inventory (£212.05.02) includes bonds of Henry Ford, Rob't Woodruff and Joseph Ogden; also money sent from Long Island by Mr. Elihu Howell. Made by Sam'll Woodruff and Joseph Ogden.

1750, Nov. 7. Woodruff, Charles, of Newark, Essex Co.; will of. Brother, James Woodruff. Sister, Sarah Blackledge. Children of brother Ichabod, deceased. £15 for use of New Jersey College. £15 to Jonathan Sergeant for use of Presbyterian Church in Newark. Real and personal estate. Executors—wife, Hanah, Eliphalet Johnson of Newark, and Paul Richards, merchant, of New York. Witnesses—Aaron Burr, Samuel Clarke, Alexander Gordon.

1750, Nov. 20. Codicil. Negro man, Caesar, to have his freedom. Proved Jan. 2, 1750-1. Lib. E, p. 506.

1732, Oct. 28. Woodruff, Daniel, of Elizabeth Town, Essex Co., cordwainer; will of. Children—Daniel, Abraham, Josiah, Stephen and Jemima. Land joining land of Edward Sale; land in partnership with my brothers. Executors—wife, Anne, and brother-in-law Thomas Price. Witnesses—Jonathan Dickinson, Joseph Woodruff, Jonathan Thompson. Proved April 15, 1741. Lib. C, p. 402.

1740, Dec. 22. Inventory (£128.09.09) includes debts from Joseph Woodruff, William Cole, Joseph Cole. Made by David Whitehead and Jonathan Thompson.

1731, Feb. 28. Woodruff, David, of Elizabeth Town, Essex Co. Int.

Mary Woodruff, the widow, declines to act and desires that her brother, Joseph Woodruff, be appointed administrator. Bond of Joseph Woodruff. Benjamin Woodruff, fellow bondsman. Witness—Wm. Chetwood. Lib. B, p. 243.

1731-2, March 7. Inventory, £17.13.06; made by Robert Ogden and John Hinds.

1749, April 24. Woodruff, David, of Elizabeth Town, Essex Co., weaver; will of. Children—Abner, David, Nathaniel, Jedediah, Jonathan, Elias, Jabesh, Usel and Eunice; all under age. Land on which my father, John Woodruff, now lives; land joining lands of Rob't Ogden and brother, John Woodruff. Executors—wife, Eunice, son Abner, brother Abner Ward of Newarke, and friend Robert Ogden. Witnesses—Jonathan Dayton, Sam'll Woodruff, Daniel Sale. Proved July 12, 1749. Lib. E, p. 329.

1749, July 19. Inventory, £201.16.09; made by Jonathan Dayton and Isaac Nuttman.

1745, Oct. 30. Woodruff, Ichabod, of Woodbridge, Middlesex Co., ship-carpenter. Int. Adm'x, Mary Woodruff, widow. Richard Fitz-Randolph, of Perth Amboy, fellow bondsman. Lib. D, p. 346.

1741-2, Jan. 15. Woodruff, Joseph, Jun'r, of Borough of Elizabeth, Essex Co., yeoman; will of. Children—John, Jonathan, William, Samuel, Abigail Gold, Thomas, Hezekiah, Banjamin (not 16), Joseph, Nathaniel, Isaac, Sarah and Joanna. Lands purchased of Daniel Talmage, deceased, Dec. 11, 1741, and Joseph Bird, deceased. Executors—wife, Hannah, friend William Miller, and son Thomas. Witnesses—George Ross, George Ross, Jun'r, Charles Hole. Proved Feb. 10, 1741. Lib. C, p. 475.

1741-2, Feb. 22. Inventory of estate (£304.05.06) includes bonds of Thomas Gold, Jonathan Marsh, Thomas Jeffery; old loom at Nath'll Woodruff's; 3 hides at Mr. Robert Ogden's; negro boy. Made by Charles Hole, schoolmaster, and George Ross, wheelwright.

1742, May 10. Accompt. Payments to John Shotwell, John Rolph, Joseph Woodruff, Isaac Terrill, Abraham Clarke, Thomas Clarke, Esq., Zebulon Jennings, John Pintard, Robert Little, Isaac Ogden, Samuel More, George Ross, Sarah Woodruff (her legacy), Ebenezer Sayre, Hezekiah Woodruff, John Clarke, Joseph Man, Samuel Woodruff, Gershom Moore, Jonathan Hampton, Josiah Crane (being his wife's legacy from her father), Caleb Jefferys, Isaac Woodruff, Sarah Jefferys, David Miller, George Stead, Henry Gathwait, Henry Bagnell, John Cleverly, Henry Shotwell, Charles Hole, Henry Jaques, Joseph Shotwell, John Cragie, John Hall, Peter Tremly, William Winans, Capt. Dehart, Nathaniel Woodruff, John Ross, William Ogden, Thomas Price, Richard Hall, John Rattan, Thomas Edgar, John Tucker, Henry Demony, Richard Clarke, Nathaniel Hubbell, John Woodruff, Thomas Scudder, Richard Hall, Robert Ogden, Jonathan Woodruff, Charles Marsh, Dennis Springer, Abraham Clarke, Edward Willmot, Ephraim Terrill, Will'm Ogden, Samuel Jaquess, Ichabod Burnet, Thomas Woodruff, William Miller; negro boy given to Benjamin Woodruff; bay mare Joseph Woodruff had given him by his mother.

1743, Aug. 9. Woods, Richard, of Morris Co. Int. Adm'r, Richard Woods, his son. Bondsman—Jonathan Osborn. Both of Morris Co. Witness—John Harrison.

1743, Aug. 6. Inventory (£49.13.6) includes note of Natl. Stillwell, smith's anvil (£8), vice (£1), bellows, etc. (£10.11.0). Appraisers—Solomon White, Nathl. Wheeler. Morris Wills, 4 N.

1746, Dec. 10. Woodward, Japheth, of Gloucester Co., hatmaker. Int. Adm'x, Eliza. Woodward, widow. Bondsmen—Alexander Morgan and Israel Hewlings. Lib. 5, p. 432.

1746, Nov. 21. Inventory (£146.9.11) includes "hat press, 4 caster hats, 2 beaver hats, 4 coarse hats," riding mare, colt, etc. Appraisers—William Griscom, Israel Heulings.

1747-8, Jan. 25. Wooledge, John, of Piscataway, Middlesex Co., yeoman; will of. James, son of Thomas Piatt, land in Woodbridge. John, son of Benjamin Stelle, 12 acres joining lands of Jeremiah Dunn and Patience Drake. Mary, wife of Eliphalet Jones. Wife, Hepzibah, executrix, and to have remainder of all estate. Witnesses—Dinah Martin, Isaac Brooks, William Rogers. Proved April 26, 1748. Lib. E, p. 165.

1739, Oct. 9. Woolever, Henry, of Amwell Township, Hunterdon Co., carpenter; will of. Wife, Ann. Son, Peter, a minor. Daughter, Elizabeth, when aged 21. Expected child. Executors—Peter Wooliever, Sr., and Peter Rockifeller, Sr., of Amwell. Witnesses—Joseph Bast, Jacob Wollever, Christopher Search. Proved Nov. 17, 1739. Lib. 4, p. 209.

———, ——, —. Account. Receipts from Henry Kitchen, Mr. Cowell, David Fetter, Henry Deardorf, Jacob Henry, Honust Trimmer, Timothy Rose, Justice Gons, Philip Ringo, Joseph Bast, Honust Beckelshammer, Martin Quinby, John Mullen, Richard Lowrey, Christopher Search, Henry Wooliever, Rindard Adler, Seth Lowry, Jacob Race, Cathrine Wooliever, John Porter, Thomas Martin, Peter Wooliever, John Swallow, Eden Burroughs, Anna Woolever.

1732, Oct. 2. Wooley, John, of Town of Shrewsbury, Monmouth Co., yeoman; will of. Wife, Rachel. Eldest son, Thomas, land and meadow on south side of Poplar Swamp Brook, adjoining said son's brother, William. Sons: Thomas, William, John and Benjamin, a Proprietary right. Land bought of Dr. Johnstone and Gabriel Stelle to be sold. Daughters—Leah Denn, Elizabeth Field and Anne Mercy Allen. Executors—wife, friend William Hartshorne, and son William Woolley. Witnesses—William Hartshorne, John Curlies, William Lippincott, Jacob Dennis.

1734, May 21. Codicil. Wife, Rachel, and friend and cousin, William Hartshorne, executors. Witnesses—Joseph Wardell, Jr., Adam Brewer, Daniel Tilton, Judah Williams. Proved May 30, 1743. Rachel Woolley, a Quaker). Lib. D, p. 69.

1743, June 8. Renunciation of William Hartshorne, of Middletown, as executor. Witnesses—William Hartshorne, Jr., Robert Hartshorne, Jr.

1743, Oct. 31. Inventory (£129.17.6) includes Bible, Sewel's History. Made by Hezekiah Williams, Ephraim Allen, Emanuel Woolley, Amos White.

1732, Nov. 3. Woolley (Wooley), Lydia, of Town of Shrewsbury, Monmouth Co., widow; will of. Son, Adam, and daughter, Ruth Wooley. Residue to children Adam and George, children of Gabriel Stelle and Elizabeth (the daughter of testatrix), Hannah Little, Content Bills and Ruth Wooley. Executors—sons Adam and George, and daughter Content Bills. Witnesses—Mehetable Scott, William Scott, George Thornborough. Proved July 20, 1732. Lib. B, p. 433.

1732, Dec. 19. Inventory, £80.02.0; made by John Scott and Abraham Russall.

1747, ——, —. Woolley, Thomas, of Town of Shrewsbury, Monmouth Co., yeoman; will of. Wife, Patience, use of all estate during widowhood. Eldest son, John, land below Mossy Swamp, now in said son's possession; land adjoining Amos White, 10 acres woodland adjoining Hog Swamp, tract bought of Stoffel Longstreet. Reversion to second and youngest son, Thomas, and also land bought of Gawin Drummond. After death of testator's wife, Thomas to pay sums to his eldest sister, Content Clayton, and sisters Lydia Borden, Abigail Longstreet, Hannah Nicholson and (youngest) Meribah Woolley. Executors—wife, and friend Job Cook, of Shrewsbury. Witnesses—Amos White, Gavine Drummond, Stoffel Longstreet. Proved March 2, 1747. (Amos White and the widow, Patience, Quakers). Lib. E, p. 152.

1747-8, March 12. Inventory, £205.11; made by Amos White and Jarvis Hance. Signed by "Patience Woolee."

1744, 2nd mo. (Apr.), 9. Woolman, Elizabeth, Jun'r, of Gloucester Co.; will of. My father, Samuel Woolman, to have my great Bible; my mother, Elizabeth Woolman, my great looking-glass. Brothers —John and Asher Woolman. Sisters—Sarah Elton and Patience Moore. £6 to my brothers, Abner, Uriah, Jonah, Abram and Eber, and younger sisters, Hannah, Esther and Rachel Woolman, to be put to interest for their uses until they will be 21. Executors—brothers, John and Asher Woolman. Witnesses—John Craig, Mary Gill, Elizabeth Estaugh. Affirmed 13 April, May 4, 1747. Lib. 5, p. 509.

1746-7, 1st mo. (Mar.), 17. Inventory, £273.11.11; made by John Craig, Saml. Mickle, Jun.

1750, 7th day, 6th mo. (Aug.). Woolman, Samuel, of Burlington Co.; will of. Wife, Elizabeth, ½ the plantation whereon I now live for 4 years and 3 months from this date, and then £5 annually, and personal estate. Sons—Asher, John, Jonah, Uriah, Abraham and Eber, lands adjoining Fred. Sipenert, Edward Hilyer and Daniel Wills, also 388 acres in Morris Co. surveyed by John Reding, and lots bought of James Southwick and Will'm Murrill. Daughters—Sarah Elton, Patience Moore, Hannah Gauntt, Esther and Rachel. Executors—sons Asher and John. Witnesses—Daniel Wills, Jun'r, Thomas Green, Joseph Green. Proved Nov. 5, 1750. Lib. 6, p. 391.

1750, 25th day, 8th mo. (Oct.). Inventory, £819.1.4; made by Joseph Burr and John Deacon. Includes books of divinity, navigation and law, £19.0.2.

1747-8, Feb. 17. Woolston, John, of Northampton, Burlington Co., yeoman; will of. My plantation on Leeds Lane divided between my brothers, William and Samuel. Sisters—Ruth Allen, Susannah and Margaret Woolston. Executor—brother, Samuel. Witnesses—Samuel Woolston, Sen'r, Benjamin Pyppit, Gab. Blond. Proved March 8, 1747. Burlington Wills, 4165-8 C.

1750, April 24. Woolston, Joseph, of Northampton, Burlington Co., yeoman. Int. Adm'x, Jane Woolston, widow. Thomas Budd, farmer, and George Briggs, yeoman, both of Nottingham, fellow bondsmen. Lib. 4, p. 16.

1734, Feb. 26. Woolston, Joshua, of Northampton, Burlington Co., yeoman; will of. Daughters—Rebeckah, Ann and Elizabeth; all under age. Real and personal estate. Executors—wife, Ann, and brother Joseph Woolston. Witnesses—Levi Shinn, Will. Allcott, James Wills. Proved March 18, 1733.

1733-4, March 16. Inventory, £126.10.7; made by Philo Leeds and James Wills. Burlington Wills, 2781-8 C.

1747, Feb. 24. Woolverton, Roger, of Hopewell, Hunterdon Co., within the corporation of Trenton, tailor; will of. Wife, Mary. Son, Isaac, a minor, eastern part of plantation in Amwell, whereon Thomas Starling dwells, bounded by lands of testator's brother, Isaac Woolverton. Son, Charles, when of age, other half of plantation in Amwell. Son, Roger, homestead plantation of 160 acres, in Hopewell. Residue to daughters, Rosannah, Mary, Sarah, Dinah, and Rosemand, when 18 or at marriage. Executors—brothers, Charles, Isaac and Dennis Woolverton. Witnesses—Mary Fox, Mary Fowler, Timothy Milburn, Andrew Smith. Proved April 21, 1748. Lib. 5, p. 444.

1748, April 18. Inventory, £132.17.1; made by Andrew Smith, Wilson Hunt.

1734, March 27. Worlidge, Joseph, of Town and Co. of Salem, cordwainer; will of. Wife, Arcadia, executrix. Sons—John and Joseph, two-thirds of personal estate as they arrive at 21. Witnesses—Renier Vanhist, Ann Coxe, William Shields. Proved 13 April, 1734. Lib. 3, p. 407.

1734, April 11. Inventory, £101.13; made by Joseph Hawks, Joseph Woodnutt.

1748-9, March 14. Wouterse, Garrett, of Second River, Essex Co. labourer. Int. Elizabeth Worster, widow, renounces right to administer, and desires that her brother-in-law, Henry Worster, be appointed. Witness—Andrew Joline.

1732, Oct. 24. Bond of Henry Worster, as administrator. James Hindes, fellow bondsman. Witness—Thomas Jackman. Lib. B, p. 305.

1739, 1st day, 6th mo. (Aug.). Worth, Giles, of Windsor, Middlesex Co.; will of. Mother, Sarah Worth. Brothers and sisters—James, Samuel, William, Sarah, Providence, Elizabeth and Ann, 300 acres of land in Bethlehem. Executors—wife, Elizabeth, and brother-in-law Aaron Hews. Witnesses—Thos. Stevenson, D. Humphrey, Elizabeth Cunningham. Proved Oct. 24, 1739. Lib. 4, p. 205.

1748-9, March 14. Wovterse, Garrett, of Second River, Essex Co. Int. Adm'r Hendrick Brine (Birnie), Jun'r, principal creditor. Robert Huston (Hewstone), fellow bondsman. Lib. E, p. 269.

1748, Aug. 18. Wright, Benjamin, of Chesterfield, Burlington Co., yeoman. Int. Mary Wright, widow, relinquishes right of administration, and requests that Peter Rose, of City of Burlington, brewer, be appointed.

1748, Aug. 19. Bond of Peter Rose as administrator. Jonathan Scott, wheelwright, and John Rose, brewer, both of same, fellow bondsmen. Lib. 6, p. 327; Lib. 7, p. 93.

1748, Aug. 22. Inventory, £26.19; made by Judah Williams and Samuel Cheshire.

1747, Jan. 26. Wright, Ebenezer (over 15 years), son of Jonathan, Esq., of Burlington, petitions that William Skeeles, of same place, yeoman, be appointed his guardian. Letters issued. Elias Hughes, fellow bondsman. Burlington Wills, 4171 C.

1737, Jan. 10. Wright, Elizabeth, of Gloucester Co., widow (deceased during minority of Richard Wright, son). Int. Adm'r John Kaighin. Bondsman—Joseph Ellis. Both of Gloucester Co. Lib. 4, p. 126.

1747, April 10. Wright, Empson, of City of Burlington, farmer. Int. Adm'r, Thomas Hartshorne, of Middleton, Monmouth Co., farmer. Samuel Wright, Esq., of Burlington, and Hugh Hartshorne, of City of Burlington, blacksmith, fellow bondsmen. Lib. 5, p. 326.

1747, April 10. Inventory, £340.15.9; made by Ralph Peart and Thos. Scattergood.

1748, Jan. 19. Account. Payments to Doc. Shaw, Mary White (nursing), Abra. Heulings (for coffin), Deborah Wright (nursing), Mary Wright, Benjamin Wheat, Benj'n Butterworth, Jonathan Wright, John Rose, Fretwell Wright, William Norcross, Richard Wright, Thomas Fox, Richard Roberts, Thomas Scattergood, John Pole, Sam'l Lovett, John Imlay, James Cobberly, Wm. Skeels.

1732, Dec. 1. Wright, John, of Burlington Co.; will of. Elizabeth Branson and her son David, that part of the saw mill I had of Thomas Fox. Personal estate of said Thomas Fox to the next six following children of Elizabeth Branson. Son, Samuel, 20 acres adjoining Thomas Earl, late widow Fox and Preserved Brown. Daughter, Mary, under age. Remainder of estate to wife, Abigail. Executors—friends, John Steward and Benjamin Kirby. Witnesses—Tho. Earl, John Marshall, Wm. Cooke. Proved Feb. 13, 1732-3. Lib. 3, p. 301.

1732-3, Jan. 5. Inventory, £356.14.3; made by Wm. Cooke and Will Montgomery. Includes bond payable March 1, 1729, for £100; bond of Rob't Lawrence (£15), and debts of Tho. Fox Estate and Anthony Woodward.

1733, April 30. John Steward and Benjamin Kirby refusing executorship, Abigail Wright, widow, appointed administratrix, with Benjamin Kirby and Silas Crispin of Burlington, taylor, fellow bondsmen.

1736, July 2. Account of Abigail Wright. Paid Ann Lamb, Sarah Cutler, Samuel Wright, Robert Hulitt, Wm. Coates, Thos. Hough, Mathew Champion, Joseph Arney (debt due his father, John Arney), Thos. Leonard, Wm. Cooke, Peter Bard, Thomas Dikes, David Curtis, Preserved Brown, Jun'r, Gilel Faizer, Margaret Stelle, Robert Lawrence, George Harrison, John Ryno, Samuel Lovett, Josiah White, Dan'l Smith, Thos. Harrison. Dubious debts due from Nicholas Mills, dec'd, Nich's Martineaux, who hath been many years removed to a distant colony, Rich'd Croxall, Thos. Fox, deceased, Jon. Wright (legatee), Wm. Webster, Thos. King, Thomas Lovelattey, who ran away, and Thos. Harrison.

1732, Nov. 24. Wright, John, of Amwell Township, Hunterdon Co., blacksmith; will of. Wife, Orka (or Orcha). Children—Harmanus, John, Hannah, William, Elizabeth, Katherine and Affea. Wife, executrix. Witnesses—Daniel Woolverton, Ruth Woolverton, Samuel Green. Proved May 3, 1733. Lib. 3, p. 305.

1732, Dec. 29. Inventory (£159.17.6) includes Bible. Made by John Holcomb and Samuel Green.

1736, Sept. 18. Wright, John, of Newton, Gloucester Co.; will of. Wife, Elizabeth, executrix. Sons—John, the 100 acres he lives on; Richard, personal estate after death of my wife. Witnesses—Tobias Holloway, Thomas Edgerton, Robert Stephens. Affirmed 9 Dec., 1736.

1736, Nov. 29. Inventory, £265.07.2; made by Tobias Holloway, Robert Stephens. Lib. 4, p. 78.

1742, 11th day, 6th mo. (Aug.). Wright, Jonathan, Esq., of City and Co. of Burlington; will of. Eldest son, Fretwell, my tan yard and houses. Sons, Jonathan and Ebenezer, plantation whereon Joseph Woodrow now dwelleth (about 700 acres) and salt marsh bought of Peter Baynton and John Douglass; also lands in little Eggharbour, grist mill in partnership with Patrick Reynolds, and lands bought of Thomas Scott at Wrightstown. Daughters, Esther and Rebecca, two tenements near Yorkshire Bridge, lands and meadows bought of Joshua Raper, and 320 acres in Hunterdon Co., near land I sold Jacob Doughty. Dwelling houses on High Street in possession of Charles Tonkin and Sarah Borradail. Lot on High Street in tenure of Daniel Smith. 260 acres in Hunterdon on Raritan River and on Musconetcong River, at an Old Indian plantation called Whopemenchonhhong. Daughter, Ellen (wife of Isaac Connarro), 300 acres in Gloucester Co. Friend, Martha Milnor, £100 and liberty of house on York Road. Granddaughter, Sarah Connarroe. Friend, Patrick Reynolds, land near Pellock Mile, being land surveyed to us and William Murrels. Land now in possession of Benjamin Butterworth; land at Black River, Morris Co., now in tenure of Aaron Starke, and 50 acres at Tom Roberts' meadow. Negro woman, Nanny, to be free and to be under care of my friend, Samuel Lovett. Executors—Caleb Raper, Samuel Lovett and Joshua Raper. Witnesses—Thomas Wetherill, Joseph Robinson, Jos. Scattergood. Proved Aug. 31, 1742. Lib. 4, p. 345.

1742, Aug. 30. Inventory, £1817.17.10 1.3; made by Thomas Wetherill and Rob. Smith. Includes bonds and bills, £320.5.0½; article with Aaron Starke, Jun'r (£81.6.5); money due on agreement with John Robinson and William Griffith, £69.18.0; also with Jacob Drake, Obadiah Seward, Atkinson, Webster & Southworth; clock, silver tankard, etc., £37.7; large quarto Bible; Denah Bard's note. Debts supposed to be insolvent and not included in inventory—James Stephenson, John Albert, Peter Vantilbury, Richard Ridgway, John Bell, John Hillas, John Bennet, John Oakford, Samuel Shinn, Jonas Cattel, Robert Newbury, Francis Collins, Francis Hickman.

1740, 7th day, 8th mo. (Oct.). Wright, Joshua, of New Hanover, Burlington Co., yeoman; will of. Son, Joshua (has already received his portion). Sons, Mahlon, Nathan and David, land, being dividends of 4th and 5th divisions after payment of 200 acres to Jonathan Wright which I borrowed. Daughters, Elizabeth Knight and Rebecca, 600 acres in Nottingham, which adjoins upon Assunpink at Bear Swamp. Plantation adjoining Joseph Steward's and widow Fowler's as surveyed by Isaac DeCow. 200 acres upon Wading River in Little Eggharbour and 590 acres in Nottingham near the Falls Pond at the mouth of Watson's Creek. Brothers—Robert, Thomas and Samuel Wright, and John Steward, to see that my land is properly divided. 10 grandchildren, £1 each. Wife, Rebeckah, remainder of estate and executrix, with son Mahlon, brother Samuel Wright, and John Steward. Witnesses—John Bower, Jos. Steward, Wm. Emley. Proved March 31, 1741. Lib. 4, p. 274.

1741, March 27. Inventory, £555.15.1; made by Isaac Horner, Benjamin Kirby, Wm. Lawrie, Sam'l Emley.

1744-5, Feb. 20. Wright, Nathan, of Salem Co., yeoman. Int. Adm'x, Sarah Wright, widow. Bondsman—Sinick Sinnickson, Peter Peterson. Witnesses—Daniel Watson, Danl. Mestayer. Lib. 5, p. 179.

1744-5, Feb. 11. Inventory (£117.12.6) includes cattle, colt, carpenter and turning tools and other things in the shop. Appraisers—Sinick Sinnickson, Peter Peterson.

1736, Oct. 30. Wright, Richard, of Woodbridge, Middlesex Co., yeoman; will of. Children—Abner, Jeremiah, Richard, David (a minor), and Mary. Real and personal estate. Executors—wife, Sarah, and Joseph FitzRandolph. Witnesses—Joseph FitzRandolph, Solomon Tharp, Charles Murray. Proved Dec. 5, 1736. Lib. C, p. 133.

1737, Jan. 10. Wright, Richard (above 14), son of Jon. Wright, late of Gloucester Co., yeoman. Guardian—Joseph Ellis, of Newton Township. Bondsman—John Kaighin. Lib. 4, p. 126.

1742, June 27. Wright, Robert, of Chesterfield, Burlington Co., yeoman; will of. Children—Robert, Joshua, James and Jane; all under age. Son-in-law and dau.-in-law, Andrew and Isabel Ware. Real and personal estate. Executors—wife, Jane, brother Samuel, and nephew Amos Wright. Witnesses—Tho. Wright, Empson Wright, Constant Woodward, Elizabeth Wright. Proved July 15, 1742. Lib. 4, p. 327.

1742, May 12. Inventory, £239.4.11; made by Michael Newbold and John Steward.

1742, 30th da., 6th mo. (Aug.). Wright, Stephen, of New Hanover, Burlington Co.; will of. Mother Wright, the dwelling house wherein she dwells, and then to be brother Benjamin's. Rachel Fowler, my wife's wearing clothes. Sons—Benjamin, Nathan and William; all under age. Real and personal estate. Negro boy, Will, to be free at 30. Executors—friend, John Steward, and Will'm Followel. Witnesses—Benja. Fowler, Mahlon Wright, Jos. Reckless. Proved July 23, 1743. Lib. 4, p. 370.

1743, July 23. Inventory, £188.19.8; made by Sam'l Emley and Mahlon Wright. Includes servant man and negro man, £21.

1744-5, Jan. 11. Wright, Thomas, of Salem Co.; will of. Wife, Elizabeth. Son, Nathan, the plantation I live on; in case of no lawful issue it shall go, after his death, to my son Joseph. If my son, Nathan, should have a child or children, then my son, Joseph, shall pay £70 to such child or children. Executor—son, Joseph, and he to have the personal estate. Witnesses—Mary Vanhist, Dennis MacCarty, Ranier Vanhist. Proved 19 April, 1745. Lib. 5, p. 182.

1745, 2 mo. (Apr.), 19. Inventory, £184.14.10; made by Sinick Sinnickson, Jonathan Bradway.

1749, June 22. Wright, Thomas, of Freehold, Monmouth Co., blacksmith; will of. Wife, Priscilla, for bringing up of children. Residue divided between wife and five children, Nancy, Abraham, Mary, Susannah and William. Executors to compound with Mrs. Kerney, widow to John Kerney, of New Brunswick, for time she has in testa-

tor's house and lot at New Brunswick, in order to make sale of it. Executors—wife, and friend Joseph Forman. Witnesses—Jemima Wright, Henry Guest, Benjamin Dassigny. Proved Aug. 29, 1749.
Lib. E, p. 324.

1749, Aug. 25. Inventory (£171.16.8) includes sword and gun, pistol, white servant girl (£5), negro man and negro woman (£55), bond on Samuel Mulford. Made by Henry Guest and Benjamin Dussigney.

1744, Sept. 22. Wright, William, of Salem Co., yeoman. Int. Adm'x, Desir Wright (relict). Bondsman—Samuel Wright and Wm. Siddons, store-keeper, all of said county. Witness—Benjamin Eaton.
Lib. 5, p. 56.

1744, Sept. 18. Inventory, £140.3.1; made by Wm. Siddons, Benj. Easton.

1730, Dec. 19. Wyckof, Jacob, of Six-Mile Run, Somerset Co., yeoman; will of. Wife, Janietje, executrix, and, during widowhood, dwelling house at Six-Mile Run, and one-half of benefits of the house at the ferry, purchased of Samuel Mulford. Son, Cornelius, land situate at the ferry, purchased of Jacob Ouky. Sons, Cornelius, Jacob and Garret, all lands possessed in the Province of New Jersey, after marriage or decease of my executrix. Daughters, Hyntje (wife of Abraham Hyert) and Geertje, £500, "within 15 years after the age of Gerret Wyckof." Executors—son, Cornelius, and John Stryker (in case of marriage or death of wife, Janietje). Witnesses—Samuel Romyn, Yoghorn Willemson, H. N. Sperling. Proved 6 Feb., 1732.
Lib. B, p. 365.

1738, Aug. 26. Wyckoff, Jacob, of Somerset Co.; will of. Wife, Frances. Son, Jacob, all real estate, unless a son should be born, then he to share equally with Jacob; if daughter, she to have suitable education out of my estate, and my son Jacob to pay her £100 at age. Executors—wife, uncle Petrus Wyckof, of Middlebush, and Reynier Fontine, of Middlesex County. Witnesses—Simon Wyckof, Abraham Heyer, Wm. Ouke. Proved 20 Dec., 1738. Lib. C, p. 226.

1738, Dec. 8. Inventory (£207.18.4½) includes negroes, boy Cuff (£42), girl Philis (£35), 3 law books. Appraisers—Elbert Stoothof, Nicholas Willemson, Frederick VanLeave (Van Liew).

1739, Aug. 17. Account. Includes bond of Jor's Bennett and note by John Piatt.

1748, April 27. Frances Pyatt, late Frances Wycof, one of the executors, qualified. Lib. C, p. 228.

1737, May 16. Wycof, Cornelius, of Somerset Co. Int. Adm'r, his brother, Jacob Wycof, the widow, Idae, having renounced her right. Fellow bondsman—Jan. Stryker. Lib. C, p. 161.

1737, May 18. Inventory, £167.6.6; made by Ryneire Fontyn, Willem Willemse, Jun.

1738-9, Feb. 2. Account of goods left out of inventory by Jacob Whycoff, of said County, adm'r, deceased, and sold by Christopher Vanarsdall, adm'r de bonis non, of said County, to Danll. Henderson, Peter Whycoff, Joseph Bennet, Saml. Freeman, Wm. Williamson, Christopher Callowbash, Simon Whicoff, Hendrick Vanangle, Stoffel Vanarsdall, (£14,04.03).

1738-9, March 23. Account of administration of Jacob Wicof, deceased, on estate of Garret Wycof, by executors of said Jacob. Includes cash paid Richd. Pippenger, Renire Fontyne, Jas. Prideaux, Francis Whycof,

Dan'l Hendrickson and Abram. Hiers. Signed by Francis Wicof, Ryniere Fontyne, Peteres Wycof.

1737, May 16. Wycof, Garrit, of Somerset Co. Int. Adm'r, his brother, Jacob. Fellow bondsman—Jan. Stryker. Lib. C, p. 161.

1737, April 27. Inventory, £54.15.6; made by Ryniere Fontyn, Peter Soullard.

1738-9, March 23. Account by Executors of Jacob Wyckoff, administrator, deceased. Payments to Nichos. Williamson, John Manley, Ryniere Fontyne, Peter Soullard, Jacob Ouke, Willim Ouke, Doct. Farquar, Garr't Degrew, Derrick Schuyler, Adrian Hegeman, Altye Stryker, James Harding, Mr. Kimble, Mr. Jas. Hude, Cornelius Whycof's daughter, Abraham Hires, John Whycof, in favour of Cornelius Whycof's (deceased) daughter. Signed by Francis Wicof, Ryniere Fontyne, Peteres Wycof.

1746, Feb. 27. Wykof, Jan (John), of Somerset Co., yeoman; will of. Wife, Neeltie, all real and personal estate in Somerset Co., or elsewhere, during widowhood. Children—Cornelius (eldest), John, Pieter, Jacob, Geertie, Neeltie and Johannes. Sons Pieter and Jacob to have outset at marriage, such as the others had. Executors—sons, Cornelis, John and brother, Symon Wyckoff. Witnesses—Frederick VanLawe (Van Liew), Aert Wyckof, Samuel Garretson. Proved 25 April, 1746. Lib. D, p. 376.

1746, April 26. Inventory (£288.10.6) includes "40 acres of weate" (£30), horses, negro girl (£30). Made by Hendrick Van Lewe and Gerrit Gerritsen.

1738-9, March 15. Wynckoop, Henry, of Salem Co., yeoman. Inventory, £201.18.9; made by William Hunt and John Thomson.

1738-9, Sept. 1. Bond of Sarah Wynckoop and Isaac Vanmeter, both of Salem Co., as administrators. Salem Wills, 602 Q.

1738-9, July 18. Inventory, £127.8.3; made by William Hancock.

1741, June 29. Inventory, £14.13.2; made by Joseph Champneys and Aaron Hill.

1738-9, Jan. 16. Wynn (Wint), John, of Second River, Essex Co. Int. Inventory (£15.06) includes debts due from Ezeciah Barker, Hudson Stevens, Manes Burger, Thomas Shengelton, Warner Richards, Phillip Row, Gysbert VanInburgh, Mrs. Jean Tongerlow, Peter Bayard, John Sidman, Ebenezer Cate, John Foster, Thomas Richards, Cornelis Tomasse, William Dyar, John Cockrinn, John Kip, Richard Doose, Charles Duran, David Poinsett, Jacobus Burgoo, Peter Bras, Robert Kelley, William King, David Andrew; made by Peter Stoutenburgh, John King.

1739, March 27. Adm'x, Johanna Wynn. Daniel Pierson, fellow bondsman. Witnesses—Andrew Joline, Nath'll Bonnell. Lib. C, p. 269.

1738, May 24. Yard, Joseph, of Wellinborough, Burlington Co., bricklayer (who deceased May 1, 1738). Int. Inventory, £242.16.11; made by John Busby and Thomas Busby.

1738, May 25. Adm'x, Susanna Yard, widow. John Busby and Thomas Busby, yeomen, both of same, fellow bondsmen. Lib. 4, p. 138.

1755, Aug. 2. Thomas Busby, surviving appraiser, affirms to inventory.

1747, May 11. Yard, Mary, late Mary Peace, of Hunterdon Co. Int.

Adm'r, William Yard of Trenton, gent. Joseph Yard and Andrew Reed, of Trenton, gents., sureties. Witness—Mary Rowland.
Lib. 5, p. 458.

1742-3, Feb. 12. Yard, William, Sr., of Trenton, Hunterdon Co., innholder; will of. Wife, Mary. Real estate in Hunterdon County to five sons, Joseph, William, John, Benjamin and Jethro, excepting one house and lot. Daughter, Elizabeth. William Justus, eldest son of daughter Elizabeth, one-third of lot on west side of road, adjoining land formerly Joseph Higbee's, in Trenton. Negro wench, Teen, then with Henry Mershon in Maidenhead, to be sold, and one-half proceeds to William Mershon, eldest son of testator's daughter, Mary, deceased; other half to Joseph and Benjamin Mershon, sons of said daughter Mary. Lands in Morris County to be sold. Executors—sons, Joseph and William Yard. Witnesses—Joseph De Cow, Andrew Reed, David Cowell. Proved July 3, 1745. Lib. 5, p. 127.

1749, April 20. Young, James, of Lebanon Township, Hunterdon Co. Int. Adm'r, Andrew Palmer, of Lebanon. John Burroughs, of Trenton, farmer, surety. Witness—Neil Livingston.
Hunterdon Wills, 273 J.

1738, March 25. Young, Johannes, of Somerset Co. Int. Adm'r, Samuel Stockton, Esq., of Somerset, the widow, Elmary, having renounced her right. Witness—Zebulon Stout. Fellow bondsman—Benjamin Price, of Middlesex. Lib. C, p. 190.

1749, 3d mo. (May), 20th. Young, Joseph, of Greenwich Township, Gloucester Co., yeoman; will of. Executors—Francis Eastlack and Joshua Lord. 420 ft. square around the graves in my garden to my daughter, Ame Yong, to remain a burying-place for my children and their children's children forever. Wife, Elizabeth, £60 in lieu of dower, and the home plantation (under care of the executors) so long as she remains my widow. Daughter, Ame Yong, to possess the same when clear from the incumbrance of my wife, provided she will be 18. Said place to be appraised and the value divided equally among all my daughters—Mary, Martha, Susannah, Phebe and Ame, as they come to age. Witnesses—Garrat Dewees, Henry Treadway, William Hanby. Proved 22 March, 1749-50. Lib. 6, p. 299.

1749-50, 1st mo. (Mar.), 13, 14. Inventory (£167.09.4½) includes small Bibles and other books (£1.03), cattle (£47.15.0), market boat and rigging, canoe. Appraisers—Wm. Wilkins, Solomon Lippincott.

1750-1, March 1. Yourison, Lawrence, of Penns Neck, Salem Co. Int. Adm'x, Mary Yourison, (widow). Bondsmen—Samuel Capner, Joseph Hawks, all of said Co.

1751, ——. —. Inventory, £132.19.4; made by Joseph Wright, Samuel Copner. Salem Wills, 929 Q.

1732, Oct. 4. Zane, Elnathan, of Gloucester Co., yeoman. Int. Adm'r, Nathaniel Zane, of said County, yeoman. John Kaighin and Amos Ashead, yeoman, both of Haddonfield, fellow bondsmen.
Lib. 3, p. 138.

1732, Oct. 14. Inventory (Newton Township), £66.7.3; made by John Kaighin, Sam'l Clement.

1750, Feb. 12. Zane, Jonathan, of Gloucester Co., merchant, guardian of Mary Bates (above 14 years), daughter of William Bates, late of Gloucester Co. Lib. 6, p. 375.

APPENDIX

Abstracts of Some Wills Referred to in Preceding Volume of Wills, but not Fully printed therein.

[NOTE.—The following abstracts of wills are, with an exception or two, noted in the preceding volume of "Wills of New Jersey" ("N. J. Archives," Vol. XXIII), but without the usual abstract of each being given. Instead, reference is made to a preceding volume of the "Archives" (Vol. XXI) for such abstract. This obliges those consulting Vol. XXIII to hunt up Vol. XXI in order to secure the information. As various possessors of Vol. XXIII, including some public libraries, have not Vol. XXI to which to refer, it has been thought advisable to incorporate in this Appendix the abstracts omitted from Vol. XXIII, in order that the two volumes of wills shall actually contain all Abstracts from 1670 to 1750.

These Abstracts have been carefully looked up and copied by Mr. Frederick A. Canfield, of Dover, one of the officers of the New Jersey Historical Society. In printing them herewith an alphabetical arrangement has been followed; also some verbal condensation has been employed, without, however, disturbing the facts.

The references given are to the original records, viz., East Jersey Deeds (E. J. D.) and West Jersey Records (W. J. R.). If sought for in Volumes XXI or XXIII of the New Jersey Archives, consult the Indices therein.—EDITOR.]

1710, Oct. 2. Ackerman, David, Sr., of Hackinsack; will of. Wife, Hillegond. Children—David, Johannes, Mary. Hereditary right in property in New York to daughter; grist-mills, saw-mills and lands to sons. Witnesses—Albert Stevensen, Lourens Van Boskerck, Jan Terhunen. Proved June 4, 1724. Unrecorded Wills, Vol. 1, pp. 147-152.

1694, Nov. 17. Aires, Obadiah, Sr., of Woodbridge; will of. Sons—Samuel, John, Joseph, Obadiah; dau. Mary. Real and personal estate. Executors—eldest sons John and Samuel. Witnesses—Ephr., Andrew, John Pike.

1694, Dec. 6. Letters issued to executors named.

E. J. D., Lib. E, pp. 140-142.

1702, Sept. 11. Baker, John, of Elizabethtown; will of. Wife, Agnes. Sons—Richard, Thomas, Derrick. Grandsons—John, Ebenezer, sons of Ebenezer Spining of Elizabethtown, dec'd. Daughter, Frances. Elizabeth, wife of son Derrick. Real and personal property. Executors—wife and son Derrick. Witnesses—Samuel Whitehead, Roger Lambert, John Littell. Proved Sept. 24, 1702.

1702, Sept. 30. Administration granted to executors.

E. J. D., Lib. C, pp. 239, 411.

1686, Aug. 30. Barker, Edward, of London, citizen and merchant tailor; will of. Children—Edward and Elizabeth. "Goods and chattels." Servants—Robert Bull, Jeremy Awdrey, maid Jane Sannum, legatees. Executors—father, Henry Barker, and father-in-law, John Pennyman, citizen and merchant tailor, both of London. Witnesses—Storie (?) Barker, John Tatham, James Gibson.

1686, Oct. 9. Letters testamentary with will annexed, issued to executors named, by the Archbishop of Canterbury. (In Latin).

E. J. D., Lib. F, pp. 619, 620.

1695, Sept. 8. Barre, James, of New York, about to sail for the Island of Barbados; will of. Wife, Mary. Children—James, Charles and Mary. Real and personal estate. The wife executrix. Witnesses—Robert Blackwell, William Lawrence, Johannes Lawrence, Daniel Lawrence. Proved at Perth Amboy May 12, 1696.

1696, May 22. Letters issued to the widow, Mary Barre.

E. J. D., Lib. E, pp. 505, 506.

1694, Nov. 15. Binglay, John; nuncupative will of, made before Nathaniel Fitzrandolph, senior and junior, and Sarah Parker, who was to become his wife, father, brother William and sister. Proved December 18, 1694.

1694-5, Jan. 28. Administration granted to his father, William Binglay of Woodbridge. E. J. D., Lib. E, p. 175.

1678-9, Feb. 16. Blomfeild, Thomas, Jr., of Woodbridge; will of. Bequeathes lands at Woodbridge and personal property to brother, Ezekiel Blomfeild; to aged father and mother; to cousin Elisabeth, dau. of John Dennis; to cousins Jonathan and David Dunham, sons of brother-in-law Jonathan Dunham; to brother Nathaniel Blumfield; to cousin John Dennis; to cousin Samuel Dennis; to cousin William Thornton; to "my boy," Mathew Moore; to brother John Blumfield. Executor, brother Ezekiel. Witnesses—Ephraim Andross, Samuel Hale.

1679, April 7. Inventory made by Samuel Dennis and Jonathan Dunham (£267.10.8). E. J. D., Lib. 3, p. 163.

1694, Nov. 6. Bond, Steven; will of. Children—Joseph and Hannah; widow Elizabeth Ogdan; brother Benjamin Bond. Real and personal estate. Executors—John Curtis and Jonathan Ogdan. Witnesses—Zophar Beech, Elizabeth Baldwin, John Curtis. Codicil mentions Benjamin Trotter. Proved Nov. 21, 1694.

1694-5, Jan. 2. Letters issued to executors named.

E. J. D., Lib. E, pp. 148, 149.

1689, Apr. 1. Broadwell, William, of Elizabeth Town; will of. Wife, Mary. Sons—John, William, Richard. Real and personal estate. The wife executrix. Witnesses—Robert Traverse, Edward Gay. (For inventory, etc., see N. J. Archives, Vol. XXIII, p. 61).

1690-1, Jan. 27. Letters granted to widow. E. J. D., Lib. D, p. 142.

1694, Oct. 20. Brown, Joseph, of Newark; will of. Wife, Hannah. Sons—Joseph, Stephen, James, Samuel. Daughters—Hannah, Mary, Sarah. Real and personal estate. The wife executrix, with brothers John and Thomas Brown as overseers. Witnesses—John Brown, Daniel Dod, Thomas Brown. Proved November 21, 1694.

1694-5, Jan. 5. Letters issued to the widow, Hannah Brown.

E. J. D., Lib. E, pp. 149, 151.

1698, Dec. 28. Browne, William, of Woodbridge; will of. John

Browne of Staten Island, John Moore, George Browne. Personal property. George Browne executor. Witnesses—Adam Hude, George Browne. Proved February 23, 1698-9.

1699, May 18. Letters issued to George Browne, of Woodbridge.

E. J. D., Lib. G, p. 2.

1696, June 9. Brymson, Daniel, of Milston River; nuncupative will of. Declared before Mary Davis, Sarah Gannett, Jonathan Davis and Samuel Davis. Wife Frances Brymson, dau. of Dr. Greenland; son Barefoot; eldest dau. Ruth, and apparently other children. Real and personal property. Proved Sept. 15, 1696.

1696, Sept. 26. Letters issued to the widow, Frances Brymson.

E. J. D., Lib. F, pp. 44, 45.

1672-3, March 19. Camfeild, Mathew; will of. Wife mentioned but not by name. Sons—Samuel, Ebinezar, Mathew, Jonathan. Daughters —Mary, Hannah, Ruth, Sarah. Lands at Norwack already given to son Samuel; other lands next to Sergeant Ward's, to Goodman Waters, to Mr. Pierson on Robard's Neck, at Wheeler's Point. Executors— the wife, brother Deten Tompkins, brother Henry Lion and son Mathew. Witnesses—John Brown, senior, and Tho. Pierson, senior. Proved June 1, 1673.

1673, June 11. Inventory made by John Brown and John Ward (£324.4.3).

1673, June 30. Administration granted to his widow, Sarah.

E. J. D., Lib. 3, pp. 88-90.

———, ———, —. Campbell, Archibald; will of. Names John Campbell as heir and executor, and leaves a legacy to Elizabeth Swan. Statement of debts due by Edwards, Richard Clarke, William Ridford, John Collins, and due to Elisha Parker, Miles Forster, John Barclay, James More, John Lee, John McCalm, George Cumins and Alexander Thomson. Personal estate. Witnesses—James More, John Foreman, Gawin Lockhart. Proved May 12, 1702.

1702, May 15. Administration issued to John Campbell.

E. J. D., Lib. C, p. 202.

1694, Nov. 11. Canfield, Ebenezer, of Newark; will of. Wife ———; son Joseph; dau. Rachel; brother Mathew Canfield mentioned. Real and personal estate. The wife executrix, with Mathew Canfield and Joseph Harison as overseers. Witnesses—John Lindsly, William Muir, Mathew Canfield. Proved Nov. 21, 1694.

1694-5, Jan. 5. Letters issued to the widow, Bathia Camfield.

E. J. D., Lib. E, pp. 152, 153.

1684-5, Jan. 31. Canfield, Jonathan; will of. Brothers—Eabenezer, Mathew, Samuel. Sisters—Sarah, Mary. Real and personal property. Witnesses—John Couch and William Shoores. Proved Dec. 5, 1688. (See also N. J. Archives, Vol. XXIII, p. 81). E. J. D., Lib. D, p. 24.

1682, Dec. 10. Carteret, Philipp, of Elizabethtown; will of. Wife Elizabeth; mother Rachel Carteret; brothers and sisters, not named. Lands in New Jersey and the Island of Jersey. Executrix—the wife, with Thomas Rudyard and Robert Vicars of Elizabethtown. Witnesses—Robert Vicars, Isaac Swinton, James Emott, George Jewell, Marth Symco.

1682, Dec. 30. Administration granted to his widow, Elizabeth.

E. J. D., Lib. A, pp. 17, 18.

1689, Oct. 15. Clark, Benjamin, of Amboy, merchant; will of. Son, Benjamin. Real and personal estate. Executor—Benjamin Griffith of Woodbridge. Witnesses—Jon. and Margaret Carrington.

1690, Dec. 11. Letters issued to Benjamin Griffith. (See also N. J. Archives, Vol. XXIII, p. 93). E. J. D., Lib. D, p. 93.

1697, Apr. 1. Clerke, Richard, of Elizabeth Town; will of. Wife, Elizabeth. Sons—Richard, John, Joshua, Samuel, Ephraim, Thomas, Benjamin. Real and personal estate. Executors—the wife and son Richard. Witnesses—William Janeway, John Glasbrooke, Mary Baker. Proved in New York, April 15.

1697, May 3. Letters with will attached issued to executors named. (For inventory, see N. J. Archives, Vol. XXIII, p. 95).

E. J. D., Lib. F, p. 281.

1671, Feb. 5. Coerten, Guert, from Voorthuysen in Guelderlant, now living at Bergen; will of (in Dutch). Made before Claes Arentsen Toers, constable of Bergen. Annuls testament made with his wife Geertje Jacobs Dueunaers January 15, 1657, because she has been unfaithful; also testament of March 24, 1664; and names as legatees the son of his sister, Pieter Hessélse, brother Thomas Jurianses, oldest son Ryckje Harmens, Mathys Hendricksen Smack, oldest son of Guertje Harmens, his brother's daughter, Jan Harmensen, brother's son, Christyntje Claes, dau. of Claes Christiansen, universal heir brother Harmen Coerten. E. J. D., Lib. 3, p. 146.

1694, Oct. 2. Compton, William, of Woodbridge. Int. Testimony of Edward Watson and Richard Smith and wife Ellener concerning the intentions expressed by William Compton of Woodbridge, who died Friday night, Sept. 21, 1694. Mentions a wife and sons—Jonathan, John, William, David.

1694, Oct. 2. Letters issued to his widow, Mary, and to Jonathan Compton. E. J. D., Lib. E, p. 143.

1678, Oct. 1. Craine, Jasper, of Newark; will of. Sons—John, Azeriah, Jasper. Daughter Hannah, wife of Thomas Huntington. Children of dau. Bell. Real and personal property. (A silver bowl, a silver cup). Executors—son John, and son-in-law Thomas Huntington. Witnesses—John Ward, senior, and Michell Tompkinse.

1681, Oct. 28. Inventory made by John Ward and Thomas Pierson (£289. 19s. 6d.).

1681, Nov. 15. Administration granted to John Craine and Thos. Huntington. E. J. D., Lib. 3, pp. 173, 174.

1694, Nov. 4. Crane, John, Sr., 59 years old; will of. Wife ———. Sons—John, Jasper, Daniel. Daughter, Sarah. Real and personal estate. The wife executrix, with John Prudden, senior, and Elder John Brown as overseers. Witnesses—Nathaniel Ward, George Harrison. Proved November 21, 1694.

1694-5, Jan. 5. Letters issued to the widow, Hanna Crane.

E. J. D., Lib. E, pp. 151, 152.

1694, Nov. 3. Denison, John; 40 years old; will of. Son of Robert Denison and wife Esther. Sisters—Esther, Hannah and Sarah, and children of dec'd sister Mary. Cousins, by Robert Douglas, viz.——John, Esther and Samuel. Real and personal estate. Executor—the mother and cousin, John Brown. Witnesses—John Prudden, John Curtis. Proved November 21, 1694.

1694-5, Jan. 5. Letters issued to the mother, Hester Dennison, and John Brown. E. J. D., Lib. E, pp. 153, 154.

1689, Aug. 26. Desmarett, David, of Essex Co., yeoman and miller; will of. Sons—John, David, and Samuel. Maid, Anna Counk, legatee of 100 acres. Real and personal property. Executors—the sons. Witnesses—Paull Richards, Giles Grandineau, Peter D'Lattoy. Proved July 30, 1697.

1697, Aug. 18. Letters issued to executors named.

E. J. D., Lib. F, pp. 400, 401.

1679, May 10. Dunham, Benaiah, of Piscataway, weaver; will of. (See N. J. Archives, Vol. XXIII, p. 146).

1684, Jan. 14. Notice. Jonas Wood and wife Elizabeth, late widow of Benaiah Donham, refuse to take the executorship of Benaiah Donham's estate.

1684-5, ——. Administration granted to son, Edmund.

E. J. D., Lib. A, pp. 181, 182.

1691-2, Jan. 23. Falconar, Patrick, of Newark; will of. Wife, Hannah, sole heiress and executrix, with father William Jones and brother John Jones as assistants, and brother James Falconar and James Emmett as overseers. Legacies to Abraham Peirson, teacher to the church at Newark, and his daughter Abigail. Real and personal property (land in N. Y., L. I., N. J. and on West side of the Hudson). Witnesses—John Browne, Robert Yongs, David Herriot. Proved Feb. 27, following.

1691-2, Feb. 27. Letters issued to the widow, Hannah.

E. J. D., Lib. D, pp. 339, 340.

1684-5, Feb. 9. Fletcher, Richard, of Newark; will of. Bequeathes personal property to Samuel Denison, Daniel Titchinor and John Curtis, and "the rest of my estate to those persons that brought me home out of the woods." Executor—John Curtis. Witnesses—John Curtis, John Browne, jun. Proved Sept. 5, 1685.

1684-5, March 9. Administration granted to John Curtis.

E. J. D., Lib. A, pp. 198, 180.

1689, Nov. 22. Forrest, Henry, late of Dublin, Ireland, now of Woodbridge, merchant; will of. Wife, Margaret. Son, John. Son-in-law, William Wolmore. Sister, Ellenor Francklen, who has son Joseph Francklen of Cork, Ireland, merchant. Mathew Moore and wife of Woodbridge, Capt. John Bischop, Nathaniel Fitzrandolph and Samuel Dennis, all of Woodbridge, apprentice boy John Markfeat. Personal estate. Executors—Capt. John Stuart of Barbadoes and Samuel Dennis. Witnesses—James Moore, Bartholomew Doud, Samuel Dennes. Proved Dec. 10, 1689. E. J. D., Lib. D, p. 110.

1693, Nov. 7. Frasey, Joseph, Jr.; nuncupative will of. Brothers Edward and William, and three younger ones; sister Mary. Real and personal estate. Witnesses—Mary Bishop and Francis Moore. Proved same day.

1693, Dec. 21. Letters issued to Joseph Frasey, Senior, of Elizabeth Town. E. J. D., Lib. E, p. 80.

1678, July 27. Fredericksen, Thomas, 67 years old; will of. (In Dutch). Wife, Maritje Ariansen, 50 yrs. old, of Bergen. Children—Frederick Tomassen, 31 yrs., Arien Tomassen, 27 yrs., Franscyntje T., 25 yrs., Cornelis T., 19 yrs., Catarin T., 15 yrs., Johannes T., 12 yrs., Jannetje T., 9 yrs., Thomas T., 6 yrs. E. J. D., Lib. 3, p. 148.

1675, June 14. Freeman, Stephen, of Newark; will of. Wife, Hannah; son, Samuel. Daughters—Hannah, Mary, Martha and Sarah.

Executors—Deacon Michel Tomkins and Lieut. Ward. Witnesses—Obediah Bruen and John Baldwin, jun.

1675, Oct. 22. Inventory, £554.19.4.

1675, Oct. 22. Administration granted to the widow, Hannah Freeman. E. J. D., Lib. 3, pp. 119, 120.

1682, Aug. 21. Groom, Samuel, Sr., of Ratcliffe, Middlesex Co. (England), mariner; will of. Wife, Elizabeth. Children—Susan, Samuel, Elizabeth Braine, Margaret Heathcott and Mary Taylor. Real estate in Ratcliffe and Lymehouse, England. Executors—wife and son. Witnesses—Ewseping Sheppard, Henry Philipps, John Allsop, servant, John Brooks, servant. Probated at London, March 1, 1683-4.

1683-4, March 10. Power of attorney. Samuel Groom, son, and Elizabeth, widow, of Samuel Groom, dec'd, to Gawen Lawry, Deputy Governour of East New Jersey, and George Heathcott of Ratcliffe, Parish of Stebonheath, alias Stepney, now of New York, to manage estate in America. E. J. D., Lib. A, pp. 122, 126.

1688, Dec. 7. Grover, Joseph, of Midletoun; will of. Son James; wife Hannah; an expected child; daughters mentioned, but not named. Real and personal property. Executors—wife and her brother, William Lawrence, junior. Witnesses—Peter Tilton, William Lawrence, Daniel Aplegate, William Leeds. Proved March 26, 1689.

1690, March 27. Letters issued to executors.
E. J. D., Lib. D, pp. 88, 91.

1685, Dec. 31. Guthrie, Samuel, of Woodbridge; will of. Sick at the house of Richard Paull in Woodbridge. David Vilant, sole heir and executor. Witnesses—John Allance, John Watkins.

1686, May 10. Administration issued to David Vilant of Amboy Perth. E. J. D., Lib. A, p. 265.

1688, June 17. Gyles, James, of Piscataway; will of. Wife, Elizabeth; son Matthew. Daughters—Eliza Olden, Anne Gyles, Mary Booth. Real and personal estate. Executors—the wife and son (-in-law?) William Olden, with Edward Slater as overseer. Witnesses—Edward Slater, William Sharpe. Proved 3d Tuesday of March, 1690.

1690, July 25. Administration on estate of Major James Gyles of Raraton River, granted to Mathew Gyles, the executors having refused to act. E. J. D., Lib. D, pp. 201, 203.

1690-1, Jan. 7. Hall, Jonas, of Shrosberry; will of. Son, James; friends, Eliza Hutton, William Goodbody, Francis Jeffry, George Hewlett, Samuel Dennes, John Tucker. Real and personal estate. John Tucker, residuary legatee and executor. Witnesses—Samuel Dennes, George Hewlett.

1691, Feb. 13. Letters to John Tucker, the executor named.
E. J. D., Lib. D, pp. 268, 269.

1696-7, Jan. 21. Hamilton, Andrew, of the Parish of St. Anne's, Westminster, Doctor in phisick; will of. Wife, Ann Dusancier; half brother, Charles Murray, Lady Ann Hamilton of Kister (?) holme, Parish of Kilbright, Clisdeall Shire, Scotland, Watkinson Taylor of said Parish of St. Anne's, William Graham of London, Capt. James Hamilton, John Cathcart of London, George Clerke of the Parish of St. Martin's in the Fields, Middlesex Co., Elizabeth, daughter of said George Clarke. Real estate in the City and Republic of Geneva and in Scotland; personal property. Executor—George Clarke. Witnesses—

Richard Duke, George Cadge, Edmund Bell, N. P., in St. James Market St.

1696-7, Jan. 26. Letters issued to George Clarke. (In Latin).

E. J. D., Lib. F, pp. 714, 715.

1678, March 25. Harmensen, Douwe, 54 years old; will of. (In Dutch). Wife, Dirkie Teunissen Outkoop, 54 years old, of Bergen. Sons—Harmen Douwessen, 21 yrs. old and Teunis Douwesen, 12 yrs. old. E. J. D., Lib. 3, p. 144.

1684, April 19. Hartfield, Mathias; will of. Wife and children spoken of, but not by name. Witnesses—George Ross, Humphrey Spinige. Proved December 13, 1687. E. J. D., Lib. B, p. 306.

1686-7, March 14. Havens, John, of Shroesberry; will of. Wife, Anna. Sons, William, John, Nicholas, Daniel. Sons-in-law, George Axtone, who has son John (?), and Thomas Wainright. Land at Sessoconneta and Little Silver. Executors—son William and son-in-law Thomas Wainright. Witnesses—Nicholas Brown and Edmond Laffetra. Proved Nov. 22, 1687. E. J. D., Lib. B, p. 229.

1688, Nov. 14. Johnson, William, Sr., of Elizabeth Town; will of. Sons—John, Daniel, Samuel, Benjamin, William, Henry. Daughters—Kathren, Hannah, Abigall. Real estate devised not to be sold from the name and generation of Johnson; personal property. Executors—Jeffry Jones and Nathaniel Tutle. Witnesses—Thomas Mullinex, Jeffry Jones. Proved October 12, 1699.

1697-8, Jan. 29. Cape May. Affidavit of Hannah, wife of Henry Leonard of Cape May, daughter of William Johnson (above) and formerly wife of Joseph Holden, concerning the preceding will and why it was not proved earlier, her father having died May 14, 1689; mentions Elizabeth as her mother's name, and threats against the mother by son William, a neighbour Simon Rouse in Elizabeth and Nicholas Martineau of Burlington. E. J. D., Lib. G, pp. 17, 18.

1683-4, Feb. 11. Kitchell, Samuel, of Newark; will of. Wife Grace, sons Samuel and Abraham, daughters Elizabeth Tompkins, Abigail Ward, Mary Kitchell, Bethia Kitchell, Grace Kitchell, Susannah Kitchell; the wife executrix; brother-in-law Abraham Pierson and friend John Browne, jun., overseers and witnesses. Proved June 20, 1690. [Erroneously entered as will of William Kitchell, in Vol. XXIII, of N. J. Archives].

1690, June 13. Administration granted to Patrick Falckener of Newark, the executrix named having died before the testator.

E. J. D., Lib. D, p. 174.

1692-3, Jan. 29. Lawrence, Sarah, of Newark; will of. Cousins—Esther Brown, Joseph Brown, Joseph Bond, Bethia Bond. Sister, ——— Brown. John and Isaack, sons of friend George Harrison, Silvester Cent. Personal property. Executor—George Harrison. Witnesses—Samuel Ross, George Harrison. Proved Feb. 1 following.

1694-5, Feb. 9. Letters issued to executor.

E. J. D., Lib. D, p. 368; Lib. E, p. 198.

1687, Aug. 12. Lawrie, Gawen, late Governour of East Jersey; will of. Brother, Arthur Lawrie. Sister Christian's children, sister Agnes' children, George and John Watt, John Swinton of Swinton, Henry Stoutt, Richard Thomas, Thomas Burr of Hartford, children of deceased son James Lawrie, of daughter Mary Haig, of daughter Rebecca Foster. Executors—George and John Watt, with Francis Campfield and Robert Barclay assistants. Witnesses—William Haig, Miles Foster, Charles Soddon.

1687, Aug. 15. Last Will and Testament of Gawen Lawrie disposes of the real estate to wife Mary and daughters Mary Haig and Rebecca Foster. Executors—the wife, with the assistance of William Haig and Miles Foster.

1687, Oct. 20. Administration on the estate of Gawen Lawrie granted to his widow Mary. E. J. D., Lib. B, p. 137.

1683, Nov. 3. Leagey, William, of Elizabethtown; will of. Provides only for payment of testator's debts to the executor, Thomas Johnson, and gives surplus to friend Benjamin Wade. Witnesses—Benj. Wade, George Jewell. Proved January 25, 1683-4.

1683-4, March 5. Administration granted to Thomas Johnson.

E. J. D., Lib. A, pp. 67, 68.

1694-5, Jan. 9. Lee, Thomas, of Elizabethtown; will of. Children—Bennone, John, Mary, Anna, Abigail. Personal property. Executors—John Litle, Aron Thomson and Nathaniel Tutill. Witnesses—John Harrick, John Erskin. Proved May 28, 1695.

1695, July 1. Letters issued to John Litle; of the other executors named, one had died, the other refused to act.

E. J. D., Lib. E, pp. 218, 219.

1694, Oct. 23. Lyon, John, of Elizabeth Town; will of. Now at Burlington. Wife, Hannah. Four children and a fifth expected. Real and personal estate. The wife executrix. Witnesses—Thomas Peachee, John Petty, James Hill. Proved November 2, 1694.

1694-5, Jan. 14. Letters issued to the widow, Hannah Lyon.

E. J. D., Lib. E, pp. 156, 157.

1681-2, Feb. 9. Masters, Francis, of Shrewsbury; will of. Wife, Mary. Children—Clemens, Poolemah, Mary, Cobas Vogden. The wife, Joseph Parker, and Abiah Edwards executors, and the last two witnesses. Proved July 24, 1684.

1684, Aug. 24. Administration granted to Mary and Clemens Masters.

1684, Aug. 24. Bond of Mary Masters, widow, and Clement Masters as executors. Willum Whitelock, of Middletown, planter, fellow bondsman. E. J. D., Lib. A, pp. 140, 141.

1690, Dec. 9. Meaker, William, of Elizabeth Town; will of. Wife Hannah. Sons Joseph, Benjamin, John. Eleven grandchildren. Real and personal estate. Executors—sons Joseph and Benjamin. Witnesses—John Harriman, Jonathan Ogden.

1691, Jan. 15. Letters granted to Joseph and Benjamin Meaker.

E. J. D., Lib. D, pp. 256, 257.

1687, Dec. 30. Mitchell, Mary, widow of James, of Elizabeth; will of. Sons John, Jacob, William, Nathaniel. Executor—Andrew Hamptone, tailor. Witnesses—Stewen Crane, Edward Gay.

1688, April 12. Administration granted to Andrew Hamptone.

E. J. D., Lib. B, p. 355.

1702, April 9. Morris, Dennes, of Elizabeth Town; will of. Wife, Jane. Sons—John, Dennes. Daughters—Deborah, Mary. Real and personal estate. The wife executrix. Witnesses—George Pack, John Bishop. Proved May 8, 1702. Administration to the widow, May 15.

E. J. D., Lib. C, p. 205.

1688-9, Jan. 22. Morris, George, of Elizabeth Town; will of. Wife

Abigall, sons George, John, Benjamin; Henry Morris mentioned as a neighbour. Real and personal property. The wife executrix. Witnesses—Isaac Whitehead, Henry Lyon.

1692, April 11. Letters granted to the widow, Abigall Morris.

E. J. D., Lib. D, pp. 280, 281.

1690-1, Feb. 12. Morris, Colonel Lewis, of New York; will of. Made at his plantation over against Haerlem. Wife, Mary, sole executrix; vice, nephew Lewis, son of dec'd brother Richard Morris. Legacies to Friends' Meeting of Shrewsbury and of New York Province, Thomas Webley of Shrewsbury, William Penn, William Bickly, William Richardson, Samuel Palmer, John Adams of Flushing, L. I., John Bowne of Flushing, Miles Forster; nephew, Lewis Morris, the principal heir. Real and personal property (includes gold and silver ware). Executrix—the wife, with Richard Jones and Miles Forster, of New York, John Bowne, of Flushing, William Richardson of Westchester, Richard Hartshorne and John Hance of Monmouth Co., William Bickley of Westchester C., as overseers. No witnesses. Examined in N. Y., May 15, 1691.

1691, May 15. Administration on the estate of Colonel Lewis Morris of Bronk's Land, Westchester Co., N. Y., granted by Gov'r Henry Sloughter of New York, to the nephew of Lewis Morris, as next of kin, the widow named as executrix having died, on the testimony of David Lilly and Susanna Roberts, two subscribing witnesses.

E. J. D., Lib. E, pp. 183, 188.

1694, July 12. Osborne, Stephen, of Elizabethtown; will of. Wife, Sarah. Sons—Jeremiah, Josiah. Daughters—Mary, wife of Joseph Frasey; Sarah, wife of John Cramer; Martha, Rebecca and Abigail. Real and personal property. Son, Jeremiah, executor, with brothers Joseph Osborn and Josiah Stanbrough as overseers. Witnesses—Elizabeth Stanbrough, Jas. Stanbrough, senior, Josiah Stanbrough, junior. Proved July 20, 1698.

1698, Sept. 5. Letters issued to Jeremiah Osborne.

E. J. D., Lib. F, p. 632.

———, ——, —. Peirce, Daniel, Sr., of Woodbridge; will of. Draft of will of Daniel Peirce, senior, of Woodbridge, disposing of real and personal property to his daughter and her children, to which the son, Capt. Daniel Peirc, gives his consent September 29, 1681.

E. J. D., Lib. E, p. 44.

1671, Aug. 10. Pierson, Abraham, of Newark; will of. Wife, Abigail. Daughters—Devenporte, Mary and two others not named. Sons—Abraham, Thomas, Theophilus, Isaac. Executors—Jasper Crane, Robert Treat, Lieut. Swaine, brother Tomkins, brother Lawrence, brother Serjant Ward. Witness—Thomas Pierson. Proved March 12, 1678.

1678-9, March 12. Inventory made by John Ward, Michel Tompkins and Thomas Pierson (£854.17.7).

1678-9, March 18. Administration granted Abigail Pierson, the widow.

E. J. D., Lib. 3, pp. 153-155.

1697-8, Jan. 12. Pierson, Thomas, Sr., of Newark; will of. Children—Samuel, Thomas (youngest son), Hannah, Abigail, Mary, Elizabeth. Real and personal estate. Son, Samuel Lyon, executor. Witnesses—Zophar Beech, Jonathan Tichnar, Benjamin Lyon. Proved March 3, 1700-1.

1701, May 1. Letters issued to Samuel Lyon, of Newark.

E. J. D., Lib. G, pp. 278, 279.

1690-1, Jan. 17. Reus, Alse, living "upon Raway;" will of. Leaves all to her kinswoman, Sarah Maninge of Boston, New England, with legacies to Frances, dau. of Samuel Moore of Woodbridge. Executors—John Herryman, preacher, and Jonathan Ogden, planter, both of Elizabeth Town. Witness—Dr. William Robinson.

1690, Sept. 10. Administration granted to executors named.

E. J. D., Lib. D, pp. 215, 225.

1683, Sept. 2. Reus, Simon; will of. Leaves all to his wife, not named, with provision for John Looker. Witnesses—Thomas Mullinax, John Mills, James Mash. Proved April 24, 1689.

E. J. D., Lib. D, p. 215.

1685, Nov. 27. Rig, William, aboard "Henry and Frances of New Castle;" will of. Son of Thomas Rig of Athorny, dec'd. Names as heirs, children of brothers Walter and James Rig of Scotland, Eupham Scott, dau. of George Scott of Pitlockey, dec'd., Rev. Archibald Riddall, James, son of said George Scott. Witnesses—James Dundas, brother of the Laird of Armestonn, James Hutchinson, apothecary, and John Fraser, writing-master. Proved February 9, 1685-6.

E. J. D., Lib. A, p. 238.

1670-1, Feb. 26. Roberts, Hugh, of Newark; will of. Wife, Mary. Sons—Samuel (eldest) and Hugh (youngest). Eldest daughter Priscilla, wife of Joseph Osburn. Executors—Robert Treat, Henry Lyon and Sargent John Ward. Witness—Robert Treat.

1671, Nov. 17. Inventory made by Michell Tomkins and Thomas Johnson. E. J. D., Lib. 3, pp. 49, 50.

1693, May 18. Robleson (Robertson), Dr. William; will of. Wife, Margaret. Children—Ann Wynnings, William, Elizabeth, Mary. Real and personal estate. Executors—the wife and Benjamin Griffith. Witnesses—John Barclay, James Walker, John Luefbourrow. Proved June 3, 1693.

1693, July 20. Letters to the executors named.

E. J. D., Lib. E, pp. 41, 42.

1680, Sept. 1. Rogers, Robert, of Woodbridge; will of. Wife, Anne. Sons—Thomas, John. Son-in-law, Henry Allword. Real and personal estate. The wife executrix, with Ephraim Andrise and Samuel Dennes as assistants. Witnesses—John Dennes, Samuel Haile, John Wilkines. Proved June 15, 1686. E. J. D., Lib. B, p. 463.

1698, May 31. Roos (Rose), Samuel, of Newark; will of. Wife, Mary. Cousins—Hannah Brant, Sarah Moris, Abigall Ball, Phebie Day. Daughters-in-law, Abigall Bunell, Hannah Carter. Personal property. The wife executrix, with George Harrison as assistant. Witnesses—Robert Young, Jonathan Sergint, Jonathan Sergint, junior. Proved Nov. 24, 1701.

1701, Dec. 3. Administration granted to his widow, Mary.

E. J. D., Lib. C, pp. 180, 181.

1689, March 26. Rouse, Simon; will of. Wife, sole heiress; Frances Moore, after her death. Real and personal estate. Witnesses—Thomas Mullinex, Issabell More, Joseph Hart, John Bishop. Proved at Philadelphia, June 8, 1693.

1693-4, Jan. 22. Letters issued to John Bishop of Raway.

E. J. D., Lib. E, pp. 81, 82.

1688, July 21. Sadler, Richard, of Middletown; will of. Wife, Jean. Stepchildren—John, Sarah, Mary, Jean Purdy, John Job, senior, George Job, senior. Witnesses—Safty Grover, Rob'd Johnes. Proved Aug. 31, 1688. E. J. D., Lib. B, p. 533.

1695, Dec. 5. Sayre, Joseph, of Elizabeth Town; will of. Wife, Martha. Sons—Thomas, Ephraim, Daniel. Dau., Sarah. Real and personal estate. Executors—Benjamin Meaker and Daniel Price. Witnesses—Benjamin Meaker, Henry Walwine, Samuel Whitehead. Proved Dec. 11, 1695.

1695-6, Jan. 16. Letters issued to the widow, Martha Sayre.

E. J. D., Lib. E, pp. 314, 316.

1688-9, 19th d., 1st m. (March). Scholey, Robert, of Nottingham Woodhouse, W. J.; will of. Wife, Sarah. Youngest son, Robert. Other children, not mentioned by name. Real and personal estate. The wife sole executrix; Mahlon Stacy and Thomas Lambert, trustees. Witnesses—Anne Pharoe, Elizabeth Lambert, William Emley, Justice.

W. J. R., Lib. B, Part I, p. 315.

1700, July 8. Scott, Alexander, of Elizabeth Town, planter; will of. Wife, Ellin. Daughter, Elizabeth. Sons—Alexander and Samuel. Real and personal property. The wife sole executrix. Witnesses—Thomas Akin, Samuel Whitehead. Proved Sept. 17, 1700.

1700, Dec. 31. Letters issued to the widow, Ellin Scott.

E. J. D., Lib. G, pp. 205, 206.

1689, July 16. Smally, John and Ann, his wife, of Piscataway; will of. Sons—Isaac, John. Sons of John, viz., John and Jonathan. Daughters—Hannah Banges, Mary Snow (who has three daughters). Real and personal property. Executor, the survivor. Witnesses—Edward Slater, Samuel Blackford. Proved June 23, 1697.

E. J. D., Lib. F, p. 395.

1685, Dec. 24. Smith, Edward, of Middletoun; will of. Bequeathes property to John, son of John Boune, dec'd., Obadiah Boune and Gershom Mott, widow of John Boune, brother-in-law Stephen Arnold, brother Philipp Smith of Newport, Rhode Island. Executor—the brother. Witnesses—Richard Stoute, senior, Andrew Boune, James Boune, Jonathan Huller. Proved April 1, 1686.

1686, April 8. Letters of administration issued to Philipp Smith.

E. J. D., Lib. A, p. 304.

1685, Nov. 1. Spence, Margaret, widow of John Verner of Dalvick; will of. Made aboard the Henry and Francis of New Castle, Capt. Richard Huttone. Sister Christian Spence, dau. of James Spence of Queensferry, Scotland, merchant, sole heiress. ——— McClelland of Barmagachan, James Armour, merchant, James Rainie, mariner, executors. William Livingstone, mariner, Alexander Adam, merchant, Alex'r Riddock, writer, witnesses.

1689, Aug. 11. Administration granted to James Clarksone of Woodbridge, her brother-in-law. E. J. D., Lib. B, pp. 475, 522.

1690, Aug. 26. Spinage, Daniel, "bachler;" will of. Names Constant, wife of George Royse, brothers John, Ebinezar, Joseph, Edward, Benjamin, sisters Abigall, Hannah and Eliza. "My estate." Executor—George Royse. Witnesses—Aron Thompson, John Lamburd, Edward Gay. Proved Sept. 9, 1690.

1690, Sept. 9. Letters granted to his executor.

E. J. D., Lib. D, p. 225.

1677, Dec. 13. Steenhuys, Engelbert, of Bergen; will of. (In Dutch). Made at Bergen before Allard Anthony, Not. Publ. at New York. Wife mentioned but not named. Sons Stephen, Joost and Pieter live in Germany, and if they do not appear to claim the estate in 10 years Gerrit Gerritson, Hans Dederick, Claes Arentsen Tours, Pieter Marcellis and Jan Arentsen Tours shall become owners of it and administrators.

1678, April 9. Administration granted to men named in will.

E. J. D., Lib. 3, p. 141.

1683, April 10. Sturridge, Samuel, of Elizabethtown, yeoman; will of. Sole heir and executor, Joseph Hart. Witnesses—James Emott, Isaac Swinton.

1683, Feb. 14. Administration granted to Joseph Hart.

E. J. D., Lib. A, p. 62.

1682, July 21. Taylor, Moses, 35 yrs. old; will of. Bequeathes personal property to Henry Browne, Edward Clarke, wife and daughter Dorothy Clarke. Wishes to be buried in the garden of Jacob Corbitt by the side of William Nobile. Proved Aug. 21, 1683.

E. J. D., Lib. A, p. 42.

1694-5, Feb. 4. Thompson, Aaron, of Elizabeth Town; will of. Wife, Hannah. Sons—Thomas, Joseph, Aaron. Daughter, Hannah. Sister, Mary Hinds. Real and personal estate. Executors—Rev. John Harriman and Nathaniel Tuttle. Witnesses—William Miller, Steven Crane. Proved October 2, 1695. (For inventory, see N. J. Archives, Vol. XXIII, p. 458).

1696, Apr. 29. Administration granted to the widow, Hannah Thompson and John Haynes, one of the executors having died and the other refusing to act. E. J. D., Lib. E, pp. 227, 489.

1690, July 17. Throgmorton, John; will of. Wife ———. Son, Joseph. Daughters—Rebeckah, Sarah, Patience, Alice, Deliverance. Real and personal estate (land inherited from brother Joseph). Wife sole executrix. Witnesses—Richard Hartshorne and Job Throgmorton. Proved August 22, 1690.

1690, Aug. 22. Administration granted to Alice, his widow.

E. J. D., Lib. D, pp. 221, 222.

1681, Oct. 19. Tichanor, Martin; will of. Children—John, Daniel, Samuel, Jonathan, Abigall. Son-in-law, John Treat. Real and personal estate. Executor—son John. Overseers—William Camp and Joseph Riggs. Witnesses—Ephraim Burwell, William Camp, Joseph Riggs.

1681, Oct. 27. Inventory made by Samuel Swaine, Wm. Camp and Ephr. Burwell (£230.11).

1681, Nov. 14. Administration granted to John Tichanor.

E. J. D., Lib. 3, pp. 172, 173.

1695, May 18. Tichenor, John, of Newark; will of. Wife, Hannah; son, Martin; an expected child. Real and personal property. The wife executrix, with brothers Ensign John Treat and Daniel Tichenor as overseers. Witnesses—John Browen, John Treat, Jonathan Tichenor. Proved September 10, 1695.

1695, Dec. 20. Letters issued to the widow, Hannah Tichenor.

E. J. D., Lib. E, pp. 270, 271.

1675, Nov. 20. Tomson, Thomas, of Elizabethtown; will of. Children—Aaron, Moses, Hur. Hannah, Elizabeth. Executor—son Aaron. Witnesses—Stephen Crane, Nathaniel Tuttell. Recorded Sept. 9, 1676.

1676, April —. Inventory made by Aaron Tomson (£152.15.6).

E. J. D., Lib. 3, pp. 126, 127.

1688, Nov. 15. Walters, Joseph, of Newark; will of. Wife ———; cousin Jonathan Seers; Elizabeth Baldwine. Real and personal estate. Overseers—John Curtis and John Brown, junior. Witnesses—the same.

1688-9, Jan. 4. Administration granted to his widow, Martha.
E. J. D., Lib. D, pp. 23, 24.

———, ———, —. Ward, John, turner; will of. Wife mentioned, but not named. Sons—Josiah, John, Samuel, John Garner. The wife executrix. Witnesses—Richard Lawrence, Stephen Davis. Proved July 16, 1684.

1684, July 16. Administration granted to his widow Sarah.
E. J. D., Lib. A, p. 139.

1695, May 2. Ward, John, of Newark; will of. First wife a daughter of Henry Lyon; present wife, Abigail. Sons—John, Jonathan, David. Daughter, Marie. Real and personal estate. Executors—the wife, with brothers Nathaniel Ward and Joseph Harrison as overseers. Witnesses—John Curtise, John Brown, Robert Young. Proved September 20, 1695. (Died May 5).

1695, Dec. 20. Letters issued to widow, Abigail Ward.
E. J. D., Lib. E, p. 267.

1690-1, March 12. Warren, John, of Elizabeth Town; will of. Wife, Grace. Mary eldest dau. of Samuel Whitehead of Southhampton. Real and personal estate. The wife executrix. Witnesses—John Parker, Isaac Whitehead. Proved March 28, 1691.

1692, March 29. Letters issued to the executrix named.
E. J. D., Lib. D, p. 283.

1687-8, Feb. 14. Weinans, John, of Elizabeth, weaver; will of. Wife, Susanna. Children—Samuel, Johannes, Conradus, Jacob, Isaac, Elisabeth, Johanna, Susanna Baker. Real and personal estate. The wife executrix. Witnesses—George Ross, Humphrey Speining, Edward Gay. Testator signs "Jan Winans." Proved Jan. 15, 1694-5.

1695, May 17. Letters issued to Henry Baker and wife, Susanna, Ebenezer Lyon and his wife, Elizabeth, all of Elizabeth Town.
E. J. D., Lib. E, pp. 155, 156.

1682, July 24. White, Robert; will of. Wife ———. Children—William Andrew, Ann Lee, Elizabeth; Mary Little. Real estate (home lot adjoining Thomas Lee) and personal property. Witnesses—Steven Crane, Isabell Moore. E. J. D., Lib. C, p. 64.

1690-1, Jan. 31. Whitehead, Isaac, of Elizabeth Town; will of. Wife, Mary. Having disposed of his lands by deeds of gift he appoints sons Isaac and Joseph with Nathaniel Bunnell executors. Witnesses—John Harriman, John Woodruffe. Proved February 26 following.

1691, Feb. 27. Letters issued to executors named.
E. J. D., Lib. D, pp. 271, 272.

1688-9, Jan. 7. Winder, Samuel, of Boston, New England; will of. Wife Margaret; daughter Sarah. Real and personal estate. The wife sole executrix.

1688-'9, Feb. 14. Letters issued to the widow, Margaret Winder, at Boston. E. J. D., Lib. F, p. 127.

1674-5, Feb. 1. Winter, Obediah (alias Grabum), of Woodbridge; will of. Wife, Margaret. Sons—Josiah and Obediah. Father-in-law, John Cromwell. Lands, 30 acres lately acquired by exchange with John Conger, and other land bought with father-in-law. Executors—the wife, John Bishop, senior, and Jonathan Dunham. Witnesses—Mathew Moore, John Conger. Entered April 17, 1675

1675, March 30. Inventory of the estate (£149.12).

1675, Apr. 12. Administration granted to Margaret Winter (alias Grabum). E. J. D., Lib. 3, p. 111.

1691, April 27. Woodruff, John, Sr., of Elizabeth Town; will of. Wife, Mary. Sons—John, Jonathan, Benjamin, Joseph, David, Daniel. Daughters—Elizabeth, Sarah, Hanna. Real and personal estate. Executors—sons John, Jonathan, David and Joseph, with John Herriman, Jonathan Ogden and John Parker as overseers. Witnesses—Isaac Whitehead, William Browne. Proved May 11, 1691.

1691, April [May?], 16. Letters issued to the executors named. E. J. D., Lib. D, pp. 283, 285.

1691, Nov. 7. Woodruff, Jonathan, of Elizabeth Town; will of. Wife, Mary; son, Jonathan. Real and personal estate. Witnesses—Joseph and Isaac Whitehead. Mem. Administration granted to the widow Dec. 20, 1691. E. J. D., Lib. D, p. 308.

1687, May 7. Woolcott, Samuel, of Shroesberry; will of. Sons—Edward Williams and Nathaniel Wolcott. Executors—Judah Allan and Thomas Webley. Witnesses—John Martein, Edmond Laffetra, Andrey Webley.

1687, Dec. 1. Administration granted to Judah Allan and Thomas Webley. E. J. D., Lib. B, p. 214.

1687, July 2. Wren, John; nuncupative will of. Made before Gawen Lawrie; names his wife as sole heiress and Edward Gay executor. John Stephen, witness.

1687, Aug. 3. Administration granted to Dr. Edward Gay of same place. E. J. D., Lib. B, pp. 133, 134.

INDEXES

I. INDEX OF NAMES OF PERSONS

II. INDEX OF PLACE-NAMES

Index of Names of Persons

NOTE.—The names of testators, intestates, etc., printed in heavy type in the preceding text, are not repeated in this Index, except in the case of alternate spellings, since they are already printed in strict alphabetical order. An exception is made as to the few names added in the Appendix.

Where surnames in common use to-day, or at least with well-known spellings, are unusually or curiously spelled in the text, the current modern spelling is substituted in this Index in order to facilitate reference. Otherwise originals are adhered to.

For any omitted names, see at end of this Index.

A

F

G

H

K

M

P

S

U

Y

Z

NAMES (OR PAGINGS) OMITTED

Index of Place-Names.

NOTE.—Where names of places are unusually or curiously spelled in the text, modern spelling is substituted in this Index, as a rule. Names of *Counties* are omitted, as their numerals would take up many pages and be of little practical use.

www.ingramcontent.com/pod-product-compliance
Lightning Source LLC
Chambersburg PA
CBHW060544280326
41932CB00011B/1401

* 9 7 8 0 7 8 8 4 0 0 4 1 4 *